STATUTORY INSTRUMENTS 1973

PART II
(in two Sections)

SECTION 1

Published by Authority

LONDON
HER MAJESTY'S STATIONERY OFFICE
1973

ISBN 0 11 840122 X*

Contents of the Volume

PART I, Section 1

PART I, Section 2

PART II, Section 1

PART II, Section 2

PART III

Preface

Scope and arrangement of the Volume

1. This volume gives the full text of the statutory instruments (**a**) registered in the year 1973 which were classified as general, and gives particulars of those which were classified as local(**b**). Other instruments are contained in the Appendix (as to which see para. 3, below).

2. The general instruments are arranged according to their S.I. numbers (**c**), that is to say, in the order of their registration as statutory instruments. The volume is published in three Parts, containing the instruments registered between 1st January and 30th April, 1st May and 31st August, and 1st September and 31st December respectively.

Contents of the Volume

3. **Parts I and II.** At the beginning of each of these Parts is a list of the instruments whose text is contained in that Part, showing their S.I. numbers and titles. The list is followed by the text of the statutory instruments registered in the relevant period and an **Appendix of Instruments not registered as Statutory Instruments** issued in that period. This Appendix includes Orders in Council issued under the royal prerogative or otherwise outside the definition of a statutory instrument, Royal Proclamations which are of a legislative nature, and Letters Patent and Royal Instructions which relate to the constitutions, etc., of overseas territories.

At the end of each Part is a Table showing the modifications to legislation and an Index. Each Table is confined to the instruments in its own Part and gives particulars of those Acts and instruments which have been amended, extended, excluded, repealed or revoked by instruments in the Part. The Index to Part II will be cumulative to both Parts.

4. **Part III.** At the beginning is a list of the instruments in Part III similar to the lists in Parts I and II. It is followed by the text of the instruments comprising Part III, as in Parts I and II.

At the end of Part III are the features which are required by reg. 10 of the Statutory Instruments Regulations 1947 to be included in the Annual Volume of Statutory Instruments. They cover the instruments in all three Parts. In the order in which they occur in the Volume, they are as follows:—

The **Classified List of Local Instruments** gives particulars, including the S.I. numbers, of all local statutory instruments registered in the S.I. series of the year to which the Annual Volume relates. They are grouped in classes according to their subject-matter.

(a) As to Orders in Council made under s. 1(3) of the Northern Ireland (Temporary Provisions) Act 1972 (c. 22), *see* para. 4A below.

(b) *See* Statutory Instruments Regulations 1947 (S.I. 1948/1 (Rev. XXI, p. 498: 1948 I, p. 4002)), reg. 4 of which provides that S.I. which are in the nature of public general Acts of Parliament shall be classified as general and those which are in the nature of local and personal or private Acts shall be classified as local.

(c) Reg. 3 of the Statutory Instruments Regulations 1947 provides for instruments to be numbered in a separate series for each calendar year. Certain instruments bear also a subsidiary number—

    C.   Commencement Orders (bringing an Act or part of an Act into operation).

    L.   Instruments relating to fees or procedure in courts in England or Wales.

    N.I.   Orders in Council made under s. 1 of the Northern Ireland (Temp. Provisions) Act 1972.

    S.   Instruments made by a Scottish rule-making authority and applying to Scotland only.

The **Tables.** " Table A " gives particulars of the Acts of Parliament, and " Table B " particulars of statutory and other instruments, the operation of which was affected by the instruments appearing in the Volume. They include the information as to amendments, repeals, revocations, etc., already given in tables of " Modifications to Legislation " in Parts I and II and corresponding information with respect to the instruments in Part III, and also give particulars of Acts or instruments modified or restricted by general instruments throughout the Volume. In addition, Table B gives particulars of general instruments whose operation was affected expressly by Public General Acts of the year in question, or which ceased to operate through becoming spent during that year as a result of legislation of the year.

The **Numerical and Issue List** gives particulars of all statutory instruments which were printed and put on sale by the Queen's Printer of Acts of Parliament under the provisions of the Statutory Instruments Act 1946(**a**), during the year, with, in each case, the date of first issue by Her Majesty's Stationery Office.

The **Index** will be cumulative to Parts I and II.

4A. **Northern Ireland.** A number of Orders in Council under s. 1(3) of the Northern Ireland (Temporary Provisions) Act 1972(**b**) are excluded in reliance upon the Statutory Instruments (Amendment) Regulations 1972(**c**). All Orders in Council made under s. 1(3), which have the same validity and effect as an Act of the Parliament of Northern Ireland, are included in the annual volumes of Northern Ireland Statutes. Particulars will be given in the Numerical and Issue List in Part III of this volume.

Definition of a statutory instrument

5. To determine whether or not any instrument is required to be a statutory instrument, reference must be made to s. 1 of the Statutory Instruments Act 1946, reg. 2 of the Statutory Instruments Regulations 1947, and arts. 1 and 2 of the Statutory Instruments (Confirmatory Powers) Order 1947(**d**).

The definition of what constitutes a statutory instrument, as respects instruments made under Acts passed before the commencement (1 Jan. 1948) of the 1946 Act, is governed by definitions contained in the Rules Publication Act 1893(**e**) (which was repealed and replaced by the 1946 Act); for those made under Acts passed after the commencement of the 1946 Act, the document is a statutory instrument if it is an Order in Council or if it is made by a Minister of the Crown and the Act provides that the power is to be exercisable by statutory instrument.

Citation

6. For the purposes of citation, statutory instruments are given a title. In addition, all statutory instruments may be identified by the year and number. The first instrument in Part I of this Volume would, by this method, be cited as " S.I. 1973/1 ". When a statutory instrument is referred to in another statutory instrument, a lettered footnote is provided in the latter, giving the identification of the first instrument as above, and also its Part and page reference in the Annual Volume. The footnote reference for the same instrument would therefore be " S.I. 1973/1 (1973 I, p. 1) ".

If the text of the instrument is set out in the current edition of *S.R. & O. and S.I. Revised* (Third Edition, as at 31st Dec., 1948) the footnote references give the volume reference in that edition as well as the page reference in the Annual Volume (see, for example, footnote (**d**) below). If a footnote contains the references of a number of instruments, they may in certain circumstances be run together, so as to give all the instrument numbers together and all the volume references together, e.g. " S.R. & O. 1946/157; S.I. 1948/1073, 1961/ 1942 (1946 II, p. 26; 1948 II, p. 13; 1961 III, p. 2650) ".

(**a**) 1946 c. 36.   (**b**) 1972 c. 22.   (**c**) S.I. 1972/1205 (1972 II, p. 3571).
(**d**) S.I. 1948/2 (Rev. XXI, p. 504: 1948 I, p. 4008).   (**e**) 1893 c. 66.

Production in Court

7. Under section 2 of the Documentary Evidence Act 1868 (a), read with section 2 of the Documentary Evidence Act 1882 (b), *prima facie* evidence of any proclamation, order or regulation made by certain rule-making authorities may be given in courts of justice by production of a copy purporting to be printed by the Government Printer or under the superintendence or authority of Her Majesty's Stationery Office. The Act of 1868 has since been extended by numerous Acts (c) to rules, etc., made thereunder by other rule-making authorities. The copies of proclamations, orders, regulations, etc., made by the authorities referred to above as printed in these volumes may therefore be produced as *prima facie* evidence.

Up to date information on statutory instruments

8. The *Index to Government Orders* contains, under subject headings, summaries of all powers to make subordinate legislation conferred by statute on H.M. in Council, the Privy Council, government departments and certain other public bodies. Below each summary appear particulars of any general instruments made in exercise of it which were in force at the date of publication of the *Index*. Details are also given of certain instruments made under prerogative powers. The work contains also a Table of Statutes showing the subject headings under which references to particular sections of enabling Acts appear. (The *Index* is published every two years by H.M.S.O.)

9. Information as to whether any instrument is still in operation, or whether anything has happened to it since it was made, can be obtained from the *Table of Government Orders*. This Table lists general statutory rules and orders and statutory instruments in numerical order, and gives the history of those which have been affected (i.e. revoked, amended, etc.) by subsequent legislation, whether statute or subordinate legislation, identifying the Act or instrument in question. Where any instrument has been amended, the Table gives particulars of the article, section, rule, etc., affected. A user who is interested in one particular provision only of the earlier instrument can thus ascertain whether or not he need consult the text of the amending enactment at all. The *Table of Government Orders* is published annually by H.M.S.O. and is cumulative. A Noter-Up is issued twice yearly.

Authority for Publication

10. The Annual Volumes of Statutory Instruments are published in pursuance of reg. 10 of the Statutory Instruments Regulations 1947 and are prepared under the direction of the Statute Law Committee. Any suggestion or communication relating to their contents should be addressed to the Editor, Statutory Publications Office, Queen Anne's Chambers, 41, Tothill Street, S.W.1.

(a) 1868 c. 37.   (b) 1882 c. 9.
(c) *See* the entries relating to extensions of the 1868 Act in the *Chronological Table of the Statutes*.

Abbreviations

Addnl. Instructions	Additional Instructions.
A.S.	Act of Sederunt.
am., amdg., amdt.	amended, amending, amendment.
appx.	appendix.
art(s).	article(s).
Authy.	Authority.
bd(s).	board(s).
c.	chapter(s).
cl(s).	clause(s).
Cmd., Cmnd.	Command Paper.
Commn.	Commission.
cont.	continued.
ct(s).	court(s).
ctee.	committee.
E.	England.
exc.	except, excepted
excl.	excluded.
expl.	explained.
ext.	extended, extension.
G.B.	Great Britain.
gen.	generally.
govt.	government.
H.C.	House of Commons Paper.
H.M.	Her Majesty, Her Majesty's.
incl.	included, including.
instrt.	instrument.
Is.	Island(s), Isle(s).
L.P.	Letters Patent.
Min(s).	Minister(s).
misc.	miscellaneous.
mod., mod(s).	modified, modification(s).
N.	North.
N.I.	Northern Ireland.
No.	number.
O.	Order(s).
O. in C., O. of C.	Order(s) in Council, Order(s) of Council.
p., pp.	page(s).
para(s).	paragraph(s).
prerog.	prerogative.
prosp.	prospectively.
prov.	provisional, proviso.
provn(s).	provision(s).
pt.	part.
r.	revoked.
R.C.	Rules of the Court of Session.
R. Instructions	Royal Instructions.
R. Warrant	Royal Warrant.
reg(s).	regulation(s).
rep.	repealed.
restr.	restricted.
retrosp.	retrospectively.
Rev.	Statutory Rules and Orders and Statutory Instruments Revised (Third Edition, 1948).

Rev. 1903 ...	...	...	Statutory Rules and Orders Revised (Second Edition, 1903).
revn.	...	...	revocation.
S. ...	...	...	Scotland.
s., ss.	...	...	section(s).
S.I. ...	...	...	Statutory Instrument(s).
S.R. & O. ...	...	...	Statutory Rule(s) and Order(s).
sch(s).	...	...	schedule(s).
Secy.	...	...	Secretary.
susp.	...	...	suspended.
temp.	...	...	temporarily, temporary.
transfd.	...	...	transferred.
Treas.	...	...	Treasury.
U.K.	...	...	United Kingdom of Great Britain and Northern Ireland.
vol.	...	...	volume.
W. ...	...	...	Wales.

Statutory Instruments in Part II

OTHER INSTRUMENTS IN PART II

STATUTORY INSTRUMENTS

1973 No. 833 (C.21)

SOCIAL SECURITY

The National Insurance Act 1972 (Commencement No. 4) Order 1973

Made - - -		*30th April* 1973
Laid before Parliament		*8th May* 1973
Coming into Operation		*10th May* 1973

The Secretary of State for Social Services, in conjunction with the Treasury, in exercise of powers conferred by section 6(5) of, and Schedule 4 to, the National Insurance Act 1972(**a**), and of all other powers enabling him in that behalf, hereby makes the following Order:—

Citation and commencement

1. This Order may be cited as the National Insurance Act 1972 (Commencement No. 4) Order 1973 and shall come into operation on 10th May 1973.

Appointed days

2. The day appointed for the coming into force, in Great Britain, of any provision of the National Insurance Act 1972 specified in column 1 of the Schedule to this Order, so far as that provision relates to any subject matter specified in column 2 of that Schedule, shall be the date specified in column 3 of that Schedule in relation to that subject matter.

Keith Joseph,
Secretary of State for Social
Services.

18th April 1973.

Tim Fortescue,
V. H. Goodhew,
Two of the Lords Commissioners
of Her Majesty's Treasury.

30th April 1973.

(**a**) 1972 c. 57.

Article 2

SCHEDULE

Provisions of the National Insurance Act 1972	Subject matter	Appointed Day
Section 1(1) and Schedule 1	Lower weekly rate of attendance allowance for persons who, under paragraph 4(3) of Schedule 4 to the National Insurance Act 1972, are of Category 2	1st October 1973
Section 2 and Schedule 4 Part II	Lower weekly rate of attendance allowance for persons who, under paragraph 4(3) of Schedule 4 to the National Insurance Act 1972, are of Category 2	10th May 1973

EXPLANATORY NOTE

(This Note is not part of the Order.)

This Order brings into operation, in Great Britain, the provisions of the National Insurance Act 1972 relating to the lower weekly rate of attendance allowance in the case of persons who are in Category 2 (i.e. persons born after the year 1956).

Under the Order, questions as to entitlement to the lower weekly rate of the allowance in the case of persons in Category 2 may be determined as from 10th May 1973, but the allowance will not become payable in respect of such persons before 1st October 1973.

STATUTORY INSTRUMENTS

1973 No. 835

SAVINGS BANKS

The Trustee Savings Banks (Interest-bearing Receipts) Order 1973

Made - - - -	*30th April* 1973
Laid before Parliament	*7th May* 1973
Coming into Operation	*21st May* 1973

The Treasury, in exercise of the powers conferred on them by section 34(2) and (4) of the Trustee Savings Banks Act 1969(**a**), as amended by section 34(3) of the Finance Act 1970(**b**), and of all other powers enabling them in that behalf, hereby make the following Order:—

1. This Order may be cited as the Trustee Savings Banks (Interest-bearing Receipts) Order 1973, and shall come into operation on 21st May 1973.

2. The Interpretation Act 1889(**c**) shall apply for the interpretation of this Order as it applies for the interpretation of an Act of Parliament, and as if this Order and the Order hereby revoked were Acts of Parliament.

3. The rate at which interest is to be paid or credited on sums standing to the credit of trustee savings banks in the Fund for the Banks for Savings shall be £5.95 per cent. per annum.

4. The Trustee Savings Banks (Interest-bearing Receipts) Order 1972(**d**) is hereby revoked.

Tim Fortescue,
Oscar Murton,

Two of the Lords Commissioners
of Her Majesty's Treasury.

30th April 1973.

(**a**) 1969 c. 50. (**b**) 1970 c. 24.
(**c**) 1889 c. 63. (**d**) S.I. 1972/1751 (1972 III, p. 5081).

EXPLANATORY NOTE

(This Note is not part of the Order.)

This Order increases the rate of interest allowed to trustee savings banks on sums standing to their credit in the Fund for the Banks for Savings from £5.65 to £5.95 per cent. per annum.

STATUTORY INSTRUMENTS

1973 No. 840

LOCAL GOVERNMENT, ENGLAND AND WALES

The Police Act 1964 (Modification of section 21) Order 1973

Made - - - -	*27th April* 1973
Laid before Parliament	*8th May* 1973
Coming into Operation	*1st June* 1973

In exercise of the powers conferred on me by section 254 of the Local Government Act 1972**(a)**, I hereby make the following Order:—

1. This Order may be cited as the Police Act 1964 (Modification of section 21) Order 1973 and shall come into operation on 1st June 1973.

2. References in this Order to the Act are references to the Police Act 1964**(b)**, as amended by any subsequent enactment.

3. An amalgamation scheme expressed to come into full operation in 1st April 1974 may be approved or made under the Act notwithstanding that it does not make provision with respect to the matters mentioned in paragraphs (*d*) and (*e*) of section 21(3) of the Act (transfer of persons, property etc.) and, accordingly, the said section 21(3) shall have effect in relation to such an amalgamation scheme as if it authorised, but did not require, the making of provision with respect to the said matters.

Robert Carr,
One of Her Majesty's Principal
Secretaries of State.

Home Office,
   Whitehall.
27th April 1973.

EXPLANATORY NOTE
(This Note is not part of the Order.)

This Order modfies section 21(3) of the Police Act 1964 in its application to police amalgamation schemes which become fully operative on 1st April 1974 (the date on which the Local Government Act 1972 becomes fully operative).

It provides that a scheme need not make such provision relating to the transfer of persons, property etc. as is mentioned in section 21(3)(*d*) and (*e*) (such provision may be made under powers conferred by the Local Government Act 1972).

(a) 1972 c. 70.   **(b)** 1964 c. 48.

STATUTORY INSTRUMENTS

1973 No. 844

CUSTOMS AND EXCISE

The Import Duties (Temporary Exemptions) (No. 13) Order 1973

Made - - -	*2nd May* 1973
Laid before the House of Commons	*2nd May* 1973
Coming into Operation	*3rd May* 1973

The Lords Commissioners of Her Majesty's Treasury, by virtue of the powers conferred on them by sections 3(6) and 13 of the Import Duties Act 1958(a) and of all other powers enabling them in that behalf, on the recommendation of the Secretary of State (b), hereby make the following Order:—

1.—(1) This Order may be cited as the Import Duties (Temporary Exemptions (No. 13) Order 1973.

(2) The Interpretation Act 1889(c) shall apply for the interpretation of this Order as it applies for the interpretation of an Act of Parliament.

(3) This Order shall come into operation on 3rd May 1973.

2.—(1) Until the beginning of 1st January 1974 or, in the case of goods in relation to which an earlier day is specified in Schedule 1 hereto, until the beginning of that day, any import duty which is for the time being chargeable on goods of a heading of the Customs Tariff 1959 specified in that Schedule shall not be chargeable in respect of goods of any description there specified in relation to that heading.

(2) The period for which goods of headings of the Customs Tariff 1959 and descriptions specified in Schedule 2 hereto are exempt from import duty shall be extended until the beginning of 3rd July 1973.

(3) Any entry in the second column of Schedule 1 or Schedule 2 hereto shall be taken to comprise all goods which would be classified under an entry in the same terms constituting a subheading (other than the final subheading) in the relevant heading of the Customs Tariff 1959.

3. For the purposes of classification under the Customs Tariff 1959, in so far as that depends on the rate of duty, any goods to which paragraph (1) or (2) of Article 2 applies shall be treated as chargeable with the same duty as if this Order had not been made.

(a) 1958 c. 6.   (b) *See* S.I. 1970/1537 (1970 III, p. 5293).   (c) 1889 c. 63.

Oscar Murton,

Hugh Rossi,

Two of the Lords Commissioners
of Her Majesty's Treasury.

2nd May 1973.

SCHEDULE 1

GOODS TEMPORARILY EXEMPT FROM IMPORT DUTY

Tariff Heading	Description
29.08	Decabromodiphenyl ether
29.34	Triethylaluminium (until 3rd July 1973)
73.09	Universal plates of iron or steel (until 1st October 1973)
73.11	Angles, shapes and sections of iron or steel, hot-rolled or extruded, not drilled, punched or otherwise fabricated or clad, in the case of I, U, H and Z sections the distance between the outer surfaces of the two parallel planes is to be not less than 70 millimetres, in the case of angles the outer length of the leg or of the longest leg is to be not less than 70 millimetres and in all other cases the greatest dimension of the cross-section is to be not less than 70 millimetres (until 1st October 1973)
73.15	Alloy steel bars, containing not less than 0·40% and not more than 0·70% by weight of nickel, not less than 0·40% and not more than 0·60% by weight of chromium, not less than 0·20% and not more than 0·30% by weight of molybdenum as the major alloying elements, being not less than 76 millimetres and not more than 215 millimetres in diameter and not less than 5 metres and not more than 8 metres in length (until 3rd July 1973)
	Alloy steel bars, containing not less than 0·90% and not more than 1·20% by weight of nickel, not less than 0·30% and not more than 0·60% by weight of chromium, not less than 0·20% and not more than 0·30% by weight of molybdenum as the major alloying elements, being not less than 76 millimetres and not more than 215 millimetres in diameter and not less than 5 metres and not more than 8 metres in length (until 3rd July 1973)
	Alloy steel bars, containing not less than 0·90% and not more than 1·20% by weight of carbon, not less than 1·30% and not more than

1·60% by weight of chromium as the major alloying elements, being not less than 76 millimetres and not more than 215 millimetres in diameter and not less than 5 metres and not more than 8 metres in length (until 3rd July 1973)

Steel sheets, rectangular or in coils, being steel containing not less than 2·0%, nor more than 3·5% by weight of silicon as the major alloying element, with a manganese content exceeding 0·1% and an aluminium not exceeding 0·01%, whether or not coated, and of a width not exceeding 1,250 millimetres and a thickness not exceeding 1·6 millimetres (until 4th September 1973)

SCHEDULE 2

GOODS FOR WHICH EXEMPTION FROM IMPORT DUTY IS EXTENDED

Tariff Heading	Description
29.01	Styrene
29.14	Undec-10-enoic acid which freezes at a temperature not lower than 23° centigrade
73.21	Steel piles in the form of longitudinally welded steel tubes, having an outside diameter of not less than 1200 millimetres and not more than 1240 millimetres, of a wall thickness of not less than 20 millimetres and not more than 55 millimetres, of a length of not less than 31,300 millimetres and not more than 32,500 millimetres, each tube having two sets of 16 lengths of mild steel angle iron in the form of splines, welded longitudinally around the periphery at two levels towards one end, each spline being of a length of not less than 1040 millimetres and not more than 2000 millimetres

EXPLANATORY NOTE

(*This Note is not part of the Order.*)

This Order provides that goods of a description specified in Schedule 1 are to be exempt from import duty until 1st January 1974 or until such earlier date as is specified in that Schedule. The Order also continues until 3rd July 1973 the temporary exemption from import duty of goods of a description specified in Schedule 2.

STATUTORY INSTRUMENTS

1973 No. 847 (L.13)

COUNTY COURTS

PROCEDURE

The County Court (Amendment No. 2) Rules 1973

Made - - - -	*17th April* 1973
Coming into Operation—	
All provisions except Rules 5, 10 *and* 11	*29th May* 1973
Rules 5, 10 *and* 11	*2nd July* 1973

1.—(1) These Rules may be cited as the County Court (Amendment No. 2) Rules 1973.

(2) In these Rules an Order and Rule referred to by number means the Order and Rule so numbered in the County Court Rules 1936**(a)**, as amended**(b)**, and a form referred to by number means the form so numbered in Appendix A to those Rules.

(3) The Interpretation Act 1889**(c)** shall apply for the interpretation of these Rules as it applies for the interpretation of an Act of Parliament.

2. In Order 7, Rule 3(*b*), for sub-paragraphs (i) and (ii) there shall be substituted the following sub-paragraphs:—

> "(i) where the land forms part of a hereditament having a net annual value for rating of an amount not exceeding the county court limit under section 51 of the Act, the net annual value of that hereditament, or
>
> (ii) in any other case, the value of the land by the year."

3. For Order 8, Rule 3, there shall be substituted the following Rule:—

No service
on Sunday
> "3. Without prejudice to the provisions of Order 35, Rule 10, no process shall be served or executed within England or Wales on a Sunday, Christmas Day or Good Friday except , in case of urgency, with the leave of the court."

(a) S.R. & O. 1936/626 (1936 I, p. 282).
(b) The relevant amending instruments are S.I. 1950/1231, 1954/1675. 1955/1799, 1956/1851, 1959/1251, 1963/403, 1969/585, 1971/836, 2152 (1950 I, p. 400; 1954 I, p. 541; 1955 I, p. 530; 1956 I, p. 545; 1959 I, p. 795; 1963 I, p. 475; 1969 I. p. 1551; 1971 II, p. 2393; III, p. 6305).
(c) 1889 c. 63.

4. Order 19 shall be amended as follows:—

(1) In the title after the word "REPORT" there shall be added the words "OR TO EUROPEAN COURT".

(2) For the first marginal note to Rule 1 there shall be substituted the words "Reference under s.93 of Act".

(3) Paragraphs (1) and (2) of Rule 2 shall be added to Rule 1 as paragraphs (3) and (4), and in paragraph (3)(*e*) as so renumbered for the figure "(2)" there shall be substituted the figure "(4)".

(4) The following Rule shall be added at the end of the Order:—

Reference to European Court

"2.—(1) In this Rule "the European Court" means the Court of Justice of the European Communities and "order" means an order referring a question to the European Court for a preliminary ruling under Article 177 of the Treaty establishing the European Economic Community, Article 150 of the Treaty establishing the European Atomic Energy Community or Article 41 of the Treaty establishing the European Coal and Steel Community.

(2) An order may be made by the judge before or at the trial or hearing of any action or matter and either of his own motion or on the application of any party.

(3) An order shall set out in a schedule the request for the preliminary ruling of the European Court, and the judge may give directions as to the manner and form in which the schedule is to be prepared.

(4) The proceedings in which an order is made shall, unless the judge otherwise orders, be stayed until the European Court has given a preliminary ruling on the question referred to it.

(5) When an order has been made, the registrar shall send a copy thereof to the Senior Master of the Supreme Court (Queen's Bench Division) for transmission to the registrar of the European Court; but, unless the judge otherwise orders, the copy shall not be sent to the Senior Master until the time for appealing to the Court of Appeal against the order has expired or, if an appeal is entered within that time, until the appeal has been determined or otherwise disposed of.

(6) Nothing in these Rules shall authorise the registrar to make an order."

5. Order 25, Rule 2, shall be amended as follows:—

(1) After paragraph (1) there shall be inserted the following paragraph:—
"(2) The application shall be made to the court for the district in which the person to be examined (or, if there are more such persons than one, any of them) resides or carries on business, and paragraphs (2) to (6) of Rule 48 of this Order shall apply with the necessary modifications as if the references in those paragraphs to a judgment summons included references to an application for oral examination."

(2) Paragraph (2) shall stand as paragraph (3) and after that paragraph there shall be inserted the following paragraph:—
"(4) The examination may be ordered to take place either before

the registrar or before any officer of the court not below the rank
of higher executive officer."

(3) Paragraphs (3), (4) and (6) shall stand as paragraphs (5), (6) and (7)
and the existing paragraph (5) shall be omitted.

(4) In paragraph (5) as so renumbered for the words "the last preceding
paragraph" there shall be substituted the words "paragraph (3) of
this Rule".

(5) In paragraph (6) as so renumbered for the words "paragraph (2)"
there shall be substituted the words "paragraph (3)".

(6) After paragraph (7) as so renumbered there shall be inserted the
following paragraphs:—

"(8) Any difficulty arising in the course of an examination before
an officer of the court, including any dispute as to the obligation
of the person being examined to answer any question put to him,
may be referred to the registrar and he may determine it or give
such directions for determining it as he thinks fit.

(9) Nothing in this Rule shall be construed as preventing the
registrar, before deciding whether to make an order under
paragraph (3), from giving the debtor an opportunity of making
a statement in writing or an affidavit as to his means."

6. Order 48, Rule 1, shall stand as paragraph (1) of that Rule and at the
end there shall be added the following paragraph:—

"(2) The Lord Chancellor may issue directions for the purpose of
securing uniformity of practice in the county courts."

7. In Form 9, for the paragraph beginning "The net annual value" there
shall be substituted the following paragraph:—

"The net annual value of the premises for rating is £   [*or, if the premises
do not consist of one or more hereditaments having a separate net annual
value for rating but form part of a hereditament having a net annual value
for rating not exceeding* [*the county court limit*] The premises form part of
a hereditament having a net annual value for rating of £   [*or in any
other case* The value of the premises by the year is £   ]]."

8. In Form 18A after the words "*Pay and Means*" in paragraph 4 of the
section headed "ADMISSION" there shall be inserted the words "(*a*) What
is your occupation?" and sub-paragraphs (*a*) to (*f*) shall be re-lettered
accordingly.

9. In Form 27(1) the words "in your absence" shall be omitted and at the
end there shall be inserted the words "In the absence of the plaintiff the
proceedings may be struck out and in the absence of the defendant judgment may be entered against him."

10. In Form 149 the words from "before the registrar" to "may appoint"
and the words from "and that the costs" to "the said registrar" shall be
omitted.

11. Form 150 shall be amended as follows:—

(1) In the marginal note for the words "Rules 2(3)" there shall be
substituted the words "Rules 2(5)".

(2) For the words "at the office of this Court" there shall be substituted the words "[*or* one of the officers] of this Court at the court office".

(3) The words "[*or* before" to "may appoint]" shall be omitted.

(4) The word "said" after the words "discretion of the" shall be omitted.

(5) The words below the line at the foot of the form shall be omitted.

12. Form 402 shall be amended as follows:—

(a) The words from "*together with*" to "*known to the Plaintiff*" shall be omitted.

(b) For the words "of   at" there shall be substituted the words "of [*employer's address for service*] at".

(c) Before the words "as a" there shall be inserted the words "[*add if known*]".

13. In Form 404 after the words "each of them" in section 1(*b*) there shall be inserted the words "If you are not employed, say so and give the name of your last employer, if any."

14.   Notwithstanding anything in Rules 8 and 9, Forms 18A and 27(1) may continue to be used in the form hitherto prescribed until the Lord Chancellor otherwise directs.

We, the undersigned members of the Rule Committee appointed by the Lord Chancellor under section 102 of the County Courts Act 1959**(a)** having by virtue of the powers vested in us in this behalf made the foregoing Rules, do hereby certify the same under our hands and submit them to the Lord Chancellor accordingly.

D. O. McKee.
Conolly H. Gage.
H. S. Ruttle.
David Pennant.
W. Granville Wingate.
E. A. Everett.
A. A. Hibbert.
K. W. Mellor.
Arnold Russell Vick.
D. A. Marshall.
D. P. Tomlin.

I allow these Rules, which shall come into operation on 29th May 1973 with the exception of Rules 5, 10 and 11 which shall come into operation on 2nd July 1973.

Dated 17th April 1973.

Hailsham of St. Marylebone, C.

EXPLANATORY NOTE

(This Note is not part of the Rules.)

These Rules make a number of miscellaneous amendments in the County Court Rules 1936. The particulars to be given in a claim for recovery of land are altered in consequence of the changes in county court jurisdiction made by section 6 of the Administration of Justice Act 1973 (c. 15) (Rules 2 and 7). The service of process on a Sunday is forbidden, as in the Supreme Court, except, in case of urgency, with the leave of the court (Rule 3). Provision is made for reference to the European Court, in consequence of the accession of the United Kingdom to the European Communities (Rule 4). An application for the oral examination of a judgment debtor must be made to the debtor's local court and the examination may be ordered to take place before a senior officer of the court (Rules 5, 10 and 11). Uniformity of practice in county courts is to be promoted by directions given by the Lord Chancellor (Rule 6). Minor alterations are made in the forms relating to attachment of earnings and other forms (Rules 8, 9, 12 and 13).

STATUTORY INSTRUMENTS

1973 No. 848

ACQUISITION OF LAND
COMPENSATION

The Acquisition of Land (Rate of Interest after Entry) (No. 3) Regulations 1973

Made - - -	*3rd May* 1973
Laid before Parliament	*10th May* 1973
Coming into Operation	*11th May* 1973

The Treasury, in exercise of the powers conferred upon them by section 32(1) of the Land Compensation Act 1961(a), and of all other powers enabling them in that behalf, hereby make the following Regulations:—

1. These Regulations may be cited as the Acquisition of Land (Rate of Interest after Entry) (No. 3) Regulations 1973, and shall come into operation on 11th May 1973.

2. The Interpretation Act 1889(b) shall apply for the interpretation of these Regulations as it applies for the interpretation of an Act of Parliament.

3. The rate of interest on any compensation in respect of the compulsory acquisition of an interest in any land on which entry has been made before the payment of the compensation shall be 10 per cent. per annum.

4. The Acquisition of Land (Rate of Interest after Entry) (No. 2) Regulations 1973(c) are hereby revoked.

Tim Fortescue,
Hugh Rossi,
Two of the Lords Commissioners
of Her Majesty's Treasury.

3rd May 1973.

EXPLANATORY NOTE
(This Note is not part of the Regulations.)

These Regulations reduce from 10½ per cent. to 10 per cent. per annum, in respect of any period after the coming into operation of these Regulations, the rate of interest payable where entry is made, before payment of compensation, on land in England and Wales which is being purchased compulsorily, and revoke the Acquisition of Land (Rate of Interest after Entry) (No. 2) Regulations 1973.

(a) 1961 c. 33.   (b) 1889 c. 63.   (c) S.I. 1973/573 (1973 I, p. 1841).

STATUTORY INSTRUMENTS

1973 No. 849

ACQUISITION OF LAND
COMPENSATION

The Acquisition of Land (Rate of Interest after Entry) (Scotland) (No. 3) Regulations 1973

Made - - -	*3rd May* 1973
Laid before Parliament	*10th May* 1973
Coming into Operation	*11th May* 1973

The Treasury, in exercise of the powers conferred upon them by section 40(1) of the Land Compensation (Scotland) Act 1963(a), and of all other powers enabling them in that behalf, hereby make the following Regulations:—

1.—(1) These Regulations may be cited as the Acquisition of Land (Rate of Interest after Entry) (Scotland) (No. 3) Regulations 1973, and shall come into operation on 11th May 1973.

(2) These Regulations shall extend to Scotland only.

2. The Interpretation Act 1889(b) shall apply for the interpretation of these Regulations as it applies for the interpretation of an Act of Parliament.

3. The rate of interest on any compensation in respect of the compulsory acquisition of an interest in any land on which entry has been made before the payment of the compensation shall be 10 per cent. per annum.

4. The Acquisition of Land (Rate of Interest after Entry) (Scotland) (No. 2) Regulations 1973(c) are hereby revoked.

Tim Fortescue,
Hugh Rossi,
Two of the Lords Commissioners
of Her Majesty's Treasury.

3rd May 1973.

EXPLANATORY NOTE
(This Note is not part of the Regulations.)

These Regulations reduce from 10½ per cent. to 10 per cent. per annum, in respect of any period after the coming into operation of these Regulations, the rate of interest payable where entry is made, before payment of compensation, on land in Scotland which is being purchased compulsorily, and revoke the Acquisition of Land (Rate of Interest after Entry) (Scotland) (No. 2) Regulations 1973.

(a) 1963 c. 51.   (b) 1889 c. 63.   (c) S.I. 1973/574 (1973 I, p.1842).

STATUTORY INSTRUMENTS

1973 No. 850

COAL INDUSTRY

The Opencast Coal (Rate of Interest on Compensation) (No. 3) Order 1973

Made - - -	3rd May 1973
Laid before Parliament	10th May 1973
Coming into Operation	11th May 1973

The Treasury, in exercise of the powers conferred upon them by sections 35(8) and 49(4) of the Opencast Coal Act 1958(a) and of all other powers enabling them in that behalf, hereby make the following Order:—

1. This Order may be cited as the Opencast Coal (Rate of Interest on Compensation) (No. 3) Order 1973, and shall come into operation on 11th May 1973.

2. The Interpretation Act 1889(b) shall apply for the interpretation of this Order as it applies for the interpretation of an Act of Parliament.

3. The rate of interest for the purposes of section 35 of the Opencast Coal Act 1958 shall be 9 per cent. per annum.

4. The Opencast Coal (Rate of Interest on Compensation) (No. 2) Order 1973(c) is hereby revoked.

Tim Fortescue,
Hugh Rossi,
Two of the Lords Commissioners
of Her Majesty's Treasury.

3rd May 1973

EXPLANATORY NOTE

(*This Note is not part of the Order.*)

Section 35 of the Opencast Coal Act 1958 provides that interest shall be payable in addition to compensation in certain circumstances. This Order reduces the rate of interest from 10 per cent. to 9 per cent. per annum and revokes the Opencast Coal (Rate of Interest on Compensation) (No. 2) Order 1973.

(a) 1958 c. 69.   (b) 1889 c. 63.   (c) S.I. 1973/572 (1973 I, p. 1840).

1973 No. 855

THERAPEUTIC SUBSTANCES

The Therapeutic Substances (Control of Sale and Supply) Regulations 1973

Made - - -	*2nd May* 1973
Laid before Parliament	*11th May* 1973
Coming into Operation	*1st June* 1973

Whereas the therapeutic substances hereinafter mentioned appear to the Secretary of State for Social Services, the Secretary of State for Wales, the Secretary of State for Scotland and the Secretary of State for Northern Ireland (hereinafter called "the Ministers") to be substances which are capable of causing danger to the health of the community if used without proper safeguards:

Now, therefore, the Ministers, in exercise of the powers conferred on them by section 8 of the Therapeutic Substances Act 1956(a), as amended by Article 2(2) of, and Schedule 1 to, the Transfer of Functions (Wales) Order 1969(b) and as having effect subject to the provisions of section 1(1)(a) of the Northern Ireland (Temporary Provisions) Act 1972(c) and of all other powers enabling them in that behalf, acting jointly, after consultation with the Medical Research Council, hereby make the following regulations:—

Citation and commencement

1. These regulations may be cited as the Therapeutic Substances (Control of Sale and Supply) Regulations 1973 and shall come into operation on 1st June 1973.

Interpretation

2. The rules for the construction of Acts of Parliament contained in the Interpretation Act 1889(d) shall apply for the purposes of the interpretation of these regulations as they apply for the purposes of the interpretation of an Act of Parliament.

Control of sale and supply

3. Part II of the Therapeutic Substances Act 1956 (which controls the sale and supply of penicillin and certain other therapeutic substances) shall also apply:—

    (*a*) to sterile aqueous solutions, sterile oily solutions and sterile suspensions of derivatives of stilbene with oestrogenic activity and such solutions and suspensions of esters of such derivatives,

---

(a) 1956 c. 25.　　　　　　　　　　(b) S.I. 1969/388 (1969 I, p. 1070).
(c) 1972 c. 22.　　　　　　　　　　(d) 1889 c. 63.

(b) to sterile aqueous solutions, sterile oily solutions and sterile suspensions of derivatives of dibenzyl with oestrogenic activity and such solutions and suspensions of esters of such derivatives,

(c) to sterile aqueous solutions, sterile oily solutions and sterile suspensions of steroid compounds with oestrogenic activity and such solutions and suspensions of esters of such compounds.

Keith Joseph,
Secretary of State for Social Services.

30th April 1973.

Peter Thomas,
Secretary of State for Wales.

30th April 1973.

Gordon Campbell,
Secretary of State for Scotland.

1st May 1973.

W. S. I. Whitelaw,
Secretary of State for Northern Ireland.

2nd May 1973.

EXPLANATORY NOTE

(This Note is not part of the Regulations.)

These Regulations bring within the scope of Part II of the Therapeutic Substances Act 1956 (which controls the sale and supply of substances to which that Part applies) the substances specified in Regulation 3.

STATUTORY INSTRUMENTS

1973 No. 856

COUNTER-INFLATION

The Counter-Inflation (Agricultural Rents) (Northern Ireland) Order 1973

Made - - -		*3rd May* 1973
Laid before Parliament		*11th May* 1973
Coming into Operation		*3rd May* 1973

In exercise of the powers conferred on me by sections 11 and 23(2) of, and paragraphs 1 and 3 of Part I of Schedule 3 to, the Counter-Inflation Act 1973(a), I hereby make the following Order:—

Citation, commencement and extent

1.—(1) This Order may be cited as the Counter-Inflation (Agricultural Rents) (Northern Ireland) Order 1973 and shall come into operation forthwith.

(2) This Order shall extend to Northern Ireland only.

Interpretation

2.—(1) The Interpretation Act 1889(b) shall apply for the interpretation of this Order as it applies for the interpretation of an Act of Parliament.

(2) In this Order, unless the context otherwise requires—

"agricultural land" has the same meaning as in the Agriculture Act (Northern Ireland) 1949(c);

"agricultural tenancy" means any tenancy where the property comprised in the tenancy is or includes agricultural land;

"enactment" includes an Act of the Parliament of Northern Ireland;

"rent" means the rent payable under an agricultural tenancy and for the purposes of any comparison under this Order excludes any sums payable by the tenant in respect of rates, repairs, maintenance or insurance;

"standard rate" in relation to any land means—

(a) where an agricultural tenancy comprising the land was subsisting on 5th November 1972, the rate at which rent was payable (whether or not then determined as to amount) under the tenancy for the land on that date;

(b) where there was no such agricultural tenancy subsisting on 5th November 1972 but an agricultural tenancy had subsisted in respect of the land in question on or after 5th November 1971, the rate at

(a) 1973 c. 9.　　　　　　　　　(b) 1889 c. 63.

(c) 1949 c. 2. (N.I.).

which rent was payable under the tenancy for the land at the date upon which the tenancy or, where there were successive tenancies, the last such tenancy came to an end;

with the addition, in either case, of any increase in that rate as a result of an increase of rent permitted by Part IV of the Counter-Inflation (Northern Ireland) Order 1972(**a**), where that Part applied.

(3) In this Order, unless the context otherwise requires, references to any enactment shall be construed as a reference to that enactment as amended or extended by or under any other enactment.

(4) In this Order, unless the context otherwise requires, any reference to a numbered Article or paragraph is a reference to the Article or paragraph bearing that number in this Order or in the Article in question, as the case may be.

Application of this Order

3.—(1) Subject to paragraph (2), this Order shall apply to any agricultural tenancy.

(2) This Order shall not apply to—

(*a*) any letting in conacre; or

(*b*) any new letting of agricultural land.

(3) In paragraph (2)(*b*) "new letting" means any agricultural tenancy granted after 6th November 1972 where the land comprised in the tenancy consists of or includes agricultural land in relation to which there is not a standard rate.

Prevention of rent increases

4. Where, in relation to any land there is a standard rate, rent under an agricultural tenancy (whether granted before or after the commencement of this Order) comprising that land shall, subject to this Order, not be payable for that land in respect of any part of the period during which this Order is in force at a rate exceeding the standard rate.

Land re-let after 29th April 1973

5. Where an agricultural tenancy comes to an end on or after 29th April 1973 and the land is re-let (whether to the previous tenant or not) the rate at which rent is payable shall not exceed the standard rate except to the extent that any such excess is properly attributable to a variation in the terms of the tenancy.

Improvements

6. Nothing in this Order shall preclude the recovery of the cost of improvements to land comprised in an agricultural tenancy by way of an increased rent—

(*a*) where the tenancy was subsisting on 5th November 1972, in accordance with the terms of that tenancy or any agreement subsisting on that date;

(*b*) in all other cases, of an amount representing a yearly increase not exceeding $12\frac{1}{2}\%$ of that cost;

and the standard rate in relation to that land shall be increased accordingly.

(a) S.I. 1972/1913 (1972 III, p. 5695).

Recovery of excess rent

7.—(1) Subject to paragraph (3), where a tenant has paid on account of rent any amount which, by virtue of this Order, he is not liable to pay he shall be entitled to recover that amount from the landlord who received it.

(2) Subject to paragraph (3), any amount which a tenant is entitled to recover under paragraph (1) may, without prejudice to any other method of recovery, be deducted by the tenant from any rent payable by him to the landlord.

(3) No amount which a tenant is entitled to recover under paragraph (1) shall be recoverable at any time after the expiration of two years from the date of payment.

Supplemental

8. Nothing in this Order shall render unlawful any agreement, determination or notice increasing a rent to which this Order applies but, subject to this Order, no increase of any such rent provided or determined by any agreement, arbitration, determination or notice shall have effect during the period while this Order is in force.

Disclosure of information

9. Unless he has a reasonable excuse for not doing so, the landlord under an agricultural tenancy shall, within 21 days of being so requested in writing by the tenant, supply him with a statement in writing of—

(*a*) the rent which was payable at the date appropriate for the purpose of establishing the standard rate in relation to the land comprised in that tenancy;

(*b*) the cost of any improvement in respect of which the landlord is requiring an increase in rent by virtue of Article 6.

Determination of questions as to rent

10. Any dispute as to a question arising under this Order in relation to rent or the application of this Order to any land, shall be determined by the Lands Tribunal for Northern Ireland.

Transitional

11. Without prejudice to paragraph 4 of Part I of Schedule 3 to the Counter-Inflation Act 1973, any right acquired or liability or obligation incurred by virtue of, or any penalty incurred for the contravention of, this Order shall not be affected by Part II of that Act ceasing to be in force, and accordingly any investigation, legal proceedings or remedy in respect of any such right, liability, obligation or penalty may be instituted, continued or enforced as though that Part had continued in force.

W. S. I. Whitelaw,
One of Her Majesty's Principal
Secretaries of State.

Northern Ireland Office.
3rd May 1973.

EXPLANATORY NOTE

(This Note is not part of the Order.)

This Order (which applies to Northern Ireland only) makes provision, while Part II of the Counter-Inflation Act 1973 is in force, for preventing rent increases under certain agricultural tenancies.

The Order also provides for the recovery by tenants of excess payments of rent.

STATUTORY INSTRUMENTS

1973 No. 857

COUNTER-INFLATION

The Counter-Inflation (Agricultural Wages and Wages Councils) (Northern Ireland) Order 1973

Made - - -	*3rd May* 1973
Laid before Parliament	11*th May* 1973
Coming into Operation	*3rd May* 1973

In pursuance of section 8(1) of, and paragraph 1 of Schedule 2 to, the Counter-Inflation Act 1973(**a**), and all other powers enabling me in that behalf, I hereby make the following Order:—

Citation, commencement and interpretation

1.—(1) This Order may be cited as the Counter-Inflation (Agricultural Wages and Wages Councils) (Northern Ireland) Order 1973, and shall come into operation forthwith.

(2) In this Order, unless the context otherwise requires—

"the Agricultural Wages Act" means the Agricultural Wages (Regulation) Act (Northern Ireland) 1939(**b**);

"Act" includes an Act of Parliament of Northern Ireland;

"the Act of 1973" means the Counter-Inflation Act 1973;

"Agricultural Wages Board" means the Agricultural Wages Board Northern Ireland;

"the Wages Councils Act" means the Wages Councils Act (Northern Ireland) 1945(**c**);

"wages council" means a wages council in Northern Ireland.

(3) In this Order references to increases in remuneration include references to improvements in the terms and conditions of employment.

(4) Any reference in this Order to an Act shall be construed as a reference to that Act as amended or extended by or under any subsequent Act.

(5) The Interpretation Act 1889(**d**) applies to the interpretation of this Order as it applies to the interpretation of an Act of Parliament.

(**a**) 1973 c. 9.
(**c**) 1945 c. 21 (N.I.).
(**b**) 1939 c. 25 (N.I.).
(**d**) 1889 c. 63.

Modification of the Agricultural Wages (Regulation) Act (Northern Ireland) 1939

2.—(1) So long as Part II of the Act of 1973 is in force, the Agricultural Wages Act shall have effect subject to paragraphs (2) to (4) below.

(2) Section 2(9) shall be subject to a prior requirement that the Agricultural Wages Board shall submit to the Pay Board for approval any proposals for increases in remuneration to be given effect to by any order proposed to be made.

(3) The Agricultural Wages Board shall not give or serve any such notice as is referred to in paragraph (2) above relating to proposals for increases in remuneration unless those proposals have been approved by the Pay Board.

(4) The Agricultural Wages Board shall not make an order giving effect to increases in remuneration unless those increases have been approved by the Pay Board in pursuance of proposals submitted by the Agricultural Wages Board under paragraph (2) above.

Modification of the Wages Councils Act (Northern Ireland) 1945

3.—(1) So long as Part II of the Act of 1973 is in force, the Wages Councils Act shall have effect subject to paragraphs (2) to (5) below.

(2) Section 10(3) shall be subject to a prior requirement that the wages council shall submit to the Pay Board any wages regulation proposals relating to increases in remuneration for approval; and accordingly a wages council shall not publish any wages regulation proposals or give notice of such proposals to persons affected thereby, under that section, until the wages regulation proposals relating to increases in remuneration have been approved by that Board.

(3) Where wages regulation proposals relating to increases in remuneration have already been published by a wages council under that section, that council may submit the proposals to the Pay Board for approval.

(4) Where pursuant to paragraph 2(2) and (3) of Schedule 2 to the Act of 1973, the Pay Board approve, subject to amendments or modifications, any proposals submitted under paragraph (3) above, section 10(3) shall not impose a duty on the wages council to re-publish, or give notice to the persons affected thereby, the proposals as so amended or modified.

(5) Section 10(4) shall not impose a duty on the Ministry of Health and Social Services to make an order giving effect to any wages regulation proposals relating to increases in remuneration which have not been approved by the Pay Board.

Approval of certain proposals for increase in remuneration

4.—(1) The Pay Board shall entertain any proposals for increases in remuneration—

    (*a*) submitted to them by the Agricultural Wages Board; or

    (*b*) contained in any wages regulation proposals submitted to them by a wages council.

(2) Where the Pay Board are satisfied that any such increases ought to be allowed, they shall approve the proposals.

(3) The Pay Board shall give their decision whether or not to approve any such proposals within 8 weeks of the date on which they receive them.

(4) Where the Pay Board do not give their decision under paragraph (3) above before the expiration of the period specified in that paragraph, they shall for the purposes of paragraph 2(1) of Schedule 2 to the Act of 1973 be deemed to have approved the proposals as submitted.

W. S. I. Whitelaw,
One of Her Majesty's Principal
Secretaries of State.

Northern Ireland Office.

3rd May 1973.

EXPLANATORY NOTE

(This Note is not part of the Order.)

This Order modifies the Agricultural Wages (Regulation) Act (Northern Ireland) 1939 and the Wages Councils Act (Northern Ireland) 1945, while Part II of the Counter-Inflation Act 1973 is in force. Under Articles 2 and 3 the Agricultural Wages Board and wages councils must submit proposals for pay increases (or improvements in the terms and conditions of employment) to the Pay Board; in addition the Ministry of Health and Social Services need not make an order giving effect to the proposals of a wages council until they have been approved by the Pay Board.

STATUTORY INSTRUMENTS

1973 No. 859 (S.67)

RATING AND VALUATION

The Rating of Industry (Scotland) Order 1973

Made - - -	4th April 1973
Laid before the Commons House of Parliament	13th April 1973
Coming into Operation	1st May 1973

In exercise of the powers conferred on me by section 10(2) of the Local Government (Financial Provisions) (Scotland) Act 1963(a) and of all other powers enabling me in that behalf, I hereby make the following order:—

1. This order may be cited as the Rating of Industry (Scotland) Order 1973 and shall come into operation on the day following the day on which it is approved by resolution of the Commons House of Parliament.

2. The Interpretation Act 1889(b) shall apply for the interpretation of this order as it applies for the interpretation of an Act of Parliament.

3. In respect of the years 1973/74 and 1974/75, the rateable value of any industrial or freight transport lands and heritages so far as occupied and used or treated as occupied and used for industrial or freight transport purposes shall be the amount produced by deducting from the net annual value thereof fifty per cent. of that value.

Gordon Campbell,
One of Her Majesty's Principal
Secretaries of State.

St. Andrew's House,
Edinburgh.
4th April 1973.

EXPLANATORY NOTE

(*This Note is not part of the Order.*)

This Order provides that the present de-rating to the extent of 50 per cent. in respect of industrial and freight transport lands and heritages shall continue for a further two years.

(a) 1963 c. 12. (b) 1889 c. 63.

STATUTORY INSTRUMENTS

1973 No. 860

INDUSTRIAL TRAINING

The Industrial Training (Road Transport Board) Order 1966 (Amendment) Order 1973

Made - - -	*3rd May* 1973
Laid before Parliament	*14th May* 1973
Coming into Operation	*8th June* 1973

The Secretary of State after consultation with the Road Transport Industry Training Board and with organisations and associations of organisations appearing to be representative respectively of substantial numbers of employers engaging in the activities hereinafter mentioned and of substantial numbers of persons employed in those activities and with the bodies established for the purpose of carrying on under national ownership industries in which the said activities are carried on to a substantial extent and in exercise of powers conferred by section 9 of the Industrial Training Act 1964(a) and now vested in him(b), and of all other powers enabling him in that behalf hereby makes the following Order : —

Citation, commencement and interpretation

1.—(1) This Order may be cited as the Industrial Training (Road Transport Board) Order 1966 (Amendment) Order 1973 and shall come into operation on 8th June 1973.

(2) In this Order—

    (*a*) "the Act" means the Industrial Training Act 1964;

    (*b*) "the Board" means the Road Transport Industry Training Board;

    (*c*) "Levy Order" includes the Industrial Training Levy (Road Transport) Order 1967(c), the Industrial Training Levy (Road Transport) Order 1968(d), the Industrial Training Levy (Road Transport) Order 1969(e), the Industrial Training Levy (Road Transport) Order 1970(f), the Industrial Training Levy (Road Transport) Order 1971(g), and the Industrial Training Levy (Road Transport) Order 1972(h);

    (*d*) "the 1972 Order" means the Industrial Training (Road Transport Board) Order 1972(i);

    (*e*) "the principal Order" means the Industrial Training (Road Transport Board) Order 1966(j).

(a) 1964 c. 16.
(b) S.I. 1968/729 (1968 II, p. 2108).
(c) S.I. 1967/1309 (1967 III, p. 3939).
(d) S.I. 1968/1835 (1968 III, p.4841).
(e) S.I. 1969/880 (1969 II, p. 2503).
(f) S.I. 1970/1062 (1970 II, p. 3305).
(g) S.I. 1971/1049 (1971 II, p. 3135).
(h) S.I. 1972/880 (1972 II, p. 2817).
(i) S.I. 1972/772 (1972 II, p. 2471).
(j) S.I. 1966/1112 (1966 III, p. 2712).

(3) The Interpretation Act 1889(**a**) shall apply to the interpretation of this Order as it applies to the interpretation of an Act of Parliament and as if this Order, the principal Order and the 1972 Order were Acts of Parliament.

Amendment of the principal Order

2. The principal Order (as amended by the 1972 Order) shall be further amended in accordance with the Schedule to this Order, and accordingly the activities in relation to which the Board exercises the functions conferred by the Act upon industrial training boards shall be the activities specified in Schedule 1 to the principal Order, as amended by the 1972 Order and this Order.

Transitional provisions

3.—(1) The chairman and other members of the Board on the day upon which this Order comes into operation shall continue to be members of the Board and to hold and vacate their offices in accordance with the terms of the instruments appointing them to be members.

(2) The provisions of this Order shall not—

    (*a*) extend the operation of a Levy Order;

    (*b*) affect the operation of a Levy Order in relation to the assessment of an employer within the meaning of that Order in respect of an establishment that was engaged in the relevant levy period wholly or mainly in activities included in Schedule 1 to the principal Order as amended by the 1972 Order and this Order.

    (*c*) affect the operation of any assessment notice served by the Board under the provisions of a Levy Order before the date upon which this Order comes into operation or any appeal or other proceedings arising out of any such notice.

Signed by order of the Secretary of State.

3rd May 1973.

R. Chichester-Clark,
Minister of State,
Department of Employment.

(**a**) 1889 c. 63.

SCHEDULE

Amendments to the Principal Order (as amended by the 1972 Order)

1. In this Schedule the expression "the Schedule" means Schedule 1 to the principal Order (as amended by the 1972 Order).

2.—(1) Paragraph 2 of the Schedule shall be amended as follows.

(2) For sub-paragraph (c)(v) there shall be substituted the following—

"(v) in the operation of taxi-cabs or private car hire;".

(3) For sub-paragraph (d)(ii) there shall be substituted the following—

"(ii) the British Gas Corporation;".

3. In paragraph 3 of the Schedule, immediately after the definition of "principal activities of the road transport industry" there shall be inserted the following—

" 'private car hire' means the provision, together with services of a driver, of a motor vehicle (other than a taxi-cab) which is designed to carry less than eight passengers;".

4. In the Appendix to the Schedule the following entry shall be substituted for the corresponding entry appearing in that Appendix—

Column 1	Column 2	Column 3
The construction industry	The Industrial Training (Construction Board) Order 1964 as amended by the Industrial Training (Construction Board) Order 1973(a).	Schedule 1 Paragraph 1(h)

EXPLANATORY NOTE

(*This Note is not part of the Order.*)

This Order further amends the Industrial Training (Road Transport Board) Order 1966 (which was amended by the Industrial Training (Road Transport Board) Order 1972) which specifies the activities in relation to which the Road Transport Industry Training Board exercises its functions.

There will henceforth be excluded from the industry the activities of any establishment engaged wholly or mainly in the operation of private car hire.

(a) S.I. 1964/1079, 1973/160 (1964 II, p. 2384; 1973 I, p. 654).

STATUTORY INSTRUMENTS

1973 No. 862

CUSTOMS AND EXCISE

The Import Duties (Temporary Reductions) (No. 2) Order 1973

Made - - -		*4th May* 1973
Laid before the House of Commons		*4th May* 1973
Coming into Operation		*4th May* 1973

The Lords Commissioners of Her Majesty's Treasury, by virtue of the powers conferred on them by sections 1, 3(6) and 13 of the Import Duties Act 1958(a) and of all other powers enabling them in that behalf, on the recommendation of the Secretary of State(b), hereby make the following Order:—

1.—(1) This Order may be cited as the Import Duties (Temporary Reductions) (No. 2) Order 1973.

(2) The Interpretation Act 1889(c) shall apply for the interpretation of this Order as it applies for the interpretation of an Act of Parliament.

(3) This Order shall come into operation on 4th May 1973.

2.—(1) Until the beginning of 14th May 1973 any import duty which is for the time being chargeable on goods of a subheading of the Customs Tariff 1959 specified in column 1 of the Schedule hereto shall be chargeable—

(*a*) at the rate, if any, specified in column 2 opposite the relevant subheading in the case of goods chargeable to import duty at the full rate and

(*b*) at the rate, if any, specified in column 3 opposite the relevant subheading in the case of goods of Austria, Finland, Iceland, Norway, Portugal, Sweden or Switzerland,

and if no rate of duty is so specified in the said column 3 no duty shall be chargeable on goods of the relevant subheading if they are goods of the kind referred to in paragraph (*a*) or (*b*) above, as the case may be.

(2) Until the beginning of 14th May 1973 no import duty shall be chargeable on goods of a subheading of the Customs Tariff 1959 specified in the said column 1 of the Schedule hereto or of subheading (B)(1) of heading 15.02 (fats of bovine cattle) if the goods qualify for Commonwealth preference.

3. For the purposes of classification under the Customs Tariff 1959, in so far as that depends on the rate of duty, any goods to which Article 2 above applies shall be treated as chargeable with the same duty as if this Order had not been made.

(a) 1958 c. 6. (b) *See* S.I. 1970/1537 (1970 III, p. 5293).
(c) 1889 c. 63.

4th May 1973.

Hugh Rossi,
V. H. Goodhew,
Two of the Lords Commissioners
of Her Majesty's Treasury.

SCHEDULE
REDUCED RATES OF DUTY

1 *Tariff subheading*	2 *Full*	3 *EFTA Countries*
02.01 (Meat and edible offals, fresh, chilled or frozen)		
(B)(II)(*b*)(1)	10%	10%
(B)(II)(*b*)(2)(*aa*)	—	—
(B)(II)(*b*)(2)(*bb*)	10%	10%
02.06 (Meat and edible meat offals, salted, in brine, dried or smoked)		
(C)(I)(*a*)(1)	£0·3110 per cwt.	£0·3110 per cwt.
(C)(I)(*a*)(2)	20%	20%
(C)(I)(*b*)(1)	—	—
(C)(I)(*b*)(2)	20%	20%
16.02 (Other prepared or preserved meat or meat offal)		
(B)(III)(*b*)(1)(*aa*)(11)	15%	—
(B)(III)(*b*)(1)(*aa*)(22)	15%	15%
(B)(III)(*b*)(1)(*bb*)(11)(*aaa*)	15%	15%
(B)(III)(*b*)(1)(*bb*)(11)(*bbb*)	10%	10%
(B)(III)(*b*)(1)(*bb*)(22)	15%	15%

EXPLANATORY NOTE
(*This Note is not part of the Order.*)

This Order reduces the full rates of import duty and the rates applicable to E.F.T.A. countries on beef and veal products specified in the Schedule until 14th May 1973. This Order also provides for no import duty to be charged until the same date on those products and on certain beef fats in the case of goods qualifying for Commonwealth preference. (The rates resulting from this Order are those which were chargeable on the relevant goods immediately before 30th April 1973.)

STATUTORY INSTRUMENTS

1973 No. 863

CUSTOMS AND EXCISE

The Import Duties (Process) Order 1973

Made - - -		*4th May* 1973
Laid before the House of Commons		*7th May* 1973
Coming into Operation		*28th May* 1973

The Secretary of State, in exercise of powers conferred by section 8(5) of the Import Duties Act 1958(**a**), as amended by paragraph 1 of Schedule 4 to the European Communities Act 1972(**b**), and of all other powers enabling him in that behalf, hereby makes the following Order:—

1.—(1) This Order may be cited as the Import Duties (Process) Order 1973.

(2) The Interpretation Act 1889(**c**) shall apply for the interpretation of this Order as it applies for the interpretation of an Act of Parliament.

(3) This Order shall come into operation on 28th May 1973.

2.—(1) Where there is imported into the United Kingdom any colour negative film, classifiable under heading 37.05 of the Customs Tariff 1959 (exposed and developed plates and film, negative or positive), being film which—

(*a*) has been previously exported from the United Kingdom; and

(*b*) after being so exported has undergone outside the United Kingdom a process of developing,

then subsection (5) of section 8 of the Import Duties Act 1958 shall not have effect so as to exclude subsections (1) to (4) of that section by reason only of any difference attributable to that process between the rate of import duty under heading 37.05 and that applicable to the like goods referred to in subsection (2) of that section.

(2) Where subsections (1) to (4) of the said section 8 would not apply but for this Order, any reduction under that section of the import duty chargeable on the imported goods shall be calculated as if the like goods referred to in subsection (2) of that section were chargeable with the rate of duty applicable to the imported goods under heading 37.05.

4th May 1973.

Limerick,
Parliamentary Under Secretary of State,
Department of Trade and Industry.

(**a**) 1958 c. 6. (**b**) 1972 c. 68.
(**c**) 1889 c. 63.

EXPLANATORY NOTE

(This Note is not part of the Order.)

This Order, made under section 8(5) of the Import Duties Act 1958, provides that colour negative film, exposed but not developed, which is sent abroad for the process of development and re-imported in bulk will be chargeable on its return with customs duty in respect only of the increased value attributable to the process.

STATUTORY INSTRUMENTS

1973 No. 864 (S.68)

EDUCATION, SCOTLAND

The Teachers (Education, Training and Registration) (Scotland) Amendment Regulations 1973

Made - - -	*3rd May* 1973
Laid before Parliament	11*th May* 1973

Coming into Operation—

for the purposes of paragraphs	
(1)(*b*), (2)(*b*), (3)(*a*) *and*	
(4) *of regulation 2*	1*st June* 1973
for all other purposes	1*st August* 1974

In exercise of the powers conferred on me by section 7(1) of the Teaching Council (Scotland) Act 1965(**a**), and by section 144(5) of the Education (Scotland) Act 1962(**b**), as applied by section 7(8) of the said Act of 1965, as amended by the Education (Scotland) Act 1969(**c**), and of all other powers enabling me in that behalf and—

(i) after affording under section 7(5) of the said Act of 1965, as amended aforesaid, to the General Teaching Council for Scotland an opportunity of considering a draft of the following regulations and no representations having been made by them; and

(ii) after causing under section 7(8A) of the said Act of 1965, as amended aforesaid, a draft of the following regulations to be published and a copy to be sent to every education authority, and no representations having been made by them or by any person interested,

I hereby make the following regulations:—

Citation, construction and commencement

1.—(1) These regulations may be cited as the Teachers (Education, Training and Registration) (Scotland) Amendment Regulations 1973 and shall be construed as one with the Teachers (Education, Training and Registration) (Scotland) Regulations 1967(**d**) as amended(**e**) (hereinafter referred to as the "principal regulations").

(a) 1965 c. 19.   (b) 1962 c. 47.   (c) 1969 c. 49.

(d) S.l. 1967/1162 (1967 II, p. 3396).

(e) S.I. 1969/1341, 1971/903 (1969 III, p. 3982; 1971 II, p. 2620).

(2) These regulations shall come into operation as follows:—

(*a*) for the purposes of paragraphs (1)(*b*), (2)(*b*), (3)(*a*) and (4) of regulation 2 on 1st June 1973;

(*b*) for all other purposes on 1st August 1974.

Amendment of Schedule 1 *to the principal regulations*

2. In Schedule 1 to the principal regulations—

(1) in paragraph 1(5)—

(*a*) head (*c*)(iii) shall be omitted;

(*b*) in proviso (i) to head (*c*) after the word "satisfactory" there shall be added the words "and in relation to any subject on the Ordinary grade of the Scottish Certificate of Education examination for any year after 1972 means a performance therein falling within band A, B or C"; and

(*c*) head (*d*)(i) shall be omitted;

(2) in paragraph 1(6)—

(*a*) head (*a*)(ii) shall be omitted;

(*b*) in proviso (i) to head (*a*) after the word "satisfactory" there shall be added the words "and in relation to any subject on the Ordinary grade of the Scottish Certificate of Education examination for any year after 1972 means a performance therein falling within band A, B or C"; and

(*c*) head (*b*)(i) shall be omitted.

(3) in paragraph 2(1)—

(*a*) in head (*g*) after the words "said sub-paragraph (5)" there shall be inserted the words ", other than proviso (i) to head (*c*) thereof,"; and

(*b*) after head (*g*) there shall be inserted the following head:—

"(*h*) for the purposes of heads (*a*) to (*f*) of this sub-paragraph—

(i) sub-paragraph (5)(*c*) of paragraph 1 of this Schedule shall be deemed to include the following sub-paragraph:—

'(iii) passes in at least 2 subjects on the Higher grade and in 3 other subjects on the Lower grade or in 4 other subjects on the Ordinary grade;'; and

(ii) sub-paragraph (5)(*d*) of paragraph 1 of this Schedule shall be deemed to include the following sub-paragraph:—

'(i) a pass in at least 1 subject at Advanced level and passes in 6 other subjects; or'".

(4) In paragraph 3(2) after the word "Council" where it occurs for the second time there shall be inserted the following words:—

": provided that the word "pass" in relation to any subject on the Ordinary grade of the Scottish Certificate of Education examination for any year after 1972 means a performance falling within band A, B or C".

Gordon Campbell,
One of Her Majesty's
Principal Secretaries of State.

St. Andrew's House,
Edinburgh.
3rd May 1973.

EXPLANATORY NOTE

(This Note is not part of the Regulations.)

These Regulations amend the Teachers (Education, Training and Registration) (Scotland) Regulations 1967, as previously amended. They provide that—

(a) from 1st June 1973, in relation to the requirements for admission to a course leading to a teaching qualification, a performance in any Ordinary grade examination of the Scottish Certificate of Education after 1972 is to be regarded as a pass if it falls within band A, B or C;

(b) from 1st August 1974, the minimum requirements for admission to a course leading to a Teaching Qualification (Primary Education) are raised to 3 passes on the Higher grade and 2 on the Lower or Ordinary grade, and in the case of the General Certificate of Education examination to 2 passes at Advanced level and 4 other passes; and for persons aged 23 or over to 3 passes on the Higher grade, and in the case of the General Certificate of Education examination, to 2 passes at Advanced level and 2 other passes;

(c) subject to the change described in (a) above, the requirements for admission to a course leading to a Teaching Qualification (Secondary Education) or a Teaching Qualification (Further Education) remain unchanged.

STATUTORY INSTRUMENTS

1973 No. 865 (S.69)

AGRICULTURE

LIVESTOCK INDUSTRIES,

The Beef Cow (Scotland) (Amendment) Scheme 1973

Made - - -	*2nd May* 1973
Laid before Parliament	11*th May* 1973
Coming into Operation	1*st June* 1973

In exercise of the powers conferred on me by section 12 of the Agriculture Act 1967(**a**) and of all other powers enabling me in that behalf, and with the approval of the Treasury, I hereby make the following scheme:—

Citation, commencement and interpretation

1. This scheme, which may be cited as the Beef Cow (Scotland) (Amendment) Scheme 1973, shall be construed as one with the Beef Cow (Scotland) Scheme 1972(**b**) (in this scheme referred to as "the principal scheme") and shall come into operation on 1st June 1973.

Amendment of the Principal Scheme

2. Paragraph 2(1) of the principal scheme shall be amended by deleting all reference to "December Return" and by substituting for the definition of "June Return" the following definition:—

" 'June Return' means the return of information required by the Secretary of State in exercise of the powers conferred on him by the Agriculture Act 1947(**c**) as amended by the Agriculture (Miscellaneous Provisions) Act 1972(**d**) to be made by occupiers of land used for agriculture with respect to a date in June."

3.—(1) Paragraph 6(*b*) of the principal scheme shall be amended to read— "the number of cows and in-calf heifers comprised in the herd on the 4th day in the immediately preceding December,"

(2) The words "or no such December" shall be deleted from sub-paragraph (i) of the proviso to paragraph 6.

(3) In paragraph 7(1)(*c*) of the principal scheme, the words "date of the December Return made in that period" shall be deleted and there shall be substituted therefor the words "4th day of the month of December in that period".

(**a**) 1967 c. 22.
(**c**) 1947 c. 48.

(**b**) S.I. 1972/727 (1972 II, p. 2292).
(**d**) 1972 c. 62.

Gordon Campbell,
One of Her Majesty's Principal
Secretaries of State.

St. Andrew's House,
Edinburgh.

30th April 1973.

We approve.

2nd May 1973.

Tim Fortescue,
Oscar Murton,
Two of the Lords Commissioners
of Her Majesty's Treasury.

EXPLANATORY NOTE

(This Note is not part of the Scheme.)

This Scheme amends the definition of "June Return" and deletes the definition of "December Return" following the amendment of the Agriculture Act 1947 by the Agriculture (Miscellaneous Provisions) Act 1972.

STATUTORY INSTRUMENTS

1973 No. 866 (S.70)

AGRICULTURE

HILL LANDS

The Hill Cattle (Scotland) Scheme 1973

Made - - -		*2nd May* 1973
Laid before Parliament		11*th May* 1973
Coming into Operation		1*st June* 1973

In exercise of the powers conferred on me by sections 13, 14 and 15 of the Hill Farming Act 1946(**a**), as extended by section 43 of the Agriculture Act 1967(**b**), and of all other powers enabling me in that behalf, and with the approval of the Treasury, I hereby make the following scheme:—

Citation and commencement

1. This scheme may be cited as the Hill Cattle (Scotland) Scheme 1973 and shall come into operation on 1st June 1973.

Interpretation

2.—(1) In this scheme, unless the context otherwise requires—

"agricultural unit", except as provided by paragraph 4(2) of this scheme, means land which is occupied as a unit for agricultural purposes, together with any other land, including land held in common, used in connection with such land for the purpose of grazing;

"applicant" means a person who makes application for a subsidy payment, and "application" shall be construed accordingly;

"breeding cow" means a female bovine animal which has borne a calf;

"crofter" means a crofter within the meaning of the Crofters (Scotland) Acts 1955 and 1961(**c**);

"eligible occupier" means a person who is for the time being an eligible occupier within the meaning of the Crofting Counties Agricultural Grants (Scotland) Scheme 1961(**d**), the Crofting Counties Agricultural Grants (Scotland) Scheme 1963(**e**), the Crofting Counties Agricultural Grants (Scotland) Scheme 1965(**f**) or the Crofting Counties Agricultural Grants (Scotland) Scheme 1972(**g**) and, except in the case of a person who is a sub-tenant as is mentioned in section 14(1)(*c*) of the Crofters (Scotland) Act 1961, who has been offered a grant under any of the said schemes;

"in-calf heifer" means a female bovine animal which is with calf for the first time;

(**a**) 1946 c. 73.
(**b**) 1967 c. 22.
(**c**) 1955 c. 21; 1961 c. 58.
(**d**) S.I. 1961/2266 (1961 III, p. 3973).
(**e**) S.I. 1963/1294 (1963 II, p. 2240).
(**f**) S.I. 1965/1519 (1965 II, p. 4399).
(**g**) S.I. 1972/407 (1972 I, p. 1499).

"June Return" means the return of information required by the Secretary of State in exercise of the powers conferred on him by the Agriculture Act 1947(a) as amended by the Agriculture (Miscellaneous Provisions) Act 1972(b) to be made by occupiers of land used for agriculture with respect to a date in June;

"qualifying day" in relation to any of the relevant years, means the day which coincides with the date of the June Return in that year;

"regular breeding herd" means a herd of cattle maintained and managed in accordance with sound herd management practice by the occupier of hill land for the production and rearing of calves and consisting mainly of breeding cows, being cows which have been grazed on hill land throughout the relevant period;

"relevant period" in relation to any of the relevant years, means the period from 1st October in the year immediately preceding that relevant year to 30th September in the relevant year or, where there occurs on or after the qualifying day in the relevant year and not later than the said 30th September a change of occupancy of the hill land (being the hill land specified in the application), the period from the said 1st October to the date of the occurrence of that change;

"relevant years" means the year 1973 and the four next succeeding years;

"subsidy payment" means a payment falling to be made in accordance with the provisions of this scheme.

(2) In this scheme:—

"hill land" means, subject to the following provisions of this sub-paragraph, land which is livestock rearing land as defined in section 1(3) of the Livestock Rearing Act 1951(c) that is to say, land situated in an area consisting predominantly of mountains, hills or heath, being land which is, or by improvement could be made, suitable for use for the breeding, rearing and maintenance of sheep or cattle but not for the carrying on, to any material extent, of dairy farming, the production, to any material extent, of fat sheep or fat cattle, or the production of crops in quantity materially greater than that necessary to feed the number of sheep or cattle capable of being maintained on the land:

Provided that in any case where an agricultural unit consists in part only of such land, such land shall be deemed not to be hill land unless, in the opinion of the Secretary of State, it comprises an area suitable to be dealt with as a unit and is capable, taking into account the numbers of any other livestock normally grazed thereon, of carrying a regular breeding herd.

(3) Where at any time after 2nd July 1968 land is hill land as defined in sub-paragraph (2) of this paragraph, the effect of any subsequent improvement to that land shall be disregarded in determining for the purposes of this scheme whether it is hill land.

(4) Any reference in this scheme to any other scheme shall be construed as a reference to such scheme as amended by any subsequent scheme, and if any scheme referred to in this scheme is replaced by any subsequent scheme, the reference shall be construed as a reference to such subsequent scheme.

(5) The Interpretation Act 1889(d) shall apply for the interpretation of this scheme as it applies for the interpretation of an Act of Parliament.

(a) 1947 c. 48.   (b) 1972 c. 62.
(c) 1951 c. 18.   (d) 1889 c. 63.

Subsidy payment

3. Subject to the provisions of this scheme, the Secretary of State may, in respect of each of the relevant years, make a subsidy payment in respect of any cow in the case of which the provisions of this scheme have been complied with.

Amount of subsidy payment and reduction in certain circumstances

4.—(1) Subject to the provisions of sub-paragraph (2) of this paragraph, a subsidy payment in respect of a cow shall be of such amount as may be prescribed by order made by the Secretary of State under section 14(3) of the Hill Farming Act 1946.

(2) There shall be reduced by the sum of £5·75 the amount of a subsidy payment as so prescribed which may be paid in respect of any of the relevant years in respect of any cow grazed and maintained on hill land—

(*a*) being land comprising or forming part of an agricultural unit in which is comprised any land in respect of which (i) an application for grant for the year commencing with 1st January of that year has been submitted under the Winter Keep (Scotland) Scheme 1969(**a**), and (ii) grant for the year commencing as aforesaid has been paid or in the opinion of the Secretary of State is payable under that scheme, or would, but for the provisions of paragraph 4 or 7 thereof, have been payable thereunder, or

(*b*) being land occupied by any person as a crofter or as an eligible occupier including, in relation to a cow grazed and maintained by any such person, any pasture or grazing land in which that person has any right, whether alone or in common with others, being a right which is deemed to form part of, or is held along with, the croft or holding of which he is the occupier.

In this sub-paragraph the expression "agricultural unit" means land, other than land occupied by any person as a crofter or as an eligible occupier, which is occupied as a unit for agricultural purposes, together with any other land, including land held in common, used in connection with such land for the purpose of grazing.

Persons eligible for subsidy payment

5.—(1) Subject to the provisions of sub-paragraph (2) of this paragraph, a subsidy payment shall be made only to the person who is the occupier as at the beginning of the qualifying day of the hill land specified in his application.

(2) Notwithstanding the provisions of sub-paragraph (1) of this paragraph where, in accordance with paragraph 6(2) of this scheme, an application is made as therein mentioned by the Clerk to a committee appointed for the management of a common grazings or common pasture or by such other person as may be authorised, the subsidy payment falling to be made by virtue of the application shall be made to the Clerk or, as the case may be, to that other person, and the Clerk or that other person shall forthwith make payment of the subsidy payment to the person referred to in sub-paragraph (1) of this paragraph.

(a) S.I. 1969/1845 (1969 III, p. 5769).

Application for subsidy payment

6.—(1) Subject to the provisions of sub-paragraph (2) of this paragraph, a subsidy payment in respect of a cow in respect in any of the relevant years shall not be made by the Secretary of State unless an application therefor has been: —

   (*a*) made, in such manner as the Secretary of State may require, by the person who is the occupier of the hill land specified in the application as at the beginning of the qualifying day in that year; and

   (*b*) received by the Secretary of State by such date as he may require;

Provided that the Secretary of State may, in the case of any such application as is not received by the date required but in regard to which it appears to him that the circumstances are exceptional and that the application should be entertained, treat the application as having been received by that date.

(2) An application made in respect of a cow belonging to the occupier of a holding to which the Small Landholders (Scotland) Acts 1886 to 1931(**a**) or the Crofters (Scotland) Acts 1955 and 1961 apply, being a holding comprised in a township having common grazings or a common pasture, may, if not made by the occupier, be made in accordance with the following provisions of this sub-paragraph, that is to say—

   (*a*) where a committee has been appointed for the management of the common grazings or common pasture, and there is in office a Clerk to that committee, by the Clerk;

   (*b*) in any other case, by a person who has been duly authorised by the occupiers of the holdings in that township, in a manner satisfactory to the Secretary of State, to make the application.

Description of cattle in respect of which subsidy payments may be made

7.—(1) Subject to the provisions of this scheme, a subsidy payment may be made in respect of any of the relevant years in respect of a cow which is a breeding cow on the qualifying day, is of a type and quality approved by the Secretary of State and in the case of which he is satisfied that it—

   (*a*) has been grazed and maintained for the production and rearing of calves in accordance with sound herd management practice by the occupier of the hill land specified in the application made by him for that year in respect of it;

   (*b*) has been so grazed and maintained on hill land throughout the relevant period; and

   (*c*) will continue to be grazed on hill land for a substantial part of its breeding life.

(2) Where a breeding cow is included in a regular breeding herd, head (*c*) of sub-paragraph (1) of this paragraph shall be deemed to be complied with in the case of that cow in any relevant year if the Secretary of State is satisfied that the said occupier intends to continue to maintain a regular breeding herd on hill land.

(**a**) 1886 c. 29; 1887 c. 24; 1891 c. 41; 1908 c. 50; 1911 c. 49; 1919 c. 97; 1931 c. 44.

Management of cattle

8.—(1) This paragraph shall have effect for the purpose of determining whether the provisions of paragraph 7(1)(*b*) have, in any of the relevant years, been complied with in the case of any cow in respect of which an application is made in respect of that year—that is to say for determining whether the cow has been grazed and maintained for the production and rearing of calves in accordance with sound herd management practice on hill land throughout the relevant period.

(2) Where the cow is owned by the occupier of a holding to which the Small Landholders (Scotland) Acts 1886 to 1931 or, as the case may be, the Crofters (Scotland) Acts 1955 and 1961 apply, being a holding comprised in a township, and has been grazed and maintained for the production and rearing of calves in accordance with sound herd management practice throughout the relevant period either on the common grazings or common pasture of the township or on that holding or partly on the common grazings or common pasture and partly on the holding, and those grazings or that pasture or holding, or both those grazings or that pasture and that holding, as the case may be, are hill land, the provisions of paragraph 7(1)(*b*) shall be deemed to have been complied with.

(3) The cow, if it is included in a regular breeding herd, shall be deemed to have been grazed and maintained on hill land throughout any period (hereafter in this paragraph referred to as "the wintering period") during which the cow has in the winter months occurring in the relevant period been grazed and maintained on land other than hill land if the Secretary of State is satisfied that—

(*a*) in all the circumstances it was necessary, other than on account of excessive stocking, to maintain all or some of the breeding cows or in-calf heifers included in the herd during the wintering period on land other than hill land during that period;

(*b*) the maintenance of the breeding cows or in-calf heifers during the wintering period conformed to sound herd management practice; and

(*c*) the wintering period was not longer than was in all the circumstances necessary.

(4) Where the cow was not being grazed and maintained at the commencement of the relevant period on hill land but was, on a date not later than 4th December in that period or by such later date as the Secretary of State may in exceptional circumstances allow, brought on to such land for the first time, the cow shall be deemed to have been grazed and maintained on that land during the period between the date of commencement of the relevant period and the date when it was brought on to that land.

(5) Where—

(*a*) a cow being grazed and maintained on hill land dies or in accordance with sound herd management practice ceases to be so grazed and maintained; and

(*b*) a suitable replacement is brought on to that land,

the provisions of paragraph 7(1)(*b*) shall be deemed to have been complied with in respect of the cow if, subject to the provisions of this scheme, at every part of the relevant period there was being grazed and maintained on the said land for the production and rearing of calves in accordance with sound herd management practice either the cow or its replacement, there being disregarded for the purposes of this sub-paragraph any interval which in the opinion of the Secretary of State was not unreasonably long between the date the cow died or ceased to be so grazed and maintained and the date its replacement was brought on to the said land.

(6) If during any period between the commencement of the relevant period and the date of the June Return made in the relevant period, the cow was an in-calf heifer, references in paragraph 7 to a breeding cow shall, in their application to that cow in respect of that period, include references to it as if it had then been a breeding cow.

Number of cows qualifying for subsidy payments

9. Subject to the provisions of this and the two next succeeding paragraphs, the number of cows in respect of which subsidy payments may be made to an occupier of hill land in respect of any of the relevant years shall be equal to—

> (*a*) the number of breeding cows grazed and maintained on hill land (being the land specified in his application or in the application made on his behalf) on the qualifying day in that year and included in the June Return required to be made as at that day in respect of that land, or

> (*b*) the number of breeding cows and in-calf heifers so grazed and maintained on the 4th day in the immediately preceding December,

whichever is the less:

Provided that where the Secretary of State is satisfied that—

> (i) no such June Return has been made, or

> (ii) any such Return which has been made is inaccurate in respect of the number of breeding cows included therein or is inappropriate for the computation of the number of cows in respect of which subsidy payments fall to be made, or

> (iii) the number of breeding cows or in-calf heifers on the qualifying day or on the 4th day in the immediately preceding December is less, having regard to the provisions of paragraph 8 of this scheme, than the number of breeding cows or in-calf heifers grazed and maintained by the occupier on hill land throughout the relevant period;

the number of cows in respect of which subsidy payments may be made as aforesaid shall be equal to such number as the Secretary of State, having regard to all the circumstances, deems to be the number of cows in respect of which subsidy payments should be made.

Reduction of number of cows in respect of which subsidy payments may be made

10.—(1) Where the Secretary of State is satisfied that the number of cows in respect of which subsidy payments would otherwise fall to be made to an applicant in respect of any of the relevant years exceeds the number of cows, being cows to which his application for that year relates, which have been grazed and maintained throughout the relevant period in accordance with the provisions of this scheme, the number of cows in respect of which subsidy payments may be made shall be such lesser number as the Secretary of State may determine but not exceeding the number of cows grazed and maintained as aforesaid.

In making a determination for the purposes of this sub-paragraph in relation to any application, the Secretary of State may have regard to the number of cows and in-calf heifers found to be grazed and maintained on the hill land specified in the application at any inspection of such cows and in-calf heifers in relation to the relevant period carried out by a person authorised by the Secretary of State in that behalf.

(2) Where the Secretary of State is of the opinion that the number of cows in respect of which subsidy payments would otherwise fall to be made to an applicant in respect of any of the relevant years exceeds the number of cows which the hill land on which the cows to which his application for that year relates were grazed and maintained during the relevant period was, taking into account the numbers of any other livestock normally grazed on that land, capable of carrying, or that the cows to which an application for any of the relevant years relates produced an unsatisfactory number of calves during the relevant period, the Secretary of State may make subsidy payments in respect of such lesser number of cows as he may determine.

Disqualification

11. A subsidy payment shall not be made in respect of any cow in respect of any of the relevant years if the Secretary of State is satisfied that—

(a) it was kept during the relevant period for production of milk for sale, for the making of milk products for sale or for a domestic milk supply; or

(b) the management of the cow, including the selection of the bull used to produce a calf, was not in accordance with sound herd management practice.

Recovery of subsidy payments

12. Where, in the opinion of the Secretary of State, any subsidy payment made to any person in respect of a cow should not have been made because the provisions of this scheme had not been complied with by that person either before or after the receipt by him of such payment, the Secretary of State may recover the subsidy payment so made and (without prejudice to any other mode of recovery available to him) may recover that payment by withholding payment of any subsequent subsidy payment which would otherwise fall to be made to that person.

Count and inspection

13. A person authorised by the Secretary of State in that behalf may require an applicant for subsidy payments to gather or cause to be gathered the cows to which his application relates for the purpose of the counting or inspection on behalf of the Secretary of State of the cows, and to give all reasonable assistance and information for the purposes of any such authority as aforesaid, and failure by the applicant to gather the cows or cause them to be gathered or to give such assistance or information as aforesaid shall be a ground upon which the Secretary of State may withhold all or any of the subsidy payments which would otherwise be payable to the applicant.

Prohibition of assignation of subsidy payments

14. Any subsidy payment in respect of any of the relevant years may be made to a person who, if such payment had been a debt which at the beginning

of the qualifying day in that year accrued due to the person who then occupied the hill land specified in the application for the payment, would have been entitled to claim the payment otherwise than by virtue of an assignation.

                                             Gordon Campbell,
                                    One of Her Majesty's Principal
                                             Secretaries of State.

St. Andrew's House,
Edinburgh.
    30th April 1973.

We approve.

                                             Tim Fortescue,
                                             Oscar Murton,
                                    Two of the Lords Commissioners
                                        of Her Majesty's Treasury.

2nd May 1973.

EXPLANATORY NOTE

(This Note is not part of the Scheme.)

The Hill Farming Act 1946 as extended by Section 43 of the Agriculture Act 1967 provides that schemes may be made for the payment of subsidy in respect of cattle grazed and maintained on hill land, such schemes being restricted to a period not exceeding five years.

This Scheme made by the Secretary of State with the approval of the Treasury applies to Scotland and makes provision for subsidy payments from 1973 to 1977. It defines hill land and the descriptions of cattle to which it applies. It also specifies the conditions under which the cattle must be grazed and maintained and contains provisions against over-stocking. It provides for the making of applications, for determining to whom payment may be made, for the computation of the number of cattle qualifying for subsidy, for reducing the amount of payment in certain circumstances, for eligible land not being rendered ineligible by improvements, and for other matters.

The principal difference in this Scheme from the Hill Cattle (Scotland) Scheme 1968 (S.I. 1968/981) as amended, (which governed the payment of hill cattle subsidy until 1972), is that the Scheme no longer provides for the payment of brucellosis incentives which are now made in respect of beef animals under the Brucellosis (Beef Incentives) Payments Scheme 1972 (S.I. 1972/1329).

The Scheme does not fix the amount of subsidy payment as the Hill Farming Act 1946 requires the Secretary of State to prescribe this by separate order; the Order for that purpose is the Hill Cattle Subsidy Payment (Scotland) Order 1973 (S.I. 1973/867).

1973 No. 867 (S.71)

AGRICULTURE

HILL LANDS

The Hill Cattle Subsidy Payment (Scotland) Order 1973

Made - - -	*2nd May* 1973
Laid before Parliament	11*th May* 1973
Coming into Operation	1*st June* 1973

In exercise of the powers conferred on me by section 14(3) of the Hill Farming Act 1946(**a**) as amended by section 8 of the Livestock Rearing Act 1951(**b**), and of all other powers enabling me in that behalf, and with the approval of the Treasury, I hereby make the following order:—

Citation, commencement and interpretation

1.—(1) This order may be cited as the Hill Cattle Subsidy Payment (Scotland) Order 1973 and shall come into operation on 1st June 1973.

(2) The Interpretation Act 1889(**c**) shall apply for the interpretation of this order as it applies for the interpretation of an Act of Parliament.

Amount of subsidy payment

2. Subject to the provisions of the Hill Cattle (Scotland) Scheme 1973(**d**), the amount which may be paid by way of subsidy payment in accordance with that scheme in respect of a breeding cow in respect of the year 1973 and each of the four next succeeding years shall be £24·50.

Gordon Campbell,
One of Her Majesty's Principal
Secretaries of State.

St. Andrew's House,
Edinburgh.
30th April 1973.

(**a**) 1946 c. 73.   (**b**) 1951 c. 18.

(**c**) 1889 c. 63.   (**d**) S.I. 1973/866 (1973 II, p. 2675).

We approve.

> *Tim Fortescue,*
> *Oscar Murton,*
> Two of the Lords Commissioners
> of Her Majesty's Treasury.

2nd May 1973.

EXPLANATORY NOTE

(This Note is not part of the Order.)

The Hill Cattle (Scotland) Scheme 1973 sets out the conditions on which subsidy payments may be made in the year 1973 and each of the next four succeeding years in respect of breeding cows grazed and maintained on hill land in Scotland. This Order prescribes the amount of subsidy payment which may be made in respect of each of those five years for each animal in the case of which the provisions of the Scheme are satisfied.

STATUTORY INSTRUMENTS

1973 No. 869 (C.22)

LANDLORD AND TENANT

The Furnished Lettings (Rateable Value Limits) Order 1973

Laid before Parliament in draft

Made - - -		*3rd May* 1973
Coming into Operation		*1st June* 1973

The Secretary of State for the Environment (as respects England, except Monmouthshire) and the Secretary of State for Wales (as respects Wales and Monmouthshire), in exercise of their powers under section 89 of the Housing Finance Act 1972(a), as amended by sections 14(3) and 23(3) of, and Schedule 6 to, the Counter-Inflation Act 1973(b), and of all other powers enabling them in that behalf, hereby make the following order in the terms of a draft which has been laid before Parliament and approved by a resolution of each House of Parliament:—

Title and Commencement

1. This order may be cited as the Furnished Lettings (Rateable Value Limits) Order 1973 and shall come into operation on 1st June 1973.

Interpretation

2.—(1) In this order—

"the Rent Act" means the Rent Act 1968(c);

"dwelling" has the meaning assigned to it by section 84(1) of the Rent Act, and

"Part VI contract" has the meaning assigned to it by section 70(6) of the Rent Act.

(2) The Interpretation Act 1889(d) shall apply for the interpretation of this order as it applies for the interpretation of an Act of Parliament.

Alteration of rateable value limits

3.—(1) Section 89(7) of the Housing Finance Act 1972 (which, for dwellings first entered in the valuation list on or after 1st April 1973, alters the rateable value limits in section 71 of the Rent Act) shall come into force on 1st June 1973.

(2) For the purposes of the said section 89(7) it is hereby determined that—

(*a*) £1,000 be the relevant amount for a dwelling in Greater London, and

(*b*) £500 be the relevant amount for a dwelling elsewhere.

(a) 1972 c. 47.   (b) 1973 c. 9.   (c) 1968 c. 23.   (d) 1889 c. 63.

Transitional provision

4. If on 1st June 1973 there is in existence a contract relating to a dwelling which becomes a Part VI contract by virtue of the said section 89(7) and of article 3 above, then in relation to that contract, paragraph (*a*) of section 79 of the Rent Act (notices to quit served by owner-occupiers) shall have effect as if for 8th December 1965 there were substituted a reference to 1st June 1973, and as if for the reference to 7th June 1966 there were substituted a reference to 30th November 1973.

Geoffrey Rippon,
Secretary of State for the Environment.

2nd May 1973.

Peter Thomas,
Secretary of State for Wales.

3rd May 1973.

EXPLANATORY NOTE

(This Note is not part of the Order.)

Section 71(1) of the Rent Act 1968 specifies the rateable value limits for dwellings to which Part VI of that Act (furnished lettings) applies. This Order brings into force on 1st June 1973 section 89(7) of the Housing Finance Act 1972. That subsection amends section 71(1) of the Rent Act by altering, in consequence of rating revaluation, the rateable value limits for dwellings first entered in the valuation list on or after 1st April 1973. Those altered limits have to be determined by an Order under section 89(1) of the 1972 Act. This Order determines those rateable value limits as £1,000 for dwellings in Greater London and £500 for dwellings elsewhere in England and Wales.

The Order also contains a transitional provision enabling "owner-occupiers" of dwellings subject to contracts to which Part VI of the Rent Act 1968 becomes applicable by virtue of section 89(7) of the Housing Finance Act 1972 and this order, to give notice in writing under section 79 of the Rent Act not later than 30th November 1973. Such a notice will prevent sections 77 and 78 of that Act (security of tenure) from applying, as provided in section 79 of that Act, where notice to quit is served.

STATUTORY INSTRUMENTS

1973 No. 870

ROAD TRAFFIC

The Road Vehicles (Registration and Licensing) (Amendment) Regulations 1973

Made - - -	*7th May* 1973
Laid before Parliament	15*th May* 1973
Coming into Operation	5*th June* 1973

The Secretary of State for the Environment, in exercise of the powers conferred on him by section 23 of the Vehicles (Excise) Act 1971(**a**) as modified by section 39(1) of, and paragraph 20 of Part I of Schedule 7 to, that Act, and as extended by section 52(11) of, and paragraph 27 of Schedule 7 to, the Finance Act 1972(**b**), and of all other enabling powers, hereby makes the following Regulations: —

1. These Regulations shall come into operation on 5th June 1973 and may be cited as the Road Vehicles (Registration and Licensing) (Amendment) Regulations 1973.

2. The Road Vehicles (Registration and Licensing) Regulations 1971(**c**) as amended(**d**) shall have effect as though after Regulation 4 there were inserted the following Regulation: —

"Restriction on registration of vehicles chargeable with car tax

4A.—(1) The Secretary of State may refuse to register a vehicle under section 19 of the Act unless there is produced to him, at the time when he would otherwise be required by that section to register the vehicle, a document purporting to be issued by, or by authority of, the Commissioners of Customs and Excise which certifies either—

(*a*) that the vehicle is not a chargeable vehicle; or

(*b*) that the tax chargeable on it has been or will be paid; or

(*c*) that tax on it has been remitted.

(2) Paragraph (1) above shall not apply in relation to the registration of a vehicle which is chargeable with duty under the Act by virtue of section 1 thereof and Schedule 1 or Schedule 3 thereto, but shall otherwise apply without prejudice to any other requirement of these Regulations.

(3) In this Regulation—

(*a*) "chargeable vehicle" has the same meaning as in section 52 of the Finance Act 1972; and

(*b*) "the tax" means car tax chargeable under the said section 52.".

(**a**) 1971 c. 10. (**b**) 1972 c. 41.
(**c**) S.I. 1971/450 (1971 I, p. 1305).
(**d**) The amending Regulations are not relevant to the subject matter of these Regulations.

Signed by authority of the Secretary of State.

7th May 1973.

John Peyton,
Minister for Transport Industries,
Department of the Environment.

EXPLANATORY NOTE

(This Note is not part of the Regulations.)

These Regulations further amend the Road Vehicles (Registration and Licensing) Regulations 1971 by providing that (subject to certain exceptions) the Secretary of State may refuse to register a vehicle under the Vehicles (Excise) Act 1971 unless a certificate issued by, or by the authority of, the Commissioners of Customs and Excise is produced stating either that the vehicle is not subject to the car tax chargeable under section 52 of the Finance Act 1972 or that the car tax chargeable on the vehicle has been or will be paid or has been remitted.

STATUTORY INSTRUMENTS

1973 No. 874

CUSTOMS AND EXCISE

The Import Duties (Cyprus) (Reductions) Order 1973

Made - - - -	7th May 1973
Laid before the House of Commons	11th May 1973
Coming into Operation	1st June 1973

The Lords Commissioners of Her Majesty's Treasury, by virtue of the powers conferred on them by sections 1, 3(6) and 13 of the Import Duties Act 1958(a), as amended by the European Communities Act 1972(b) and of all other powers enabling them in that behalf, on the recommendation of the Secretary of State (c), hereby make the following Order:

1.—(1) This Order may be cited as the Import Duties (Cyprus) (Reductions) Order 1973.

(2) The Interpretation Act 1889(d) shall apply for the interpretation of this Order as it applies for the interpretation of an Act of Parliament.

(3) This Order shall operate from the beginning of 1st June 1973 until the beginning of 1st January 1974.

2.—(1) Any import duty which is for the time being chargeable on goods of any heading or subheading of the Customs Tariff 1959 specified in:

(a) Schedule 1 hereto, shall be chargeable at 80 per cent. of the full rate, and

(b) Schedule 2 hereto, shall be chargeable at the relevant rate there specified instead of the full rate

in the case of goods which are to be regarded under the Agreement, signed on 19th December 1972, between the European Economic Community and Cyprus as products originating in Cyprus.

(2) Paragraph (1) above shall operate without prejudice to any reduction in or exemption or relief from duties which may be available in the case of goods qualifying for Commonwealth preference or goods of developing countries.

3. For the purposes of classification under the Customs Tariff 1959, insofar as that depends on the rate of duty, any goods to which Article 2 above applies shall be treated as chargeable with the same duty as if this Order had not been made.

7th May 1973.

V. H. Goodhew,
Tim Fortescue,
Two of the Lords Commissioners
of Her Majesty's Treasury.

(a) 1958 c. 6.   (b) 1972 c. 68.
(c) See S.I. 1970/1537 (1970 III, p. 5293).   (d) 1889 c. 63.

SCHEDULE 1

HEADINGS AND SUBHEADINGS SUBJECT TO REDUCTION OF 20% IN DUTY FROM 1ST JUNE
1973

05.02(C); 05.03(A)(II), (B)(II); 05.05(B); 05.07(B)(III); 05.08(B); 05.11

13.02; 13.03(A); 13.03(B)(I)(*b*), (B)(II)(*b*), (C)

All headings of Chapter 14

15.05; 15.06; 15.09 to 15.11 (inclusive); 15.15; 15.16

17.04(A)

19.08

21.01(A)(1), (B)(1); 21.02 to 21.05 (inclusive); 21.06(A)(I), (A)(III), (B), (C); 21.07
(F)(I)(*a*)(1)

22.01; 22.02(A)

All headings and subheadings of Chapter 25 except 25.19(A) and 25.24

All headings and subheadings of Chapter 27 except 27.10(B)(III)(*b*)(2), (C)(I)(*c*)(2),
(C)(II)(*c*)(2), (C)(III)(*c*)(2), (C)(III)(*d*)(2); 27.11(B)(I)(*c*); 27.12A(III)(*b*), (B)(II);
27.13 (B)(I)(*a*)(2), (B)(I)(*b*)(2), (B)(I)(*c*), (B)(II); 27.14(C)

All headings and subheadings of Chapter 28 except 28.04(B); 28.40(N); 28.40(O)

All headings and subheadings of Chapter 29 except 29.04(C)(II), (C)(III)

All headings and subheadings of Chapter 30 except 30.03

All headings and subheadings of Chapters 31 to 34 (inclusive) except 32.01(B);
(C)(II), (D)(II); 32.05(D); 33.01(A)(3)(*a*)(i), (*b*)

35.01(B); 35.02(A)(I); 35.02(A)(II)(*b*), (B); 35.03; 35.04; 35.06

All headings and subheadings of Chapters 36 to 72 (inclusive) except 38.11(B)(1);
38.12(A)(I); 38.14(B); 38.18(B)(1)(*a*), (B)(1)(*b*); 38.19(1J)(1); 39.01(D)(1); 41.02;
41.03(A)(2), (B); 41.04 to 41.08 (inclusive); 43.02; 44.15(A)(1); 45.01; 45.03(C)(1);
45.04(A), (B), (C); 46.03(B); 54.01; 55.05(B); 55.06(B); 55.07 to 55.09 (inclusive) 56.04;
57.01; 57.06(B)(2); 57.07(B)(2); 57.10(B); 58.01(A)(2), (B)(3); 58.02(A), (B)(3); 58.05(B)
59.02(B)(2); 59.04(B)(3); 60.05(B)(2); 61.01; 61.05(C); 61.06(C); 62.01(B); 62.02(B);
62.03(B)(2)(*b*); 62.05(B); 67.01; 68.01(B)

All headings and subheadings of Chapter 73 except 73.01(A), (B), (C), (D)(II);
73.02(A)(I); 73.03; 73.05(B); 73.06; 73.07(A)(I), (B)(I); 73.08; 73.09; 73.10(A), (D)(I)(*a*),
73.11(A)(I), (A)(IV)(*a*)(1), (B); 73.12(A), (B)(I), (C)(III)(*a*), (C)(V)(*a*)(1); 73.13(A),
(B)(I), (B)(II)(*b*), (B)(III), (B)(IV)(*b*), (B)(IV)(*c*), (B)(IV)(*d*), (B)(V)(*a*)(2); 73.15(A)(I)(*b*),
(A)(III), (A)(IV), (A)(V)(*b*); 73.15(A)(V)(*d*)(1)(*aa*), (A)(VI)(*a*), (A)(VI)(*c*)(1)(*aa*),
(A)(VII)(*a*), (A)(VII)(*b*)(2), (A)(VII)(*c*), (A)(VII)(*d*)(1), (B)(I)(*b*), (B)(III), (IV), (B)(V)
(*b*), (B)(V)(*d*)(1)(*aa*), (B)(VI)(*a*), (B)(VI)(*c*)(1)(*aa*), (B)(VII)(*a*), (B)(VII)(*b*)(1), (B)(VII)
(*b*)(2)(*bb*), (B)(VII)(*b*)(3), (B)(VII)(*b*)(4)(*aa*); 73.16(A)(II), (B), (C), (D)(I)

All headings and subheadings of Chapters 74 to 99 (inclusive) except 79.01(A); 87.02;
87.04; 97.06(B), (C), (D); 97.07; 98.02(B)(3); 98.10(A)(I).

SCHEDULE 2

Specific Reductions

28.04(B)	2·8%
32.05(D)	8%
38.11(B)(I), 38.14(B)	6·4% or such greater rate as is equal to four-fifths of the amount or aggregate amount of the duty chargeable, apart from this Order, on such constituents as are mentioned in that subheading
38.18(B)(1)(*a*)	2·4% or such greater rate as is equal to four-fifths of the amount or aggregate amount by which the duty chargeable, apart from this Order, on such constituents as are mentioned in subheading 38.18(B)(1) exceeds 7%, in addition to any hydrocarbon oil duty
38.18(B)(1)(*b*)	6·4% or such greater rate as is equal to four-fifths of the amount or aggregate amount of the duty chargeable, apart from this Order, on such constituents as are mentioned in subheading 38.18(B)(1)
38.19(IJ)(1)	6·4% or such greater rate as is equal to four-fifths of the amount or aggregate amount of the duty chargeable apart from this Order, on such constituents as are mentioned in that subheading
39.01(D)(1)	4·8%
44.15(A)(1)	3·9%
45.03(C)(1); 45.04(A), (B), (C)	4·8%
98.02(B)(3)	4·2%

EXPLANATORY NOTE

(This Note is not part of the Order.)

This Order, which comes into operation on 1st June 1973, implements obligations of the United Kingdom concerning import duties in 1973 under the Agreement between the European Economic Community and Cyprus.

Article 3 provides for the full rate of duty to be reduced by 20 per cent. in the case of the goods listed in Schedule 1, on condition that they originate in Cyprus in terms of the Agreement. Different reduced rates apply in the case of goods listed in Schedule 2. (These are the first of a number of reductions in import duties which are to be made under the Agreement.)

The Order does not affect preferences or reliefs in respect of import duties which may be available in the case of goods of Cyprus qualifying for Commonwealth preference or goods of developing countries.

STATUTORY INSTRUMENTS

1973 No. 886

HOUSING, ENGLAND AND WALES

The Isles of Scilly (Housing) (No. 2) Order 1973

Made - - - -	*8th May* 1973
Laid before Parliament	*17th May* 1973
Coming into Operation	*7th June* 1973

The Secretary of State for the Environment, in exercise of his powers under section 103 of the Housing Finance Act 1972(a) and of all other powers enabling him in that behalf, hereby makes the following order:—

1.—(1) This order may be cited as the Isles of Scilly (Housing) (No. 2) Order 1973 and shall come into operation on 7th June 1973.

(2) The Interpretation Act 1889(b) shall apply for the interpretation of this order as it applies for the interpretation of an Act of Parliament.

2. The Housing (Amendment) Act 1973(c) shall extend to the Isles of Scilly subject to the adaptation that any reference to a local authority shall, unless the context otherwise requires, include the Council of the Isles of Scilly.

Geoffrey Rippon,
Secretary of State for the Environment.

8th May 1973.

EXPLANATORY NOTE

(*This Note is not part of the Order.*)

This Order extends the Housing (Amendment) Act 1973 to the Isles of Scilly. That Act contains amendments of the Housing Act 1957 (c. 56) and the Housing Act 1971 (c. 76), both of which have been extended to the Isles. (See the Isles of Scilly (Housing) Order 1972 (S.I. 1972/1204)).

(a) 1972 c. 47.   (b) 1889 c. 63.   (c) 1973 c. 5.

STATUTORY INSTRUMENTS

1973 No. 887

INDUSTRIAL TRAINING

The Industrial Training Levy (Hotel and Catering) Order 1973

Made - - -	*9th May* 1973
Laid before Parliament	*21st May* 1973
Coming into Operation	*13th June* 1973

The Secretary of State after approving proposals submitted by the Hotel and Catering Industry Training Board for the imposition of a further levy on employers in the hotel and catering industry and in exercise of powers conferred by section 4 of the Industrial Training Act 1964(**a**) and now vested in him(**b**), and of all other powers enabling him in that behalf hereby makes the following Order:—

Title and commencement

1. This Order may be cited as the Industrial Training Levy (Hotel and Catering) Order 1973 and shall come into operation on 13th June 1973.

Interpretation

2.—(1) In this Order unless the context otherwise requires:—

(*a*) "agriculture" has the same meaning as in section 109(3) of the Agriculture Act 1947(**c**) or, in relation to Scotland, as in section 86(3) of the Agriculture (Scotland) Act 1948(**d**);

(*b*) "an appeal tribunal" means an industrial tribunal established under section 12 of the Industrial Training Act 1964;

(*c*) "assessment" means an assessment of an employer to the levy;

(*d*) "the Board" means the Hotel and Catering Industry Training Board;

(*e*) "British Airways Group" means the British Airways Board, the British Overseas Airways Corporation, the British European Airways Corporation and all subsidiaries and joint subsidiaries, and "member of the British Airways Group" shall be construed accordingly;

(*f*) "charity" has the same meaning as in section 360 of the Income and Corporation Taxes Act 1970(**e**);

(*g*) "emoluments" means all emoluments assessable to income tax under Schedule E (other than pensions), being emoluments from which tax under that Schedule is deductible, whether or not tax in fact falls to be deducted from any particular payment thereof;

(*h*) "employer" means a person who is an employer in the hotel and catering industry at any time in the seventh levy period;

(*i*) "establishment" (except in sub-paragraphs (*j*) and (*k*) of this paragraph) means an establishment comprising catering activities or a hotel and catering establishment;

(a) 1964 c. 16.   (b) S.I. 1968/729 (1968 II, p. 2108).
(c) 1947 c. 48.   (d) 1948 c. 45.
(e) 1970 c. 10.

(*j*) "establishment comprising catering activities" means an establishment in Great Britain at or from which persons were employed in the seventh base period in the supply of food or drink to persons for immediate consumption, but does not include—

  (i) a hotel and catering establishment; or

  (ii) an establishment in which the employer supplied for immediate consumption light refreshments to persons employed at or from the same where the employer was not otherwise engaged at or from the establishment in any activities to which paragraph 1 of the Schedule to the industrial training order applies or in the manufacture of any chocolate or flour confectionery so supplied as light refreshments;

(*k*) "hotel and catering establishment" means an establishment in Great Britain that was engaged in the seventh base period wholly or mainly in the hotel and catering industry;

(*l*) "hotel and catering industry" means any one or more of the activities which, subject to the provisions of paragraph 2 of the Schedule to the industrial training order, are specified in paragraph 1 of that Schedule as the activities of the hotel and catering industry;

(*m*) "the industrial training order" means the Industrial Training (Hotel and Catering Board) Order 1969(**a**);

(*n*) "the levy" means the levy imposed by the Board in respect of the seventh levy period;

(*o*) "notice" means a notice in writing;

(*p*) "the seventh base period" means the period of twelve months that commenced on 6th April 1972;

(*q*) "the seventh levy period" means the period commencing with the day upon which this Order comes into operation and ending on 31st March 1974;

(*r*) "subsidiary" and "joint subsidiary" have the same meanings as in section 60(1) of the Civil Aviation Act 1971(**b**);

(*s*) "the supply of food or drink to persons for immediate consumption" means such a supply either by way of business or by a person carrying on a business to persons employed in the business;

(*t*) other expressions have the same meanings as in the industrial training order.

(2) In the case where an establishment is taken over (whether directly or indirectly) by an employer in succession to, or jointly with, another person, a person employed at any time in the seventh base period at or from the establishment shall be deemed, for the purposes of this Order, to have been so employed by the employer carrying on the said establishment on the day upon which this Order comes into operation, and any reference in this Order to persons employed by an employer in the seventh base period at or from an establishment shall be construed accordingly.

(3) Any reference in this Order to an establishment that ceases to carry on business shall not be taken to apply where the location of the establishment is changed but its business is continued wholly or mainly at or from the new location, or where the suspension of activities is of a temporary or seasonal nature.

(4) The Interpretation Act 1889(**c**) shall apply to the interpretation of this

---

(**a**) S.I. 1969/1405 (1969 III, p. 4132). (**b**) 1971 c. 75. (**c**) 1889 c. 63.

Order as it applies to the interpretation of an Act of Parliament.

Imposition of the levy

3.—(1) The levy to be imposed by the Board on employers in respect of the seventh levy period shall be assessed in accordance with the provisions of this and the next following Article.

(2) Subject to the provisions of the next following Article, the levy shall be assessed by the Board separately in respect of each establishment of an employer (not being an employer who is exempt from the levy by virtue of paragraph (3) of this Article), but in agreement with the employer one assessment may be made in respect of any number of hotel and catering establishments or of establishments comprising catering activities, in which case such establishments shall be deemed for the purposes of the assessment to constitute one establishment.

(3) There shall be exempt from the levy—

(*a*) an employer in whose case the sum of the emoluments of all the persons employed by him in the seventh base period in the hotel and catering industry at or from the establishment or establishments of the employer was less than £8,000;

(*b*) a charity.

Assessment of the levy

4.—(1) Subject to the provisions of this Article, the levy assessed in respect of an establishment shall be an amount equal to 0·8 per cent, of the sum of the emoluments of the following persons, being persons employed by the employer at or from the establishment in the seventh base period, that is to say—

(*a*) in the case of a hotel and catering establishment, all such persons;

(*b*) in the case of an establishment comprising catering activities, all such persons employed wholly or mainly in the supply of food or drink to persons for immediate consumption.

(2) In the case of one establishment only of an employer, the sum of the emoluments determined in accordance with the last foregoing paragraph shall be treated for the purpose of the assessment of the levy in respect of that establishment as if that sum were reduced by £1,000.

(3) For the purposes of the application of the provisions of the last foregoing paragraph, the Board shall, if necessary—

(*a*) select the establishment in relation to which the provisions of the said paragraph are to apply; or

(*b*) aggregate the sum total of the emoluments of the persons employed at or from any two or more establishments of the employer (each sum first being determined separately in accordance with paragraph (1) of this Article) in which case the said establishments shall be deemed for the purposes of the assessment thereof to constitute one establishment.

(4) The amount of the levy imposed in respect of an establishment that ceases to carry on business in the seventh levy period shall be in the same proportion to the amount that would otherwise be due under the foregoing provisions of this Article as the number of days between the commencement of the said levy period and the date of cessation of business (both dates inclusive) bears to the number of days in the said levy period.

(5) For the purposes of this Article, no regard shall be had to the emoluments of any person employed as follows—

(*a*) wholly in the supply (except at or in connection with an hotel, restaurant, café, snack bar, canteen, mess room or similar place of refreshment) of—

(i) ice cream, chocolate confectionery, sugar confectionery or soft drink;

(ii) shellfish or eels; or

(iii) food or drink by means of an automatic vending machine;

(*b*) wholly in agriculture;

(*c*) otherwise than wholly in the supply of food or drink to persons for immediate consumption, where the employment is at or from an establishment engaged mainly in any activities of an industry specified in column 1 of the Schedule to this Order by virtue of the relevant industrial training order specified in column 2 of that Schedule or in any activities of two or more such industries;

(*d*) as a member of the crew of an aircraft, or as the master or a member of the crew of a ship or, in the case of a person ordinarily employed as a seaman, in or about a ship in port by the owner or charterer thereof on work of a kind ordinarily done by a seaman on a ship while it is in port;

(*e*) by a local authority in any activities mentioned in sub-paragraph (*d*) or (*e*) of paragraph 1 of the Schedule to the industrial training order, not being activities mentioned in head (ii) or head (iv) of paragraph 3(*l*) of that Schedule; or

(*f*) in any activities mentioned in sub-paragraph (*b*), (*c*)(ii), (*d*) or (*e*) of paragraph 1 of the Schedule to the industrial training order when carried out by—

(i) a harbour authority while acting in that capacity;

(ii) the Electricity Council, the Central Electricity Generating Board or an Area Electricity Board;

(iii) the North of Scotland Hydro-Electric Board or the South of Scotland Electricity Board;

(iv) the British Gas Corporation;

(v) statutory water undertakers within the meaning of the Water Act 1945(**a**) or regional water boards or water development boards within the meaning of the Water (Scotland) Act 1967(**b**), being the activities of such undertakers or boards in the exercise of their powers or duties as such;

(vi) the British Airports Authority or a member of the British Airways Group;

(vii) a marketing board; or

(viii) the United Kingdom Atomic Energy Authority.

Assessment notices

5.—(1) The Board shall serve an assessment notice on every employer assessed to the levy, but one notice may comprise two or more assessments.

(2) An assessment notice shall state the Board's address for the service of a notice of appeal or of an application for an extension of time for appealing.

(**a**) 1945 c. 42.   (**b**) 1967 c. 78.

(3) An assessment notice may be served on the person assessed to the levy either by delivering it to him personally or by leaving it, or sending it to him by post, at his last known address or place of business in the United Kingdom or, if that person is a corporation, by leaving it, or sending it by post to the corporation, at such address or place of business or at its registered or principal office.

Payment of the levy

6.—(1) Subject to the provisions of this Article and of Articles 7 and 8, the amount of the levy payable under an assessment notice served by the Board shall be payable to the Board in two equal instalments, and the first such instalment shall be due one month after the date of the assessment notice and the second such instalment shall be due one month after the date (not being earlier than five months after the date of the assessment notice) of a notice requiring payment of that instalment, which notice shall be served by the Board on the person assessed to the levy in the same manner as an assessment notice.

(2) The amount of an instalment mentioned in the last foregoing paragraph may be rounded up or down by the Board to a convenient figure, but so that the aggregate amount of both instalments shall be equal to the amount of the levy stated in the assessment notice.

(3) An instalment of an assessment shall not be recoverable by the Board until there has expired the time allowed for appealing against the assessment by Article 8(1) of this Order and any further period or periods of time that the Board or an appeal tribunal may have allowed for appealing under paragraph (2) or (3) of that Article or, where an appeal is brought, until the appeal is decided or withdrawn.

Withdrawal of assessment

7.—(1) The Board may, by a notice served on the person assessed to the levy in the same manner as an assessment notice, withdraw an assessment if that person has appealed against that assessment under the provisions of Article 8 of this Order and the appeal has not been entered in the Register of Appeals kept under the appropriate Regulations specified in paragraph (5) of that Article, and such withdrawal may be extended by the Board to any other assessment appearing in the assessment notice.

(2) The withdrawal of an assessment shall be without prejudice—

(a) to the power of the Board to serve a further assessment notice in respect of any establishment to which that assessment related and, where the withdrawal is made by reason of the fact that an establishment has ceased to carry on business in the seventh levy period, the said notice may provide that the whole amount payable thereunder in respect of the establishment shall be due one month after the date of the notice; or

(b) to any other assessment included in the original assessment notice and not withdrawn by the Board, and such notice shall thereupon have effect as if any assessment withdrawn by the Board had not been included therein.

Appeals

8.—(1) A person assessed to the levy may appeal to an appeal tribunal against the assessment within one month from the date of the service of the assessment notice or within any further period or periods of time that may be allowed by the Board or an appeal tribunal under the following provisions of this Article.

(2) The Board by notice may for good cause allow a person assessed to the levy to appeal to an appeal tribunal against the assessment at any time within the period of four months from the date of the service of the assessment notice or within such further period or periods as the Board may allow before such time as may then be limited for appealing has expired.

(3) If the Board shall not allow an application for extension of time for appealing, an appeal tribunal shall upon application made to the tribunal by the person assessed to the levy have the like powers as the Board under the last foregoing paragraph.

(4) In the case of an establishment that ceases to carry on business in the seventh levy period on any day after the date of the service of the relevant assessment notice, the foregoing provisions of this Article shall have effect as if for the period of four months from the date of the service of the assessment notice mentioned in paragraph (2) of this Article there were substituted the period of six months from the date of the cessation of business.

(5) An appeal or an application to an appeal tribunal under this Article shall be made in accordance with the Industrial Tribunals (England and Wales) Regulations 1965(**a**) as amended by the Industrial Tribunals (England and Wales) (Amendment) Regulations 1967(**b**) except where the establishment to which the relevant assessment relates is wholly in Scotland in which case the appeal or application shall be made in accordance with the Industrial Tribunals (Scotland) Regulations 1965(**c**) as amended by the Industrial Tribunals (Scotland) (Amendment) Regulations 1967(**d**).

(6) The powers of an appeal tribunal under paragraph (3) of this Article may be exercised by the President of the Industrial Tribunals (England and Wales) or by the President of the Industrial Tribunals (Scotland) as the case may be.

Evidence

9.—(1) Upon the discharge by a person assessed to the levy of his liability under an assessment the Board shall if so requested issue to him a certificate to that effect.

(2) The production in any proceedings of a document purporting to be certified by the Secretary of the Board to be a true copy of an assessment or other notice issued by the Board or purporting to be a certificate such as is mentioned in the foregoing paragraph of this Article shall, unless the contrary is proved, be sufficient evidence of the document and of the facts stated therein.

Signed by order of the Secretary of State.
9th May 1973.

R. Chichester-Clark,
Minister of State,
Department of Employment.

(**a**) S.I. 1965/1101 (1965 II, p. 2805).   (**b**) S.I. 1967/301 (1967 I, p. 1040).
(**c**) S.I. 1965/1157 (1965 II, p. 3266).   (**d**) S.I. 1967/302 (1967 I, p. 1050).

SCHEDULE

THE INDUSTRIES REFERRED TO IN ARTICLE 4(5)(c) OF THIS ORDER

Column 1	Column 2
The wool, jute and flax industry	The Industrial Training (Wool Industry Board) Order 1964 as amended by the Industrial Training (Wool, Jute and Flax Board) Order 1968(a)
The iron and steel industry	The Industrial Training (Iron and Steel Board) Order 1964 as amended by the Industrial Training (Iron and Steel Board) Order 1969(b)
The construction industry	The Industrial Training (Construction Board) Order 1964 as amended by the Industrial Training (Construction Board) Order 1973(c)
The engineering industry	The Industrial Training (Engineering Board) Order 1964 as amended by the Industrial Training (Engineering Board) Order 1971(d)
The shipbuilding industry	The Industrial Training (Shipbuilding Board) Order 1964 as amended by the Industrial Training (Shipbuilding Board) Order 1968(e)
The electricity supply industry	The Industrial Training (Electricity Supply Board) Order 1965(f)
The gas industry	The Industrial Training (Gas Industry Board) Order 1965(g)
The water supply industry	The Industrial Training (Water Supply Board) Order 1965(h)
The ceramics, glass and mineral products industry	The Industrial Training (Ceramics, Glass and Mineral Products Board) Order 1965 as amended by the Industrial Training (Ceramics, Glass and Mineral Products Board) Order 1969(i)

(a) S.I. 1964/907, 1968/898 (1964 II, p. 1928; 1968 II, p. 2376).
(b) S.I. 1964/949, 1969/884 (1964 II, p. 2127; 1969 II, p. 2517).
(c) S.I. 1964/1079, 1973/160 (1964 II, p. 2384; 1973 I, p. 654).
(d) S.I. 1964/1086, 1971/1530 (1964 II, p. 2402; 1971 III, p. 4309).
(e) S.I. 1964/1782, 1968/1614 (1964 III, p. 3928; 1968 III, p. 4432).
(f) S.I. 1965/1256 (1965 II, p. 3548).
(g) S.I. 1965/1257 (1965 II, p. 3552).
(h) S.I. 1965/1258 (1965 II, p. 3556).
(i) S.I. 1965/1391, 1969/689 (1965 II, p. 4062; 1969 II, p. 1860).

Column 1	Column 2
The furniture and timber industry	The Industrial Training (Furniture and Timber Industry Board) Order 1965 as amended by the Industrial Training (Furniture and Timber Industry Board) Order 1969 and the Industrial Training (Furniture and Timber Industry Board) Order 1969 (Amendment) Order 1970**(a)**
The man-made fibres producing industry	The Industrial Training (Man-made Fibres Producing Industry Board) Order 1966 as amended by the Industrial Training (Man-made Fibres Producing Industry Board) Order 1969**(b)**
The carpet industry	The Industrial Training (Carpet Board) Order 1966 as amended by the Industrial Training (Carpet Board) Order 1968**(c)**
The knitting, lace and net industry	The Industrial Training (Knitting, Lace and Net Industry Board) Order 1966**(d)**
The cotton and allied textiles industry	The Industrial Training (Cotton and Allied Textiles Board) Order 1966**(e)**
The agricultural, horticultural and forestry industry	The Industrial Training (Agricultural, Horticultural and Forestry Board) Order 1966 as amended by the Industrial Training (Agricultural, Horticultural and Forestry Board) Order 1970**(f)**
The road transport industry	The Industrial Training (Road Transport Board) Order 1966 as amended by the Industrial Training (Road Transport Board) Order 1972**(g)**
The air transport and travel industry	The Industrial Training (Civil Air Transport Board) Order 1967 as amended by the Industrial Training (Air Transport and Travel Industry Board) Order 1970**(h)**
The petroleum industry	The Industrial Training (Petroleum Board) Order 1967 as amended by the Industrial Training (Petroleum Board) Order 1970**(i)**
The rubber and plastics processing industry	The Industrial Training (Rubber and Plastics Processing Board) Order 1967**(j)**

(a) S.I. 1965/2028, 1969/1290, 1970/1634 (1965 III, p. 5998; 1969 III, p. 3820; 1970 III, p. 5372).
(b) S.I. 1966/143, 1969/1210 (1966 I, p. 257; 1969 II, p. 3545).
(c) S.I. 1966/245, 1968/1882 (1966 I, p. 499; 1968 III, p. 5017).
(d) S.I. 1966/246 (1966 I, p. 506).　　　**(e)** S.I. 1966/823 (1966 II, p. 1907).
(f) S.I. 1966/969, 1970/1886 (1966 II, p. 2333; 1970 III, p. 6227).
(g) S.I. 1966/1112, 1972/772 (1966 III, p. 2712; 1972 II, p. 2471).
(h) S.I. 1967/263, 1970/252 (1967 I, p. 968; 1970 I, p. 983).
(i) S.I. 1967/648, 1970/205 (1967 I, p. 2032; 1970 I, p. 926).
(j) S.I. 1967/1062 (1967 II, p. 3151).

Column 1	Column 2
The chemical and allied products industry	The Industrial Training (Chemical and Allied Products Board) Order 1967 as amended by the Industrial Training (Chemical and Allied Products Board) Order 1970(a)
The paper and paper products industry	The Industrial Training (Paper and Paper Products Board) Order 1968(b)
The printing and publishing industry	The Industrial Training (Printing and Publishing Board) Order 1968(c)
The distributive industry	The Industrial Training (Distributive Board) Order 1968 as amended by the Industrial Training (Distributive Board) Order 1970 and the Industrial Training (Distributive Board) Order 1970 (Amendment) Order 1971(d)
The food, drink and tobacco industry	The Industrial Training (Food, Drink and Tobacco Board) Order 1968 as amended by the Industrial Training (Food, Drink and Tobacco Board) Order 1971(e)
The footwear, leather and fur skin industry	The Industrial Training (Footwear, Leather and Fur Skin Board) Order 1968 as amended by the Industrial Training (Footwear, Leather and Fur Skin Board) Order 1968 (Amendment) Order 1972(f)
The clothing and allied products industry	The Industrial Training (Clothing and Allied Products Board) Order 1969(g)

(a) S.I. 1967/1386, 1970/1743 (1967 III, p. 4049; 1970 III, p. 5706).
(b) S.I. 1968/787 (1968 II, p. 2194).   (c) S.I. 1968/786 (1968 II, p. 2185).
(d) S.I. 1968/1032, 1970/1053, 1971/1876 (1968 II, p. 2709; 1970 II, p. 3273; 1971 III, p. 5109).
(e) S.I. 1968/1033, 1971/648 (1968 II, p. 2721; 1971 I, p. 1709).
(f) S.I. 1968/1763, 1972/597 (1968 III, p. 4785; 1972 I, p. 1966).
(g) S.I. 1969/1375 (1969 III, p. 4094).

EXPLANATORY NOTE

(This Note is not part of the Order.)

This Order gives effect to proposals submitted by the Hotel and Catering Industry Training Board to the Secretary of State for Employment for the imposition of a further levy upon employers in the hotel and catering industry for the purpose of raising money towards the expenses of the Board.

The levy is to be imposed in respect of the seventh levy period commencing with the day upon which this Order comes into operation and ending on 31st March 1974. The levy will be assessed by the Board and there will be a right of appeal against an assessment to an industrial tribunal.

STATUTORY INSTRUMENTS

1973 No. 889 (C.23)

HARBOURS, DOCKS, PIERS AND FERRIES

The Docks and Harbours Act 1966 (Commencement No. 12) Order 1973

Made	- - -		*9th May* 1973

The Secretary of State for the Environment in exercise of the powers conferred by section 60 of the Docks and Harbours Act 1966(**a**) and now vested in him(**b**) and of all other enabling powers hereby makes the following Order:—

1. Section 1 of the Docks and Harbours Act 1966 shall come into operation in the port specified in the Schedule to this Order on 23rd May 1973.

2. This Order may be cited as the Docks and Harbours Act 1966 (Commencement No. 12) Order 1973.

Signed by authority of the Secretary of State.
9th May 1973.

> *J. E. Sanderson,*
> An Under Secretary in
> the Department of the Environment.

SCHEDULE

Aberdeen

EXPLANATORY NOTE

(This Note is not part of the Order.)

This Order brings into operation section 1 of the Docks and Harbours Act 1966 in the port specified in the Schedule to the Order, and thus introduces in this port the system of licensing of employers of dock workers provided for by Part I of the Act.

(**a**) 1966 c. 28. (**b**) S.I. 1970/1681 (1970 III, p. 5551).

STATUTORY INSTRUMENTS

1973 No. 890

NORTHERN IRELAND

The Northern Ireland Assembly (Election) Order 1973

Made - - - -	*9th May* 1973
Laid before Parliament	*14th May* 1973
Coming into Operation	*15th May* 1973

In exercise of the powers conferred on me by sections 2(5) and 3(3) of the Northern Ireland Assembly Act 1973(a) and of all other powers enabling me in that behalf, I hereby make the following Order:—

Citation, commencement and extent

1.—(1) This Order may be cited as the Northern Ireland Assembly (Election) Order 1973 and shall come into operation on 15th May 1973.

(2) This Order shall apply only to the first election to the Northern Ireland Assembly.

(3) This Order, except Article 4, extends to Northern Ireland only.

Interpretation

2.—(1) In this Order—

"the Assembly" means the Northern Ireland Assembly;

"the election" means the first election to the Assembly;

"the principal Act" means the Electoral Law Act (Northern Ireland) 1962(b);

and any expression used in this Order and in the principal Act has the same meaning as in that Act.

(2) The Interpretation Act (Northern Ireland) 1954(c) shall apply to Article 1, paragraph (1) and the following provisions of this Order as it applies to an Act of the Parliament of Northern Ireland.

Application of principal Act

3. Parts IV to VII and IX to XI of, and Schedules 7 to 9 to the principal Act shall apply to the election and to persons entitled to vote and voting at the election in like manner as they apply respectively to a parliamentary election and to persons entitled to vote and voting at such an election but with the adaptations specified in Schedule 1.

(a) 1973 c. 17.
(b) 1962 c. 14 (N.I.).
(c) 1954 c. 33 (N.I.).

Effect etc. of disqualification for membership of the Assembly

4.—(1) Sections 6 and 7 of the House of Commons Disqualification Act, 1957**(a)** (effects of disqualification, provision for relief and jurisdiction of Privy Council) shall, subject to the modifications specified in paragraphs (2) and (3), apply to the Assembly as they apply to the House of Commons of Northern Ireland, and as if any reference to that Act were a reference to that Act as applied by section 3 of the Northern Ireland Assembly Act 1973.

(2) In section 6 of that Act—

(*a*) for any reference to the House of Commons of Northern Ireland there shall be substituted a reference to the Assembly;

(*b*) subsections (1) and (4) to (6) shall be omitted;

(*c*) in subsection (3) the words "Senate or" and "as the case may be" and, in the proviso, the words from "and this subsection" onwards shall be omitted.

(3) Section 7(6) of that Act shall be omitted.

(4) In this Article, references to sections 6 and 7 of that Act of 1957 are references to those sections as modified by section 10(1) of and Schedule 3 to that Act.

Deputy and assistant returning officers

5.—(1) The Chief Electoral Officer shall not, under section 14A of the principal Act delegate functions conferred on him regarding the furnishing of accounts and returns to the Ministry or conferred on him by section 57(4) of the principal Act.

(2) Where the Chief Electoral Officer under section 14A of the principal Act appoints a deputy returning officer or one or more assistant returning officers for a constituency—

(*a*) he shall not delegate to an assistant returning officer any of the following giving functions:—

(i) the receipt of nominations and deposits and withdrawal of nominations and sending of notices to candidates concerning nomination;

(ii) publishing the statement of candidates validly nominated and notice of poll;

(iii) publishing the summary of the return regarding candidates' expenses;

(iv) publishing the result of the poll in the constituency;

(*b*) the deputy returning officer shall appoint to be his principal office (in this Order referred to as "the principal office") for the purpose of the election for the constituency for which he has been appointed a place within the constituency or within the area of a local authority which wholly or partly contains the constituency and may appoint subsidiary offices under the control of assistant returning officers to deal with specified matters which have been delegated to those officers; and

---

(a) 1957 c. 20.

(c) in the principal Act and this Order, unless the context otherwise requires, any reference to the returning officer or a person acting as returning officer shall, in relation to any functions delegated to a deputy returning officer or an assistant returning officer be construed as a reference respectively to the deputy returning officer or an assistant returning officer for the relevant constituency.

Polling station scheme for the election

6. The Chief Electoral Officer may prepare a polling station scheme designating the polling stations to be used at the election and where he does so the polling stations so designated shall, subject to section 65(6) of the principal Act, be the polling stations to be used at the election.

Postal voting at the election

7. A person who submits or has submitted a valid application to vote by post at the border poll on 8th March 1973 or at the local general elections on 30th May 1973 may if he complies with Rule 22 in Schedule 2 vote by post at the election.

Conduct of the election

8.—(1) The election shall be conducted in accordance with the timetable and Rules contained in Schedule 2.

(2) The forms contained in Schedule 3 shall be used at the election for the purposes for which they are expressed to be applicable and the returning officer may make any adaptation in any form which may be necessary for its use in particular circumstances.

W. S. I. Whitelaw,
One of Her Majesty's Principal
Secretaries of State.

Northern Ireland Office.

9th May 1973.

Article 3 **SCHEDULE 1**

ADAPTATIONS OF PRINCIPAL ACT IN ITS APPLICATION TO ELECTION TO THE NORTHERN IRELAND ASSEMBLY

General adaptations of references

1. For any such reference in the principal Act as is specified in column 1 of the Table set out below there shall be substituted the reference specified in column 2.

TABLE

Reference	Substituted reference
an election	the election
a parliamentary candidate	a candidate at the election
a parliamentary election	the election
a parliamentary election court	an Assembly election court
a parliamentary election petition	an Assembly election petition
a parliamentary general election	the election
a parliamentary elector	an elector for the election

Specific adaptations

2. The following specific adaptations shall be made in the principal Act:—

Provision	Adaptation
Section 22	In subsection (2), for the words "charged on and paid out of the Consolidated Fund" there shall be substituted the words "paid by the Ministry". In subsection (4) for the word "prescribe" there shall be substituted the word "determine".
Section 28	Shall not apply.
Section 29(8)	For the words "Rules 38, 42 and 44 of the Parliamentary Elections Rules" there shall be substituted the words "Rules 39, 43 and 45 in Schedule 2 to the Northern Ireland Assembly (Election) Order 1973".
Section 41(6)	For the words "2 and 3 in the Tenth Schedule" there shall be substituted the words "AE 8 and AE 9 in Schedule 3 to the Northern Ireland Assembly (Election) Order 1973".
Section 46(1)	For the words "4 in the Tenth Schedule" there shall be substituted the words "AE 10 in Schedule 3 to the Northern Ireland Assembly (Election) Order 1973".
Section 47(1)	For the words "5 in the Tenth Schedule" there shall be substituted the words "AE 11 in Schedule 3 to the Northern Ireland Assembly (Election) Order 1973".
Section 48(1) and (2)	For the words "House of Commons" in both places where they occur there shall be substituted the word "Assembly".
Section 57	In subsection (1) for the words "Parliamentary Elections Rules" there shall be substituted the words "the Northern Ireland Assembly Act 1973 and the Northern Ireland Assembly (Election) Order 1973" and subsection (3) shall not apply.
Section 61	In subsection (1)(*a*) for the words "Parliamentary Elections Rules" there shall be substituted the words "Rules contained in the Northern Ireland Assembly (Election) Order 1973"; subsection (2) shall not apply; in subsection (3)(*a*) for the words from "candidate" to "member" there shall be substituted the words "the candidate's name or signature has been entered in the records of the Assembly indicating his attendance at a meeting of the Assembly" and for the words from "until" to "taken" there shall be substituted the words "until such entry has been made"; in subsection (4) for the words "take the oath" there shall be substituted the words "attend the Assembly" and the word "respectively" shall be omitted; in subsection (5)(*a*) for the word "Parliament" there shall be substituted the words "the Assembly"; and in subsection (8)(*b*) the words "and paid into the Exchequer" shall be omitted.
Section 63	At the beginning there shall be inserted the words "Except where Article 5(2)(*b*) of the Northern Ireland Assembly (Election) Order 1973 applies,".

Provision	Adaptation
Section 65	Subsections (1) to (5) shall not apply.
Section 66	Shall not apply.
Section 67	Subsection (3) shall not apply.
Section 74(1)	For the word "Parliament" there shall be substituted the words "the Assembly".
Section 77	In subsection (1) after the words "member" (wherever it occurs) and "person" there shall be inserted respectively the words "or members" and "or persons"; after the word "was" where it occurs for the first, third and fourth times there shall be inserted the words "or were"; in subsections (1) to (5) for the word "Speaker" there shall be substituted the words "person presiding over the Assembly" and in subsections (3) and (5) for the words "House of Commons" there shall be substituted the word "Assembly".
Section 83	In subsection (3) for the word "Speaker" there shall be substituted the words "person presiding over the Assembly".
Section 88	For the word "Speaker" there shall be substituted the words "person presiding over the Assembly".
Section 90	In subsections (1)(a) and (2) for the words "the House of Commons" there shall be substituted the words "the Assembly" and in subsection (2) for the word "Speaker" there shall be substituted the words "person presiding over the Assembly".
Section 95	In subsection (2) for the words "House of Commons" there shall be substituted the word "Assembly" and for the word "Parliament" there shall be substituted the word "Assembly".
Section 96	In subsection (3) for the words "House of Commons" there shall be substituted the word "Assembly".
Section 110	In subsection (1) for the words "Rule 44 of the Parliamentary Election Rules" there shall be substituted the words "Rule 45 in Schedule 2 to the Northern Ireland Assembly (Election) Order 1973".
Section 126	Shall not apply.
Section 128	Shall not apply.
Section 130	In subsection (1)— (a) the following definitions shall be inserted at the appropriate places in alphabetical order— "Assembly" means the Northern Ireland Assembly; "Assembly election" and Assembly "elector" mean respectively an election in a constituency of members to serve in the Assembly, and a person entitled to vote at an Assembly election; (b) for the definition of "constituency" there shall be substituted the following definition:— "constituency" means a constituency specified in the Schedule to the Northern Ireland Assembly Act 1973 and "borough constituency" and "county constituency" mean respectively the constituencies so specified in the enactment which constituted them;

Provision	Adaptation
Section 130 (*cont.*)	(*c*) the definitions of "postal voting area" and "Speaker" shall be omitted; In subsection (3), in paragraph (*a*) ,for the word "Parliament" there shall be substituted the words "the Assembly" and for the words from 'writ for" onwards there shall be substituted the words "notice of election" and in subsection (5) paragraphs (*a*) and (*b*) and in paragraph (*c*) the words to "local election" shall be omitted.
Schedule 8	For any reference to the House of Commons or Parliament there shall be substituted a reference to the Assembly and in addition the following specific adaptations shall be made:— in paragraph 3(2) the words "out of moneys provided by Parliament" shall be omitted; in paragraph 5, in sub-paragraph (3)(*a*) for the words "the Clerk of the Parliaments" there shall be substituted "such officer of the Assembly as the Secretary of State may specify" and in sub-paragraph (3)(*b*) for the word "Speaker" there shall be substituted the words "person presiding over the Northern Ireland Assembly"; in paragraph 11(6) for the words from "Parliamentary" to "may be" there shall be substituted the words "Rules contained in Schedule 2 to the Northern Ireland Assembly (Election) Order 1973".

SCHEDULE 2   Article 8(1)

ELECTION RULES

PART I

TIME-TABLE AND COMPUTATION OF TIME

Time-table

1. The proceedings at the election shall be conducted in accordance with the following Table:—

	Proceeding (1)	Time fixed or allowed at the Election (2)
1	Publication of notice of election	Not later than 22nd May 1973.
2	Delivery of nomination papers and candidates' statements and lodgment of deposits under section 60 of the principal Act as applied by this Order	Subject to Rule 12, during the period between 10 a.m. and 5 p. m. on 5th June 1973.
3	Delivery of withdrawal of candidature	Within the period allowed for proceeding 2 above.
4	The making of objections to nomination papers	Within the time specified in Rule 11(11).
5	Notice to candidates— (*a*) of valid nomination; (*b*) of invalid nomination	As soon as practicable after the expiration of the time allowed by Rule 11(11) for the making of objections to nomination papers.
6	Publication of statement of candidates validly nominated	As soon after the close of the time allowed for proceeding 4 above as the validity of all nomination papers has been determined.
7	Notice of poll	Not later than 15th June 1973.
8	Poll	Between 8 a.m. and 8.30 p.m. on 28th June 1973.

Computation of time

2. In the computation of any period of time for the purpose of these Rules, a Sunday or public holiday shall be disregarded and shall not be treated as a day for the purposes of any proceedings up to the completion of the poll, nor shall the returning officer be obliged to proceed with the count on such a day.

PART II

STAGES COMMON TO CONTESTED AND UNCONTESTED ELECTIONS

Publication of notices

3. Any public notice required by these Rules to be given shall, unless these Rules otherwise provide, or the Chief Electoral Officer otherwise directs, be given by means of—

    (*a*) advertisement in one or more than one newspaper circulating in the area to which the notice relates; or

    (*b*) posters exhibited in suitable positions throughout that area; or

    (*c*) any other method which the Chief Electoral Officer thinks necessary or desirable for the purpose of bringing to the attention of persons interested the matter so required to be notified; or

    (*d*) two or more of the above-mentioned methods.

Notice of election

4. The returning officer shall, in accordance with the timetable in **Rule 1**, give public notice of the election in the form numbered AE1 in Schedule 3 which shall state—

    (*a*) the principal and, if any, the subsidiary offices from which nomination forms can be obtained;

    (*b*) the number of members to be returned for the constituency;

    (*c*) the date, times and place for receiving nominations;

    (*d*) the amount of the deposit;

    (*e*) the date and time up to which withdrawal of candidature may be made;

    (*f*) the date and the period of time fixed for the holding of the poll, if the election is contested.

Nomination forms

5. Nomination forms and copies of candidates' statements referred to in Rule 9 shall be available at the principal and, if any, the subsidiary offices from 9.30 a.m. to 5 p.m. on Mondays to Fridays inclusive between the date of the publication of the notice of election and up to 4.30 p.m. on the day fixed for receiving nominations and such nomination papers and statements shall be supplied free of charge to any person applying therefor but it shall not be necessary for a nomination or such statements to be on a form obtained or supplied under this Rule.

Nomination and description of candidates

6.—(1) Each candidate shall be nominated by means of a separate nomination paper in the form numbered AE2 in Schedule 3.

(2) The nomination paper shall be subscribed by two persons as proposer and seconder and by eight other persons as assenting to the nomination (all such persons being registered in the current register).

(3) Where a nomination paper bears the signatures of more than the required number of persons as proposing, seconding or assenting to the nomination of a candidate, the signature or signatures (up to the required number) appearing first on the paper in each category shall be taken into account to the exclusion of any others in that category.

(4) The number in the register of each person subscribing the nomination paper shall be stated in the paper.

(5) No person shall subscribe more than one nomination paper at the same election and, if he does, his signature shall be inoperative on any paper other than the one first delivered but a person shall not be prevented from subscribing a nomination paper by reason only of his having subscribed that of a candidate who has died or withdrawn before delivery of the first-mentioned paper.

Description of candidate on nomination paper

7.—(1) A nomination paper may, subject to paragraph (2) include a description of the candidate.

(2) The description shall not exceed six words in length.

Consent to nomination

8.—(1) A person shall, subject to paragraph (2), not be validly nominated unless his consent to nomination, given in writing on or within one month before the nomination day and attested by one witness, is delivered at the principal office within the nomination period as defined in Rule 10.

(2) If the returning officer is satisfied that, owing to the absence of a person from Northern Ireland, it has not been reasonably practicable for his consent in writing to be given as aforesaid, a telegram consenting to his nomination and purporting to have been sent by him shall for the purpose of this Rule be deemed to be consent in writing given by him on the day on which it purports to have been sent, and attestation of his consent shall not be required.

Statement by candidate

9. A candidate's consent given under Rule 8 shall contain a statement—

(a) that he is aware of the provisions of the House of Commons Disqualification Act 1957 as they apply to the Assembly; and

(b) that to the best of his knowledge and belief he is not disqualified by those provisions or otherwise for membership of the Assembly.

Attendance of returning officer to receive nominations and deposits

10.—(1) The returning officer shall on nomination day attend at the principal office, between 10 a.m. and 5 p.m. (in these Rules referred to as "the nomination period") for the purpose of receiving nominations from or on behalf of candidates nominated for the constituency.

(2) The returning officer shall also receive during the nomination period the deposit of £150 (required by section 2(4) of the Northern Ireland Assembly Act 1973 to be made by or on behalf of each candidate).

Delivery and determination of validity of nomination papers and attendance at nomination

11.—(1) Every nomination paper shall be delivered by or on behalf of the candidate to the returning officer at the principal office during the nomination period.

(2) The returning officer shall endorse on the first nomination paper received in respect of each candidate, and shall sign, a statement of the time of receipt thereof and of the due lodgment of the candidate's statement under Rule 9 and of the candidate's deposit and shall annex to that paper a second or any subsequent paper in the order in which it is received but shall not be required to endorse any such second or subsequent paper.

(3) The returning officer shall as soon as practicable examine and determine the validity of the first nomination paper received in respect of each candidate, and if he determines it to be valid shall mark it accordingly; and where a paper in respect of any candidate is so marked, the returning officer shall not be required to mark a second or any subsequent paper in respect of that candidate.

(4) Where the returning officer determines that the first of several nomination papers received in respect of any candidate is invalid, he shall examine, in the order of their receipt, the subsequent papers in respect of that candidate and shall mark in accordance with paragraph (3) the first such paper that he determines to be valid; and thereupon shall not be required to examine any subsequent paper in respect of that candidate.

(5) The returning officer shall for the purpose of paragraph (3) determine a nomination paper to be valid if—

    (a) it is in the form numbered AE2 in Schedule 3;

    (b) the instructions in that form have been duly complied with; and

    (c) it is accompanied by the candidate's consent, statement and deposit in accordance with Rules 8 to 10;

and otherwise shall determine the nomination paper to be invalid.

(6) Where the returning officer determines a nomination paper to be valid his decision shall be final and shall not be questioned in any proceedings.

(7) Every person in respect of whom a nomination paper has under this Rule been determined to be valid and whose candidature is not withdrawn under Rule 13 shall stand validly nominated as a candidate.

(8) Nothing in this Rule shall prevent the validity of the nomination of any candidate from being questioned on an election petition.

(9) Except for the purpose of assisting the returning officer, no person shall be entitled to attend the proceedings during the time for delivery of nomination papers or for making objections thereto, unless he is a person nominated as a candidate or is the election agent, proposer or seconder of such a person or, where such a person intends to be his own election agent, another person designated by such person.

(10) Where more than one nomination paper is delivered in respect of any candidate, the persons entitled to attend as his proposer and seconder shall be those only who have, as such, subscribed such one of the papers as the candidate may designate or, in default of such designation, the paper first received (whether marked under paragraph (3) or not).

(11) Any person lawfully present at the nomination proceedings may, at any time before the returning officer determines the validity of a nomination paper but not later than one hour after the nomination period, inspect and object to the validity of that nomination paper or the candidate's statement accompanying it on the ground that it ought to be determined to be invalid under paragraph (5), and the returning officer shall take any such objection into consideration and shall give his decision thereon as soon as practicable.

Adjournment of nomination proceedings in case of riot etc.

12.—(1) Where any proceedings for or in connection with the nomination of candidates at the election are obstructed or interrupted by riot, open violence or any form of civil disorder or disobedience, the returning officer may adjourn the proceedings to the next following day and if he considers it necessary, may further adjourn the proceedings until the obstruction or interruption has ceased.

(2) If the Chief Electoral Electoral Officer is satisfied that any proceedings for or in connection with the nomination of candidates at the election are likely to be obstructed or interrupted as specified in paragraph (1) at or in the general vicinity of the nomination place, he may adjourn the proceedings to the next following day and if he considers it necessary further adjourn the nomination proceedings.

(3) Where any proceedings for or in connection with nominations for a constituency are adjourned under this Rule, the Chief Electoral Officer shall make such amendment to the time-table for the election in that constituency as he considers necessary.

Withdrawal of candidate

13.—(1) A candidate may withdraw his candidature by notice of withdrawal signed by him and authenticated by one witness and delivered to the returning officer at the principal office within the nomination period.

(2) Where a candidate is out of Northern Ireland, a notice of withdrawal signed by his proposer and accompanied by a written declaration, also so signed, of the candidate's absence from Northern Ireland shall have the same effect as a notice under paragraph (1), but where, upon the examination of all the nomination papers received in respect of a candidate, more than one valid nomination paper is found to have been so received a notice of withdrawal under this paragraph, in respect of that candidate, shall be effective if, and only if—

  (a) that notice and the accompanying declaration are signed by all the proposers except any who is and is stated in the declaration to be out of Northern Ireland; or

  (b) it is accompanied, in addition to the said declaration, by a written statement signed by the candidate that the proposer giving the notice is authorised to do so on behalf of the candidate during the candidate's absence from Northern Ireland.

Publication of statement of candidates nominated

14.—(1) As soon as practicable after the determination of the validity of all the nomination papers, the returning officer shall prepare and publish a statement setting out separately—

  (a) the candidates who stand validly nominated;

  (b) the persons who having been validly nominated have withdrawn their candidatures.

(2) The statement shall with respect to such candidates and persons set out—

  (a) their surnames arranged in alphabetical order, and, as between two or more candidates bearing the same surname, in the alphabetical order of their other names;

  (b) the address and description, if any, of each as shown in his nomination paper, or where there is more than one nomination paper, in that paper marked valid by the returning officer under Rule 11, and the names of the person subscribing such paper.

(3) Where the number of candidates standing validly nominated for a constituency is greater than the number of members to be returned by that constituency, the statement shall also include a notice of the poll in accordance with Rule 18 and a poll shall be taken in accordance with Part IV.

Death of a candidate

15.—(1) Where during the nomination period the returning officer is given proof to his satisfaction that a candidate standing nominated has died, he shall immediately give public notice to that effect and the candidature of the candidate shall be deemed to have been withdrawn.

(2) Subject to paragraph (3), where, at any time after the close of the nomination period and before the close of the poll, the returning officer is given proof to his satisfaction that a candidate standing nominated for election in the constituency has died, the following provisions shall have effect in relation to the election for that constituency:—

　　(a) the returning officer shall give public notice to that effect;

　　(b) votes given for that candidate shall not be counted; and

　　(c) the preferences shown for that candidate shall be ignored and subsequent preferences for other candidates shall be taken to be one figure lower than that shown on the ballot paper, so that a second such preference will then become a first preference, a third a second and so on.

(3) Where candidates in a constituency have been declared elected under Rule 16, the death of one of those candidates, proof of which to the satisfaction of the returning officer is received by the returning officer after the declaration, shall not affect the declaration and that candidate shall be deemed to have vacated his seat on the day following that on which the poll would have been held if there had been an election in that constituency.

(4) The death of a candidate, proof of which to the satisfaction of the returning officer has not been received by the returning officer before the close of the poll, shall not affect the election or the counting of the votes and if that candidate is elected he shall be deemed to have vacated his seat on the day following that on which the poll was held.

Part III

Uncontested Elections

Declaration of result of election

16. Where the number of candidates standing validly nominated for a constituency is equal to or less than the number of members to be returned by that constituency, the statement referred to in Rule 14(1) and (2) shall also declare those candidates to have been elected.

Part IV

Contested Elections

Poll to be taken by ballot

17.—(1) The votes at the poll shall be given by secret ballot.

(2) The votes given to each candidate shall be counted and the result of the poll shall be determined in accordance with Part V.

Notice of poll

18.—(1) The returning officer shall in the statement of candidates standing validly nominated include a notice of the poll, stating the day on which and the hours during which the poll will be taken and the number of members to be returned for the constituency.

(2) The returning officer shall also give public notice (which may be combined with the above-mentioned statement) of the situation of each polling station and the description of voters entitled to vote thereat and of the mode in which voters are to vote.

Ballot papers

19.—(1) The ballot of every voter shall consist of a ballot paper and the persons named in the statement published under Rule 14 as standing validly nominated, and no others, shall be entitled to have their names inserted in the ballot paper.

(2) Every ballot paper shall be in the form numbered AE 3 in Schedule 3 and shall be printed in accordance with the directions therein, and—

(*a*) shall contain the names and other particulars of the candidates standing validly nominated, as shown in the above-mentioned statement;

(*b*) shall be capable of being folded up;

(*c*) shall have a serial number printed on the back; and

(*d*) shall have attached a counterfoil having the same serial number printed on the face.

(3) The order of the names in the ballot paper shall be the same as in the above-mentioned statement.

(4) The colour of the ordinary ballot papers shall be white and the colour of the tendered ballot papers issued in accordance with Rule 44 shall be pink.

(5) All ballot papers shall be made up in books which—

(*a*) for ordinary ballot papers shall each contain, at the discretion of the returning officer, either fifty or one hundred papers;

(*b*) for tendered ballot papers shall each contain not more than twenty-five papers;

(*c*) shall be so bound that at the close of the poll the counterfoils of the issued papers can be detached from those of the unused papers.

(6) It shall be the duty of the returning officer to make arrangements for the printing for the election of such number of ballot papers of each appropriate colour as he thinks adequate, the ballot papers of each colour to be numbered consecutively.

The official mark

20.—(1) Every ballot paper shall at the time of issue be marked with an official mark, which shall be either embossed or perforated so as to be visible on both sides of the paper, and for this purpose the returning officer shall provide a sufficient number of marking instruments.

(2) The official mark to be used on postal ballot papers (in these Rules referred to as the "postal voting mark") shall be different from that to be used for ballot papers issued to electors voting in person; and where the postal voting mark is embossed the other official mark shall be perforated and vice versa.

(3) It shall be the duty of the returning officer to ensure that the official mark is kept secret.

Polling information cards

21.—(1) Polling information cards in the form numbered AE4 in Schedule 3 shall be prepared by the returning officer in respect of all the electors registered in the constituency and shall be issued by post to those electors.

(2) A polling information card shall be sent to the elector in sufficient time to be delivered in the ordinary course of post not later than 6th June 1973.

Postal voting list

22.—(1) A voter who—

(*a*) submits or has submitted a valid application to vote by post, either—

(i) at the Border Poll on 8th March 1973; or

(ii) at the local government elections on 30th May 1973; and

(*b*) desires to vote by post at the election,

shall, not later than 5 p.m. on 12th June 1973, so inform the returning officer by completing the appropriate part of the polling information card sent to him and returning it to that officer.

(2) Where the returning officer is informed as mentioned in paragraph (1) he shall, if an application so mentioned which is submitted on or before 17th May 1973 by that voter to vote by post has already been accepted, and the voter gives an address in the United Kingdom to which a ballot paper may be sent, place his name on the postal voting list for the election.

General provisions as to postal ballot papers

23.—(1) No person other than—

(*a*) the returning officer, his deputy, his assistants and his clerks;

(*b*) the candidates;

(*c*) the election agents or persons appointed by those agents;

(*d*) such other persons as the returning officer may admit,

shall, subject to paragraph (2), be present at the proceedings on the issue of postal ballot papers or the opening of the postal voters ballot boxes (in these Rules referred to as "postal ballot boxes") and of the envelopes therein contained.

(2) Where by reason of the number of postal voters the returning officer decides that the issue of the ballot papers or the opening of the envelopes containing ballot papers is to be carried out in two or more batches simultaneously, the returning officer shall authorise the election agent of each candidate to appoint one additional person to be present with or on behalf of the election agent at each such issue or opening.

(3) The returning officer shall—

(*a*) give to the election agent of each candidate reasonable notice of the time and place at which the issue of postal ballot papers will commence and of the number of persons who may be appointed to be present thereat; and

(*b*) where he intends to issue those papers on more than one day, shall also indicate the date and hour of commencement of the final issue.

(4) The returning officer may if he thinks fit (and taking due precautions for the safe-keeping of the marked copy of the postal voting list, the unused ballot papers and the counterfoils of those issued) adjourn from day to day the proceedings on any day other than that of the final issue and the intimation at the time of such adjournment of the date and hour of resumption shall be sufficient notice to all persons concerned.

(5) All proceedings under paragraphs (3) and (4) shall be conducted at the same place.

(6) The returning officer shall ensure that postal ballot papers are issued not later than such time as will enable them to be marked and returned to him before the close of the poll.

(7) The time fixed for the commencement of the issue of postal ballot papers may, if the returning officer thinks fit, be earlier than the latest time for the receipt of applications to vote by post; but the time of the final issue of postal ballot papers shall be so fixed as to ensure that the postal voting list is complete and that postal ballot papers are issued to all electors entitled thereto.

(8) The returning officer shall provide at the principal office a sufficient number of postal ballot boxes constructed in accordance with Rule 29(3)(a) and such boxes shall have the words "Postal Ballot Box" and the name of the constituency for which the boxes are to be used marked on them.

(9) As soon as the first issue of postal ballot papers has been completed the boxes shall be exhibited empty to, and shall be locked and sealed in the presence of, the election or other agents of the candidates and any such agent so requiring may also affix his seal.

(10) The returning officer shall give to the election agent of each candidate not less than twenty-four hours' notice in writing of—

(a) the time and place at which the postal ballot boxes and the envelopes therein contained will be opened; and

(b) the number of persons who may be appointed to be present thereat.

(11) The returning officer shall make provision for the safe custody of every postal ballot box.

(12) No proceedings under this Rule or Rule 25 or 26 shall be invalidated by reason of the non-attendance of any candidate, agent or other person appointed to be present at the proceedings if any notice required by this Rule has been given.

Declaration of secrecy

24.—(1) Every person attending the proceedings at either the issue or receipt of postal ballot papers shall before being admitted to the proceedings make a declaration of secrecy.

(2) Before the opening of the poll a declaration of secrecy shall be made by—

(a) the Chief Electoral Officer and persons appointed by him as deputy and assistant returning officers;

(b) every officer or clerk authorised to attend at a polling station or at the count;

(c) every candidate attending at a polling station or at the count and every election agent so attending;

(d) every polling agent and counting agent; and

(e) every person permitted by the returning officer to attend at the poll or the count.

(3) Notwithstanding anything in paragraph (2), the following persons attending only at the count, that is to say—

(a) any candidate;

(b) any election agent;

(c) any person permitted by the returning officer to attend;

need not make the declaration before the opening of the poll but shall make it before being permitted to attend the count; and a polling or counting agent appointed after the opening of the poll shall make the declaration before acting as such agent.

(4) Any messenger sent by or on behalf of the returning officer shall before entering a polling station or being admitted to a count make a declaration of secrecy.

(5) The declaration shall be made and signed—

(a) by the Chief Electoral Officer in the presence of and countersigned by a justice of the peace;

(b) by a deputy returning officer in the presence of and countersigned by a justice of the peace or the Chief Electoral Officer;

(c) by every other person in the presence of and countersigned by either a justice of the peace or the returning officer or deputy returning officer;

and a copy of paragraph 27 of Schedule 9 to the principal Act shall be given to the declarant by the person taking the declaration.

(6) The declaration of secrecy to be made under this Rule shall be made on a form supplied by the returning officer and shall be as follows:—

"I solemnly promise and declare that I will not do anything forbidden by paragraph 27 of Schedule 9 to the Electoral Law Act (Northern Ireland) 1962 and I hereby acknowledge receipt of a copy of that paragraph which has been given to me at the time of making this declaration.".

Proceedings on the issue and return of postal ballot papers

25.—(1) The ballot papers to be sent to postal voters shall be marked with the postal voting mark as provided by Rule 20 but in other respects shall be the same as those to be issued to electors voting in person.

(2) A printed declaration in the form numbered AE5 in Schedule 3 (in these Rules referred to as a "voter's declaration") shall be sent with each postal ballot paper and shall have printed on the back thereof the instructions to the voter set out in that form and shall be marked with the postal voting mark.

(3) The returning officer shall cause—

(a) the serial number and the particulars of each elector as shown in the postal voting list to be called out;

(b) each such serial number to be marked on the counterfoil of a ballot paper;

(c) a mark to be placed in a copy of the postal voting list against the number of the elector to denote that a ballot paper has been issued to him, but without identifying the ballot paper.

(4) The returning officer shall for each postal voter place in an envelope addressed to the voter at the address recorded in the postal voting list—

(a) the ballot paper duly marked in accordance with paragraph (1);

(b) the form of voter's declaration duly marked in accordance with paragraph (2);

(c) an envelope addressed to the returning officer (in these Rules referred to as the "covering envelope");

(d) a smaller envelope marked "Ballot Paper Envelope";

and shall effectually close the first-mentioned envelope.

(5) If the returning officer is satisfied that two or more entries in the postal voting list relate to the same person he shall not issue more than one ballot paper in respect of such entries.

(6) The returning officer shall count all envelopes addressed to postal voters and forthwith deliver the envelopes to the nearest head post office or such other office as may be arranged by him with the head postmaster; and the returning officer shall obtain from the postmaster a duly stamped receipt stating the number of envelopes so delivered.

(7) As and when the covering envelopes are received from postal voters the returning officer shall place them unopened in one of the boxes which have been locked and sealed under Rule 23(9) and one such box shall be kept available for that purpose until the close of the poll but not later.

(8) If the returning officer on receiving and opening an envelope, other than a covering envelope, addressed to him as returning officer, finds therein any documents appropriate to a covering envelope, he shall, without examining such documents,—

(a) effectually close the envelope so received;

(b) endorse thereon and sign a statement that it has been closed with its contents intact;

(c) place the closed envelope in a ballot box in accordance with paragraph (7); and

(d) treat such envelope for all purposes as a covering envelope.

(9) The returning officer may, at any time before the close of the poll, open the postal ballot boxes other than that kept available under paragraph (7) and that box shall be opened as soon as may be after the close of the poll and before the beginning of the count, and in relation to that box the same procedure, as nearly as may be, shall be followed as in relation to the other ballot boxes under these Rules.

(10) At the hour fixed for the close of the poll the returning officer shall in the presence of the election or other agents of the candidates either—

(a) seal any postal ballot box then remaining open for the insertion of covering envelopes so that no further such envelopes can be inserted therein; or

(b) forthwith open such box and extract and deal with the contents in accordance with Rule 26.

Proceedings on the opening of the postal ballot boxes containing covering envelopes

26.—(1) Before opening the postal ballot boxes the returning officer shall exhibit to any candidates or agents then present the boxes duly locked and sealed and shall then—

(a) open the ballot boxes in succession and remove the contents from each;

(b) close and lock and seal each empty ballot box and permit it to be sealed by any election or other agent so requiring; and

(c) count and note the number of covering envelopes removed from the ballot boxes.

(2) The covering envelopes removed from each ballot box shall each be opened separately and, where any such envelope is found to contain one voter's declaration and one ballot paper envelope or one such declaration and one ballot paper and only such declaration and envelope or only such declaration and ballot paper as the case may be, such contents shall be dealt with as provided in the succeeding paragraphs of this Rule but, subject to paragraph (6), in every other case the envelope and its contents shall be set aside and disregarded.

(3) If on complying with paragraph (2)—

(a) the returning officer is satisfied that the voter's declaration has been duly signed and authenticated and bears the postal voting mark he shall—

(i) place the declaration in a receptacle specially provided for accepted declarations; and

(ii) open the ballot paper envelope and if it contains one ballot paper, and only such ballot paper, place it, or where the ballot paper is not enclosed in an envelope place that paper, in a ballot box which has been locked and sealed under paragraph (1) and if a ballot paper envelope does not contain a ballot paper mark the envelope "empty";

(b) the returning officer is not satisfied that the voter's declaration has been duly signed and authenticated or if the said declaration does not bear the postal voting mark, he shall endorse on the declaration the words "vote rejected" and shall attach thereto the ballot paper envelope unopened or if there is no such envelope, place the ballot paper in a ballot paper envelope and effectually close it and attach it to the declaration.

(4) Where the returning officer proposes to reject a voter's declaration, he shall permit it to be examined by the election or other agents then present, and, if any such agent objects to the proposed rejection, shall add to the endorsement the words "rejection objected to".

(5) The decision of the returning officer on any question arising in respect of a voter's declaration shall be final, but shall be subject to review on an election petition.

(6) If, in any covering envelope opened under paragraph (2), there is found only a ballot paper envelope, the returning officer shall open the ballot paper envelope and, if one voter's declaration and one ballot paper and only such declaration and ballot paper are found therein, the returning officer shall immediately deal with such declaration and ballot paper in accordance with paragraphs (3) and (4).

(7) The returning officer shall take due precautions to ensure the secrecy of the ballot with regard to any ballot paper not enclosed in, or removed from, a ballot paper envelope.

(8) All documents set aside and disregarded under paragraph (2) shall be endorsed with the word "rejected" and all such documents and all rejected declarations with the attached envelopes shall be kept by the returning officer separate from all other documents.

(9) As soon as the contents of any postal ballot box have been dealt with in accordance with the preceding paragraphs of this Rule, the ballot box in which the ballot papers have under paragraph (3)(a) been placed shall be sealed by the returning officer so that no further ballot papers can be inserted therein.

Disposal by returning officer of postal voting documents

27.—(1) As soon as practicable after completing the issue of postal ballot papers, the returning officer shall in the presence of the several election or other agents make up in separate packets, sealed with his own seal and with that of any such agent so requiring, the marked copy of the postal voting list and the counterfoils of the ballot papers issued.

(2) Notwithstanding paragraph (1), where any further issue of postal ballot papers is to be made, the returning officer may for that purpose open the packet containing the copy of the postal voting list, and, on the completion of such further issue, that copy and the counterfoils of the ballot papers so issued shall be dealt with in accordance with paragraph (1).

(3) The returning officer shall make up in separate packets (to be sealed by him)—

(a) the voters' declarations which accompanied the accepted ballot papers;

(b) any rejected voters' declarations, with any envelopes thereto attached;

(c) any rejected ballot papers, with any envelopes thereto attached;

(d) any ballot paper envelopes marked "empty" under Rule 26(3); and

(e) all documents marked "rejected" under Rule 26(8).

(4) The returning officer shall make up, unopened, in separate packets (to be sealed by him)—

(*a*) any covering envelopes received by him after the close of the poll;

(*b*) any envelopes addressed to postal voters and returned as undelivered.

(5) The returning officer shall transmit to the Clerk of the Crown together with the documents referred to in Rule 66—

(*a*) any such packets as are referred to in this Rule; and

(*b*) a statement in the form numbered AE6 in Schedule 3 setting out the number of postal ballot papers issued, and such other particulars as are required by that form.

(6) Where after the returning officer has complied with paragraph (5) any envelopes sent to postal voters are returned as undelivered, or any covering envelopes are received by him, the returning officer shall retain all such envelopes unopened and shall subsequently transmit them in a sealed packet to the Clerk of the Crown.

(7) Before transmitting any packet referred to in this Rule to the Clerk of the Crown, the returning officer shall mark thereon particulars of its contents, the date of the election to which they relate and the name of the constituency for which the election was held.

Use of schools and public rooms

28.—(1) The returning officer may for the purpose of the taking of the poll or the counting of the votes use, free of charge—

(*a*) a room in a school to which this Rule applies;

(*b*) a room the expense of maintaining which is payable out of any rate.

(2) This Rule applies to a school in receipt of a grant out of moneys appropriated for the purpose, not being a school adjoining or adjacent to any church or other place of worship or connected with a nunnery or other religious establishment.

(3) The returning officer shall make good any damage to, and defray any expense incurred by the persons having control over, any such room as aforesaid by reason of its being used under paragraph (1).

(4) The use of any unoccupied premises or any part thereof for the purpose of the taking of the poll or the counting of the votes shall not render any person liable to be rated or to pay any rate for the premises.

Polling stations and ballot boxes

29.—(1) The returning officer shall make adequate provision for the heating, lighting and cleaning of each polling station.

(2) The returning officer shall provide at each polling station a sufficient number of ballot boxes, one or more than one of which may be provided in any room in the polling station and a polling station in which there is so provided—

(*a*) one ballot box is in these Rules referred to as a "single box station";

(*b*) more than one ballot box is in these Rules referred to as a "multiple station".

(3) Every ballot box so provided—

(*a*) shall be so constructed that—

(i) it will adequately withstand the wear and tear of transit;

(ii) it will contain the ballot papers of such number of electors as are allotted to it;

(iii) it can be securely locked and that while it is so locked ballot papers can be inserted therein but cannot be extracted;

(iv) the lock and aperture for the insertion of ballot papers can be sealed after the close of the poll;

(b) shall be clearly marked with a distinctive number and with the name and number of the polling station in which it is to be used.

(4) The returning officer shall allot the electors to the polling stations in such manner as, in his opinion, will be most convenient for them, and shall suitably divide the electors allotted to each multiple station among the ballot boxes at that station.

(5) The returning officer shall provide at each polling station such number of compartments as may be necessary to enable the voters to mark their ballot papers screened from observation.

(6) In any room in a polling station in which two or more ballot boxes are provided the compartment to be used by the electors allotted to any box shall be so fixed in relation to that box as to render it inconvenient for a voter after marking his ballot paper to place it in any ballot box other than that to which he is allotted.

Appointment of presiding officers, poll clerks, etc.

30.—(1) The returning officer shall for every polling station appoint a presiding officer for each ballot box therein provided, and in a multiple station may designate as senior presiding officer one of the presiding officers who in addition to his functions as presiding officer shall perform such functions as are by these Rules conferred on a senior presiding officer and such other duties as may be assigned to him by the returning officer.

(2) The returning officer shall appoint a poll clerk to assist each presiding officer.

(3) The returning officer shall appoint such clerks and other assistants as he considers necessary for the due conduct of the election.

(4) The returning officer shall not employ in any capacity for the purposes of the election a person who has been employed by or on behalf of a candidate in or about the election.

(5) The returning officer shall, on the due performance of the duties for which they were appointed, pay to presiding officers and other persons appointed under this Rule remuneration in accordance with the scale determined under section 22 of the principal Act.

(6) The returning officer may in the absence or incapacity of a presiding officer, or where in the opinion of the returning officer the circumstances so warrant or require, perform all or any of the functions of that officer, and while so doing shall be subject to these Rules in like manner as if he had been appointed a presiding officer.

(7) Subject to any direction of the returning officer, a presiding officer may perform any of his functions by any person appointed under these Rules to assist him.

Appointment of polling agents and counting agents, etc., and non-attendance of candidates and their election or other agents

31.—(1) The election agent of each candidate may before the commencement of the poll appoint in accordance with this Rule polling agents to attend at polling stations on behalf of the candidate for the purpose of detecting personation, and counting agents to attend the count on his behalf.

(2) The number of polling agents who may be appointed to attend at any polling station on behalf of any candidate shall be one more than the number of ballot boxes provided at that station.

(3) One counting agent may be appointed on behalf of a candidate.

(4) Each election agent shall, not later than the time of the opening of the poll, give written notice to the presiding officer at each polling station (or in a multiple station, the senior presiding officer) of the name and address of every polling agent appointed by him to attend at that station.

(5) Each election agent shall, not later than two days before the polling day give written notice to the returning officer of the name and address of the counting agent appointed by him.

(6) If any polling agent or counting agent dies or becomes incapable of acting, the election agent who appointed him may appoint another agent in his place and shall forthwith give written notice of the name and address of the person so appointed to the returning officer who shall in the case of a polling agent forthwith give particulars of such notice to the presiding officer at the appropriate polling station or, in a multiple station, to the senior presiding officer.

(7) A candidate may lawfully do or assist in the doing of any act or thing which might lawfully be done on his behalf by a polling agent or counting agent.

(8) Any act or thing by these Rules required or authorised to be done in the presence of the candidates or their election or other agents shall not be invalidated by reason only of the non-attendance of any candidate or any such agent or agents at the time and place appointed for so doing.

Marking of register

32. In the copy of the current register to be used at the election in connection with the issue of postal or other ballot papers, the returning officer shall before the polling day—

(a) mark the letter "A" against the name of every elector entered on the postal voting list;

(b) mark the letters "PS" against the name of every elector registered by virtue of a service qualification who has appointed a proxy; and

(c) mark the letters "PC" against the name of every other elector who has appointed a proxy.

Election equipment, etc.

33.—(1) The returning officer shall provide at each polling station—

(a) such furniture as he thinks necessary for the efficient conduct of the poll, regard being had to the convenience and comfort of the officers and clerks concerned;

(b) for each compartment therein, such materials as he thinks necessary for the purpose of enabling voters to mark their ballot papers;

(c) copies of directions for the guidance of voters (in the form numbered AE7 in Schedule 3) which he shall cause to be conspicuously displayed—

(i) in every room in the polling station in which a ballot box is provided; and

(ii) in every compartment;

(d) sufficient copies of such directions as will enable voters to proceed without difficulty to the ballot boxes to which they are allotted, which directions he shall cause to be conspicuously displayed;

(e) for the presiding officer for each ballot box—

    (i) such number of ballot papers as the returning officer thinks adequate for the due conduct of the poll, a record being kept by him of the serial numbers of the ballot papers so provided;

    (ii) one marking instrument;

    (iii) that part of the marked copy of the register which contains the names of the electors allotted to the box;

    (iv) a copy of so much of the list of proxies as relates to such part of the register as aforesaid;

    (v) such other documents and forms as may be appropriate;

    (vi) such stationery and other materials as the returning officer thinks necessary for the due conduct of the poll.

(2) The returning officer shall provide such furniture, stationery and other materials as he thinks necessary for the efficient counting of the votes.

(3) In paragraphs (4) to (7) "election equipment" means ballot boxes, compartments and such furniture as is referred to in paragraph (1)(a) or (2) and such other of the materials and things referred to in paragraphs (1) and (2) as are capable of being used at a subsequent election.

(4) All election equipment in the custody of a local authority shall—

    (a) be duly stored by that local authority on behalf of the Ministry so as to minimise depreciation thereof;

    (b) be made available, free of charge, to the returning officer for any election thereafter held in the area of that local authority.

(5) The Ministry shall provide any election equipment which is necessary in addition to or for the replacement of any such election equipment as is referred to in paragraph (4).

(6) It shall be the duty of a returning officer to ensure that all election equipment provided by him is fit for use and in good order, and after the election to return in good order any equipment made available under paragraph (4) to the local authority from whom he obtained it and to send any other equipment for safe custody to such local authority as he thinks fit.

(7) A returning officer may make such arrangements (including arrangements with the Ministry of Finance) as he thinks fit for the repair of election equipment; and any expenditure incurred in pursuance of such arrangements, in accordance with the scale determined under section 22 of the principal Act, shall be part of the election expenses of the returning officer.

(8) Arrangements shall be made by the Ministry of Finance with Her Majesty's Stationery Office for the issue on loan free of charge to the returning officer on demand, of such number of marking instruments as may be adequate for the purpose of the election.

Opening of poll

34.—(1) Immediately before the commencement of the poll the presiding officer for each ballot box shall show the box, empty, to such persons, if any, as are present in the polling station and shall then lock that box and place his seal on it in such manner as to prevent its being opened without breaking the seal, and shall place it in his view for the deposit of ballot papers, and keep it so locked and sealed.

(2) The senior presiding officer at a multiple station and the presiding officer at a single box station shall cause the door of the station to be opened for the admittance of voters at the precise hour fixed by Rule 1 for the opening of the poll, and no person shall before that hour be admitted to the polling station for the purpose of recording his vote.

Admission to polling station

35.—(1) Except for the purpose of recording his vote, no person shall be admitted to a polling station, other than—

(a) the returning officer and any deputy or assistant of his;

(b) any messengers sent by or on behalf of the returning officer;

(c) the presiding officers and poll clerks for the ballot boxes in the station;

(d) the candidates and their election agents and polling agents;

(e) a person admitted under Rule 41(3);

(f) constables and members of Her Majesty's forces on duty;

(g) a person permitted by the returning officer to observe the conduct of the poll.

(2) Subject to Rule 42, a person shall not be admitted to vote at any polling station other than that to which he is allotted.

(3) The presiding officer for any ballot box shall regulate the number of voters to be admitted at the same time for the purpose of recording their votes in that box.

Meaning of polling station

36. For the purposes of these Rules a polling station shall include—

(a) any entrance porch, vestibule, corridor, ante-room or passageway whereby entrance to the polling station can lawfully be effected;

(b) any road or path connecting the polling station with a public road or street;

(c) any other place within the same curtilage as the polling station.

Maintenance of order in polling station

37.—(1) It shall be the duty of the senior presiding officer assisted by the other presiding officers in a multiple station and of the presiding officer in a single box station to keep order in that polling station.

(2) If a person misconducts himself in a polling station or fails to obey the lawful orders of a presiding officer, he may immediately, by order of the presiding officer, be removed from the polling station by a constable or member of Her Majesty's forces in or near that station or by any other person authorised in writing by the returning officer to remove him, and a person so removed shall not re-enter the polling station without the permission of the presiding officer.

(3) Any person so removed may, if charged with the commission in the polling station of an offence, be dealt with as a person taken into custody by a constable for an offence without a warrant.

(4) The powers conferred by this Rule shall not be exercised so as to prevent a voter who is otherwise entitled to vote at a polling station from having an opportunity of voting at that station.

Where poll cannot be held or completed at time and place appointed

38.—(1) Where the proceedings at any polling station are obstructed or interrupted or voters are prevented from coming to the polling station by riot, open violence or any form of civil disobedience, the returning officer or the presiding officer may adjourn the proceedings to the next following day and, where the presiding officer does so, shall forthwith inform the returning officer and, where he considers it necessary, the returning officer or, if he obtains the approval of the returning officer, the presiding officer, may further adjourn the proceedings until the obstruction or interruption has ceased.

(2) Where under paragraph (1) the poll is adjourned at any polling station—

(*a*) the hours of polling on the day to which it is adjourned shall be the same as for the original day; and

(*b*) references in this Order to the close of the poll shall be construed accordingly.

(3) Where a polling station is damaged by fire or in any other manner and by reason of such damage a poll cannot be held or completed at the time and place appointed by or under these Rules, the Chief Electoral Officer may order another poll to be held and may so far as may appear to him to be necessary or expedient modify Rule 1 and give directions for the purposes of such other poll and the election to which that poll relates.

Voting procedure

39.—(1) Subject to Rules 43 to 45, a ballot paper shall be delivered—

(*a*) to a voter who applies therefor declaring his surname and other names or their initials, his qualifying address and his number in the register (if known to him); and

(*b*) subject to paragraph 3(3) of Schedule 7 to the principal Act, to a person who applies therefor as proxy declaring the surname and other names or their initials and the address of himself and of the elector who has appointed him as a proxy;

and immediately before delivery—

(i) the number, name and description of the elector as stated in the marked copy of the register shall be called out;

(ii) the number of the elector shall be marked on the counterfoil;

(iii) the ballot paper shall be stamped with the official mark;

(iv) a short horizontal line shall be placed in the marked copy of the register against the number of the elector to denote that a ballot paper has been issued to that elector or his proxy but without showing the number of the ballot paper so issued; and

(v) where a person applies for a ballot paper as proxy, a mark shall also be placed against his name in the list of proxies.

(2) A presiding officer shall not issue a ballot paper—

(*a*) to a person claiming to vote in person where the entry in the register relating to that person is marked with the letter "A";

(*b*) to any person other than the duly appointed proxy claiming to vote in person where the relevant entry in the register is marked with the letters "PC".

(3) Where the relevant entry in the register is marked with the letters "PS" a presiding officer shall issue a ballot paper either to the elector or to his proxy, whoever first applies.

(4) The voter, on receiving the ballot paper, shall, subject to Rule 41, forthwith proceed alone into one of the compartments provided for the ballot box to which he is allotted and shall—

(a) secretly record his vote by placing on the ballot paper the figure 1 opposite the name of the candidate for whom he votes and in addition, if he so wishes, by placing the figure 2 opposite the name of the candidate of his second choice, the figure 3 opposite the candidate of his third choice and so on in the order of his preference;

(b) fold the paper so that his vote is concealed;

(c) return to the presiding officer's table and show the back of the folded paper to the presiding officer so as to disclose the official mark; and

(d) put the folded paper into the ballot box in the presence of the presiding officer.

(5) The voter shall vote without undue delay and shall leave the polling station as soon as he has put his ballot paper into the ballot box.

Spoilt ballot papers

40.—(1) A voter who has inadvertently spoilt his ballot paper may, on delivering it to the presiding officer and proving to his satisfaction the fact of the inadvertance, obtain another ballot paper in place of the spoilt ballot paper so delivered and the spoilt ballot paper and the counterfoil thereof shall immediately be marked "cancelled" in bold characters.

(2) For the purposes of this Rule a ballot paper shall be spoilt and void if when recording his vote a voter—

(a) adds to the ballot paper any such writing or symbol as would enable him to be identified; or

(b) marks his ballot paper in such a manner as to render his intention uncertain; or

(c) damages his ballot paper in such manner that it cannot conveniently be used as a ballot paper.

Blind and other assisted voters

41.—(1) This Rule shall have effect as respects any voter who states to a presiding officer that by reason of total or partial blindness, defective vision or illiteracy he is unable to read, or that for one of those reasons or by reason of any other physical disability, or of any religious belief, he is unable without assistance or unwilling to record his vote in accordance with these Rules.

(2) The presiding officer shall—

(a) verify the entry in the register;

(b) record in a list of assisted voters (in these Rules referred to as the "assisted voters list") the name and particulars of the voter;

(c) comply with Rule 39(1)(i) to (v);

(d) deliver a ballot paper to the voter;

(e) in the presence of the polling agents, mark the ballot paper as instructed by the voter, taking such steps as the presiding officer thinks necessary to ensure the secrecy of the ballot; and

(f) deposit the ballot paper in the ballot box.

(3) A person accompanying a voter who by reason of total or partial blindness or other physical disability requires guidance or assistance may be admitted to the polling station for the purpose of giving such guidance or assistance.

(4) If a voter who is totally or partially blind so requests and the person accompanying him makes a declaration of secrecy, but not otherwise, that person may remain with the voter while the presiding officer records his vote under paragraph (2).

(5) The declaration of secrecy to be made under paragraph (4) shall be made in the presence of, and given to, the presiding officer who shall thereupon attest it.

(6) The declaration and form of attestation shall be as follows:—

I,   , of   , having been permitted to remain with   , of   , while the presiding officer records a vote in accordance with that person's instructions, hereby declare that I will not divulge to any person whomsoever the name of the candidates for or against whom the said vote is recorded.

Signature..

Date ....

I, the undersigned, being the presiding officer for   ballot box in the polling station situate at   , hereby certify that the above declaration, having been first read to the above-named declarant, was signed by him in my presence.

Signature ....

Date ....

Voting by constables and other persons on duty

42.—(1) Where a constable will be, or is likely by reason of discharging his duty to be, prevented from voting at an election at his allotted polling station,—

(a) the constable may, within the period of seven days before the day on which the poll is to be taken, apply to an officer of the Royal Ulster Constabulary not below the rank of chief inspector for a certificate to that effect; and

(b) the officer shall in the form numbered AE 12 in Schedule 3 certify under his hand—

(i) the full name and number of the constable;

(ii) the number and description of the constable appearing in the register; and

(iii) the fact that the constable will or is likely to be so prevented as aforesaid.

(2) Where an elector is employed by the returning officer for any purpose connected with an election at which that elector is entitled to vote, and the circumstances of his employment are such as to prevent that elector from voting at his allotted polling station, the returning officer may and at the request of the elector shall so certify in the form numbered AE13 in Schedule 3.

(3) Where a constable or other elector presents a certificate issued respectively under paragraph (1) or (2) above at any polling station for the same constituency as his allotted polling station the presiding officer to whom it is presented shall permit him to vote and shall forthwith cancel the certificate and retain it for disposal at the close of the poll in accordance with Rule 46(5).

(4) This Rule shall not apply to a voter when acting as proxy.

Questions to be put to voters

43.—(1) A presiding officer may, and if required by a candidate or his election agent or polling agent present in the station shall, put to any person applying for a ballot paper at the time of his application, but not afterwards, such one or more than one of the following question as may be appropriate, that is to say—

(a) to a person applying at the election as an elector—

(i) "Are you the person registered in the register of electors for this constituency as follows......?" (*The whole entry from the register is to be read aloud by the presiding officer*);

(ii) "Have you already voted on your own behalf either here or elsewhere in this constituency or any other constituency at this election?";

(*b*) to a person applying at the election as proxy—

(i) "Are you the person whose name appears as AB [in this proxy paper] [*or where the proxy is permitted to vote without producing a proxy paper* on the list of proxies for this election] as entitled to vote as proxy on behalf of CD?";

(ii) "Have you already voted as proxy on behalf of CD either here or elsewhere in this constituency or any other constituency at this election?";

(iii) "Are you the husband [*or*, wife], parent, grandparent brother [*or*, sister], child or grandchild of CD?" and if that question is not answered in the affirmative, then

(iv) "Have you at this election already voted on behalf of more than one person of whom you are not the husband [*or*, wife], parent, grandparent, brother [*or*, sister], child or grandchild?".

(2) Where a person is required to answer any of the foregoing questions a ballot paper shall not be delivered to him unless he has satisfactorily answered such question or questions.

(3) Save as authorised by this Rule, no inquiry shall be made as to the right of any person to vote.

Tendered ballot papers

44.—(1) Where—

(*a*) a ballot paper has been issued to a person representing himself to be a particular elector or proxy; and

(*b*) another person representing himself to be that elector or proxy—

(i) applies for a ballot paper; and

(ii) satisfactorily answers any questions put to him under Rule 43;

that other person shall be entitled to receive, mark and place in the ballot box, in like manner as another voter, a ballot paper (to be known as a "tendered ballot paper") differing only in colour from the ordinary ballot papers.

(2) The name of the elector and his number in the register shall be entered on a list (to be known as the "tendered votes list").

Challenge of voter for personation

45.—(1) If at the time a person applies for a ballot paper for the purpose of voting either in person or as proxy, or after he has applied for a ballot paper for such purpose and before he has left the polling station, a polling agent orally declares to the presiding officer to whom the application was made, that he has reasonable cause to believe that the applicant has committed an offence of personation, and undertakes to substantiate the charge in a court of law, the presiding officer shall order a constable to arrest the applicant, and the order of the presiding officer shall be sufficient authority for the constable so to do.

(2) Where a person in respect of whom a declaration is made under paragraph (1) satisfactorily answers any appropriate question put to him under Rule 43, that paragraph shall not be construed as authorising a presiding officer to prevent that person from voting or to reject his vote; but in such event the presiding officer shall cause the words "Protested against for personation" to be entered against the name of that person in the marked copy of the register or, as the case may be, the list of proxies, used at the polling station.

(3) Where a person is arrested under paragraph (1), the presiding officer—

(a) before that person is removed from the polling station; and

(b) if that person has voted, before any such entry is made as is required by paragraph (2);

shall require the polling agent concerned to make in the form numbered AE 14 in Schedule 3 and sign a declaration confirming his oral declaration; and if such agent fails to comply with such requirement that person shall be released and if he has not already voted shall be permitted to vote, subject to his answering satisfactorily any questions put to him under Rule 43.

(4) A person arrested under paragraph (1) shall be dealt with as a person taken into custody by a constable for an offence without a warrant but a preliminary investigation of the charge shall not be conducted by a justice of the peace who is not a resident magistrate.

Procedure on close of poll

46.—(1) At the time fixed for the close of the poll, the presiding officer shall take steps to ensure that no further voters are admitted to a room within a polling station containing a ballot box but any voter who is in such a room at that time shall, subject to the provisions of these Rules, be entitled to receive a ballot paper and to vote.

(2) The presiding officer or, in a multiple station, the senior presiding officer shall as soon as may be after the time aforesaid and after the voters referred to in paragraph (1) have had an opportunity of voting cause the polling station to be cleared of all persons other than—

(a) the returning officer and any deputy or assistants of his;

(b) any messengers sent by or on behalf of the Chief Electoral Officer or returning officer;

(c) the presiding officers and poll clerks for the ballot boxes in the station and any other polling station assistants appointed by the returning officer;

(d) the candidates and their election agents and polling agents;

(e) constables and members of Her Majesty's forces on duty;

(f) a person admitted to the polling station under Rule 35(1)(g);

and forthwith thereafter cause the doors of the polling station to be closed and to remain closed.

(3) As soon as the polling station is closed, each presiding officer shall seal the ballot box in his charge so that no further ballot papers can be inserted therein and any polling agent so requiring may also affix his seal.

(4) Each presiding officer shall complete a statement in the form numbered AE 15 in Schedule 3 (in these Rules referred to as the "ballot paper account") showing the number of ordinary and tendered ballot papers entrusted to him and accounting for them all under the several heads following, that is to say, used, unused and spoilt.

(5) Each presiding officer shall make up in separate packets (to be sealed by him)—
(a) the ballot paper account;

(b) the counterfoils of all ordinary and tendered ballot papers used, and any certificates presented under Rule 42;

(c) the marked copy of the register, all ordinary and tendered ballot papers unused, all spoilt ballot papers, the lists of tendered votes and of proxies, the assisted voters list, and all declarations of secrecy made under Rules 24 and 41;

and shall place in a separate parcel the marking instrument, and the unused residue of the equipment provided by the returning officer for the conduct of the poll.

(6) Where any person has been taken into custody in a polling station the presiding officer who ordered the arrest shall complete a statement and shall insert therein any such observations or particulars as he may consider necessary or expedient, and shall place that statement in an envelope together with any relevant declaration of a polling agent, and shall keep that envelope in safe custody pending any proceedings.

(7) The presiding officer or, in a multiple station, the senior presiding officer, after the foregoing provisions of this Rule have been complied with, shall proceed to the place where the votes are to be counted, or such other place as may be designated by the returning officer, and shall there deliver to the returning officer or his deputy, or a messenger appointed for the purpose by the returning officer, the ballot box or boxes together with the sealed packets and parcel appropriate to each box; and a presiding officer or senior presiding officer may direct one or more of the clerks or constables on duty to accompany him and assist him in the performance of his duty under this paragraph.

(8) The returning officer shall make adequate arrangements for the safe custody of the ballot boxes and of all documents connected with the poll from the time of their delivery to him until the beginning of the count.

PART V

COUNTING OF THE VOTES AND RETURN OF PERSONS ELECTED

Definitions

47. In this Part—

"candidate's vote" means the value of voting papers credited to a candidate at any stage of the count;

"continuing candidate" means any candidate not deemed to be elected and not excluded;

"count" means all the operations involved in the counting of the first preferences recorded for candidates, the transfer of the surpluses of elected candidates, and the transfer of the votes of excluded candidates.

"deemed to be elected" means deemed to be elected for the purpose of the counting of the votes but without prejudice to the declaration of the result of the poll;

"determine by lot" means determine as follows:—the names of the candidates concerned having been written on similar slips of paper, and the slips having been folded so as to prevent identification and mixed and drawn at random, the candidate whose name is drawn shall be the candidate—

(i) who is next excluded, or

(ii) whose surplus is next transferred, as the case may be.

"mark" means a figure, a word written in the English language or a mark such as "X";

"non-transferable paper" means a ballot paper on which no second or subsequent preference is recorded for a continuing candidate, but a paper shall be deemed to have become a non-transferable paper whenever—

(a) the names of two or more candidates (whether continuing candidates or not) are marked with marks which, in the opinion of the returning officer, indicate the same order of preference and are next in order of preference; or

(b) the name of the candidate next in order of preference (whether a continuing candidate or not) is marked with a mark which, in the opinion of the returning officer, does not follow consecutively after some other mark on the ballot paper, or with two or more marks; or (*c*) it is void for uncertainty;

"original vote" in regard to any candidate means a vote derived from a ballot paper on which a first preference is recorded for that candidate;

"preference" shall be interpreted as follows—

(*a*) "first preference" means the figure "1" or any mark which, in the opinion of the returning officer. clearly indicates a first preference;

"second preference" means the figure "2" or any mark which, in the opinion of the returning officer, clearly indicates a second preference standing in succession to a first preference;

"third preference" means the figure "3" or any mark which, in the opinion of the returning officer, clearly indicates a third preference standing in succession to a second preference; and so on;

(*b*) "next available preference" means a preference which, in the opinion of the returning officer, is a second or subsequent preference recorded in consecutive order for a continuing candidate, the preference next in order on the ballot paper for candidates already deemed to be elected or excluded being ignored;

"surplus" means the number of votes by which the total number of the votes, original and transferred, credited to any candidate, exceeds the quota;

"stage of the count" means the determination of—

(*a*) the first preference vote for each candidate "the first stage"; or

(*b*) the transfer of a surplus of a candidate deemed to be elected; or

(*c*) the exclusion of one or more candidates at the same time;

"transferable paper" means a ballot paper on which, following a first preference, a second or subsequent preference is recorded in consecutive numerical order for a continuing candidate;

"transferred vote" in regard to any candidate, means a vote derived from a ballot paper on which a second or subsequent preference is recorded for that candidate.

Place and time for the counting of the votes

48.—(1) The returning officer shall appoint a place within the constituency or convenient to the constituency as the place at which he will count the votes and shall, at the place so appointed, provide suitable accommodation and all furniture and equipment necessary for counting the votes in accordance with these Rules.

(2) The counting of the votes shall begin at 9 a.m. on the day following that on which the poll is held.

Attendance at the counting of the votes

49.—(1) Not less than six days before the polling day, the returning officer shall give to the election agent of each candidate notice in writing of the time and places at which he will begin to count the votes.

(2) No person other than—

(*a*) the returning officer, his deputy, his assistants and his clerks;

(*b*) the candidates;

(*c*) the election agents;

(*d*) the counting agents;

(e) constables and members of Her Majesty's forces on duty;

(f) such other persons as the returning officer may admit;

may be present at the counting of the votes, but a person admitted under sub-paragraph (f) shall not be permitted in any way to participate in the proceedings.

(3) The returning officer shall give the election and counting agents of the candidates all such reasonable facilities for overseeing the proceedings at the counting of the votes (including, in particular, facilities for satisfying themselves that the ballot papers are correctly sorted) and all such information with respect thereto as he can give them consistently with the orderly conduct of the proceedings and the performance of his functions.

(4) Where the Chief Electoral Officer has delegated the functions in relation to the counting of the votes in a constituency to a deputy returning officer, that deputy returning officer shall not less than three days before the polling day, inform the Chief Electoral Officer of the place at which he proposes to conduct the count.

Preliminary proceedings

50.—(1) Before proceeding to the count the returning officer shall, in the presence of the several counting agents, ascertain in accordance with the following provisions of this Rule the total number of ballot papers to be admitted to the count:—

(a) the postal ballot boxes shall be opened and the number of ballot papers therein contained shall be counted and recorded;

(b) every ballot box other than a postal ballot box shall be opened, and—

(i) the ballot papers shall be extracted;

(ii) any ballot papers found therein which bear the postal voting mark shall be rejected;

(iii) all tendered ballot papers shall be set aside until the completion of the count;

(iv) the remaining ballot papers found therein shall be counted and their total number shall be compared with that shown in the ballot paper account as having been issued by the presiding officer for deposit in that ballot box.

(2) During the conduct of proceedings in accordance with paragraph (1) the returning officer may, in his discretion—

(a) conduct a scrutiny of the ballot papers for the purpose of discovering any papers liable to be rejected; and

(b) conduct a preliminary sorting of the ballot papers.

(3) If, when paragraph (1) has been complied with, the number of ballot papers in each of the ballot boxes (other than the postal ballot boxes) is the same as that shown in the respective ballot paper account the returning officer shall forthwith proceed to the count.

Special provisions

51.—(1) If during the proceedings under Rule 50 the returning officer finds that any ballot box—

(a) is missing; or

(b) has been tampered with and the contents thereof wholly or partly abstracted, defaced or destroyed; or

(c) has from any other cause suffered such damage that its contents are wholly or partly defaced or destroyed;

he shall designate such box a reserved box.

1e

(2) If for any reason the ballot paper account for any ballot box is destroyed or not immediately available the returning officer shall, if possible, determine the number of ballot papers that could properly have been deposited in the box, by reference—

(a) to the marked copy of the portion of the register relevant to that box; and

(b) to the number of ballot papers remaining unused out of the number supplied to the presiding officer;

and if the number of papers found in the box is equal to or less than the number so determined, he shall inform the several election agents then present and, subject to Rule 53, shall admit the papers to the count.

(3) If for any reason it is not possible to comply with paragraph (2) the returning officer shall forthwith, in the presence of the candidates or their election agents, cause each ballot paper found in the box to be examined; and if no such paper bears—

(a) a serial number not borne by any of the ballot papers supplied to the polling station; or

(b) the same serial number as that borne by another paper found in the box; or

(c) no serial number,

the number of papers found in that box shall be deemed to be the number of ballot papers issued by the presiding officer for deposit in that box and the returning officer shall admit to the count the papers so found.

(4) If any such ballot papers as are referred to in paragraph (3)(a),(b) or (c) are found in the box, the returning officer shall designate that ballot box a reserved box.

(5) If in any ballot box brought from a single box station the number of ballot papers found exceeds that shown in the relevant ballot paper account or determined under paragraph (2), the returning officer shall forthwith in the presence of the candidates or their election agents, cause each such ballot paper to be re-examined, and any papers to be abstracted which do not bear the official mark or which bear no serial number or a serial number not borne by any of the ballot papers supplied to that polling station; and if after such abstraction the number of ballot papers found in that box is still excessive and, on further examination, it appears that two or more ballot papers bearing the same serial number and marked with the official mark have been deposited in that box, the returning officer shall designate that ballot box a reserved box.

(6) If in any ballot box brought from a multiple station the number of ballot papers found exceeds that shown in the relevant ballot paper account or determined under paragraph (2), and the returning officer, after ascertaining the number of ballot papers found in the other box or boxes brought from that station—

(a) is satisfied that the discrepancy was caused solely by the deposit by voters of their ballot papers in the wrong ballot box, he shall admit to the count the ballot papers contained in the box in question;

(b) is not satisfied that the discrepancy was so caused as aforesaid, he shall forthwith carry out the procedure provided in paragraph (5).

(7) If the number of ballot papers found in any ballot box is less than the number of papers shown in the relevant ballot paper account, the returning officer shall inform the several election agents then present of the deficiency but shall admit those ballot papers to the count.

(8) Where under this Rule a ballot box has been designated a reserved box and it has not been possible to determine by reference to the ballot paper account or to the other documents referred to in paragraph (2) the number of ballot papers that could properly have been deposited in the box, all the electors allotted to that box shall be deemed to have duly voted and their ballot papers shall be deemed to have been deposited in that box.

(9) Where a ballot box has been designated a reserved box under paragraph (1)(*b*) or (*c*), the returning officer shall, in the presence of the several election agents—

(*a*) extract from the box singly as many as possible of the ballot papers which are intact or not wholly destroyed; and

(*b*) examine each ballot paper so extracted, and, subject to Rule 53, admit as valid any such paper which is intact or of which a sufficient portion remains decipherable to satisfy him, after consultation with the several election agents then present—

(i) that it is a genuine ballot paper; and

(ii) that the intention of the voter can be determined notwithstanding that by reason of damage that portion either does not bear the official mark or does not bear a serial number; and

(*c*) sort and count the ballot papers so admitted in accordance with these Rules.

(10) Where any ballot box has been designated a reserved box—

(*a*) under paragraph (1)(*b*) or (*c*), and the procedure specified in paragraph (9) has been complied with; or

(*b*) under paragraph (1)(*a*) or under paragraph (4), (5) or (6);

and, after the ballot papers from all other ballot boxes have been counted, it appears to the returning officer that all the votes cast by the uncounted papers deemed to have been deposited in that box—

(i) could not, irrespective of the candidate or candidates for whom they were given, affect the result of the election, the returning officer shall disregard those uncounted papers and, subject to paragraph (11), the number of votes counted as having been given for a candidate shall for all purposes be regarded as the number of votes given for that candidate;

(ii) could, if they had all given a preference for any one candidate at any stage of the count, affect the result of the election, the returning officer shall declare the election in that constituency null and void.

(11) If in any constituency the number of ballot boxes designated reserved boxes is such as to give the returning officer reasonable grounds to suspect that corrupt or illegal practices or other contraventions of the law have prevailed in the election to such an extent as would preclude the securing of a valid result of the election, he may at his discretion declare the election in that constituency null and void.

(12) Where the functions of returning officer are being performed by a deputy returning officer and, pursuant to this Rule, the deputy returning officer declares an election to be null and void he shall immediately inform the Chief Electoral Officer and with his approval shall then—

(*a*) publish a notice stating that the election in that constituency is void and that all acts done in connection with it other than the nomination of the candidates is void;

(*b*) taking all necessary precautions to ensure the secrecy of the ballot, destroy all ballot papers used at the election;

(*c*) hold a fresh election in the constituency in accordance with a time-table prepared by the Chief Electoral Officer and with the rules contained in this Schedule but such rules may be modified for the purposes of that election to the extent that the Chief Electoral Officer considers necessary,

and Rule 16(2) of Schedule 4 to the principal Act shall apply with the substitution for the reference in paragraph (2)(*c*) of that Rule to paragraph (1)(*b*) of a reference to sub-paragraph (*a*) of this paragraph.

(13) Where, by virtue of paragraph (10)(i), the returning officer determines that a new election is unnecessary, then an unsuccessful candidate shall not forfeit his deposit unless the number of votes necessary to prevent such forfeiture would not be attained by the addition to the number of votes counted as given for him at any stage of the count of the total number of uncounted votes.

Conduct of the counting of the votes

52.—(1) The returning officer shall cause the ballot papers to be scrutinised for the purpose of discovering any papers liable to be rejected as invalid and shall, in accordance with these Rules, ascertain and record the number of votes given to each candidate.

(2) The returning officer, while counting and recording the number of ballot papers, shall cause those papers to be kept face upwards and due precautions to be taken to prevent any person from seeing the numbers printed on the backs of the papers.

(3) The returning officer shall, so far as practicable, proceed continuously with the counting of the votes, allowing only time for refreshment and excluding (except so far as he and the candidates otherwise agree) the hours between 11 p.m. and 9 a.m. on the following day.

(4) During the excluded time the returning officer shall place the ballot boxes and documents relating to the election under his seal and the seals of such of the counting agents as desire to affix their seals and shall take due precautions for the security of the said boxes and documents.

Invalid ballot papers

53.—(1) Any ballot paper—

 (a) which does not bear the official mark; or

 (b) on which the figure 1 standing alone is not placed so as to indicate a first preference for some candidate; or

 (c) on which the figure 1 standing alone indicating a first preference is set opposite the name of more than one candidate; or

 (d) on which anything (other than the printed number on the back) is written or marked by which the voter can be identified; or

 (e) which is void for uncertainty;

shall be invalid and not counted, but the ballot paper shall not be invalid by reason only of carrying the words "one", "two", "three", (and so on) or any other mark which, in the opinion of the returning officer, clearly indicates a preference or preferences.

(2) The returning officer shall endorse "Rejected" on any ballot paper which under this Rule is not to be counted and if an election agent objects to his decision shall add to the endorsement the words "rejection objected to".

(3) The returning officer shall prepare a statement showing the number of ballot papers rejected by him under each of sub-paragraphs (a), (b), (c), (d) and (e) of paragraph (1) and shall, on request, allow any candidate or agent of a candidate to copy such statement.

(4) The decision of the returning officer on any question arising in respect of a ballot paper shall be final but shall be subject to review on an election petition.

First stage

54.—(1) After any action necessary under the provisions of Rule 51 has been taken, the returning officer shall, after rejecting any that are invalid, arrange the ballot papers in parcels according to the first preferences recorded for each candidate.

(2) The returning officer shall then count the number of papers in each parcel and credit each candidate with a number of votes equal to the number of valid papers on which a first preference has been recorded for that candidate and he shall then ascertain the number of all valid papers.

(3) The number of first preference votes for each candidate shall then be recorded on the result sheet.

The quota

55.—(1) The returning officer shall then divide the number of valid papers by a number exceeded by one the number of members to be elected.

(2) The result, increased by one, of the division under paragraph (1) (any fractional remainder being disregarded) shall be the number of votes sufficient to secure the election of a candidate (in these Rules referred to as "the quota").

Transfer of surplus

56.—(1) Where at the end of any stage of the count the number of votes credited to a candidate is greater than the quota, the surplus shall be transferred in accordance with this Rule to the continuing candidate or candidates indicated on the ballot papers in the parcel or sub-parcel of the candidate deemed to be elected according to the next available preferences recorded thereon.

(2) Where the votes credited to a candidate whose surplus is to be transferred consist of original votes only, the returning officer shall examine all the papers in the parcel of that candidate and shall arrange the transferable papers in sub-parcels according to the next available preferences for continuing candidates recorded thereon.

(3) Where the votes credited to a candidate whose surplus is to be transferred consist of original and transferred votes, or of transferred votes only, the returning officer shall examine the papers contained in the sub-parcel last received by that candidate and shall arrange the transferable papers therein in further sub-parcels according to the next available preferences for continuing candidates recorded thereon.

(4) In either of the cases referred to in paragraphs (2) and (3) the returning officer shall make a separate sub-parcel of the non-transferable papers and shall ascertain the number of papers in each sub-parcel of transferable papers and in the sub-parcel of non-transferable papers.

(5) If—

(a) at any stage of the count two or more of the candidates have surpluses, the largest surplus shall be transferred first;

(b) the surpluses determined in respect of two or more candidates are equal, the surplus of the candidate who had the highest recorded vote at the earliest preceding stage at which they had unequal votes shall be transferred first; and

(c) the votes credited to two or more candidates were equal at all stages of the count, the returning officer shall determine by lot which surplus is to be transferred first.

(6) In transferring the surplus of any candidate deemed to be elected each ballot paper of that candidate shall be transferred either—

(a) at a calculated value equal to the total of the surplus divided by the number of transferable papers, the calculation being made to two decimal places (ignoring the remainder if any); or

(b) at the value at which such a paper had been received by the candidate from whom is it being transferred;

whichever is the less.

(7) All papers transferred in accordance with the provisions of paragraph (6) shall be clearly marked with the transfer value accorded to each paper either singly or as a sub-parcel of such transferred papers.

(8) The returning officer in carrying out such a transfer of a surplus shall at each such stage enter on the election result sheet the value of the papers transferred to each continuing candidate.

(9) In carrying out a transfer under paragraph (6), the returning officer shall add the value of transferred papers to the previous vote recorded in each case and then determine and record on the result sheet the new total vote received by each candidate at that stage of the count.

(10) The returning officer shall also—

(a) enter on the result sheet as non-transferable votes the difference between the surplus and the total value of the transferred papers; and

(b) add that difference to the recorded total of the previous non-transferable vote.

(11) At each stage of the count when a transfer of a surplus has been effected the returning officer shall reconcile from his result sheet the total of votes at that stage credited to all candidates, together with the total non-transferable vote, with the already determined total valid vote.

(12) When at any stage the transfer of a surplus has been effected and the procedures at paragraphs (8) to (11) have been completed, the returning officer shall deem to be elected any candidate whose total vote, at that stage, then equals or is in excess of the declared quota.

(13) The transfer of a surplus constitutes a further stage in the count.

(14) The returning officer shall, subject to paragraph (15), proceed to transfer surpluses until no surplus remains to be transferred.

(15) A surplus shall not be subject to transfer where that surplus, together with any other surpluses at that particular stage of the count not already transferred, is—

(a) less than the difference between the total vote then credited to the continuing candidate with the lowest recorded vote and the vote of the candidate with the next lowest recorded vote; or

(b) less than the difference between the total votes of the two or more continuing candidates, credited at that stage of the count with the lowest recorded total numbers of votes and the candidate next above such candidates.

Exclusion of candidate

57.—(1) If, after completion of the transfer of surpluses in accordance with Rule 56, one or more vacancies remain to be filled, the returning officer shall exclude from the election at that stage of the count the candidate then credited with the lowest vote.

(2) Where a candidate is excluded in accordance with paragraph (1), the returning officer shall then arrange the papers attributed at that stage to that candidate in sub-parcels according to their transfer value.

(3) The returning officer shall then examine the sub-parcel of papers with the highest transfer value and transfer the papers in it, examine the sub-parcel with the next highest transfer value and transfer those papers and so deal with each sub-parcel.

(4) The papers in each sub-parcel shall be sorted and transferred at the value at which they were received in accordance with the next available preference expressed on the papers for the continuing candidates, passing over preferences for candidates who at such a stage have either been deemed to be elected or have been excluded.

(5) Any papers on which no next available preferences have been expressed shall be then set aside as non-transferable papers.

(6) After the transfer of papers of any one transfer value the returning officer shall deem to be elected any candidate whose total vote equals or is in excess of the quota.

(7) When the procedures required at paragraphs (1) to (5) have been completed and all sub-parcels of papers of an excluded candidate have been transferred, the returning officer shall record on the result sheet the total value of the papers transferred to each continuing candidate, adding such totals to the candidate's previously recorded total vote in each case, thus determining the new total vote for each continuing candidate at that stage.

(8) The returning officer shall then record on the result sheet the value of the non-transferable papers and add such total to the previous non-transferable papers total.

(9) The total number of votes at that stage of the count credited to all candidates, together with the total of the non-transferable vote, shall be reconciled with the total valid vote.

(10) Where the total of the votes of the two or more lowest candidates, together with any surpluses not transferred, is less than the number of votes credited to the next lowest candidate, the returning officer shall in one operation exclude such two or more candidates.

(11) If, when a candidate has to be excluded under this Rule, two or more candidates have each the same number of votes and are lowest—
> (a) regard shall be had to the total numbers of votes credited to those candidates at the earliest stage of the count at which they had an unequal number of votes and the candidate with the lowest number of votes at that stage shall be excluded; and

> (b) where the numbers of votes credited to those candidates were equal at all stages, the returning officer shall determine by lot which candidate shall be excluded.

(12) The exclusion of a candidate, or two or more candidates together constitutes a further stage in the count.

Transfer of votes

58.—(1) Where the transfer of votes is made under Rule 56 or 57 each sub-parcel of papers transferred (marked as to the transfer value) shall be placed on top of the parcel, if any, of papers of the candidate to whom the tranfer is made and that candidate shall be credited with a total number of votes equal to the transferred value of the papers transferred to him.

(2) If after any transfer of votes a candidate has a surplus that surplus shall be dealt with in accordance with and subject to Rule 56 before any other candidate is excluded.

Filling of last vacancies

59.—(1) Where the number of continuing candidates is equal to the number of vacancies remaining unfilled the continuing candidates shall there upon be deemed to be elected.

(2) Where only one vacancy remains unfilled and the votes of some one continuing candidate are equal to or greater than the total of votes credited to another or other continuing candidates together with any surplus not transferred, that candidate shall thereupon be deemed to be elected.

(3) Where the last vacancies can be filled under this Rule, no further transfer of votes shall be made.

Recount

60.—(1) The returning officer on completion of each stage of the count shall, before proceeding with the next stage involved, inform all the candidates and their election agents then present of his intention, subject to a request for a recount, to proceed to the next stage.

(2) Before the returning officer so proceeds, any candidate or his election agent may request that a recount be undertaken of the immediate preceding stage.

(3) If a request is made under paragraph (2), the returning officer shall then proceed to carry out the recount of the immediate preceding stage, but, if no such request is made, he shall proceed with the next subsequent stage of the count.

(4) The returning officer may also, if he thinks fit, recount papers either once or more often if he is not satisfied as to the accuracy of any stage.

(5) Nothing in this Rule shall require the returning officer to recount the same parcel or sub-parcel more than once.

(6) Where as a result of a recount an error is discovered, the returning officer shall, where necessary, amend any results previously announced by him.

Order of election of candidates

61.—(1) The order in which candidates credited with a number of votes equal to or greater than the quota shall be deemed to be elected shall be the order in which their respective surpluses were transferred, or would have been transferred but for Rule56(15).

(2) A candidate credited with a number of votes equal to and not greater than the quota shall, for the purpose of this Rule, be regarded as having had the smallest surplus at the count at which he obtained the quota.

(3) Where the surpluses of two or more candidates are equal and need not be transferred, regard shall be had to the total number of votes credited to such candidates at the earliest stage of the count at which they had an unequal number of votes and the surplus of the candidates credited with the greatest number of votes at that stage shall be deemed to be the largest.

(4) Where the numbers of votes credited to two or more candidates were equal at all counts, the returning officer shall determine by lot the order in which such candidates shall be deemed to have been elected.

Declaration of the result of the poll

62. On the completion of the counting of the votes the returning officer shall declare the result of the poll and the candidates deemed to be elected shall thereupon stand elected in the order ascertained in accordance with Rule 61.

Decisions of the returning officer

63. The decision of the returning officer, whether expressed or implied by his acts, on any question which arises in relation to the exclusion of any candidate under Rule 57 or to any ballot paper or transfer of votes shall be final, but may be reviewed on an election petition.

Return of persons elected

64.—(1) The returning officer for each constituency shall give public notice of the names of the candidates elected and also, in the case of a contested election, of the total number of votes for each candidate, whether elected or not, of any transfer of votes, of the total number of votes credited to each candidate at the end of each stage of the count at which such transfer took place, and the order in which the candidates were elected.

(2) Where the Chief Electoral Officer has delegated the functions under this Rule in relation to any constituency to a deputy returning officer, that deputy returning officer shall send a copy of the said notice, together with any other information which may be required, to the Chief Electoral Officer.

(3) The notice under paragraph (1) relating to a contested election shall be in the form numbered AE 16 in Schedule 3.

(4) The Chief Electoral Officer shall return to the Clerk of the Crown the names of the persons elected in each constituency.

(5) The Clerk of the Crown shall from the return made to him under paragraph (4) enter in a book to be kept by him the names of those persons.

(6) The book kept by the Clerk of the Crown under paragraph (5) shall be open to public inspection at reasonable times and any person may, on payment of a reasonable fee, take copies from the book.

Election report by Chief Electoral Officer

65.—(1) The Chief Electoral Officer shall as soon as practicable after receipt of the returns of the elections for each constituency, prepare and publish a report of the results of the election.

(2) Such report shall include the detailed election results for each consitituency together with details of the total election expenses and any other matter which the Chief Electoral Officer may consider to be relevant and appropriate.

PART VI

DISPOSAL, PRODUCTION AND INSPECTION OF DOCUMENTS AND RETURNS TO THE MINISTRY

Disposal of documents, etc., by returning officer

66.—(1) On the completion of the count, the returning officer shall place in separate sealed packets—

(a) the counted ballot papers including the sealed packets of damaged ballot papers counted from any reserved ballot box;

(b) the rejected ballot papers;

(c) the counterfoils of all ordinary ballot papers used, with the certificates (if any) presented under Rule 42;

(d) the tendered ballot papers used and their counterfoils;

(e) the ballot papers found in any reserved box which under these Rules have not been counted;

and shall mark on each packet the nature of the contents thereof and shall place the several packets in a parcel which he shall seal and on which he shall mark particulars of its contents, the date of the election to which they relate and the name of the constituency for which that election was held.

(2) The returning officer shall also place in a parcel—

(a) the marked copy of the register used at each polling station;

(b) the ballot paper accounts;

(c) the lists of tendered votes;

(d) the assisted voters lists;

(e) the statement of the number of votes given for each candidate and the number of rejected ballot papers;

(f) the statement of the contents of the ballot boxes;

(g) all declarations of secrecy;

(h) the list of proxies; and

(i) the candidates' nomination papers (whether valid or not);

and shall mark on the parcel particulars of its contents, the date of the election to which they relate and the name of the constituency for which that election was held.

(3) The returning officer shall then transmit both those parcels to the Clerk of the Crown, either by delivering them by himself or his agent or by sending them by post; but if he sends them by post—

(a) he shall send a letter to the Clerk of the Crown by the same post, specifying the number and description of the documents so sent;

(b) a copy of the receipt given him by the postmaster or deputy postmaster shall be signed by him for retention by the postmaster or deputy postmaster.

(4) The Clerk of the Crown shall on receiving the documents give a receipt to the person delivering them, and shall register them in his books specifying the date and time of receipt.

(5) Any receipt to be given for the documents shall show the date and time of their receipt.

Orders for production of documents

67.—(1) An order—

(a) for the inspection or production of any rejected ballot papers; or

(b) for the opening of a sealed packet of counterfoils and certificates presented under Rule 42; or

(c) for the inspection of any tendered or counted or uncounted ballot papers; or

(d) for the inspection of covering envelopes received by the returning officer after the close of the poll and of voters' declarations;

in the custody of the Clerk of the Crown may be made—

(i) by the Assembly; or

(ii) if satisfied by evidence on oath that the order is required for the purpose of instituting or maintaining a prosecution for an offence in relation to ballot papers, or for the purpose of an election petition, by the High Court or a county court.

(2) An order for the opening of a sealed packet of counterfoils and certificates or for the inspection of any counted or uncounted ballot papers in the said custody may be made by an election court.

(3) An order under this Rule may be made subject to such conditions as to persons, time, place and mode of inspection, production or opening as the Assembly or court making the order may think expedient, but in making and carrying into effect an order for the opening of a packet of counterfoils and certificates or for the inspection of counted or uncounted or tendered ballot papers, care shall be taken that the way in which the vote of any particular elector has been given shall not be disclosed until it has been proved that his vote was given and that the vote has been declared by a competent court to be invalid.

(4) An appeal shall lie to the High Court from any order of a county court made under this Rule.

(5) Where an order is made for the production by the Clerk of the Crown of any document in his possession relating to any specified election, the production in compliance with the order by him or his agent of that document shall be conclusive evidence that the document relates to the specified election; and any endorsement on any packet of ballot papers so produced shall be prima facie evidence that the elector whose vote was given by that ballot paper was the person to whose name in the register at the time of the election there was affixed the same number as the number written on the counterfoil.

(7) Save as provided by this Rule, no person shall be allowed to inspect any rejected or counted or uncounted ballot papers in the possession of the Clerk of the Crown or to open any sealed packets of counterfoils and certificates.

Retention and public inspection of documents

68.—(1) The Clerk of the Crown shall retain for a year all documents relating to an election forwarded to him by a returning officer in pursuance of these Rules and then, unless otherwise directed by order of the Assembly or the High Court, shall cause them to be destroyed.

(2) The said documents, except ballot papers, counterfoils, certificates presented under Rule 42, covering envelopes received by the returning officer after the close of the poll and voters' declarations, shall be open to public inspection at such time and subject to such conditions as may be determined by the Clerk of the Crown with the consent of the person presiding over the Assembly.

(3) The Clerk of the Crown shall, on request, supply copies of or extracts from the documents open to public inspection on payment of such fees and subject to such conditions as may be sanctioned by the Ministry of Finance.

Returns to be made by returning officer to Ministry

69. Within twenty-eight days after the declaration of the result of the election the returning officer shall furnish to the Chief Electoral Officer and the Ministry—

(*a*) particulars of the number of service and other electors respectively entitled to vote by proxies whose appointments were valid for the purposes of the election; and

(*b*) a copy of the notice of the result of a contested election published under Rule 64 or, where the election was uncontested, a copy of the statement of the result of the election published under Rule 16;

(*c*) a copy of the statement referred to in Rule 27(5)(*b*);

(*d*) a copy of each of the statements specified in Rule 66(2)(*e*) and (*f*).

SCHEDULE 3　　　　　　　Article 7(2)

FORMS

FORM AE 1

ELECTION TO NORTHERN IRELAND ASSEMBLY　　Schedule 2
　　　　　　　　　　　　　　　　　　　　　　　　　　Rule 4(1)
Form of notice of election to be used in election to Northern Ireland Assembly

Constituency of ....

1. An election is to be held for [state number] members for this constituency to serve in the Northern Ireland Assembly.

2. Nomination papers may be delivered by the candidate or his proposer or seconder to the returning officer at　　　　　　　　　　　　　(which is his principal office for the purposes of the election) between 10 a.m. and 5 p.m. on 5th June 1973.

3. Forms of nomination papers may be obtained at the above address [or at the subsidiary office[s]] situated at　　　　　　　　　　　　　　　　　　．

4. £150 must be deposited with the returning officer by or on behalf of each candidate within the period specified in paragraph 2.

5. The returning officer will at the request of an elector prepare a nomination paper for signature.

6. A candidature may be withdrawn at any time before 5 p.m. on 5th June 1973.

7. If the election is contested, the poll will take place on 28th June 1973.

Signed ....

Returning Officer

day of　　　　　　　　　　　　　　　　1973

NOTE.

1. The attention of candidates and electors is drawn to the rules for filling up nomination papers and other provisions relating to nominations contained in Schedule 2 to the Northern Ireland Assembly (Election) Order 1973.

2. A person guilty of a corrupt or illegal practice will, on conviction, be liable to the penalties imposed by Part X of Schedule 9 to the Electoral Law Act (Northern Ireland) 1962(a).

3. Every person having a claim against the returning officer for any debt incurred by or on behalf of the returning officer for the purposes of the election shall, within twenty-one days after the day on which public notice is given of the result of the election, send to the returning officer detailed particulars in writing of such claim and the returning officer shall not be liable in respect of anything which is not duly stated in such particulars.

FORM AE 2

Schedule 2
Rule 6(1)

Form of nomination paper for an election to the Northern Ireland Assembly

ELECTION OF A MEMBER to serve in the Northern Ireland Assembly for the .... constituency.

We, the undersigned, being electors for the said constituency, do hereby nominate the undermentioned person as a candidate at the said election.

Candidate's Surname	Other Names in full	Home Address in full	Description (if any)

Signature	Electoral Number (See note 3)
Proposer..	....
Seconder...	....
We, the undersigned, being electors for the said constituency, do hereby assent to the foregoing nomination. 1..	....
2..	....
3..	....
4..	....
5..	....
6..	....
7..	....
8..	....

Received by the returning officer at
............................m. on the......
day of..........................., 19......
together with the candidate's declaration and a deposit of £150.
　　(Signed) ....

NOTE.

1. The attention of candidates and electors is drawn to the rules for filling up nomination papers and other provisions relating to nomination contained in Schedule 2 to the Northern Ireland Assembly (Election) Order 1973.

2. Where a candidate is commonly known by some title he may be described by his title as if it were his surname.

3. A person's electoral number is his number in the register to be used at the election (including the distinguishing number of the polling district in which he is registered).

4. An elector may not subscribe more than one nomination paper for the election.

(a) 1962 c. 14. (N.I.).

FORM AE 3

Schedule 2
Rule 19(2)

Form of ballot paper for election to Northern Ireland Assembly

Mark order of preference in space below		COUNTER-FOIL No.
	BLACK—CONSTRUCTION PARTY (James Black of 5 Down Street, Bangor, Co. Down— Engineer)	
	BLUE—CONCERT PARTY (Joan Blue of 9 Mourne View, Donaghadu, Co. Down— Singer)	*(The counterfoil is to have a number to correspond with that on the back of the ballot paper)*
	BROWN—THIRD PARTY (Rupert Brown of 8 Magilligan Drive, Portaferry, Co. Down—Solicitor)	
	GOLD—NON-PARTY (John Gold of 29 Gilford Place, Millisle, Co. Down— Driver)	ELECTOR'S REGISTRATION No.
	HAZEL—GARDEN PARTY (Maurice Hazel of Glen Cottage, Banbridge, Co. Down —Nurseryman)	
	LIME—THIRD PARTY (Henry Lime of 7 Gortin Mansions, Dromara, Co. Down —Insurance Broker)	
	PLUM—INDEPENDENT (Robert Plum of 3 Strangford Road, Killinchy, Co. Down—Greengrocer)	
	ROSE—GARDEN PARTY (Ruth Rose of 41 Devenish Drive, Ballynahinch, Co. Down—Florist)	
	SILVER—CONSTRUCTION PARTY (Anthony Silver of 3 Mourne View, Bangor, Co. Down— Architect)	
	WRIGHT—WORKING PARTY (Frank Wright of 11 Moira Terrace, Newry, Co. Down— Dispenser)	

BACK OF BALLOT PAPER

No. ELECTION FOR THE CONSTITUENCY OF

DIRECTIONS AS TO PRINTING THE BALLOT PAPER

1. Nothing is to be printed on the ballot paper except in accordance with these directions.

2. The following arrangements shall be observed in the printing of the ballot paper—

    (*a*) apart from the instructions to "Mark Order of Preference in space below" no other word or words shall be printed on the face except the particulars of the candidates;

(b) no rule shall be printed on the face except the horizontal rules separating the particulars of the candidates from one another and the vertical rule separating those particulars from the spaces on the left side of the paper where the order of preference is to be marked;

(c) the whole space between the top and the bottom of the paper shall be equally divided between the candidates by the rules separating these particulars.

4. (a) The ballot paper shall contain the names, addresses, occupations and descriptions, if any, of the candidates standing nominated, as shown in their respective nomination paper. The names shall be arranged alphabetically in the order of surnames, or if there are two or more candidates bearing the same surname, in alphabetical order of their other names, or if their other names are the same, in the alphabetical order of their occupations;

(b) the surname of each candidate and the name of his political party, group, organization or other body, or if the candidate has described himself as "Independent" or "New Party" shall be printed in large characters and his full name, address and description, if any, as appearing in his nomination paper, shall be printed in small characters;

(c) where the surnames of two or more candidates are the same there shall also be printed in large characters the other names of such candidates and so much of the descriptions of such candidates appearing in their respective nomination papers, as will, in the opinion of the returning officer, distinguish such candidates;

(d) the list of candidates shall be arranged either in one continuous column or in two or more columns in such manner (without departing from the alphabetical order) as, in the opinion of the returning officer, is best for marking and counting;

(e) the ballot papers shall be numbered consecutively and the back of the ballot paper and the front of the counterfoil attached to it shall bear the same number. The numbers on the ballot papers shall be printed in the smallest characters compatible with legibility and shall be printed on or about the centre of the paper.

Schedule 2
Rule 21

FORM AE 4

ELECTION TO THE NORTHERN IRELAND ASSEMBLY

Form of polling information card

POLLING INFORMATION CARD

(FRONT OF CARD)

POLLING INFORMATION CARD

Election to Northern Ireland Assembly 1973	
Constituency of................................	
Your Polling Station is at	
....	....
Polling Day is Thursday 28th June 1973	....
Hours of Poll—from 8 a.m. to 8.30 p.m.	....
.... **Returning Officer** **(Address)**	No. on Register

(BACK OF CARD)

THIS POLLING INFORMATION CARD DOES NOT AUTHORISE ANY PERSON TO VOTE WHO IS PROHIBITED FROM VOTING NOR DOES IT ESTABLISH THE IDENTITY OF THE PERSON IN WHOSE POSSESSION IT MAY BE.

UNLESS YOU ARE ELIGIBLE TO VOTE BY POST AND WISH TO DO SO, KEEP THIS CARD CAREFULLY FOR REFERENCE ON POLLING DAY; IT WILL ASSIST YOU IN CLAIMING YOUR BALLOT PAPER AT YOUR POLLING STATION.

If you submitted by 17th May 1973 a valid application to vote by post at the border poll on 8th March 1973 or the local general elections on 30th May 1973, you may vote by post at this election. If you wish to do so sign this card below and return it in an unstamped envelope to the deputy returning officer (address overleaf) to reach him by 12th June 1973.

Signed..

Address in ....
United Kingdom
(to which ....
further
correspondence.......................................
should be sent)

FORM AE 5   Schedule 2
                                             Rule 25(2)

FORM OF DECLARATION BY A PERSON VOTING BY POST AT AN ELECTION TO THE NORTHERN IRELAND ASSEMBLY

Form of front of voter's declaration

I declare that I am the person to whom the envelope which I have produced and shown to the witness whose attestation appears below was addressed by the returning officer.

I have given my vote on the ballot paper in the sealed envelope enclosed herewith, which contains nothing but the said ballot paper. I have shown the said sealed envelope to the witness.

I declare that I have given no other vote on my own behalf at this election in this or any other constituency.

(Signed) ....
                              Elector.

ATTESTATION BY WITNESS

I certify that this declaration was signed in my presence by the elector who has permitted me to examine the particulars on the envelope received by him and has shown me the sealed envelope stated in his declaration to contain the ballot paper.

I further declare that the said elector is personally known to me and to the best of my knowledge and belief is the person described by the particulars on the envelope received by him.

(Signed) ....
                              Witness.

Address of witness ....

....

Form on back of voter's declaration

INSTRUCTIONS TO THE VOTER

1. You should place the figure 1 opposite the name of the candidate for whom you wish to vote and in addition you may, if you wish, place the figure 2 opposite the name of the candidate of your second choice, the figure 3 opposite the name of the candidate of your third choice and so on in the order of your preference. You may indicate by figures as many or as few preferences as you wish.

2. The figure or figures should be placed in the space provided at the left-hand side of the paper opposite the name of the candidate for whom you intend it.

3. In no circumstances write anything else on the paper; if you do you destroy your vote.

4. Immediately after voting you must place the marked ballot paper in the enclosed small envelope on which are printed the words "Ballot paper envelope" and fasten it up.

5. Then take the envelope addressed to you by the returning officer together with the sealed ballot paper envelope and the voter's declaration to the witness and sign the declaration in his presence. He should then attest your signature on the declaration.

6. Enclose the signed and witnessed paper and the sealed ballot paper envelope in the larger enclosed envelope addressed to the returning officer and despatch the same by post without delay. Unless you return the ballot paper at once it may be received by the returning officer too late to be counted.

7. If you receive more than one ballot paper it must be remembered that you can vote only once on your own behalf at this election.

8. If you lose or destroy the stamped addressed envelope provided for the return of your vote you may use another envelope but any such envelope should be addressed and marked as nearly as possible in the same way as the printed envelope provided.

9. In no circumstances should you share your return envelope with another voter nor share his. If more than one voter's declaration or more than one ballot paper are received together in one covering envelope, the whole contents of the envelope will be disregarded by the returning officer and your vote will be lost.

10. If you inadvertently spoil your postal ballot paper, you can apply to the deputy returning officer for another one. With your application you must return (in a fresh envelope) the spoilt ballot paper, the declaration of identity and the two envelopes sent to you with your ballot paper. Remember that there is little time available if a fresh postal ballot paper is to be issued to you for completion and return before the close of the poll.

Form AE 6

Schedule 2
Rule 27(5)

Election to the Northern Ireland Assembly

.... constituency

.... 19......

Statement of the number of Postal Ballot Papers issued

Postal voting documents issued and returned	Number	Disposal of postal voting documents returned before the close of poll	Number
1. Total number of ballot papers issued.		1. Number of covering envelopes received by the returning officer before the close of the poll.	
2. Number of covering envelopes received by the returning officer *before* the close of the poll.		2. Number of ballot papers returned by postal voters which were included in the count.	
3. Number of covering envelopes received by the returning officer *after* the close of the poll.		3. Number of cases in which any postal voting documents were marked "empty", "vote rejected" or "rejected" in pursuance of Rule 26 in Schedule 2 to the Northern Ireland Assembly (Election) Order 1973.	
4. Number of covering envelopes which were returned as undelivered.			
5. Number of covering envelopes which have not been received by the returning officer at the date of this statement.			

....

Returning Officer.

Dated this   day of   19   .

Note: In each column the figure entered against the first item should equal the sum of the figures entered against the remaining items in the column.

Form AE 7

Schedule 2
Rule 33(1)(c)

Form of Directions for the Guidance of Voters in Voting at Elections to the Northern Ireland Assembly

*This form is to be printed in bold characters

1. Make sure that the ballot paper you have received from the presiding officer has the official mark stamped on it. It is useless without it.

2. Go into one of the compartments provided; look at the ballot paper carefully and in the space provided at the left-hand side of the paper place the figure 1 opposite the name of the candidate for whom you wish to vote and, if you wish, the figure 2 opposite the name of the candidate of your second choice, the figure 3 opposite the name of the candidate of your third choice and so on in the order of your preference. You may indicate by figures as many or as few preferences as you wish.

3. Under no circumstances write anything else on the paper; if you do you destroy your vote. If by accident you damage your paper, or if you mark it in such a way that it may be rejected as spoilt, or if you mark it in the wrong place, take the paper back to the presiding officer, tell him what has happened and ask him for a fresh paper.

4. When you have marked your paper fold it so that the front of the paper is inwards, hiding your vote, and take it back to the table of the presiding officer from whom you got it. Hold out the folded paper so that the presiding officer can see the stamped official mark showing through the back. You will see on the table a ballot box. Put the paper into the box.

5. You must not take your ballot paper out of the polling station nor put any other paper into the ballot box. If you do you will commit a serious offence and will be liable to heavy penalties.

6. When you have voted leave the polling station at once.

Schedule 1

FORM AE 8

FORM OF RETURN OF EXPENSES REQUIRED BY SECTION 41 OF THE ELECTORAL LAW ACT (NORTHERN IRELAND) 1962 AS APPLIED BY THE NORTHERN IRELAND ASSEMBLY (ELECTION) ORDER 1973 TO BE AUTHORISED BY AN ELECTION AGENT

Election in the.. constituency.

Date of publication of notice of election..

The expenses incurred at the above election in support of...............................
............................., a candidate thereat, by ....
.... (*insert name of person or association or body of persons incurring the expenses*) being expenses required by section 41 of the Electoral Law Act (Northern Ireland) 1962, as applied by the Northern Ireland Assembly (Election) Order 1973, to be authorised by the election agent, amounted to £............

The written authority of the election agent is annexed hereto.

Signature ....

Date ....

Schedule 1

FORM AE 9

FORM OF DECLARATION AS TO EXPENSES REQUIRED BY SECTION 41 OF THE ELECTORAL LAW ACT (NORTHERN IRELAND) 1962 AS APPLIED BY THE NORTHERN IRELAND ASSEMBLY (ELECTION) ORDER 1973 TO BE AUTHORISED BY AN ELECTION AGENT

Election in the.. constituency.

Date of publication of notice of election..

I hereby declare that—

1. I am the person [*or* a director, general manager, secretary or other like officer of the association or body of persons] named as incurring expenses in the accompanying return, marked.................................... of expenses required by section 41 of the Electoral Law Act (Northern Ireland) 1962, as applied by the Northern Ireland Assembly (Election) Order 1973, to be authorised by an election agent.

2. To the best of my knowledge and belief the said return is complete and correct.

3. The matters for which the expenses referred to in the said return were incurred were as follows ....
....
....

Signature of declarant..............................

Office held by declarant..........................
(in the case of an association or body of persons)

Date.....................................

Form AE 10

Form of Return of Expenses required by Section 46 of the Electoral Law Act (Northern Ireland) 1962 as applied by the Northern Ireland Assembly (Election) Order 1973

Election in the.. constituency.

Date of publication of notice of election ....

Name of candidate..

1. I am the election agent of the person named above as a candidate at this election [am the person named above as a candidate at this election and was my own election agent].

(*Where there has been a change of election agent suitable variations may be introduced here and elsewhere in the return*).

2. I hereby make the following return of the candidate's [my] election expenses at this election.

Receipts

(*Include all money, securities or equivalent of money received in respect of expenses incurred on account of or in connection with or incidental to the above election*).

Received of the above-named candidate (*or, if the candidate is his own election agent,* paid by me)   ...   . £

Received of (*set out separately the name and description of each person, club, society or association and the amount received from him or them*)   ...   . £

Expenditure

NOTE.—*The return shall deal under a separate heading or sub-heading with any expenses included therein as respects which a return is required by section 46.*

Candidate's personal expenses—

paid by him [by me as candidate]   ...   . £

paid by me [by me acting as my election agent]...   ...   ... £

Received by me for my services as election agent (*omit if candidate is his own election agent*)   ...   . £

Paid to *as sub-agent of the polling district of .... £

Paid to *†as polling agent.. £

Paid to *†as clerk [messenger] for   days services   ...   ... £

Paid to the following persons in respect of goods supplied or work and labour done—

to *†(*set out the nature of the goods supplied or work and labour done thus:*—

[printing], [advertising], [stationery])   ...   . £

Paid to *†as a speaker at a public meeting at
on   19   , as remuneration [expenses]   ... £

Paid for the hire of rooms—

for holding public meetings—

paid to *†for hire of (*identify the rooms by naming or describing them*)   ...   . £

for committee rooms—

paid to *†for hire of (*identify the rooms by naming or describing them*)   ...   . £

Paid for hire of vehicles ... ... £

Paid for postage ... ... £

Paid for telegrams ... ... £

Paid for miscellaneous matters—

    to *†(*set out the reasons for the payment*) ... ... £

    In addition to the above I am aware (*unless the*

candidate is his own election agent *add* as election agent for the above-named candidate) of the following disputed and unpaid claims—

    Disputed claims—

        by *for (*set out the goods, work and labour, or other matter on the ground of which the claim is based*) ... ... £

Unpaid claims allowed by the   court to be paid after the proper time or in respect of which application has been or is about to be made to the   court (*state in each case whether the High Court or some other court*)—

        by *for (*set out the goods, work and labour, or other matter on the ground of which the claim is due*) ... ... £

Signature of person making return..

---

*Set out separately the name and description of each person with the amount paid to or claimed by him.

†These particulars may be set out in a separate list annexed to and referred to in the account thus e.g., "Paid to polling agents as per annexed list £.........................".

Schedule 1

Form AE 11

Form of Declaration as to Expenses required by Section 47 of the Electoral Law Act (Northern Ireland) 1962 as Applied by the Northern Ireland Assembly (Election) Order 1973

Election in the... constituency.

Date of publication of notice of election...

Name of candidate...

I solemnly and sincerely declare as follows:—

1. I am the person named above as a candidate at this election [and was my own election agent] *or* I was at this election the election agent of the person named above as a candidate.

2. I have examined the return of election expenses [about to be] transmitted by my election agent [by me] to the returning officer, of which a copy is now shown to me and marked   , and to the best of my knowledge and belief it is a complete and correct return as required by law.

3. To the best of my knowledge and belief, all expenses shown in the return as paid were paid by my election agent [by me], except as otherwise stated in relation to my [the candidate's] personal expenses.

4. I understand that the law does not allow any election expenses not mentioned in this return to be defrayed except in pursuance of a court order.

Signature of declarant...

Signed and declared by the above-named declarant on the   day of   , before me,

(Signed) ....

Justice of the Peace for..............................

(NOTE.—*Where there has been a change of election agent, suitable variations may be introduced into the declaration as to expenses.*)

FORM AE 12

Schedule 2
Rule 42(1)(b

ELECTION TO NORTHERN IRELAND ASSEMBLY

Form of certificate of employment as constable

CONSTITUENCY OF...

CERTIFICATE OF EMPLOYMENT AS CONSTABLE

I certify that *...
who is numbered .... in the register of electors for the above-mentioned
constituency will or is likely to be prevented from voting at his allotted polling station
at the election on.................................... by reason of discharging his duty as a
constable.

....
(Being Chief Inspector or above)

Royal Ulster Constabulary District of...

Dated this   day of   1973.

(*Insert name, rank and police number).

NOTE: The person named above is entitled to vote at any polling station for the
constituency on production and surrender of this certificate to the presiding
officer.

FORM AE 13

Schedule 2
Rule 42(2)

ELECTION TO THE NORTHERN IRELAND ASSEMBLY

Form of certificate of employment by returning officer

CONSTITUENCY OF ....

CERTIFICATE OF EMPLOYMENT BY RETURNING OFFICER

I, a returning officer for the above election, hereby certify that ....

who is numbered .... in the register of electors for the constituency

named above is employed by me for the purposes of the election on ....

and that the circumstances of his employment are such as to prevent him from voting

at his allotted polling station.

....
Returning Officer.

Dated this   day of   1973.

....
Principal Office for the purpose of the Election

NOTE: The person named above is entitled to vote at any polling station for the
constituency on production and surrender of this certificate to the presiding officer

Schedule 2
Rule 45(3)

FORM AE 14

ELECTION TO THE NORTHERN IRELAND ASSEMBLY

Form of declaration made by the polling agent

CONSTITUENCY OF ....

POLLING DISTRICT ....

POLLING STATION .... BALLOT BOX NO.....................

DATE OF POLL...

DECLARATION TO BE MADE BY THE POLLING AGENT BEFORE A PERSON
ARRESTED FOR AN ALLEGED OFFENCE OF PERSONATION IS REMOVED
FROM THE POLLING STATION BY A CONSTABLE

I, ... of ....

appointed under Rule 31 in Schedule 2 to the Northern Ireland Assembly (Election)

Order 1973 as polling agent for ....

a candidate at this election, do hereby declare that I have reasonable cause to believe

that the person applying for a ballot paper in the name of ....

of .... has by so applying committed an

offence of personation as defined in paragraph 4 of Schedule 9 to the Electoral Law

Act (Northern Ireland) 1962 as applied by that Order, and I undertake to subtantiate

this charge in a court of law.

....

POLLING AGENT

WITNESS ....

....
Presiding Officer

Date ....

NOTE: This declaration, together with the statement of persons taken into custody
should be placed in an envelope and kept in safe custody by the presiding officer
pending any proceedings.

FORM AE 15

Schedule 2
Rule 46(4)

ELECTION TO THE NORTHERN IRELAND ASSEMBLY

Form of ballot paper account

CONSTITUENCY..

POLLING DISTRICT ....

POLLING STATION .... BALLOT BOX NO..................

DATE OF POLL..

BALLOT PAPER ACCOUNT

ORDINARY BALLOT PAPERS

Number of ballot papers entrusted to presiding officer		*Number of ballot papers issued and not returned as spoilt*	
Serial numbers		*Number of ballot papers not issued*	
From		*Number of ballot papers issued but returned as spoilt*	
To			
Colour		TOTAL	

TENDERED BALLOT PAPERS

Number of tendered ballot papers entrusted to presiding officer		*Number of tendered ballot papers issued and not returned as spoilt*	
Serial numbers		*Number of tendered ballot papers not issued*	
From		*Number of tendered ballot papers issued but returned as spoilt*	
To			
Colour		TOTAL	

....
Presiding Officer

Date..

Schedule 2
Rule 64(3)

FORM AE 16

ELECTION TO THE NORTHERN IRELAND ASSEMBLY

Form of declaration of result of Poll

CONSTITUENCY OF ....

DECLARATION OF RESULT OF POLL

DATE OF POLL ....

I, the undersigned, being the Returning Officer at the poll for the election of [   ] members held on the .... day of .... 1973, do hereby give notice that the result of the poll and of the transfer of votes is as follows:

Number of valid votes ....

Number of members to be elected ....

Quota (number of votes sufficient to secure the election of a candidate) ....

Names of candidates	FIRST COUNT	SECOND COUNT		THIRD COUNT		FOURTH COUNT		FIFTH COUNT		SIXTH COUNT		Names of candidates elected and the order of their election
	Votes	*Transfer of*	*Result*	*Transfer of*	*Result*	*Transfer of*	*Result*	*Transfer of*	*Result*	*Transfer of*	*Result*	
non-transferable papers												

And I do hereby declare the said Members duly elected for the said Constituency.

Dated this   day of   1973.

....
Returning Officer

EXPLANATORY NOTE

(This Note is not part of the Order.)

This Order makes provision with respect to the first election to the Northern Ireland Assembly, which is to be conducted in accordance with the Rules in Schedule 2. Rules 54 to 61 in that Schedule specify the method of counting and transferring votes. The Order applies specified provisions of the Electoral Law Act (Northern Ireland) 1962 to the election and applies, with certain modifications, sections 6 and 7 of the House of Commons Disqualification Act 1957 in relation to the Assembly. Provision is made for persons who were entitled to vote by post at the Border Poll or the 1973 local general elections to vote by post at this election, if they give notice to that effect.

STATUTORY INSTRUMENTS

1973 No. 892

CUSTOMS AND EXCISE

The Import Duties (Developing Countries) (No. 2) Order 1973

Made - - -		*10th May* 1973
Laid before the *House of Commons*		*11th May* 1973
Coming into Operation		*1st June* 1973

The Lords Commissioners of Her Majesty's Treasury, by virtue of the powers conferred on them by section 1 of the Finance Act 1971(a) and of all other powers enabling them in that behalf, on the recommendation of the Secretary of State, hereby make the following Order:

1.—(1) This Order may be cited as the Import Duties (Developing Countries) (No 2) Order 1973.

(2) The Interpretation Act 1889(b) shall apply for the interpretation of this Order as it applies for the interpretation of an Act of Parliament.

(3) This Order shall come into operation on 1st June 1973.

2.—(1) So much of Article 3 of the Import Duties (Developing Countries) Order 1971(c), as amended(d), as provides that payment shall not be required of any import duty chargeable under heading 41.02 of the Customs Tariff 1959 (certain bovine cattle leather and equine leather) in respect of goods of a country specified in Part I of Schedule 1 to that Order shall have no effect with respect to goods which fall within sub-heading (A) of that heading (box and willow calf, etc.) and which are goods of any of the following countries, namely:

The Argentine Republic,

The Federative Republic of Brazil,

The Republic of Colombia, and

The Oriental Republic of Uruguay.

(2) Any import duty for the time being chargeable on goods of the above-mentioned heading 41.02(A) shall be chargeable at 12 per cent. instead of the full rate if they are of any of the four above-mentioned countries.

(a) 1971 c. 68.   (b) 1889 c. 63.
(c) S.I. 1971/1882 (1971 III, p. 5125).
(d) The relevant amending order is S.I. 1972/1791 (1972 III, p. 5177).

3. The Import Duties (Developing Countries) Order 1972(**a**) is hereby revoked.

P. L. Hawkins,
Hugh Rossi,
Two of the Lords Commissioners
of Her Majesty's Treasury.

10th May 1973.

EXPLANATORY NOTE

(*This Note is not part of the Order.*)

This Order, which comes into operation on 1st June 1973, revokes the Import Duties (Developing Countries) Order 1972 and provides that import duty chargeable under the Import Duties Act 1958 is now reduced to 12% in respect of certain leathers when imported from four specified developing countries into the United Kingdom under the provisions of the Generalised System of Tariff Preferences.

(a) S.I. 1972/1620 (1972 III, p. 4775).

STATUTORY INSTRUMENTS

1973 No. 894

NORTHERN IRELAND

The Northern Ireland Assembly (Polling Day) Order 1973

Made - - - -   10*th May* 1973
Coming into Operation   10*th May* 1973

In exercise of the powers conferred on me by section 2(1) of the Northern Ireland Assembly Act 1973(**a**), I hereby make the following Order :—

1. This Order may be cited as the Northern Ireland Assembly (Polling Day) Order 1973 and shall come into operation forthwith.

2. The poll for the election of members of the Northern Ireland Assembly shall be held on 28th June 1973.

W. S. I. Whitelaw,
One of Her Majesty's Principal
Secretaries of State.

Northern Ireland Office.
10th May 1973.

EXPLANATORY NOTE

(*This Note is not part of the Order.*)

This Order provides that polling day for the first election to the Northern Ireland Assembly is 28th June 1973.

(**a**) 1973 c. 17.

STATUTORY INSTRUMENTS

1973 No. 895

LOCAL GOVERNMENT, ENGLAND AND WALES

The Rate Support Grant (Amendment) Regulations 1973

Made - - - -	11*th May* 1973
Laid before Parliament	22*nd May* 1973
Coming into Operation	12*th June* 1973

The Secretary of State for the Environment, in exercise of powers conferred by section 5(1)(*a*) of the Local Government Act 1966(**a**) and now vested in him(**b**), and of all other powers enabling him in that behalf, hereby makes the following regulations:—

Title and commencement

1. These regulations may be cited as the Rate Support Grant (Amendment) Regulations 1973 and shall come into operation on 12th June 1973.

Interpretation

2.—(1) The Interpretation Act 1889(**c**) shall apply for the interpretation of these regulations as it applies for the interpretation of an Act of Parliament.

(2) In these regulations "the principal regulations" means the Rate Support Grant Regulations 1967(**d**) as amended(**e**).

Amendment of the schedule to the principal regulations

3. In the schedule to the principal regulations (which provides for calculating the number of education units for an area) for the table set out in paragraph 1 there shall be substituted the following table:—

(1)	(2)
(*a*) Primary and nursery school pupil	1·00
(*b*) Secondary and special school pupil—	
under 16 years of age...	1·78
16 years of age and over	3·02
(*c*) Further education establishment student	2·88
(*d*) University or other student award	2·68
(*e*) 1,000 main mid-day meals for day pupils provided in any year in	
maintained schools	0·65

(**a**) 1966 c. 42.   (**b**) S.I. 1970/1681 (1970 III, p. 5551).
(**c**) 1889 c. 63.   (**d**) S.I. 1967/363 (1967 I, p. 1235).
(**e**) The relevant amending instruments are S.I. 1969/105, 1971/1898 (1969 I, p. 339; 1971 III, p. 5151).

Transitional Provision

4. Nothing in regulation 3 of these regulations shall affect any calculation required to be made in connection with the payment of rate support grants for any year earlier than 1973–74.

Geoffrey Rippon,
Secretary of State for the Environment.

11th May 1973.

EXPLANATORY NOTE

(This Note is not part of the Regulations.)

The Rate Support Grant Regulations 1967 provide for the carrying into effect of sections 1 to 4 of the Local Government Act 1966 (under which rate support grants are paid to local authorities). They determine, inter alia, the method of calculating the number of education units for any area for the purpose of assessing the amounts payable to individual authorities in respect of the needs element of rate support grants. These Regulations amend the method of calculating education units for the years 1973-74 onwards by providing a new table specifying the number of education units to be constituted by each of the persons and items indicated.

STATUTORY INSTRUMENTS

1973 No. 898

CHILDREN AND YOUNG PERSONS

The Cessation of Approved Institutions (St. Peter's School)
Order 1973

Made - - -	*11th May* 1973
Coming into Operation	*1st June* 1973

The Secretary of State for Social Services in exercise of his power under
section 46 of the Children and Young Persons Act 1969(a) and of all other
powers enabling him in that behalf, hereby makes the following order:—

Citation and commencement

1. This order may be cited as the Cessation of Approved Institutions (St.
Peter's School) Order 1973, and shall come into operation on 1st June 1973.

Interpretation

2.—(1) In this order unless the context otherwise requires—

"approved institution" has the meaning assigned to it under section 46 of
the Children and Young Persons Act 1969;

"a protected person" means a person employed by the Hexham and Newcastle Diocesan Rescue Society in respect of the school;

"the school" means the school as approved by the Secretary of State under
section 79(1) of the Children and Young Persons Act 1933(b) and known as
St. Peter's School;

"the specified date" means 1st June 1973;

"the tribunal" means a tribunal established under section 12 of the Industrial Training Act 1964(c), and referred to in section 100 of the Industrial
Relations Act 1971(d);

"the voluntary organisation" means the Hexham and Newcastle Diocesan
Rescue Society.

"Planning Area No. 1" means the area so designated in the Schedule to
the Children and Young Persons (Planning Areas) Order 1970(e).

(2) The Interpretation Act 1889(f) shall apply to the interpretation of this
order as it applies to the interpretation of an Act of Parliament.

Cessation as an approved institution

3. It having appeared to the Secretary of State that in consequence of the
establishment of community homes in Planning Area No. 1 the school is no
longer required he hereby orders that it shall cease to be an approved institution as from the specified date.

(a) 1969 c. 54.	(b) 1933 c. 12.
(c) 1964 c. 16.	(d) 1971 c. 72.
(e) S.I. 1970/335 (1970 I, p. 1220).	(f) 1889 c. 63.

Safeguarding of interests

4.—(1) A protected person shall, until he is served with a statement in writing referring to this order and specifying new terms and conditions of employment, enjoy terms and conditions of employment not less favourable than those he enjoyed immediately before the specified date.

(2) Any new terms and conditions of employment contained in such a statement as aforesaid shall be such that—

(*a*) so long as the person is engaged in duties reasonably comparable to those in which he was engaged immediately before the specified date, the scale of his salary or remuneration; and

(*b*) the other terms and conditions of his employment, shall not be less favourable than those he enjoyed immediately before the specified date.

(3) Any question whether duties are reasonably comparable or whether terms and conditions of employment are less favourable as mentioned in paragraph (2) of this article shall where necessary be determined by the tribunal.

(4) A written statement given in accordance with section 4(1) of the Contracts of Employment Act 1972(**a**) shall not be regarded as a statement of new terms and conditions of employment for the purposes of this article unless the statement so indicates; and such a statement for the purposes of this article shall draw the attention of the person concerned to his right to have any question as to comparability of duties or terms and conditions of employment determined in accordance with the preceding paragraph and give him the address to which the reference of any such questions for determination should be sent.

(5) For the purposes of this article any reference to terms and conditions of employment includes a reference to any restriction, arising under any Act or any instrument made under any Act, on the termination of the employment of any person.

(6) Any determination made by the tribunal as provided under paragraph (3) of this article shall be made in accordance with the Industrial Tribunals (Industrial Relations, etc.) Regulations 1972(**b**), and this order, and in respect of any hearing of the tribunal for purposes of any such determination a person or persons may be appointed to sit with the tribunal as assessor or assessors.

(7) Any determination of the tribunal as mentioned in paragraph (6) of this article shall, subject to any modification that may be required in consequence of any appeal from that determination on a point of law, be given effect to by the voluntary organisation.

Financial provisions

5. The voluntary organisation shall repay to the Secretary of State such sum as he may determine in accordance with paragraph 9(4) of Schedule 3 to the Children and Young Persons Act 1969, such sum to be paid before the expiry of three months from the date it is notified to the voluntary organisation, but so that with the consent of the Treasury the Secretary of State may reduce the sum to be so paid to him to such sum as he may think fit, in which case the sum so reduced shall be paid to the Secretary of State before the expiry of three months from its notification to the voluntary organisation.

(**a**) 1972 c. 53.   (**b**) S.I. 1972/38 (1972 I, p. 91).

Signed by authority of the Secretary of State for Social Services.

M. G. Russell,
Assistant Secretary,
Department of Health and Social Security.

11th May 1973.

EXPLANATORY NOTE

(This Note is not part of the Order.)

This Order makes provision for the cessation as an approved institution of St. Peter's approved school, for the protection of the interests of the staff after the school becomes an assisted community home and for the repayment to the Secretary of State by the Hexham and Newcastle Diocesan Rescue Society of grants which had been made to them in respect of the school.

STATUTORY INSTRUMENTS

1973 No. 900

INCOME TAX

The Clerks to General Commissioners (Compensation) Regulations 1973

Made - - - -		11*th May* 1973
Laid before Parliament		21*st May* 1973
Coming into Operation		12*th June* 1973

ARRANGEMENT OF REGULATIONS

PART I

PRELIMINARY

PART II

ENTITLEMENT TO COMPENSATION

PART III

RESETTLEMENT COMPENSATION

PART IV

LONG-TERM COMPENSATION

Part V

Adjustment, Review and Compounding of Compensation

Part VI

Procedure and Miscellaneous

Schedule

Table mentioned in Regulation 2(2).

The Commissioners of Inland Revenue, in exercise of the powers conferred on them by section 130 of the Finance Act 1972(a), and with the concurrence of the Minister for the Civil Service, hereby make the following Regulations:—

Part I

Preliminary

Citation and commencement

1. These Regulations may be cited as the Clerks to General Commissioners (Compensation) Regulations 1973 and shall come into operation on 12th June 1973.

Interpretation

2.—(1) In these Regulations, unless the context otherwise requires, the following expressions have the meanings hereby respectively assigned to them, that is to say:—

"compensating authority" means the Commissioners of Inland Revenue;

"compensation question" means a question arising under these Regulations—

(*a*) as to a person's entitlement to compensation for loss of employment, or for loss or diminution of emoluments; or

(*b*) as to the manner of a person's employment or the comparability of his duties;

(a) 1972 c. 41.

"gross emoluments" means all remuneration paid or payable to a Clerk to General Commissioners under section 3(2) of the Taxes Management Act 1970(a) but does not include any payments relating to the cost of providing accommodation for meetings of General Commissioners or any travelling or subsistence allowance in respect of expenses incurred personally by the Clerk;

"net emoluments" in relation to any employment which has been lost or the emoluments of which have been diminished means 40 per cent of the gross emoluments payable in respect of the twelve months ending on the material date;

"enactment" means any Act or any instrument made under an Act;

"full time Clerk" means a Clerk as regards whom the Commissioners of Inland Revenue are satisfied that he is required to devote substantially the whole of his time to the duties of his office;

"division" means the area of jurisdiction of a body of General Commissioners;

"General Commissioners" means the Commissioners for the general purposes of the income tax;

"long-term compensation" means compensation payable in accordance with the provisions of Part IV of these Regulations for loss of employment or loss or diminution of emoluments;

"material date", in relation to any person who has suffered loss of employment or loss or diminution of emoluments, means the date on which he suffers that loss or diminution or on which the relevant event happens, whichever date is the earlier;

"national service" means service which is relevant service within the meaning of the Reserve and Auxiliary Forces (Protection of Civil Interests) Act 1951(b) and includes service immediately following such service as aforesaid being service in any of Her Majesty's naval, military or air forces pursuant to a voluntary engagement entered into with the consent of the General Commissioners under whom an officer held his last relevant employment;

"normal retiring age" means seventy years;

"reckonable service", in relation to a person, means any period of part-time employment in any relevant employment and includes any period of war service or national service undertaken on his ceasing to hold any such employment;

"relevant employment" means employment as a Clerk to General Commissioners other than as a full-time Clerk, but except as provided in Regulations 6(1) and 12(1) does not include service in the armed forces of the Crown;

"relevant event" in relation to any person who has suffered loss of employment or loss or diminution of emoluments, means the date of the coming into operation of any order under section 2(6) of the Taxes Management Act 1970, which gives rise to any of the matters referred to in Regulation 4, being matters to which the said loss of employment or loss or diminution of emoluments is attributable;

"resettlement compensation" means compensation payable in accordance with Part III of these Regulations for loss of employment;

"tribunal" means a tribunal established under section 12 of the Industrial Training Act 1964(c);

(a) 1970 c. 9.   (b) 1951 c. 65.
(c) 1964 c. 16.

"war service" means war service within the meaning of the Local Government Staffs (War Service) Act 1939(a), the Teachers Superannuation (War Service) Act 1939(b), the Police and Firemen (War Service) Act 1939(c), or employment for war purposes within the meaning of the Superannuation Schemes (War Service) Act 1940(d).

(2) (a) Where under any provision of these Regulations a capital value is to be assigned to an annual amount, it shall be ascertained in accordance with the table set out in the schedule to these Regulations.

(b) For the purpose of determining the application of the table the headings and the note to the table shall be treated as part of the table.

(3) Unless the context otherwise requires, references in these Regulations to the provisions of any enactment shall be construed as references to those provisions as amended, re-enacted or modified by any subsequent enactment.

(4) References in these Regulations to a numbered regulation shall, unless the reference is to a regulation of specified regulations, be construed as references to the regulation bearing that number in these Regulations.

(5) References in any of these Regulations to a numbered paragraph shall, unless the reference is to a paragraph of a specified regulation, be construed as references to the paragraph bearing that number in the first mentioned regulation.

(6) The Interpretation Act 1889(e) shall apply to the interpretation of these Regulations as it applies to the interpretation of an Act of Parliament.

PART II

ENTITLEMENT TO COMPENSATION

Persons to whom the regulations apply

3. These Regulations shall apply to any person other than a full-time Clerk who, for part only of his time, immediately before the material date was employed as a Clerk to General Commissioners in a non-pensionable capacity.

Grounds of entitlement to compensation

4. Subject to the provisions of these Regulations, any person to whom these Regulations apply and who suffers loss of employment or loss or diminution of emoluments which is attributable to the creation of a new division, the abolition of an existing division, or the alteration in any other respect of a division or its boundaries under an Order made under section 2(6) of the Taxes Management Act 1970(f) shall be entitled to have his case considered for the payment of compensation under these Regulations, and such compensation shall be determined in accordance with these Regulations.

PART III

RESETTLEMENT COMPENSATION

Resettlement compensation for loss of employment

5. The compensating authority shall, subject to the provisions of these Regulations, pay resettlement compensation to any person to whom these Regulations apply and who satisfies the conditions set out in Regulation 6.

(a) 1939 c. 94.	(b) 1939 c. 95.
(c) 1939 c. 103.	(d) 1940 c. 26.
(e) 1889 c. 63.	(f) 1970 c. 9.

Conditions for payment of resettlement compensation

6.—(1) Without prejudice to any other requirement of these Regulations, the conditions for the payment of resettlement compensation to any person are that—

(*a*) he has suffered loss of employment attributable to any of the matters referred to in Regulation 4 on or after the material date but not later than ten years after that date;

(*b*) he had not at the date of the loss attained normal retiring age;

(*c*) he had been for a period beginning on the date three years immediately before the material date and ending on the date when the loss of employment occurred continuously engaged (disregarding breaks not exceeding in the aggregate six months) in relevant employment; and for this purpose the expression "relevant employment" includes any period of national service immediately following such employment;

(*d*) he has made a claim for such compensation in accordance with the provisions of Part VI of these Regulations not later than thirteen weeks after the loss of employment which is the cause of his claim, or thirteen weeks after the coming into operation of these Regulations, whichever is the later, or within such longer period as the compensating authority may allow in any particular case where they are satisfied that the delay in making the claim was due to ill-health or other circumstances beyond the claimant's control;

(*e*) the loss of employment which is the cause of his claim has occurred for some reason other than misconduct or incapacity to perform such duties as, immediately before the loss, he was performing or might reasonably have been required to perform; and

(*f*) he has not, subject to paragraph (2), been offered any reasonably comparable employment as a Clerk to the General Commissioners of another division.

(2) No account shall be taken for the purposes of this Regulation of an offer of employment where the compensating authority is satisfied—

(*a*) that acceptance would have involved undue hardship to the person, or

(*b*) that he was prevented from accepting the offer by reason of ill-health or other circumstances beyond his control.

Amount of resettlement compensation

7.—(1) The amount of resettlement compensation which may be paid to a person shall, for each week for which such compensation is payable, be a sum ascertained by taking two-thirds of the weekly rate of the net emoluments which that person has lost and deducting therefrom such of the following items as may be applicable—

(*a*) unemployment, sickness or injury benefit under any Act relating to National Insurance claimable by him in respect of such week (excluding any amount claimable by him in respect of a dependant); and

(*b*) two-thirds of the net emoluments received by him in respect of such week from work or employment undertaken as a result of the loss of employment.

(2) For the purposes of this Regulation the weekly rate of a person's net emoluments shall be deemed to be seven three hundred and sixty-fifths of those emoluments.

Period for payment of resettlement compensation

8. Subject to the provisions of these Regulations, resettlement compensation shall be payable to a person only in respect of the period of thirteen weeks next succeeding the week in which he lost the employment in respect of which his claim has been made or, in the case of a person who has attained the age of forty-five years, the said thirteen weeks and one additional week for every year of his age after attaining the age of forty-five years and before the date of the loss of employment, subject to a maximum addition of thirteen such weeks.

Additional provisions relating to resettlement compensation

9.—(1) Resettlement compensation shall be payable to a person at intervals equivalent to those at which the emoluments of his employment were previously paid or at such other intervals as may be agreed between the person and the compensating authority.

(2) Resettlement compensation shall be terminated by the compensating authority—

(*a*) if without reasonable cause the recipient fails to comply with any of the provisions of Regulation 10, or

(*b*) if on being requested to do so, he fails to satisfy the compensating authority that, so far as he is able, he is seeking suitable employment.

Claimant for resettlement compensation to furnish particulars of employment

10. Every person claiming or in receipt of resettlement compensation shall (after as well as before the compensation begins to be paid) forthwith supply the compensating authority in writing with particulars of any employment which he obtains or of any change in his earnings from any such employment.

PART IV

LONG-TERM COMPENSATION

Long-term compensation for loss of employment or loss or diminution of emoluments

11. The compensating authority shall, subject to the provisions of these Regulations, pay long-term compensation to any person to whom these Regulations apply and who satisfies the conditions set out in Regulation 12.

Conditions for payment of long-term compensation

12.—(1) Without prejudice to any other requirement of these Regulations, the conditions for the payment of long-term compensation to any person are that—

(*a*) he has suffered loss of employment or loss or diminution of emoluments attributable to any of the matters referred to in Regulation 4 on or after the material date, but not later than ten years after the material date;

(*b*) he had not at the date of the loss or diminution attained normal retiring age;

(c) he had been for a period beginning on a date not less than eight years immediately before the material date and ending on the date when the loss or diminution occurred continuously engaged (without a break of more than twelve months at any one time) in relevant employment; and for this purpose the expression "relevant employment" includes any period of national service immediately following such employment;

(d) he has made a claim for such compensation in accordance with the provisions of Part VI of these Regulations not later than two years after the loss or diminution which is the cause of the claim or two years after the coming into operation of these Regulations whichever is the later; and

(e) if the cause of the claim for compensation is loss of employment—

(i) the loss has occurred for some reason other than misconduct or incapacity to perform such duties as, immediately before the loss, he was performing or might reasonably have been required to perform; and

(ii) he has not been offered any reasonably comparable employment as a Clerk to the General Commissioners of another division.

(2) No account shall be taken for the purposes of this Regulation of an offer of employment where the compensating authority is satisfied—

(a) that acceptance would have involved undue hardship to the person, or

(b) that he was prevented from accepting the offer by reason of ill-health or other circumstances beyond his control.

(3) Claims for long-term compensation for loss of employment shall in all respects be treated as claims for such compensation for the loss of emoluments occasioned thereby and the provisions of these Regulations shall apply to all such claims accordingly.

Factors to be considered in determining payment of long-term compensation

13.—(1) For the purpose of determining the amount (subject to the limits set out in these Regulations) of long-term compensation, if any, payable under these Regulations to any person for loss or diminution of emoluments, the compensating authority shall have regard to such of the following factors as may be relevant, that is to say—

(a) the conditions upon which the person held the employment which he has lost, including in particular its security of tenure, whether by law or practice;

(b) the emoluments and other conditions, including security of tenure, whether by law or practice, of any work or employment undertaken by the person as a result of the loss of employment;

(c) the extent to which he has sought suitable employment and the emoluments which he might have acquired by accepting other suitable employment offered to him;

(d) all the other circumstances of his case.

(2) In ascertaining for the purposes of paragraph (1)(c) whether a person has been offered suitable employment, Regulation 6(2) shall apply.

Amount of long-term compensation payable for loss of emoluments

14.—(1) Long-term compensation for loss of emoluments shall, subject to the provisions of these Regulations, be payable until the normal retiring age or death of a person to whom it is payable, whichever first occurs, and shall not exceed a maximum annual sum calculated in accordance with the provisions of paragraphs (2) and (3).

(2) The said maximum annual sum shall, subject as hereinafter provided, be the aggregate of the following sums, namely—

    (*a*) for every year of the person's reckonable service, one sixtieth of the net emoluments which he has lost; and

    (*b*) in the case of a person who has attained the age of forty years at the date of the loss, a sum calculated in accordance with the provisions of paragraph (3) appropriate to his age at that date,

but the said maximum annual sum shall in no case exceed two-thirds of the net emoluments which the person has lost.

(3) The sum referred to in paragraph (2)(*b*) shall be—

    (*a*) in the case of a person who has attained the age of forty years but has not attained the age of fifty years at the date of the loss, the following fraction of the net emoluments which he has lost—

        (i) where his reckonable service is less than ten years, one sixtieth for each year of such service, after attaining the age of forty years; or

        (ii) where his reckonable service amounts to ten years but is less than fifteen years, one sixtieth for each year of such service after attaining the age of forty years and one additional sixtieth; or

        (iii) where his reckonable service amounts to fifteen years but is less than twenty years, one sixtieth for each year of such service after attaining the age of forty years and two additional sixtieths; or

        (iv) where his reckonable service amounts to twenty years or more, one sixtieth for each year of such service after attainng the age of forty years and three additional sixtieths;

    but the sum so calculated shall not in any case exceed one sixth of the said net emoluments;

    (*b*) in the case of a person who has attained the age of fifty years but has not attained the age of sixty years at the date of the loss, one sixtieth of the said net emoluments for each year of his reckonable service after attaining the age of forty years, up to a maximum of fifteen such years; and

    (*c*) in the case of a person who has attained the age of sixty years at the date of the loss, one sixtieth of the said net emoluments for each year of his reckonable service after attaining the age of forty-five years.

(4) Where long-term compensation is payable in respect of any period and resettlement compensation is also payable in respect of that period, the long-term compensation shall be limited to the amount (if any) by which it exceeds the resettlement compensation payable as aforesaid.

(5) Long-term compensation shall be payable to a person at intervals equivalent to those at which the emoluments of his employment were previously paid or at such other intervals as may be agreed between the person and the compensating authority.

Long-term compensation for diminution of emoluments

15. Long-term compensation for diminution of emoluments in respect of any employment shall, subject to the provisions of these Regulations, be awarded and paid in accordance with the following provisions:—

(*a*) the compensation shall consist of an annual sum which shall be payable to a person at intervals equivalent to those at which the emoluments of his employment are or were previously paid or at such other intervals as may be agreed between the person and the compensating authority, and shall, subject to the provisions of these Regulations, be payable until normal retiring age or death, whichever first occurs; and

(*b*) the said annual sum shall not exceed the maximum annual sum which could have been awarded under Regulation 14 if the person had suffered loss of employment and the loss of emoluments occasioned thereby had been equivalent to the amount of the diminution:

Provided that no compensation shall be payable if the emoluments have been diminished by less than two and one half per cent.

Date from which long-term compensation is to be payable

16.—(1) Long-term compensation shall be payable with effect from the date of the claim or from any earlier date permitted by the succeeding provisions of this regulation.

(2) Where a claim for long-term compensation is duly made within thirteen weeks of the occurrence of the loss or diminution which is the cause of the claim, or within thirteen weeks of the coming into operation of these Regulations, whichever is the later, the award shall be made retrospective to the date on which the loss or diminution occurred.

(3) Where a claim for long-term compensation is made after the expiry of the period mentioned in paragraph (2), the award may, at the discretion of the compensating authority, be made retrospective to a date not earlier than thirteen weeks prior to the date on which the claim was made:

Provided that if the compensating authority are satisfied that the failure to make the claim within the period mentioned in paragraph (2) was due to ill-health or other circumstances beyond the claimant's control, the award may be made retrospective to a date not earlier than that on which the loss or diminution occurred.

PART V

ADJUSTMENT, REVIEW AND COMPOUNDING OF COMPENSATION

Reduction of compensation in certain cases

17.—(1) Where in any week a person is entitled to long-term compensation for loss or diminution of emoluments and is also entitled to unemployment, sickness or injury benefit under any Act relating to National Insurance, other than a benefit claimable by him in respect of a dependant, there shall be deducted from the long-term compensation payable for that week a sum not exceeding the amount by which the aggregate of such National Insurance benefits claimable in respect of that week and the weekly rate at which the long-term compensation would be payable but for this Regulation exceeds two-thirds of the weekly rate of the net emoluments of the employment which he has lost or in which the emoluments have been diminished:

Provided that this paragraph shall not apply in relation to any such sickness or injury benefit in so far as—

    (*a*) an equivalent sum is deducted from the emoluments of his current employment, and

    (*b*) such deduction from those emoluments has not occasioned an increase in his long-term compensation.

(2) In paragraph (1) the expression "weekly rate" means seven three hundred and sixty-fifths of the relevant annual rate.

Notification of change of circumstances

18. Where—

    (*a*) a person entitled to long-term compensation enters employment the remuneration whereof is payable out of public funds, or ceases to hold such employment, or receives any increase in his remuneration in such employment, or

    (*b*) a person entitled to long-term compensation starts to receive any benefit, any increase in benefit or any further benefit, under any Act relating to National Insurance,

he shall forthwith inform the compensating authority in writing of that fact.

Review of awards of long-term compensation

19.—(1) The compensating authority shall, within a period of two years after the date on which any decision on a claim for long-term compensation for loss of employment is notified to a claimant under Regulation 21, or within such longer period as is specified in the subsequent provisions of this Regulation, and at intervals of not more than six months, review its decision or, where the claim has been the subject of an appeal, the decision of the tribunal, and these Regulations shall apply in relation to any such review as they apply in relation to the initial determination of the claim; and on such review, in the light of any material change in the circumstances of the case, compensation may be awarded, or compensation previously awarded may be increased, reduced or discontinued, subject to the limits set out in these Regulations.

(2) The person to whom the decision relates may require the compensating authority to carry out the review mentioned in paragraph (1) at any time within the period of two years mentioned in that paragraph if he considers that there has been a change in the circumstances of his case which is material for the purposes of these Regulations.

(3) The compensating authority shall carry out a review in accordance with paragraph (1), notwithstanding the expiration of the period mentioned in that paragraph, if—

    (*a*) the emoluments of employment or work undertaken as a result of the loss of employment had been taken into account in determining the amount of any compensation awarded, and

    (*b*) such employment or work has been lost or the emoluments thereof reduced, otherwise than by reason of misconduct or incapacity to perform such duties as the person might reasonably have been required to perform, and

    (*c*) the compensating authority is satisfied that such loss or reduction is causing him hardship, and where any decision is so reviewed, the decision shall be subject to further review in accordance with paragraph (1) as if the review carried out under this paragraph had been the initial determination of the claim.

(4) Paragraphs (1) and (2) shall apply in relation to any decision on a claim for long-term compensation in respect of diminution of emoluments as they apply in relation to any decision mentioned in the said paragraph (1):

Provided that—

(i) where the person to whom the decision relates ceases to hold the employment in which his emoluments were diminished, a review shall be held within three months after that date, but no further review shall be held after the expiry of that period, and

(ii) while that person continues to hold that employment, there shall be no limit to the period within which a review may take place.

(5) Notwithstanding anything contained in the foregoing provisions of this Regulation, the compensating authority shall review a decision, whether of the authority or the tribunal, on a claim for long-term compensation for loss of employment or diminution of emoluments after the expiration of any period within which a review is required to be made if at any time—

(a) the person to whom the decision relates becomes engaged in employment (hereinafter referred to as "his current employment") the remuneration whereof is payable out of public funds and which he has undertaken subsequent to the loss or diminution, and

(b) the aggregate of the net emoluments of his current employment and the long-term compensation payable to him exceeds the net emoluments of the employment which he has lost or, as the case may be, in which the emoluments have been diminished.

(6) The compensating authority shall further review any decision reviewed under paragraph (5) whenever the net emoluments of the person's current employment are increased.

(7) If on any review under paragraph (5) or (6) the compensation is reduced it shall not be reduced below the amount by which the net emoluments of the person's current employment falls short of the net emoluments of the employment which he has lost, or, as the case may be, in which the emoluments have been diminished.

(8) The compensating authority shall give to a person to whom a decision relates not less than fourteen days' notice of any review of that decision to be carried out under this Regulation unless the review is carried out at his request.

(9) Nothing in this Regulation shall preclude the making of any adjustment of compensation required by Regulation 17.

Compounding of awards

20.—(1) In a case where an annual sum which has been or might be awarded under these Regulations does not exceed £39, the compensating authority may, at its discretion, compound its liability in respect thereof by paying a lump sum equivalent to the capital value of the annual sum.

(2) In any other case, if the person who has been awarded long-term compensation requests it to do so, the compensating authority may, after having regard to the state of health of that person and the other circumstances of the case, compound up to one quarter of its liability to make payments under the award by the payment of an equivalent amount as a lump sum.

(3) The making of a composition under paragraph (2) in relation to an award of long-term compensation shall not prevent the subsequent making of a composition under paragraph (1) in relation to that award but, subject as aforesaid, not more than one composition may be made in relation to any award.

PART VI

PROCEDURE AND MISCELLANEOUS

Procedure on making claims

21.—(1) Every claim for compensation under these Regulations and every request for a review of an award of long-term compensation shall be made in accordance with this Regulation.

(2) Every such claim or request, shall be made to the compensating authority in a form approved by that authority and shall state whether any other claim for compensation has been made by the claimant under these Regulations.

(3) Resettlement compensation shall be claimed separately from long-term compensation.

(4) The compensating authority shall consider any such claim or request in accordance with the relevant provisions of these Regulations and shall notify the person making the claim or request in writing of its decision—

(a) in the case of a claim for resettlement compensation not later than one month after the receipt of the claim, and

(b) in the case of a claim for, or request for the review of an award of, compensation under Part IV of these Regulations, not later than thirteen weeks after the receipt of the claim or request, and

(c) in any other case, as soon as possible after the decision;
but the decision of the compensating authority shall not be invalidated by reason of the fact that notice of the decision is given after the expiry of the period mentioned in this paragraph.

(5) Every notification of a decision by the compensating authority (whether granting or refusing compensation or reviewing an award, or otherwise affecting any compensation under these Regulations) shall contain a statement—

(a) giving reasons for the decision;

(b) showing how any compensation has been calculated and, in particular, if the amount is less than the maximum which could have been awarded under these Regulations, showing the factors taken into account in awarding that amount; and

(c) directing the attention of the claimant to his right under Regulation 27, if he is aggrieved by the decision, to institute proceedings before a tribunal and giving him the address to which the application instituting such proceedings should be sent.

Claimants to furnish information

22.—(1) Any person claiming or receiving compensation or whose award of compensation is being reviewed shall furnish all such information as the compensating authority may at any time reasonably require; and he shall verify the same in such manner, including the production of books or of original documents in his possession or control, as may be reasonably so required.

(2) Any such person shall, on receipt of reasonable notice, present himself for interview at such place as the compensating authority may reasonably require; and any person who attends for interview may, if he so desires, be represented by his adviser.

Procedure on death of claimant

23.—(1) In the event of the death of a claimant or of a person who, if he had survived, could have been a claimant, a claim for compensation under these Regulations may be continued or made, as the case may be, by his personal representatives.

(2) Where any such claim is continued or made as aforesaid by personal representatives, the personal representatives shall, as respects any steps to be taken or thing to be done by them in order to continue to make the claim, be deemed for the purposes of these Regulations to be the person entitled to claim, but, save as aforesaid, the person in whose right they continue or make the claim shall be deemed for the purposes of these Regulations to be such person, and the relevant provisions of these Regulations shall be construed accordingly:

Provided that the compensating authority may in any such case extend the period within which a claim is required to be made by Regulation 6 or Regulation 12.

Calculation of service

24. For the purpose of making any calculations under these Regulations in respect of a person's reckonable service, all periods of such service shall be aggregated and, except where reference is made to completed years of service, if the aggregated service includes a fraction of a year, that fraction shall, if it equals or exceeds six months, be treated as a year, and shall, in any other case be disregarded.

Emoluments of part-time employments

25. In ascertaining for the purposes of these Regulations whether, and how far, the remuneration of alternative employment falls short of emoluments which have been lost where those emoluments were payable in respect of two or more part-time employments, the remuneration of the alternative employment or of the aggregate of two or more such employments shall be apportioned in the proportion which the emoluments of the part-time employments bore to each other.

Compensation not assignable

26. Subject to any statutory provision in that behalf, any compensation to which a person becomes entitled under these Regulations shall be paid by the compensating authority and shall be payable to, or in trust for, the person who is entitled to receive it, and shall not be assignable:

Provided that, without prejudice to any other right of recovery, any compensation paid in error may be recovered by the compensating authority by deduction from any compensation payable under these Regulations.

Right of appeal from decision of compensating authority

27.—(1) Every person who is aggrieved by any decision of the compensating authority with respect to a compensation question or by any failure on the part of the compensating authority to notify him of any such decision within the appropriate time prescribed by these Regulations, may within thirteen weeks of the notification to him of the decision or the expiry of the prescribed time, as the case may be, institute proceedings for the determination of the question by a tribunal in accordance with the Industrial Tribunals (Industrial Relations, etc) Regulations 1972**(a)** or in Scotland the Industrial Tribunals (Industrial Relations, etc) (Scotland) Regulations 1972**(b)** and these Regulations; and the tribunal shall determine the question accordingly.

(2) For the purpose of any such proceedings a person or persons may be appointed to sit with the tribunal as assessor or assessors.

(3) The compensating authority shall give effect to the decision of a tribunal subject to any modifications that may be required in consequence of any appeal from that decision on a point of law.

By Order of the Commissioners of Inland Revenue.

                                             J. Webb,

10th May 1973.   Secretary.

Concurrence of the Minister for the Civil Service given under his Official Seal on 11th May 1973.

(L.S.)   *K. H. McNeill,*
                                              Authorised by the
                               Minister for the Civil Service.

(a) S.I. 1972/38 (1972 I, p. 91).   (b) S.I. 1972/39 (1972 I, p. 102).

SCHEDULE

TABLE

Capital value, according to the age of employee, of each £100 of the total amount of long-term compensation payable to age 70.

Age last birthday of employee	Capital value of each £100 of the total amount of long-term compensation	
	Female	Male
	£ p	£ p
30	30·55	30·35
31	31·20	30·95
32	31·85	31·60
33	32·55	32·25
34	33·25	32·95
35	34·00	33·65
36	34·80	34·40
37	35·60	35·15
38	36·40	35·95
39	37·25	36·75
40	38·15	37·60
41	39·10	38·50
42	40·10	39·40
43	41·10	40·35
44	42·15	41·35
45	43·25	42·40
46	44·40	43·45
47	45·60	44·55
48	46·85	45·75
49	48·15	47·00
50	49·55	48·30
51	51·00	49·65
52	52·50	51·05
53	54·10	52·55
54	55·75	54·15
55	57·50	55·80
56	59·35	57·60
57	61·30	59·50
58	63·35	61·50
59	65·55	63·65
60	67·90	65·95
61	70·35	68·45
62	73·00	71·15
63	75·85	74·05
64	78·90	77·20
65	82·20	80·65
66	85·75	84·45
67	89·55	88·60
68	93·65	93·05
69	97·90	97·75

NOTE: The total amount of the annual long-term compensation which is to be compounded must first be calculated, i.e. the amount which the employee would receive on account of that compensation, or the part of it which is to be compounded, if it were paid until age 70. For each £100 so calculated, the lump sum payment will be the amount shown in the table according to the age of the employee at which the compounding is taking place.

Example: if long-term compensation of £20 per annum is paid to a male officer aged 39 years 5 months until he is aged 70 the amount payable would be

$$30\frac{7}{12} \times £20 \times \frac{£36\cdot75}{£100} = £224\cdot79$$

EXPLANATORY NOTE

(*This Note is not part of the Regulations.*)

1. These Regulations made under section 130, Finance Act 1972, provide for the payment of compensation to or in respect of part-time Clerks to General Commissioners who suffer loss of employment or loss or diminution of emoluments in consequence of adjustments (under section 2(6), Taxes Management Act 1970) of the divisions for which the General Commissioners act.

2. Part I of the Regulations contains definitions. Part II specifies the persons to whom the Regulations apply and the grounds of entitlement to compensation.

3. The compensation payable is—

    (*a*) resettlement compensation for loss of employment (Part III);

    (*b*) long-term compensation for loss of employment or loss or diminution of emoluments (Part IV).

4. Resettlement compensation is payable for a period not exceeding 26 weeks to Clerks with at least three years' service in relevant employment. The qualifying conditions and factors to be considered are set out in Regulation 6. The method of calculating the amount of compensation is contained in Regulation 7.

5. Long-term compensation is payable to Clerks with at least eight years' service in relevant employment. The qualifying and other conditions are set out in Regulation 12.

6. The method of calculating the maximum amount of long-term compensation is laid down in Regulation 14 (loss of emoluments) and Regulation 15 (diminution of emoluments). This amount is a proportion, not exceeding two-thirds, of the net emoluments lost or of the amount by which emoluments have been diminished, as the case may be. This compensation is payable from a date determined under Regulation 16 and can be payable up to normal retiring age.

STATUTORY INSTRUMENTS

1973 No. 905

SOCIAL SECURITY

The National Insurance (Industrial Injuries) (Claims and Payments) Amendment Regulations 1973

Made - - - -	*14th May* 1973
Laid before Parliament	*22nd May* 1973
Coming into Operation	*12th June* 1973

The Secretary of State for Social Services, in exercise of powers conferred by sections 25(2)(c), 27(1) and 31(2) of the National Insurance (Industrial Injuries) Act 1965**(a)** and now vested in him**(b)**, and of all other powers enabling him in that behalf, and after reference to the Industrial Injuries Advisory Council, hereby makes the following regulations:—

Citation, interpretation and commencement

1. These regulations, which may be cited as the National Insurance (Industrial Injuries) (Claims and Payments) Amendment Regulations 1973, amend the National Insurance (Industrial Injuries) (Claims and Payments) Regulations 1964**(c)** as amended**(d)** (hereinafter referred to as "the principal regulations"), and shall come into operation on 12th June 1973.

Revocation of regulations

2. Regulation 4(1)(c) of the principal regulations is hereby revoked.

Amendment of regulation 15 *of the principal regulations*

3. In regulation 15(2)(b) of the principal regulations the word "only" shall be omitted and in regulation 15(2)(b) and (c) thereof the word "approved" shall be omitted.

Amendment of regulation 19 *of the principal regulations*

4. In regulation 19(3) of the principal regulations the words "or any course which he is so required to attend" shall be omitted.

Amendment of column 3 *of paragraph* 2 *of Schedule* 2 *to the principal regulations*

5. In column 3 of paragraph 2 of Schedule 2 to the principal regulations, for the word "Benefit" there shall be substituted the words "Disablement pension (including disablement pension paid in lieu of gratuity)".

(a) 1965 c. 52.
(b) *See* Ministry of Social Security Act 1966, section 2 (1966 c. 20) and Secretary of State for Social Services Order 1968, Article 2 (S.I. 1968/1699 (1968 III, p. 4585)).
(c) S.I. 1964/73 (1964 I, p. 115).
(d) There is no amendment which relates expressly to the subject matter of these regulations.

Signed by authority of the Secretary of State for Social Services.

Paul Dean,
Parliamentary Under-Secretary of State,
Department of Health and Social Security

14th May 1973.

EXPLANATORY NOTE

(This Note is not part of the Regulations.)

Regulation 1 is formal.

Regulation 2 revokes Regulation 4(1)(*c*) of the National Insurance (Industrial Injuries) (Claims and Payments) Regulations 1964, which is no longer required and which will cease to have effect upon the repeal of section 25(2)(*c*) of the National Insurance (Industrial Injuries) Act 1965.

The amendment made by Regulation 5 limits to disablement pension (including disablement pension paid in lieu of gratuity) the provisions for disqualification for receipt of benefit not claimed in due time which are contained in paragraph 2 of Schedule 2 to the said Regulations.

The other amendments are of a minor or consequential character.

STATUTORY INSTRUMENTS

1973 No. 912

INDUSTRIAL TRAINING

The Industrial Training Levy (Distributive Board) Order 1973

Made - - -	*15th May* 1973
Laid before Parliament	*24th May* 1973
Coming into Operation	*1st July* 1973

The Secretary of State after approving proposals submitted by the Distributive Industry Training Board for the imposition of a further levy on employers in the distributive industry and in exercise of powers conferred by section 4 of the Industrial Training Act 1964(a) and now vested in him(b), and of all other powers enabling him in that behalf hereby makes the following Order:—

Title and commencement

1. This Order may be cited as the Industrial Training Levy (Distributive Board) Order 1973 and shall come into operation on 1st July 1973.

Interpretation

2.—(1) In this Order unless the context otherwise requires:—

(*a*) "an appeal tribunal" means an industrial tribunal established under section 12 of the Industrial Training Act 1964;

(*b*) "assessment" means an assessment of an employer to the levy;

(*c*) "the Board" means the Distributive Industry Training Board;

(*d*) "business" means any activities of industry or commerce;

(*e*) "distributive establishment" means an establishment in Great Britain engaged in the fifth base period wholly or mainly in the distributive industry for a total of twenty-seven or more weeks or, being an establishment that commenced to carry on business in the fifth base period, for a total number of weeks exceeding one half of the number of weeks in the part of the said period commencing with the day on which business was commenced and ending on the last day thereof;

(*f*) "the distributive industry" means any one or more of the activities which, subject to the provisions of paragraph 2 of the Schedule to the industrial training order, are specified in paragraph 1 of that Schedule as the activities of the distributive industry;

(a) 1964 c. 16.   (b) S.I. 1968/729 (1968 II, p. 2108).

(*g*) "emoluments" means all emoluments assessable to income tax under Schedule E (other than pensions), being emoluments from which tax under that Schedule is deductible, whether or not tax in fact falls to be deducted from any particular payment thereof;

(*h*) "employer" means a person who is an employer in the distributive industry at any time in the fifth levy period;

(*i*) "the fifth base period" means the period of twelve months that commenced on 6th April 1972;

(*j*) "the fifth levy period" means the period commencing with the day upon which this Order comes into operation and ending on 31st March 1974;

(*k*) "the industrial training order" means the Industrial Training (Distributive Board) Order 1970(**a**) as amended by the Industrial Training (Distributive Board) Order 1970 (Amendment) Order 1971(**b**);

(*l*) "the levy" means the levy imposed by the Board in respect of the fifth levy period;

(*m*) "notice" means a notice in writing;

(*n*) other expressions have the same meanings as in the industrial training order.

(2) Any reference in this Order to an establishment that commences to carry on business or that ceases to carry on business shall not be taken to apply where the location of the establishment is changed but its business is continued wholly or mainly at or from the new location, or where the suspension of activities is of a temporary or seasonal nature.

(3) In the case where a distributive establishment is taken over (whether directly or indirectly) by an employer in succession to, or jointly with, another person, a person employed at any time in the fifth base period at or from the establishment shall be deemed for the purposes of this Order to have been so employed by the employer carrying on the said establishment on the day upon which this Order comes into operation, and any reference in this Order to persons employed by the employer at or from a distributive establishment in the fifth base period shall be construed accordingly.

(4) The Interpretation Act 1889(**c**) shall apply to the interpretation of this Order as it applies to the interpretation of an Act of Parliament.

Imposition of the levy

3.—(1) The levy to be imposed by the Board on employers in respect of the fifth levy period shall be assessed in accordance with the provisions of this Article.

(2) Subject to the provisions of this Article, the levy shall be assessed by the Board in respect of each employer and the amount thereof shall be equal to 0·7 per cent. of the sum (less £3,000) of the emoluments of all the persons employed by the employer at or from the distributive establishment or establishments of the employer in the fifth base period.

(a) S.I 1970/1053 (1970 II, p. 3273).   (b) S.I. 1971/1876 (1971 III, p. 5109).
(c) 1889 c. 63.

(3) Where any persons whose emoluments are taken into account for the purposes of this Article were employed at or from an establishment that ceases to carry on business in the fifth levy period, the sum of the emoluments of those persons shall be reduced in the same proportion as the number of days between the commencement of the said levy period and the date of cessation of business (both dates inclusive) bears to the number of days in the said levy period.

(4) For the purposes of this Article no regard shall be had to the emoluments of—

(a) any person who, being a registered pharmacist or a registered optician, is employed wholly or mainly in activities undertaken by him personally in the exercise of his profession;

(b) any person employed as a member of the crew of an aircraft or as the master or member of the crew of a ship or any person ordinarily employed as a seaman who is employed in or about a ship in port by the owner or charterer thereof on work of a kind ordinarily done by a seaman on a ship while it is in port;

(c) a registered dock worker employed on dock work;

(d) any person wholly employed in agriculture;

(e) any person wholly employed in the supply of food or drink to persons being a supply—

   (i) for immediate consumption;

   (ii) of hot fried fish or hot chipped potatoes; or

   (iii) by means of an automatic vending machine at or in connection with an hotel, restaurant, café, snack bar, canteen, mess room or similar place of refreshment; or

(f) any person engaged wholly or mainly in the work of a consultant or valuer in connection with antiques and works of fine art.

(5) There shall be exempt from the levy an employer in whose case—

(a) the number of all the persons employed by him on 5th April 1973 at or from the distributive establishment or establishments of the employer was less than ten; or

(b) the sum of the emoluments of all the persons employed by him at or from the distributive establishment or establishments of the employer in the fifth base period was less than £8,000.

Assessment notices

4.—(1) The Board shall serve an assessment notice on every employer assessed to the levy.

(2) The amount of an assessment shall be rounded down, where necessary, to the nearest £1.

(3) An assessment notice shall state the Board's address for the service of a notice of appeal or of an application for an extension of time for appealing.

(4) An assessment notice may be served on the person assessed to the levy either by delivering it to him personally or by leaving it, or sending it to him

by post, at his last known address or place of business in the United Kingdom or, if that person is a corporation, by leaving it, or sending it by post to the corporation, at such address or place of business or at its registered or principal office.

Payment of the levy

5.—(1) Subject to the provisions of this Article and of Articles 6 and 7, the amount of the assessment payable under an assessment notice served by the Board shall be payable to the Board in two instalments equal to one-fifth and four-fifths of the said amount respectively, and the said instalments shall be due respectively one month and four months after the date of the notice.

(2) The amount of an instalment mentioned in the last foregoing paragraph may be rounded up or down by the Board to a convenient figure, but so that the aggregate amount of both instalments shall be equal to the amount of the assessment.

(3) An instalment of an assessment shall not be recoverable by the Board until there has expired the time allowed for appealing against the assessment by Article 7(1) of this Order and any further period or periods of time that the Board or an appeal tribunal may have allowed for appealing under paragraph (2) or (3) of that Article or, where an appeal is brought, until the appeal is decided or withdrawn.

Withdrawal of assessment

6.—(1) The Board may, by a notice served on the person assessed to the levy in the same manner as an assessment notice, withdraw an assessment if that person has appealed against that assessment under the provisions of Article 7 of this Order and the appeal has not been entered in the Register of Appeals kept under the appropriate Regulations specified in paragraph (5) of that Article.

(2) The withdrawal of an assessment shall be without prejudice to the power of the Board to serve a further assessment notice on the employer.

Appeals

7.—(1) A person assessed to the levy may appeal to an appeal tribunal against the assessment within one month from the date of the service of the assessment notice or within any further period or periods of time that may be allowed by the Board or an appeal tribunal under the following provisions of this Article.

(2) The Board by notice may for good cause allow a person assessed to the levy to appeal to an appeal tribunal against the assessment at any time within the period of four months from the date of the service of the assessment notice or within such further period or periods as the Board may allow before such time as may then be limited for appealing has expired.

(3) If the Board shall not allow an application for extension of time for appealing, an appeal tribunal shall upon application made to the tribunal by the person assessed to the levy have the like powers as the Board under the last foregoing paragraph.

(4) In the case of an assessment that has reference to an establishment that ceases to carry on business in the fifth levy period on any day after the date of the service of the assessment notice, the foregoing provisions of this Article shall have effect as if for the period of four months from the date of the service of the assessment notice mentioned in paragraph (2) of this Article there were substituted the period of six months from the date of the cessation of business.

(5) An appeal or an application to an appeal tribunal under this Article shall be made in accordance with the Industrial Tribunals (England and Wales) Regulations 1965(a) as amended by the Industrial Tribunals (England and Wales) (Amendment) Regulations 1967(b) except where the assessment has reference to persons employed at or from one or more establishments that are wholly in Scotland and to no other persons, in which case the appeal or application shall be made in accordance with the Industrial Tribunals (Scotland) Regulations 1965(c) as amended by the Industrial Tribunals (Scotland) (Amendment) Regulations 1967(d).

(6) The powers of an appeal tribunal under paragraph (3) of this Article may be exercised by the President of the Industrial Tribunals (England and Wales) or by the President of the Industrial Tribunals (Scotland) as the case may be.

Evidence

8.—(1) Upon the discharge by a person assessed to the levy of his liability under an assessment the Board shall if so requested issue to him a certificate to that effect.

(2) The production in any proceedings of a document purporting to be certified by the Secretary of the Board to be a true copy of an assessment or other notice issued by the Board or purporting to be a certificate such as is mentioned in the foregoing paragraph of this Article shall, unless the contrary is proved, be sufficient evidence of the document and of the facts stated therein.

Signed by order of the Secretary of State.
15th May 1973.

R. Chichester-Clark,
Minister of State,
Department of Employment.

(a) S.I. 1965/1101 (1965 II, p. 2805).   (b) S.I. 1967/301 (1967 I, p. 1040).
(c) S.I. 1965/1157 (1965 II, p. 3266).   (d) S.I. 1967/302 (1967 I, p. 1050).

EXPLANATORY NOTE

(This Note is not part of the Order.)

This Order gives effect to proposals submitted by the Distributive Industry Training Board to the Secretary of State for Employment for the imposition of a further levy on employers in the distributive industry for the purpose of raising money towards the expenses of the Board.

The levy is to be imposed in respect of the fifth levy period commencing with the date upon which this Order comes into operation and ending on 31st March 1974. The levy will be assessed by the Board and there will be a right of appeal against an assessment to an industrial tribunal.

STATUTORY INSTRUMENTS

1973 No. 914 (S.72)

FOOD AND DRUGS

The Separated Milk (Scotland) Regulations 1973

Made - - - -	*8th May* 1973
Laid before Parliament	*24th May* 1973
Coming into Operation	*14th June* 1973

In exercise of the powers conferred on me by section 56 and 56A of the Food and Drugs (Scotland) Act 1956(a) as read with section 4(1) of, and paragraph 3(2)(a) and (b) of Schedule 4 to, the European Communities Act 1972 (b) and of all other powers enabling me in that behalf, and after consultation with such organisations as appear to me to be representative of interests substantially affected by these regulations I hereby make the following regulations:—

Citation and commencement

1. These regulations may be cited as the Separated Milk (Scotland) Regulations 1973 and shall come into operation on 14th June 1973.

Interpretation

2.—(1) In these regulations, unless the context otherwise requires—

"the Act" means the Food and Drugs (Scotland) Act 1956;

"the Act of Accession" means the Act annexed to the Treaty relating to the accession of the United Kingdom to the European Economic Community signed at Brussels on 22nd January 1972;

"human consumption" does not include use in the preparation of food for human consumption;

"milk", "raw milk", "whole milk", "semi-skimmed milk" and "skimmed milk" have the same respective meanings as in regulation No. 1411/71 of the Council of the European Communities(c);

"sale" in relation to milk, does not include sale to a milk processor for heat treatment or for an authorised treatment of equivalent effect;

"separated milk" means milk other than raw milk and whole milk.

(2) The Interpretation Act 1889(d) shall apply for the interpretation of these regulations as it applies for the interpretation of an Act of Parliament.

(a) 1956 c. 30.   (b) 1972 c. 68.

(c) OJ No. L148/4 of 3.7.71 (S.E. 1971 II, p. 412).

(d) 1889 c. 63.

(3) Any reference in these regulations to regulation No. 1411/71 of the Council of the European Communities shall be construed as a reference to that regulation—

(a) as specified in and as adapted by Article 29 of and Annex I Part II paragraph I.11 to the Act of Accession (which permit Member States to provide for an additional high fat whole milk category) and as read with Article 89.1 of the Act of Accession (which until 31st December 1975, permits the supply to consumers as whole milk of unskimmed milk with a fat content of less than 3·5 per cent.);

(b) as replaced or amended by any subsequent directly applicable Community instrument.

Delivery of separated milk

3. No person shall deliver, or cause or permit to be delivered, on or in pursuance of any sale for human consumption any separated milk which is not semi-skimmed milk or skimmed milk delivered, in either case, as such.

Enforcement

4.—(1) The local authority of any area shall enforce and execute the provisions of these regulations within their area.

(2) In this regulation "local authority" means the council of a county or of a large burgh within the meaning of the Local Government (Scotland) Act 1947**(a)**; and any small burgh within the meaning of that Act shall, for the purposes of these regulations, be included in the county in which it is situated.

Penalties

5. If any person contravenes or fails to comply with the foregoing provisions of these regulations he shall be guilty of an offence under these regulations.

Application of various sections of the Act

6.—(1) Without prejudice to the provisions of the Act which specifically apply in respect of regulations made thereunder section 40(1) (which relates to penalties) of the Act shall apply for the purposes of these regulations as if the reference therein to an offence against the Act included a reference to an offence against these regulations.

(2) Without prejudice to the provisions of the Act which specifically apply in respect of regulations made thereunder sections 41(2) and (5) (which relate to proceedings), 42(1), (2) and (3) (which relate to evidence of certificates of analysis), 44 (which relates to the power of a Court to require analysis by the Government Chemist) and 47 (which relates to offences in relation to warranties and certificates of analysis) of the Act shall apply for the purposes of these regulations as if references therein to proceedings, or a prosecution, under or taken under the Act included references to proceedings, or a prosecution as the case may be, for an offence against these regulations and in addition as if—

(a) 1947 c. 43.

(*a*) in the case of section 44(1) of the Act, the reference therein to section 41(5) of the Act included a reference to said section 41(5) as applied by these regulations; and

(*b*) in the case of section 47(1) and (2) of the Act, the references therein to an offence against the Act included references to an offence against these regulations.

(3) Section 41(4) of the Act shall apply for the purposes of these regulations as if the reference therein to section 47 of the Act included a reference to said section 47 as applied by these regulations.

Gordon Campbell,

One of Her Majesty's Principal Secretaries of State.

St. Andrew's House,
Edinburgh.
8th May 1973.

EXPLANATORY NOTE

(This Note is not part of the Regulations.)

These Regulations, which apply to Scotland only, supplement EEC regulation No. 1411/71 in so far as it relates to semi-skimmed milk and skimmed milk.

The Regulations prohibit the delivery on or in pursuance of sale for human consumption of separated milk other than semi-skimmed milk or skimmed milk delivered as such.

1973 No. 916

DEFENCE
The Royal Navy Terms of Service (Amendment) Regulations 1973

Made - - - -	16*th May* 1973
Laid before Parliament	24*th May* 1973
Coming into Operation	1*st July* 1973

The Defence Council, in exercise of the powers conferred upon them by section 2 of the Armed Forces Act 1966(a) and of all other powers enabling them in that behalf, hereby make the following Regulations:—

Citation, Commencement and Interpretation

1.—(1) These Regulations may be cited as the Royal Navy Terms of Service (Amendment) Regulations 1973 and shall come into operation on 1st July 1973.

(2) The Interpretation Act 1889(b) shall apply to the interpretation of these Regulations as it applies to the interpretation of an Act of Parliament.

Competent Naval Authorities

2. The Royal Navy Terms of Service Regulations 1967(c), as amended (d), shall have effect as though in the Schedule thereto, in Column 3, for the words "The Director General of Naval Manpower" there were substituted the words "The Director General of Naval Manpower and Training" and for the words "The Head of Naval Personnel Division 1, Ministry of Defence" there were substituted the words "The Head of Naval Personnel Division 2, Ministry of Defence".

On behalf of the Defence Council,

M. P. Pollock,

Antony Buck,
Members of the Defence Council.

Dated 16th May, 1973.

(a) 1966 c. 45.   (b) 1889 c. 63.
(c) S.I. 1967/1821 (1967 III, p. 4855).
(d) There are no relevant amending instruments.

EXPLANATORY NOTE

(This Note is not part of the Regulations.)

The Royal Navy Terms of Service Regulations 1967 specify certain persons to be competent naval authorities, in addition to the Defence Council and the Admiralty Board, for the purposes of some of those Regulations. The present Regulations amend the names of those authorities in two respects. One of the authorities for the purpose of approving the continuance in service of a person in naval service is now known as the Director General of Naval Manpower and Training and the authority for the purpose of publishing and providing forms of consent and notices is now the Head of Naval Personnel, Division 2, in the Ministry of Defence.

STATUTORY INSTRUMENTS

1973 No. 921

CORONERS

EXPENSES

The Coroners (Fees and Allowances) (Amendment) Rules 1973

Made - - -		*15th May* 1973
Coming into Operation		*11th June* 1973

In exercise of the powers conferred upon me by section 1(1) of the Coroners Act 1954(**a**), I hereby make the following Rules:—

1. These Rules may be cited as the Coroners (Fees and Allowances) (Amendment) Rules 1973 and shall come into operation on 11th June 1973.

2. Rule 4(3) of the Coroners (Fees and Allowances) Rules 1971(**b**), as amended(**c**), shall be amended by the substitution of the words "5·6p" for the words "5p".

3. For Rule 7 of the said Rules there shall be substituted the following Rule:—

"7. A witness at an inquest to whom the preceding Rules do not apply, who attends to give evidence whether at one or more inquests and thereby—

(*a*) necessarily incurs any expenditure (other than on travelling, lodging or subsistence) to which he would not otherwise be subject, or

(*b*) suffers any loss of earnings, or of benefit under the enactments relating to National Insurance, which he would otherwise have received,

may be paid a loss allowance not exceeding £4·75 a day in respect of that loss or expense;

Provided that if the period during which the witness is necessarily absent from his place of residence, business or employment to attend as aforesaid does not exceed four hours, his loss allowance shall not exceed £2·375 unless he necessarily loses more than half a day's remuneration or the expense necessarily incurred exceeds £2·375.".

4. Rule 8 of the said Rules shall be amended by the substitution of the words "57p", "£1·25", "£2·20", "£3·12", "£3·75", "£8·00" and "75p" for the words "45p", "95p", "£1·75", "£2·50", "£2·95", "£5·50" and "50p" respectively.

5. Rule 9 of the said Rules shall be amended by the substitution of the words "£5·80" and "75p" for the words "£3·75" and "50p" respectively.

6. Rule 10 of the said Rules shall be amended by the substitution for paragraph (3) of the following paragraphs:—

(**a**) 1954 c. 31.   (**b**) S.I. 1971/108 (1971 I, p. 200).
(**c**) S.I. 1971/1260, 1972/980 (1971 II, p. 3625; 1972 II, p. 3061).

"(3) Subject to paragraph (3A) below, where a witness at an inquest travels to or from the inquest by a private conveyance, he may be paid in respect thereof—

    (*a*) in any case where the witness travels by motor-cycle, a sum not exceeding—

        (i) in the case of a motor-cycle of engine capacity not exceeding 150 c.c., 1·2p a mile each way;

        (ii) in the case of a motor-cycle of engine capacity exceeding 150 c.c. but not exceeding 245 c.c., 1·8p a mile each way;

        (iii) in the case of a motor-cycle of engine capacity exceeding 245 c.c., 2·2p a mile each way;

    (*b*) in any case where the witness travels by motor car and the coroner is satisfied that the use of the motor car results in a substantial saving of time or is otherwise reasonable, a sum not exceeding—

        (i) in the case of a motor car of engine capacity not exceeding 1000 c.c., 4·1p a mile each way;

        (ii) in the case of a motor car of engine capacity exceeding 1000 c.c. but not exceeding 1750 c.c., 5·1p a mile each way;

        (iii) in the case of a motor car of engine capacity exceeding 1750 c.c., 5·6p a mile each way; and

    (*c*) in any other case, a sum not exceeding 2·6p a mile each way.

(3A) The rates specified in paragraph (3) above shall be increased—

    (*a*) by a supplement of 0·5p a mile for each passenger carried and to whom an allowance would otherwise have been payable under this Rule;

    (*b*) by the amount of any expenditure necessarily incurred on parking fees, provided the use of the motor car results in a substantial saving of time, or is otherwise reasonable.".

Robert Carr,
One of Her Majesty's Principal
Secretaries of State.

Home Office,
  Whitehall.

15th May 1973.

EXPLANATORY NOTE

(This Note is not part of the Rules.)

These Rules provide for an increase in subsistence and travelling allowances payable to witnesses attending at an inquest; in particular they provide for the payment of motor car parking fees and for allowances for travel by motor-cycle.

STATUTORY INSTRUMENTS

1973 No. 922

CRIMINAL PROCEDURE, ENGLAND AND WALES

COSTS AND EXPENSES

The Witnesses' Allowances (Amendment) Regulations 1973

Made	- - -	*15th May* 1973
Coming into Operation		*11th June* 1973

In exercise of the powers conferred upon me by section 12 of the Costs in Criminal Cases Act 1952(**a**), as amended by section 52 of, and Schedule 5 to, the Criminal Appeal Act 1968(**b**), and by section 51 of, and Schedule 6 to, the Courts Act 1971(**c**), I hereby make the following Regulations: —

1. These Regulations may be cited as the Witnesses' Allowances (Amendment) Regulations 1973 and shall come into operation on 11th June 1973.

2. For Regulation 7 of the Witnesses' Allowances Regulations 1971(**d**), as amended(**e**), there shall be substituted the following Regulation: —

"7. There may be allowed in respect of a witness, who attends to give evidence (other than professional or expert evidence), whether in one or more cases, and thereby—

(*a*) incurs any expenditure (other than on travelling, lodging or subsistence) to which he would not otherwise be subject, or

(*b*) suffers any loss of earnings, or of benefit under the enactments relating to National Insurance, which he would otherwise have received,

a loss allowance not exceeding £4·75 a day in respect of that expense or loss:

Provided that if the period during which the witness is necessarily absent from his place of residence, business or employment to attend as aforesaid does not exceed four hours, his loss allowance shall not exceed £2·375 unless he necessarily loses more than half a day's remuneration or the expense necessarily incurred exceeds £2·375.".

3. Regulation 8 of the said Regulations shall be amended by the substitution of the words "57p", "£1·25", "£2·20", "£3·12", "£3·75", "£8·00" and "75p" for the words "45p", "95p", "£1·75", "£2·50", "£2·95", "£5·50" and "50p" respectively.

4. Regulation 9 of the said Regulations shall be amended by the substitution of the words "£5·80" and "75p" for the words "£3·75" and "50p" respectively.

5. Regulation 11 of the said Regulations shall be amended by the substitution for paragraph (3) of the following paragraphs: —

(**a**) 1952 c.48. (**b**) 1968 c.19.
(**c**) 1971 c.23. (**d**) S.I. 1971/107 (1971 I, p.195).
(**e**) S.I. 1971/1259, 1972/49, (1971 II, p. 3624; 1972 I, p. 124).

"(3) Subject to paragraph (3A) below, where a witness travels to or from court by a private conveyance there may be allowed in respect thereof—

(a) in any case where the witness travels by motor-cycle, a sum not exceeding—

   (i) in the case of a motor-cycle of engine capacity not exceeding 150 c.c., 1·2p a mile each way;

   (ii) in the case of a motor-cycle of engine capacity exceeding 150 c.c. but not exceeding 245 c.c., 1·8p a mile each way;

   (iii) in the case of a motor-cycle of engine capacity exceeding 245 c.c., 2·2p a mile each way;

(b) in any case where the witness travels by motor car and the court is satisfied that the use of the motor car results in a substantial saving of time or is otherwise reasonable, a sum not exceeding—

   (i) in the case of a motor car of engine capacity not exceeding 1000 c.c., 4·1p a mile each way;

   (ii) in the case of a motor car of engine capacity exceeding 1000 c.c. but not exceeding 1750 c.c., 5·1p a mile each way;

   (iii) in the case of a motor car of engine capacity exceeding 1750 c.c., 5·6p a mile each way; and

(c) in any other case a sum not exceeding 2·6p a mile each way.

(3A) The rates specified in paragraph (3) above shall be increased—

(a) by a supplement of 0·5p a mile for each passenger carried and to whom an allowance would otherwise have been payable under this Regulation;

(b) by the amount of any expenditure necessarily incurred on parking fees, provided the use of the motor car results in a substantial saving of time, or is otherwise reasonable.".

Robert Carr,
One of Her Majesty's Principal
Secretaries of State.

Home Office,
  Whitehall.
15th May 1973.

EXPLANATORY NOTE

(This Note is not part of the Regulations.)

These Regulations provide for an increase in subsistence and travelling allowances payable to witnesses under the Costs in Criminal Cases Act 1952; in particular they provide for the payment of motor car parking fees and for allowances for travel by motor-cycle.

STATUTORY INSTRUMENTS

1973 No. 923

CUSTOMS AND EXCISE

The Import Duties (Quota Relief) (Cyprus) Order 1973

Made - - - -	17*th May* 1973
Laid before the House of Commons	18*th May* 1973
Coming into Operation	1*st June* 1973

The Secretary of State, in exercise of powers conferred on him by section 5(1) and (4) of the Import Duties Act 1958(a), as amended by paragraph 1 of Schedule 4 to the European Communities Act 1972(b), and of all other powers enabling him in that behalf, hereby makes the following Order:

1.—(1) This Order may be cited as the Import Duties (Quota Relief) (Cyprus) Order 1973 and shall come into operation on 1st June 1973.

(2) The Interpretation Act 1889(c) shall apply for the interpretation of this Order as it applies for the interpretation of an Act of Parliament.

2. For the purposes of this Order "goods of Cyprus" means goods which under the Agreement, signed on 19th December 1972, between the European Economic Community and Cyprus are to be regarded as originating in Cyprus, but does not include any goods in respect of which import duty has not been charged or has been charged at less than the full rate by virtue of the goods qualifying for Commonwealth preference.

3.—(1) Until the date specified in paragraph (2) below, any import duty which is for the time being chargeable on goods of a heading or subheading of the Customs Tariff 1959 specified in column 1 of the Schedule hereto shall be chargeable at the relevant rate specified in column 2 of that Schedule, instead of the full rate, in the case of goods of Cyprus.

(2) The provisions of the foregoing paragraph shall cease to operate in the case of goods of any aforementioned heading or subheading on 1st January 1974 or at such time, if earlier, as the quantity of goods of Cyprus of that heading or subheading entered for home use after the commencement of this Order first exceeds the quantity specified in relation to that heading or subheading in column 3 of the Schedule hereto (being the quota of goods of Cyprus allocated to the United Kingdom by Regulations approved by the Council of the European Communities on 14th May 1973).

(a) 1958 c. 6.	(b) 1972 c. 68.
(c) 1889 c. 63.	

(3) In paragraph (2) above the expression "entered for home use" has the same meaning as in the Customs and Excise Act 1952(a).

Limerick,
Parliamentary Under Secretary of State,
17th May 1973.   Department of Trade and Industry.

SCHEDULE

Tariff Heading	Rates of duty	Size of United Kingdom share of tariff quota by weight
56.04 (*Man-made fibres (discontinuous or waste) carded, combed or otherwise prepared for spinning*)	8%	10 metric tons
61.01 (A) (*Men's and boys' outer garments containing more than 20% by weight of silk, of man-made fibres, or of both together*)	£0·2000 per lb or 16% whichever is greater	280 metric tons (of goods of subheading 61.01(A), (B) or (C) as a whole)
61.01 (B) and (C) (*Other men's and boys' outer garments*)	16%	

EXPLANATORY NOTE

(This Note is not part of the Order.)

This Order, which comes into operation on 1st June 1973, provides for the implementation and administration of the United Kingdom's share of two tariff quotas opened by the European Economic Community for certain textile goods from Cyprus under the provisions of Council Regulations.

The Order specifies the reduced rates of duty applicable up to and including 31st December 1973 to imports of the relevant goods within the United Kingdom's share of the quotas. It also provides that goods shall not be debited to the United Kingdom's share of the quotas if Commonwealth preference is claimed in respect of them, and that any goods which constitute part of each quota do so as soon as they are entered for home use in the United Kingdom.

(a) 1952 c. 44.

1973 No 924

MONOPOLIES AND MERGERS

The Restriction of Merger (No. 1) Order 1973

Made - - - - -	18*th May* 1973
Laid before Parliament -	18*th May* 1973
Coming into Operation -	19*th May* 1973

Whereas the Secretary of State in exercise of powers conferred by section 6(7) of the Monopolies and Mergers Act 1965(a) and now vested in him by virtue of the Transfer of Functions (Monopolies, Mergers and Restrictive Practices) Order 1969(b) has referred to the Monopolies Commission for investigation and report, the matter of the proposed acquisition by Whessoe Limited of Capper-Neill Limited:

Now, therefore, the Secretary of State with a view to preventing action which may prejudice the reference or impede the taking of any remedial action which may be warranted by the Commission's Report and in exercise of powers conferred by sections 3(5) and 6(11) of the said Act and now so vested in him hereby orders as follows:—

1.—(1) This Order may be cited as the Restriction of Merger (No. 1) Order 1973 and shall come into operation on 19th May 1973.

(2) The Interpretation Act 1889(c) shall apply to the interpretation of this Order as it applies to the interpretation of an Act of Parliament.

2. It shall be unlawful for Whessoe Limited or any subsidiary thereof to acquire any shares or any interest in shares of Capper-Neill Limited if such acquisition would or might result in Whessoe Limited and Capper-Neill Limited becoming interconnected bodies corporate:

Provided that this Article shall not apply to anything done in pursuance of a legally enforceable agreement to acquire shares made before the commencement of this Order other than an agreement made in pursuance of any general offer addressed to the members of Capper-Neill Limited by Guinness-Mahon and Company Limited on behalf of Whessoe Limited.

Dated 18th May 1973.

Geoffrey Howe,

Minister for Trade and Consumer Affairs,

Department of Trade and Industry.

(a) 1965 c. 50.   (b) S.I. 1969/1534 (1969 III p. 4991).   (c) 1889 c. 63.

EXPLANATORY NOTE

(This Note is not part of the Order.)

This Order imposes a standstill on any acquisition by Whessoe Limited or its subsidiaries of shares of Capper-Neill Limited which would or might result in Capper-Neill Limited becoming a subsidiary of Whessoe Limited. The proposed merger of these two companies has been referred to the Monopolies Commission.

An exemption is provided for any acquisition of shares in pursuance of an agreement made before the commencement of this Order other than an agreement resulting from a general offer to acquire shares of Capper-Neill Limited made by Guinness-Mahon and Company Limited on behalf of Whessoe Limited.

The Order, unless previously revoked, will cease to have effect—

(*a*) 40 days after the report of the Monopolies Commission on the proposed merger is laid before Parliament; or

(*b*) on the failure of the Commission to report within the period allowed.

STATUTORY INSTRUMENTS

1973 No. 925

MONOPOLIES AND MERGERS

The Regulation of Prices (Tranquillising Drugs) (No. 2) Order 1973

Made - - - -	18*th May* 1973
Laid before Parliament	18*th May* 1973
Coming into Operation	20*th May* 1973

Whereas it appears to the Secretary of State on the facts found by the Monopolies Commission as stated in their report entitled " A report on the supply of chlordiazepoxide and diazepam " that the prices charged in the case of goods of the classes to which the report relates, being goods to which this Order applies, are or have been such as to operate against the public interest:

Now, therefore, the Secretary of State in exercise of the powers conferred by section 3(3)(*a*) and (*d*) and (4)(*c*) of the Monopolies and Mergers Act 1965(**a**) and section 10(3) of the Monopolies and Restrictive Practices (Inquiry and Control) Act 1948(**b**) and now in him vested(**c**) and of all other powers enabling him in that behalf and with a view to remedying or preventing mischiefs which in his opinion result or may be expected to result from the things which according to the said report as laid before Parliament on 11th April 1973 operate or may be expected to operate against the public interest hereby orders as follows:—

1.—(1) This Order may be cited as the Regulation of Prices (Tranquillising Drugs) (No. 2) Order 1973 and shall come into operation on 20th May 1973.

(2) In this Order—

" container " has the same meaning in relation to a preparation mentioned in the Schedule hereto as it has in relation to a medicinal product in the Medicines Act 1968(**d**); and

references to chlordiazepoxide include references to its salts and references to diazepam include references to its salts.

(3) For the purposes of this Order a body corporate shall be regarded as having a controlling interest in another body corporate if it can—

(i) directly or indirectly determine the manner in which more than one half of the votes which could be cast at a general meeting of the other body corporate are to be cast; or

(ii) by the exercise of a power which does not require the consent or concurrence of any other person appoint or remove the holders of all or a majority of the directorships.

(4) The Interpretation Act 1889(**e**) shall apply to the interpretation of this Order as it applies to the interpretation of an Act of Parliament.

(**a**) 1965 c. 50.   (**b**) 1948 c. 66.
(**c**) By the Transfer of Functions (Monopolies, Mergers and Restrictive Practices) Order 1969 (S.I. 1969/1534 (1969 III, p.4991)).   (**d**) 1968 c. 67.   (**e**) 1889 c. 63.

2. This Order applies to F Hoffmann-La Roche and Co. AG, a body corporate incorporated in Switzerland, the SAPAC Corporation Ltd., a body corporate incorporated under the laws of New Brunswick, Canada, to Roche Products Limited, a body corporate incorporated in England, and to any other body corporate (wherever incorporated) in which any of the said bodies corporate has a controlling interest.

3.—(1) Subject to paragraph (2) hereof, the prices charged on the sale in the United Kingdom after the commencement of this Order of any pharmaceutical preparations mentioned in the Schedule hereto shall not exceed the relevant price specified in the third column of the appropriate table in that Schedule, or, if the goods are packed in a container holding a nominal quantity which is not mentioned in that table, the maximum price calculated in accordance with paragraph 2 of that Schedule.

(2) Nothing in paragraph (1) shall apply in relation to—

(*a*) a sale by a person to whom this Order does not apply;

(*b*) a sale of goods which are to be exported from the United Kingdom.

4. It shall be unlawful for any person to whom this Order applies who supplies any pharmaceutical preparation mentioned in the Schedule hereto in the United Kingdom to require as a condition of such supply otherwise than by or for export from the United Kingdom the purchase of any other pharmaceutical preparation.

5.—(1) It shall be unlawful for any person mentioned in Article 4 of this Order to enter into any agreement or arrangement under which any other person is precluded from reselling, or required to preclude any other person from reselling, in the United Kingdom and otherwise than by way of export, except at a price above the price mentioned in paragraph (2) of this Article, any preparation mentioned in the Schedule hereto which has been sold in the United Kingdom on or after 23rd April 1973 by a person to whom this Order applies.

(2) For the purposes of paragraph (1) the highest price at which a person may be required by a minimum resale price condition to resell any goods is—

(*a*) in the case of a resale to a retailer or to any other person purchasing in the course of trade, the relevant price set out in the final column of the appropriate table in the Schedule hereto or, if the goods are not packed in a container in a nominal quantity mentioned in that table, a price which when reduced by 12½ per cent. does not exceed the appropriate maximum selling price calculated in accordance with paragraph 2 of that Schedule;

(*b*) in the case of a resale by retail, a price which does not exceed by more than 50 per cent the highest price which a seller may be required to charge on such a resale as is mentioned in subparagraph (*a*) of this paragraph.

Geoffrey Howe ,
Minister for Trade and Consumer Affairs,
Department of Trade and Industry.

Dated 18th May 1973.

SCHEDULE

MAXIMUM PRICES FOR GOODS TO WHICH THE ORDER APPLIES

Standard Packs

1. (a) *Preparations of chlordiazepoxide (" Librium ")*

Form of preparation	Nominal quantity in container	Maximum price	Maintainable resale price (wholesale)
		£	£
Tablets or capsules, nominal chlordiazepoxide content 5mg	100	0·28	0·32
	500	1·14	1·30
Tablets or capsules, nominal chlordiazepoxide content 10mg	100	0·35	0·40
	500	1·44	1·64
Tablets (or capsules), nominal chlordiazepoxide content 25mg	100	0·70	0·80
	500	2·87	3·28

(b) *Preparations of diazepam (" Valium ")*

Form of preparation	Nominal quantity in container	Maximum price	Maintainable resale price (wholesale)
		£	£
Tablets or capsules, nominal diazepam content 2mg	100	0·18	0·21
	500	0·73	0·83
Tablets or capsules, nominal diazepam content 5mg	100	0·26	0·30
	500	1·08	1·23
Tablets (or capsules), nominal diazepam content 10mg	100	0·39	0·45
	500	1·59	1·82

(c) *Preparations of chlordiazepoxide in combination with theophylline and ephedrine hydrochloride ("Brontrium")*

Form of preparation	Nominal quantity in container	Maximum price	Maintainable resale price (wholesale)
		£	£
Capsules (or tablets), nominal chlordiazepoxide content 10mg	100	0·48	0·55
Capsules (or tablets), nominal chlordiazepoxide content 5mg	100	0·32	0·37

(d) *Preparations of chlordiazepoxide in combination with clidinium bromide ("Libraxin")*

Form of preparation	Nominal quantity in container	Maximum price	Maintainable resale price (wholesale)
		£	£
Tablets (or capsules), nominal chlordiazepoxide content 5mg	100	0·41	0·47
	500	1·69	1·93

(e) *Preparations of chlordiazepoxide in combination with pentaerythritol tetranitrate ("Pentrium")*

Form of preparation	Nominal quantity in container	Maximum price	Maintainable resale price (wholesale)
		£	£
Tablets (or capsules), nominal chlordiazepoxide content 5mg	100	0·42	0·48

(f) Preparations of chlordiazepoxide in combination with amitriptyline (" Limbitrol ")

Form of preparation	Nominal quantity in container	Maximum price	Maintainable resale price (wholesale)
		£	£
Capsules (or tablets), nominal chlordiazepoxide content 5mg	100	0·56	0·64
	500	2·32	2·65
Capsules (or tablets), nominal chlordiazepoxide content 10mg	100	0·84	0·97
	500	3·59	4·10

Other Packs

2. For the purposes of Article 3, the maximum price chargeable for any preparations mentioned in the preceding tables when sold in a container holding a nominal quantity which is not so mentioned shall be—

(i) in a case where only one quantity is mentioned in the relevant table or where two quantities are so mentioned and the nominal quantity in the container is greater than the smaller of those two quantities, a price equal to such a fraction or multiple of the relevant price, or of the greater of the two relevant prices, mentioned in column 3 as appropriately reflects the difference in the quantities;

(ii) in a case where two quantities are so mentioned and the nominal quantity in the container is less than the smaller of those two quantities, a price equal to such a fraction of the price mentioned in column 3 in relation to the smaller quantity as appropriately reflects the difference between the nominal quantity in the container and that smaller quantity.

EXPLANATORY NOTE

(This Note is not part of the Order.)

This Order reproduces the provisions of the Regulation of Prices (Tranquillising Drugs) Order 1973 (S.I. 1973/720) other than those provisions relating to the determination of agreements within 7 days of its commencement. The only other changes take account of the different date of commencement.

The Order regulates the prices at which certain tranquillising drugs may be sold in the United Kingdom when sold by Roche Products Limited, F Hoffmann-La Roche and Co. AG (a Swiss company) and SAPAC Corporation Ltd. (a Canadian company) and other companies controlled by them.

The Order only relates to drugs sold in the form of tablets or capsules and there are exceptions for exports.

Maximum prices for the quantities in which the drugs are commonly made up are set out in the third column of the tables in the Schedule. For other quantities maximum prices are to be calculated by reference to these prices in accordance with paragraph 2 of the Schedule.

The brand names under which the drugs in question are commonly sold by Roche Products Limited in the United Kingdom are mentioned in the Schedule.

The Order also precludes the companies to which it applies from imposing on the sale of the relevant drugs any condition requiring the buying of other pharmaceutical products or from imposing resale price conditions which would require goods which are subject to price control to be resold to trade buyers or by retail at prices which reflect a greater percentage increase over the original selling price than the percentages mentioned in the report of the Monopolies Commission as secured by resale price conditions.

In accordance with section 3(11)(*b*) of the Monopolies and Mergers Act 1965, the Regulation of Prices (Tranquillising Drugs) Order 1973 ceased to have effect on 19th May 1973 for want of approval by resolution of each House of Parliament.

Copies of the report of the Monopolies Commission referred to in this Order (H.C. 197 Session 1972–73) may be obtained from Her Majesty's Stationery Office.

STATUTORY INSTRUMENTS

1973 No. 927

CUSTOMS AND EXCISE

The Import Duties (Temporary Exemptions) (No. 14) Order 1973

Made - - -	18*th May* 1973
Laid before the House of Commons	21*st May* 1973
Coming into Operation	23*rd May* 1973

The Lords Commissioners of Her Majesty's Treasury, by virtue of the powers conferred on them by sections 1, 3(6) and13 of the Import Duties Act 1958(a) as amended by paragraph 1 of Schedule 4 to the European Communities Act 1972(b) and of all other powers enabling them in that behalf, on the recommendation of the Secretary of State(c), hereby make the following Order:

1.—(1) This Order may be cited as the Import Duties (Temporary Exemptions) (No. 14) Order 1973 and shall come into operation on 23rd May 1973.

(2) The Interpretation Act 1889(d) shall apply for the interpretation of this Order as it applies for the interpretation of an Act of Parliament.

2.—(1) Up to and including 30th September 1973 or in the case of goods in relation to which an earlier day is specified in the Schedule hereto, up to and including that day, any import duty which is for the time being chargeable on goods of a heading of the Customs Tariff 1959 specified in that Schedule shall not be chargeable in respect of goods of any description there specified in relation to that heading.

(2) Any entry in the second column in the Schedule to this Order shall be taken to comprise all goods which would be classified under an entry in the same terms constituting a subheading (other than the final subheading) of the relevant heading in the Customs Tariff 1959.

(3) For the purposes of classification under the Customs Tariff 1959, insofar as that depends on the rate of duty, any goods to which paragraph (1) or (2) above applies shall be treated as chargeable with the same duty as if this Order had not been made.

(a) 1958 c. 6. (b) 1972 c. 68.
(c) *See* S.I. 1970/1537 (1970 III, p. 5293). (d) 1889 c. 63.

Tim Fortescue,
Oscar Murton,

Two of the Lords Commissioners
of Her Majesty's Treasury.

18th May 1973.

SCHEDULE
GOODS TEMPORARILY EXEMPT FROM IMPORT DUTY

Tariff Heading	Description
44.09	Cleft pales, stub-pointed, not less than 914 millimetres nor more than 1·91 metres in length, split from stems or branches of sweet chestnut of not less than 101 millimetres girth (up to and including 3rd September 1973)
73.07	Blooms, billets, slabs and sheet bars of iron or steel, rolled but not forged
73.10	Bars and rods of iron or steel, of circular or square cross-section or ribbed, in straight lengths or in coils and not further worked than hot-rolled or extruded; containing not more than 0·25 per cent. carbon, not more than 0·06 per cent. sulphur and not more than 0·06 per cent. phosphorus; in all cases the greatest dimension of the cross-section is not to exceed 44 millimetres and in the case of square cross-section the corners may be either square or rounded Wire rod (ECSC), of iron or steel and of round section
73.15	Bars and rods of high carbon steel, in coils, not further worked than hot-rolled, of circular cross-section and having a diameter of not less than 13 millimetres and not more than 28·5 millimetres Wire rod (ECSC), of high carbon steel and of round section

---

EXPLANATORY NOTE
(*This Note is not part of the Order.*)

This Order provides that the goods listed in the Schedule shall be temporarily exempt from import duty up to and including 30th September 1973 or, in the case of certain items, up to and including such earlier day as is specified.

STATUTORY INSTRUMENTS

1973 No. 928 (C.24)

SEEDS

The Plant Varieties and Seeds Act 1964 (Commencement No. 3) Order 1973

Made - - - *17th May* 1973

The Minister of Agriculture, Fisheries and Food and the Secretary of State for Scotland, in exercise of the powers vested in them by section 41(2) of the Plant Varieties and Seeds Act 1964(a) and of all other powers enabling them in that behalf, hereby make the following order:—

1. This order may be cited as the Plant Varieties and Seeds Act 1964 (Commencement No. 3) Order 1973.

2. Sections 16 to 19, inclusive, sections 24 to 30, inclusive, and section 32 of the Plant Varieties and Seeds Act 1964, as amended by section 4(1) of and paragraph 5 (1), (2), (3) and (4) of Schedule 4 to the European Communities Act 1972(b), shall come into force on 1st July 1973.

In Witness whereof the Official Seal of the Minister of Agriculture, Fisheries and Food is hereunto affixed on 17th May 1973.

(L.S.)

Joseph Godber,
Minister of Agriculture, Fisheries and Food.

Gordon Campbell,
16th May 1973.   Secretary of State for Scotland.

EXPLANATORY NOTE

(This Note is not part of the Order.)

This Order brings into force sections 16 to 19, 24 to 30 and 32 of the Plant Varieties and Seeds Act 1964 which, as amended by the European Communities Act 1972, are concerned with the making of seeds regulations for the whole of Great Britain and matters connected with such regulations.

(a) 1964 c. 14.   (b) 1972 c. 68.

STATUTORY INSTRUMENTS

1973 No. 934

TRANSPORT

The Transport Tribunal (Amendment) Rules 1973

Made - - -		*18th May* 1973
Coming into Operation		*25th May* 1973

The Transport Tribunal, in exercise of the powers conferred upon them by paragraph 11 of the Tenth Schedule to the Transport Act 1962(**a**), as read with Article 5(2) of the Secretary of State for the Environment Order 1970(**b**) and Article 2(2) of the Transfer of Functions (Secretary of State and Lord Advocate) Order 1972(**c**) and all other powers them enabling in this behalf, with the approval of the Lord Chancellor, the Secretary of State for the Environment and the Lord Advocate after consultation with the Council on Tribunals in accordance with the requirements of section 10 of the Tribunals and Inquiries Act 1971(**d**), hereby make the following Rules:—

1.—(1) These Rules may be cited as the Transport Tribunal (Amendment) Rules 1973 and shall come into operation on 25th May 1973.

(2) In these Rules, a Rule referred to by number means the Rule so numbered in the Transport Tribunal Rules 1965(**e**), as amended(**f**).

(3) The Interpretation Act 1889(**g**) shall apply for the interpretation of these Rules as it applies for the interpretation of an Act of Parliament.

2. Rule 2(1) shall be amended as follows:—

(1) For the definition of "Bank holiday" there shall be substituted the following definition:—

"Bank holiday" means a day which is, or is appointed to be, a bank holiday under the Banking and Financial Dealings Act 1971(**h**) in England and Wales or in Scotland, as the case may be;

(2) After the definition of "sealed" there shall be inserted the following definition:—

"the spring holiday" means the bank holiday falling on the last Monday in May or any day appointed instead of that day under section 1(2) of the Banking and Financial Dealings Act 1971.

(**a**) 1962 c. 46.
(**c**) S.I. 1972/2002 (1972 III, p. 5957).
(**e**) S.I. 1965/1687 (1965 III, p. 4785).
(**g**) 1889 c. 63.

(**b**) S.I. 1970/1681 (1970 III, p. 5551).
(**d**) 1971 c. 62.
(**f**) S.I. 1970/491 (1970 I, p. 1648).
(**h**) 1971 c. 80.

3. In Rule 50, for the words "Whit Sunday", in each place where they occur, there shall be substituted the words "the spring holiday".

Dated 18th May 1973.

Approved.

> *G. D. Squibb.*
> *W. Morton.*
> *G. W. Quick Smith.*
>
> *Hailsham of St. Marylebone,* C.
> *John Peyton.*
> *Norman R. Wylie.*

EXPLANATORY NOTE

(This Note is not part of the Rules.)

These Rules amend the Transport Tribunal Rules 1965 so as to make provision for the sittings of the Transport Tribunal to coincide with those of the High Court and the Court of Appeal as altered by the Supreme Court (Spring Holiday) Order 1972 (S.I. 1972/968).

STATUTORY INSTRUMENTS

1973 No. 935
JURIES

The Jurors' (Coroners' Courts) Allowances (Amendment) Regulations 1973

Made - - -		18*th May* 1973
Coming into Operation		11*th June* 1973

In exercise of the powers conferred on me by section 1 of the Juries Act 1949(**a**), as amended by section 1 of the Juries Act 1954(**b**), section 36 of the Courts Act 1971(**c**) and section 27 of the Criminal Justice Act 1972(**d**), I hereby, with the consent of the Minister for the Civil Service, make the following Regulations : —

1. These Regulations may be cited as the Jurors' (Coroners' Courts) Allowances (Amendment) Regulations 1973 and shall come into operation on 11th June 1973.

2. Regulation 6 of the Jurors' (Coroners' Courts) Allowances Regulations 1972(**e**) shall be amended by the substitution of the words "57p", "£1·25", "£2·20", "£3·12", "£3·75" and "£8·00" for the words "£0·45", "£0·95", "£1·75", "£2·50", "£2·95" and £5·50" respectively.

3. For Regulation 7 of the said Regulations there shall be substituted the following Regulation : —

"7.—(1) Where, in consequence of his attendance, a juror has incurred—

    (i) any expenditure (other than on travelling or subsistence) to which he would not otherwise be subject, or

    (ii) any loss of earnings, or of benefits under the enactments relating to National Insurance, which he would otherwise have received,

the financial loss allowance, to which he is entitled under section 1 of the Act (as amended by the Criminal Justice Act 1972) shall, subject to paragraph (2) of this Regulation, be the amount of the said expenditure or loss.

(2) The amount payable under this Regulation to a person in respect of any one day shall not exceed—

    (*a*) where the period of time over which the expenditure is incurred or earnings or benefits are lost does not exceed four hours, the sum of £2·375; or

    (*b*) where that period of time exceeds four hours, the sum of £4·75.".

4. The Schedule to the said Regulations shall be amended by the substitution for paragraph 3 of the following paragraphs : —

"3. Subject to paragraph 4 below, where a person travels by private conveyance, the allowance shall—

    (*a*) in any case where the juror travels by motor-cycle, be at a rate not exceeding—

        (i) in the case of a motor-cycle of engine capacity not exceeding

---

(**a**) 1949 c.27.   (**b**) 1954 c.41.
(**c**) 1971 c.23.   (**d**) 1972 c.71.
(**e**) S.I. 1972/1001 (1972 II, p.3084).

150 c.c., 1·2p a mile each way;

    (ii) in the case of a motor-cycle of engine capacity exceeding 150 c.c. but not exceeding 245 c.c., 1·8p a mile each way;

    (iii) in the case of a motor-cycle of engine capacity exceeding 245 c.c., 2·2p a mile each way;

(b) in any case where the juror travels by motor car and the coroner is satisfied that the use of the motor car results in a substantial saving of time or is otherwise reasonable, be at a rate not exceeding—

    (i) in the case of a motor car of engine capacity not exceeding 1000 c.c., 4·1p a mile each way;

    (ii) in the case of a motor car of engine capacity exceeding 1000 c.c., but not exceeding 1750 c.c., 5·1p a mile each way;

    (iii) in the case of a motor car of engine capacity exceeding 1750 c.c., 5·6p a mile each way; and

(c) in any other case, be at a rate not exceeding 2·6p a mile each way.

4. The rates specified in paragraph 3 above shall be increased—

(a) by a supplement of 0·5p a mile for each passenger carried and to whom an allowance would otherwise have been payable under this Schedule;

(b) by the amount of any expenditure necessarily incurred on parking fees, provided the use of the motor car results in a substantial saving of time, or is otherwise reasonable.".

Robert Carr,
One of Her Majesty's Principal
Secretaries of State.

15th May 1973.

Consent of the Minister for the Civil Service given under his official seal on 18th May 1973.

(L.S.)

P. F. Clifton,
Authorised by the Minister
for the Civil Service.

EXPLANATORY NOTE

(This Note is not part of the Regulations.)

These Regulations provide for an increase in subsistence and travelling allowances in respect of jury service in a coroner's court; in particular they provide for the payment of motor car parking fees and for allowances for travel by motor-cycle.

STATUTORY INSTRUMENTS

1973 No. 936

EDUCATION, ENGLAND AND WALES

The Teachers' Superannuation (Family Benefits) (Amendment) Regulations 1973

Made - - -	*21st May* 1973
Laid before Parliament	*4th June* 1973
Coming into Operation	*26th June* 1973

ARRANGEMENT OF REGULATIONS

Miscellaneous and supplementary

Schedule 1

Deemed additional service.

Schedule 2

Contributions and deductions.

Schedule 3

Modifications relating to teachers with service in Scotland or Northern Ireland.

Schedule 4

Minor and consequential amendments and revocations.

The Secretary of State for Education and Science, with the consent of the Minister for the Civil Service and after consultation with representatives of local education authorities and of teachers and with such representatives of other persons likely to be affected as appear to her to be appropriate, in exercise of the powers conferred on her by section 9 of the Superannuation Act 1972(a) hereby makes the following regulations:—

Introductory

Citation and commencement

1.—(1) These regulations may be cited as the Teachers' Superannuation (Family Benefits) (Amendment) Regulations 1973.

(2) The Teachers' Superannuation (Family Benefits) Regulations 1970 to 1972(b) and these regulations may be cited together as the Teachers' Superannuation (Family Benefits) Regulations 1970 to 1973.

(3) These regulations shall come into operation on 26th June 1973.

Interpretation

2.—(1) In these regulations, except where the context otherwise requires—

"the Actuary" means the Government Actuary;

"child" in reference to the child of a person, means a child (including an illegitimate child or adopted child) of that person, or a child accepted by that person as a member of the family and wholly or mainly dependent on

(a) 1972 c. 11.
(b) S.I. 1970/862, 1971/679, 1972/360 (1970 II, p. 2736; 1971 I, p. 1787; 1972 I, p. 1425).

him, who has not attained the age of seventeen or, having attained the age of seventeen, is receiving full-time education or attending a course of not less than two years full-time training for a trade, profession or calling—

but does not include a married woman nor a person who is for the time being in receipt of a disqualifying income;

"disqualifying income" means remuneration payable to a person attending a course of full-time training at a rate not less than the annual rate for the time being payable of an official pension (within the meaning of the Pensions (Increase) Act 1971(a)) which began on 1st April 1972 at the annual rate of £250;

"member" means a teacher employed in reckonable service on or after 1st April 1972 who immediately before that date had service counting for benefit within the meaning of regulation 40 of the Family Benefits Regulations but does not include a teacher to whom regulation 23 below (teachers in admitted schools) applies;

"non-member" means a teacher employed in reckonable service on or after 1st April 1972 who immediately before that date had no such service counting for benefit as is referred to above;

"the Family Benefits Regulations" means the Teachers' Superannuation (Family Benefits) Regulations 1970(b) as amended(c);

"the principal Teachers' Regulations" means the Teachers' Superannuation Regulations 1967(d) as amended(e);

"the Teachers and Teachers' Families Regulations" means the Superannuation (Teachers and Teachers' Families) (Amendment) Regulations 1972(f);

other expressions have the meanings assigned to them by the Family Benefits Regulations.

(2) References to a teacher's widow do not include a woman who married him after the day on which he was last employed in reckonable service.

(3) The Interpretation Act 1889(g) shall apply for the interpretation of these regulations as it applies for the interpretation of an Act of Parliament.

Service before 1st April 1972

3.—(1) Subject to paragraph (2) below, the service before 1st April 1972 counting for benefit for the purposes of these regulations of a member shall, unless he retires without making an election for those purposes within the time prescribed by regulation 7(1) below, be the aggregate of—

(*a*) two-thirds of any such service in respect of which the full amount of normal contributions is held in the Fund ("deemed normal service");

(*b*) the number of years determined in accordance with Schedule 1 as the actuarial value of any additional contributions held in the Fund on 31st March 1972 in respect of such service ("deemed additional service"); and

---

(a) 1971 c. 56. (b) S.I. 1970/862 (1970 II, p. 2736).
(c) S.I. 1971/679, 1972/360 (1971 I, p. 1787; 1972 I, p. 1425).
(d) S.I. 1967/489 (1967 I, p. 1562).
(e) S.I. 1967/1286, 1968/1353, 1969/80, 1970/10, 753, 1971/403, 1972/568, 1092, 1960, 1973/215 (1967 II, p. 3721; 1968 II, p. 3753; 1969 I, p. 241; 1970 I, p. 11; II, p. 2394; 1971 I, p. 1206; 1972 I, p. 1892; II, p. 3223; III, p. 5853; 1973 I, p. 825).
(f) S.I. 1972/1960 (1972 III, p. 5853). (g) 1889 c. 63.

(c) the number of years determined by the Actuary as the actuarial value of his interest in the balance (so determined) of the Fund as at 31st March 1972 ("notional service").

(2) For the purposes of these regulations the service before 1st April 1972 counting for benefit of a member who retired on pension after 31st March 1972 and before 26th June 1973, or after that date but without making an election for thoset purposes within the time prescribed by regulation 7(1) below, shall be the aggregate of—

(a) two-thirds of any such service in respect of which contributions were paid to the Fund; and

(b) twice his notional service (within the meaning of paragraph (1)(c) above).

Non-member's contributions

4.—(1) Subject to paragraph (2) below, a non-member shall, if he so elects, pay contributions in accordance with these regulations, in respect of his reckonable service before 1st April 1972.

(2) Any election for the purposes of this regulation shall relate to the whole of the reckonable service of the teacher before 1st April 1972 or, if that service amounts to five years or more, five or more complete years of that service, as he may elect.

(3) For the purposes of paragraph (2) above references in this regulation to reckonable service do not include such service in an admitted school as is mentioned in regulation 16 below.

Member's contributions

5.—(1) As from 1st May 1974 contributions payable by teachers for the purposes of family benefits in respect of service before 1st April 1972 may, and as from 1st November 1974 shall, be paid in accordance with this regulation and not in accordance with regulations 31, 32, 33 and 38 of the Family Benefits Regulations.

(2) A member whose service counting for benefit under the Family Benefits Regulations began on or after 1st April 1966 and who had no previous service in respect of which additional contributions were payable by Method I or II shall pay contributions in respect of so much (if any) as he elects of his reckonable service before 1st April 1972, not exceeding one half of the length of the period ("the excess period") by which his reckonable service between 1st April 1966 and 31st March 1972 ("the first period") exceeds the aggregate of his deemed normal service and twice his notional service ("the second period").

(3) Paragraph (2) shall apply to a member who elected to pay additional contributions by Method I or II subject to—

(a) the substitution of a reference to five-sixths for the reference to one half of the excess period; and

(b) the addition to the first period of the number of years in respect of which he elected to pay additional contributions and to the second period of his deemed additional service.

(4) A member who elected to pay additional contributions in respect of his previous service by Method III may, if he is employed in reckonable service on 1st May 1974, by notice in writing delivered to the Secretary of State before 1st November 1974 revoke his election to pay such contributions; and any such member who is not so employed or does not so revoke that election shall pay contributions in respect of so much (if any) as he elects of his reckonable service before 1st April 1972, not exceeding five-sixths of the length of the period by which that service exceeds the aggregate of his service counting for benefit for the purposes of these regulations and six-fifths of the period (if any) in respect of which he elects to pay contributions under paragraph (2) as modified by paragraph (3) above.

(5) A member with service counting for benefit under the Family Benefits Regulations before 1st April 1966 who did not elect to pay additional contributions in respect of that service shall pay contributions in respect of so much (if any) as he elects of that service.

Retired member's contributions

6. A member who, having been employed in reckonable service on or after 1st April 1972 retires from such service before 26th June 1973, or after that date but without making an election for the purposes of these regulations within the time prescribed by regulation 7(1) below, shall, if he so elects, pay contributions in the form of a lump sum equal to the actuarial equivalent of the contributions payable in respect of so much of his service before 1st April 1972 as does not exceed one half of the amount by which one-third of the service in respect of which normal and additional contributions are held in the Fund on 31st March 1972 exceeds twice his notional service.

Elections

Time for making elections

7.—(1) Subject to paragraph (3) below, the first election for the purposes of regulation 4, 5 or 6 above shall be made so as to be received by the Secretary of State—

(a) for the purposes of regulation 4, if the teacher is employed in reckonable service on 26th June 1973, before 26th December 1973;

(b) for the purposes of regulation 5, if the teacher is employed in reckonable service on 1st May 1974, before 1st November 1974;

(c) for the purposes of regulation 6, before 1st November 1974; and

(d) for the purposes of regulations 4 and 5 in any case not falling within sub-paragraph (a) or (b) above, not later than six months from the date of the teacher becoming employed or as the case may be again employed in reckonable service or of the award to him of superannuation allowances under the principal Teachers' Regulations.

(2) For the purposes of regulation 6, the election may, if the member dies before 1st November 1974, be made by his widow and the provisions of these regulations relating to the payment of contributions for the purposes of that regulation shall be construed accordingly.

(3) A man teacher who does not make an election within the time specified by paragraph (1) above may, notwithstanding that paragraph, make a first election for the purposes of regulation 4 or 5 within the six months next following the first to occur of any of the following events—

    (i) his marriage if he is then employed in reckonable service;

    (ii) his becoming again employed in reckonable service after his marriage while not so employed;

    (iii) the nomination by him of an adult dependant under regulation 19 below;

and a woman teacher who does not make an election within the time specified by paragraph (1) above may, notwithstanding that paragraph, make a first election for the purposes of regulation 4 or 5 within the six months next following the nomination by her of an adult dependant under regulation 19 below.

Form of elections

8.—(1) The first election by any teacher for the purposes of these regulations shall specify—

    (a) the number of years in respect of which the teacher elects to pay contributions; and

    (b) the rate at which the teacher elects to pay contributions expressed as a percentage, being a whole number not exceeding eight, of the rate of his salary from time to time.

(2) An election shall be made in writing and delivered to the Secretary of State and shall be effective from the date of its receipt by her.

(3) In so far as it specifies the number of years in respect of which contributions are to be paid an election shall be irrevocable; but in so far as it specifies the rate at which contributions are to be paid it may from time to time be varied by a subsequent election to pay contributions at a higher rate (expressed as is specified in paragraph (1)(b) above) taking effect from 1st April in the year following the end of the year in which that subsequent election is received by the Secretary of State.

(4) The Secretary of State may treat as an election made for the purposes of this regulation any notification in writing received from a teacher before 26th June 1973 which—

    (a) states the teacher's intention to pay contributions in respect of any such benefits as are payable under these regulations; and

    (b) specifies the matters required by this regulation to be specified by an election—

and any notification so treated shall be effective as such an election from 26th June 1973.

Effect of elections

9.—(1) Subject to paragraph (2) below, regulations 24, 25 and 27 of the Teachers and Teachers' Families Regulations shall, as regards any teacher, cease to have effect as from the date upon which any election by him under regulation 8 above is effective or the time specified by regulation 7(1) above for the making of election expires without his having made an election.

(2) The Secretary of State may, having regard to the special circumstances of a particular teacher, direct that paragraph (1) above shall not apply to him; and in any such case regulations 24, 25 and 27 of the Teachers and Teachers' Families Regulations shall continue to apply in relation to that teacher until such time as is specified in the direction.

Contributions

Payment of contributions

10. Subject to regulation 14 below contributions shall be paid, at the rate for the time being specified by the teacher in an election under these regulations, for so long as he continues to be employed, or is for purposes of the principal Teachers' Regulations treated as if he were employed, in reckonable service.

Restriction on amount of contributions

11. Regulation 73 of the Family Benefits Regulations shall be construed as if the contributions specified in paragraph (1) included contributions payable under these regulations and for the references in paragraph (2)(a)(ii) to six per cent. and thirteen per cent. there were substituted references to 6·75 per cent. and 14·25 per cent. respectively.

Determination of contributions, etc.

12.—(1) The Secretary of State shall as soon as may be after the receipt of any election made by a teacher for the purposes of these regulations determine—

(a) in accordance with table 1 of schedule 2 the period for which contributions are required to be paid by the teacher; and

(b) the amount (if any) of any deduction that will fall to be made from the terminal sum payable to or in respect of the teacher under regulation 15 below by reason of the fact that the teacher will attain the age of sixty before the end of the period determined under sub-paragraph (a) above.

(2) A determination under paragraph (1) may be varied by a subsequent determination, and shall be so varied if—

(a) payment of contributions is interrupted by a break in service; or

(b) the amount of his contributions is reduced by reason of the teacher being for the time being employed in part-time reckonable service or (in the case of a teacher so employed) being so employed for a smaller proportion of his time; or

(c) a contribution payable in accordance with regulation 10 is not paid.

Notices

13. The Secretary of State shall as soon as may be after making a determination under regulation 12 above serve a notice in writing on the teacher specifying as may be appropriate—

(a) the day on which, in accordance with regulation 14 below, the payment of contributions is to begin;

(b) the period determined under regulation 12 above for which contributions are required to be paid;

(c) any liability of the teacher to a deduction from the terminal sum payable to or in respect of him by virtue of regulation 15 below.

Duration of contributions

14. Contributions shall begin to be paid by a teacher on the first day of the month next following the date of the notice served on him by the Secretary of State under regulation 13 above and shall cease to be paid on whichever is the earlier of the day he retires from reckonable service and the day specified in that notice as the last day on which contributions are required to be paid by him.

Deduction from terminal sum

15.—(1) If a member who elected to pay contributions by Method III and did not revoke his election to pay such contributions either—

(a) does not elect to pay contributions under regulation 5(4) above; or

(b) elects to pay such contributions in respect of a period which is less than two-thirds of the period in respect of which he elected to pay contributions by Method III—

there shall be deducted from the terminal sum payable to or in respect of him the amount determined by the Actuary as the sum necessary to defray the cost of the benefits payable under these regulations in so far as they relate to his reckonable service before 1st April 1972.

(2) If, as regards any teacher, the period determined under regulation 12 above ends after whichever is the later of his sixtieth birthday and the award to him of superannuation allowances under regulation 41(1)(a) or (b) of the principal Teachers' Regulations there shall be deducted from the terminal sum payable to or in respect of him the amount determined in accordance with table 2 of schedule 2 as outstanding for payment.

(3) There shall be deducted from any terminal sum payable to or in respect of a teacher before his sixtieth birthday the amount determined by the Actuary as the actuarial equivalent of the amount which would have been outstanding for payment on that birthday if he had continued to pay contributions at the last rate specified by him until he attained the age of sixty; and if any such teacher becomes again employed in reckonable service he shall be treated as having paid those contributions.

Benefits

"Reckonable service"

16. For the purposes of regulations 17 to 22 below the expression "reckonable service" does not include service which is treated as if it were reckonable by virtue of Part VIII of the principal Teachers' Regulations or as contributory service by virtue of the Teachers Superannuation (Independent Schools) Scheme 1963(a) or any scheme revoked by that scheme.

(a) S.I. 1963/577 (1963 I, p. 668).

Service counting for pension

17.—(1) A pension shall be paid in accordance with regulations 18 to 22 below upon the death of any person who was employed in reckonable service on or after 1st April 1972 and whose service to which this regulation applies amounts to not less than five years.

(2) This regulation applies to—

(*a*) any reckonable service since the beginning of April 1972;

(*b*) any such service before 1st April 1972 in respect of which the person elected to pay contributions under regulation 4 or 5 above or paid or elected to pay contributions under the Family Benefits Regulations.

Entitlement to pension

18. A pension shall be paid under these regulations—

(*a*) in respect of a man teacher—

(i) if he is survived by his wife, to her in accordance with regulation 20 below;

(ii) if he is survived by a child or children, subject to regulation 22(6) below to or for the benefit of that child or those children in accordance with regulation 21 below;

(iii) if he is not survived by his wife or a child of his but is survived by a person nominated by him in pursuance of regulation 19 below ("the nominated beneficiary"), to the nominated beneficiary in accordance with regulation 20 (if the beneficiary is an adult) or in accordance with regulation 21 (if the beneficiary is a child).

(*b*) in respect of a woman teacher—

(i) if she is survived by her husband and he is the nominated beneficiary, to him in accordance with regulation 20 below;

(ii) if she is survived by a child or children, subject to regulation 22(6) below to or for the benefit of that child or those children in accordance with regulation 21 below;

(iii) if she is not survived by her husband or a child, but is survived by the nominated beneficiary, to the nominated beneficiary in accordance with regulation 20 (if the beneficiary is an adult) or in accordance with regulation 21 (if the beneficiary is a child).

Nomination of beneficiaries

19.—(1) A teacher to whom this regulation applies may at any time when—

(*a*) he is employed in reckonable service; and

(*b*) there is not in force a nomination made by him for the purposes of Part V of the Family Benefits Regulations—

nominate to receive a pension under these regulations a person who at the time of the nomination is wholly or mainly dependent on the teacher and is—

(i) the teacher's parent; or

(ii) an unmarried descendant of either of the teacher's parents; or

(iii) the teacher's widowed stepmother or stepfather; or

(iv) any unmarried descendant of the deceased wife of a man teacher; or

(v) the husband of a woman teacher.

(2) This regulation applies to a man teacher who is unmarried and to any woman teacher.

(3) The nomination of a beneficiary under this regulation shall become void—

(a) on the receipt by the Secretary of State of a written notice of revocation by the teacher;

(b) on the death or marriage of the nominated beneficiary;

(c) if the teacher is a man, on his marriage;

(d) if the beneficiary was a child, on his ceasing to be a child.

Amount of pension for widow or adult beneficiary

20.—(1) The annual amount of a pension payable to a widow or an adult nominated beneficiary shall be equal to one one-hundred and sixtieth of the teacher's average salary in respect of every year of his reckonable service counting for benefit for the purposes of this regulation.

(2) The reckonable service of a teacher counting for benefit for the purposes of this regulation is—

(a) his reckonable service since the beginning of April 1972;

(b) any reckonable service before 1st April 1972 in respect of which the teacher elected to pay contributions under regulation 4 above;

(c) any service (whether or not it is reckonable service) before 1st April 1972 in respect of which he paid contributions or elected to pay (and did not revoke his election to pay) additional contributions under the Family Benefits Regulations—

(i) augmented by so much of the service as is specified in an election by him to pay contributions under regulation 5; or

(ii) in any case where the service counting for benefit is not augmented under sub-paragraph (c)(i) above, reduced by six-fifths of the period (if any) of his service before 1st April 1972 in respect of which he did not elect to pay contributions under regulation 5;

(d) if the teacher died while employed in reckonable service or while in receipt of an annual superannuation allowance to which he became entitled by virtue of regulation 41(1)(c) of the principal Teachers' Regulations, such number of years as bears to any period which was or could have been added to his reckonable service by virtue of regulation 42 of the principal Teachers' Regulations the same proportion as the aggregate number of years of his reckonable service under sub-paragraphs (a), (b) and (c) of paragraph (2) of regulation 20 above bears to his total reckonable service.

Amount of child's pension

21.—(1) The annual amount of a pension payable to or for the benefit of a child or children shall be—

(*a*) if the teacher is survived by a widow or dependent husband—

(i) for so long as there are two or more children, an amount equal to one one-hundred and sixtieth of the teacher's average salary for every year of the teacher's service counting for benefit for the purposes of regulation 20 above;

(ii) for so long as there is one child, an amount equal to one three-hundred and twentieth of the teacher's average salary for each such year;

(*b*) if (in the case of a man teacher) he is not survived by his wife or (in the case of a woman teacher) immediately before her death she was not married—

(i) for so long as there are two or more children, an amount equal to one one-hundred and twentieth of the teacher's average salary for every year of his reckonable service counting for benefit for the purposes of this regulation;

(ii) for so long as there is one child, an amount equal to one two-hundred and fortieth of the teacher's average salary for each such year.

(2) The reckonable service of a teacher counting for benefit for the purposes of this regulation is—

(*a*) his reckonable service; and

(*b*) if the teacher died while employed in reckonable service or while in receipt of an annual superannuation allowance to which he became entitled by virtue of regulation 41(1)(*c*) of the principal Teachers' Regulations such number of years as bears to any period which was or could have been added to his reckonable service by virtue of regulation 42 of the principal Teachers' Regulations the same proportion as the aggregate number of years of his reckonable service under sub-paragraphs (*a*), (*b*) and (*c*) of paragraph (2) of regulation 20 above bears to his total reckonable service.

Duration of pensions

22.—(1) A pension payable to a teacher's widow, or to the husband of a deceased woman teacher, shall subject to paragraph (2) below, if a short term pension is payable under regulation 20 or 21 of the Teachers and Teachers' Families Regulations, begin to accrue on the termination of that pension and, if no such pension is payable under those regulations, on the day following the death of the teacher.

(2) If the annual rate of the pension payable to a widow or widower under these regulations exceeds the annual rate of the pension payable under regulation 20 or 21 of the Teachers and Teachers' Families Regulations the pension provided for by these regulations shall be paid in substitution for the pension payable under those regulations.

(3) The amount payable to or for the benefit of a child by virtue of regulation 21(1)(*a*) above shall, if a short term pension is payable under regulation 20 or 21 of the Teachers and Teachers' Families Regulations to the child's parent begin to accrue on the termination of the short term pension and, if no such short term pension is payable, on the day following the death of the teacher.

(4) A pension payable to or for the benefit of a child of a teacher shall, if the teacher is survived by a widow or widower, begin to accrue on the day following the death of that widow or widower and otherwise on the day following the death of the teacher.

(5) Subject to paragraph (6) below a pension payable under these regulations or under regulation 24 or 25 of the Teachers and Teachers' Families Regulations shall cease to be paid upon the death of the person to whom it is payable or, unless the Secretary of State otherwise directs, upon that person marrying or commencing to cohabit with a person to whom he or she is not married; but any pension which has ceased to be payable under the above provisions by reason of marriage or cohabitation may, if the Secretary of State so decides, be paid upon the person again becoming a widow or widower or as the case may be ceasing to cohabit.

(6) A pension payable to or for the benefit of a child shall cease on the death of the child or when the child ceases to be a child within the meaning of these regulations, whichever first occurs.

Miscellaneous and Supplementary

Teachers in admitted schools

23.—(1) This regulation applies to a teacher who—

(*a*) on the commencement of these regulations is employed in service to which Part VIII of the principal Teachers' Regulations applies; and

(*b*) was by virtue of that employment a member of the scheme administered in accordance with Part IV of the Family Benefits Regulations.

(2) A teacher to whom this regulation applies may, with the approval of the Secretary of State, pay for so long as he is employed as is mentioned in paragraph (1)(*a*) above in such manner as may be agreed contributions at a rate appearing to the Secretary of State to be a rate at which that teacher could have elected to pay if regulation 5 above had applied to him.

(3) Upon the death of any teacher to whom this regulation applies who—

(*a*) has paid contributions in pursuance of paragraph (1) above; and

(*b*) has been employed for not less than five years in service counting for benefit for the purpose of this regulation—

there shall be paid to or for the benefit of his widow and any child or children of his surviving him a pension at an annual rate certified by the Government Actuary as the actuarial equivalent of the contributions paid by him under this regulation.

(4) The service counting for benefit for the purposes of this regulation is—

(*a*) reckonable service (including service to which Part VIII of the principal Teachers' Regulations applies) since the beginning of April 1972;

(*b*) the aggregate of his service counting for benefit for the purposes of these regulations (within the meaning of regulation 3 above);

(c) any service during which he has paid contributions under this regulation; and

(d) any service before 1st April 1972 to which either Part VIII of the principal Teachers' Regulations or the scheme of 1963 applied and in respect of which he was a contributor within the meaning of regulation 23 of the Family Benefits Regulations.

Special provision for widows of certain non-members

24.—(1) A pension of an amount specified in paragraph (2) below may be paid to the widow of any non-member who dies without having made an election for the purposes of regulation 4 above if a death gratuity is payable to his personal representatives under regulation 47 of the principal Teachers' Regulations.

(2) The amount of a pension under paragraph (1) above shall be equal to one one-hundred and sixtieth of the teacher's average salary for every year of the service by reference to which the gratuity under regulation 47 of the principal Teachers' Regulations falls to be calculated.

(3) There shall be deducted from the terminal sum payable to or in respect of the teacher, or paid to the Secretary of State in such manner as may be agreed, the actuarial equivalent of the pension paid under this regulation.

(4) Paragraphs (1) and (5) of regulation 22 above shall apply to a pension paid under this regulation.

Application of Family Benefits Regulations

25. Except in so far as other provision is made by these regulations Part VI (Miscellaneous and Supplementary) of the Family Benefits Regulations shall, with the necessary modifications, apply for the purposes of these regulations as it applies for the purposes of those regulations.

Repayment of contributions

26.—(1) There shall, as soon as may be, be repaid the amount, together with compound interest thereon calculated at three per cent. per annum with yearly rests, certified by the Actuary as the amount by which the contributions paid under regulation 39A(1) of the Family Benefits Regulations before the commencement of these regulations exceeds the amount payable under that provision as affected by these regulations.

(2) If a teacher to whom regulation 5 applies does not elect to pay contributions under that regulation, such sums as are prescribed by regulations 42 to 44 of the Family Benefits Regulations, reduced in any case by a sum equal to the tax chargeable on that repayment under paragraph 2 of Part II of schedule 5 to the Finance Act 1970(a) (charge to tax on repayment of employee's contributions), shall be paid to him by way of repayment of contributions paid by him—

(a) on his being repaid his superannuation contributions after ceasing to be employed in reckonable service;

(b) on his transfer to other employment if interchange rules apply to him on that transfer;

(a) 1970 c. 24.

(c) on his becoming eligible for superannuation allowances if on his death no pension will be payable to his widow, or other adult beneficiary nominated by him, under any provision relating to the superannuation of teachers except a provision contained in Part VI of the principal Teachers' Regulations.

Special provision for teachers with certain external service

27.—(1) On the death of a teacher or former teacher who is a former external contributor to an external scheme relating to such service as is mentioned in paragraph 1 (Scotland) or 2 (Northern Ireland) of schedule 2 to the principal Teachers' Regulations the Secretary of State may in accordance with this regulation pay a pension to or for the benefit of any widow, widower, child or other nominated beneficiary of that teacher to or for whose benefit a pension is payable under the preceding provisions of these regulations.

(2) The annual amount of a pension payable under this regulation shall be equal to the amount that would have been payable under those provisions of the external scheme which correspond to these regulations if that part of the election under regulation 8(1)(a) above as is made in pursuance of paragraph 2(1) of schedule 3 below had formed part of an election to the like effect for the purposes of the external scheme.

(3) There shall be deducted from the terminal sum payable to or in respect of the teacher, or paid to the Secretary of State in such manner as may be agreed, an amount equal to the sum of any contributions outstanding for payment in respect of the service to which the part of the election referred to in paragraph (2) above relates.

(4) In connection with the provisions of the preceding paragraphs of this regulation, schedule 3 to these regulations shall have effect for the modification

(a) in accordance with paragraph 1 of that schedule, of the Teachers and Teachers' Families Regulations in their application to a former external contributor to such a scheme as is mentioned in paragraph (1) above who dies within the time prescribed for making an election under regulation 8(1)(a) above without making such an election; and

(b) in accordance with paragraph 2 of that schedule, of these regulations in their application to a teacher or former teacher to whom paragraph (1) above applies.

Short term pensions for dependants of women teachers

28. Regulations 20 (widow's short term pension) and 21 (retired teacher's widow's short term pension) of the Teachers and Teachers' Families Regulations shall with the necessary modifications apply on the death after 31st March 1972 of a woman teacher whose husband is her nominated beneficiary as they apply on the death of a man teacher; and regulation 22 (children's short term pension) of those regulations shall so apply on the death after 31st March 1972, survived by a child or children, of a woman teacher who immediately before her death was not married as it applies on the death of a man teacher survived by a child or children.

Minor and consequential amendments and revocations

29. The minor and consequential amendments and revocations specified in schedule 4 shall have effect.

Regulation 3(1)(b)

SCHEDULE 1

DEEMED ADDITIONAL SERVICE

The deemed additional service of any teacher shall be determined in accordance with the formula $\frac{ab}{c}$ where—

a is the factor shown in the appropriate entry of column B of the table below;

b is the amount (in pounds) of his additional contributions held in the Fund at 31st March 1972;

and

c is the amount (in pounds) of his annual salary at that date.

A Age of teacher at last birthday before 1st April 1972	B Factor	A Age of teacher at last birthday before 1st April 1972	B Factor
18	23·8	43	55·3
19	26·5	44	55·1
20	29·1	45	54·9
21	31·6	46	54·8
22	34·0	47	54·7
23	36·2	48	54·6
24	38·3	49	54·5
25	40·3	50	54·5
26	42·2	51	54·4
27	44·0	52	54·4
28	45·7	53	54·3
29	47·3	54	54·3
30	48·8	55	54·2
31	50·2	56	54·2
32	51·5	57	54·1
33	52·7	58	54·1
34	53·8	59	54·0
35	54·7		
36	55·3	60 and over	54·0
37	55·6		
38	55·8		
39	55·9		
40	55·9		
41	55·8		
42	55·6		

Regulations 12 and 15

SCHEDULE 2

CONTRIBUTIONS AND DEDUCTIONS

TABLE 1

CONTRIBUTIONS

A	B							
	Period in years for which contributions are required to be paid in respect of each year of service (regulation 8(1)(*a*))							
Age on the date from which additional contributions begin to be paid	Rate of contributions elected (regulation 8(1)(*b*))							
	1%	2%	3%	4%	5%	6%	7%	8%
27 and under	2·90	1·45	·97	·73	·58	·48	·41	·36
28—37	2·95	1·48	·98	·74	·59	·49	·42	·37
38—42	3·00	1·50	1·00	·75	·60	·50	·43	·375
43—47	3·05	1·52	1·02	·76	·61	·51	·435	·38
48 and over	3·10	1·55	1·03	·77	·62	·52	·44	·39

Notes:—1. A teacher who before the day specified in relation to him under regulation 13(*a*) pays in accordance with the Family Benefits Regulations additional contributions so payable after 31st March 1972 shall be taken to have paid contributions in accordance with regulation 5 at the rate specified by him in accordance with regulation 8(1)(*b*) for the number of years equal to the fraction of which the denominator is that rate and the numerator is the amount of those contributions expressed as a percentage of his annual salary on the day specified; and, as regards any such teacher, that number shall accordingly be deducted from the period determined in accordance with the table above.

2. The necessary interpolations are to be made where the period elected under regulation 8(1)(*a*) is not an exact number of years.

TABLE 2

DEDUCTIONS

As regards any teacher the deduction to be made is the annual amount of his contributions at the last rate payable multiplied by the factor shown in column B against the entry in column A which specifies the number of further years during which contributions would have been payable.

A Number of further years during which contributions would have been payable	B Factor
1	·990
2	1·961
3	2·913
4	3·846
5	4·760
6	5·657
7	6·536
8	7·398
9	8·244
10	9·072
11	9·884
12	10·681
13	11·461
14	12·227
15	12·977
16	13·713
17	14·434
18	15·141
19	15·835
20	16·514

Note: The necessary interpolations are to be made where the further period for which contributions would have been payable is not an exact number of years.

Regulation 27

SCHEDULE 3

MODIFICATIONS RELATING TO TEACHERS WITH SERVICE IN SCOTLAND OR NORTHERN IRELAND

Modification of the Teachers and Teachers' Families Regulations

1.—(1) In computing the period of service of a non-contributor for the purposes of regulation 24(1)(*a*) (non-contributor's widow's pension) any period of external service in Scotland or Northern Ireland shall be treated as a period of reckonable service.

(2) The references in regulations 24(1) (non-contributor's widow's pension) and 25(1) (retired non-contributor's widow's pension) to the annual superannuation allowance payable to the teacher shall, if his widow so elects, be construed as including references to the allowance that would have been payable to the teacher if in computing it any external service in Scotland or Northern Ireland had been treated as reckonable service.

(3) The reference in regulation 26(1) (adjustment of terminal sum) to the teacher's reckonable service before 1st April 1972 shall, if his widow has so elected as is mentioned in sub-paragraph (2) above, be construed as including a reference to his external service in Scotland or Northern Ireland.

Modifications of the Regulations

2.—(1) Any election under regulation 8(1) shall in addition specify the period of external service in Scotland or Northern Ireland which the teacher elects to be treated as reckonable service for the purposes of regulation 20 in the event of his death in, or after retirement from, reckonable service.

(2) There shall be added at the end of regulation 15 as a new paragraph—

"(4) There shall be deducted from the terminal sum payable to or in respect of the teacher, or paid to the Secretary of State in such manner as may be agreed, the actuarial equivalent of the cost of defraying any pension payable in pursuance of regulation 27 below."

(3) The references in sub-paragraph (*a*) of each of regulations 17(2) and 20(2) to reckonable service since the beginning of April 1972 shall be construed as including references to external service since that date in Scotland or Northern Ireland; and the references in sub-paragraph (*b*) of each of those provisions to reckonable service before 1st April 1972 shall be construed as including references to such external service as is specified in that part of an election under regulation 8(1) of these regulations as is made in pursuance of paragraph 2(1) above.

Regulation 29

SCHEDULE 4

Minor and Consequential Amendments and Revocations

Amount of pensions under the Teachers' Widows' and Children's Scheme

1. The words "and before 14th January 1973" shall be inserted immediately after the words "before 17th March 1972" in regulations 47(2)(*d*) (amount of widow's pension), 50(*d*) (amount of short service widow's pension) and 53(1)(*d*) (amount of children's pension) of the Family Benefits Regulations.

Additional contributions

2. No contributions shall be payable by a teacher under regulations 31, 32, 33 and 38 of the Family Benefits Regulations as from any date before 1st November 1974 upon which he commences to pay contributions in accordance with regulation 5 above or as the case may be revokes his election to pay contributions under regulation 33 of the Family Benefits Regulations; and regulations 31, 32, 33 and 38 of those regulations shall cease to have effect on 1st November 1974.

Nomination of dependants

3. Regulation 58 (nomination of dependants) of the Family Benefits Regulations shall cease to have effect, but without prejudice to the validity of any nomination made under that regulation which had not become void before the commencement of these regulations.

Teachers' contribution

4. Regulation 5(2) (teacher's contribution towards financing of benefits) of the Teachers' Superannuation (Financial Provisions) Regulations 1972(**a**) as amended by regulation 3 of the Teachers' Superannuation (Financial Provisions and Family Benefits) (Amendment) Regulations 1972(**b**) shall have effect subject to the substitution—

(*a*) for the reference to the Teachers' Superannuation (Family Benefits) Regulations 1970 to 1972 of a reference to the Teachers' Superannuation (Family Benefits) Regulations 1970 to 1973; and

(*b*) for the words "six and three quarters per cent. of his salary for the time being" of the words—

"the aggregate of—

(*a*) six and three quarters per cent. of his salary for the time being; and

(*b*) any contributions which he has elected to pay under Part V of the Family Benefits Regulations or the Teachers' Superannuation (Family Benefits) (Amendment) Regulations 1973."

Short term pensions

5.—(1) In regulations 20 (widow's short term pension) and 21 (retired teacher's widow's short term pension) of the Teachers and Teachers' Families Regulations references to the annual rate of a teacher's salary are to be construed as references to his salary as calculated under regulation 3(1) of the Teachers' Superannuation (Financial Provisions) Regulations 1972.

(**a**) S.I. 1972/568 (1972 I, p. 1892).   (**b**) S.I. 1972/1092 (1972 II, p. 3223).

(2) Regulation 21 of the Teachers and Teachers' Families Regulations shall have effect as from 1st April 1972 with the insertion of the words "24(1)(*b*) or" immediately after the word "regulation".

Service in European School

6. There shall be inserted as a new paragraph immediately after paragraph 18A of Part I of schedule 1 (reckonable service) to the principal Teachers' Regulations—

"18B. Service as a teacher in pursuance of arrangements made by the Secretary of State with the governors of any establishment to which the European Communities (European Schools) Order 1972(a) for the time being applies."

Deduction from terminal sum

7. There shall be deducted from the terminal sum payable to or in respect of a teacher who, after being employed in reckonable service, is last employed in reckonable service in Scotland or Northern Ireland the actuarial equivalent of the benefits payable under the relevant external scheme in respect of his external service.

Given under the Official Seal of the Secretary of State for Education and Science on 16th May 1973.

(L.S.)

Margaret Thatcher,
Secretary of State for Education
and Science.

Consent of the Minister for the Civil Service given under his Official Seal on 21st May 1973.

(L.S.)

K. H. McNeill,
Authorised by the Minister for the
Civil Service.

(a) S.I. 1972/1582 (1972 III, p. 4586).

EXPLANATORY NOTE

(This Note is not part of the Regulations.)

These Regulations amend the provisions contained in the Teachers' Superannuation (Family Benefits) Regulations 1970 to 1972 relating to the payment of pensions to the widows or widowers of teachers and their families and other dependants.

The Regulations enable all teachers employed in reckonable service on or after 1st April 1972 to elect to pay contributions or, as the case may be, further contributions in respect of their reckonable service before that date and make new provision with respect to the amount of pensions payable.

Special provision is made with regard to teachers in admitted schools (regulation 23) and teachers with external service in Scotland or Northern Ireland (regulation 27). The Regulations also make a number of minor amendments to the existing regulations and one amendment of the principal Teachers' Regulations (paragraph 6 of schedule 4) which has the effect of treating service in a European school as reckonable service.

Regulation 28 and paragraph 5(2) of schedule 4 have retrospective effect by virtue of section 12(1) of the Superannuation Act 1972.

STATUTORY INSTRUMENTS

1973 No. 942

PENSIONS

The Pensions Increase (Power Jets) Regulations 1973

Made - - -	*22nd May* 1973
Laid before Parliament	*31st May* 1973
Coming into Operation	*22nd June* 1973

The Minister for the Civil Service, in exercise of the powers conferred on him by section 13(2) and (5) of the Pensions (Increase) Act 1971(a) and of all other powers enabling him in that behalf, hereby makes the following Regulations:—

Citation and commencement

1. These Regulations may be cited as the Pensions Increase (Power Jets) Regulations 1973, and shall come into operation on 22nd June 1973.

Interpretation

2.—(1) In these Regulations—

"the civil service pension scheme" means, in relation to a person whose reckonable service ended not later than 29th February 1972, the Superannuation Acts 1965 and 1967(b) and, in relation to a person whose reckonable service ended after that date, the principal civil service pension scheme within the meaning of section 2 of the Superannuation Act 1972(c);

"the Power Jets pension scheme", in relation to any male person, means the pension scheme established by Power Jets Limited for its male employees and, in relation to any female person, means the pension scheme established by Power Jets (Research and Development) Limited for its female employees;

"reckonable service", in relation to any person, means the period after 30th June 1946 in respect of which, while he was employed by Power Jets (Research and Development) Limited or in the civil service of the State, contributions were paid in his case under the Power Jets pension scheme.

(2) The Interpretation Act 1889(d) shall apply for the interpretation of these Regulations as it applies for the interpretation of an Act of Parliament.

(3) Any reference in these Regulations to the provisions of any enactment shall be construed, unless the context otherwise requires, as a reference to those provisions as amended by any subsequent enactment.

(a) 1971 c. 56.
(c) 1972 c. 11.
(b) 1965 c. 74; 1967 c. 28.
(d) 1889 c. 63.

Persons to whom the Regulations apply

3. These Regulations apply to any person who—

(*a*) has been employed in the civil service of the State after ceasing to be employed by Power Jets (Research and Development) Limited; and

(*b*) has, while employed by Power Jets (Research and Development) Limited and in the civil service of the State, been a participant in the Power Jets pension scheme; and

(*c*) has been such a participant for a continuous period of not less than ten years; and

(*d*) either—

    (i) has retired from the civil service of the State after attaining the age of sixty years or on account of physical or mental infirmity; or

    (ii) having retired from the civil service of the State not earlier than 14th July 1949 in circumstances other than those described above, has attained the age of sixty years or satisfies the Minister for the Civil Service that he is disabled by physical or mental infirmity; or

    (iii) having been transferred from the civil service of the State to employment which is approved employment for the purposes of the civil service pension scheme, has retired from such employment after attaining the age of sixty years or on account of physical or mental infirmity; and

(*e*) has received, or become entitled to receive, retirement benefit under the Power Jets pension scheme.

Notional pension and lump sum

4.—(1) There shall be ascribed to each person to whom these Regulations apply a notional pension equal to the amount of the annual pension for which he would have been eligible under the civil service pension scheme if he had during the period of his employment in the civil service of the State been subject to that scheme and his reckonable service had been reckonable for the purposes of that scheme.

(2) Where a person to whom these Regulations apply has retired from the civil service of the State in such circumstances that, if the civil service pension scheme applied to him, a lump sum would be payable to him by way of retiring allowance upon his subsequently attaining a particular age or becoming disabled by physical or mental infirmity before that age, there shall be ascribed to him a notional lump sum, treated as if it became payable on his attaining that age or becoming so disabled, as the case may be, of an amount equal to the lump sum for which he would have been eligible under the civil service pension scheme if he had during the period of his employment in the civil service of the State been subject to that scheme and his reckonable service had been reckonable for the purposes of that scheme.

Payment of benefit equivalent to pension increase

5. The Minister for the Civil Service may, in respect of any period beginning on or after 1st September 1971, pay to any person to whom these Regulations apply an amount equal to the increase which would be payable to him under the Pensions (Increase) Act 1971 if there were payable to him—

(*a*) an annual pension under the civil service pension scheme of an amount equal to the notional pension ascribed to him under Regulation 4(1) above and beginning on the day following the end of the period of his reckonable service, and

(*b*) in a case where a notional lump sum is ascribed to him under Regulation 4(2) above, a lump sum under the civil service pension scheme of an amount equal to, and becoming payable at the same time as, that notional lump sum and beginning on the day following the end of the period of his reckonable service.

Given under the official seal of the Minister for the Civil Service on 22nd May 1973.

(L.S.)

Kenneth Baker,
Parliamentary Secretary to
the Civil Service Department.

EXPLANATORY NOTE

(This Note is not part of the Regulations.)

These Regulations apply to certain persons who have retired from the civil service and were formerly employed by Power Jets (Research and Development) Limited, and who receive retirement benefits under certain pension schemes providing benefits by means of insurance policies.

The Regulations provide for the payment of allowances corresponding to the increases for which the persons concerned would have been eligible under the Pensions (Increase) Act 1971 if they had been pensionable in the normal way under the principal civil service pension scheme. The allowances will be calculated on a "notional pension" and, in certain circumstances, a "notional lump sum" corresponding to the pension and lump sum a person would have received if he had been subject to the civil service pension scheme and entitled to reckon under that scheme his service during which he was subject to the insurance policy scheme.

In accordance with the power conferred by section 13(5) of the 1971 Act, the Regulations provide for the increase to take effect from 1st September 1971.

STATUTORY INSTRUMENTS

1973 No. 943

LOCAL GOVERNMENT, ENGLAND AND WALES

The Local Government (Interim Provision) Order 1973

Made - - - -	*22nd May* 1973
Laid before Parliament	*29th May* 1973
Coming into Operation	*30th May* 1973

The Secretary of State for the Environment, in relation to England, and the Secretary of State for Wales, in relation to Wales, in exercise of the powers conferred on them by section 254(1)(*a*) and (2)(*c*) and (*d*) of the Local Government Act 1972**(a)** and of all other powers enabling them in that behalf, hereby make the following order:—

Title and commencement

1. This order may be cited as the Local Government (Interim Provision) Order 1973 and shall come into operation on 30th May 1973.

Interpretation

2.—(1) The Interpretation Act 1889**(b)** shall apply for the interpretation of this order as it applies for the interpretation of an Act of Parliament.

(2) In this order—

"the Act" means the Local Government Act 1972; and

"Wales" means the area consisting of the counties established by section 20 of the Act (new local government areas in Wales), and England does not include any area included in any of those counties.

Superannuation contributions of former clerks of the peace, etc.

3. Where a person who—

(*a*) is, under sub-paragraph (2) of paragraph 13 of Schedule 10 to the Courts Act 1971**(c)**, contributing to the superannuation fund (within the meaning of Part I of the Local Government Superannuation Act 1937**(d)**) specified in that sub-paragraph the amount therein specified;

(*b*) would, apart from the appointment mentioned below, be transferred on 1st April 1974 under section 255 of the Act to the employment of any local authority,

is appointed by a county council before 1st April 1974 to hold any office or employment before or as from that date, the said sub-paragraph (2) shall have

---

(a) 1972 c. 70.	(b) 1889 c. 63.
(c) 1971 c. 23.	(d) 1937 c. 68.

effect with the substitution for "maintained by the authority referred to in sub-paragraph (1)(*b*) above" of "which is the appropriate superannuation fund in respect of him in that office or employment".

The references in this article to provisions of the said Acts of 1937 and 1971 are references thereto as having effect by virtue of paragraph 5(1) of Schedule 7 to the Superannuation Act 1972**(a)**.

Election of councillors of the parish of Bawtry

4. An election of councillors of the parish of Bawtry as enlarged by paragraph 2 of Part IV of Schedule 1 to the Act shall be held on 25th November 1973 and the Parish Council Election Rules 1973**(b)** shall apply thereto with the necessary modifications. The persons elected as the result of the said election shall not act in their offices before 1st April 1974 except for the purpose of taking any action with a view to enabling the parish council to exercise their functions on and after that date.

Wards of the parish of Abbots Langley

5. The New Parishes Order 1973**(c)** shall have effect as if in Schedule 2 (Wards), in columns (2), (3) and (4), the following entries had been inserted—

"No. 5 | The Abbots Langley ward of the | 3 "
(Abbots Langley) | existing parish of Abbots Langley |

Geoffrey Rippon,
Secretary of State for the Environment.

22nd May 1973.

Peter Thomas,
Secretary of State for Wales.

21st May 1973.

EXPLANATORY NOTE

(*This Note is not part of the Order.*)

This Order deals with three matters—
(*a*) Paragraph 13 of Schedule 10 to the Courts Act 1971 made provision in relation to certain contributory employees within the meaning of the Local Government Superannuation Act 1937 affected by the Act of 1971: in the context of this order the more important of such persons are clerks and deputy clerks of the peace. Sub-paragraph (2) enabled such persons to pay the same contributions as they had paid before the paragraph came into operation. These contributions were to be paid to the superannuation fund maintained by the authority by whom the person in question was

(a) 1972 c. 11. (b) S.I. 1973/166(1973 I, p. 670).
(c) S.I. 1973/688.

employed or paid. As a result of the Local Government Act 1972 some of the persons covered by paragraph 13 will come to be employed by new county councils Article 3 of this order therefore provides for the substitution of references to the appropriate superannuation fund:

(b) Provision for elections of councillors of parishes to which parts of other parishes are added by paragraph 2 of Part IV of Schedule 1 to the Local Government Act 1972 on 12th April 1973 was made by the New Parishes Order 1973. That provision was ineffective in one parish as the necessary action could not be taken in time. Article 4 of this order makes new provision for an election;

(c) The New Parishes Order 1973 (see (b)) provided for four wards in the parish of Abbots Langley. A fifth ward was in error omitted. Article 5 of this order provides that the earlier order shall have effect with additional entries, to rectify the omission.

STATUTORY INSTRUMENTS

1973 No. 944

SEEDS

The Forest Reproductive Material Regulations 1973

Made - - - -	*22nd May* 1973
Laid before Parliament	*7th June* 1973
Coming into Operation	*1st July* 1973
	(subject to regulation 1(3))

The Minister of Agriculture, Fisheries and Food, and the Secretary of State for Scotland, in exercise of the powers vested in them by section 7(1) of the Seeds Act 1920(a), and after consultation with the Forestry Commissioners and with representatives of the interests concerned, and the Minister of Agriculture, Fisheries and Food, the Secretary of State for Scotland and the Secretary of State for Wales, acting jointly, in exercise of the powers vested in them by subsections (1), (1A), (2), (3), (4) and (8) of section 16 of the Plant Varieties and Seeds Act 1964(b) as amended by section 4(1) of, and subparagraphs (1), (2), (3), (4) and (5) of paragraph 5 of Schedule 4 to, the European Communities Act 1972(c), and all other powers enabling them in that behalf, after consultation with the Council on Tribunals and with representatives of such interests as appear to them to be concerned, hereby make the following regulations:—

PART I

GENERAL

Citation and commencement

1.—(1) These regulations may be cited as the Forest Reproductive Material Regulations 1973.

(2) These regulations, except the regulations mentioned in paragraph (3) of this regulation to the extent of the application of those regulations as therein specified, shall come into operation on 1st July 1973.

(3) Regulations 10, 11, 12, and 13(1)(*a*),—

(*a*) in so far as they apply to seed and cones of such of the genera and species listed in Schedule 1 as are coniferous collected before 1st July 1973, shall come into operation on 1st July 1975; and

(*b*) in so far as they apply to young plants raised from seed collected, or parts of plants taken, before 1st July 1973, shall come into operation on 1st July 1977.

Restriction of the Seeds Regulations 1961 *and of the Seeds* (*Scotland*) *Regulations* 1961.

2. The Seeds Regulations 1961(d) shall cease to have effect in relation to the forest tree seeds specified in Part I of the First Schedule thereto, and the Seeds (Scotland) Regulations 1961(e) shall cease to have effect in relation to the forest tree seeds specified in Part I of the First Schedule thereto.

(a) 1920 c. 54.   (b) 1964 c. 14.
(c) 1972 c. 68.   (d) S.I. 1961/212 (1961 I, p. 362).
(e) S.I. 1961/274 (1961 I, p. 446).

Interpretation

3.—(1) The Interpretation Act 1889(a) shall apply for the interpretation of these regulations as it applies for the interpretation of an Act of Parliament.

(2) In these regulations, unless the context otherwise requires,—

"the Act" means the Plant Varieties and Seeds Act 1964 as amended by section 43 of, and Schedule 7 to, the Agriculture (Miscellaneous Provisions) Act 1968(b) and section 4(1) of, and paragraph 5 of Schedule 4 to, the European Communities Act 1972;

"basic material" means—

(a) in relation to forest reproductive material produced by sexual means, stands of trees and conservation seed orchards, and

(b) in relation to forest reproductive material produced by vegetative means, clones;

"Commissioners" means Forestry Commissioners;

"cones" means cones containing seed;

"conservation seed orchard" means an orchard raised artificially from one or more officially approved stands of trees in the same region of provenance and intended for the production of seed;

"forest reproductive material" means—

(a) seed and cones intended for the production of plants,

(b) parts of plants intended for the production of plants, and

(c) young plants raised from seed or from parts of plants, natural seedlings and sets,

derived from basic material of the genera and species specified in Schedule 1;

"marketing" means exposure for sale, offer for sale, sale or delivery, and "marketed" shall be construed accordingly;

"Member State" means a state, other than the United Kingdom, which is a member of the European Communities;

"National Register" means the National Register of Basic Material for the Production of Forest Reproductive Material established in accordance with regulation 5;

"official testing station" means the official testing station for forest reproductive material in Great Britain established by the Commissioners;

"origin" means the place in which an indigenous stand of trees is growing, or the place from which a non-indigenous stand was originally introduced;

"parts of plants" means cuttings, layers and scions;

"percentage of germination" means the percentage by number of pure seed which in the course of a germination test produce seedlings which have developed structures which indicate the ability to produce mature plants under favourable conditions in the field;

"percentage of purity" means the percentage by weight of pure seed as ascertained in a seed test;

"provenance" means the place in which any stand of trees, whether indigenous or non-indigenous, is growing;

"pure seed" means whole seeds of the kind which the seed purport to be (including any such seeds which are immature, shrivelled, sprouted, cracked, insect-damaged, diseased or otherwise injured provided they can be definitely

---

(a) 1889 c. 63.   (b) 1968 c. 34.

identified as the species under consideration) and pieces of such seeds larger than one-half of the original size of the whole seed but excluding, in the case of conifers, seeds and pieces of seeds from which the seed coat is entirely removed;

"region of provenance" means—

(*a*) for a species, a sub-species or distinct variety, the area or group of areas subject to sufficiently uniform ecological conditions in which are found stands whose genetic or morphological characteristics are similar and of equal value for the production of wood, and

(*b*) for a conservation seed orchard, the region of provenance of the basic material used for the creation of the orchard;

"seed" includes fruits;

"Test Certificate" means a test certificate issued under regulation 8;

"the Tribunal" means the Plant Varieties and Seeds Tribunal established by section 10 of, and Schedule 4 to, the Act.

(3) Any references in these regulations to a numbered regulation or a schedule are references to the regulation or schedule so numbered in these regulations.

Application

4.—(1) These regulations shall not apply to—

(*a*) seed or cones collected or marketed for export to countries other than Member States; or

(*b*) parts of plants or young plants taken, raised or marketed for purposes other than the production of wood.

(2) Regulations 10, 11, 12 and 13(1)(*a*) shall not apply to parts of plants or young plants taken, raised or marketed for export to countries other than Member States.

PART II

REGISTRATION OF BASIC MATERIAL, TESTING OF SEED AND DELINEATION OF REGIONS OF PROVENANCE

National Register of Basic Material

5.—(1) The Commissioners shall establish and maintain an official register of basic material in Great Britain to be known as the National Register of Basic Material for the Production of Forest Reproductive Material (hereafter in these regulations referred to as "the National Register") which shall be kept at the Commissioners' principal office and in which shall be recorded the particulars of such basic material as may be approved and accepted by the Commissioners for registration.

(2) A copy of the National Register shall be held at the official testing station, and at every Forestry Commission Conservancy Office in Great Britain.

(3) The Commissioners shall provide reasonable facilities for inspecting the National Register and each of the copies thereof mentioned in paragraph (2) of this regulation, and for taking copies of and extracts from them.

Registration of basic material

6.—(1) An owner of basic material seeking approval and registration thereof in the National Register shall apply in writing to the Commissioners who, upon receiving payment of their fee for their services in connection with such application, shall arrange for an inspection of the basic material to be made by a Forestry Commission officer.

(2) The Commissioners shall not approve basic material for registration unless they are satisfied, having regard to the inspecting officer's report and to the criteria set out in Schedule 2, that its qualities are such as to make it suitable for reproductive purposes and that it has no characteristics undesirable for the production of wood.

(3) If the basic material inspected is approved for registration the Commissioners shall register it in the National Register.

(4) The Commissioners may at any time remove basic material from the National Register if they are satisfied that it should be so removed having regard to the matters mentioned in paragraph (2) of this regulation.

Appeals against refusal to register or removal from the National Register

7.—(1) Where the Commissioners propose to make a decision

    (*a*) to refuse to register basic material submitted for registration, or

    (*b*) to remove basic material from the National Register,

the Commissioners shall give to the owner of the basic material notice of the proposal together with the reasons for it; and the owner may, within 28 days from the day on which the notice is given, submit to the Commissioners representations in writing or a written request to be permitted to appear before them to make oral representations with respect to the proposal.

(2) Where, within the period specified in paragraph (1) above, the owner of the basic material shall request permission to make oral representations, the Commissioners shall give him an opportunity to be heard either in person or by any person authorised by him in that behalf.

(3) The Commissioners shall not decide to refuse to register the basic material submitted for registration or, as the case may be, to remove the basic material from the National Register until after the expiration of the said period and, before deciding whether or not to do so, shall consider any representations made to them by or on behalf of the owner of the basic material.

(4) For the purpose of making a decision in any such case a quorum of the Commissioners shall be one Commissioner, and the procedure to be followed at an oral hearing before the Commissioners shall be such as the Commissioners may direct.

(5) Where the Commissioners decide to refuse to register basic material submitted for registration or to remove basic material from the National Register, they shall notify the owner accordingly and shall at the same time furnish a statement of their reasons for the decision.

(6) An appeal shall lie to the Tribunal from any decision of the Commissioners as to a matter mentioned in paragraph (1) of this regulation.

(7) Where an appeal is brought against a decision of the Commissioners under the foregoing provisions of this regulation, the operation of such decision shall be suspended pending the final determination of the appeal; and the Commissioners shall take such steps as may be necessary to give effect to any decision given on the final determination of an appeal.

Seed testing

8.—(1) Seed testing in Great Britain for the purposes of these regulations shall be carried out at the official testing station.

(2) An application for a seed test and Test Certificate shall be made in accordance with the procedure laid down in Part I of Schedule 3 and shall be accompanied by a sample representative of the bulk of the seed to which the application relates and by the fee charged by the Commissioners for their services in connection with the application.

(3) A sample of the seed to which the application relates shall be taken in accordance with the rules laid down in Part II of Schedule 3.

(4) If the test made as a result of the application establishes that the sample sent therewith satisfies the conditions specified in Part III of Schedule 3 the officer in charge of the official testing station shall, on behalf of the Commissioners, issue to the applicant a Test Certificate in the form set out in Part IV of Schedule 3.

Map of Regions of Provenance

9.—(1) The Commissioners shall prepare a map of the regions of provenance of forest reproductive material in Great Britain delineating their boundaries by reference to boundaries of local government areas or geographic or altitudinal features.

(2) The map shall be held at the Commissioners' principal office, and a copy thereof shall be kept at the official testing station and at every Forestry Commission Conservancy Office in Great Britain; and the Commissioners shall provide reasonable facilities for inspecting the said map and the said copies thereof, and for taking copies of and extracts from them.

(3) The Commissioners may from time to time alter the map so as to show any change which has occurred to any of the boundaries of the regions of provenance, and the said copies thereof shall be altered accordingly.

PART III

Marketing of Forest Reproductive Material

Collection and taking of forest reproductive material

10.—(1) Except in the case of forest reproductive material authorised for marketing under regulation 13(2), no seed or cones shall be collected, and no parts of plants shall be taken, for the purpose of marketing unless they are derived from basic material which has been approved by the Commissioners and registered by them in the National Register.

(2) Any person proposing to collect seed or cones or to take parts of plants for the purpose of marketing shall inform the Commissioners of the proposed collection or taking at least 28 days before the date on which the collection or taking is to commence stating—

  (*a*) his name, his address and (if any) his telephone number,

  (*b*) the place of collection or of taking, and

  (*c*) the proposed date of commencement, and the approximate date of completion, of the collection or taking.

(3) On completion of the collection of any lot of seed or of the taking of any lot of parts of plants the owner thereof shall inform the Commissioners in writing

of the kind and the quantity of seed collected or of parts of plants taken, and the Commissioners shall,—

(a) if satisfied that the seed or parts of plants are derived from basic material approved and registered in accordance with regulation 6, issue to the owner in respect of the lot a Master Certificate of Provenance or Clonal Identity in the form set out in Schedule 4, or

(b) if the seed or parts of plants have been authorised for marketing under regulation 13(2), issue to the owner in respect of the lot a certificate of provenance or clonal identity in the form set out in Schedule 8, or in a form to the like effect.

(4) On completion of the collection of any lot of cones the owner thereof shall inform the Commissioners in writing of the quantity of cones collected, and on completion of extraction of seed therefrom the owner of the seed shall inform the Commissioners in writing of the kind and the quantity of seed extracted, and the Commissioners shall,—

(a) if satisfied that the seed is derived from basic material approved and registered in accordance with regulation 6, issue to the owner in respect of the seed extracted from the lot a Master Certificate of Provenance in the form set out in Schedule 4, or

(b) if the seed has been authorised for marketing under regulation 13(2), issue to the owner in respect of the seed extracted from the lot a certificate of provenance in the form set out in Schedule 8, or in a form to the like effect.

Identification criteria

11.—(1) Forest reproductive material shall during collection, taking, extraction, processing, storage, transporation and raising, for the purpose of marketing, and while being marketed, be kept by the person in possession thereof in separate lots distinguished from each other by reference to the following criteria (hereafter in this regulation referred to as the "identification criteria"), namely,—

(a) the genus and species, the sub-species (if any) and the variety (if any) to which it belongs;

(b) in the case of forest reproductive material produced by vegetative means, its clone;

(c) in the case of forest reproductive material produced by sexual means, its region of provenance;

(d) in the case of forest reproductive material which, although not derived from officially approved basic material, has been authorised for marketing under regulation 13(2), its place of provenance and the altitude of that place;

(e) its origin: whether indigenous or non-indigenous;

(f) in the case of seed, the year in which it shall have ripened; and

(g) (i) in the case of seedlings, the length of time the seedlings have been in the seed bed, and also,

(ii) in the case of transplants, the length of time they have existed as seedlings and as transplants, respectively, and the number of times transplanted.

(2) The person in possession of any such lot shall,—

(a) if it is not marked as mentioned in this paragraph when it comes into his possession, mark it, and

(b) secure that until it leaves his possession it continues to be marked,

with the particulars of the identification criteria relating to it, and such marking shall be effected in accordance with regulation 12.

Marking of forest reproductive material for the purposes of regulation 11

12. The marking of each lot of forest reproductive material required by regulation 11 to be marked shall be effected as follows, that is to say, there shall be indelibly marked in writing, printing, stencilling or by any other appropriate means—

(a) where the lot is in a single bundle or sack or package or in a single container of any other kind whatsoever, the bundle, sack, package or container, or a label securely attached thereto;

(b) where the lot comprises more than one bundle or sack or package or container, either—

(i) each bundle or sack or package or container or a label securely attached thereto, or

(ii) a notice displayed in such a manner that it shall be readily observable and be unequivocally associated with the lot; and

(c) where the lot is not in a bundle or sack or package or other container, a notice displaying the mark in such a manner that it shall be both readily observable and unequivocally associated with the lot.

Marketing of forest reproductive material

13.—(1) Except as provided by paragraph (2) of this regulation—

(a) no forest reproductive material shall be marketed unless

(i) it is derived from basic material approved and registered by the Commissioners in accordance with regulation 6, or

(ii) it is derived from basic material officially approved and registered under the corresponding legislation of a Member State or Northern Ireland relating to forest reproductive material;

(b) no seed shall be marketed—

(i) except under the description "EEC Standard";

(ii) unless a Test Certificate in the form set out in Part IV of Schedule 3 has been issued in respect of it establishing that it complies with the conditions laid down in Part III of Schedule 3, or, in the case of seed imported from a Member State or Northern Ireland it has been established by documentary evidence that it complies with the conditions laid down in Part III of Schedule 3;

(iii) except in a sealed package, the sealing device of which shall be such as shall become unserviceable when the package is opened; and

(iv) in any seed testing year unless either—

(aa) it has been officially tested and a Test Certificate issued in respect of it during the same seed testing year as that in which it is marketed, or

(bb) in the case of seed imported from a Member State or Northern Ireland, the seed has been tested for the purpose of giving the results required to be given in a Test Certificate during the same seed testing year as that in which it is marketed,

provided that seed marketed during August or September of any seed testing year shall be deemed to comply with the foregoing provisions of this subparagraph if the seed was tested in any of the months of the preceding seed testing year other than the month of August.

(2) Any forest reproductive material, the marketing of which is prohibited under paragraph (1) of this regulation may, if the Commissioners so authorise by licence in writing, be marketed during such period or periods and subject to such conditions as the Commissioners may prescribe or impose.

(3) No parts of plants shall be marketed under the description "EEC Standard" unless they comply with the conditions set out in Schedule 5.

(4) No young plants shall be marketed under the description "EEC Standard" unless they comply with the conditions set out in Schedule 6.

(5) Paragraph (1)(*a*) of this regulation shall not apply to reproductive material intended for use in tests or for scientific purposes or for selection work, and paragraph (1)(*b*) of this regulation shall not apply to seed intended for use in tests or for scientific purposes.

(6) In this regulation "seed testing year" means the period beginning with the 1st day of August in any calendar year and ending with the 31st day of July in the next calendar year.

Supplier's Certificate

14.—(1) A person who sells any lot of forest reproductive material shall at the time of sale or delivery of the lot or within a reasonable period thereafter furnish to the buyer a supplier's certificate relating to that lot.

(2) Subject to paragraph (3) of this regulation, a supplier's certificate, for the purpose of this regulation, means a document in writing giving the particulars specified in Part I of Schedule 7 and, in addition,—

(*a*) in the case of seed, the particulars specified in Part II of Schedule 7, or

(*b*) in the case of young plants or parts of plants sold or delivered under the description "EEC Standard", the particulars specified in Part III of Schedule 7.

(3) It shall not be necessary for a supplier's certificate—

(*a*) in relation to parts of plants or young plants taken, raised or marketed for export to countries other than Member States, to give the particulars specified in items 1, 5, 6, 7, 8, 9 and 10 of Part I of Schedule 7;

(*b*) in relation to seed or cones of such of the genera and species listed in Schedule 1 as are coniferous collected before 1st July 1973, to give the particulars referred to in subparagraph (*a*) of this paragraph until 1st July 1975; or

(*c*) in relation to young plants raised from seed collected, or parts of plants taken, before 1st July 1973, to give the particulars referred to in the said subparagraph (*a*) until 1st July 1977.

(4) The particulars required to be furnished in a supplier's certificate relating to seed shall, in relation to items 3, 4, 5 and 6 of Part II of Schedule 7,—

(*a*) in the case of seed imported from a Member State or Northern Ireland, correspond to the relevant information set out in a test certificate, a supplier's certificate or an equivalent document relating to that seed, or

(b) in the case of any other seed, correspond to the test results declared in the Test Certificate relating to that seed.

PART IV

IMPORTATION OF FOREST REPRODUCTIVE MATERIAL

Importation of forest reproductive material from Member States

15. Forest reproductive material shall not be imported into Great Britain from a Member State unless accompanied by an official certificate of provenance or clonal identity issued by a competent authority of that State in the form set out in Schedule 8, or in a form to the like effect, which shall be produced by the importer or consignee to the proper officer of Customs and Excise at the time of importation.

Importation from countries not being Member States

16.—(1) Forest reproductive material shall not be imported into Great Britain from a country which is not a Member State unless—

(a) it is accompanied by an official certificate of provenance or clonal identity issued by a competent authority of that State in the form set out in Schedule 8, or a form to the like effect, and

(b) an import licence in respect of it has been issued by the Commissioners, and

(c) both the said certificate and the said import licence are produced by the importer or consignee to the proper officer of Customs and Excise at the time of importation.

(2) An application for an import licence shall be made to the Commissioners, who may grant the licence, grant it subject to conditions, or refuse it.

PART V

MISCELLANEOUS

Keeping and retention of records

17. Any person concerned in the collection, taking, extraction, processing, storage, transportation, raising or marketing of forest reproductive material shall

(a) keep or cause to be kept, if so required by a notice in writing served on him by the Commissioners, such records relating to those activities and in such form as may be specified in the said notice, and shall retain or cause to be retained all such records for the period of time specified in the said notice, and

(b) furnish to the Commissioners on request such information relating to those records as they may require.

Production of records

18. Any person concerned in the collection, taking, extraction, processing, storage, transportation, raising or marketing of forest reproductive material shall on request produce to an authorised officer of the Commissioners, and allow the officer to take copies of,—

(a) records kept by him or on his behalf in pursuance of regulation 17,

(b) certificates or licences issued to him under these regulations, and copies in his possession of such certificates or licences the originals of which have been issued to other persons, and

(c) books or records (other than those kept in pursuance of regulation 17) in his possession or control relating to those activities.

Sampling

19.—(1) A sample of seed to be taken by an authorised officer of the Commissioners in exercise of the powers conferred by section 25(5) of the Act for the purposes of enforcement of these regulations shall be taken in accordance with the rules laid down in Part II of Schedule 3.

(2) A sample of seed taken by an authorised officer shall be divided by him into four parts, of which one part shall be delivered or sent by him to the owner of the seed or his representative, two parts shall be delivered or sent to the officer in charge of the official testing station, and the remaining part shall be retained by the authorised officer and be available for production to a court in accordance with section 26(7) of the Act.

(3) A certificate of the result of a test of a sample of seed taken by an authorised officer for the purposes of Part II of the Act shall be in the form set out in Schedule 9.

In Witness whereof the official seal of the Minister of Agriculture, Fisheries and Food is hereunto affixed on

L.S.   *Joseph Godber*,
                              Minister of Agriculture, Fisheries and Food.

21st May 1973.

                                                    Gordon Campbell,
                                          Secretary of State for Scotland.

22nd May 1973.

                                                    Peter Thomas,
                                          Secretary of State for Wales.

22nd May 1973.

SCHEDULE 1

Regulation 3(2).

Forest Reproductive Material to which these Regulations apply

1. Reproductive material derived from:

English Name	Botanical Name	Synonym
Silver fir	*Abies alba* Mill.	*Abies pectinata* D C
Beech	*Fagus sylvatica* L.	
European larch	*Larix decidua* Mill.	
Japanese larch	*Larix leptolepis* (Sieb. & Zucc.) Gord.	
Norway spruce	*Picea abies* Karst.	*Picea excelsa* Link
Sitka spruce	*Picea sitchensis* Trautv. et Mey.	*Picea menziesii* Carr.
Austrian and Corsican pine	*Pinus nigra* Arn.	*Pinus laricio* Poir.
Scots pine	*Pinus sylvestris* L.	
Weymouth pine	*Pinus strobus* L.	
Douglas fir	*Pseudotsuga taxifolia* (Poir.) Britt.	*Pseudotsuga douglasii* Carr. *Pseudotsuga menziesii* (Mirb.) Franco
Red Oak	*Quercus borealis* Michx.	*Quercus rubra* Du Roi
Pedunculate oak	*Quercus pedunculata* Ehrh.	*Quercus robur* L.
Sessile oak	*Quercus sessiliflora* Sal.	*Quercus petraea* Liebl.

2. Vegetative reproductive material derived from:

Poplar	*Populus* species	

SCHEDULE 2

Regulation 6.

Criteria for the Approval of Basic Material

A. *Stands*

1. Location—Stands shall be situated at a sufficient distance from poor stands of the same species or from stands of a related species which can form hybrids with the species in question.

2. Uniformity—Stands shall show no more than a normal degree of individual variation in respect of morphological characteristics.

3. Volume production—Where volume production is an essential criterion for approval it must be superior to the accepted mean under similar ecological conditions.

4. Wood quality—The quality of wood shall be taken into account and may in certain circumstances be an essential criterion.

5. Morphology—Stands must show particulary good morphological features, especially in respect of stem straightness, branch habit, branch size and natural pruning.

6. Health—Stands shall be generally healthy and show maximum resistance to harmful organisms and to adverse external conditions.

7. Effective size of population—Stands shall consist of a sufficient number of trees to ensure adequate interpollination and avoid the unfavourable effects of inbreeding.

8. Age—Stands shall consist of trees of such an age that the above criteria can be clearly judged.

B. *Conservation Seed Orchards*

Conservation seed orchards shall be established in a manner that will ensure that the seed collected will represent at least the average genetic quality of the basic material forming the seed orchard.

C. *Clones*

1. Items 3, 4, 5, 6 and 8 of Part A shall apply in so far as they are appropriate.

2. Clones must be identifiable by distinctive characteristics.

3. The value of clones shall be established by experience or be demonstrated by sufficiently prolonged tests.

Regulations 8, 13(1) and 19(1).

SCHEDULE 3

Seed Testing

Regulation 8.

PART I

Procedure for Applying for a Seed Test

1. Applications for a seed test shall be made in writing to the officer in charge of the official testing station at the Forestry Commission Research Station, Alice Holt Lodge, Wrecclesham, Farnham, Surrey.

2. The sample of the seed to be tested shall be enclosed in one of the standard seed envelopes obtainable from the official testing station or in an envelope of a similar kind and having an equivalent durability, which envelope shall be packed in a protective outer cover to prevent damage during transit.

3. The following particulars shall be written on the outside of the seed envelope:—

    (i) Full name and address of sender.

    (ii) Date of sampling.

    (iii) Species, and sub-species (if any) and variety (if any) of the seed.

    (iv) Stock number or reference.

    (v) Quantity of seed represented by the sample.

    (vi) The number of the master or other certificate of provenance (if any).

    (vii) A statement as to whether or not the seed is or has been kept in cold storage.

Regulations 8 and 19(1).

PART II

Rules for the Sampling of Seed

A. *Sampling Procedure*

1. Prior to sampling a seed lot shall be well mixed so as to be as uniform among its parts as is practicable.

2. When the seed lot is in sacks or containers of similar size the number of sacks or containers to be sampled shall be in accordance with the following table:—

No. of sacks or other containers	Minimum No. of sacks or other containers to be sampled
1—5 (inclusive)	Sample each container
6—30 (inclusive)	Sample at least 1 in every 3 containers, but never less than 5.
31 or more	Sample at least 1 in every 5 containers but never less than 10.

3. The samples shall be taken in the following manner:—

(*a*) Seed in full sacks or other containers:

The sampled sacks or other containers shall be chosen at random and in all cases seed shall be taken from the top, middle and bottom of each selected sack or container.

Wherever practicable seed in sacks or other containers shall be sampled with a stick trier designed for the kind of seed of which and size of container from which the sample is being taken, and of sufficient length to reach beyond the middle of the sack when inserted from the side.

The trier shall consist of a hollow metal tube inside a closely-fitting outer shell or sleeve which has a solid pointed end. Internally the tube shall be divded by transverse partitions into a number of compartments, and the tube and sleeve shall have open slots in their walls so arranged that when the tube is turned until the slots in the tube and sleeve are in line, seed can flow into the compartments of the tube and when the sleeve is turned the openings are closed. The closed trier should be inserted diagonally across the container, opened and gently agitated so that its compartments fill with seed, then closed carefully to avoid damage to the seed, and withdrawn and emptied. When it is not practicable to use a stick trier portions may be taken by hand, care being taken to keep the fingers tightly closed about the seed so that none may escape as the hand is withdrawn.

If necessary, in order to reach the lower levels, parts of the contents shall be emptied into another sack or other container.

(*b*) Seed in a partly filled sack or other container:

The seed shall be thoroughly mixed by hand and small portions taken from at least five different positions.

(*c*) Seed in bulk:

Portions of seed shall be taken with a stick sampler or by hand from at least the number of positions indicated in the following table:—

Size of bulk	Number of positions to be sampled
Up to 50 kg	Not less than 3
51 to 1500 kg	Not less than 5
1501 to 3000 kg	At least 1 for each 300 kg
over 3000 kg	Not less than 10

Samples shall be taken at random so that portions are taken from different depths.

(*d*) Seed in a cleaning, mixing or dressing machine:

Portions of seed shall be drawn during the cleaning, mixing or dressing process so that the entire cross section of the seed stream is uniformly sampled at regular intervals throughout the whole of the process. The frequency shall be at least as indicated in the following table:—

Size of lot	Number of times to be sampled
Up to 50 kg	Not less than 3
51 to 1500 kg	Not less than 5
1501 to 3000 kg	At least 1 for each 300 kg
Over 3000 kg	Not less than 10

4. When individual portions taken from the bulk together exceed the amounts required, they shall be put together in a clean receptacle and well mixed. Where the aggregate sample so obtained exceeds the amount required it shall be reduced by using an efficient mechanical seed divider or by employing the "halving method", that is to say by dividing the aggregate sample into two equal parts, rejecting one of them, and so on in this manner until the amount required is attained.

B. *Minimum Weights of or Number of Seeds in Samples to be Submitted for Testing and Maximum Weights of or Number of Seeds in Lots Sampled*

The minimum weights or numbers of seeds to be submitted for testing and the maximum weights of or the maximum number of seeds in lots sampled shall be as set out in the table which follows:—

Species	Minimum sample weight (gm)	Maximum lot weight (kg)
(a) *Abies alba* Mill.	240	
Fagus sylvatica L.	1000	
Larix decidua Mill.	25	
Larix leptolepis (Sieb. & Zucc.) Gord.	25	
Picea abies Karst.	25	
Picea sitchensis Trautv. et Hey.	25	1000
Pinus nigra Arn.	80	
Pinus sylvestris L.	40	
Pinus strobus L.	90	
Pseudotsuga taxifolia (Poir.) Britt.	60	

Species	Minimum number of seeds in sample	Maximum number of seeds in lots
(b) *Quercus borealis* Michx.	500	
Quercus pedunculata Ehrh.	500	5000
Quercus sessiliflora Sal.	500	

Regulations 8 and 13(1).   PART III

Conditions which Seed must Satisfy

1. Seed shall comply with the conditions as to maximum permitted percentage by weight of seed of other forest tree species set out in the following table:—

Species from which seed derived	Maximum permitted percentage by weight of seed of other forest tree species
Abies alba Mill.	0·1%
Fagus sylvatica L.	0·1%
Larix decidua Mill.	0·5% (or 1·0% of other *Larix* seed)
Larix leptolepis (Sieb. & Zucc.) Gord.	0·5% (or 1·0% of other *Larix* seed)
Picea abies Karst.	0·5%
Picea sitchensis Trautv. et Mey.	0·5%
Pinus nigra Arn.	0·5%
Pinus sylvestris L.	0·5%
Pinus strobus L.	0·5%
Pseudotsuga taxifolia (Poir.) Britt.	0·5%
Quercus borealis Michx.	0·1% (or 1% of other *Quercus* seed)
Quercus pedunculata Ehrh.	0·1% (or 1% of other *Quercus* seed)
Quercus sessiliflora Sal.	0·1% (or 1% of other *Quercus* seed)

2. Seed shall, as far as practicable, be free from harmful organisms which might reduce its quality.

PART IV Regulations 8 and 13(1).

Test Certificate

No.............................

The Official Seed Testing Station for Forest Reproductive
Material for Great Britain

Forestry Commission Research Station
Alice Holt Lodge
Wrecclesham, Farnham, Surrey.

Sender of Sample: Name:

Address:

Description of Sample: Species:

Stock No. or reference:

Quantity represented:

Number of master or other certificate of
provenance (if any):

Date of sampling:

Date received:

It is hereby certified that the results of the official test are as follows:—

1. Percentage by weight of seed of other forest species:

2. Other particulars:

    (*a*) Percentage of purity:

    (*b*) Percentage of germination:

    (*c*) Number per kilogramme of live seeds capable of germinating:

    (*d*) Weight of 1000 pure seeds in grammes:

3. Remarks:

Officer in Charge
Date

SCHEDULE 4 Regulation 10(3) and (4).

Master Certificate of Provenance(1)

Master Certificate of Clonal Identity(1)

Certificate No..

This is to certify that the forest reproductive material listed below is correctly described
and is approved for marketing in accordance with the Forest Reproductive Material
Regulations 1973.

1. Type of Material: Seed/Young Plants/Parts of Plants(1):

2. Genus and species, sub-species, variety (1):

    (*a*) Common name:

    (*b*) Botanical name:

3. Clone, for vegetative reproductive material(1):

4. Region of Provenance (1):

5. Origin: Indigenous/Non-indigenous(1):

6. Year in which the seed shall have ripened(1):

7. Quantity of material:

8. Additional information (1):

Signed:
(Authorised by the Forestry
    Commission)
Address:

(Stamp of Forestry Commission)

Date:

Note:
(¹) Delete words which do not apply

Regulation 13(3).   **SCHEDULE 5**

Conditions which Parts of Plants must satisfy

1. Lots shall include at least 95% of parts of plants of fair marketable quality.

2. Fair marketable quality shall be determined by reference to the criteria relating to general characteristics, health and, where appropriate size, set out in the two following paragraphs.

3. Populus species:

(1) General characteristics and health

Parts of plants shall not be considered to be of fair marketable quality if:

(a) the wood is unripe;

(b) the wood is more than two seasons old;

(c) they have abnormalities of form, such as forking, branching or excessive bending;

(d) they have less than two well-formed buds;

(e) they have not been severed with a clean cut;

(f) they are partly or totally dried out, injured or have the bark detached from the wood;

(g) they are affected by necroses or damage caused by harmful organisms;

(h) they have any other defects wihch reduce their value for reproductive purposes;

except that paragraphs (a), (b), (c) and (d) shall not apply to root cuttings and soft wood cuttings.

(2) Minimum dimensions of parts of the plants of the Aigeiros section, other than root cuttings and soft wood cuttings:

(a)—minimum length: 20 cm.

(b)—minimum top diameter:

    8 mm for those described as Class 1/EEC

    10 mm for those described as Class 2/EEC

4. Forest Species other than Populus:

General characteristics and health

Parts of plants shall not be considered to be of fair marketable quality if:

(a) they have abnormalities of form or insufficient vigour;

(b) they have not been severed by a clean cut;

(c) their age or size makes them unsuitable for propagation purposes;

(d) they are partially or totally dried out or show injury other than wounds incurred in the taking of cuttings;

(e) they are affected by necroses or are damaged by harmful organisms;

(f) they have any other defects which reduce their value for reproductive purposes.

NOTE: All these criteria shall be considered in relation to the species or clones in question.

SCHEDULE 6 Regulation 13(4).

Conditions which Young Plants must satisfy

1. Lots shall include at least 95% of young plants of fair marketable quality.

2. Fair marketable quality shall be determined by reference to the criteria relating to general characteristics, health, age and size, set out in paragraphs 3 and 4 below.

3. General characteristics and health

An asterisk in the following table shows for each genus and species in question the defects which prevent young plants from being classified as of fair marketable quality. All these criteria shall be considered in relation to the species or clone in question and to the suitability of the reproductive material for forestry purposes.

Defects which prevent young plants from being classed as of fair marketable quality	Abies alba, Picea	Larix	Pinus	Pseudotsuga taxifolia	Fagus sylvatica, Quercus	Populus sp
(a) young plants with unhealed wounds						
—except cutting wounds where excess leaders have been removed	*	*	*	*	*	*
—except other such wounds incurred in the taking of cuttings	*	*	*	*		*
—except branch wounds	*	*	*	*	*	*
(b) young plants partially or totally dried out	*	*	*	*	*	*
(c) stem showing considerable bending	*			*		*
(d) multiple stem	*	*	*	*	*	*
(e) stem with several leaders	*	*	*			*
(f) stem and branches incompletely ripened	*(1)		*(1)			*(2)
(g) stem without a healthy terminal bud	*(1)	*(1)	*(1)	*(1)		
(h) branching either absent or clearly insufficient	*			*		
(i) youngest needles so seriously damaged as to endanger the survival of the plant	*		*	*		
(k) damaged root collar(4)	*	*	*	*	*	*(3)
(l) main roots seriously entwined or twisted(4)	*	*	*	*	*	
(m) secondary roots either absent or severely cut	*	*	*	*	*(5)	
(n) young plants showing serious damage caused by harmful organisms	*	*	*	*	*	*
(o) young plants showing signs of heating, fermentation or mould following storage in the nursery.	*	*	*	*	*	*

(1) Except where the young plants were taken from the nursery during the first growing season.
(2) Not applicable to clones of *Populus deltoides angulata*.
(3) Not applicable to *Populus* plants butt trimmed in the nursery.
(4) Not applicable to sets.
(5) Not applicable to *Quercus borealis*.

4. Age and size

A *Species other than Populus*

(a) Criteria of age and size of young plants shall not apply to young plants which have not been transplanted.

(b) Minimum standards for age and size are listed in the table below:

	Normal young plants			Stocky young plants		
	Max. age in years (See Note 1 below)	Height in cm (See Note 2 below)	Min. diameter of root collar (mm)	Max. age in years (See Note 1 below)	Height in cm (See Note 2 below)	Min. diameter of root collar (mm)
Abies alba	4	10–15	4	4	10–15	4
	5	15–25	5	4	15–20	5
	5	25–35	5	5	20–25	6
	5	35–45	6	5	25–35	7
	5	45–60	8	5	35–40	8
	—	60 and over	10	—	40 and over	10
Larix	2	20–35	4			
	3	35–50	5			
	4	50–65	6			
	4	65–80	7			
	5	80–90	8			
	5	90 and over	10			
Picea abies	3	15–25	4	4	15–20	4
	4	25–40	5	4	20–30	5
	5	40–55	6	5	30–40	6
	5	55–65	7	5	40–50	8
	5	65–80	9	5	50–60	9
	—	80 and over	10	—	60 and over	10
Picea sitchensis	3	20–30	4			
	4	30–50	5			
	4	50–65	6			
	5	65–75	8			
	5	75–85	9			
	—	85 and over	10			
Pinus sylvestris	2	6–15	3	2	6–10	3
	3	15–25	4	3	10–20	4
	3	25–35	5	3	20–30	5
	3	35–45	6	3	30–40	6
	4	45–55	7	4	40–50	7
				—	50 and over	8
Pinus nigra (forma *austriaca*)	2	6–15	3	2	6–10	3
	3	15–25	4	3	10–20	4
	4	25–35	5	4	20–30	5
	4	35–45	6	4	30–40	6
	4	45–55	7	4	40–50	7
				—	50 and over	8
Pinus nigra (other than forma *austriaca*)	2	5–10	3			
	3	10–20	4			
	3	20–30	5			
	4	30–40	6			
	4	40–50	7			
	—	50 and over	8			

	Normal young plants			Stocky young plants		
	Max. age in years (See Note 1 below)	Height in cm (See Note 2 below)	Min. diameter of root collar (mm)	Max. age in years (See Note 1 below)	Height in cm (See Note 2 below)	Min. diameter of root collar (mm)
Pinus strobus	2	6–10	3			
	3	10–20	4			
	4	20–30	5			
	4	30–40	6			
	5	40–50	7			
	5	50–60	8			
	5	60 and over	10			
Pseudotsuga taxifolia	2	20–25	3	3	20–25	4
	3	25–30	4	4	25–35	5
	3	30–40	5	4	35–40	6
	4	40–50	6	4	40–45	6
	4	50–60	7	4	45–55	7
	4	60–70	8	4	55–65	8
	4	70–80	9	4	65–70	9
	4	80–100	12	—	70 and over	12
	—	100 and over	14			
Fagus sylvatica, Quercus	2	15–25	4			
	3	25–40	5			
	4	40–55	6			
	4	55–70	7			
	5	70–85	9			
	—	85 and over	11			

NOTES:

1. Age: Age is expressed in complete years. Each growing season or part thereof shall count as a complete year. The growing season shall be considered as having begun:

—in the case of plants with a terminal shoot not yet containing a dormant terminal bud, when this shoot is not less than one quarter of the length of the previous year's shoot.

—in the case of young plants with a shorter terminal shoot, when this shoot contains a dormant bud.

2. Height: Height shall be measured to within plus or minus 1 centimetre in the case of young plants not exceeding 30 centimetres in height, and to within plus or minus 2·5 centimetres in the case of young plants exceeding 30 centimetres in height.

B *Populus*

(a) Age of young plants

The maximum age shall be four years for the stem and, where appropriate, five years for the root.

(b) Size standards shall apply only to *Populus* plants of the *Aigeiros* section, and shall be as set out in the following table:

Age	Point of diameter measure- ment	EEC Classifi- cation Number	Diameter (mm)	Height (m)	
				min.	max.
0 + 1	0·50 m	N 1 a	6 to 8	1·00	1·50
		N 1 b	more than 8 but not more than 10	1·00	1·75
		N 1 c	more than 10 but not more than 12	1·00	2·00
		N 1 d	more than 12 but not more than 15	1·00	2·25
		N 1 e	more than 15 but not more than 20	1·00	2·50
		N 1 f	20	1·00	—
more than 1 year	1 m	N 2	more than 8 but not more than 10	1·75	2·50
		N 3	more than 10 but not more than 15	1·75	3·00
		N 4	more than 15 but not more than 20	1·75	3·50
		N 5	more than 20 but not more than 25	2·25	4·00
		N 6	more than 25 but not more than 30	2·25	4·75
		N 7	more than 30 but not more than 40	2·75	5·75
		N 8	more than 40 but not more than 50	2·75	6·75
		N 9	50	4·00	—

Regulation 14.

SCHEDULE 7

Particulars required in a Supplier's Certificate

PART I

Particulars to be furnished in every case

1. The number of the Master Certificate, if any, or the number, if any, of the certificate of provenance or clonal identity and the name of the country issuing it.

2. Type of material, whether seed, cones, parts of plants or young plants.

3. Quantity of material being marketed.

4. Botanical name: genus and species.

5. Clone, in the case of vegetative material.

6.   (i) Region of provenance, in the case of material produced by sexual means from basic material registered in accordance with regulation 6 or otherwise officially approved for marketing within the Member States.

  (ii) Place of provenance and its altitude, in the case of material produced by sexual means from basic material not registered in accordance with regulation 6 or otherwise officially approved within the Member States, but which has been authorised for marketing in accordance with regulation 13(2).

7. Origin: whether indigenous or non-indigenous.

8. If the forest reproductive material although not derived from officially approved basic material is authorised for marketing under regulation 13(2), a statement to that effect.

9. If derived from conservation seed orchards a statement that the reproductive material is so derived.

10. Length of time, if any, in the seed bed and in transplant lines and the number of times transplanted.

11. Name and address of the supplier.

PART II

Further particulars to be furnished in the case of seed

1. Number of Test Certificate (if any).

2. The description "EEC Standard", OR, where the seed does not comply with the conditions laid down in Part III of Schedule 3, and is authorised for marketing under regulation 13(2), a statement that it does not so comply.

3. Percentage of purity.

4. Percentage of germination.

5. Number per kilogramme of live seeds capable of germinating.

6. Weight of 1000 pure seeds in grammes.

7. Year in which the seed shall have ripened.

8. If the seed has been kept in cold storage, a statement to that effect.

PART III

Particulars to be furnished in the case of young plants and parts of plants

1. The description "EEC Standard".

2. EEC classification number, in the case of the genus *Populus*.

3. Location of nursery in which the young plants were raised during their last growing season.

4. Age, in the case of parts of plants of the genus *Populus* which have had more than one growing season.

5. The size of the young plants.

SCHEDULE 8 Regulations 15 and 16(1).

Certificate of Provenance([1])

Certificate of Clonal Identity([1])

.... Certificate No......................
(Country)

It is certified that the forest reproductive material described below has been controlled by the competent authority and that, according to the findings made and the documents submitted, it conforms to the information given below:

1. Type of material: Seed/parts of plants/young plants([1]):

2. Genus and species, sub-species, variety, clone([1]):
   (*a*) Common name:
   (*b*) Botanical name:

3. Region of provenance([1]):
   OR
   Place of provenance and altitude([1])([2]):

4. Origin: whether indigenous or non-indigenous:

5. Year in which the seed shall have ripened([1]):

6. Length of time in nursery seed bed and in transplant lines and number of times tranplanted(^{1}):

7. Quantity of material:

8. Number and nature of packages or bundles(^{3}):

9. Marking of packages or bundles(^{3}):

10. Additional information:

.... (Signature)

(Stamp of Competent   ....(Position or rank)

Authority)

.....................................(Place and date)

Notes:

(^{1}) Delete words which do not apply.

(^{2}) For forest reproductive material not derived from basic material officially approved within the European Communities.

(^{3}) Not required when certificate is issued under regulation 10(3)(*b*) or (4)(*b*).

Regulation 19(3).   **SCHEDULE 9**

Certificate of the Result of a Test of Seeds

PLANT VARIETIES AND SEEDS ACT 1964
THE FOREST REPRODUCTIVE MATERIAL REGULATIONS 1973
REPORT
OF THE
OFFICIAL TESTING STATION FOR FOREST
REPRODUCTIVE MATERIAL IN GREAT BRITAIN
ON A SAMPLE TAKEN UNDER SECTION 25(5) OF THE ACT

on the premises of

Date received   Name:

at station:

Address:

Date of sampling: Quantity represented:
Quantity of sample: Stock No. or reference:

Description of seed given by the person on whose premises the sample was taken
Species: Country in which grown:
Sub-species (if any)   Number of test
or variety (if any):   certificate:

It is hereby certified that the results of the official test are as follows:—

1. Species:

2. Sub-species (if any) and variety (if any):

3. Percentage by weight of other forest species:

4. Percentage of purity:

5. Percentage of germination:

6. Number per kilogramme of live seeds capable of germination:

7. Weight of 1000 pure seeds in grammes:

Other particulars:

Remarks:

....
Officer in Charge
....
Date

EXPLANATORY NOTE

(This Note is not part of the Regulations.)

These Regulations, which apply to Great Britain and are made under Part II of the Plant Varieties and Seeds Act 1964 as amended by the European Communities Act 1972, are concerned with forest reproduction material (seed, cones, parts of plants and young plants) of the genera and species of tree specified in Schedule 1.

The Regulations provide that forest reproductive material may not be marketed unless it is derived from basic material (stands of trees, seed orchards and clones) which has been approved and registered in Great Britain or in Northern Ireland or in another Member State of the European Communities, or has been authorised for marketing by the Forestry Commissioners. In addition they provide that seed may not (except with the authority of the Forestry Commissioners) be marketed other than under the description "EEC Standard" and unless it has been established, by a test in the official testing station in Great Britain or a test in Northern Ireland or another Member State, that it is of a certain standard. They also provide that young plants and parts of plants shall not be marketed under the description "EEC Standard" unless they satisfy certain conditions.

The Regulations further provide for the marking of forest reproductive material marketed or intended for marketing with certain particulars as to its nature and source, for the giving by sellers of supplier's certificates, for the controlling of importation, and for the keeping of records by persons trading in forest reproductive material. They also provide rules for the sampling of seed.

The Regulations do not apply to seed or cones to be exported to countries other than Member States, or to parts of plants or young plants intended for purposes other than the production of wood. Certain provisions do not apply to parts of plants or young plants to be exported to countries other than Member States.

Any contravention of these Regulations will be an offence under Part II of the Plant Varieties and Seeds Act 1964.

STATUTORY INSTRUMENTS

1973 No. 945

CUSTOMS AND EXCISE

The Import Duties (Temporary Exemptions) (No. 15) Order 1973

Made - - -	*23rd May* 1973
Laid before the House of Commons	*23rd May* 1973
Coming into Operation	*28th May* 1973

The Lords Commissioners of Her Majesty's Treasury, by virtue of the powers conferred on them by sections 1, 3(6) and 13 of the Import Duties Act 1958(a), as amended by paragraph 1 of Schedule 4 to the European Communities Act 1972(b), and of all other powers enabling them in that behalf, on the recommendation of the Secretary of State(c), hereby make the following Order:

1.— (1) This Order may be cited as the Import Duties (Temporary Exemptions) (No. 15) Order 1973 and shall come into operation on 28th May 1973.

(2) The Interpretation Act 1889(d) shall apply for the interpretation of this Order as it applies for the interpretation of an Act of Parliament.

2. The period for which, by virtue of the Import Duties (Temporary Exemptions) (No. 12) Order 1973(e):

(a) goods of subheading (A)(II) of heading 01.02 (live domestic bovine animals) of, and

(b) goods of subheading (A)(II)(a) of heading 02.01 (certain beef and veal) of,

the Customs Tariff 1959, are exempt from import duty, shall be extended up to and including 16th September 1973.

3. For the purposes of classification under the Customs Tariff 1959, insofar as that depends on the rate of duty, any goods to which Article 2 above applies shall be treated as chargeable with the same duty as if this Order had not been made.

(a) 1958 c. 6.
(c) *See* S.I. 1970/1537 (1970 III, p. 5293).
(d) 1889 c. 63.

(b) 1972 c. 68.

(e) S.I. 1973/832 (1973 I, p. 2630).

Tim Fortescue,

V. H. Goodhew,

23rd May 1973.

Two of the Lords Commissioners
of Her Majesty's Treasury.

EXPLANATORY NOTE

(This Note is not part of the Order.)

This Order continues up to and including 16th September 1973 the temporary exemption from import duty of fresh, chilled or frozen beef and veal and of live domestic bovine animals.

STATUTORY INSTRUMENTS

1973 No. 950

RESTRICTIVE TRADE PRACTICES

The Registration of Restrictive Trading Agreements (EEC Documents) Regulations 1973

Made - - -	*22nd May* 1973
Laid before Parliament	*4th June* 1973
Coming into Operation	*25th June* 1973

The Registrar of Restrictive Trading Agreements (in these regulations referred to as "the Registrar") in exercise of the powers conferred upon him by sections 11 and 19 of the Restrictive Trade Practices Act 1956(**a**) (hereinafter referred to as "the Act of 1956") and subsection (2) of section 10 of the European Communities Act 1972(**b**) hereby orders that the following regulations shall have effect: —

1.—(1) These regulations may be cited as the Registration of Restrictive Trading Agreements (EEC Documents) Regulations 1973 and shall come into operation on the 25th June 1973.

(2) The Interpretation Act 1889(**c**) shall apply to the interpretation of these regulations as it applies to the interpretation of an Act of Parliament.

2.—(1) Where in relation to any agreement which is subject to registration under the Act of 1956 any such step or any such decision as is specified in paragraph (2) hereof is or has been taken or given under or for the purposes of any directly applicable Community provision affecting that agreement, there shall be delivered or sent to the Registrar by or on behalf of the parties to that agreement the information so specified in respect of that step or decision within 30 days of the taking or giving thereof or within 30 days of the coming into operation of these regulations, whichever is the later.

(2) The steps, decisions and information referred to are the following: —

(*a*) applying for negative clearance for or notifying the agreement to the Commission of the European Communities—a copy of the application or notification submitted to the Commission;

(*b*) notification by the Commission to the parties to the agreement of the opportunity to be heard in relation to objections raised against them— a memorandum to that effect specifying the date of the notification;

(*c*) a decision of the Commission giving negative clearance in respect of the agreement—four copies of such part of the decision as sets out the effects thereof;

(**a**) 1956 c. 68. (**b**) 1972 c. 68.
(**c**) 1889 c. 63.

(*d*) a decision of the Commission pursuant to article 85(3) of the EEC Treaty given in respect of the agreement—four copies of such part of the decision as sets out the effects thereof;

(*e*) a decision of the Commission finding infringement of article 85 of the EEC Treaty by the agreement—four copies of such part of the decision as sets out the effects thereof;

(*f*) a decision of the European Court relating to any decision of the Commission hereinbefore described—four copies of such part of the decision as sets out the effects thereof.

3. The particulars of an agreement subject to registration under the Act of 1956 to be entered or filed in the register shall include a copy of any such part of a decision of the Commission of the European Communities or the European Court affecting that agreement furnished in·pursuance of regulation 2 hereof.

4. Anything required by these regulations to be delivered or sent to the Registrar shall be addressed to:—

The Registrar of Restrictive Trading Agreements (Branch R)
    Chancery House
        Chancery Lane
           London WC2A 1SP.

Rupert Sich,
Registrar of Restrictive Trading Agreements.

22nd May 1973.

EXPLANATORY NOTE
(This Note is not part of the Regulations.)

Section 10 of the European Communities Act 1972 enables the Registrar to refrain from taking proceedings before the Restrictive Practices Court in respect of an agreement where appropriate having regard to the operation of Community provisions, and by regulations to require information as to any steps taken or decisions given under or for the purpose of a Community provision affecting an agreement.

These Regulations require parties to agreements to inform the Registrar when notifying an agreement to the Commission or seeking negative clearance therefor and when proceedings are instituted and decisions given in respect of an agreement. Decisions are to be entered on the register with other particulars of the agreement and accordingly four copies are required.

STATUTORY INSTRUMENTS

1973 No. 953

WAGES COUNCILS

The Wages Regulation (General Waste Materials Reclamation) Order 1973

Made - - - -		*23rd May* 1973
Coming into Operation		*27th June* 1973

Whereas the Secretary of State has received from the General Waste Materials Reclamation Wages Council (Great Britain) the wages regulation proposals set out in the Schedule hereto;

Now, therefore, the Secretary of State in exercise of powers conferred by section 11 of the Wages Councils Act 1959(a), as modified by Article 2 of the Counter-Inflation (Modification of Wages Councils Act 1959) Order 1973(b), and now vested in him(c), and of all other powers enabling him in that behalf, hereby makes the following Order:—

1. This Order may be cited as the Wages Regulation (General Waste Materials Reclamation) Order 1973.

2.—(1) In this Order the expression "the specified date" means the 27th June 1973, provided that where, as respects any worker who is paid wages at intervals not exceeding seven days, that date does not correspond with the beginning of the period for which the wages are paid, the expression "the specified date" means, as respects that worker, the beginning of the next such period following that date.

(2) The Interpretation Act 1889(d) shall apply to the interpretation of this Order as it applies to the interpretation of an Act of Parliament and as if this Order and the Order hereby revoked were Acts of Parliament.

3. The wages regulation proposals set out in the Schedule hereto shall have effect as from the specified date and as from that date the Wages Regulation (General Waste Materials Reclamation) Order 1971(e) shall cease to have effect.

Signed by order of the Secretary of State.
23rd May 1973.

> *K. Barnes,*
> Deputy Secretary,
> Department of Employment.

(a) 1959 c. 69.   (b) S.I. 1973/661 (1973 I, p. 2141).
(c) S.I. 1959/1769, 1968/729 (1959 I, p. 1795; 1968 II, p. 2108).
(d) 1889 c. 63.   (e) S.I. 1971/2129 (1971 III, p. 6289).

ARRANGEMENT OF SCHEDULE

Article 3

SCHEDULE

The following minimum remuneration shall be substituted for the statutory minimum remuneration fixed by the Wages Regulation (General Waste Materials Reclamation) Order 1971 (Order D.B. (76)).

STATUTORY MINIMUM REMUNERATION

PART I—GENERAL

1. The minimum remuneration payable to a worker to whom this Schedule applies for all work except work to which a minimum overtime rate applies under Part IV is:—

(1) in the case of a time worker, the general minimum time rate payable to the worker under Part II or Part III of this Schedule;

(2) in the case of a male worker employed on piece work, piece rates each of which would yield, in the circumstances of the case, to an ordinary worker at least the same amount of money as the general minimum time rate which would be payable to the worker under Part II of this Schedule if he were a time worker;

(3) in the case of a female worker employed on piece work, piece rates each of which would yield, in the circumstances of the case, to an ordinary worker at least the same amount of money as the piece work basis time rate applicable to the worker under Part III of this Schedule:

Provided that where a guaranteed time rate is applicable to a female worker under paragraph 8 and the remuneration calculated on a time work basis at that rate exceeds the remuneration calculated under sub-paragraph (3) of this paragraph on the basis of the said piece rates, the worker shall be paid not less than that guaranteed time rate.

PART II

MALE WORKERS

GENERAL MINIMUM TIME RATES

2. The general minimum time rates payable to male workers employed in any section of the trade are:—

	Per hour p
Aged under 16 years	21
„ 16 and under 16½ years	25
„ 16½ „ „ 17 „	27
„ 17 „ „ 17½ „	32
„ 17½ „ „ 18 „	37
„ 18 years or over	41

PART III

FEMALE WORKERS

GENERAL MINIMUM TIME RATES

3. Subject to the provisions of paragraphs 4 and 9, the general minimum time rates payable to female workers employed—

(1) wholly or mainly on one or more of the operations of the sorting or grading of either woollen rags or woollen and worsted waste materials, or of both such rags and materials, to shade or quality or to both shade and quality, or

(2) in receiving, stripping, packing, compressing, teagling, craning, despatching or warehousing, when carried on in, or in association with, or in conjunction with, any establishment or department in which the sorting or grading of either woollen rags or woollen and worsted waste materials, or of both such rags and materials, to shade or quality or to both shade and quality, constitutes the sole or main work of the establishment or department,

are as follows:—

	Per hour p
Aged under 16 years	18
„ 16 and under 16½ years	23
„ 16½ „ „ 17 „	25
„ 17 „ „ 17½ „	30
„ 17½ „ „ 18 „	32
„ 18 years or over	37

4. Notwithstanding the provisions of paragraph 3, where a worker is employed for the first time after reaching the age of 18 years on any work therein mentioned and her employer causes her to be well and sufficiently instructed in the sorting and grading of woollen rags or woollen and worsted waste materials or of both such rags and materials, to shade or quality or to both shade and quality, the general minimum time rate payable during the periods following shall be:—

	Per hour p
during the first six months of such employment	36

5. Subject to the provisions of paragraphs 6 and 9, the general minimum time rates payable to female workers other than the workers specified in paragraph 3 or 4 are as follows:—

	Per hour p
Aged under 16 years	18
„ 16 and under 16½ years	22
„ 16½ „ „ 17 „	25
„ 17 „ „ 17½ „	29
„ 17½ „ „ 18 „	32
„ 18 years or over	36

6. Notwithstanding the provisions of paragraph 5, where a worker is employed for the first time after reaching the age of 18 years and her employer causes her to be well and sufficiently instructed in the sorting and grading of waste paper, rags, and paper-making materials, or of paper-making materials, the general minimum time rate payable shall be:—

	Per hour p
during the first six months of such employment	35

PIECE WORK BASIS TIME RATES

7. The following piece work basis time rates are applicable to female workers employed on piece work:—

	Per hour p
(1) the workers specified in paragraph 3 or 4	37
(2) all other workers	36

GUARANTEED TIME RATE

8. The guaranteed time rate applicable to a female worker specified in paragraph 4 or 6 when employed on piece work during the period of six months therein mentioned is a rate equal to the general minimum time rate which would be payable to her if she were employed on time work.

DETERMINATION OF AGE RATES

9. The general minimum time rate payable under paragraph 3 or 5 to a female worker aged under 18 years shall be determined (1) during the period 1st January to 30th June in any year by reference to her age or prospective age on 31st March in that year; and (2) during the period 1st July to 31st December in any year by reference to her age or prospective age on 30th September in that year:

Provided that the rate for a female worker aged $17\frac{1}{2}$ and under 18 years having become payable under the provisions of this paragraph shall continue to be payable only until her 18th birthday.

PART IV

OVERTIME AND WAITING TIME

MINIMUM OVERTIME RATES

10. Minimum overtime rates are payable to a worker to whom this Schedule applies as follows:—

(1) On any day other than a Saturday, Sunday or customary holiday—

for all time worked in excess of $7\frac{1}{4}$ hours ... ... time-and-a-half

Provided that where it is, or may become, the established practice of the employer to require the worker's attendance only on Monday, Tuesday, Wednesday, Thursday and Friday in the week, the overtime rate of time-and-a-half shall be payable—

after 8 hours' work on any of these days.

(2) On a Saturday, not being a customary holiday—
for all time worked in excess of $3\frac{3}{4}$ hours ... ... time-and-a-half

(3) On a Sunday or a customary holiday, for all time worked ... double time

(4) In any week, for all time worked in excess of 40 hours, exclusive of any time for which a minimum overtime rate is payable under the foregoing provisions of this paragraph ... time-and-a-half

11. In this Part of this Schedule—

(1) The expression "customary holiday" means—

(a) (i) in England and Wales—
Christmas Day;
26th December if it be not a Sunday;
27th December in a year when 25th or 26th December is a Sunday;
Good Friday;
Easter Monday;
the last Monday in May;
the last Monday in August; (or, where a day is substituted for any of
the above days by national proclamation, that day); and any day
proclaimed as an additional bank holiday or as a public holiday
throughout England and Wales;

(ii) in Scotland—
New Year's Day (or, if New Year's Day falls on a Sunday, the following Monday);
the local Spring holiday;
the local Autumn holiday;
three other days (being days on which the worker normally works) in the course of a calendar year, to be fixed by the employer and notified to the worker not less than three weeks before the holiday, and any day proclaimed *as an additional bank holiday or as a public holiday throughout Scotland;* or

(b) in the case of each of the said days (other than a day fixed by the employer in Scotland and notified to the worker as aforesaid) a day substituted by the employer therefor, being either a day recognised by local custom as a day of holiday in substitution for the said day, or a day agreed between the employer and the worker or his representative.

(2) The expressions "time-and-a-half" and "double time" mean respectively:—

(a) in the case of a time worker:—
one and a half times and twice the general minimum time rate otherwise applicable to the worker;

(b) in the case of a female worker employed on piece work:—
(i) a time rate equal respectively to one half and the whole of the piece work basis time rate otherwise applicable to the worker, and, in addition thereto,
(ii) the minimum remuneration otherwise applicable to the worker under paragraph 1(3);

(c) in the case of a male worker employed on piece work:—
(i) a time rate equal respectively to one half and the whole of the general minimum time rate which would be applicable to the worker if he were a time worker and a minimum overtime rate did not apply, and, in addition thereto,
(ii) the minimum remuneration otherwise applicable to the worker under paragraph 1(2).

WAITING TIME

12.—(1) A worker is entitled to payment of the minimum remuneration specified in this Schedule for all time during which he is present on the premises of his employer, unless he is present thereon in any of the following circumstances:—

(a) without the employer's consent, express or implied;
(b) for some purpose unconnected with his work and other than that of waiting for work to be given to him to perform;
(c) by reason only of the fact that he is resident thereon;
(d) during normal meal times in a room or place in which no work is being done, and he is not waiting for work to be given to him to perform.

(2) The minimum remuneration payable under sub-paragraph (1) of this paragraph to a piece worker when not engaged on piece work is that which would be payable if he were a time worker.

PART V

APPLICABILITY OF STATUTORY MINIMUM REMUNERATION

13. This Schedule does not apply to male workers engaged in the loading or discharging of water-borne craft in any section of the trade, but, save as aforesaid, this Schedule applies to workers in relation to whom the General Waste Materials Reclamation Wages Council (Great Britain) operates, that is to say, workers employed in Great Britain in the Waste Materials Reclamation Trade (General Waste Branch) specified in the Schedule to the General Waste Materials Reclamation Wages Council (Great Britain) (Variation) Order 1970(a), which Schedule reads as follows:—

"1. For the purposes of this Schedule:—

The expression 'reclamation' means all operations (including the operations of willowing and garnetting) performed on any waste material or waste article.

The expression 'general waste materials establishment' means an establishment in which the operations specified in paragraph 2(a) hereof and operations connected therewith constitute the principal business carried on.

The expression 'establishment' means any establishment or any branch or department of an establishment.

2. Subject to the provisions of this Schedule the General Waste Branch of the Waste Materials Reclamation trade consists of the following operations:—

(a) reclamation wherever performed of any of the following waste materials or waste articles, that is to say:— rags, waste paper and paper salvage (including paper damaged by fire, newspaper reel-ends, damaged paper reels, outer wrappers of reels and news off-cuts), paper stock, woollen, worsted, flax, or other textile waste (not being jute or cotton waste), textile clippings or cuttings, used bags, used sacks, used sackings, or used tares, scrap rubber, scrap iron or other scrap metals (other than unbroken heavy machinery or plant), fur cuttings, rabbit skins, bones and fat, used tins, used bottles or jars, old ropes or string and broken glass or earthenware;

(b) reclamation of any other waste material or article where performed in or in connection with a general waste materials establishment;

(c) making (whether from new or waste material) or repairing sacks or bags in a general waste materials establishment except where the bags are made or repaired:—

(i) otherwise than for use in the establishment, and

(ii) in an establishment wholly or mainly engaged in the making or repairing of sacks or bags;

and operations connected therewith.

3. Notwithstanding anything in this Schedule the following operations are not operations in the General Waste Branch of the Waste Materials Reclamation trade:—

(a) reclamation of any waste material or waste article in an establishment (other than a general waste materials establishment) in which that material or article is produced or is used as material for manufacture or as container or wrapper for other articles manufactured in the establishment; and operations connected therewith;

(b) reclamation of any waste material or waste article produced in the business of breaking up ships or breaking up or dismantling buildings or machinery or tramway or railway installations or heavy plant when performed in the course of such business; and operations connected therewith;

(c) reclamation of scrap rubber in an establishment in which the scrap rubber is broken down or devulcanised; and operations connected therewith;

(a) S.I. 1970/1175 (1970 II, p. 3956).

(d) reclamation of rabbit skins where performed in an establishment in which such reclamation constitutes the principal business carried on or in connection with an establishment in which the principal business carried on is the manufacture of hatters' fur; and operations connected therewith;

(e) reclamation of bottles or jars preliminary to their use in the same establishment as containers, or when such bottles or jars are the property of a trader and are used by him for the purpose of delivering the contents to a customer and are recovered when empty from the customer by or on behalf of the trader; and operations connected therewith;

(f) reclamation of jute textile cuttings and clippings where carried on in an establishment mainly engaged in operations included in the Trade Boards (Jute) Order, 1919(a), or any amendment thereof;

(g) production of shoddy or mungo or woollen flock (including sorting, willowing or garnetting) or any operations performed in an establishment in which the production of shoddy or mungo or woollen flock is the principal business carried on;

(h) de-tinning of metal or refining of old gold or silver;

(i) repairing or overhauling machinery or plant;

(j) collecting, transporting, packing, warehousing or despatching, when performed by workers in the direct employment of an employer who is not otherwise engaged in the Waste Materials Reclamation trade;

(k) cleaning or washing when performed in an establishment where the cleaning or washing is mainly of articles other than those specified in paragraph 2 hereof;

(l) cleaning of premises by charwomen;

(m) caretaking;

(n) clerical work;

(o) operations performed in or in connection with a cotton waste establishment as defined in the Schedule to the Trade Boards (Waste Materials Reclamation Trade, Great Britain) (Cotton Waste Branch) (Constitution and Proceedings) Regulations, 1929(b);

(p) all operations performed in an establishment in which the manual sorting to shade and quality of the wastes and by-products of the woollen and worsted textile processes is the sole or main activity."

EXPLANATORY NOTE

(This Note is not part of the Order.)

This Order, which has effect from 27th June 1973, sets out the statutory minimum remuneration payable in substitution for that fixed by the Wages Regulation (General Waste Materials Reclamation) Order 1971 (Order D.B. (76)), which Order is revoked.

New provisions are printed in italics.

(a) S.R. & O. 1919/859 (1919 II, p. 517).   (b) S.R. & O. 1929/3 (1929, p. 1378).

STATUTORY INSTRUMENTS

1973 No. 954

WAGES COUNCILS

The Wages Regulation (General Waste Materials Reclamation) (Holidays) Order 1973

Made - - - -	23rd *May* 1973
Coming into Operation	27th *June* 1973

Whereas the Secretary of State has received from the General Waste Materials Reclamation Wages Council (Great Britain) the wages regulation proposals set out in the Schedule hereto;

Now, therefore, the Secretary of State in exercise of powers conferred by section 11 of the Wages Councils Act 1959(a), as modified by Article 2 of the Counter-Inflation (Modification of Wages Councils Act 1959) Order 1973(b), and now vested in him(c), and of all other powers enabling him in that behalf, hereby makes the following Order:—

1. This Order may be cited as the Wages Regulation (General Waste Materials Reclamation) (Holidays) Order 1973.

2.—(1) In this Order the expression "the specified date" means the 27th June 1973, provided that where, as respects any worker who is paid wages at intervals not exceeding seven days, that date does not correspond with the beginning of the period for which the wages are paid, the expression "the specified date" means, as respects that worker, the beginning of the next such period following that date.

(2) The Interpretation Act 1889(d) shall apply to the interpretation of this Order as it applies to the interpretation of an Act of Parliament and as if this Order and the Order hereby revoked were Acts of Parliament.

3. The wages regulation proposals set out in the Schedule hereto shall have effect as from the specified date and as from that date the Wages Regulation (General Waste Materials Reclamation) (Holidays) Order 1970(e), shall cease to have effect.

Signed by order of the Secretary of State.
23rd May 1973.

K. Barnes,
Deputy Secretary,
Department of Employment.

(a) 1959 c. 69.   (b) S.I. 1973/661 (1973 I, p. 2141).
(c) S.I. 1959/1769, 1968/729 (1959 I, p. 1795; 1968 II, p. 2108).
(d) 1889 c. 63.   (e) S.I. 1970/1315 (1970 III, p. 4404).

Article 3

SCHEDULE

The following provisions as to holidays and holiday remuneration shall be substituted for the provisions as to holidays and holiday remuneration set out in the Wages Regulation (General Waste Materials Reclamation) (Holidays) Order 1970 (Order D.B. (74)).

PART I

APPLICATION

1. This Schedule applies to every worker for whom statutory minimum remuneration has been fixed.

PART II

CUSTOMARY HOLIDAYS

2.—(1) An employer shall allow to every worker to whom this Schedule applies a holiday (hereinafter referred to as a "customary holiday") in each year on the days specified in the following sub-paragraph provided that the worker has been in his employment for a period of not less than four weeks immediately preceding the customary holiday and (unless excused by the employer or absent by reason of the proved illness of, or accident to, the worker) has worked for the employer throughout the last working day on which work was available to him immediately preceding the customary holiday.

(2) The said customary holidays are:—

(a) (i) In England and Wales—

Christmas Day;
26th December if it be not a Sunday;
27th December in a year when 25th or 26th December is a Sunday;
Good Friday;
Easter Monday;
the last Monday in May;
the last Monday in August; (or, where a day is substituted for any of the above days by national proclamation, that day); and any day proclaimed as an additional bank holiday or as a public holiday throughout England and Wales;

(ii) In Scotland—

New Year's Day (or, if New Year's Day falls on a Sunday, the following Monday);
the local Spring holiday;
the local Autumn holiday; and
three other days (being days on which the worker normally works for the employer) in the course of a calendar year to be fixed by the employer and notified to the worker not less than three weeks before the holiday; *and any day proclaimed as an additional bank holiday or as a public holiday throughout Scotland;*

or (b) in the case of each of the said days (other than a day fixed by the employer in Scotland and notified to the worker as aforesaid) a day substituted by the employer therefor, being a day recognised by local custom as a day of holiday in substitution for the said day, or a day substituted therefor by mutual agreement between the employer and the worker or his representative.

PART III

ANNUAL HOLIDAY

3.—(1) Subject to the provisions of this paragraph and paragraph 4, in addition to the holidays specified in Part II of this Schedule an employer shall, between the date on which this Schedule becomes effective, and 30th September 1973, and between 1st May and 30th September in each succeeding year allow a holiday (hereinafter referred to as an "annual holiday") to every worker in his employment to whom this Schedule applies who has been employed by him during the 12 months immediately preceding the commencement of the holiday season for any of the periods of employment (calculated in accordance with the provisions of paragraph 10) set out in the appropriate column of the Table below and the duration of the annual holiday shall in the case of each such worker be related to his period of employment during that 12 months as follows:—

Workers with a normal working week of six days		Workers with a normal working week of five days or less	
Period of employment	Duration of annual holiday	Period of employment	Duration of annual holiday
At least 48 weeks	18 days	At least 48 weeks	15 days
„ „ 44 „	11 „	„ „ 43 „	9 „
„ „ 40 „	10 „	„ „ 38 „	8 „
„ „ 36 „	9 „	„ „ 33 „	7 „
„ „ 32 „	8 „	„ „ 28 „	6 „
„ „ 28 „	7 „	„ „ 24 „	5 „
„ „ 24 „	6 „	„ „ 19 „	4 „
„ „ 20 „	5 „	„ „ 14 „	3 „
„ „ 16 „	4 „	„ „ 9 „	2 „
„ „ 12 „	3 „	„ „ 4 „	1 day
„ „ 8 „	2 „		
„ „ 4 „	1 day		

(2) Notwithstanding the provisions of the last foregoing sub-paragraph, the number of days of annual holiday which an employer is required to allow to a worker in respect of a period of employment during the 12 months immediately preceding 1st May 1973 and during the 12 months immediately preceding 1st May in any succeeding year shall not exceed in the aggregate three times the number of days constituting the worker's normal working week.

(3) The duration of the worker's annual holiday during the holiday season ending on 30th September 1973, shall be reduced by any days of annual holiday duly allowed to him by the employer under the provisions of Order D.B. (74) between 1st May 1973 and the date on which the provisions of this Schedule become effective.

(4) In this Schedule the expression "holiday season" means in relation to the year 1973 the period commencing on 1st May 1973 and ending on 30 September 1973 and, in each succeeding year, the period commencing on 1st May and ending on 30th September of the same year.

4.—(1) Subject to the provisions of this paragraph, an annual holiday shall be allowed on consecutive working days, being days on which the worker is normally called upon to work for the employer.

(2)(a) Where the number of days of annual holiday for which a worker has qualified exceeds the number of days constituting his normal working week, but does not exceed twice that number, the holiday may be allowed in two periods of consecutive working days; so, however, that when a holiday is so allowed, one of the periods shall consist of a number of such days not less than the number of days constituting the worker's normal working week.

(b) Where the number of days of annual holiday for which a worker has qualified exceeds twice the number of days constituting his normal working week the holiday may be allowed as follows:—

    (i) as to two periods of consecutive working days, each such period not being less than the period constituting the worker's normal working week, during the holiday season; and

    (ii) as to the additional days, on working days, to be fixed by agreement between the employer or his representative, and the worker or his representative, either during the holiday season or within the period ending on 30th April immediately following the holiday season.

(3) For the purposes of this paragraph, days of annual holiday shall be treated as consecutive notwithstanding that a customary holiday or a day upon which the worker does not normally work for the employer intervenes.

(4) Where a customary holiday immediately precedes a period of annual holiday or occurs during such a period and the total number of days of annual holiday required to be allowed in the period under the foregoing provisions of this paragraph, together with any such customary holiday, exceeds the number of days constituting the worker's normal working week then, notwithstanding the foregoing provisions of this paragraph, the duration of that period of annual holiday may be reduced by one day and in such a case one day of annual holiday may be allowed on any working day (not being the worker's weekly short day) in the holiday season.

(5) Subject to the provisions of the foregoing sub-paragraphs of this paragraph, any day of annual holiday under this Schedule may be allowed on a day on which the worker is entitled to a day of holiday or to a half-holiday under any enactment other than the Wages Councils Act 1959.

5. An employer shall give to a worker reasonable notice of the commencing date or dates and duration of the period or periods of his annual holiday. Such notice may be given individually to the worker or by the posting of a notice in the place where the worker is employed.

PART IV

HOLIDAY REMUNERATION

A—CUSTOMARY HOLIDAYS

6.—(1) Subject to the provisions of this paragraph, for each day of customary holiday to which a worker is entitled under Part II of this Schedule he shall be paid by the employer holiday remuneration equal to the appropriate statutory minimum remuneration to which he would have been entitled as a time worker if the day had not been a day of holiday and he had been employed on work for which statutory minimum remuneration is payable for the time usually worked by him on that day of the week:

Provided, however, that payment of the said holiday remuneration is subject to the condition that the worker (unless excused by the employer or absent by reason of the proved illness of, or accident to, the worker) presents himself for employment at the usual starting hour on the first working day following the customary holiday and works throughout the remainder of that day.

(2) The holiday remuneration in respect of any customary holiday shall be paid by the employer to the worker on the pay day on which the wages for the week including the first working day following the customary holiday are paid.

B—ANNUAL HOLIDAY

7.—(1) Subject to the provisions of paragraph 8, a worker qualified to be allowed an annual holiday under this Schedule shall be paid by his employer in respect thereof, on the last pay day preceding such annual holiday, one day's holiday pay (as defined in paragraph 11) in respect of each day of annual holiday.

(2) Where under the provisions of paragraph 4 an annual holiday is allowed in more than one period, the holiday remuneration shall be apportioned accordingly.

8. Where any accrued holiday remuneration has been paid by the employer to the worker in accordance with paragraph 9 of this Schedule, or in accordance with the provisions of Order D.B. (74), in respect of employment during any of the periods

referred to in that paragraph, or that Order respectively, the amount of holiday remuneration payable by the employer in respect of any annual holiday for which the worker has qualified by reason of employment during the said period shall be reduced by the amount of the said accrued holiday remuneration unless that remuneration has been deducted from a previous payment of holiday remuneration made under the provisions of this Schedule.

ACCRUED HOLIDAY REMUNERATION PAYABLE ON TERMINATION OF EMPLOYMENT

9. Where a worker ceases to be employed by an employer after the provisions of this Schedule become effective the employer shall, immediately on the termination of the employment, pay to the worker as accrued holiday remuneration:—

(1) in respect of employment in the 12 months up to and including the preceding 30th April, a sum equal to the holiday remuneration for any days of annual holiday for which he has qualified except days of annual holiday which he has been allowed or has become entitled to be allowed before leaving the employment; and

(2) in respect of any employment since the said 30th April, a sum equal to the holiday remuneration which would have been payable to him if he could have been allowed an annual holiday in respect of that employment at the time of leaving it:

Provided that—

(a) no worker shall be entitled to the payment by his employer of accrued holiday remuneration if he is dismissed on the grounds of misconduct and is so informed in writing by the employer at the time of dismissal;

(b) where a worker is employed under a contract of service under which not less than one week's notice on either side is required to terminate the employment and the worker without the consent of his employer terminates his employment—

(i) without having given not less than one week's notice, or

(ii) before one week has expired from the beginning of such notice, the amount of accrued holiday remuneration payable to the worker shall be the amount payable under the foregoing provisions of this paragraph, less an amount equal to the holiday remuneration which would be payable to the worker for one day of annual holiday multiplied, in the case of (i) by the number of days constituting the worker's normal working week or, in the case of (ii), by the number of days which at the termination of the employment would complete a normal working week commencing at the beginning of the notice.

PART V

GENERAL

10. For the purposes of calculating any period of employment qualifying a worker for an annual holiday or for any accrued holiday remuneration under this Schedule, the worker shall be treated—

(1) as if he were employed for a week in respect of any week in which—

(a) he has worked for the employer for not less than 24 hours and has performed some work for which statutory minimum remuneration is payable; or

(b) he has been absent throughout the week by reason of the proved illness of, or accident to, the worker, or for a like reason has worked for the employer for less than 24 hours: provided that the number of weeks which may be treated as weeks of employment for such reasons shall not exceed six in the aggregate in the period of 12 months immediately preceding the commencement of the holiday season; or

(c) he has been suspended throughout the week owing to shortage of work: provided that the number of weeks which may be treated as weeks of employment for such reason shall not exceed four in the aggregate in the period of 12 months last mentioned; and

(2) as if he were employed on any day of holiday allowed under the provisions of this Schedule or of Order D.B. (74), and, for the purposes of the provisions of sub-paragraph (1) of this paragraph, a worker who is absent on such a holiday shall be treated as having worked thereon the number of hours ordinarily worked by him for the employer on that day of the week on work for which statutory minimum remuneration is payable.

11. In this Schedule, unless the context otherwise requires, the following expressions have the meanings hereby respectively assigned to them, that is to say:—

"normal working week" means the number of days on which it has been usual for the worker to work in a week in the employment of the employer in the 12 months immediately preceding the commencement of the holiday season or, where under paragraph 9 accrued holiday remuneration is payable on the termination of the employment, during the 12 months immediately preceding the date of the termination of the employment:

Provided that—

(1) part of a day shall count as a day;

(2) no account shall be taken of any week in which the worker did not perform any work for which statutory minimum remuneration has been fixed.

"one day's holiday pay" means—

the appropriate proportion of the amount which the worker would be entitled to receive from his employer, at the beginning of the holiday or the first period of the holiday, as the case may be, for a week's work, if working his normal working week and the number of daily hours usually worked by him (exclusive of overtime), and if paid—

(a) in the case of a time worker, at the appropriate rate of statutory minimum remuneration for time work, for work to which that rate applies and at the same rate for work (if any) to which that rate does not apply;

(b) in the case of a piece worker, at the appropriate general minimum time rate that would have been applicable to him if he had been employed as a time worker.

In this definition "appropriate proportion" means—

where the worker's normal working week is six days ... one-sixth
   "   "   "   "   "   " " five days
or less ...   . one-fifth.

"statutory minimum remuneration" means minimum remuneration (other than holiday remuneration) fixed by a wages regulation order made by the Secretary of State to give effect to proposals submitted to him by the General Waste Materials Reclamation Wages Council (Great Britain).

"week" in paragraphs 3, 6 and 10 means "pay week".

12. The provisions of this Schedule are without prejudice to any agreement for the allowance of any further holidays with pay or for the payment of additional holiday remuneration.

EXPLANATORY NOTE

(This Note is not part of the Order.)

This Order, which has effect from 27th June 1973, sets out the holidays which an employer is required to allow to workers and the remuneration payable for those holidays, in substitution for the holidays and holiday remuneration fixed by the Wages Regulation (General Waste Materials Reclamation) (Holidays) Order 1970 (Order D.B. (74)), which Order is revoked.

New provisions are printed in italics.

STATUTORY INSTRUMENTS

1973 No. 955

CUSTOMS AND EXCISE

The Customs Duty (Personal Reliefs) (No. 1) Order 1973

Made - - - -	*24th May* 1973
Laid before the House of Commons	*1st June* 1973
Coming into Operation	*22nd June* 1973

The Commissioners of Customs and Excise, in exercise of the powers conferred upon them by section 7 of the Finance Act 1968(a) and of all other powers enabling them in that behalf, hereby make the following Order:—

1. This Order may be cited as the Customs Duty (Personal Reliefs) (No. 1) Order 1973 and shall come into operation on the 22nd June 1973.

2. In this Order—

"Accompanied baggage" in relation to a person entering the United Kingdom means baggage which he brings with him when he enters;

"Commonwealth preference" and "Commonwealth preference area" have the same meanings respectively as in the Import Duties Act 1958(b);

"Convention rate of duty" means the rate of duty applicable to goods originating in a country which at the end of 1972 was part of the Convention area within the meaning of the European Free Trade Association Act 1960(c) and "Convention area" shall be construed accordingly;

"E.E.C. rate" means the rate of duty applicable to goods originating or in free circulation in a State which is a member of the European Economic Community.

3. The Interpretation Act 1889(d) shall apply for the interpretation of this Order as it applies for the interpretation of an Act of Parliament.

4. The Customs Duty (Personal Reliefs) (No. 4) Order 1968(e), The Customs Duty (Personal Reliefs) (No. 4) Order 1968 (Amendment) Order 1971(f) and The Customs Duty (Personal Reliefs) (No. 4) Order 1968 (Amendment) Order 1972(g) are hereby revoked.

5.—(1) Subject to paragraph (3) hereof, this Article shall apply to personal effects to a total value not exceeding £25 being dutiable goods or goods on the importation of which value added tax is charged and payable by virtue of the Finance Act 1972(h) and which are carried with or contained in the accompanied baggage of a person entering the United Kingdom.

(a) 1968 c. 44.	**(b)** 1958 c. 6.
(c) 1960 c. 19.	**(d)** 1889 c. 63.
(e) S.I. 1968/1561 (1968 III, p. 4349).	**(f)** S.I. 1971/1974 (1971 III, p. 5646).
(g) S.I. 1972/872 (1972 II, p. 2800).	**(h)** 1972 c. 41.

(2) The aggregate amount payable by way of duty and value added tax in respect of goods to which this Article applies shall, unless the person entering the United Kingdom otherwise requests, be:—

(*a*) 10 per cent of the value thereof in the case of

    (i) goods which qualify for a Commonwealth preference or a Convention rate of duty or a rate of duty applicable to goods of the Republic of Ireland, or which would so qualify if consigned to the United Kingdom from a place in the Commonwealth preference area, the Convention area or the Republic of Ireland as the case may be;

    (ii) goods on the importation of which value added tax only is charged and payable; and

    (iii) goods which are relieved wholly or partly from duty by Orders made under section 1 of the Finance Act 1971(a) or which would be so relieved if consigned to the United Kingdom from a place specified in such Orders;

(*b*) 15 per cent of the value thereof in the case of goods chargeable with an E.E.C. rate of duty; and

(*c*) 20 per cent of the value thereof in the case of any other goods.

(3) This Article shall not apply to spirits, wine, tobacco or mechanical lighters.

(4) (*a*) The reference in this Article to effects to a total value not exceeding £25 is a reference either to a single thing the value of which does not exceed £25 or to two or more things the value of which taken together does not exceed £25.

(*b*) The total value of £25 shall be determined in relation to personal effects on which duty is payable after any other reliefs have been afforded.

6. Any personal effects of a person entering the United Kingdom in respect of which he is not either afforded relief from payment of duty and value added tax by virtue of any Order made under section 7 of the Finance Act 1968 or entitled by virtue of this Order to pay duty and tax at aggregate rates shall, on importation by him, be treated as though qualified for—

(*a*) Commonwealth preference;

(*b*) A Convention rate of duty;

(*c*) A rate of duty applicable to goods of the Republic of Ireland;

(*d*) An E.E.C. rate of duty; or

(*e*) Relief under section 1 of the Finance Act 1971,

in any case in which they do not so qualify by reason only of the fact that they have not been consigned to the United Kingdom from a place in the Commonwealth preference area or the Convention area or from the Republic of Ireland or from the European Economic Community or from a place designated under section 1 of the Finance Act 1971 as the case may be.

(a) 1971 c. 68.

7. Section 258 of the Customs and Excise Act 1952**(a)** (Valuation of goods) as amended by paragraph 2(8) of Schedule 4 to the European Communities Act 1972**(b)** shall apply for the purposes of this Order.

24th May 1973.

E. A. Knight,
Commissioner of Customs and Excise.

King's Beam House,
Mark Lane,
London, EC3R 7HE.

EXPLANATORY NOTE

(*This Note is not part of the Order.*)

This Order consolidates with amendments the existing simplified rules for assessing customs duty and tax on personal effects imported in passengers' baggage. The amendments are consequential upon the introduction of value added tax and upon the entry of the United Kingdom into the European Economic Community.

STATUTORY INSTRUMENTS

1973 No. 956

EDUCATION, ENGLAND AND WALES

The Remuneration of Teachers (Primary and Secondary Schools) Order 1973

Made - - -	24th May 1973
Coming into Operation	25th May 1973

Whereas—

(1) the Committee constituted under section 1 of the Remuneration of Teachers Act 1965(a) ("the Act") for the purpose of considering the remuneration of teachers in primary and secondary schools maintained by local education authorities ("the Committee") have, in pursuance of section 2(2) of the Act, transmitted to the Secretary of State for Education and Science ("the Secretary of State") recommendations agreed on by them with respect to the remuneration of such teachers;

(2) the Committee have, in pursuance of section 2(2) of the Act as modified by the Counter-Inflation (Modification of the Remuneration of Teachers Act 1965) Order 1973(b), also transmitted to the Pay Board established under section 1(1) of the Counter-Inflation Act 1973(c) ("the Pay Board") the proposals contained in those recommendations for increases in the remuneration of such teachers;

(3) the Pay Board have approved the said proposals;

(4) the Secretary of State has, as required by section 2(3) of the Act as modified as aforesaid, prepared a draft document setting out the scales and other provisions required for determining the remuneration of such teachers in the form in which, in her opinion, those scales and provisions should be so as to give effect to the recommendations;

(5) the Secretary of State has, as required by section 2(4) of the Act, consulted the Committee with respect to the draft document and has made such modifications thereof as were requisite for giving effect to representations (not being representations involving increases in remuneration in excess of those approved by the Pay Board) made by the Committee;

(6) the Secretary of State has arranged for a document setting out the requisite scales and other provisions in the form of the draft as modified as aforesaid to be published by Her Majesty's Stationery Office on 24th May 1973 under the title "SCALES OF SALARIES FOR TEACHERS IN PRIMARY AND SECONDARY SCHOOLS, ENGLAND AND WALES, 1973."

Now therefore the Secretary of State, in pursuance of section 2(4) of the Act, hereby makes the following Order:—

(a) 1965 c. 3. (b) S.I. 1973/616 (1973 I, p. 1950). (c) 1973 c. 9.

Citation and Commencement

1. This Order may be cited as the Remuneration of Teachers (Primary and Secondary Schools) Order 1973 and shall come into operation on 25th May 1973.

Interpretation

2. The Interpretation Act 1889(**a**) shall apply for the interpretation of this Order as it applies for the interpretation of an Act of Parliament.

Remuneration of Teachers

3. The remuneration payable from 1st April 1973 to teachers in primary and secondary schools maintained by local education authorities shall be determined in accordance with the scales and other provisions set out in the document published by Her Majesty's Stationery Office as aforesaid.

Revocation

4. The Remuneration of Teachers (Primary and Secondary Schools) Order 1972(**b**) is hereby revoked and section 38(2) of the Interpretation Act 1889 (which section relates to the effect of repeals) shall have effect in relation to that Order as if both it and this Order were Acts of Parliament.

Given under the Official Seal of the Secretary of State for Education and Science on 24th May 1973.

(L.S.)   *Margaret H. Thatcher,*
                              Secretary of State for Education and Science.

EXPLANATORY NOTE

(*This Note is not part of the Order.*)

This Order brings into operation the scales and other provisions relating to the remuneration of teachers in primary and secondary schools maintained by local education authorities set out in a document published by Her Majesty's Stationery Office, which document contains the recommendations of the committee constituted under the Remuneration of Teachers Act 1965 for the purpose of considering the remuneration of such teachers. Increases in remuneration resulting from the Order have been approved by the Pay Board.

The Order has effect from 1st April 1973 by virtue of section 7(3) of the Act.

(**a**) 1889 c. 63.   (**b**) S.I. 1972/1082 (1972 II, p. 3194).

STATUTORY   INSTRUMENTS

1973 No. 958

DIPLOMATIC AND INTERNATIONAL IMMUNITIES AND PRIVILEGES

The African Development Fund (Immunities and Privileges) Order 1973

Laid before Parliament in draft

Made - - - -   *24th May* 1973
Coming into Operation   On a date to be notified
                         in   the   London,
                         Edinburgh,   and
                         Belfast Gazettes

At the Court at Buckingham Palace, the 24th day of May 1973

Present,

The Queen's Most Excellent Majesty in Council

Whereas a draft of this Order has been laid before Parliament in accordance with section 10 of the International Organisations Act 1968(a) and has been approved by a resolution of each House of Parliament:

Now, therefore, Her Majesty, by virtue and in exercise of the powers conferred on Her by section 1 of the said Act or otherwise in Her Majesty vested, is pleased, by and with the advice of Her Privy Council, to order, and it is hereby ordered, as follows:—

PART I

GENERAL

1. This Order may be cited as the African Development Fund (Immunities and Privileges) Order 1973. It shall come into operation on the date on which the Agreement establishing the African Development Fund(b), signed at Abidjan on 29th November 1972, enters into force in respect of the United Kingdom. This date shall be notified in the London, Edinburgh and Belfast Gazettes.

2.—(1) In this Order "the 1961 Convention Articles" means the Articles (being certain Articles of the Vienna Convention on Diplomatic Relations signed in 1961) which are set out in Schedule 1 to the Diplomatic Privileges Act 1964(c).

(2) The Interpretation Act 1889(d) shall apply for the interpretation of this Order as it applies for the interpretation of an Act of Parliament.

(a) 1968 c. 48.   (b) Cmnd. 5230.   (c) 1964 c. 81.   (d) 1889 c. 63.

PART II

THE FUND

3. The African Development Fund (hereinafter referred to as the Fund) is an organisation of which the United Kingdom and foreign sovereign powers are members.

4. The Fund shall have the legal capacities of a body corporate.

5.—(1) The Fund shall have immunity from suit and legal process except:

(a) to the extent that the Board of Directors of the Fund shall have expressly waived such immunity in a particular case ;

(b) in relation to a civil action arising out of an accident caused by a motor vehicle belonging to the Fund or operated on its behalf or to a traffic offence committed by the driver of such a vehicle ; and

(c) if the Fund has appointed an agent for the purpose of accepting service or notice of process, in respect of any proceedings (other than proceedings brought against the Fund by any participant or by any agency or instrumentality of a participant, or by any entity or person directly or indirectly acting for or deriving claims from a participant or from any agency or instrumentality of a participant) arising out of or in connection with the exercise of its powers to receive loans.

(2) The provisions of paragraph (1) of this Article shall not prevent the taking of such measures as may be permitted by law in relation to the execution of judgment against the Fund.

6. The Fund shall have the like inviolability of official archives as, in accordance with the 1961 Convention Articles, is accorded in respect of the official archives of a diplomatic mission. Premises of the Fund shall be immune from search, requisition, confiscation, expropriation or any other form of taking or foreclosure.

7. The Fund shall have the like exemption or relief from taxes, other than customs duties and taxes on the importation of goods, as is accorded to a foreign sovereign power.

8. The Fund shall have the like relief from rates on its official premises as in accordance with Article 23 of the 1961 Convention Articles is accorded in respect of the premises of a diplomatic mission.

9. The Fund shall have exemption from customs duties and taxes on the importation of goods imported by or on behalf of the Fund for its official use in the United Kingdom, or on the importation of any publications of the Fund imported by it or on its behalf, such exemption to be subject to compliance with such conditions as the Commissioners of Customs and Excise may prescribe for the protection of the Revenue.

10. The Fund shall have exemption from prohibitions and restrictions on importation or exportation in the case of goods imported or exported by the Fund for its official use and in the case of any publications of the Fund imported or exported by it.

11. The Fund shall have relief, under arrangements made by the Commissioners of Customs and Excise, by way of refund of customs duty paid on any hydrocarbon oil (within the meaning of the Hydrocarbon Oil (Customs

& Excise) Act 1971(**a**)) which is bought in the United Kingdom and used for the official purposes of the Fund, such relief to be subject to compliance with such conditions as may be imposed in accordance with the arrangements.

12. The Fund shall have relief, under arrangements made by the Secretary of State, by way of refund of car tax paid on any vehicles and value added tax paid on the supply of any goods which are used for the official purposes of the Fund, such relief to be subject to compliance with such conditions as may be imposed in accordance with the arrangements.

PART III

OFFICERS, SERVANTS AND EXPERTS

13. Except in so far as in any particular case any privilege or immunity is waived by the Board of Directors or the President of the Fund, any governor, director, alternate, officer and servant of the Fund and any expert performing a mission for the Fund shall enjoy: —

(*a*) immunity from suit and legal process in respect of things done or omitted to be done by him in the course of the performance of his official duties, except in relation to a civil action arising out of an accident caused by a motor vehicle belonging to the Fund or operated on its behalf or to a traffic offence committed by him when driving such a vehicle ; and

(*b*) unless he is a citizen of the United Kingdom and Colonies or resident in the United Kingdom, exemption from income tax in respect of emoluments received by him as an officer or servant of the Fund or as an expert performing a mission for the Fund.

W. G. Agnew.

EXPLANATORY NOTE

(*This Note is not part of the Order.*)

This Order confers privileges and immunities upon the African Development Fund, its officers, servants and experts performing missions on its behalf. It will enable the United Kingdom to give effect to Chapter VIII of the Agreement establishing the Fund (Cmnd. 5230) signed at Abidjan on 29th November 1972, as limited by the declarations permitted by Article 58 which will accompany the instrument of ratification. It will come into operation on the date on which the Agreement enters into force with respect to the United Kingdom.

(a) 1971 c. 12.

STATUTORY INSTRUMENTS

1973 No. 959

POST OFFICE

The Postal Services (Isle of Man) Order 1973

Made - - -	*24th May* 1973
Coming into Operation	*5th July* 1973

At the Court at Buckingham Palace, the 24th day of May 1973

Present,

The Queen's Most Excellent Majesty in Council

Whereas an agreement has been concluded between the Minister of Posts and Telecommunications and the Government of the Isle of Man providing for the surrender by the Post Office, as regards the Isle of Man, of the privilege conferred on the Post Office by section 3 of the Post Office Act 1953(a) and the administration in that Island of postal services by, or under the authority of, the Government of the Island instead of by the Post Office:

Now, therefore, Her Majesty, in exercise of the powers conferred upon Her by section 87(1) of the Post Office Act 1969(b), is pleased, by and with the advice of Her Privy Council, to order, and it is hereby ordered, as follows:—

1. This Order may be cited as the Postal Services (Isle of Man) Order 1973 and shall come into operation on 5th July 1973.

2. This Order applies only to the Isle of Man.

3.—(1) The Interpretation Act 1889(c) shall apply for the interpretation of this Order as it applies for the interpretation of an Act of Parliament, and section 38 of that Act (effect of repeals) shall apply as if this Order were an Act of Parliament.

(2) Any reference in this Order to any enactment shall, except so far as the context otherwise requires, be construed as a reference to that enactment as amended, and as including a reference to it as extended or applied, by or under any other enactment, including the Post Office Act 1969, or by this Order.

4. The agreement mentioned in the preamble to this Order and set out in Schedule 1 thereto shall have the force of law.

5. Sections 12, 13, 20, 23, 30, 64, 66, 67, 73, 79 and 84 of the Post Office Act 1969 are hereby repealed.

(a) 1953 c. 36. (b) 1969 c. 48.
(c) 1889 c. 63.

6. The provisions of the Post Office Act 1969 specified in Schedule 2 to this Order shall be amended in the manner specified in relation thereto in that Schedule.

7. The provisions of the Post Office Act 1953, except section 65A as inserted by paragraph 8 of Schedule 2 to the Theft Act 1968(**a**) (fraudulent use of public telephone and telex system), and those specified in Schedule 3 to this Order, are hereby repealed and the provisions so specified shall be amended in the manner specified in relation thereto in that Schedule.

W. G. Agnew.

SCHEDULE 1

Article 4

AGREEMENT BETWEEN THE MINISTER OF POSTS AND TELECOMMUNICATIONS AND THE GOVERNMENT OF THE ISLE OF MAN

This Agreement made the fourth day of May One thousand nine hundred and seventy three between the Right Honourable Sir John Eden Bt., M.P. Her Majesty's Minister of Posts and Telecommunications in exercise of the powers conferred on him by the Post Office Act 1969 and on behalf of Her Majesty of the one part and the Government of the Isle of Man acting by and through George Victor Harris Kneale, Esquire, Member of the House of Keys, Chairman of the Isle of Man Post Office Authority of the other part.

Whereas subsection (1) of section 87 of the Post Office Act 1969 makes provision in the event of the conclusion of an agreement between the Minister of Posts and Telecommunications and the Government of the Isle of Man for the surrender by the Post Office as regards that Isle of the privilege conferred on the Post Office by section 3 of the Post Office Act 1953, as amended by section 23 of the Post Office Act 1969, and for the administration in that Isle of postal services by or under the authority of that Government instead of by the Post Office.

Now it is hereby agreed as follows:

1. This Agreement takes effect on the fifth day of July One thousand nine hundred and seventy three.

2. The Post Office surrenders as regards the Isle of Man the exclusive privilege conferred on the Post Office by section 3 of the Post Office Act 1953 as amended by section 23 of the Post Office Act 1969, and the postal services shall be administered in that Isle by or under the authority of the Government of the Isle of Man instead of by the Post Office.

3. If, in the opinion of the Minister of Posts and Telecommunications, it is requisite or expedient in the interests of national security or relations with the government of a country or territory outside the British Islands or, in relation to the Isle of Man, in order to discharge or facilitate the discharge of an obligation of Her Majesty's Government in the United Kingdom by virtue of its being a member of an international organisation or a party to an international agreement, to attain, or facilitate the attainment of, any other object in view of that Government being a member or party as aforesaid, or to enable that Government to become a member or party as aforesaid, that any thing should be done or not done, the Government of the Isle of Man will do what is necessary to secure that it is done or not, as the case may be.

(a) 1968 c. 60.

4. The Isle of Man Post Office Authority will receive, collect and deliver written telegrams transmitted or to be transmitted by the Post Office, in accordance with (and at the tariffs prescribed by or under) the relevant schemes made from time to time by the Post Office under section 28 of the Post Office Act 1969.

5. (i) The Isle of Man Post Office Authority will perform the services described in paragraph (ii) for and on behalf of the Post Office if, and in such manner, and for so long as, the Minister of Posts and Telecommunications, after consultation with the Post Office and the Isle of Man Post Office Authority, may from time to time require for the purpose of the provision by the Post Office in the Isle of Man of its inland and international telegram services.

    (ii) The Authority will in accordance with paragraph (i):

      (a) collect charges payable under the tariffs referred to in Article 4;

      (b) by means of telecommunication equipment provided for that purpose by the Post Office (and with the licence of the Post Office under section 27 of the said Act where required) transmit and receive telegrams within the Island and from and at places in the Island to and from Post Office establishments in the United Kingdom.

In witness whereof the Minister of Posts and Telecommunications has hereunto set his hand and seal and the said George Victor Harris Kneale has signed these presents for and on behalf of the Government of the Isle of Man, the day and year first above written.

Signed sealed and delivered
by the said Sir John Eden in
the presence of:—   }   *John Eden*
  A. Fortnam
  Civil Servant.

Signed by the said George
Victor Harris Kneale in
the presence of:—   }   *G. V. H. Kneale*
  S. V. Thomas.

Article 6   SCHEDULE 2

AMENDMENTS TO THE POST OFFICE ACT 1969 IN ITS APPLICATION TO THE
ISLE OF MAN

1. Section 9 (general duty of the Post Office) shall apply only in relation to the power to provide and the provision of telecommunication services.

2. Section 14 (the Post Office Users' Councils) shall apply only in relation to telecommunication services.

3. Section 15 (duty of the Post Office to consult the Post Office Users' National Council about certain proposals) shall apply only in relation to proposals relating to telecommunication services.

4. In section 28 (schemes for determining charges and other terms and conditions applicable to services) in subsection (1) for the words "any of the services" there shall be substituted the words "any of the telecommunication services".

5. In section 29 (exclusion of liability of the Post Office, its officers and servants, in relation to posts and telecommunications) in subsection (1) there shall be omitted the words "Save as provided by the next following section," and in subsection (3) after the words "No person engaged" there shall be inserted the words "by or on behalf of the Post Office".

6. Section 80 (provision of information to persons holding office under the Crown) shall apply in relation to postal services as if the words "provided by the Post Office" were omitted and as if for the words "laid on the Post Office for the like purposes and in the like manner" there were substituted the words "laid on an officer of the Isle of Man Post Office Authority by the Lieutenant Governor of the Isle of Man for the like purposes".

7. In Schedule 9 (general transitional provisions) in paragraph 3 sub-paragraphs (1)(c) and (2), and sub-paragraph (4) so far as it relates thereto, shall be omitted.

SCHEDULE 3   Article 7

AMENDMENTS TO THE POST OFFICE ACT 1953 IN ITS APPLICATION TO
THE ISLE OF MAN

1. Section 50 (indemnity on account of extending Post Office accommodation) shall extend to the Isle of Man only in relation to any telegraph office or the accommodation of the telegraphic services.

2. Subsection (2) of section 58 (opening or delaying of postal packets by officers of the Post Office) shall extend to the Isle of Man only for the purposes specified in paragraph 1 of Schedule 5 of the Post Office Act 1969.

3. Section 60 (prohibition of placing injurious substances in or against post office letter boxes or telephone kiosks) shall extend to the Isle of Man only in relation to any telephone kiosk or cabinet.

4. Section 61 (prohibition of affixing placards, notices, etc. on post office letter boxes, etc.) shall extend to the Isle of Man only in relation to any telegraph post or other property used by or on behalf of the Post Office for telecommunication services.

5. Section 64 (prohibition of false notice as to reception of letters etc.) shall extend to the Isle of Man only in relation to the words "public telephone call office" or to any words, letters or marks which signify or imply or may reasonably lead the public to believe that any place is a place where the public may make telephone calls.

6. Section 65 (obstruction and molestation of officers of the Post Office) shall extend to the Isle of Man only in relation to telecommunication services.

EXPLANATORY NOTE

(This Note is not part of the Order.)

This Order gives the force of law to an agreement between the Minister of Posts and Telecommunications and the Government of the Isle of Man for the administration of postal services in the Isle of Man by or under the authority of the Government of the Isle of Man and consequentially repeals or adapts certain provisions of the Post Office Act 1969 and the Post Office Act 1953 in their application to the Isle of Man.

STATUTORY INSTRUMENTS

1973 No. 960

POST OFFICE

The Postal Services (Isle of Man Consequential Provisions) Order 1973

Made - - -	*24th May* 1973
Coming into Operation	*5th July* 1973

At the Court at Buckingham Palace, the 24th day of May 1973

Present,

The Queen's Most Excellent Majesty in Council

Whereas an agreement has been concluded between the Minister of Posts and Telecommunications and the Government of the Isle of Man providing for the surrender by the Post Office, as regards the Isle of Man, of the privilege conferred on the Post Office by section 3 of the Post Office Act 1953(**a**) and the administration in that Island of postal services by, or under the authority of, the Government of the Island instead of by the Post Office:

Now, therefore, Her Majesty, in exercise of the powers conferred upon Her by section 87(1) of the Post Office Act 1969(**b**), is pleased, by and with the advice of Her Privy Council, to order, and it is hereby ordered, as follows:—

1. This Order may be cited as the Postal Services (Isle of Man Consequential Provisions) Order 1973 and shall come into operation on 5th July 1973.

2. This Order applies—

(*a*) to the United Kingdom;

(*b*) so far as it relates to an enactment extending to the Channel Islands, to those Islands;

(*c*) so far as it relates to an enactment extending to the Isle of Man, to that Isle.

3.—(1) Any reference in this Order to any enactment shall, except so far as the context otherwise requires, be construed as a reference to that enactment as amended, and as including a reference to it as extended or applied, by or under any other enactment, including the Post Office Act 1969, or by this Order.

(2) The Interpretation Act 1889(**c**) shall apply for the interpretation of this Order as it applies for the interpretation of an Act of Parliament, and section 38 of that Act (effect of repeals) shall apply as if this Order were an Act of Parliament.

(**a**) 1953 c. 36.   (**b**) 1969 c. 48.
(**c**) 1889 c. 63.

4. The privilege conferred by section 3 of the Post Office Act 1953 with respect to the conveyance of letters and the performance of services of receiving, collecting, despatching and delivering letters which, by virtue of section 23 of the Post Office Act 1969, has become that of the Post Office, shall not extend to the Isle of Man.

5. In section 30(7) of the Post Office Act 1969 (the Post Office to be subject to limited liability in respect of registered inland packets) the following definition shall be substituted for the definition of "inland packet":—

' "inland packet" means anything which is posted in the United Kingdom for delivery at a place in the United Kingdom to the person to whom it is addressed;'.

6. In section 66 of the Post Office Act 1969—

(*a*) in subsection (4), the words "or the Isle of Man" shall be omitted; and

(*b*) subsection (6) shall be repealed.

7. Section 69(3) of the Post Office Act 1969 (documentary evidence as to sums due for services) shall have effect, in relation to a rate at which a charge was levied in respect of a service other than a telecommunication service, as if the Isle of Man were not included in the definition of the expression "the British Islands" in section 86(1) thereof (interpretation).

8. Section 70 of the Post Office Act 1969 (provisions as to money and postal orders) and section 71 thereof (recoupment of losses on money orders wrongly paid to bankers) shall have effect as if the Isle of Man were not included in the last-mentioned definition.

9. Section 86(1) of the Post Office Act 1969 (interpretation) shall be amended by the deletion in the definitions of "harbour", "harbour authority" and "statutory provision" of the words "or the Isle of Man" and the words from "and, in relation to the Isle of Man" to the end of the definition in each case.

10. Section 133 of the Post Office Act 1969 as amended by the Postal Services (Channel Islands Consequential Provisions) Order 1969(**a**) and the Telecommunication Services (Channel Islands Consequential Provisions) Order 1972(**b**) shall be further amended as follows:—

(*a*) in subsection (2)(*a*) at the end of sub-paragraph (iv) the word "and" shall be omitted, and at the end of sub-paragraph (v) there shall be added the word "and" and the following sub-paragraph:—

"(vi) without prejudice to the generality of (i) above, persons who, having been officers or servants of the Post Office, are or have been in consequence of such an agreement as is mentioned in paragraph (*a*)(i) of subsection (1) of section 87 of this Act and of such an Order in Council as is mentioned in that subsection, employed by the Isle of Man Post Office Authority.".

(*b*) in subsection (2)(*b*), there shall be omitted the words "or, as the case may be", and after the words "the States of Guernsey" there shall be inserted the words "or, as the case may be, employment by the Isle of Man Post Office Authority".

(**a**) S.I. 1969/1368 (1969 III, p. 4082).   (**b**) S.I. 1972/1816 (1972 III, p. 5235).

11.—(1) Article 9(*c*) and (*e*) of the Postal Services (Channel Islands Consequential Provisions) Order 1969 shall be revoked, and for subsection (1) of section 16 of the Post Office Act 1953 (application of Customs Acts to postal packets) there shall be substituted the following subsection:—

"(1) Subject to the provisions of this section, the enactments for the time being in force relating to customs shall apply in relation to goods contained in postal packets to which this section applies brought into or sent out of the United Kingdom by post from or to any place outside the United Kingdom as they apply in relation to goods otherwise imported, exported or removed into or out of the United Kingdom from or to any such place.".

(2) Subsection 2(*d*) of the said section 16 shall have effect as if the Isle of Man were included in the expression "any other country".

12. In section 17 of the Post Office Act 1953 (power to detain postal packets containing contraband) the words "or the Isle of Man" shall be omitted.

13. Section 24 of the Post Office Act 1953 (arrangements with other countries as to money orders) shall have effect as if the Isle of Man were included in the expression "any other country".

14. Section 63 of the Post Office Act 1953 (prohibition of fictitious stamps) shall have effect as if the Isle of Man were a country outside the British postal area; and, in subsection (5) of that section, the words "or the Isle of Man" shall be omitted.

15. In section 70(2) of the Post Office Act 1953, as substituted by paragraph 10 of Schedule 2 to the Theft Act 1968(**a**) (prosecution of certain offences in any jurisdiction of British postal area) and as amended by the Postal Services (Channel Islands Consequential Provisions) Order 1969 the words "and of the Isle of Man" shall be omitted.

16. In section 87(1) of the Post Office Act 1953 (interpretation) in the definition of "British postal area" the words "and the Isle of Man" shall be omitted.

W. G. Agnew.

EXPLANATORY NOTE
(*This Note is not part of the Order.*)

This Order amends the Post Office Act 1969 and the Post Office Act 1953 and the Postal Services (Channel Islands Consequential Provisions) Order 1969 to take account of the fact that the postal services in the Isle of Man are to be administered by or under the authority of the Government of that Isle (*see* the Postal Services (Isle of Man) Order 1973 (S.I. 1973/959.)).

(**a**) 1968 c. 60.

STATUTORY INSTRUMENTS

1973 No. 963

COPYRIGHT

The Copyright (International Conventions) (Amendment No. 3) Order 1973

Made - - -	*24th May* 1973
Laid before Parliament	*24th May* 1973
Coming into Operation	*27th May* 1973

At the Court at Buckingham Palace, the 24th day of May 1973

Present,

The Queen's Most Excellent Majesty in Council

Her Majesty, by and with the advice of Her Privy Council, and by virtue of the authority conferred upon Her by sections 31, 32 and 47 of the Copyright Act 1956(a) and of all other powers enabling Her in that behalf, is pleased to order, and it is hereby ordered, as follows:—

1.—(1) This Order may be cited as the Copyright (International Conventions) (Amendment No. 3) Order 1973, and shall come into operation on 27th May 1973.

(2) The Interpretation Act 1889(b) shall apply to the interpretation of this Order as it applies to the interpretation of an Act of Parliament.

2. The Copyright (International Conventions) Order 1972(c) (hereinafter referred to as "the principal Order"), as amended(d), shall be further amended by including in Schedule 2 (which names the countries party to the Universal Copyright Convention but not Members of the Berne Union) a reference to the Union of Soviet Socialist Republics and a related reference to 27th May 1973.

3. This Order shall extend to all the countries mentioned in Schedule 6 to the principal Order and to Hong Kong.

W. G. Agnew.

(a) 1956 c. 74.   (b) 1889 c. 63.   (c) S.I. 1972/673 (1972 I, p. 2172).
(d) The amendments are not relevant to the subject matter of this Order.

EXPLANATORY NOTE

(*This Note is not part of the Order.*)

This Order further amends the Copyright (International Conventions) Order 1972. It takes account of the accession by the U.S.S.R. to the Universal Copyright Convention.

This Order extends to dependent countries of the Commonwealth to which the 1972 Order extends.

STATUTORY INSTRUMENTS

1973 No. 964

MERCHANT SHIPPING

The Merchant Shipping (Light Dues) Order 1973

Laid before Parliament in draft

Made - - -		*24th May* 1973
Coming into Operation		*7th June* 1973

To be laid before Parliament

At the Court at Buckingham Palace, the 24th day of May 1973

Present,

The Queen's Most Excellent Majesty in Council

Her Majesty in exercise of the powers conferred upon Her by section 5 of the Merchant Shipping (Mercantile Marine Fund) Act 1898(a), and of all other powers enabling Her in that behalf, is pleased, by and with the advice of Her Privy Council, to order, and it is hereby ordered, as follows:—

1.—(1) This Order shall come into operation 14 days after the making thereof and may be cited as the Merchant Shipping (Light Dues) Order 1973.

(2) The Interpretation Act 1889(b) shall apply to the interpretation of this Order as it applies to the interpretation of an Act of Parliament.

2. There shall be substituted for the scale of payments relating to light dues contained in Schedule 2 of the Merchant Shipping (Light Dues) Order 1972(c) the following scale of payments:—

SCALE OF PAYMENTS

1. Home-trade sailing ships: 34p per 10 tons per voyage

2. Foreign-going sailing ships: 78p per 10 tons per voyage

3. Home-trade steamers:
   Full rate: 52p per 10 tons per voyage
   Reduced rate (visiting cruise ships): 26p per 10 tons per voyage

4. Foreign-going steamers:
   Full rate: 95p per 10 tons per voyage
   Reduced rate (visiting cruise ships): 53p per 10 tons per voyage

---

(a) 1898 c. 44.　　　　　　　　　　(b) 1889 c. 63.
(c) S.I. 1972/456 (1972 I, p. 1689).

5. In the place of payments per voyage, the following payments : —

(*a*) for pleasure yachts which the general lighthouse authority is satisfied are ordinarily kept or used outside any of the following countries and territories (including the territorial waters adjacent thereto), namely the United Kingdom, Isle of Man, Republic of Ireland, a payment in respect of any visit of 34p per 10 tons for every period of 30 days or less comprised in such visit;

(*b*) for tugs and pleasure yachts not included in sub-paragraph (*a*) of this paragraph an annual payment of £4·09 per 10 tons.

3. The rules contained in the said Schedule 2 shall be amended as follows : —

(*a*) In the proviso to Rule 1 for "£5·16" and "£4·26" there shall be substituted respectively "£5·70" and "£4·68".

(*b*) In Rule 7 for "31p" there shall be substituted "34p".

W. G. Agnew.

EXPLANATORY NOTE

(This Note is not part of the Order.)

This Order increases the scale of light dues set out in the Merchant Shipping (Light Dues) Order 1972 by about 10% overall.

STATUTORY INSTRUMENTS

1973 No. 965

PENSIONS

The Increase of Pensions (Police and Fire Services) (Amendment) (No. 2) Regulations 1973

Made - - - -	*23rd May* 1973
Laid before Parliament	*8th June* 1973
Coming into Operation	*1st July* 1973

In exercise of the powers conferred on me by section 5(3) and (4) of the Pensions (Increase) Act 1971(a), I hereby, with the consent of the Minister for the Civil Service, make the following Regulations:—

1. These Regulations may be cited as the Increase of Pensions (Police and Fire Services) (Amendment) (No. 2) Regulations 1973.

2. These Regulations shall come into operation on 1st July 1973 and shall have effect as from 1st April 1972.

3. For paragraph (1) of Regulation 4 of the Increase of Pensions (Police and Fire Services) Regulations 1971(b), as amended (c), (pensions reduced on account of additional benefit), there shall be substituted the following provision:—

"(1) This Regulation shall apply to a pension payable to or in respect of a person who retired, or ceased to serve, before 1st April 1972, being a pension payable in accordance with—

(*a*) the Police Pensions Regulations;

(*b*) the Special Constables (Pensions) Regulations;

(*c*) the Police Cadets (Pensions) Regulations, or

(*d*) the Firemen's Pension Scheme,

which is reduced in amount or is not payable on account of the payment of some additional benefit.".

Robert Carr,
One of Her Majesty's Principal
Secretaries of State.

23rd May 1973.

(a) 1971 c. 56.
(c) S.I. 1973/432 (1973 I, p. 1520).
(b) S.I. 1971/1330 (1971 II, p. 3813).

Consent of the Minister for the Civil Service given under his official Seal on 22nd May 1973.

(L.S.) *K. H. McNeill,*
Authorised by the
Minister for the Civil Service.

EXPLANATORY NOTE

(*This Note is not part of the Regulations.*)

These Regulations amend the Increase of Pensions (Police and Fire Services) Regulations 1971 and have effect as from 1st April 1972, the date from which certain changes take effect in the provisions governing fire service pensions (retrospective effect is authorised by section 5(4) of the Pensions (Increase) Act 1971).

Pensions payable to firemen with service on or after 1st April 1972 are excluded from the operation of Regulation 4 of the Regulations of 1971.

STATUTORY INSTRUMENTS

1973 No. 966

FIRE SERVICES

The Firemen's Pension Scheme Order 1973

Made - - - -	*23rd May* 1973
Laid before Parliament	*8th June* 1973
Coming into Operation	*1st July* 1973

In exercise of the powers conferred on me by section 26 of the Fire Services Act 1947(a), as amended and extended by sections 1 and 2(1) of the Fire Services Act 1951(b), section 42 of the Reserve and Auxiliary Forces (Protection of Civil Interests) Act 1951(c), section 8 of the Fire Services Act 1959(d) and sections 12 and 16 of the Superannuation Act 1972(e), and with the approval of the Minister for the Civil Service (f) and after consultation with the Central Fire Brigades Advisory Council and the Scottish Central Fire Brigades Advisory Council and so far as concerns Article 86(4) to (6) of the Scheme set out in Appendix 2 to the following Order, with the Council on Tribunals, I hereby make the following Order:—

1.—(1) This Order may be cited as the Firemen's Pension Scheme Order 1973.

(2) This Order shall come into operation on 1st July 1973 and shall have effect as from 1st April 1972.

2.—(1) The Firemen's Pension Scheme 1971 (set out in Appendix 2 to the Firemen's Pension Scheme Order 1971(g)) and the Orders set out in Appendix 1 to this Order shall cease to have effect except in old cases, that is to say, except in the case of an award or payment to or in respect of, or relating to—

(*a*) a person who retired or otherwise ceased to be a member of a fire brigade before 1st April 1972, or

(*b*) a person, being a serviceman who did not resume service as a member of a fire brigade, whose period of relevant service in the armed forces ended before 1st April 1972,

including an award on the death of such a person on or after the said date.

This paragraph shall be construed as one with the Firemen's Pension Scheme 1973.

(2) The Firemen's Pension Scheme (Amendment) Order 1973(h) is hereby revoked.

3. The Pension Scheme set out in Appendix 2 to this Order (herein referred to as the Firemen's Pension Scheme 1973) is hereby brought into operation.

(a) 1947 c. 41. (b) 1951 c. 27.
(c) 1951 c. 65. (d) 1959 c. 44.
(e) 1972 c. 11.
(f) Formerly the Treasury; *see* S.I. 1968/1656 (1968 III, p. 4485).
(g) S.I. 1971/145 (1971 I, p. 320). (h) S.I. 1973/318 (1973 I, p. 1112).

4. The Firemen's Pension Scheme 1973 shall have effect subject to the transitory provisions set out in Appendix 3 to this Order.

Robert Carr,
One of Her Majesty's Principal
Secretaries of State.

23rd May 1973.

Approval of the Minister for the Civil Service given under his Official Seal on 22nd May 1973.

(L.S.)

K. H. McNeill,
Authorised by the
Minister for the Civil Service.

APPENDIX 1 Article 2

OLD CASES ORDERS

The Firemen's Pension Scheme Order 1971	S.I. 1971/145 (1971 I, p. 320).
The Firemen's Pension Scheme (Amendment) Order 1971	S.I. 1971/1329 (1971 II, p. 3801).
The Firemen's Pension Scheme (Amendment) (No. 2) Order 1971	S.I. 1971/1468 (1971 III, p. 4144).
The Firemen's Pension Scheme (Amendment) Order 1972	S.I. 1972/522 (1972 I, p. 1798).
The Firemen's Pension Scheme (Amendment) (No. 2) Order 1972	S.I. 1972/1643 (1972 III, p. 4833).

Article 3

APPENDIX 2

THE FIREMEN'S PENSION SCHEME 1973
ARRANGEMENT OF ARTICLES

PART I
CITATION, INTERPRETATION ETC.

Article

1. Citation, effect, transitional provisions etc.
2. Meaning of "regular fireman".
3. Meaning of "qualifying injury".
4. Meaning of infirmity or death occasioned by an injury and of disablement.
5. Meaning of "aggregate contributions".
6. Meaning of reference to awards.
7. Meaning of certain expressions related to the operation of the National Insurance Acts.
8. Meaning of certain expressions.
9. Construction of references to provisions of Scheme.
10. Construction of references to enactments and instruments.
11. Application of the Interpretation Act 1889.

PART II
AWARDS ON RETIREMENT OF REGULAR FIREMEN

12. Fireman's ordinary pension.
13. Fireman's short service award.
14. Fireman's ill-health award.
15. Fireman's injury awards.
16. Deferred pension and award where no other award payable.
17. Minimum aggregate amount of payments in respect of fireman's pension.
18. Cancellation of fireman's ill-health and injury pensions on recovery.
19. Reassessment of fireman's injury pension.
20. Reduction of award in case of default.
21. Commutation of pension.

PART III
AWARDS ON DEATH OF REGULAR FIREMEN
Widows

22. Widow's ordinary pension.
23. Widow's special award.
24. Widow's augmented award.
25. Widow's accrued pension.
26. Widow's gratuity by way of commuted pension.
27. Widow's award where no other award payable.
28. Right to widow's pension dependent on date of marriage.
29. Special provisions where widow was living apart from her husband.
30. Effect of remarriage.

PART XII

PERSONS WHO WERE SERVING ON 10th JULY 1956

PART XIII

MISCELLANEOUS PROVISIONS

SCHEDULES

SCHEDULE 5

Sums to be paid by firemen in respect of previous service.

SCHEDULE 6

Part   I   Civil service, metropolitan civil staffs, education, health, police and Belfast fire service.

Part   II   Other service or employment.

SCHEDULE 7—ADDITIONAL AND FURTHER PAYMENTS

Part   I   Contributions.

Part   II   Lump sums.

SCHEDULE 8

Appeals to medical referees.

SCHEDULE 9

Transfer values.

SCHEDULE 10

Modifications to Scheme in its application to firemen serving on 10th July 1956.

PART I

CITATION, INTERPRETATION ETC.

Citation, effect, transitional provisions etc.

1.—(1) This Scheme may be cited as the Firemen's Pension Scheme 1973 and shall have effect as from 1st April 1972.

(2) Nothing in this Scheme shall apply in the case of an award or payment to or in respect of, or relating to—

(*a*) a person who retired or otherwise ceased to be a member of a fire brigade before 1st April 1972, or

(*b*) a person, being a serviceman who did not resume service as a member of a fire brigade, whose period of relevant service in the armed forces ended before 1st April 1972,

including an award on the death of such a person on or after the said date.

(3) Subject as aforesaid and to the transitory provisions contained in Appendix 3 to the Firemen's Pension Scheme Order 1973, this Scheme shall have effect as if anything done or treated as done under or for the purposes of the Firemen's Pension Scheme 1971(a), as amended, had been done under or for the purposes of the corresponding provision of this Scheme.

(4) Without prejudice to the generality of paragraph (3), references therein to anything done shall include—

(*a*) the determination of a question;

(*b*) the exercise of a discretion;

(*c*) the making of a payment; and

(*d*) the giving of a notice.

(5) For the purpose of determining the amount payable on account of an award for a period ending before 1st December 1972, this Scheme shall have effect subject to the transitory provisions referred to in paragraph (3).

(a) *See* S.I. 1971/145 (1971 I, p. 320).

Meaning of "regular fireman"

2. In this Scheme the expression "regular fireman" means—

(a) a whole-time member of a brigade who was appointed on terms under which he is or may be required to engage in fire-fighting, not being a person whose employment is temporary only; or

(b) a whole-time member of a brigade whc—

(i) was, immediately before the appointed day, subject to the Fire Brigade Pensions Act 1925(a);

(ii) became, on that day, a whole-time member of a brigade serving the whole or any part of the area of the local authority by whom he was last employed as a member of a fire brigade before the appointed day; and

(iii) has not since the appointed day ceased to be a whole-time member of that brigade.

Meaning of "qualifying injury"

3.—(1) In this Scheme the expression "qualifying injury" means an injury received by a person without his own default in the execution of his duties—

(a) as a regular fireman;

(b) as a professional fireman within the meaning of the Fire Brigade Pensions Act 1925, whether or not a member of the London Fire Brigade, or as a member of a police force employed whole-time on fire brigade duties within the meaning of the Fire Brigades Act 1938(b); or

(c) as a whole-time member of the National Fire Service to whom the National Fire Service (Preservation of Pensions) (Act of 1925) Regulations 1941(c), the National Fire Service (Preservation of Pensions) (London and West Ham) Regulations 1941(d), the National Fire Service (Preservation of Pensions) (Birmingham and Leicester) Regulations 1941(e), the National Fire Service (Preservation of Pensions) (Bolton and Derby) Regulations 1941(f) or the National Fire Service (Preservation of Pensions) (Police Firemen) Regulations 1941(g) applied,

except that, save where the context otherwise requires, in Part X of this Scheme the said expression means an injury so received by a person in the execution of his duties as a part-time member of a brigade.

(2) For the purposes of this Scheme an injury shall be treated as received without the default of the person concerned unless the injury is wholly or mainly due to his own serious and culpable negligence or misconduct.

Meaning of infirmity or death occasioned by an injury and of disablement

4.—(1) A person shall be deemed for the purposes of this Scheme to have died from the effects of a particular injury if it appears that if he had not suffered that injury he would not have died at the time he in fact died.

(2) Infirmity of mind or body shall be deemed for the purposes of this Scheme to be occasioned by a particular injury—

(a) where a person dies while serving as a fireman, if it appears that the injury has so substantially aggravated the infirmity of mind or body that if he had not received that injury he would not have died at the time he in fact died;

(b) where a person has ceased to be a fireman, if it appears that the injury has so substantially aggravated the infirmity of mind or body that if he had not received that injury he would not have had to retire at the time when he in fact retired.

(a) 1925 c. 47. (b) 1938 c. 72.
(c) S.R. & O. 1941/1268 (1941 I, p. 320). (d) S.R. & O. 1941/1272 (1941 I, p. 333).
(e) S.R. & O. 1941/1273 (1941 I, p. 337). (f) S.R. & O. 1941/1274 (1941 I, p. 342).
(g) S.R. & O. 1941/1271 (1941 I, p. 328).

(3) Any reference in this Scheme to a person being permanently disabled is to be taken as a reference to that person being disabled at the time when the question arises for decision and to that disability appearing, at that time, likely to be permanent.

(4) Subject to paragraph (5) disablement means incapacity, occasioned by infirmity of mind or body, for the performance of duty except that, in relation to a child, it means incapacity, occasioned as aforesaid, to earn a living.

(5) Where it is necessary to determine the degree of a person's disablement, it shall be determined by reference to the degree to which his earning capacity has been affected as a result of a qualifying injury:

Provided that a person shall be deemed to be totally disabled if, as a result of a qualifying injury, he is receiving in-patient treatment at a hospital.

(6) Where a person has retired before becoming disabled and the date on which he becomes disabled cannot be ascertained, it shall be taken to be the date on which the claim that he is disabled is first made known to the fire authority.

Meaning of "aggregate contributions"

5.—(1) In this Scheme the expression "aggregate contributions" means in relation to a regular fireman—

   (a) all payments made by him to a fire authority under this Scheme or a previous Scheme which relate to a period of service he is entitled to reckon as pensionable service for the purposes of this Scheme and have not been refunded to him including such payments made—

   (i) by way of rateable deductions from pay,

   (ii) by way of such additional and further contributions as are mentioned in Articles 57 and 58,

   (iii) by way of such a lump sum as is mentioned in Article 59, and

   (iv) in pursuance of such an undertaking as is mentioned in Schedule 4; and

   (b) the amount of any award by way of return of contributions which would have been made to him at the end of any period of service or employment, otherwise than as a regular fireman, by virtue of which he was subject to superannuation arrangements, being a period which he is entitled to reckon as pensionable service for the purposes of this Scheme, had he then voluntarily retired in circumstances entitling him to such an award under those arrangements.

(2) In this Article the expression "award by way of return of contributions" shall include—

   (a) a payment under section 18 of the Fire Brigade Pensions Act 1925;

   (b) a payment under section 10 of the Local Government Superannuation Act 1937(a);

   (c) a payment under section 10 of the Local Government Superannuation (Scotland) Act 1937(b);

   (d) a payment under section 12 of the Teachers (Superannuation) Act 1925(c);

   (e) any analogous payment.

Meaning of reference to awards

6.—(1) Except where the context otherwise requires and subject to paragraph (2), any reference in this Scheme to a pension or other award is a reference to a pension or other award, as the case may be, under this Scheme.

(2) Any reference to a pension or other award to a regular fireman in Articles 48, 49 or 56(4) includes a reference to a pension or other award, as the case may be, under a previous Scheme.

(a) 1937 c. 68.   (b) 1937 c. 69.
(c) 1925 c. 59.

(3) Any reference in this Scheme to a widow's pension, however expressed, shall be construed as excluding a reference to a pension payable to a widow under Article 41.

Meaning of certain expressions related to the operation of the National Insurance Acts

7.—(1) In this Scheme the following expressions shall have the meanings respectively which they have for the purposes of the National Insurance Act 1965(a):—

"employed contributor's employment";

"graduated contribution";

"graduated retirement benefit";

"non-participating employment";

"payment in lieu of contributions".

(2) In this Scheme any reference to a participating period of relevant employment is a reference to a period of employed contributor's employment after 5th April 1961 and before insured pension age other than—

    (*a*) relevant service in the armed forces; and

    (*b*) non-participating employment at the end of which no payment in lieu of contributions falls to be made,

and for the purposes of this paragraph a period of employed contributor's employment or of non-participating employment shall be treated as continuing during periods of holiday, temporary incapacity for work and similar temporary interruptions.

(3) In this Scheme any reference to the secured portion of a pension is a reference to the portion of the pension which equals the graduated retirement benefit which would be payable to the pensioner, on the assumption that he retired from regular employment on attaining insured pensionable age, in return for a payment in lieu of contributions in respect of the whole of any period of non-participating employment by virtue of which he is entitled to reckon pensionable service for the purposes of the pension, being a period of non-participating employment at the end of which no payment in lieu of contributions in fact fell to be made; and any reference to the unsecured portion of a pension shall be construed accordingly.

For the purposes of this paragraph a period of non-participating employment shall be treated as continuing during periods of holiday, temporary incapacity for work and similar temporary interruptions.

(4) For the purposes of this Scheme, the annual rate of graduated retirement benefit shall be determined as if there were $52\frac{1}{8}$ weeks in each year.

(5) In the case of a person entitled to reckon a period of pensionable service by virtue of service or employment otherwise than as a regular fireman in respect of which he was subject to superannuation arrangements, being service or employment in Northern Ireland or the Isle of Man, this Scheme shall have effect as if any reference to the National Insurance Act 1946(b) or the National Insurance Act 1965 or any enactment contained therein included a reference to any enactment of the Parliament of Northern Ireland or, as the case may be, any enactment of Tynwald, making provision for corresponding purposes.

Meaning of certain expressions

8.—(1) In this Scheme, unless the context otherwise requires, the following expressions have the meanings hereby respectively assigned to them, that is to say:—

"appointed day" means, in relation to England and Wales, 1st April 1948, and in relation to Scotland, 16th May 1948;

"award" means a pension, allowance, gratuity or award by way of return of aggregate contributions;

(a) 1965 c. 51.   (b) 1946 c. 67.

"brigade" means a fire brigade maintained under the principal Act;

"child" means (without regard to age) legitimate or illegitimate child, step-child or adopted child and any other child who is substantially dependent on the person concerned and either is related to him or is the child of his spouse; and the expressions "father", "mother", "parent" and "grandparent" shall be construed accordingly;

"fireman" means, subject to paragraph (2), a member of a brigade including a regular fireman;

"former brigade" means the brigade in which a serviceman was serving immediately before undertaking relevant service in the armed forces;

"injury" includes disease;

"previous Scheme" means the Firemen's Pension Scheme 1971, the Firemen's Pension Scheme 1966(a), the Firemen's Pension Scheme 1964(b), the Firemen's Pension Scheme 1956(c), the Firemen's Pension Scheme 1952(d) or the Firemen's Pension Scheme 1948(e), as from time to time in force;

"principal Act" means the Fire Services Act 1947;

"rank" includes the post of chief officer or, in Scotland, of firemaster;

"relative" means wife, widow, parent, grandparent or child, or any person who is a child of such a relative;

"relevant service in the armed forces" means—

(a) service specified in Schedule 1 to the Reserve and Auxiliary Forces (Protection of Civil Interests) Act 1951, other than service specified in sub-paragraph (b) of paragraph 5 thereof;

(b) part-time service under the National Service Act 1948(f), otherwise than pursuant to a training notice under that Act; and

(c) service for the purpose of training only performed by a person mentioned in paragraph 7 of Schedule 1 to the Reserve and Auxiliary Forces (Protection of Civil Interests) Act 1951 for a period shorter than 7 days;

"serviceman" means a person who immediately before undertaking relevant service in the armed forces was a regular fireman;

"service pension" means any armed forces pension or allowance payable in pursuance of any Royal Warrant or other instrument.

(2) Any reference in this Scheme to a member of a brigade or regular fireman shall, where appropriate, be construed as, or be construed as including, a reference to a person who has been a member of a brigade or, as the case may be, a regular fireman.

(3) Any reference in this Scheme to 1p or 6p a week less than a percentage of a person's pensionable pay shall, in relation to a period before 15th February 1971, be construed as a reference to 2d. or 1s. 2d. a week, as the case may be, less than that percentage.

(4) For the purposes of this Scheme a member of a fire brigade shall be taken to retire immediately following his last day of service.

Construction of references to provisions of Scheme

9. In this Scheme, unless the context otherwise requires, a reference to an Article shall be construed as a reference to an Article of this Scheme, a reference to a Schedule shall be construed as a reference to a Schedule to this Scheme, a reference to a paragraph shall be construed as a reference to a paragraph in the same Article or, as the case may be, the same Part of the same Schedule and a reference to a sub-paragraph shall be construed as a reference to a sub-paragraph in the same paragraph.

(a) *See* S.I. 1966/1045 (1966 II, p. 2504). (b) *See* S.I. 1964/1148 (1964 II, p. 2574).
(c) *See* S.I. 1956/1022 (1956 I, p. 953). (d) *See* S.I. 1952/944 (1952 I, p. 1003).
(e) *See* S.I. 1948/604 (Rev. VII, p. 776: 1948 I, p. 1091).
(f) 1948 c. 64.

Construction of references to enactments and instruments

10. In this Scheme, unless the contrary intention appears, a reference to any enactment or instrument shall be construed as including a reference to that enactment or instrument as amended, extended or applied by any other enactment or instrument.

Application of the Interpretation Act 1889

11. The Interpretation Act 1889(a) shall apply for the purpose of the interpretation of this Scheme as it applies for the purpose of the interpretation of an Act of Parliament.

PART II

AWARDS ON RETIREMENT OF REGULAR FIREMEN

Fireman's ordinary pension

12.—(1) Every regular fireman who has attained the age of 50 years and retires, being entitled to reckon at least 25 years' pensionable service, shall be entitled to a fireman's ordinary pension of an amount calculated in accordance with Part I of Schedule 1, subject however to Parts VII and VIII of that Schedule.

(2) Notwithstanding anything in paragraph (1), a chief officer or in Scotland a firemaster who retires before attaining the age of 55 years shall not be entitled to a pension under this Article unless his notice of retirement was given with the permission of the fire authority.

Fireman's short service award

13.—(1) Every regular fireman who is required to retire on account of age, but is not entitled to an ordinary pension under Article 12 shall be entitled to a fireman's short service award as hereinafter provided.

(2) In the case of a fireman entitled to reckon at least 5 years' pensionable service, the award under paragraph (1) shall be a short service pension calculated in accordance with Part II of Schedule 1, subject however to Parts VII and VIII of that Schedule.

(3) In the case of any other fireman, the award under paragraph (1) shall be a short service gratuity calculated in accordance with Part IV of Schedule 1, subject however to Part IX of that Schedule.

(4) Every regular fireman who retires at or over the age of 65 years and is entitled to reckon at least 5 years' pensionable service but is not entitled to a pension or gratuity under any other provision of this Part of this Scheme shall be entitled to a short service pension calculated in accordance with Part II of Schedule 1, subject however to Parts VII and VIII of that Schedule.

Fireman's ill-health award

14.—(1) Every regular fireman who is permanently disabled and retires on that account shall be entitled to an ill-health award as hereinafter provided.

(2) In the case of a fireman—

    (*a*) who is entitled to reckon at least 5 years' pensionable service; or

    (*b*) whose infirmity of mind or body is occasioned by a qualifying injury,

the award under paragraph (1) shall be an ill-health pension calculated in accordance with Part III of Schedule 1, subject however to Parts VII and VIII of that Schedule.

(3) In the case of any other fireman the award under paragraph (1) shall be an ill-health gratuity calculated in accordance with Part IV of Schedule 1, subject however to Part IX of that Schedule.

(a) 1889 c. 63.

Fireman's injury awards

15.—(1) This Article shall apply to a regular fireman who retires or has retired and is permanently disabled where his infirmity of mind or body is occasioned by a qualifying injury.

(2) A fireman to whom this Article applies shall be entitled to a gratuity and, in addition, to an injury pension, in both cases calculated in accordance with Part V of Schedule 1; but payment of an injury pension shall be subject to the provisions of paragraph 5 of the said Part V and, where the fireman retired before becoming permanently disabled, no payment shall be made in respect of the period before he became so disabled.

Deferred pension and award where no other award payable

16.—(1) This Article shall apply to a regular fireman who retires in circumstances in which no transfer value is payable in respect of him and which do not entitle him to any award other than such as is mentioned in this Article.

(2) A regular fireman to whom this Article applies who—

(a) has attained the age of 26 years,

(b) is entitled to reckon at least 5 years' pensionable service or, though not so entitled, is entitled to reckon pensionable service by virtue of service or employment aggregating at least 5 years, and

(c) elects that this paragraph shall apply in his case by notice in writing given to the fire authority within 3 months of 1st July 1973 or the date on which he ceased to be a member of a fire brigade whichever is the later, or within such longer period as the authority may allow in the circumstances of his case,

shall, on retirement, be entitled to a deferred pension calculated in accordance with Part VI of Schedule 1, subject however to Parts VII and VIII of that Schedule; but no payments shall be made on account of the pension—

(i) in respect of the period before he attains the age of 60 years or, if he sooner becomes permanently disabled, before he becomes so disabled, or

(ii) if he sooner relinquishes his entitlement to the pension by written notice given to the fire authority, in respect of any period thereafter.

(3) In the case of a regular fireman who retired before 1st July 1973, an election under paragraph (2)(c) shall be of no effect unless within the period there mentioned he repays to the fire authority any award made in his case under Article 55(1) of the Firemen's Pension Scheme 1971.

(4) A regular fireman to whom this Article applies who, on retirement, is not granted a pension under paragraph (2) shall be entitled to an award by way of repayment of his aggregate contributions.

(5) In the case of a regular fireman—

(a) who retired on or after 6th April 1973, and

(b) whose annual pensionable pay has at any time exceeded £5,000,

this Article shall have effect as if sub-paragraph (c) of paragraph (2) and paragraphs (3) and (4) were omitted.

Minimum aggregate amount of payments in respect of fireman's pension

17.—(1) Where a regular fireman dies while in receipt of an ordinary, short service or ill-health pension, then if the aggregate of—

(a) the sums paid in respect of the pension;

(b) any gratuity payable in respect of his death; and

(c) the actuarial value of any widow's pension or child's allowance payable in respect of his death,

is less than his aggregate contributions, there shall be paid to his estate the difference by way of adjustment of the amount of the pension.

(2) Where a regular fireman does not resume service in his brigade before the expiration of a month from the termination, under Article 18, of the unsecured portion of his ill-health pension, then if the aggregate of—

(a) the sums paid in respect of the pension; and

(b) the actuarial value of the secured portion of the pension (in so far as it is payable under Article 18(4)),

is less than his aggregate contributions, there shall be paid to him the difference by way of adjustment of the amount of the pension.

(3) For the purposes of this Article—

(a) where a person was in receipt of both an ill-health pension and an injury award, the sums paid in respect of the gratuity and pension under Article 15 shall be treated as if they had been paid in respect of the ill-health pension;

(b) the actuarial value of a widow's pension, of a child's allowance or of the secured portion of an ill-health pension shall be calculated in accordance with the tables prepared from time to time by the Government Actuary;

(c) where a fireman's pension is reduced under Article 21 the lump sum paid to him under that Article shall be deemed to have been paid in respect of the pension; and

(d) where a fireman's pension is reduced under Article 41, any reference in this Article to the aggregate amount paid to him in respect of the pension shall be construed as a reference to the aggregate amount which would have been so paid had the pension not been so reduced.

Cancellation of fireman's ill-health and injury pensions on recovery

18.—(1) As long as a person—

(a) is in receipt of an ill-health pension;

(b) would not, if he had continued to serve as a regular fireman instead of retiring with an ill-health pension, have become entitled to retire with an ordinary pension; and

(c) if he had continued so to serve, could not have been required to retire on account of age,

the fire authority may, if they wish to exercise the powers conferred by this Article, consider, at such intervals as they in their discretion think proper, whether he has become capable of performing the duties of a regular fireman.

(2) If on any such consideration it is found that he has become capable of performing the duties of a regular fireman, the fire authority may terminate the unsecured portion of the ill-health pension.

(3) Where the unsecured portion of a person's ill-health pension is terminated under this Article, the fire authority shall, if he presents himself for service in the brigade at any time before the expiration of a month from its termination, permit him to resume service in the brigade forthwith in a rank not lower than that which he held when he retired with the pension; and if the fire authority fail to comply with the requirements of this paragraph the termination shall be void and shall be deemed never to have taken effect.

(4) Where the unsecured portion of a person's ill-health pension is terminated under this Article—

(a) the secured portion of that pension shall not be payable in respect of any period before he attains the age of 65 years; and

(b) if the person is also in receipt of an injury pension under Article 15, the injury pension shall be terminated.

Reassessment of fireman's injury pension

19.—(1) Where a person is in receipt of a fireman's injury pension, the fire authority shall, at such intervals as they think fit, consider whether the degree of his disablement has substantially altered, and if they find that it has, the pension shall be reassessed accordingly.

(2) Where the person concerned is not also in receipt of an ordinary, ill-health or short service pension, if on any such reconsideration it is found that his disability has ceased, his injury pension shall be terminated.

(3) This Article shall cease to have effect with respect to a particular injury pension if, at any time after the expiration of 5 years from the time when the pension first became payable, the fire authority so resolve.

Reduction of award in case of default

20. Where a person is permanently disabled and he has brought about or contributed to his infirmity by his own default or his vicious habits, the fire authority may reduce the amount of any ill-health or injury award or deferred pension payable to him by them by an amount not exceeding a half of that to which he would otherwise be entitled.

Commutation of pension

21.—(1) A regular fireman may in accordance with the provisions of this Article commute for a lump sum a portion of any ordinary, ill-health, short service or deferred pension to which he is or may become entitled, provided in the case of an ordinary pension—

(a) that he retires when entitled to reckon at least 30 years' pensionable service; or

(b) that he is required to retire on account of age; or

(c) that the notice of commutation referred to in paragraph (3) is given with the consent of the fire authority and that he retires when entitled to reckon at least 25 years' pensionable service and on or after attaining the age of 55 years.

(2) In the case of a deferred pension, the following provisions of this Article shall have effect as if any reference therein to retirement or the date thereof were a reference to the coming into payment of the deferred pension or the date thereof.

(3) For the purpose of commuting a portion of his pension a person shall give notice in writing (in this Article called "notice of commutation") to the fire authority of his wish to commute for a lump sum such portion of his pension not exceeding a quarter thereof as (subject to the limitation contained in Article 42) he may specify.

(4) The notice of commutation shall be given by a person not earlier than 2 months before his intended retirement nor later than 6 months after his retirement.

(5) The notice of commutation given by a person shall become effective—

(a) as from the date on which it is received by the fire authority, or

(b) as from the date of his retirement,

whichever is the later:

Provided that the said notice shall not become effective if—

(i) it was given more than 2 months before his retirement, or

(ii) it relates to an ill-health pension and the unsecured portion of that pension has sooner been terminated under Article 18.

(6) Where a person retires or has retired and a notice of commutation given by him has become or becomes effective, the fire authority shall reduce the pension to which the notice relates in accordance with the notice as from the time from which the notice is effective and shall pay to him a lump sum of such amount as is the actuarial equivalent of the surrendered portion of the pension at the date of his retirement, calculated from tables prepared by the Government Actuary:

Provided that where the notice is effective as from the time mentioned in paragraph (5)(*a*), the lump sum shall be reduced by an amount equal to the difference between the aggregate payments made in respect of the pension and the aggregate payments which would have been so made had it been reduced from the date of the retirement.

(7) For the purposes of this Article no account shall be taken of any increase under Article 73(3) or 76 in an award to a serviceman.

(8) Without prejudice to the generality of Article 1(3) but subject to the transitory provisions contained in Appendix 3 to the Firemen's Pension Scheme Order 1973, the commutation of a pension, the giving of a notice or any other thing done under Article 20 of the Firemen's Pension Scheme 1971 shall have effect for the purposes of this Article as if done thereunder.

PART III

AWARDS ON DEATH OF REGULAR FIREMEN

Widows

Widow's ordinary pension

22.—(1) This Article shall apply to a widow of a regular fireman entitled to reckon at least 3 years' pensionable service who—

(*a*) dies while serving as such a fireman;

(*b*) having retired with a pension, other than a deferred pension, granted in respect of service as such a fireman, dies while still in receipt of the pension; or

(*c*) having retired from service as such a fireman on account of any injury, subsequently (without any intervening period of service as such) dies in consequence of that injury.

(2) A widow to whom this Article applies shall be entitled to an ordinary pension calculated in accordance with Part I and V of Schedule 2 subject, however, to the provisions of paragraph (3).

(3) Where the husband was serving as a regular fireman or entitled to a pension other than a deferred pension either—

(*a*) on 1st July 1973, or

(*b*) at the date of his death where that date is before 1st October 1973,

and he or, as the case may be, his widow has not excercised the rights of election accorded by Articles 58, 59, 60 and 61 for the purpose of avoiding the application to the calculation of the widow's ordinary pension—

(i) of paragraphs 2 and 3 of Part II of Schedule 2 where, before 1st April 1972, he last paid pension contributions at a rate related to 5% of his pensionable pay, or

(ii) of paragraph 3, in any other case,

then the said Part II shall apply and, accordingly, for the purposes of calculating the widow's ordinary pension, Part I of Schedule 2 shall have effect subject to the provisions of Part II.

Widow's special award

23.—(1) This Article shall apply to a widow of a regular fireman who dies from the effects of a qualifying injury or from the effects of infirmity of mind or body occasioned by such an injury.

(2) A widow to whom this Article applies shall be entitled to a widow's special pension and, in addition but subject to paragraph (5), to a gratuity.

(3) Without prejudice to Article 24(2), a widow's special pension shall be calculated in accordance with Parts III and V of Schedule 2.

(4) Without prejudice to Article 24(3), a gratuity under paragraph (2) shall be of an amount, subject to paragraph (5) equal to 25% of the husband's average annual pensionable pay.

(5) Where the husband was entitled to an injury gratuity under Article 15—

 (a) if it equalled, or exceeded, 25% of his average annual pensionable pay, the gratuity under paragraph (2) shall not be payable;

 (b) in any other case, the gratuity under paragraph (2) shall be reduced by the amount of the husband's gratuity.

Widow's augmented award

24.—(1) This Article shall apply to a widow of a regular fireman who dies from the effects of a qualifying injury or from the effects of infirmity of mind or body occasioned by such an injury where one of the following conditions is satisfied, namely that—

 (a) the injury was received in the execution of duties which were performed by the fireman—

  (i) for the immediate purpose of saving the life of another person or of preventing loss of human life, and

  (ii) in circumstances in which there was an intrinsic likelihood of his receiving a fatal injury, or

 (b) the fire authority are of the opinion that the preceding condition may be satisfied, and that this Article should apply, or

 (c) the fire authority are of the opinion that the injury was received otherwise than as aforesaid but in the course of duties performed in such circumstances that it would be inequitable if there were not payable in respect of him such an award as would have been payable had the condition specified in sub-paragraph (a) been satisfied.

(2) For the purpose of calculating the special pension payable to a widow to whom this Article applies, Part III of Schedule 2 shall have effect as if for the reference in paragraph 1 thereof to 45% of the husband's average pensionable pay there were substituted a reference to 50% thereof.

(3) The gratuity payable under Article 23(2) to a widow to whom this Article applies shall not be less than it would have been had this Article not so applied but, subject as aforesaid, Article 23(4) and (5) shall not apply to the gratuity which shall be of an amount equal to twice the annual pensionable pay, at the date of the husband's death, of a regular fireman—

 (a) holding the rank of fireman in the fire brigade maintained by the Greater London Council, and

 (b) entitled to reckon 30 years' service for the purposes of pay.

Widow's accrued pension

25.—(1) This Article shall apply to a widow of a regular fireman who dies while entitled to a deferred pension, whether or not that pension has come into payment.

(2) A widow to whom this Article applies shall be entitled to an accrued pension calculated in accordance with Parts IV and V of Schedule 2.

Widow's gratuity by way of commuted pension

26.—(1) Where a widow is entitled to an ordinary or special pension and the fire authority are satisfied that there are sufficient reasons for granting her a gratuity in lieu thereof, they may, subject to the provisions of Article 40, in their discretion and with her consent commute the pension for a gratuity of an amount calculated in accordance with Part VI of Schedule 2.

(2) Where the fire authority are precluded by reason of the provisions of Article 40 from exercising their discretion under the preceding paragraph in the manner in which they would, but for those provisions, exercise it, they may, subject to those provisions, exercise that discretion in relation to part only of the pension.

Widow's award where no other award payable

27.—(1) This Article shall apply to a widow of a regular fireman who dies while serving as such.

(2) A widow to whom this Article applies shall, unless she is a widow to whom Article 22 or 23 applies, be entitled to an award under this Article.

(3) An award under this Article shall comprise—

(a) in respect of the first 13 weeks following the husband's death, a temporary pension of such amount as secures that, in respect of each such week, the aggregate amount of the payment under this sub-paragraph and of any children's allowances payable in respect of the husband's death is of the like amount as his pensionable pay for a week immediately before he died, and

(b) an ordinary gratuity of an amount equal to the husband's average annual pensionable pay.

Right to widow's pension dependent on date of marriage

28. A woman shall not be entitled to a widow's award if she married her husband after he last ceased to serve as a regular fireman.

Special provisions where widow was living apart from her husband

29.—(1) Where a woman was living apart from her husband at the time of his death, no widow's award shall be paid to her unless—

(a) he was then making regular contributions for her support or to her for the support of her child;

(b) he was then liable to make such contributions by virtue of an agreement or of the order or decree of a competent court; or

(c) the fire authority determine that, in the circumstances of the case, the award should be payable.

(2) Where a pension is payable under paragraph (1)(a) or (b), it shall be payable at a rate not exceeding the rate at which the husband was making or was liable to make such contributions as are therein mentioned:

Provided that if the fire authority in the circumstances of the case so determine, the pension shall be payable for such period as they think fit, at such increased rate as they think fit not exceeding the rate at which it would be payable but for this Article.

(3) Where a gratuity is payable under paragraph (1)(c), it shall be payable in whole or in such part, as the fire authority think fit, and where a pension is so payable, it shall be payable for such period and at such rate as they think fit, not exceeding the rate at which it would be payable but for this Article.

Effect of remarriage

30.—(1) Where a widow's pension becomes payable to a woman, then, if she subsequently remarries, she shall not be entitled to receive any payment on account of the pension in respect of any period after her remarriage:

Provided that if at any time after her remarriage the woman again becomes a widow, or that marriage is dissolved, the fire authority may pay the whole or any part of the pension for such period after that time as they think fit.

(2) Where a widow's gratuity becomes payable to a woman, then, if she subsequently remarries, so much of the gratuity as has not been paid before her remarriage shall not be payable thereafter:

Provided that if at any time after her remarriage the woman again becomes a widow, or that marriage is dissolved, the fire authority may pay to her the whole or any part of the sums which they were actually or contingently liable to pay to her in respect of the gratuity immediately before her remarriage.

Adult Dependent Relatives

Dependent relative's special pension

31.—(1) This Article shall apply where a regular fireman dies from the effects of a qualifying injury or from the effects of infirmity of mind or body occasioned by such an injury and, in such case, shall apply—

(*a*) to a parent or (without prejudice to the following sub-paragraph) to a brother or sister of the fireman who had attained the age of 19 years before the fireman's death, or

(*b*) subject to his having attained the age of 19 years, to any child of the fireman whether or not he had attained that age before the fireman's death,

being a person who was substantially dependent on the fireman immediately before his death (in this Article referred to as a dependent relative).

(2) A dependent relative to whom this Article applies may be granted a special pension if the fire authority, having regard to all the circumstances of the case, in their discretion so determine.

(3) A dependent relative's special pension shall be calculated in accordance with Part VII of Schedule 2 and, subject to paragraph 3 thereof, shall be payable for such period or periods as the fire authority may, in their discretion, from time to time determine.

Dependent relative's gratuity

32.—(1) This Article shall apply where a regular fireman—

(*a*) dies while serving as such a fireman; or

(*b*) having retired with a pension other than a deferred pension granted in respect of service as such a fireman, dies while still in receipt of the pension,

and, in such case, shall apply to any relative of the fireman, being a person who was substantially dependent on him immediately before his death and is not entitled to an award under any other provision of this Scheme (in this Article referred to as a dependent relative).

(2) A dependent relative to whom this Article applies may, if the fire authority think fit, be granted a gratuity.

(3) The aggregate of all gratuities paid under this Article in respect of the death of any one person shall not exceed the amount of his aggregate contributions.

Children

Child's ordinary allowance

33.—(1) This Article shall apply to a child of a regular fireman who—

(*a*) dies while serving as such a fireman;

(*b*) having retired with a pension other than a deferred pension granted in respect of service as such a fireman, dies while still in receipt of the pension; or

(*c*) having retired from service as such a fireman on account of any injury, subsequently (without any intervening period of service as such) dies in consequence of that injury.

(2) A child to whom this Article applies shall be entitled to a child's ordinary allowance calculated in accordance with Parts I and IV of Schedule 3.

Child's special allowance

34.—(1) This Article shall apply to a child of a regular fireman who dies from the effects of a qualifying injury or from the effects of infirmity of mind or body occasioned by such an injury.

(2) A child to whom this Article applies shall be entitled to a child's special allowance calculated in accordance with Parts II and IV of Schedule 3.

Child's special gratuity

35.—(1) This Article shall apply to a child of a regular fireman who dies from the effects of a qualifying injury or from the effects of infirmity of mind or body occasioned by such an injury where one of the conditions set out in Article 24(1) is satisfied and the fireman does not leave a widow entitled to a gratuity under Article 23(2).

(2) A child to whom this Article applies shall be entitled to a gratuity, as hereinafter provided, in addition to a child's special allowance.

(3) The gratuity under paragraph (2) shall be of the amount mentioned in paragraph (4) except that, where two or more such gratuities are payable in respect of the same person, each gratuity shall be of the said amount divided by the number of such gratuities.

(4) The said amount shall be of an amount equal to twice the annual pensionable pay, at the date of the father's death, of a regular fireman—

(a) holding the rank of fireman in the fire brigade maintained by the Greater London Council, and

(b) entitled to reckon 30 years' service for the purposes of pay.

Child's accrued allowance

36.—(1) This Article shall apply to a child of a regular fireman who dies while entitled to a deferred pension, whether or not that pension has come into payment.

(2) A child to whom this Article applies shall be entitled to an accrued allowance calculated in accordance with Parts III and IV of Schedule 3.

Child's gratuity by way of commuted allowance

37.—(1) Where a child is entitled to an allowance, and the fire authority are satisfied that there are sufficient reasons for the grant of a gratuity in lieu of an allowance, they may, subject to the provisions of Article 40, in their discretion and with the consent of the child's guardian commute the allowance for a gratuity of an amount calculated in accordance with Part V of Schedule 3.

(2) Where the fire authority are precluded by reason of the provisions of Article 40 from exercising their discretion under the preceding paragraph in the manner in which they would but for those provisions exercise it, they may, subject to those provisions exercise that discretion in relation to part only of the allowance.

Duration of child's allowance

38. A child's allowance shall not be payable in respect of the death of a regular fireman—

(a) after the child has attained the age of 16 years unless he is undergoing full-time education or is an apprentice or is permanently disabled;

(b) after the child has attained the age of 19 years, unless he is permanently disabled and has been so disabled since attaining that age or, where later, since the death of the fireman.

Limitation on child's award

39. A child's allowance or gratuity (other than a gratuity in lieu of an allowance) shall not be granted in respect of the death of a regular fireman—

(a) to a child born on or after the date on which the fireman last ceased to be a regular fireman otherwise than of a marriage which took place before that date (hereinafter referred to as "the relevant date");

(b) by virtue of his being a step-child, to a child whose mother married the fireman on or after the relevant date;

(c) by virtue of his being substantially dependent on the fireman, to a child who was not so dependent before the relevant date;

(d) by virtue only of his being an adopted child, to a child adopted or on after the relevant date;

(e) except in the case of a legitimate child of the fireman, to a child who was not substantially dependent on the fireman at the time of his death, or

(f) to a child who had attained the age of 19 years before the date of the fireman's death unless at that date he is permanently disabled;

and, wi'hout prejudice as aforesaid, a child's gratuity shall not be granted to a child who had attained the age of 16 years before the date of the fireman's death unless at that date he is undergoing full-time education or is an apprentice or is permanently disabled.

General

Limitation on discretion to grant a gratuity in lieu of a pension or allowance

40.—(1) Where a person has died while in receipt of an ordinary, ill-health, short service or deferred pension (in this Article referred to as "the principal pension"), the fire authority shall not under Article 26 or 37 substitute for the whole or any part of a widow's pension or child's allowance payable in respect of him a gratuity the actuarial value of which, when added to that of—

(a) any other gratuity so substituted under Article 26 or 37, and

(b) any lump sum paid under Article 21 by reason that a portion of the principal pension was commuted,

exceeds a quarter of the actuarial value of the principal pension, any reduction therein under the said Article 21 being ignored.

(2) For the purposes of this Article the actuarial value of a gratuity, lump sum or pension shall be the actuarial value at the time of the husband's or father's retirement as calculated by the Government Actuary.

(3) For the purposes of this Article no account shall be taken of an increase under Article 73(3) or 76 in an award to a serviceman.

PART IV

ALLOCATION OF PENSIONS AND GENERAL PROVISIONS AFFECTING RIGHTS TO AWARDS

Allocation

41.—(1) A regular fireman may, subject to and in accordance with this Article, allocate a portion of any pension, other than an injury pension, and notwithstanding that he has already allocated a portion of such a pension, he may—

(a) where he is entitled to retire with an ordinary pension—

(i) allocate a further portion of his pension in favour of the beneficiary of a previous allocation, or

(ii) where that beneficiary has died, allocate a further portion of his pension in favour of some other beneficiary, and

(b) in any case where (not having attained the age of 70 years) he proposes to marry or remarry, allocate a further portion of his pension in favour of his wife by that marriage.

(2) For the purpose of allocating a portion of his pension a person shall—

  (a) within the time limits mentioned in paragraph (3), give notice in writing (in this Article called "notice of surrender") to the fire authority maintaining the fire brigade in which he is serving or by whom his pension is payable stating—

  (i) his wish to surrender such portion of his pension as, subject to the limitations contained in paragraph (4) and in Article 42, he may specify,

  (ii) the person in whose favour the surrender is to take effect (in this Article called "the beneficiary") being his wife or some other person who the fire authority are satisfied is substantially dependent on him; and

  (b) provide the fire authority with such evidence of his good health as they consider satisfactory.

(3) Notice of surrender shall be given—

  (a) where a person has not retired but is entitled to retire with an ordinary pension, before the person's intended retirement;

  (b) where a person in receipt of a pension who has not attained the age of 70 years proposes to marry or remarry and the beneficiary is his wife by that marriage, before but not earlier than 2 months before his intended marriage;

  (c) where the pension is a deferred pension but the preceding sub-paragraph does not apply, before but not earlier than 2 months before the pension comes into payment;

  (d) in any other case, before but not earlier than 2 months before the person's intended retirement.

(4) The total portion of a fireman's pension which he may surrender in accordance with this Article shall not exceed a third thereof.

(5) Where a person has complied with the provisions of sub-paragraphs (a) and (b) of paragraph (2), the fire authority shall forthwith send to him a written notification that they have accepted the notice of surrender, which shall become effective—

  (a) in such case as is mentioned in paragraph (3)(a)—

  (i) as from the time when the notification is received by him or, if sent by post, as from the time when it would be received by him in the ordinary course of post, or

  (ii) as from the date of his retirement,
  whichever is the earlier;

  (b) in such case as is mentioned in paragraph (3)(b), if, and only if, the proposed marriage takes place within 2 months of giving the notice of surrender and in that event as from the date of the marriage;

  (c) in such case as is mentioned in paragraph (3)(c), if, and only if, the deferred pension comes into payment within 2 months of giving the notice of surrender and in that event as from the date it comes into payment;

  (d) in any other case, if, and only if, the person retired within 2 months of giving the notice of surrender and in that event as from the date of retirement.

(6) Where a person retires or has retired and a notice of surrender given by him becomes effective—

  (a) the pension to which the notice relates shall be reduced in accordance with the notice (notwithstanding the previous death of the beneficiary) as from the date from which the pension is payable or on which the notice becomes effective, whichever is the later; and

  (b) the fire authority shall, as from the person's death, pay to the beneficiary specified in the notice, if that person survives him, a pension of such amount as is the actuarial equivalent of the surrendered portion of the pension so specified.

(7) For the purposes of paragraph (6)(b) the actuarial equivalent of the surrendered portion of the pension shall be calculated from tables prepared by the Government Actuary and in force at the time when the notice of surrender became effective, which tables shall—

(a) take account of the age of the regular fireman and of the age of the beneficiary at that time; and

(b) make different provision according to whether or not the notice of surrender became effective in accordance with paragraph (5)(a),

and separate calculations shall be made in respect of separate allocations.

(8) Where a person has allocated an ordinary pension and the allocation has taken effect and he was entitled to retire with an ordinary pension when he gave the notice of surrender, then—

(a) if he dies before retiring, the fire authority shall pay to the beneficiary specified in the notice of surrender the like pension as they would have paid by virtue of that allocation if the fireman had retired immediately before he died;

(b) if he retires with an ill-health pension, the foregoing provisions of this Article shall apply as if the allocation related to such pension.

(9) In the case of a chief officer or in Scotland a firemaster, in determining for the purposes of this Article—

(a) whether he is entitled to retire with an ordinary pension; or

(b) where he dies before retiring, the pension which would have been paid if he had retired immediately before he died,

no account shall be taken of the restriction on entitlement to an ordinary pension contained in Article 12(2).

(10) For the purposes of this Article no account shall be taken of an increase under Article 73(3) or 76 in an award to a serviceman.

(11) Without prejudice to the generality of Article 1(3) but subject to the transitory provisions contained in Appendix 3 to the Firemen's Pension Scheme Order 1973, the allocation of a pension, the giving of a notice or any other thing done under, or having effect for the purposes of Article 37 of the Firemen's Pension Scheme 1971(a) shall have effect for the purposes of this Article as if done thereunder.

Limitation on right to commute or allocate part of a pension

42.—(1) A regular fireman shall not under Article 21 commute for a lump sum nor under Article 41 allocate in favour of his wife or other dependant such a portion of his pension that that pension becomes payable at a rate less than 2 thirds of the rate at which it would have been payable but for the provisions of the said Articles and of Part VIII of Schedule 1.

(2) For the purposes of this Article no account shall be taken of an increase under Article 73(3) or 76 in an award to a serviceman.

Prevention of duplication

43. Where, apart from the provisions of this Article, a person would be entitled to receive two or more pensions or allowances under this Scheme in respect of any particular period, he shall be entitled in respect of that period to receive that one only of those pensions or allowances which is for the time being greater than the others, or, if for the time being they are all equal, one only of the said pensions or allowances shall be paid:

Provided that, for the purposes of this Article, where a person is entitled to both an injury pension and either an ill-health, ordinary, short service or deferred pension, those pensions shall be treated as one, and there shall be disregarded—

(a) a pension payable under Article 41(6) or (8);

(b) a pension payable under Part X of this Scheme;

(c) the secured portion of an ill-health pension the unsecured portion of which was terminated in the circumstances mentioned in Article 18(2), in so far as it is payable under Article 18(4).

(a) *See* S.I. 1971/145 (1971 I, p. 320).

Award not payable in case of transfer

44.—(1) Where a regular fireman retires from a brigade in pursuance of a written notice to the fire authority of his intention to retire for the purpose of joining another brigade, then, notwithstanding anything in Part II of this Scheme, he shall not, on the occasion of that retirement, be entitled to an award under that Part.

(2) Where paragraph (1) does not apply but a regular fireman retires or has retired from a brigade and after again becoming such a fireman in that or another brigade becomes entitled, in the circumstances mentioned in Article 48(1) or (4), to reckon as pensionable service the period of pensionable service he was entitled to reckon on retiring, then, subject to paragraph (4), any award to which he has become entitled on the occasion of that retirement shall cease to be payable.

(3) Where a regular fireman retires or has retired from a brigade and enters other pensionable employment in such circumstances that a transfer value becomes payable by the fire authority in respect of him, then, subject to paragraph (4), any award to which he has become entitled on the occasion of that retirement shall cease to be payable.

(4) Where an award under Article 16(4) ceases to be payable under paragraph (2) or (3), there shall continue to be payable—

(a) where the award ceases to be payable under paragraph (2) or (3), so much of the award as is unpaid and represents a return of such additional or further payments by way of contributions or lump sum as are mentioned in Articles 57, 58 and 59;

(b) where the award ceases to be payable under paragraph (3), so much of the award as is unpaid and would not have been payable had he paid pension contributions at a rate related to 5% of his pensionable pay.

Withdrawal of pension or allowance for misconduct

45.—(1) Where any person to whom a pension or allowance is payable—

(a) is sentenced for any offence to imprisonment for a term exceeding 12 months;
or

(b) becomes or continues to be engaged in any business, occupation or employment which is illegal,

the fire authority may, in relation to that pension or allowance, excercise the powers conferred by this Article.

(2) In the case of an ordinary, short service, ill-health or deferred pension, the fire authority may—

(a) withdraw the unsecured portion of the pension in whole or in part and either temporarily or permanently;

(b) withdraw the secured portion of the pension in whole or in part for a period before the pensioner attains the age of 65 years or during his imprisonment or detention in legal custody.

(3) In the case of any other pension or of an allowance, the fire authority may withdraw the award in whole or in part and either temporarily or permanently.

(4) So much of any pension or allowance as is withdrawn under this Article may, to such extent as the fire authority at any time think fit—

(a) be applied by that authority for the benefit of any dependant of the person to whom but for its withdrawal it would be payable;

(b) be restored to that person.

Withdrawal of pension during employment as a regular fireman

46. The fire authority by whom a pension is payable may, in their discretion, withdraw the whole or any part of the pension for any period during which the pensioner is employed as a regular fireman in any fire brigade.

PART V

PENSIONABLE SERVICE OF REGULAR FIREMEN

Current service in the brigade

47. A regular fireman shall be entitled to reckon as pensionable service—

(a) any period of service as such, in the brigade in which he is serving, on or after 1st April 1972; and

(b) where he was serving in that brigade both on and immediately before 1st April 1972, any period of pensionable service which he was entitled to reckon immediately before that date:

Provided that, subject as hereinafter provided, there shall not be reckonable as pensionable service—

(i) where he has left and rejoined the brigade on or after 1st April 1972 any period of service before he last rejoined the brigade;

(ii) any period of absence from duty as a fireman as a result of sickness or injury which is certified by a duly qualified medical practitioner to be due to his own misconduct or vicious habits; or

(iii) any period of absence from duty as a fireman without pay, including any period of suspension from duty terminating with the fireman having been found guilty of an offence against discipline or a criminal offence. .

Previous service in a brigade

48.—(1) Subject to paragraph (3) and to Article 59(4), where a regular fireman—

(a) retires or has retired from a brigade—

(i) without a pension or with a deferred pension which he has relinquished under Article 16(2), and

(ii) without a transfer value becoming payable by the fire authority (otherwise than under Article 71), and

(b) within twelve months of so retiring and without any intervening service as a regular fireman rejoins or has rejoined that brigade or joins or has joined another brigade,

he shall be entitled to reckon as pensionable service the period of pensionable service he was entitled to reckon on so retiring, but subject to his undertaking, within 6 months of rejoining or, as the case may be, joining the brigade or within such longer period as the fire authority may in his case allow, to pay in accordance with Schedule 4 the sum, if any, mentioned in paragraph (2).

(2) The sum referred to in paragraph (1) shall be equal to the aggregate of—

(a) any sum paid to him by way of gratuity or return of aggregate contributions on retirement less so much of such sum, if any, as represents a return of such additional or further payments by way of contributions or lump sum as are mentioned in Articles 57, 58 and 59; and

(b) the balance of any sum he had undertaken to pay, in accordance with the provisions of Schedule 4 or the corresponding provisions of a previous Firemen's Pension Scheme, which was outstanding immediately before his retirement.

(3) In the case of a person who has completed less than 2 years' service as a regular fireman, paragraph (1) shall apply only where he retires or has retired from one brigade for the purpose of joining another brigade and joins that brigade with the written consent of the fire authority maintaining the first-mentioned brigade, and such consent may be given after he has left the first-mentioned brigade if he has applied to the fire authority for such consent while still a member of the brigade.

(4) Where a regular fireman—

(a) retires or has retired from a brigade with an ill-health pension; and (*b*) resumes service in the brigade in the circumstances and within the period mentioned in Article 18(3),

he shall be entitled to reckon as pensionable service the period of pensionable service he was entitled to reckon on so retiring.

(5) Where a regular fireman—

(*a*) retires or has retired from a brigade without a pension, other than an ill-health pension the unsecured portion of which has been terminated in the circumstances mentioned in Article 18(2);

(*b*) without any intervening service as a regular fireman rejoins or has rejoined that brigade or joins or has joined another brigade; and

(*c*) cannot under paragraph (1) or (4) reckon as pensionable service the period of pensionable service he was entitled to reckon on so retiring,

he shall be entitled to reckon that period as pensionable service, but subject to his undertaking, within 6 months of rejoining or, as the case may be, joining the brigade, or within such longer period as the fire authority may in his case allow, to pay in accordance with Schedule 4 a sum calculated in accordance with Schedule 5.

Period during which an injury or a special pension was payable

49.—(1) Subject to Article 59(4), where a regular fireman—

(*a*) retires or has retired from a brigade with an injury pension or, before 1st April 1972, with a special pension; and

(*b*) resumes or has resumed service in the brigade in the circumstances and within the period mentioned in Article 18(3),

he shall be entitled to reckon as pensionable service the period for which that pension was payable, but subject to his undertaking, within 6 months of resuming service in the brigade or within such longer period as the fire authority may in his case allow, to pay in accordance with Schedule 4 a sum equal to the aggregate of the pension contributions (other than such additional or further contributions as are mentioned in Articles 57 and 58) which would have been payable by him for that period had he continued to serve as a regular fireman in the brigade in the rank he held immediately before his retirement.

(2) For the purposes of this Article a person shall be treated as having been entitled to, and in receipt of, an injury or, as the case may be, special pension if such a pension would have been payable but for the amount of some benefit payable to him under the enactments relating to national insurance (including industrial injuries).

Absence from duty in the brigade without pay

50.—(1) Where a regular fireman is or has been absent from duty without pay, the fire authority may, at any time while he is such a fireman in their brigade, resolve that the whole or any part of the period of absence shall be reckoned as pensionable service for the purposes of this Scheme.

(2) Where by virtue of any such resolution as aforesaid any period is reckoned as pensionable service, the fireman shall become liable to pay to the fire authority the contributions (including such additional or further contributions as are mentioned in Articles 57 and 58) which would have been payable by him for that period if he had been paid at the rate applicable to his case.

Previous local government service

51.—(1) Subject to Article 59(4), this Article shall apply in the case of a person—

(*a*) who before becoming a regular fireman was in employment by virtue of which he was or was deemed to be a contributory employee or a local Act contributor within the meaning of the Local Government Superannuation Act 1937(**a**); and

(*b*) in respect of whom a transfer value relating to his former employment is paid to the fire authority under rules made under sections 2 and 15 of the Superannuation (Miscellaneous Provisions) Act 1948(**b**).

(**a**) 1937 c. 68.   (**b**) 1948 c. 33.

(2) Subject to paragraphs (3) and (4) such a person as is mentioned in the preceding paragraphs shall be entitled to reckon as pensionable service the aggregate of—

    (*a*) 3 quarters of the period of contributing service; and

    (*b*) 3 eighths of the period of non-contributing service,

which he would have been entitled to reckon had he on becoming a regular fireman become a contributory employee within the meaning of the Local Government Superannuation Act 1937 entitled to the benefit of section 13 of that Act.

(3) Where he would have been entitled in the circumstances mentioned in the preceding paragraph to reckon a period as contributing service subject to his making certain payments by way of—

    (*a*) additional contributory payments in discharge of a fixed sum; or

    (*b*) additional contributions for added years,

whether on giving notice in that behalf or otherwise, then he shall and shall only be entitled to reckon 3 quarters of that period as pensionable service if within 3 months of his becoming a regular fireman or within such longer period as the fire authority may in his case allow, he undertakes to pay in accordance with Schedule 4 a sum equal to the capital value of those additional payments or contributions as the case may be, as determined by the fire authority.

(4) Where in the exercise of their discretion under rules made under the Superannuation (Miscellaneous Provisions) Act 1948 the authority by whom he was employed in his former employment increase his service for the purposes of those rules, then for the purposes of this Article the service reckonable by him immediately before ceasing to hold his former employment shall be deemed to have been correspondingly increased.

(5) Any reference in this Article to the Local Government Superannuation Act 1937 shall be construed as including a reference to the Local Government Superannuation (Scotland) Act 1937(a).

Previous service other than fire or local government service

52.—(1) Subject to Article 59(4), this Article shall apply in the case of a regular fireman—

    (*a*) who before becoming a regular fireman was in such service or employment as is mentioned in Schedule 6 (hereafter referred to in this Article as "former service") by virtue of which he was subject to superannuation arrangements;

    (*b*) who last became a regular fireman within 12 months of the termination of his former service or within such longer period as may be agreed, in the circumstances of his case, between the fire authority and the authority specified in Schedule 6 in relation to his former service;

    (*c*) in respect of whom such a transfer value relating to his former service as is mentioned in Schedule 6 is paid to the fire authority;

    (*d*) who, within 3 months of his becoming a regular fireman or (subject to paragraph 2 of Part I of Schedule 6) within 6 months of the date specified in Schedule 6 in relation to his former service, whichever is the later, or within such longer period as the fire authority may allow in his case, undertakes to pay in accordance with Schedule 4—

        (i) a sum equal to the balance of any liability outstanding immediately before the termination of his former service in respect of payments or contributions he was then making as a condition of reckoning past service as contributing service or otherwise for the purposes of the said superannuation arrangements, being service of which account has been taken in the calculation of the said transfer value, together with

        (ii) a sum equal to the amount, if any, by which the said transfer value falls to be reduced on account of any gratuity or award by way of return of contributions made under the said arrangements on the termination of his former service.

(a) 1937 c. 69.

(2) Where under the superannuation arrangements mentioned in paragraph (1)—

    (*a*) a maximum pension is provided (otherwise than on retirement occasioned by injury or ill-health) for a person entitled to reckon 30 years' service for the purposes thereof, or

    (*b*) after 20 years' service each year of service is reckonable as 2 years' service for the purposes thereof,

then such a person as is mentioned in paragraph (1) who was subject to those arrangements shall be entitled to reckon as pensionable service the whole of the period specified in paragraph (4), so, however, that, where under those arrangements such provision as is mentioned in sub-paragraph (*a*) or (*b*) is made in relation only to service or employment of a description designated therein (in this paragraph referred to as "designated service") and the former service included designated service, there shall be reckonable as aforesaid—

    (i) the whole of that part of the period specified in paragraph (4) as is referable to designated service, and

    (ii) 3 quarters of that part of that period as is not so referable.

(3) In any other case, such a person as is mentioned in paragraph (1) shall be entitled to reckon 3 quarters of the period specified in paragraph (4).

(4) The period referred to in paragraphs (2) and (3) is—

    (*a*) the period of service which is or was reckonable for the purpose of calculating the transfer value; or

    (*b*) where separate calculations are or were made in respect of contributing and non-contributing service reckonable for the purpose of calculating the said transfer value, the aggregate of the period of contributing service and a half of the period of non-contributing service which is so reckonable.

(5) In this Article the expression "award by way of return of contributions" has the meaning assigned thereto by Article 5(2).

Certificates of pensionable service

53.—(1) Where a regular fireman becomes entitled to reckon a period of service as pensionable service for the purposes of this Scheme by virtue of Article 48, 49, 51, 52 or 78, then the fire authority shall, within a period of 6 months, supply him with a certificate showing the pensionable service he was entitled to reckon on the date on which he became entitled to reckon the said period of such service.

(2) Where a fireman is dissatisfied with a certificate supplied to him in accordance with the provisions of the preceding paragraph, he may, within 3 months of being supplied with it, appeal to the Secretary of State who shall either confirm or vary the said certificate.

(3) Where in accordance with the preceding provisions of this Article a certificate has been supplied to a fireman and he has not appealed to the Secretary of State within the period of 3 months aforesaid, or where a certificate has been confirmed or varied on such an appeal, then the certificate as supplied, confirmed or varied, as the case may be, shall be conclusive as to the pensionable service which the fireman was entitled to reckon on the date to which it refers.

(4) Where a fireman is entitled to a certificate under paragraph (1) but claims a pension or gratuity or dies—

    (*a*) before the certificate has been supplied, then the obligation to supply a certificate shall cease;

    (*b*) after the certificate has been supplied but before it has become conclusive, then the certificate shall cease to have effect and no further proceedings under paragraph (2) shall take place.

(5) For the purposes of this Article a fireman shall be treated as only becoming entitled to reckon service under Article 78 if and when he resumes service in his former brigade.

Prevention of double reckoning

54. A regular fireman who is entitled to reckon a period as pensionable service under any provision of this Part of this Scheme shall not be entitled also to reckon that period under some other such provision.

PART VI

PENSIONABLE PAY, CONTRIBUTIONS AND OTHER ADDITIONAL AND FURTHER PAYMENTS

Pensionable pay and average pensionable pay

55.—(1) In this Scheme the expression "pensionable pay" means the pay of a regular fireman as determined in relation to his rank or, in the case of a chief officer or an assistant chief officer or, in Scotland, a firemaster or an assistant firemaster, his pay as determined for the post.

(2) For the purpose of determining the benefits payable under this Scheme on the death or retirement of a regular fireman—

(*a*) the expression "average annual pensionable pay" means, subject to paragraphs (3) and (4), the aggregate of his pensionable pay during the period of a year ending with the relevant date:

Provided that where he was in receipt of pensionable pay for part only of that period, the said aggregate shall be multiplied by the reciprocal of the fraction of the year for which he was in receipt of pensionable pay; and

(*b*) the expression " average pensionable pay" means the average annual pensionable pay divided by $52\frac{1}{6}$.

(3) Where the amount of a fireman's average annual pensionable pay, determined in accordance with paragraph (2), is less than the amount it would have been had he not suffered a reduction of pay during sick leave or a stoppage of pay by way of punishment, it shall be increased by the difference between the two said amounts.

(4) Where the amount of a fireman's average annual pensionable pay, determined in accordance with paragraphs (2) and (3), is less than the amount it would have been had the relevant date been the corresponding date in one of the two preceding years (whichever year yields the higher amount), it shall be increased by the difference between the two said amounts.

(5) Where an award is made to or in respect of a regular fireman the relevant date for the purpose of determining his average annual pensionable pay shall be the date of his last day of service as such a fireman.

Rate of payment of pension contributions

56.—(1) Subject to the provisions of this Scheme, a regular fireman shall pay pension contributions to the fire authority at the rate of 6p a week less than 6·75% of his pensionable pay.

(2) In the case of a person who—

(*a*) served before the appointed day in a fire brigade maintained by a local authority or in the National Fire Service;

(*b*) became a regular fireman on the appointed day or, where he was then a member of the armed forces of the Crown, after next ceasing to be such a member and without any intervening service in another capacity; and

(*c*) did not elect to pay pension contributions at the lower rate under Article 38 of the Firemen's Pension Scheme 1948(a),

this Article shall, subject to the proviso to paragraph (4), apply subject to the provisions of that paragraph.

(3) In the case of a person who—

(*a*) is entitled to reckon a period as pensionable service by virtue of service or employment otherwise than as a regular firemen in respect of which he was subject to superannuation arrangements; and

(*b*) has been excepted from the operation of any regulations made under section 69(4) of the National Insurance Act 1946(b) or section 110(1) of the National

---

(a) *See* S.I. 1948/604 (Rev. VII, p. 776: 1948 I, p. 1091).   (b) 1946 c. 67.

Insurance Act 1965(a) or of any other provisions modifying the said arrangements in connection with the passing of the said Act of 1946, this Article shall, subject to the proviso to paragraph (4), apply subject to the provisions of that paragraph.

(4) In the case of a person such as is mentioned in paragraph (2) or (3), this Article shall apply as if for any reference to a rate of 6p a week less than a percentage of his pensionable pay there were substituted a reference to the rate of 1p a week less than that percentage of his pensionable pay:

Provided that in the case of a person who has previously retired from service as a regular fireman, otherwise than with an ill-health pension, and resumed service as such later than a year after that retirement this paragraph shall have effect only if he is such a person as is mentioned in paragraph (3) by reason of his being entitled to reckon pensionable service by virtue of such service or employment as is there mentioned which he entered after his previous retirement.

Additional contributions—preserved provisions

57.—(1) Where a man elected, in accordance with Article 40 of the Firemen's Pension Scheme 1966(b), to pay additional pension contributions and has not since he so elected become entitled to reckon 25 years' pensionable service or retired, he shall pay such contributions at a rate calculated in accordance with paragraph 1 of Part I of Schedule 7 until such time as he becomes entitled to reckon 25 years' pensionable service or retires, whichever is the earlier.

(2) In this Article a reference to a person's retirement is a reference to his retirement otherwise than in pursuance of a written notice to the fire authority of his intention to retire for the purpose of joining another brigade.

Additional and further payments by way of contributions—current provisions

58.—(1) This Article shall apply to a regular fireman who—

(a) is, on 1st July 1973, serving as such, and entitled to reckon less than 41 years' and 3 months' pensionable service, and

(b) cannot, before 1st April 1977, be required to retire on account of age in accordance with Article 96.

(2) A man to whom this Article applies who, before 1st April 1972, last paid pension contributions at a rate related to 5% of his pensionable pay may, for the purpose of avoiding the application of paragraph 2 of Part II of Schedule 2 to the calculation of his widow's ordinary pension, elect to pay additional contributions at a rate calculated in accordance with paragraph 2 of Part I of Schedule 7.

(3) Subject to Article 62(2), a man to whom this Article applies may, for the purpose of avoiding the application of paragraph 3 of Part II of Schedule 2 to the calculation of his widow's ordinary pension, elect to pay further pension contributions at a rate calculated in accordance with paragraph 3 of Part I of Schedule 7

(4) Where a man elects as mentioned in paragraph (2) or (3), he shall pay additional or, as the case may be, further pension contributions as from 1st April 1973 until, subject to paragraph (5), the following date, namely—

(a) if, on 1st July 1973, he was entitled to reckon less than 19 years' pensionable service otherwise than by virtue of service as a regular fireman on or after 1st April 1972, the date on which he becomes entitled to reckon 25 years' pensionable service so, however, in determining the said date there shall be disregarded pensionable service reckonable by virtue of such service or employment before 1st July 1973 which he was not then entitled to reckon;

(b) in any other case, 1st April 1978.

(5) Additional or further pension contributions payable under this Article shall cease to be payable on retirement; but where a regular fireman was paying such

(a) 1965 c. 51.   (b) *See* S.I. 1966/1045 (1966 II, p. 2504).

contributions immediately before retiring with an ordinary pension that pension shall be reduced in accordance with paragraph 6 of Part VIII of Schedule 1.

(6) Notwithstanding anything in paragraphs (2) and (3), a man shall not so exercise the rights of election accorded by those paragraphs that the aggregate rate at which he is liable to pay pension contributions (including additional contributions under Article 57 or this Article and further contributions under this Article) exceeds 15% of his pensionable pay.

Additional and further payments by way of lump sum or reduction of pension

59.—(1) This Article shall apply to a regular fireman who is, on 1st July 1973—

    (*a*) serving as such, or

    (*b*) entitled to an ordinary, short service or deferred pension, having retired on or after 1st April 1972.

(2) A man to whom this Article applies who, before 1st April 1972, last paid pension contributions at a rate related to 5% of his pensionable pay may, for the purpose mentioned in Article 58(2), elect either—

    (*a*) to make an additional payment by way of a lump sum calculated in accordance with paragraph 2 of Part II of Schedule 7, or

    (*b*) that any ordinary, ill-health, short service or deferred pension payable to him shall be reduced in accordance with paragraph 2 of Part VIII of Schedule 1.

(3) Subject to Article 62(2), a man to whom this Article applies may, for the purpose mentioned in Article 58(3), elect either—

    (*a*) to make a further payment by way of a lump sum calculated in accordance with paragraph 3 of Part II of Schedule 7, or

    (*b*) that any ordinary, ill-health, short service or deferred pension payable to him shall be reduced in accordance with paragraph 3 of Part VIII of Schedule 1.

(4) In the case of a regular fireman to whom this Article applies by virtue of paragraph (1)(*a*), Article 48, 49, 51 or 52 shall only apply by virtue of the conditions specified in the Article in question being satisfied on or after 1st July 1973—

    (*a*) where he has not elected as mentioned in paragraph (2)(*b*), if he agrees that any ordinary, ill-health, short service or deferred pension payable to him shall be reduced in accordance with paragraph 2 of Part VIII of Schedule 1;

    (*b*) where he has not elected as mentioned in paragraph (3)(*b*), if he agrees that any such pension shall be reduced in accordance with paragraph 3 of the said Part VIII,

and, in the case of Article 51 or 52, so agrees within the period mentioned in Article 51(3) or, as the case may be, Article 52(1)(*d*).

Additional and further payments etc. in the case of an ill-health pensioner

60.—(1) This Article shall apply to a regular fireman who is, on 1st July 1973 entitled to an ill-health pension, having retired on or after 1st April 1972.

(2) A man to whom this Article applies who, before 1st April 1972, last paid pension contributions at a rate related to 5% of his pensionable pay may, for the purpose mentioned in Article 58(2), elect—

    (*a*) to make additional payments in accordance with this Article, or

    (*b*) that his ill-health pension be reduced in accordance with paragraph 2 of Part VIII of Schedule 1.

(3) Subject to Article 62(2), a man to whom this Article applies may, for the purpose mentioned in Article 58(3), elect either—

    (*a*) to make further payments in accordance with this Article, or

    (*b*) that his ill-health pension be reduced in accordance with paragraph 3 of Part VIII of Schedule 1.

(4) Where a man elects as mentioned in paragraph (2)(*a*) or (3)(*a*), he shall make additional or, as the case may be, further payments in respect of the period beginning with the date of his election which corresponds in duration with that of his service as a regular fireman on or after 1st April 1972, being payments equivalent to the payments by way of additional or further pension contributions in respect of that period of service which he would have made had he been liable to make such contributions calculated in accordance with paragraph 2 or, as the case may be, paragraph 3 of Part I of Schedule 7 so, however, that should he die before completing his additional or further payments, no such payments shall be due in respect of the period following his death.

(5) Where a man elects as mentioned in paragraph (2)(*a*) or (3)(*a*), the additional, or, as the case may be, further payments shall be made to the fire authority by whom his pension is payable and may, without prejudice to any other method of payment, be discharged by way of deductions of appropriate amounts made by that authority from instalments of his pension.

Additional and further payments in the case of deceased fireman

61.—(1) This Article shall apply in the case of a regular fireman who dies or has died on or after 1st April 1972 but before 1st October 1973—

   (*a*) either while serving as such or having retired on or after 1st April 1972, and

   (*b*) not having exercised any right of election accorded by Article 58, 59 or 60.

(2) The widow of a man in whose case this Article applies who, before 1st April 1972, last paid pension contributions at a rate related to 5% of his pensionable pay may, for the purpose of avoiding the application of paragraph 2 of Part II of Schedule 2 to the calculation of her widow's ordinary pension elect to make additional payments in accordance with this Article.

(3) Subject to Article 62(2), the widow of a man in whose case this Article applies may, for the purpose of avoiding the application of paragraph 3 of Part II of Schedule 2 to the calculation of her widow's ordinary pension, elect to make further payments in accordance with this Article.

(4) Where a widow elects as mentioned in paragraph (2) or (3), the provisions of paragraphs (4) and (5) of Article 60 shall apply, subject to the necessary adaptations, as they apply where a man elects as mentioned in paragraph (2)(*a*) or (3)(*a*) of the said Article.

Provisions supplemental to Articles 57 to 61

62.—(1) In the case of a regular fireman to whom both Articles 58 and 59 apply, the rights of election accorded by paragraph (2) or, as the case may be, paragraph (3) of each of those Articles shall be alternative rights.

(2) Where a regular fireman last paid pension contributions before 1st April 1972 at a rate related to 5% of his pensionable pay—

   (*a*) he shall not exercise the right of election accorded by either Article 58(3) or Article 59(3) unless he also exercises the right of election accorded by either Article 58(2) or Article 59(2);

   (*b*) he shall not exercise the right of election accorded by paragraph (3) of Article 60 unless he also exercises the right of election accorded by paragraph (2) thereof;

   (*c*) his widow shall not exercise the right of election accorded by paragraph (3) of Article 61 unless she also exercises the right of election accorded by paragraph (2) thereof.

(3) Any election under Article 58, 59, 60 or 61 shall be made by notice in writing to the fire authority maintaining the fire brigade in which the man is serving or by whom his or his widow's pension is payable.

(4) Any such election, and any payment of a lump sum in pursuance of an election under Article 59, shall be made before 1st October 1973 except that a widow of a man who has died before the said date may exercise a right of election accorded by Article 61 on or after the said date if she does so within 3 months of his death.

(5) Where a regular fireman elects under Article 59 or Article 60 that his pension shall be reduced and, on the date on which he so elects, he is in receipt of an ordinary, ill-health, short service or deferred pension, that pension shall be recalculated as from the date from which it became payable.

(6) Any reference in Articles 57 and 58 to retirement shall be construed as excluding a reference to a man's retirement in pursuance of a written notice to the fire authority of his intention to retire for the purpose of joining another brigade.

Method of payment of pension contributions

63. The pension contributions (including additional and further contributions, if any) upon each instalment of pay shall fall due at the same time as that instalment and may, without prejudice to any other method of payment, be discharged by way of a deduction of an appropriate amount made by the fire authority from the said instalment.

Repayment of contributions on death

64. Where a regular fireman dies while serving as such and either no pension, allowance or gratuity is payable in respect of his death or the aggregate of—

(a) any gratuity so payable; and

(b) the actuarial value of any pension or allowance so payable (calculated in accordance with the tables prepared from time to time by the Government Actuary),

is less than his aggregate contributions, an award shall be made to his estate by way of repayment of his aggregate contributions or of so much thereof as represents the difference, as the case may be.

Repayment of contributions on dismissal

65.—(1) Where a regular fireman is dismissed from the brigade otherwise than for one of the offences mentioned in paragraph (3), the fire authority shall repay to him his aggregate contributions.

(2) Where a regular fireman is dismissed from the brigade for one of the offences mentioned in paragraph (3), the fire authority may in their discretion—

(a) repay to him his aggregate contributions wholly or in part;

(b) apply his aggregate contributions wholly or in part for the benefit of his dependants;

(c) retain his aggregate contributions wholly or in part.

(3) The offences referred to in paragraphs (1) and (2) are the following disciplinary offences:—

(a) by carelessness or neglect suffering any loss, damage or injury to occur to any person or property (which offence is specified in paragraph (4)(b) of the code of disciplinary offences set out in the Schedule to the Fire Services (Discipline) Regulations 1948(a) and in the Schedule to the Fire Services (Discipline) (Scotland) Regulations 1953(b));

(b) failing to account for, or to make a true return of any money or property which comes into the fireman's possession in the course of his duties (which offence is specified in paragraph (7)(b) of the said code), and

(c) wilfully or negligently damaging any article of clothing or personal equipment with which the fireman has been provided or entrusted or failing to take proper care thereof (which offence is specified in paragraph (9)(a) of the said code).

(a) S.I. 1948/545 (Rev. VII, p. 757: 1948 I, p. 1059).
(b) S.I. 1953/1086 (1953 I, p. 766).

PART VII

DETERMINATION OF QUESTIONS AND APPEALS

General functions of fire authority

66.—(1) Subject as hereinafter provided, the question whether a person is entitled to any and if so what awards shall be determined in the first instance by the fire authority.

(2) Subject to the provisions of this Scheme, the fire authority shall consider the medical evidence of at least one duly qualified medical practitioner selected by the authority before determining for the purposes of this Scheme—

(*a*) whether a person has been disabled;

(*b*) whether any such disablement appears likely to be permanent;

(*c*) whether a person's disablement has been occasioned by a qualifying injury;

(*d*) whether a person has become capable of performing the duties of a fireman;

(*e*) the degree to which a person has been disabled;

(*f*) any other question which ought to be determined in whole or in part on medical grounds:

Provided that where an authority are unable to obtain such evidence by reason of the refusal or the wilful or negligent failure of any person to submit to medical examination by a duly qualified medical practitioner selected by the authority, the authority may dispense with such evidence and may give such decision on the question at issue as they may in their discretion choose to give, either without medical evidence or upon such medical evidence as they think fit.

Appeal against opinion of fire authority's medical practitioner

67.—(1) Where for the purposes of any decision which falls to be made by a fire authority under this Scheme any person is medically examined by a medical practitioner selected by the authority, the opinion of the practitioner shall be given in writing to the authority.

(2) If within 14 days of being informed by the fire authority of the decision the said person applies to the authority for a copy of the opinion, the authority shall supply him with a copy thereof.

(3) If he is dissatisfied with the opinion of which a copy has been so supplied to him, he may, subject to and in accordance with the provisions of Schedule 8, appeal against the opinion to an independent person nominated by the Secretary of State (hereinafter referred to as a "medical referee").

(4) A fire authority shall be bound by any decision on a medical question duly given on any such appeal.

Appeal against decision of fire authority

68.—(1) Where any person claims that he is entitled to an award or to any payment on account of an award and the fire authority do not admit the claim at all, or do not admit the claim to the full extent thereof, the person aggrieved may apply to the fire authority for reconsideration of the case, and, if aggrieved by the decision on such reconsideration, may appeal to the Crown Court.

(2) Subject as hereinafter provided, the Crown Court may, on an appeal under paragraph (1), make such order or declaration as appears to the court to be just.

(3) Nothing in this Article shall authorise the Crown Court—

(*a*) to make an order or declaration controlling or restricting the exercise of any discretion which by this Scheme is vested in a fire authority;

(*b*) to reopen any decision on a medical question which has been given on an appeal under Article 67; or

(c) to question any certificate of pensionable service given under Article 53 or any corresponding provision of the Firemen's Pension Scheme then in operation, which is deemed to be conclusive thereby.

(4) In the application of this Article to Scotland, for any reference to the Crown Court there shall be substituted a reference to the sheriff having jurisdiction in the place where the person concerned last served as a regular fireman.

PART VIII

PAYMENT OF AWARDS AND FINANCIAL PROVISIONS

Payment of awards generally

69.—(1) An award which is payable to or in respect of a person by reason of his having been employed as a regular fireman shall be payable by the fire authority by whom he was last employed as such.

(2) An award which is payable to or in respect of a person by reason of his having received an injury while employed as a member of a brigade otherwise than as a regular fireman, shall be payable by the fire authority by whom he was employed when he received the injury.

(3) Subject to the provisions of this Scheme, every pension or allowance shall be payable in respect of each week and shall, subject to such delay as may be necessary for the purpose of determining any question as to the liability of the fire authority in respect thereof, be discharged by payments in advance at such reasonable intervals as the fire authority may determine.

(4) Where a person dies after receiving a sum paid in advance on account of a pension or allowance, no claim for repayment shall be made on the ground that the said sum or any part thereof is referable to a period after his death.

(5) Where a widow remarries after receiving a sum paid in advance on account of a pension, no claim for repayment shall be made on the ground that the said sum or any part thereof is referable to a period after her remarriage.

(6) Subject to the provisions of this Scheme and, in particular, of Article 15 (injury pension) and of Article 16 (deferred pension), a pension payable to a fireman shall be payable as from the date of his retirement.

(7) A pension or allowance payable to the widow or child of a fireman shall be payable as from his death, or, in the case of an allowance payable to a posthumous child as from the birth of the child, except—

(a) where the fireman was in receipt of a pension and he died during a period in respect of which he had already received his pension, in which case the pension or allowance shall not be payable before the end of that period;

(b) where the fireman received a gratuity other than an injury gratuity under Article 15, in which case the pension or allowance shall be payable as from the first anniversary of his death or such earlier date as the fire authority, in the circumstances of the case, think fit.

(8) Subject to the provisions of this Scheme, every gratuity shall be paid in one sum: Provided that where a fire authority are satisfied that it would be to the advantage of the beneficiary to pay a gratuity in instalments, they may pay it in instalments of such reasonable amounts and over such reasonable period as they think fit.

(9) Without prejudice to the provisions of any such regulations as are mentioned in section 60(5) of the National Insurance Act 1965 and for the time being in force, where a regular fireman is entitled under Article 16(4) to an award by way of repayment of his aggregate contributions the fire authority shall be under no obligation to make payment until the expiration of a year from the date of his retirement or until he requests payment, whichever first occurs.

(10) From any payment on account of an award made to a fireman during his lifetime which constitutes a repayment of contributions within the meaning of paragraph 2 of Part II of Schedule 5 to the Finance Act 1970(a) the fire authority may deduct the tax for the time being chargeable thereon under the said paragraph 2.

(a) 1970 c. 24.

Payment of awards in special cases

70.—(1) Where any sum is due on account of a pension, and any debt is due to the fire authority from the pensioner, so much of the said sum as does not exceed the debt may be applied by the authority in or towards the satisfaction of the debt:

Provided that where the pension is an ordinary, ill-health or short service pension, and the sum due is in respect of a period beyond the age of 65 years, only so much of the sum as is due on account of the unsecured portion of the pension may be applied as mentioned in this paragraph.

(2) If it appears to the fire authority that a pensioner is by reason of mental disorder or otherwise incapable of managing his affairs, the authority may in their discretion pay the pension or any part thereof to any person having the care of the pensioner, and, in so far as they do not dispose of the pension in that manner, may apply it in such manner as they think fit for the benefit of the pensioner or his dependants.

(3) On the death of a person to whom or to whose estate a sum not exceeding £500 is due on account of a pension, the fire authority may, without probate, confirmation or any other formality or proof of title, pay the said sum to the persons appearing to the authority to be beneficially entitled to the personal estate of the deceased, or, as the authority think fit, pay the said sum to one or more of those persons or distribute it among all or any of those persons in such proportions as the authority may determine.

(4) Where any sum is payable to a minor on account of a pension, the authority may, if they think fit, in lieu of paying the said sum to the minor, pay it to such other person as they may determine.

A person who receives any sum paid under this paragraph shall, subject to and in accordance with any directions of the fire authority, apply the said sum for the minor's benefit.

(5) Every assignment or charge on a pension shall be void to the extent that—

(a) it is in favour of a person other than a relative of the pensioner, or

(b) it relates to a sum due to an ordinary, ill-health, short service or deferred pensioner, in respect of a period beyond the age of 65 years, on account of the secured portion of the pension.

(6) A pension shall not pass to a trustee in bankruptcy or any other person acting on behalf of creditors of the pensioner.

(7) This Article shall apply with respect to awards other than pensions as it applies with respect to pensions, and accordingly any reference in this Article to a pension shall be construed as including a reference to any such award, and any reference therein to a pensioner shall be construed as including a reference to a person to whom any such award is payable.

(8) In the application of this Article to Scotland—

(a) the reference in paragraph (3) to the personal estate of the deceased shall be construed as a reference to his movable estate;

(b) any reference in paragraph (4) to a minor shall be construed as including a reference to a pupil.

Payment of transfer values

71. Where a regular fireman retires or has retired from a brigade and after again becoming such a fireman in another brigade becomes entitled under Article 48(1) to reckon as pensionable service the period of pensionable service he was entitled to reckon on retiring, the fire authority maintaining the first-mentioned brigade shall pay to the fire authority maintaining the other brigade a sum by way of transfer value calculated in accordance with Schedule 9.

Expenses and receipts of fire authorities

72.—(1) Every fire authority shall maintain an account showing all sums received or paid by the authority under, or for the purposes of this Scheme or a previous Firemen's Pension Scheme.

(2) If and so long as the fire authority maintain a pension reserve account in accordance with paragraph (3) the account mentioned in paragraph (1) shall be separate from any account maintained by the fire authority which shows sums received or paid by the authority (not being such sums as are there mentioned) other than sums received or paid under rules made by virtue of section 9 of the Fire Services Act 1959(a), or payments in lieu of contributions made in respect of regular firemen.

(3) A fire authority which maintained a pension reserve account immediately before 1st July 1973 shall continue to maintain such an account on and after that day until it is exhausted in accordance with paragraph (4).

(4) Where in any year the payments debited to the account mentioned in paragraph (1) exceed the receipts credited thereto, and the fire authority maintain a pension reserve account, the balance shall be met out of the pension reserve account to the extent thereof.

(5) In this Article the expression "year" means a year beginning on the anniversary of the appointed day.

PART IX

SERVICEMEN

Awards to servicemen

73.—(1) This Article shall apply in the case of a serviceman who at the end of his period of relevant service in the armed forces is permanently disabled.

(2) Such a person shall be entitled to the same award on the same conditions in all respects as if he had retired from his former brigade at the end of the said period on the ground that he had been so disabled.

(3) Where the infirmity of mind or body is occasioned by an injury received during the person's period of relevant service in the armed forces or by a qualifying injury, the fire authority may, in their discretion—

(a) pay him, in lieu of a gratuity, a pension at the rate of a twelfth of his average pensionable pay; and

(b) increase any pension payable under this Article, so however that the increased pension, when aggregated with any service pension other than an allowance for constant attendance, wear and tear of clothing, or comforts, shall not be payable at a rate exceeding that of the aggregate of the pensions to which he would have been entitled had the injury been treated, for the purposes of the preceding paragraph, as if it were a qualifying injury.

Awards on death of servicemen

74.—(1) This Article shall apply in the case of a serviceman who—

(a) dies during his period of relevant service in the armed forces; or

(b) having been permanently disabled at the end of the said period (without any intervening period of service as such a fireman) dies from the effects of the injury that resulted in his disablement or while in receipt of a pension.

(2) Such a person's widow shall—

(a) if he was entitled to reckon 3 years' pensionable service, be entitled to a pension as though he were a person mentioned in Article 22(1); or

(b) if she is not so entitled to a pension and if her husband died during his period of relevant service in the armed forces, be entitled to an award under Article 27 as though he died while serving as a regular fireman.

(3) Any child of such a person shall be entitled to an allowance as though he were mentioned in Article 33.

(a) 1959 c. 44.

(4) Where such a person dies from the effects of an injury received during his period of relevant service in the armed forces or of a qualifying injury, the fire authority may, in their discretion—

(a) pay to the widow, in lieu of a gratuity, a pension at the rate of £163.81 a year; and

(b) increase any pension or allowance payable under this Article, so however that the increased award, when aggregated with any service pension payable to or for the widow or child, as the case may be, in respect of the serviceman, shall not be payable at a rate exceeding that of the award to which the widow or child, as the case may be, would have been entitled had the serviceman died from the effects of a qualifying injury.

Gratuities for dependants other than widows and children

75. In relation to a serviceman who dies during his relevant service in the armed forces, Article 32 shall apply as though he died while serving as a regular fireman.

Servicemen who resume service as regular firemen

76. If a serviceman who resumes service as a regular fireman—

(a) is permanently disabled; or

(b) dies (whether while serving as such a fireman or otherwise),

as a result of an injury received during his period of relevant service in the armed forces, the fire authority may, in relation to any award payable to or in respect of him, exercise the like discretions as are conferred on them by Article 73 or by Article 74.

Servicemen who do not resume service in their former brigade

77. If a serviceman within one month of the end of his period of relevant service in the armed forces does not resume service in his former brigade, he shall be treated for the purposes of Articles 16, 28, 39, 44, 48, 55 and 88(3) as having left his former brigade at the end of that period:

Provided that he may apply to the fire authority for the consent mentioned in Article 48(3) at any time within a month of the end of the said period.

Pensionable service, contributions and pay

78.—(1) A serviceman shall be entitled to reckon his period of relevant service in the armed forces as pensionable service in his former brigade for the purposes of this Scheme.

(2) A serviceman shall pay pension contributions (including additional and further contributions under Articles 57 and 58) to the fire authority of his former brigade in respect of his period of relevant service in the armed forces as though he had remained a regular fireman in that brigade:

Provided that pension contributions shall not be payable by a serviceman in respect of any period during which he is in receipt of service pay which when aggregated with any payments under Part V of the Reserve and Auxiliary Forces (Protection of Civil Interests) Act 1951(a) is less than his pensionable pay.

(3) For the purpose of calculating pensionable pay, a serviceman shall be deemed to receive during his period of relevant service in the armed forces the pay which he would have received if he had continued to serve in his former brigade.

Servicemen deemed not to have retired

79. Except where the context otherwise requires, a reference in this Scheme to a regular fireman retiring or ceasing to be such does not include a reference to his so doing for the purpose of undertaking relevant service in the armed forces.

Application to regular firemen with war service

80.—(1) A regular fireman who received any injury during a period of war service at a time when section 1 of the Police and Firemen (War Service) Act 1939(b) applied

(a) 1951 c. 65.   (b) 1939 c. 103.

to him shall be deemed to be a serviceman and his period of war service shall be deemed to be a period of relevant service in the armed forces; and Article 76 shall have effect accordingly.

(2) In this Article any reference to "a period of war service" is a reference to a period of service in the armed forces of the Crown or to a period, beginning before 1st January 1948 and ending before 1st April 1948, of work which the Secretary of State directed should be treated as war work for the purpose of Regulation 60DA of the Defence (General) Regulations 1939, and the reference to the Police and Firemen (War Service) Act 1939 includes a reference to that Act as extended by the said Regulation 60DA.

PART X

MEMBERS OF BRIGADES WHO ARE NOT REGULAR FIREMEN

Awards to and in respect of whole-time firemen

81.—(1) Where, while in attendance at a fire and without his own default, a whole-time member of a brigade who is not a regular fireman suffers or has suffered any injury in the execution of his duties as a member of the brigade, the provisions of this Article shall have effect in his case.

(2) If he retires in consequence of the injury, the fire authority may grant him such pension and such gratuity as they think fit so, however, that the said pension or gratuity, when aggregated with any relevant additional benefit which may be payable to him, shall not exceed the injury pension or, as the case may be, gratuity to which he would have been entitled under Article 15, disregarding paragraph 3 of Part V of Schedule 1, had he been a regular fireman of the rank of fireman and retired on account of a qualifying injury during his first year of service.

(3) If he dies from the effects of the injury, either before or after retiring from the brigade, the fire authority may grant his widow such pension and gratuity, and his child such allowance, as they think fit so, however, that the said pension, gratuity or allowance, when aggregated with any relevant additional benefit which may be payable to the recipient, shall not exceed the special pension or, as the case may be, gratuity to which the widow would have been entitled under Article 23 or the special allowance to which the child would have been entitled under Article 34, had he been a regular fireman of the rank of fireman who died or retired during his first year of service and died from the effects of a qualifying injury.

(4) In this Article the expression "additional benefit" means any payments of whatever nature which are made by the fire authority otherwise than under this Article, by any other local authority or by a Minister of the Crown so, however, that the said expression does not include any benefit payable under the National Insurance Act 1965 or the National Insurance (Industrial Injuries) Act 1965(a); and the expression "relevant additional benefit" means, in relation to a pension or allowance, additional benefit by way of periodical payments and, in relation to a gratuity, additional benefit otherwise than by way of such payments.

(5) This Article shall have effect in the case of a woman member of a brigade subject to Article 85(1).

Part-time firemen: injury award

82.—(1) Where a part-time member of a brigade who retires or has retired is permanently disabled by infirmity of mind or body occasioned by a qualifying injury, he shall be entitled to an injury award as hereinafter provided.

(2) The award under paragraph (1) shall consist of an ill-health pension and an injury pension and gratuity which shall be payable at the like rates and be subject to the like conditions as they would have been if the part-time member concerned had been such a regular fireman as is mentioned in Article 85(2) disabled as aforesaid in the like circumstances; and, accordingly, Articles 14, 15, 18, 19, 20, 21, 41 and 42 shall have effect subject to any necessary modifications.

(a) 1965 c. 52.

Widow of part-time fireman: injury award

83.—(1) Where a part-time member of a brigade dies from the effects of a qualifying injury or from the effects of infirmity of mind or body occasioned by such an injury, his widow shall be entitled to a widow's injury award as hereinafter provided.

(2) The award under paragraph (1) shall consist of a widow's special pension and a gratuity which shall be payable at the like rates and be subject to the like conditions as they would have been had the member been such a regular fireman as is mentioned in Article 85(2), and had died from the effects of a qualifying injury received in the like circumstances; and, accordingly, Articles 23, 24, 26, 28, 29 and 30 shall have effect subject to any necessary modifications.

Child of part-time fireman: injury award

84.—(1) Where a part-time member of a brigade dies from the effects of a qualifying injury or from the effects of infirmity of mind or body occasioned by such an injury, any child of his shall be entitled to, or in the case of a woman member, any child of hers may be granted, an injury award as hereinafter provided.

(2) The award under paragraph (1) shall comprise a child's special allowance and, where one of the conditions set out in Article 24(1) is satisfied and the member does not leave a widow entitled to a gratuity under Article 83, a child's special gratuity which shall be payable at the like rates and be payable subject to the like conditions as they would have been had the member been such a regular fireman as is mentioned in Article 85(2) and had died from the effects of a qualifying injury received in the like circumstances; and, accordingly, Articles 34, 35, 37, 38 and 39 shall have effect subject to any necessary modifications.

(3) This Article shall have effect in the case of a woman member of a brigade subject to Article 85(1) and in such case an allowance which falls to be calculated in accordance with paragraph (2) shall be payable at such rate as the fire authority from time to time think fit, not exceeding the rate at which it would have been payable but for this paragraph.

Auxiliary provisions

85.—(1) In the case of a woman member of a brigade who is not a regular fireman this Part of this Scheme shall have effect—

(a) as if for any reference in Article 81(2) or (3) to the rank of fireman there were substituted a reference to the rank of firewoman;

(b) as if for any reference in Article 81(3) or 84(1) to a child there were substituted a reference to a child of the member substantially dependent upon her at the time of her death;

(c) as if in Article 39(b) for the reference to the mother there were substituted a reference to the father.

(2) For the purposes of the injury award payable to or in respect of a part-time member of a brigade, any reference in this Part of this Scheme to a regular fireman is a reference to such a fireman who—

(a) held the same rank as the part-time member in fact held and had the same service in that rank,

(b) was entitled to reckon as pensionable service a period equal to the part-time member's service as such, and

(c) paid pension contributions at the rate of 6p a week less than 6·75% of his pensionable pay.

(3) The provisions of Article 45 and of Parts I, VII, VIII and XIII of this Scheme (in so far as they are applicable) shall apply to a member of a fire brigade who is not a regular fireman and to a pension, allowance or gratuity granted to or in respect of him, but, save as provided in this Part of this Scheme, the provisions of this Scheme shall not apply to such a member or to such a pension, allowance or gratuity.

Part XI

Persons who are not Members of Brigades

Temporary employment in connection with the provision of fire services

86—(1) This Article shall apply in the case of a person who ceases or has ceased to perform duties as a regular fireman in order to enter temporary employment on duties connected with the provision of fire services, being—

(a) employment as an instructor at the central training institution or any training centre maintained by the Secretary of State;

(b) employment as an inspector, assistant inspector or other officer appointed under section 24 of the principal Act;

(c) employment entered upon in pursuance of arrangements made by the Secretary of State in connection with the training in fire-fighting of members of the armed forces of the Crown; or

(d) employment entered upon in pursuance of arrangements made by the Secretary of State in connection with the training and organisation of fire-fighting forces in any country or territory outside the United Kingdom,

(hereafter in this Article referred to as "the relevant employment").

(2) In the case of a person to whom this Article applies the relevant employment shall be treated for the purposes of this Scheme as employment as a member of a fire brigade and, without prejudice to the following provisions of this Article, this Scheme shall apply in relation thereto as if—

(a) he were a regular fireman and his duties were his duties as such;

(b) his pay and rank were the same as they would have been had he not ceased to perform duties as such a fireman or, where section 10 of the Fire Services Act 1959 applies in his case, the same as his pay and rank as a member of a fire brigade;

(c) any reference to a brigade were a reference to the relevant employment;

(d) Articles 72, 96 and 97 were omitted; and

(e) any reference to a fire authority were a reference to the Secretary of State.

(3) Except where the relevant employment is such as is mentioned in paragraph (1)(d), this Scheme shall have effect as aforesaid as if the reference to the sheriff in Article 68(4) were a reference to the sheriff having jurisdiction in the place where the person concerned served as a fireman immediately before entering the relevant employment.

(4) Where the relevant employment is such as is mentioned in paragraph (1)(d), this Scheme shall have effect as aforesaid as if a reference in Article 68 to the Crown Court were a reference to an appeal tribunal appointed by the Secretary of State and consisting of three persons including—

(a) a retired member of a fire brigade who before he retired held a rank not lower than that of Divisional Officer (Grade I), and

(b) a barrister or solicitor of seven years' standing or, where the person ceased to perform duties in a Scottish fire brigade in order to enter the relevant employment, an advocate or a solicitor of seven years' standing,

and paragraph (4) were omitted from the said Article.

(5) In the case of an appeal to such a tribunal as is mentioned in paragraph (4)—

(a) the time and place for the hearing, or the postponed or adjourned hearing, shall be determined by the tribunal, which shall give reasonable notice thereof to the appellant and to the Secretary of State (hereinafter described as "the parties");

(b) either party may be represented before the tribunal by counsel or by solicitor or by some other person approved by the tribunal, adduce evidence and cross-examine witnesses;

(c) the tribunal shall apply the rules of evidence applicable in the case of an appeal to the Crown Court under Article 68 or, where the person ceased to perform duties in a Scottish fire brigade in order to enter the relevant employment, in the case of such an appeal to the sheriff, and

(d) subject to the preceding provisions of this paragraph, the tribunal shall determine its own procedure.

(6) Subject to and in accordance with rules of court, an appeal on a point of law from a decision of such a tribunal as is mentioned in paragraph (4) shall lie to the High Court or, where the person ceased to perform duties in a Scottish fire brigade in order to enter the relevant employment, to the Court of Session.

(7) For the purposes of paragraph (1)(d), any arrangements made by the Minister of Overseas Development on or after 1st April 1968 but before 15th November 1970 shall be treated as if they had been made by the Secretary of State.

Permanent employment as an instructor

87.—(1) This Article shall apply in the case of a person who ceases or has ceased to perform duties as a regular fireman in order to enter employment on duties connected with the provision of fire services, being permanent employment as an instructor at the central training institution or any training centre maintained by the Secretary of State.

(2) In the case of such a person as is mentioned in paragraph (1), the employment therein mentioned (hereafter in this paragraph referred to as "the relevant employment") shall be treated for the purposes of this Scheme as employment as a member of a brigade and this Scheme shall apply in relation to that employment as if—

(a) he were a regular fireman and his duties were his duties as such;

(b) any reference to a brigade were a reference to the relevant employment;

(c) any reference to a fire authority were a reference to the Secretary of State;

(d) the reference to the sheriff in Article 68(4) were a reference to the sheriff having jurisdiction in the place where the central training institution is situate; and

(e) Articles 72, 96 and 97 were omitted.

PART XII

PERSONS WHO WERE SERVING ON 10TH JULY 1956

Persons to whom Part XII applies etc.

88.—(1) Subject to paragraphs (2) and (3) and to Articles 89 and 90, this Part shall apply in the case of a person who—

(a) was, on 10th July 1956, a regular fireman or a serviceman performing relevant service in the armed forces; or

(b) was, on 10th July 1956, in receipt of an ill-health pension and subsequently, but before 1st August 1964, resumed service in his brigade in the circumstances and within the period mentioned in Article 18(3).

(2) This Part shall not apply in the case of such a person as is mentioned in paragraph (1) who exercised the right of election accorded by—

(a) Article 60 of the Firemen's Pension Scheme 1956(a);

(b) Article 39(2) of the Firemen's Pension Scheme 1966(b); or

(c) Article 52(2) of the Firemen's Pension Scheme 1971(c) as amended by the Firemen's Pension Scheme (Amendment) Order 1973(d),

---

(a) *See* S.I. 1956/1022 (1956 I, p. 953).   (b) *See* S.I. 1966/1045 (1966 II, p. 2504).
(c) *See* S.I. 1971/145 (1971 I, p. 320).   (d) S.I. 1973/318 (1973 I, p. 1112).

unless, in the case of a person who exercised the right of election accorded by the said Article 52(2), before 1st October 1973 he elects hereunder that, with effect from 1st April 1972, this Part shall apply in his case.

(3) Where such a person as is mentioned in paragraph (1) ceases or has ceased to serve as a regular fireman in any particular brigade, this Part shall not apply to him in relation to any subsequent period during which he serves as a regular fireman in the same or another brigade, beginning on or after 1st August 1964, unless in the circumstances mentioned in Article 48(1) or (4), he becomes or has become entitled to reckon as pensionable service the period so reckonable on his ceasing to serve.

(4) Any election under this Part shall be made by notice in writing to the fire authority maintaining the fire brigade in which the man is serving or by whom his, or his widow's, pension is payable.

Election by serving member, pensioner or widow

89.—(1) This Article shall apply in the case of a regular fireman in whose case this Part applies on 1st July 1973 and who—

(a) is on that date serving as such or entitled to a pension having retired on or after 1st April 1972, or

(b) dies or has died on or after 1st April 1972 but before 1st October 1973, either while serving or having retired as aforesaid.

(2) A regular fireman in whose case this Article applies or his widow may elect that, with effect from 1st April 1972, this Part shall not apply in his case.

(3) Where a regular fireman or his widow so elects, in consequence thereof the arrears of pension contributions in respect of his service on or after 1st April 1972 shall be paid by him or his widow and any award in payment to or in respect of him shall be recalculated as from the date from which it became payable.

(4) Any election or payment under this Article shall be made before 1st October 1973 except that where made by a widow of a man who has died before the said date it may be made later if made within 3 months of his death.

Election on resuming service

90.—(1) This Article shall apply to a regular fireman—

(a) who, having ceased to serve as such before 1st July 1973, in a particular brigade, becomes a regular fireman, on a date (in this Article referred to as the relevant date) subsequent to 1st July 1973, in the same or another brigade, and

(b) to whom this Part applies having regard to the provisions of Article 88(3).

(2) A regular fireman to whom this Article applies may, within 3 months of the relevant date, elect that, with effect from the relevant date, this Part shall not apply in his case.

(3) Where a regular fireman so elects—

(a) the arrears of pension contributions payable by him in respect of his service on and after the relevant date in consequence of his election shall be paid within three months of the relevant date, and

(b) paragraphs 2(1)(a) and 3(1) of Part VIII of Schedule 1, paragraph 1(1)(a) and (4)(a) of Part IV of Schedule 2 and paragraph 3(1)(a) of Part III of Schedule 3 shall have effect in his case as if the references therein to 1st April 1972 were references to the relevant date and, for the purposes of Articles 22(3) and 60 and paragraph 4(1) of Part I of Schedule 3, his entitlement (if any) to an ill-health pension on 1st July 1973 shall be disregarded.

Modification of Scheme

91. In the case of a person to whom this Part applies, this Scheme shall have effect subject to the modifications set out in Schedule 10.

PART XIII

MISCELLANEOUS PROVISIONS

Auxiliary firemen not subject to Scheme

92.—(1) This Scheme shall not apply in relation to a member of a brigade who is an auxiliary fireman.

(2) In this Article the expression "auxiliary fireman" means a member of a brigade who is enrolled for service therein which is restricted except in a war emergency to such duties as are desirable for training.

Exclusive application of Scheme in relation to regular firemen

93. Subject to the provisions of section 27 of the principal Act, the provisions of this Scheme (and, in so far as they continue to have effect, of the previous Schemes) shall have effect in relation to regular firemen, their wives and dependants to the exclusion of any provision for pension allowance or gratuity in respect of a person's employment as such a fireman (whether in respect of a person's ceasing to be so employed or in respect of his death) contained in or in force under any enactment:

Provided that nothing in this Article shall affect the operation of—

(a) any such provision in respect of a person's employment or service otherwise than as a member of a fire brigade which is treated for the purposes of this Scheme as employment as a regular fireman; or

(b) the National Insurance Act 1965(a) or the National Insurance (Industrial Injuries) Act 1965.

Application of Scheme to persons affected by local government reorganisation or a combination scheme

94.—(1) In relation to a member of a fire brigade who is or has been transferred to, or otherwise becomes or has become a member of, another fire brigade by virtue of an instrument mentioned in paragraph (4)—

(a) this Scheme shall apply as though the brigade of which he becomes a member and the authority maintaining that brigade were, respectively, the same brigade and authority as the brigade first mentioned in this paragraph and the authority maintaining that brigade;

(b) where he held the rank of assistant divisional officer or any higher rank in the brigade first mentioned in this paragraph but suffers or has suffered reduction in rank attributable to the provisions of such an instrument, Article 96 shall apply as though he had not suffered such reduction in rank, unless he elects otherwise by notice in writing to the fire authority.

(2) In relation to a member of a fire brigade who suffers or has suffered loss of employment as a regular fireman which is attributable to the provisions of an instrument mentioned in paragraph (4)—

(a) this Scheme shall apply as though he had retired from the brigade after having given due notice of retirement to the fire authority and, if the fire authority so agree, as though the notice of retirement had been given with their permission, and

(b) where he becomes a regular fireman in another brigade before the end of his resettlement period, Article 47 shall apply as though he had become a member of that other brigade immediately after ceasing to be a member of the brigade first mentioned in this paragraph.

(a) 1965 c. 51.

(3) In relation to a member of a fire brigade who is or has been transferred to, or otherwise becomes or has become a member of, another fire brigade by virtue of the London Government Act 1963(a) or of any instrument mentioned in paragraph (4)—

(a) in whose case this Scheme has effect subject to the modifications set out in Schedule 10;

(b) whose last change of rank during the relevant period for the purposes of Article 55(3) (as modified by paragraph 13 of Schedule 10) was a reduction in rank attributable to the provisions of the said Act of 1963 or of any instrument mentioned in paragraph (4), and

(c) whose average pensionable pay during the said relevant period was less than his pensionable pay immediately before his death or retirement,

Article 55 (as modified as aforesaid) shall apply as though paragraph (3) were omitted therefrom.

(4) The reference in paragraphs (1), (2) and (3) to an instrument mentioned in this paragraph are references to—

(a) an order under Part VI of the Local Government Act 1933(b), Part II of the Local Government Act 1958(c) or section 85 of the London Government Act 1963, or

(b) a scheme under section 5, 6 or 9 of the principal Act or, in Scotland, an order under section 36(8) of that Act;

and the reference in paragraph (2) to a person's resettlement period is a reference to the period of 13 weeks next succeeding the week in which he ceased to be a member of the brigade first mentioned in that paragraph or, in the case of a person who has attained the age of 45 years, the said 13 weeks extended by an additional week for every year of his age after attaining the age of 45 years and before he ceased to be a member of that brigade, subject to a maximum extension of 13 such weeks.

Application of Scheme where modified by section 27 of principal Act

95.—(1) This Article shall apply in the case of a person in relation to whom this Scheme is modified as mentioned in section 27(3) of the principal Act.

(2) Where such a person as aforesaid is entitled to both an ill-health and an injury pension, then, for the purposes of Articles 21, 40, 41 and 42, his entitlement to, and the amount of, the ill-health pension shall be deemed to be the same as they would have been had he not been entitled to an injury pension.

(3) Where in relation to such a person as aforesaid this Scheme is modified by reference to regulations made under either the Metropolitan Fire Brigade Act 1865(d) or the West Ham Corporation Act 1925(e), Article 21(1) shall apply in relation to him as if for the reference to 30 years' pensionable service there were substituted a reference to 28 years' pensionable service.

Age of compulsory retirement

96.—(1) Subject to paragraphs (2) and (3), retirement shall be compulsory for a male whole-time member of a brigade appointed on terms under which he is or may be required to engage in fire-fighting—

(a) in the case of a member of the rank of assistant divisional officer or any higher rank, on attaining the age of 60 years; and

(b) in the case of a member of the rank of station officer or any lower rank, on attaining the age of 55 years,

except that in special cases the fire authority may extend any such member's service for a further period on being satisfied that such extension would be in the interests of efficiency.

(a) 1963 c. 33. (b) 1933 c. 51.
(c) 1958 c. 55. (d) 1865 c. 90.
(e) 1925 c. cxii.

(2) Without prejudice to the extension under paragraph (1) of the service of such a member of a brigade as is therein mentioned, in the case of a regular fireman of the rank of station officer or any lower rank, if the fireman so elects by notice in writing to the fire authority, that authority may extend his service by such period, if any, not exceeding 6 months from his attaining the age of 55 years as is requisite to enable him to reckon—

(a) an additional completed year of pensionable service, in the case of a member who will be entitled to reckon less than 20 years' pensionable service on attaining that age, or

(b) an additional completed half year of pensionable service, in any other case.

(3) Nothing in paragraph (1) shall apply to a member in whose case any regulations made for the purposes set out in paragraph 7 of the Schedule to the Fire Services (Emergency Provisions) Act 1941(a) had effect immediately before 1st April 1948 unless and until—

(a) he is entitled without a medical certificate to retire and receive a pension at the rate of 2 thirds of his average pensionable pay; or

(b) he elects that the provisions of paragraph (1) should apply to him, by notice in writing to the fire authority maintaining the brigade of which he is a member.

(4) Subject to paragraph (5), retirement shall also be compulsory for any male whole-time member of a brigade who has attained the age of 50 years and completed 25 years' pensionable service if he is required to retire by the fire authority on the grounds that his retention in the brigade would not be in the general interests of its efficiency.

(5) Nothing in paragraph (4) shall apply to a member of the brigade in whose case the National Fire Service (Preservation of Pensions) (Police Firemen) Regulations 1941(b), the National Fire Service (Preservation of Pensions) (Birmingham and Leicester) Regulations 1941(c) or the National Fire Service (Preservation of Pensions) (Bolton and Derby) Regulations 1941(d) had effect immediately before 1st April 1948, or to a member who, immediately before 18th August 1941, was a professional fireman within the meaning of the Fire Brigade Pensions Act 1925(e) as amended by the Fire Brigades Act 1938(f) and in whose case the National Fire Service (Preservation of Pensions) (General Pension Funds) Regulations 1941(g) had effect immediately before 1st April 1948.

(6) This Article shall apply to a member of a Scottish fire brigade as if paragraphs (3) and (5) were omitted, but nothing in this Article shall apply to such a member in whose case any regulations made for the purposes set out in paragraph 7 of the Schedule to the Fire Services (Emergency Provisions) Act 1941 had effect immediately before 16th May 1948, unless and until—

(a) he could have been compelled to retire under the statutory provisions or regulations applicable to him immediately before 18th August 1941, or

(b) he elects that the provisions of paragraph (1) should apply to him, by notice in writing to the fire authority maintaining the brigade of which he is a member.

Compulsory retirement on grounds of incapacity

97. A regular fireman may be required to retire on the date on which the fire authority determine he ought to retire on the ground that he is permanently disabled:

Provided that a retirement in accordance with this Article shall be void if after the said date, on an appeal against the medical opinion on which the fire authority acted in determining that he ought to retire, the medical referee decides that the appellant is not disabled as aforesaid.

(a) 1941 c. 22. (b) S.R. & O. 1941/1271 (1941 I, p. 328).
(c) S.R. & O. 1941/1273 (1941 I, p. 337). (d) S.R. & O. 1941/1274 (1941 I, p. 342).
(e) 1925 c. 47. (f) 1938 c. 72.
(g) S.R. & O. 1941/1270 (1941 I, p. 325).

SCHEDULE 1

Article 12

PART I

FIREMAN'S ORDINARY PENSION

Subject as hereafter in this Schedule provided, an ordinary pension shall be of an amount equal to 30 sixtieths of the fireman's average pensionable pay, with the addition, subject to a maximum of 40 sixtieths, of a sixtieth for each completed half year by which his pensionable service exceeds 25 years.

Article 13

PART II

FIREMAN'S SHORT SERVICE PENSION

Subject as hereafter in this Schedule provided, a short service pension shall be equal to a sixtieth of the fireman's average pensionable pay for each completed year of pensionable service up to 20 years with the addition of a sixtieth for each completed half year by which his pensionable service exceeds 20 years.

Article 14

PART III

FIREMAN'S ILL-HEALTH PENSION

1. Subject as hereafter in this Schedule provided, the amount of the ill-health pension shall be determined in accordance with paragraph 2, 3 or 4 as the case may require.

2. Where the fireman has not completed 5 years' pensionable service, the amount of the pension shall not be less than a sixtieth of his average pensionable pay and, subject as aforesaid, shall be equal to a sixtieth of his average pensionable pay for each completed year of pensionable service.

3. Where the fireman has completed 5 years' but less than 11 years' pensionable service, subject to paragraph 5, the amount of the pension shall be equal to 2 sixtieths of his average pensionable pay for each completed year of pensionable service.

4. Where the fireman has completed at least 11 years' pensionable service, the amount of the pension shall not be less than 20 sixtieths of his average pensionable pay and, subject as aforesaid and to paragraph 5, shall be equal to 7 sixtieths of his average pensionable pay with the addition—

   (a) of a sixtieth for each completed year of pensionable service up to 20 years, and

   (b) of a sixtieth for each completed half year by which his pensionable service exceeds 20 years.

5. In the case of a fireman who, had he continued to serve until he could be required to retire on account of age, would have become entitled to an ordinary or short service pension, a pension calculated in accordance with paragraph 3 or 4 shall not exceed the pension to which he would so have become entitled calculated, however, by reference to the average pensionable pay by reference to which the ill-health pension is calculated.

Articles 13 and 14

PART IV

FIREMAN'S SHORT SERVICE OR ILL-HEALTH GRATUITY

1. Where the fireman is entitled to reckon at least a years' pensionable service, the short service or ill-health gratuity shall be whichever is the greater of the two following amounts:—

Sch. 1 (*contd.*)

(*a*) a twelfth of his average annual pensionable pay multiplied by the number of completed years of pensionable service which he is entitled to reckon; or

(*b*) his aggregate contributions.

2. Where the fireman is not entitled to reckon at least a years' pensionable service, the gratuity shall be of an amount equal to his aggregate contributions.

PART V   Article 15

FIREMAN'S INJURY AWARDS

1. A gratuity under Article 15 shall be calculated by reference to the person's degree of disablement and his average annual pensionable pay and shall be the amount specified as appropriate to his degree of disablement in column (2) of the following Table.

2. An injury pension shall be calculated by reference to the person's degree of disablement, his average pensionable pay and the number of his completed years of pensionable service, and, subject to the following paragraphs, shall be of the amount specified as appropriate to his degree of disablement in column (3), (4), (5) or (6) of the following Table, whichever is applicable to his completed years of pensionable service.

TABLE

Degree of disablement	Gratuity expressed as % of average annual pensionable pay	Pension expressed as % of average pensionable pay			
		Less than 5 years' service	5 or more but less than 15 years' service	15 or more but less than 25 years' service	25 or more years' service
(1)	(2)	(3)	(4)	(5)	(6)
25% or less (slight disablement)	12·5%	15%	30%	45%	60%
More than 25% but not more than 50% (minor disablement)	25%	40%	50%	60%	70%
More than 50% but not more than 75% (major disablement)	37·5%	65%	70%	75%	80%
More than 75% (very severe disablement)	50%	85%	85%	85%	85%

3.—(1) The amount of an injury pension shall be reduced by three-quarters of the amount of any other pension payable to the person concerned which is calculated by reference to pensionable service reckonable by virtue of the period of service during which he received the qualifying injury.

(2) For the purposes of sub-paragraph (1), such other pension as is there mentioned which is reduced in accordance with the provisions of Article 21 or 41 or of Part VIII of Schedule 1 shall be deemed not to have been so reduced.

Sch. 1 (contd.)

4.—(1) The amount of the injury pension in respect of any week shall be reduced on account of any such additional benefit as is mentioned in sub-paragraph (3) which is payable to the person concerned in respect of the same week.

(2) Where the provisions governing scales of additional benefits have changed after the person concerned ceased to be a regular fireman, the amount of the reduction in respect of any week on account of a particular benefit shall not exceed the amount which would have been the amount thereof in respect of that week had those provisions not changed, it being assumed, in the case of such benefit as is mentioned in sub-paragraph (3)(b)(ii), that it would have borne the same relationship to the former maximum amount thereof.

(3) The following benefits are the additional benefits referred to in this paragraph—

   (a) any injury benefit payable under the National Insurance (Industrial Injuries) Act 1965 which relates to the relevant injury together with any supplement payable therewith under section 2 of the National Insurance Act 1966(a);

   (b) any disablement pension payable under section 12 of the National Insurance (Industrial Injuries) Act 1965 in respect of the relevant injury or so much of any such pension as relates to that injury (hereinafter referred to as the relevant part of the pension), together with—

      (i) any increase in such pension payable by way of unemployability supplement under section 13 of the said Act or so much of any such increase as is proportionate to the relevant part of the said pension so, however, that where he is entitled to an unemployability supplement which is increased under section 13A of the said Act, the unemployability supplement shall be deemed not to have been so increased;

      (ii) any increase in such pension payable under section 14 of the said Act (special hardship) or so much of any such increase as is proportionate to the relevant part of the said pension,

      (iii) any increase in such pension payable under section 17 or 18 of the said Act (dependants) or so much of any such increase as is proportionate to the relevant part of the said pension, and

      (iv) so long as he is receiving treatment as an in-patient at a hospital as a result of that injury, any increase in such pension payable under section 16, 17 or 18 of the said Act (hospital treatment and dependants),

   so, however, that an increase (or the proportionate part thereof) under each of the sections aforesaid shall be treated as a particular benefit for the purposes of sub-paragraph (2);

   (c) until the first day after his retirement which is not or is deemed not to be a day of incapacity for work under section 20 of the National Insurance Act 1965—

      (i) any sickness benefit payable under the said Act of 1965, together with any increase therein payable under section 40 or 43 of the said Act of 1965 (dependants) and any supplement thereto payable under section 2 of the National Insurance Act 1966 (short-term earnings related benefit), or

      (ii) any invalidity pension payable under the said Act of 1965 together with any increase therein payable under section 40 or 43A of that Act (dependants),

   so, however, that the benefits aforesaid shall not constitute separate particular benefits but a single benefit for the purposes of sub-paragraph (2).

(4) Where a person has received a disablement gratuity under the National Insurance (Industrial Injuries) Act 1965 this paragraph shall apply as if he were entitled during the relevant period to a disablement pension under the said Act of 1965 of such amount as would be produced by converting the gratuity into an annuity for that period.

In this sub-paragraph the expression "the relevant period" means the period taken into account, in accordance with section 12 of the said Act of 1965, for the purpose of making the assessment by reference to which the gratuity became payable.

(a) 1966 c. 6.

5. No payment shall be made in respect of an injury pension for any week in which the aggregate reductions under paragraphs 3 and 4 exceed the amount of the pension calculated in accordance with paragraph 2.

6. In the case of a person who—

   (*a*) received the qualifying injury during a period of service which included 1st April 1972 or ended before 1st July 1973, and

   (*b*) is entitled to reckon less than 5 years' pensionable service,
an injury pension shall be calculated and payable in accordance with the preceding provisions of this Part or in accordance with the provisions of Article 15 of the Firemen's Pension Scheme 1971**(a)**, as from time to time amended, (which provisions govern special pensions), whichever are the more favourable in his case when he first becomes entitled to the pension.

PART VI   Article 16

FIREMAN'S DEFERRED PENSION

1. The amount of a fireman's deferred pension shall be calculated by reference to—

   (*a*) the pensionable service he is entitled to reckon (here referred to as "actual service");

   (*b*) the pensionable service he would have become entitled to reckon had he continued to serve until he could retire with a maximum ordinary pension (disregarding Article 12(2)) or until he could be required to retire on account of age, whichever is the earlier, (here referred to as "hypothetical service"), and

   (*c*) his average pensionable pay.

2. Subject as hereafter in this Schedule provided, the fireman's pension shall be such that it is the same proportion of the hypothetical pension referred to in paragraph 3 as his actual service is of his hypothetical service, in both cases calculated in completed years, as respects the first 20 years of service, and in completed half years, as respects service in excess of 20 years.

3. The hypothetical pension referred to in paragraph 2 is a pension of an amount equal to a sixtieth of his average pensionable pay for each completed year of his hypothetical service up to 20 years with the addition of a sixtieth for each completed half year by which his hypothetical service exceeds 20 years.

PART VII   Articles 12, 13, 14 and 16

REDUCTION OF FIREMAN'S PENSION AT AGE 65

1.—(1) Subject as hereafter in this paragraph provided, the unsecured portion of an ordinary, ill-health, short service or deferred pension shall be reduced in respect of any period beyond the age of 65 years by an amount calculated at an annual rate obtained by multiplying £1·70 by the number of years specified in sub-paragraph (4).

(2) In the case of a person who immediately before he retired and was granted a pension was paying pension contributions at a rate of 1p a week less than the appropriate percentage of his pensionable pay there shall not be any reduction in the pension under this paragraph.

(3) Subject as hereafter in this paragraph provided, in the case of a person who immediately before he retired and was granted a pension was paying pension contributions at a rate of 6p a week less than the appropriate percentage of his pensionable pay by reason of his having elected so to do as mentioned in Article 56(2) the reduction under sub-paragraph (1) shall be calculated not as therein stated but at an annual rate obtained by multiplying the sum in the second column of the following Table set opposite to his age on the appointed day in the first column of the said Table by the number of years specified in sub-paragraph (4):—

(a) *See* S.I. 1971/145 (1971 I, p. 320).

Sch. 1 (*contd.*)

TABLE

Age in years					Sum to be multiplied
					£
Under 23	...	...	...	...	1·700
23 but under 24		...	...	...	1·650
24 ,, ,, 25		...	...	...	1·600
25 ,, ,, 26		...	...	...	1·550
26 ,, ,, 27		...	...	...	1·525
27 ,, ,, 28		...	...	...	1·500
28 ,, ,, 29		...	...	...	1·475
29 ,, ,, 30		...	...	...	1·450
30 ,, ,, 31		...	...	...	1·425
31 ,, ,, 32		...	...	...	1·400
32 ,, ,, 33		...	...	...	1·375
33 , ,, 34		...	...	...	1·350
34 ,, ,, 35		...	...	...	1·325
35 ,, ,, 37		...	...	...	1·300
37 ,, ,, 38		...	...	...	1·275
38 ,, ,, 40		...	...	...	1·250
40 ,, ,, 42		...	...	...	1·225
42 ,, ,, 44		...	...	...	1·200
44 and over	...	...	...	...	1·175

(4) The number of years referred to in sub-paragraph (1) and in sub-paragraph (3), by which the sums therein respectively specified are to be multiplied for the purposes of those sub-paragraphs, is the number of complete years during which the person concerned has served as a regular fireman:

Provided that no account shall be taken of any service which is not reckonable as pensionable service.

(5) In the case of a person who is entitled to reckon a period as pensionable service for the purposes of the pension in question by virtue of service or employment otherwise than as a regular fireman in respect of which he was subject to superannuation arrangements—

(a) if he was subject to the operation of any regulations made under section 69(4) of the National Insurance Act 1946(a) or section 110(1) of the National Insurance Act 1965 or of other provisions modifying the said superannuation arrangements in connection with the passing of the said Act of 1946, otherwise than by virtue of an election made or notice given, then, for the purposes of sub-paragraph (1), sub-paragraph (4) shall apply as though the period he is so entitled to reckon as pensionable service were a period of service as a regular fireman;

(b) if he was subject to the operation of such regulations or other provisions by virtue of an election made or notice given, then sub-paragraph (3) shall apply in his case as if for the reference therein to his age on the appointed day there were substituted a reference to his age on the date on which the said election or notice became effective and, for the purposes of the said sub-paragraph, sub-paragraph (4) shall apply as though the period he is so entitled to reckon as pensionable service were a period of service as a regular fireman:

Provided that no account shall be taken of any period he is so entitled to reckon as pensionable service which is not attributable to service or employment which would have been taken into account for the purposes of the said regulations as provisions.

(6) The rate of reduction of a pension under this paragraph shall not in any case exceed £51 a year.

(a) 1946 c. 67.

2.—(1) Where a person in receipt of an ordinary, ill-health, short service or deferred pension has been in service or employment otherwise than as a regular fireman—

(*a*) in respect of which he was subject to superannuation arrangements;

(*b*) by virtue of which he is entitled to reckon pensionable service for the purposes of the pension; and

(*c*) the period of which includes a participating period of relevant employment, then, for the purpose of abating the pension in relation to that participating period of relevant employment, any provision of the said arrangements in operation when he left the said service or employment the effect of which is that pensions payable thereunder are to be reduced in connection with the operation of the National Insurance Act 1959**(a)** or of any provision of the National Insurance Act 1965 relating to graduated contributions or graduated retirement benefit shall apply, subject to the necessary adaptations and modifications, as though the provision were contained in this paragraph and as if—

(i) the pension were payable under the said arrangements, and

(ii) any other period of service or employment by virtue of which he is entitled to reckon pensionable service for the purposes of the pension were a period of non-participating employment at the end of which no payment in lieu of contributions falls to be made.

(2) A fire authority, in determining any question arising under sub-paragraph (1) and relating to a particular service or employment, shall be entitled to treat as conclusive any relevant certificate issued, with the agreement of the person concerned, by his employer in that service or employment.

(3) Where for the purposes of the superannuation arrangements applicable to such service or employment as is mentioned in sub-paragraph (1) the person concerned was entitled to reckon service by virtue of some previous service or employment, that previous service or employment shall be treated for the purposes of this paragraph as if it were part of the service or employment first mentioned in this sub-paragraph.

3.—(1) Where a person in receipt of an ordinary, ill-health, short service or deferred pension is entitled to reckon as pensionable service for the purposes of the pension a period of employment as a regular fireman which is a participating period of relevant employment, then in relation to that period the unsecured portion of the pension shall be reduced in accordance with the provisions of sub-paragraph (2).

(2) Where the unsecured portion of a pension is reduced in accordance with the provisions of this sub-paragraph, the annual rate of that portion of the pension shall be reduced in respect of any period beyond the age of 65 years by the annual rate of the graduated retirement benefit which would be payable to the pensioner on the assumption that he retired from regular employment on attaining that age, in return for a payment in lieu of contributions in respect of the whole of the period referred to in sub-paragraph (1).

4.—(1) Where a person in receipt of the secured portion of an ill-health pension, (under this or a previous Scheme), the unsecured portion of which has been terminated in the circumstances mentioned in Article 18, is also in receipt of some other pension (being an ordinary, ill-health, short service or deferred pension) and is entitled to reckon for the purposes of that other pension the period of pensionable service reckonable for the purposes of the ill-health pension, then the unsecured portion of that other pension shall be reduced in accordance with the provisions of sub-paragraph (2).

(2) Where the unsecured portion of an ordinary, ill-health, short service or deferred pension is reduced in accordance with the provisions of this sub-paragraph, the annual rate of that portion shall be reduced in respect of any period beyond the age of 65 years by the annual rate of the secured portion of the ill-health pension first mentioned in this paragraph.

(a) 1959 c. 47.

Sch. 1 (*contd.*)

Articles 12, 13, 14 and 16 PART VIII

REDUCTION OF PENSION IN SPECIFIED CASES

1. An ordinary, ill-health, short service or deferred pension payable to a fireman shall, in the cases mentioned in this Part, be reduced in accordance therewith; and any reference in this Part to a pension is a reference to such a pension.

2.—(1) This paragraph shall apply in the case of a fireman entitled to reckon pensionable service otherwise than—

(*a*) by virtue of service as a regular fireman on or after 1st April 1972, or

(*b*) by virtue of such service before that date in respect of which he has paid pension contributions at a rate related to 6% of his pensionable pay;

except that this paragraph shall not apply in the case of a man to whom Article 59 or 60 applies who last paid pension contributions before 1st April 1972 at a rate related to 5% of his pensionable pay unless he elected or agreed under Article 59(2)(*b*) or (4)(*a*) or Article 60(2)(*b*) that his pension be reduced.

(2) The pension of a fireman in whose case this paragraph applies shall, subject to the provisions of this Part, be reduced by that percentage specified in the second column of the following Table opposite the number of completed years of pensionable service he is entitled to reckon otherwise than as mentioned in sub-paragraph (1)(*a*) or (*b*) being, where he agreed to the reduction under Article 59(4)(*a*), pensionable service which he became so entitled to reckon under Article 48, 49, 51 or 52 on or after 1st July 1973.

(3) If the fireman elected to pay additional contributions as mentioned in Article 57 and paid such contributions until he became entitled to reckon 25 years' pensionable service or retired with a pension, in calculating the amount of the reduction under this paragraph no account shall be taken of any service which was taken into account for the purpose of calculating the rate at which the additional contributions were payable.

3.—(1) This paragraph shall apply in the case of a fireman entitled to reckon pensionable service otherwise than by virtue of service as a member of a fire brigade on or after 1st April 1972; except that this paragraph shall not apply in the case of a man to whom Article 59 or 60 applies unless he elected or agreed under Article 59(3)(*b*) or (4)(*b*) or 60(3)(*b*) that his pension be reduced.

(2) The pension of a fireman in whose case this paragraph applies shall, subject to the provisions of this Part, be reduced by the percentage specified in the third column of the following Table opposite the number of completed years of pensionable service he is entitled to reckon otherwise than as mentioned in sub-paragraph (1), being, where he agreed to the reduction under Article 59(4)(*b*), pensionable service which he became so entitled to reckon under Article 48, 49, 51 or 52 on or after 1st July 1973.

4. In calculating the amount of a reduction in a fireman's pension under paragraph 2 or 3 no account shall be taken of any such service as is mentioned in the proviso to Article 78(2) which he is entitled to reckon as pensionable service by virtue of Article 78(1).

5. In calculating the amount of a reduction in a fireman's pension under paragraph 2 or 3 no account shall be taken of any reduction in the amount of the pension in accordance with the provisions of Article 21 or 41 or of Part VII of this Schedule, and, where the pension falls to be reduced under both those paragraphs, for the purpose of calculating each reduction, no account shall be taken of the other reduction.

6.—(1) In the case of a fireman who elected under Article 58 to pay additional or further pension contributions and was still paying such contributions immediately before retiring with an ordinary pension, the annual amount of that pension shall be reduced for the period mentioned in sub-paragraph (2) by the annual amount of those contributions immediately before his retirement, calculated by reference to his pensionable pay at that time so, however, that no account of the said reduction shall be taken for the purposes of calculating any other reduction in the pension under this Scheme.

(2) The period referred to in sub-paragraph (1) shall be one corresponding to that for which the additional or further contributions would have remained payable had the man not retired.

TABLE

Completed years of pensionable service taken into account	Percentage reduction in pension	
	Under paragraph 2	Under paragraph 3
1	0·2	0·2
2	0·4	0·4
3	0·6	0·5
4	0·8	0·7
5	1·0	0·8
6	1·2	0·9
7	1·3	1·0
8	1·4	1·1
9	1·6	1·2
10	1·7	1·3
11	1·8	1·4
12	1·9	1·5
13	2·1	1·6
14	2·2	1·6
15	2·3	1·7
16	2·4	1·8
17	2·5	1·9
18	2·6	2·0
19	2·7	2·0
20	2·8	2·1
21	2·9	2·1
22	3·0	2·2
23	3·1	2·2
24	3·2	2·3
25	3·2	2·3
26	3·3	2·4
27	3·4	2·4
28	3·4	2·5
29	3·5	2·5
30 or more	3·5	2·5

PART IX   Articles 13 and 14

REDUCTION OF FIREMAN'S GRATUITY

1. Where a payment in lieu of contributions falls to be made by a fire authority in respect of a regular fireman and—

(*a*) a short service gratuity is payable by that authority on his retitement, or

(*b*) an ill-health gratuity is so payable and the fire authority determine that the provisions of this Part of this Schedule shall apply,

the gratuity in question shall be reduced by an amount equal to the amount which could be retained out of the gratuity by the fire authority under section 60(4) of the National Insurance Act 1965 if the gratuity were a refund of payments to which that subsection applies.

Sch. 1 (*contd.*)

2. Where a payment in lieu of contributions may fall to be made by a fire authority in respect of a regular fireman and such a gratuity as is mentioned in paragraph 1 is payable as mentioned therein, the fire authority may reduce the amount of the gratuity in question by the amount by which it would be reduced under the said paragraph 1 if the payment in lieu of contributions in fact fell to be made, so however that, if the said payment does not fall to be made within the period of 78 weeks from the date when the person concerned ceases to be a regular fireman or within such shorter period as the fire authority may determine, then any reduction in the amount of the gratuity under this paragraph shall cease to have effect and the difference between the full and the reduced amounts thereof shall become payable.

SCHEDULE 2

WIDOWS AND ADULT DEPENDANTS

PART I

Article 22

WIDOWS ORDINARY PENSION

1. Subject to paragraph 2, the amount of a widow's ordinary pension shall equal a half of that of her husband's pension or notional pension referred to in paragraph 3.

2.—(1) Where in respect of any period a widow so elects, then, subject to sub-paragraph (2), the annual rate of her ordinary pension in respect of that period shall be, if her husband at the time when he ceased to be a regular fireman—

  (*a*) held a rank not higher than that of sub-officer, £163·81 a year;

  (*b*) held a rank higher than that of sub-officer but not higher than that of divisional officer (Grade I) £213·37 a year;

  (*c*) held a rank higher than that of divisional officer (Grade I), £256·66 a year.

(2) Where the husband was entitled to reckon at least 10 years' pensionable service, the preceding sub-paragraph shall have effect as if for the rates of £163·81, £213·37 and £256·66 there were substituted, respectively ,the rates of £175·28, £224·84 and £268·14 a year.

3.—(1) The husband's pension or notional pension mentioned in paragraph 1 shall be—

  (*a*) where he died while entitled to an ordinary, short service or ill-health pension, that pension;

  (*b*) in any other case, the ill-health pension to which he would have been entitled had he retired with such a pension immediately before he died,
calculated, in either case, in accordance with the following sub-paragraph.

(2) For the purposes of paragraph 1, in calculating the husband's pension or notional pension the following provisions shall be disregarded, that is to say the provisions for the reduction of a pensiom contained in Articles 21(6) and 41(6) and in Parts VII and VIII of Schedule 1.

Article 22

PART II

TRANSITIONAL MODIFICATIONS OF PART I

1.—(1) Where this Part of this Schedule applies, Part I of this Schedule (hereinafter referred to as Part I) shall have effect as if the relevant provisions of this Part were substituted for paragraph 1 thereof and paragraph 3 of Part I shall have effect accordingly.

(2) In this Part "pre-1972 pensionable service" means the pensionable service the husband was entitled to reckon otherwise than by virtue of—

(*a*) service as a regular fireman on or after 1st April 1972, or

(*b*) Article 51 or 52, where the conditions specified in paragraph (1) of the Article in question are satisfied on or after 1st July 1973.

2.—(1) This paragraph shall apply where—

(*a*) the husband, before 1st April 1972, last paid pension contributions at a rate related to 5% of his pensionable pay, and

(*b*) neither he nor the widow exercised a right of election accorded by Article 58(2), 59(2), 60(2) or 61(2).

(2) Subject to paragraph 2(1) of Part I but disregarding paragraph 2(2) thereof, where this paragraph applies the amount of the widow's ordinary pension shall equal a half of the amount specified in paragraph 4 of this Part:

Provided that the amount payable in respect of any week shall not be less than it would have been had the weekly amount of the pension been calculated as provided in Scheme II of Part II of Schedule 2 to the Fireman's Pension Scheme 1971.

3.—(1) This paragraph shall apply where—

(*a*) paragraph 2 does not apply since either the husband did not pay pension contributions as mentioned in sub-paragraph (1)(*a*) thereof, or, if he did, he or the widow exercised a right of election mentioned in sub-paragraph (1)(*b*) thereof, and

(*b*) neither the husband nor the widow exercised a right of election accorded by Article 58(3), 59(3), 60(3) or 61(3).

(2) Subject to paragraph 2 of Part I, the amount of the widow's ordinary pension shall, subject to sub-paragraph (3), equal a third of the amount of her husband's pension or notional pension with the addition of a sixth of the amount specified in paragraph 4 of this Part.

(3) Except where the husband dies while in receipt of an ordinary or short service pension, his widow's ordinary pension shall be of an amount not less than a half of the amount specified in paragraph 5.

4. The amount specified in this paragraph shall be the difference between the two following amounts, subject, however to paragraph 6—

(*a*) an amount equal to a sixtieth of the husband's average pensionable pay for each completed year of pensionable service up to 20 years with the addition of a sixtieth for each completed half year by which his pensionable service exeeds 20 years;

(*b*) an amount calculated as aforesaid but by reference only to the husband's pre-1972 pensionable service.

5.—(1) In this paragraph the following expressions have the meanings hereby respectively assigned to them that is to say:—

"relevant number of years" means the number of years (if any) by which the fireman's completed years of pre-1972 pensionable service fall short of 20 years;

"relevant pensionable service" means a fireman's pensionable service reduced by his completed years of pre-1972 pensionable service;

"weighted relevant pensionable service" means a fireman's completed years of relevant pensionable service up to the relevant number of years with the addition of a year for each completed half year by which his relevant pensionable service exceeds the relevant number of years.

Sch. 2 (*contd.*)

(2) The amount specified in this paragraph shall be the amount of the husband's ill-health or notional pension calculated in accordance with Part III of Schedule 1 but, subject to paragraph 6—

(*a*) where his weighted relevant pensionable service does not exceed 20 years, by reference thereto;

(*b*) where that service exceeds 20 years, by reference to his relevant pensionable service with the addition of a half year for each completed year of pre-1972 service,

instead of by reference to his pensionable service.

6. Where the husband's completed years of pensionable service exceed 30 years, then there shall be reduced by that excess—

(*a*) his completed years of pensionable service taken into account for the purposes of paragraph 4(*a*);

(*b*) his completed years of pre-1972 pensionable service taken into account for the purposes of paragraph 4(*b*);

(*c*) his completed years of pre-1972 pensionable service taken into account for the purposes of paragraph 5(2)(*b*) (otherwise than for the purpose of determining his relevant pensionable service).

Article 23

PART III

WIDOW'S SPECIAL PENSION

1. Subject to paragraphs 2 and 3, the weekly amount of a widow's special pension calculated in accordance with this Part of this Schedule shall be equal to 45% of her husband's average pensionable pay.

2.—(1) Where, in respect of any week, a pension under section 19 of the National Insurance (Industrial Injuries) Act 1965 is payable to the widow in consequence of her husband's death and the amount of that pension exceeds that of a widow's pension under the National Insurance Act 1965 as specified in Part I of Schedule 3 thereto at the time of the husband's death, then the amount of her special pension in respect of that week shall be reduced by that excess.

(2) Where the provisions governing the amounts of pensions under section 19 of the National Insurance (Industrial Injuries) Act 1965 have changed after the death of the husband, the reduction under sub-paragraph (1) in respect of any week shall not exceed the amount which would have been the amount thereof in respect of that week had those provisions not changed.

Article 25

PART IV

WIDOW'S ACCRUED PENSION

1.—(1) In this Part the husband's half-rate service means the aggregate of—

(*a*) his pensionable service reckonable by virtue of service as a regular fireman on or after 1st April 1972;

(*b*) his pensionable service (if any) reckonable by virtue of such service as is mentioned in the proviso to Article 78(2) and the provisions of Article 78(1);

(*c*) if, immediately before he retired, he was paying further contributions under Article 58 in pursuance of an election thereunder, the proportion specified in sub-paragraph (3) of the pensionable service taken into account under Part I of Schedule 7 in calculating those contributions;

Sch. 2 (*contd.*)

(*d*) if he had elected under Article 59 to make a further payment by way of a lump sum, the pensionable service taken into account under Part II of Schedule 7 in calculating that lump sum;

(*e*) if his deferred pension fell to be reduced in accordance with paragraph 3 of Part VIII of Schedule 1 the proportion specified in sub-paragraph (4) of the pensionable service taken into account in calculating the reduction.

(2) In this Part the husband's mixed-rate service means the aggregate of—

(*a*) his pensionable service reckonable by virtue of service as a regular fireman in respect of which he has paid pension contributions at a rate related to 6% of his pensionable pay;

(*b*) his pensionable service reckonable as mentioned in sub-paragraph (1)(*a*) and (*b*);

(*c*) if, immediately before he retired, he was paying additional contributions under Article 57 or 58 in pursuance of such an election as is mentioned in the Article in question, the proportion mentioned in sub-paragraph (3) of the pensionable service taken into account, under Part I of Schedule 7 in calculating those contributions;

(*d*) if he had elected under Article 59 to make an additional payment by way of a lump sum, the pensionable service taken into account under Part II of Schedule 7 in calculating that lump sum;

(*e*) if his deferred pension fell to be reduced in accordance with paragraph 2 of Part VIII of Schedule 1, the proportion mentioned in sub-paragraph (4) of the pensionable service taken into account in calculating the reduction.

(3) The proportion referred to in sub-paragraph (1)(*c*) or sub-paragraph (2)(*c*) shall be the proportion which the period for which the husband paid further contributions or, as the case may be, additional contributions, bore to the period by which the pensionable service he was entitled to reckon at the time when he made the election referred to in the sub-paragraph in question fell short of 25 years or, where that period is less than 5 years, to a period of 5 years, each period being reckoned in completed years and completed months.

(4) The proportion referred to in sub-paragraph (1)(*e*) or sub-paragraph (2)(*e*) shall be the proportion which the period of the man's actual service—

(*a*) on or after 1st April 1972, in the case of sub-paragraph (1)(*e*), or

(*b*) on or after 26th August 1966, in the case of sub-paragraph (2)(*e*),

as a regular fireman, bears to the period of such service as he would have had if (irrespective of the date of his death) he had not retired until entitled to an ordinary pension or until he could be required to retire on account of age, whichever is the earlier each period being reckoned in completed years and completed months.

2.—(1) Subject to paragraphs 3 and 4, the amount of a widow's accrued pension shall equal the aggregate of the following amounts, namely:—

(*a*) in respect of the husband's half-rate service, a sixth of the corresponding proportion of his deferred pension;

(*b*) in respect of his mixed-rate service, a third of the corresponding proportion of his deferred pension.

(2) For the purposes of sub-paragraphs (1)(*a*) and (*b*), the corresponding proportion means the proportion which the husband's half-rate or, as the case may be, mixed-rate service bears to the pensionable service reckonable by him, each period being reckoned in completed years up to 20 years and in completed half years in so far as it exceeds 20 years.

3. Where in respect of any period a widow so elects, then the annual rate of her accrued pension in respect of that period shall be, if her husband at the time when he ceased to be a regular fireman—

Sch. 2 (*contd.*)

(*a*) held a rank not higher than that of sub-officer, £163·81 a year;

(*b*) held a rank higher than that of sub-officer but not higher than that of divisional officer (Grade I), £213·37 a year;

(*c*) held a rank higher than that of divisional officer (Grade I), £256·66 a year.

Articles 22, 23 and 25   PART V

INCREASE IN WIDOW'S PENSION DURING FIRST 13 WEEKS

1. This Part shall apply unless, immediately before his death, the husband was neither—

(*a*) serving as a regular fireman, nor

(*b*) in receipt of a pension.

2.—(1) Where this Part applies, a widow's ordinary, special or accrued pension shall, so far as necessary, be increased in respect of the first 13 weeks for which it is payable so as to secure that, in respect of each such week, the aggregate amount of the pension and of any children's allowances payable in respect of the husband's death is not less than—

(*a*) his pensionable pay for a week immediately before he died, where he was then serving as a regular fireman, or

(*b*) the weekly amount of his pension immediately before he died in any other case.

(2) For the purposes of this paragraph there shall be disregarded any reduction in the husband's pension in consequence of—

(*a*) Part VIII of Schedule 1, or

(*b*) his entitlement to any additional benefit within the meaning of paragraph 4 of Part V of Schedule 1.

Article 26   PART VI

WIDOW'S GRATUITY BY WAY OF COMMUTED PENSION

A widow's gratuity by way of commuted pension shall be such sum as may be agreed between the fire authority and the widow, not exceeding the capitalised value of the pension or, as the case may be, of that part of the pension which is commuted, calculated in accordance with tables prepared from time to time by the Government Actuary.

                                        PART VII
Article 31
DEPENDENT RELATIVE'S SPECIAL PENSION

1.—(1) Where a regular fireman in respect of whose death a dependent relative's special pension is granted (in this Part referred to as the "deceased") was married and his widow is alive, the pension shall, subject to paragraph 3, be determined in accordance with this paragraph.

(2) A pension determined in accordance herewith shall be of an amount equal to 20% of the deceased's average pensionable pay.

2.—(1) Where the deceased was not married or in respect of any period after the death of the widow, the amount of the dependent relative's special pension shall, subject to paragraph 3, be determined in accordance with this paragraph.

(2) A pension determined in accordance herewith shall be of an amount equal to 45% of the deceased's average pensionable pay.

3.—(1) Where in respect of any week the aggregate amount of—

(*a*) any widow's special pension, and

(*b*) any child's special allowance,

payable in respect of the deceased's death equals or exceeds the amount of his average pensionable pay, no dependent relative's special pension shall be payable in respect of that week.

(2) Where in respect of any week the aggregate amount of—

(*a*) any widow's special pension,

(*b*) any child's special allowance, and

(*c*) any dependent relative's special pension,

payable in respect of the deceased's death would exceed the amount of his average pensionable pay, the dependent relative's pension shall be reduced by such factor as will ensure that the said aggregate does not exceed the said amount.

SCHEDULE 3

CHILDREN

PART I   Article 33

CHILD'S ORDINARY ALLOWANCE

1.—(1) Where the mother of the child is alive, the child's ordinary allowance in respect of the death of a regular fireman shall, subject to paragraph 5, be determined in accordance with this paragraph.

(2) Subject to sub-paragraphs (3) and (4), an allowance determined in accordance herewith shall be of an amount equal to 12·5% of the amount specified in paragraph 3 or 4, as the case may be.

(3) Subject to sub-paragraph (4), where 4 or more children's ordinary allowances are payable in respect of the death of the same person, an allowance determined in accordance herewith shall be of an amount equal to 37·5% of the amount specified in paragraph 3 or 4, as the case may be, divided by the total number of allowances so payable.

(4) Where in respect of any period a person to whom there is paid an allowance determined in accordance herewith so elects, then, in respect of that period, the allowance shall be payable as hereinafter provided, that is to say—

(*a*) where the father's last rank was not higher than that of sub-officer, at the rate of £45·91 a year;

(*b*) where the father's last rank was higher than that of sub-officer but not higher than that of divisional officer (Grade I), at the rate of £54·78 a year; or

(*c*) where the father's last rank was higher than that of divisional officer (Grade I), at the rate of £67·30 a year.

2.—(1) Where the father was the child's only surviving parent or in respect of the period after the death of the mother, the child's ordinary allowance shall, subject to paragraph 5, be determined in accordance with this paragraph.

(2) Subject to sub-paragraphs (3) and (4), an allowance determined in accordance herewith shall be of an amount equal to 25% of the amount specified in paragraph 3 or 4, as the case may be.

(3) Subject to sub-paragraph (4), where 3 or more children's ordinary allowances are payable in respect of the death of the same person, an allowance determined in accordance herewith shall be of an amount equal to 50% of the amount specified in paragraph 3 or 4, as the case may be, divided by the total number of allowances so payable.

Sch. 3 (*contd.*)

(4) Where in respect of any period a person to whom there is paid an allowance determined in accordance herewith so elects, then, in respect of that period, the allowance shall be payable as hereinafter provided, that is to say—

(*a*) where the father's last rank was not higher than that of sub-officer, at the rate of £67·82 a year or such higher rate not exceeding £89·73 a year as the fire authority may from time to time determine;

(*b*) where the father's last rank was higher than that of sub-officer but not higher than that of divisional officer (Grade I), at the rate of £80·86 a year or such higher rate not exceeding £107·47 a year as the fire authority may from time to time determine; or

(*c*) where the father's last rank was higher than that of divisional officer (Grade I), at the rate of £100·69 a year or such higher rate not exceeding £134·07 a year as the fire authority may from time to time determine.

3.—(1) Except where the father is such a person as is mentioned in paragraph 4(1), the specified amount shall be that of his pension or notional pension, that is to say—

(*a*) where he dies while entitled to an ordinary, short service or ill-health pension, that pension;

(*b*) in any other case, the ill-health pension to which he would have been entitled had he retired with such a pension immediately before he died,

calculated, in either case, in accordance with the following sub-paragraph.

(2) For the purposes of paragraph 1 or 2, in calculating the father's pension or notional pension the following provisions shall be disregarded, that is to say the provisions for the reduction of a pension contained in Articles 21(6) and 41(6) and in Parts VII and VIII of Schedule 1.

4.—(1) This paragraph shall apply where the father was serving as a regular fireman or entitled to a pension other than a deferred pension either—

(*a*) on 1st July 1973, or

(*b*) at the date of his death where that date is before 1st October 1973,

and he or, as the case may be, his widow has not exercised the rights of election accorded by Articles 58, 59, 60 and 61 for the purpose of avoiding the application to the calculation of his widow's ordinary pension (if any)—

(i) of paragraphs 2 and 3 of Part II of Schedule 2, where, before 1st April 1972, he last paid pension contributions at a rate related to 5% of his pensionable pay, or

(ii) of paragraph 3 of the said Part II, in any other case.

(2) Where this paragraph applies, the specified amount shall be the difference between the two following amounts, subject, however, to sub-paragraph (3):—

(*a*) an amount equal to a sixtieth of the father's average pensionable pay for each completed year of pensionable service up to 20 years with the addition of a sixtieth for each completed half year by which his pensionable service exceeds 20 years;

(*b*) an amount calculated as aforesaid but by reference only to the father's pre-1972 pensionable service, that is to say the pensionable service he was entitled to reckon otherwise than by virtue of—

(i) service as a regular fireman on or after 1st April 1972, or

(ii) Article 51 or 52, where the conditions specified in paragraph (1) of the Article in question are satisfied on or after 1st July 1973.

(3) Where the father's completed years of pensionable service exceed 30 years, then there shall be reduced by that excess—

Sch. 3 (*contd.*)

(*a*) his completed years of pensionable service taken into account for the purposes of sub-paragraph (2)(*a*);

(*b*) his completed years of pre-1972 pensionable service taken into account for the purposes of sub-paragraph (2)(*b*).

5.—(1) Where in respect of any week the aggregate rate at which—

(*a*) any widow's ordinary pension, and

(*b*) any children's ordinary allowances determined in accordance with sub-paragraph (2) or (3) of paragraph 1,

are payable in respect of a fireman who died while entitled to a pension other than a deferred pension exceeds the rate at which that pension was payable immediately before his death, the children's allowances shall be reduced by such factor as will ensure that the said aggregate rate does not exceed the last-mentioned rate.

(2) For the purposes of this paragraph there shall be ignored any reduction in the deceased fireman's pension other than a reduction under Article 21(6) or 41(6) or (in the case of an injury pension) under paragraph 3(1) of Part V of Schedule 1.

PART II   Article 34

CHILD'S SPECIAL ALLOWANCE

1.—(1) Where the mother of the child is alive, the child's special allowance in respect of the death of a regular fireman shall be determined in accordance with this paragraph.

(2) Subject to sub-paragraph (3), an allowance determined in accordance herewith shall be of an amount equal to 10% of the father's average pensionable pay.

(3) Where 5 or more children's special allowances are payable in respect of the death of the same person, an allowance determined in accordance herewith shall be of an amount equal to 40% of the father's average pensionable pay divided by the total number of allowances so payable.

2.—(1) Where the father was the child's only surviving parent or in respect of the period after the death of the mother, the child's special allowance shall be determined in accordance with this paragraph.

(2) Subject to sub-paragraph (3), an allowance determined in accordance herewith shall be of an amount equal to 20% of the father's average pensionable pay.

(3) Where 5 or more children's special allowances are payable in respect of the death of the same person, an allowance determined in accordance herewith shall be of an amount equal to 80% of the father's average pensionable pay divided by the total number of allowances so payable.

PART III   Article 36

CHILD'S ACCRUED ALLOWANCE

1. Subject as hereinafter provided, a child's accrued allowance shall be determined in like manner as an ordinary allowance would be determined under Part I of this Schedule if the child were entitled to such an allowance.

2. Except where the child's father is such a person as is referred to in paragraph 3, the specified amount, for the purposes of paragraph 1 or 2 of the said Part I as applied hereby, shall be the amount of the father's deferred pension and not the amount specified in the said Part I.

Sch. 3 (*contd.*)

3.—(1) This paragraph shall apply where the father is entitled to reckon pensionable service otherwise than by virtue of—

  (*a*) service as a regular fireman on or after 1st April 1972;

  (*b*) by virtue of such service as is mentioned in the proviso to Article 78(2) and the provisions of Article 78(1);

  (*c*) Article 51 or 52, where the conditions specified in paragraph (1) of the Article in question are satisfied on or after 1st July 1973.

(2) Where this paragraph applies, the specified amount, for the purposes of paragraph 1 or 2 of Part I of this Schedule as applied hereby, shall be the following proportion of the amount of the father's deferred pension, that is to say, the proportion which his half-rate service (within the meaning of Part IV of Schedule 2) bears to the pensionable service reckonable by him, each period being reckoned in completed years up to 20 years and in completed half years in so far as it exceeds 20 years, and not the amount specified in the said Part I.

4. For the purposes of paragraph 1 or 2 of Part I of this Schedule as applied hereby, in calculating the father's deferred pension the following provisions shall be disregarded, that is to say:—

  (*a*) the restrictions on payment contained in Article 16(2), and

  (*b*) the provisions for the reduction of a pension contained in Articles 21(6) and 41(6) and in Parts VII and VIII of Schedule 1.

5. For the purposes of Part I of this Schedule as applied hereby, paragraph 5 thereof shall have effect as if for sub-paragraph (1) thereof there were substituted the following provision, namely, that where in respect of any week the aggregate rate at which—

  (*a*) any widow's accrued pension, and

  (*b*) any children's accrued allowances determined in accordance with sub-paragraph (2) or (3) of paragraph 1 of the said Part I,

exceeds the rate at which the husband and father's deferred pension was payable immediately before his death, or would have been so payable had he attained the age of 60 years, the children's allowances shall be reduced by such factor as will ensure that the said aggregate rate does not exceed the last-mentioned rate.

Articles 33, 34 and 36

PART IV

INCREASE IN CHILD'S ALLOWANCE IN CERTAIN CASES DURING FIRST 13 WEEKS

1. This Part shall apply where the regular fireman in respect of whose death the allowance is payable did not leave a widow entitled to a pension which was payable for a continuous period of 13 weeks unless, immediately before his death, he was neither—

  (i) serving as a regular fireman, nor

  (ii) in receipt of a pension.

2. Where this Part applies, a child's ordinary, special or accrued allowance shall, so far as necessary, be increased in respect of the first 13 weeks for which it is payable so as to secure that, in respect of each such week, it is not less than the amount specified in paragraph 2(1)(*a*) or (*b*) of Part V of Schedule 2 except that, where two or more such allowances are payable in respect of the death of the same fireman, each allowance shall be so increased that it is of that amount divided by the number of such allowances:

Provided that where a widow's pension is payable in respect of any such week, a child's allowance in respect of the death of the same person shall not be so increased in respect of that week.

CHILD'S GRATUITY BY WAY OF COMMUTED ALLOWANCE

A child's gratuity by way of commuted allowance shall be such sum as may be agreed between the fire authority and the child's guardian, not exceeding the capitalised value of the allowance or, as the case may be, of that part of the allowance which is commuted, calculated in accordance with tables prepared from time to time by the Government Actuary.

SCHEDULE 4   Articles 48, 49, 51 and 52

PAYMENTS BY FIREMEN IN RESPECT OF PREVIOUS SERVICE

1. Where a fireman undertakes to make payments in accordance with this Schedule, he shall pay by regular instalments of such an amount that the payment will be completed within a period of 5 years and before he can be required to retire under Article 96:

Provided that—

   (*a*) he may on giving the said undertaking or at any later date discharge his liability thereunder, in whole or in part by paying the whole or part of the sum, or balance of the sum then outstanding, as the case may be;

   (*b*) if he retires and is not entitled to an award other than one of an amount equal to his aggregate contributions, or dies, all further liability under the said undertaking shall cease;

   (*c*) if he retires before his liability under the said undertaking is discharged and his liability does not cease in accordance with the provisions of proviso (*b*) to this paragraph, the fire authority shall be empowered to deduct the balance of the sum then outstanding from payments of any award payable to him.

2. Where a fireman undertakes to make payments in accordance with this Schedule, he shall make payment to the authority by whom he is employed when he gives the undertaking and, without prejudice to any other method of payment, this liability may be discharged by way of a deduction by the said authority from his pay.

SCHEDULE 5   Article 48

SUMS TO BE PAID BY FIREMEN IN RESPECT OF PREVIOUS SERVICE

1.—(1) Subject to the provisions of this Schedule, the sum to be paid by a regular fireman under an undertaking given under Article 48(5) shall be, in respect of each year of pensionable service reckonable under Article 48(5) and in respect of £100 of annual pensionable pay, the sum shown in the second column of the following Table in relation to an age which corresponds with that of the fireman, and the total sum to be paid as aforesaid shall be calculated proportionately be reference to the pensionable service so reckonable and to his annual pensionable pay:—

Sch. 5 (*contd.*)

TABLE

Age in years	Amount for £100 of annual pensionable pay
	£
Under 38	9·50
38 but under 39	9·60
39 „ „ 40	9·70
40 „ „ 41	9·80
41 „ „ 42	9·90
42 „ „ 43	10·05
43 „ „ 44	10·20
44 „ „ 45	10·40
45 „ „ 46	10·55
46 „ „ 47	10·70
47 „ „ 48	10·90
48 „ „ 49	11·05
49 „ „ 50	11·25
50 „ „ 51	11·40
51 „ „ 52	11·60
52 „ „ 53	11·80
53 „ „ 54	12·00
54 „ „ 55	12·30
55 and over	12·60

(2) In this paragraph a reference to the age or annual pensionable pay of a fireman is a reference to his age or, as the case may be, the annual rate of his pensionable pay on joining or, as the case may be, rejoining the brigade, any retrospective increase in his pensionable pay granted after that time being ignored.

2. The sum to be paid by the fireman, calculated in accordance with the preceding provisions of this Schedule, shall be reduced by a half of the amount, if any, by which the sum which would have been payable in his case by way of transfer value under Article 71 would have been reduced under paragraphs 3, 4 and 5 of Schedule 9 had the pensionable service reckonable under Article 48(5) been reckonable under Article 48(1).

SCHEDULE 6

Article 52

PART I

CIVIL SERVICE, METROPOLITAN CIVIL STAFFS, EDUCATION, HEALTH, POLICE AND BELFAST FIRE SERVICE

1. This Part shall apply in relation to service or employment—

(*a*) as a civil servant,

(*b*) in the metropolitan civil staffs within the meaning of section 15 of the Superannuation (Miscellaneous Provisions) Act 1967(a),

(*c*) such as is mentioned in section 2(2)(*e*) and (*ee*) of the Superannuation (Miscellaneous Provisions) Act 1948(b) (education service),

(*d*) in respect of which awards may be made under regulations for the time being in force under section 10 of the Superannuation Act 1972(c), section 67 of the National Health Service Act 1946(d) or section 66 of the National Health Service (Scotland) Act 1947(e),

---

(a) 1967 c. 28.   (b) 1948 c. 33.   (c) 1972 c. 11.
(d) 1946 c. 81.   (e) 1947 c. 27.

Sch. 6 (*contd.*)

(*e*) as a regular policeman within the meaning of the regulations for the time being in force under section 1 of the Police Pensions Act 1948(**a**), (hereinafter referred to as the Police Pensions Regulations), or

(*f*) in the Belfast Fire Force.

2. In relation to the said service or employment Article 52(1)(*d*) shall have effect as if the words "or (subject to paragraph 2 of Part I of Schedule 6) within 6 months of the date specified in Schedule 6 in relation to his former service, whichever is the later," were omitted.

3. In relation to the said service or employment the transfer value for the purposes of Article 52 shall be one payable under—

(*a*) rules made under sections 2 and 15 of the Superannuation (Miscellaneous Provisions) Act 1948;

(*b*) such regulations as are mentioned in paragraph 1(*d*);

(*c*) the Police Pensions Regulations;

(*d*) the Scheme for the time being in force under section 13 of the Fire Services (Amendment) Act (Northern Ireland) 1950(**b**); or

(*e*) a scheme made under section 1, or regulations made under section 9 or 10 of the Superannuation Act 1972.

4. The specified authority for the purposes of Article 52 shall be—

(*a*) in relation to service or employment as a civil servant, the Minister for the Civil Service;

(*b*) in relation to service or employment as a regular policeman, the police authority within the meaning of the Police Pensions Regulations;

(*c*) in relation to service in the Belfast Fire Force, the Corporation of the city of Belfast;

(*d*) in relation to any other service or employment, the Secretary of State.

Part II

Other Service or Employment

1. This Part shall apply in relation to such service or employment as is mentioned in paragraphs 3 and 4 of Schedule 1 to the Superannuation (Fire and Specified Services) Interchange Rules 1972(**c**).

2.—(1) Subject to sub-paragraph (2), in relation to any such service or employment the specified date for the purposes of Article 52 and of paragraph 3(2)(*b*) shall be 1st May 1972.

(2) Where in relation to a particular service or employment no provisions are in operation on 1st May 1972 for the payment of a transfer value to the fire authority, as mentioned in Article 52(1)(*c*) then in relation thereto the specified date for the purposes aforesaid shall be the date on which such provisions first thereafter come into operation.

3.—(1) In relation to any such service or employment the transfer value for the purposes of Article 52 shall, subject to sub-paragraphs (2) and (3), be one of the like amount, and calculated in the like manner, as the transfer value which would have been receivable under Part III of the Superannuation (Local Government and Approved Employment) Interchange Rules 1969(**d**) (as originally made) had the person concerned

---

(**a**) 1948 c. 24.   (**b**) 1950 c. 4 (N.I.).

(**c**) S.I. 1972/521 (1972 I, p. 1786).   (**d**) S.I. 1969/997 (1969 II, p. 2906).

Sch. 6 (*contd.*)

entered local government employment, within the meaning of those Rules, on the date on which he became a regular fireman and in circumstances in which the said Part III applied.

(2) For the purposes of sub-paragraph (1)—

(*a*) to the extent that the Table in Schedule 1 to the said Rules of 1969 does not contain entries relating to a particular service or employment, it shall be deemed to do so, and

(*b*) paragraph 6 of Schedule 1 to the said Rules of 1969 shall have effect as if any references therein to 18th August 1969 and 18th August 1968 were, respectively, references to the specified date and to a date 12 months before the specified date and sub-paragraphs (1)(*a*) and (*b*) and (3) were omitted.

(3) In relation to service in which a person is subject to the Isle of Man Police Pension Regulations, that is to say, the Regulations for the time being in operation under section 16 of the Police (Isle of Man) Act 1962 (an Act of Tynwald) the transfer value shall be one payable under those Regulations.

4. In relation to any such service or employment, the specified authority for the purposes of Article 52 shall be the persons having the general management of the superannuation arrangements to which the person concerned was subject in the service or employment in question.

SCHEDULE 7

Additional and Further Payments

Articles 57 and 58   Part I

Contributions

1. Where additional pension contributions are payable by a man under Article 57 in pursuance of such an election as is there mentioned, he shall pay such contributions at the rate specified in the second column of the Table in Schedule 7 to the Firemen's Pension Scheme 1971(**a**) opposite to the number of completed years of service reckonable by him, at the time he made his election, by virtue of a period of service, or a period for which a special pension was payable, before 26th August 1966.

2. Where additional pension contributions are payable by a man in pursuance of an election under Article 58(2), he shall pay such contributions at the rate specified in the second column of the following Table opposite to the number of completed years of pensionable service reckonable by him immediately before 1st July 1973 otherwise than by virtue of service as a regular fireman on or after 1st April 1972.

3. Where further pension contributions are payable by a man in pursuance of an election under Article 58(3), he shall pay such contributions at the rate specified in the third column of the following Table opposite to the number of completed years of pensionable service reckonable by him immediately before 1st July 1973 otherwise than by virtue of service as a regular fireman on or after 1st April 1972.

(**a**) *See* S.I. 1971/145 (1971 I, p. 320).

TABLE

Completed years of pensionable service taken into account	Rate expressed as a percentage of pensionable pay	
	Additional contributions	Further contributions
1	0·1	0·1
2	0·1	0·1
3	0·2	0·2
4	0·2	0·2
5	0·3	0·3
6	0·4	0·3
7	0·5	0·4
8	0·6	0·5
9	0·7	0·6
10	0·8	0·7
11	1·0	0·8
12	1·2	0·9
13	1·4	1·1
14	1·7	1·3
15	2·0	1·5
16	2·4	1·8
17	2·9	2·2
18	3·6	2·7
19	4·2	3·1
20	4·4	3·3
21	4·6	3·4
22	4·8	3·5
23	5·0	3·6
24	5·1	3·8
25	5·3	3·9
26	5·5	4·0
27	5·6	4·2
28	5·8	4·3
29	6·0	4·4
30	6·1	4·5
31	6·1	4·5
32	6·2	4·6
33	6·3	4·6
34	6·4	4·7
35	6·4	4·7
36	6·5	4·8
37	6·6	4·9
38	6·6	4·9
39	6·7	5·0

PART II   Article 59

LUMP SUMS

1. Where a payment by way of a lump sum is payable by a man in pursuance of an election under Article 59(2) or (3), it shall be calculated by reference to his annual pensionable pay immediately before 1st April 1972 or, if he was not then in receipt of pensionable pay, on the date on which he was thereafter first in receipt of such pay.

Sch. 7 (*contd.*)

2. Where an additional payment by way of a lump sum is payable by a man in pursuance of an election under Article 59(2), the sum shall be of an amount equal to the percentage of his said pensionable pay specified in the second column of the following Table opposite to the number of completed years of pensionable service reckonable by him immediately before 1st July 1973 otherwise than by virtue of service as a regular fireman on or after 1st April 1972.

3. Where a further payment by way of a lump sum is payable by a man in pursuance of an election under Regulation 59(3), the sum shall be of an amount equal to the percentage of his said pensionable pay specified in the third column of the following Table opposite to the number of years of pensionable service reckonable by him immediately before 1st July 1973 otherwise than by virtue of service as a regular fireman on or after 1st April 1972.

TABLE

Completed years of pensionable service taken into account	Payment expressed as a percentage of annual pensionable pay	
	Additional payment	Further payment
1	1·2	1·0
2	2·0	1·6
3	2·8	2·3
4	3·6	3·0
5	4·5	3·7
6	5·4	4·4
7	6·4	5·2
8	7·4	5·9
9	8·4	6·6
10	9·4	7·3
11	10·4	8·1
12	11·4	8·8
13	12·4	9·6
14	13·4	10·3
15	14·5	11·1
16	15·6	11·8
17	16·7	12·6
18	17·8	13·3
19	18·9	14·0
20	20·0	14·8
21	21·1	15·5
22	22·2	16·3
23	23·3	17·1
24	24·4	17·9
25	25·3	18·6
26	26·1	19·2
27	26·8	19·7
28	27·4	20·2
29	28·0	20·6
30	28·5	20·9
31	28·7	21·1
32	28·8	21·2
33	28·9	21·3
34	29·1	21·4
35	29·2	21·5
36	29·4	21·6
37	29·5	21·7
38	29·7	21·8
39 or more	29·9	22·0

SCHEDULE 8   Article 67

APPEALS TO MEDICAL REFEREES

1. The person seeking to appeal must institute his appeal within 14 days from the date on which he is supplied by the fire authority with a copy of the opinion in pursuance of Article 67:

Provided that where the fire authority are of opinion that a person's failure to institute his appeal within the time allowed was not due to his own default, they may (notwithstanding that the said time has expired) extend it by so much as they think fit, but so that the appeal shall in any event be instituted before the expiration of 6 months from the aforesaid date.

2. He must institute his appeal by giving to the fire authority a notice in writing informing them of his intention to appeal and stating the grounds on which he proposes to appeal.

Any such notice shall state the appellant's name and his place of residence.

3.—(1) Upon receiving the said notice the fire authority shall supply the Secretary of State with 2 copies thereof and 2 copies of the opinion in question.

(2) The Secretary of State shall supply a copy of the said notice and a copy of the said opinion to the medical referee nominated by the Secreatry of State for the purposes of the appeal.

4.—(1) The medical referee so nominated shall forthwith after his nomination inform the appellant and the fire authority that he has been nominated to act as medical referee for the purposes of the appeal.

(2) It shall be the duty of the medical referee to secure that the appellant and the fire authority are at all material times aware of an address at which communications may be delivered to the referee for the purposes of the appeal.

5.—(1) Subject to the provisions of this Schedule, the medical referee shall interview the appellant at least once, and may interview him or cause him to be interviewed on such further occasions as the referee thinks necessary for the purpose of determining the appeal.

(2) The medical referee shall appoint a time and place for any such interview and shall give reasonable notice thereof to the appellant and to the fire authority.

(3) Where the medical referee is satisfied that the appellant is unable to travel, the place appointed for any such interview shall be the place where the appellant resides.

(4) It shall be the duty of the appellant to attend at the time and place appointed for any such interview and to submit himself at the interview to medical examination by the medical referee or by any person appointed by the referee for that purpose.

(5) If the appellant fails to comply with sub-paragraph (4), the medical referee may, unless satisfied that there was reasonable cause for the failure, dispense with the interview required by the preceding provisions of this Schedule, or, as the case may be, with any further interview, and give his decision upon such information as is then available.

(6) Any such interview may be attended by a person appointed for the purpose by the fire authority and by a person so appointed by the appellant.

6. At any time before the interview, or before the last interview if there is more than one, either party may submit to the medical referee a statement relating to the subject matter of the appeal, and the referee shall take account of any such statement and give to the other party such opportunity as he thinks necessary of replying thereto.

Sch. 8 (*contd.*)

7. The decision of the medical referee shall take the form of an opinion on the medical questions which appear to him to be relevant, and the opinion shall be delivered in writing to both parties.

8.—(1) The medical referee shall be entitled to such fees and allowances as the Secretary of State may from time to time determine.

(2) The said fees and allowances shall be paid by the fire authority, and shall be treated as part of the fire authority's expenses for the purposes of the following provisions of this Schedule.

9.—(1) Save as hereinafter provided, the expenses of each party to the appeal shall be borne by that party.

(2) Where the medical referee decides in favour of the fire authority, the authority may, unless the referee otherwise directs, require the appellant to pay toward the cost of the appeal such sum not exceeding the referee's total fees and allowances as the authority think fit.

(3) Where the medical referee decides in favour of the appellant, the fire authority shall, unless the referee otherwise directs, refund to the appellant any personal expenses actually and reasonably incurred by the appellant in respect of any such interview as is mentioned in paragraph 5 and, if any duly qualified medical practitioner chosen by the appellant has attended any such interview, any fees and expenses reasonably paid by the appellant in respect of such attendance.

(4) If in connection with any payment claimed under this paragraph any question arises as to whether the decision of the medical referee is in favour of the fire authority or the appellant, that question shall be decided by the referee, or, in default of a decision by the referee, by the Secretary of State.

10. An appellant shall be deemed to have received any information, notice or document which he is entitled to receive for the purposes of this Schedule if that information, notice or document has been duly posted in a letter addressed to the appellant at his last known place of residence.

Article 71

SCHEDULE 9

TRANSFER VALUES

1.—(1) The sum to be paid by a fire authority under Article 71 shall be calculated in accordance with this paragraph.

(2) The amounts shown in the second and third columns of the following Table in relation to an age which corresponds with that of the fireman are to be multiplied respectively by the number of completed years and the number of completed months aggregating less than a year which the fireman is entitled to reckon as pensionable service immediately before he ceases to be employed by the said authority:

Provided that in calculating the number of completed years and completed months which he is entitled to reckon as pensionable service—

(a) any period by which his pensionable service exceeds 20 years but does not exceed 30 years shall be counted twice;

(b) any period by which his pensionable service exceeds 30 years shall be ignored.

(3) The sum of the products aforesaid is an amount appropriate in respect of £100 of annual pensionable pay.

(4) The total sum referred to in sub-paragraph (1) is to be calculated proportionately by reference to the annual pensionable pay of the fireman.

(5) In this paragraph the expression "annual pensionable pay" means the annual value of the fireman's pensionable pay immediately before he ceases to be employed by the authority, any retrospective increase therein granted after that time being ignored.

TABLE

Age in years	Amount for £100 of annual pensionable pay in respect of each completed	
	Year	Month
	£	£
Under 35	18·20	1·50
35 but under 36	18·30	1·55
36 „ „ 37	18·45	1·55
37 „ „ 38	18·65	1·55
38 „ „ 39	18·90	1·60
39 „ „ 40	19·20	1·60
40 „ „ 41	19·45	1·60
41 „ „ 42	19·75	1·65
42 „ „ 43	20·05	1·65
43 „ „ 44	20·40	1·70
44 „ „ 45	20·75	1·75
45 „ „ 46	21·10	1·75
46 „ „ 47	21·45	1·80
47 „ „ 48	21·80	1·80
48 „ „ 49	22·15	1·85
49 „ „ 50	22·50	1·90
50 „ „ 51	22·85	1·90
51 „ „ 52	23·20	1·95
52 „ „ 53	23·60	1·95
53 „ „ 54	24·05	2·00
54 „ „ 55	24·60	2·05
55 and over	25·20	2·10

2. The sum to be paid by a fire authority under Article 71, calculated in accordance with the preceding provisions of this Schedule, shall be reduced by the amount he has, under Article 48(1), undertaken to pay in accordance with Schedule 4.

3. Except in the case of a fireman who is paying pension contributions at the rate of 1p a week less than the appropriate percentage of his pensionable pay, the sum to be paid by a fire authority under Article 71, calculated in accordance with the preceding provisions of this Schedule, shall be reduced by an amount calculated in accordance with paragraph 5.

4. In the case of a fireman entitled to reckon pensionable service, immediately before he ceases to be employed by a fire authority, by virtue of a participating period of relevant employment, the sum to be paid by that authority under Article 71, calculated in accordance with the preceding provisions of this Schedule, shall be reduced by an amount calculated in accordance with paragraph 5.

5.—(1) The amount shown in the second column of the following Table in relation to an age which corresponds with that of the fireman immediately before he ceases to be employed by the authority is the amount of the reduction referred to in paragraph 3 or, as the case may be, paragraph 4 in respect of each £1 by which the annual value of his pension would be reduced—

(a) under paragraph 1 of Part VII of Schedule 1, in a case in which paragraph 3 applies;

(b) under paragraphs 2 and 3 of the said Part VII, in a case in which paragraph 4 applies,

Sch. 9 (*contd.*)

in respect of any period beyond the age of 65 years, if he had retired immediately before he ceased to be employed by the authority and had been entitled to a pension.

(2) The total reduction is to be calculated proportionately by reference to the amount by which the annual value of such a pension would be so reduced.

TABLE

Age in years	Amount of the reduction in respect of each £1 by which the annual value of a pension would be reduced
	£
Under 25	1·70
25 but under 26	1·80
26 ,, ,, 27	1·90
27 ,, ,, 28	2·00
28 ,, ,, 29	2·10
29 ,, ,, 30	2·20
30 ,, ,, 31	2·35
31 ,, ,, 32	2·45
32 ,, ,, 33	2·55
33 ,, ,, 34	2·65
34 ,, ,, 35	2·75
35 ,, ,, 36	2·90
36 ,, ,, 37	3·00
37 ,, ,, 38	3·10
38 ,, ,, 39	3·25
39 ,, ,, 40	3·35
40 ,, ,, 41	3·50
41 ,, ,, 42	3·65
42 ,, ,, 43	3·75
43 ,, ,, 44	3·90
44 ,, ,, 45	4·05
45 ,, ,, 46	4·20
46 ,, ,, 47	4·35
47 ,, ,, 48	4·50
48 ,, ,, 49	4·70
49 ,, ,, 50	4·90
50 ,, ,, 51	5·05
51 ,, ,, 52	5·25
52 ,, ,, 53	5·45
53 ,, ,, 54	5·65
54 ,, ,, 55	5·85
55 ,, ,, 56	6·10
56 ,, ,, 57	6·40
57 ,, ,, 58	6·70
58 ,, ,, 59	7·00
59 ,, ,, 60	7·30

Article 91   **SCHEDULE 10**

MODIFICATIONS TO SCHEME IN ITS APPLICATION TO FIREMEN SERVING ON 10TH JULY 1956

1. For the words "average pensionable pay" wherever they occur, there shall be substituted the words "pensionable pay".

2. For the words "average annual pensionable pay" wherever they occur, there shall be substituted the words "annual pensionable pay".

3. In Article 12(1)—

(*a*) the words "has attained the age of 50 years and" shall be omitted, and

(*b*) for the words "Parts VII and VIII" there shall be substituted the words "Part VII".

4. In Article 13(2) and (4) for the words "Parts VII and VIII", in both places, there shall be substituted the words "Part VII".

5. In Article 14(2)—

(*a*) for the words "Part III" there shall be substituted the words "Part II", and

(*b*) for the words "Parts VII and VIII" there shall be substituted the words "Part VII".

6. In Article 16(2) for the words "Parts VII and VIII" there shall be substituted the words "Part VII".

7. For Article 22(2) and (3) there shall be substituted the following provision:—

"(2) A widow to whom this Article applies shall be entitled to an ordinary pension calculated in accordance with Part I of Schedule 2.".

8. In Article 23(3) for the words "Parts III and V" there shall be substituted the words "Part III".

9. In Article 25(2) for the words "Parts IV and V" there shall be substituted the words "Scheme I of Part I".

10. In Article 27(3) sub-paragraph (*a*) shall be omitted.

11. In Article 34(2) for the words "Parts II and IV" there shall be substitted the words "Part II".

12. In Article 36(2) for the words "Parts III" there shall be substituted the words "Parts I".

13. For Article 55(2), (3), (4) and (5) there shall be substituted the following provisions:—

"(2) For the purpose of determining the benefits payable under this Scheme on the death or retirement of a regular fireman—

(*a*) the expression "pensionable pay" means his pensionable pay immediately before the death or retirement or, in a case where he was not serving as such a fireman when he died, his pensionable pay immediately before he last ceased to serve as such; and

(*b*) the expression "annual pensionable pay" means the annual value of his said pensionable pay.

(3) Where during the relevant period before his death or retirement a regular fireman's rank has changed, paragraph (2) shall have effect in his case as if his pensionable pay immediately before the death or retirement were his average pensionable pay during that period:

Provided that where during the relevant period—

(*a*) he reverted to a rank from which he had been temporarily promoted (whether before or during that period), or

(*b*) the last change of rank was a promotion,

and the said average is less than his pensionable pay would have been, immediately before his death or retirement, had he continued to hold the rank he held before the promotion until he reverted thereto or, as the case may be, until his death or retirement,

Sch. 10 (*contd.*)

then paragraph (2) shall have effect in his case as though he had continued to hold that rank.

In this paragraph the expression "the relevant period" means the period of 3 years ending with the death or retirement.".

14. In Article 56(1) for the percentage "6·75%" there shall be substituted the percentage "5%".

15. Articles 57 to 62 shall be omitted.

16. In Article 74(4)(*a*) for the words "£163·81 a year" there shall be substituted the words "£123·12 a year".

17. In Article 96(2) for sub-paragraphs (*a*) and (*b*) there shall be substituted the words "an additional completed year of pensionable service".

18. For Part I of Schedule 1 there shall be substituted the following Part:—

"Part I

Subject as hereafter in this Schedule provided an ordinary pension shall be of an amount equal to 30 sixtieths of the fireman's pensionable pay with the addition of 2 sixtieths for each completed year by which his pensionable service exceeds 25 years up to the maximum set opposite his age at retirement in the following Table:—

Table

Years of age of fireman at retirement	Maximum pension expressed in 60ths of pensionable pay
Less than 51	30
Less than 52 but 51 or over	32
Less than 53 but 52 or over	34
Less than 54 but 53 or over	36
Less than 55 but 54 or over	38
55 or over	40"

19. For Part II of Schedule 1 there shall be substituted the following Part:—

"Part II

Fireman's Short Service or Ill-Health Pension

Subject as hereafter in this Schedule provided, the amount of the short service or ill-health pension shall be not less than a sixtieth nor more than 40 sixtieths of the fireman's pensionable pay and subject as aforesaid shall be equal to a sixtieth of his pensionable pay for each completed year of pensionable service up to 20 years, with the addition of 2 sixtieths for each completed year by which his pensionable service exceeds 20 years.".

20. In Part VI of Schedule 1—

(*a*) in paragraph 2 for the words "as respects the first" to the end shall be omitted; and

(*b*) in paragraph 3 for the words "a sixtieth for each completed half year" there shall be substituted the words "2 sixtieths for each completed year".

21. Part VIII of Schedule 1 shall be omitted.

22. For Part I of Schedule 2 there shall be substituted the following Part:—

"Part I

Widow's Ordinary or Accrued Pension

The amount of a widow's ordinary or accrued pension in respect of each week shall be the amount calculated according to Scheme I set out below, or, in the case of an ordinary pension, where the fireman was entitled to reckon at least 10 years' pensionable service, according to whichever of the two Schemes set out below would yield to the widow the higher pension.

Scheme I

The pension shall be of such amount that the rate of payment is—

(*a*) where the husband's last rank was not higher than that of sub-officer, £123·12 a year;

(*b*) where the husband's last rank was higher than that of sub-officer but not higher than that of divisional officer (Grade I), £160·16 a year; or

(*c*) where the husband's last rank was higher than that of divisional officer (Grade I), £196·67 a year.

Scheme II

The pension shall be of such amount that, when it is added to any widow's benefit or retirement pension payable to the widow under the National Insurance Act 1965 in right of her husband's insurance, the total weekly rate of payment is equal to the percentage of his average pensionable pay specified in the second column of the following Table being the percentage set out opposite to the number of his completed years of pensionable service in the first column of the said Table:—

Table

Husband's completed years of pensionable service	Total weekly rate
10, 11, 12, 13 and 14	5·0 per cent.
15, 16, 17, 18 and 19	7·5 per cent.
20, 21, 22, 23 and 24	10·0 per cent.
25, 26, 27, 28 and 29	12·5 per cent.
30 or more	16·0 per cent."

23. Parts II, IV and V of Schedule 2 shall be omitted.

24. For Part I of Schedule 3 there shall be substituted the following Part:—

"Part I

Child's Ordinary or Accrued Allowance

1. Subject to Part IV of this Schedule, where the mother of the child is alive the child's ordinary or accrued allowance shall be payable at the following rate:—

(*a*) where the father's last rank was not higher than that of sub-officer, £45·91 a year;

(*b*) where the father's last rank was higher than that of sub-officer but not higher than that of divisional officer (Grade I), £54·78 a year; or

(*c*) where the father's last rank was higher than that of divisional officer (Grade I), £67·30 a year.

Sch. 10 (*contd.*)

2. Subject to Part IV of this Schedule, where the father was the child's only surviving parent or in respect of the period after the death of the mother, the child's ordinary or accrued allowance shall be payable at the following rate:—

(*a*) where the father's last rank was not higher than that of sub-officer, £67·82 a year, or such higher rate not exceeding £89·73 a year as the fire authority may from time to time determine;

(*b*) where the father's last rank was higher than that of sub-officer but not higher than that of divisional officer (Grade I), £80·86 a year, or such higher rate not exceeding £107·47 a year as the fire authority may from time to time determine; or

(*c*) where the father's last rank was higher than that of divisional officer (Grade I), £100·69 a year, or such rate not exceeding £134·07 a year as the fire authority may from time to time determine.".

25. Part III of Schedule 3 shall be omitted.

26. For Part IV of Schedule 3 there shall be substituted the following Part:—

"PART IV

VARIATION OF CHILD'S ALLOWANCE

1.—(1) Subject as hereinafter provided, where under any enactment specified in the first column of the following Table a payment specified in the second column is made to the recipient mentioned in the third column thereof, a child's ordinary or accrued allowance shall be reduced by so much as is necessary to reduce the allowance by the weekly amount specified in the fourth column, and where that reduction is greater than the allowance determined under the preceding provisions of this Schedule, that allowance shall not be payable.

TABLE

1 Enactment	2 Type of Payment	3 Recipient	4 Weekly Reduc- tion
National Insurance Act 1965**(a)**, s. 27	Widowed mother's allow-ance	Child's mother	37p
National Insurance Act 1965, s. 29	Guardian's allowance in respect of the child ...	Child's guardian	60p
National Insurance Act 1965, s. 40	Increased widow's allow-ance	Child's mother	37p
National Insurance Act 1965, s. 40	Increased retirement pen-sion	Child's mother	37p
Family Allowances Act 1965**(b)**	Family allowance in re-spect of the child ...	Any person	25p

(2) Where a woman has 2 or more children who would apart from the provisions of this paragraph be entitled to a child's allowance, only the allowance of the elder or eldest of those children shall be reduced in respect of the payment to her of a widowed mother's allowance, increased widow's allowance or increased retirement pension.".

(a) 1965 c. 51.   (b) 1965 c. 53.

APPENDIX 3

TRANSITORY PROVISIONS

Interpretation

1.—(1) In this Appendix references to the Scheme of 1971 and to the Scheme of 1973 are, respectively, references to the Firemen's Pension Scheme 1971, as amended(a) and to the Firemen's Pension Scheme 1973.

(2) This Appendix shall be construed as one with the Scheme of 1973.

Commutation—variation of notice

2.—(1) This paragraph shall apply to a regular fireman who retired on or after 1st April 1972 but before 1st July 1973, not being a fireman to whom Part XII of the Scheme of 1973 applies.

(2) Where a regular fireman to whom this paragraph applies has given notice of commutation under Article 20 of the Scheme of 1971 (in this paragraph referred to as the "original notice") he may give further notice to the fire authority of his wish to increase the portion of his pension commuted for a lump sum to such portion, not exceeding a quarter of the pension which would be payable but for the provisions of Article 41 of the Scheme of 1973 as (subject to the limitation contained in Article 42 thereof) he may specify.

(3) Where a further notice has been given under sub-paragraph (2) of this paragraph the original notice shall have effect for the purposes of Article 21 of the Scheme of 1973 as if given thereunder but as if the portion of the pension specified therein were that specified in the further notice.

Allocation—variation of notice

3.—(1) This paragraph shall apply to a regular fireman who retired on or after 1st April 1972 but before 1st July 1973, not being a fireman to whom Part XII of the Scheme of 1973 applies.

(2) Where a regular fireman to whom this paragraph applies has given notice of surrender under Article 37 of the Scheme of 1971 (in this paragraph referred to as the "original notice") he may give further notice to the fire authority of his wish to increase the portion of his pension surrendered to such portion as he may specify so, however, that the total portion of the pension which may be surrendered for the purposes of allocation shall not exceed a third of the pension which would be payable but for the provisions of Articles 21 and 41 of the Scheme of 1973 and Part VIII of Schedule 1 thereto.

(3) Where a further notice has been given under sub-paragraph (2) of this paragraph the original notice shall have effect for the purposes of Article 41 of the Scheme of 1973 as if given thereunder but as if the portion of the pension specified therein were that specified in the further notice.

(4) Nothing in this paragraph shall be construed as derogating from any right of a regular fireman under Article 41(1) of the Scheme of 1973 to allocate a further portion of his pension notwithstanding that he has already allocated a portion of that pension.

Allocation—cancellation of notice

4.—(1) This paragraph shall apply to a regular fireman who—

   (*a*) was serving as such immediately before 1st April 1972 or, though not so serving, is entitled to reckon pensionable service otherwise than by virtue of service as a regular fireman on or after that date, and

   (*b*) has exercised the right of election accorded by either Article 58(3), Article 59(3) or Article 60(3) of the Scheme of 1973.

(a) The amending instruments are not relevant to the subject matter hereof.

(2) Where a regular fireman to whom this paragraph applies has given notice of surrender under Article 37 of the Scheme of 1971 (in this paragraph referred to as the "original notice") and the beneficiary specified therein is his wife and she is still alive, he may give further notice to the fire authority of his wish to cancel the original notice.

(3) Where a further notice has been given under paragraph (2) of this paragraph the original notice shall not have effect for the purposes of Article 41 of the Scheme of 1973.

Provisions supplemental to paragraphs 2, 3 and 4

5. Notice to the fire authority under any of the preceding paragraphs shall be given in writing to the fire authority of the brigade in which the man is serving or by whom his pension is payable and shall be given before 1st October 1973.

Awards for a period ending before 1st December 1972

6.—(1) For the purpose of determining the amount payable on account of an award for a period ending before 1st December 1972, the Scheme of 1973 shall have effect subject to the modifications set out in this paragraph.

(2) In Article 74(4)(a) (awards on death of servicemen) for the sum "£163·81" there shall be substituted the sum "£148·27".

(3) In paragraph 2 of Part I of Schedule 2 (widow's ordinary pension) for the sums "£163·81", "£213·37" and "£256·66", in each place where they occur, there shall be substituted, respectively, the sums "£148·27", "£193·62" and "£233·03", and for the sums "£175·28", "£224·84" and "£268·14" there shall be substituted, respectively, the sums "£158·27", "£203·62" and "£243·03".

(4) In paragraph 3 of Part IV of Schedule 2 (widow's accrued pension) for the sums "£163·81", "£213·37" and "£256·66" there shall be substituted, respectively, the sums "£148·27", "£193·62" and "£233·03".

(5) In paragraph 1(4) of Part I of Schedule 3 (child's ordinary allowance) for the sums "£45·91", "£54·78" and "£67·30" there shall be substituted, respectively, the sums "£41·26", "£49·26" and "£60·96".

(6) In paragraph 2(4) of the said Part I for the sums "£67·82", "£89·73", "£80·86", "£107·47", "£100·69" and "£134·07" there shall be substituted, respectively, the sums "£61·58", "£81·28", "£73·27", "£97·29", "£91·13" and "£121·30".

(7) In paragraph 16 of Schedule 10 (firemen serving on 10th July 1956) for the sum "£123·12" there shall be substituted the sum "£111·20".

(8) In paragraph 22 of Schedule 10 for the sums "£123·12", "£160·16" and "£196·67" there shall be substituted, respectively, the sums "£111·20", "£145·22" and "£178·27".

(9) In paragraph 24 of Schedule 10 for the sums "£45·91", "£54·78", "£67·30", "£67·82", "£89·73", "£80·86", "£107·47", "£100·69" and "£134·07" there shall be substituted, respectively, the sums "£41·26", "£49·26", "£60·96", "£61·58", "£81·28", "£73·27", "£97·29", "£91·13" and "£121·30".

EXPLANATORY NOTE

(This Note is not part of the Order.)

This Order, which has effect as from 1st April 1972 (retrospective effect is authorised by sections 12 and 16 of the Superannuation Act 1972), brings the Firemen's Pension Scheme 1973, set out in Appendix 2, into operation.

The Scheme of 1973 applies to the exclusion of the Firemen's Pension Scheme 1971 (*see* S.I. 1971/145) in the case of firemen with service on or after 1st April 1972 (Article 2 of the Order and Article 1 of the Scheme). It has effect subject to the transitory provisions contained in Appendix 3 (Article 1(3) of the Scheme). The main differences between the Schemes of 1973 and of 1971 are described below.

The normal qualifying period of service for an ill-health or short service pension is reduced from 10 to 5 years (Articles 13 and 14). Ill-health pensions are payable at enhanced rates (Part III of Schedule 1).

A fireman disabled as a result of an injury received in the execution of duty is entitled not only to an injury pension (corresponding to a special pension under the Scheme of 1971) but also to a gratuity (Article 15). Injury pensions are payable at enhanced rates (Part V of Schedule 1).

A person with 5 years' service who has attained the age of 26 years may, on retiring in circumstances in which no other award is payable, elect to be granted a deferred pension instead of a return of contributions (Article 16).

Widows' pensions and children's allowances are payable at enhanced rates (Schedules 2 and 3), in particular in respect of the first 13 weeks for which they are payable. Where a fireman dies as the result of an injury received in the execution of duty a gratuity is normally payable in addition to a special pension (Article 23(2)). Provision is made for the payment of pensions and allowances to the widows and children of men who have elected to be granted deferred pensions (Articles 25 and 36).

Where a fireman dies as a result of an injury received in the execution of duty, the fire authority may, in their discretion, grant a special pension to an adult relative who was substantially dependent on him (Article 31).

Awards are normally calculated on pensionable pay averaged over the last year, instead of the last 3 years, of service (Article 55).

Only where a fireman has paid pension contributions throughout his period of service at a rate related to 6.75% of his pensionable pay, or equivalent "additional" or "further" payments are made, are his widow and children entitled to the full benefit of the enhanced rates of dependants' awards. Articles 58 to 62 enable a person to elect to make these equivalent payments.

The Scheme of 1973 (like that of 1971) contains special provisions applicable to certain firemen who were serving on 10th July 1956 (Part XII). Unless they otherwise elect under Article 89 or 90, the Scheme applies subject to specified modifications (Article 91 and Schedule 10) and not all the changes mentioned above have effect in relation to them.

STATUTORY INSTRUMENTS

1973 No. 967

COUNTER-INFLATION

The Counter-Inflation (Notification of Increases in Prices and Charges) (No. 2) Order 1973

Made - - - -	*24th May* 1973
Laid before Parliament	*25th May* 1973
Coming into Operation	*30th May* 1973

The Secretary of State, in exercise of powers conferred on him by sections 5 and 15 of and paragraphs 1(1) and (2), 2(4) and 3 of Schedule 2 to and paragraphs 1(1), (2), (4) and (6), and 2(2) of Schedule 3 to the Counter-Inflation Act 1973(**a**), and of all other powers enabling him in that behalf, hereby makes the following Order:—

1.—(1) This Order may be cited as the Counter-Inflation (Notification of Increases in Prices and Charges) (No. 2) Order 1973 and shall come into operation on 30th May 1973.

(2) The Interpretation Act 1889(**b**) shall apply for the interpretation of this Order as it applies for the interpretation of an Act of Parliament.

2. The Counter-Inflation (Notification of Increases in Prices and Charges) Order 1973(**c**) is hereby amended in article 1(2) by the substitution for the definition of " provider of services " of the following definition—

" " provider of services " means a person who carries on in the course of business activities falling within minimum list headings 864 and 865 of Order XXIV or within Order XXVI (other than minimum list heading 894) of the Standard Industrial Classification or the repairing of motor vehicles ".

Geoffrey Howe,

Minister for Trade and Consumer Affairs,
Department of Trade and Industry.

24th May 1973.

(**a**) 1973 c. 9.   (**b**) 1889 c. 63.   (**c**) S.I. 1973/664 (1973 I, p. 2151.)

EXPLANATORY NOTE

(This Note is not part of the Order.)

This Order amends the Counter-Inflation (Notification of Increases in Prices and Charges) Order 1973. It amends the definition of " provider of services " so as to include therein the business activities of garage proprietors only in relation to the repairing of motor vehicles.

STATUTORY INSTRUMENTS

1973 No. 968

COUNTER-INFLATION

The Counter-Inflation (Prices and Charges) (Information) (No. 2) Order 1973

Made - - - 24th May 1973
Coming into operation 30th May 1973

The Secretary of State, in exercise of powers conferred on him by section 15 of the Counter-Inflation Act 1973(**a**), and of all other powers enabling him in that behalf, hereby makes the following Order:—

1.—(1) This Order may be cited as the Counter-Inflation (Prices and Charges) (Information) (No. 2) Order 1973 and shall come into operation on 30th May 1973.

(2) The Interpretation Act 1889(**b**) shall apply for the interpretation of this Order as it applies for the interpretation of an Act of Parliament.

2. The Counter-Inflation (Prices and Charges) (Information) Order 1973(**c**) (in this Order called " the principal Order ") is hereby amended—

(*a*) in article 1(2) by the substitution for the definition of " distributor " of the following definition—
" " distributor " means a person who carries on in the course of business activities falling within Order XXIII (other than the wholesale slaughtering of animals for human consumption, leasing industrial or office machinery or the hiring of furniture, radio and television sets and other domestic appliances) or falling within minimum list heading 894 of Order XXVI (other than the repairing of motor vehicles) of the Standard Industrial Classification ";

(*b*) in article 1(2) by the substitution for the definition of " provider of services " of the following definition—
" " provider of services " means a person who carries on in the course of business activities falling within minimum list headings 864 and 865 of Order XXIV or within Order XXVI (other than minimum list heading 894) of the Standard Industrial Classification or the hiring of furniture, radio and television sets and other domestic appliances or the repairing of motor vehicles "; and

(*c*) in article 8(1)(*a*), by the addition after the words " by virtue of Schedule 2 " of the words " (except paragraph 12(*c*)) ".

3. For the application of the requirements in article 5 of the principal Order in relation to the cases affected by the amendments made by this Order, there shall be substituted for the references to 31st May 1973 in article 5(1)(*a*) and (*b*) references to the time when the person in question is required to furnish his first return under article 3 of the principal Order.

Geoffrey Howe,

Minister for Trade and Consumer Affairs,
Department of Trade and Industry.

24th May 1973.

(**a**) 1973 c. 9.   (**b**) 1889 c. 63.   (**c**) S.I. 1973/778 (1973 I, p. 2463).

EXPLANATORY NOTE

(This Note is not part of the Order.)

This Order amends the Counter-Inflation (Prices and Charges) (Information) Order 1973. It amends the definitions therein of " distributor " and " provider of services " and places the business activities of garage proprietors, apart from the repairing of motor vehicles, in the former instead of in the latter definition so as to conform with the treatment of such activities under the Counter-Inflation (Price and Pay Code) Order 1973 (S.I. 1973/658). The Order also amends the requirements as respects the making of returns and the keeping of records so as to include particulars relating to contracts formed by the acceptance of a competitive tender.

STATUTORY INSTRUMENTS

1973 No. 973

CUSTOMS AND EXCISE

The Import Duties (General) (No. 4) Order 1973

Made - - - -	24th May 1973
Laid before the House of Commons	29th May 1973
Coming into Operation	1st June 1973

The Lords Commissioners of Her Majesty's Treasury, by virtue of the powers conferred on them by sections 1 and 13 of the Import Duties Act 1958(a), as amended by section 5(5) of, and paragraph 1 of Schedule 4 to, the European Communities Act 1972(b), and of all other powers enabling them in that behalf, on the recommendation of the Secretary of State(c), hereby make the following Order:

1.—(1) This Order may be cited as the Import Duties (General) (No. 4) Order 1973 and shall come into operation on 1st June 1973.

(2) The Interpretation Act 1889(d) shall apply to the interpretation of this Order as it applies to the interpretation of an Act of Parliament.

2. The Import Duties (General) (No. 7) Order 1971(e), as amended(f), shall have effect subject to the following further amendments:

    (a) in Article 2(4) (relating to the definition of the unit of account), for rule (b) there shall be substituted the following:
        "until (and on) such day as is referred to in rule (a), the unit of account shall be taken as equal to £0·46202.";

    (b) in Schedule 1 (which by reference to the Customs Tariff 1959 sets out the import duties chargeable under the Import Duties Act 1958), Additional Note 6(c) to Chapter 4, subheading 02.02(A) (whole dead poultry) and heading 04.04 (cheese and curd) shall be amended as specified in the Schedule to this Order.

24th May 1973.

P. L. Hawkins,
Tim Fortescue,
Two of the Lords Commissioners
of Her Majesty's Treasury.

(a) 1958 c. 6.
(b) 1972 c. 68.
(c) See S.I. 1970/1537 (1970 III, p. 5293).
(d) 1889 c. 63.
(e) S.I. 1971/1971 (1971 III, p. 5330).
(f) The relevant amending Order is S.I. 1972/1909 (1972 III, p. 5549).

SCHEDULE

(a) For subheading 02.02(A)(II) there shall be substituted the following: —

"(II) Ducks:

    (a) Plucked, bled, gutted but not drawn,   —   —
    with heads and feet, known as "85%
    ducks" ..   ..

    (b) Plucked and drawn, without heads and   —   —
    feet, but with hearts, livers and gizz-
    ards, known as "70% ducks" ..

    (c) Plucked and drawn, without heads   —   —".
    and feet and without hearts, livers and
    gizzards, known as "63% ducks" ..

(b) For Additional Note 6(c) to Chapter 4 there shall be substituted the following:

    "(c) In the form of slices wrapped separately in aluminium foil or artificial plastic wrappings, the net weight of each slice not exceeding 30g.".

(c) For subheading 04.04(A)(i) there shall be substituted the following: —

    "(A) Emmentaler, Gruyère, Sbrinz, Bergkäse and Appenzell, not grated or powdered:

    (1) Of a minimum fat content of 45% by weight, referred to dry matter, matured for at least 3 months:

        (a) Whole cheeses of a free-at-frontier value per 100 kg net weight of:

        (1) 134 UA or more, but less than   —   —
        154 UA ..   ..   ..
        (2) 154 UA or more ..   ..   —   —

        (b) Pieces packed in vacuum or in inert gas:

        (1) With rind on at least one side, of a net weight:

        (aa) Of not less than 1 kg but less   —   —
        than 5 kg and of a free-at-frontier value of not less than 154 UA but less than 182 UA per 100 kg net weight ..

        (bb) Of not less than 450 g and of   —   —
        a free-at-frontier value of not less than 182 UA per 100 kg net weight ..   ..   ..

        (2) Other, of a net weight of not   —   —".
        less than 75 g but not more than 250 g and of a free-at-frontier value of not less than 202 UA per 100 kg net weight ..

(d) In subheading 04.04(E)(I)(b)(2), for the description there shall be substituted the following: —

    "(2) Tilsit and Butterkäse, of a fat content, by weight, referred to dry matter: ".

EXPLANATORY NOTE

(This Note is not part of the Order.)

This Order, which comes into operation on 1st June 1973, further amends the Import Duties (General) (No. 7) Order 1971, which sets out the United Kingdom Customs Tariff and the protective import duties chargeable in accordance with it.

The Order provides for certain changes in additional note 6(*c*) to Chapter 4 and in tariff descriptions affecting subheadings 02.02(A)(II) (whole ducks) and 04.04(A) and (E) (cheeses and curds), in order to conform with the Common Customs Tariff of the European Economic Community (as amended by Regulation (EEC) 988/73 (O.J. No. L99, 13.4.73, p. 6) and a Regulation approved by the Council of the European Communities on 14th May 1973).

The Order also alters the method presently used for converting units of account into pounds sterling in cases where goods are classified in the Customs Tariff by reference to values expressed in units of account. The rate of conversion conforms with that specified in Regulation (EEC) 222/73 (O.J. No. L27, 1.2.73, p. 4) as amended by Regulation (EEC) 560/73 (O.J. No. L55, 28.2.73, p. 5).

These amendments do not affect the amount of import duties actually chargeable on any goods.

STATUTORY INSTRUMENTS

1973 No. 974

AGRICULTURE

The Hill Farming (Cottages) (England and Wales) (Amendment) Regulations 1973

Made - - -	*22nd May* 1973
Laid before Parliament	*6th June* 1973
Coming into Operation	*2nd July* 1973

The Minister of Agriculture, Fisheries and Food and the Secretary of State, acting jointly, in exercise of the powers conferred by section 10 of the Hill Farming Act 1946(**a**), as amended by section 1 of the Hill Farming Act 1954(**b**), and now vested in them(**c**), and of all their other enabling powers, hereby make the following regulations: —

Citation, extent, commencement and interpretation

1.—(1) These regulations, which may be cited as the Hill Farming (Cottages) (England and Wales) (Amendment) Regulations 1973, apply to England and Wales, and shall come into operation on 2nd July 1973.

(2) These regulations shall be construed as one with the Hill Farming (Cottages) (England and Wales) Regulations 1954(**d**), hereinafter referred to as the "principal regulations".

Amendment of principal regulations

2. Regulation 3(*a*) of the principal regulations (which specifies the persons who may occupy a cottage in respect of which an improvement grant has been made) shall be amended by adding after subparagraph (iv) thereof the following subparagraph: —

"(v) a person who occupies the cottage otherwise than under a protected tenancy or statutory tenancy within the meaning of the Rent Act 1968(**e**) during any part of a period in respect of which the Minister has given his consent to the cottage being occupied in that manner."

Application of regulations

3. These regulations shall apply to any cottage in respect of which an improvement grant has been made under section 1 of the Hill Farming Act 1946, whether that grant was made before or after the coming into operation of these regulations.

(**a**) 1946 c. 73.   (**b**) 1954 c. 23.
(**c**) S.I. 1969/388 (1969 I, p. 1070).   (**d**) S.I. 1954/670 (1954 I, p. 89).
(**e**) 1968 c. 23.

In Witness whereof the Official Seal of the Minister of Agriculture, Fisheries and Food is hereunto affixed on 22nd May 1973.

Joseph Godber,
Minister of Agriculture, Fisheries and Food.

(L.S.)

Given under my hand on 22nd May 1973.

Peter Thomas,
Secretary of State for Wales.

EXPLANATORY NOTE
(This Note is not part of the Regulations.)

These Regulations amend the Hill Farming (Cottages) (England and Wales) Regulations 1954 by adding a further subparagraph to regulation 3(a) setting out an additional category of persons who may occupy a cottage in respect of which an improvement grant has been made under the Hill Farming and Livestock Rearing Acts 1946 to 1959. The subparagraph enables the Minister of Agriculture, Fisheries and Food to allow such a cottage to be occupied for a specified period by a person, or a succession of persons, whose occupation thereof does not amount to a protected or statutory tenancy within the meaning of the Rent Act 1968.

STATUTORY INSTRUMENTS

1973 No. 975

AGRICULTURE

The Hill Farming (Cottages) (Northern Ireland) (Amendment) Regulations 1973

Made - - -	*22nd May* 1973
Laid before Parliament	*6th June* 1973
Coming into Operation	*2nd July* 1973

The Minister of Agriculture, Fisheries and Food, in exercise of the powers conferred on him by section 10 of the Hill Farming Act 1946(a), as amended by section 1 of the Hill Farming Act 1954(b), and of all his other enabling powers, hereby makes the following regulations:—

Citation, extent, commencement and interpretation

1.—(1) These regulations, which may be cited as the Hill Farming (Cottages) (Northern Ireland) (Amendment) Regulations 1973, apply to Northern Ireland, and shall come into operation on 2nd July 1973.

(2) These regulations shall be construed as one with the Hill Farming (Cottages) (Northern Ireland) Regulations 1954(c), hereinafter referred to as the "principal regulations".

Amendment of principal regulations

2. Regulation 3(a) of the principal regulations (which specifies the persons who may occupy a cottage in respect of which an improvement grant has been made) shall be amended by adding after subparagraph (iv) thereof the following subparagraph:—

"(v) a person who occupies the cottage, in circumstances which do not give rise to a statutory restriction on the owner's right to recover possession, during any part of a period in respect of which the Minister has given his consent to the cottage being occupied in that manner."

Application of regulations

3. These regulations shall apply to any cottage in respect of which an improvement grant has been made under section 1 of the Hill Farming Act 1946, whether that grant was made before or after the coming into operation of these regulations.

(a) 1946 c. 73. (b) 1954 c. 23.
(c) S.I. 1954/671 (1954 I, p. 93).

In Witness whereof the Official Seal of the Minister of Agriculture, Fisheries and Food is hereunto affixed on 22nd May 1973.

(L.S.)

Joseph Godber,
Minister of Agriculture, Fisheries and Food.

EXPLANATORY NOTE

(This Note is not part of the Regulations.)

These Regulations amend the Hill Farming (Cottages) (Northern Ireland) Regulations, 1954 by adding a further subparagraph to Regulation 3(*a*) setting out an additional category of persons who may occupy a cottage in respect of which an improvement grant has been made under the Hill Farming and Livestock Rearing Acts 1946 to 1959. The subparagraph enables the Minister of Agriculture, Fisheries and Food to allow such a cottage to be occupied for a specified period by a person, or succession of persons, whose occupation thereof would not give rise to a statutory restriction on the owner's right to recover possession.

STATUTORY INSTRUMENTS

1973 No. 976

AGRICULTURE

AGRICULTURAL GRANTS, GOODS AND SERVICES

The Fertilisers (United Kingdom) (Amendment) Scheme 1973

Laid before Parliament in draft

Made - - -		*23rd May* 1973

The Minister of Agriculture, Fisheries and Food, the Secretary of State for Wales and the Secretary of State for Scotland, acting jointly, in exercise of powers conferred by sections 1 and 4 of the Agriculture (Fertilisers) Act 1952(a) and sections 4 and 5(1) of the Agriculture (Miscellaneous Provisions) Act 1963(b) and now vested in them jointly(c) and of all other powers enabling them in that behalf, with the approval of the Treasury, hereby make the following scheme, a draft whereof has been laid before Parliament and has been approved by resolution of each House of Parliament:—

Citation, extent and interpretation

1.—(1) This scheme, which may be cited as the Fertilisers (United Kingdom) (Amendment) Scheme 1973, shall apply to England and Wales, Scotland and Northern Ireland.

(2) The Interpretation Act 1889(d) shall apply to the interpretation of this scheme as it applies to the interpretation of an Act of Parliament.

Amendment of the principal scheme

2. The Fertilisers (United Kingdom) Scheme 1972(e) shall be amended as follows:—

> (*a*) by substituting in paragraph 3 thereof for the words "and ending with 31st May 1973" the words "and ending with 31st May 1974";

> (*b*) by inserting in paragraph 6(3) thereof immediately after the word "spreading" the words "and any value added tax".

In Witness whereof the Official Seal of the Minister of Agriculture, Fisheries and Food is hereunto affixed on 21st May 1973.

(L.S.)

Joseph Godber,
Minister of Agriculture, Fisheries and Food.

(**a**) 1952 c. 15.　　　　　　　　　　(**b**) 1963 c. 11.
(**c**) S.I. 1969/388 (1969 I, p. 1070).　　(**d**) 1889 c. 63.
(**e**) S.I. 1972/815 (1972 II, p. 2623.)

Given under my hand on 21st May 1973.

Peter Thomas,
Secretary of State for Wales.

22nd May 1973.

Gordon Campbell,
Secretary of State for Scotland.

Approved on 23rd May 1973.

Tim Fortescue,
P. L. Hawkins,
Two of the Lords Commissioners of
Her Majesty's Treasury.

EXPLANATORY NOTE
(This Note is not part of the Scheme.)

This amending Scheme extends for a period of one year the operation of the Fertilisers (United Kingdom) Scheme 1972. That Scheme provides for the payment of contributions towards the cost of nitrogenous and phosphatic fertilisers applied to agricultural land or to crops thereon or used for the growing of mushrooms. The period within which such fertilisers are to be delivered in order to qualify for contributions in accordance with that Scheme, as now amended, is a period of 2 years ending on 31st May 1974.

STATUTORY INSTRUMENTS

1973 No. 979

INDUSTRIAL TRAINING

The Industrial Training Levy (Footwear, Leather and Fur Skin) Order 1973

Made - - -		*24th May* 1973
Laid before Parliament		*6th June* 1973
Coming into Operation		*3rd July* 1973

The Secretary of State after approving proposals submitted by the Footwear, Leather and Fur Skin Industry Training Board for the imposition of a further levy on employers in the footwear, leather and fur skin industry and in exercise of powers conferred by section 4 of the Industrial Training Act 1964(**a**) and now vested in him(**b**), and of all other powers enabling him in that behalf hereby makes the following Order:—

Title and commencement

1. This Order may be cited as the Industrial Training Levy (Footwear, Leather and Fur Skin) Order 1973 and shall come into operation on 3rd July 1973.

Interpretation

2.—(1) In this Order unless the context otherwise requires:—

(*a*) "agriculture" has the same meaning as in section 109(3) of the Agriculture Act 1947(**c**) or, in relation to Scotland, as in section 86(3) of the Agriculture (Scotland) Act 1948(**d**);

(*b*) "an appeal tribunal" means an industrial tribunal established under section 12 of the Industrial Training Act 1964;

(*c*) "assessment" means an assessment of an employer to the levy;

(*d*) "the Board" means the Footwear, Leather and Fur Skin Industry Training Board;

(*e*) "business" means any activities of industry or commerce;

(*f*) "charity" has the same meaning as in section 360 of the Income and Corporation Taxes Act 1970(**e**);

(a) 1964 c. 16. (b) 1968/729 (1968 II, p. 2108).
(c) 1947 c. 48. (d) 1948 c. 45.
(e) 1970 c. 10.

(g) "emoluments" means all emoluments assessable to income tax under Schedule E (other than pensions), being emoluments from which tax under that Schedule is deductible, whether or not tax in fact falls to be deducted from any particular payment thereof;

(h) "employer" means a person who is an employer in the footwear, leather and fur skin industry at any time in the fourth levy period;

(i) "footwear, leather and fur skin establishment" means an establishment in Great Britain engaged in the fourth base period wholly or mainly in the footwear, leather and fur skin industry for a total of twenty-seven or more weeks or, being an establishment that commenced to carry on business in the fourth base period, for a total number of weeks exceeding one half of the number of weeks in the part of the said period commencing with the day on which business was commenced and ending on the last day thereof;

(j) "footwear, leather and fur skin industry" means any one or more of the activities which, subject to the provisions of paragraph 2 of Schedule 1 to the industrial training order, are specified in paragraph 1 of that Schedule as the activities of the footwear, leather and fur skin industry;

(k) "the fourth base period" means the period of twelve months that commenced on 6th April 1971;

(l) "the fourth levy period" means the period commencing with the day upon which this Order comes into operation and ending on 31st March 1974;

(m) "the industrial training order" means the Industrial Training (Footwear, Leather and Fur Skin Board) Order 1968(a), as amended by the Industrial Training (Footwear, Leather and Fur Skin Board) Order 1968 (Amendment) Order 1972(b);

(n) "the levy" means the levy imposed by the Board in respect of the fourth levy period;

(o) "notice" means a notice in writing.

(2) In the case where a footwear, leather and fur skin establishment is taken over (whether directly or indirectly) by an employer in succession to, or jointly with, another person, a person employed at any time in the fourth base period at or from the establishment shall be deemed, for the purposes of this Order, to have been so employed by the employer carrying on the said establishment on the day upon which this Order comes into operation, and any reference in this Order to persons employed by the employer at or from a footwear, leather and fur skin establishment in the fourth base period shall be construed accordingly.

(3) Any reference in this Order to an establishment that commences to carry on business or that ceases to carry on business shall not be taken to apply where the location of the establishment is changed but its business is continued wholly or mainly at or from the new location, or where the suspension of activities is of a temporary or seasonal nature.

(4) The Interpretation Act 1889(c) shall apply to the interpretation of this Order as it applies to the interpretation of an Act of Parliament.

(a) S.I. 1968/1763 (1968 III, p. 4785).   (b) S.I. 1972/597 (1972 I, p. 1966).
(c) 1889 c. 63.

Imposition of the levy

3.—(1) The levy to be imposed by the Board on employers in respect of the fourth levy period shall be assessed in accordance with the provisions of this Article.

(2) Subject to the provisions of this Article, the levy shall be assessed by the Board in respect of each employer and the amount thereof shall be equal to 0·8 per cent. of the sum (less £3,000) of the emoluments of all the persons employed by the employer at or from the footwear, leather and fur skin establishment or establishments of the employer in the fourth base period.

(3) There shall be exempt from the levy—

    (*a*) an employer in respect of whom the sum of the emoluments of the persons mentioned in the last foregoing paragraph is less than £10,000;

    (*b*) a charity.

(4) Where any persons whose emoluments are taken into account for the purpose of this Article were employed at or from an establishment that ceases to carry on business in the fourth levy period, the sum of the emoluments of those persons shall be reduced in the same proportion as the number of days between the commencement of the said levy period and the date of cessation of business (both dates inclusive) bears to the number of days in the said levy period.

(5) For the purposes of this Article no regard shall be had to the emoluments of any person wholly engaged in agriculture or in the supply of food or drink for immediate consumption.

Assessment notices

4.—(1) The Board shall serve an assessment notice on every employer assessed to the levy.

(2) The amount of an assessment shall be rounded down to the nearest £1.

(3) An assessment notice shall state the Board's address for the service of a notice of appeal or of an application for an extension of time for appealing.

(4) An assessment notice may be served on the person assessed to the levy either by delivering it to him personally or by leaving it, or sending it to him by post, at his last known address or place of business in the United Kingdom or, if that person is a corporation, by leaving it, or sending it by post to the corporation, at such address or place of business or at its registered or principal office.

Payment of the levy

5.—(1) Subject to the provisions of this Article and of Articles 6 and 7, the amount of the levy payable under an assessment notice served by the Board shall be due and payable to the Board one month after the date of the notice.

(2) The amount of an assessment shall not be recoverable by the Board until there has expired the time allowed for appealing against the assessment by Article 7(1) of this Order and any further period or periods of time that the Board or an appeal tribunal may have allowed for appealing under paragraph (2) or (3) of that Article or, where an appeal is brought, until the appeal is decided or withdrawn.

Withdrawal of assessment

6.—(1) The Board may, by a notice served on the person assessed to the levy in the same manner as an assessment notice, withdraw an assessment if that person has appealed against that assessment under the provisions of Article 7 of this Order and the appeal has not been entered in the Register of Appeals kept under the appropriate Regulations specified in paragraph (5) of that Article.

(2) The withdrawal of an assessment shall be without prejudice to the power of the Board to serve a further assessment notice on the employer.

Appeals

7.—(1) A person assessed to the levy may appeal to an appeal tribunal against the assessment within one month from the date of the service of the assessment notice or within any further period or periods of time that may be allowed by the Board or an appeal tribunal under the following provisions of this Article.

(2) The Board by notice may for good cause allow a person assessed to the levy to appeal to an appeal tribunal against the assessment at any time within the period of four months from the date of the service of the assessment notice or within such further period or periods as the Board may allow before such time as may then be limited for appealing has expired.

(3) If the Board shall not allow an application for extension of time for appealing, an appeal tribunal shall upon application made to the tribunal by the person assessed to the levy have the like powers as the Board under the last foregoing paragraph.

(4) In the case of an assessment that has reference to an establishment that ceases to carry on business in the fourth levy period on any day after the date of the service of the assessment notice the foregoing provisions of this Article shall have effect as if for the period of four months from the date of the service of the assessment notice mentioned in paragraph (2) of this Article there were substituted the period of six months from the date of the cessation of business.

(5) An appeal or an application to an appeal tribunal under this Article shall be made in accordance with the Industrial Tribunals (England and Wales) Regulations 1965(a) as amended by the Industrial Tribunals (England and Wales) (Amendment) Regulations 1967(b), except where the assessment relates to persons employed at or from an establishment which is wholly in Scotland and to no other persons, in which case the appeal or application shall be made in accordance with the Industrial Tribunals (Scotland) Regulations 1965(c) as amended by the Industrial Tribunals (Scotland) (Amendment) Regulations 1967(d).

(6) The powers of an appeal tribunal under paragraph (3) of this Article may be exercised by the President of the Industrial Tribunals (England and Wales) or by the President of the Industrial Tribunals (Scotland) as the case may be.

(a) S.I. 1965/1101 (1965 II, p. 2805).   (b) S.I. 1967/301 (1967 I, p. 1040).
(c) S.I. 1965/1157 (1965 II, p. 3266).   (d) S.I. 1967/302 (1967 I, p. 1050).

Evidence

8.—(1) Upon the discharge by a person assessed to the levy of his liability under an assessment the Board shall if so requested issue to him a certificate to that effect.

(2) The production in any proceedings of a document purporting to be certified by the Secretary of the Board to be a true copy of an assessment or other notice issued by the Board or purporting to be a certificate such as is mentioned in the foregoing paragraph of this Article shall, unless the contrary is proved, be sufficient evidence of the document and of the facts stated therein.

Signed by order of the Secretary of State.

24th May 1973.

R. Chichester-Clark,
Minister of State,
Department of Employment.

EXPLANATORY NOTE

(This Note is not part of the Order.)

This Order gives effect to proposals submitted by the Footwear, Leather and Fur Skin Industry Training Board to the Secretary of State for Employment for the imposition of a further levy upon employers in the industry for the purpose of raising money towards the expenses of the Board.

The levy is to be imposed in respect of the fourth levy period commencing on the day upon which this Order comes into operation and ending on 31st March 1974. The levy will be assessed by the Board and there will be a right of appeal against an assessment to an industrial tribunal.

STATUTORY INSTRUMENTS

1973 No. 980

INDUSTRIAL TRAINING

The Industrial Training Levy (Petroleum) Order 1973

Made - - -		*24th May* 1973
Laid before Parliament		*6th June* 1973
Coming into Operation		*3rd July* 1973

The Secretary of State after approving proposals submitted by the Petroleum Industry Training Board for the imposition of a further levy on employers in the petroleum industry and in exercise of powers conferred by section 4 of the Industrial Training Act 1964(a) and now vested in him(b), and of all other powers enabling him in that behalf hereby makes the following Order: —

Title and commencement

1. This Order may be cited as the Industrial Training Levy (Petroleum) Order 1973 and shall come into operation on 3rd July 1973.

Interpretation

2.—(1) In this Order unless the context otherwise requires: —

(*a*) "agriculture" has the same meaning as in section 109(3) of the Agriculture Act 1947(c) or, in relation to Scotland, as in section 86(3) of the Agriculture (Scotland) Act 1948(d);

(*b*) "an appeal tribunal" means an industrial tribunal established under section 12 of the Industrial Training Act 1964;

(*c*) "assessment" means an assessment of an employer to the levy;

(*d*) "average number" in relation to the persons employed at or from a petroleum establishment of an employer means the number that is equal to the average (calculated to the lowest whole number) of the numbers of the persons employed at or from the establishment by the employer on the relevant dates;

(*e*) "the Board" means the Petroleum Industry Training Board;

(*f*) "business" means any activities of industry or commerce;

(*g*) "charity" has the same meaning as in section 360 of the Income and Corporation Taxes Act 1970(e);

(*h*) "employer" means a person who is an employer in the petroleum industry at any time in the fifth levy period;

(*i*) "the fifth levy period" means the period commencing with the day upon which this Order comes into operation and ending on 31st March 1974;

(*j*) "the industrial training order" means the Industrial Training (Petroleum Board) Order 1970(f);

(a) 1964 c. 16.   (b) S.I. 1968/729 (1968 II, p. 2108).
(c) 1947 c. 48.   (d) 1948 c. 45.
(e) 1970 c. 10.   (f) S.I. 1970/205 (1970 I, p. 926).

(k) "the levy" means the levy imposed by the Board in respect of the fifth levy period;

(l) "notice" means a notice in writing;

(m) "petroleum establishment" means an establishment in Great Britain engaged wholly or mainly in the petroleum industry for a total of twenty-seven or more weeks in the period of twelve months that commenced on 1st June 1972 or, being an establishment that commenced to carry on business in the said period, for a total number of weeks exceeding one half of the number of weeks in the part of the said period commencing with the day on which business was commenced and ending on the last day thereof;

(n) "the petroleum industry" means any one or more of the activities which, subject to the provisions of paragraph 2 of the Schedule to the industrial training order, are specified in paragraph 1 of that Schedule as the activities of the petroleum industry;

(o) "the relevant dates" means 18th December 1972 and 18th June 1973.

(2) Any reference in this Order to persons employed at or from a petroleum establishment shall in any case where the employer is a company be construed as including a reference to any director of the company (or any person occupying the position of director by whatever name he was called) who devoted substantially the whole of his time to the service of the company.

(3) For the purposes of this Order no regard shall be had—

(a) to any person employed at or from a petroleum establishment, being on either or both of the relevant dates—

(i) a person normally employed by the employer for less than twenty-two hours a week; or

(ii) a male person aged sixty-five years or more or a female person aged sixty years or more;

(b) to any person employed wholly in agriculture or in the supply of food or drink for immediate consumption; or

(c) to any person who is employed as the master or a member of the crew of a ship or who, being ordinarily employed as a seaman, is employed in or about a ship in port by the owner or charterer thereof on work of a kind ordinarily done by a seaman on a ship while it is in port.

(4) In the case where a petroleum establishment is taken over (whether directly or indirectly) by an employer in succession to, or jointly with, another person, a person employed at or from the establishment on either or both of the relevant dates by a person other than the employer carrying on the establishment on the day upon which this Order comes into operation shall be deemed for the purposes of this Order to have been employed by the last mentioned employer, and any reference in this Order to persons employed by an employer at or from a petroleum establishment on either or both of the relevant dates shall be construed accordingly.

(5) Any reference in this Order to an establishment that commences to carry on business or that ceases to carry on business shall not be taken to apply where the location of the establishment is changed but its business is continued wholly or mainly at or from the new location, or where the suspension of activities is of a temporary or seasonal nature.

(6) The Interpretation Act 1889(a) shall apply to the interpretation of this Order as it applies to the interpretation of an Act of Parliament.

Imposition of the levy

3.—(1) The levy to be imposed by the Board on employers in respect of the fifth levy period shall be assessed in accordance with the provisions of this Article.

(2) The levy shall be assessed by the Board separately in respect of each petroleum establishment of an employer, not being an employer who is exempt from the levy by virtue of paragraph (5) of this Article.

(3) Subject to the provisions of this Article, the levy in respect of a petroleum establishment of an employer shall be assessed by reference to the average number of the persons employed at or from the establishment by the employer as follows—

    (*a*) where the said average number of persons exceeded ten but did not exceed twenty, by multiplying the sum of £10 by that average number and by subtracting from the amount so obtained the sum of £60; or

    (*b*) where the said average number of persons exceeded twenty, by multiplying the sum of £7 by the said average number of persons.

(4) The amount of the levy imposed in respect of a petroleum establishment that ceases to carry on business in the fifth levy period shall be in the same proportion to the amount that would otherwise be due under paragraph (3) of this Article as the number of days between the commencement of the said levy period and the date of cessation of business (both dates inclusive) bears to the number of days in the said levy period.

(5) There shall be exempt from the levy—

    (*a*) an employer in whose case the average number of all the persons employed by him at or from the petroleum establishment or establishments of the employer (including any persons employed at or from a petroleum establishment by an associated company of the employer) was less than eleven;

    (*b*) a charity.

Assessment notices

4.—(1) The Board shall serve an assessment notice on every employer assessed to the levy, but one notice may comprise two or more assessments.

(2) An assessment notice shall state the Board's address for the service of a notice of appeal or of an application for an extension of time for appealing.

(3)An assessment notice may be served on the person assessed to the levy either by delivering it to him personally or by leaving it, or sending it to him by post, at his last known address or place of business in the United Kingdom or, if that person is a corporation, by leaving it, or sending it by post to the corporation, at such address or place of business or at its registered or principal office.

Payment of the levy

5.—(1) Subject to the provisions of this Article and of Articles 6 and 7, the amount of each assessment appearing in an assessment notice served by the

---

(a) 1889 c. 63.

Board shall be payable to the Board in two instalments equal to three sevenths and four sevenths of the said amount respectively, and the said instalments shall be due respectively one month and seven months after the date of the notice.

(2) An instalment of an assessment shall not be recoverable by the Board until there has expired the time allowed for appealing against the assessment by Article 7(1) of this Order and any further period or periods of time that the Board or an appeal tribunal may have allowed for appealing under paragraph (2) or (3) of that Article or, where an appeal is brought, until the appeal is decided or withdrawn.

Withdrawal of assessment

6.—(1) The Board may, by a notice served on the person assessed to the levy in the same manner as an assessment notice, withdraw an assessment if that person has appealed against that assessment under the provisions of Article 7 of this Order and the appeal has not been entered in the Register of Appeals kept under the appropriate Regulations specified in paragraph (5) of that Article.

(2) The withdrawal of an assessment shall be without prejudice to the power of the Board to serve a further assessment notice in respect of any establishment to which that assessment related and, where the withdrawal is made by reason of the fact that an establishment has ceased to carry on business in the fifth levy period, the said notice may provide that the whole amount payable thereunder in respect of the establishment shall be due one month after the date of the notice.

Appeals

7.—(1) A person assessed to the levy may appeal to an appeal tribunal against the assessment within one month from the date of the service of the assessment notice or within any further period or periods of time that may be allowed by the Board or an appeal tribunal under the following provisions of this Article.

(2) The Board by notice may for good cause allow a person assessed to the levy to appeal to an appeal tribunal against the assessment at any time within the period of four months from the date of the service of the assessment notice or within such further period or periods as the Board may allow before such time as may then be limited for appealing has expired.

(3) If the Board shall not allow an application for extension of time for appealing an appeal tribunal shall upon application made to the tribunal by the person assessed to the levy have the like powers as the Board under the last foregoing paragraph.

(4) In the case of an establishment that ceases to carry on business in the fifth levy period on any day after the date of the service of the relevant assessment notice the foregoing provisions of this Article shall have effect as if for the period of four months from the date of the service of the assessment notice mentioned in paragraph (2) of this Article there were substituted the period of six months from the date of the cessation of business.

(5) An appeal or an application to an appeal tribunal under this Article shall be made in accordance with the Industrial Tribunals (England and

Wales) Regulations 1965(a) as amended by the Industrial Tribunals (England and Wales) (Amendment) Regulations 1967(b), except where the establishment to which the relevant assessment relates is wholly in Scotland, in which case the appeal or application shall be made in accordance with the Industrial Tribunals (Scotland) Regulations 1965(c) as amended by the Industrial Tribunals (Scotland) (Amendment) Regulations 1967(d).

(6) The powers of an appeal tribunal under paragraph (3) of this Article may be exercised by the President of the Industrial Tribunals (England and Wales) or by the President of the Industrial Tribunals (Scotland) as the case may be.

Evidence

8.—(1) Upon the discharge by a person assessed to the levy of his liability under an assessment the Board shall if so requested issue to him a certificate to that effect.

(2) The production in any proceedings of a document purporting to be certified by the Secretary of the Board to be a true copy of an assessment or other notice issued by the Board or purporting to be a certificate such as is mentioned in the foregoing paragraph of this Article shall, unless the contrary is proved, be sufficient evidence of the document and of the facts stated therein.

Signed by order of the Secretary of State.
24th May 1973.

R. Chichester-Clark,
Minister of State,
Department of Employment.

EXPLANATORY NOTE

(*This Note is not part of the Order.*)

This Order gives effect to proposals submitted by the Petroleum Industry Training Board to the Secretary of State for Employment for the imposition of a further levy on employers in the petroleum industry for the purpose of raising money towards the expenses of the Board.

The levy is to be imposed in respect of the fifth levy period commencing with the day upon which this Order comes into operation and ending on 31st March 1974. The levy will be assessed by the Board and there will be a right of appeal against an assessment to an industrial tribunal.

(a) S.I. 1965/1101 (1965 II, p. 2805).   (b) S.I. 1967/301 (1967 I, p. 1040).
(c) S.I. 1965/1157 (1965 II, p. 3266).   (d) S.I. 1967/302 (1967 I, p. 1050).

STATUTORY INSTRUMENTS

1973 No. 981 (L.14)

SHERIFF, ENGLAND

The Sheriffs' Fees (Amendment) Order 1973

Made - - - -	24*th May* 1973
Coming into Operation	25*th June* 1973

The Lord Chancellor, in exercise of the powers conferred on him by section 20(2) of the Sheriffs Act 1887(a) and with the advice and consent of the Judges of the Court of Appeal and the High Court and with the concurrence of the Treasury, hereby makes the following Order:—

1.—(1) This Order may be cited as the Sheriffs' Fees (Amendment) Order 1973 and shall come into operation on 25th June 1973.

(2) In this Order "the Order of 1921" means the Order made under section 20(2) of the Sheriffs Act 1887 and dated 2nd May 1921(b), as amended (c).

(3) The Interpretation Act 1889(d) shall apply to the interpretation of this Order as it applies to the interpretation of an Act of Parliament.

2. In Fee No. 7B in the Table of Fees set out in Part I of the Schedule to the Order of 1921 for the words "$7\frac{1}{2}$ per cent." there shall be substituted the words "3 per cent.".

Dated 23rd May 1973.

Hailsham of St. Marylebone, C.

Widgery, C. J.
Denning, M. R.
George Baker, P.

We concur.
Dated 24th May 1973.

Tim Fortescue,
P. L. Hawkins,
Two of the Lords Commissioners
of Her Majesty's Treasury.

(a) 1887 c. 55. (b) S.R. & O. 1921/827 (Rev. XX, p. 736: 1921, p. 1226).
(c) S.I. 1971/808 (1971 II, p. 2307). (d) 1889 c. 63.

EXPLANATORY NOTE

(This Note is not part of the Order.)

This Order provides for the fee payable to a sheriff for executing a writ of possession to be reduced from 7½ per cent. to 3 per cent. of the net annual value for rating of the property, so as to take into account the revaluation for rating.

STATUTORY INSTRUMENTS

1973 No. 982

MAGISTRATES' COURTS

The Petty Sessional Divisions (North-East London) Order 1973

Made - - -	*24th May* 1973
Coming into Operation	*1st June* 1973

Whereas the magistrates' courts committee for the north-east London area of Greater London (which area is deemed to be a county for all purposes of the law relating to magistrates' courts and matters connected with magistrates' courts by section 2 of the Administration of Justice Act 1964(a)) has, in pursuance of subsection (1) of section 18 of the Justices of the Peace Act 1949(b), submitted to the Secretary of State a draft order making provision about the division of part of the said area into petty sessional divisions:

And whereas by subsections (3)(*a*) and (4)(*a*) of the said section 18 it is provided that the Secretary of State may by statutory instrument make the Order either in the terms of the said draft or with such modifications as he thinks fit and that the said Order may contain transitional and other consequential provisions:

And whereas the provisions of subsections (5), (6) and (7) of the said section have been complied with:

Now, therefore, in exercise of the powers conferred upon me by subsections (3) and (4) of the said section 18, I hereby make the following Order:—

1. This Order may be cited as the Petty Sessional Divisions (North-East London) Order 1973 and shall come into operation on 1st June 1973, except that for the purposes of paragraph 2 of the Schedule thereto this Order shall come into operation forthwith.

2.—(1) In this Order, except where the context otherwise requires, the expression "division" means petty sessional division and any reference to a justice for a division shall be construed as a reference to a justice of the peace who ordinarily acts, or, as the case may be, will on or after 1st June 1973 ordinarily act, in and for that division.

(2) The Interpretation Act 1889(c) shall apply to the interpretation of this Order as it applies to the interpretation of an Act of Parliament.

3.—(1) The division of Chingford, which consists of part of the London borough of Waltham Forest, shall be abolished.

(a) 1964 c. 42.   (b) 1949 c. 101.   (c) 1889 c. 63.

(2) The London borough of Barking and the remainder of the London borough of Waltham Forest, shall cease to form part of the Beacontree division which accordingly shall consist of the London borough of Redbridge.

(3) The London borough of Waltham Forest shall form a new division which shall be known as the Waltham Forest division.

(4) The London borough of Barking shall form a new division which shall be known as the Barking division.

4. The transitional and other consequential provisions set out in the Schedule to this Order shall have effect in connection with the provisions of Article 3 of this Order.

Robert Carr,
One of Her Majesty's Principal
Secretaries of State.

Home Office,
 Whitehall.
24th May 1973.

SCHEDULE

Article 4

TRANSITIONAL AND OTHER CONSEQUENTIAL PROVISIONS

1. In this Schedule—

"existing Beacontree division" means the Beacontree division as constituted before the coming into effect of this Order;

"Beacontree division" means the Beacontree division as reduced in area by this Order;

"new division" means a division constituted by Article 3 of this Order;

"probation order" means a probation order made or having effect as if made under section 3 of the Criminal Justice Act 1948(a);

"supervision order" means a supervision order within the meaning of section 11 of the Children and Young Persons Act 1969(b) or to which paragraph 12 of Schedule 4 to that Act applies or an order under section 2(1)(f) of the Matrimonial Proceedings (Magistrates' Courts) Act 1960(c).

2.—(1) The justices for each new division shall appoint, in the prescribed manner, so far as may be applicable, and for the prescribed term, to take office on 1st June 1973—

(*a*) a chairman and one or more deputy chairmen;

(*b*) a juvenile court panel;

(*c*) one or more case committees;

(*d*) three justices to serve as members of the probation and after-care committee for the north-east London combined probation and after-care area;

(*e*) two justices to serve as members of the magistrates' courts committee for the north-east London area;

(*f*) a betting licensing committee.

(2) In the foregoing sub-paragraph, the expression "the prescribed manner" and "the prescribed term" mean, respectively—

(a) in relation to the election of a chairman or deputy chairman, the manner prescribed by rules made under section 13 of the Justices of the Peace Act 1949 and a term ending at the expiration of the month of December 1973;

(b) in relation to the election of a juvenile court panel, the manner prescribed by rules made under section 15 of that Act and section 61 of the Children and Young Persons Act 1969 and a term ending at the expiration of the month of October 1973;

(c) in relation to the appointment of a case committee, the manner prescribed by rules made under Schedule 5 to the Criminal Justice Act 1948 and a term ending at the expiration of the month of December 1973;

(d) in relation to the appointment of the members of the probation and after-care committee, the manner prescribed by the Outer London Probation Areas Order 1964(a), as amended (b), and a term ending in the case of one such member from each new division at the expiration of the month of December 1973, in the case of one such member from each new division at the expiration of the month of December 1974 and in the case of one such member from each new division at the expiration of the month of December 1975, the first two such members from each new division being chosen by lot;

(e) in relation to the appointment of the members of the magistrates' courts committee, the manner prescribed by regulations made under Schedule 4 to the Justices of the Peace Act 1949 and a term ending at the expiration of the month of November 1973;

(f) in relation to the appointment of the betting licensing committee, the manner prescribed in Regulation 1 of the Betting (Licensing) Regulations 1960(c) and a term ending at the expiration of the month of December 1973.

(3) In relation to the appointment of a justices' clerk for a new division, any consultation with the justices for that division required by section 19(9) of the Justices of the Peace Act 1949 may take place before 1st June 1973.

3. The three justices appointed by the justices for each of the divisions of Havering and Newham and for the existing Beacontree division, who serve as members of the magistrates' courts committee for the north-east London area shall agree among themselves, or, in default of agreement, draw lots to determine, which one of them from each division shall cease to serve as a member of that committee on 1st June 1973.

4.—(1) The existing Beacontree division and the Chingford division shall, notwithstanding the provisions of Article 3 of this Order, continue until the expiration of the month of December 1973 to constitute separate licensing districts for the purposes of the Licensing Act 1964(d) and, until the expiration of the said month, the said Act shall apply in relation to those divisions and the divisional licensing committees appointed therefor shall continue to carry out their functions as licensing authorities in relation thereto as if this Order had not been made.

(2) Sub-paragraph (1) of this paragraph shall continue to have effect after the expiration of the said month for the purpose of continuing in force the permitted hours in the Chingford division and in that part of the London borough of Waltham

---

(a) S.I. 1964/1834.

(b) The amending orders are not relevant to the subject matter of this Order.

(c) S.I. 1960/1701 (1960 I, p. 363).   (d) 1964 c. 26.

Forest which forms part of the existing Beacontree division until there is in operation an order under section 60 of the Licensing Act 1964 fixing permitted hours made at the general annual licensing meeting of the licensing justices for the Waltham Forest division to be held in 1974.

(3) The said sub-paragraph shall continue to have effect after the expiration of the said month for the purpose of continuing in force the permitted hours in the London borough of Barking until there is in operation an order under the said section fixing permitted hours made at the general annual licensing meeting of the licensing justices for the Barking division to be held in 1974.

(4) Nothing in the foregoing provisions of this paragraph shall be construed as preventing the justices for a new division from exercising on and after 1st June 1973 in relation to the area thereof any powers relating to the grant of occasional licences, orders of exemption or protection orders conferred on them by the Licensing Act 1964.

5. Anything required by virtue of the foregoing provisions of this Schedule to be done on or after 1st June 1973 by, or in relation to, the clerk to the justices for the Chingford division shall be done by, or in relation to, the clerk to the justices for the Waltham Forest division.

6. Subject to the foregoing provisions of this Schedule, any process issued, order made, sentence passed, appeal brought, case stated, licence granted, recognizance entered into, proceeding begun, appointment made or other thing done (whether before 1st June 1973 or in pursuance of paragraph 4 of this Schedule) by, from, to or before any justices for the Chingford division or their clerk shall be deemed to have been issued, made, passed, brought, stated, granted, entered into, begun or done by, from, to or before those justices as justices for the Waltham Forest division or their clerk, as the case may be.

7. Any order made by a magistrates' court directing the payment of money to the clerk or any other officer of a magistrates' court acting for the Chingford division shall have effect as if it had directed payment to be made to the clerk to the justices for the Waltham Forest division.

8.—(1) Any process, record or other document in the custody, by virtue of his office as such, of the clerk to the justices for the Chingford division, shall be retained by that clerk in his capacity as clerk to the justices for the Waltham Forest division, or if he does not hold that clerkship, be transferred to the custody of the clerk to the justices for the Waltham Forest division.

(2) Copies of, and extracts from, any such record or other document as aforesaid made or certified by the clerk to the justices for the Waltham Forest division, shall be of the same effect as if they had been made or certified by the clerk to the justices for the Chingford division.

9.—(1) Where the Chingford division is named in a probation order or in a supervision order, the powers and functions of the justices for such division as supervising court shall vest in and be discharged by the justices for the Waltham Forest division; and such orders, unless amended in regard to the division named, shall have effect in all respects as if the Waltham Forest division were named therein.

(2) Where on 1st June 1973 a probation order or a supervision order is in force and the probationer or person under supervision is residing in the London borough of Barking or in that part of the London borough of Waltham Forest which forms part of the existing Beacontree division, the justices for the Beacontree division as supervising court may, if the Beacontree division is named in the order, amend the order in regard to the division named as if the probationer or person under supervision had changed his residence.

10.—(1) Any process issued, order made, sentence passed, appeal brought, case stated, recognizance entered into, proceeding begun or other thing done before 1st June 1973 by, from, to or before any justices for the existing Beacontree division or their clerk in any proceedings before a magistrates' court sitting in the courthouse in East Street, Barking, or in relation to any such proceedings shall be deemed to have been issued, made, passed, brought, stated, entered into, begun or done by, from, to or before those justices as justices for the Barking division or their clerk, as the case may be.

(2) Any process, record or other document relating to any matter to which sub-paragraph (1) of this paragraph applies which is in the custody, by virtue of his office as such, of the clerk to the justices for the Beacontree division, shall be transferred to the custody of the clerk to the justices for the Barking division.

(3) Copies of, and extracts from, any such record or other document as aforesaid made or certified by the clerk to the justices for the Barking division, shall be of the same effect as if they had been made or certified by the clerk to the justices for the Beacontree division.

11. Where on 1st June 1973 periodical payments are payable under section 52 of the Magistrates' Courts Act 1952(a) through the clerk to the justices for the Beacontree division to a person who resides in the London borough of Barking or in that part of the London borough of Waltham Forest which forms part of the existing Beacontree division, that clerk may amend the order so as to require payments to be made through the clerk to the justices for the Barking division or for the Waltham Forest division, as the case may require, and if he does so, shall give notice of the amendment to the person entitled to the payments, to the person required to make the payments and to the justices' clerk through whom the payments are to be made.

(a) 1952 c. 55.

EXPLANATORY NOTE

(This Note is not part of the Order.)

This Order gives effect to a draft order submitted by the magistrates' courts committee for the north-east London area and provides for the abolition of the petty sessional division of Chingford, the reduction in size of the petty sessional division of Beacontree so that it consists of the London borough of Redbridge, and the formation of the new petty sessional divisions of Waltham Forest and Barking consisting respectively of the London boroughs of Waltham Forest and Barking.

STATUTORY INSTRUMENTS

1973 No. 984 (S.74)

COURT OF SESSION, SCOTLAND

Act of Sederunt (Rules of Court Amendment No. 5 1973) (Alteration of Fees to Shorthand Writers) 1973

Made - - - -	*24th May* 1973
Coming into Operation	*5th July* 1973

The Lords of Council and Session, under and by virtue of the powers conferred upon them by section 16 of the Administration of Justice (Scotland) Act 1933(a) and of all other powers competent to them in that behalf, do hereby enact and declare as follows:—

1. Chapter IV of the Schedule to Rule 347 of the Rules of Court (b) is hereby amended by deleting the first two lines thereof and by substituting therefor:—

"1. Attending trials, proofs and commissions per hour, with a minimum fee of £6 per day   £2.00".

2. This Act of Sederunt may be cited as the Act of Sederunt (Rules of Court Amendment No. 5 1973) (Alteration of Fees to Shorthand Writers) 1973 and shall come into operation on 5th July 1973.

And the Lords appoint this Act of Sederunt to be inserted in the books of Sederunt.

G. C. Emslie,

Edinburgh,
24th May 1973.   I.P.D.

EXPLANATORY NOTE

(This Note is not part of the Act of Sederunt.)

This Act of Sederunt amends the Rules of Court by increasing to £6 per day the minimum fee payable to Shorthand Writers in the Court of Session for attending trials, proofs and commissions to equate it to the minimum fee for such work in the Sheriff Court.

(a) 1933 c. 41.   (b) S.I. 1970/1746 (1970 III, p. 5718).

STATUTORY INSTRUMENTS

1973 No. 988

ANIMALS

DISEASES OF ANIMALS

The Brucellosis (Eradication Areas) (Wales) Order 1973

Made - - - -	*24th May* 1973
Coming into Operation	*1st July* 1973

The Minister of Agriculture, Fisheries and Food, in exercise of the powers conferred on him by section 5 of the Diseases of Animals Act 1950(a), as read with the Diseases of Animals (Extension of Definitions) Order 1971(b), and as extended by section 106(3) of the Agriculture Act 1970(c), and of all his other enabling powers, hereby orders as follows:—

Citation and commencement

1. This order may be cited as the Brucellosis (Eradication Areas) (Wales) Order 1973, and shall come into operation on 1st July 1973.

Interpretation

2.—(1) In this order, unless the context otherwise requires—

"approved landing place" means a landing place for the time being approved by the Minister for the purposes of the Animals (Landing from Channel Islands, Isle of Man, Northern Ireland and Republic of Ireland) Order 1955(d), as amended (e), or the Importation of Canadian Cattle Order of 1933(f), as amended (g);

"the Minister" means the Minister of Agriculture, Fisheries and Food;

"veterinary inspector" means a veterinary inspector appointed by the Minister.

(2) The Interpretation Act 1889(h) applies to the interpretation of this order as it applies to the interpretation of an Act of Parliament.

Declaration of brucellosis eradication areas

3. The areas respectively described in the Schedule hereto, being areas as respects which the Minister is satisfied in each case that a substantial majority of the cattle therein are free from brucellosis, are hereby declared to be eradication areas for purposes connected with the control of brucellosis, and shall be known for such purposes by the names by which they are referred to in the said Schedule.

(a) 1950 c. 36. (b) S.I. 1971/531 (1971 I, p. 1530).
(c) 1970 c. 40. (d) S.I. 1955/1310 (1955 I, p. 190).
(e) S.I. 1962/757, 1963/736, 1967/171 (1962 I, p. 752; 1963 I, p. 892; 1967 I, p. 281).
(f) S.R. & O. 1933/15 (Rev. II, p. 377: 1933, p. 361).
(g) S.I. 1963/224, 1972/1644 (1963 I, p. 202; 1972 III, p. 4841). (h) 1889 c. 63.

Restrictions on vaccination

4.—(1) No cattle shall be vaccinated against brucellosis in an area declared by this order to be an eradication area, except—

    (*a*) by an officer of the Minister or a person acting on the Minister's behalf; or

    (*b*) where a licence has been issued for the purpose by a veterinary inspector, and the vaccination is carried out in accordance with the terms and conditions (if any) of the licence.

(2) This Article shall not apply to an approved landing place.

Application of the Brucellosis (Area Eradication) (England and Wales) Order 1971, as amended

5.—(1) Subject to the following provisions of this Article, the provisions of the Brucellosis (Area Eradication) (England and Wales) Order 1971**(a)**, as amended **(b)**, shall apply to, and have effect in,—

    (*a*) the Wales No. 3 Eradication Area, as from the 1st March 1974; and

    (*b*) the Wales Nos. 4, 5 and 6 Eradication Areas, as from the 4th November 1974.

(2) Article 4 (movement of cattle into or through eradication areas or attested areas) and Article 5 (movement of cattle within an eradication area or attested area) of the said order shall not apply to cattle being moved direct to any premises within the areas which are for the purposes of this order approved from time to time by a veterinary inspector for the temporary accommodation of cattle immediately before their exportation from Great Britain.

(3) Any such approval as is referred to in the preceding paragraph may be given subject to compliance by the owner or occupier of the premises to which it relates with such conditions as may be specified therein, and may, by notice in writing, be withdrawn or varied at any time, but without prejudice to anything lawfully done pursuant to the approval before such withdrawal or variation took effect.

Offences

6. Any person who vaccinates cattle, or causes or permits cattle to be vaccinated, in contravention of Article 4 of this order, or who fails to comply with a condition of a licence granted thereunder, or with a condition subject to which premises are approved under paragraph (3) of the preceding Article, commits an offence against the Diseases of Animals Act 1950.

Enforcement

7. This order shall, except where otherwise expressly provided, be enforced by the local authority.

In Witness whereof the Official Seal of the Minister of Agriculture, Fisheries and Food is hereunto affixed on 24th May 1973.

    (a) S.I. 1971/1717 (1971 III, p. 4673).   **(b)** S.I. 1972/1173 (1972 II, p. 3486).

(L.S.)

Joseph Godber,
Minister of Agriculture, Fisheries and Food.

SCHEDULE* | Article 3

Wales No. 3 Eradication Area

An area comprising:—

In the administrative county of Glamorgan

In the petty sessional division of Pontardawe
The parishes of Llanguicke and Rhyndwyclydach.

In the petty sessional division of Swansea
The parishes of Llandeilo Tal-y-Bont, Llangyfelach and Mawr.

Wales No. 4 Eradication Area

An area comprising (except as hereinafter mentioned):—

The administrative county of Pembroke.

In the administrative county of Cardigan
Bathouse slaughterhouse and so much of the borough of Cardigan as lies outside the Wales No. 1 Eradication Area.

In the administrative county of Carmarthen
So much of the borough of Carmarthen as lies outside the Wales No. 1 Eradication Area.

The petty sessional divisions of St. Clears and Whitland.

In the petty sessional division of Carmarthen County
The parishes of Abernant, Llangain, Llangynog, Llanstephen and Trelech a'r Betws and so much of the parishes of Cynwyl Elfed and Newchurch as lie outside the Wales No. 1 Eradication Area.

In the petty sessional division of Newcastle Emlyn
Llandyssul livestock market; the parishes of Cenarth and Newcastle Emlyn and so much of the parish of Llangeler as lies outside the Wales No. 1 Eradication Area.

Wales No. 5 Eradication Area

An area comprising (except as hereinafter mentioned):—

The administrative county of Anglesey, excluding the approved landing place for cattle at the port of Holyhead.

In the administrative county of Caernarvon
So much of the royal borough of Caernarvon as lies outside the Wales No. 2 Eradication Area.

The petty sessional divisions of Bangor, Conway and Llandudno and Nant Conway.

In the petty sessional division of Caernarvon County

The parishes of Llanberis, Llanddeiniolen and Llanfairisgaer and so much of the parishes of Betws Garmon, Llanrug and Waunfawr as lie outside the Wales No. 2 Eradication Area.

In the petty sessional division of Eifionydd

So much of the parish of Beddgelert as lies outside the Wales No. 2 Eradication Area.

In the administrative county of Denbigh

In the petty sessional division of Uwchddulas and Uwchaled

The parishes of Eglwysbach, Llanddoget, Llansantffraid Glan Conway, Llanrwst Rural, Llanrwst Urban and Tir Ifan.

Wales No. 6 Eradication Area

An area comprising (except as hereinafter mentioned):—

The administrative counties of Brecon and Radnor excluding Hay and Knighton livestock markets.

In the administrative county of Glamorgan

In the petty sessional division of Neath County

The parishes of Dylais Higher and Neath Higher.

In the administrative county of Montgomery

The petty sessional divisions of Deytheur, Llanfyllin, Llanidloes, Mathrafal, Montgomery, Newtown Upper and Welshpool.

In the petty sessional division of Machynlleth

The parishes of Isygarreg, Llanbrynmair, Machynlleth, Penegoes and Uwchygarreg and so much of the parishes of Caereinion Fechan, Cemmaes, Darowen and Llanwrin as lie outside the Wales No. 2 Eradication Area.

EXPLANATORY NOTE
(*This Note is not part of the Order.*)

Under section 5 of the Diseases of Animals Act 1950, the Minister of Agriculture, Fisheries and Food may make Orders declaring an area to be an eradication area for purposes connected with the control of any disease of cattle if he is satisfied that a substantial majority of the cattle therein are free from that disease. Under the same section, as amended by section 106(3) of the Agriculture Act 1970, the Minister may make Orders imposing such prohibitions or requirements with respect to cattle in eradication areas as he may consider necessary or desirable for the purpose of eradicating brucellosis.

The present Order declares four further areas in Wales to be eradication areas, and prohibits the vaccination against brucellosis of cattle in those areas, unless undertaken on behalf of the Minister, or under a licence issued by a veterinary inspector employed by him. The Order also provides that the provisions of the Brucellosis (Area Eradication) (England and Wales) Order 1971, as amended, shall come into effect in the first of these areas (the Wales No. 3 Eradication Area) as from 1st March 1974, and in the others, as from 4th November 1974.

1973 No. 990   (S. 75)

AGRICULTURE

HILL LANDS

The Hill Farming (Cottages) (Amendment) (Scotland) Regulations 1973

Made - - -	*24th May* 1973
Laid before Parliament	*7th June* 1973
Coming into Operation	*2nd July* 1973

In exercise of the powers conferred upon me by section 10 of the Hill Farming Act 1946**(a)**, as amended by section 1 of the Hill Farming Act 1954**(b)**, and of all other powers enabling me in that behalf, I hereby make the following regulations:—

Citation, Commencement and Interpretation

1.—(1) These regulations may be cited as the Hill Farming (Cottages) (Amendment) (Scotland) Regulations 1973 and shall come into operation on 2nd July 1973.

(2) These regulations shall be construed as one with the Hill Farming (Cottages) (Scotland) Regulations 1954**(c)**, hereinafter referred to as "the principal regulations".

Amendment of the principal regulations

2. Regulation 3(b) of the principal regulations and paragraph (b) of the First Schedule thereto (which specify the persons who may occupy a cottage in respect of which an improvement grant has been made) shall be amended by adding after sub-paragraph (iii) thereof the following sub-paragraph:—

"(iv) by a person who occupies the cottage otherwise than under a protected tenancy or a statutory tenancy within the meaning of the Rent (Scotland) Act 1971**(d)** during any part of a period in respect of which the Secretary of State has given his consent to the cottage being occupied in that manner".

(a) 1946 c. 73.   **(b)** 1954 c. 23.   **(c)** S.I. 1954/672 (1954 I, p. 96).
(d) 1971 c. 28.

Application

3. These regulations shall apply to any cottage in respect of which an improvement grant has been made, whether made before or after the coming into operation of these regulations.

Gordon Campbell,
One of Her Majesty's Principal
Secretaries of State.

St. Andrew's House,
Edinburgh.
24th May 1973.

EXPLANATORY NOTE

(*This Note is not part of the Regulations.*)

These Regulations amend the conditions as to the occupation of cottages grant-aided under the Hill Farming and Livestock Rearing Acts 1946-59. They enable the Secretary of State to allow such cottages to be occupied for a specified period, provided that such occupation does not constitute a protected or statutory tenancy within the meaning of the Rent (Scotland) Act 1971.

The occupancy requirements for grant-aided cottages under Regulation 3(b) of the Hill Farming (Cottages) (Scotland) Regulations 1954 are otherwise unchanged.

STATUTORY INSTRUMENTS

1973 No. 991

JURIES

The Jurors' Allowances (Amendment) Regulations 1973

Made - - - - 30th May 1973

Coming into Operation 2nd July 1973

The Lord Chancellor, in exercise of the powers conferred on him by section 1 of the Juries Act 1949(**a**), as amended by section 1 of the Juries Act 1954(**b**), section 36 of the Courts Act 1971(**c**) and section 27 of the Criminal Justice Act 1972(**d**), and with the consent of the Minister for the Civil Service, hereby makes the following Regulations :—

1. These Regulations may be cited as the Jurors' Allowances (Amendment) Regulations 1973 and shall come into operation on 2nd July 1973.

2. Regulation 5 of the Jurors' Allowances Regulations 1972(**e**) shall be amended as follows :—

(a) in paragraph (2)(a), for the words " the sum of £2·37½ " there shall be substituted the words " the sum of £2·75 ; "

(b) in paragraph (2)(b), for the words " the sum of £4·75 " there shall be substituted the words " the sum of £5·50 ; "

(c) in paragraph (3), for the expression " £9·50 " there shall be substituted the expression " £11 ".

Dated 24th May 1973.

Hailsham of St. Marylebone, C.

Consent of the Minister for the Civil Service given under his official seal on 30th May 1973.

(L.S.)

P. M. Blake,
Authorised by the Minister
for the Civil Service.

EXPLANATORY NOTE

(This Note is not part of the Regulations.)

These Regulations provide for an increase in the allowances payable to jurors for financial loss or loss of earnings, or of benefit under the enactments relating to national insurance.

(**a**) 1949 c. 27. (**b**) 1954 c. 41. (**c**) 1971 c. 23. (**d**) 1972 c. 71.
(**e**) S.I. 1972/1976 (1972 III, p. 5889).

STATUTORY INSTRUMENTS

1973 No. 994

SEEDS

The Seeds (National Lists of Varieties) Regulations 1973

Made - - - -	31*st May* 1973
Laid before Parliament	8*th June* 1973
Coming into Operation	1*st July* 1973

The Minister of Agriculture, Fisheries and Food, the Secretary of State for Scotland and the Secretary of State for Northern Ireland (being the Secretary of State concerned with agriculture in Northern Ireland), acting jointly, in exercise of the powers vested in them by section 16(1), (1A) and (8) of the Plant Varieties and Seeds Act 1964(a) as amended by section 4(1) of and paragraph 5(1), (2) and (3) of Schedule 4 to the European Communities Act 1972(b) (extended to Northern Ireland by the Plant Varieties and Seeds (Northern Ireland) Order 1964(c) and the Plant Varieties and Seeds (Northern Ireland) Order 1973(d)) and of all other powers enabling them in that behalf, after consultation with the Council on Tribunals in accordance with section 10(1) of the Tribunals and Inquiries Act 1971(e) as applied to the Plant Varieties and Seeds Tribunal and with representatives of such interests as appear to them to be concerned, hereby make the following Regulations.

Citation and commencement

1. These Regulations may be cited as the Seeds (National Lists of Varieties) Regulations 1973 and shall come into operation on the 1st July 1973.

Interpretation

2.—(1) The Interpretation Act 1889(f) shall apply to the interpretation of these Regulations as it applies to the interpretation of an Act of Parliament.

(2) In these Regulations—

"the Act" means the Plant Varieties and Seeds Act 1964 as amended by section 43 of and Schedule 7 to the Agriculture (Miscellaneous Provisions) Act 1968(g) and by section 4(1) of and paragraph 5 of Schedule 4 to the European Communities Act 1972;

(a) 1964 c. 14.	(b) 1972 c. 68.
(c) S.I. 1964/1574 (1964 III, p. 3543).	(d) S.I. 1973/609 (1973 I, p. 1934).
(e) 1971 c. 62.	(f) 1889 c. 63.
(g) 1968 c. 34.	

"Common Catalogue" means, as the case may be, either the Common Catalogue of varieties of kinds of agricultural plants or the Common Catalogue of varieties of vegetables, published or to be published in the Official Journal of the European Communities;

"the gazette" means the Plant Varieties and Seeds Gazette published in accordance with section 34(1) of the Act;

"Member State" means a member of the European Communities other than the United Kingdom;

"the Ministers" means the Minister of Agriculture, Fisheries and Food, the Secretary of State for Scotland and the Secretary of State concerned with agriculture in Northern Ireland;

"National List" means a list of plant varieties prepared and published in accordance with Regulation 3 of these Regulations;

"plant breeders' rights" means rights which may be granted in accordance with Part I of the Act;

"plant variety" means any clone, line, hybrid or genetic variant;

"the Tribunal" means the Plant Varieties and Seeds Tribunal established by section 10 of and Schedule 4 to the Act as respectively amended by paragraph 5(5) of Schedule 4 to the European Communities Act 1972.

National Lists

3.—(1) The Ministers shall for the purposes of these Regulations prepare and publish in the gazette National Lists of the plant varieties (not being plant varieties which are intended for use only as hereditary sources of hybrid or synthetic plant varieties) of the kinds specified in Parts I and II of Schedule 1 to these Regulations.

(2) A plant variety may be entered in a National List when it is first published notwithstanding that the Ministers are not satisfied that it conforms with the requirements of Schedule 2 to these Regulations.

4.—(1) At any time after the publication of a National List the Ministers may—

(*a*) entertain applications from persons seeking additions to, corrections in or removals from any such list and, subject to the succeeding provisions of these Regulations and to the payment of any fee imposed by Regulations made under the Act, may grant or refuse such applications;

(*b*) in relation to plant varieties which have been entered in a list of a Member State corresponding to a National List, make such additions to the National List as appear to them to be desirable.

(2) If more than one application for the addition of the same plant variety to a National List is made the Ministers shall entertain the application which was the first to be made.

(3) The Ministers shall publish in the gazette any additions to, corrections in or removals from a National List.

5. The Ministers shall publish in the gazette in respect of each plant variety in relation to which there is an obligation to maintain such plant variety either the name and address of the person responsible for such maintenance or, where a number of persons are so responsible, an indication of the source from which their names and addresses may be obtained.

6. The Ministers may for the purposes of a National List establish or arrange for the establishment of a reference collection of plant material.

7. The Ministers shall conduct or make arrangements for such tests and trials of a plant variety which is the subject of an application for entry in a National List as appear to them to be necessary to establish that it conforms with the requirements of Schedule 2 to these Regulations.

Period of Entry in a National List

8.—(1) Subject to paragraph (2) of this Regulation and to Regulations 9 and 12 of these Regulations a plant variety entered in a National List shall, subject to the payment of any fee imposed by Regulations made under the Act, remain in that list until the end of the tenth calendar year following the calendar year in which it was so entered and at the end of that period it shall be removed from the list.

(2) Where a plant variety was entered in a National List when it was first published and the Ministers have not been satisfied that it conforms with the requirements of Schedule 2 to these Regulations the plant variety shall, unless it has previously been removed and subject to the payment of any fee imposed by Regulations made under the Act, remain in that list until 30th June, 1980 and no longer.

Renewal of Period of Entry in a National List

9.—(1) The Ministers may, upon an application made not later than two years before the expiry of the period during which a plant variety may remain in a National List, whether such period is that for which the plant variety was first entered in the National List or is an extension of that period, and subject to the payment of any fee imposed by Regulations made under the Act, renew such period for a further period not exceeding ten years from the date when it would otherwise expire provided that they are satisfied that the scale of the cultivation in the United Kingdom of the plant variety is such as to justify such an extension and that the plant variety continues to conform with the requirements of Schedule 2 to these Regulations as regards its distinctness, uniformity and stability or, being a plant variety falling within Regulation 8(2) of these Regulations, conforms with the requirements of the said Schedule 2.

(2) The Ministers may extend the period during which a plant variety may remain in a National List until such time as a decision is made upon an application in accordance with paragraph (1) of this Regulation.

Refusal of Applications for Entry in a National List

10. The Ministers shall refuse an application for the entry of a plant variety in a National List if:—

(a) it appears to them that the plant variety does not conform with the requirements of Schedule 2 to these Regulations; or

(b) it appears to them that the cultivation in the United Kingdom of the plant variety is likely to affect adversely the health of any persons, animals or plants.

Naming of Plant Varieties in a National List

11.—(1) A plant variety shall be entered in a National List under a name submitted by the person applying for the entry of the plant variety in such list, which name shall if it is otherwise suitable be that, if any, under which the plant variety is already known, whether in connection with a grant of plant breeders' rights or by reason of the entry of the plant variety in the list of a Member State corresponding to a National List, and in any other case shall be a name appearing to the Ministers to be suitable.

(2) If the Ministers are not satisfied that a suitable name for the plant variety has been submitted they may refuse to enter the plant variety in a National List until a name appearing to them to be suitable has been submitted by the person making the application.

(3) A person applying for the entry of a plant variety in a National List may propose a name for the plant variety in substitution for one already submitted and a person responsible for the maintenance of the plant variety in accordance with Regulation 13 of these Regulations may, subject to the payment of any fee imposed by Regulations made under the Act, propose a name for the plant variety in substitution for that under which the plant variety is already entered in the National List and the Ministers, if they consider that it is desirable that the proposal should be given effect, may substitute it for the name already submitted or entered.

Removal of a Plant Variety from a National List

12.—(1) The Ministers shall at any time remove a plant variety from a National List:—

(a) if it appears to them that the plant variety does not conform with the requirements of Schedule 2 to these Regulations as regards its distinctness, uniformity and stability, to the extent that such matters were taken into account when the plant variety was first entered in the National List or that the plant variety being a plant variety falling within Regulation 8(2) of these Regulations, does not conform with the requirements of the said Schedule as regards its value for cultivation and use;

(b) upon the application of the person responsible for the maintenance of the plant variety in accordance with Regulation 13 of these Regulations where no other person is able and willing to assume such responsibility; or

(c) if a fee payable in respect of the addition to or retention of a plant variety in a National List, imposed by Regulations made under the Act, shall not have been paid as required by such Regulations.

(2) The Ministers may at any time remove a plant variety from a National List if:—

(a) it appears to them that false information was given to them before the plant variety was entered in the National List being information which was material to the decision to enter the plant variety in such List;

(b) it appears to them that the person responsible for the maintenance of the plant variety in accordance with Regulation 13 of these Regulations has failed to comply in a material respect with the requirements of these Regulations or the terms of the undertaking given by him in pursuance of Regulation 13(1) of these Regulations;

(c) it appears to them that the scale of cultivation of the plant variety is such that the retention of the plant variety in the National List would be unreasonable, due regard being had, *inter alia*, to the length of time during which the plant variety has been entered in the National List; or

(d) it appears to them that the cultivation in the United Kingdom of the plant variety is likely to affect adversely the health of any persons, animals or plants.

(3) The Ministers may at any time remove the name of a plant variety from a National List if the plant variety is also entered in that List under another name.

(4) The Ministers may, if it appears to them to be necessary or desirable to do so, allow a period of not more than three years following the removal of a plant variety from a National List during which seed of that variety, being seed which was in the course of being produced or which was produced before the date of such removal, may be marketed in such a manner as would have been lawful had the plant variety remained in the National List during such period.

Maintenance of Plant Varieties in a National List

13.—(1) In respect of each plant variety which is entered in a National List a person (in this Regulation referred to as "the maintainer") shall be indicated therein as responsible for the maintenance of the plant variety and a plant variety shall not be entered in a National List unless the breeder of the plant variety or a person appointed or approved by him has agreed to be so indicated and has undertaken to maintain the plant variety in accordance with the morphological, physiological and other characteristics to which regard was had when the plant variety was so entered: Provided that the provisions of this paragraph shall not apply to a vegetable variety whose existence was a matter of common knowledge on 1st January, 1973 and of which the seed may be controlled only as standard seed in accordance with Regulations made under the Act.

(2) The maintainer may maintain the plant variety either in the United Kingdom or in a Member State or, in a case where the Ministers or the Council of the European Communities are satisfied that official examinations and inspections of the maintenance procedures are adequate, elsewhere and such person shall give to the Ministers an address in the United Kingdom as that at which any notices or other documents may be delivered to or served on him.

(3) The maintainer shall keep records of all the generations in his maintenance of the plant variety and shall on demand produce such records for inspection by or on behalf of the Ministers and shall also, if so required at any time, deliver to the Ministers samples of seed of the plant variety.

(4) The maintainer shall, when required to do so, afford to an officer authorised by one of the Ministers facilities for the inspection or examination of plants, plant material, trial grounds or other land or premises and permit him to take a sample of the seed of the plant variety which is in the possession or under the control of the maintainer.

(5) If in relation to a plant variety a maintainer is one of two or more maintainers and fails to comply in a material respect with the requirements of these Regulations or the terms of the undertaking given by him in pursuance of paragraph (1) of this Regulation the Ministers may remove his name from the record referred to in Regulation 33 of these Regulations and thereafter the rights of the said maintainer in relation to the maintenance of the plant variety shall cease and no further obligations in relation thereto shall be incurred by him.

Applications

14. An application made in pursuance of these Regulations shall be made in writing on a form supplied by the Ministers.

15. Where any document submitted in support of an application is in a language other than the English language it shall, unless the Ministers otherwise direct, be accompanied by a complete and adequate translation thereof into the English language.

16. The application and any documents submitted in support thereof shall be delivered or sent by post in a properly addressed pre-paid letter to the Ministry of Agriculture, Fisheries and Food.

17. Where an application is made by a person who does not reside in the United Kingdom he shall, on making the application, give to the Ministers an address in the United Kingdom as that at which any notices or other documents may be delivered to or served upon him.

18. Any application, notice or other document, given, delivered to or served upon the Ministers in accordance with these Regulations may be signed, and all attendances upon the Ministers may be made, by an agent in the United Kingdom appointed so to act by an authorisation in writing which shall have been delivered to the Ministers.

19. Any document required or authorised by these Regulations to be delivered to or served upon any person other than the Ministers may be delivered or served by being delivered to him personally or left at or sent by post to his last known address in the United Kingdom, at or to that of his agent or at or to the address referred to in Regulation 17 of these Regulations.

20.—(1) Any person making an application for the entry of a plant variety on a National List or for the renewal of such an entry shall—

 (*a*) give to the Ministers such information and produce and deliver to them such documents, records and illustrations as they may from time to time require, and

 (*b*) deliver to the Ministers such reproductive and other material of the plant variety and, in the case of a hybrid or synthetic plant variety, of any of its hereditary sources, in the quantity and of the description and quality, and packed and in such condition, as they may from time to time require and such further reproductive and other material of the plant variety or hereditary source, as the case may be, in the quantity and of the description and quality, and packed and in such condition, as they may require to replace any material already delivered as may have been damaged in transit or damaged or lost in the course of tests and trials or which is, or has in the course of tests or trials been shown to be, unhealthy or otherwise unsuitable,

being information, documents, records, illustrations and material relevant to the application and in the possession, control or power of the person making the application.

(2) Anything required to be given, produced or delivered in accordance with paragraph (1) of this Regulation shall be given, produced or delivered to the Ministers at such place as they shall require within 14 days of the requirement,

which shall be made by the Ministers in writing, or within such longer time as the Ministers may allow and if it is not so given, produced or delivered, the Ministers shall not be obliged to take any further steps in relation to the application until the said requirement has been complied with.

Representations and Hearings

21.—(1) The Ministers shall, before taking a decision—

(*a*) upon an application for the addition of a plant variety to a National List in accordance with Regulation 4 of these Regulations or for the renewal of the period during which a plant variety may remain in a National List in accordance with Regulation 9(1) of these Regulations,

(*b*) to remove a plant variety from a National List in accordance with Regulation 12(1)(*a*) or (*b*) or Regulation 12(2) of these Regulations,

(*c*) to remove from the record referred to in Regulation 33 of these Regulations, in accordance with Regulation 13(5) of these Regulations, the name of a person responsible for the maintenance of a plant variety, or

(*d*) to enter in a National List, in accordance with Regulation 4(1)(*b*) of these Regulations, a plant variety which has been entered in a list of a Member State corresponding to a National List,

give notice of their proposed decision to, as the case may be, the applicant, the person responsible for the maintenance of the plant variety and such other persons as appear to the Ministers to have a substantial interest in the decision, including persons or organisations appearing to the Ministers to be representative of classes of persons likely to be affected by the decision, and shall afford to each of such persons or organisations, subject to the payment of any fee imposed by Regulations made under the Act, an opportunity of making representations to them in writing or of being heard by a person appointed by them for the purpose or of both making such representations and being so heard.

(2) The Ministers may afford to any or to all of the persons or organisations entitled to make representations in accordance with paragraph (1) of this Regulation an opportunity to make representations to them on more than one occasion if in the circumstances it appears to them to be necessary or desirable to do so.

22. The Ministers shall publish in the gazette a notice indicating the nature of the matter under consideration and of their proposed decision together with a statement of the descriptions of persons entitled to make representations and to be heard and of the manner in which and the time (not being less than 14 days) within which representations may be made to them in writing and an application made for an opportunity to be heard.

23. The Ministers shall give to the applicant or to the person responsible for the maintenance of the plant variety, as the case may be, and to the other persons or organisations referred to in Regulation 21(1) of these Regulations a notice informing them of their right to make representations, of the manner in which and the time (not being less than 14 days) within which representations may be made and of their right to be heard and of the manner in which and the time (not being less than 14 days) within which they may apply for an opportunity to be heard.

24. The Ministers shall serve on each of the persons or organisations entitled to make representations in accordance with Regulation 21(1) of these Regulations of whom they are aware, other than the party making the representations, a copy of any representations made in accordance with the said Regulation 21(1).

25. If no person or organisation within the time limited for the purpose has made any representations to the Ministers in writing or has applied to be heard the Ministers shall proceed to take their decision.

26. Any person or organisation making representations to the Ministers in writing shall with the representations, and any person or organisation applying to be heard shall not later than 7 days before the day appointed for the hearing, deliver to the Ministers two copies of any documents which such person or organisation proposes to rely upon, and the Ministers shall deliver copies thereof to each of the other persons or organisations who appear to them to be concerned in the matter.

27.—(1) If any person or organisation so entitled shall apply to be heard the Ministers shall, subject to the payment of any fee imposed by Regulations made under the Act, appoint a time and place in the United Kingdom at which that person or organisation and any other such persons or organisations so applying shall be heard.

(2) In appointing such time and place the Ministers shall have regard to the convenience of the parties and their witnesses, the situation of any land or premises to be viewed in connection with the matter and to the other circumstances of the case, including the wishes of and expense to the parties.

(3) The Ministers shall give to each of the parties at least 14 days notice of the time and place of the hearing.

(4) The hearing may be adjourned from time to time, and, if an adjournment is announced in the course of the hearing, no further notice thereof to the parties shall be required.

(5) Any of the parties may be represented at the hearing by a person chosen by him.

(6) Any of the parties attending the hearing may give evidence and he or his representative may call witnesses and produce documents and shall be given an opportunity of putting questions directly to any witness called at the hearing: Provided that except with the leave of the person conducting the hearing no document shall be produced unless copies thereof were delivered to the Ministers in accordance with Regulation 26 of these Regulations.

(7) The person conducting the hearing may require any witness to give his evidence on oath or affirmation and may for that purpose administer an oath or affirmation in due form.

(8) The hearing shall be in public unless the person conducting the hearing, after consultation with the parties or their representatives, otherwise directs.

28. Where any document or thing is to be delivered, served or given or any act is to be done within a time prescribed or required by or under these Regulations such time may, if in all the circumstances of the case they consider it reasonable to do so, be extended by the Ministers for such period and upon such terms, if any, as they think fit: Provided that this Regulation shall not have effect so as to permit an extension of the time for the making of an application in pursuance of Regulation 9(1) of these Regulations or to allow a period exceeding three years for the marketing of seed in accordance with Regulation 12(4) of these Regulations.

29.—(1) The Ministers shall not take their decision until they have considered, in addition to the submissions made and evidence adduced at the hearing, any representations made to them in writing.

(2) The Ministers shall give to each of the parties notice of their decision together with their reasons for it and also a sufficient indication of the time within which and manner in which an appeal may be brought.

Appeals

30.—(1) An appeal shall lie to the Tribunal against any decision of the Ministers relating to one of the matters referred to in Regulation 21 of these Regulations and may be brought, as the case may be, by the applicant, a person responsible for the maintenance of the plant variety, or by any person who or organisation which made representations in writing to the Ministers in accordance with Regulation 21 of these Regulations or who or which attended or was represented at a hearing conducted by a person appointed by the Ministers.

(2) The hearing of an appeal by the Tribunal shall take place in such part of the United Kingdom as shall be determined by the Chairman of the Tribunal appointed by the Lord Chancellor who shall have regard to the matters referred to in Regulation 27(2) of these Regulations as well as to the convenience of the members of the Tribunal.

(3) Where an appeal is brought against any decision of the Ministers the operation of the decision shall be suspended pending the final determination of the appeal except in a case where the appeal is from a decision to renew the period during which a plant variety may remain in a National List and in a case where the appeal is from a decision to refuse to renew such a period any extension of the period granted in accordance with Regulation 9(2) of these Regulations shall continue until the final determination of the appeal.

(4) The Ministers shall publish in the gazette a notice of the proposed appeal, of any suspension of the operation of their decision and of any withdrawal of the appeal, as the case may be.

(5) The Ministers shall take such steps as may be necessary to give effect to any decision given on the final determination of the appeal.

Dealings in Seeds of Plant Varieties

31.—(1) No person shall offer or expose for sale or sell seed of a plant variety (not being a plant variety which is intended for use only as one of the hereditary sources of a hybrid or synthetic plant variety) of a kind specified in Part I or Part II of Schedule 1 to these Regulations unless the plant variety:

    (*a*) is entered in a National List, or

    (*b*) is entered in a Common Catalogue, or

(c) is entered in a list of a member State corresponding to a National List of plant varieties of the kinds specified in Part I of Schedule 1 to these Regulations and two complete calendar years following the calendar year in which the plant variety was so entered have expired: Provided that the marketing in the United Kingdom of seed of the plant variety has not been prohibited by the Ministers and that no proposal to prohibit such marketing, made before the expiration of the two complete calendar years referred to above, is under consideration.

(2) No person shall advertise, offer or expose for sale or sell seed of a plant variety of a kind specified in Part I or Part II of Schedule 1 to these Regulations which is entered in a National List or in a Common Catalogue except under the name given in the National List or the Common Catalogue for that variety.

(3) For the purposes of this Regulation "sale" includes any transaction effected in the course of business—

(a) under which the property in the seed passes from one person to another, or

(b) under which the seed is made over by one person to another in pursuance of a contract under which he will use the seeds for growing further seed,

and paragraph (b) of this paragraph shall apply irrespective of whether the contract provides that the property in the crop will be in the person to be regarded as the seller, or the person to be regarded as the purchaser, or a third party; and any reference to "sell" shall be construed accordingly.

(4) Paragraphs (1) and (2) of this Regulation shall not apply where the seed is or is intended to be delivered in pursuance of the sale or proposed sale elsewhere than in the United Kingdom or a Member State.

(5) For the purposes of paragraphs (1) and (2) of this Regulation the entry of a plant variety in a Common Catalogue shall be disregarded if the Common Catalogue provides that seed of that variety may not be marketed in the United Kingdom.

(6) Where a person makes arrangements under which some other person uses seed under the control of the first-mentioned person, for the purpose of increasing the first-mentioned person's stock or of carrying out tests or trials and under which the whole of the material produced, directly or indirectly, from the seed, and any unused seed, becomes or remains the property of the first-mentioned person paragraphs (1) and (2) of this Regulation shall not apply to a sale or an offer for sale of the seed by the first-mentioned person to the other person as part of the arrangements or to a sale by that other person to the first-mentioned person of seed produced, directly or indirectly, from that seed.

(7) Paragraphs (1) and (2) of this Regulation shall not apply to a sale or an offer for sale of seed which is undergoing a process of selection or which is to be used for experiment or research or for a purpose which does not involve the reproduction of the seed.

(8) Paragraphs (1) and (2) of this Regulation shall not apply to a sale or an offer for sale of seed to a person purchasing it with a view to cleaning it.

Publication of Notices

32.—(1) The Ministers shall publish in the gazette, in addition to the matters which they are so required to publish in accordance with the preceding provisions of these Regulations, notices of the following matters—

(*a*) any applications made in accordance with these Regulations;

(*b*) any decision made by the Ministers in relation to such an application;

(*c*) the entry of a plant variety in the Common Catalogue where the Common Catalogue does not provide that seed of that variety may not be marketed in the United Kingdom;

(*d*) the fact that in respect of a specified plant variety the requirements of paragraph 1(*c*) of Regulation 31 of these Regulations have been fulfilled;

(*e*) any decision made by the Ministers to remove a plant variety from a National List; and

(*f*) any decision made by the Tribunal consequent upon an appeal made in pursuance of these Regulations.

(2) It shall be no defence in civil or criminal proceedings to show that at any time a person did not know of an entry in a National List or a Common Catalogue or did not know that a National List or a Common Catalogue had come into force or did not know of a fact of a kind mentioned in paragraph (1)(*d*) of this Regulation, if before that time notice of that entry or fact had been published in the gazette.

National List Record

33.—(1) The Ministers shall keep in respect of each of the plant varieties entered in a National List a record of—

(*a*) the name of the plant variety and any other name under which the plant variety is marketed in another country;

(*b*) the kind to which the plant variety belongs;

(*c*) an indication of the morphological, physiological and other characteristics of the plant variety including (except in the case of vegetables and of grasses where the person responsible for the maintenance of the plant variety has declared that seeds of the plant variety are not intended for use as forage crops) those determining its value for cultivation and use;

(*d*) the date of entry of the plant variety in the National List and the date of any renewal of such entry;

(*e*) the date of the expiry of such entry; and

(*f*) the name and address of the person responsible for the maintenance of the plant variety or, where a number of persons are so responsible, an indication of the source from which their names and addresses may be obtained.

(2) The record kept in accordance with paragraph (1) of this Regulation shall, subject to the payment of any fee prescribed by Regulations made under the Act, be available for inspection by any person.

Plant Variety Files

34.—(1) The Ministers shall maintain a file for each plant variety entered in a National List.

(2) The file shall include a description of the plant variety and a summary of the facts in reliance on which the plant variety was entered in the List.

(3) The file shall, subject to the payment of any fee prescribed by Regulations made under the Act, be available for inspection by any person who is able to satisfy the Ministers that his particular interest in the plant variety is such that its production to him is justified: Provided that in the case of a plant variety which is a hybrid or synthetic variety where knowledge of hereditary sources is necessary for an understanding of the plant variety, and the breeder has so requested, particulars of those sources shall not be disclosed to any other person except on a confidential basis to Member States and to the Commission of the European Communities.

In Witness whereof the Official Seal of the Minister of Agriculture, Fisheries and Food is hereunto affixed on 24th May 1973.

(L.S.)

Joseph Godber,
Minister of Agriculture, Fisheries and Food.

25th May 1973.

Gordon Campbell,
Secretary of State for Scotland.

31st May 1973.

W. S. I. Whitelaw,
Secretary of State for Northern Ireland.

Regulations 3 and 31

SCHEDULE 1

KINDS OF PLANT VARIETIES IN NATIONAL LISTS

PART I

Agricultural Crop Varieties

Plants conforming with the characteristics of cultivated plant varieties of the following kinds:

Cereals

Name	Common Name
Avena sativa L.	Oats
Hordeum distichum L.	2 row barley
Hordeum polystichum L.	6 row barley
Oryza sativa L.	Rice
Phalaris canariensis L.	Canary Grass
Secale cereale L.	Rye
Triticum aestivum L.	Wheat
Triticum durum L.	Durum wheat
Triticum spelta L.	Spelt
Zea mais L., except for	Maize (except for Sweetcorn and Popcorn)
Zea mais convar. *saccharata* (Koern.) and	
Zea mais convar. *microsperma* (Koern.)	

Potatoes

Solanum tuberosum L. *sens lat.*	Potatoes

Beet

Beta vulgaris L.	Sugar beet, fodder beet, mangels

Fodder Plants

(a) Grasses

Agrostis canina L. ssp. *canina* Hwd	Velvet bent
Agrostis gigantea Roth	Red top
Agrostis stolonifera L.	Creeping bent
Agrostis tenuis Sibth	Brown top
Alopecurus pratensis L.	Meadow foxtail
Arrhenatherum elatius (L.) J et c Presl	Tall oatgrass
Dactylis glomerata L.	Cocksfoot
Festuca arundinacea Schreb	Tall fescue
Festuca ovina L.	Sheep's fescue, Fine-leaved Sheep's fescue and Hard fescue
Festuca pratensis Huds.	Meadow fescue
Festuca rubra L.	Red fescue, Chewings fescue
Lolium multiflorum Lam.	Italian and Westerwolds ryegrass
Lolium perenne L.	Perennial ryegrass
Lolium X Hybridum Hausskn.	Hybrid ryegrass
Phleum pratense L.; *Phleum bertolonii* DC.	Timothy
Poa annua L.	Annual meadow-grass

Name	Common Name
(a) Grasses (contd.)	
Poa nemoralis L.	Wood meadow-grass
Poa palustris L.	Swamp meadow-grass
Poa pratensis L.	Smooth stalked meadow-grass
Poa trivialis L.	Rough stalked meadow-grass
Trisetum flavescens (L) Pal Beauv.	Yellow oatgrass
(b) Legumes	
Hedysarum coronarium L.	Sulla
Lotus corniculatus L.	Birdsfoot trefoil
Lupinus albus L.	White lupin
Lupinus angustifolius L.	Blue lupin
Lupinus luteus L.	Yellow lupin
Medicago lupulina L.	Yellow trefoil
Medicago sativa L.	Lucerne
Medicago varia Martyn	Lucerne
Onobrychis sativa Lam.	Sainfoin
Pisum arvense L.	Field peas
Trifolium alexandrinum L.	Berseem, Egyptian clover
Trifolium hybridium L.	Alsike clover
Trifolium incarnatum L.	Crimson clover
Trifolium pratense L.	Red clover
Trifolium repens L.	White clover
Trifolium resupinatum L.	Persian clover
Trigonella foenum-Graecum L.	Fenugreek
Vicia faba L. ssp faba var. equina Pers.	Horse beans
Vicia faba L. var. minor (Peterm.) Bull	Tick beans
Vicia pannonica Crantz	Hungarian vetch
Vicia sativa L.	Common vetch
Vicia villosa Roth	Hairy vetch
(c) Other fodder plants	
Brassica napus L. var. napobrassica Peterm	Swedes
Brassica oleracea L. convar. acephala (DC)	Fodder kale
Raphanus sativus L. ssp. oleifera (DC) Metzg.	Fodder radish

Oleaginous and fibrous plants

Name	Common Name
Arachis hypogaea L.	Groundnut, peanut
Brassica campestris L. ssp oleifera (Metzg.) Sinsk.	Oil rape
Brassica juncea L.	Brown mustard
Brassica napus L. ssp. oleifera (Metzg.) Sinsk.	Forage (Swede) Rape
Brassica nigra (L) W. Koch	Black mustard
Cannabis sativa L.	Hemp
Carum carvi L.	Caraway
Gossypium sp.	Cotton
Helianthus annuus L.	Sunflower
Linus usitatissimum L.	Flax, linseed
Papaver somniferum L.	Opium poppy
Sinapis alba L.	White mustard
Soia hispida L.	Soya bean

PART II

Vegetable Varieties

Plants conforming with the characteristics of cultivated plant varieties of the following kinds intended for agricultural or horticultural production but not for ornamental use:

Name	Common Name
Allium cepa L.	Onions
Allium porrum L.	Leeks
Anthriscus cerefolium (L.) Hoffm.	Chervils
Apium graveolens L.	Celery, Celeriac
Beta vulgaris L. var. *cycla* (L.) Ulrich	Leaf beet
Beta vulgaris L. var. *esculenta* L.	Red beet or beetroot
Brassica oleracea L. var. *acephala* DC. subvar. *laciniata* L.	Curly kale or borecole
Brassica oleracea L. convar. *botrytis* (L.) Alef var. *botrytis*	Cauliflowers
Brassica oleracea L. convar. *botrytis* (L.) Alef. var. *italica* Plenck	Sprouting Broccoli, Calabrese
Brassica oleracea L. var. *bullata* subvar. *gemmifera* DC	Brussels sprouts
Brassica oleracea L. var. *bullata* DC. et. var. *subauda* L.	Savoy Cabbage
Brassica oleracea L. var. *capitata* L.f. *alba* DC.	White Cabbage
Brassica oleracea L. var. *capitata* L.f. *rubra* (L.) Thell	Red Cabbage
Brassica oleracea L. var. *gongylodes* L.	Kohlrabi
Brassica rapa L. var. *rapa* (L.) Thell	Turnips
Capsicum annuum L.	Chili, Pepper, Capsicum
Cichorium endivia L.	Endives
Citrullus vulgaris L.	Water melons
Cucumis melo L.	Melons
Cucumis sativus L.	Cucumber, Gherkin
Cucurbita pepo L.	Marrows
Daucus carota L. ssp. *sativus* (Hoffm.) Hayek	Carrots
Lactuca sativa L.	Lettuce
Petroselinum hortense Hoffm.	Parsley
Phaseolus coccineus L.	Runner beans
Phaseolus vulgaris L.	French beans
Pisum sativum L. (excl. *P. arvense* L.)	Peas
Raphanus sativus L.	Radish
Solanum lycopersicum L. (*Lycopersicum esculentum* Mill.)	Tomatoes
Solanum melongena L.	Aubergine or Egg plant
Spinacia oleracea L.	Spinach
Valerianella locusta (L.) Betcke (*V. olitoria* Polt.)	Corn-salad, Lamb's Lettuce
Vicia faba major L.	Broad beans

Regulations 7, 8, 10 and 12　　　　SCHEDULE 2

REQUIREMENTS WITH WHICH A PLANT VARIETY IS TO COMPLY FOR ENTRY IN A NATIONAL LIST

Distinctness

1. The plant variety shall be clearly distinguishable, by one or more important morphological, physiological or other characteristics, from any other plant variety entered or submitted for entry in a National List or entered in the Common Catalogue.

Uniformity

2. The plant variety shall be such that the plants (derived from its seed) are, disregarding rare aberrations and taking into account the particular reproductive system of the plants, similar or identical as regards its essential characteristics.

Stability

3. The plant variety shall, after successive reproductions or at the end of each cycle of reproduction where the breeder has defined a particular cycle of reproduction, continue to exhibit its essential characteristics.

Value for Cultivation and Use

4. The qualities of the plant variety shall, in comparison with other plant varieties in a National List, constitute, either generally or as far as production in a specific area is concerned, a clear improvement either as regards crop farming or the use made of harvested crops or of products produced from those crops. The qualities of the plant variety shall for this purpose be taken as a whole and inferiority in respect of certain characteristics may be offset by other favourable characteristics.

Exceptions

5. Consideration of the plant variety in accordance with paragraph 4 of this Schedule shall not be undertaken in respect of—

(*a*) plant varieties of vegetables, and

(*b*) plant varieties of grasses not intended for use as forage crops.

EXPLANATORY NOTE

(*This Note is not part of the Regulations.*)

These Regulations are made under Part II of the Plant Varieties and Seeds Act 1964 as amended by the European Communities Act 1972. They require the Minister of Agriculture, Fisheries and Food and the Secretaries of State for Scotland and Northern Ireland jointly to prepare and publish National Lists of varieties of specified kinds of agricultural and vegetable crops.

The Regulations indicate the requirements to be met before a plant variety can be placed on a National List. They make provision for applications for additions to Lists and for the renewal of entries in Lists at 10-yearly intervals. A plant variety may be removed from a List if it no longer meets the necessary requirements, if no person is available to maintain it with its own characteristics or if a person who has undertaken so to maintain it fails to meet his obligations under the Regulations.

The Regulations provide for the making of written and oral representations by all interested parties before the Ministers make decisions concerning additions to or removals from National Lists and there is provision for appeals from the Ministers to the Plant Varieties and Seeds Tribunal.

It will be an offence to sell seed of a plant variety not entered in a National List or in a Common Catalogue published in the Official Journal of the European Communities. The use of the registered name will be obligatory.

STATUTORY INSTRUMENTS

1973 No. 997

CUSTOMS AND EXCISE

The Process (Temporary Importation) (Revocation) Regulations 1973

Made - - -		*31st May* 1973
Laid before Parliament		*8th June* 1973
Coming into Operation		*1st July* 1973

The Commissioners of Customs and Excise in exercise of the powers conferred on them by section 40 of the Customs and Excise Act 1952(a), and of all other powers enabling them in that behalf, hereby make the following Regulations:—

1. These Regulations may be cited as the Process (Temporary Importation) (Revocation) Regulations 1973 and shall come into operation on 1st July 1973.

2. The Interpretation Act 1889(b) shall apply for the interpretation of these Regulations as it applies for the interpretation of an Act of Parliament.

3. The Process (Temporary Importation) Regulations 1958(c) are hereby revoked.

31st May 1973.

H. F. Christopherson,
Commissioner of Customs and Excise.

King's Beam House,
Mark Lane,
London EC3R 7HE.

EXPLANATORY NOTE

(This Note is not part of the Regulations.)

These Regulations revoke the Process (Temporary Importation) Regulations 1958 which are no longer necessary as the relief from import duties and import charges under the Common Agricultural Policy on goods imported for process and re-exportation hitherto available under those Regulations, will, from 1st July 1973, be governed instead by section 7 of the Import Duties Act 1958 (c.6). This change is in pursuance of an obligation under EEC Directive 69/73 of 4th March 1969.

(a) 1952 c. 44.   (b) 1889 c. 63.   (c) S.I. 1958/1642 (1958 I, p. 811).

STATUTORY INSTRUMENTS

1973 No. 1000

CIVIL AVIATION

The Rules of the Air and Air Traffic Control (Fifth Amendment) Regulations 1973

Made -	-	-	-	*31st May* 1973
Coming into Operation				*21st June* 1973

The Secretary of State, in exercise of his powers under Article 61(1) of the Air Navigation Order 1972**(a)**, as amended **(b)**, and of all other powers enabling him in that behalf, hereby makes the following Regulations:

1. These Regulations may be cited as the Rules of the Air and Air Traffic Control (Fifth Amendment) Regulations 1973 and shall come into operation on 21st June 1973.

2. The Interpretation Act 1889**(c)** applies for the purpose of the interpretation of these Regulations as it applies for the purpose of the interpretation of an Act of Parliament.

3. The Schedule to the Rules of the Air and Air Traffic Control Regulations 1972**(d)**, as amended **(e)**, shall be further amended as follows:

(1) In Rule 24 for paragraph (*a*) there shall be substituted,

"*Outside controlled airspace*

(i) An aircraft flying outside controlled airspace above 3,000 feet above mean sea level shall remain at least one nautical mile horizontally and 1,000 feet vertically away from cloud and in a flight visibility of at least five nautical miles;

(ii) An aircraft, other than a helicopter, flying outside controlled airspace at or below 3,000 feet above mean sea level shall remain at least 1 nautical mile horizontally and 1,000 feet vertically away from cloud and in a flight visibility of at least three nautical miles:

Provided that this sub-paragraph shall be deemed to be complied with if the aircraft is flown at a speed which according to its air speed indicator is 140 knots or less and remains clear of cloud, in sight of the surface and in a flight visibility of at least 1 nautical mile;

(a) S.I. 1972/129 (1972 I, p. 366).   (b) There are no relevant amendments.
(c) 1889 c. 63.   (d) S.I. 1972/321 (1972 I, p. 1258).
(e) S.I. 1972/699 (1972 II, p. 2232).

(iii) a helicopter flying outside controlled airspace at or below 3,000 feet above mean sea level shall remain either clear of cloud and in sight of the surface, or at least 1 nautical mile horizontally and 1,000 feet vertically away from cloud and in a flight visibility of at least 3 nautical miles."

(2) For Rule 26 there shall be substituted,

"*Minimum Height*

Without prejudice to the provisions of Rule 5 of these Rules, in order to comply with the Instrument Flight Rules an aircraft shall not fly at a height of less than 1,000 feet above the highest obstacle within a distance of five nautical miles of the aircraft unless:

(a) the aircraft is flying on a route notified for the purposes of this Rule; or

(b) the aircraft has been otherwise authorised by the competent authority; or

(c) it is necessary for the aircraft to do so in order to take off or land; or

(d) the aircraft is flying at an altitude not exceeding 3,000 feet above mean sea level and remains clear of cloud and in sight of the surface."

(3) In sub-paragraph (a) of Rule 37(12) after "aircraft" where it first occurs there shall be inserted:

"which is equipped with radio capable of operating on the notified radio frequency";

(4) In sub-paragraph (b) of Rule 37(12) for "the aircraft" where it first occurs there shall be substituted:

"an aircraft which is equipped with radio capable of operating on the notified radio frequency";

(5) After sub-paragraph (b) of Rule 37(12) and before the proviso there shall be inserted:

"(c) an aircraft which is not equipped with radio capable of operating on the notified radio frequency shall not fly at less than 2,000 feet above the notified elevation of the aerodrome within five nautical miles of the notified aerodrome reference point unless it flies on a route notified for the purposes of this sub-paragraph and the commander of the aircraft, before so flying, obtains the permission of the air traffic control unit at the aerodrome."

(6) Sub-paragraph (ii) of the proviso to Rule 37(12) shall be deleted.

(7) In sub-paragraph (i) of Rule 37(14)(b) after "aircraft" where it first occurs there shall be inserted:

"which is equipped with radio capable of operating on the notified radio frequency".

(8) In sub-paragraph (ii) of Rule 37(14)(*b*) for "the aircraft" where it first occurs there shall be substituted:

"an aircraft which is equipped with radio capable of operating on the notified radio frequency".

(9) After sub-paragraph (ii) of Rule 37(14)(*b*) and before the proviso there shall be inserted:

"(iii) an aircraft which is not equipped with radio capable of operating on the notified radio frequency shall not fly within the relevant airspace unless it flies on a route notified for the purposes of this sub-paragraph and the commander of the aircraft, before so flying, obtains the permission of the air traffic control unit at the aerodrome".

(10) The proviso to Rule 37(14)(*b*) shall be deleted.

G. R. Sunderland,
An Assistant Secretary,
31st May 1973.   Department of Trade and Industry.

EXPLANATORY NOTE

(*This Note is not part of the Regulations.*)

These Regulations further amend the Schedule to the Rules of the Air and Air Traffic Control Regulations 1972, by amending the Visual Flight Rules in so far as they apply outside controlled airspace, the Instrument Flight Rules, applicable outside and within controlled airspace, and the special rules applicable to Prestwick and Edinburgh Airports.

STATUTORY INSTRUMENTS

1973 No. 1006

ROAD TRAFFIC

The Road Vehicles Lighting (Amendment) Regulations 1973

Made - - -	*4th June* 1973
Laid before Parliament	*8th June* 1973
Coming into Operation	*30th June* 1973

The Secretary of State for the Environment in exercise of the powers conferred on him by sections 40, 71, 73 and 78(2) of the Road Traffic Act 1972(a), and of all other enabling powers, and after consultation with representative organisations in accordance with the provisions of section 199(2) of that Act, hereby makes the following Regulations:—

1.—(1) These Regulations may be cited as the Road Vehicles Lighting (Amendment) Regulations 1973 and shall come into operation on 30th June 1973.

(2) The Interpretation Act 1889(b) shall apply for the interpretation of these Regulations as it applies for the interpretation of an Act of Parliament.

2. The Road Vehicles Lighting Regulations 1971(c) shall have effect as though:—

(*a*) in paragraph (2) of Regulation 14 there were inserted after sub-paragraph (*f*) the following sub-paragraph:—

"(*ff*) to a vehicle manufactured in Great Britain, the supply of which has been zero rated under Regulation 44 or 45 of the Value Added Tax (General) Regulations 1972(d); or";

(*b*) in paragraphs (5) and (7) of Regulation 25 each reference to "1st January 1973" were a reference to "1st August 1973" and each reference to "1st July 1973" were a reference to "1st January 1974";

(*c*) in paragraph (6)(*b*) of Regulation 25 there were inserted after the word "symbol" the words " "R-S1" or";

(*d*) in paragraph (1)(*a*) of Regulation 64:—

(i) in sub-paragraph (vii) for the words "Coast Life Saving Corps" there were substituted the words "Coastguard Auxiliary Service";

(ii) after sub-paragraph (viii) there were inserted the following sub-paragraphs—

"(ix) motor vehicles owned by the Secretary of State for Defence and used by the Royal Air Force Mountain Rescue Service for the purposes of rescue operations in connection with crashed aircraft or any other emergencies;

(**a**) 1972 c. 20. (**b**) 1889 c. 63.
(**c**) S.I. 1971/694 (1971 I, p. 1833). (**d**) S.I. 1972/1147 (1972 II, p. 3362).

(x) motor vehicles owned by the Royal National Lifeboat Institution and used for launching lifeboats; and";

(e) in paragraph (1) of Regulation 70:—

(i) for sub-paragraph (b) there were substituted the following sub-paragraph:—

"(b) every motor vehicle (except a motor vehicle to which sub-paragraph (a) of this paragraph applies) which was manu-factured before 1st August 1973 or first used before 1st Jan-uary 1974 shall be fitted with direction indicators in accord-ance with the provisions of Part III of Schedule 5,";

(ii) in sub-paragraph (c) the reference to "1st July 1973" were a refer-ence to "1st January 1974";

(f) in paragraph (2) of Regulation 71 the reference to "1st July 1973" were a reference to "1st January 1974";

(g) in paragraph (3) of Regulation 71 the reference to "1st January 1973" were a reference to "1st August 1973";

(h) in paragraph (5)(b) of Regulation 71 the words " "2a" or" were in-serted after the word "number";

(i) in paragraph (6) of Regulation 71 for the words from the beginning to the words "illumination and" (where they first occur) there were substituted the words:—

"Where a rear direction indicator fitted to a vehicle in accordance with paragraph (4) of this Regulation is capable of being operated on either of the two levels of illumination it shall";

and for the proviso there were substituted:—

"Provided that nothing in this paragraph shall apply to a rear direction indicator fitted to a trailer mentioned in Regulation 70(2)(b)(iii) or which is being drawn by a motor vehicle which is equipped with rear direction indicators not marked with the number "2b" above an approval mark.";

(j) in paragraph (7) of Regulation 71 the number " "2a"," were inserted after the words "said numbers "1",";

(k) in paragraph (1) of Regulation 75 the reference to "1st July 1973" were a reference to "1st January 1974";

(l) in paragraph (2) of Regulation 75:—

(i) in sub-paragraph (a) the reference to "1st January 1973" were a reference to "1st August 1973";

(ii) sub-paragraph (c) were omitted;

(m) in Schedule 6 for Part III there were substituted the following:—
"Conditions to be complied with by stop lamps fitted to motor veh-icles first used on or after 1st January 1974 and trailers manufactured on or after that date.

1. Every stop lamp fitted to a motor vehicle or to a trailer shall be marked with an approval mark and,—

(a) in the case of a stop lamp not combined with a rear lamp, the symbol "S1" or "S2" enclosed in a square above that mark, or

(b) in the case of a stop lamp combined with a rear lamp, the symbol "R-S1" or "R-S2" enclosed in a rectangle above such mark.

2. Where a stop lamp fitted to a motor vehicle or to a trailer is capable of being operated on either of two levels of illumination, it shall be wired in such a way that, when the obligatory front and obligatory rear lamps of the motor vehicle on which the stop lamp is fitted, or of the motor vehicle which is drawing the trailer on which the stop lamp is fitted, are switched off, the stop lamp when operated is lit at the higher level of illumination, and when the obligatory front and obligatory rear lamps of the motor vehicle are switched on, the stop lamp when operated is lit at the lower level of illumination, so, however, that the foregoing provisions shall not preclude each stop lamp and the obligatory front and obligatory rear lamps of the motor vehicle being wired in such a way that, when such obligatory lamps are switched on and any fog lamp on that motor vehicle is switched on, the stop lamp when operated is lit at the higher level of illumination, and when such obligatory lamps are switched on but no fog lamp is switched on, the stop lamp when operated is lit at the lower level of illumination:

Provided that nothing in this paragraph shall apply to a stop lamp on a trailer which is being drawn by a motor vehicle which is not required to be fitted with stop lamps or is equipped with stop lamps not marked with the symbol "S2" or "R-S2" enclosed in the square or rectangle above an approval mark.

3. Nothing in this Part of this Schedule shall be taken to authorise any person to apply an approval mark, the said symbol "S1", the said symbol "S2", the said symbol "R-S1" or the said symbol "R-S2" to any stop lamp in contravention of the Trade Descriptions Act 1968(a).

4. In this paragraph "approval mark" means a marking designated as an approval mark by Regulation 2(2) of the Motor Vehicles (Designation of Approval Marks) Regulations 1968(b).".

Signed by authority of the Secretary of State.

4th June 1973.

John Peyton,
Minister for Transport Industries,
Department of the Environment.

(a) 1968 c. 29.   (b) S.I. 1968/171 (1968 I, p. 403).

EXPLANATORY NOTE

(This Note is not part of the Regulations.)

These Regulations amend the Road Vehicles Lighting Regulations 1971. The principal changes are as follows. Vehicles manufactured in Great Britain which have been zero rated for VAT purposes as being vehicles intended for personal export are exempted from Part III of those Regulations (which contains provisions governing headlamps) (Regulation 2(*a*)). The requirements for certain markings on rear lamps (Regulation 2(*b*)), direction indicators (Regulation 2(*e*)—(*g*)) and stop lamps (Regulation 2(*k*) and (*l*)) have been postponed. Single level of illumination rear direction indicators and stop lamps are permitted to be used as an alternative to ones with dual levels of illumination (Regulation 2(*c*), (*h*), (*i*) and (*m*)). Certain vehicles used by the Royal Air Force Mountain Rescue Service and the Royal National Lifeboat Institution are permitted to be fitted with a blue flashing light (Regulation 2(*d*)).

STATUTORY INSTRUMENTS

1973 No. 1009

LAND REGISTRATION

The Land Registration Fee Order 1973

Made - - - -	*4th June* 1973
Coming into Operation	*2nd July* 1973

The Lord Chancellor, with the advice and assistance of the Rule Committee appointed in pursuance of section 144 of the Land Registration Act 1925(a) and with the concurrence of the Treasury, in exercise of the powers conferred on him by section 145 of that Act, hereby makes the following Order:—

1.—(1) This Order may be cited as the Land Registration Fee Order 1973 and shall come into operation on 2nd July 1973.

(2) The Interpretation Act 1889(b) shall apply to the interpretation of this Order as it applies to the interpretation of an Act of Parliament.

2. Paragraph 5 of the Land Registration Fee Order 1970(c) shall be amended as follows:—

(i) For Abatement 2 there shall be substituted the following:—

"Abatement 2. Where a charge by the transferee under a transfer for value of registered land is delivered with the application to register the transfer, no fee shall be payable for the registration of the charge."

(ii) At the end there shall be added the following Abatement:—

"Fees fixed by reference to value

Abatement 4. Every fee payable under scale 1, 2, 3 or 4 or under paragraph VI of the Schedule shall be reduced by 10%:

Provided that where such a reduction results in a fee which is not a multiple of 5 pence the fee payable shall be further reduced to the nearest lower multiple of 5 pence."

Dated 1st June 1973.

Hailsham of St. Marylebone, C.

We concur.
Dated 4th June 1973.

V. H. Goodhew,
Hugh Rossi,
Two of the Lords Commissioners
of Her Majesty's Treasury.

(a) 1925 c. 21.   (b) 1889 c. 63.   (c) S.I. 1970/557 (1970 I, p. 1779).

EXPLANATORY NOTE

(This Note is not part of the Order.)

This Order, which amends the Land Registration Fee Order 1970, abolishes the fee payable for the registration of a charge accompanying an application for a transfer of registered land and reduces *ad valorem* fees by 10%.

STATUTORY INSTRUMENTS

1973 No. 1012

FOOD AND DRUGS

The Butter Subsidy Regulations 1973

Made - - -	*5th June* 1973
Laid before Parliament	*12th June* 1973
Coming into Operation	*1st July* 1973

The Secretary of State for Social Services and the Minister of Agriculture, Fisheries and Food, being Ministers designated (a) for the purposes of section 2(2) of the European Communities Act 1972(b) in relation to the Common Agricultural Policy of the European Economic Community, in exercise of the powers conferred on them by the said section 2(2), hereby make the following regulations: —

Citation, commencement and interpretation

1.—(1) These regulations may be cited as the Butter Subsidy Regulations 1973 and shall come into operation on 1st July 1973.

(2) In these regulations, unless the context otherwise requires, "butter token" means a token issued in accordance with these regulations or valid in Great Britain by virtue of regulation 3(5) below, and "supplier" means a person who sells butter.

(3) The Interpretation Act 1889(c) shall apply for the interpretation of these regulations as it applies for the interpretation of an Act of Parliament.

Persons entitled to butter tokens

2. Subject to the provisions of regulation 3 below, a person shall be entitled to butter tokens for any month during the period from 1st July 1973 to 31st December 1973 (inclusive of both dates) in which he is—

    (*a*) for the purposes of the Family Income Supplements Act 1970(d), a member of a family for which a family income supplement is paid under that Act; or

    (*b*) paid a supplementary pension or a supplementary allowance under the Ministry of Social Security Act 1966(e) and he is either—

        (i) a person whose pension or allowance is paid by means of an order which is one of a series of orders for the payment of sums on account of benefit, which is, or has been, contained in a book of such orders, or

---

(a) S.I. 1972/1811 (1972 III, p. 5216).   (b) 1972 c. 68.
(c) 1889 c. 63.   (d) 1970 c. 55.
(e) 1966 c. 20.

(ii) such other person as the Secretary of State may decide; or

(c) any other person whose requirements are taken into account in the calculation of the supplementary pension or supplementary allowance payable to a person mentioned in sub-paragraph (b) above.

Issue and validity of butter tokens

3.—(1) Where a person is entitled to butter tokens, the Secretary of State shall issue to, or in respect of, him 2 butter tokens for each month for which he is so entitled; and the Secretary of State may issue a butter token in advance where it appears to him appropriate to do so.

(2) Each butter token shall be valid for the purchase, in accordance with the provisions of these regulations, of one half pound of butter at a price 5 pence below the price at which it would otherwise have been sold.

(3) Butter tokens shall only be issued under paragraph (1) above on application for them being made by the person to whom the family income supplement, supplementary pension or supplementary allowance, as the case may be, is payable and any such application shall be made on a form provided for this purpose by the Secretary of State; but the Secretary of State may dispense with any or all of the requirements of this paragraph in such cases or classes of cases as he may decide.

(4) Each butter token shall be valid only for such period as may be stated on it.

(5) A token issued by a department of the Government of Northern Ireland for purposes corresponding to those of these regulations shall be valid in Great Britain as if it were a butter token issued by the Secretary of State under these regulations.

Use of butter tokens

4.—(1) Only the person to, or in respect of whom, a butter token is issued, or someone acting on his behalf, shall be entitled to use it.

(2) A person entitled to use a butter token shall not use it except by surrendering it to a supplier who sells him one half pound of butter at a price 5 pence below that at which he would have sold it but for his acceptance of the token.

Payment by Secretary of State to suppliers

5.—(1) Where a supplier has accepted a valid butter token in accordance with the provisions of regulation 4 above and has complied with the following provisions of this regulation he shall be entitled to payment by the Secretary of State of 5 pence in respect of that token.

(2) A supplier shall, in accordance with any general or special directions of the Secretary of State, submit to him any token which he has accepted under regulation 4 above.

Miscellaneous provisions relating to butter tokens

6.—(1) Every butter token shall remain the property of the Secretary of State.

(2) Any person ceasing to be entitled to a butter token, or who is in possession of a butter token on behalf of a person so ceasing, shall return it forthwith to an office of the Department of Health and Social Security.

(3) The Secretary of State may, in his discretion, replace any butter token which has been lost; and where the person to whom a replacement butter token has been issued subsequently finds the token which had been lost, he shall not be entitled to use it and shall deliver it forthwith to an office of the Department of Health and Social Security.

(4) Where a person entitled to butter tokens dies, any person who has or obtains possession of any token issued in respect of the deceased shall deliver it forthwith to an office of the Department of Health and Social Security.

Recovery by Secretary of State in cases of misuse of butter tokens

7. Where a butter token is used whether fraudulently or otherwise, by a person not entitled to use it, the Secretary of State may recover the value of it from that person or from any other person who has dealt with the token contrary to the provisions of these regulations.

Keith Joseph,
Secretary of State for Social Services.

4th June 1973.

In witness whereof the official seal of the Minister of Agriculture, Fisheries and Food is hereunto affixed on 5th June 1973.

(L.S.)

Joseph Godber,
Minister of Agriculture, Fisheries and Food.

EXPLANATORY NOTE

(This Note is not part of the Regulations.)

These Regulations make the necessary arrangements to take advantage of the right conferred on Member States of the European Economic Community by Commission Decision of 29th December 1972(a) authorising the grant of a subsidy to allow certain persons to buy butter at a reduced price (the cost of the subsidy being recouped from Community funds).

(a) 73/10/EEC, O.J. No. L.40, as corrected by O.J. No. L.78 and as amended by 73/35/EEC, O.J. No. L.77.

The Regulations provide for the issue by the Secretary of State of butter tokens to enable certain persons to purchase 2 one-half pounds of butter a month at a price of 5 pence a half pound below that at which it would otherwise have been sold. The persons are those who at any time during the period 1st July to 31st December 1973 are in receipt of Family Income Supplement, Supplementary Benefit paid by order book and certain other persons in receipt of Supplementary Benefit, and in each case the dependants of such persons.

Provision is made for the Secretary of State to reimburse the seller for tokens which he accepts in accordance with the Regulations, and for incidental matters.

STATUTORY INSTRUMENTS

1973 No. 1013

SOCIAL SECURITY

The National Insurance (Assessment of Graduated Contributions) Regulations 1973

Made - - - -	*6th June* 1973
Laid before Parliament	*15th June* 1973
Coming into Operation	*5th July* 1973

The Secretary of State for Social Services(a), in exercise of powers conferred by sections 4(3), (4), (5), (6) and (7) and 106(2) of the National Insurance Act 1965(b) and section 8 of the National Insurance Act 1969(c) and of all other powers enabling him in that behalf, and for the purpose only of consolidating the regulations hereby revoked, hereby makes the following regulations:—

Citation, commencement and interpretation

1.—(1) These regulations, which may be cited as the National Insurance (Assessment of Graduated Contributions) Regulations 1973, shall come into operation on 5th July 1973.

(2) In these regulations, unless the context otherwise requires—

"the Act" means the National Insurance Act 1965;

"aggregation" means the aggregating and treating as a single payment, under section 4(3) of the Act, of two or more payments, and "aggregated" shall be construed accordingly;

"apportionment" means the apportioning and treating as two or more separate payments, under section 4(3) of the Act, of any single payment;

"cumulative emoluments" has the same meaning as in the Income Tax (Employments) Regulations 1973(d);

"the employer" means, in relation to any payment, the employer in the employment in which that payment is made or is payable;

"graduated contribution period" has the meaning assigned to it in paragraph (3) of this regulation;

"payment" means a payment on account of a person's remuneration in any employment, except any employment such that graduated contributions are not payable in respect of it, and includes any part of a payment which is calculated separately from the remainder thereof;

"regular payment" means any payment made, or falling under these regulations to be treated for the purpose of graduated contributions as made, at regular intervals;

and other expressions have the same meaning as in the Act.

(a) For transfer of functions from Minister of Pensions and National Insurance to (eventually) the Secretary of State, see Ministry of Social Security Act 1966 (c. 20) and S.I. 1968/1699 (1968 III, p. 4585).

(b) 1965 c. 51. (c) 1969 c. 44.

(d) S.I. 1973/334 (1973 I, p. 1147).

(3) "Graduated contribution period" in relation to any person means a period—

  (a) the length of which is—

    (i) in the case of a person any part of whose remuneration is paid in regular payments at intervals of a week or more, the length of the shortest interval at which any such part is paid or treated as paid; and

    (ii) in the case of any other person, one week; and

  (b) which is one of a succession of periods of the same length beginning in the case of the first such period in any income tax year on the first day of that year, and in the case of each subsequent period immediately upon the ending of the period which last precedes it:

Provided that in any income tax year the period, if any, between the end of the last graduated contribution period of normal length and the beginning of the next income tax year shall itself be treated as a graduated contribution period of normal length.

(4) References in these regulations to any enactment or regulations shall, except in so far as the context otherwise requires, be construed as including references to such enactment or regulations as amended or extended by or under any other enactment, order or regulations and as including references to any enactment or regulations thereby consolidated.

(5) The rules for the construction of Acts of Parliament contained in the Interpretation Act 1889(a) shall apply in relation to this instrument and in relation to the revocations effected by it as if this instrument and the regulations revoked by it and any regulations revoked by the regulations so revoked were Acts of Parliament, and as if each revocation were a repeal.

Equivalent amounts

2.—(1) The equivalent amounts for the purposes of section 4(1) of the Act (under which in respect of any payment exceeding £9 or the equivalent amount for remuneration not paid weekly, the graduated contributions are calculated on certain specified amounts, or on the equivalent amounts for remuneration not paid weekly) shall be determined in accordance with the provisions of this regulation.

(2) The respective equivalent amounts shall be—

  (a) where the graduated contribution period is a week, £9 and the amount, up to £9, by which the payment exceeds £9, and the amount, up to £30, by which the payment exceeds £18;

  (b) where the graduated contribution period is a multiple of a week, the amounts calculated by applying sub-paragraph (a) of this paragraph with the substitution for any reference to a sum specified in pounds of a reference to the corresponding multiple of that sum;

  (c) where the graduated contribution period is a month, £39 and the amount, up to £39, by which the payment exceeds £39, and the amount up to £130, by which the payment exceeds £78;

  (d) where the graduated contribution period is a multiple of a month, the amounts calculated by applying sub-paragraph (c) of this paragraph with the substitution for any reference to a sum specified in pounds of a reference to the corresponding multiple of that sum; and

---

(a) 1889 c. 63.

(*e*) in any other case, the amounts calculated by applying sub-paragraph (*a*) of this paragraph with the substitution for any reference to a sum specified in pounds of a reference to one-seventh of that sum multiplied by the number of days in the graduated contribution period in question.

Calculation of graduated contributions

3.—(1) Subject to the provisions of paragraph (3) of this regulation, where the graduated contribution period is a week or a month the graduated contributions payable by the employer and the employed person respectively, in respect of any payment of an amount shown in the first column of Part I or, as the case may be, Part II of the appropriate Schedule to these regulations, shall be the amount opposite thereto in the second column and, in respect of any payment of an amount not so shown, shall be the amount in the second column opposite to the next smaller amount, if any, which is so shown.

(2) Where the graduated contribution period is a multiple of a week or of a month, paragraph (1) of this regulation shall apply subject to the substitution for the references to the amounts in the respective columns of the said appropriate Schedule of references to the corresponding multiples of those amounts.

(3) Where, in the case of any payments to which the provisions of paragraph (1) or paragraph (2) of this regulation apply, it would, having regard to the means by which the net sums payable are to be calculated, be unduly difficult or inconvenient to calculate the graduated contributions payable in respect of those payments in accordance with those provisions, the amounts of those contributions may be calculated as if those provisions did not apply; and in any case in which the amount of any graduated contribution payable is not calculated in accordance with those provisions, whether by virtue of the foregoing provisions of this paragraph or because the graduated contribution period is not a week or a month or a multiple of either a week or a month, that amount shall be calculated to the nearest £0·01, any amount of £0·005 being disregarded:

Provided that 4·75 per cent., 4·35 per cent., 4·25 per cent., 3·85 per cent., 3·25 per cent., 2·75 per cent., 1·6 per cent., 1·1 per cent., 0·5 per cent., and 0·4 per cent. of any amount (other than the amount of the graduated contribution), or of any equivalent amount, referred to in section 4(1)(*c*) of the Act, as from time to time in force, or of the total of more than any one such amount or equivalent amount, may be calculated to the nearest £0·01, any amount of £0·005 being disregarded:

And provided that under paragraph (3) of this regulation no amount shall be payable which is in excess of the maximum weekly or, as the case might be, monthly amount specified in the second column of the appropriate Schedule, or, where the graduated contribution period is a multiple of a week or a month, of a sum equal to the same multiple of the said maximum amount.

(4) In this regulation "appropriate Schedule" means Schedule 1 to these regulations in the case of an employment which is not a non-participating employment and means Schedule 2 to these regulations in the case of an employment which is a non-participating employment.

Payments treated as made at regular intervals

4.—(1) If on any occasion a payment which would normally fall to be made at a regular interval is made otherwise than at that regular interval, it shall for the purpose of graduated contributions be treated, subject to the provisions of regulations 7 and 8, as if it were a payment made at that regular interval.

(2) Where payments are made at irregular intervals of the amounts due for regular intervals, the payments shall for the purpose of graduated contributions be treated, subject to the provisions of regulations 7 and 8, as if they were payments made at those regular intervals.

(3) Where payments are normally made at intervals which secure that one and only one payment is made in each of a succession of periods consisting of the same number of days, weeks or months, those payments shall for the purpose of graduated contributions be treated, subject to the provisions of regulations 7 and 8, as if they were payments made at the regular interval of one of those periods; and where the intervals for which payments are normally due are such as to secure that one and only one such interval ends in each of a succession of like periods, those intervals shall be treated as regular intervals of the length of those periods for the purpose of paragraph (2) of this regulation.

General provisions as to aggregation and apportionment

5.—(1) Where on one or more occasions the whole or any part of a person's remuneration is not paid weekly (whether or not it is treated for the purpose of graduated contributions as paid weekly), section 4(3) of the Act (determination of the graduated contributions payable in any income tax week by the aggregation of separate payments and the apportionment of single payments in certain cases) shall apply subject to the modifications prescribed in this regulation.

(2) In every case to which this regulation applies the said section 4(3) shall have effect as if for the references therein to "income tax week" and "week" there were substituted references to "graduated contribution period".

(3) Where a regular payment is made in a graduated contribution period other than that in which it would normally have fallen to be made, the said section 4(3) shall, subject to the provisions of this regulation, have effect as if that payment (together with any other payment which on that occasion is, and which normally falls to be, made on the same day as that regular payment) had been made in the graduated contribution period in which it would normally have fallen to be made:

Provided that where the graduated contribution period in which it is made and the graduated contribution period in which it would normally have fallen to be made are in different income tax years, the preceding provisions of this paragraph shall not apply and that regular payment shall not be aggregated with any payment other than one which on that occasion is, and which normally falls to be, made on the same day as that regular payment.

(4) For the purposes of paragraph (3) of this regulation—

    (a) if a payment is one of a series of regular payments and if the intervals at which payments of that series are made are such that the graduated contribution period in which that payment would normally have fallen to be made cannot be otherwise identified, that graduated contribution period shall be determined in the following manner, namely—

        (i) by ascertaining the graduated contribution period in which the first payment of that series in the same income tax year was made or, alternatively, in which the first payment of the corresponding series in that income tax year was made on account of the remuneration of other persons employed by the same employer on account of whose remuneration regular payments are normally made at the same intervals and on the same days; and

    (ii) by treating all other payments of that series made in the same income tax year as normally falling to be made in the respective graduated contribution periods in which they would have been made if they had in fact all been made at the regular interval at which under the provisions of regulation 4 they fall to be treated as made; and

  (b) in the application of sub-paragraph (a) of this paragraph—

    (i) for the purposes of head (i) thereof, where the said first payment comprised two or more parts being payments of that series separately calculated, the part attributable to the latest interval to which any such part related shall alone be treated as the first payment of that series; and

    (ii) for the purposes of head (ii) thereof, any payment (whether or not due to be made) which has been wholly omitted from a series shall be treated as if it had been made.

Aggregation of payments in separate employments under the same employer

6. Payments in any employment shall not be aggregated with payments in any other employment under the same employer if—

  (a) such aggregation is not reasonably practicable because—

    (i) any of the employments is of a casual nature, or

    (ii) the remuneration in the respective employments is calculated at different places; or

  (b) having regard to the arrangements which are or might reasonably be made for the calculation and payment of the remuneration in the respective employments, it is not reasonably practicable at or before the time of payment for any of the persons calculating or making the payments in any one such employment to have such information about the other employment or employments and the payments made or to be made therein as would be required for the calculation of the graduated contributions payable if the payments made in the respective employments fell to be aggregated.

Change of graduated contribution period

7.—(1) The provisions of this regulation apply where, by reason of a change in the shortest regular interval at which any part of a person's remuneration is paid or treated as paid (hereinafter referred to as "the shortest regular interval of payment"), that person's graduated contribution period in any employment or employments under the same employer is, or is in process of being, changed.

  (2) In this regulation—

  (a) the shortest regular interval of payment which has been, or is to be, discontinued is referred to as "the old interval" and the interval which has, or is to, become the shortest regular interval of payment is referred to as "the new interval"; and

  (b) the graduated contribution period determined according to the old interval is referred to as "the old period", that determined according to the new interval is referred to as "the new period", and whichever of those two periods is the longer is referred to as "the longer period".

  (3) During the first longer period, if any, in which payments are made at both the old and the new intervals, the provisions of these regulations shall apply subject to the following modifications, namely—

(a) the graduated contribution period shall be determined according to the interval of the first regular payment, being a payment at either the old or the new interval, made in that first longer period or, if the first such regular payment at the old interval and the first such regular payment at the new interval are made on the same day, according to the old or the new interval whichever is the longer;

(b) any payment made, or which but for this provision would be treated for the purpose of graduated contributions as made, at a regular interval shorter than the interval of the graduated contribution period determined in accordance with the provisions of sub-paragraph (a) of this paragraph, shall for the purpose aforesaid be treated as not being a regular payment;

(c) any interval between the beginning of the said first longer period and the beginning of the first graduated contribution period determined in accordance with the provisions of sub-paragraph (a) of this paragraph shall be combined with the interval, if any, between the end of the last complete old period and the beginning of the said first longer period, and the first-mentioned interval or, as the case may be, the intervals so combined shall be treated as a complete old period or a complete new period, whichever is the shorter; and

(d) any interval between the end of the last complete graduated contribution period determined in accordance with the provisions of sub-paragraph (a) of this paragraph and the end of the said first longer period shall, subject to the provisions of paragraph (4)(b) of this regulation, be treated as a complete graduated contribution period of the same length as that last complete one:

Provided that if in any case where the new period is the longer period it would, having regard to the means by which the net sums payable are to be calculated, be unduly difficult or inconvenient to give effect to the foregoing modifications, there shall be substituted therefor the following modifications, namely—

(i) the graduated contribution period shall be determined according to the new interval; and

(ii) any payment made, or which but for this provision would be treated for the purpose of graduated contributions as made, at the old interval shall for the purpose aforesaid be treated as not being a regular payment.

(4) After the end of the said first longer period, the provisions of these regulations shall apply subject to the following modifications, namely—

(a) any payment made, or which but for this provision would be treated for the purpose of graduated contributions as made, at the old interval, shall for the purpose aforesaid be treated as not being a regular payment; and

(b) any interval between the end of the said first longer period and the beginning of the next new period shall, if there was no such interval as is specified in paragraph (3)(d) of this regulation, be treated as a complete new period, and if there was any such interval shall be treated as if it formed part thereof.

Holiday payments

8.—(1) For the purposes only of regulation 5, where a payment in respect of a period of holiday of a week or more is made in any case in which the graduated contribution period is a week or a multiple of a week, such payment—

(a) if it is a regular payment may be treated as if the graduated contribution period in which it is made were that in which it would normally have fallen to be made; and

(b) if it is not a regular payment shall be treated as if it were a regular payment and as if the graduated contribution period in which it is made were that in which it would normally have fallen to be made.

(2) In determining the graduated contributions payable in respect of any payment treated in accordance with the provisions of paragraph (1) of this regulation (together with any payment required to be aggregated therewith), regulations 2 and 3 shall apply as if the graduated contribution period were—

(a) if the payment is required to be aggregated with any regular payment according to the interval of which the graduated contribution period is determined, the sum of the number of weeks in that graduated contribution period and the number of complete weeks in the said period of holiday; and

(b) in any other case, the number of complete weeks in the said period of holiday.

(3) In so far as a payment in respect of a period of holiday of a week or more (hereinafter called a "holiday payment"), not being a regular payment, replaces one or more regular payments which would normally have fallen to be made in respect of, or for work done on, any days occurring during that period, the provisions of regulations 4 and 5 and the foregoing paragraphs of this regulation shall apply as if that holiday payment were or, as the case may be, comprised the payment or payments so replaced.

Annual maximum

9. For the purposes of section 4(4) of the Act (by which where the graduated contributions paid by a person in respect of his remuneration from two or more employments in any income tax year exceed a prescribed amount the excess shall, for certain purposes, be treated as contributions of the wrong class paid in error and as not properly payable) the prescribed amount—

(a) in respect of any income tax year ending before 6th April 1963 shall, if the graduated contributions so paid in that year amount to £14 or more, be £13 10s.;

(b) in respect of any income tax year ending after 6th April 1963 and before 6th April 1966—

(i) in relation to a person who is employed in non-participating employment in each contribution week during that year, if it is a year in which only 52 such weeks commence and if the graduated contributions so paid in that year amount to £20 8s. 8d. or more, shall be £19 18s. 8d.; and

(ii) in any other case shall, if the graduated contributions so paid in that year amount to £20 16s. 4d. or more, be £20 6s. 4d.;

(c) in respect of the income tax year beginning on 6th April 1966 shall, if the graduated contributions so paid in that year amount to £23 12s. 7d. or more, be £23 2s. 7d.;

(d) in respect of any income tax year ending after 6th April 1967 and before 6th April 1969 shall, if the graduated contributions so paid in that year amount to £26 6s. 9d. or more, be £25 16s. 9d.;

(e) in respect of the income tax year ending on 5th April 1970 shall, if the graduated contributions so paid in that year amount to £33 11s. 7d. or more, be £33 1s. 7d.;

(f) in respect of the income tax year ending on 5th April 1971 shall, if the graduated contributions so paid in that year amount to £43·96 or more, be £43·46;

(g) in respect of the income tax year ending on 5th April 1972 shall, if the graduated contributions so paid in that year amount to £62·81 or more, be £62·31;

(h) in respect of the income tax year ending on 5th April 1973 shall, if the graduated contributions so paid in that year amount to £88·67 or more, be £88·17;

(i) in respect of any income tax year ending on or after 5th April 1974 shall, if the graduated contributions so paid in that year amount to £98·55 or more, be £98·05.

Remuneration to be disregarded

10.—(1) A sum deducted from any payment on account of a person's remuneration which is or would but for the deduction be made shall not be treated for the purpose of graduated contributions as paid on account of that person's remuneration unless—

(a) it is included in that person's cumulative emoluments, or

(b) it is a sum in respect of which relief from income tax is allowable by way of deduction from that person's emoluments.

(2) In so far as any payment on account of a person's remuneration comprises or represents, and does not exceed in amount, sums deducted from any previous payments on account of his remuneration (whether or not remuneration in an employment such that graduated contributions were payable in respect of it), that payment shall be treated for the purposes of section 4(5) of the Act (disregard of payments) as coming from sums comprised in a previous payment:

Provided that the provisions of this paragraph shall apply only in so far as—

(a) the payment comprising or representing the sums deducted is not included in that person's cumulative emoluments or comprises or represents sums specified in paragraph (1)(b) of this regulation; and

(b) those sums have not been comprised in or represented by any previous payment to or to the order or for the benefit of that person (whether or not a payment on account of remuneration in an employment such that graduated contributions were payable in respect of it).

(3) There shall be excluded from the computation of a person's remuneration any payment in so far as it is—

(a) a payment in respect of a period of holiday, where the sum paid is derived directly or indirectly from a fund to which more than one employer contributes and the management and control of which are not vested in those employers, or where the person making the payment is entitled to be reimbursed from such a fund;

(b) a payment of or in respect of a gratuity, where the payment is not made directly or indirectly by the employer and the sum paid does not comprise or represent sums previously paid to the employer;

(*c*) a payment made before it is due, where the sum paid is to be deducted from a subsequent regular payment made or treated as made at an interval not exceeding one week (including such a regular payment which but for any deduction would be made) and for the purpose of graduated contributions the sum so deducted will fall to be treated as paid;

(*d*) a payment made solely to adjust to a more convenient amount the sum paid on any occasion, and in so far as a compensating deduction has been or is to be made from a payment (whether or not a payment on account of remuneration in an employment such that graduated contributions are or were payable in respect of it) made on another occasion; or

(*e*) a payment made to or by trustees, where—

(i) in the case of a payment made to trustees, the share thereof which that person is entitled to have paid to him; or

(ii) in the case of a payment made by trustees, the amount to be so paid;

is or may be dependent upon the exercise by the trustees of a discretion or the performance by them of a duty arising under the trust, and where not more than two payments under the trust are ordinarily made by the trustees to any one person in any income tax year.

(4)(*a*) Subject to the provisions of sub-paragraph (*b*) of this paragraph, where by an arrangement approved by the Secretary of State for the purposes of this provision and made between an employed person and his employer the employed person draws pay unabated by any deduction as on account of a specified benefit for a period in respect of which under the arrangement he has undertaken not to claim such benefit, there shall, for the purposes of computing his and his employer's liability for graduated contributions under section 4 of the Act, be excluded from the computation of the employed person's remuneration in each graduated contribution period in which such deduction would have been made but for the arrangement a sum equal to the specified benefit which would have been payable if the employed person had claimed it and in respect of which such deduction would have been made.

(*b*) In this paragraph "specified benefit" means sickness benefit, invalidity benefit, maternity allowance or, as the case may be, under the National Insurance (Industrial Injuries) Act 1965**(a)**, injury benefit.

Abnormal pay practices

11.—(1) The provisions of this regulation shall not apply for the purpose of any decision of the Secretary of State in so far as that decision relates to contributions based on payments made more than one year before the beginning of the income tax year in which that decision is given.

(2) With a view to securing that liability for the payment of graduated contributions is not avoided or reduced by an employer's following in the payment of persons employed any practice which is abnormal for their employments (hereinafter referred to as an "abnormal pay practice"), the Secretary of State may, if he thinks fit, determine any question relating to a person's graduated contributions where any such practice has been or is being followed, as if the employer concerned had not followed any abnormal pay practice but had followed a practice or practices normal for the employment or employments in question.

(a) 1965 c. 52.

(3) With the view aforesaid the Secretary of State, in any case in which he has reason to believe that any abnormal pay practice has been or is being followed, may determine any such question, if he is satisfied that it ought properly to be so determined, as if application had been duly made to him for the determination thereof.

Revocation and transitional provisions

12.—(1) The regulations specified in column 1 of Schedule 3 to these regulations are hereby revoked to the extent mentioned in column 3 of that Schedule.

(2) Anything whatsoever done under or by virtue of any regulation revoked by these regulations shall be deemed to have been done under or by virtue of the corresponding provision of these regulations, and anything whatsoever begun under any such regulation may be continued under these regulations as if begun under these regulations.

(3) Nothing in paragraph (2) of this regulation shall be taken as affecting the general application by regulation 1(5) of these regulations of the rules for the construction of Acts of Parliament contained in section 38 of the Interpretation Act 1889 (effect of repeals) with regard to the effect of revocations.

Keith Joseph,
Secretary of State for Social Services.

6th June 1973.

Regulation 3   SCHEDULE 1

EMPLOYMENT WHICH IS NOT A NON-PARTICIPATING EMPLOYMENT

PART I

WEEKLY SCALE

Amount of payment	Amount of contribution
£	£
9·01	0·01
9·25	0·02
9·50	0·04
10·00	0·06
10·50	0·08
11·00	0·11
11·50	0·13
12·00	0·15
12·50	0·18
13·00	0·20
13·50	0·23
14·00	0·25
14·50	0·27
15·00	0·30
15·50	0·32
16·00	0·34
16·50	0·37
17·00	0·39
17·50	0·42
18·00	0·45
19·00	0·50
20·00	0·55
21·00	0·59
22·00	0·64
23·00	0·69
24·00	0·74
25·00	0·78
26·00	0·83
27·00	0·88
28·00	0·93
29·00	0·97
30·00	1·02
31·00	1·07
32·00	1·12
33·00	1·16
34·00	1·21
35·00	1·26
36·00	1·31
37·00	1·35
38·00	1·40

Amount of payment	Amount of contribution
£	£
39·00	1·45
40·00	1·50
41·00	1·54
42·00	1·59
43·00	1·64
44·00	1·69
45·00	1·73
46·00	1·78
47·00	1·83
48·00	1·85
or more	

PART II

MONTHLY SCALE

Amount of payment	Amount of contribution
£	£
39·02	0·02
40·00	0·09
42·00	0·19
44·00	0·28
46·00	0·38
48·00	0·47
50·00	0·57
52·00	0·66
54·00	0·76
56·00	0·85
58·00	0·95
60·00	1·04
62·00	1·14
64·00	1·23
66·00	1·33
68·00	1·42
70·00	1·52
72·00	1·61
74·00	1·71
76·00	1·80
78·00	1·95
82·00	2·14
86·00	2·33
90·00	2·52
94·00	2·71
98·00	2·90
102·00	3·09
106·00	3·28
110·00	3·47
114·00	3·66
118·00	3·85
122·00	4·04

Amount of payment	Amount of contribution
£	£
126·00	4·23
130·00	4·42
134·00	4·61
138·00	4·80
142·00	4·99
146·00	5·18
150·00	5·37
154·00	5·56
158·00	5·75
162·00	5·94
166·00	6·13
170·00	6·32
174·00	6·51
178·00	6·70
182·00	6·89
186·00	7·08
190·00	7·27
194·00	7·46
198·00	7·65
202·00	7·84
206·00	7·98
208·00 or more	8·03

Regulation 3

SCHEDULE 2

NON-PARTICIPATING EMPLOYMENT

PART I

WEEKLY SCALE

Amount of payment	Amount of contribution
£	£
9·01	0·01
12·00	0·02
15·00	0·04
18·00	0·07
19·00	0·12
20·00	0·16
21·00	0·21
22·00	0·26
23·00	0·31
24·00	0·35
25·00	0·40
26·00	0·45
27·00	0·50
28·00	0·54
29·00	0·59

Amount of payment	Amount of contribution
£	£
30·00	0·64
31·00	0·69
32·00	0·73
33·00	0·78
34·00	0·83
35·00	0·88
36·00	0·92
37·00	0·97
38·00	1·02
39·00	1·07
40·00	1·11
41·00	1·16
42·00	1·21
43·00	1·26
44·00	1·30
45·00	1·35
46·00	1·40
47·00	1·45
48·00	1·47
or more	

PART II

MONTHLY SCALE

Amount of payment	Amount of contribution
£	£
39·01	0·01
40·00	0·03
50·00	0·08
60·00	0·13
70·00	0·17
78·00	0·29
82·00	0·48
86·00	0·67
90·00	0·86
94·00	1·05
98·00	1·24
102·00	1·43
106·00	1·62
110·00	1·81
114·00	2·00
118·00	2·19
122·00	2·38
126·00	2·57

Amount of payment	Amount of contribution
£	£
130·00	2·76
134·00	2·95
138·00	3·14
142·00	3·33
146·00	3·52
150·00	3·71
154·00	3·90
158·00	4·09
162·00	4·28
166·00	4·47
170·00	4·66
174·00	4·85
178·00	5·04
182·00	5·23
186·00	5·42
190·00	5·61
194·00	5·80
198·00	5·99
202·00	6·18
206·00	6·32
208·00	6·37
or more	

Regulation 12 **SCHEDULE 3**

Column 1 Regulations revoked	Column 2 References	Column 3 Extent of revocations
The National Insurance (Assessment of Graduated Contributions) Regulations 1967.	S.I. 1967/844 (1967 II, p. 2513).	The whole regulations.
The National Insurance (Assessment of Graduated Contributions) Amendment Regulations 1969.	S.I. 1969/1133 (1969 II, p. 3363).	The whole regulations.
The Family Allowances, National Insurance, Industrial Injuries and Miscellaneous Provisions (Decimalisation of the Currency) Regulations 1970.	S.I. 1970/46 (1970 I, p. 243).	Regulation 17.
The National Insurance (Assessment of Graduated Contributions) Amendment Regulations 1971.	S.I. 1971/1202 (1971 II, p. 3522).	The whole regulations.

Column 1 Regulations revoked	Column 2 References	Column 3 Extent of revocations
The National Insurance (Assessment of Graduated Contributions) Amendment Regulations 1972.	S.I. 1972/235 (1972 I, p. 835).	The whole regulations.
The National Insurance (Assessment of Graduated Contributions) Amendment (No. 2) Regulations 1972.	S.I. 1972/1259 (1972 II, p.3771).	The whole regulations.
The National Insurance (Graduated Contributions) Amendment Regulations 1973.	S.I. 1973/548 (1973 I, p. 1754).	Regulation 2.

EXPLANATORY NOTE

(This Note is not part of the Regulations.)

These Regulations are made for the purpose only of consolidating the Regulations hereby revoked and accordingly by virtue of section 108(9)(*c*) of the National Insurance Act 1965, no reference of them has been made to the National Insurance Advisory Committee.

The Regulations consolidate the regulations relating to the assessment of graduated contributions hitherto in force for the purposes of the National Insurance Acts 1965 to 1972.

STATUTORY INSTRUMENTS

1973 No. 1014

CUSTOMS AND EXCISE

The Import Duties (Cyprus) (Reductions) (No. 2) Order 1973

Made - - -	*6th June* 1973
Laid before the House of Commons	*11th June* 1973
Coming into Operation	*1st July* 1973

The Lords Commissioners of Her Majesty's Treasury, by virtue of the powers conferred on them by sections 1, 3(6) and 13 of the Import Duties Act 1958(a), as amended by section 5(5) of, and paragraph 1 of Schedule 4 to, the European Communities Act 1972(b), and of all other powers enabling them in that behalf, on the recommendation of the Secretary of State(c), hereby make the following Order:

1.—(1) This Order may be cited as the Import Duties (Cyprus) (Reductions) (No. 2) Order 1973 and shall come into operation on 1st July 1973.

(2) The Interpretation Act 1889(d) shall apply for the interpretation of this Order as it applies for the interpretation of an Act of Parliament.

2.—(1) Up to and including 31st December 1973 any import duty which is for the time being chargeable on goods of any heading or subheading of the Customs Tariff 1959 specified in:

(a) Schedule 1 hereto, shall be chargeable at 80 per cent. of the full rate, and

(b) Schedule 2 hereto, shall be chargeable at the relevant rate there specified instead of the full rate

in the case of goods which are to be regarded under the Agreement, signed on 19th December 1972, between the European Economic Community and Cyprus as products originating in Cyprus.

(2) Paragraph (1) above shall operate without prejudice to any reduction in, or exemption or relief from, duties which may be available in the case of (a) goods qualifying for Commonwealth preference or (b) goods of developing countries.

3. For the purposes of classification under the Customs Tariff 1959, insofar as that depends on the rate of duty, any goods to which Article 2 above applies shall be treated as chargeable with the same duty as if this Order had not been made.

(a) 1958 c. 6.
(c) *See* S.I. 1970/1537 (1970 III, p. 5293).

(b) 1972 c. 68.
(d) 1889 c. 63.

V. H. Goodhew,

Oscar Murton,

Two of the Lords Commissioners

6th June 1973 of Her Majesty's Treasury.

SCHEDULE 1

HEADINGS AND SUBHEADINGS SUBJECT TO REDUCTION OF 20% IN DUTY
FROM 1st JULY 1973

05.07(A), (B)(I), (II), (IV); 05.08(C); 05.09; 05.14(B)
12.08(A)
13.01(D)
15.08; 15.14
19.03
25.19(A); 25.24
27.13(B)(I)(a)2, (b)2
32.01(B), (C)(II), (D)(II)
33.01(A)(3)(a)(i), (b)
41.02; 41.03(A)(2), (B); 41.04 to 41.08 (inclusive)
43.02
55.05(B); 55.06(B); 55.07 to 55.09 (inclusive)
57.06(B)(2); 57.07(B)(2); 57.10(B)
58.01(A)(2), (B)(3); 58.02(A), (B)(3); 58.05(B)
59.02(B)(2); 59.04(B)(3)
60.05(B)(2)
61.05(C); 61.06(C)
62.01(B); 62.02(B); 62.03(B)(2)(b); 62.05(B)
67.01
68.01(B)
79.01(A)
97.06(B), (C), (D); 97.07

SCHEDULE 2

SPECIFIC REDUCTIONS

Tariff Heading	*Rate of Import Duty*
32.01(A), (C)(I)	2·7%

EXPLANATORY NOTE

(This Note is not part of the Order.)

This Order, which comes into operation on 1st July 1973, implements obligations of the United Kingdom concerning import duties in 1973 under the Agreement between the European Economic Community and Cyprus.

Article 2 provides for the full rate of duty to be reduced up to and including 31st December 1973 by 20 per cent. in the case of goods listed in Schedule 1, on condition that they originate in Cyprus in terms of the Agreement. Different reduced rates apply in the case of goods listed in Schedule 2. (These are the second in a number of reductions in import duties which are to be made under the Agreement).

The Order does not affect preferences or reliefs in respect of import duties which may be available in the case of goods of Cyprus qualifying for Commonwealth preference or goods of developing countries.

STATUTORY INSTRUMENTS

1973 No. 1015

INDUSTRIAL TRAINING

The Industrial Training Levy (Electricity Supply) Order 1973

Made - - -		*5th June* 1973
Laid before Parliament		*14th June* 1973
Coming into Operation		*11th July* 1973

The Secretary of State after approving proposals submitted by the Electricity Supply Industry Training Board for the imposition of a further levy on employers in the electricity supply industry and in exercise of powers conferred by section 4 of the Industrial Training Act 1964(a) and now vested in him(b), and of all other powers enabling him in that behalf hereby makes the following Order:—

Title and commencement

1. This Order may be cited as the Industrial Training Levy (Electricity Supply) Order 1973 and shall come into operation on 11th July 1973.

Interpretation

2.—(1) In this Order unless the context otherwise requires:—

(*a*) "activities of the electricity supply industry" means any activities (not being in agriculture) which, subject to the provisions of paragraph 2 of Schedule 1 to the industrial training order, are specified in paragraph 1 of that Schedule as activities of the electricity supply industry;

(*b*) "agriculture" has the same meaning as in section 109(3) of the Agriculture Act 1947(c) or, in relation to Scotland, as in section 86(3) of the Agriculture (Scotland) Act 1948(d);

(*c*) "an appeal tribunal" means an industrial tribunal established under section 12 of the Industrial Training Act 1964;

(*d*) "assessment" means an assessment of an employer to the levy;

(*e*) "the eighth base period" means the period of twelve months that commenced on 1st April 1971;

(*f*) "the eighth levy period" means the period commencing with the day on which this Order comes into operation and ending on 31st March 1974;

(*g*) "emoluments" means all emoluments assessable to income tax under Schedule E (other than pensions), being emoluments from which tax under that Schedule is deductible, whether or not tax in fact falls to be deducted from any particular payment thereof;

(a) 1964 c. 16.
(c) 1947 c. 48.

(b) S.I. 1968/729 (1968 II, p. 2108).
(d) 1948 c. 45.

(*h*) "employer" means any of the following employers in the electricity supply industry, that is to say—

  (i) the Electricity Council;

  (ii) the Central Electricity Generating Board;

  (iii) an Area Electricity Board;

  (iv) the North of Scotland Hydro-Electric Board;

  (v) the South of Scotland Electricity Board;

  (vi) the London Transport Executive;

(*i*) "the Industrial Training Board" means the Electricity Supply Industry Training Board;

(*j*) "the industrial training order" means the Industrial Training (Electricity Supply Board) Order 1965(**a**);

(*k*) "the levy" means the levy imposed by the Industrial Training Board in respect of the eighth levy period;

(*l*) "notice" means a notice in writing.

(2) The Interpretation Act 1889(**b**) shall apply to the interpretation of this Order as it applies to the interpretation of an Act of Parliament.

Imposition of the levy

3.—(1) The levy to be imposed by the Industrial Training Board on employers in respect of the eighth levy period shall be assessed in accordance with the provisions of this Article.

(2) The levy shall be assessed by the Industrial Training Board in respect of each employer.

(3) The amount of the levy imposed on an employer shall be a sum equal to 0·03 per cent. of the emoluments of all persons employed by the employer in activities of the electricity supply industry in the eighth base period, the said sum being rounded down to the nearest £1.

(4) In the event of the industrial training order being revoked under section 9 of the Industrial Training Act 1964 at any time during the eighth levy period, the amount of the levy imposed on an employer shall be in the same proportion to the amount that would otherwise be due under paragraph (3) of this Article as the number of days between the commencement of the said levy period and the date of revocation (both dates inclusive) bears to the number of days in the said levy period.

Assessment notices

4.—(1) The Industrial Training Board shall serve an assessment notice on every employer.

(2) An assessment notice shall state the Industrial Training Board's address for the service of a notice of appeal or of an application for an extension of time for appealing.

(3) An assessment notice may be served on an employer by sending it by post to the employer's principal office.

  (**a**) S.I. 1965/1256 (1965 II, p. 3548).   (**b**) 1889 c. 63.

Payment of the levy

5.—(1) Subject to the provisions of this Article and of Articles 3, 6 and 7, the amount of an assessment appearing in an assessment notice served by the Industrial Training Board shall be payable by the employer to the Board in two equal instalments, and the said instalments shall be due respectively one month and four months after the date of the notice.

(2) An instalment of an assessment shall not be recoverable by the Industrial Training Board until there has expired the time allowed for appealing against the assessment by Article 7(1) of this Order and any further period or periods of time that the Industrial Training Board or an appeal tribunal may have allowed for appealing under paragraph (2) or (3) of that Article or, where an appeal is brought, until the appeal is decided or withdrawn.

Withdrawal of assessment

6.—(1) The Industrial Training Board may, by a notice served on the employer in the same manner as an assessment notice, withdraw an assessment if the employer has appeal against that assessment under the provisions of Article 7 of this Order and the appeal has not been entered in the Register of Appeals kept under the appropriate Regulations specified in paragraph (4) of that Article.

(2) The withdrawal of an assessment shall be without prejudice to the power of the Board to serve a further assessment notice on the employer.

Appeals

7.—(1) An employer assessed to the levy may appeal to an appeal tribunal against the assessment within one month from the date of the service of the assessment notice or within any further period or periods of time that may be allowed by the Industrial Training Board or an appeal tribunal under the following provisions of this Article.

(2) The Industrial Training Board by notice may for good cause allow an employer assessed to the levy to appeal to an appeal tribunal against the assessment at any time within the period of four months from the date of the service of the assessment notice or within such further period or periods as the said Board may allow before such time as may then be limited for appealing has expired.

(3) If the Industrial Training Board shall not allow an application for extension of time for appealing, an appeal tribunal shall upon application made to the tribunal by the employer assessed to the levy have the like powers as the said Board under the last foregoing paragraph.

(4) An appeal or an application to an appeal tribunal under this Article shall be made in accordance with the Industrial Tribunals (England and Wales) Regulations 1965(**a**) as amended by the Industrial Tribunals (England and Wales) (Amendment) Regulations 1967(**b**), except where the employer is the North of Scotland Hydro-Electric Board or the South of Scotland Electricity Board in which case the appeal or application shall be made in accordance with the Industrial Tribunals (Scotland) Regulations 1965(**c**) as amended by the Industrial Tribunals (Scotland) (Amendment) Regulations 1967(**d**).

(**a**) S.I. 1965/1101 (1965 II, p. 2805). (**b**) S.I. 1967/301 (1967 I, p. 1040).
(**c**) S.I. 1965/1157 (1965 II, p. 3266). (**d**) S.I. 1967/302 (1967 I, p. 1050).

(5) The powers of an appeal tribunal under paragraph (3) of this Article may be exercised by the President of the Industrial Tribunals (England and Wales) or by the President of the Industrial Tribunals (Scotland) as the case may be.

Evidence

8.—(1) Upon the discharge of an employer's liability under an assessment the Industrial Training Board shall if so requested issue to the employer a certificate to that effect.

(2) The production in any proceedings of a document purporting to be certified by the Secretary of the Industrial Training Board to be a true copy of an assessment or other notice issued by the Board or purporting to be a certificate such as is mentioned in the foregoing paragraph of this Article shall, unless the contrary is proved, be sufficient evidence of the document and of the facts stated therein.

Signed by order of the Secretary of State.
5th June 1973.

Dudley Smith,
Parliamentary Under Secretary of State,
Department of Employment.

EXPLANATORY NOTE

(*This Note is not part of the Order.*)

This Order gives effect to proposals submitted by the Electricity Supply Industry Training Board to the Secretary of State for Employment for the imposition of a further levy on employers in the electricity supply industry for the purpose of raising money towards the expenses of the Board.

The levy is to be imposed in respect of the eighth levy period commencing with the day on which this Order comes into operation and ending on 31st March 1974. The levy will be assessed by the industrial training board and there will be a right of appeal against an assessment to an industrial tribunal.

STATUTORY INSTRUMENTS

1973 No. 1016

WAGES COUNCILS

The Wages Regulation (Sack and Bag) Order 1973

Made	-	-	-	5th June 1973
Coming into Operation				28th June 1973

Whereas the Secretary of State has received from the Sack and Bag Wages Council (Great Britain) the wages regulation proposals set out in the Schedule hereto;

Now, therefore, the Secretary of State in exercise of powers conferred by section 11 of the Wages Councils Act 1959(a), as modified by Article 2 of the Counter-Inflation (Modification of Wages Councils Act 1959) Order 1973(b), and now vested in him(c), and of all other powers enabling him in that behalf, hereby makes the following Order:—

1. This Order may be cited as the Wages Regulation (Sack and Bag) Order 1973.

2.—(1) In this Order the expression "the specified date" means the 28th June 1973, provided that where, as respects any worker who is paid wages at intervals not exceeding seven days, that date does not correspond with the beginning of the period for which the wages are paid, the expression "the specified date" means, as respects that worker, the beginning of the next such period following that date.

(2) The Interpretation Act 1889(d) shall apply to the interpretation of this Order as it applies to the interpretation of an Act of Parliament and as if this Order and the Order hereby revoked were Acts of Parliament.

3. The wages regulation proposals set out in the Schedule hereto shall have effect as from the specified date and as from that date the Wages Regulation (Sack and Bag) Order 1972(e) shall cease to have effect.

Signed by Order of the Secretary of State.
5th June 1973.

W. H. Marsh,
Assistant Secretary,
Department of Employment.

(a) 1959 c. 69. (b) S.I. 1973/661 (1973 I, p. 2141).
(c) S.I. 1959/1769, 1968/729 (1959 I, p. 1795; 1968 II, p. 2108).
(d) 1889 c. 63. (e) S.I. 1972/854 (1972 II, p. 2735).

SCHEDULE
Article 3

The following minimum remuneration shall be substituted for the statutory minimum remuneration fixed by the Wages Regulation (Sack and Bag) Order 1972 (Order S.B. (73)).

STATUTORY MINIMUM REMUNERATION

PART I

GENERAL

1. The minimum remuneration payable to a worker to whom this Schedule applies for all work except work to which a minimum overtime rate applies under Part IV of this Schedule is:—

(1) in the case of a time worker, the general minimum time rate payable to the worker under Part II or Part III of this Schedule;

(2) in the case of a male worker employed on piece work, piece rates each of which would yield, in the circumstances of the case, to an ordinary worker at least the same amount of money as the general minimum time rate which would be payable under Part II of this Schedule if he were a time worker;

(3) in the case of a female worker employed on piece work, piece rates each of which would yield, in the circumstances of the case, to an ordinary worker at least the same amount of money as the piece work basis time rate applicable to the worker under Part III of this Schedule.

PART II

MALE WORKERS

GENERAL MINIMUM TIME RATES

2. The general minimum time rates payable to male workers are as follows:—

(1) Workers aged 21 years or over and employed during the whole or part of their time:—

                          Per hour
                                p

    (a) as superintendents of packing presses (hand or machine) or as press foremen (hand or machine), or

    (b) in setting up or minding or in setting up and minding, branding or printing machines or both such machines ... ...   40·5

        Provided that the general minimum time rate payable during his first six months' employment in the trade to a worker who enters, or who has entered, the trade for the first time at or over the age of 21 years shall be ... ...   40·2

(2) All other workers aged—

	Per hour p
21 years or over	39·4
20 and under 21 years	36·0
19 „ „ 20 „	35·5
18 „ „ 19 „	35·0
17 „ „ 18 „	28·7
16 „ „ 17 „	25·3
under 16 years	23·3

    Provided that the general minimum time rate payable during his first two months' employment in the trade to a worker who enters, or who has entered, the trade for the first time at or over the age of 18 years shall be 0·2p per hour less than the minimum rate otherwise payable under this sub-paragraph.

PART III

FEMALE WORKERS

GENERAL MINIMUM TIME RATES

3. The general minimum time rates payable to female workers are as follows:—

	Per hour p
(1) *Workers aged 18 years or over and employed as examiners of mended work, allocators, forewomen, selectors or graders of mixed loads or setters-up on branding machines*	*35·7*
Provided that the general minimum time rate payable during her first six months' employment in the trade to a worker who enters, or who has entered, the trade for the first time at or over the age of 18 years shall be	*35·2*
(2) All other workers aged—	
18 years or over	*35·0*
17 and under 18 years	*28·7*
16 „ „ 17 „	*25·3*
under 16 years	*23·3*

Provided that the general minimum time rate payable during her first two months' employment in the trade to a worker who enters, or who has entered, the trade for the first time at or over the age of 16 years shall be 0·2p per hour less than the minimum rate otherwise payable under this sub-paragraph.

PIECE WORK BASIS TIME RATES

4. The piece work basis time rates applicable to female workers of any age employed on piece work are as follows:—

	Per hour p
(1) *Workers employed as examiners of mended work, allocators, fore-women, selectors or graders of mixed loads or setters-up on branding machines*	*36·4*
(2) All other workers	*35·8*

PART IV

OVERTIME AND WAITING TIME

MINIMUM OVERTIME RATES

5. Minimum overtime rates are payable to any worker, not being a male worker employed on piece work, as follows:—

(1) on any day other than a Saturday, Sunday or customary holiday—

    (a) for the first two hours worked in excess of $8\frac{1}{2}$ hours   time-and-a-quarter

    (b) thereafter ... ...   time-and-a-half

Provided that, where the employer normally requires the worker's attendance on five days only in the week, the foregoing minimum overtime rates of time-and-a-quarter and time-and-a-half shall be payable after 9 and 11 hours' work respectively.

(2) on a Saturday, not being a customary holiday—

(*a*) where the worker is normally required to attend on six days in the week—

for the first 2 hours worked in excess of 4 hours ...	time-and-a-quarter
thereafter	time-and-a-half

(*b*) where the worker is normally required to attend on five days only in the week—

for the first 2 hours worked	time-and-a-quarter
thereafter	time-and-a-half

(3) on a Sunday or a customary holiday—

for all time worked	double time

(4) in any week exclusive of any time for which a minimum overtime rate is payable under the foregoing provisions of this paragraph—

for all time worked in excess of 40 hours	time-and-a-quarter.

6. In this Part of this Schedule—

(1) the expressions "time-and-a-quarter", "time-and-a-half" and "double time" mean respectively—

(*a*) in the case of a time worker, one and a quarter times, one and a half times and twice the general minimum time rate otherwise payable to the worker;

(*b*) in the case of a female worker employed on piece work—

(i) a time rate equal respectively to one-quarter, one-half and the whole of the piece work basis time rate otherwise applicable to the worker under Part III of this Schedule and, in addition thereto—

(ii) the piece rates otherwise applicable to the worker under paragraph 1(3).

(2) the expression "customary holiday" means

(*a*) (i) in England and Wales—

Christmas Day;
26th December if it be not a Sunday;
27th December in a year when 25th or 26th December is a Sunday;
Good Friday;
Easter Monday;
the last Monday in May;
the last Monday in August;
or where a day is substituted for any of the above days by national proclamation, that day;

(ii) in Scotland—

New Year's Day and the following day:

Provided that if New Year's Day falls on a Sunday the holidays shall be the following Monday and Tuesday, and if New Year's Day falls on a Saturday the holidays shall be New Year's Day and the following Monday;

the local Spring holiday;

the local Autumn holiday; and

two other days (being days on which the worker would normally work) in the course of a calendar year, to be fixed by the employer and notified to the worker not less than three weeks before the holiday;

or (*b*) in the case of each of the said days (other than a day fixed by the employer in Scotland and notified to the worker as aforesaid) such weekday as may be substituted therefor by the employer being either—

(i) a day which is by local custom recognised as a day of holiday, or

(ii) a day (being a day on which the worker would normally work) which falls within three weeks of the day for which it is substituted and i mutually agreed between the employer and the worker.

WAITING TIME

7.—(1) A worker is entitled to payment of the minimum remuneration specified in this Schedule for all time during which he is present on the premises of his employer unless he is present thereon in any of the following circumstances:—

(a) without the employer's consent, express or implied;

(b) for some purpose unconnected with his work and other than that of waiting for work to be given to him to perform;

(c) by reason only of the fact that he is resident thereon;

(d) during normal meal times in a room or place in which no work is being done and he is not waiting for work to be given to him to perform.

(2) The minimum remuneration payable under sub-paragraph (1) of this paragraph to a piece worker when not engaged on piece work is that which would be payable if he were a time worker.

Part V

APPLICATION

8. This Schedule applies to workers in relation to whom the Sack and Bag Wages Council (Great Britain) operates, namely, workers employed in Great Britain in the trade specified in the Schedule to the Trade Boards (Sack and Bag Trade, Great Britain) (Constitution and Proceedings) Regulations 1933(a), that is to say:—

The making from woven fabrics of corn sacks, flour sacks, coal sacks, sugar sacks, cement bags, sand bags, nail bags, potato bags, seed bags and similar sacks or bags, or the repairing thereof:

including:—

(a) the following and similar operations (whether performed by hand or machine) known in the trade as:—

(i) Folding (or hooking), cutting, machining, turning;

(ii) Brushing, selecting, mending;

(iii) Branding, tarring, bundling;

(b) the warehousing of, the packing of, and similar operations in regard to sacks or bags of the kind mentioned above when carried on in association with or in conjunction with the making or repairing thereof;

(c) the warehousing of, the packing of, and similar operations in regard to any other articles when carried on in or in association with or in conjunction with any business, establishment, branch or department mainly engaged in any of the operations mentioned in paragraph (b) above;
excluding:—

(i) any of the operations mentioned above when carried on in association with or in conjunction with the weaving of jute, flax or hemp, or the dyeing, bleaching or finishing of jute, flax or hemp yarn or cloth;

(ii) any of the operations mentioned above when carried on in or in association with or in conjunction with any business, establishment, branch or department mainly engaged in a business in which the sacks or bags are used as containers for other articles the production or sale of which forms part of the business;

(iii) the making of rope-bound coal or coke sacks when carried on in association with or in conjunction with any business, establishment, branch or department engaged in the making of made-up textile articles other than sacks or bags, whether rope-bound or not, of the kind mentioned';

(a) S.R. & O. 1933/1157 (1933, p. 2052).

(iv) any of the operations mentioned in paragraph (*b*) above when carried on in or in association with or in conjunction with any business, establishment, branch or department mainly engaged in the warehousing of, the packing of, and similar operations in regard to made-up textile articles other than sacks or bags, whether rope-bound or not, of the kind mentioned;

(v) operations included in the Trade Boards (Waste Materials Reclamation) Order 1920**(a)**.

EXPLANATORY NOTE

(*This Note is not part of the Order.*)

This Order which has effect from 28th June 1973, sets out the statutory minimum remuneration payable in substitution for that fixed by the Wages Regulation (Sack and Bag) Order 1972 (Order S.B. (73)), which Order is revoked.

New provisions are printed in italics.

(a) S.R. & O. 1920/305 (1920 II, p. 794).

STATUTORY INSTRUMENTS

1973 No. 1017

WAGES COUNCILS

The Wages Regulation (Sack and Bag) (Holidays) Order 1973

Made - - - -	*5th June* 1973
Coming into Operation	*28th June* 1973

Whereas the Secretary of State has received from the Sack and Bag Wages Council (Great Britain) (hereinafter referred to as "the Wages Council") the wages regulation proposals set out in the Schedule hereto;

Now, therefore, the Secretary of State in exercise of powers conferred by section 11 of the Wages Councils Act 1959(a), as modified by Article 2 of the Counter-Inflation (Modification of Wages Councils Act 1959) Order 1973(b), and now vested in him (c), and of all other powers enabling him in that behalf, hereby makes the following Order:—

1. This Order may be cited as the Wages Regulation (Sack and Bag) (Holidays) Order 1973.

2.—(1) In this Order the expression "the specified date" means the 28th June 1973, provided that where, as respects any worker who is paid wages at intervals not exceeding seven days, that date does not correspond with the beginning of the period for which the wages are paid, the expression "the specified date" means, as respects that worker, the beginning of the next such period following that date.

(2) The Interpretation Act 1889(d) shall apply to the interpretation of this Order as it applies to the interpretation of an Act of Parliament and as if this Order and the Order hereby revoked were Acts of Parliament.

3. The wages regulation proposals set out in the Schedule hereto shall have effect as from the specified date and as from that date the Wages Regulation (Sack and Bag) (Holidays) Order 1969(e) as amended by Schedule 2 to the Wages Regulation (Sack and Bag) Order 1972(f) shall cease to have effect.

Signed by Order of the Secretary of State.
5th June 1973.

W. H. Marsh,
Assistant Secretary,
Department of Employment.

(a) 1959 c. 69.   (b) S.I. 1973/661 (1973 I, p. 2141).
(c) S.I. 1959/1769, 1968/729 (1959 I, p. 1795; 1968 II, p. 2108).
(d) 1889 c. 63.   (e) S.I. 1969/1740 (1969 III, p. 5463).
(f) S.I. 1972/854 (1972 II, p. 2735).

Article 3
SCHEDULE

The following provisions as to holidays and holiday remuneration shall be substituted for the provisions as to holidays and holiday remuneration set out in the Wages Regulation (Sack and Bag) (Holidays) Order 1969 (hereinafter referred to as "Order S.B. (69)"), as amended by Schedule 2 to the Wages Regulation (Sack and Bag) Order 1972 (Order S.B. (73)).

PART I

APPLICATION

1.—(1) This Schedule applies to every worker (other than an outworker) for whom statutory minimum remuneration has been fixed.

(2) For the purposes of this Schedule an outworker is a worker who works in his own home or in some other place not under the control or management of the employer.

PART II

CUSTOMARY HOLIDAYS

2.—(1) An employer shall allow to every worker to whom this Schedule applies a holiday (hereinafter referred to as a "customary holiday") in each year on the days specified in the following sub-paragraph, provided that the worker was in his employment and (unless excused by the employer or absent by reason of the proved illness of, or accident to, the worker) has worked for the employer throughout the last working day on which work was available to him prior to the customary holiday.

(2) The said customary holidays are:—

(a) (i) In England and Wales—

Christmas Day;
26th December if it be not a Sunday;
27th December in a year when 25th or 26th December is a Sunday;
Good Friday;
Easter Monday;
the last Monday in May;
the last Monday in August;
or where a day is substituted for any of the above days by national proclamation.
that day;

(ii) In Scotland—
New Year's Day and the following day:

Provided that if New Year's Day falls on a Sunday the holidays shall be the following Monday and Tuesday, and if New Year's Day falls on a Saturday the holidays shall be New Year's Day and the following Monday;
the local Spring holiday;
the local Autumn holiday; and
two other days (being days on which the worker would normally work) in the course of a calendar year to be fixed by the employer and notified to the worker not less than three weeks before the holiday;

or (b) in the case of each of the said days (other than a day fixed by the employer in Scotland and notified to the worker as aforesaid) such weekday as may be substituted therefor by the employer being either—

(i) a day which is by local custom recognised as a day of holiday, or

(ii) a day (being a day on which the worker would normally work) which falls within three weeks of the day for which it is substituted and is mutually agreed between the employer and the worker.

(3) Notwithstanding the preceding provisions of this paragraph, where by reason of the circumstances in which the work is carried on in an establishment the allowing of the customary holiday is rendered impracticable, a worker may be required to work on a customary holiday (except where in the case of a woman or young person such a requirement would be unlawful) and, if so required, shall be paid for all time worked thereon the statutory minimum remuneration appropriate to him for work on a customary holiday.

PART III

ANNUAL HOLIDAY

3.—(1) Subject to the provisions of paragraph 4, in addition to the holidays specified in Part II of this Schedule an employer shall between the date on which this Schedule becomes effective and 30th September 1973, and in each succeeding year between 6th April and 30th September allow a holiday (hereinafter referred to as an "annual holiday") to every worker in his employment to whom this Schedule applies who has been employed by him during the 12 months immediately preceding the commencement of the holiday season for any of the periods of employment (calculated in accordance with the provisions of paragraph 10) set out in the table below and the duration of the annual holiday shall, in the case of each such worker, be related to his period of employment during that 12 months as follows:—

Workers with a normal working week of 6 days		Workers with a normal working week of 5 days or less	
Period of employment	Duration of annual holiday	Period of employment	Duration of annual holiday
At least 48 weeks	18 days	At least 48 weeks	15 days
„ „ 45 „	17 „	„ „ 45 „	14 „
„ „ 43 „	16 „	„ „ 42 „	13 „
„ „ 40 „	15 „	„ „ 38 „	12 „
„ „ 37 „	14 „	„ „ 35 „	11 „
„ „ 35 „	13 „	„ „ 32 „	10 „
„ „ 32 „	12 „	„ „ 29 „	9 „
„ „ 29 „	11 „	„ „ 25 „	8 „
„ „ 27 „	10 „	„ „ 22 „	7 „
„ „ 24 „	9 „	„ „ 19 „	6 „
„ „ 21 „	8 „	„ „ 16 „	5 „
„ „ 19 „	7 „	„ „ 12 „	4 „
„ „ 16 „	6 „	„ „ 9 „	3 „
„ „ 13 „	5 „		
„ „ 11 „	4 „		
„ „ 8 „	3 „		

(2) Notwithstanding the provisions of sub-paragraph (1) of this paragraph, the number of days of annual holiday which an employer is required to allow to a worker in any holiday season shall not exceed in the aggregate three times the number of days constituting the worker's normal working week.

(3) In this Schedule the expression "holiday season" means in relation to the year 1973 the period commencing on 6th April 1973 and ending on 30th September 1973, and, in each succeeding year, the period commencing on 6th April and ending on 30th September of the same year.

(4) The duration of the worker's annual holiday during the holiday season ending on 30th September 1973 shall be reduced by any days of annual holiday allowed to him by the employer under the provisions of Order S.B. (69), as amended, between 6th April 1973 and the date on which the provisions of this Schedule become effective.

4.—(1) Subject to the provisions of this paragraph, an annual holiday shall be allowed on consecutive working days, being days on which the worker is normally called upon to work for the employer.

(2) (a) Where the number of days of annual holiday for which a worker has qualified exceeds the number of days constituting his normal working week but does not exceed twice that number the holiday may be allowed in two periods of consecutive working days; so, however, that when a holiday is so allowed, one of the periods shall consist of a number of such days not less than the number of days constituting the worker's normal working week.

(b) Where the number of days of annual holiday for which a worker has qualified exceeds twice the number of days constituting his normal working week the holiday may be allowed as follows:—

  (i) as to two periods of consecutive working days, each such period not being less than the period constituting the worker's normal working week, during the holiday season; and

  (ii) as to any additional days, on working days which need not be consecutive, to be fixed by agreement between the employer and the worker or his representative, either during the holiday season or before 6th April next following the holiday season.

(3) For the purposes of this paragraph, days of annual holiday shall be treated as consecutive notwithstanding that a day of holiday allowed to a worker under Part II of this Schedule or a day upon which he does not normally work for the employer intervenes.

(4) Where a day of holiday allowed to a worker under Part II of this Schedule immediately precedes a period of annual holiday or occurs during such a period and the total number of days of annual holiday required to be allowed in the period under the foregoing provisions of this paragraph, together with any such day of holiday allowed under Part II of this Schedule, exceeds the number of days constituting the worker's normal working week then, notwithstanding the foregoing provisions of this paragraph, the duration of that period of annual holiday may be reduced by one day and in such a case one day of annual holiday may be allowed on any working day (not being the worker's weekly short day) in the holiday season.

(5) Subject to the provisions of sub-paragraph (1) of this paragraph, any day of annual holiday under this Schedule may be allowed on a day on which the worker is entitled to a day of holiday or to a half-holiday under any enactment other than the Wages Councils Act 1959.

5. An employer shall give to a worker reasonable notice of the commencing date or dates and duration of the period or periods of his annual holiday. Such notice shall be given at least 21 days before the first day of the annual holiday or before the first day of each period of annual holiday, as the case may be, and may be given individually to the worker or by the posting of a notice in the place where the worker is employed.

PART IV

HOLIDAY REMUNERATION

A.—CUSTOMARY HOLIDAYS

6.—(1) Subject to the provisions of this paragraph, for each day of holiday to which a worker is entitled under Part II of this Schedule he shall be paid by the employer as holiday remuneration whichever of the following sums is the greater, that is to say either:—

(a) a sum equal to the worker's average hourly earnings for the hours worked by him for the employer in the week immediately preceding that in which the holiday occurs; or

(b) a sum equal to the hourly general minimum time rate (being statutory minimum remuneration) which is applicable to the worker (or which would be applicable to him if he were a time worker);

multiplied in either case by the number of hours (exclusive of overtime) normally worked by him for the employer on that day of the week.

(2) Payment of the said holiday remuneration is subject to the condition that the worker presents himself for employment at the usual starting hour on the first working day following the holiday and works throughout that day or, if he fails to do so, failure is by reason of the proved illness of, or accident to, the worker or with the consent of the employer.

(3) The holiday remuneration in respect of any customary holiday shall be paid by the employer to the worker on the pay day on which the wages for the week including the first working day following the customary holiday are paid.

B.—ANNUAL HOLIDAY

7.—(1) Subject to the provisions of this paragraph and of paragraph 8, a worker qualified to be allowed an annual holiday under this Schedule shall be paid as holiday remuneration by his employer in respect thereof, on the last pay day preceding such annual holiday, in respect of the annual holiday to be allowed during the holiday season commencing on 6th April 1973 and during the holiday season in each succeeding year an amount equal to 6·0 per cent. of the total remuneration paid by the employer to the worker during the 12 months immediately preceding the commencement of the holiday season.

(2) Where under the provisions of paragraph 4 an annual holiday is allowed in more than one period, the holiday remuneration shall be apportioned accordingly.

8. Where any accrued holiday remuneration has been paid by the employer to the worker (in accordance with paragraph 9 of this Schedule or with Order S.B. (69)), in respect of employment during any of the periods referred to in that paragraph or that Order, the amount of holiday remuneration payable by the employer in respect of any annual holiday for which the worker has qualified by reason of employment during the said period shall be reduced by the amount of the said accrued holiday remuneration unless that remuneration has been deducted from a previous payment of holiday remuneration made under the provisions of this Schedule or of Order S.B. (69).

ACCRUED HOLIDAY REMUNERATION PAYABLE ON TERMINATION OF EMPLOYMENT

9. Where a worker ceases to be employed by an employer after the provisions of this Schedule become effective, the employer shall, immediately on the termination of the employment (hereinafter called "the termination date"), pay to the worker as accrued holiday remuneration:—

(1) in respect of employment in the 12 months up to and including 5th April immediately preceding the termination date, a sum equal to the holiday remuneration for any days of annual holiday for which he has qualified except days of annual holiday which he has been allowed or has become entitled to be allowed before leaving the employment; and

(2) in respect of any employment since 5th April immediately preceding the termination date, an amount equal to the holiday remuneration which would have been payable to him if he could have been allowed an annual holiday in respect of that employment at the time of leaving it:

Provided that no worker shall be entitled to the payment by his employer of accrued holiday remuneration if he is dismissed on the grounds of industrial misconduct and is so informed by the employer at the time of dismissal.

PART V

GENERAL

10. For the purpose of calculating any period of employment qualifying a worker for an annual holiday under this Schedule, the worker shall be treated—

(1) as if he were employed for a week in respect of any week in which—

    (*a*) in the case of a worker other than a part-time worker, he has worked for the employer for not less than 24 hours and has performed some work for which statutory minimum remuneration is payable;

    (*b*) in the case of a part-time worker, he has worked for the employer and has performed some work for which statutory minimum renumeration is payable;

    (*c*) (i) in the case of a worker other than a part-time worker, he has worked for the employer for less than 24 hours by reason of the proved illness of, or accident to, the worker or, in the case of any worker, for a like reason he has been absent throughout the week:

    Provided that the number of weeks which may be treated as weeks of employment for such reason shall not exceed four in the aggregate in any such period;   or

    (ii) in the case of any worker, he has been suspended throughout the week owing to shortage of work:

    Provided that the number of weeks which may be treated as weeks of employment for such reason shall not exceed four in the aggregate in any such period;

(2) as if he were employed on any day of holiday allowed under the provisions of this Schedule, or of Order S.B. (69), and for the purposes of the provisions of sub-paragraph (1) of this paragraph, a worker who is absent on any such holiday shall be treated as having worked thereon for the employer on work for which statutory minimum remuneration is payable for the number of hours normally worked by him on that day of the week.

DEFINITIONS

11. In this Schedule, unless the context otherwise requires, the following expressions have the meanings hereby respectively assigned to them, that is to say:—

"AVERAGE HOURLY EARNINGS" means the total remuneration paid by the employer to the worker in the week preceding the holiday divided by the number of hours (including overtime) worked for the employer in that week:

Provided that where a worker has been allowed any day as holiday in that week he shall be deemed to have worked thereon for the number of hours normally worked by him on that day of the week.

"NORMAL WORKING WEEK" means the number of days on which it has been usual for the worker to work in a week in the employment of the employer in the 12 months immediately preceding the commencement of the holiday season, or, where under paragraph 9 accrued holiday remuneration is payable on the termination of the employment in the 12 months immediately preceding the termination date: Provided that—

(1) part of a day shall count as a day;

(2) no account shall be taken of any week in which the worker did not perform any work for which statutory minimum remuneration has been fixed.

"PART-TIME WORKER" means a worker who normally works for the employer for less than 24 hours a week by reason only of the fact that he does not hold himself out as normally available for work for more than the number of hours he normally works in the week.

"STATUTORY MINIMUM REMUNERATION" means minimum remuneration (other than holiday remuneration) fixed by a wages regulation order made by the Secretary of State to give effect to proposals submitted to him by the Wages Council.

"TOTAL REMUNERATION" means any payments paid or payable to the worker under his contract of employment, for time worked or piece work done by him, holiday remuneration, any productivity, long service or other bonus payable to the worker on a weekly, fortnightly or monthly basis and merit payments so payable but does not include any other payments.

"WEEK" means "pay week".

12. The provisions of this Schedule are without prejudice to any agreement for the allowance of any further holidays with pay or for the payment of additional holiday remuneration.

EXPLANATORY NOTE

(This Note is not part of the Order.)

This Order, which has effect from 28th June 1973, sets out the holidays which an employer is required to allow to workers and the remuneration payable for those holidays in substitution for the holidays and holiday remuneration set out in the Wages Regulation (Sack and Bag) (Holidays) Order 1969 (Order S.B. (69)), as amended, which Order is revoked.

New provisions are printed in italics.

STATUTORY INSTRUMENTS

1973 No. 1018

CUSTOMS AND EXCISE

The Import Duties (Temporary Exemptions) (No. 16) Order 1973

Made - - - -	*6th June* 1973
Laid before the House of Commons	*12th June* 1973
Coming into Operation	*3rd July* 1973

The Lords Commissioners of Her Majesty's Treasury, by virtue of the powers conferred on them by sections 1, 3(6) and 13 of the Import Duties Act 1958**(a)**, as amended by paragraph 1 of Schedule 4 to the European Communities Act 1972**(b)**, and of all other powers enabling them in that behalf, on the recommendation of the Secretary of State**(c)**, hereby make the following Order:

1.—(1) This Order may be cited as the Import Duties (Temporary Exemptions) (No. 16) Order 1973 and shall come into operation on 3rd July 1973.

(2) The Interpretation Act 1889**(d)** shall apply for the interpretation of this Order as it applies for the interpretation of an Act of Parliament.

2.—(1) Up to and including 31st December 1973 or, in the case of goods in relation to which an earlier day is specified in Schedule 1 to this Order, up to and including that day, any import duty which is for the time being chargeable on goods of a heading of the Customs Tariff 1959 specified in that Schedule shall not be chargeable in respect of goods of any description there specified in relation to that heading.

(2) The period for which goods of headings of the Customs Tariff 1959 and descriptions specified in Schedule 2 to this Order are exempt from import duty shall be extended up to and including 31st December 1973 or, in the case of goods in relation to which an earlier day is specified in that Schedule, up to and including that day.

(3) Any entry in the second column in Schedule 1 or Schedule 2 to this Order shall be taken to comprise all goods which would be classified under an entry in the same terms constituting a subheading (other than the final subheading) of the relevant heading in the Customs Tariff 1959.

(4) For the purposes of classification under the Customs Tariff 1959, insofar as that depends on the rate of duty, any goods to which paragraph (1) or (2) above applies shall be treated as chargeable with the same duty as if this Order had not been made.

(a) 1958 c. 6.
(c) *See* S.I. 1970/1537 (1970 III, p. 5293).
(b) 1972 c. 68.
(d) 1889 c. 63.

Hugh Rossi,

Oscar Murton,

Two of the Lords Commissioners
of Her Majesty's Treasury.

6th June 1973.

SCHEDULE 1

GOODS TEMPORARILY EXEMPT FROM IMPORT DUTY

Tariff Heading	Description
28.24	Cobaltous hydroxide
28.30	Cobaltous chloride
28.38	Sodium persulphate
29.02	2-Chloro-6-fluorotoluene (up to and including 3rd September 1973)
29.07	diPotassium 7-hydroxynaphthalene-1, 3-disulphonate
29.08	Di-α-propylene glycol monomethyl ether
29.13	17β-Hydroxy-7β,17α-dimethylandrost-4-en-3-one
29.14	Cyclohexyl acrylate
29.16	Triethyl citrate
29.20	Diethyl carbonate
29.21	Iodofenphos
29.23	2-Aminophenol 2,4-Diaminophenol dihydrochloride Sodium hydrogen 4-amino-5-hydroxynaphthalene-2,7-disulphonate
29.25	Di-(4-phenoxycarbonylaminophenyl)methane 3-Hydroxy-N-2-naphthyl-2-naphthamide
29.31	S-Methyl N′N′-dimethyl-N-(methylcarbamoyloxy)thio oxamimidate
29.32	Sodium hydrogen p-arsanilate

Tariff Heading	Description
29.35	Ethyl 4-(3,4,5-trimethoxycinnamoyl)piperazin-1-ylacetate hydrogen maleate
29.39	Flumethasone 17,21-diacetate
29.42	Theophylline
58.02	"Synthetic grass", being a woven pile fabric with a pile of green polyamide strip of not less than 220 decitex of heading number 51·02 and a ground of polypropylene strip of heading number 51·02 sealed on the back with a layer of synthetic rubber or artificial plastic material, and weighing not less than 1·4 kilogrammes per square metre (up to and including 3rd September 1973)
59.02	Fawn/grey needleloom felt of man-made fibres (mainly polyamide) impregnated with polyurethane resin, having an overall thickness between 1·5 millimetres and 2·5 millimetres, not made up White needleloom felt of man-made fibres (mainly polyamide) impregnated with polyurethane resin and covered on one side with a smooth coating of a polyurethane resin, having an overall thickness between 1·0 millimetre and 1·5 millimetres, not made up
73.18	Spirally double welded linepipe in lengths of not more than 16 metres with an outside diameter of not less than 911·2 millimetres and not more than 917·6 millimetres and a wall thickness of not less than 9·044 millimetres and not more than 10·472 millimetres containing not more than 0·14 per cent. by weight of carbon, not more than 1·5 per cent. by weight of manganese, not more than 0·015 per cent. by weight of sulphur with a yield strength of not less than 45·7 Kg/mm^2 and not more than 59·8 Kg/mm^2 in a direction transverse to the pipe axis and a Charpy V notch value at minus 10°C of not less than 61 joule in parent material with the specimen length orientated in a direction transverse to the pipe axis (up to and including 30th September 1973)
85.21	Digital displays consisting of a printed circuit board of a size not exceeding 30 millimetres by 90 millimetres with a single line of digits, not less than 3 in number, comprising light emitting diodes manufactured from gallium based semi-conductor compounds mounted thereon; the line of digits having a protective cover of translucent plastic (up to and including 3rd September 1973)
90.09	Photo-reduction apparatus capable of step and repeat operation at a speed of 5 millimetres per second in increments of integer multiples of 25·4 micrometres or less; having an intrinsic repeatable positional accuracy in two axial directions of plus or minus ·254 micrometres, or better, relative to an alignment datum over an area not less than 76·2 millimetres by 76·2 millimetres and a resolution of 650 line pairs per millimetre, or better, over a projected area of 8 millimetres in diameter; the overall accuracy of the system being plus or minus 2·032 micrometres in two axial directions over an exposable area of 101·6 millimetres by 101·6 millimetres (up to and including 3rd September 1973)

Tariff Heading	Description
90·12	Reticle alignment apparatus having an alignment accuracy of plus or minus 1·016 micrometres, or better, incorporating two independently adjustable matched microscopes having a magnification of 340 times, or better, to enable a master mask to be positioned to an accuracy of 1 micrometre when using a fiducial spacing of not less than 40·64 millimetres and not more than 66·04 millimetres (up to and including 3rd September 1973)

SCHEDULE 2

GOODS FOR WHICH EXEMPTION FROM IMPORT DUTY IS EXTENDED

Tariff Heading	Description
28.15	Phosphorus pentasulphide, containing less than 15 parts per million by weight of arsenic calculated as As_2O_3, and containing less than 35 parts per million by weight of iron calculated as Fe
28.51	Deuterated potassium dihydrogen orthophosphate in the form of of single crystals
28.52	Mixed rare earth chlorides which, when precipitated as oxalates and calcined yield not less than 45 per cent. by weight of rare earth oxides, of which the content of cerium expressed as CeO_2 is not less than 45 per cent. by weight and the content of samarium expressed as Sm_2O_3 is not more than 3 per cent. by weight
29.01	Ethylene (up to and including 31st October 1973) Styrene (up to and including 3rd September 1973)
29.02	1,2-Dichloroethane Octabromobiphenyl, mixed isomers (up to and including 3rd September 1973) Vinyl chloride
29.04	n-Pentan-2-ol
29.06	2-tertButyl-4-ethylphenol (up to and including 3rd September 1973) Di-(3,5-ditertbutyl-4-hydroxyphenyl)methane (up to and including 3rd September 1973)
29.07	4-Chloro-m-cresol (-OH at 1) (up to and including 3rd September 1973) 2,2-Di-(3,5-dibromo-4-hydroxyphenyl)propane Zinc 4-hydroxybenzenesulphonate
29.14	Methyl n-dodecanoate Undec-10-enoic acid which freezes at a temperature not lower than 23° centigrade (up to and including 3rd September 1973)
29.15	Succinic acid

Tariff Heading	Description
29.16	Cyclandelate
29.22	3,4-Dichloroaniline
29.23	Potassium 4-aminobenzoate of which an aqueous solution containing 100 grammes per litre has a pH not greater than 8·5 Sodium picramate
29.25	2-Iodobenzanilide
29.30	1-Chloro-3-*iso*cyanatobenzene 1-Chloro-4-*iso*cyanatobenzene 1,2-Dichloro-4-*iso*cyanatobenzene
29.31	Diethyl sulphide Dimethyl sulphide 2-Methylpropane-2-thiol
29.34	2-Chloroethylphosphonic acid Triethylaluminium (up to and including 3rd September 1973)
29.35	Cyanuric acid (up to and including 3rd September 1973) 1,6-Hexanolactam (up to and including 3rd September 1973) 1,6-Hexanolactone 1-Methyl-2-pyrrolidone
29.39	Mestanolone
32.07	Pigments, white, dry, containing not less than 90 per cent. but less than 94 per cent. by weight of titanium dioxide, and which, when dispersed in four times their weight of a solution containing 50 per cent. by weight of a melamine formaldehyde resin having a mole ratio of 0·5 to 1, cause no visible greying on a filter paper which has been dipped in the dispersion, dried, cured and exposed to ultra-violet radiation sufficient to initiate fading of the number 5 reference standard of British Standard 1006 : 1953
39.01	Polyurethanes of wholly aliphatic composition, uncompounded and in the forms covered by Note 3(*b*) of Chapter 39 (up to and including 3rd September 1973) Resins, being products of the condensation of adipic acid with a mixture of propane-1,2-diol and ethanediol of which the ethanediol content is not less than 50 per cent. by weight, and having— (*a*) an acetyl value not less than 34 and not more than 38, (*b*) an acid value not more than 1, (*c*) a colour not deeper than 50 Hazen units, and (*d*) a viscosity at 40° centigrade of not less than 70 seconds and not more than 125 seconds, for a free fall of 20 centimetres of a steel sphere ⅛ inch in diameter, in a tube of internal diameter 3·5 centimetres, when determined by the method of British Standard 188 : 1957, part 3, as amended up to and including September 1964 (up to and including 3rd September 1973)

Tariff Heading	Description
48.07	Electrophotographic base paper, barrier coated, of a substance not less than 50 grammes per square metre, being resistant to toluene solvent on either or both sides which, when subjected for 24 hours to 50 per cent. relative humidity at 17° centigrade, has an apparent surface resistance, of not less than 10 megaohms and not more than 5,000 megaohms, measured under the same conditions between two electrodes 1 inch wide and 1 inch apart and using a Keithley model 600B electrometer (up to and including 3rd September 1973)
51.01	Yarn wholly of polytetrafluoroethylene
51.02	Monofil wholly of fluorocarbon polymer
56.02	"Synthetic hair" being continuous filament tow of co-polymerised vinyl chloride and acrylonitrile, dyed and having a total weight of more than 60 grammes per metre (60,000 tex/540,000 denier), the individual filaments having an irregular cross-section, a specific gravity of less than 1·32 at 20° centigrade and weighing more than 5·0 milligrammes per metre (50dtex/45 denier) (up to and including 3rd September 1973)
59.17	Yarn or tow of polytetrafluoroethylene fibre impregnated with polytetrafluoroethylene dispersion whether or not treated with a lubricant
68.13	Asbestos paper, rubber impregnated, in rolls, being not less than 0·55 millimetre and not more than 0·85 millimetre in thickness, weighing not less than 500 grammes and not more than 780 grammes per square metre, and having a loss on ignition at 1,000° centigrade of not less than 24 per cent. by weight and not more than 32 per cent. by weight (up to and including 31st October 1973)
73.08	Iron or steel coils for re-rolling (up to and including 30th September 1973)
73.12	Strip of iron or steel, coated with tin, of a width not less than 304 millimetres and not more than 500 millimetres, of a thickness of not less than 0·12 millimetre and not more than 0·5 millimetre, and of a length of not more than 1,016 millimetres (up to and including 30th September 1973)
Strip of iron or steel, in coil form, coated with tin, of a width of not less than 140 millimetres and not more than 500 millimetres, and of a thickness of not less than 0·12 millimetre and not more than 0·5 millimetre (up to and including 30th September 1973)
73.13	Sheets of iron or steel, coated with tin, of a width exceeding 500 millimetres but not more than 966 millimetres, of a thickness of not less than 0·12 millimetre and not more than 0·5 millimetre, and of a length of not more than 1,016 millimetres (up to and including 30th September 1973)
Sheets of iron or steel, in coil form, coated with tin, or a width exceeding 500 millimetres but not more than 966 millimetres, and of a thickness of not less than 0·12 millimetres and not more than 0·5 millimetre (up to and including 30th September 1973)
Sheets or plates of iron or steel, cold-rolled but not coated or otherwise worked (up to and including 30th September 1973)
Sheets or plates of iron or steel, in coils, hot-rolled but not coated or otherwise worked (up to and including 30th September 1973)

Tariff Heading	Description
73.14	Iron-nickel alloy wire, copper clad and nickel plated, having an overall diameter of not less than 200 micrometres and not more than 600 micrometres, the nickel plating being not less than 2 micrometres and not more than 15 micrometres in thickness; the whole containing not less than 18 per cent. by weight of copper, not less than 25 per cent. by weight of nickel and not less than 40 per cent, by weight of iron, and having, when measured on an 0·20 metre length, a percentage elongation not less than 16 and not more than 25, and a tensile strength not less than 430 newtons per square millimetre and not more than 590 newtons per square millimetres, the rate of straining being 50 millimetres per minute
73.15	Alloy steel bars, containing not less than 0·40 per cent. and not not more than 0·70 per cent. by weight of nickel; not less than 0·40 per cent. and not more than 0·60 per cent. by weight of chromium; not less than 0·20 per cent. and not more than 0·30 per cent. by weight of molybdenum as the major alloying elements; being not less than 76 millimetres and not more than 215 millimetres in diameter and not less than 5 metres and not more than 8 metres in length (up to and including 30th September 1973)
	Alloy steel bars, containing not less than 0·90 per cent. and not more than 1·20 per cent. by weight of nickel; not less than 0·30 per cent. and not more than 0·60 per cent. by weight of chromium; not less than 0·20 per cent. and not more than 0·30 per cent. by weight of molybdenum as the major alloying elements; being not less than 76 millimetres and not more than 215 millimetres in diameter and not less than 5 metres and not more than 8 metres in length (up to and including 30th September 1973)
	Alloy steel bars, containing not less than 0·90 per cent. and not more than 1·20 per cent. by weight of carbon; not less than 1·30 per cent. and not more than 1·60 per cent. by weight of chromium as the major alloying elements; being not less than 76 millimetres and not more than 215 millimetres in diameter and not less than 5 metres and not more than 8 metres in length (up to and including 30th September 1973)
	Alloy steel wire having a diameter of not less than 2·514 millimetres and not more than 2·590 millimetres, containing not less than 11·0 per cent. and not more than 14·0 per cent. chromium by weight, as the major alloying element, with not less than 0·10 per cent. and not more than 0·40 per cent. sulphur by weight, not more than 1·0 per cent. silicon by weight, not more than 1·25 per cent. manganese by weight and not more than 0·15 per cent. carbon by weight, the tensile strength being not less than 75·6 and not more than 86·625 kilogrammes per square millimetre and the yield strength being not less than 44·1 kilogrammes per square millimetre (up to and including 3rd September 1973)
	Cold-rolled steel strip, with dressed edges, in coils, the strip being not less than 0·002 inch nor more than 0·007 inch in thickness and not less than ¼ inch nor more than 4 inches in width, containing not less than 16 per cent. by weight nor more than 18 per cent. by weight of chromium and not less than 6 per cent. by weight nor more than 8 per cent. by weight of nickel and being of a tensile strength of not less than 115 tons per square inch

Tariff Heading	Description
	Cold-rolled steel strip, with dressed edges, in coils, the strip being not less than 0·002 inch nor more than 0·040 inch in thickness and not less than $\frac{1}{16}$ inch nor more than 4 inches in width, containing not less than 16 per cent. by weight nor more than 18 per cent. by weight of chromium and not less than 6 per cent. by weight not more than 8 per cent. by weight of nickel, and being of a tensile strength of not less than 120 tons per square inch
76.16	Circular aluminium can ends scored for opening with incorporated ring-pull device and having an overall diameter of not less than 106 millimetres and not more than 110 millimetres Circular aluminium can ends spirally wound for opening with incorporated lift and pull tab and having an overall diameter of not less than 106 millimetres and not more than 110 millimetres.
83.13	Tinplate caps for sealing jars, of an internal diameter on the rim of not less than 1·580 inches and not more than 1·610 inches and a maximum depth of not less than 0·415 inch and not more than 0·425 inch stamped from tinplate of nominal thickness of 0·0055 inch or of 0·0066 inch, with an internal curl, a vinyl coating applied to the internal surface and a plasticised lining compound deposited on the internal side wall and top sealing panel to form a sealing gasket
85.15	The following apparatus for use in aircraft: (a) automatic radio direction finding apparatus covering a frequency range of at least 200 KHz to 850KHz; (b) distance measuring apparatus for determining the slant range from aircraft to ground transponter and operating within the frequency range of 960MHz to 1,215 MHz; (c) panel-mounted secondary surveillance radar transponder apparatus, operating within a 12 or 24 volt electrical power system, having an integral control panel and capable of interrogation at a frequency of 1,030 MHz on each of the modes A and C and replying on these modes at a frequency of 1,090 MHz (d) very high frequency omni-directional radio range apparatus (VOR), instrument landing system localised apparatus (ILS/LOC), instrument landing system glide path apparatus (ILS/G. PATH); (e) very high frequency communication apparatus (VHF/COM) (transmitters, receivers, or combined transmitter/receivers) covering a frequency band of at least 118 to 135·95 MHz, with not less than 180 channels and capable of operating in areas where 50 KHz channel spacing is in force; (f) apparatus combining the functions and capabilities of any of the apparatus specified in (d) and (e) above but excluding apparatus combining any of those functions and capabilities with any other function or capabilitity; being in each case apparatus of a type approved by the Civil Aviation Authority, at the date of this Order under Article 14(5) of the Air Navigation Order 1972, for use in aircraft of not more than 5,700 kilogrammes maximum total weight authorised, flying in controlled airspace in accordance with the Instrument Flight Rules as defined in the said Air Navigation Order, but not for use in other aircraft (up to and including 3rd September 1973)

Tariff Heading	Description
85.21	Containers for electronic micro-circuits, consisting of square or rectangular laminations, built up from a bottom sheet of glass, metal or ceramic composition; from a middle frame of glass with embedded metal alloy leads extending to a lead frame along one, two or all four sides; and from a top sealing frame of glass, metal or ceramic composition, all three laminae being fused together. Separate solder frames and metal alloy lids for subsequent sealing to the top sealing frame.
90.01	Lenses, prisms, mirrors and other optical elements, not optically worked, of barium fluoride
91.03	Electric clocks of the instrument panel type designed to be permanently mounted in a motor vehicle with the power source provided by the battery of the vehicle
91.08	Movements for electric clocks of the instrument panel type designed to be permanently mounted in a motor vehicle with the power source provided by the battery of the vehicle.

EXPLANATORY NOTE
(This Note is not part of the Order.)

This Order provides that the goods listed in Schedule 1 shall be temporarily exempt from import duty, and those listed in Schedule 2 shall continue to be exempt from import duty, up to and including 31st December 1973 or, in the case of certain items up to and including such earlier day as is specified.

As regards the exemption for equipment for use in aircraft under heading 85.15, apparatus of a type approved by the Civil Aviation Authority is listed in Civil Aviation Publication CAP 208, Airborne Radio Apparatus Vol. 2, published by Her Majesty's Stationery Office. This publication is subject to amendment, and confirmation that apparatus is of a type approved at the date of this Order should be obtained from the Civil Aviation Authority, Controllerate of National Air Traffic Services, Tels.N2(c), 19-29 Woburn Place, London, WC1H 0LX.

STATUTORY INSTRUMENTS

1973 No. 1019 (C. 25)

SUGAR

The Sugar Act 1956 (Repeals) (Appointed Day) (No. 2) Order 1973

Made - - - -	*6th June* 1973
Coming into Operation	*1st July* 1973

The Minister of Agriculture, Fisheries and Food and the Secretary of State acting jointly in exercise of the powers conferred upon them by section 4 of, and Part II of Schedule 3 to, the European Communities Act 1972(a), and of all other powers enabling them in that behalf, hereby make the following order:—

1.—(1) This order may be cited as the Sugar Act 1956 (Repeals) (Appointed Day) (No. 2) Order 1973, and shall come into operation on 1st July 1973.

(2) The Interpretation Act 1889(b) shall apply to the interpretation of this order as it applies to the interpretation of an Act of Parliament.

2. The repeal of the enactments mentioned in the Schedule to this order shall take effect, to the extent specified in column 3 of the Schedule, on 1st July 1973.

In Witness whereof the Official Seal of the Minister of Agriculture, Fisheries and Food is hereunto affixed on 5th June 1973.

(L.S.)   *Joseph Godber*,
                        Minister of Agriculture, Fisheries and Food.

                                          Gordon Campbell,
                        Secretary of State for Scotland.

6th June 1973.

(a) 1972 c. 68.   (b) 1889 c. 63.

SCHEDULE

REPEALS

Chapter	Short Title	Extent of Repeal
4 & 5 Eliz. 2. c. 48.	The Sugar Act 1956.	Sections 7 to 16. In section 20, subsection (6). In section 33, in subsection (1), the words " regulations or ", in subsection (2), the words " Every instrument containing any such regulations, and,". In section 34, " or the Commissioners ". In section 35, in subsection (2), the definitions of " the Commissioners ", " composite sugar products ", " distribution payments ", " distribution repayments ", " manufacture ", " refiner ", " surcharge " and " surcharge repayment ", subsections (4) to (6). In section 36, subsection (2).
10 & 11 Eliz. 2. c. 44.	Finance Act 1962.	In section 3(6) the words from " the Sugar Act 1956 " onwards. Part II of Schedule 5.
1964 c. 49.	Finance Act 1964.	Section 22.
1966 c. 18.	Finance Act 1966.	Section 52.

EXPLANATORY NOTE

(This Note is not part of the Order.)

This Order, made under section 4 of, and Part II of Schedule 3 to, the European Communities Act 1972, appoints a day for the repeal of specified provisions of the Sugar Act 1956 and of associated legislation which will no longer be required following adoption by the United Kingdom of the Common Agricultural Policy of the European Community.

STATUTORY INSTRUMENTS

1973 No. 1022

NATIONAL HEALTH SERVICE, ENGLAND AND WALES

HOSPITAL AND SPECIALIST SERVICES

The National Health Service (Designation of Teaching Hospitals) Amendment Order 1973

Made - - -	*6th June* 1973
Coming into Operation	*5th July* 1973

The Secretary of State for Social Services, in exercise of powers conferred by sections 11(8), 11(9) and 75(4) of the National Health Service Act 1946(a), and now vested in him(b), and of all other powers enabling him in that behalf, and after consultation with the University of Cambridge hereby orders as follows: —

1. This order may be cited as the National Health Service (Designation of Teaching Hospitals) Amendment Order 1973 and shall come into operation on 5th July 1973.

2.—(1) In this order—

"the Act" means the National Health Service Act 1946;

"the appointed day" means 5th July 1973;

"the First Board" means the Board of Governors of The United Cambridge Hospitals;

"the Second Board" means the East Anglian Regional Hospital Board;

"the Committee" means the Papworth—Huntingdon Hospital Management Committee;

"the transferred hospital" means the hospital named in article 3 hereof.

(2) The Interpretation Act 1889(c) shall apply to the interpretation of this order as it applies to the interpretation of an Act of Parliament.

3. In column (2) of the Schedule to the National Health Service (Designation of Teaching Hospitals) Order 1959(d) as amended(e) (which Schedule lists designated teaching hospitals) opposite the name "The United Cambridge Hospitals" in column (1) the words "Brookfields Hospital, Cambridge" shall be deleted.

4.—(1) All officers of the First Board employed immediately before the appointed day solely at or for the purposes of the transferred hospital shall on that day be transferred to and become officers of the Second Board.

(a) 1946 c. 81.
(c) 1889 c. 63.
(e) The relevant amending instrument is S.I. 1972/1779 (1972 III, p. 5149).

(b) S.I. 1968/1699 (1968 III, p. 4585).
(d) S.I. 1959/748 (1959 I, p. 1813).

(2) Any officer of the First Board who is employed immediately before the appointed day partly at or for the purposes of the transferred hospital and who does not receive before that day notice in writing from the First Board that he is not to be transferred to the Second Board shall on that day be transferred to and become an officer of the Second Board.

(3) Any officer who is transferred to the Second Board under this article and whose employment was whole-time shall continue to be subject to the remuneration and other conditions of service applicable to a whole-time officer so long as his employment for both the First Board and the Second Board amounts in the aggregate to whole-time employment.

5. On the appointed day there shall be transferred to and vest without further conveyance in the Committee—

(*a*) any property held immediately before the appointed day by the First Board

    (i) under section 59 of the Act solely for the purposes of the transferred hospital, and

    (ii) under section 60 of the Act so far as practicable for the purposes of the transferred hospital; and

(*b*) any other property held by the First Board and any rights and liabilities to which the Board was entitled or subject immediately before the appointed day so far as these relate solely to the transferred hospital.

6. Any action or proceeding or any cause of action or proceeding, pending or existing at the appointed day by, or against, the First Board solely in respect of any property, right or liability transferred by this order shall not be prejudicially affected by reason of this order, and may be continued, prosecuted and enforced by or against, the Committee.

Signed by authority of the Secretary of State for Social Services.

G. Beltram,
Under Secretary,
Department of Health and Social Security.

6th June 1973.

EXPLANATORY NOTE
(*This Note is not part of the Order.*)

This Order amends the National Health Service (Designation of Teaching Hospitals) Order 1959—by removing Brookfields Hospital Cambridge from the group of hospitals designated as The United Cambridge Hospitals and providing for consequential matters relating to officers and property connected with Brookfields Hospital Cambridge.

STATUTORY INSTRUMENTS

1973 No. 1027

TRADE DESCRIPTIONS

The Trade Descriptions (Indication of Origin) (Exemptions) (Amendment) Directions 1973

Made	-	-	-	*6th June* 1973
Coming into Operation				*29th June* 1973

The Secretary of State, in exercise of the powers conferred on him by section 1(5) of the Trade Descriptions Act 1972(**a**), hereby gives the following Directions : —

1. These Directions may be cited as the Trade Descriptions (Indication of Origin) (Exemptions) (Amendment) Directions 1973, and shall come into operation on 29th June 1973.

2. The Trade Descriptions (Indication of Origin) (Exemptions No. 2) Directions 1972(**b**), shall have effect as if in paragraph 2(2)(*a*) thereof for the date "29th June 1973" there were substituted the date "29th June 1974".

C. E. Coffin,
An Under Secretary of the
Department of Trade and Industry.

6th June 1973.

EXPLANATORY NOTE

(*This Note is not part of the Directions.*)

These Directions extend the period during which section 1(2) of the Trade Descriptions Act 1972 (which required that a United Kingdom name or mark applied to imported goods be accompanied by an indication of the country of origin of those goods) is excluded in relation to prepacked food until 29th June 1974.

(**a**) 1972 c. 34. (**b**) S.I. 1972/1887 (1972 III, p. 5511)

STATUTORY INSTRUMENTS

1973 No. 1028

ROAD TRAFFIC

The Secretary of State's Traffic Orders (Procedure) (England and Wales) Regulations 1973

Made - - - -	*7th June* 1973
Laid before Parliament	*19th June* 1973
Coming into Operation	*10th July* 1973

The Secretary of State for the Environment (as respects England and Wales in relation to orders under section 15 or 33 of the Road Traffic Regulation Act 1967(a), and as respects England excluding Monmouthshire in relation to all other matters) and the Secretary of State for Wales (as respects Wales and Monmouthshire in relation to all matters other than orders under the said section 15 or 33) make these Regulations in exercise of the powers conferred by section 84C of the said Act, as amended by Part IX of the Transport Act 1968(b) and as read with section 32 of the Countryside Act 1968(c), and now vested in them (d), and of all other enabling powers, after consultation with representative organisations in accordance with section 107(2) of the said Act of 1967:—

PART I

GENERAL

Citation and Commencement

1. These Regulations may be cited as the Secretary of State's Traffic Orders (Procedure) (England and Wales) Regulations 1973, and shall come into operation on 10th July 1973.

Interpretation

2.—(1) In these Regulations the following expressions have the meanings hereby respectively assigned to them:—

"the Act" means the Road Traffic Regulation Act 1967 as amended by Part IX of the Transport Act 1968 and as read with section 32 of the Countryside Act 1968;

"consolidation order" means an order which revokes provisions of one or more existing orders, reproduces those provisions without any change in substance and makes no other provision, but so, however, that for the purpose of this definition the inclusion in the order (by way of addition to the provisions of any existing order or orders) of an exemption of the same kind as

---

(a) 1967 c. 76.   (b) 1968 c. 73.   (c) 1968 c. 41.
(d) As respects the Secretary of State for the Environment—S.I. 1970/1681 (1970 III, p. 5551).

is mentioned in the Local Authorities' Traffic Orders (Exemptions for Disabled Persons) (England and Wales) Regulations 1971(a) in respect of a disabled person's vehicle, or of a provision for conferring on a traffic warden functions similar to those conferred by the existing order or orders on a police constable in uniform, or of both such exemption and such provision, shall not be regarded as constituting a change in substance;

"countryside road order" has the meaning given to that expression in Regulation 3 of these Regulations;

"local newspaper", for the purposes of the procedure for any order relating to any road or other place in Greater London, includes any newspaper published in Greater London and circulating throughout the whole of Greater London (whether or not that newspaper also circulates outside Greater London);

"the notice of proposals" and "the notice of making", in relation to an order, mean respectively the notices required to be published under Regulations 5 and 12 of these Regulations;

"the objection period" means the period within which objections to an order may be made in accordance with Regulation 6 of these Regulations;

"the order" means, in relation to anything occurring or falling to be done before its making, the order as proposed to be made, and in relation to anything occurring or falling to be done on or after its making, the order as made;

"the relevant local authority" means:—

(a) in relation to a reserve power order—

(i) where the order is made or proposed to be made by virtue of section 84A(2) of the Act, the Greater London Council or other local authority to whom there has been given under section 84A(1) of the Act the direction, for the purpose of securing the object of which the order is made or proposed to be made,

(ii) where the order is made or proposed to be made under section 84A(4) of the Act, the Greater London Council or other local authority whose order is or is proposed to be varied or revoked by the reserve power order,

(b) in relation to a trunk road order—

(i) where the order applies or will apply to a road in Greater London, the Greater London Council,

(ii) where the order applies or will apply to a road outside Greater London, the local authority who would have the power under the Act to make the order if the road were not a trunk road,

(c) in relation to a countryside road order, the local authority who have power under section 1 of the Act to make such an order as respects the road to which the countryside road order applies or will apply,

and where under the foregoing provisions of this definition there would in relation to any particular order be more than one relevant local authority, that expression shall in the case of that order include all of those authorities;

"reserve power order" and "trunk road order" have the meanings respectively given to those expressions in Regulation 3 of these Regulations; and

---

(a) S.I. 1971/1493 (1971 III, p. 4185).

"road" includes any length of road and any part of the width of a road and, in relation to an order under section 6 of the Act, any length of a street as defined in section 6(12) of the Act and any part of the width of such a street.

(2) Any reference in these Regulations to an order under any particular section of the Act includes—

(*a*) a reference to an order (whether made by virtue of section 84D, or under section 84A(4), of the Act) varying or revoking an order made, or having effect as if made, under the section in question, and

(*b*) a reference to an order under the section in question made or proposed to be made by virtue of section 84A(2) of the Act.

(3) Any reference in these Regulations to any enactment shall be construed as a reference to that enactment as amended by or under any subsequent enactment.

(4) The Interpretation Act 1889(a) shall apply for the interpretation of these Regulations as it applies for the interpretation of an Act of Parliament.

Application of Regulations

3.—(1) These Regulations apply to:—

(*a*) orders made or proposed to be made by the Secretary of State by virtue of subsection (2) or under subsection (4) of section 84A of the Act (any such order being in these Regulations referred to as a "reserve power order");

(*b*) orders made or proposed to be made by the Secretary of State with respect to trunk roads under any of the following provisions of the Act, that is to say, sections 1(1) to (7), 6, 9, 73 and 74 (any such order being in these Regulations referred to as a "trunk road order"); and

(*c*) orders made or proposed to be made by the Secretary of State with respect to roads which are not trunk roads under section 32(3) of the Countryside Act 1968 (any such order being in these Regulations referred to as a "countryside road order").

(2) Except where otherwise stated, each Regulation applies to every such order.

(3) Where, in connection with an order to which these Regulations apply, procedural steps which accord substantially with the relevant requirements of these Regulations have been taken before the coming into operation of these Regulations or are in the course of being taken when these Regulations come into operation (whether or not they were taken or are being taken in the sequence required by these Regulations), but the order has not been made before these Regulations come into operation, then those steps need not be repeated and for the purpose of these Regulations they shall be deemed to have been taken under and in accordance with these Regulations, and any remaining procedural steps in connection with the order shall be determined by, and carried out or completed in accordance with, these Regulations as nearly as may be.

(4) Nothing in these Regulations shall apply to any order made before the coming into operation of these Regulations.

(a) 1889 c. 63.

PART II

PROCEDURE BEFORE MAKING THE ORDER

Consultation with Police

4.—(1) Before making any order to which these Regulations apply, other than an order under section 6 of the Act, the Secretary of State shall consult with the chief officer of police of any police area in which any road or other place to which the order is to relate is situated.

(2) The consultation referred to in paragraph (1) of this Regulation is additional to any consultation required by the Act or, in the case of a countryside road order, by section 32 of the Countryside Act 1968.

(3) This Regulation has effect subject to Regulation 13 below.

Publication of proposals

5.—(1) Before making the order the Secretary of State shall:—

(*a*) publish once at least in a local newspaper circulating in the area in which any road or other place to which the order relates is situated a notice of proposals containing the particulars specified in Part I of Schedule 1 to these Regulations;

(*b*) publish a similar notice in the London Gazette;

(*c*) serve upon the relevant local authority a copy of the notice of proposals containing the particulars aforesaid and a copy of the order as drafted;

(*d*) except where the order is an order under section 6 of the Act, comply with the relevant requirements of Schedule 2 to these Regulations as to the notices to be displayed in each road or other place to which the order relates;

(*e*) comply with the relevant requirements of Schedule 3 to these Regulations as to the availability of documents for inspection.

(2) Where the order is one which relates to a road, or to roads, situated in more than one locality, it shall be sufficient for the purposes of this Regulation if the notice published in each local newspaper states the general nature and effect of the order so far as it affects the road or roads situated in the locality in which that newspaper circulates and names or otherwise describes only the road or roads so affected in that locality, but the notice in the London Gazette shall state the general nature and effect of the entire order and name or otherwise describe the whole road, or all the roads, to which the order relates.

(3) This Regulation has effect subject to Regulations 13 and 14 below.

Objections

6.—(1) The period during which objections to the order can be made shall begin not earlier than the date on which the Secretary of State has complied with the requirements of paragraph (1)(*a*), (*b*) and (*c*) of Regulation 5 above and (where such display is required) has begun to display the notices required by paragraph 1(*d*) of that Regulation, and shall continue, in the case of orders under section 73 or 74 of the Act, for not less than 28 days, and in the case of all other orders, for not less than 21 days.

(2) Any person desiring to object to the Secretary of State's proposals to make the order shall send within the period, and to the address, specified in the notice of proposals published as required by Regulation 5 above a written statement of his objection and of the grounds thereof.

(3) This Regulation has effect subject to Regulations 13 and 14 below.

Notice of public inquiry

7.—(1) Where the Secretary of State decides, before publishing the notice of proposals under Regulation 5 above, that a public inquiry shall be held, the notice of proposals shall contain, in addition to the particulars required by that Regulation, the particulars specified in Part II of Schedule 1 to these Regulations.

(2) In any case where the Secretary of State decides that a public inquiry shall be held in connection with an order to which these Regulations apply but the published notice of proposals has not contained the particulars specified in Part II of Schedule 1 aforesaid, the Secretary of State shall:—

(*a*) publish once at least in a local newspaper circulating in the area in which any road or other place to which the order relates is situated a notice of the inquiry containing the particulars specified in Part III of Schedule 1 to these Regulations;

(*b*) publish a similar notice in the London Gazette;

(*c*) serve upon the relevant local authority a copy of the notice of the inquiry containing the particulars aforesaid;

(*d*) except where the order is an order under section 6 or 9 of the Act, comply with the relevant requirements of Schedule 2 to these Regulations as to the notices to be displayed in each road or other place to which the order relates;

(*e*) comply with the relevant requirements of Schedule 3 to these Regulations as to the availability of documents for inspection;

(*f*) not later than the date of the first publication of the notice required by sub-paragraph (*a*) of this paragraph, inform in writing any person who has objected to the order in accordance with Regulation 6 above and who has not withdrawn the objection, of the date, time and place of the inquiry.

(3) The provisions of paragraph (2) of Regulation 5 above shall apply in relation to the publication of a notice under paragraph (2) of this Regulation as they apply in relation to the publication of a notice of proposals under the said Regulation 5.

(4) Where the notice of proposals announces the holding of a public inquiry, there shall be at least 42 days between the date on which the publication of that notice in the local newspaper and the London Gazette under the foregoing provisions of these Regulations is completed and the date on which the inquiry is due to begin, and in all other cases there shall be at least 21 days between the date on which the publication as aforesaid of the notice announcing the holding of the public inquiry is completed or the date of the expiration of the objection period (whichever is later) and the date on which the inquiry is due to begin.

Procedure at public inquiry

8.—(1) Any person interested in the subject matter of a public inquiry may appear at the inquiry either in person or by counsel, solicitor or other representative.

(2) Any person so interested may, whether or not he proposes to appear at the inquiry, send to the address given in the notice of proposals for the receipt of objections, such written representations as he may wish to make in relation to the subject matter of the inquiry with a view to their transmission to and consideration by the person appointed to hold the inquiry.

(3) The person holding the inquiry may refuse to hear any person, or to consider any objection or representation made by any person, if he is satisfied that the views of that person or the objection or representation are frivolous or that such views have already been adequately stated by some other person at the inquiry.

(4) Subject as aforesaid, the procedure at the inquiry shall be in the discretion of the person holding it.

Consideration of objections

9. Before making the order the Secretary of State shall consider all objections duly made in accordance with Regulation 6 above and not withdrawn and also the report and recommendations (if any) of the person holding any public inquiry in connection with the order.

Modifications

10. The Secretary of State may make the order with modifications (whether in consequence of any objections or otherwise), but where the modifications which the Secretary of State proposes to make appear to him substantially to affect the character of the order as drafted, then, before making the order, he shall take such steps as appear to him to be appropriate for informing the persons likely to be concerned of the effect of the proposed modifications and for giving to those persons an opportunity to make representations in connection therewith, and shall consider any such representations which are made to him.

PART III

MAKING THE ORDER AND SUBSEQUENT PROCEDURE

Operative date of order

11.—(1) The order shall specify the date on which it comes into operation or, in a case where different operative dates are provided for different provisions of the order, each of the dates on which a provision of the order comes into operation.

(2) No date on which an order, or a provision of an order, comes into operation shall be earlier than the date on which the notice of the making of the order is published in the local newspaper under Regulation 12 below.

Notice of the making of the order

12.—(1) When the Secretary of State has made the order, he shall:—

(*a*) forthwith give notice in writing of the making of the order to the relevant local authority and to the chief officer of police for the police area in which any road or other place to which the order relates is situated;

(*b*) except where such notification has previously been given to such person, notify in writing each person who has duly objected to the order in accordance with Regulation 6 above and has not withdrawn his objection, of the Secretary of State's decision in relation to the objection and, where the objection has not been, or not wholly been, acceded to, of the Secretary of State's reasons therefor;

(*c*) within 14 days of the making of the order publish once in a local newspaper circulating in the area in which any road or other place to which the order relates is situated a notice of the making of the order containing the particulars specified in Part IV of Schedule 1 to these Regulations;

(*d*) within the same period publish a similar notice in the London Gazette;

(*e*) comply with the relevant requirements of Schedule 3 to these Regulations as to the availability of documents for inspection;

(*f*) where the order relates to any road, forthwith take such steps as it is practicable for the Secretary of State to take to ensure, before the order comes into operation—

(i) the placing on or near the road of such traffic signs in such positions as the Secretary of State may consider requisite for the purpose of securing that adequate information as to the effect of the order is made available to persons using the road, and

(ii) in a case where the order contains provisions for revoking, or altering the application of, a previous order, such removal or replacement of existing traffic signs as the Secretary of State may consider requisite for the purpose of avoiding confusion to users of the road or the continuance of traffic signs in incorrect positions.

(2) The provisions of paragraph (2) of Regulation 5 above shall apply in relation to the publication of a notice of making under paragraph (1) of this Regulation as they apply in relation to the publication of a notice of proposals under the said Regulation 5.

(3) The provisions of paragraph (1)(*f*) above are without prejudice to section 75 of the Act.

(4) This Regulation has effect subject to Regulation 13 below.

PART IV

SPECIAL PROCEDURAL PROVISIONS FOR CERTAIN ORDERS

Special provisions for consolidation orders and for certain variation orders

13.—(1) Regulations 4, 5 and 6 above shall not apply to any trunk road order which is a consolidation order and Regulation 12 above shall have effect in relation to such an order with the following modifications, namely, that the particulars to be contained in the notice of the making of the order shall consist only of:—

(i) the title of the order;

(ii) a statement of the titles of the orders the provisions of which are reproduced in the order;

(iii) the operative date or dates of the order; and

(iv) the items numbered 6 and (if necessary) 7 in Part IV of Schedule 1 to these Regulations.

(2) A trunk road order which is a consolidation order shall be framed so as to come into operation on a date not less than 14 days after the publication in the local newspaper of the notice of the making of the order.

(3) Regulations 4, 5 and 6 above shall not apply to an order the sole effect of which would be:—

(*a*) to postpone for a period of not more than 6 months the coming into operation of any provision of an existing order; or

(*b*) to vary an order under section 1, 6 or 9 of the Act so as to include in the order being varied an exemption in respect of a disabled person's vehicle of the same kind as is mentioned in Regulation 3 of the Local Authorities' Traffic Orders (Exemptions for Disabled Persons) (England and Wales) Regulations 1971, or a provision for conferring on a traffic warden functions similar to those conferred by the order being varied on a police constable in uniform, or both such exemption and such provision.

Special provisions for certain experimental traffic orders and other orders

14.—(1) This Regulation applies to the following orders, that is to say:—

(*a*) a trunk road order under section 9 of the Act;

(*b*) a reserve power order under section 84A(4) of the Act which provides only for one or more of the following matters:—

    (i) the revocation of an order made, or having effect as if made, under section 9(1) of the Act;

    (ii) the variation of an order made, or having effect as if made, under the said section 9(1) so as to reduce the extent of its application or the stringency of any prohibition or restriction imposed by it;

(*c*) a reserve power order under section 9(3) of the Act by virtue of section 84A(2) thereof;

(*d*) an order under section 1 or 6 of the Act where the sole effect of the order would be to—

    (i) prohibit the riding of cycles or mopeds on a footbridge or in a pedestrian subway or in the approaches to such bridge or subway, or

    (ii) restrict the driving of vehicles into a boxed area, or

    (iii) revoke or vary the provision of an order, being a provision the sole effect of which is as mentioned in (i) or (ii) of this sub-paragraph.

(2) Regulations 5 and 6 above shall not apply to any order to which this Regulation applies, but where the order is a reserve power order the Secretary of State shall, not less than 14 days before making the order, serve upon the relevant local authority a notice of his proposal to make the order, a copy of the order as drafted and a statement of his reasons for proposing to make the order.

(3) In paragraph (1)(*d*) of this Regulation—

"boxed area" means an area of the carriageway of a road, at or near its junction with another road, marked or to be marked by a traffic sign consisting of cross hatched yellow lines, bounded by a yellow line, placed on the carriageway to indicate that a vehicle must not be driven into the area at a time when, by reason of the presence of one or more other vehicles in or near to that area, it cannot be driven out of that area without stopping;

"cycle" means a pedal cycle which is not a motor vehicle; and

"moped" means a motorcycle which is equipped with pedals by means whereof it is capable of being propelled and which has an engine with a cylinder capacity not exceeding 50 cubic centimetres.

Signed by authority of the Secretary of State.

John Peyton,
Minister for Transport Industries,
Department of the Environment.

6th June 1973.

Peter Thomas,
Secretary of State for Wales.

7th June 1973.

SCHEDULE 1

PARTICULARS TO BE INCLUDED IN PRESS NOTICES

Part I—Particulars to be included in the notice of proposals

1. The title of the order.

2. A statement of the general nature and effect of the order.

3. Where the order relates to any road, the name or other brief description of the road and, in a case where the order is an order under section 73 or 74 of the Act, a statement of the approximate length of that road to which the order will apply.

4. Where the order does not relate to a road, a brief description of the place to which it does relate and of the location of that place.

5. Where the order is a reserve power order to be made under section 84A(4) of the Act, a statement of the title, date and general nature of the order proposed to be varied or revoked and of the name of the authority who made that order.

6. A statement of all the documents required by Regulation 5(1)(e) of these Regulations to be available for inspection, of each address at which those documents can be inspected and of the times when inspection can take place at each such address.

7. The period during which, and the address to which, objections to the order can be made, and a statement that all objections must be made in writing and must specify the grounds thereof.

Part II—Additional Particulars to be included in the notice of proposals which announces the holding of a public inquiry

1. A statement that a public inquiry will be held in connection with the order.

2. The date, time and place of the inquiry.

Part III—Particulars to be included in the separate notice of a public inquiry

1. The title of the order.

2. A statement which refers to the published notice of proposals for the order and which indicates that a public inquiry will be held in connection with the order.

3. A brief statement of the general nature and effect of the order and of the name or other brief description of any road or other place to which the order will apply.

4. The date, time and place of the inquiry.

5. A statement of all the documents required by Regulation 7(2)(e) of these Regulations to be available for inspection, of each address at which those documents can be inspected and of the times when inspection can take place at each such address.

Part IV—Particulars to be included in the notice of making the order

1. The title of the order.

2. A statement of the general nature and effect of the order and of its operative date or dates.

3. Where the order relates to any road, the name or other brief description of the road.

4. Where the order does not relate to a road, a brief description of the place to which it does relate and of the location of that place.

5. Where the order is a reserve power order made under section 84A(4) of the Act, a statement of the title, date and general nature of the order varied or revoked and of the name of the authority who made that order.

6. A statement of all the documents required by Regulation 12(1)(*e*) of these Regulations to be available for inspection, of each address at which those documents can be inspected and of the times when inspection can take place at each such address.

7. In the case of an order under section 1, 5, 6, 9, 15, 28, 33 or 35 of the Act, a statement that any person who desires to question the validity of the order or of any provision contained in the order on the ground that it is not within the powers of the relevant section of the Act or on the ground that any requirement of that section or of section 84A, 84B or 84C of the Act or of any regulations made under the said section 84C has not been complied with in relation to the order, may, within 6 weeks of the date on which the order is made (such date being stated in the notice) make application for the purpose to the High Court.

SCHEDULE 2

REQUIREMENTS AS TO NOTICES TO BE DISPLAYED IN A ROAD OR OTHER PLACE

Part I—Particulars to be included in the notice

1. The title of the order.

2. A brief statement of the effect of the order in relation to the road or other place where it is displayed.

3. A statement of all the documents required by Regulation 5(1)(*e*) or 7(2)(*e*) of these Regulations to be available for inspection, of each address at which those documents can be inspected and of the times when inspection can take place at each such address.

4. Where the notice is a notice of proposals, the address to which, and the period during which, objections to the order can be made, and a statement that all objections must be made in writing and must specify the grounds thereof.

5. Where the notice announces the holding of a public inquiry, the date, time and place of the inquiry.

Part II—Other requirements as to the display of the notice

1. Where the order relates to any road, the notice shall be displayed in a prominent position at or near each end of the road and in such other positions (if any) as the Secretary of State thinks requisite for securing that adequate information about the subject matter of the notice is made available to persons using the road.

2. Where the order does not relate to a road, the notice shall be displayed in one or more prominent positions in the road or roads giving access to the place to which it does relate, and, where that place is in public use, in that place itself.

3. The notice shall first be displayed as aforesaid not later than the first publication of the corresponding notice in the local newspaper and the Secretary of State shall take all steps which it is reasonably practicable for him to take to ensure that it remains in a legible condition and continues to be so displayed:—

    (*a*) in the case of a notice of proposals not announcing the holding of a public inquiry, until the end of the objection period;

    (*b*) in the case of a notice announcing the holding of a public inquiry, until the date on which the inquiry begins.

SCHEDULE 3

REQUIREMENTS AS TO THE AVAILABILITY OF DOCUMENTS FOR INSPECTION

1. There shall be available for inspection at such address or addresses, and during such times, as may be specified in the notice in connection with which they are required to be made available (one such address being, so far as practicable, an address in the area in which any road or other place to which the order relates is situated) the following documents:—

(a) a copy of the order as proposed to be made or made (as the case may be);

(b) in the case of an order which varies, revokes, applies or suspends a previous order or which modifies, suspends or revokes regulations made or having effect as if made under section 11 of the Act, a copy of that order or, as the case may be, of those regulations;

(c) in the case of a reserve power order made or proposed to be made by virtue of section 84A(2) of the Act, a copy of the direction for the purpose of securing the object of which the order is made or proposed to be made;

(d) in the case of a proposed order, a copy of a statement setting out the Secretary of State's reasons for proposing to make the order; and

(e) in the case of an order made after the holding of a public inquiry, a copy of the report and the recommendations (if any) of the person appointed to hold the inquiry.

2. The said documents shall be made available as aforesaid not later than the date of the first publication in the local newspaper of the notice in connection with which they are required to be made available, and they shall continue to be so available:—

(a) where the notice is a notice of proposals not announcing the holding of a public inquiry, until the end of the objection period;

(b) where the notice is one announcing the holding of a public inquiry, until the date on which the inquiry begins; and

(c) where the notice is a notice of making the order, until the end of 6 weeks from the date on which the order is made.

EXPLANATORY NOTE

(This Note is not part of the Regulations.)

1. These Regulations lay down the procedure to be followed by the Secretary of State for the Environment and the Secretary of State for Wales in connection with the making by them of various types of traffic orders under the Road Traffic Regulation Act 1967, as amended by Part IX of the Transport Act 1968, and under section 32(3) of the Countryside Act 1968.

2. Regulation 3 specifies the orders to which the Regulations apply. These include traffic regulation orders, experimental traffic orders and speed limit orders in respect of trunk roads and orders being made in respect of non-trunk roads whether under the Countryside Act 1968 or under the reserve powers of the Secretaries of State under Section 84A of the 1967 Act.

3. Regulations 4 to 10 lay down the procedure to be followed before the order is made. They provide for preliminary consultation with the police (Regulation 4), publication of the proposals (Regulation 5), objections to the order (Regulations 6 and 9), public inquiries (Regulations 7 and 8) and the modification of the proposals (Regulation 10).

4. Provisions as to the making of the order and the subsequent procedure, including the publication of a notice of its making, the notification of the police, the local authority and objectors, and the provision of traffic signs, are contained in Regulations 11 and 12.

5. Certain of the above-mentioned requirements are modified in relation to certain classes of order by virtue of Regulations 13 and 14.

6. Schedules 1 to 3 contain particulars of the details to be included in the press notices of an order, of the requirements as to the display of notices of an order in the road itself, and of the requirements about making documents relating to an order available for public inspection.

STATUTORY INSTRUMENTS

1973 No. 1029

CUSTOMS AND EXCISE

The Import Duty Drawbacks (Revocation) Order 1973

Made - - -	*7th June* 1973
Laid before the House of Commons	*8th June* 1973
Coming into Operation	*1st July* 1973

The Secretary of State, by virtue of the powers conferred on him by sections 9 and 13 of the Import Duties Act 1958(**a**) as amended by paragraph 1 of Schedule 4 to the European Communities Act 1972(**b**) and of all other powers enabling him in that behalf, hereby makes the following Order:

1.—(1) This Order may be cited as the Import Duty Drawbacks (Revocation) Order 1973 and shall come into operation on 1st July 1973.

(2) The Interpretation Act 1889(**c**) shall apply to the interpretation of this Order as it applies to the interpretation of an Act of Parliament and as if this Order and the Orders hereby revoked were Acts of Parliament.

2. The following Orders are hereby revoked:

The Import Duty Drawbacks (No. 1) Order 1971(**d**);

The Import Duty Drawbacks (No. 2) Order 1971(**e**);

The Import Duty Drawbacks (No. 3) Order 1971(**f**);

The Import Duty Drawbacks (No. 1) Order 1972(**g**);

The Import Duty Drawbacks (No. 2) Order 1972(**h**).

Limerick,
Parliamentary Under Secretary of State,
Department of Trade and Industry.

7th June 1973.

(**a**) 1958 c. 6.
(**c**) 1889 c. 63.
(**e**) S.I. 1971/1186 (1971 II, p. 3480).
(**g**) S.I. 1972/406 (1972 I, p. 1497).

(**b**) 1972 c. 68.
(**d**) S.I. 1971/274 (1971 I, p. 939).
(**f**) S.I. 1971/2009 (1971 III, p. 5738).
(**h**) S.I. 1972/1664 (1972 III, p. 4889).

EXPLANATORY NOTE

(*This Note is not part of the Order.*)

This Order revokes the Orders providing for the allowance of drawback of import duty on exportation under the Import Duties Act 1958. As a result of the Directive of the Council of the European Communities of 4th March 1969 (69/73/EEC) any relief on goods imported for processing or for use in the production of exported products will henceforth be granted by way of remission or repayment of import duty under section 7 of the Act.

STATUTORY INSTRUMENTS

1973 No. 1031 (S.77)

LOCAL GOVERNMENT, SCOTLAND

The Local Government (Financial Loss Allowance) (Scotland) Amendment Regulations 1973

Made - - -	*4th June* 1973
Laid before Parliament	*15th June* 1973
Coming into Operation	*6th July* 1973

In exercise of the powers conferred on me by sections 112 and 117 as read with section 118 of the Local Government Act 1948(**a**) and as amended by section 16 of the Local Government (Miscellaneous Provisions) Act 1953(**b**), and of all other powers enabling me in that behalf, I hereby make the following regulations: —

1. These regulations may be cited as the Local Government (Financial Loss Allowance) (Scotland) Amendment Regulations 1973 and shall come into operation on 6th July 1973.

2. The Interpretation Act 1889(**c**) shall apply for the interpretation of these regulations as it applies for the interpretation of an Act of Parliament.

3. For "£2·37½" in paragraph (i) and "£4·75" in paragraph (ii) of Schedule 1 to the Local Government (Financial Loss Allowance) (Scotland) Regulations 1970(**d**) as amended by the Local Government (Financial Loss Allowance) (Scotland) Amendment Regulations 1971(**e**), there shall be substituted "£2·75" and "£5·50" respectively.

Gordon Campbell,
One of Her Majesty's Principal
Secretaries of State.

St. Andrew's House,
Edinburgh.
4th June 1973.

(**a**) 1948 c. 26. (**b**) 1953 c. 26.
(**c**) 1889 c. 63. (**d**) S.I. 1970/106 (1970 I, p. 454).
(**e**) S.I. 1971/2130 (1971 III, p. 6296).

EXPLANATORY NOTE

(This Note is not part of the Regulations.)

These Regulations prescribe in pursuance of section 16 of the Local Government (Miscellaneous Provisions) Act 1953, revised maximum amounts which may be paid to members of any body, to which Part VI of the Local Government Act 1948 applies, by way of financial loss allowance for loss of earnings or additional expenses (other than travelling or subsistence) incurred in the performance of their duties as such members.

1973 No. 1032

SEEDS

The Seeds (EEC) General Licence 1973

Made - - - -	*8th June* 1973
Coming into Operation	*1st July* 1973

Whereas the Minister of Agriculture, Fisheries and Food is satisfied that the circumstances connected with the sale or exposure for sale of the seeds described in the Schedule hereto (hereinafter called " the said seeds ") in containers labelled and sealed with the official labels and seals of the European Economic Community are such that compliance with the provisions of section 1 of the Seeds Act 1920(a), as amended by section 12 of the Agriculture (Miscellaneous Provisions) Act 1954(b) and section 24 of the Agriculture (Miscellaneous Provisions) Act 1963(c), cannot reasonably be enforced and that an exemption should be granted so as to apply generally to all persons as regards such provisions in relation to such sales or exposure for sale of the said seeds.

Now the Minister of Agriculture, Fisheries and Food in exercise of the powers vested in him by section 1(7) of the Seeds Act 1920, and of all other powers enabling him in that behalf and in accordance with Regulation 9 of the Seeds Regulations 1961(d) hereby grants the following licence:—

1. This licence which may be cited as the Seeds (EEC) General Licence 1973 shall come into operation on 1st July 1973 and shall cease to have effect on 30th June 1974.

2. On the sale or exposure for sale of the said seeds in containers labelled and sealed with the official labels and seals of the European Economic Community the seller is hereby exempted from compliance with the provisions of section 1 of the Seeds Act 1920.

In Witness whereof the Official Seal of the Minister of Agriculture, Fisheries and Food is hereunto affixed on 8th June 1973.

(L.S.)

Joseph Godber,
Minister of Agriculture, Fisheries and Food.

THE SCHEDULE ABOVE REFERRED TO

The seeds of the following kinds:—Barley, maize, oats, rye, wheat, cocksfoot, meadow fescue, red fescue, tall fescue, meadow foxtail, smooth-stalked meadowgrass, rough-stalked meadowgrass, hybrid ryegrass, Italian ryegrass, perennial ryegrass, Westerwolds ryegrass, timothy, birdsfoot trefoil, alsike clover, crimson clover, red clover, white clover, lucerne, sainfoin, field pea, field (horse or tic) bean, fodder kale, mustard (black, brown or white), fodder radish, swede rape, turnip rape, swede, flax, linseed, lupin, sunflower, vetch, fodder beet, sugar beet.

(a) 1920 c. 54.	(b) 1954 c. 39.
(c) 1963 c. 11.	(d) S.I. 1961/212 (1961 I, p. 362).

EXPLANATORY NOTE

(This Note is not part of the Licence.)

This Licence relieves sellers of seeds from the obligations imposed by the Seeds Act 1920 to test and give prescribed particulars of the kinds of seeds set out in the Schedule to the Licence, provided that the containers of such seeds bear the official labels and seals of the European Economic Community.

STATUTORY INSTRUMENTS

1973 No. 1033

CUSTOMS AND EXCISE

The Export of Goods (Control) (Amendment No. 3) Order 1973

Made - - -	*8th June* 1973
Coming into Operation	*1st July* 1973

The Secretary of State, in exercise of powers conferred by section 1 of the Import, Export and Customs Powers (Defence) Act 1939(a) and now vested in him(b), hereby orders as follows:

1. This Order may be cited as the Export of Goods (Control) (Amendment No. 3) Order 1973 and shall come into operation on 1st July 1973.

2. The Interpretation Act 1889(c) shall apply to the interpretation of this Order as it applies to the interpretation of an Act of Parliament and as if this Order and the Orders hereby revoked were Acts of Parliament.

3. The Export of Goods (Control) Order 1970(d), as amended(e), shall have effect as if:

(*a*) in Article 5(1)(*f*) after the words "the said Schedule" the following was deleted namely:

"and (iii) goods falling within the entry relating to sugar in Group 8 of the said Schedule";

(*b*) in Group 8 of Schedule 1, the following was deleted, namely:

(i) "Potatoes ... ... A";

(ii) "Sugar, invert sugar and composite sugar products, qualifying for a distribution payment payable under section 14 of the Sugar Act 1956(f) ... ... A other than—

(*a*) goods produced or manufactured in the United Kingdom;

(*b*) goods exported as a single shipment or consignment in a quantity not exceeding 112 pounds or 10 gallons;

(*c*) goods exported by post;

(*d*) goods transhipped or exported from bonded warehouse;

(*e*) goods which were entered with the proper officer of Customs and Excise for home use or delivered from bonded warehouse for home use before 1st February 1972."

(a) 1939 c. 69.   (b) *See* S.I. 1970/1537 (1970 III, p. 5293).
(c) 1889 c. 63.   (d) S.I. 1970/1288 (1970 III, p. 4270).
(e) The relevant amending Orders are S.I. 1972/89, 1973/532 (1972 I, p. 253; i3; 1973 I, p. 1705).   (f) 1956 c. 48.

4. The Export of Goods (Control) (Amendment) Order 1972 and the Export of Goods (Control) (Amendment No. 2) Order 1973 are hereby revoked.

B. M. Eyles,
An Assistant Secretary,
Department of Trade and Industry.

8th June 1973.

EXPLANATORY NOTE
(This Note is not part of the Order.)

This Order amends the Export of Goods (Control) Order 1970. It removes the export control on potatoes and on certain sugar, invert sugar and composite sugar products.

STATUTORY INSTRUMENTS

1973 No. 1034

CUSTOMS AND EXCISE

The Import Duties (European Free Trade Association Countries) (Reductions and Exemptions) (No. 2) Order 1973

Made - - - -	*11th June* 1973
Laid before the House of Commons	*11th June* 1973
Coming into Operation	*1st July* 1973

The Lords Commissioners of Her Majesty's Treasury, by virtue of the powers conferred on them by sections 1, 3(6) and 13 of the Import Duties Act 1958(a), as amended by section 5(5) of, and paragraph 1 of Schedule 4 to, the European Communities Act 1972(b), and of all other powers enabling them in that behalf, on the recommendation of the Secretary of State(c), hereby make the following Order:

Operation, citation, interpretation

1.—(1) This Order may be cited as the Import Duties (European Free Trade Association Countries) (Reductions and Exemptions) (No. 2) Order 1973.

(2) The Interpretation Act 1889(d) shall apply for the interpretation of this Order as it applies for the interpretation of an Act of Parliament.

(3) This Order shall come into operation on 1st July 1973 and shall operate up to and including 31st December 1973.

2. In this Order:

"the Agreements" means:

(a) the Agreements, signed on 22nd July 1972, between the European Economic Community (hereinafter referred to as "the Community") and, respectively, Austria, Iceland, Portugal, Sweden and Switzerland,

(b) the Agreement, signed on 14th May 1973, between the Community and Norway and

(c) any provisions of those Agreements as applied by any Community instrument to trade with Finland(e);

references to a heading or subheading are references to a heading or sub-heading of the Customs Tariff 1959.

(a) 1958 c. 6.
(c) *See* S.I. 1970/1537 (1970 III, p. 5293).
(e) (EEC) No. 984/73 (O.J. NoL101, p.1).

(b) 1972 c. 68.
(d) 1889 c. 63.

3. The Import Duties (European Free Trade Association Countries) (Reductions and Exemptions) Order 1973**(a)** is hereby revoked.

4. The Import Duties (General) (No. 7) Order 1971**(b)**, as amended**(c)**, shall be further amended by the substitution, for paragraph (c) of the proviso to Article 3(1), of the following:

"(c) in the case of goods which,

(i) under the provisions relating to origin of goods of the Agreements, signed on 22nd July 1972, between the European Economic Community and, respectively, Austria, Iceland, Portugal, Sweden and Switzerland or the Agreement, signed on 14th May 1973, between the Community and Norway or under those provisions as applied by any instrument of the Community to trade with Finland, are entitled to the benefit of the prohibition of new customs duties on import into the United Kingdom or,

(ii) not being goods of a class to which those Agreements apply, are goods of one of the aforementioned countries,

no import duty shall be charged unless a rate is shown in the said column 3 prefixed by the letter "E" and, if a rate is so shown, import duty shall be charged at that rate;".

5. Any import duty which is for the time being chargeable on goods of any heading or subheading specified in Schedule 1 hereto shall be chargeable at 80 per cent. of the full rate in the case of goods of a description there specified in relation to the heading or subheading if they are to be regarded as originating products under the Agreements but are not entitled to the benefit of the prohibition of new customs duties on import into the United Kingdom.

6. Any import duty which is for the time being chargeable on goods of a subheading specified in Schedule 2 hereto:

(a) shall be chargeable at the relevant rate there specified instead of the full rate or,

(b) if no rate is so specified, shall not be chargeable in the case of goods which are to be regarded as originating products under the Agreements but are not entitled to the benefit of the prohibition of new customs duties on import into the United Kingdom.

7. Any import duty which is for the time being chargeable on goods of a heading or subheading specified in Schedule 3 hereto shall be chargeable at the relevant rate specified in column 3 of that Schedule in the case of goods of a description specified in column 2 if they are to be regarded as originating products under the Agreements referred to in Article 2(a) and (b) above with Austria, Iceland, Norway, Portugal, Sweden and Switzerland.

8. Any import duty which is for the time being chargeable on goods of any heading or subheading specified on Part I or II of Schedule 4 hereto shall be chargeable:

(a) at 80 per cent. of the full rate in the case of goods of a description specified in relation to the heading or subheading in Part I of the Schedule and

---

(a) S.I. 1973/652 (1973 I, p. 2071).   (b) S.I. 1971/1971 (1971 III, p. 5330).
(c) The relevant amending order is that revoked by this Order.

(b) at the rate specified in Part II of the Schedule instead of the full rate

if (in either case) the goods are to be regarded as originating products under the Agreement, referred to in Article 2(a) above, with Portugal.

9.—(1) Any description in column 2 of Schedules 1, 3, or 4 hereto (other than a description covering a whole heading or subheading) shall be taken to comprise all goods which would be classified under an entry in the same terms constituting a subheading (other than the final subheading) in the relevant heading in the Customs Tariff 1959.

(2) For the purposes of classification under the Customs Tariff 1959, insofar as that depends on the rate of duty, any goods to which Articles 4 to 8 above apply shall be treated as chargeable with the same duty as if this order had not been made.

Tim Fortescue,
Oscar Murton.
Two of the Lords Commissioners
11th June 1973.   of Her Majesty's Treasury.

Article 5

SCHEDULE 1

Tariff Heading	Description
15.10 (C)	Products obtained from pinewood, with a fatty acid content of 90% or more by weight
17.04 18.06 19.01 19.02 19.05 19.06	All goods of these headings
19.07 (D)	Ships' biscuits, crumbs and rusks
19.08 (A)	Gingerbread and the like without covering or filling
19.08 (B) (I)	Biscuits, wafers, rusks and cakes without covering or filling
19.08 (B)(II) to (B)(V) (inclusive)	Biscuits, wafers, rusks, cakes without covering or filling, and pastry of the kind known as Danish pastry
21.01 (A)(II) (B)(II)	All goods of these subheadings
21.04 (B)	All goods of this subheading not containing tomato
21.05 (A)	All goods of this subheading not containing tomato
21.06 (A)(II) (B)	All goods of these subheadings

Tariff Heading	Description
21.07 (A)(I) (A)(II) (A)(III) 21.07 (B)(II)(*b*)	All goods of these subheadings
21.07 (C)(I)	Ice-cream (not including ice-cream powder) and other ices containing no fats
21.07 (D)(I)	Prepared yoghourt other than yoghourt with added flavouring or fruit
21.07 (D)(II)	All goods of this subheading
21.07 (E)	All goods of this subheading
21.07 (F)(I)(*a*)(1)(*cc*)	Hydrolysates of proteins; autolysates of yeast
21.07 (F)(I)(*a*)(2)(*aa*) (F)(I)(*a*)(2)(*bb*) (F)(I)(*b*)(2)(*aa*) (F)(I)(*b*)(2)(*bb*) (F)(I)(*c*)(2)(*aa*) (F)(I)(*c*)(2)(*bb*) (F)(I)(*d*)(2)(*aa*) (F)(I)(*d*)(2)(*bb*) (F)(I)(*e*)(2) (F)(II)(*a*)(2)(*aa*) (F)(II)(*a*)(2)(*bb*) (F)(II)(*b*)(2)(*aa*) (F)(II)(*b*)(2)(*bb*) (F)(II)(*c*)(2)(*aa*) (F)(II)(*c*)(2)(*bb*) (F)(II)(*d*)(2) (F)(III)(*a*)(2)(*aa*) (F)(III)(*a*)(2)(*bb*) (F)(III)(*b*)(2) (F)(III)(*c*)(2) (F)(III)(*d*)(2) (F)(IV)(*a*)(2) (F)(IV)(*b*)(2) (F)(V)(*a*)(2) (F)(VI)(*a*)(2) (F)(VI)(*b*)(2) (F)(VII)(*a*)(2) (F)(VII)(*b*)(2)	Food preparations other than coffee pastes (mixtures of ground, roasted coffee with vegetable fats, with or without other ingredients)

(F)(I)(*b*)(1)
(F)(I)(*c*)(1)
(F)(I)(*d*)(1)
(F)(I)(*e*)(1)
(F)(II)(*b*)(1)
(F)(II)(*c*)(1)
(F)(II)(*d*)(1)
(F)(III)(*b*)(1)
(F)(III)(*c*)(1)
(F)(III)(*d*)(1)
(F)(IV)(*b*)(1)
	Food preparations other than—
	   (*a*) sweetfat (mixtures of edible fats and sugar) and
	   (*b*) coffee pastes (mixtures of ground, roasted coffee with vegetable fats, with or without other ingredients)

Tariff Heading	Description
(F)(IV)(c) (F)(V)(b) (F)(VI)(b)(1) (F)(VI)(c) (F)(VII)(b)(1)	
21.07 (F)(I)(f) (F)(II)(e) (F)(III)(e) (F)(VIII)(b)	Food preparations other than sweetfat (mixtures of edible fats and sugar)
21.07 (F)(II)(a)(1) (F)(III)(a)(1) (F)(IV)(a)(1) (F)(V)(a)(1) (F)(VI)(a)(1) (F)(VII)(a)(1)	Food preparations other than— (a) mixtures of water and emulsifying agents with fats or oil and (b) Coffee pastes (mixtures of ground, roasted coffee with vegetable fats, with or without other ingredients)
21.07 (F)(VIII)(a)	Food preparations other than mixtures of water and emulsifying agents with fat or oil (not including synthetic cream)
21.07 (F)(IX)	Food preparations other than— (a) sweetfat (mixtures of edible fats and sugar) and (b) mixtures of water, and emulsifying agents with fat or oil (not including synthetic cream)
21.07 (F)(I)(a)(2)(cc) (F)(I)(b)(2)(cc) (F)(I)(c)(2)(cc) (F)(II)(a)(2)(cc)	All goods of these subheadings
22.02 (A)	All goods of this subheading containing sugar (sucrose or invert sugar)
22.02 (B)	All goods of this subheading

All headings and subheadings of Chapters 25 to 38 (inclusive) except
28.04 (B)
29.43 (B)(2)
30.03 (A)(2)
32.01 (A)
   (C)(1)
32.05 (D)
35.01 (A)(III)
   (B)
38.11 (B)(1)
38.14 (B)
38.18 (B)(1)(a)
38.18 (B)(1)(b)
38.19 (IJ)(1)
38.19 (IJ)(2)
	All goods of these headings and subheadings

38.19 (IJ)(2)	(a) Foundry core binders based on synthetic resin (b) Products of sorbitol cracking

Tariff Heading	Description
All headings of Chapters 39 and 40	All goods of these headings
All headings of Chapter 41 except 41.01 and 41.09	All goods of these headings
All headings and subheadings of Chapters 42 to 99 (inclusive) except 43.01 44.15 (A)(I) 54.01 57.01	All goods of these headings and subheadings

Article 6

SCHEDULE 2

Description of goods	Rate of Import Duty (if any)
Goods of subheading 28.04(B)	—
Goods of subheading 30.03(A)(2)	5.2% or such greater rate as is equal to four-fifths of the amount or aggregate amount of the duty chargeable, apart from this Order, on such constituents as are mentioned in that subheading
Goods of subheading 32.01(A) (C)(1)	— —
Goods of subheading 32.05(D)	8%
Goods of subheadings 38.11 (B)(1) and 38.14 (B)	6·4% or such greater rate as is equal to four-fifths of the amount or aggregate amount of the duty chargeable, apart from this Order, on such constituents as are mentioned in that subheading
Goods of subheading 38.18 (B)(1)(a)	2·4% or such greater rate as is equal to four-fifths of the amount or aggregate amount by which the duty chargeable, apart from this Order, on such constituents as are mentioned in subheading 38.18 (B)(1) exceeds 7%, in addition to any hydrocarbon oil duty
Goods of subheading 38.18 (B)(1)(b)	6·4% or such greater rate as is equal to four-fifths of the amount or aggregate amount of the duty chargeable, apart from this Order, on such constituents as are mentioned in subheading 38.18 (B)(1)
Goods of subheading 38.19 (IJ)(1)	6·4% or such greater rate as is equal to four-fifths of the amount or aggregate amount of the duty chargeable, apart from this Order, on such constituents as are mentioned in that subheading
Goods of subheading 44.15 (A)(1)	—

SCHEDULE 3

Tariff Heading	Description	Rate of Import Duty (if any)
19.03	All goods of this subheading	8%
19.07 (A) to (C) (inclusive)	All goods of these subheadings	8%
19.07 (D)	All goods of this subheading other than ships' biscuits, crumbs and rusks	8%
19.08 (A)	All goods of this subheading other than gingerbread and the like without covering or filling	8%
19.08 (B)(I)	All goods of this subheading other than biscuits, wafers, rusks and cakes without covering or filling	8%
19.08 (B)(II) to (B)(V) (inclusive)	All goods of these subheadings other than biscuits, wafers, rusks, cakes without covering or filling, and pastry of the kind known as Danish pastry	8%
21.07 (B)(I) (B)(II)(a) (B)(II)(a)	All goods of this subheading Ravioli All goods of this subheading other than ravioli	8% 4% 5·1%
21.07 (C)	Ice-cream containing fat	8%
21.07 (D)(I)	Prepared yoghourt with added flavouring or fruit	8%
21.07 (F)(I)(a)(2)(aa) (F)(I)(a)(2)(bb) (F)(I)(b)(2)(aa) (F)(I)(b)(2)(bb) (F)(I)(c)(2)(aa) (F)(I)(c)(2)(bb) (F)(I)(d)(2)(aa) (F)(I)(d)(2)(bb) (F)(I)(e)(2) (F)(II)(a)(2)(aa) (F)(II)(a)(2)(bb) (F)(II)(b)(2)(aa) (F)(II)(b)(2)(bb) (F)(II)(c)(2)(aa) (F)(II)(c)(2)(bb) (F)(II)(d)(2) (F)(III)(a)(2)(aa) (F)(III)(a)(2)(bb) (F)(III)(b)(2) (F)(III)(c)(2)	Coffee pastes (mixtures of ground, roasted coffee with vegetable fats, with or without other ingredients)	7·2%

Tariff Heading	Description	Rate of Import Duty (if any)
(F)(III)(*d*)(2) (F)(IV)(*a*)(2) (F)(IV)(*b*)(2) (F)(V)(*a*)(2)		
21.07 (F)(IV)(*a*)(2) (F)(VI)(*b*)(2) (F)(VII)(*a*)(2) (F)(VII)(*b*)(2)	Coffee pastes (mixtures of ground, roasted coffee with vegetable fats, with or without other ingredients)— (*a*) in immediate packings of a net capacity of 1 kg or less (*b*) other	7·2% 8·4%
21.07 (F)(I)(*b*)(1) (F)(I)(*c*)(1) (F)(I)(*d*)(1) (F)(I)(*e*)(1) (F)(II)(*b*)(1) (F)(II)(*c*)(1) (F)(II)(*d*)(1) (F)(III)(*b*)(1) (F)(III)(*c*)(1) (F)(III)(*d*)(1) (F)(IV)(*b*)(1) (F)(IV)(*c*) (F)(V)(*b*)	Sweetfat (mixtures of edible fats and sugar) and coffee pastes (mixtures of ground, roasted coffee with vegetable fats, with or without other ingredients)	7·2%
(F)(VI)(*b*)(1) (F)(VI)(*c*) (F)(VII)(*b*)(1)	Sweetfat (mixtures of edible fats and sugar) and coffee pastes (mixtures of ground, roasted coffee with vegetable fats, with or without other ingredients)— (*a*) in immediate packings of a net capacity of 1 kg or less (*b*) other	7·2% 8·4%
21.07 (F)(I)(*f*) (F)(II)(*e*) (F)(III)(*e*)	Sweetfat (mixtures of edible fats and sugar)	7·2%
(F)(VIII)(*b*)	Sweetfat (mixtures of edible fats and sugar) (*a*) in immediate packings of a net capacity of 1 kg or less (*b*) other	7·2% 8·4%
21.07 (F)(II)(*a*)(1) (F)(III)(*a*)(1) (F)(IV)(*a*)(1) (F)(V)(*a*)(1)	Mixtures of water and emulsifying agents with fat or oil and— coffee pastes (mixtures of ground, roasted coffee with vegetable fats, with or without other ingredients)	7·2%
(F)(VI)(*a*)(1) (F)(VII)(*a*)(1)	Mixtures of water and emulsifying agents with fat or oil and— coffee pastes (mixtures of ground, roasted coffee with vegetable fats, with or without other ingredients)— (*a*) in immediate packings of a net capacity of 1 kg or less (*b*) other	7·2% 8·4%

Tariff Heading	Description	Rate of Import Duty (if any)
21.07 (F)(VIII)(a)	Mixtures of water and emulsifying agents with fat or oil (not including synthetic cream)— (a) in immediate packings of a net capacity of 1 kg or less (b) other	 7·2% 8·4%
21.07 (F)(IX)	Sweetfat (mixtures of edible fats and sugar) and— mixtures of water and emulsifying agents with fat or oil (not including synthetic cream)— (a) in immediate packings of a net capacity of 1 kg or less (b) other	 7·2% 8·4%

35.01 (A)(I)
    (A)(II)
    (C)
	All goods of these subheadings	8%

Article 8

SCHEDULE 4

PART I

Tariff Heading or subheading	Description of Goods
02.04 (C)(I)(a)	All goods of this subheading
03.01 (B)(I)(q)	Barbel mullet and rock mullet; sea perch and sea dace: sole
03.03 (B)(I)(b)	All goods of this subheading
(B)(IV)(a)(4)	Clams or cockles (Scrobicularia plana)
(B)(IV)(b)(2)	Clams or cockles (Scrobicularia plana)
05.04	Pigs' guts, suitable for use as sausage casings of a c.i.f. value on importation exceeding £10 per cwt (50·8 kg) or of an equivalent value expressed in other currencies, and edible guts of sheep, pigs or bovine animals, other than those suitable for use as sausage casings.
05.15 (A)(II)	Salted roes
(B)(II)	All goods of this subheading
07.01 (A)(II)(a)	All goods of this subheading
07.05	All goods of this heading
12.03 (B)(I)	Seeds of pine trees
12.07 (A)	All goods of these subheadings
(B)	
(C)	
(D)(I)	
(II)	
(IV)	
12.08 (A)	All goods of these subheadings
(B)(II)	

Tariff Heading or subheading	Description of Goods
15.04 (A)(I)	All goods of these subheadings
16.03 (A)(II)	All goods of these subheadings
(B)(II)	
(C)(II)	
16.04 (A)	All goods of this subheading,
16.05 (A)	All goods of these subheadings
(B)(I)	
(B)(II)(b)(2)	
23.01	All goods of this heading
23.07 (A)(I)	All goods of this subheading
54.01	All goods of this heading
57.01	All goods of this heading

PART II

Tariff Subheading	Rate of Import Duty
16.04 (B)(III)	9·1%

EXPLANATORY NOTE

(This Note is not part of the Order.)

This Order, which comes into operation on 1st July 1973, revokes and re-enacts, with amendments, the Import Duties (European Free Trade Association Countries) (Reductions and Exemptions) Order 1973. That Order provided for the implementation of the United Kingdom's obligations concerning import duties under the Agreements between the European Community and Austria, Iceland, Portugal, Sweden and Switzerland and a like Agreement with Norway has now come into force and is added to the Agreements covered by this Order. The implementation of Community arrangements for trade with Finland, until such time as an Agreement with that country comes into force, will continue.

Likewise, this Order provides for continuing duty-free or preferential treatment until the end of 1973 for certain goods which have hitherto been subject to such treatment as goods originating in the area of the European Free Trade Association (EFTA), but which are not covered by the Agreements.

Continued exemption from import duty or a continued preferential rate of duty is provided for by Article 4 of the Order for all goods so treated hitherto under the EFTA Convention. If such goods are of a class covered by the Agreements or the Agreements as applied by an instrument of the Community to Finland, they must satisfy the conditions specified in the Agreements (in the Protocols relating to origin) for goods which are to benefit from the prohibition of new customs duties between the United Kingdom and the above-mentioned countries.

Goods of a class covered by the EFTA Convention which do not satisfy those conditions are entitled (Articles 5 and 6 of the Order) to a reduction of 20 per cent. of the full rate or duty in the case of goods listed in Schedule 1 or to a specified reduction in, or exemption from, duty in the case of goods listed in Schedule 2.

In the case of goods (listed in Schedule 3) not covered by the EFTA Convention but covered by the Agreements, a reduced rate of duty (equal in most cases to 80 per cent. of the full rate) is given provided that they are originating products for the purposes of the Agreements with Austria, Iceland, Norway, Portugal, Sweden or Switzerland (Article 7) of the Order, and a new reduced rate of duty (equal in most cases to 80 per cent. of the full rate) is now given in the case of certain Portuguese goods (listed in Schedule 4).

The Agreements with Austria, Sweden, Switzerland, Iceland and Portugal are annexed respectively to Community Regulations (EEC) Nos 2836/72 (OJ No. L300, p.1), 2838/72 (OJ No. L300, p. 96), 2840/72 (OJ No. L300, p. 188), 2842/72 (OJ No. L301, p.1) and 2844/72 (OJ No. L301, p. 167). The Agreement between the European Economic Community and Norway has yet to be published in the Official Journal of the European Communities.

STATUTORY INSTRUMENTS

1973 No. 1038

SEA FISHERIES

LANDING AND SALE OF SEA-FISH

The North Sea Herring (Restrictions on Landing) Order 1973

Made - - -	*8th June* 1973
Laid before Parliament	*15th June* 1973
Coming into Operation	*16th June* 1973

The Minister of Agriculture, Fisheries and Food, and the Secretaries of State respectively concerned with the sea-fishing industry in Scotland and Northern Ireland in exercise of the powers conferred on them by sections 6 and 15 of the Sea Fish (Conservation) Act 1967(a) as the latter section is amended by section 22(1) of, and paragraph 38 of Part II of Schedule 1 to, the Sea Fisheries Act 1968(b) and all other powers enabling them in that behalf, after consultation with the Secretary of State for Trade and Industry (c), hereby make the following order: —

Citation, commencement and interpretation

1.—(1) This order may be cited as the North Sea Herring (Restrictions on Landing) Order 1973 and shall come into operation on 16th June 1973.

(2) The Interpretation Act 1889(d) shall apply for the interpretation of this order as it applies for the interpretation of an Act of Parliament.

Prohibition of Landings

2. The landing in the United Kingdom, during the period from 16th June 1973 to 31st January 1974, both dates inclusive, of any herring (clupae harengus) caught in the waters comprised in the North Sea being the area described in the Schedule to this order, is prohibited, but this prohibition shall not apply to the landing of herring so caught, which are landed within 24 hours of being so caught, and herring which, though not so landed, were, immediately on being so caught, packed in ice in boxes, stored in a refrigerated sea water tank or otherwise processed in such a way as to secure preservation for human consumption.

(a) 1967 c. 84.   (b) 1968 c. 77.
(c) For transfer of functions from the Board of Trade to the Secretary of State for Trade and Industry *see* the Secretary of State for Trade and Industry Order 1970 (S.I. 1970/1537 (1970 III, p. 5293).   (d) 1889 c. 63.

Powers of British Sea-Fishery Officers

3. For the purposes of the enforcement of this order there are hereby conferred on every British sea-fishery officer all the powers of a British sea-fishery officer under section 8(2) to (4) of the Sea Fisheries Act 1968.

In Witness whereof the Official Seal of the Minister of Agriculture, Fisheries and Food is hereunto affixed on 6th June 1973.

(L.S.)   *Joseph Godber,*
                    Minister of Agriculture, Fisheries and Food.

                                Gordon Campbell,
                         Secretary of State for Scotland.
6th June 1973.

                              W. S. I. Whitelaw,
                    Secretary of State for Northern Ireland.
8th June 1973.

                                                    Article 2.
SCHEDULE
THE NORTH SEA

The area of sea contained within a line drawn from a position having the co-ordinates of 62° north latitude and 4° west longitude, due south to the north coast of Scotland, thence generally south-eastwards along the north and east coasts of Scotland and the east coast of England, thence westwards along the south coast of England to the meridian of 1° west longitude, thence due south to the coast of France, thence generally in a north-easterly direction along the coasts of France, Belgium, the Netherlands, the Federal Republic of Germany and Denmark to Skagen Point, thence along a rhumb line to the Pater Noster Lighthouse on the coast of Sweden, thence generally in a north-westerly, south-westerly and northerly direction along the coasts of Sweden and Norway to the parallel of 62° north latitude, thence due west to the meridian of 4° west longitude.

EXPLANATORY NOTE

(This Note is not part of the Order.)

This Order bans the landing in the United Kingdom of North Sea herring during the period 16th June 1973—31st January 1974 (both dates inclusive) unless such herring were landed within 24 hours of being caught or if landed later were, on being caught, immediately packed in ice in boxes, stored in refrigerated sea water tanks or otherwise processed in such a way as to secure preservation for human consumption.

STATUTORY INSTRUMENTS

1973 No. 1039 (S.78)

FOOD AND DRUGS

COMPOSITION

The Arsenic in Food (Scotland) Amendment Regulations 1973

Made - - - -	*6th June* 1973
Laid before Parliament	*18th June* 1973
Coming into Operation	*9th July* 1973

In exercise of the powers conferred upon me by sections 4 and 56 of the Food and Drugs (Scotland) Act, 1956(a), and of all other powers enabling me in that behalf, and after consultation with such organisations as appear to me to be representative of interests substantially affected by these regulations, I hereby make the following regulations:—

Citation, commencement and interpretation

1.—(1) These regulations may be cited as the Arsenic in Food (Scotland) Amendment Regulations 1973, and shall come into operation on 9th July 1973.

(2) The Interpretation Act 1889(b) shall apply for the interpretation of these regulations as it applies for the interpretation of an Act of Parliament.

Amendment of principal regulations

2. The Arsenic in Food (Scotland) Regulations 1959(c), as amended **(d)**, shall be further amended by substituting for sub-paragraph (*d*) of regulation 4(2) thereof the following sub-paragraph:—

> "(*d*) to any food in respect of which the maximum permitted arsenic content is prescribed by any regulations, other than these regulations or any amendment to these regulations, made under the Food and Drugs (Scotland) Act 1956 or by any order having effect as if contained in regulations so made.".

Gordon Campbell,
One of Her Majesty's Principal
Secretaries of State.

St. Andrew's House,
Edinburgh.
6th June 1973.

(a) 1956 c. 30.   (b) 1889 c. 63.
(c) S.I. 1959/928 (1959 I, p. 1296).
(d) The relevant amending instrument is S.I. 1966/1384 (1966 III, p. 3715).

EXPLANATORY NOTE
(This Note is not part of the Regulations.)

These Regulations, which come into operation on 9th July 1973, amend the Arsenic in Food (Scotland) Regulations 1959, as amended by the Colouring Matter in Food (Scotland) Regulations 1966 (S.I. 1966 I, 1384). They extend exemption from arsensic limits already specified, to food for which the maximum permitted arsenic content is prescribed by any other instrument made, or having effect as if made, under the Food and Drugs (Scotland) Act 1956.

STATUTORY INSTRUMENTS

1973 No. 1040 (S.79)

FOOD AND DRUGS
COMPOSITION

The Lead in Food (Scotland) Amendment Regulations 1973

Made - - - -	*6th June* 1973
Laid before Parliament	*18th June* 1973
Coming into Operation	*9th July* 1973

In exercise of the powers conferred upon me by sections 4 and 56 of the Food and Drugs (Scotland) Act 1956**(a)**, and of all other powers enabling me in that behalf, and after consultation with such organisations as appear to me to be representative of interests substantially affected by these regulations, I hereby make the following regulations:—

Citation, commencement and interpretation

1.—(1) These regulations may be cited as the Lead in Food (Scotland) Amendment Regulations 1973, and shall come into operation on 9th July 1973.

(2) The Interpretation Act 1889**(b)** shall apply for the interpretation of these regulations as it applies for the interpretation of an Act of Parliament.

Amendment of principal regulations

2. The Lead in Food (Scotland) Regulations 1961**(c)**, as amended **(d)**, shall be further amended by substituting for paragraph (4) of regulation 4 thereof the following paragraph:—

"(4) the foregoing provisions of this regulation shall not apply to any food in respect of which the maximum permitted lead content is prescribed by any regulations, other than these regulations or any amendment to these regulations, made under the Food and Drugs (Scotland) Act 1956 or by any order, other than the Food Standards (Edible Gelatine) Order 1951**(e)**, as amended**(f)**, having effect as if contained in regulations so made.".

Gordon Campbell,
One of Her Majesty's Principal
Secretaries of State.

St. Andrew's House,
Edinburgh.
6th June 1973.

(**a**) 1956 c. 30.   (**b**) 1889 c. 63.
(**c**) S.I. 1961/1942 (1961 III, p. 3650).
(**d**) The relevant amending instrument is S.I. 1966/1384, (1966 III, p. 3715).
(**e**) S.I. 1951/1196 (1951 III, p. 14).   (**f**) S.I. 1961/1942 (1961 III, p. 3650).

EXPLANATORY NOTE

(This Note is not part of the Regulations.)

These Regulations, which come into operation on 9th July 1973, amend the Lead in Food (Scotland) Regulations 1961, as amended by the Colouring Matter in Food (Scotland) Regulations 1966 (S.I. 1966 I, 1384). They extend exemption from the lead limits specified by the principal regulations, to food (other than edible gelatine) for which the maximum permitted lead limit is prescribed by any other instrument made, or having effect as if made, under the Food and Drugs (Scotland) Act 1956.

STATUTORY INSTRUMENTS

1973 No. 1047

LOCAL GOVERNMENT, ENGLAND AND WALES

The Local Government (Financial Loss Allowance) Regulations 1973

Made - - -	*12th June* 1973
Laid before Parliament	*21st June* 1973
Coming into Operation	*12th July* 1973

The Secretary of State for the Environment, in exercise of powers conferred by sections 112 and 117 of the Local Government Act 1948(**a**), as having effect by virtue of section 16 of the Local Government (Miscellaneous Provisions) Act 1953(**b**), and now vested in him(**c**), and of all other powers enabling him in that behalf, hereby makes the following regulations:—

Title and commencement

1. These regulations may be cited as the Local Government (Financial Loss Allowance) Regulations 1973 and shall come into operation on 12th July 1973.

Interpretation

2. The Interpretation Act 1889(**d**) shall apply for the interpretation of these regulations as it applies for the interpretation of an Act of Parliament.

Financial loss allowance

3. The amount which a member of a body to which Part VI of the Local Government Act 1948 applies shall be entitled to be paid by way of financial loss allowance within the meaning of section 112 of the said Act in respect of any one period of 24 hours shall not exceed—

    (*a*) where the period of time over which earnings are lost or additional expense (other than expense on account of travelling or subsistence) is incurred is not more than 4 hours, the sum of £2·75;

    (*b*) where the said period of time is more than 4 hours, the sum of £5·50.

(**a**) 1948 c. 26. (**b**) 1953 c. 26.
(**c**) S.I. 1951/142, 1900, 1970/1681 (1951 I, pp. 1348, 1347; 1970 III, p. 5551).
(**d**) 1889 c. 63.

Revocation

4. The Local Government (Financial Loss Allowance) Regulations 1971(a)
are hereby revoked.

12th June 1973.

Geoffrey Rippon,
Secretary of State for the Environment.

EXPLANATORY NOTE

(This Note is not part of the Regulations.)

These Regulations increase the maximum amounts which members of local
authorities and certain other bodies may claim by way of financial loss allowance.

(a) S.I. 1971/2096 (1971 III, p. 6182).

STATUTORY INSTRUMENTS

1973 No. 1049

SEEDS

The Vegetable Seeds Regulations 1973

Made - - - -	*12th June* 1973
Laid before Parliament	*22nd June* 1973
Coming into Operation	*16th July* 1973

The Minister of Agriculture, Fisheries and Food and the Secretary of State in exercise of the powers vested in them by section 7(1) of the Seeds Act 1920(a) and, acting jointly, in exercise of the powers vested in them by sections 16(1), (1A), (2), (3), (4), (5) and (8), 17(1), (2), (3) and (4), 26(2) and 36 of the Plant Varieties and Seeds Act 1964(b), as amended by section 4(1) of and paragraph 5(1), (2) and (3) of Schedule 4 to the European Communities Act 1972(c) and of all other powers enabling them in that behalf, after consultation with representatives of such interests as appear to them to be concerned, hereby make the following Regulations.

Application, citation and commencement

1. These Regulations, which apply to Great Britain, may be cited as the Vegetable Seeds Regulations 1973 and shall come into operation on the 16th July 1973.

Restriction of Seeds Regulations 1961 *and Seeds (Scotland) Regulations* 1961

2. The Seeds Regulations 1961(d), and the Seeds (Scotland) Regulations 1961(e) and, in particular, Schedules 1, 2, 3, 4 and 8 thereof shall cease to have effect in relation to root and vegetable seeds of the following kinds—

Beetroot	Kohl rabi
Broad bean	Leek
Brussels sprout	Lettuce
Cabbage	Melon
Carrot	Onion
Cauliflower (including winter and spring heading forms commonly known as broccoli)	Parsley
	Parsnip
	Radish
Chicory	Runner bean
Celeriac	Savoy
Celery	Spinach
Cress	Spinach beet (including chard)

(a) 1920 c. 54.   (b) 1964 c. 14.
(c) 1972 c. 68.   (d) S.I. 1961/212 (1961 I, p. 362).
(e) S.I. 1961/274 (1961 I, p. 446).

Cucumber
Dwarf bean (including climbing French
  or pole bean)
Endive
Garden kale (including borecole)
Garden pea

Sprouting broccoli
  (including calabrese)
Sweet corn
Tomato
Turnip
Vegetable marrow

Interpretation

3.—(1) In these Regulations, unless the context otherwise requires—

"the Act" means the Plant Varieties and Seeds Act 1964 as amended by section 4(1) of and Schedule 4 to the European Communities Act 1972;

"authorised officer" means an officer appointed by the Minister of Agriculture, Fisheries and Food or the Secretary of State for the execution of Part II of the Act;

"basic seeds" has the meaning assigned to that expression by Regulation 5(2) of these Regulations;

"certified seeds" has the meaning assigned to that expression by Regulation 5(2) of these Regulations;

"Common Catalogue" means the Common Catalogue of varieties of vegetables published or to be published in the Official Journal of the European Communities;

"marketing" includes, as the context shall permit, the offering for sale, exposing for sale, sale and possession with a view to sale of seeds, and any transaction in the course of business under which the property in seeds is transferred from one person to another and "market" and "marketed" shall be construed accordingly;

"Member State" means a member State of the European Communities;

"the Ministers" means the Minister of Agriculture, Fisheries and Food and the Secretary of State;

"National List" means the list of varieties of vegetables published in accordance with the Seeds (National Lists of Varieties) Regulations 1973(**a**);

"official examination" means an examination carried out by or on behalf of the Ministers, subject to the payment of any fee imposed by Regulations made under the Act or, in relation to seeds harvested elsewhere than in the United Kingdom, an examination approved by the Ministers;

"official label" and "official notice" mean respectively a label and a notice prepared by or on behalf of the Ministers;

"percentage of germination" means the percentage by number of pure seeds or pure pellets which produce seedlings which have developed the structures which indicate the ability to produce mature plants under favourable conditions in the field;

"percentage of purity" means the percentage by weight of pure seeds;

"pure" in relation to seeds means wholly comprised of seeds of the kind of which the seeds purport to be;

"small package" means a package containing no more than a net weight of seeds of 5 kilograms as regards pulses, 500 grams as regards onion, chervil, asparagus, spinach beet, leaf beet or chard, red beet or beetroot, turnip,

---

(**a**) S.I. 1973/994 (1973II, p.3024).

marrow, carrot, radish, and corn salad or lamb's lettuce and 100 grams as regards other kinds of vegetables;

"standard seeds" has the meaning assigned to that expression by Regulation 5(2) of these Regulations.

(2) The Interpretation Act 1889(a) shall apply to the interpretation of these Regulations as it applies to the interpretation of an Act of Parliament and as if these Regulations and the Regulations partially revoked hereby were Acts of Parliament.

Seeds to which the Regulations apply

4.—(1) Subject to paragraph (2) of this Regulation these Regulations apply to vegetable seeds of the kinds set out in Schedule 1 to these Regulations being seeds intended to be used only for the production of agricultural or horticultural crops.

(2) These Regulations shall not apply to any seeds which are marketed for delivery elsewhere than in a Member State.

Marketing of seeds

5.—(1) Subject to the provisions of this Regulation no person shall market any seeds of a variety of a kind to which these Regulations apply unless they are basic seeds, certified seeds or standard seeds of that variety.

(2) For the purposes of this Regulation—

"basic seeds" means seeds which have been produced by or under the authority of a person who is indicated in the National List or in the Common Catalogue as responsible for the maintenance of that variety being seeds which are intended to be used for the production of certified seeds and which, subject to paragraphs (6) and (7) of this Regulation, satisfy the requirements for basic seeds set out in Schedule 2 to these Regulations and which have on official examination satisfied those requirements;

"certified seeds" means seeds—

(a) which have been produced directly from basic seeds or, with the approval of a person who is indicated in the National List or in the Common Catalogue as responsible for the maintenance of that variety, from seeds of a generation earlier than that of basic seeds where the seeds of such earlier generation have on official examination satisfied the requirements for basic seeds set out in Schedule 2 to these Regulations,

(b) which are intended to be used mainly for the production of plants or parts of plants for human or animal consumption, and

(c) which, subject to paragraphs (3) and (6) of this Regulation satisfy the requirements for certified seeds set out in Schedule 2 to these Regulations and which have on official examination satisfied those requirements;

"standard seeds" means seeds which are intended to be used mainly for the production of plants or parts of plants for human or animal consumption and which satisfy the requirements for standard seeds set out in Schedule 2 to these Regulations.

(a) 1889 c. 63.

(3) The Ministers may, by a general licence taking effect during a period of 3 years beginning with the 16th July 1973, permit any person to market as certified seeds, seeds which have been examined in accordance with the licence notwithstanding that the requirements of the definition of "certified seeds" in paragraph (2) of this Regulation have not been fully met:

Provided that in all other respects the provisions of these Regulations shall apply in relation to the marketing of the seeds as they apply to the marketing of certified seeds.

(4) The Ministers may, by a general licence taking effect during a period specified in the licence and, subject to any conditions imposed by the licence, authorise any person to market, as basic seeds, certified seeds, standard seeds or otherwise, seeds which fail in some respect to satisfy the requirements for basic seeds, certified seeds or standard seeds set out in Schedule 2 to these Regulations or which, notwithstanding the requirements of the Seeds (National Lists of Varieties) Regulations 1973 are of a variety not entered in the National List or in the Common Catalogue:

Provided that in all other respects the provisions of these Regulations shall apply in relation to the marketing of the seeds.

(5) Notwithstanding paragraph (1) of this Regulation any person may market in relation to a sale or a proposed sale to a person engaged in the business of trading in seeds otherwise than by way of retail sale seeds which have been imported from a country other than a Member State.

(6) Notwithstanding the requirement in Schedule 2 to these Regulations that basic seeds attain the minimum standards of germination specified in the said Schedule the Ministers may by licence authorise any person to market, as basic seeds, seeds of a kind specified in the licence which attain a lower percentage of germination than that specified in the said Schedule in relation to seeds of that kind.

(7) In a case where the official examination in respect of the germination of a proposed consignment of seeds has not been completed and the Ministers have been supplied with a provisional report in respect of such germination they may, if the seeds in other respects satisfy the appropriate requirements of Schedule 2 to these Regulations, authorise the sale of the seeds as basic seeds or as certified seeds, as the case may be, to the first consignee.

(8) Paragraphs (6) and (7) of this Regulation shall not apply to seeds which have been imported from a country other than a Member State unless they were (a) produced directly from basic seeds certified in a Member State or (b) produced directly from seeds of a generation earlier than that of basic seeds where the seeds of such earlier generation have on an official examination satisfied the requirements for basic seeds set out in Schedule 2 to these Regulations.

(9) (a) Except as provided in sub-paragraph (b) of this paragraph no person shall market any seeds comprising a mixture of varieties of seeds of the same kind.

(b) Subject to compliance with the additional requirement as to labelling in Part III of Schedule 5 to these Regulations, mixtures of varieties of standard seeds of lettuce or of radish may be marketed in packages containing no more than 50 grams of seed.

(10) Paragraph (1) of this Regulation shall not take effect in relation to—

(a) seeds of any generation earlier than that of basic seeds;

(b) seeds used or to be used for research or experiment;

(c) seeds used or to be used in the course of a process of selection;

(d) seeds which have not been cleaned which are marketed with a view to processing, treatment or cleaning, provided that the identity of the seeds is stated by the person by whom they are marketed.

Sampling

6.—(1) A sample of seeds for the purposes of the enforcement of these Regulations shall be taken by an authorised officer in accordance with the procedure set out in Part I of Schedule 3 to these Regulations.

(2) Subject to paragraph (3) of this Regulation the minimum weight of each part into which a sample of seeds is divided in accordance with paragraph (4) of this Regulation and the maximum weight of the lot or quantity of seeds from which a sample may be taken shall be respectively equal to the weights set out opposite the reference to the particular kind of seeds in Part II of the said Schedule 3.

(3) Where the seeds of which a sample is to be taken are contained in small packages the sample may consist of fifteen of such packages.

(4) A sample of seeds shall be divided by the authorised officer into three parts of which one part shall be delivered or sent by him to the owner of the seeds or his representative, one part shall be delivered or sent to the Chief Officer of an Official Seed Testing Station and the remaining part shall be retained by the authorised officer and be available for production to a court in accordance with section 26(7) of the Act.

Certificate of test of sample

7. A certificate of the result of a test of a sample of seeds taken by an authorised officer for the purposes of Part II of the Act shall be in the form set out in Schedule 4 to these Regulations.

Sealing of packages

8.—(1) No person shall market a package of basic seeds or a package, other than a small package, of certified seeds unless it has been sealed with a sealing device by an authorised officer in such a manner that when the package is opened the sealing device will be broken and cannot be replaced except by a further sealing device affixed by an authorised officer.

(2) No person shall market a package of standard seeds or a small package of certified seeds unless it has been sealed by the person affixing the label required by Regulation 9(6) or 9(7) of these Regulations with a sealing device approved by the Ministers and in such a manner that when the package is opened the sealing device will be broken and cannot be replaced.

Labelling of packages

9.—(1) No person shall market a package of seeds unless it is labelled, inscribed or otherwise dealt with in accordance with this Regulation.

(2) (*a*) Subject to the exception in sub-paragraph (*c*) of this paragraph, a package of basic seeds or a package, other than a small package, of certified seeds shall have affixed on the outside an official label which shall be either an adhesive label or a label secured to the package by a sealing device and shall be affixed in either case by an authorised officer.

(*b*) The official label shall be of the minimum size and of the colour specified, and shall contain particulars of the matters also specified, in Part I of Schedule 5 to these Regulations.

(*c*) The official label referred to in sub-paragraph (*a*) of this paragraph shall not be required when all of the particulars required by sub-paragraph (*b*) are included in the official notice placed in the package in accordance with paragraph (5) of this Regulation and the package is sufficiently transparent to enable such particulars to be readily legible through it.

(3) If the Ministers shall have authorised the marketing of basic seeds or of certified seeds in accordance with Regulation 5(6) or 5(7) of these Regulations a special label affixed to the outside of the package shall contain a statement of the germination of the seeds together with the name and address of the seller and the reference number of the lot.

(4) If a package of basic seeds or certified seeds shall have been officially re-sealed the fact shall be stated together with the date of re-sealing either on the official label referred to in paragraph (2) of this Regulation or on the official notice in the circumstances referred to in the said paragraph (2).

(5) A package of basic seeds, or a package, other than a small package, of certified seeds shall contain an official notice which shall be coloured white in the case of basic seeds and blue in the case of certified seeds containing particulars of the matters specified in the items numbered 4, 5 and 6 in Part I of Schedule 5 to these Regulations:

Provided that if such particulars are printed indelibly on the outside of the package or on an adhesive label affixed on the outside of the package the official notice referred to in this paragraph shall not be required.

(6) A package, other than a small package, of standard seeds shall have affixed on the outside a label which shall be of the minimum size and of the colour specified in Part II of Schedule 5 to these Regulations and shall contain particulars of the matters also specified in the said Part II:

Provided that if such particulars are indelibly printed on the outside of the package the said label shall not be required.

(7) A small package of certified seeds and a small package of standard seeds shall have affixed on the outside a label which shall be of the colour and shall contain the particulars appropriate to the seeds of the matters specified in Part III of Schedule 5 to these Regulations:

Provided that if such particulars are indelibly printed on the outside of the package the said label shall not be required.

(8) If any seeds have been subjected to any chemical treatment the fact, the nature of the treatment and the proprietary name of the chemical employed shall be stated either—

(*a*) on the label referred to in paragraphs (2), (6) or (7) of this Regulation or, where such a label is not required, with the particulars otherwise given in accordance with those paragraphs, or

(*b*) on a separate label

and also (except where the label referred to in the said paragraphs (2), (6) or (7) of this Regulation is not required) either on the outside of the package or in a statement enclosed in the package.

(9) If the Ministers shall have authorised the marketing of seeds of a lower standard in accordance with Regulation 5(4) of these Regulations the official label referred to in paragraph (2) of this Regulation or the label referred to in paragraphs (6) or (7) of this Regulation shall state the respect in which the seeds are of a lower standard and if the seeds shall not have been authorised to be marketed as basic seeds, certified seeds or standard seeds the label shall be coloured brown and shall contain such particulars as shall be required by the general licence referred to in the said Regulation 5(4).

(10) The particulars and information given in accordance with this Regulation may be accompanied by further particulars and information relating to the seeds except that a reference to a particular selection may only be made in respect of an approved selection and in respect of standard seeds of a variety which was entered on the 1st January 1973 either in a list of a Member State other than the United Kingdom corresponding to a National List or in the Common Catalogue or in the National List when it was first published without any reference to any particular properties of that selection, the selection name in such a case being made to appear after the name of the variety of the seeds and with no greater prominence than that of the name of the variety.

(11) During the period expiring on the 1st July 1975 a statement of the testing of the seeds in accordance with the requirements of the Seeds Act 1920 may be substituted for the items numbered 1 in Part III of Schedule 5 to these Regulations.

(12) No person shall sell any seeds otherwise than in a package which is labelled, inscribed or otherwise dealt with in accordance with this Regulation unless they are sold by way of retail sale, in a quantity not exceeding the appropriate maximum weight indicated in Schedule 6 to these Regulations, and are taken in the presence of the purchaser from a container on or in the proximity of which there is clearly and visibly marked or displayed a statement containing the particulars of the matters specified in Part IV of Schedule 5 to these Regulations.

(13) The particulars and information given in accordance with this Regulation shall be given in the official language of one of the Member States.

Records etc. of transactions concerning standard seeds

10.—(1) A person who in the course of marketing any standard seeds affixes or causes to be affixed, in accordance with Regulation 9(6) of these Regulations, a label on the outside of a package of standard seeds or prints or stamps or causes to be printed or stamped on the outside of such a package the particulars referred to in the said Regulation 9(6) shall maintain and keep available for inspection by an authorised officer a record of the dates on which and of the packages on which such labels were affixed or particulars printed or stamped and shall, if so required by the Ministers, furnish them from time to time with a copy of such record.

(2) A person referred to in paragraph (1) of this Regulation shall keep and retain for a period of at least three years a record of the lots of standard seeds marketed by him, and shall take and retain for a period of at least two years

a sample of each such lot of at least the appropriate minimum weight specified in Part II of Schedule 3 to these Regulations and, if so required by the Ministers, or by an authorised officer, shall produce such record or deliver any such sample to them or to him.

Civil liabilities of sellers of seeds

11.—(1) The particulars given to a purchaser by the seller of basic seeds or certified seeds to which these Regulations apply, whether given in pursuance of these Regulations expressly or by implication arising from the description under which the seeds are sold, shall constitute a statutory warranty for the purpose of section 17 of the Act in so far as they relate to the percentage of germination of the seeds, the percentage of analytical purity of the seeds, the content of seeds of other plant species or the varietal purity of the seeds.

(2) Section 17(2) of the Act shall apply to any particulars given to a purchaser by the seller of seeds, being particulars given or implied as in paragraph (1) of this Regulation, in so far as they relate to the percentages of germination, of analytical purity, or of the content of seeds of other plant species and there are hereby prescribed in respect of such matters the limits of variation set out in Schedule 7 to these Regulations.

(3) Section 17(3) of the Act shall apply to any particulars given to a purchaser by the seller of seeds, being particulars given or implied as in paragraph (1) of this Regulation, in so far as they relate to the percentages of germination, of analytical purity or of the content of seeds of other plant species.

(4) A purchaser who intends to obtain a test of seeds for the purposes of section 17(3) of the Act shall, not more than 10 days after delivery to him of the seeds and statutory statement, give to the seller written notice of his intention and thereupon the seller may indicate a day (not being more than 21 days after delivery to the purchaser of the seeds and statutory statement) and a reasonable time on that day at which a sample of the seeds may be taken in the presence of himself or of his representative and the purchaser shall afford to the seller reasonable facilities for that purpose.

(5) On the day and at the time appointed by the seller in accordance with paragraph (4) of this Regulation or, if the seller shall have failed to appoint such a day and time, on a day not more than 28 days after delivery to the purchaser of the seeds and statutory statement the purchaser may, and if the seller or his representative is present shall, take a sample of the seeds in accordance with the procedure set out in Part I of Schedule 3 to these Regulations and shall divide the sample so taken into two parts, each being of at least the appropriate minimum weight specified in Part II of Schedule 3 to these Regulations, of which one part shall be sent to the chief officer of the official testing station for the purpose of being tested and the other part delivered or tendered to the seller or his representative or, if he or his representative was not present when the sample was taken, sent to him by post.

In Witness whereof the Official Seal of the Minister of Agriculture, Fisheries and Food is hereunto affixed on 8th June 1973.

(L.S.)

Joseph Godber,
Minister of Agriculture, Fisheries and Food.

Gordon Campbell,
Secretary of State for Scotland.

12th June 1973.

Regulation 4(1)

SCHEDULE 1

KINDS OF SEEDS TO WHICH THE REGULATIONS APPLY

Latin Name	Common Name
Allium cepa L.	Onion
Allium porrum L.	Leek
Anthriscus cerefolium (L.) Hoffm.	Chervil
Apium graveolens L.	Celery and celeriac
Asparagus officinalis L.	Asparagus
Beta vulgaris L. var. cicla (L.) Ulrich	Spinach beet, leaf beet or chard
Beta vulgaris L. var. esculenta L.	Red beet or beetroot
Brassica oleracea L. var. acephala DC. subvar. laciniata L.	Curly kale or borecole
Brassica oleracea L. convar. botrytis (L.) Alef. var. botrytis	Cauliflower
Brassica oleracea L. convar, botrytis (L.) Alef. var. italica Plenck	Sprouting broccoli and calabrese
Brassica oleracea L. var. bullata subvar. gemmifera DC.	Brussels sprout
Brassica oleracea L. var. bullata DC. et var. sabauda L.	Savoy cabbage
Brassica oleracea L. var capitata L.f. alba DC.	Cabbage
Brasscia oleracea L. var. capitata L.f. rubra (L.) Thell.	Red Cabbage
Brassica oleracea L. var. gongylodes L.	Kohl rabi
Brassica rapa L. var. rapa (L.) Thell.	Turnip
Capsicum annuum L.	Chili, pepper and capsicum
Cichorium endivia L.	Endive
Cichorium intybus L. var. foliosum Bisch.	Chicory
Cucumis melo L.	Melon
Cucumis sativus L.	Cucumber or gherkin
Cucurbita pepo L.	Marrow
Daucus carota L. ssp. sativus (Hoffm.) Hayek	Carrot
Lactuca sativa L.	Lettuce
Petroselinum hortense Hoffm.	Parsley
Phaseolus coccineus L.	Runner bean
Phaseolus vulgaris L.	French bean, dwarf and climbing
Pisum sativum L. (excluding P. arvense L.)	Pea
Raphanus sativus L.	Radish,
Solanum lycopersicum L. (Lycopersicum esculentum Mill.)	Tomato
Solanum melongena L.	Aubergine or egg plant
Spinacia oleracea L.	Spinach
Valeria nella locusta (L.) Betcke (V. olitoria Poll.)	Corn-salad or lamb's lettuce
Vicia faba L. var. major	Broad bean

SCHEDULE 2 Regulation 5(2)

REQUIREMENTS FOR BASIC SEEDS, CERTIFIED SEEDS AND STANDARD SEEDS

PART I

Conditions relating to the crop from which the seeds are obtained.

1. So far as it can be ascertained at crop inspection, allowing for the variation expected in the particular kind of vegetable, the plants shall conform to the characteristics of the variety established when the variety was included in the UK National List of Varieties or the EEC Common Catalogue of varieties.

2. For basic seeds, at least one official field inspection shall be carried out. For certified seeds, at least one field inspection shall be carried out of which at least 20% of the area of each species shall be officially check inspected.

3. The cultural condition of the field and the stage of development of the crop shall be such that sufficient varietal identity and varietal purity and health can be adequately checked.

4. The minimum distances from neighbouring plants which might cause undesirable foreign pollination are as follows:—

A. *Beta and Brassica species*

Distance from other sources of foreign pollen likely to cross-fertilise with varieties of Beta or Brassica species:

(a) for basic seeds   1000 metres

(b) for certified seeds   600 metres

B. *Other species*

Distance from other sources of foreign pollen likely to cross-fertilise with varieties of these species:

(a) for basic seeds   500 metres

(b) for certified seeds   300 metres

These distances may be disregarded if there is adequate protection against any undesirable foreign pollination.

5. The crop shall be of a satisfactory state of health insofar as seed-borne diseases and organisms affecting the seeds are concerned.

PART II

Conditions relating to the seeds.

1. The seeds and the plants produced from them shall conform to the characteristics of the variety established when the variety was included in the UK National List of Varieties or the EEC Common Catalogue of varieties.

2. The seeds shall be of a satisfactory state of health insofar as seed-borne diseases and organisms affecting the seeds are concerned. In particular all basic seeds of brassica and of beta vegetables must be subject to a test for Phoma lingam and Phoma betae respectively and infected seeds must be appropriately treated before they can be used to produce certified seeds. For basic seeds and certified seeds the number of lettuce seeds infected with lettuce mosaic virus must not exceed 0·1 %.

3. The seeds shall also comply with the following conditions:

(a) Standards

Kind		Minimum analytical purity (% by weight)	Maximum content of seeds of other plant species (% by weight)	Minimum germination (% of pure seeds, clusters or pellets)
Allium cepa	Onion	97	0·5	70
Allium porrum	Leek	97	0·5	65
Anthriscus cerefolium	Chervil	96	1	70
Apium graveolens	Celery and celeriac	97	1	70
Asparagus officinalis	Asparagus	96	0·5	70
Beta vulgaris	Cheltenham beet	97	0·5	50 (clusters)
	Other kinds	97	0·5	70 (clusters)
Brassica oleracea convar botrytis	Cauliflower, sprouting broccoli	97	1	70
Brassica oleracea (other kinds)	Other brassica kinds (curly kale, Brussels sprout, Savoy cabbage, cabbage, red cabbage, kohl rabi)	97	1	75
Brassica rapa	Turnip	97	1	80
Capsicum annuum	Chili, pepper and capsicum	97	0·5	65
Cichorium endivia	Endive	95	1	65
Cichorium intybus	Chicory	95	1·5	65
Cucumis melo	Melon	98	0·1	75
Cucumis sativus	Cucumber or gherkin	98	0·1	80
Cucurbita pepo	Marrow	98	0·1	75
Daucus carota	Carrot	95	1	65
Lactuca sativa	Lettuce	95	0·5	75
Petroselinum hortense	Parsley	97	1	65
Phaseolus coccineus	Runner bean	98	0·1	80
Phaseolus vulgaris	French bean, dwarf and climbing	98	0·1	75
Pisum sativum	Pea	98	0·1	80
Raphanus sativus	Radish	97	1	70
Solanum lycopersicum	Tomato	97	0·5	75
Solanum melongena	Aubergine or egg plant	96	0·5	65
Spinacia oleracea	Spinach	97	1	75
Valerianella locusta	Corn-salad or lamb's lettuce	95	1	65
Vicia faba	Broad bean	98	0·1	80

(b) Additional requirements

(i) seeds of pulses must not be contaminated by the following pea and bean seed beetles:

Acanthoscelides obtectus Say.

Bruchus affinis Fro.

Bruchus atomarius L.

Bruchus pisorum L.

Bruchus rufimanus Boh.

(ii) Seeds must not be contaminated with live mite (Acarina).

Regulations 6(1) and (2), 10(2) and 11(5).

SCHEDULE 3

PART I

PROCEDURE FOR THE TAKING OF SAMPLES

1. The following paragraphs numbered 2-5 inclusive shall not apply where the seeds to be sampled are in small packages as defined in Regulation 3(1) of these Regulations.

2. Prior to sampling a seed lot shall be well mixed so as to be as uniform among its parts as is practicable.

3. When the seed lot is in sacks or other similar sized containers, the number of sacks or containers to be sampled shall be in accordance with the following table:—

Number of sacks or other containers in the Bulk	*Minimum number of sacks or other containers to be sampled*
1— 5 (inclusive)	Each sack or other container, portions being taken from at least five positions
6—14　　,,	Not less than 5 sacks or other containers
15—30　　,,	At least 1 sack in 3
31—49　　,,	Not less than 10 sacks
50 or more	At least 1 sack in 5

When there are more than 5 sacks or other containers in the lot the sacks to be sampled must be selected at random.

For sampling seed lots in containers weighing less than 50 kg, a 100 kg weight of seed is taken as the basic unit. Containers are combined to form sampling units weighing a maximum of 100 kg (e.g., 5 containers of 20 kg each form 1 unit). For sampling purposes each unit is regarded as one container and the sampling intensity prescribed above is used.

4. The samples shall be taken in the following manner:

SEEDS IN FULL SACKS OR OTHER CONTAINERS

The sacks or containers shall be sampled at random and samples taken from either the top, middle or bottom of each selected sack or container. The position from which the seed is taken shall be varied from sack to sack and seed shall be taken from different horizontal positions. Wherever practicable, seed in sacks shall be sampled with a metal spear, trier or probe with a solid point which shall be of sufficient length to reach beyond the middle of the sack when inserted from the side and shall have an oval aperture so placed that the instrument removes portions of seed of equal volume from each part of the container through which it travels. The instrument shall be inserted into the container in an upward direction at an angle of approximately 30° to the horizontal, with its aperture downwards until the aperture reaches the centre of the container. It shall then be rotated so as to bring the aperture uppermost and withdrawn at once at a decreasing speed so that the quantity of seed obtained from successive locations increases progressively from the centre to the side of the container.

Alternatively, a longer instrument may be inserted until the aperture reaches the farther side of the container, rotated in the manner described above and then withdrawn at a uniform speed.

A stick sampler may be used in place of the instrument mentioned above. It may be used horizontally or vertically. If there is more than one aperture it must have transverse partitions so that each aperture opens into a separate compartment; it shall be inserted diagonally into the container in the closed position, then opened, gently agitated to allow it to fill completely, closed again, with drawn and emptied.

Seeds in containers other than sacks shall wherever practicable be sampled with an instrument as aforesaid, which shall be used as already described. Where it is not practicable to sample seeds in sacks or other containers in the manner already described, portions may be taken by hand, care being taken to keep the fingers tightly closed about the seeds so that none may escape as the hand is withdrawn. If necessary, in order to reach the lower levels, part of the contents shall be emptied into another sack or other container.

SEEDS IN A PARTLY FILLED SACK

The seeds shall be thoroughly mixed by hand and small portions then taken from at least five different positions.

SEEDS IN BULK

Portions of seed shall be taken with a stick sampler from at least the number of positions indicated in the table below:—

Size of bulk	Number of positions to be sampled
Up to 50 kg	Not less than 3
51 to 1,500 kg	„ „ „ 5
1,501 to 3,000 kg	At least 1 for each 300 kg
3,001 to 5,000 kg	Not less than 10
5,001 to 20,000 kg	At least 1 for each 500 kg

Sampling positions must be selected at random in both vertical and horizontal planes. If the sampler has more than one aperture it shall have transverse partitions so that each aperture opens into a separate compartment.

SEEDS IN A CLEANING, MIXING OR DRESSING MACHINE

Portions of seed shall be drawn during the cleaning, mixing or dressing process so that the entire cross section of the seed stream is uniformly sampled at regular intervals throughout the whole of the process. The frequency shall be at least as indicated in the table below:

Size of lot	Number of times to be sampled
Up to 50 kg	Not less than 3
51 to 1,500 kg	„ „ „ 5
1,501 to 3,000 kg	At least 1 for each 300 kg
3,001 to 5,000 kg	Not less than 10
5,001 to 20,000 kg	At least 1 for each 500 kg

5. When the individual portions taken from the lot already exceed the amount required they shall be put together in a clean receptacle and well mixed. Where the composite sample so obtained exceeds the amount required, it shall be reduced by using an efficient seed divider.

Part II

Minimum Weights of Samples and Maximum Weights of Lots Sampled

Kind		Mini-mum Sample Weight (in grams)	Maxi-mum Lot Weight (in tons)	Kind		Mini-mum Sample Weight (in grams)	Maxi-mum Lot Weight (in tons)
Allium cepa	Onion	25	10	Daucus carota	Carrot	25	10
Allium porrum	Leek	25	10	Lactuca sativa	Lettuce	25	10
Anthriscus cerefolium	Chervil	25	10	Petroselinum hortense	Parsley	25	10
Apium graveolens	Celery, Celeriac	25	10	Phaseolus coccineus	Runner bean	1,000	20
Asparagus officinalis	Asparagus	100	10	Phaseolus vulgaris	French bean	500	20
Beta vulgaris	Beet (all kinds)	100	20	Pisum sativum	Pea	500	20
Brassica oleracea	Brassica (all kinds)	25	10	Raphanus sativus	Radish	50	10
Brassica rapa	Turnip	50	10	Solanum lycopersicum	Tomato	25	10
Capsicum annum	Chili, capsicum, pepper	50	10	Solanum melongena	Aubergine	25	10
Cichorium endivia	Endive	25	10	Spinacia oleracea	Spinach	100	10
Cichorium intybus	Chicory	25	10	Valerianella locusta	Corn-salad	25	10
Cucumis melo	Melon	100	20	Vicia faba	Broad bean	1,000	20
Cucumis sativus	Cucumber, gherkin	25	20				
Cucurbita pepo	Marrow	150	20				

In the case of F1 hybrid varieties of the above kinds, the minimum weight of the sample may be reduced to a quarter of the weight specified for the variety. The number of seeds per sample must be at least 200.

Regulation 7

SCHEDULE 4

Certificate of the Result of a Test of Seeds

Station No...

Control Sample No..................................

MINISTRY OF AGRICULTURE, FISHERIES AND FOOD

DEPARTMENT OF AGRICULTURE AND FISHERIES FOR SCOTLAND

PLANT VARIETIES AND SEEDS ACT 1964

The Vegetable Seeds Regulations 1973

Final report of the Official Seed Testing Station for England and Wales/ Scotland on a Sample Taken under Section 25(5) of the Act

on the premises of

Name ....

Address ....

....

....

Date received at Station...

Date of sampling ....

Quantity sampled ....

Quantity represented ....

Description of seed

Kind ....%

Variety ....%

Category ....%

Certificate or
reference number ....

Result of Official Test

Purity ....

Weed seeds ....

Other crop seeds ....

Germination ....

Remarks

Date ....

Chief Officer

Regulations 5(9), 9(2), (5), (6), (7) and (11)

SCHEDULE 5

Part 1

Official Label for a Package of Basic Seeds of any Size or for a Package of Certified Seeds, other than a Small Package as Defined in Regulation 3

(a) Prescribed Contents

1. "EEC rules and standards"

2. Certification service and Member State or its mark

3. Month and year when officially sealed

4. Reference number of the lot

5. Kind

6. Variety

7. Category

8. Country of production

9. Declared net or gross weight or declared number of seeds

(b) MINIMUM SIZE OF THE LABEL

110 mm x 67 mm

(c) The label shall be white for basic seeds and blue for certified seeds

PART II

SUPPLIER'S LABEL FOR A PACKAGE OF STANDARD SEEDS, OTHER THAN A SMALL PACKAGE AS DEFINED IN REGULATION 3

(a) PRESCRIBED CONTENTS

1. "EEC rules and standards"

2. Name and address of the supplier responsible for affixing the labels or his identification mark

3. Month and year when sealed

4. Kind

5. Variety

6. "Standard seeds"

7. Lot reference number given by the supplier responsible for affixing the labels

8. Country of production

9. Declared net or gross weight or declared number of seeds

(b) MINIMUM SIZE OF THE LABEL

110 mm x 67 mm

(c) The label shall be dark yellow

PART III

SMALL PACKAGES AS DEFINED IN REGULATION 3

A. SUPPLIER'S LABEL FOR A SMALL PACKAGE OF CERTIFIED SEEDS

(a) PRESCRIBED CONTENTS

1. "EEC rules and standards"

2. Name and address of the supplier responsible for affixing the labels or his identification mark

3. Year of sealing

4. Kind

5. Variety

6. "Certified seeds"

7. Reference number enabling the certified lot to be identified

8. Declared net or gross weight or declared number of seeds, except in the case of packages not exceeding 500 grams

(b) The label shall be blue

B. Supplier's Label for a small Package of Standard Seeds

(a) Prescribed Contents

1. "Complies with legal standards"
2. Kind
3. Variety
4. Name and address of packeter or his identifying reference number
5. Declared net or gross weight or declared number of seeds, except in the case of packages not exceeding 500 grams
6. "Standard seeds"
7. Year of sealing (packeting)

(b) Where the seeds comprise a mixture of seeds of varieties of lettuce or of radish the label shall also state the names of the constituent varieties

(c) The label shall be dark yellow

Part IV

Particulars to be Marked or Displayed on the Sale of Unpacketed Seeds

1. "Complies with legal standards"
2. Kind
3. Variety

Regulation 9(12)

SCHEDULE 6

Maximum Weights for Retail Sales of Unpacketed Seeds

Allium cepa	Onion	
Allium porrum	Leek	
Anthriscus cerefolium	Chervil	
Apium graveolens	Celery and celeriac	
Asparagus officinalis	Asparagus	
Beta vulgaris	Spinach beet, leaf beet or chard	
Beta vulgaris	Red beet or beetroot	
Brassica oleracea	Cauliflower, broccoli and other brassica species	
Brassica rapa	Turnip	
Capsicum annuum	Chili, pepper and capsicum	1 kg
Cichorium endivia	Endive	
Cichorium intybus	Chicory	
Cucumis melo	Melon	
Cucumis sativus	Cucumber or gherkin	
Cucurbita pepo	Marrow	
Daucus carota	Carrot	
Lactuca sativa	Lettuce	
Petroselinum hortense	Parsley	
Raphanus sativus	Radish	
Solanum lycopersicum	Tomato	
Solanum melongena	Aubergine	
Spinacia oleracea	Spinach	
Valerianella locusta	Corn-salad or lamb's lettuce	
Phaseolus coccineus	Runner bean	
Phaseolus vulgaris	French bean, dwarf and climbing	3 kg
Pisum sativum	Pea	
Vicia faba	Broad bean	

Regulation 11(2)

SCHEDULE 7

LIMITS OF VARIATION

PART I

PURITY

Minimum Percentage of Purity Per cent	Limit of Variation Per cent
95·0	0·93
96·0	0·84
97.0	0·75
98·0	0·63

PART II

CONTENT OF SEEDS OF OTHER PLANT SPECIES

Maximum Content of Seeds of Other Plant Species Per cent	Limit of Variation Per cent
0·1	0·16
0·5	0·34
1·0	0·46
1·5	0·54

PART III

GERMINATION

Minimum Percentage of Germination Per cent	Limit of Variation Per cent
50	11
65	10
70	9
75	9
80	8

EXPLANATORY NOTE

(This Note is not part of the Regulations.)

These Regulations, which apply to Great Britain, are made under Part II of the Plant Varieties and Seeds Act 1964, as amended by the European Communities Act. The Regulations restrict the marketing of vegetable seeds to specified grades of seeds namely basic seeds, certified seeds and standard seeds as defined in the Regulations. By virtue of the Seeds (National Lists of Varieties) Regulations 1973 (S.I. 1973/994) only varieties of seeds entered in the National List of vegetable seeds, in the Common Catalogue of vegetable seeds published in the Official Journal of the European Communities or, in certain circumstances, in the National List of vegetable seeds of another Member State of the European Communities may be so marketed.

The seeds may only be sold in sealed packages which are to be labelled with prescribed particulars.

Samples of seeds may be taken in a prescribed manner for the enforcement of the Regulations and of the civil rights of a purchaser. The Regulations provide that certain particulars given on the sale of seeds are deemed to be warranted by the seller to be true.

A contravention of any of the provisions of the Regulations will be an offence under Part II of the Plant Varieties and Seeds Act 1964.

The Regulations do not apply to the marketing of seeds for delivery elsewhere than in a Member State of the European Communities.

STATUTORY INSTRUMENTS

1973 No. 1050

SEEDS

The Seeds (Fees) Regulations 1973

Made - - -	*6th June* 1973
Laid before Parliament	*22nd June* 1973
Coming into Operation	*16th July* 1973

The Minister of Agriculture, Fisheries and Food and the Secretary of State for Scotland, acting jointly, in exercise of the powers vested in them by section 16(1A) of the Plant Varieties and Seeds Act 1964(a), as amended by section 4(1) of and paragraph 5(1) and (2) of Schedule 4 to the European Communities Act 1972(b) and of all other powers enabling them in that behalf, hereby make the following Regulations:—

Citation and commencement

1. These Regulations may be cited as the Seeds (Fees) Regulations 1973 and shall come into operation on 16th July 1973.

Fees

2. There shall be paid in respect of matters arising under regulations made under Part II of the Plant Varieties and Seeds Act 1964, as amended by the European Communities Act 1972, being the matters specified in the first column of the Schedule to these Regulations, the fees specified in the second column of the said Schedule opposite the respective references to such matters.

3. Any such fees in respect of matters arising—

(a) in England and Wales shall be payable to the Minister of Agriculture, Fisheries and Food;

(b) in Scotland shall be payable to the Secretary of State.

In Witness whereof the official seal of the Minister of Agriculture, Fisheries and Food is hereunto affixed on 5th June 1973.

(L.S.)
Joseph Godber,
Minister of Agriculture, Fisheries and Food.

Gordon Campbell,
Secretary of State for Scotland.

6th June 1973.

(a) 1964 c. 14.   (b) 1972 c. 68.

SCHEDULE

MATTERS ARISING UNDER THE VEGETABLE SEEDS REGULATIONS 1973(a) IN
RELATION TO THE CERTIFICATION OF BASIC SEEDS AND CERTIFIED SEEDS.

Matter	Fee
	£
Crop entry, that is to say, application for certification when a sample of the seeds to be used for the production of the crop is already in the possession of the certifying authority. In the case of such an application relating to a biennial species, no fee will be payable if the application is withdrawn before 1st November in the year of sowing ..	5·00
Stock entry, that is to say, application for certification when a sample of the seeds to be used for the production of the crop is not in the possession of the certifying authority ..	10·00
Seed levy, that is to say, the certification fee payable at the appropriate rate according to their kind on the final weight of seeds that have undergone the certification process, being seeds of one of the following kinds: —	
Turnip	0·08 per cwt.
Red beet	0·60 per cwt.
Cabbage	0·75 per cwt.
Lettuce	2·00 per cwt.
Brussels sprout	1·50 per cwt.
Tomato	1·00 per lb.
Cauliflower	0·08 per lb.
Labelling	0·05 per label
Drawing of sample for the official examination mentioned in regulation 5(2) of the Vegetable Seeds Regulations 1973	4·75 per sample

EXPLANATORY NOTE

(This Note is not part of the Regulations.)

These Regulations indicate the fees payable in respect of matters arising under the Vegetable Seeds Regulations 1973 (S.I. 1973/1049).

(a) S.I. 1973/1049 (1973 II, p. 3142).

STATUTORY INSTRUMENTS

1973 No. 1052

FOOD AND DRUGS

COMPOSITION

The Arsenic in Food (Amendment) Regulations 1973

Made - - -	*14th June* 1973
Laid before Parliament	*22nd June* 1973
Coming into Operation	*14th July* 1973

The Minister of Agriculture, Fisheries and Food and the Secretary of State for Social Services, acting jointly, in exercise of the powers conferred on them by sections 4 and 123 of the Food and Drugs Act 1955(**a**), as read with the Secretary of State for Social Services Order 1968(**b**), and of all other powers enabling them in that behalf, hereby make the following regulations after consultation with such organisations as appear to them to be representative of interests substantially affected by the regulations:—

Citation, commencement and interpretation

1.—(1) These regulations may be cited as the Arsenic in Food (Amendment) Regulations 1973, and shall come into operation on 14th July 1973.

(2) The Interpretation Act 1889(**c**) shall apply to the interpretation of these regulations as it applies to the interpretation of an Act of Parliament.

Amendment of principal regulations

2. The Arsenic in Food Regulations 1959(**d**), as amended(**e**), shall be further amended by substituting for sub-paragraph (*d*) of regulation 3(2) thereof the following sub-paragraph:—

"(*d*) to any food in respect of which the maximum permitted arsenic content is prescribed by any regulations, other than these regulations or any amendment to these regulations, made under the Food and Drugs Act 1955 or by any order having effect as if contained in regulations so made.".

(**a**) 4 & 5 Eliz. 2. c. 16.　　　　　(**b**) S.I. 1968/1699 (1968 III, p. 4585).
(**c**) 1889 c. 63.　　　　　　　　　(**d**) S.I. 1959/831 (1959 I, p. 1293).
(**e**) The relevant amending instrument is S.I. 1966/1203 (1966 III, p. 3203).

In Witness whereof the Official Seal of the Minister of Agriculture, Fisheries and Food is hereunto affixed on 14th June 1973.

(L.S.)
                                                    Joseph Godber,
                                        Minister of Agriculture, Fisheries
                                                    and Food.

                                                    Keith Joseph,
                                        Secretary of State for Social Services.
12th June 1973.

EXPLANATORY NOTE

(This Note is not part of the Regulations.)

These Regulations, which come into operation on 14th July 1973, amend the Arsenic in Food Regulations 1959 as amended by the Colouring Matter in Food Regulations 1966 (S.I. 1966/1203). They extend exemption from arsenic limits already specified, to food for which the maximum permitted arsenic content is prescribed by any other instrument made, or having effect as if made, under the Food and Drugs Act 1955.

STATUTORY INSTRUMENTS

1973 No. 1053

FOOD AND DRUGS

COMPOSITION

The Lead in Food (Amendment) Regulations 1973

Made - - -	14*th June* 1973
Laid before Parliament	22*nd June* 1973
Coming into Operation	14*th July* 1973

The Minister of Agriculture, Fisheries and Food and the Secretary of State for Social Services, acting jointly, in exercise of the powers conferred on them by sections 4 and 123 of the Food and Drugs Act 1955(a), as read with the Secretary of State for Social Services Order 1968(b), and of all other powers enabling them in that behalf, hereby make the following regulations after consultation with such organisations as appear to them to be representative of interests substantially affected by the regulations: —

Citation, commencement and interpretation

1.—(1) These regulations may be cited as the Lead in Food (Amendment) Regulations 1973, and shall come into operation on 14th July 1973.

(2) The Interpretation Act 1889(c) shall apply to the interpretation of these regulations as it applies to the interpretation of an Act of Parliament.

Amendment of principal regulations

2. The Lead in Food Regulations 1961(d), as amended(e), shall be further amended by substituting for paragraph (4) of regulation 3 thereof the following paragraph: —

"(4) The foregoing provisions of this regulation shall not apply to any food in respect of which the maximum permitted lead content is prescribed by any regulations, other than these regulations or any amendment to these regulations, made under the Food and Drugs Act 1955 or by any order, other than the Food Standards (Edible Gelatine) Order 1951(f), as amended(g), having effect as if contained in regulations so made.".

(a) 4 & 5 Eliz. 2. c. 16.   (b) S.I. 1968/1699 (1968 III, p. 4585).
(c) 1889 c. 63.   (d) S.I. 1961/1931 (1961 III, p. 3631).
(e) The relevant amending instrument is S.I. 1966/1203 (1966 III, p. 3203).
(f) S.I. 1951/1196 (1951 III, p. 14).   (g) S.I. 1961/1931 (1961 III, p. 3631).

In Witness whereof the Official Seal of the Minister of Agriculture, Fisheries and Food is hereunto affixed on 14th June 1973.

(L.S.)

Joseph Godber,
Minister of Agriculture, Fisheries and Food.

Keith Joseph,
Secretary of State for Social Services.

12th June 1973.

EXPLANATORY NOTE

(This Note is not part of the Regulations.)

These Regulations, which come into operation on 14th July 1973, amend the Lead in Food Regulations 1961 as amended by the Colouring Matter in Food Regulations 1966 (S.I. 1966/1203). They extend exemption from the lead limits specified by the principal regulations, to food (other than edible gelatine) for which the maximum permitted lead limit is prescribed by any other instrument made, or having effect as if made, under the Food and Drugs Act 1955.

STATUTORY INSTRUMENTS

1973 No. 1055

LANDLORD AND TENANT

The Rent Book (Forms of Notice) (Amendment) Regulations 1973

Made - - - -	*15th June* 1973
Laid before Parliament	*25th June* 1973
Coming into Operation	*16th July* 1973

The Secretary of State for the Environment, in exercise of powers conferred by section 2(1) of the Landlord and Tenant Act 1962(**a**) (as amended by section 117(2) of, and Schedule 15 to, the Rent Act 1968(**b**)) and now vested in him(**c**), and in exercise of all other powers enabling him in that behalf, hereby makes the following regulations:—

1. These regulations may be cited as the Rent Book (Forms of Notice) (Amendment) Regulations 1973 and shall come into operation on 16th July 1973.

2. The Interpretation Act 1889(**d**) shall apply for the interpretation of these regulations as it applies for the interpretation of an Act of Parliament.

3. The Schedule to the Rent Book (Forms of Notice) Regulations 1972(**e**) shall be amended in the manner mentioned in the Schedule to these regulations.

SCHEDULE

1. In Part I (rent book for controlled tenancy), in paragraph 17, for the date "30th June 1973" there shall be substituted the date "30th September 1973".

2. In Part II (rent book for regulated tenancy), in paragraph 16, for the date "30th June 1973" there shall be substituted the date "30th September 1973".

3. In Part III (rent book for furnished lettings), in paragraph 11, the words "to the police or" shall be omitted.

(**a**) 1962 c. 50. (**b**) 1968 c. 23.
(**c**) S.I. 1970/1681 (1970 III, p. 5551). (**d**) 1889 c. 63.
(**e**) S.I. 1972/1827 (1972 III, p. 5276).

4. In Part III, at the end thereof, there shall be added the following paragraph—

"12. A tenant who has difficulty in affording his rent may apply to his local authority for a rent allowance. When the rent is payable weekly, the landlord is obliged to insert in this rent book a leaflet describing your local authority's rent allowance scheme; he is obliged to do this by 30th September 1973 and whenever a new rent book is issued. If the leaflet is not already in this book it can be obtained from your local council offices where you should also be able to obtain a leaflet on rate rebates if you require one."

Geoffrey Rippon,
15th June 1973. Secretary of State for the Environment.

EXPLANATORY NOTE

(This Note is not part of the Regulations.)

The Rent Book (Forms of Notice) Regulations 1972 prescribe the forms of notice to be inserted in rent books or other similar documents in pursuance of section 1 of the Landlord and Tenant Act 1962 (i.e. where the rent is payable weekly) in the cases of controlled tenancies, regulated tenancies and contracts to which Part VI of the Rent Act 1968 applies (furnished lettings).

Among the matters referred to in the forms of notice for controlled and regulated tenancies is the date upon which (under section 24(11) of the Housing Finance Act 1972 (c. 47) (as enacted)) the landlord is obliged to insert the statutory particulars of the rent allowance scheme operated by the local authority. The date has been altered by the Furnished Lettings (Rent Allowances) Act 1973 (c.6), which also provides for the payment of rent allowances in the case of contracts to which Part VI of the Rent Act applies.

These Regulations substitute the new date in the case of the forms of notice for controlled and regulated tenancies, and add a paragraph referring to rent allowances in the form of notice for contracts to which Part VI of the Rent Act applies. They also make a small alteration to the last-mentioned notice.

STATUTORY INSTRUMENTS

1973 No. 1058

INDUSTRIAL TRAINING

The Industrial Training Levy (Shipbuilding) Order 1973

Made - - - -	14*th June* 1973
Laid before Parliament	25*th June* 1973
Coming into Operation	1*st August* 1973

The Secretary of State after approving proposals submitted by the Shipbuilding Industry Training Board for the imposition of a further levy on employers in the shipbuilding industry and in exercise of powers conferred by section 4 of the Industrial Training Act 1964(a) and now vested in him (b), and of all other powers enabling him in that behalf hereby makes the following Order:—

Title and commencement

1. This Order may be cited as the Industrial Training Levy (Shipbuilding) Order 1973 and shall come into operation on 1st August 1973.

Interpretation

2.—(1) In this Order unless the context otherwise requires:—

(*a*) "agriculture" has the same meaning as in section 109(3) of the Agriculture Act 1947(c) or, in relation to Scotland, as in section 86(3) of the Agriculture (Scotland) Act 1948(d);

(*b*) "an appeal tribunal" means an industrial tribunal established under section 12 of the Industrial Training Act 1964;

(*c*) "assessment" means an assessment of an employer to the levy;

(*d*) "the Board" means the Shipbuilding Industry Training Board;

(*e*) "business" means any activities of industry or commerce;

(*f*) "charity" has the same meaning as in section 360 of the Income and Corporation Taxes Act 1970(e);

(*g*) "emoluments" means all emoluments assessable to income tax under Schedule E (other than pensions), being emoluments from which tax under that Schedule is deductible, whether or not tax in fact falls to be deducted from any particular payment thereof;

(*h*) "employer" means a person who is an employer in the shipbuilding industry at any time in the ninth levy period;

(*i*) "the industrial training order" means the Industrial Training (Shipbuilding Board) Order 1968(f);

(**a**) 1964 c. 16.	(**b**) S.I. 1968/729 (1968 II, p. 2108).
(**c**) 1947 c. 48.	(**d**) 1948 c. 45.
(**e**) 1970 c. 10.	(**f**) S.I. 1968/1614 (1968 III, p. 4432).

(*j*) "the levy" means the levy imposed by the Board in respect of the ninth levy period;

(*k*) "the ninth base period" means the period of twelve months that commenced on 6th April 1972;

(*l*) "the ninth levy period" means the period commencing with the day upon which this Order comes into operation and ending on 31st July 1974;

(*m*) "notice" means a notice in writing;

(*n*) "shipbuilding establishment" means an establishment in Great Britain engaged in the ninth base period wholly or mainly in the shipbuilding industry for a total of twenty-seven or more weeks or, being an establishment that commenced to carry on business in the ninth base period, for a total number of weeks exceeding one-half of the number of weeks in the part of the said period commencing with the day of which business was commenced and ending on the last day thereof;

(*o*) "the shipbuilding industry" means any one or more of the activities which, subject to the provisions of paragraph 2 of the Schedule to the industrial training order, are specified in paragraph 1 of that Schedule as the activities of the shipbuilding industry.

(2) Any reference in this Order to an establishment that commences to carry on business or that ceases to carry on business shall not be taken to apply where the location of the establishment is changed but its business is continued wholly or mainly at or from the new location, or where the suspension of activities is of a temporary or seasonal nature.

(3) The Interpretation Act 1889(a) shall apply to the interpretation of this Order as it applies to the interpretation of an Act of Parliament.

Imposition of the levy

3.—(1) The levy to be imposed by the Board on employers in respect of the ninth levy period shall be assessed in accordance with the provisions of this Article.

(2) The levy shall be assessed by the Board separately in respect of each shipbuilding establishment of an employer, not being an employer who is exempt from the levy by virtue of paragraph (6) of this Article.

(3) Subject to the provisions of this Article, the levy assessed in respect of a shipbuilding establishment of an employer shall be an amount equal to 0·95 per cent. of the sum of the emoluments of all the persons following, that is to say—

(*a*) any persons employed by the employer at or from that establishment in the ninth base period;

(*b*) any persons deemed to have been so employed under the provisions of paragraph (4) of this Article.

(a) 1889 c. 63.

(4) In the case where a shipbuilding establishment is taken over (whether directly or indirectly) by an employer in succession to, or jointly with, another person, a person employed at any time in the ninth base period at or from the establishment shall be deemed for the purposes of this Article, to have been so employed by the employer carrying on the said establishment on the day upon which this Order comes into operation.

(5) The amount of the levy imposed in respect of a shipbuilding establishment that ceases to carry on business in the ninth levy period shall be in the same proportion to the amount that would otherwise be due under the foregoing provisions of this Article as the number of days between the commencement of the said levy period and the date of cessation of business (both dates inclusive) bears to the number of days in the said levy period.

(6) There shall be exempt from the levy—

(a) an employer in whose case the sum of the emoluments of all the persons employed by him in the ninth period at or from the shipbuilding establishment or establishments of the employer (including any persons employed in that period at or from a shipbuilding establishment by an associated company of the employer) is less than £15,000;

(b) a charity.

(7) For the purposes of this Article no regard shall be had to be emoluments of any person—

(a) employed as the master or a member of the crew of a ship or any person ordinarily employed in or about a ship in port on work of a kind ordinarily done by a seaman on a ship while it is in port;

(b) engaged wholly in any operations mentioned in paragraph 1(a) or 1(b) of the Schedule to the industrial training order being a person undergoing a course of training as a sea-going officer or rating (otherwise than in a sea-fishing service) under an agreement in writing with an employer in the shipping industry or with any organisation of employers in that industry or any association of such organisations;

(c) engaged wholly in agriculture; or

(d) engaged wholly in the supply of food or drink for immediate consumption.

Assessment notices

4.—(1) The Board shall serve an assessment notice on every employer assessed to the levy, but one notice may comprise two or more assessments.

(2) The amount of any assessment payable under an assessment notice shall be rounded down to the nearest £1.

(3) An assessment notice shall state the Board's address for the service of a notice of appeal or of an application for an extension of time for appealing.

(4) An assessment notice may be served on the person assessed to the levy either by delivering it to him personally or by leaving it, or sending it to him by post, at his last known address or place of business in the United Kingdom or, if that person is a corporation, by leaving it, or sending it by post to the corporation, at such address or place of business or at its registered or principal office.

Payment of the levy

5.—(1) Subject to the provisions of this Article and of Articles 6 and 7, the amount of each assessment appearing in an assessment notice served by the Board shall be due and payable to the Board in four instalments, the first three each being equal to one-sixth and the fourth equal to three-sixths of the said amount respectively, and the said instalments shall be due respectively, one month, five months, eight months and fifteen months after the date of the assessment notice.

(2) An instalment of an assessment shall not be recoverable by the Board until there has expired the time allowed for appealing against the assessment by Article 7(1) of this Order and any further period or periods of time that the Board or an appeal tribunal may have allowed for appealing under paragraph (2) or (3) of that Article or, where an appeal is brought, until the appeal is decided or withdrawn.

Withdrawal of assessment

6.—(1) The Board may, by a notice served on the person assessed to the levy in the same manner as an assessment notice, withdraw an assessment if that person has appealed against that assessment under the provisions of Article 7 of this Order and the appeal has not been entered in the Register of Appeals kept under the appropriate Regulations specified in paragraph (5) of that Article.

(2) The withdrawal of an assessment shall be without prejudice to the power of the Board to serve a further assessment notice in respect of any establishment to which that assessment related and, where the withdrawal is made by reason of the fact that an establishment has ceased to carry on business in the ninth levy period, the said notice may provide that the whole amount payable thereunder in respect of the establishment shall be due one month after the date of the notice.

Appeals

7.—(1) A person assessed to the levy may appeal to an appeal tribunal against the assessment within one month from the date of the service of the assessment notice or within any further period or periods of time that may be allowed by the Board or an appeal tribunal under the following provisions of this Article.

(2) The Board by notice may for good cause allow a person assessed to the levy to appeal to an appeal tribunal against the assessment at any time within the period of four months from the date of the service of the assessment notice or within such further period or periods as the Board may allow before such time as may then be limited for appealing has expired.

(3) If the Board shall not allow an application for extention of time for appealing, an appeal tribunal shall upon application made to the tribunal by the person assessed to the levy have the like powers as the Board under the last foregoing paragraph.

(4) In the case of an establishment that ceases to carry on business in the ninth levy period on any day after the date of the service of the relevant assessment notice the foregoing provisions of this Article shall have effect as if for the

period of four months from the date of the service of the assessment notice mentioned in paragraph (2) of this Article there were substituted the period of six months from the date of the cessation of business.

(5) An appeal or an application to an appeal tribunal under this Article shall be made in accordance with the Industrial Tribunals (England and Wales) Regulations 1965(a) as amended by the Industrial Tribunals (England and Wales) (Amendment) Regulations 1967(b), except where the establishment to which the relevant assessment relates is wholly in Scotland, in which case the appeal or application shall be made in accordance with the Industrial Tribunals (Scotland) Regulations 1965(c) as amended by the Industrial Tribunals (Scotland) (Amendment) Regulations 1967(d).

(6) The powers of an appeal tribunal under paragraph (3) of this Article may be exercised by the President of the Industrial Tribunals (England and Wales) or by the President of the Industrial Tribunals (Scotland) as the case may be.

Evidence

8.—(1) Upon the discharge by a person assessed to the levy of his liability under an assessment the Board shall if so requested issue to him a certificate to that effect.

(2) The production in any proceedings of a document purporting to be certified by the Secretary to the Board to be a true copy of an assessment or other notice issued by the Board or purporting to be a certificate such as is mentioned in the foregoing paragraph of this Article shall, unless the contrary is proved, be sufficient evidence of the document and of the facts stated therein.

Signed by order of the Secretary of State.

14th June 1973.

R. Chichester-Clark,
Minister of State,
Department of Employment.

(a) S.I. 1965/1101 (1965 II, p. 2805).   (b) S.I. 1967/301 (1967 I, p. 1040).
(c) S.I. 1965/1157 (1965 II, p. 3266).   (d) S.I. 1967/302 (1967 I, p. 1050).

EXPLANATORY NOTE

(This Note is not part of the Order.)

This Order gives effect to proposals submitted by the Shipbuilding Industry Training Board to the Secretary of State for Employment for the imposition of a further levy on employers in the shipbuilding industry for the purpose of raising money towards the expenses of the Board.

The levy is to be imposed in respect of the ninth levy period commencing with the day on which this Order comes into operation and ending on 31st July 1974. The levy will be assessed by the Board, and there will be a right of appeal against an assessment to an industrial tribunal.

STATUTORY INSTRUMENTS

1973 No. 1059

PLANT HEALTH

The Potato Cyst Eelworm (Great Britain) Order 1973

Made - - -	*14th June* 1973
Laid before Parliament	*25th June* 1973
Coming into Operation	*1st August* 1973

The Minister of Agriculture, Fisheries and Food and the Secretary of State, in exercise of the powers conferred on them respectively by section 3(1), (2), (3) and (4) of the Plant Health Act 1967(a), as amended by section 92(2) of, and Part II of Schedule 3 to, the Criminal Justice Act 1967(b) and by section 4(1) of, and paragraph 8 of Schedule 4 to, the European Communities Act 1972(c) and as read with section 20 of the Agriculture (Miscellaneous Provisions) Act 1972(d), and of all other powers enabling them in that behalf, hereby make the following order:—

Citation, extent and commencement

1. This order, which may be cited as the Potato Cyst Eelworm (Great Britain) Order 1973, shall apply to England and Wales and Scotland and shall come into operation on 1st August 1973.

Interpretation

2.—(1) In this order, unless the context otherwise requires—

"appropriate Minister" means, in the application of this order to England and Wales, the Minister of Agriculture, Fisheries and Food and, in its application to Scotland, the Secretary of State;

"approved resistant cultivar" means a cultivar approved for the time being by the appropriate Minister as being resistant to one or more pathotypes of potato cyst eelworm;

"inspector" means an officer authorised by the appropriate Minister for the purposes of this order;

"potato" means the tuber, or part thereof, or any part of the plant of *Solanum tuberosum* L. or other tuber-forming species or hybrids of *Solanum;*

"potato tuber" includes part thereof;

"potato cyst eelworm" means cyst-forming nematodes of the genus *Heterodera* that infest and multiply on potatoes, and includes all strains and pathotypes thereof;

"premises" includes any vehicle, vessel, aircraft, hovercraft or freight container.

(2) The Interpretation Act 1889(e) shall apply to the interpretation of this order as it applies to the interpretation of an Act of Parliament.

(a) 1967 c.8.	(b) 1967 c. 80.	(c) 1972 c. 68.
(d) 1972 c. 62.	(e) 1889 c. 63.	

(3) Any reference in this order to a numbered article shall be construed as a reference to the article bearing that number in this order.

Declaration of contaminated land

3.—(1) If it appears to the appropriate Minister in consequence of the examination of a sample of soil taken from any land for the purpose of preventing the spread of potato cyst eelworm or for any other purpose of this order that that land is infested with potato cyst eelworm, that Minister may serve on the occupier or other person in charge of the land a notice in writing declaring the land to be land on which potato cyst eelworm is present.

(2) Any notice served under paragraph (1) of this article may define by reference to a map or plan or otherwise the extent of the land declared in the notice to be land on which potato cyst eelworm is present.

(3) A notice served under paragraph (1) of this article may, if it appears to the appropriate Minister, after examination of a sample of soil taken from the land to which the notice relates at such interval of time after the service of the notice or after a previous sampling as appears to that Minister to be appropriate, that potato cyst eelworm is no longer present on the land to which the notice relates, be withdrawn by that Minister by a notice in writing served on the occupier or other person in charge of that land.

Restrictions on the planting and disposal of potatoes and plants

4.—(1) No person shall plant or cause or permit to be planted any potatoes in any land in his occupation or under his charge to which a notice served under article 3(1) relates.

(2) No person shall remove for transplanting elsewhere from any land to which a notice served under article 3(1) relates any plants which have been grown or stored in or on that land.

5.—(1) If in consequence of the examination of a sample of the soil taken from any land by an inspector for the purposes of this order that land appears not to be contaminated by potato cyst eelworm, an inspector may issue a written certificate to that effect in relation to that land.

(2) Unless previously amended, modified or withdrawn, such a certificate shall remain in force until the expiration of 24 months from the taking of the sample mentioned in the certificate or until potatoes are planted in the land to which the certificate relates, whichever is the earlier.

(3) No person shall sell, offer or expose for sale, deliver or cause to be delivered or otherwise pass from his possession any potatoes grown by him and intended for planting unless immediately before the planting of the potatoes from which those potatoes were produced there was in force in relation to the land in which they were grown a written certificate issued in accordance with paragraph (1) of this article.

(4) The provisions of paragraph (3) of this article shall not apply in relation to any potatoes planted before the commencement of this order.

Misdescription of potatoes

6.—(1) No person shall sell or offer or expose for sale as being of approved resistant cultivars any potatoes which are not of approved resistant cultivars.

(2) A person shall not be liable to conviction for a failure to comply with,

or a contravention of, the terms or conditions of a notice or licence served or granted under this order relating to the planting of approved resistant cultivars if he proves to the satisfaction of the court that the potatoes were sold to him as potatoes of approved resistant cultivars and that he did not know that the potatoes were not of approved resistant cultivars.

Prohibition of keeping and release or disposal of potato cyst eelworm

7. No person shall keep, or release, deliver or otherwise dispose of, or cause to be kept, or released, delivered or otherwise disposed of, any culture of potato cyst eelworm except under and in accordance with the conditions of a licence granted by the appropriate Minister:

Provided that nothing in this article shall be deemed to prohibit the carrying out of tests to determine the presence or absence of potato cyst eelworm nor the delivery or release to or the keeping and disposal by the appropriate Minister of any culture of potato cyst eelworm for the purpose of laboratory examination or research.

Information to be given

8. The owner or occupier or other person in charge of land in respect of which there has been served a notice under article 3(1) shall, if so required in writing by an inspector, give him any information he may possess as to the crops grown on the land at any time, including the names of the varieties of any potatoes grown thereon and shall produce for inspection by the inspector any licences, declarations, certificates, records or invoices relating to the planting, sale or purchase of potatoes grown on the land.

Powers of entry and examination and sampling

9. An inspector, upon production if so required of his authority, may for the purpose of preventing the spread of potato cyst eelworm or for any other purpose of this order enter any land and any premises and examine and take and remove samples of any potatoes and plants and of any soil on that land or those premises.

Service of notices

10. For the purposes of this order a notice shall be deemed to be served on or given to any person if it is delivered to him personally or left for him at his last known place of abode or business, or sent through the post in a letter addressed to him there.

Licences

11. Notwithstanding any provisions of this order, any potatoes may be planted, sold, offered or exposed for sale or delivered or caused to be delivered and any plants may be removed under and in accordance with the conditions of a licence granted by the appropriate Minister or by an inspector.

Offences

12. Any person who fails to comply with, or acts in contravention of, this order or the terms or conditions of a notice or licence served or granted thereunder or who wilfully obstructs an inspector in the exercise of his powers under this order shall be liable on summary conviction to a penalty not exceeding £100 or, in respect of a second or subsequent offence, to a penalty not exceeding £200.

In Witness whereof the Official Seal of the Minister of Agriculture, Fisheries and Food is hereunto affixed on 14th June 1973.

(L.S.)

Joseph Godber,
Minister of Agriculture,
Fisheries and Food.

12th June 1973.

Gordon Campbell,
Secretary of State for Scotland.

EXPLANATORY NOTE

(This Note is not part of the Order.)

This Order, which applies throughout Great Britain, implements Directive 69/465/EEC of the Council (O.J. No. L. 323, 24.12.69, p.3 (O.J./S.E. 1969 (II), p. 563)) on the control of potato cyst eelworm.

This Order requires that seed potatoes intended for marketing may be produced only on land which is recognised after official soil examination to be free from potato cyst eelworm. It prohibits the planting of any potatoes in, or the removal of any plants for transplanting from, land declared by notice to be land infested with potato cyst eelworm. It also prohibits the keeping of cultures of potato cyst eelworm except under licence.

STATUTORY INSTRUMENTS

1973 No. 1060

PLANT HEALTH

The Wart Disease of Potatoes (Great Britain) Order 1973

Made - - - -	*14th June* 1973
Laid before Parliament	*25th June* 1973
Coming into Operation	
Article 8	*1st July* 1974
Remainder	*1st August* 1973

The Minister of Agriculture, Fisheries and Food and the Secretary of State, by virtue and in exercise of the powers vested in them repectively by section 3(1), (2) and (4) of the Plant Health Act 1967**(a)**, as amended by section 92(2) of, and Part II of Schedule 3 to, the Criminal Justice Act 1967**(b)**, and by section 4(1) of, and paragraph 8 of Schedule 4 to, the European Communities Act 1972**(c)** and as read with section 20 of the Agriculture (Miscellaneous Provisions) Act 1972**(d)**, and of every other power enabling them in that behalf, hereby make the following order:—

Citation, extent and commencement

1. This order, which may be cited as the Wart Disease of Potatoes (Great Britain) Order 1973, shall apply to England and Wales and Scotland and shall come into operation as respects article 8 on 1st July 1974 and as respects the remainder on 1st August 1973.

Revocation of previous orders

2. The Wart Disease of Potatoes Order 1958**(e)**, the Wart Disease of Potatoes (Scotland) Order of 1941**(f)** and the Wart Disease of Potatoes (General Licence) (Scotland) Order 1954**(g)** are hereby revoked.

Interpretation

3.—(1) In this order, unless the context otherwise requires—

"allotment garden"means an allotment not exceeding $\frac{1}{4}$ acre in extent which is wholly or mainly cultivated by the occupier for the production of vegetables and fruit for consumption by himself or his family;

(a) 1967 c. 8.   (b) 1967 c. 80.
(c) 1972 c. 68.   (d) 1972 c. 62.
(e) S.I. 1958/308 (1958 II. p. 1883).
(f) S.R. & O. 1941/1587 (Rev. V, p. 807: 1941 I, p. 223).
(g) S.I. 1954/235 (1954 II, p. 1772).

"appropriate Minister" means, in the application of this order to England and Wales, the Minister of Agriculture, Fisheries and Food and, in its application to Scotland, the Secretary of State;

"approved immune variety" means a variety approved for the time being by the appropriate Minister as being immune from wart disease;

"inspector" means an officer authorised by the appropriate Minister for the purposes of this order;

"potato" means the tuber, or part thereof, or any part of the plant of *Solanum tuberosum* L. or other tuber-forming species or hybrids of *Solanum;*

"potato tuber" includes part thereof;

"wart disease" means either the disease affecting potatoes which is caused by *Synchytrium endobioticum* (Schilb.) Perc. and known as wart disease of potatoes or the organism *Synchytrium endobioticum*, as the context may require.

(2) The Interpretation Act 1889(a) shall apply to the interpretation of this order as it applies to the interpretation of an Act of Parliament and as if this order and the orders hereby revoked were Acts of Parliament.

(3) Any reference in this order to a numbered article shall be construed as a reference to the article bearing that number in this order.

Notification of disease

4.—(1) The occupier or other person in charge of any land on which wart disease is present or appears to be present, and any person having in his possession or under his charge potatoes which are affected with wart disease, shall forthwith give to the appropriate Minister written notification of the fact.

(2) If on land in respect of which such a notification of disease has been given wart disease is present or appears to be present on potatoes in any subsequent year or years, a further notification of disease shall be so given in each of such years.

Declaration of contaminated land or a safety zone

5.—(1) If it appears to the appropriate Minister that wart disease is present on any land, that Minister may serve on the occupier or other person in charge of the land a notice in writing declaring the land to be land on which wart disease is present and thereafter, until the said notice is withdrawn in accordance with paragraph (4) of this article, the land shall be deemed for the purposes of this order to be land on which wart disease is present.

(2) The appropriate Minister may serve on the occupier or other person in charge of land which surrounds, adjoins or is in close proximity to land on which wart disease is present a notice declaring the first mentioned land to be a safety zone.

(3) Any notice served under paragraph (1) or (2) of this article may define by reference to a map or plan or otherwise the extent of the land declared in the notice to be land on which wart disease is present or to be a safety zone, as the case may be.

(a) 1889 c. 63.

(4) Any notice served, or having effect as if served, under any order which is revoked by this order, being a notice declaring land to be land on which wart disease is present or a notice applying the provisions of any such order to land, shall continue to have effect as if it were a notice served under paragraph (2) of this article and any such notice or any notice served under paragraph (1) of this article may, if it appears to the appropriate Minister that wart disease is no longer present on the land, or any part of the land, to which the notice relates, be withdrawn as respects that land, or that part of the land, by that Minister by a notice in writing served on the occupier or other person in charge of that land and the last mentioned notice may impose such conditions, if any, as appear to the appropriate Minister expedient to prevent a further occurrence of wart disease and that last mentioned notice may be amended, modified or withdrawn by the appropriate Minister by a further notice in writing served on the occupier or other person in charge of the land to which the further notice relates.

(5) Any notice served under paragraph (2) of this article may, if it appears to the appropriate Minister that wart disease is no longer present on the land surrounded by or adjoining or in close proximity to the land to which the notice relates, be withdrawn by that Minister by a notice in writing served on the occupier or other person in charge of that land.

Restrictions on the planting and disposal of potatoes and plants

6.—(1) No person shall plant or cause or permit to be planted any potatoes in any land in his occupation or under his charge on which wart disease is present.

(2) No person shall plant or cause or permit to be planted in any land in his occupation or under his charge—

(a) to which a notice served under article 5(2), or deemed by virtue of article 5(4) to have been so served, relates, or

(b) as respects land in England or Wales, in respect of which a notification of the presence or apparent presence of wart disease was given before the commencement of the Wart Disease of Potatoes Order 1958 by the occupier or other person then in charge of the land or by the appropriate Minister

any potatoes which are not of an approved immune variety, or, in the case of any land which surrounds, adjoins or is in close proximity to land on which wart disease of any race other than the common European race is present and in respect of which the appropriate Minister so directs by notice in writing served on the person aforesaid, any potatoes whatsoever except such variety or varieties, if any, as the appropriate Minister may authorise in writing to be planted in the said land:

Provided that the provisions of this paragraph shall not apply as respects any land of a kind described in sub-paragraph (b) hereof if the appropriate Minister has served on the occupier or other person in charge of that land a notice in writing declaring that the provisions of this paragraph shall not apply as respects that land.

(3) No person shall remove for transplanting elsewhere from any land on which wart disease is present any plants which have been grown or stored in or on that land.

(4) No person shall sell or offer or expose for sale or deliver or cause or permit to be delivered or otherwise pass from his possession for any purpose or

plant or cause or permit to be planted any potatoes visibly affected with wart disease:

Provided that nothing in this paragraph shall be deemed to prohibit the delivery, or giving of possession, of any such potatoes to the appropriate Minister or to an inspector.

(5) No person shall sell or offer or expose for sale for planting or deliver or cause to be delivered for planting or cause or permit to be planted any potatoes from a crop in any part of which wart disease has been found to be present.

7.—(1) No person shall permit potatoes to remain in or on land in his occupation or under his charge if they have been planted in contravention of this order and their removal or destruction is required by notice in writing served on him by the appropriate Minister. Any such notice may state the time within which and the manner in which the removal or destruction shall be completed.

(2) If any person shall fail to remove or destroy any potatoes in compliance with a notice served on that person under paragraph (1) of this article, without prejudice to any proceedings under this order consequent upon such failure, an inspector or a person authorised by him for the purpose may remove or destroy them and the cost of so doing shall be recoverable by the appropriate Minister as a debt due from the person on whom the notice was served.

Restrictions on the planting of potatoes in gardens or allotments

8. No person shall plant or cause or permit to be planted in any private garden or in any allotment garden any potatoes which are not of an approved immune variety.

Misdescription of potatoes

9.—(1) No person shall sell or offer or expose for sale as potatoes of an approved immune variety any potatoes which are not of an approved immune variety.

(2) A person shall not be liable to conviction for a contravention of article 6(2) or 8 if he proves to the satisfaction of the court that the potatoes were sold to him as potatoes of an approved immune variety and that he did not know that the potatoes were not of an approved immune variety.

Power to require the fencing off and treatment of land contaminated by wart disease

10.—(1) Where the appropriate Minister or an inspector becomes aware of or has reasonable cause to suspect the presence in or on land of a race of wart disease other than the common European race, he may serve on the occupier or other person in charge of that land a notice in writing requiring him to erect and at all times thereafter to maintain on that land such fences, and to treat that land, in such manner and within such time as may be specified in the notice.

(2) A notice served under this article may at any time be amended, modified or withdrawn by the appropriate Minister or by an inspector by a further notice in writing served on the occupier or other person in charge of the land to which the further notice relates.

Restriction on the removal of soil from land contaminated by wart disease

11. No person shall remove, or cause or permit to be removed, any soil from land on which wart disease is present, or from any premises on such land, so that it may be used or disposed of where wart disease is not present, except in accordance with the conditions of a licence granted by the appropriate Minister.

Powers of entry, examination and sampling

12.—(1) An inspector upon production if so required of his authority may, for the purposes of this order, enter any land and any premises and examine and take samples of any potatoes and of any soil on that land or those premises.

(2) In this article and in article 13 the expression "premises" includes any vehicle, vessel, aircraft, hovercraft or freight container.

Power to deal with diseased or suspected potatoes, potato plants and certain plant and equipment

13.—(1) An inspector may at any time serve on the occupier or other person in charge of land on which wart disease is present a notice in writing requiring him to destroy to the satisfaction of an inspector potato plants grown on the land on which wart disease is present.

(2) An inspector may at any time serve on—

(*a*) any person having in his possession or under his charge potato tubers which are affected with wart disease, or which are on any premises or in a store, clamp, pit, bag or other receptacle with potato tubers so affected, or which the inspector has reason to believe to have been on any premises or in a store, clamp, pit, bag or other receptacle with potato tubers so affected or otherwise exposed to infection with wart disease;

(*b*) the occupier or other person in charge of land on which the inspector has reason to believe there have been potato tubers which are or have been affected with wart disease or potato tubers which have been on any premises or in a store, clamp, pit, bag or other receptacle with potato tubers so affected or otherwise exposed to infection with wart disease;

a notice in writing—

(i) requiring the aforesaid occupier or person to treat in such manner and within such time as may be specified in the notice the premises on which the potato tubers are or are reasonably believed to have been in any of the aforesaid circumstances and such plant or equipment as may be so specified, being plant or equipment which has been used in connection with the potato tubers, and

(ii) requiring the aforesaid occupier or person to treat or destroy such of the potato tubers and such packing materials and receptacles used for the storage or conveyance of the potato tubers in such manner and within such time as may be specified in the notice, and

(iii) prohibiting the removal of the potato tubers, the soil and debris riddled from the potato tubers and any packing materials, plant, equipment or receptacles used for the storage, conveyance or handling of the potato tubers or otherwise used in connection with the potato tubers from the premises on which they are when the notice is served and prohibiting the moving of any vehicle or freight container from the place where it is when the notice is served except, in each case, under such conditions, prescribed in the notice, as the inspector may consider necessary to prevent the spread of wart disease.

(3) If any person shall fail to carry out the destruction of any potato plants or to treat any premises, plant or equipment or to treat or destroy any potato tubers, packing materials or receptacles used for the storage or conveyance of potato tubers in accordance with the requirements of a notice served in pursuance of paragraph (1) or (2) of this article, then, without prejudice to any proceedings under this order consequent upon such failure, an inspector or a person authorised by him for the purpose may enter the premises and treat the premises, plant or equipment and may enter any premises on which the potato plants, potato tubers, packing materials or receptacles or any of them may be and, at his discretion, either destroy such potato plants or treat or destroy such potato tubers, packing materials or receptacles on the said premises or remove them and take such action elsewhere, and the cost of taking such steps shall be recoverable by the appropriate Minister as a debt due from the aforesaid person.

Service of notices

14. For the purpose of this order a notice shall be deemed to be served on or given to any person if it is delivered to him personally or left for him at his last known place of abode or business, or sent through the post in a letter addressed to him there.

Information to be given

15.—(1) The owner or occupier or other person in charge of land in respect of which there has been served a notice under article 5(1) or (2) or a notice which is deemed, by virtue of article 5(4), to have been served under article 5(2) shall, if so required in writing by an inspector, give him any information he may possess as to the crops grown on the land at any time, including the names of the varieties of any potatoes grown thereon, and as to the persons in whose possession or under whose charge any potatoes grown on the land are or have been and shall produce for inspection by the inspector any licences, declarations, certificates, records or invoices relating to the planting, sale or purchase of potatoes grown on the land.

(2) Every person who has or has had in his possession or under his charge any potatoes whether affected with wart disease or not and every person who as auctioneer, salesman or otherwise has sold or offered for sale any potatoes shall, if so required in writing by an inspector, give any information he may possess as to the persons in whose possession or under whose charge they are or have been and shall produce for inspection by an inspector any licences, declarations, certificates, records or invoices relating to the planting, sale or purchase of potatoes.

(3) Any information given under this article shall not be available as evidence against the person giving the same in any prosecution under this order except in respect of an alleged failure to comply with this article.

Licences

16. Notwithstanding any provisions of this order, any potatoes may be planted, moved, consigned, sold, offered for sale or kept for scientific purposes under and in accordance with the conditions of a licence granted by the appropriate Minister.

Offences

17. Any person who fails to comply with, or acts in contravention of, this order or the terms or conditions of a notice or licence served or granted thereunder or who wilfully obstructs an inspector in the exercise of his powers under this order shall be liable on summary conviction to a penalty not exceeding £100 or, in respect of a second or subsequent offence, to a penalty not exceeding £200.

In Witness whereof the Official Seal of the Minister of Agriculture, Fisheries and Food is hereunto affixed on 14th June 1973.

(L.S.)   *Joseph Godber*,
                              Minister of Agriculture, Fisheries and Food.

                                                  Gordon Campbell,
12th June 1973.   Secretary of State for Scotland.

EXPLANATORY NOTE

(This Note is not part of the Order.)

This Order, which applies throughout Great Britain, supersedes the Wart Disease of Potatoes Order 1958 (which applied to England and Wales only) and the Wart Disease of Potatoes (Scotland) Order of 1941, as amended. It implements Directive 69/464/EEC of the Council (O.J. No. L. 323, 24.12.69, p. 1 (O.J./S.E. 1969 (II), p. 561)) on the control of potato wart disease.

This Order prohibits the planting of potatoes in, and the removal of plants for transplanting from, any land which is declared by a notice served under this Order to be land on which wart disease is present (articles 5(1), 6(1) and (3)). It also prohibits the planting of potatoes which are not of an approved immune variety in land which is declared by a notice served under this Order to be a safety zone surrounding land on which wart disease is present or in land on which wart disease has previously occurred (article 6(2)). Provision is no longer made for "protected areas", first established in 1929, within which the planting, and the sale for planting, of potatoes was controlled.

The requirement that only potatoes of an approved immune variety may be planted in private gardens and allotments, already in force in Scotland, is extended to England and Wales (article 8). Power is given, in certain cases, to require the fencing off and treatment of land contaminated by wart disease (article 10).

This Order re-enacts the prohibition against selling diseased or suspected potatoes (article 6(4) and (5)) and, with amendments, the power of an inspector to deal with diseased or suspected potatoes (article 13).

STATUTORY INSTRUMENTS

1973 No. 1063 (S.80)

NATIONAL HEALTH SERVICE, SCOTLAND

The National Health Service (General Medical and Pharmaceutical Services) (Scotland) Amendment Regulations 1973

Made - - -	*13th June* 1973
Laid before Parliament	*25th June* 1973
Coming into Operation	*1st August* 1973

In exercise of the powers conferred on me by sections 34 and 40 of the National Health Service (Scotland) Act 1947(a) as amended(b) and of all other powers enabling me in that behalf I hereby make the following regulations:—

1.—(1) These regulations may be cited as the National Health Service (General Medical and Pharmaceutical Services) (Scotland) Amendment Regulations 1973 and shall come into operation on 1st August 1973.

(2) The Interpretation Act 1889(c) shall apply for the interpretation of these regulations as it applies for the interpretation of an Act of Parliament.

2. The National Health Service (General Medical and Pharmaceutical Services) (Scotland) Regulations 1966(d) as amended(e) shall be further amended as follows:—

In Part I of Schedule 3 (which part specifies the appliances to be supplied to persons receiving general medical services) there shall be inserted after the item "Colostomy apparatus: repairs and replacement only" the item "Contraceptive devices for women".

(Sgd.) *Gordon Campbell,*

One of Her Majesty's Principal Secretaries of State.

St. Andrew's House,
Edinburgh
13th June 1973.

(a) 1947 c. 27.
(b) The amendments do not expressly relate to the subject matter of these regulations.
(c) 1889 c. 63.　　　　　　　　　　　　(d) S.I. 1966/1233 (1966 III, p. 3330).
(e) S.I. 1966/1618, 1971/472 (1966 III, p. 5057, 1971 I, p. 1405).

EXPLANATORY NOTE

(*This Note is not part of the Regulations.*)

The Regulations further amend the 1966 Regulations by adding contraceptive devices for women to the list of appliances which may be supplied to persons receiving general medical services.

STATUTORY INSTRUMENTS

1973 No. 1064

FOOD AND DRUGS

MILK AND DAIRIES

The Milk and Dairies (Semi-skimmed and Skimmed Milk) (Heat Treatment and Labelling) Regulations 1973

Made - - - -	*15th June* 1973
Laid before Parliament	*26th June* 1973
Coming into Operation	*18th July* 1973

The Minister of Agriculture, Fisheries and Food and the Secretary of State for Social Services acting jointly, in exercise of the powers conferred on them by sections 29, 87(3) and 123 of the Food and Drugs Act 1955(a), as read with the Secretary of State for Social Services Order 1968(b) and all other powers enabling them in that behalf, hereby make the following regulations after consultation with such organisations as appear to them to be representative of interests substantially affected by the regulations:—

Citation and commencement

1. These regulations may be cited as the Milk and Dairies (Semi-skimmed and Skimmed Milk) (Heat Treatment and Labelling) Regulations 1973, and shall come into operation on 18th July 1973.

Interpretation

2.—(1) In these regulations, unless the context otherwise requires—

"the Act" means the Food and Drugs Act 1955;

"atmospheric shade box" means a well ventilated box or cupboard so situated on the outside of a wall on the north side of a building or in a comparable position that it is at all times in the shade, such box or cupboard being not less than three feet above the ground at its lowest point and having inside it a maximum thermometer and a minimum thermometer of the meteorological type, accurate to within $0 \cdot 2 \, °C.$;

"atmospheric shade temperature" means the temperature inside an atmospheric shade box;

"consumer" means any person to whom milk is supplied and who neither sells it nor uses it in the manufacture of milk products for sale;

"local authority" has the meaning assigned to it by section 85 of the Act;

(a) 4 & 5 Eliz. 2. c. 16.　　　　(b) S.I. 1968/1699 (1968 III, p. 4585).

"milk" means cows' milk intended for sale or sold for human consumption, but does not include such milk intended for manufacture into products for sale for human consumption;

"milk processor" means any milk pasteuriser, milk steriliser or person treating milk by the ultra high temperature method;

"milk purveyor" includes any person who sells milk, whether wholesale or by retail;

"the Minister" means the Minister of Agriculture, Fisheries and Food;

"sample" means a sample procured by a person duly authorised in that behalf by a local authority;

"sell" includes offer or agree to sell or expose for sale; and "sold" shall be construed accordingly;

"semi-skimmed milk" means milk the fat content of which has been brought to at least 1·50 per cent. and at the most 1·80 per cent. calculated by weight;

"skimmed milk" means milk the fat content of which has been brought to not more than 0·30 per cent. calculated by weight.

(2) The Interpretation Act 1889(a) shall apply to the interpretation of these regulations as it applies to the interpretation of an Act of Parliament and as if these regulations and the regulations hereby partially revoked were Acts of Parliament.

Heat treatment of semi-skimmed and skimmed milk

3.—(1) No person shall sell any semi-skimmed milk or skimmed milk unless the requirements specified in the following paragraph are satisfied:

Provided that this paragraph shall not apply where any such milk is sold to a milk processor for heat treatment in accordance with these regulations.

(2) The requirements to be satisfied are the general requirements of Schedule 1 to these regulations in connection with the heat treatment of semi-skimmed milk and skimmed milk and the special requirements of Part I, II or III of Schedule 2 to these regulations in relation to and in connection with such heat treatment by pasteurisation, sterilisation or the ultra high temperature method respectively:

Provided that where semi-skimmed or skimmed milk is brought from Scotland into England and Wales, the requirements of Schedules 1 and 2 to these regulations in relation to that milk shall, so far as they would relate to anything to be done before the milk enters England and Wales, be deemed to be satisfied if the corresponding requirements of any provisions made by statutory instrument by the Secretary of State and providing in Scotland for the heat treatement of semi-skimmed or skimmed milk are satisfied.

Labelling of semi-skimmed and skimmed milk containers

4. No person shall sell any semi-skimmed milk or skimmed milk, which has been subjected to heat treatment by pasteurisation, sterilisation or treatment by the ultra high temperature method, in a container unless that container is labelled in accordance with the requirements of Part I, II or III respectively of Schedule 4 to these regulations.

(a) 1889 c. 63.

Penalties and enforcement

5.—(1) If any person contravenes or fails to comply with any of the foregoing provisions of these regulations he shall be guilty of an offence and shall be liable to a fine not exceeding one hundred pounds or to imprisonment for a term not exceeding three months, or to both, and, in the case of a continuing offence, to a further fine not exceeding five pounds for each day during which the offence continues after conviction.

(2) Each local authority shall enforce and execute such provisions in their area.

(3) Every local authority shall give such assistance and information to any other local authority as that other local authority may reasonably require for the purpose of carrying out their duties under these regulations.

Application of various sections of Act

6.—(1) Sections 108(3) (which relates to prosecutions), 110(1), (2) and (3) (which relate to evidence of analysis), 113 (which relates to a contravention due to some person other than the person charged), 115(2)(*a*) and (*b*) (which relate to the conditions under which a warranty may be pleaded as a defence) and 116 (which relates to offences in relation to warranties and certificates of analysis) of the Act shall apply for the purposes of these regulations as if references therein to proceedings, or a prosecution, under or taken or brought under the Act included references to proceedings, or a prosecution as the case may be, taken or brought for an offence under these regulations.

(2) Paragraph (*b*) of the proviso to section 108(1) of the Act shall apply for the purposes of these regulations as if the reference therein to section 116 of the Act included a reference to that section as applied by these regulations.

Revocation

7. Regulation 29 of the Milk and Dairies (General) Regulations 1959**(a)** as amended **(b)**, is hereby revoked.

In Witness whereof the Official Seal of the Minister of Agriculture, Fisheries and Food is hereunto affixed on 15th June 1973.

Joseph Godber,
(L.S.)   Minister of Agriculture, Fisheries and Food.

Keith Joseph,
5th June 1973.   Secretary of State for Social Services.

(a) S.I. 1959/277 (1959 I, p. 1351).

(b) The amendment does not relate expressly to the subject matter of these regulations.

SCHEDULE 1 Regulation 3(2)

General requirements in connection with the heat treatment of semi-skimmed and skimmed milk

1. Every milk processor shall take such measures as are adequate to ensure that any semi-skimmed milk or skimmed milk which has been heat treated by pasteurisation, sterilisation or the ultra high temperature method shall be kept apart from all other milk at all times except when in separate sealed containers.

2. Every milk processor and every milk purveyor shall—

(a) keep accurate records of the quanities of the semi-skimmed milk and skimmed milk purchased and sold by him, as the case may be, and of the names and addresses of the persons from whom that milk was purchased and to whom it was sold otherwise than by retail;

(b) retain such records for a period of twelve months from the date of the transaction to which the record relates;

(c) permit any person duly authorised by the local authority—

(i) to inspect the arrangements and processes for the handling, treatment, storage and distribution of semi-skimmed milk and skimmed milk at any place at which the milk is in the possession of the milk processor or milk purveyor as the case may be;

(ii) to procure samples of the milk at any such place; and

(iii) to inspect any records which the milk processor or the milk purveyor as the case may be, is required to keep by these regulations.

SCHEDULE 2 Regulation 3(2)

Special requirements in relation to and in connection with the heat treatment of semi-skimmed milk and skimmed milk

PART I.—PASTEURISATION

1. The milk shall be pasteurised, that is to say,—

(a) retained at a temperature of not less than 62·8 °C. and not more than 65·6 °C. for at least thirty minutes and be immediately cooled to a temperature of not more than 10 °C.; or

(b) retained at a temperature of not less than 71·7 °C. for at least fifteen seconds and be immediately cooled to a temperature of not more than 10 °C.

2. The whole of the apparatus in which the milk is pasteurised, including the cooler, shall be so constructed as to secure the protection of the milk from risk of atmospheric contamination by dust or otherwise.

3. Any apparatus in which the milk is to be heated to and maintained at a temperature of more than 65·6 °C. shall be provided with a device which shall automatically divert the flow of any milk which is not raised to the authorised temperature:

Provided that this paragraph shall only apply when the milk is heated by a continuous-flow method and is pasteurised in accordance with the provisions of sub-paragraph (b) of paragraph 1 of this Part of this Schedule.

4.—(1) Such indicating and recording thermometers shall be installed in suitable places in the apparatus in which the milk is pasteurised as are necessary to register the temperatures at which the milk is retained and to which the milk is cooled.

(2) The records of recording thermometers shall be marked with graduations adequately spaced to give clear readings, and they shall be dated and shall be preserved for a period of not less than one month.

5.—(1) A sample of the milk procured in accordance with Part I of Schedule 3 to these regulations after pasteurisation and before delivery to the consumer shall satisfy the phosphatase test prescribed in Part II of that Schedule.

(2) A sample of the milk procured in accordance with Part I of Schedule 3 to these regulations after pasteurisation and on the day of but before delivery to the consumer shall, if it is kept in an insulated container without artificial cooling until it reaches the laboratory, satisfy the methylene blue test prescribed in Part III of that Schedule.

6.—(1) Milk which is pasteurised in bottles shall be supplied to the consumer in those bottles, and milk which is pasteurised in containers other than bottles shall be put into the containers in which it is to be supplied to the consumer at the premises at which it is pasteurised, and as soon as possible after pasteurisation.

(2) Every container in which the milk is sold shall be so closed and securely fastened that it is airtight.

Part II.—Sterilisation

1. The milk shall be sterilised, that is to say, filtered or clarified, and (except in the case of skimmed milk) homogenised, and thereafter heated to and maintained at such a temperature, not less than 100°C. for such a period as to ensure that it will comply with the turbidity test prescribed in Part IV of Schedule 3 to these regulations—

    (*a*) in glass bottles and in such a manner that on or before completion of the treatment the bottles shall be sealed with an airtight seal; or

    (*b*) by a continuous-flow method and immediately after such treatment shall be put into the sterile containers in which it is to be supplied to the consumer. Such containers shall be filled and sealed at the premises at which the treatment has been carried out with such aseptic precautions as will ensure the protection of the milk from risk of contamination.

2.—(1) There shall be installed in suitable places in the apparatus, in the case of sterilisation of the milk in bottles, such thermometers and pressure gauges or, in the case of sterilisation of the milk by a continuous-flow method, such indicating and recording thermometers, as are necessary to register the temperature or pressure to which the milk is raised or subjected as the case may be.

(2) The records of recording thermometers shall be marked with graduations adequately spaced to give clear readings, and they shall be dated and shall be preserved for a period of not less than three months.

3. Any apparatus in which the milk is to be sterilised by a continuous-flow method shall be provided with a device which shall automatically divert the flow of any milk which is not raised to the authorised temperature.

4.—(1) A sample of the milk procured in accordance with Part I of Schedule 3 to these regulations after treatment and before delivery to the consumer shall satisfy the turbidity test prescribed in Part IV of that Schedule.

(2) A sample of the milk sterilised by a continuous-flow method which is procured in accordance with Part I of Schedule 3 to these regulations after treatment and before delivery to the consumer shall satisfy the colony count test prescribed in Part V of that Schedule.

5. Every container in which milk sterilised by a continous-flow method is sold shall be so closed and securely fastened that it is airtight.

Part III.—Treatment by the Ultra High Temperature Method

1. The milk shall be treated by the ultra high temperature method, that is to say retained at a temperature of not less than 132·2°C. for not less than one second.

2. Any apparatus in which the milk is to be heated to and maintained at a temperature of not less than 132·2°C. shall be provided with a device which shall automatically divert the flow of any milk which is not raised to the authorised temperature.

3.—(1) Such indicating and recording thermometers shall be installed in suitable places in the apparatus in which the milk is treated by the ultra high temperature method as are necessary to register the temperatures to which the milk is heated.

(2) The records of recording thermometers shall be marked with graduations adequately spaced to give clear readings, and they shall be dated and shall be preserved for a period of not less than three months.

4. A sample of the milk procured in accordance with Part I of Schedule 3 to these regulations after treatment by the ultra high temperature method and before delivery to the consumer shall satisfy the colony count test prescribed in Part V of that Schedule.

5.—(1) Milk which is treated by the ultra high temperature method shall immediately after such treatment be put into the sterile containers in which it is to be supplied to the consumer. Such containers shall be filled and sealed at the premises at which the treatment has been carried out with such aseptic precautions as will ensure the protection of the milk from risk of contamination.

(2) Every container in which the milk is sold shall be so closed and securely fastened that it is airtight.

SCHEDULE 3   Schedule 2

Part I.—Provisions as to Sampling

Procuring of sample

1. A sample shall be procured at any time when the semi-skimmed milk or skimmed milk is in the possession of a milk processor or a milk purveyor.

2. When the milk is in containers not exceeding one quart in capacity, or when milk has been treated by the ultra high temperature method whether or not such milk is in containers exceeding one quart in capacity, the sample shall consist of one such container which shall be delivered intact to the testing laboratory.

3. When the milk (other than milk which has been treated by the ultra high temperature method) is in containers exceeding one quart in capacity, the sample shall consist of not less than two fluid ounces of the milk. The milk shall be thoroughly stirred before sampling and the sample shall be taken from well below the surface of the milk. The instruments used for stirring and sampling shall be sterile and the sample shall be poured into a sterile bottle which shall thereupon be immediately stoppered. The part of the stopper which may come into contact with the milk shall be sterile. Where the person procuring the sample breaks the seal on a container he shall, after taking the sample, re-seal the container and attach to it a label certifying that it has been opened and re-sealed by him.

Identification of sample

4. For the purpose of identification in the testing laboratory, the person procuring the sample shall mark the container of the sample with a number or other suitable identification mark at the time of sampling and shall enter in a book or on a paper, which shall accompany the sample, the following particulars:—

(a) the identification number or mark;

(*b*) the name and address of the person by whom the milk was consigned, or by whom it was being delivered, or on whose premises the sample was procured.

Transport of sample

5. The container holding any sample of milk shall be transferred forthwith to an insulated container, which shall not be artificially cooled, for transport to the testing laboratory. The sample shall be transported to the testing laboratory with the least possible delay. Any sample which does not arrive at the testing laboratory on the day on which it is procured shall be discarded.

PART II.—THE PHOSPHATASE TEST FOR PASTEURISED SEMI-SKIMMED AND SKIMMED MILK

Examination of sample

1. The sample of milk shall be examined as soon as possible after arrival at the testing laboratory. If it is not examined immediately on arrival at the testing laboratory, it shall be kept at a temperature of between 3 °C. and 5 °C. until examined. The sample shall be raised to room temperature immediately before being tested.

Precautions

2. The following precautions shall be taken:—

(*a*) A sample which shows evidence of taint or souring shall not be tested.

(*b*) All glassware shall be clean immediately before use.

(*c*) A fresh pipette shall be used for each sample of milk. Pipettes shall not be contaminated with saliva.

(*d*) The test shall not be carried out in direct sunlight.

(*e*) Distilled water shall be used throughout.

Reagents

3.—(1) Whenever possible, reagents of analytical quality shall be used.

(2) The buffer-substrate solution shall be prepared as follows:—

(*a*) Buffer solution: 3·5g. of anhydrous sodium carbonate and 1·5g. of sodium bicarbonate shall be dissolved in distilled water, and made up to one litre.

(*b*) Substrate: Disodium p-nitrophenyl phosphate. The solid substrate shall be kept in a refrigerator.

(*c*) Buffer-substrate solution: 0·15g. of the substrate shall be placed in a 100 ml. measuring cylinder, and made up to 100 ml. with the buffer solution. The solution shall be stored in a refrigerator and protected from light. It shall give a reading of less than the standard marked 10 on the comparator disc A.P.T.W. or A.P.T.W.7 when viewed in transmitted light through a 25 mm. cell in the "all purposes" comparator, distilled water being used for comparison. The solution shall not be used for more than one week.

Apparatus

4. The following apparatus shall be used:—

(*a*) A Lovibond "all purposes" comparator complete with stand for work in reflected light.

(*b*) A Lovibond comparator disc A.P.T.W. or A.P.T.W.7.

(*c*) Two fused glass cells, 25 mm. depth.

(*d*) A water bath or incubator capable of being maintained at 37·5 °C. ±0·5 °C.

(*e*) A pipette to deliver 5·0 ml.

(*f*) A supply of 1·0 ml. straight-sided pipettes of an accuracy equal to that of N.P.L. grade B.

(g) A 1000 ml. graduated flask.

(h) A 100 ml. measuring cylinder.

(i) A supply of test tubes conforming to British Standard 625:1959 nominal size 150/16, with rubber stoppers to fit.

Care of apparatus

5.—(1) After use, each test tube shall be emptied, rinsed in water, well washed in hot water containing soda, rinsed in warm water, rinsed in distilled water and finally dried.

(2) If after treatment in accordance with sub-paragraph (1) hereof a test tube does not appear to be clean, the treatment shall be repeated with the addition that after being rinsed in warm water it shall be soaked in 50 per cent. commercial hydrochloric acid and then rinsed again in warm water before being rinsed in distilled water and finally dried.

(3) New glassware shall be cleaned by soaking in chromic acid solution prepared as follows—

5 volumes of 8 per cent. W/V potassium bichromate

4 volumes of concentrated sulphuric acid.   This should be added slowly and carefully to the mixture of bichromate and water.

The solution shall be kept covered and shall be discarded when it beomes green. After cleaning in chromic acid solution, new glassware shall be rinsed in warm water, rinsed in distilled water and finally dried.

(4) Pipettes shall be well rinsed in cold water and then cleaned by soaking for 24 hours in chromic acid solution in a 250 ml. glass cylinder or other suitable container. The pipettes shall then be well rinsed in warm water, rinsed in distilled water and finally dried.

(5) Glassware used for the test shall not be used for any other purpose and shall be kept apart from all other apparatus in the laboratory.

Method of carrying out the test

6. 5 ml. of the buffer-substrate solution shall be transferred to a test tube using a pipette and the test tube shall be stoppered and brought to a temperature of 37°C. 1 ml. of the milk to be tested shall be added, the test tube stopper replaced and the contents well mixed by shaking.   The test tube shall then be incubated for exactly 2 hours at 37°C.   One blank prepared from boiled milk of the same type as those undergoing the test shall be incubated with each series of samples.   (Where the sample consists of highly coloured milk, such as homogenised milk or milk from Channel Island cows, a separate blank of such milk shall be prepared).   After incubation the test tube shall be removed from the water bath and its contents shall be well mixed. The blank shall be placed on the left hand ramp of the stand and the test sample on the right.   Readings shall be taken in reflected light by looking down on to the two apertures with the comparator facing a good source of daylight (preferably north light). If artificial light is needed for matching, a "daylight" type of illumination must be used.   The disc shall be revolved until the test sample is matched.   Readings falling between two standards shall be recorded by affixing a plus or minus sign to the figure for the nearest standard.

Interpretation

7. The test shall be deemed to be satisfied by milk which gives a reading of 10 µg. or less of p-nitrophenol/ml. of milk.

PART III.—THE METHYLENE BLUE TEST FOR PASTEURISED SEMI-SKIMMED AND SKIMMED MILK

Treatment of sample

1.—(1) On arrival at the testing laboratory the sample of milk shall at once be removed from the insulated container.   Thereafter it shall be stored as follows:—

(*a*) a sample procured at any time during the period from 1 May to 31 October, inclusive, in any year shall be kept at atmospheric shade temperature until 9.30 a.m. on the following day.

(*b*) a sample procured at any time during the period from 1 November to 30 April, inclusive, in any year shall be kept in its original container or in a sterile 3 oz. sample bottle at atmospheric shade temperature until 5.0 p.m. on the day of sampling and thereafter at a constant temperature at $18\cdot3°C. \pm 1°C.$ until 9.30 a.m. on the following day.

(2) If during the period of storage at atmospheric shade temperature to which a sample is subject this temperature at any time exceeds 21 °C., the test shall not be applied.

(3) The test shall be begun between 9.30 and 10.00 a.m. on the day after the sample is procured.

Reagent—Methylene Blue

2.—(1) Tablets manufactured under arrangements made by the Minister shall be used for the test. A solution shall be prepared aseptically by adding one tablet to 200 ml. of cold, sterile, glass-distilled water in a sterile flask, shaking until the tablet is completely dissolved, and making up the solution to 800 ml. with cold, sterile, glass-distilled water. The resultant solution shall be stored in a stoppered sterile flask in a cool, dark place, and shall not be used if—

(*a*) it has been exposed to sunlight, or

(*b*) a period of two months has elapsed since the date of preparation.

(2) The amount of methylene blue required for a day's work shall be poured off from the stock bottle into a suitable glass container. The pipette used for transferring the methylene blue solution to the tubes of milk shall not be introduced into the stock bottle.

Apparatus

3.—(1) Test tubes shall conform to British Standard 625:1959, nominal size 150/16 and shall be accurately marked at 10 ml. They shall be plugged with cotton wool or covered with closely fitting aluminium caps or stored in such a way as to prevent contamination.

(2) Pipettes shall be 1·0 ml. straight-sided blow out delivery pipettes, and shall be plugged with cotton wool at the upper end.

(3) Glassware and rubber stoppers shall be sterile immediately before use.

(4) The water bath shall be fitted with a reliable automatic thermo-regulator capable of maintaining the water at a temperature of $37\cdot5°C. \pm 0\cdot5°C.$

Method of carrying out the test

4.—(1) The sample shall be mixed thoroughly by inverting and shaking and the milk shall be transferred to a test tube up to the 10 ml. mark in such a manner that one side of the interior of the test tube is not wetted with milk. 1 ml. of methylene blue solution shall be added without letting the pipette come into contact with the milk in the tube or with the wetted side of the interior of the tube. After a lapse of 3 seconds, the solution remaining in the tip of the pipette shall be blown out. The test tube shall be closed with a rubber stopper, aseptic precautions being taken, and shall then be inverted twice slowly, so that the whole column of contained air rises above the level of the milk. Within a period of 5 minutes the test tube shall be placed in a water bath. The water in the bath shall be kept above the level of the milk in the test tube, and its temperature, which shall be between 37 °C. and 38 °C., shall be maintained as nearly uniform as possible by means of a reliable automatic thermo-regulator. The interior of the bath shall be kept completely dark.

(2) A control tube shall be used for comparison with each batch of experimental tubes to indicate when decolourisation is complete. The control tube shall be pre-

pared by immersing in boiling water for 3 minutes a stoppered test tube containing 1 ml. of tap water and 10 ml. of mixed milk having a fat content and colour similar to that of the milk being tested.

(3) The milk shall be regarded as decolourised when the whole column of milk is completely decolourised or is decolourised up to within 5 mm. of the surface. A trace of colour at the bottom of the tube may be ignored provided that it does not extend upwards for more than 5 mm.

Interpretation

5. The test shall be deemed to be satified by milk which fails to decolourise methylene blue in 30 minutes.

PART IV.—THE TURBIDITY TEST FOR STERILISED SEMI-SKIMMED AND SKIMMED MILK

Examination of sample

1. The sample of milk may be examined at any time after delivery to the testing laboratory but shall be at room temperature when the test is begun.

Reagent

2. Ammonium sulphate A.R. shall be used.

Apparatus

3. The following apparatus shall be used:—

    (*a*) Conical flasks of 50 ml. capacity.

    (*b*) Graduated cylinders of 25 ml. capacity.

    (*c*) Test tubes conforming to British Standard 625:1959, nominal size 150/16.

    (*d*) Filter funnels of 6 cm. diameter.

    (*e*) Beakers of 400 ml. capacity.

    (*f*) 12·5 cm. No. 12 Whatman folded filter papers.

Method of carrying out the test

4. $4 \pm 0·1$ g. of ammonium sulphate shall be weighed into a 50 ml. conical flask. $20 \pm 0·5$ ml. of the milk sample shall be measured out and poured into the conical flask, the flask being shaken for 1 minute to ensure that the ammonium sulphate dissolves. The mixture shall be left for not less than 5 minutes and then filtered through a folded filter paper into a test tube. When not less than 5 ml. of a clear filtrate have collected, the tube shall be placed in a beaker of water, which has been kept boiling, and kept therein for 5 minutes. The tube shall be transferred to a beaker of cold water, and when the tube is cool, the contents shall be examined for turbidity by moving the tube in front of an electric light shaded from the eyes of the observer.

Interpretation

5. The test shall be deemed to be satisfied when a sample of milk treated as in paragraph 4 hereof gives a filtrate showing no sign of turbidity.

PART V.—THE COLONY COUNT TEST FOR SEMI-SKIMMED AND SKIMMED MILK STERILISED BY A CONTINUOUS-FLOW METHOD AND SEMI-SKIMMED AND SKIMMED MILK TREATED BY THE ULTRA HIGH TEMPERATURE METHOD

Apparatus

1. The following apparatus shall be used:—

    (*a*) McCartney bottles of 1 fl.oz. capacity.

    (*b*) Test tubes plugged with cotton wool or covered with closely fitting aluminium caps or stored in such a way as to prevent contamination.

(*c*) A standard iridium platinum loop of 4 mm. internal diameter made from gauge wire conforming to British Standard 19 and containing 10 per cent. iridium. The loop, when used as directed, should transfer about 0·01 ml. of milk to the molten medium in a tube or a McCartney bottle.

(*d*) An incubator capable of operating at a preselected temperature within the range 30 °C. to 37 °C. and of maintaining the preselected temperature within ±1 °C.

(*e*) A water bath capable of maintaining the water at a temperature of not less than 45 °C. and not more than 50 °C.

(*f*) A refrigerator fitted with a reliable automatic thermo-regulator capable of maintaining a temperature of between 3 °C. and 5 °C.

Culture medium

2. A culture medium prepared as follows should be used:—

(*a*) Yeastrel milk agar constituted as follows:—

Yeastrel	3g.
Peptone	5g.
Agar	15g.
(If New Zealand agar is used 12g. is normally sufficient.)	
Fresh whole milk	10 ml.
Distilled water	1,000 ml.

(*b*) The yeastrel and peptone shall be dissolved in the distilled water in a steamer and the reaction at room temperature adjusted to pH 7·4, using phenol red as an indicator or using a pH meter. When phenol red is used, a brightness screen must be employed with Lovibond phenol red disc 2/IJ. The agar and the milk shall then be added to the broth and autoclaved at 121 °C. for 25 minutes. If shredded agar is used, it shall be wrapped in muslin and washed in running water for 15 minutes, the excess water being squeezed out before the agar is added to the broth. To ensure thorough mixing and that heat treatment of the bulk at this stage is equivalent to the final sterilisation of the tubed medium, quantities of not more than 2 litres shall be autoclaved in 3-litre conical flasks. The hot medium shall then be filtered through paper pulp in a Buchner funnel.

(*c*) The pulp shall be prepared by mashing up small pieces of filter paper in water and boiling. The funnel shall be inserted into an Erlenmeyer flask fitted with a side piece and a single layer of filter paper laid on the top of the Buchner funnel to prevent the pulp being sucked through. The hot pulp shall then be poured on to the filter paper and a filter pump applied to suck through the excess water, which shall then be poured away. The pulp should be firmly packed down just before the last of the water is sucked through. At this stage a layer of filter paper shall be laid on the filter bed, so that the hot medium can subsequently be poured on to it without disturbing the pulp. The filter when ready for use should have a total depth of about 1·5 mm. (A pulp layer of suitable and approximately the same depth for any size of funnel is obtained by pulping an area of filter paper equal to four times the square of the diameter of the funnel. With ordinary grade filter paper 1g. of the dry paper will be required for every 20 sq. cm. of filtering area).

(*d*) The flask and funnel shall be thoroughly hot before filtering commences and these and the medium shall be kept hot during filtering. The medium shall be taken direct from the autoclave, poured on to the pulp where the filter paper is laid and the vacuum pump connected.

(*e*) The reaction of the filtrate shall be tested at 50 °C. and adjusted if necessary to pH 7·0. Adjustment at this stage should not normally be necessary, and if it is needed at all frequently, the method of preparation should be checked.

(*f*) The medium shall be distributed in 5 ml. quantities in 6 x $\frac{5}{8}$ in. test-tubes or in 1 oz. McCartney bottles and autoclaved at 121 °C. for 15 minutes.

(*g*) The final reaction of the medium at room temperature shall be pH 7·2.

Alternative medium

3. A dehydrated medium of the same composition may be used provided that it has been shown to give similar results.

Incubation of sample

4. On arrival at the laboratory the sample shall be placed unopened in the incubator at a temperature of between 30°C. and 37°C. and retained at that temperature for 24 hours.

Mixing of sample prior to examination

5. At the end of the 24-hour incubation period, the sample shall be removed from the incubator and shall be mixed thoroughly by inverting the container and shaking it.

Method of carrying out the test

6. (*a*) After the sample has been thoroughly mixed as described above, it shall be opened with aseptic precautions as follows:—

    (i) If the sample is contained in a carton, one of the corners or edges of the carton shall be thoroughly swabbed with alcohol and the excess burnt off. The carton shall then be opened by cutting off this corner or edge using a pair of sterile scissors.

    (ii) If the sample is contained in a bottle, the closure and neck of the bottle shall be thoroughly swabbed with alcohol and the excess burnt off. The closure shall then be removed by means of a sterile opener.

    (iii) If the sample is in a container other than a carton or bottle a suitable surface of the container shall be thoroughly swabbed with alcohol and the excess burnt off. A hole in that sterile surface shall then be punched using a sterile tool.

(*b*) Immediately after opening the sample container, the cap from a sterile McCartney bottle shall be removed and approximately 10 ml. of the sample transferred by means of a sterile pipette to the bottle, the cap replaced and the McCartney bottle put in the refrigerator. A further 10 ml. (approximately) of the sample shall be transferred to a sterile test-tube after removing the plug. The plug shall then be replaced.

(*c*) With as little delay as possible, a loopful of milk from the test-tube sample shall be transferred to a sterile test-tube or 1 oz. McCartney bottle containing about 5 ml. of melted yeastrel milk agar medium at 45°C. to 50°C. The loop, after being flame-sterilised and cooled, shall be lowered into the milk about 1 inch below the surface and a loopful of milk withdrawn and transferred to the molten medium in the tube or McCartney bottle. The contents of the tube or bottle shall then be carefully mixed, the tube or bottle placed in a sloping position (the medium being at least half an inch from the closure) and the medium allowed to set. The tube or bottle shall then be incubated in a sloping position at a temperature of between 30°C. and 37°C. for 48 hours and at the end of that time it shall be examined for the presence of colonies.

Counting of colonies

7. Colonies shall be counted within 4 hours of the expiry of the incubation period.

Interpretation

8. The test shall be deemed to be satisfied by a sample if the number of colonies is found to be less than 10. If there is any doubt about the result, the test should be repeated using the sample in the McCartney bottle placed in the refrigerator.

Regulation 4 SCHEDULE 4

Requirements as to labelling of containers of heat treated semi-skimmed and skimmed milk

PART I.—PASTEURISED

Every container in which semi-skimmed milk or skimmed milk which has been pasteurised is sold shall be conspicuously and legibly labelled or marked with the words "Pasteurised Semi-skimmed Milk" or "Pasteurised Skimmed Milk" as appropriate.

PART II.—STERILISED

Every container in which semi-skimmed or skimmed milk which has been sterilised is sold shall be conspicuously and legibly labelled or marked with the words "Sterilised Semi-skimmed Milk" or "Sterilised Skimmed Milk" as appropriate.

PART III.—ULTRA HEAT TREATED

Every container in which semi-skimmed milk or skimmed milk which has been treated by the ultra high temperature method is sold shall be conspicuously and legibly labelled or marked with the address of the premises at which the milk was put into the container and with the words "Ultra Heat Treated Semi-skimmed Milk" or "Ultra Heat Treated Skimmed Milk" as appropriate, so however that the letters "U.H.T." may be substituted for the words "Ultra Heat Treated".

EXPLANATORY NOTE

(This Note is not part of the Regulations.)

These Regulations apply to England and Wales only and come into operation on 18th July 1973. They—

(*a*) require that semi-skimmed milk or skimmed milk sold for human consumption (other than milk intended for manufacture into products for sale for human consumption or sold to a processor for heat treatment under the regulations) shall have been heat treated by pasteurisation, sterilisation or the ultra high temperature method in accordance with the prescribed requirements (Regulation 3 and Schedules 1 and 2);

(*b*) specify sampling provisions for heat treated semi-skimmed milk and skimmed milk and tests which it must satisfy after pasteurisation, sterilisation or treatment by the ultra high temperature method (Schedule 3);

(*c*) require that containers in which pasteurised, sterilised or ultra heat treated semi-skimmed milk or skimmed milk is sold for human consumption shall be labelled in the prescribed manner (Regulation 4 and Schedule 4).

STATUTORY INSTRUMENTS

1973 No. 1065

COUNTER-INFLATION

The Counter-Inflation (Designated Officers) (No. 2) Order 1973

Made - - - - 18*th June* 1973

Coming into Operation:

Articles 1 *and* 2 - 20*th June* 1973

Article 3 - - - 1*st July* 1973

The Secretary of State and the Minister of Agriculture, Fisheries and Food, for the purpose of conferring on designated persons the powers of their respective officers, in exercise of the powers conferred on them by section 23(2) of, and paragraph 2 (1) and (4) of Schedule 4 to, the Counter-Inflation Act 1973(**a**), and of all other powers enabling them in that behalf, hereby make the following Order:—

1.—(1) This Order may be cited as the Counter-Inflation (Designated Officers) (No. 2) Order 1973 and, except article 3, shall come into operation on 20th June 1973.

(2) The Interpretation Act 1889(**b**) shall apply for the interpretation of this Order as it applies for the interpretation of an Act of Parliament and as if this Order and the Order hereby revoked were Acts of Parliament.

2.—(1) The persons specified in paragraph (2) below are hereby designated as persons to execute the Counter-Inflation Act 1973 in the United Kingdom in accordance with paragraph 2 of Schedule 4 to that Act by doing what may be done by officers of the Secretary of State or the Minister of Agriculture, Fisheries and Food.

(2) The persons referred to in paragraph (1) above are all officers of the Price Commission of or above the rank of higher executive officer or equivalent rank.

3.—(1) The Counter-Inflation (Designated Officers) Order 1973(**c**) is hereby revoked.

(2) This article shall come into operation on 1st July 1973.

Geoffrey Howe,
Minister for Trade and Consumer Affairs,
Department of Trade and Industry.

18th June 1973.

In witness whereof the Official Seal of the Minister of Agriculture, Fisheries and Food is hereunto affixed on 18th June 1973.

(L.S.)

A. D. Neale,
Permanent Secretary,
Ministry of Agriculture, Fisheries and Food.

(**a**) 1973 c. 9.   (**b**) 1889 c. 63.   (**c**) S.I. 1973/645 (1973 I, p. 2009).

EXPLANATORY NOTE

(This Note is not part of the Order.)

By this Order, officers of the Price Commission of or above the rank of higher executive officer or equivalent are designated officers for the purposes of enforcement in accordance with Schedule 4 of the Counter-Inflation Act 1973.

This Order also revokes on 1st July 1973 the Counter-Inflation (Designated Officers) Order 1973 by which Inspectors of Weights and Measures were designated officers for the purposes of the Act.

STATUTORY INSTRUMENTS

1973 No. 1067

CUSTOMS AND EXCISE

The Import Duties (Temporary Exemptions) (No. 17) Order 1973

Made	- - -	18*th June* 1973
Laid before the House of Commons		19*th June* 1973
Coming into Operation		20*th June* 1973

The Lords Commissioners of Her Majesty's Treasury, by virtue of the powers conferred on them by sections 1, 3(6) and 13 of the Import Duties Act 1958(a), as amended by paragraph 1 of Schedule 4 to the European Communities Act 1972(b), and of all other powers enabling them in that behalf, on the recommendation of the Secretary of State(c), hereby make the following Order:

1.—(1) This Order may be cited as the Import Duties (Temporary Exemptions) (No. 17) Order 1973 and shall come into operation on 20th June 1973.

(2) The Interpretation Act 1889(d) shall apply for the interpretation of this Order as it applies for the interpretation of an Act of Parliament.

2.—(1) Up to and including 31st December 1973 no import duty shall be chargeable on flax sliver falling within heading 54.01 of the Customs Tariff 1959.

(2) For the purposes of classification under the Customs Tariff 1959, insofar as that depends on the rate of duty, any goods to which paragraph (1) of this Article applies shall be treated as chargeable with the same duty as if this Order had not been made.

> *Tim Fortescue,*
> *Oscar Murton,*
> Two of the Lords Commissioners of
> Her Majesty's Treasury.

18th June 1973.

EXPLANATORY NOTE

(This Note is not part of the Order.)

This Order provides that flax sliver falling within tariff heading 54.01 is to be exempt from import duty up to and including 31st December 1973.

(a) 1958 c.6.   (b) 1972 c.68.

(c) *See* S.I. 1970/1537 (1970 III, p. 5293).   (d) 1889 c.63.

STATUTORY INSTRUMENTS

1973 No. 1068

PENSIONS

The Pensions Increase (Federated Superannuation Scheme for Nurses and Hospital Officers) (Civil Service) (Amendment) Regulations 1973

Made - - -	*18th June* 1973
Laid before Parliament	*26th June* 1973
Coming into Operation	*18th July* 1973

The Minister for the Civil Service, in exercise of the powers conferred on him by section 13(2) and (5) of the Pensions (Increase) Act 1971(**a**) and of all other powers enabling him in that behalf, hereby makes the following Regulations:—

1. These Regulations may be cited as the Pensions Increase (Federated Superannuation Scheme for Nurses and Hospital Officers) (Civil Service) (Amendment) Regulations 1973, and shall come into operation on 18th July 1973.

2.—(1) In these Regulations "the principal Regulations" means the Pensions Increase (Federated Superannuation Scheme for Nurses and Hospital Officers) (Civil Service) Regulations 1972(**b**).

(2) The Interpretation Act 1889(**c**) shall apply for the interpretation of these Regulations as it applies for the interpretation of an Act of Parliament.

3. The principal Regulations shall be amended, in Regulation 2(1), by substituting for the definition of "the civil service pension scheme" the following definition:—

" "the civil service pension scheme" means, in relation to a person whose service in the civil service of the state ended not later than 29th February 1972, the Superannuation Acts 1965 and 1967(**d**) and, in relation to a person whose reckonable service ended after that date, the principal civil service pension scheme within the meaning of section 2 of the Superannuation Act 1972(**e**) and for the time being in force;".

4. The principal Regulations shall be amended, in Regulation 4, by substituting for paragraphs (1) and (2) the following paragraphs:—

(**a**) 1971 c. 56.   (**b**) S.I. 1972/395 (1972 **I**, p. 1486).   (**c**) 1889 c. 63.

(**d**) 1965 c. 74;   (**e**) 1972 c. 11.

"(1) There shall be ascribed to every person to whom these Regulations apply a notional pension equal to the amount of the annual pension for which he would have been eligible under the civil service pension scheme if he had during the period of his employment in the civil service of the state been subject to that scheme and his reckonable service had been reckonable for the purposes of that scheme.

(2) Where a person to whom these Regulations apply has retired from the civil service of the State in such circumstances that, if the civil service pension scheme applied to him, a lump sum would become payable to him by way of retiring allowance upon his subsequently attaining a particular age or becoming disabled by physical or mental infirmity before that age, there shall be ascribed to him a notional lump sum, treated as if it became payable on his attaining that age or becoming so disabled, as the case may be, of an amount equal to the lump sum for which he would have been eligible under the civil service pension scheme if he had during the period of his employment in the civil service of the State been subject to that scheme and his reckonable service had been reckonable for the purposes of that scheme".

5. The principal Regulations shall be amended, in Regulation 5, by substituting for paragraph (*a*) the following paragraph: —

"(*a*) there were payable to him—

(i) an annual pension under the civil service pension scheme of an amount equal to the notional pension ascribed to him under Regulation 4(1) above and beginning on the day following the end of the period of his service in the civil service of the State, and

(ii) in a case where a lump sum is ascribed to him under Regulation 4(2) above, a lump sum under the civil service pension scheme of an amount equal to, and becoming payable at the same time as, the notional lump sum and beginning on the day following the end of the period of his service in the civil service of the State, and".

6. Any increase of benefit attributable to these Regulations shall take effect in respect of any period beginning on or after 1st December 1972.

Given under the official seal of the Minister for the Civil Service on 18th June 1973.

(L.S.)

Kenneth Baker,
Parliamentary Secretary of
the Civil Service Department.

EXPLANATORY NOTE

(This Note is not part of the Regulations.)

These Regulations amend the Pensions Increase (Federated Superannuation Scheme for Nurses and Hospital Officers) (Civil Service) Regulations 1972, which provide for the payment of allowances corresponding to pension increases under the Pensions (Increase) Act 1971 to persons who have retired from the civil service and receive superannuation benefits under a scheme operated under the Federated Superannuation Scheme for Nurses and Hospital Officers.

The principal change is that, in the case of a person who has retired after 29th February 1972, the notional pension and notional lump sum on which his allowances are based are to be calculated, in accordance with the principal civil service pension scheme, by reference to the year's salary in his last three years of service which is most favourable to him, instead of on the average of his salary for such last three years. His reckonable service will also be counted in years and days, instead of in completed years.

The Regulations also make it clear that the notional pension and lump sum are to be treated as "beginning", for the purposes of applying the Pensions (Increase) Act 1971, on the day following the end of a person's service in the civil service.

In accordance with the power conferred by section 13(5) of the 1971 Act, the Regulations provide for any increase in allowances attributable to the Regulations to take effect from 1st December 1972.

STATUTORY INSTRUMENTS

1973 No. 1069 (C.26)

TOWN AND COUNTRY PLANNING, ENGLAND AND WALES

The Town and Country Planning Act 1971 (Commencement No. 17) (Oxford—Oxfordshire etc.) Order 1973

Made -   -   -   -   18*th June* 1973

The Secretary of State for the Environment in exercise of the power conferred on him by section 21 of the Town and Country Planning Act 1971**(a)** hereby makes the following order:—

1.—(1) This order may be cited as the Town and Country Planning Act 1971 (Commencement No. 17) (Oxford-Oxfordshire etc.) Order 1973.

(2) In this order:—

"the Act" means the Town and Country Planning Act 1971; and

"the Order area" means the area described in Schedule 1 to this order.

2. The provisions of the Act specified in the first column of Schedule 2 hereto (which relate to the matters specified in the second column of the said Schedule) shall come into operation in the Order area on 17th July 1973.

3. Pending the repeal of Part I of Schedule 5 and Schedule 6 to the Act as respects the Order area, any reference in the Act to the carrying out of a survey or the preparation, approval, making or amendment of a development plan under the said Schedule 5 or to a plan or amendment approved or made thereunder shall be construed as respects the Order area as including a reference to the carrying out of a survey or the preparation, approval, adoption, making or amendment of a structure or local plan under Part II of the Act or, as the case may be, to a plan or amendment approved, adopted or made thereunder.

SCHEDULE 1

THE ORDER AREA

The county borough of Oxford.

The administrative county of Oxford.

In the administrative county of Berkshire—
the boroughs of Abingdon and Wallingford;
the urban district of Wantage;
the rural districts of Abingdon, Faringdon and Wallingford;
in the rural district of Wantage, the parishes of Ardington, Blewbury, Childrey, Chilton, Denchworth, East Challow, East Hanney, East Hendred, Goosey, Grove, Harwell, Letcombe Bassett, Letcombe Regis, Lockinge, Sparsholt, Upton, West Challow, West Hanney and West Hendred.

(a) 1971 c. 78.

SCHEDULE 2

PROVISIONS COMING INTO OPERATION IN THE ORDER AREA ON 17TH JULY 1973.

Provisions of the Act	Subject matter of provisions
Part II, except sections 9(4), 18, 19, 20 and 21, and except so far as it enables any matter or thing to be prescribed.	New provisions as to development plans.

18th June 1973.

Geoffrey Rippon,
Secretary of State for the Environment.

EXPLANATORY NOTE

(This Note is not part of the Order.)

This Order brings into force for the county borough of Oxford, the administrative county of Oxford and certain adjacent areas in the administrative county of Berkshire as described in Schedule 1 to the Order the provisions of Part II of the Town and Country Planning Act 1971 (as amended by sections 1, 2 and 3 of the Town and Country Planning (Amendment) Act 1972 (1972 c. 42.)) which are set out in Schedule 2.

The provisions which are brought into force are the substantive provisions for the new development plan system of structure and local plans.

The provisions require a local planning authority to institute a survey, prepare a report of the survey and prepare and submit to the Secretary of State for his approval a structure plan for their area, and enable two or more local planning authorities, with the consent of the Secretary of State, to carry out their duties under Part II of the Act of 1971 by instituting a joint survey, preparing a joint report and preparing and submitting a joint structure plan for a combined area consisting of their areas or any part of their areas. The provisions also empower a local planning authority to prepare a local plan for any part of their area within the area of the structure plan.

1973 No. 1070

FOOD AND DRUGS
MILK AND DAIRIES

The Milk and Dairies (Milk Bottle Caps) (Colour) Regulations 1973

Made - - -		18*th June* 1973
Laid before Parliament		26*th June* 1973
Coming into Operation		1*st December* 1973

The Minister of Agriculture, Fisheries and Food and the Secretary of State for Social Services, acting jointly, in exercise of the powers conferred on them by sections 29 and 123 of the Food and Drugs Act 1955(**a**) as read with the Secretary of State for Social Services Order 1968(**b**), and of all other powers enabling them in that behalf, hereby make the following regulations after consultation with such organisations as appear to them to be representative of interests substantially affected by the regulations: —

Commencement and citation

1. These regulations may be cited as the Milk and Dairies (Milk Bottle Caps) (Colour) Regulations 1973, and shall come into operation on 1st December 1973.

Interpretation

2.—(1) In these regulations, unless the context otherwise requires—

"the Act" means the Food and Drugs Act 1955;

"bottle" means any container which is closed and fastened by a cap of aluminium foil, but does not include a container which is closed and fastened by any other means;

"food and drugs authority" has the meaning assigned to it by section 83 of the Act;

"milk" means cows' milk intended for sale or sold for human consumption but does not include cream, or separated, dried, condensed or evaporated milk, or butter milk;

"milk description" means, in relation to milk, any description specified in column 1 of the Schedule to these regulations and includes, in each case where appropriate, that description expressed by the same words in a different order.

(2) The Interpretation Act 1889(**c**) shall apply to the interpretation of these regulations as it applies to the interpretation of an Act of Parliament.

(**a**) 4 & 5 Eliz. 2. c. 16.   (**b**) S.I. 1968/1699 (1968 III, p. 4585).
(**c**) 1889 c. 63.

Labelling of milk bottles

3. No person shall sell or offer or expose for sale any milk contained in a bottle which is labelled with any milk description (whether or not it is labelled in any other way or with any other words) unless—

(*a*) the bottle is so labelled in embossed lettering or in lettering of a colour specified in relation to that description in column 2 of the Schedule to these regulations or partly in embossed lettering and partly in lettering of such a colour, on a cap of the colour specified in relation thereto in column 3 of that Schedule; and

(*b*) any symbol, marking or lettering other than that of the milk description, which appears on the cap, is embossed or is of a colour specified in relation to that description in column 2 of the Schedule to these regulations or is partly embossed and partly of such a colour.

Penalties and enforcement

4.—(1) If any person contravenes or fails to comply with any of the foregoing provisions of these regulations he shall be guilty of an offence and shall be liable to a fine not exceeding one hundred pounds or to imprisonment for a term not exceeding three months, or to both, and in the case of a continuing offence, to a further fine not exceeding five pounds for each day during which the offence continues after conviction.

(2) Each food and drugs authority shall enforce and execute such provisions in their area.

Application of provisions of the Act

5.—(1) Sections 108(3) and (4) (which relate to prosecutions), 110(1), (2) and (3) (which relate to evidence of analysis), 112 (which relates to the power of a court to require analysis by the Government Chemist), 113 (which relates to a contravention due to some person other than the person charged), 115(2) (which relates to the conditions under which a warranty may be pleaded as a defence) and 116 (which relates to offences in relation to warranties and certificates of analysis) of the Act shall apply for the purposes of these regulations as if references therein to proceedings, or a prosecution, under or taken or brought under the Act included references to proceedings, or a prosecution as the case may be, taken or brought for an offence under these regulations and as if the reference in the said section 112 to subsection (4) of section 108 included a reference to that subsection as applied by these regulations.

(2) Paragraph (*b*) of the proviso to section 108(1) of the Act shall apply for the purposes of these regulations as if the reference therein to section 116 of the Act included a reference to that section as applied by these regulations.

In Witness whereof the Official Seal of the Minister of Agriculture, Fisheries and Food is hereunto affixed on 13th June 1973.

(L.S.)

Joseph Godber,
Minister of Agriculture, Fisheries
and Food.

Keith Joseph,
Secretary of State for Social Services.

18th June 1973.

SCHEDULE

regulations 2(1) and 3

Column 1 Milk Description	Column 2 Colour of Lettering	Column 3 Colour of Cap
Pasteurised Channel Islands Pasteurised Jersey Pasteurised Guernsey Pasteurised South Devon (whether or not the bottle is also labelled "Homogenised") ...	Black Silver	Gold
Pasteurised Homogenised	Black Silver	Red
Pasteurised Kosher (whether or not the bottle is also labelled with any of the following words:— "Channel Islands", "Jersey", "Guernsey", "South Devon", "Homogenised")	Black	Blue and Silver Stripes
Pasteurised Kedassia (whether or not the bottle is also labelled with any of the following words:— "Channel Islands", "Jersey", "Guernsey", "South Devon", "Homogenised")	Black	Purple and Silver Stripes
Pasteurised (except where it forms part of one of the foregoing milk descriptions) ...	Black	Silver
Untreated Channel Islands Untreated Jersey Untreated Guernsey Untreated South Devon (whether or not the bottle is also labelled "Kosher" or "Kedassia")	Black Silver	Green with single gold stripe not exceeding 10 mm. in width
Untreated (except where it forms part of one of the foregoing milk descriptions and whether or not the bottle is also labelled "Kosher" or "Kedassia")	Black Silver	Green

EXPLANATORY NOTE

(*This Note is not part of the Regulations.*)

These Regulations apply to England and Wales only and come into operation on 1st December 1973. They prescribe the colours of caps and lettering which shall be used in labelling, with the descriptions specified in relation to those colours, milk which is sold in bottles.

STATUTORY INSTRUMENTS

1973 No. 1076

BETTING AND GAMING

The Pool Competitions (Fee for Renewal of Licence) Order 1973

Made - - - -	16*th June* 1973
Laid before Parliament	27*th June* 1973
Coming into Operation	25*th July* 1973

In pursuance of section 5(1)(*c*) and (2) of the Pool Competitions Act 1971(**a**), I hereby make the following Order:—

1. This Order may be cited as the Pool Competitions (Fee for Renewal of Licence) Order 1973 and shall come into operation on 25th July 1973.

2. In respect of the grant, by way of renewal, of a licence under the Pool Competitions Act 1971, there shall be payable to the Gaming Board for Great Britain a fee of such amount, being not less than £50 nor more than £2,500, as the Board may determine.

Robert Carr,
One of Her Majesty's Principal
Secretaries of State.

Home Office,
 Whitehall.
16th June 1973.

EXPLANATORY NOTE

(*This Note is not part of the Order.*)

This Order makes provision for the fee to be payable upon the renewal of a licence under the Pool Competitions Act 1971. The fee payable upon the grant of such a licence otherwise than on renewal is regulated by the Pool Competitions (Licence Fees) Order 1971 (S.I. 1971/2167).

(**a**) 1971 c. 57.

STATUTORY INSTRUMENTS

1973 No. 1077

NURSES AND MIDWIVES

The Nurses and Enrolled Nurses (Amendment) Rules Approval Instrument 1973

Made - - - -	*20th June* 1973
Laid before Parliament	*28th June* 1973
Coming into Operation	*18th July* 1973

The Secretary of State for Social Services, in exercise of powers conferred by section 32 of the Nurses Act 1957(a) and now vested in him (b) and of all other powers enabling him in that behalf, hereby approves the rules made by the General Nursing Council for England and Wales as set out in Schedules 1 and 2 hereto.

This Instrument may be cited as the Nurses and Enrolled Nurses (Amendment) Rules Approval Instrument 1973, and shall come into operation on 18th July 1973.

Keith Joseph,
Secretary of State for Social Services.

20th June 1973.

SCHEDULE 1

THE GENERAL NURSING COUNCIL FOR ENGLAND AND WALES

The Nurses Acts 1957 *to* 1969

The General Nursing Council for England and Wales, in exercise of the powers conferred on them by sections 3, 6, 7, 10, 23 and 30 of the Nurses Act 1957, and all other powers enabling them in that behalf, having consulted with the General Nursing Council for Scotland and the Northern Ireland Council for Nurses and Midwives, hereby make the following rules:—

Citation and Interpretation

1.—(1) These Rules may be cited as the Nurses (Amendment) Rules 1973.

(2) In these rules "the principal rules" means the Nurses Rules 1969(c), as amended (d).

(3) The Interpretation Act 1889(e) applies to the interpretation of these Rules as it applies to the interpretation of an Act of Parliament.

(a) 1957 c. 15.　　　　　　　　　(b) S.I. 1968/1699 (1968 III, p. 4585).
(c) S.I. 1969/1675 (1969 III, p. 5245).
(d) The amending Rules are not relevant to the subject matter of these Rules.
(e) 1889 c. 63.

Amendment of rule 2 of the principal rules

2. In rule 2 of the principal rules after the definition of "the Secretary of State" there shall be added the following definition:—

"specified practical experience" means practical experience specified by the Council.

Amendment of rule 11 of the principal rules

3. For paragraph (1) of rule 11 of the principal rules there shall be substituted the following paragraph:—

"(1) Subject to the provisions of these Rules the Council shall hold examinations for admission to the parts of the register at such times and subject to such conditions as they may from time to time determine."

Revocation of rule 12 of the principal rules

4. Rule 12 of the principal rules is hereby revoked.

Amendment of rule 14 of the principal rules

5.—(1) Rule 14 of the principal rules shall be amended in accordance with the following provisions of this rule.

(2) For paragraph (*b*) there shall be substituted the following paragraph:—

"(*b*) 52 weeks in the case of an enrolled general nurse with specified practical experience; or"

(3) For paragraph (*c*) there shall be substituted the following paragraph:—

"(*c*) 26 weeks in the case of a person who is:—

(i) an enrolled general nurse without specified practical experience; or

(ii) an enrolled mental nurse; or

(iii) an enrolled nurse for the mentally subnormal; or

(iv) a certified midwife; or

(v) a person who when starting training is a person qualified in ophthalmic nursing; or

(vi) a person who when starting training is a person qualified in orthopaedic nursing; or"

Amendment of rule 16 of the principal rules

6. For paragraph (*c*) of rule 16 of the principal rules there shall be substituted the following paragraph:—

"(*c*) 52 weeks in the case of an enrolled mental nurse or an enrolled nurse for the mentally subnormal; or"

Amendment of rule 18 of the principal rules

7. For paragraph (*c*) of rule 18 of the principal rules there shall be substituted the following paragraph:—

"(*c*) 52 weeks in the case of an enrolled mental nurse or an enrolled nurse for the mentally subnormal; or"

Amendment of rule 20 of the principal rules

8.—(1) Rule 20 of the principal rules shall be amended in accordance with the following provisions of this rule.

(2) For paragraph (*b*) there shall be substituted the following paragraph:—

"(*b*) 52 weeks in the case of an enrolled general nurse with specified practical experience; or"

(3) For paragraph (*c*) there shall be substituted the following paragraph:—

"(*c*) 26 weeks in the case of a person who is:—

(i) an enrolled general nurse without specified practical experience; or

    (ii) an enrolled mental nurse; or

    (iii) an enrolled nurse for the mentally subnormal; or

    (iv) a certified midwife; or

    (v) a person who when starting training is a person qualified in ophthalmic nursing; or

    (vi) a person who when starting training is a person qualified in orthopaedic nursing; or"

(4) After paragraph (c) there shall be added the following paragraph:—

    "(d) 13 weeks in the case of a person who when starting such training is a person qualified in thoracic nursing."

Amendment of rule 22 of the principal rules

9. Subject to the provisions of rules 21 and 22 of these Rules, for rule 22 of the principal rules there shall be substituted the following rule:—

"22.—(1) The final examination for each part of the register shall relate to the syllabus of training prescribed in Schedule 4 to these Rules in relation to that part, and shall consist of:—

    (a) a practical section consisting of such number of tests of practical nursing ability conducted by an approved training institution in accordance with the requirements of the Council as is specified in Schedule 4A to these Rules; and

    (b) a written section.

(2) Subject to the provisions of paragraphs (4) to (6) of this rule, a person may enter for the practical section of the final examination for a part of the register if she satisfies the following conditions:—

    (a) that she is on the index of student nurses; and

    (b) that she has reached the standard required by the approved training institution.

(3) Subject to the provisions of paragraphs (4) to (6) of this rule, a person may enter for the written section of the final examination for a part of the register if she satisfies the following conditions:—

    (a) that she has finished, or is due to finish by the last day of the month following the month in which that section is to be completed, the training appropriate to her case specified in rules 13 to 20 of these Rules, and, if she has failed 3 times to pass that section, she has undergone at least 26 weeks further training since her third failure; and

    (b) that she has undergone systematic instruction in each of the subjects included in the syllabus of training prescribed in Schedule 4 to these Rules in relation to that part; and

    (c) that she is honest and of good character and her conduct has been satisfactory during the period of her training; and

    (d) that she has deposited with the Registrar a certificate signed by two officers, acceptable to the Council, of the institution or institutions in which she was trained, verifying that the conditions specified in sub-paragraphs (a) to (c) of this paragraph have been satisfied.

(4) Subject to the provisions of paragraph (5) of this rule no person shall enter, or remain a candidate, for the final examination for any part of the register if she has failed 3 times to pass any one of the tests of the practical section for that part or has failed 4 times to pass the written section for that part.

(5) For the purposes of paragraph (4) of this rule a failure to pass the final examination for any part of the register maintained by the General Nursing Council for Scotland or the Northern Ireland Council for Nurses and Midwives shall be treated as a failure to pass the written section of the final examination for the corresponding part of the register.

(6) No person who has failed 3 times to pass any one of the tests of the practical section of the final examination may undergo the period of further training prescribed in paragraph (3)(*a*) of this rule."

Amendment of rule 24 of the principal rules

10. For paragraph (1) of rule 24 of the principal rules there shall be substituted the following:—

"(1) A person other than a person to whom rules 27, 28, 29 or 30 of these Rules applies, shall, subject to paragraph (2) of this rule, be entitled to be admitted to a part of the register and to be issued with a certificate to that effect if she complies with the following conditions:—

(*a*) that she has completed the appropriate training; and

(*b*) that she has passed the final examination for that part of the register."

Amendment of rule 25 of the principal rules

11. Subject to the provisions of rule 23 of these Rules in paragraph (4) of rule 25 of the principal rules for "£5 5s. 0d." there shall be substituted "£5" and the words from "and an additional sum" to the end of that paragraph shall be omitted.

Amendment of rule 28 of the principal rules

12. Subject to the provisions of rule 23 of these Rules in paragraph (2) of rule 28 of the principal rules for "£3 3s. 0d." there shall be substituted "£5".

Amendment of rule 30 of the principal rules

13. Subject to the provisions of rule 23 of these Rules in rule 30 of the principal rules for "£9 9s. 0d." there shall be substituted "£9".

Amendment of rule 31 of the principal rules

14. In rule 31 of the principal rules for "£1 1s. 0d" there shall be substituted "£2".

Amendment of rule 36 of the principal rules

15. For head (iii) of rule 36(2)(*b*) of the principal rules there shall be substituted the following head:—

"(iii) Teacher's Certificate of the City and Guilds No. 394, 395, or 730; or"

Amendment of rule 37 of the principal rules

16. In rule 37 of the principal rules for "£5 5s. 0d." there shall be substituted "£5" and for "£1 1s. 0d" there shall be substituted "£2".

Amendment of rule 39 of the principal rules

17. In rule 39 of the principal rules for the words and figures "10s. 6d. or on or after 15th February 1971 53p." there shall be substituted "£5".

Amendment of rule 54 of the principal rules

18. Subject to the provisions of rule 23 of these Rules in rule 54 of the principal rules for "£5 5s. 0d." there shall be substituted "£5" and sub-paragraph (*b*) shall be omitted.

Amendment of rule 91 of the principal rules

19. In rule 91 of the principal rules for "£1 1s. 0d." there shall be substituted "£4".

Addition of Schedule 4A to the principal rules

20. After Schedule 4 to the principal rules there shall be inserted the following schedule:—

"
Rule 22(1)(*a*)
SCHEDULE 4A
TESTS OF PRACTICAL NURSING ABILITY

The number of tests of practical nursing ability shall be as follows:—

(1) In the case of a person to whom one of the following rules applies, that is to say, rules 13, 14(*d*), 15, 17, 19 and 20(*d*) ...   .   4 tests.

(2) In the case of a person to whom one of the following rules applies, that is to say, rules 14(*b*), 14(*c*), 16(*d*), 18(*d*), 20(*b*) and 20(*c*) ... ... 3 tests.

(3) In the case of a person to whom one of the following rules applies, that is to say, rules 14(*a*), 16(*a*), 16(*b*), 16(*c*), 18(*a*), 18(*b*), 18(*c*) and 20(*a*) ... ... 2 tests."

Transitional provision in relation to the final examination for the general part of the register and for the part of the register for sick children's nurses

21. The condition prescribed in rule 24(1)(*b*) of the principal rules, as amended by these Rules, shall be deemed to be satisfied in the case of a person who before the coming into operation of these Rules has failed to pass the final examination for the general part of the register or for the part of the register for sick children's nurses if before 1st November 1974 she has passed in respect of the appropriate part of the register, the final examination which was prescribed for that part immediately before the coming into operation of these Rules.

Transitional provisions in relation to the final examination for the part of the register for mental nurses and the part of the register for nurses for the mentally subnormal

22.—(1) Rule 22 of the principal rules, as amended by these Rules, shall not apply in the case of a person training for entry for the part of the register for mental nurses or the part of the register for nurses for the mentally subnormal who elects to enter the examination prescribed for either of those parts immediately before the coming into operation of these Rules, being such an examination held before 1st November 1976.

(2) In relation to any examination for the parts of the register for mental nurses and for nurses for the mentally subnormal held between the date of the coming into operation of these Rules and 1st November 1976 the following rule shall apply in substitution for rule 22 of the principal rules in the case of a person making an election under paragraph (1) of this rule.

"(1) Subject to the provisions of paragraph (2) of this rule, a person may enter for the final examination for a part of the register if she complies with the following conditions:—

(*a*) that she is on the index of student nurses; and

(*b*) that she has reached the standard required by the approved training institution; and

(*c*) that she has finished or is due to finish by the last day of the month following the month in which the final examination is to be completed the training appropriate to her case specified in rules 15 to 18 of these Rules and if she has failed 3 times to pass the final examination she has undergone at least 26 weeks further training since her third such failure; and

(*d*) she has undergone systematic instruction in each of the subjects included in the syllabus of training prescribed in Schedule 4 to the principal rules for the final examination for which she is entering; and

(*e*) she is honest and of good character and her conduct has been satisfactory during the period of training; and

(*f*) she has deposited with the Registrar a certificate signed by two officers, acceptable to the Council, of the institution or institutions in which she was trained, verifying that the requirements specified in this rule have been satisfied.

(2) No person shall enter for the final examination for a part of the register if she has failed 4 times to pass the final examination for that part."

(3) Notwithstanding the provisions of paragraph (1) of this rule, the condition prescribed in rule 24(1)(*b*) of the principal rules, as amended by these Rules, shall be deemed to be satisfied in the case of a person who between the date of coming into operation of these Rules and 1st November 1976 has failed to pass the final examination for the part of the register for mental nurses or for the part of the register for nurses for the mentally subnormal, if before 1st November 1978 she has passed, in respect of the

appropriate part of the register, the final examination which was prescribed for that part immediately before the date of coming into operation of these Rules.

Transitional provision in relation to rules 11, 12, 13 *and* 18 *of these Rules*

23. The provisions of rules 11, 12, 13 and 18 of these Rules shall not come into operation until 30th July 1973.

(L.S.)

Margaret J. Cooper,
Chairman of the Council.

The seal of the General Nursing Council for England and Wales was hereunto affixed on 4th June 1973.

M. Henry,
Registrar.

SCHEDULE 2

THE GENERAL NURSING COUNCIL FOR ENGLAND AND WALES

The Nurses Acts 1957 to 1969

The General Nursing Council for England and Wales, in exercise of the powers conferred on them by sections 3, 6, 7, 10, 23 and 30 of the Nurses Act 1957(a), and of all other powers enabling them in that behalf, having consulted with the General Nursing Council for Scotland and the Northern Ireland Council for Nurses and Midwives, hereby make the following rules:—

Citation and Interpretation

1.—(1) These Rules may be cited as the Enrolled Nurses (Amendment) Rules 1973.

(2) In these Rules "the principal rules" means the Enrolled Nurses Rules 1969(b), as amended(c).

(3) The Interpretation Act 1889(d) applies to the interpretation of these Rules as it applies to the interpretation of an Act of Parliament.

Amendment of rule 11 of the principal rules

2. For rule 11 of the principal rules there shall be substituted the following rule:—
"11. Subject to rules 12, 12A and 16A of these Rules the training required for admission to the general part of the roll shall be not less than 104 weeks training in accordance with the syllabus prescribed in Part 1 of Schedule 2 to these Rules in an approved training institution for enrolled general nurses."

Amendment of rule 12 of the principal rules

3. For rule 12 of the principal rules there shall be substituted the following rule:—
"12. The period of training required by rule 11 of these Rules for admission to the general part of the roll shall be reduced as follows:—

(*a*) in the case of a person who has undergone training for the part of the register for registered mental nurses or the part of the register for registered nurses for the mentally subnormal—

    (i) where the period of such training was not less than 104 weeks the reduction shall be 78 weeks; or

---

(a) 1957 c. 15.   (b) S.I. 1969/1674 (1969 III, p. 5217).
(c) The amending Rules are not relevant to the subject matter of these Rules.
(d) 1889 c. 63.

(ii) where the period of such training was not less than 52 weeks but less than 104 weeks the reduction shall be 52 weeks; or

(b) in the case of a person who has undergone not less than 52 weeks training for the general part of the register or for the part of the register for sick children's nurses the reduction shall be a period equal to the total number of weeks of such training completed by that person; or

(c) in the case of a person who is an enrolled mental nurse or an enrolled nurse for the mentally subnormal the reduction shall be 52 weeks; or

(d) in the case of a person who is qualified in ophthalmic nursing, orthopaedic nursing or thoracic nursing the reduction shall be 52 weeks; or

(e) in the case of a person who is a certified midwife the reduction shall be 26 weeks."

Addition of rule 12A to the principal rules

4. After rule 12 of the principal rules there shall be added the following rule:—

"12A. A person who has served or who has been qualified to serve in the Royal Navy as a senior naval nurse (or leading medical assistant) or in the Army as an army nurse class I (or army male nurse class I) shall be treated as having completed the training required by rule 11 of these Rules for admission to the general part of the roll."

Amendment of rule 13 of the principal rules

5. For rule 13 of the principal rules there shall be substituted the following rule:—

"13. Subject to rules 14 and 16A of these Rules the training required for admission to the part of the roll for enrolled mental nurses shall be not less than 104 weeks training in accordance with the syllabus of training prescribed in Part 2 of Schedule 2 to these Rules in an approved training institution for enrolled mental nurses."

Amendment of rule 14 of the principal rules

6. For rule 14 of the principal rules there shall be substituted the following rule:—

"14. The period of training required by rule 13 of these Rules for admission to the part of the roll for enrolled mental nurses shall be reduced as follows:—

(a) in the case of a person who has undergone training for any part of the register other than the part for registered mental nurses—

(i) where the period of such training was not less than 104 weeks the reduction shall be 78 weeks; or

(ii) where the period of such training was not less than 52 weeks but was less than 104 weeks, the reduction shall be 52 weeks; or

(b) in the case of a person who has undergone not less than 52 weeks training for the part of the register for registered mental nurses the reduction shall be a period equal to the total number of weeks of such training completed by that person; or

(c) in the case of a person who is an enrolled nurse for the mentally subnormal the reduction shall be 65 weeks; or

(d) in the case of a person who is an enrolled general nurse the reduction shall be 52 weeks."

Amendment of rule 15 of the principal rules

7. For rule 15 of the principal rules there shall be substituted the following rule—

"15. Subject to rules 16 and 16A of these Rules the training required for admission to the part of the roll for enrolled nurses for the mentally subnormal shall be not less than 104 weeks training in accordance with the syllabus of training prescribed in Part 3 of Schedule 2 to these Rules in an approved training institution for enrolled nurses for the mentally subnormal."

Amendment of rule 16 *of the principal rules*

8. For rule 16 of the principal rules there shall be substituted the following rule:—

"16. The period of training required by rule 15 of these Rules for admission to the part of the roll for enrolled nurses for the mentally subnormal shall be reduced as follows:—

(*a*) in the case of a person who has undergone training for any part of the register other than the part for registered nurses for the mentally subnormal—

(i) where the period of such training was not less than 104 weeks the reduction shall be 78 weeks; or

(ii) where the period of such training was not less than 52 weeks but less than 104 weeks, the reduction shall be 52 weeks; or

(*b*) in the case of a person who has undergone not less than 52 weeks training for the part of the register for registered nurses for the mentally subnormal the reduction shall be a period equal to the total number of weeks of such training completed by that person; or

(*c*) in the case of a person who is an enrolled mental nurse the reduction shall be 65 weeks; or

(*d*) in the case of a person who is an enrolled general nurse the reduction shall be 52 weeks."

Addition of rule 16A *to the principal rules*

9. After rule 16 of the principal rules there shall be added the following rule:—

"16A. A person who has completed not less than 104 weeks training for admission to a part of the register and has passed the practical section of the final examination for that part and has failed the written section thereof shall be treated as having completed the training required and passed the examination for admission to the corresponding part of the roll."

Addition of rule 16B *to the principal rules*

10. After rule 16A of the principal rules there shall be added the following rule:—

"16B. For the purposes of rules 11 to 16A of these Rules training for admission to any part of the register maintained by the General Nursing Council for Scotland or the Northern Ireland Council for Nurses and Midwives at a training institution approved by either of those Councils shall be treated as training for admission to the corresponding part of the register maintained by the General Nursing Council for England and Wales."

Amendment of rule 17 *of the principal rules*

11. For rule 17 of the principal rules there shall be substituted the following rule:—

"17. Subject to rules 18 and 19 of these Rules a person who has satisfied the requirements of training prescribed in rules 13 and 15 of these Rules shall be entitled to enter for the examination for admission to the part of the roll for mental nurses or the part of the roll for nurses for the mentally subnormal, as the case may be, held under rule 19 of these Rules if she also satisfies the following conditions:—

(*a*) that her name is in the index of pupil nurses kept under rule 10 of these Rules; and

(*b*) that she is honest and of good character and her conduct has been satisfactory during the period of training, if any; and

(*c*) that she has received instruction in each of the subjects contained in the appropriate syllabus of training prescribed in Schedule 2 to these Rules and that—

(i) she has or will have completed by the last day of the month in which the examination is held, not less than 78 weeks training; or

(ii) where the period of training required is reduced by rules 14 or 16 of these Rules she will, not later than 13 weeks after the first day in which the examination is held, have completed that reduced period of training; and (*d*) that she has deposited with the Registrar a certificate signed by two officers, acceptable to the Council, of the institution or institutions in which she was trained verifying that the conditions specified in sub-paragraphs (*a*) to (*c*) of this rule have been satisfied;

provided that if a candidate fails an examination for a second time she may be required to undergo further training for such period not exceeding 13 weeks as the Education Committee may decide, before being permitted to enter again for that examination."

Addition of rule 17A to the principal rules

12. After rule 17 of the principal rules there shall be added the following rule:—

"17A.—(1) Subject to the provisions of this rule and to rules 18 and 19 of these Rules a person who has satisfied the requirements of rule 11 of these Rules shall be entitled to enter for the examination for admission to the general part of the roll if she also satisfies the following conditions:—

(*a*) that her name is in the index of pupil nurses kept under rule 10 of these Rules; and

(*b*) that she is honest and of good character and her conduct has been satisfactory during the period of training, if any; and

(*c*) that she has deposited with the Registrar a certificate signed by two officers, acceptable to the Council, of the institution or institutions in which she was trained verifying that the conditions specified in sub-paragraphs (*a*) and (*b*) of this paragraph have been satisfied.

(2) No person shall enter for the written section of the examination for admission to the general part of the roll unless she has completed at least 78 weeks training except where the period of training required under rule 11 of these Rules is reduced by rule 12 thereof to less than 78 weeks, in which case entry shall not be made earlier than 13 weeks before the end of such period of training.

(3) Subject to the provisions of paragraph (4) of this rule no person shall enter, or remain a candidate, for the examination for admission to the general part of the roll if she has failed 3 times to pass any one of the tests of the practical section of that examination or has failed 3 times to pass the written section thereof.

(4) For the purposes of paragraph (3) of this rule a failure to pass the examination for any part of the roll maintained by the General Nursing Council for Scotland or the Northern Ireland Council for Nurses and Midwives shall be treated as a failure to pass the written section of the examination for admission to the corresponding part of the roll."

Addition of rule 17B to the principal rules

13. After rule 17A of the principal rules there shall be added the following rule:—

"17B. No person who has undergone training for admission to any part of the register shall enter an examination for admission to the corresponding part of the roll unless she has ceased that training and has not passed the final examination for that part of the register."

Amendment of rule 19 of the principal rules

14. For rule 19 of the principal rules there shall be substituted the following rule:—

"19.—(1) Subject to the provisions of these Rules the Council shall hold examinations for admission to the parts of the roll at such times and subject to such conditions as they may from time to time determine.

(2) Any fee payable to the Council under the provisions of section 3(3) of the Act of 1957 in respect of an application to be examined shall be paid to the Council by the applicant before the Council enters her name for the examination.

(3) The examinations held under this rule shall relate to the appropriate syllabus of training prescribed in Schedule 2 to these Rules.

(4) The examination for admission to the part of the roll for enrolled mental nurses and to the part of the roll for enrolled nurses for the mentally subnormal shall consist of a simple written test together with a test of practical efficiency and shall be held in an approved training institution.

(5) Subject to the provisions of sub-paragraph (6) of this rule the examination for admission to the general part of the roll shall consist of:—

    (*a*) a practical section consisting of such number of tests of practical nursing ability conducted by an approved training institution in accordance with the requirements of the Council as is specified in Schedule 2A to these Rules; and

    (*b*) a written section.

(6) A person who has passed any of the tests of practical nursing ability for any part of the register may, in accordance with the requirements of the Council, be exempted by an approved training institution from any part of the practical section of the examination for admission to the general part of the roll."

Amendment of rule 21 of the principal rules

15. Subject to the provisions of rule 21(1) of these Rules for paragraph (1) of rule 21 of the principal rules there shall be substituted the following paragraph:—

"(1) A person other than a person to whom rule 25 or rule 28 applies, shall, subject to paragraph (2) of this rule, be entitled to be admitted to the appropriate part or parts of the roll and be issued with a certificate or certificates to that effect if she complies with the following conditions:—

    (*a*) that she has completed the appropriate training;

    (*b*) that she has passed any appropriate examination in accordance with Part IV of these Rules;

    (*c*) that she is honest and of good character and her conduct has been satisfactory during the period of her training;

    (*d*) that she has deposited with the Registrar a certificate signed by two officers, acceptable to the Council, of the institution or institutions in which she was trained verifying that the conditions specified in sub-paragraphs (*a*) to (*c*) of this paragraph have been satisfied."

Amendment of rule 22 of the principal rules

16. Subject to the provision of rule 21(2) of these Rules in paragraph (4) of rule 22 of the principal rules for "£4 4s. 0d." there shall be substituted "£5" and the words from "and an additional sum" to the end of that paragraph shall be omitted.

Amendment of rule 32 of the principal rules

17. In rule 32 of the principal rules for "£1 1s. 0d." there shall be substituted "£2".

Amendment of rule 48 of the principal rules

18. Subject to the provisions of rule 21(2) of these Rules in rule 48 of the principal rules for "£4 4s. 0d." there shall be substituted "£5" and sub-paragraph (*b*) shall be omitted.

Amendment of rule 66 of the principal rules

19. In rule 66 of the principal rules for "10s. 6d." there shall be substituted "£4" and· the words and figures "or on or after 15th February 1971 53p." shall be omitted.

Additon of Schedule 2A to the principal rules

20. After Schedule 2 to the principal rules there shall be inserted the following schedule.

SCHEDULE 2A

Rule 19(4)(*a*)

TESTS OF PRACTICAL NURSING ABILITY

The number of tests of practical nursing ability shall be as follows:—

(1) In the case of a person to whom one of the following rules applies, that is to say, rules 11, 12(*a*)(ii), 12(*b*), 12(*d*) and 12(*e*) ... ... 3 Tests

(2) In the case of a person to whom one of the following rules applies, that is to say, rules 12(*a*)(i) and 12(*c*) ... ... 2 Tests

(3) In the case of a person to whom rule 12A applies... ... ... 1 Test"

Transitional provisions

21.—(1) The condition prescribed in rule 21(1)(*b*) of the principal rules as amended by these Rules shall be deemed to be satisfied in the case of a person who in relation to an examination held before 1st November 1976 elects to enter the examination which was prescribed for the general part of the roll immediately before the coming into operation of these Rules and passes that examination.

(2) The provisions of rules 16 and 18 of these Rules shall not come into operation until 26th November 1973.

(L.S.)

Margaret J. Cooper,
Chairman of the Council.

The seal of the General Nursing Council for England and Wales was hereunto affixed on 4th June 1973.

M. Henry,
Registrar.

EXPLANATORY NOTE
(*This Note is not part of the Instrument*)

The Rules approved by this Instrument amend the Nurses Rules 1969 and the Enrolled Nurses Rules 1969.   The amendments include in particular:—

(*a*) a reduction in the period of training for the part of the register for sick children's nurses in the case of a certified midwife and persons qualified in orthopaedic, ophthalmic and thoracic nursing;

(*b*) the introduction of a new final examination for admission to the register which comprises practical tests taken over the period of training and a written section;

(*c*) the deletion of the requirement that a person shall have attained the age of 21 before admission to the register.

(*d*) the deletion of the requirement that a person shall have attained the age of 20 before admission to the roll.

(*e*) a further reduction in the period of training required to qualify for enrolment in the case of persons who have undergone at least 52 weeks training for registration as a nurse and a provision that training in Scotland and Northern Ireland shall be taken into account for that purpose;

(*f*) the introduction of a new examination for admission to the general part of the roll which comprises 3 tests of practical nursing ability and a written section;

(*g*) a variation in the amount of certain fees payable to the Council.

STATUTORY INSTRUMENTS

1973 No. 1078

SOCIAL SECURITY

The National Insurance (Guardian's Allowances) Regulations 1973

Made	-	-	-	*20th June* 1973
Laid before Parliament			*27th June* 1973
Coming into Operation			*19th July* 1973

The National Insurance Joint Authority, in exercise of powers conferred by section 29(2) of the National Insurance Act 1965(a), and now vested in them(b), and the Secretary of State for Social Services, in exercise of powers conferred by sections 29(3) and 113(2) of that Act, which powers are now vested in him(c), in each case in exercise of all other powers enabling them in that behalf, and for the purpose only of consolidating the regulations hereby revoked, hereby make the following regulations: —

Citation, commencement and interpretation

1.—(1) These regulations may be cited as the National Insurance (Guardian's Allowances) Regulations 1973 and shall come into operation on 19th July 1973.

(2) In these regulations, unless the context otherwise requires—

"the Act" means the National Insurance Act 1965;

"the determining authority" means, as the case may require, the Chief National Insurance Commissioner appointed under section 9 of the National Insurance Act 1966(d) and any other National Insurance Commissioner so appointed or any tribunal constituted under subsection (3) of that section, a local tribunal constituted under section 77 of the Act or an insurance officer appointed under section 68(1) of the Act;

"British Islands" means the United Kingdom, the Channel Islands and the Isle of Man;

and other expressions have the same meanings as in the Act.

(3) References in these regulations to any enactment or regulation shall include references to such enactment or regulation as amended or extended by any subsequent enactment, order or regulation and as including references to any enactment or regulation thereby consolidated.

(4) The rules for the construction of Acts of Parliament contained in the Interpretation Act 1889(e) shall apply in relation to this instrument (including any instrument read as one therewith) and in relation to any revocation effected

---

(a) 1965 c. 51.
(b) *See* S.I. 1948/211 (Rev. XVI, p. 367: 1948 I, p. 2905) and sections 104(4)(b) and 117(1) of the National Insurance Act 1965 (c. 51).
(c) *See* Ministry of Social Security Act 1966 (c. 20) and S.I. 1968/1699 (1968 III, p. 4585).
(d) 1966 c. 6.   (e) 1889 c. 63.

by it as if this instrument, the regulations revoked by it and any regulations revoked by the regulations so revoked were Acts of Parliament, and as if each revocation were a repeal.

Adopted children

2. Subject to the provisions of regulation 8 of these regulations, where a child has been adopted in pursuance of an order made in the British Islands or is the subject of an overseas adoption within the meaning of section 4 of the Adoption Act 1968(a), there shall be substituted for the condition contained in section 29(1)(a) of the Act that the parents of the child are dead that condition set out below which is appropriate to the circumstances of the case, namely—

(a) if the child was adopted by a person who was not married at the date of the adoption, the condition that that person is dead; or

(b) if the child was adopted by two spouses jointly, the condition that both of those spouses are dead; or

(c) if the child was adopted by one of two spouses with or without the consent of the other, the condition that the spouse who adopted the child is dead.

Illegitimate children

3. Subject as aforesaid, where a child (other than a child to whom the preceding regulation applies) is illegitimate, there shall be substituted for the said condition that the parents of the child are dead that condition set out below which is appropriate to the circumstances of the case, namely—

(a) if any person has been found by a court of competent jurisdiction to be the father of the child, or if there is no such finding but in the opinion of the determining authority the paternity of the child has been admitted or established, the condition that the father and the mother of the child are dead; or

(b) in any other case, the condition that the mother is dead.

Children of divorced persons, etc.

4.—(1) Subject as aforesaid, where the marriage of a child's parents was terminated by divorce and where, at the death of one of the parents, the child was not in the custody of, or being maintained by, the other parent and there was no order of a court imposing any liability for custody or maintenance of the child on the other parent, there shall be substituted for the said condition that the parents of the child are dead the condition that one parent is dead.

(2) In the application of this regulation, the expression "parents" shall include persons who adopt children in the circumstances specified in regulation 2 of these regulations.

(3) For the purposes of this regulation, a voidable marriage which has been annulled, whether before or after the date when this regulation comes into force, shall be treated as if it had been a valid marriage which was terminated by divorce at the date of the annulment.

Children whose parents' whereabouts are unknown

5.—(1) Subject as aforesaid, where one of the child's parents is dead and the person claiming the guardian's allowance shows that he was at the date of the

---

(a) 1968 c. 53.

death unaware of, and has failed after all reasonable efforts to discover, the whereabouts of the other parent, there shall be substituted for the said condition that the parents of the child are dead the condition that one of the parents is dead.

(2) For the purposes of this regulation, the provisions of regulation 4(2) of these regulations shall apply.

Children whose surviving parents are in prison or legal custody

6.—(1) Subject to the following provisions of this regulation and to the provisions of regulation 8 of these regulations, where one of a child's parents is dead and the survivor of them is serving a sentence of imprisonment of not less than 5 years or of imprisonment for life, or is in legal custody as a person sentenced or ordered to be kept in custody during Her Majesty's pleasure or until the directions of Her Majesty are known, any guardian's allowance which would be payable in respect of the child if both his parents were dead shall be payable as if they were dead.

(2) For the purposes of this regulation, in relation to any sentence of imprisonment—

(*a*) no account shall be taken of any period of the sentence served before the death of the deceased parent;

(*b*) no account shall be taken of any reduction in the period of the sentence by virtue of any enactment providing for it to be treated as reduced in respect of any period of custody before sentence;

(*c*) any continuous period (other than a period before the death of the deceased parent) immediately preceding the imposition of the sentence, being a period throughout which the offender was in custody and not serving a sentence of imprisonment, shall be aggregated with the sentence;

(*d*) consecutive sentences shall be aggregated, so however that there shall be excluded from aggregation with a later sentence such period (if any) of an earlier sentence (not being a sentence of 5 years or more) as was served before the imposition of the later sentence.

(3) A guardian's allowance awarded by virtue of the provisions of this regulation shall not be payable for any period after the surviving parent has ceased to be serving such a sentence of imprisonment or to be in such legal custody as is referred to in paragraph (1) of this regulation.

(4) Subject to the provisions of the next following paragraph, a person shall be deemed not to have ceased to be serving such a sentence or to be in such custody as is referred to in paragraph (1) of this regulation if he is transferred to a hospital or is temporarily released or is unlawfully at large.

(5) A person shall be deemed to have ceased to be serving such a sentence as is referred to in paragraph (1) of this regulation if—

(*a*) he is at any time after the commencement of his sentence not in prison and there has expired a period which, measured from the date on which he was last in prison, is equal to the length of his sentence which on that date remained to be served; or

(*b*) he is released on licence or the remainder of his sentence is remitted:
Provided that if he thereafter returns to prison to resume service of the sentence he shall be treated as serving a sentence of the length which remains to be served at the time of his return.

(6) Where the sentence (or the conviction by virtue of which it is imposed) or order for custody referred to in paragraph (1) of this regulation is subject to a right of appeal or a right to apply for leave to appeal, no award of a guardian's allowance in respect thereof by virtue of the provisions of this regulation shall be made until the time limited for the making of that appeal or application has expired, or, if such an appeal is made, until the appeal has been adjudicated upon or withdrawn, and no benefit shall be payable by virtue of such an award in respect of any period before the earliest date on which that award could have been made.

(7) In determining whether for the purpose of any right to guardian's allowance by virtue of the provisions of this regulation a child is to be treated as a child of the claimant's family, no account shall be taken of any contributions made by the surviving parent towards the cost of providing for that child.

(8) Where a surviving parent contributes towards the cost of providing for his child, the weekly rate of any guardian's allowance payable by virtue of the provisions of this regulation shall be reduced by an amount equal to the rate of that contribution for the calendar week ending last before the week for which the allowance is payable:

Provided that for this purpose—

(a) if the surviving parent normally so contributes at the weekly rate specified in column 2 of Part I of Schedule 3 to the Act, he shall be treated as continuously so contributing at that rate notwithstanding that for occasional weeks he does not so contribute at that rate or at all;

(b) the provisions of section 18(2) of the Family Allowances Act 1965(a) shall apply as they apply for the purpose of that Act.

(9) The Secretary of State may require repayment to the National Insurance Fund by a surviving parent to whom paragraph (1) of this regulation applies of any sums paid in respect of guardian's allowance due in accordance with the provisions of this regulation in respect of a child of that parent.

(10) In a case for which the conditions for payment of guardian's allowance are modified by the foregoing provisions of these regulations so as to make guardian's allowance payable in respect of a child not on the death of a child's parents but on the death of two persons who are not the child's parents, or of whom one is not the child's parent, this regulation shall apply as if those persons were the child's parents.

(11) This regulation shall apply, subject to the necessary modifications, in relation to surviving parents outside Great Britain only where they are serving a sentence of imprisonment of not less than 5 years or of imprisonment for life.

Insurance condition

7. Except in relation to regulation 4 or regulation 5 of these regulations, there shall be substituted for the condition contained in section 29(1)(b) of the Act that one at least of the parents of the child was an insured person, the condition that the person or, as the case may be, one at least of the persons to whom the appropriate substituted condition contained in these regulations is applicable, was an insured person.

Special saving

8. Notwithstanding anything contained in these regulations, the parent of a child shall not be entitled to a guardian's allowance in respect of that child.

(a) 1965 c. 53.

Revocations and transitional provisions

9.—(1) The regulations specified in column (1) of the Schedule to these regulations are hereby revoked to the extent mentioned in column (3) of that Schedule.

(2) Anything whatsoever done under or by virtue of any regulation revoked by these regulations shall be deemed to have been done under or by virtue of the corresponding provision of these regulations, and anything whatsoever begun under any such regulation may be continued under these regulations as if begun under these regulations.

(3) Nothing in paragraphs (1)-(2) of this regulation shall be taken as affecting the general application by regulation 1(4) of these regulations of the rules for the construction of Acts of Parliament contained in section 38 of the Interpretation Act 1889 (effect of repeal) with regard to the effect of revocations.

Given under the official seal of the National Insurance Joint Authority.

(L.S.)   *Keith Joseph,*
                          Secretary of State for Social Services,
                          a member of the National Insurance
                          Joint Authority.
20th June 1973.

                          Keith Joseph,
                          Secretary of State for Social Services.
20th June 1973.

Regulation 9(1)   SCHEDULE

Regulations revoked (1)	Reference (2)	Extent of revocation (3)
The National Insurance (Guardian's Allowances) Regulations 1948	S.I. 1948/2687 (Rev. XVI, p. 189: 1948 I, p. 2781)	The whole regulations
The National Insurance (Guardian's Allowances) Amendment Regulations 1957	S.I. 1957/1830 (1957 I, p. 1542)	The whole regulations
The National Insurance (Guardian's Allowances) Amendment Regulations 1962	S.I. 1962/1270 (1962 II, p. 1373)	The whole regulations
The National Insurance (Increase of Benefit and Miscellaneous Provisions) Regulations 1965	S.I. 1965/40 (1965 I, p. 47)	The entry in Schedule L under the heading "The National Insurance (Guardian's Allowances) Regulations 1948"

EXPLANATORY NOTE

(This Note is not part of the Regulations.)

These Regulations consolidate the National Insurance (Guardian's Allowances) Regulations 1948 with subsequent amending Regulations. They are made for the purpose only of consolidation and accordingly, by virtue of section 108(9)(c) of the National Insurance Act 1965, have not been referred to the National Insurance Advisory Committee.

Regulation 1 contains various definitions; regulations 2, 3, 4, 5 and 6 provide substitute conditions for the condition in section 29(1)(a) of the National Insurance Act 1965 (that the parents of a child are dead) in respect of adopted children, illegitimate children, children of divorced persons, children whose parents' whereabouts are unknown and children whose surviving parents are in prison or legal custody; regulation 7 modifies the insurance condition contained in section 29(1)(b) of the 1965 Act; regulation 8 provides that a parent of a child shall not be entitled to a guardian's allowance in respect of that child; and regulation 9 and the Schedule contain revocation and transitional provisions.

STATUTORY INSTRUMENTS

1973 No. 1080

CARIBBEAN AND NORTH ATLANTIC TERRITORIES

The Bahamas Independence Order 1973

Made - - - -	*20th June* 1973
Laid before Parliament	*26th June* 1973
Coming into Operation	*10th July* 1973

At the Court at Windsor Castle, the 20th day of June 1973

Present,

The Queen's Most Excellent Majesty in Council

Her Majesty, by virtue and in exercise of the powers vested in Her by section 1 of the Bahama Islands (Constitution) Act 1963(a) and of all other powers enabling Her in that behalf, is pleased, by and with the advice of Her Privy Council, to order, and it is hereby ordered, as follows:

1.—(1) This Order may be cited as The Bahamas Independence Order 1973.

(2) Subject to the provisions of the next following subsection this Order shall come into operation on 10th July 1973 (in this Order referred to as " the appointed day ").

(3) The Governor and Commander-in-Chief of the Bahama Islands may at any time after 20th June 1973 exercise any of the powers conferred on the Governor-General by section 4(3) of this Order or Article 39(4) of the Constitution set out in the Schedule to this Order (in this Order referred to as " the Constitution ") to such an extent as may be necessary or expedient to enable the Constitution to function as from the appointed day.

(4) (*a*) For the purposes of the exercise by the Governor under subsection (3) of this section of the powers conferred by section 4(3) of this Order the Governor shall act in accordance with the advice of the Prime Minister.

(*b*) For the purposes of the exercise by the Governor under the said subsection of the powers conferred by Article 39(4) of the Constitution the Governor shall act in accordance with the advice of the Prime Minister after consultation with the Leader of the Opposition.

(*c*) For the purposes of this subsection references to the Prime Minister and Leader of the Opposition shall be construed as references to the persons performing the functions of those offices under the

Citation, commencement and construction.

(a) 1963 c. 56.

Bahama Islands (Constitution) Order 1969(a) (in this Order referred to as " the existing Order "), and in relation to the exercise by virtue of this subsection of the powers conferred by Article 39(4) of the Constitution the provisions of Article 40 of the Constitution shall apply as they would apply in relation to the exercise of those powers by virtue of Article 39(4) of the Constitution.

(5) Save where the context otherwise requires, expressions used in sections 1 to 17 of this Order shall have the same meaning as in the Constitution and the provisions of Articles 127 and 137 of the Constitution shall apply for the purposes of interpreting those sections as they apply for the purposes of interpreting the Constitution.

Revocation. **2.** The existing Order is revoked ; but the revocation of the existing Order shall not affect the operation on and after the appointed day of any law made or having effect as if made in pursuance of the existing Order or continued in force thereunder and having effect as part of the law of the Bahama Islands immediately before the appointed day (including any law made before the appointed day and coming into operation on or after that day).

Establishment of Constitution. **3.** Subject to the provisions of this Order, the Constitution shall come into effect on the appointed day.

Existing laws. **4.**—(1) Subject to the provisions of this section, the existing laws shall be construed with such modifications, adaptations, qualifications and exceptions as may be necessary to bring them into conformity with the Bahamas Independence Act 1973(b) and this Order.

(2) Where any matter that falls to be prescribed or otherwise provided for under the Constitution by Parliament or by any other authority or person is prescribed or provided for by or under an existing law (including any amendment to any such law made under this section) or is otherwise prescribed or provided for immediately before the appointed day by or under the existing Order, that prescription or provision shall, as from that day, have effect (with such modifications, adaptations, qualifications and exceptions as may be necessary to bring it into conformity with the Bahamas Independence Act 1973 and this Order) as if it had been made under the Constitution by Parliament or, as the case may require, by the other authority or person.

(3) The Governor-General may by Order made at any time before 10th July 1974 make such amendments to any existing law as may appear to him to be necessary or expedient for bringing that law into conformity with the provisions of the Bahamas Independence Act 1973 and this Order or otherwise for giving effect to or enabling effect to be given to those provisions.

(4) An Order made by the Governor-General under subsection (3) of this section shall have effect from such day, not earlier than the appointed day, as may be specified therein.

(5) The provisions of this section shall be without prejudice to any powers conferred by this Order or by any other law upon any person or authority to make provision for any matter, including the amendment or repeal of any existing law.

(a) S.I. 1969/590 (1969 I, p. 1567). (b) 1973 c. 27.

(6) In this section "existing law" means any law having effect as part of the law of the Bahama Islands immediately before the appointed day (including any law made before the appointed day and coming into operation on or after that day).

5.—(1) The persons who immediately before the appointed day are Parliament. members of the Senate established by the existing Order (in this section referred to as "the existing Senate"), having been appointed as such under paragraphs (*a*) and (*b*) respectively of section 30(2) of the Schedule to the existing Order, shall as from the appointed day be members of the Senate established by the Constitution as if they had been appointed as such under paragraphs (2) and (3) respectively of Article 39 of the Constitution and shall hold their seats as Senators in accordance with the provisions of the Constitution.

(2) The persons who immediately before the appointed day are members of the House of Assembly then established for the Bahama Islands (in this section referred to as "the existing Assembly") shall as from the appointed day be members of the House of Assembly established by the Constitution as if elected as such in pursuance of Article 46(2) of the Constitution and shall hold their seats in that House in accordance with the provisions of the Constitution.

(3) The persons who immediately before the appointed day are Speaker and Deputy Speaker of the existing Assembly shall as from the appointed day be Speaker and Deputy Speaker respectively of the House of Assembly established by the Constitution as if elected as such by that House in pursuance of Article 50(1) of the Constitution and shall hold office in accordance with the provisions of that Article.

(4) Any person who is a member of the Senate or the House of Assembly established by the Constitution by virtue of the preceding provisions of this section and who, since he was last appointed or elected as a member of the existing Senate or the existing Assembly before the appointed day, has taken the oath of allegiance in pursuance of section 45 of the Schedule to the existing Order shall be deemed to have complied with the requirements of Article 64 of the Constitution relating to the taking of the oath of allegiance.

(5) The rules of procedure of the existing Senate and the existing Assembly as in force immediately before the appointed day shall, except as may be otherwise provided in pursuance of Article 55(1) of the Constitution, be the rules of procedure respectively of the Senate and the House of Assembly established by the Constitution, but they shall be construed with such modifications, adaptations, qualifications and exceptions as may be necessary to bring them into conformity with the Constitution.

(6) Notwithstanding anything contained in Article 66(3) of the Constitution (but subject to the provisions of paragraphs (4) and (5) of that Article) Parliament shall, unless sooner dissolved, stand dissolved on the expiration of five years from the first sitting of the existing Assembly after the general election of members of the existing Assembly last preceding the appointed day.

(7) For the purposes of Articles 41 and 47 of the Constitution any period of ordinary residence in the Bahama Islands immediately before the appointed day shall be deemed to be residence in The Bahamas.

Ministers and Parliamentary Secretaries.

6.—(1) The person who immediately before the appointed day holds the office of Prime Minister under the existing Order shall, as from the appointed day, hold office as Prime Minister as if he had been appointed thereto under Article 73(1) of the Constitution.

(2) The persons (other than the Prime Minister) who immediately before the appointed day hold office as Ministers under the existing Order shall, as from the appointed day, hold the like offices as if they had been appointed thereto under Article 73(2) of the Constitution.

(3) Any person holding the office of Prime Minister or other Minister by virtue of subsection (1) or (2) of this section who immediately before the appointed day was charged with responsibility for any matter or department of government shall, as from the appointed day, be deemed to have been charged with responsibility for the corresponding business or administration of the corresponding department of the Government under Article 77 of the Constitution.

(4) The persons who immediately before the appointed day hold office as Parliamentary Secretaries under the existing Order shall, as from the appointed day, hold the like offices as if they had been appointed thereto under Article 81(1) of the Constitution.

(5) Any person who holds office as Prime Minister or other Minister or Parliamentary Secretary as from the appointed day by virtue of the provisions of this section shall be deemed to have complied with the requirements of Article 84 of the Constitution relating to the taking of oaths.

Leader of the Opposition.

7. The person who immediately before the appointed day is the Leader of the Opposition (as defined for the purposes of the Schedule to the existing Order) shall, as from the appointed day, hold office as Leader of the Opposition as if he had been appointed thereto under Article 82 of the Constitution.

Existing officers.

8. Subject to the provisions of this Order and of the Constitution, every person who immediately before the commencement of this Order holds or is acting in a public office shall, as from the commencement of this Order, continue to hold or act in the like office as if he had been appointed thereto in accordance with the provisions of the Constitution.

Supreme Court and Court of Appeal Judges.

9.—(1) The Supreme Court and the Court of Appeal in existence immediately before the appointed day shall, as from the appointed day be the Supreme Court and the Court of Appeal for the purposes of the Constitution and the Chief Justice and the Judges of the Supreme Court and the President of the Court of Appeal and the Justices of Appeal holding office immediately before that day shall, as from that day, hold offices as Chief Justice or Justices of the Supreme Court or President of the Court of Appeal or Justices of Appeal, as the case may be, as if they had been appointed under the provisions of Chapter VII of the Constitution.

(2) Any proceedings pending before the Supreme Court immediately before the appointed day may be continued and any judgment of that Court given but not satisfied before that day may be enforced as if it were the judgment of the Supreme Court established by the Constitution.

Pending appeals.

10.—(1) Any proceedings pending immediately before the appointed day on appeal from the Supreme Court to the Court of Appeal for the Bahama Islands may be continued after the appointed day before the Court of Appeal for The Bahamas established by the Constitution.

(2) Any judgment of the Court of Appeal for the Bahama Islands in an appeal from a court of the Colony of the Bahama Islands given, but not satisfied, before the appointed day may be enforced after the appointed day as if it were a judgment of the Court of Appeal for The Bahamas established by the Constitution.

11. A court of appeal for the Turks and Caicos Islands may, under arrangements between the Government of that territory and the Government of The Bahamas, sit in The Bahamas and exercise there such jurisdiction and powers in respect of the Turks and Caicos Islands as may be conferred upon it by any law for the time being in force in the Turks and Caicos Islands. Without prejudice to the generality of the foregoing, persons committed to custody in the Turks and Caicos Islands when present in The Bahamas in connection with any proceedings in a court of appeal for the Turks and Caicos Islands may be held in custody in The Bahamas and persons may be committed to custody in The Bahamas by order of such a court.

Exercise of jurisdiction by Court of Appeal for Turks and Caicos Islands.

12. Until provision is made under and in accordance with Article 135 of the Constitution, the salaries and allowances of the holders of each of the offices to which that Article applies, other than the Governor-General, shall be the salaries and allowances to which the holders of each of those offices or of the offices corresponding thereto were entitled immediately before the appointed day, and the salary and allowances of the Governor-General shall be the salary and allowances to which the Governor and Commander-in-Chief of the Bahama Islands was entitled immediately before such day.

Remuneration of certain persons.

13.—(1) Any power of the Governor and Commander-in-Chief of the Bahama Islands acting on the recommendation of the Public Service Commission established by the existing Order which has been validly delegated to any public officer under that Order shall, as from the appointed day, be deemed to have been delegated to that public officer to the extent that that power could be so delegated under Article 110 of the Constitution.

Transitional provisions relating to existing Commissions.

(2) Any matter which, immediately before the appointed day, is pending before an existing Commission or, as the case may be, before any person or authority on whom the power to deal with such matter has been conferred under the existing Order shall as from the appointed day be continued before the Public Service Commission established by the Constitution, or the Public Service Board of Appeal, or the Judicial and Legal Service Commission, or the Police Service Commission, so established or, as the case may be, the said person or authority :

Provided that where an existing Commission or, as the case may be, any person or authority as aforesaid has, immediately before the appointed day, partly completed the hearing of a disciplinary proceeding (in this section referred to as " the original hearing "), no person shall take part in the continued hearing unless he has also taken part in the original hearing ; and where by virtue of this subsection the original hearing cannot be so continued the hearing of the disciplinary proceeding shall be recommenced.

(3) A person who immediately before the appointed day holds the office of Chairman or other member of an existing Commission shall, as from the appointed day, continue to hold the like office as if he had been appointed thereto in accordance with the provisions of the Constitution and shall be deemed to have been duly appointed to such office under the Constitution.

(4) The provisions of Articles 107(3), 114(3), 116(3) or 118(3), as the case may be, of the Constitution shall have effect in relation to such a person as if the date of his appointment under the existing Order were the date of his appointment under the Constitution.

(5) Until Parliament otherwise prescribes under Article 117(2) of the Constitution the public offices to which Article 117(1) thereof applies shall be the offices of Solicitor-General, Registrar of the Supreme Court, Legal Draftsman, Senior Crown Counsel, Chief Magistrate, Registrar General, Stipendiary and Circuit Magistrate, Crown Counsel, Assistant Legal Draftsman, Assistant Registrar, Deputy Registrar General and Assistant Crown Counsel.

(6) In this section "an existing Commission" means the Public Service Commission established under the existing Order or, as the case may be, the Public Service Board of Appeal, or the Judicial and Legal Service Commission, or the Police Service Commission, so established.

Emergency Powers Order in Council 1939.

14.—(1) The Emergency Powers Order in Council 1939(a) and any Order in Council amending that Order(b) shall cease to have effect as part of the law of The Bahamas on 10th July 1974 or such earlier date as Parliament may prescribe.

(2) Until such time as the said Orders cease to have effect under subsection (1) of this section they shall continue to have effect in respect of The Bahamas as they had effect in respect of the former Colony of the Bahama Islands immediately before the appointed day, except that the powers exercisable by the Governor thereunder shall be exercisable by the Governor-General acting in accordance with the advice of the Prime Minister.

Transfer of Crown Lands Fund for Development to Consolidated Fund.

15. All sums standing to the credit of the Crown Lands Fund for Development immediately before the appointed day shall as from that day form part of the Consolidated Fund, and all sums charged on the Crown Lands Fund for Development immediately before that day shall as from that day stand charged on the Consolidated Fund.

Transitional provisions relating to compensation etc.

16. Any compensation, gratuity, grant or allowance paid or payable, whether before or after the appointed day, under any regulations made by the Governor under section 15 of the Bahama Islands (Constitution) Order in Council 1963(c) or under section 9 of the Bahama Islands (Constitution) Order 1969, which under those regulations as in force immediately prior to the appointed day was or would have been exempt from tax in the Bahama Islands, shall be exempt from tax to the same extent in The Bahamas after the appointed day.

Alteration of this Order.

17.—(1) Parliament may alter any of the provisions of this Order (in so far as those provisions form part of the law of The Bahamas), other than those mentioned in subsections (2) and (3) of this section, in the same manner as it may alter the provisions of the Constitution other than those specified in paragraphs (2) and (3) of Article 54 of the Constitution.

(a) *See* S.I. 1952 I at p. 621.
(b) The relevant amending instruments are S.I. 1956/731, 1963/88, 1633, 1964/267, 1199, 1965/131, 1968/724, 1973/759 (1956 I, p. 512; 1963 I, p. 105; III, p. 3084; 1964 I, p. 467, II, p. 2781; 1965 I p. 270; 1968 II, p. 2077; 1973 I, p. 2417).
(c) S.I. 1963/2084 (1963 III, p. 4403).

(2) Parliament may alter subsection (6) of section 5 of this Order and this section in the same manner as it may alter the provisions specified in Article 54(3) of the Constitution.

(3) Parliament may alter sections 8, 9, 12, subsections (3), (4) and (5) of section 13 and section 16 of this Order in the same manner as it may alter the provisions specified in Article 54(2) of the Constitution.

(4) In this section "alter" has the same meaning as in Article 54(4)(*b*) of the Constitution.

W. G. Agnew.

SCHEDULE TO THE ORDER

THE CONSTITUTION OF THE COMMONWEALTH OF THE BAHAMAS

ARRANGEMENT OF ARTICLES

CHAPTER I

THE CONSTITUTION

CHAPTER II

CITIZENSHIP

CHAPTER III

PROTECTION OF FUNDAMENTAL RIGHTS AND FREEDOMS OF THE INDIVIDUAL

CHAPTER IV

THE GOVERNOR-GENERAL

CHAPTER V

PARLIAMENT

PART 1

Composition of Parliament

PART 2

The Senate

PART 3

House of Assembly

PART 4

Powers and Procedure of Parliament

CHAPTER VII

The Judicature

Part 1

The Supreme Court

CHAPTER VIII

The Public Service

Part 1

The Public Service Commission

THE CONSTITUTION OF THE COMMONWEALTH OF THE BAHAMAS

WHEREAS Four hundred and eighty-one years ago the rediscovery of this Family of Islands, Rocks and Cays heralded the rebirth of the New World ;

AND WHEREAS the People of this Family of Islands recognise that the preservation of their Freedom will be guaranteed by a national commitment to Self-discipline, Industry, Loyalty, Unity and an abiding respect for Christian values and the Rule of Law ;

NOW KNOW YE THEREFORE:

We the Inheritors of and Successors to this Family of Islands, recognising the Supremacy of God and believing in the Fundamental Rights and Freedoms of the Individual, DO HEREBY PROCLAIM IN SOLEMN PRAISE the Establishment of a Free and Democratic Sovereign Nation founded on Spiritual Values and in which no Man, Woman or Child shall ever be Slave or Bondsman to anyone or their Labour exploited or their Lives frustrated by deprivation, AND DO HEREBY PROVIDE by these Articles for the indivisible Unity and Creation under God of the Commonwealth of The Bahamas.

CHAPTER I

THE CONSTITUTION

1. The Commonwealth of The Bahamas shall be a sovereign democratic State.

2. This Constitution is the supreme law of the Commonwealth of The Bahamas and, subject to the provisions of this Constitution, if any other law is inconsistent with this Constitution, this Constitution, shall prevail and the other law shall, to the extent of the inconsistency, be void.

CHAPTER II

CITIZENSHIP

3.—(1) Every person who, having been born in the former Colony of the Bahama Islands, is on 9th July 1973 a citizen of the United Kingdom and Colonies shall become a citizen of The Bahamas on 10th July 1973.

(2) Every person who, having been born outside the former Colony of the Bahama Islands, is on 9th July 1973 a citizen of the United Kingdom and Colonies shall, if his father becomes or would but for his death have become a citizen of The Bahamas in accordance with the provisions of the preceding paragraph, become a citizen of The Bahamas on 10th July 1973.

(3) Every person who on 9th July 1973 is a citizen of the United Kingdom and Colonies having become such a citizen under the British Nationality Act 1948 by virtue of his having been registered in the former Colony of the Bahama Islands under that Act shall become a citizen of The Bahamas on 10th July 1973 :

Provided that this paragraph shall not apply to any citizen of the United Kingdom and Colonies—

(a) who was not ordinarily resident in that Colony on 31st December 1972, or

(b) who became registered in that Colony on or after 1st January 1973, or

(c) who on 9th July 1973 possesses the citizenship or nationality of some other country.

Persons who become citizens on 9th July 1974.

4. Every person who on 9th July 1973 is a citizen of the United Kingdom and Colonies—

(a) having become such a citizen under the British Nationality Act 1948 by virtue of his having been naturalised in the former Colony of the Bahama Islands before that Act came into force ; or

(b) having become such a citizen by virtue of his having been naturalised in the former Colony of the Bahama Islands under that Act,

shall become a citizen of The Bahamas on 9th July 1974, unless, prior to that date, he has in such manner as may be prescribed declared that he does not desire to become a citizen of The Bahamas :

Provided that this section shall not apply to a citizen of the United Kingdom and Colonies who on 9th July 1973 possesses the citizenship or nationality of some other country.

Persons entitled to be registered as citizens.

5.—(1) Any woman who, on 9th July 1973, is or has been married to a person—

(a) who becomes a citizen of The Bahamas by virtue of Article 3 of this Constitution ; or

(b) who, having died before 10th July 1973, would, but for his death, have become a citizen of The Bahamas by virtue of that Article,

shall be entitled, upon making application and upon taking the oath of allegiance or such declaration in such manner as may be prescribed, to be registered as a citizen of The Bahamas :

Provided that the right to be registered as a citizen of The Bahamas under this paragraph shall be subject to such exceptions or qualifications as may be prescribed in the interests of national security or public policy.

(2) Any person who, on 9th July 1973, possesses Bahamian Status under the provisions of the Immigration Act 1967(a) and is ordinarily resident in the Bahama Islands, shall be entitled, upon making application before 10th July 1974, to be registered as a citizen of The Bahamas.

(3) Notwithstanding anything contained in paragraph (2) of this Article, a person who has attained the age of eighteen years or who is a woman who is or has been married shall not, if he is a citizen of some country other than The Bahamas, be entitled to be registered as a citizen of The Bahamas under the provisions of that paragraph unless he renounces his citizenship of that other country, takes the oath of allegiance and makes and registers such declaration as may be prescribed :

Provided that where a person cannot renounce his citizenship of the other country under the law of that country he may instead make such declaration concerning that citizenship as may be prescribed.

(a) Statute Law of the Bahama Islands. No. 25 of 1967.

(4) Any application for registration under paragraph (2) of this Article shall be subject to such exceptions or qualifications as may be prescribed in the interests of national security or public policy.

(5) Any woman who on 9th July 1973 is or has been married to a person who subsequently becomes a citizen of The Bahamas by registration under paragraph (2) of this Article shall be entitled, upon making application and upon taking the oath of allegiance or such declaration as may be prescribed, to be registered as a citizen of The Bahamas:

Provided that the right to be registered as a citizen of The Bahamas under this paragraph shall be subject to such exceptions or qualifications as may be prescribed in the interests of national security or public policy.

(6) Any application for registration under this Article shall be made in such manner as may be prescribed as respects that application:

Provided that such an application may not be made by a person who has not attained the age of eighteen years and is not a woman who is or has been married, but shall be made on behalf of that person by a parent or guardian of that person.

6. Every person born in The Bahamas after 9th July 1973 shall become a citizen of The Bahamas at the date of his birth if at that date either of his parents is a citizen of The Bahamas. *Persons born in The Bahamas after 9th July 1973.*

7.—(1) A person born in The Bahamas after 9th July 1973 neither of whose parents is a citizen of The Bahamas shall be entitled, upon making application on his attaining the age of eighteen years or within twelve months thereafter in such manner as may be prescribed, to be registered as a citizen of The Bahamas: *Persons born in The Bahamas after 9th July 1973 of non-citizen parents.*

Provided that if he is a citizen of some country other than The Bahamas he shall not be entitled to be registered as a citizen of The Bahamas under this Article unless he renounces his citizenship of that other country, takes the oath of allegiance and makes and registers such declaration of his intentions concerning residence as may be prescribed.

(2) Any application for registration under this Article shall be subject to such exceptions or qualifications as may be prescribed in the interests of national security or public policy.

8. A person born outside The Bahamas after 9th July 1973 shall become a citizen of The Bahamas at the date of his birth if at that date his father is a citizen of The Bahamas otherwise than by virtue of this Article or Article 3(2) of this Constitution. *Persons born outside The Bahamas after 9th July 1973.*

9.—(1) Notwithstanding anything contained in Article 8 of this Constitution, a person born legitimately outside The Bahamas after 9th July 1973 whose mother is a citizen of The Bahamas shall be entitled, upon making application on his attaining the age of eighteen years and before he attains the age of twenty-one years, in such manner as may be prescribed, to be registered as a citizen of The Bahamas: *Further provisions for persons born outside The Bahamas after 9th July 1973.*

Provided that if he is a citizen of some country other than The Bahamas he shall not be entitled to be registered as a citizen of The

Bahamas under this Article unless he renounces his citizenship of that other country, takes the oath of allegiance and makes and registers such declaration of his intentions concerning residence as may be prescribed.

(2) Where a person cannot renounce his citizenship of some other country under the law of that country, he may instead make such declaration concerning that citizenship as may be prescribed.

(3) Any application for registration under this Article shall be subject to such exceptions or qualifications as may be prescribed in the interests of national security or public policy.

Marriage to citizens of The Bahamas.
10. Any woman who, after 9th July 1973, marries a person who is or becomes a citizen of The Bahamas shall be entitled, provided she is still so married, upon making application in such manner as may be prescribed and upon taking the oath of allegiance or such declaration as may be prescribed, to be registered as a citizen of The Bahamas :

Provided that the right to be registered as a citizen of The Bahamas under this Article shall be subject to such exceptions or qualifications as may be prescribed in the interests of national security or public policy.

Deprivation of citizenship.
11.—(1) If the Governor-General is satisfied that any citizen of The Bahamas has at any time after 9th July 1973 acquired by registration, naturalisation or other voluntary and formal act (other than marriage) the citizenship of any other country, the Governor-General may by order deprive that person of his citizenship.

(2) If the Governor-General is satisfied that any citizen of The Bahamas has at any time after 9th July 1973 voluntarily claimed and exercised in any other country any rights available to him under the law of that country, being rights accorded exclusively to its citizens, the Governor-General may by order deprive that person of his citizenship.

Renunciation of citizenship.
12. Any citizen of The Bahamas who has attained the age of twenty-one years and who—

(a) is also a citizen or national of any other country ; or

(b) intends to become a citizen or national of any other country,

shall be entitled to renounce his citizenship of The Bahamas by a declaration made and registered in such manner as may be prescribed :

Provided that—

(a) in the case of a person who is not a citizen or national of any other country at the date of registration of his declaration or renunciation, if he does not become such a citizen or national within six months from the date of registration he shall be, and shall be deemed to have remained, a citizen of The Bahamas notwithstanding the making and registration of his declaration of renunciation ; and

(b) the right of any person to renounce his citizenship of The Bahamas during any period when The Bahamas is engaged in any war shall be subject to such exceptions or qualifications as may be prescribed in the interests of national security or public policy.

13. Parliament may make provision—

(a) for the acquisition of citizenship of The Bahamas by persons who do not become citizens of The Bahamas by virtue of the provisions of this Chapter ;

(b) for depriving of his citizenship of The Bahamas any person who is a citizen of The Bahamas otherwise than by virtue of paragraphs (1) or (2) of Article 3 or Articles 6 or 8 of this Constitution ; or

(c) for the certification of citizenship of The Bahamas for persons who have acquired that citizenship and who desire such certification.

Power of Parliament.

14.—(1) Any reference in this Chapter to the father of a person shall, in relation to any person born out of wedlock other than a person legitimated before 10th July 1973, be construed as a reference to the mother of that person.

Interpretation.

(2) For the purposes of this Chapter, a person born aboard a registered ship or aircraft, or aboard an unregistered ship or aircraft of the government of any country, shall be deemed to have been born in the place in which the ship or aircraft was registered or, as the case may be, in that country.

(3) Any reference in this Chapter to the national status of the father of a person at the time of that person's birth, shall, in relation to a person born after the death of the father, be construed as a reference to the national status of the father at the time of the father's death ; and where that death occurred before 10th July 1973 and the birth occurred after 9th July 1973 the national status that the father would have had if he had died on 10th July 1973 shall be deemed to be his national status at the time of his death.

CHAPTER III

PROTECTION OF FUNDAMENTAL RIGHTS AND FREEDOMS OF THE INDIVIDUAL

15. Whereas every person in The Bahamas is entitled to the fundamental rights and freedoms of the individual, that is to say, has the right, whatever his race, place of origin, political opinions, colour, creed or sex, but subject to respect for the rights and freedoms of others and for the public interest, to each and all of the following, namely—

Fundamental rights and freedoms of the individual.

(a) life, liberty, security of the person and the protection of the law ;

(b) freedom of conscience, of expression and of assembly and association ; and

(c) protection for the privacy of his home and other property and from deprivation of property without compensation,

the subsequent provisions of this Chapter shall have effect for the purpose of affording protection to the aforesaid rights and freedoms subject to such limitations of that protection as are contained in those provisions, being limitations designed to ensure that the enjoyment of the said rights and freedoms by any individual does not prejudice the rights and freedoms of others or the public interest.

Protection of right to life.

16.—(1) No person shall be deprived intentionally of his life save in execution of the sentence of a court in respect of a criminal offence of which he has been convicted.

(2) A person shall not be regarded as having been deprived of his life in contravention of this Article if he dies as the result of the use, to such extent and in such circumstances as are permitted by law, of such force as is reasonably justifiable—

(a) for the defence of any person from violence or for the defence of property ;

(b) in order to effect a lawful arrest or to prevent the escape of a person lawfully detained ;

(c) for the purpose of suppressing a riot, insurrection or mutiny ; or

(d) in order to prevent the commission by that person of a criminal offence,

or if he dies as a result of a lawful act of war.

Protection from inhuman treatment.

17.—(1) No person shall be subjected to torture or to inhuman or degrading treatment or punishment.

(2) Nothing contained in or done under the authority of any law shall be held to be inconsistent with or in contravention of this Article to the extent that the law in question authorises the infliction of any description of punishment that was lawful in the Bahama Islands immediately before 10th July 1973.

Protection from slavery and forced labour.

18.—(1) No person shall be held in slavery or servitude.

(2) No person shall be required to perform forced labour.

(3) For the purposes of this Article, " forced labour " does not include—

(a) any labour required in consequence of the sentence or order of a court ;

(b) any labour required of a member of a disciplined force in pursuance of his duties as such or, in the case of a person who has conscientious objections to service in a naval, military or air force, any labour which that person is required by law to perform in place of such service ;

(c) labour required of any person while he is lawfully detained which, though not required in consequence of the sentence or order of a court, is reasonably necessary in the interests of hygiene or for the maintenance of the place in which he is detained ; or

(d) any labour required during a period of public emergency (that is to say, a period to which Article 29 of this Constitution applies) or in the event of any other emergency or calamity that threatens the life or well-being of the community, to the extent that the requiring of such labour is reasonably justifiable, in the circumstances of any situation arising or existing during that period or as a result of that other emergency or calamity, for the purpose of dealing with that situation.

19.—(1) No person shall be deprived of his personal liberty save Protection from arbitrary arrest or detention. as may be authorised by law in any of the following cases—

(*a*) in execution of the sentence or order of a court, whether established for The Bahamas or some other country, in respect of a criminal offence of which he has been convicted or in consequence of his unfitness to plead to a criminal charge or in execution of the order of a court on the grounds of his contempt of that court or of another court or tribunal ;

(*b*) in execution of the order of a court made in order to secure the fulfilment of any obligation imposed upon him by law ;

(*c*) for the purpose of bringing him before a court in execution of the order of a court ;

(*d*) upon reasonable suspicion of his having committed, or of being about to commit, a criminal offence ;

(*e*) in the case of a person who has not attained the age of eighteen years, for the purpose of his education or welfare ;

(*f*) for the purpose of preventing the spread of an infectious or contagious disease or in the case of a person who is, or is reasonably suspected to be, of unsound mind, addicted to drugs or alcohol, or a vagrant, for the purpose of his care or treatment or the protection of the community ;

(*g*) for the purpose of preventing the unlawful entry of that person into The Bahamas or for the purpose of effecting the expulsion, extradition or other lawful removal from The Bahamas of that person or the taking of proceedings relating thereto ; and, without prejudice to the generality of the foregoing, a law may, for the purposes of this sub-paragraph, provide that a person who is not a citizen of The Bahamas may be deprived of his liberty to such extent as may be necessary in the execution of a lawful order requiring that person to remain within a specified area within The Bahamas or prohibiting him from being within such an area.

(2) Any person who is arrested or detained shall be informed as soon as is reasonably practicable, in a language that he understands, of the reasons for his arrest or detention and shall be permitted, at his own expense, to retain and instruct without delay a legal representative of his own choice and to hold private communication with him ; and in the case of a person who has not attained the age of eighteen years he shall also be afforded a reasonable opportunity for communication with his parent or guardian.

(3) Any person who is arrested or detained in such a case as is mentioned in sub-paragraph (1)(*c*) or (*d*) of this Article and who is not released shall be brought without undue delay before a court ; and if any person arrested or detained in such a case as is mentioned in the said sub-paragraph (1)(*d*) is not tried within a reasonable time he shall (without prejudice to any further proceedings that may be brought against him) be released either unconditionally or upon reasonable conditions, including in particular such conditions as are reasonably necessary to ensure that he appears at a later date for trial or for proceedings preliminary to trial.

(4) Any person who is unlawfully arrested or detained by any other person shall be entitled to compensation therefor from that other person.

(5) Where a person is detained by virtue of such a law as is referred to in Article 29 of this Constitution, the following provisions shall apply—

(a) he shall, as soon as reasonably practicable and in any case not more than five days after the commencement of his detention, be furnished with a statement in writing, in a language that he understands, of the grounds upon which he is detained :

(b) not more than fourteen days after the commencement of his detention, a notification shall be published in the Gazette stating that he has been detained and giving particulars of the provision of law under which his detention is authorised ;

(c) he may from time to time request that his case be reviewed under sub-paragraph (d) of this paragraph but, where he has made such a request, no subsequent request shall be made before the expiration of three months from the making of the previous request ;

(d) where a request is made under sub-paragraph (c) of this paragraph, the case shall, within one month of the making of the request, be reviewed by an independent and impartial tribunal established by law, presided over by the Chief Justice or another Justice of the Supreme Court appointed by him, and consisting of persons who are Justices of the Supreme Court or who are qualified to be appointed as Justices of the Supreme Court ;

(e) he shall be afforded reasonable facilities to consult and instruct, at his own expense, a legal representative of his own choice, and he and any such legal representative shall be permitted to make written or oral representations or both to the tribunal appointed for the review of his case.

(6) On any review by a tribunal in pursuance of paragraph (5) of this Article of the case of any detained person, the tribunal may make recommendations concerning the necessity or expediency of continuing his detention to the authority by whom it was ordered, but, unless it is otherwise provided by law, that authority shall not be obliged to act in accordance with any such recommendations.

(7) When any person is detained by virtue of such a law as is referred to in Article 29 of this Constitution the Prime Minister or a Minister authorised by him shall, not more than thirty days after the commencement of the detention and thereafter not more than thirty days after the making of the previous report, make a report to each House stating the number of persons detained as aforesaid and the number of cases in which the authority that ordered the detention has not acted in accordance with the recommendations of a tribunal appointed in pursuance of paragraph (5) of this Article :

Provided that in reckoning any period of thirty days for the purposes of this paragraph no account shall be taken of any period during which Parliament stands prorogued or dissolved.

Provisions to secure protection of law.

20.—(1) If any person is charged with a criminal offence, then, unless the charge is withdrawn, the case shall be afforded a fair hearing within a reasonable time by an independent and impartial court established by law.

(2) Every person who is charged with a criminal offence—

(a) shall be presumed to be innocent until he is proved or has pleaded guilty ;

(*b*) shall be informed as soon as reasonably practicable, in a language that he understands and in detail, of the nature of the offence charged ;

(*c*) shall be given adequate time and facilities for the preparation of his defence ;

(*d*) shall be permitted to defend himself before the court in person or, at his own expense, by a legal representative of his own choice or by a legal representative at the public expense where so provided by or under a law in force in The Bahamas ;

(*e*) shall be afforded facilities to examine in person or by his legal representative the witnesses called by the prosecution before the court, and to obtain the attendance and carry out the examination of witnesses to testify on his behalf before the court on the same conditions as those applying to witnesses called by the prosecution ;

(*f*) shall be permitted to have without payment the assistance of an interpreter if he cannot understand the language used at the trial . of the charge ; and

(*g*) shall, when charged on information in the Supreme Court, have the right to trial by jury ;

and except with his own consent the trial shall not take place in his absence unless he so conducts himself in the court as to render the continuance of the proceedings in his presence impracticable and the court has ordered him to be removed and the trial to proceed in his absence.

(3) When a person is tried for any criminal offence, the accused person or any person authorised by him in that behalf shall, if he so requires and subject to payment of such reasonable fee as may be prescribed by law, be given within a reasonable time after judgment a copy for the use of the accused person of any record of the proceedings made by or on behalf of the court.

(4) No person shall be held to be guilty of a criminal offence on account of any act or omission that did not, at the time it took place, constitute such an offence, and no penalty shall be imposed for any criminal offence that is severer in degree or description than the maximum penalty that might have been imposed for that offence at the time when it was committed.

(5) No person who shows that he has been tried by a competent court for a criminal offence and either convicted or acquitted shall again be tried for that offence or for any other criminal offence of which he could have been convicted at the trial for that offence, save upon the order of a superior court in the course of appeal or review proceedings relating to the conviction or acquittal.

(6) No person shall be tried for a criminal offence if he shows that he has been pardoned for that offence.

(7) No person who is tried for a criminal offence shall be compelled to give evidence at the trial.

(8) Any court or other adjudicating authority prescribed by law for the determination of the existence or extent of any civil right or obligation shall be established by law and shall be independent and impartial ; and where proceedings for such a determination are

instituted by any person before such a court or other adjudicating authority, the case shall be given a fair hearing within a reasonable time.

(9) All proceedings instituted in any court for the determination of the existence or extent of any civil right or obligation, including the announcement of the decision of the court, shall be held in public.

(10) Nothing in paragraph (9) of this Article shall prevent the court from excluding from the proceedings persons other than the parties thereto and their legal representatives to such extent as the court—

(a) may be empowered by law so to do and may consider necessary or expedient in circumstances where publicity would prejudice the interests of justice, or in interlocutory proceedings or in the interests of public morality, the welfare of persons under the age of eighteen years or the protection of the private lives of persons concerned in the proceedings ;

(b) may be empowered or required by law to do so in the interests of defence, public safety or public order ; or

(c) may be empowered or required to do so by rules of court and practice existing immediately before 10th July 1973 or by any law made subsequently to the extent that it makes provision substantially to the same effect as provision contained in any such rules.

(11) Nothing contained in or done under the authority of any law shall be held to be inconsistent with or in contravention of—

(a) sub-paragraph (2)(a) of this Article to the extent that the law in question imposes upon any person charged with a criminal offence the burden of proving particular facts ;

(b) sub-paragraph (2)(e) of this Article to the extent that the law in question imposes conditions that must be satisfied if witnesses called to testify on behalf of an accused person are to be paid their expenses out of public funds ;

(c) paragraph (5) of this Article to the extent that the law in question authorises a court to try a member of a disciplined force for a criminal offence notwithstanding any trial and conviction or acquittal of that member under the disciplinary law of that force, so, however, that any court so trying such a member and convicting him shall in sentencing him to any punishment take into account any punishment awarded him under that disciplinary law.

Protection for privacy of home and other property.

21.—(1) Except with his consent, no person shall be subjected to the search of his person or his property or the entry by others on his premises.

(2) Nothing contained in or done under the authority of any law shall be held to be inconsistent with or in contravention of this Article to the extent that the law in question makes provision—

(a) which is reasonably required—

(i) in the interests of defence, public safety, public order, public morality, public health, town and country planning, the development of mineral resources, or the development or utilisation of any other property in such a manner as to promote the public benefit ; or

(ii) for the purpose of protecting the rights and freedoms other persons ;

(b) to enable an officer or agent of the Government of The Bahamas, a local government authority or a body corporate established by law for public purposes to enter on the premises of any person in order to inspect those premises or anything thereon for the purpose of any tax, rate or due or in order to carry out work connected with any property that is lawfully on those premises and that belongs to that Government, authority or body corporate, as the case may be ; or

(c) to authorise, for the purpose of enforcing the judgment or order of a court in any civil proceedings, the search of any person or property by order of a court or the entry upon any premises by such order,

and except so far as that provision or, as the case may be, the thing done under the authority thereof is shown not to be reasonably justifiable in a democratic society.

22.—(1) Except with his consent, no person shall be hindered in the enjoyment of his freedom of conscience, and for the purposes of this Article the said freedom includes freedom of thought and of religion, freedom to change his religion or belief and freedom, either alone or in community with others, and both in public and in private, to manifest and propagate his religion or belief in worship, teaching, practice and observance. Protection of freedom of conscience.

(2) Except with his consent (or, if he is a person who has not attained the age of eighteen years, the consent of his guardian) no person attending any place of education shall be required to receive religious instruction or to take part in or attend any religious ceremony or observance if that instruction, ceremony or observance relates to a religion other than his own.

(3) No religious body or denomination shall be prevented from or hindered in providing religious instruction for persons of that body or denomination in the course of any education provided by that body or denomination whether or not that body or denomination is in receipt of any government subsidy, grant or other form of financial assistance designed to meet, in whole or in part, the cost of such course of education.

(4) No person shall be compelled to take any oath which is contrary to his religion or belief or to take any oath in a manner which is contrary to his religion or belief.

(5) Nothing contained in or done under the authority of any law shall be held to be inconsistent with or in contravention of this Article to the extent that the law in question makes provision which is reasonably required—

(a) in the interests of defence, public safety, public order, public morality or public health ; or

(b) for the purpose of protecting the rights and freedoms of other persons, including the right to observe and practise any religion without the unsolicited interference of members of any other religion, and except so far as that provision or, as the case may be, the thing done under the authority thereof is shown not to be reasonably justifiable in a democratic society.

Protection of freedom of expression.

23.—(1) Except with his consent, no person shall be hindered in the enjoyment of his freedom of expression, and for the purposes of this Article the said freedom includes freedom to hold opinions, to receive and impart ideas and information without interference, and freedom from interference with his correspondence.

(2) Nothing contained in or done under the authority of any law shall be held to be inconsistent with or in contravention of this Article to the extent that the law in question makes provision—

   (a) which is reasonably required—

      (i) in the interests of defence, public safety, public order, public morality or public health ; or

      (ii) for the purpose of protecting the rights, reputations and freedoms of other persons, preventing the disclosure of information received in confidence, maintaining the authority and independence of the courts, or regulating telephony, telegraphy, posts, wireless broadcasting, television, public exhibitions or public entertainment ; or

   (b) which imposes restrictions upon persons holding office under the Crown or upon members of a disciplined force,

and except so far as that provision or, as the case may be, the thing done under the authority thereof is shown not to be reasonably justifiable in a democratic society.

Protection of freedom of assembly and association.

24.—(1) Except with his consent, no person shall be hindered in the enjoyment of his freedom of peaceful assembly and association, that is to say, his right to assemble freely and associate with other persons and in particular to form or belong to political parties, or to form or belong to trade unions or other associations for the protection of his interests.

(2) Nothing contained in or done under the authority of any law shall be held to be inconsistent with or in contravention of this Article to the extent that the law in question makes provision—

   (a) which is reasonably required—

      (i) in the interests of defence, public safety, public order, public morality or public health ; or

      (ii) for the purpose of protecting the rights and freedoms of other persons ; or

   (b) which imposes restrictions upon persons holding office under the Crown or upon members of a disciplined force,

and except so far as that provision or, as the case may be, the thing done under the authority thereof is shown not to be reasonably justifiable in a democratic society.

Protection of freedom of movement.

25.—(1) Except with his consent, no person shall be hindered in the enjoyment of his freedom of movement, and for the purposes of this Article the said freedom means the right to move freely throughout The Bahamas, the right to reside in any part thereof, the right to enter The Bahamas, the right to leave The Bahamas and immunity from expulsion therefrom.

(2) Nothing contained in or done under the authority of any law shall be held to be inconsistent with or in contravention of this Article to the extent that the law in question makes provision—

(a) which is reasonably required—

    (i) in the interests of defence, public safety, public order, public morality, public health, town and country planning or the prevention of plant or animal diseases ; or

    (ii) for the purpose of protecting the rights and freedoms of other persons,

and except so far as that provision or, as the case may be, the thing done under the authority thereof is shown not to be reasonably justifiable in a democratic society ;

(b) for the removal of a person from The Bahamas to be tried outside The Bahamas for a criminal offence or to undergo imprisonment in some other country in respect of a criminal offence of which he has been convicted ;

(c) for the imposition of restrictions upon the movement or residence within The Bahamas of public officers or members of a disciplined force that are reasonably required for the purpose of the proper performance of their functions ; or

(d) for the imposition of restrictions on the movement or residence within The Bahamas of any person who is not a citizen of The Bahamas or the exclusion or expulsion therefrom of any such person ; or

(e) for the imposition of restrictions on the right of any person to leave The Bahamas in the public interest, or for securing compliance with any international obligation of the Government of The Bahamas particulars of which have been laid before Parliament.

(3) Any restriction on a person's freedom of movement which is involved in his lawful detention shall not be held to be inconsistent with or in contravention of this Article.

(4) For the purposes of sub-paragraph (c) of paragraph (2) of this Article " law " in that paragraph includes directions in writing regarding the conduct of public officers generally or any class of public officer issued by the Government of The Bahamas.

26.—(1) Subject to the provisions of paragraphs (4), (5) and (9) of this Article, no law shall make any provision which is discriminatory either of itself or in its effect. Protection from discrimination on the grounds of race, etc.

(2) Subject to the provisions of paragraphs (6), (9) and (10) of this Article, no person shall be treated in a discriminatory manner by any person acting by virtue of any written law or in the performance of the functions of any public office or any public authority.

(3) In this Article, the expression " discriminatory " means affording different treatment to different persons attributable wholly or mainly to their respective descriptions by race, place of origin, political opinions, colour or creed whereby persons of one such description are subjected to disabilities or restrictions to which persons of another such description are not made subject or are accorded privileges or advantages which are not accorded to persons of another such description.

(4) Paragraph (1) of this Article shall not apply to any law so far as that law makes provision—

(a) for the appropriation of revenues or other funds of The Bahamas or for the imposition of taxation (including the levying of fees for the grant of licences) ; or

(b) with respect to the entry into or exclusion from, or the employment, engaging in any business or profession, movement or residence within, The Bahamas of persons who are not citizens of The Bahamas ; or

(c) with respect to adoption, marriage, divorce, burial, devolution of property on death or other matters of personal law ; or

(d) whereby persons of any such description as is mentioned in paragraph (3) of this Article may be subjected to any disability or restriction or may be accorded any privilege or advantage which, having regard to its nature and to special circumstances pertaining to those persons or to persons of any other such description, is reasonably justifiable in a democratic society ; or

(e) for authorising the granting of licences or certificates permitting the conduct of a lottery, the keeping of a gaming house or the carrying on of gambling in any of its forms subject to conditions which impose upon persons who are citizens of The Bahamas disabilities or restrictions to which other persons are not made subject.

(5) Nothing contained in any law shall be held to be inconsistent with or in contravention of paragraph (1) of this Article to the extent that it makes provision with respect to standards or qualifications (not being a standard or qualification specifically relating to race, place of origin, political opinions, colour or creed) in order to be eligible for service as a public officer or as a member of a disciplined force or for the service of a local government authority or a body corporate established by law for public purposes.

(6) Paragraph (2) of this Article shall not apply to anything which is expressly or by necessary implication authorised to be done by any such provision of law as is referred to in paragraphs (4) or (5) of this Article.

(7) Subject to the provisions of sub-paragraph (4)(e) and of paragraph (9) of this Article, no person shall be treated in a discriminatory manner in respect of access to any of the following places to which the general public have access, namely, shops, hotels, restaurants, eating-houses, licensed premises, places of entertainment or places of resort.

(8) Subject to the provisions of this Article no person shall be treated in a discriminatory manner—

(a) in respect of any conveyance or lease or agreement for, or in consideration of, or collateral to, a conveyance or lease of any freehold or leasehold hereditaments which have been offered for sale or lease to the general public ;

(b) in respect of any covenant or provisions in any conveyance or lease or agreement for, or in consideration of, or collateral to, a conveyance or lease restricting by discriminatory provisions the transfer, ownership, use or occupation of any freehold or leasehold hereditaments which have been offered for sale or lease to the general public.

(9) Nothing contained in or done under the authority of any law shall be held to be inconsistent with or in contravention of this Article to the extent that the law in question makes provision whereby persons of any such description as is mentioned in paragraph (3) of this Article may be subjected to any restriction on the rights and freedoms guaranteed by Articles 21, 22, 23, 24 and 25 of this Constitution, being such a restriction as is authorised by Article 21(2)(a), 22(5), 23(2), 24(2) or 25(2)(a) or (e), as the case may be.

(10) Nothing in paragraph (2) of this Article shall affect any discretion relating to the institution, conduct or discontinuance of civil or criminal proceedings in any court that is vested in any person by or under this Constitution or any other law.

27.—(1) No property of any description shall be compulsorily taken possession of, and no interest in or right over property of any description shall be compulsorily acquired, except where the following conditions are satisfied, that is to say— *Protection from deprivation of property.*

(a) the taking of possession or acquisition is necessary in the interests of defence, public safety, public order, public morality, public health, town and country planning or the development or utilisation of any property in such manner as to promote the public benefit or the economic well-being of the community ; and

(b) the necessity therefor is such as to afford reasonable justification for the causing of any hardship that may result to any person having an interest in or right over the property ; and

(c) provision is made by a law applicable to that taking of possession or acquisition—

(i) for the making of prompt and adequate compensation in the circumstances ; and

(ii) securing to any person having an interest in or right over the property a right of access to the Supreme Court, whether direct or on appeal from any other authority, for the determination of his interest or right, the legality of the taking of possession or acquisition of the property, interest or right, and the amount of any compensation to which he is entitled, and for the purpose of obtaining prompt payment of that compensation ; and

(d) any party to proceedings in the Supreme Court relating to such a claim is given by law the same rights of appeal as are accorded generally to parties to civil proceedings in that Court sitting as a court of original jurisdiction.

(2) Nothing in this Article shall be construed as affecting the making or operation of any law so far as it provides for the taking of possession or acquisition of property—

(a) in satisfaction of any tax, rate or due ;

(b) by way of penalty for breach of the law, whether under civil process or after conviction of a criminal offence under the law of The Bahamas ;

(c) as an incident of a lease, tenancy, mortgage, charge, bill of sale, pledge or contract ;

(d) upon the attempted removal of the property in question out of or into The Bahamas in contravention of any law ;

(e) by way of the taking of a sample for the purposes of any law ;

(f) where the property consists of an animal upon its being found trespassing or straying ;

(g) in the execution of judgments or orders of courts ;

(h) by reason of its being in a dilapidated or dangerous state or injurious to the health of human beings, animals or plants ;

(i) in consequence of any law making provision for the validation of titles to land or (without prejudice to the generality of the foregoing words) the confirmation of such titles, or for the extinguishment of adverse claims, or with respect to prescription or the limitation of actions ;

(j) for so long only as may be necessary for the purposes of any examination, investigation, trial or inquiry or, in the case of land, the carrying out thereon—

    (i) of work or reclamation, drainage, soil conservation or the conservation of other natural resources ; or

    (ii) of agricultural development or improvement that the owner or occupier of the land has been required, and has, without reasonable and lawful excuse, refused or failed to carry out ; or

(k) to the extent that the law in question makes provision for the vesting or taking of possession or acquisition or administration of—

    (i) enemy property ;

    (ii) property of a deceased person, a person of unsound mind or a person who has not attained the age of twenty-one years, for the purpose of its administration for the benefit of the persons entitled to the beneficial interest therein ;

    (iii) property of a person adjudged insolvent or a defunct company that has been struck off the Register of Companies, or a body corporate in liquidation, for the purpose of its administration for the benefit of the creditors of that insolvent person or body corporate and, subject thereto, for the benefit of other persons entitled to the beneficial interest in the property ; or

    (iv) property subject to a trust, for the purpose of vesting the property in persons appointed as trustees under the instrument creating the trust or by a court or, by order of a court, for the purpose of giving effect to the trust.

(3) Nothing contained in or done under the authority of any law shall be held to be inconsistent with or in contravention of this Article to the extent that the law in question makes provision for the orderly marketing or production or growth or extraction of any agricultural or fish product or mineral or water or any article or thing prepared for market or manufactured therefor or for the reasonable restriction of the use of any property in the interest of safeguarding the interests of others or the protection of tenants, licensees or others having rights in or over such property.

(4) Nothing contained in or done under the authority of any law shall be held to be inconsistent with or in contravention of this Article to the extent that the law in question makes provision for the compulsory taking possession in the public interest of any property, or the compulsory acquisition in the public interest of any interest in or right over property, where that property, interest or right is held by a body corporate established directly by law for public purposes in which no monies have been invested other than monies provided by Parliament or by any Legislature established for the former Colony of the Bahama Islands.

28.—(1) If any person alleges that any of the provisions of Articles 16 to 27 (inclusive) of this Constitution has been, is being or is likely to be contravened in relation to him then, without prejudice to any other action with respect to the same matter which is lawfully available, that person may apply to the Supreme Court for redress. *Enforcement of fundamental rights.*

(2) The Supreme Court shall have original jurisdiction—

(*a*) to hear and determine any application made by any person in pursuance of paragraph (1) of this Article ; and

(*b*) to determine any question arising in the case of any person which is referred to it in pursuance of paragraph (3) of this Article,

and may make such orders, issue such writs and give such directions as it may consider appropriate for the purpose of enforcing or securing the enforcement of any of the provisions of the said Articles 16 to 27 (inclusive) to the protection of which the person concerned is entitled :

Provided that the Supreme Court shall not exercise its powers under this paragraph if it is satisfied that adequate means of redress are or have been available to the person concerned under any other law.

(3) If, in any proceedings in any court established for The Bahamas other than the Supreme Court or the Court of Appeal, any question arises as to the contravention of any of the provisions of the said Articles 16 to 27 (inclusive), the court in which the question has arisen shall refer the question to the Supreme Court.

(4) No law shall make provision with respect to rights of appeal from any determination of the Supreme Court in pursuance of this Article that is less favourable to any party thereto than the rights of appeal from determinations of the Supreme Court that are accorded generally to parties to civil proceedings in that Court sitting as a court of original jurisdiction.

(5) Parliament may make laws to confer upon the Supreme Court such additional or supplementary powers as may appear to be necessary or desirable for enabling the Court more effectively to exercise the jurisdiction conferred upon it by paragraph (2) of this Article and may make provision with respect to the practice and procedure of the Court while exercising that jurisdiction.

29.—(1) This Article applies to any period when— *Provisions for time of war or emergency.*

(*a*) The Bahamas is at war ; or

(*b*) there is in force a proclamation (in this section referred to as a " proclamation of emergency ") made by the Governor-General and published in the Gazette declaring that a state of public emergency exists for the purposes of this section.

(2) Nothing contained in or done under the authority of any law shall be held to be inconsistent with or in contravention of Article 19, any provision of Article 20 other than paragraph (4) thereof, or any provision of Articles 21 to 26 (inclusive) of this Constitution to the extent that the law in question makes in relation to any period to which this Article applies provision, or authorises the doing during any such period of anything, which is reasonably justifiable in the circumstances of any situation or existing during that period for the purpose of dealing with that situation.

(3) Where any proclamation of emergency has been made, copies thereof shall as soon as practicable be laid before both Houses of Parliament, and if for any cause those Houses are not due to meet within five days the Governor-General shall, by proclamation published in the Gazette, summon them to meet within five days and they shall accordingly meet and sit upon the day appointed by the proclamation and shall continue to sit and act as if they had stood adjourned or prorogued to that day:

Provided that if the proclamation of emergency is made during the period between a dissolution of Parliament and the next ensuing general election—

(a) the Houses to be summoned as aforesaid shall be the Houses referred to in Article 66 of this Constitution unless the Governor-General is satisfied that it will be practicable to hold that election within seven days of the making of the proclamation of emergency ; and

(b) if the Governor-General is so satisfied, he shall (instead of summoning the Houses so referred to meet within five days of the making of the proclamation) summon the Houses of the new Parliament to meet as soon as practicable after the holding of that election.

(4) A proclamation of emergency shall, unless it is sooner revoked by the Governor-General, cease to be in force at the expiration of a period of fourteen days beginning on the date on which it was made or such longer period as may be provided under paragraph (5) of this Article, but without prejudice to the making of another proclamation of emergency at or before the end of that period.

(5) If at any time while a proclamation of emergency is in force (including any time while it is in force by virtue of the provisions of this paragraph) a resolution is passed by each House of Parliament approving its continuance in force for a further period, not exceeding six months, beginning on the date on which it would otherwise expire, the proclamation shall, if not sooner revoked, continue in force for that further period.

Saving of existing law.

30.—(1) Subject to paragraph (3) of this Article, nothing contained in or done under the authority of any written law shall be held to be inconsistent with or in contravention of any provision of Articles 16 to 27 (inclusive) of this Constitution to the extent that the law in question—

(a) is a law (in this Article referred to as " an existing law ") that was enacted or made before 10th July 1973 and has continued to be part of the law of The Bahamas at all times since that day ;

(b) repeals and re-enacts an existing law without alteration ; or

(c) alters an existing law and does not thereby render that law inconsistent with any provision of the said Articles 16 to 27 (inclusive) in a manner in which, or to an extent to which, it was not previously so inconsistent.

(2) In sub-paragraph (1)(c) of this Article the reference to altering an existing law includes references to repealing it and re-enacting it with modifications or making different provisions in lieu thereof, and to modifying it ; and in paragraph (1) of this Article " written law " includes any instrument having the force of law and in this paragraph and the said paragraph (1) references to the repeal and re-enactment of an existing law shall be construed accordingly.

(3) This Article does not apply to any regulation or other instrument having legislative effect made, or to any executive act done, after 9th July 1973 under the authority of any such law as is mentioned in paragraph (1) of this Article.

31.—(1) In this Chapter— Interpre-
tation.

" contravention ", in relation to any requirement, includes a failure to comply with that requirement ; and cognate expressions shall be construed accordingly ;

" court " means any court of law having jurisdiction in The Bahamas other than a court established by a disciplinary law, and includes the Judicial Committee of Her Majesty's Privy Council or any court substituted therefore by any law made under Article 105 of this Constitution and—

(a) In Article 16, Article 18, Article 19, paragraphs (2), (3), (5), (8), (9) and (10) of Article 20, Article 26 and paragraph (3) of Article 28 of this Constitution includes, in relation to an offence against a disciplinary law, a court established by such a law ; and

(b) In Article 18, Article 19 and paragraph (3) of Article 28 of this Constitution includes, in relation to an offence against a disciplinary law, any person or authority empowered to exercise jurisdiction in respect of that offence ;

" disciplinary law " means a law regulating the discipline of any disciplined force ;

" disciplined force " means—

(a) a naval, military or air force ;

(b) the Police Force of The Bahamas ;

(c) the Prison Service of The Bahamas ; or

(d) any other force or service specified by Act of Parliament to·be a disciplined force for the purposes of this Chapter ;

" legal representative " means a person entitled to practise in The Bahamas as Counsel and Attorney of the Supreme Court ;

" member " in relation to a disciplined force includes any person who, under the law regulating the discipline of that force, is subject to that discipline.

(2) Any reference in Articles 16, 19, 25 and 27 of this Constitution to a criminal offence shall be construed as including an offence against disciplinary law, and any such reference in paragraphs (2) to (7)

(inclusive) of Article 20 of this Constitution shall, in relation to proceedings before a court constituted by or under disciplinary law, be construed in the same manner.

(3) In relation to any person who is a member of a disciplined force raised under a law of any country other than The Bahamas and lawfully present in The Bahamas, nothing contained in or done under the authority of the disciplinary law of that force shall be held to be inconsistent, with or in contravention of any of the provisions of this Chapter.

CHAPTER IV

THE GOVERNOR-GENERAL

Establishment of office of Governor-General.

32. There shall be a Governor-General of The Bahamas who shall be appointed by Her Majesty and shall hold office during Her Majesty's pleasure and who shall be Her Majesty's representative in The Bahamas.

Acting Governor-General.

33.—(1) Whenever the office of Governor-General is vacant or the holder of the office is absent from The Bahamas or is for any other reason unable to perform the functions of his office, those functions shall be performed—

(a) by any person for the time being designated by Her Majesty in that behalf who is in The Bahamas and able to perform those functions ; or

(b) at any time when there is no person in The Bahamas so designated and able to perform those functions, by the holder of the office of Chief Justice ; or

(c) at any time referred to in sub-paragraph (b) of this paragraph when the office of Chief Justice is vacant or the holder thereof is absent from The Bahamas or is for any other reason unable to perform those functions, by the President of the Senate.

(2) The holder of the office of Governor-General or any person designated under sub-paragraph (1)(a) of this Article or by sub-paragraph (1)(b) of this Article shall not, for the purposes of this Article, be regarded as absent from The Bahamas or as unable to perform the functions of the office of Governor-General at any time when there is a subsisting appointment of a deputy under Article 34 of this Constitution.

Deputy to Governor-General.

34.—(1) Whenever the Governor-General—

(a) has occasion to be absent from The Bahamas for a period which he has reason to believe will be of short duration ; or

(b) is suffering from an illness that he has reason to believe will be of short duration,

he may, acting in accordance with the advice of the Prime Minister, by instrument under the Public Seal, appoint any person in The Bahamas to be his deputy during such absence or illness and in that capacity to perform on his behalf such of the functions of the office of Governor-General as may be specified in that instrument.

(2) The power and authority of the Governor-General shall not be abridged, altered or in any way affected by the appointment of a deputy under this Article, and in the exercise of any function that is

exercisable by the Governor-General acting in accordance with his own deliberate judgment or after consultation with any person or authority a deputy shall conform to and observe any instructions that the Governor-General, acting in like manner, may address to him:

Provided that the question whether or not a deputy has conformed to or observed any such instructions shall not be enquired into in any court.

(3) A person appointed as a deputy under this Article shall hold that appointment for such period as may be specified in the instrument by which he is appointed, and his appointment may be revoked at any time by the Governor-General acting in accordance with the advice of the Prime Minister.

35.—(1) Parliament may prescribe the offices that are to constitute the personal staff of the Governor-General, the salaries and allowances that are to be paid to the members of the staff and the other sums that are to be paid in respect of the expenditure attaching to the office of Governor-General.

Personal staff of Governor-General.

(2) Any salaries or other sums prescribed under paragraph (1) of this Article are hereby charged on and shall be paid out of the Consolidated Fund.

(3) Subject to the provisions of paragraph (4) of this Article, power to make appointments to the offices for the time being prescribed under paragraph (1) of this Article as offices that are to constitute the personal staff of the Governor-General, and to remove and to exercise disciplinary control over persons holding or acting in any such office, is hereby vested in the Governor-General acting in accordance with his own deliberate judgment.

(4) The Governor-General, acting in accordance with his own deliberate judgment, may appoint to any of the offices prescribed under paragraph (1) of this Article such public officers as he may select from a list submitted by the Public Service Commission, but—

(*a*) the provisions of paragraph (3) of this Article shall apply in relation to an officer so appointed as respects his service on the personal staff of the Governor-General but not as respects his service as a public officer;

(*b*) an officer so appointed shall not, during continuance on the personal staff of the Governor-General, perform the functions of any public office; and

(*c*) an officer so appointed may at any time be appointed by the Governor-General, if the Public Service Commission so recommend, to assume or resume the functions of a public office and he shall thereupon vacate his office on the personal staff of the Governor-General, but the Governor-General may, in his own deliberate judgment, decline to release the officer for that appointment.

(5) All offices prescribed under paragraph (1) of this Article as offices that are to constitute the personal staff of the Governor-General shall, for the purposes of Chapter VIII, be deemed to be public offices.

Public Seal.

36. The Governor-General shall keep and use the Public Seal for sealing all things that shall pass the Public Seal.

Oaths to be taken by Governor-General.

37. A person appointed to the office of Governor-General or assuming the functions of that office under Article 33 of this Constitution shall, before entering upon the duties of that office, take and subscribe the oath of allegiance and an oath for the due execution of the office of Governor-General in such form as is prescribed by any law in force in The Bahamas, such oaths being administered by the Chief Justice or such other Justice of the Supreme Court as may be designated by the Chief Justice.

CHAPTER V

PARLIAMENT

PART 1

Composition of Parliament

Establishment of Parliament.

38. There shall be a Parliament of The Bahamas which shall consist of Her Majesty, a Senate and a House of Assembly.

PART 2

The Senate

Composition of Senate.

39.—(1) The Senate shall consist of sixteen members (in this Constitution referred to as " Senators ") who shall be appointed by the Governor-General by instrument under the Public Seal in accordance with the provisions of this Article.

(2) Nine Senators shall be appointed by the Governor-General acting in accordance with the advice of the Prime Minister.

(3) Four Senators shall be appointed by the Governor-General acting in accordance with the advice of the Leader of the Opposition.

(4) Three Senators shall be appointed by the Governor-General acting in accordance with the advice of the Prime Minister after consultation with the Leader of the Opposition.

(5) Whenever any person vacates his seat as a Senator for any reason other than a dissolution of Parliament, the Governor-General shall as soon as practicable appoint a person to fill the vacancy under the same provisions of this Article as those under which the person whose seat has became vacant was appointed.

Purpose of appointment of certain Senators.

40. In the exercise of the functions conferred upon him by Article 39(4) of this Constitution, the purpose of the Prime Minister shall be to secure that the political balance of the Senate reflects that of the House of Assembly at the time.

Qualifications for appointment as Senator.

41. Subject to the provisions of Article 42 of this Constitution, a person shall be qualified to be appointed as a Senator if, and shall not be qualified to be so appointed unless, he is a citizen of The Bahamas, of the age of thirty years or upwards and has ordinarily resided in The Bahamas for a period of not less than one year immediately before the date of his appointment.

42.—(1) No person shall be qualified to be appointed as a Senator who— Disqualifications for appointment as Senator.

(a) is a citizen of a country other than The Bahamas having become such a citizen voluntarily ;

(b) is, by virtue of his own act, under any acknowledgement of allegiance, obedience or adherence to a foreign power or state ;

(c) is disqualified for membership of the Senate by any law in force in The Bahamas enacted in pursuance of paragraph (2) of this Article ;

(d) is a member of the House of Assembly ;

(e) has been adjudged or otherwise declared bankrupt under any law in force in The Bahamas and has not been discharged ;

(f) is a person certified to be insane or otherwise adjudged to be of unsound mind under any law in force in The Bahamas ;

(g) is under sentence of death imposed on him by a court in The Bahamas, or is serving a sentence of imprisonment (by whatever name called) exceeding twelve months imposed on him by such a court or substituted by competent authority for some other sentence imposed on him by such a court, or is under such a sentence of imprisonment the execution of which has been suspended ;

(h) is disqualified for membership of the House of Assembly by virtue of any law in force in The Bahamas by reason of his having been convicted of any offence relating to elections ; or

(i) is interested in any government contract and has not disclosed to the Governor-General the nature of such contract and of his interest therein.

(2) Parliament may by law provide that, subject to such exceptions and limitations (if any) as may be prescribed therein, a person shall be disqualified for membership of the Senate by virtue of—

(a) his holding or acting in any office or appointment specified (either individually or by reference to a class of office or appointment) by such law ;

(b) his belonging to any armed force of The Bahamas or to any class of person so specified that is comprised in any such force ; or

(c) his belonging to any police force of The Bahamas or to any class of person so specified that is comprised in any such force.

(3) For the purposes of sub-paragraph (1)(g) of this Article—

(a) two or more sentences of imprisonment that are required to be served consecutively shall be regarded as separate sentences if none of those sentences exceeds twelve months, but if any one of such sentences exceeds that term they shall be regarded as one sentence ; and

(b) no account shall be taken of a sentence of imprisonment imposed as an alternative to or in default of the payment of a fine.

43.—(1) The seat of a Senator shall became vacant— Tenure of office of Senators.

(a) upon the next dissolution of Parliament after he has been appointed ;

(b) if he resigns by writing under his hand addressed to the President of the Senate, or, if the office of President is vacant or the President is absent from The Bahamas, to the Vice-President ;

(c) if, with his consent, he is nominated as a candidate for election to the House of Assembly ;

(d) if he is absent from The Bahamas for a period exceeding forty days at any time when the Senate is sitting, without the leave of the President given in accordance with the provisions of paragraph (2) of this Article ;

(e) if he ceases to be a citizen of The Bahamas ;

(f) subject to the provisions of paragraph (3) of this Article, if any circumstances arise that, if he were not a Senator, would cause him to be disqualified for appointment as such by virtue of sub-paragraph (a), (b), (c), (e), (f), (g) or (h) of Article 42(1) of this Constitution or of any law enacted in pursuance of Article 42(2) of this Constitution ;

(g) in the case of a Senator who was appointed as such in accordance with the advice of the Prime Minister or in accordance with the advice of the Leader of the Opposition or on the advice of the Prime Minister after consultation with the Leader of the Opposition, if the Governor-General, acting in accordance with the advice of the Prime Minister or in accordance with the advice of the Leader of the Opposition or on the advice of the Prime Minister after consultation with the Leader of the Opposition, as the case may be, by instrument under the Public Seal, declares the seat of that Senator to be vacant ; or

(h) if he becomes interested in any government contract:
Provided that—

    (i) if in the circumstances it appears to the Senate to be just so to do, the Senate may exempt any Senator from vacating his seat under the provisions of this sub-paragraph, if that Senator, before becoming interested in such contract as aforesaid or as soon as practicable after becoming so interested, discloses to the Senate the nature of such contract and his interest therein ;

    (ii) if proceedings are taken under a law made under Article 45 of this Constitution to determine whether a Senator has vacated his seat under the provisions of this sub-paragraph he shall be declared by the court not to have vacated his seat if he establishes to the satisfaction of the court that he, acting reasonably, was not aware that he was or had become interested in such contract ; and

    (iii) no proceedings under the preceding sub-paragraph shall be instituted by any person other than a Senator or Member of the House of Assembly.

(2) The President of the Senate may grant leave to any Senator to be absent from The Bahamas for any period not exceeding six months at any one time.

(3) If the circumstances such as are referred to in sub-paragraph (1)(f) of this Article arise because a Senator is under sentence of death or imprisonment, adjudged to be of unsound mind, declared bankrupt or convicted or reported guilty of a corrupt or illegal practice at elections

and if it is open to the Senator to appeal against the decision (either with the leave of a court of other authority or without such leave), he shall forthwith cease to perform his functions as a senator but, subject to paragraph (4) of this Article, he shall not vacate his seat until the expiration of a period of thirty days thereafter:

Provided that the President of the Senate may, at the request of the said Senator, from time to time extend that period for further periods of thirty days to enable the Senator to pursue an appeal against the decision, so, however, that extensions of time exceeding in the aggregate one hundred and fifty days shall not be given without the approval, signified by resolution, of the Senate.

(4) If, on the determination of any appeal, such circumstances continue to exist and no further appeal is open to the Senator, or if, by reason of the expiration of any period for entering an appeal or notice thereof or the refusal of leave to appeal or for any other reason, it ceases to be open to the Senator to appeal, he shall forthwith vacate his seat.

(5) If at any time before the Senator vacates his seat such circumstances as aforesaid cease to exist, his seat shall not become vacant on the expiration of the period referred to in paragraph (3) of this Article and he may resume the performance of his functions as a Senator.

44.—(1) When the Senate first meets after this Constitution comes into operation or after any general election and before it proceeds to the despatch of any other business, the Senate shall, in accordance with such procedure as may be prescribed by the rules of procedure of the Senate, elect a Senator to be President of the Senate ; and, if the office of President falls vacant at any time, the Senate shall, as soon as practicable, proceed in like manner to fill the vacant office. *President and Vice-President.*

(2) When the Senate first meets after this Constitution comes into operation or after any general election and before it proceeds to the despatch of any other business except the election of the President, it shall elect a Senator to be Vice-President of the Senate ; and if the office of Vice-President falls vacant at any time, the Senate shall, as soon as practicable, elect a Senator to that office.

(3) The Senate shall not elect a Senator who is a Minister or Parliamentary Secretary to be the President or Vice-President of the Senate.

(4) A person shall vacate the office of President or Vice-President of the Senate—

(a) if he ceases to be a Senator ;

(b) if he is appointed to be a Minister or Parliamentary Secretary ;

(c) if he announces the resignation of his office to the Senate or if, by writing under his hand addressed, in the case of the President, to the Clerk of the Senate and, in the case of the Vice-President, to the President (or, if the office of President is vacant or the President is absent from The Bahamas, to the Clerk), he resigns that office ; or

(d) in the case of the Vice-President, if he is elected to be President.

(5) If, by virtue of Article 43(3) of this Constitution, the President or Vice-President is required to cease to perform his functions as a Senator he shall also cease to perform his functions as President or

Vice-President, as the case may be, and those functions shall, until he vacates his seat in the Senate or resumes the performance of the functions of his office, be performed—

(a) in the case of the President, by the Vice-President or, if the office of Vice-President is vacant or the Vice-President is required to cease to perform his functions as a Senator by virtue of Article 43(3) of this Constitution, by such Senator (not being a Minister or Parliamentary Secretary) as the Senate may elect for the purpose ;

(b) in the case of the Vice-President, by such Senator (not being a a Minister or Parliamentary Secretary) as the Senate may elect for the purpose.

(6) If the President or Vice-President resumes the performance of his functions as a Senator in accordance with the provisions of Article 43(5) of this Constitution, he shall also resume the performance of his functions as President or Vice-President, as the case may be.

Determination of questions as to membership.

45.—(1) The Supreme Court shall have jurisdiction to hear and determine any question whether—

(a) any person has been validly appointed as a Senator ; or

(b) any Senator has vacated his seat or is required under Article 43(3) of this Constitution to cease to perform his functions as a Senator.

(2) Subject to the following provisions of this Article and to the provisions of Article 43(1) of this Constitution, Parliament may by law make provision with respect to—

(a) the institution of proceedings for the determination of any question referred to in paragraph (1) of this Article ; and

(b) the powers, practice and procedure of the Supreme Court in relation to any such proceedings.

(3) Proceedings for the determination of any question referred to in paragraph (1) of this Article shall not be instituted except with the leave of a Justice of the Supreme Court.

(4) No appeal shall lie from the decision of a Justice of the Supreme Court granting or refusing leave to institute proceedings in accordance with paragraph (3) of this Article.

PART 3

House of Assembly

Composition of House of Assembly.

46.—(1) The House of Assembly shall consist of thirty-eight members or such greater number of members as may be specified by an Order made by the Governor-General in accordance with the provisions of Article 70 of this Constitution.

(2) The members of the House shall be known as " Members of Parliament " and shall be persons who, being qualified for election as Members of Parliament in accordance with the provisions of this Constitution, have been so elected in the manner provided by any law in force in The Bahamas.

47. Subject to the provisions of Article 48 of this Constitution, a person shall be qualified to be elected as a member of the House of Assembly if, and shall not be qualified to be so elected unless, he—

(a) is a citizen of The Bahamas of the age of twenty-one years or upwards ; and

(b) has ordinarily resided in The Bahamas for a period of not less than one year immediately before the date of his nomination for election.

48.—(1) No person shall be qualified to be elected as a member of the House of Assembly who—

(a) is a citizen of a country other than The Bahamas having become such a citizen voluntarily ;

(b) is, by virtue of his own act, under any acknowledgment of allegiance, obedience or adherence to a foreign power or state ;

(c) is disqualified for membership of the House of Assembly by any law enacted in pursuance of paragraph (2) of this Article ;

(d) has been adjudged or otherwise declared bankrupt under any law in force in The Bahamas and has not been discharged ;

(e) is a person certified to be insane or otherwise adjudged to be of unsound mind under any law in force in The Bahamas ;

(f) is under sentence of death imposed on him by a court in The Bahamas, or is serving a sentence of imprisonment (by whatever name called) exceeding twelve months imposed on him by such a court or substituted by competent authority for some other sentence imposed on him by such a court, or is under such a sentence of imprisonment the execution of which has been suspended ;

(g) is disqualified for membership of the House of Assembly by any law in force in The Bahamas by reason of his holding, or acting in, any office the functions of which involve—

　(i) any responsibility for, or in connection with, the conduct of any election ; or

　(ii) any responsibility for the compilation or revision of any electoral register ;

(h) is disqualified for membership of the House of Assembly by virtue of any law in force in The Bahamas by reason of his having been convicted of any offence relating to elections ;

(i) is a Senator ; or

(j) is interested in any government contract and has not disclosed the nature of such contract and of his interest therein by publishing a notice in the Gazette within one month before the day of election.

(2) Parliament may by law provide that, subject to such exceptions and limitations (if any) as may be prescribed therein, a person shall be disqualified for membership of the House of Assembly by virtue of—

(a) his holding or acting in any office or appointment specified (either individually or by reference to a class of office or appointment) by such law ;

(b) his belonging to any armed force of The Bahamas or to any class of person so specified that is comprised in any such force ; or (*c*) his belonging to any police force or to any class of person that is comprised in any such force.

(3) For the purposes of sub-paragraph (1)(*f*) of this Article—

(*a*) two or more sentences of imprisonment that are required to be served consecutively shall be regarded as separate sentences if none of those sentences exceeds twelve months, but if any one of such sentences exceeds that term they shall be regarded as one sentence ; and

(*b*) no account shall be taken of a sentence of imprisonment imposed as an alternative to or in default of the payment of a fine.

Tenure of office of members of House of Assembly.

49.—(1) Every member of the House of Assembly shall vacate his seat in the House—

(*a*) upon a dissolution of Parliament ;

(*b*) if he resigns it by writing under his hand addressed to the Speaker or, if the office of Speaker is vacant or the Speaker is absent from The Bahamas, to the Deputy Speaker ;

(*c*) if he is absent from the sittings of the House for such period and and in such circumstances as may be prescribed in the rules of procedure of the House ;

(*d*) if he ceases to be a citizen of The Bahamas ;

(*e*) subject to the provisions of paragraph (2) of this Article, if any circumstances arise that, if he were not a member of the House, would cause him to be disqualified for election as such by virtue of sub-paragraph (*a*), (*b*), (*c*), (*d*), (*e*), (*f*), (*g*) or (*h*) of Article 48(1) of this Constitution ; or

(*f*) if he becomes interested in any government contract :

Provided that—

(i) if in the circumstances it appears to the House of Assembly to be just to do so, the House of Assembly may exempt any member of the House from vacating his seat under the provisions of this sub-paragraph, if that member, before becoming interested in such contract as aforesaid or as soon as practicable after becoming so interested, discloses to the House the nature of such contract and his interest therein ;

(ii) if proceedings are taken under a law made under Article 51 of this Constitution to determine whether a member of the House has vacated his seat under the provisions of this sub-paragraph he shall be declared by the court not to have vacated his seat if he establishes to the satisfaction of the court that he, acting reasonably, was not aware that he was or had become interested in such contract ; and

(iii) no proceedings under the preceding sub-paragraph shall be instituted by any person other than a Senator or member of the House of Assembly.

(2) If circumstances such as are referred to in sub-paragraph (1)(*e*) of this Article arise because any member of the House is under sentence of death or imprisonment, declared bankrupt, adjudged to be of unsound mind or convicted of an offence relating to elections and it is open to the member to appeal against the decision (either with the leave of a court or other authority or without such leave), he shall

forthwith cease to perform his functions as a member of the House but, subject to paragraph (3) of this Article, he shall not vacate his seat until the expiration of a period of thirty days thereafter:

Provided that the Speaker may, at the request of the member, from time to time extend that period for further periods of thirty days to enable the member to pursue an appeal against the decision, so, however, that extensions of time exceeding in the aggregate one hundred and fifty days shall not be given without the approval, signified by resolution, of the House of Assembly.

(3) If, on the determination of any appeal, such circumstances continue to exist and no further appeal is open to the member, or if, by reason of the expiration of any period for entering an appeal or notice thereof or the refusal of leave to appeal or for any other reason, it ceases to be open to the member to appeal, he shall forthwith vacate his seat.

(4) If at any time before the member vacates his seat such circumstances as aforesaid cease to exist, his seat shall not become vacant on the expiration of the period referred to in paragraph (2) of this Article and he may resume the performance of his functions as a member of the House.

50.—(1) When the House of Assembly first meets after any general election and before it proceeds to the despatch of any other business, the House shall, in accordance with such procedure as may be prescribed by the rules of procedure of the House, elect from among the members who are not Ministers or Parliamentary Secretaries one member to be the Speaker of the Assembly and another member to be Deputy Speaker; and, if the office of Speaker or Deputy Speaker falls vacant at any time before the next dissolution of the House of Assembly, the House shall, as soon as practicable, proceed in like manner to fill the vacant office.

Speaker and Deputy Speaker.

(2) A person shall vacate the office of Speaker or Deputy Speaker—

(a) if he ceases to be a member of the House of Assembly:
Provided that the Speaker shall not vacate his office by reason only that he has ceased to be a member on a dissolution of Parliament, until the House of Assembly first meets after that dissolution;

(b) if he is appointed to be a Minister or Parliamentary Secretary;

(c) if he announces the resignation of his office to the House of Assembly or if, by writing under his hand addressed, in the case of the Speaker, to the Clerk of the House and, in the case of the Deputy Speaker, to the Speaker (or, if the office of Speaker is vacant or the Speaker is absent from The Bahamas, to the Clerk), he resigns that office; or

(d) in the case of the Deputy Speaker, if he is elected to be Speaker.

(3) If by reason of Article 49(2) of this Constitution the Speaker or Deputy Speaker is required to cease to perform his functions as a member of the House of Assembly, he shall also cease to perform his functions as Speaker or Deputy Speaker and those functions shall, until he vacates his seat in the House or resumes the performance of the functions of his office, be performed—

(a) in the case of the Speaker, by the Deputy Speaker or, if the office of Deputy Speaker is vacant or the Deputy Speaker is required to cease to perform his functions as a member of the House of Assembly by virtue of Article 49(2) of this Constitution, by such member (not being a Minister or Parliamentary Secretary) as the House may elect for the purpose ;

(b) in the case of the Deputy Speaker, by such member (not being a Minister or Parliamentary Secretary) as the House may elect for the purpose.

(4) If the Speaker or Deputy Speaker resumes the performance of his functions as a member of the House in accordance with the provisions of Article 49(4) of this Constitution, he shall also resume the performance of his functions as Speaker or Deputy Speaker, as the case may be.

Determination of questions as to membership.

51.—(1) An Election Court, consisting of two Justices of the Supreme Court appointed by the Chief Justice or, if for any reason two such Justices are not available, one such Justice and the Chief Magistrate or a Stipendiary and Circuit Magistrate appointed by the Chief Justice, shall have jurisdiction to hear and determine any question whether—

(a) any person has been validly elected as a member of the House of Assembly ; or

(b) any member of the House of Assembly has vacated his seat or is required, under the provisions of Article 49(2) of this Constitution, to cease to perform his functions as a member.

(2) Subject to the following provisions of this Article and to the provisions of Article 49(1) of this Constitution, Parliament may make, or provide for the making of provision, with respect to—

(a) the institution of proceedings for the determination of any question referred to in paragraph (1) of this Article ; and

(b) the powers, practice and procedure of an Election Court in relation to any such proceedings.

(3) The determination by an Election Court of any question referred to in paragraph (1) of this Article shall be final.

(4) Proceedings for the determination of any question referred to in paragraph (1) of this Article shall not be instituted except with the leave of a Justice of the Supreme Court.

(5) An appeal shall lie to the Court of Appeal on a point of law from the decision of a Justice of the Supreme Court granting or refusing leave to institute proceedings in accordance with this Article ; but, subject as aforesaid, that decision shall be final.

PART 4

Powers and Procedure of Parliament

Power to make laws.

52.—(1) Subject to the provisions of this Constitution, Parliament may make laws for the peace, order and good government of The Bahamas.

(2) Subject to the provisions of Articles 60, 61 and 62 of this Constitution, the power of Parliament to make laws shall be exercised by Bills passed by both Houses, either without amendment or with such

amendments only as are agreed to by both Houses, and assented to by the Governor General in accordance with Article 63 of this Constitution.

53.—(1) Without prejudice to the generality of Article 52(1) of this Constitution and subject to the provisions of paragraph (2) of this Article, Parliament may by law determine the privileges, immunities and powers of the Senate and the House of Assembly and the members thereof.

Privileges of Parliament.

(2) No process issued by any court in the exercise of its civil juris-diction shall be served or executed within the precincts of the Senate or the House of Assembly while it is sitting, or through the President or the Speaker, the Clerk or any other officer of either House.

54.—(1) Subject to the provisions of this Article, Parliament may, by an Act of Parliament passed by both Houses, alter any of the provisions of this Constitution or (in so far as it forms part of the law of The Bahamas) any of the provisions of The Bahamas In-dependence Act, 1973.

Alteration of this Con-stitution.

(2) In so far as it alters—

(*a*) Articles 32, 33, 34, 35, 41, 42, 43, 47, 48, 49, 79, 107, 108, 109, 110, 111, 112, 113, 114, 115, 116, 117, 118, 119, 120, 121, 122, 123, 124, 125, 126, 128, 129, 130, 131, 132, 133, 134, 135 or 136 of this Constitution ; or

(*b*) Articles 127 or 137 of this Constitution in their application to any of the provisions specified in sub-paragraph (*a*) of this paragraph,

a Bill for an Act of Parliament under this Article shall not be passed by Parliament unless :—

(i) at the final voting thereon in each House it is supported by the votes of not less than two-thirds of all the members of each House, and

(ii) the Bill, after its passage through both Houses, has been sub-mitted to the electors qualified to vote for the election of members of the House of Assembly and, on a vote in such manner as Parliament may prescribe the majority of the electors voting have approved the Bill.

(3) In so far as it alters—

(*a*) this Article ;

(*b*) Articles 2, 3, 4, 5, 6, 7, 8, 9, 10, 11, 12, 13, 14, 15, 16, 17, 18, 19, 20, 21, 22, 23, 24, 25, 26, 27, 28, 29, 30, 31, 38, 39, 40, 45, 46, 51, 52, 60, 61, 62, 65, 66, 67, 68, 69, 70, 71, 72, 93, 94, 95, 96, 97, 98, 99, 100, 101, 102, 103, 104 or 105 of this Constitution ; or

(*c*) Articles 106, 127 or 137 of this Constitution in their application to any of the provisions specified in sub-paragraphs (*a*) or (*b*) of this paragraph ; or

(*d*) any of the provisions of The Bahamas Independence Act 1973, a Bill for an Act of Parliament under this Article shall not be passed by Parliament unless :—

(i) at the final voting thereon in each House it is supported by the votes of not less than three-quarters of all the members of each House, and

(ii) the Bill, after its passage through both Houses has been submitted to the electors qualified to vote for the election of members of the House of Assembly and, on a vote taken in such manner as Parliament may prescribe the majority of the electors voting have approved the Bill.

(4) In this Article—

(a) references to any of the provisions of this Constitution or the Bahamas Independence Act 1973 include references to any law that amends or replaces that provision ; and

(b) references to the alteration of any of the provisions of this Constitution or The Bahamas Independence Act 1973 include references to the amendment, modification or re-enactment with or without amendment or modification, of that provision, the suspension or repeal of that provision and the making of a different provision in lieu of that provision.

(5) No Act of Parliament shall be construed as altering this Constitution unless it is stated in the Act that it is an Act for that purpose.

Regulation of procedure in Parliament.
55.—(1) Subject to the provisions of this Constitution, each House may regulate its own procedure and for this purpose may make rules of procedure.

(2) Each House may act notwithstanding any vacancy in its membership, and the presence or participation of any person not entitled to be present at or to participate in the proceedings of the House shall not invalidate those proceedings.

Presiding in the Senate and House of Assembly.
56.—(1) The President of the Senate or, in his absence, the Vice-President or, if they are both absent, a Senator (not being a Minister or Parliamentary Secretary) elected by the Senate for that sitting shall preside at each sitting of the Senate.

(2) The Speaker or, in his absence, the Deputy Speaker or, if they are both absent, a member (not being a Minister or Parliamentary Secretary) elected by the House for that sitting shall preside at each sitting of the House of Assembly.

(3) References in this Article to circumstances in which the President, Vice-President, Speaker or Deputy Speaker is absent include references to circumstances in which the office of President, Vice-President, Speaker or Deputy Speaker is vacant.

Quorum.
57.—(1) If at any time during a sitting of either House objection is taken by a member that there is not a quorum present and, after such interval as may be prescribed by the rules of procedure of that House, the person presiding ascertains that there is still not a quorum present, he shall thereupon adjourn the House.

(2) For the purposes of this Article—

(a) a quorum of the Senate shall consist of six Senators including the person presiding ; and

(b) a quorum of the House of Assembly shall consist of ten members including the person presiding, or of such greater number of members as may be specified by an Order made by the Governor-General in accordance with the provisions of Article 70 of this Constitution.

58.—(1) Save as is otherwise provided in this Constitution, all questions proposed for decision in either House shall be determined by a majority of the votes of the members thereof present and voting.

Voting.

(2) The person presiding in either House shall not vote—

(*a*) unless on any question the votes are equally divided, in which case he shall have and exercise a casting vote ; or

(*b*) except in the case of the final vote on a Bill for an Act of Parliament under Article 54 of this Constitution in which case he shall have an original vote.

59.—(1) Subject to the provisions of this Constitution and of the rules of procedure of the Senate or the House of Assembly, as the case may be, any member of either House may introduce any Bill or propose any motion for debate in, or may present any petition to, that House, and the same shall be debated and disposed of according to the rules of procedure of that House.

Introduction of Bills, etc.

(2) A Bill other than a Money Bill may be introduced in either House, but a Money Bill shall not be introduced in the Senate.

(3) Except on the recommendation of the Cabinet signified by a Minister, the House of Assembly shall not—

(*a*) proceed upon any Bill (including any amendment to a Bill) which, in the opinion of the person presiding, makes provision for imposing or increasing any tax, for imposing any charge on the Consolidated Fund or any other public fund or altering any such charge otherwise than by reducing it or for compounding or remitting any debt due to The Bahamas ; or

(*b*) proceed upon any motion (including any amendment to a motion) the effect of which, in the opinion of the person presiding, is that provision shall be made for any of the purposes aforesaid.

(4) The Senate shall not—

(*a*) proceed upon any Bill, other than a Bill sent from the House of Assembly, or any amendment to a Bill which, in the opinion of the person presiding, makes provision for imposing or increasing any tax, for imposing any charge on the Consolidated Fund or any other public fund or altering any such charge otherwise than by reducing it or for compounding or remitting any debt due to The Bahamas ; or

(*b*) proceed upon any motion (including any amendment to a motion) the effect of which, in the opinion of the person presiding, is that provision shall be made for any of the purposes aforesaid.

60.—(1) Subject to the provisions of this Constitution, if a Money Bill, having been passed by the House of Assembly and sent to the Senate at least one month before the end of the session, is not passed by the Senate without amendment within one month after it is sent to that House, the Bill shall, unless the House of Assembly otherwise resolves, be presented to the Governor-General for his assent notwithstanding that the Senate has not consented to the Bill.

Restriction on powers of Senate as to Money Bills.

(2) There shall be endorsed on every Money Bill when it is sent to the Senate the certificate of the Speaker signed by him that it is a Money Bill ; and there shall be endorsed on any Money Bill that is

presented to the Governor-General for assent in pursuance of paragraph (1) of this Article the certificate of the Speaker signed by him
that it is a Money Bill and that the provisions of that paragraph have
been complied with.

Restriction
on powers
of Senate as
to Bills
other than
Money Bills.

61.—(1) If any Bill other than a Money Bill is passed by the House
of Assembly in two successive sessions (whether or not Parliament is
dissolved between those sessions) and, having been sent to the Senate
in each of those sessions at least one month before the end of the
session, is rejected by the Senate in each of those sessions, that Bill
shall, on its rejection for the second time by the Senate, unless the
House of Assembly otherwise resolves, be presented to the Governor-
General for assent notwithstanding that the Senate has not consented
to the Bill:

Provided that the foregoing provisions of this paragraph shall not
have effect unless at least nine months have elapsed between the date
on which the Bill is passed by the House of Assembly in the first
session and the date on which it is passed by the House of Assembly in
the second session.

(2) For the purposes of this Article a Bill that is sent to the Senate
from the House of Assembly in any session shall be deemed to be
the same Bill as a former Bill sent to the Senate in the preceding session
if, when it is sent to the Senate, it is identical with the former Bill
or contains only such alterations as are certified by the Speaker to be
necessary owing to the time that has elapsed since the date of the
former Bill or to represent any amendments which have been made
by the Senate in the former Bill in the preceding session.

(3) The House of Assembly may, if it thinks fit, on the passage
through the House of a Bill that is deemed to be the same Bill as a
former Bill sent to the Senate in the preceding session, suggest any
amendments without inserting the amendments in the Bill, and any
such amendments shall be considered by the Senate, and, if agreed to
by the Senate, shall be treated as amendments made by the Senate
and agreed to by the House of Assembly ; but the exercise of this
power by the House of Assembly shall not affect the operation of this
Article in the event of the rejection of the Bill in the Senate.

(4) There shall be inserted in any Bill that is presented to the
Governor-General for assent in pursuance of this Article any amendments that are certified by the Speaker to have been made in the Bill
by the Senate in the second session and agreed to by the Assembly.

(5) There shall be endorsed on any Bill that is presented to the
Governor-General for assent in pursuance of this Article the certificate
of the Speaker signed by him that the provisions of this Article have
been complied with.

(6) The provisions of this Article shall not apply to a Bill which
is required by Article 54 of this Constitution to be passed by both
Houses.

Provisions
relating to
Articles 59,
60 and 61.

62.—(1) In Articles 59, 60 and 61 of this Constitution " Money Bill "
means a public Bill which, in the opinion of the Speaker, contains only
provisions dealing with all or any of the following matters, namely, the
imposition, repeal, remission, alteration or regulation of taxation ; the
imposition, for the payment of debt or other financial purposes, of

charges on the Consolidated Fund or any other public funds or on monies provided by Parliament or the variation or repeal of any such charges ; the grant of money to the Crown or to any authority or person, or the variation or revocation of any such grant, the appropriation, receipt, custody, investment, issue or audit of accounts of public money ; the raising or guarantee of any loan or the repayment thereof, or the establishment, alteration, administration or abolition of any sinking fund provided in connection with any such loan ; or subordinate matters incidental to any of the matters aforesaid ; and in this paragraph the expressions " taxation ", " debt ", " public fund ", " public money ", and " loan " do not include any taxation imposed, debt incurred, fund or money provided or loan raised by any local authority or body for local purposes.

(2) For the purposes of Article 61 of this Constitution, a Bill shall be deemed to be rejected by the Senate if—

(*a*) it is not passed by the Senate without amendment ; or

(*b*) it is passed by the Senate with any amendment which is not agreed to by the House of Assembly.

(3) Whenever the office of Speaker is vacant or the Speaker is for any reason unable to perform any function conferred upon him by paragraph (1) of this Article or by Articles 60 or 61 of this Constitution, that function may be performed by the Deputy Speaker.

(4) Any certificate of the Speaker or Deputy Speaker given under Article 60 or 61 of this Constitution shall be conclusive for all purposes and shall not be questioned in any court.

63.—(1) A Bill shall not become law until the Governor-General has assented thereto in Her Majesty's name and on Her Majesty's behalf and has signed it in token of such assent. Assent to Bills.

(2) Subject to the provisions of Articles 60 and 61 of this Constitution, a Bill shall be presented to the Governor-General for assent if, and shall not be so presented unless, it has been passed by both Houses either without amendment or with such amendments only as are agreed to by both Houses.

(3) Any Bill to which Article 54(2) or (3) of this Constitution applies shall be presented to the Governor-General endorsed with certificates of the President of the Senate and the Speaker that it has been passed by the requisite majorities in accordance with whichever of those paragraphs applies to the Bill, and with a certificate of the Parliamentary Registrar that it has been approved by the majority of the electors voting on the Bill.

(4) When a Bill is presented to the Governor-General for assent he shall signify that he assents or that he withholds assent.

64. No member of either House shall take part in the proceedings thereof unless he has taken the oath of allegiance in such manner as is prescribed by any law in force in The Bahamas : Oath of allegiance.

Provided that the election of a President of the Senate or the election of a Speaker of the House of Assembly may take place before the members of the Senate or the House of Assembly, as the case may be, have taken such oath.

PART 5

Summoning, Prorogation and Dissolution

Sessions of
Parliament.

65.—(1) Each session of Parliament shall be held at such place and commence at such time as the Governor-General may by proclamation appoint.

(2) The time appointed for the commencement of any session of Parliament shall be such that a period of twelve months does not intervene between the end of one session and the first sitting of Parliament in the next session.

Prorogation
and
dissolution
of
Parliament.

66.—(1) The Governor-General, acting in accordance with the advice of the Prime Minister, may at any time by proclamation prorogue Parliament.

(2) The Governor-General, acting in accordance with the advice of the Prime Minister, may at any time by proclamation dissolve Parliament:

Provided that if the office of Prime Minister is vacant and the Governor-General considers that there is no prospect of his being able within a reasonable time to appoint to that office a person who can command the confidence of a majority of the members of the House of Assembly, he shall dissolve Parliament.

(3) Subject to the provisions of paragraph (4) of this Article, Parliament, unless sooner dissolved, shall continue for five years from the date of its first sitting after any dissolution and shall then stand dissolved.

(4) At any time when The Bahamas is at war, Parliament may extend the period of five years specified in paragraph (3) of this Article for not more than twelve months at a time:

Provided that the life of Parliament shall not be extended under this paragraph for more than two years.

(5) If, between a dissolution of Parliament and the next ensuing general election of members to the House of Assembly, an emergency arises of such a nature that, in the opinion of the Prime Minister, it is necessary for the two Houses or either of them to be summoned before that general election can be held, the Governor-General, acting in accordance with the advice of the Prime Minister, may summon the two Houses of the preceding Parliament, and that Parliament shall thereupon be deemed (except for the purposes of Article 67 of this Constitution) not to have been dissolved but shall be deemed (except as aforesaid) to be dissolved on the date on which the polls are held in the next ensuing general election.

General
elections,
bye-elections
and
appointment
of Senators.

67.—(1) After every dissolution of Parliament the Governor-General shall issue writs for a general election of members of the House of Assembly returnable within ninety days from that dissolution.

(2) As soon as may be after every general election the Governor-General shall proceed under Article 39 of this Constitution to the appointment of Senators.

(3) Whenever any person vacates his seat as a member of the House of Assembly for any reason other than a dissolution of Parliament, the

Governor-General shall issue a writ for the election of a member to fill the vacancy and such election shall be held within sixty days after the occurrence of the vacancy or, where the question whether a vacancy has occurred is determined under Article 51 of this Constitution, after that determination, unless Parliament is sooner dissolved or the date by which Parliament will be dissolved under the provisions of Article 66 of this Constitution is less than four months after the occurrence of the vacancy or, as the case may be, that determination.

PART 6

Delimitation of Constituencies

68. The Bahamas shall be divided into thirty-eight constituencies or such greater number as may be provided for by an Order made by the Governor-General in accordance with the provisions of Article 70 of this Constitution and each such constituency shall return one member to the House of Assembly.

Constituencies.

69.—(1) There shall be a Constituencies Commission for The Bahamas (in this and the next following Article referred to as " the Commission ").

Constituencies Commission.

(2) The Members of the Commission shall be—

(*a*) the Speaker who shall be Chairman ;

(*b*) a Justice of the Supreme Court who shall be Deputy Chairman and shall be appointed by the Governor-General acting on the recommendation of the Chief Justice ;

(*c*) two members of the House of Assembly who shall be appointed by the Governor-General acting in accordance with the advice of the Prime Minister ; and

(*d*) one member of the House of Assembly who shall be appointed by the Governor-General acting in accordance with the advice of the Leader of the Opposition.

(3) The office of a member of the Commission shall become vacant—

(*a*) if he ceases to be the Speaker, a Justice of the Supreme Court or a member of the House of Assembly, as the case may be ; or

(*b*) in the case of a member appointed under sub-paragraph (2)(*b*), (*c*) or (*d*) of this Article, if his appointment is revoked by the Governor-General.

(4) If the office of a member of the Commission, appointed under sub-paragraph (2)(*b*), (*c*) or (*d*) of this Article is vacant or any such member is for any reason unable to perform the functions of his office, the Governor-General may appoint a person qualified for appointment under the said sub-paragraph (*b*), (*c*) or (*d*), as the case may be, to act in the office of that member and any person so appointed may continue so to act until his appointment is revoked.

(5) In revoking the appointment of a member of the Commission under sub-paragraph (3)(*b*) of this Article, and in making or revoking an appointment to act in the office of a member of the Commission under paragraph (4) of this Article, the Governor-General shall act

in the same manner as he would act if he were making an appointment to the office of that member under paragraph (2) of this Article.

(6) Any decision of the Commission shall require the concurrence of not less than three members of the Commission.

(7) Subject to the provisions of paragraph (6) of this Article, the Commission may act notwithstanding a vacancy in its membership, and no proceedings of the Commission shall be invalidated by reason only that some person not entitled to do so has taken part in them.

Procedure for review of constituencies.

70.—(1) The Commission shall in accordance with the provisions of this Article, at intervals of not more than five years, review the number and boundaries of the constituencies into which The Bahamas is divided and shall submit to the Governor-General a single report either—

(a) stating that in the opinion of the Commission, no change is required ; or

(b) recommending certain changes,

and the Governor-General shall cause such report to be laid before the House of Assembly forthwith.

(2) In carrying out a review for the purposes of this Article, the Commission shall be guided by the general consideration that the number of voters entitled to vote for the purposes of electing every member of the House of Assembly shall, so far as is reasonably practicable, be the same and the need to take account of special considerations such as the needs of sparsely populated areas, the practicability of elected members maintaining contact with electors in such areas, size, physical features, natural boundaries and geographical isolation.

(3) When the Commission intends to proceed under paragraph (1) of this Article, it shall, by notice in writing, inform the Prime Minister, who shall cause a copy of that notice to be published in the Gazette.

(4) As soon as may be after the Commission has submitted a report recommending changes in the boundaries of any constituencies, the Prime Minister shall lay before the House of Assembly for its approval a draft of an Order by the Governor-General for giving effect, whether with or without modifications, to the recommendations contained in the report, and that draft may make provision for any matters (including variation of the quorum specified in Article 57 of this Constitution) which appear to the Prime Minister to be incidental to or consequential upon the other provisions of the draft.

(5) Where any draft Order laid under this Article would give effect to any such recommendations with modifications, the Prime Minister shall lay before the House of Assembly together with the draft a statement of the reasons for the modifications.

(6) If the motion for the approval of any draft Order laid under this Article is rejected by the House of Assembly, or is withdrawn by leave of the House, an amended draft shall be laid without undue delay by the Prime Minister before the House of Assembly.

(7) If any draft Order laid under this Article is approved by resolution of the House of Assembly, the Prime Minister shall submit it to the Governor-General who shall make an Order (which shall be published

in the Gazette) in terms of the draft ; and that Order shall come into force on such day as may be specified therein and, until revoked by a further Order made by the Governor-General in accordance with the provisions of this Article, shall have the force of law in The Bahamas :

Provided that the coming into force of any such Order shall not affect any election to the House of Assembly until a proclamation is made by the Governor-General appointing the date for the holding of a general election of members of the House of Assembly or affect the constitution of the House of Assembly then in being.

(8) Save as provided in the next following paragraph the question of the validity of any Order by the Governor-General purporting to be made under this Article and reciting that a draft thereof has been approved by resolution of the House of Assembly shall not be inquired into in any court of law.

(9) Parliament may by law provide for an appeal to the Supreme Court against a statement or recommendation submitted by the Commission in pursuance of sub-paragraph (1)(*a*) or (*b*) of this Article.

CHAPTER VI

The Executive

71.—(1) The executive authority of The Bahamas is vested in Her Majesty. Executive Authority.

(2) Subject to the provisions of this Constitution, the executive authority of The Bahamas may be exercised on behalf of Her Majesty by the Governor-General, either directly or through officers subordinate to him.

(3) Nothing in this Article shall prevent Parliament from conferring functions on persons or authorities other than the Governor-General.

72.—(1) There shall be a Cabinet for The Bahamas which shall have the general direction and control of the government of The Bahamas and shall be collectively responsible therefor to Parliament. The Cabinet.

(2) The Cabinet shall consist of the Prime Minister and not less than eight other Ministers (of whom one shall be the Attorney-General), as may be appointed in accordance with the provisions of Article 73 of this Constitution.

73.—(1) Whenever there shall be occasion for the appointment of a Prime Minister, the Governor-General shall appoint as Prime Minister— Appointment of Ministers.

(*a*) the member of the House of Assembly who is the leader of the party which commands the support of the majority of the members of that House, or

(*b*) if it appears to him that that party does not have an undisputed leader in that House or that no party commands the support of such a majority, the member of the House of Assembly who, in his judgment, is most likely to command the support of the majority of members of that House,

and who is willing to accept the office of Prime Minister.

(2) Subject to the provisions of paragraph (3) of this Article, the Ministers other than the Prime Minister shall be such persons as the Governor-General, acting in accordance with the advice of the Prime Minister, shall appoint from among the Senators and the members of the House of Assembly.

(3) If the Attorney-General is appointed from among the members of the House of Assembly, not more than three Ministers shall be appointed from among the Senators, and if the Attorney-General is appointed from among the Senators, not more than two other Ministers shall be appointed from among the Senators.

(4) If occasion arises for making an appointment to the office of Prime Minister while Parliament is dissolved, a person who was a member of the House of Assembly immediately before the dissolution may, notwithstanding any other provision of this Article, be appointed as Prime Minister.

(5) If occasion arises for making an appointment to the office of any other Minister while Parliament is dissolved, a person who, immediately before the dissolution, was a Senator or a member of the House of Assembly may, subject to the provisions of paragraph (3) of this Article, be appointed as a Minister.

Tenure of office of Ministers.

74.—(1) If the House of Assembly passes a resolution, supported by the votes of a majority of all the members of the House, declaring that it has no confidence in the Prime Minister and the Prime Minister does not within seven days of the passing of such a resolution either resign or advise the Governor-General to dissolve Parliament, the Governor-General shall revoke the appointment of the Prime Minister.

(2) The Prime Minister shall also vacate his office—

(a) if at any time between the holding of a general election and the first sitting of the House of Assembly thereafter he is informed by the Governor-General that the Governor-General in pursuance of Article 73(1) of this Constitution is about to re-appoint him as Prime Minister or to appoint another person as Prime Minister ; or

(b) if for any reason other than a dissolution of Parliament he ceases to be a member of the House of Assembly.

(3) A Minister other than the Prime Minister shall vacate his office—

(a) when any person is appointed or re-appointed as Prime Minister ;

(b) if for any reason other than a dissolution of Parliament he ceases to be a member of the House from among the members of which he was appointed ; or

(c) if his appointment is revoked by the Governor-General acting in accordance with the advice of the Prime Minister.

(4) If at any time the Prime Minister is required under the provisions of paragraphs (2), (3) and (4) of Article 49 of this Constitution to cease to perform his functions as a member of the House of Assembly, he shall cease during such time to perform any of his functions as Prime Minister.

(5) If at any time a Minister other than the Prime Minister is required under the provisions of paragraphs (3), (4) and (5) of Article 43 or paragraphs (2), (3) and (4) of Article 49 of this Constitution to cease to

perform his functions as a member of the House to which he belongs, he shall cease during such time to perform any of his functions as a Minister.

75.—(1) Whenever the Prime Minister is absent from The Bahamas or is unable by reason of illness or of the provisions of paragraph (4) of Article 74 of this Constitution to perform the functions conferred upon him by this Constitution, the Governor-General may authorise some other member of the Cabinet to perform those functions (other than the functions conferred by this Article) and that member may perform those functions until his authority is revoked by the Governor-General.

Performance of functions of Prime Minister during absence, illness or suspension.

(2) The powers of the Governor-General under this Article shall be exercised by him in accordance with the advice of the Prime Minister:

Provided that if the Governor-General considers that it is impracticable to obtain the advice of the Prime Minister owing to his absence or illness, or if the Prime Minister is unable to tender advice by reason of the provisions of paragraph (4) of Article 74 of this Constitution, the Governor-General may exercise those powers without the advice of the Prime Minister.

76.—(1) Whenever a Minister other than the Prime Minister is unable, by reason of his illness or absence from The Bahamas or absence from his duties on leave, to perform the functions of his office, the Governor-General may, in writing, authorise another Minister to perform those functions or appoint a person to be a temporary Minister:

Temporary Ministers.

Provided that if occasion arises for the making of an appointment between a dissolution of Parliament and the next following general election, the preceding provisions of this Article shall have effect for the purpose as if Parliament had not been dissolved.

(2) Subject to the provisions of Article 74 of this Constitution, a temporary Minister shall hold office until he is notified by the Governor-General in writing that the Minister on account of whose inability to perform the functions of his office he was appointed is again able to perform those functions or that Minister vacates his office.

(3) The powers conferred on the Governor-General by this Article shall be exercised by him in accordance with the advice of the Prime Minister.

77. The Governor-General, acting in accordance with the advice of the Prime Minister, may, by directions in writing, charge the Prime Minister or any other Minister with responsibility for any business of the Government of The Bahamas, including the administration of any department of Government:

Allocation of portfolios to Ministers.

Provided that a Minister appointed from among members of the House of Assembly shall be charged with responsibility for finance.

78.—(1) The Attorney-General shall have power in any case in which he considers it desirable so to do—

Functions of Attorney-General.

(a) to institute and undertake criminal proceedings against any person before any court in respect of any offence against the law of The Bahamas;

(*b*) to take over and continue any such criminal proceedings that may have been instituted by any other person or authority ; and

(*c*) to discontinue, at any stage before judgment is delivered, any such criminal proceedings instituted or undertaken by himself or any other person or authority.

(2) The powers of the Attorney-General under paragraph (1) of this Article may be exercised by him in person or through other persons acting under and in accordance with his general or special instructions.

(3) The powers conferred upon the Attorney-General by sub-paragraphs (1) (*b*) and (*c*) of this Article shall be vested in him to the exclusion of any other person or authority :

Provided that, where any other person or authority has instituted criminal proceedings, nothing in this Article shall prevent the withdrawal of those proceedings by or at the instance of that person or authority at any stage before the person against whom the proceedings have been instituted has been charged before the court.

(4) In the exercise of powers conferred upon him by this Article the Attorney-General shall not be subject to the direction or control of any other person or authority.

(5) For the purposes of this Article, any appeal from any determination in any criminal proceedings before any court or any case stated or question of law reserved for the purpose of any such proceedings to any other court shall be deemed to be part of those proceedings.

Exercise of Governor-General's powers.

79.—(1) The Governor-General shall, in the exercise of his functions, act in accordance with the advice of the Cabinet or a Minister acting under the general authority of the Cabinet, except in cases where by this Constitution or any other law he is required to act in accordance with the recommendation or advice of, or with the concurrence of, or after consultation with, any person or authority other than the Cabinet :

Provided that the Governor-General shall act in accordance with his own deliberate judgment in the performance of the following functions—

(*a*) in the exercise of the power to appoint the Prime Minister conferred upon him by paragraphs (1) or (4) of Article 73 of this Constitution ;

(*b*) in the exercise of the powers conferred upon him by Article 75 of this Constitution (which relates to the performance of the functions of the Prime Minister during absence, illness or suspension) in the circumstances described in the proviso to paragraph (2) of that Article ;

(*c*) in the exercise of the power to appoint the Leader of the Opposition and to revoke any such appointment conferred upon him by Article 82 of this Constitution ;

(*d*) in the exercise of the powers conferred on him by Article 83(*a*) of this Constitution during any vacancy in the office of Leader of the Opposition ;

(*e*) in the exercise of the power to dissolve Parliament conferred upon him by the proviso to Article 66(2) of this Constitution ;

(*f*) in removing a Justice of the Supreme Court from office under Article 96(5) of this Constitution ;

(g) in removing a Justice of Appeal from office under Article 102(5) of this Constitution ;

(h) in the powers relating to appointment, removal and disciplinary control over members of his personal staff, conferred on him by Article 35 of this Constitution.

(2) Where the Governor-General is directed to exercise any function on the recommendation of any person or authority, he shall exercise that function in accordance with such recommendation :

Provided that—

(a) before he acts in accordance therewith, he may, acting in accordance with his own deliberate judgment, once refer that recommendation back for reconsideration by the person or authority concerned ; and

(b) if that person or authority, having reconsidered the original recommendation under sub-paragraph (a) of this proviso, substitutes therefor a different recommendation, the provisions of this paragraph shall apply to that different recommendation as they apply to the original recommendation.

(3) Where the Governor-General is directed to exercise any function after consultation with any person or authority he shall not be obliged to exercise that function in accordance with the advice or recommendation of that person or authority.

(4) Where the Governor-General is directed to exercise any function on the recommendation or advice of, or with the concurrence of, or after consultation with, any person or authority, the question whether he has so exercised that function shall not be enquired into in any court.

(5) Where the Governor-General is directed to exercise any function on the recommendation of the Prime Minister after consultation with the Leader of the Opposition, the following steps shall be taken—

(a) the Prime Minister shall first consult the Leader of the Opposition and thereafter tender his recommendation to the Governor-General ;

(b) the Governor-General shall then inform the Leader of the Opposition of that recommendation and if the Leader of the Opposition concurs therein the Governor-General shall act in accordance with the recommendation ;

(c) if the Leader of the Opposition does not concur in the recommendation the Governor-General shall so inform the Prime Minister and refer the recommendation back to him ;

(d) the Prime Minister shall then advise the Governor-General and the Governor-General shall act in accordance with that advice.

(6) Any reference in this Constitution to the functions of the Governor-General shall be construed as a reference to his powers and duties in the exercise of the executive authority of The Bahamas and to any other powers and duties conferred or imposed on him as Governor-General by or under this Constitution or any other law.

Governor-General to be informed concerning matters of Government.

80. The Prime Minister shall keep the Governor-General fully informed concerning the general conduct of the government of The Bahamas and shall furnish the Governor-General with such information as he may request with respect to any particular matter relating to the government of The Bahamas.

Parliamentary Secretaries.

81.—(1) The Governor-General, acting in accordance with the advice of the Prime Minister, may appoint Parliamentary Secretaries from among the Senators and the members of the House of Assembly to assist Ministers in the performance of their duties:

Provided that, if occasion arises for making an appointment while Parliament is dissolved, a person who was a Senator or a member of the House of Assembly immediately before the dissolution may be appointed as a Parliamentary Secretary.

(2) The office of a Parliamentary Secretary shall become vacant—

(*a*) if for any reason other than a dissolution of Parliament he ceases to be a member of the House from among the members of which he was appointed ;

(*b*) upon the appointment or re-appointment of any person as Prime Minister ; or

(*c*) if the Governor-General, acting in accordance with the advice of the Prime Minister, so directs.

Leader of the Opposition.

82.—(1) There shall be a Leader of the Opposition who shall be appointed by the Governor-General.

(2) Whenever there shall be occasion for the appointment of a Leader of the Opposition, the Governor-General shall appoint the member of the House of Assembly who, in his judgment, is best able to command the support of the majority of the members of the House in opposition to the Government ; or if there is no such person, the member of the House who, in his judgment, commands the support of the largest single group of members in opposition to the Government who are prepared to support one leader:

Provided that this paragraph shall have effect in relation to any period between a dissolution of Parliament and the day on which the next election of members of the House of Assembly is held as if Parliament had not been dissolved.

(3) The Leader of the Opposition shall vacate his office if—

(*a*) after an election of members of the House of Assembly following any dissolution of Parliament he is informed by the Governor-General that the Governor-General is about to appoint another person as Leader of the Opposition ;

(*b*) for any reason other than a dissolution of Parliament he ceases to be a member of the House of Assembly ;

(*c*) under the provisions of paragraphs (2), (3) and (4) of Article 49 of this Constitution he is required to cease to perform his functions as a member of the House of Assembly ; or

(*d*) his appointment is revoked under the provisions of paragraph (4) of this Article.

(4) If in the judgment of the Governor-General the Leader of the Opposition is no longer the member of the House of Assembly best

able to command the support of the majority of members of the House in opposition to the Government or the member of the House who commands the support of the largest single group of members in opposition to the Government who are prepared to support one leader, the Governor-General shall revoke the appointment of the Leader of the Opposition.

(5) Paragraph (4) of this Article shall not have effect while Parliament is dissolved.

83. During any period in which there is a vacancy in the office of Leader of the Opposition by reason of the fact that no person is both qualified in accordance with this Constitution for, and willing to accept appointment to, that office, the Governor-General shall— *Certain vacancies in office of Leader of the Opposition.*

(a) act in accordance with his own deliberate judgment in the exercise of any function in respect of which it is provided in this Constitution that the Governor-General shall act in accordance with the advice of the Leader of the Opposition ; and

(b) act on the recommendation of the Prime Minister in the exercise of any function in respect of which it is provided in this Constitution that the Governor-General shall act on the recommendation of the Prime Minister after consultation with the Leader of the Opposition.

84. A Minister or Parliamentary Secretary shall not enter upon the duties of his office unless he has taken and subscribed the oath of allegiance and such oath for the due execution of his office as may be prescribed by Parliament. *Oaths to be taken by Ministers, etc.*

85. The Governor-General, acting in accordance with the advice of the Prime Minister, may grant leave of absence from his duties to any Minister or Parliamentary Secretary. *Leave of absence for Ministers, etc.*

86.—(1) The Cabinet shall not be summoned except by the authority of the Prime Minister. *Summoning of and presiding in Cabinet.*

(2) The Prime Minister shall, so far as is practicable, attend and preside at all meetings of the Cabinet and in his absence such other Minister shall preside as the Prime Minister shall appoint.

87.—(1) No business shall be transacted at any meeting of the Cabinet if there are present at the meeting less than a majority of the members for the time being of the Cabinet. *Quorum.*

(2) Subject to paragraph (1) of this Article, the Cabinet shall not be disqualified for the transaction of business by reason of any vacancy in the membership of the Cabinet (including any vacancy not filled when the Cabinet is first constituted or is reconstituted at any time) and the validity of the transaction of business in the Cabinet shall not be affected by reason only of the fact that some person who was not entitled so to do took part in those proceedings.

88. Where any Minister has been charged with responsibility for any department of Government, he shall exercise general direction and control over that department ; and, subject to such direction and control, the department shall be under the supervision of a public officer (in this Constitution referred to as a Permanent Secretary) appointed for the purpose : *Permanent Secretaries.*

Provided that two or more Government departments may be placed under the supervision of one Permanent Secretary.

Constitution of offices, etc.

89. Subject to the provisions of this Constitution and of any Act of Parliament, the Governor-General may constitute offices for The Bahamas, make appointments to any such office and terminate any such appointment.

Powers of pardon, etc.

90.—(1) The Governor-General may, in Her Majesty's name and on Her Majesty's behalf—

(a) grant to any person convicted of any offence against the law of The Bahamas a pardon, either free or subject to lawful conditions ;

(b) grant to any person a respite, either indefinite or for a specified period, from the execution of any punishment imposed on that person for such an offence ;

(c) substitute a less severe form of punishment for that imposed by any sentence for such an offence ; or

(d) remit the whole or any part of any sentence passed for such an offence or any penalty or forfeiture otherwise due to Her Majesty on account of such an offence.

(2) The powers of the Governor-General under paragraph (1) of this Article shall be exercised by him in accordance with the advice of a Minister designated by him, acting in accordance with the advice of the Prime Minister.

Advisory Committee on Prerogative of Mercy.

91. There shall be an Advisory Committee on the Prerogative of Mercy which shall consist of—

(a) the Minister referred to in paragraph (2) of Article 90 of this Constitution, who shall be Chairman ;

(b) the Attorney-General ; and

(c) not less than three or more than five other members appointed by the Governor-General.

Functions of Advisory Committee.

92.—(1) Where an offender has been sentenced to death by any court for an offence against the law of The Bahamas, the Minister shall cause a written report of the case from the trial Justice of the Supreme Court, together with such other information derived from the record of the case or elsewhere as the Minister may require, to be taken into consideration at a meeting of the Advisory Committee.

(2) The Minister may consult with the Advisory Committee before tendering any advice to the Governor-General under paragraph (2) of Article 90 of this Constitution in any case not falling within paragraph (1) of this Article.

(3) The Minister shall not be obliged in any case to act in accordance with the advice of the Advisory Committee.

(4) The Advisory Committee may regulate its own procedure.

(5) In this Article " the Minister " means the Minister referred to in paragraph (2) of Article 90 of this Constitution.

CHAPTER VII

THE JUDICATURE

PART I

The Supreme Court

93.—(1) There shall be a Supreme Court for The Bahamas which shall have such jurisdiction and powers as may be conferred upon it by this Constitution or any other law. Establishment of Supreme Court.

(2) The Justices of the Supreme Court shall be the Chief Justice and such number of other Justices as may be prescribed by Parliament.

(3) No office of Justice of the Supreme Court shall be abolished while there is a substantive holder thereof.

(4) The Supreme Court shall be a superior court of record and, save as otherwise provided by Parliament, shall have all the powers of such a court.

94.—(1) The Chief Justice shall be appointed by the Governor-General by instrument under the Public Seal on the recommendation of the Prime Minister after consultation with the Leader of the Opposition. Appointment of Justices of Supreme Court.

(2) The other Justices of the Supreme Court shall be appointed by the Governor-General by instrument under the Public Seal acting on the advice of the Judicial and Legal Service Commission.

(3) The qualifications for appointment as a Justice of the Supreme Court shall be such as may be prescribed by any law for the time being in force:

Provided that a person who has been appointed as a Justice of the Supreme Court may continue in office notwithstanding any subsequent variations in the qualifications so prescribed.

95.—(1) If the office of Chief Justice is vacant or if the Chief Justice is for any reason unable to perform the functions of his office, then, until a person has been appointed to that office and assumed its functions or, as the case may be, until the Chief Justice has resumed those functions, they shall be performed by such other person, qualified under paragraph (3) of Article 94 of this Constitution for appointment as a Justice, as the Governor-General, acting in accordance with the advice of the Prime Minister may appoint for that purpose by instrument under the Public Seal. Acting Justices.

(2) If the office of a Justice of the Supreme Court is vacant, or if any such Justice is appointed to act as Chief Justice or as a Justice of Appeal, or is for any reason unable to perform the functions of his office, the Governor-General, acting on the advice of the Judicial and Legal Service Commission, may by instrument under the Public Seal appoint a person qualified under paragraph (3) of Article 94 of this Constitution for appointment as a Justice to act as a Justice of the Supreme Court, and any person so appointed shall, subject to the provisions of paragraph (5) of Article 96 of this Constitution, continue

to act for the period of his appointment or, if no such period is specified, until his appointment is revoked by the Governor-General acting on the advice of the Judicial and Legal Service Commission.

(3) Any person appointed to act as a Justice under the provisions of this Article may, notwithstanding that the period of his appointment has expired or his appointment has been revoked, sit as a Justice for the purpose of delivering judgment or doing any other thing in relation to proceedings which were commenced before him while he was so acting.

Tenure of office of Justices of Supreme Court.

96.—(1) Subject to the provisions of paragraphs (4) to (7) (inclusive) of this Article, a Justice of the Supreme Court shall hold office until he attains the age of sixty-five years:

Provided that the Governor-General, acting on the recommendation of the Prime Minister after consultation with the Leader of the Opposition, may permit a Justice who attains the age of sixty-five years to continue in office until he has attained such later age, not exceeding sixty-seven years, as may (before the Justice has attained the age of sixty-five years) have been agreed between them.

(2) Notwithstanding that he has attained the age at which he is required by or under the provisions of this Article to vacate his office, a person holding the office of Justice of the Supreme Court may, with the permission of the Governor-General, acting in accordance with the advice of the Prime Minister, continue in office for such period after attaining that age as may be necessary to enable him to deliver judgment or to do any other thing in relation to proceedings that were commenced before him before he attained that age.

(3) Nothing done by a Justice of the Supreme Court shall be invalid by reason only that he has attained the age at which he is required by this Article to vacate his office.

(4) A Justice of the Supreme Court may be removed from office only for inability to discharge the functions of his office (whether arising from infirmity of body or mind or any other cause) or for misbehaviour, and shall not be so removed except in accordance with the provisions of paragraph (5) of this Article.

(5) A Justice of the Supreme Court shall be removed from office by the Governor-General by instrument under the Public Seal if the question of the removal of that Justice from office has, at the request of the Governor-General, made in pursuance of paragraph (6) of this Article, been referred by Her Majesty to the Judicial Committee of Her Majesty's Privy Council and the Judicial Committee has advised Her Majesty that the Justice ought to be removed from office for inability as aforesaid or for misbehaviour.

(6) If the Prime Minister (in the case of the Chief Justice) or the Chief Justice after consultation with the Prime Minister (in the case of any other Justice) represents to the Governor-General that the question of removing a Justice of the Supreme Court from office for inability as aforesaid or for misbehaviour ought to be investigated, then—

(a) the Governor-General shall appoint a tribunal, which shall consist of a Chairman and not less than two other members, selected by the Governor-General acting in accordance with the advice of the Prime Minister (in the case of the Chief Justice) or of the Chief Justice (in the case of any other Justice) from among persons who hold or have held high judicial office ;

(b) that tribunal shall enquire into the matter and report on the facts thereof to the Governor-General and recommend to the Governor-General whether he should request that the question of the removal of that Justice should be referred by Her Majesty to the Judicial Committee ; and

(c) if the tribunal so recommends, the Governor-General shall request that the question should be referred accordingly.

(7) The provisions of the Commissions of Inquiry Act(a) as in force immediately before the appointed day shall, subject to the provisions of this Article, apply as nearly as may be in relation to tribunals appointed under paragraph (6) of this Article or, as the context may require, to the members thereof as they apply in relation to the Commissions or Commissioners appointed under that Act, and for that purpose shall have effect as if they formed part of this Constitution.

(8) If the question of removing a Justice of the Supreme Court from office has been referred to a tribunal appointed under paragraph (6) of this Article, the Governor-General, acting in accordance with the advice of the Prime Minister (in the case of the Chief Justice) or of the Chief Justice after the Chief Justice has consulted with the Prime Minister (in the case of any other Justice), may suspend the Justice from performing the functions of his office.

(9) Any such suspension may at any time be revoked by the Governor-General, acting in accordance with the advice of the Prime Minister or the Chief Justice (as the case may be), and shall in any case cease to have effect—

(a) if the tribunal recommends to the Governor-General that he should not request that the question of the removal of the Justice from office should be referred by Her Majesty to the Judicial Committee ; or

(b) the Judicial Committee advises Her Majesty that the Justice ought not to be removed from office.

(10) The provisions of this Article shall be without prejudice to the provisions of paragraph (2) of Article 95 of this Constitution.

97. A Justice of the Supreme Court shall not enter upon the duties of his office unless he has taken and subscribed the oath of allegiance and a judicial oath in such form as is prescribed by any law in force in The Bahamas.

Oaths to be taken by Justices of Supreme Court.

PART 2

Court of Appeal

98.—(1) There shall be a Court of Appeal for The Bahamas which shall have such jurisdiction and powers as may be conferred upon it by this Constitution or any other law.

Establishment of Court of Appeal.

(a) Statute Law of the Bahama Islands, Revised Edition 1965. Cap. 180.

(2) The Justices of Appeal of the Court of Appeal shall be—

(*a*) a President ;

(*b*) the Chief Justice by virtue of his office as head of the Judiciary but who, however, shall not sit in the Court of Appeal, unless he has been invited so to sit by the President of the Court ; and

(*c*) such number of other Justices of Appeal as may be prescribed by Parliament.

(3) No office of Justice of Appeal shall be abolished while there is a substantive holder thereof.

(4) The Court of Appeal shall be a superior court of record and, save as otherwise provided by Parliament, shall have all the powers of such a court.

Justices of the Court of Appeal.
99.—(1) The President of the Court of Appeal and other Justices of Appeal shall be appointed by the Governor-General by instrument under the Public Seal on the recommendation of the Prime Minister after consultation with the Leader of the Opposition.

(2) The qualifications for appointment as a Justice of Appeal shall be such as may be prescribed by any law for the time being in force:

Provided that—

(i) a person shall not be qualified for appointment as a Justice of Appeal unless he holds or has held high judicial office ; and

(ii) a person who has been appointed as a Justice of Appeal may continue in office notwithstanding any subsequent variations in the qualifications so prescribed.

Other arrangements for appeals.
100.—(1) Notwithstanding anything contained in this Part of this Chapter, Parliament may make provision—

(*a*) for implementing arrangements made between the Government of The Bahamas and the Government or Governments of any other part or parts of the Commonwealth relating to the establishment of a court of appeal to be shared by The Bahamas with that part or those parts of the Commonwealth, and for the hearing and determination by such a court of appeal of appeals from decisions of any court in The Bahamas ; or

(*b*) for the hearing and determination of appeals from decisions of any court in The Bahamas by a court established for any other part of the Commonwealth.

(2) A law enacted in pursuance of paragraph (1) of this Article may provide that the jurisdiction conferred on any such court as is referred to in that paragraph shall be to the exclusion, in whole or in part, of the jurisdiction of the Court of Appeal established by this Part of this Chapter ; and during any period when jurisdiction is so conferred to the exclusion of the whole jurisdiction of the said Court of Appeal, Parliament may suspend the provisions of this Part establishing that Court.

(3) In paragraph (1) of this Article the expression " any court in The Bahamas " includes the Court of Appeal established by this Part of this Chapter.

101.—(1) If the office of President of the Court of Appeal is vacant or if the President of the Court of Appeal is for any reason unable to perform the functions of his office, then, until a person has been appointed to that office and assumed its functions or, as the case may be, until the President of the Court of Appeal has resumed those functions, they shall be performed by such other person, qualified under paragraph (2) of Article 99 of this Constitution for appointment as a Justice of Appeal, as the Governor-General, acting in accordance with the advice of the Prime Minister, may appoint for that purpose by instrument under the Public Seal.

Acting Justices of Court of Appeal.

(2) If the office of a Justice of Appeal (other than the President) is vacant, or if any such Justice is appointed to act as President of the Court of Appeal, or is for any reason unable to perform the functions of his office, the Governor-General, acting on the advice of the Judicial and Legal Service Commission, may by instrument under the Public Seal appoint a person qualified under paragraph (2) of Article 99 of this Constitution for appointment as a Justice of Appeal to act as a Justice of Appeal, and any person so appointed shall, subject to the provisions of paragraph (5) of Article 102 of this Constitution, continue to act for the period of his appointment or, if no such period is specified, until his appointment is revoked by the Governor-General acting on the advice of the Judicial and Legal Service Commission.

(3) Any person appointed to act as a Justice of Appeal under the provisions of this Article may, notwithstanding that the period of his appointment has expired or his appointment has been revoked, sit as a Justice for the purpose of delivering judgment or doing any other thing in relation to proceedings which were commenced before him while he was so acting.

102.—(1) Subject to the provisions of paragraph (4) to (7) (inclusive) of this Article, a Justice of Appeal shall hold office until he attains the age of sixty-eight years:

Tenure of office of Justices of Appeal.

Provided that the Governor-General, acting on the recommendation of the Prime Minister after consultation with the Leader of the Opposition, may permit a Justice of Appeal who attains the age of sixty-eight years to continue in office until he has attained such later age, not exceeding seventy years, as may (before the Justice of Appeal has attained the age of sixty-eight years) have been agreed between them.

(2) Notwithstanding that he has attained the age at which he is required by or under the provisions of this Article to vacate his office, a person holding the office of Justice of Appeal may, with the permission of the Governor-General, acting in accordance with the advice of the Prime Minister, continue in office for such period after attaining that age as may be necessary to enable him to deliver judgment or to do any other thing in relation to proceedings that were commenced before him before he attained that age.

(3) Nothing done by a Justice of Appeal shall be invalid by reason only that he has attained the age at which he is required by this Article to vacate his office.

(4) A Justice of Appeal may be removed from office only for inability to discharge the functions of his office (whether arising from infirmity

of body or mind or any other cause) or for misbehaviour, and shall not be so removed except in accordance with the provisions of paragraph (5) of this Article.

(5) A Justice of Appeal shall be removed from office by the Governor-General by instrument under the Public Seal if the question of the removal of that Justice of Appeal from office has, at the request of the Governor-General made in pursuance of paragraph (6) of this Article, been referred by Her Majesty to the Judicial Committee of Her Majesty's Privy Council and the Judicial Committee has advised Her Majesty that the Justice of Appeal ought to be removed from office for inability as aforesaid or for misbehaviour.

(6) If the Prime Minister (in the case of the President of the Court of Appeal) or the President of the Court of Appeal or the Chief Justice after consultation with the Prime Minister (in the case of any other Justice of Appeal) represents to the Governor-General that the question of removing a Justice of Appeal from office for inability as aforesaid or for misbehaviour ought to be investigated, then—

(a) the Governor-General shall appoint a tribunal, which shall consist of a Chairman and not less than two other members, selected by the Governor-General acting in accordance with the advice of the Prime Minister (in the case of the President of the Court of Appeal) or of the President of the Court of Appeal (in the case of any other Justice of Appeal) from among persons who hold or have held high judicial office ;

(b) that tribunal shall enquire into the matter and report on the facts thereof to the Governor-General and recommend to the Governor-General whether he should request that the question of the removal of that Justice of Appeal should be referred by Her Majesty to the Judicial Committee ; and

(c) if the tribunal so recommends, the Governor-General shall request that the question should be referred accordingly.

(7) The provisions of the Commissions of Inquiry Act(a) as in force immediately before the appointed day shall, subject to the provisions of this Article, apply as nearly as may be in relation to tribunals appointed under paragraph (6) of this Article or, as the context may require, to the members thereof as they apply in relation to Commissions or Commissioners appointed under that Act, and for that purpose shall have effect as if they formed part of this Constitution.

(8) If the question of removing a Justice of Appeal from office has been referred to a tribunal appointed under paragraph (6) of this Article, the Governor-General acting in accordance with the advice of the Prime Minister (in the case of the President of the Court of Appeal) or of the President of the Court of Appeal after the President of the Court of Appeal has consulted with the Prime Minister (in the case of any other Justice of Appeal), may suspend the Justice of Appeal from performing the functions of his office.

(9) Any such suspension may at any time be revoked by the Governor-General, acting in accordance with the advice of the Prime Minister or the President of the Court of Appeal (as the case may be), and shall in any case cease to have effect if—

(a) Statute Law of the Bahama Islands, Revised Edition 1965, Cap. 180.

(*a*) the tribunal recommends to the Governor-General that he should not request that the question of the removal of the Justice of Appeal from office should be referred by Her Majesty to the Judicial Committee ; or

(*b*) the Judicial Committee advises Her Majesty that the Justice of Appeal ought not to be removed from office.

(10) The provisions of this Article shall be without prejudice to the provisions of paragraph (2) of Article 101 of this Constitution.

(11) The provisions of this Article and of Article 103 of this Constitution shall not apply to the Chief Justice.

103. A Justice of Appeal shall not enter upon the duties of his office unless he has taken and subscribed the oath of allegiance and a judicial oath in such form as is prescribed by any law in force in The Bahamas. *Oaths to be taken by Justices of Appeal.*

Part 3

Appeals to Court of Appeal and Her Majesty in Council

104.—(1) An appeal to the Court of Appeal shall lie as of right from final decisions of the Supreme Court given in exercise of the jurisdiction conferred on the Supreme Court by Article 28 of this Constitution (which relates to the enforcement of fundamental rights and freedoms). *Appeals relating to fundamental rights and freedoms.*

(2) An appeal shall lie as of right to the Judicial Committee of Her Majesty's Privy Council or to such other court as may be prescribed by Parliament under Article 105(3) of this Constitution from any decision given by the Court of Appeal in any such case.

105.—(1) Parliament may provide for an appeal to lie from decisions of the Court of Appeal established by Part 2 of this Chapter to the Judicial Committee of Her Majesty's Privy Council or to such other court as may be prescribed by Parliament under this Article, either as of right or with the leave of the said Court of Appeal, in such cases other than those referred to in Article 104(2) of this Constitution as may be prescribed by Parliament. *Appeals to Her Majesty in Council in other cases.*

(2) Nothing in this Constitution shall affect any right of Her Majesty to grant special leave to appeal from decisions such as are referred to in paragraph (1) of this Article.

(3) Parliament may by law provide for the functions required in this Chapter to be exercised by the Judicial Committee of Her Majesty's Privy Council to be exercised by any other court established for the purpose in substitution for the Judicial Committee.

106. References in this Part to " the Court of Appeal " include references to a shared court of appeal established under Article 100(1) of this Constitution when exercising jurisdiction in respect of The Bahamas. *Interpretation of " Court of Appeal ".*

CHAPTER VIII

THE PUBLIC SERVICE

PART 1

The Public Service Commission

Establish-
ment and
composition
of Public
Service
Commission.

107.—(1) There shall be a Public Service Commission for The Bahamas which shall consist of a Chairman and not less than two nor more than four other members, who shall be appointed by the Governor-General, acting on the recommendation of the Prime Minister after consultation with the Leader of the Opposition, by instrument under the Public Seal.

(2) No person shall be qualified to be appointed as a member of the Public Service Commission if he is a member of either House or a public officer.

(3) Subject to the provisions of Article 126 of this Constitution the office of a member of the Public Service Commission shall become vacant—

(*a*) at the expiration of three years from the date of his appointment or such earlier time as may be specified in the instrument by which he was appointed ;

(*b*) if he becomes a member of either House or a public officer.

(4) If the office of Chairman of the Public Service Commission is vacant or the holder thereof is for any reason unable to perform the functions of his office then, until a person has been appointed to and has assumed the functions of that office or until the person holding that office has resumed those functions, as the case may be, they shall be performed by such one of the other members of the Commission as may for the time being be designated in that behalf by the Governor-General, acting on the recommendation of the Prime Minister after consultation with the Leader of the Opposition.

(5) If the office of a member of the Public Service Commission other than the Chairman is vacant or the holder thereof is for any reason unable to perform the functions of his office, the Governor-General, acting on the recommendation of the Prime Minister after consultation with the Leader of the Opposition, may appoint a person who is qualified for appointment as a member of the Commission to act in the office of that member ; and any person so appointed shall, subject to the provisions of sub-paragraph (3)(*b*) of this Article and Article 126 of this Constitution, continue so to act until a person has been appointed to the office in which he is acting and has assumed the functions thereof or, as the case may be, the holder thereof resumes those functions or until his appointment so to act is revoked by the Governor-General, acting as aforesaid.

(6) A former member of the Public Service Commission shall not, within a period of five years commencing with the date on which he last held or acted in that office, be eligible for appointment to any office power to make appointments to which is vested by this Constitution in the Governor-General acting on the recommendation or in accordance with the advice of the Public Service Commission.

PART 2

Appointments etc. of Public Officers

108. Subject to the provisions of this Constitution power to make appointments to public offices and to remove and to exercise disciplinary control over persons holding or acting in such offices is hereby vested in the Governor-General, acting in accordance with the advice of the Public Service Commission.

109.—(1) Notwithstanding anything contained in the preceding Article of this Chapter—

(*a*) power to make appointments to the office of Permanent Secretary or Head of a Department of Government (or to be the holder of any such other office of similar status as the Governor-General may, acting in accordance with the advice of the Prime Minister, specify by notice in the Gazette) is hereby vested in the Governor-General acting on the recommendation of the Public Service Commission after the Commission has consulted the Prime Minister ;

(*b*) power to make appointments to the office of Permanent Secretary on transfer from another such office carrying the same salary is hereby vested in the Governor-General acting on the advice of the Prime Minister.

(2) In this Article " Permanent Secretary " includes the Secretary of the Cabinet and the Financial Secretary.

110. The Governor-General acting in accordance with the advice of the Public Service Commission, may by directions given by instrument under the Public Seal delegate, to such extent and subject to such conditions as may be specified in those directions, the powers vested in him by Article 108 of this Constitution (other than powers to make appointments to the offices referred to in Article 109 of this Constitution and to remove or exercise disciplinary control over persons holding or acting in such offices) to such public officers as may be so specified.

111.—(1) Power to appoint persons to hold or act in the offices to which this Article applies (including power to make appointments on promotion and transfer and to confirm appointments) and to remove persons so appointed from any such office shall vest in the Governor-General, acting in accordance with the advice of the Prime Minister.

(2) Before tendering any advice for the purposes of this Article in relation to any person who holds or acts in any public office other than an office to which this Article applies, the Prime Minister shall consult the Service Commission which is responsible for advising in respect of appointments to the office which the person concerned holds or in which he is acting.

(3) The offices to which this Article applies are the offices of Ambassador, High Commissioner or any other principal representative of The Bahamas in any other country or accredited to any international organisation.

112.—(1) Power to make appointments on transfer to the offices to which this Article applies shall vest in the Prime Minister.

(2) The offices to which this Article applies are—

(*a*) offices, the holders of which are required to reside outside The Bahamas for the proper discharge of their functions ;

Marginal notes:

Appointments, etc. of public officers.

Appointments of Permanent Secretaries and certain other public officers.

Delegation of Governor-General's powers.

Appointments, etc. of principal representatives of The Bahamas abroad.

Appointments on transfer in respect of certain offices.

(b) such offices in the Ministry responsible for the conduct of the external affairs of The Bahamas as may, from time to time, be designated by the Prime Minister.

Appointment of Secretary to the Cabinet.

113.—(1) There shall be a Secretary to the Cabinet whose office shall be a public office.

(2) Power to appoint any person to the office of Secretary to the Cabinet and to remove such person from that office shall vest in the Governor-General acting in accordance with the advice of the Prime Minister.

(3) Before tendering advice for the purposes of this Article, the Prime Minister shall consult the Public Service Commission.

(4) The Secretary to the Cabinet shall have charge of the Cabinet Office and shall be responsible, in accordance with such instructions as may be given to him by the Prime Minister, for the supervision of any department of the Government for which the Prime Minister has responsibility.

PART 3

The Public Service Board of Appeal

Public Service Board of Appeal.

114.—(1) There shall be a Public Service Board of Appeal for The Bahamas which shall consist of the following members, who shall be appointed by instrument under the Public Seal—

(a) one member appointed by the Governor-General acting in accordance with the advice of the Chief Justice from among persons who hold or have held high judicial office or are qualified to hold high judicial office, who shall be Chairman ;

(b) one member appointed by the Governor-General acting in accordance with the advice of the Prime Minister ; and

(c) one member appointed by the Governor-General acting in accordance with the advice of the appropriate representative body.

(2) A person shall not be qualified for appointment as a member of the Board if he is a member of either House.

(3) Subject to the provisions of this Article and of Article 126 of this Constitution, the office of a member of the Board shall become vacant—

(a) at the expiration of three years from the date of his appointment ;

(b) if he becomes a member of either House.

(4) If at any time any member of the Board is for any reason unable to exercise the functions of his office, the Governor-General may appoint a person who is qualified to be appointed as a member of the Board to act as a member, and any person so appointed shall, subject to the provisions of sub-paragraph (3)(b) of this Article and Article 126 of this Constitution, continue to act until the office in which he is acting has been filled or, as the case may be, until the holder thereof has resumed his functions or until his appointment to act has been revoked by the Governor-General.

(5) The Board shall, in the exercise of its functions under this Constitution, not be subject to the direction or control of any other person or authority.

(6) In this Article " the appropriate representative body " means such body representing the interests of public officers as the Governor-General may, by Order, designate.

115.—(1) Subject to the provisions of this Article, an appeal shall lie to the Public Service Board of Appeal at the instance of the officer in respect of whom the decision is made from any decision of the Governor-General, acting in accordance with the advice of the Public Service Commission, that any public officer shall be removed from office or that any penalty should be imposed on him by way of disciplinary control. Appeals in discipline cases.

(2) Upon an appeal under paragraph (1) of this Article the Board may affirm or set aside the decision appealed from or may make any other decision which the authority or person from whom the appeal lies could have made.

(3) Every decision of the Board shall require the concurrence of a majority of all its members.

(4) Subject to the provisions of paragraph (3) of this Article, the Board may by regulations make provision for—

(a) the procedure of the Board ;

(b) the procedure in appeals under this Article ;

(c) excepting from the provisions of paragraph (1) of this Article decisions in respect of public officers holding offices whose emoluments do not exceed such sum as may be prescribed or such decisions to exercise disciplinary control, other than decisions to remove from office, as may be prescribed.

(5) Regulations made under this Article may, with the consent of the Prime Minister, confer powers or impose duties on any public officer or any authority of the Government of The Bahamas for the purpose of the exercise of the functions of the Board.

(6) The Board may, subject to the provisions of this Article and to its rules of procedure, act notwithstanding any vacancy in its membership or the absence of any member.

PART 4

The Judicial and Legal Service Commission

116.—(1) There shall be a Judicial and Legal Service Commission for The Bahamas. Establishment and composition of the Judicial and Legal Service Commission.

(2) The members of the Judicial and Legal Service Commission shall be—

(a) the Chief Justice, who shall be Chairman ;

(b) such other Justice of the Supreme Court or Justice of Appeal as may be designated by the Governor-General, acting on the recommendation of the Chief Justice, by instrument under the Public Seal ;

(c) the Chairman of the Public Service Commission ; and

(d) two persons appointed by the Governor-General by instrument under the Public Seal, acting on the recommendation of the Prime Minister after consultation with the Leader of the Opposition.

(3) Subject to the provisions of Article 126 of this Constitution, the office of a member of the Judicial and Legal Service Commission referred to in sub-paragraph (2)(*d*) of this Article shall become vacant—

(*a*) at the expiration of three years from the date of his appointment or such earlier time as may be specified in the instrument by which he was appointed ;

(*b*) if he becomes a member of either House.

(4) A person shall not be qualified to be appointed as a member of the Commission under subparagraph (2)(*d*) of this Article unless he holds or is qualified to hold or has held high judicial office ; and a person shall be disqualified for appointment as such if he is a member of either House.

(5) If the office of Chairman of the Judicial and Legal Service Commission is vacant or the holder thereof is for any reason unable to perform the functions of his office, then, until a person has been appointed to and has assumed the functions of that office or until the person holding that office has resumed those functions, as the case may be, they shall be performed by such one of the other members of the Commission as may for the time being be designated in that behalf by the Governor-General, acting on the recommendation of the Chief Justice, or, if he is for any reason incapacitated from making a recommendation, of the other Justice of the Supreme Court or Justice of Appeal who is a member of the Commission.

(6) If at any time one of the members of the Commission referred to in sub-paragraphs (2)(*b*), (*c*) or (*d*) of this Article is for any reason unable to exercise the functions of his office, the Governor-General, in the case of the Chairman of the Public Service Commission, may appoint another member of the Public Service Commission to act as a member, and in the case of a member referred to in sub-paragraphs (2)(*b*) or (*d*) of this Article may, acting on the same recommendation as for the appointment of that member, appoint a person who is qualified to be appointed as a member of the Commission to act as a member. Any person so appointed shall, subject to the provisions of sub-paragraph (3)(*b*) of this Article and Article 126 of this Constitution, continue to act until the office in which he is acting has been filled or, as the case may be, until the holder thereof has resumed his functions or until his appointment to act has been revoked by the Governor-General, acting as aforesaid.

Appointments, etc. of judicial and legal officers.

117.—(1) Subject to the provisions of this Constitution, power to make appointments to public offices to which this Article applies and to remove and to exercise disciplinary control over persons holding or acting in such offices is hereby vested in the Governor-General acting in accordance with the advice of the Judicial and Legal Service Commission.

(2) This Article applies to such public offices for appointment to which persons are required to possess legal qualifications as may be prescribed by Parliament.

PART 5

The Police Service Commission

118.—(1) There shall be a Police Service Commission for the Bahamas which shall consist of a Chairman and two other members appointed by the Governor-General acting on the recommendation of the Prime Minister after consultation with the Leader of the Opposition, by instrument under the Public Seal.

(2) No person shall be qualified to be appointed as a member of the Police Service Commission if he is a member of either House or a public officer.

(3) Subject to the provisions of Article 126 of this Constitution, the office of a member of the Police Service Commission shall become vacant—

(*a*) at the expiration of three years from the date of his appointment or at such earlier time as may be specified in the instrument by which he was appointed ;

(*b*) if he becomes a member of either House or a public officer.

(4) If the office of Chairman of the Police Service Commission is vacant or the holder thereof is for any reason unable to perform the functions of his office, then, until a person has been appointed to and has assumed the functions of that office or until the person holding that office has resumed those functions, as the case may be, they shall be performed by such one of the other members of the Commission as may for the time being be designated in that behalf by the Governor-General, acting on the recommendation of the Prime Minister after consultation with the Leader of the Opposition.

(5) If the office of a member of the Police Service Commission other than the Chairman is vacant or the holder thereof is for any reason unable to perform the functions thereof, the Governor-General, acting on the recommendation of the Prime Minister after consultation with the Leader of the Opposition, may appoint a person who is qualified for appointment as a member of the Commission to act in the office of that member ; and any person so appointed shall, subject to the provisions of sub-paragraph (3)(*b*) of this Article and Article 126 of this Constitution, continue so to act until a person has been appointed to the office in which he is acting and has assumed the functions thereof or, as the case may be, the holder thereof resumes those functions or until his appointment so to act is revoked by the Governor-General, acting as aforesaid.

Establishment and composition of the Police Service Commission.

119.—(1) Power to make appointments to the offices of Commissioner of Police and Deputy Commissioner of Police shall be vested in the Governor-General acting on the recommendation of the Prime Minister after consultation with the Leader of the Opposition.

(2) Save as provided under paragraph (1) of this Article power to make appointments to offices in the Police Force of or above the rank of Assistant Commissioner of Police is vested in the Governor-General acting on the recommendation of the Prime Minister after consultation with the Police Service Commission.

Appointment of Commissioner of Police and other officers of the Police Force.

(3) Save as provided in the preceding paragraphs of this Article, power to make appointments to offices in the Police Force of or above the rank of Inspector is vested in the Governor-General, acting on the advice of the Police Service Commission.

(4) There shall be in the Police Force such number of Police Promotion Boards, each consisting of officers in the Police Force above the rank of Inspector, as may be prescribed by regulations made under this paragraph.

(5) Power to make appointments to offices in the Police Force below the rank of Inspector shall be vested in the Commissioner of Police acting after consultation with a Police Promotion Board.

(6) Power to make postings and appointments on transfer within the Police Force of officers in that Force shall be vested in the Commissioner of Police.

Removal of the Commissioner and Deputy Commissioner of Police.

120.—(1) The Commissioner of Police and Deputy Commissioner of Police may be removed from office by the Governor-General but shall not be removed except in accordance with the provisions of paragraph (2) of this Article.

(2) The Commissioner of Police or Deputy Commissioner of Police shall be removed from office by the Governor-General if the question of his removal from office has been referred to a tribunal appointed under paragraph (3) of this Article and the tribunal has recommended to the Governor-General that he ought to be removed from office.

(3) If the Prime Minister represents to the Governor-General that the question of removing the Commissioner of Police or Deputy Commissioner of Police from office ought to be investigated, then—

(a) the Governor-General acting in accordance with the advice of the Prime Minister shall suspend the Commissioner of Police or Deputy Commissioner of Police from performing the functions of his office, as the case may be ;

(b) the Governor-General shall appoint a tribunal, which shall consist of a chairman and not less than two other members, selected by the Governor-General, acting in accordance with the advice of the Judicial and Legal Service Commission, from among persons who hold or have held or are eligible to hold high judicial office ; and

(c) the tribunal shall enquire into the matter and report on the facts thereof to the Governor-General whether the Commissioner of Police or Deputy Commissioner of Police ought to be removed from office.

(4) If the question of removing the Commissioner of Police or Deputy Commissioner of Police from office has been referred to a tribunal under paragraph (3) of this Article, the Governor-General shall revoke any such suspension if the tribunal recommends to the Governor-General that the Commissioner of Police or Deputy Commissioner of Police should not be removed from office.

Removal and discipline of members of the Force.

121.—(1) Save as provided under Article 120 of this Constitution, power to remove and to exercise disciplinary control over persons holding or acting in the offices of or above the rank of Assistant

Commissioner in the Police Force is vested in the Governor-General acting in accordance with the advice of the Police Service Commission after consultation with the Prime Minister.

(2) Save as provided in Article 120 of this Constitution and paragraphs (1) and (3) of this Article, power to remove and exercise disciplinary control over persons holding or acting in offices in the Police Force is vested in the Governor-General acting in accordance with the advice of the Police Service Commission.

(3) The following powers are vested in the Commissioner of Police—

(a) in respect of officers of or above the rank of Assistant Superintendent, the power to administer reprimands ;

(b) in respect of Inspectors, the power to exercise disciplinary control other than removal or reduction in rank ; and

(c) in respect of officers below the rank of Inspector, the power to exercise disciplinary control including the power of removal.

(4) The Commissioner of Police may, by directions in writing, and subject to such conditions as he thinks fit, delegate to any officer of the Police Force of or above the rank of Inspector any of his powers under sub-paragraph (3)(c) of this Article other than the power of removal ; but an appeal from any award of punishment by such officer shall lie to the Commissioner.

(5) Parliament may by law provide that an appeal shall lie to the Governor-General from a decision of the Commissioner of Police to remove or exercise disciplinary control over persons holding or acting in offices in the Police Force in such cases as may be prescribed by such law, and in determining any such appeal the Governor-General shall act in accordance with the advice of the Police Service Commission.

PART 6

Pensions

122.—(1) Subject to the provisions of Articles 123 and 124 of this Constitution, the law applicable to the grant and payment to any officer, or to his widow, children, dependants or personal representatives, of any pension, compensation, gratuity or other like allowance (in this Article and Articles 123 and 124 of this Constitution referred to as an " award ") in respect of the service of that officer in a public office shall be that in force on the relevant date or any later law that is not less favourable to that person.

Protection of pension rights.

(2) In paragraph (1) of this Article " the relevant date " means—

(a) in relation to an award granted before 10th July 1973, the date on which the award was granted ;

(b) in relation to an award granted or to be granted on or after 10th July 1973 to or in respect of any person who was a public officer before that date, 9th July 1973 ;

(c) in relation to an award granted or to be granted to or in respect of any person who becomes a public officer on or after 10th July 1973, the date on which he becomes a public officer.

(3) Where a person is entitled to exercise an option as to which of two or more laws shall apply in his case, the law specified by him in exercising the option shall, for the purposes of this Article, be deemed to be more favourable to him than the other law or laws.

(4) Awards granted under any law in respect of service in a public office (not being awards that are a charge upon some other public fund of The Bahamas) are hereby charged on the Consolidated Fund.

(5) For the purposes of this Article and of Articles 123 and 124 of this Constitution, service as a Justice of the Supreme Court or Justice of Appeal shall be deemed to be service in the public service.

Grant and withholding of pensions, etc.

123.—(1) The power to grant any award under any pensions law for the time being in force in The Bahamas (other than an award to which, under that law, the person to whom it is payable is entitled as of right) and, in accordance with any provisions in that behalf contained in any such law, to withhold, reduce in amount or suspend any award payable under any such law is hereby vested in the Governor-General.

(2) The power vested in the Governor-General by paragraph (1) of this Article shall be exercised by him on the recommendation of the appropriate Service Commission.

(3) The appropriate Service Commission shall not recommend to the Governor-General that any award for which a person who holds or has held the office of a Justice of the Supreme Court or Justice of Appeal or Auditor-General is eligible shall not be granted, or that any award payable to him shall be withheld, reduced in amount or suspended, on the ground that he has been guilty of misbehaviour unless he has been removed from office by reason of such misbehaviour.

(4) In this Article and in Article 124 of this Constitution " the appropriate Service Commission " means—

(a) in the case of an award that may be granted or is payable to a person who, having been a public officer, was immediately before the date on which he ceased to hold public office serving—

(i) as a Justice of the Supreme Court or Justice of Appeal ;

(ii) in any public office to which the provisions of Article 117 of this Constitution applied on that date,

the Judicial and Legal Service Commission ;

(b) in the case of an award that may be granted or is payable to a person who, having been a public officer, was immediately before the date on which he ceased to hold public office, serving as a member of the Police Force, the Police Service Commission ;

(c) in any other case the Public Service Commission.

(5) In this Article " pension law " means any law relating to the grant to any person or to the widow, children, dependants or personal representatives of that person, of an award of any pension, compensation, gratuity or other like allowance in respect of the service of that person in a public office and includes any instrument made under any such law.

124.—(1) The provisions of this Article shall have effect for the purpose of enabling an officer or his personal representatives to appeal against any of the following decisions, that is to say :— Appeals in respect of certain decisions affecting pensions benefits.

(a) a decision of the appropriate Service Commission embodying a recommendation in respect of an officer, under Article 123(2) of this Constitution, not to grant, or to withhold, reduce in amount or suspend, an award ;

(b) a decision of any authority to remove an officer from office if the consequence of the removal is that an award cannot be granted in respect of the officer's service in a public office ; or

(c) a decision of any authority to take some other disciplinary action in relation to such an officer if the consequence of the action is or in the opinion of the authority might be, to reduce the amount of any award that may be granted in respect of the officer's service in a public office.

(2) Where any such decision as is referred to in paragraph (1) of this Article is taken by any Commission or authority, the Commission or authority shall cause to be delivered to the officer concerned, or to his personal representatives, a written notice of that decision stating the time, not being less than twenty-eight days from the date on which the notice is delivered, within which he, or his personal representatives, may apply to the Commission or authority for the case to be referred to the Public Service Board of Appeal.

(3) The Board shall inquire into the facts of the case, and for that purpose—

(a) shall, if the applicant so requests in writing, hear the applicant either in person or by a legal representative of his choice, according to the terms of the request, and shall consider any representations that he wishes to make in writing ;

(b) may hear any other person who, in the opinion of the Board, is able to give the Board information on the case ; and

(c) shall have access to, and shall consider, all documents that were available to the Commission or authority concerned and shall also consider any further document relating to the case that may be produced by or on behalf of the applicant or the Commission or authority.

(4) When the Board has completed its consideration of the case, then—

(a) if the decision that is the subject of reference to the Board is such a decision as is mentioned in sub-paragraph (1)(a) of this Article, the Board shall advise the appropriate Service Commission or authority whether the decision should be affirmed, reversed or modified and the Commission or authority shall act in accordance with that advice ; and

(b) if the decision that is the subject of the reference to the Board is such a decision as is referred to in sub-paragraph (1)(b) or (c) of this Article, the Board shall not have power to advise the Commission or authority concerned to affirm, reverse or modify the decision but—

(i) where the officer has been removed from office the Board may direct that there shall be granted all or any part of the award that, under any law, might have been granted in respect of his service in a public office if he had retired voluntarily at the date of his removal and may direct that any law with respect to awards shall in any other respect that the Board may specify have effect as if he had so retired ; and

(ii) where some other disciplinary action has been taken in relation to the officer the Board may direct that, on the grant of any award under any law in respect of the officer's service in a public office, that award shall be increased by such amount or shall be calculated in such manner as the Board may specify in order to offset all or any part of the reduction in the amount of that award that, in the opinion of the Board, would or might otherwise be a consequence of the disciplinary action,

and any direction given by the Board under this sub-paragraph shall be complied with notwithstanding the provisions of any other law.

(5) If the appeal relates to a case in which the officer exercises his right of appeal to the Board under Article 115(1) of this Constitution, the Board shall first consider his appeal under that Article and only if it decides to affirm the decision or to make some other decision the consequence of which would be to affect the officer's award, shall the Board proceed to consider the officer's appeal under this Article.

(6) For the purposes of this Article—

(a) " legal representative " means a person entitled to practise in The Bahamas as a Counsel and Attorney of the Supreme Court ; and

(b) a notice shall be deemed to have been delivered to an officer one week after it has been posted if, in the case of an officer on pension and resident outside The Bahamas whose residential address cannot be ascertained, it has been posted addressed to him at the address to which his pension is being paid.

PART 7

Miscellaneous

Procedure of Commissions.

125.—(1) In relation to any Commission established by this Chapter, the Governor-General, acting in accordance with the advice of the Commission, may by regulation or otherwise regulate its procedure and, subject to the consent of the Prime Minister, confer powers and impose duties on any public officer or any authority of the Government for the purpose of the discharge of the functions of the Commission.

(2) At any meeting of any Commission established by this Chapter a quorum shall be constituted if a majority of the members are present ; and, if a quorum is present, the Commission shall not be disqualified for the transaction of business by reason of any vacancy among its members or the absence of any member, and any proceedings of the Commission shall be valid notwithstanding that some person who was not entitled so to do took part therein.

(3) Any question proposed for decision at any meeting of any Commission established by this Chapter shall be determined by a majority of the votes of the members thereof present and voting, and if on any such question the votes are equally divided the member presiding shall have and exercise a casting vote.

(4) Any question whether—

(a) any Commission established by this Chapter has validly performed any function vested in it by or under this Chapter ;

(b) any person has validly performed any function delegated to him ; or

(c) any member of such a Commission or any other person or authority has validly performed any other function in relation to the work of the Commission,

shall not be enquired into in any court.

126.—(1) A member of a Commission established under this Chapter may be removed from office only for inability to exercise the functions of his office (whether arising from infirmity of body or mind or any other cause) or for misbehaviour and shall not be so removed except in accordance with the provisions of this Article.

Removal from office of certain persons.

(2) A member of a Commission shall be removed from office by the Governor-General if the question of his removal from office has been referred to a tribunal appointed under paragraph (3) of this Article and the tribunal has recommended to the Governor-General that he ought to be removed from office for inability as aforesaid or for misbehaviour.

(3) If the Governor-General, acting in accordance with the advice of the prescribed authority, considers that the question of removing a member of a Commission under this Article ought to be investigated, then—

(a) the Governor-General, acting in accordance with the advice of the prescribed authority shall appoint a tribunal which shall consist of a chairman and not less than two other members, selected by the Chief Justice, or where the question concerns the Chairman of the Judicial and Legal Service Commission by the President of the Court of Appeal, from among persons who hold or have held or are qualified to hold office as a Justice of the Supreme Court ; and

(b) the tribunal shall enquire into the matter and report on the facts thereof to the Governor-General and recommend to him whether the member ought to be removed under this Article.

(4) If the question of removing a member of a Commission has been referred to a tribunal under this Article, the Governor-General, acting in accordance with the advice of the prescribed authority, may suspend that member from the exercise of the functions of his office and any such suspension may be at any time revoked by the Governor-General, and shall in any case cease to have effect if the tribunal recommends to the Governor-General that that member should not be removed.

(5) In this Article—

" Commission " includes the Public Service Board of Appeal ;

" the prescribed authority " means—

(a) in relation to the Public Service Commission or the Judicial and Legal Service Commission, the Prime Minister when the question concerns the Chairman of either of those Commissions, and the Chairman of the Commission concerned when the question concerns any other member of either of those Commissions ; and

(b) in relation to the Public Service Board of Appeal or the Police Service Commission, the Prime Minister.

Public Service.

127. In this Constitution references to the public service shall not be construed as including service in—

(a) the office of Governor-General, Prime Minister or other Minister, Parliamentary Secretary, Leader of the Opposition, President and Vice-President of the Senate, Senator, Speaker and Deputy Speaker of the House of Assembly, or member of the House of Assembly ;

(b) the office of a member of the Public Service Commission, the Public Service Board of Appeal, the Judicial and Legal Service Commission or the Police Service Commission ;

(c) the staff of the Department of Tourism or of any other department or agency of the Government established for special purposes by any law which specifies that offices therein shall not be public offices for the purposes of this Constitution ;

(d) the office of a member of any board, committee or other similar body (whether incorporated or not) established by any law in force in The Bahamas ; or

(e) except as otherwise provided in this Constitution the office of a Justice of the Supreme Court, a Justice of Appeal or any office on the personal staff of the Governor-General.

CHAPTER IX

FINANCE

Consolidated Fund.

128. There shall be in and for The Bahamas a Consolidated Fund, into which, subject to the provisions of any law for the time being in force in The Bahamas, shall be paid all revenues of The Bahamas.

Estimates.

129.—(1) The Minister of Finance shall, before the end of each financial year, cause to be prepared annual estimates of revenue and expenditure for public services during the succeeding financial year, which shall be laid before the House of Assembly.

(2) The estimates of expenditure shall show separately the sums required to meet statutory expenditure (as defined in Article 130(7) of this Constitution) and the sums required to meet other expenditure proposed to be paid out of the Consolidated Fund.

Authority for Public Expenditure.

130.—(1) The Minister of Finance shall, in respect of each financial year, at the earliest convenient moment before the commencement of that financial year, introduce in the House of Assembly an Appropriation Bill containing, under appropriate heads for the several services required, the estimated aggregate sums which are proposed to be expended (otherwise than by way of statutory expenditure) during that financial year.

(2) Subject to paragraphs (4) and (6) of this Article, the sums set out in the Appropriation Act in respect of a financial year shall represent the limit and extent of the public expenditure for that financial year.

(3) Where any sum is set out in the Appropriation Act in respect of a financial year and at the end of that year there is an unexpended balance of that sum, the unexpended balance shall lapse.

(4) The Minister of Finance may, in case of necessity, from time to time cause to be prepared supplementary estimates of expenditure which shall be laid before and voted on by the House of Assembly.

(5) In respect of all supplementary expenditure voted on by the House of Assembly in pursuance of paragraph (4) of this Article, the Minister of Finance may, at any time before the end of the financial year, introduce into the House of Assembly a Supplementary Appropriation Bill containing, under appropriate heads, the aggregate sums so voted and shall, as soon as possible after the end of each financial year, introduce into the House of Assembly a final Appropriation Bill containing any such sums which have not yet been included in any Appropriation Bill.

(6) That part of any estimate of expenditure laid before the House of Assembly which shows statutory expenditure shall not be voted on by the House, and such expenditure shall, without further authority of Parliament, be paid out of the Consolidated Fund.

(7) For the purposes of this Article and Article 129 of this Constitution—

(a) " financial year " means any period of twelve months beginning on 1st January in any year or such other date as Parliament may prescribe ; and

(b) " statutory expenditure " means expenditure charged on the Consolidated Fund or on the general revenues and assets of The Bahamas by any provision of this Constitution or of any other law for the time being in force in The Bahamas.

131. No sum shall be paid out of the Consolidated Fund except upon the authority of a warrant under the hand of the Minister of Finance or under the hand of some person authorised by him in writing ; and sums so issued shall be disposed of for meeting public expenditure authorised under Article 130 of this Constitution or, in the case of statutory expenditure, for the purposes appointed by law. *Withdrawal of money from the Consolidated Fund.*

132. Where at any time for any justifiable reason, the Appropriation Bill in respect of any financial year has not come into operation by the beginning of that financial year, the Minister of Finance may, to such an extent and subject to such conditions as may be prescribed, or if no conditions have been prescribed on a resolution to that effect passed by the House of Assembly, issue a warrant for the payment out of the Consolidated Fund or other public funds of The Bahamas of such sums as he may consider necessary for the continuance of the public service, but a statement of the sums so authorised shall, as soon as practicable, be laid before and voted on by the House of Assembly and the aggregate sums so voted shall be included, under the appropriate heads, in the next Appropriation Bill immediately following. *Withdrawal of money in advance of Appropriation Act.*

Contingencies Fund.

133.—(1) Parliament may by law provide for the establishment of a Contingencies Fund and may authorise the Minister of Finance to make advances from that Fund if he is satisfied that there is an unforeseen need for expenditure for which no provision or no sufficient provision has been made by an Appropriation Act.

(2) Where any advances are made by virtue of an authorisation conferred under paragraph (1) of this Article, a supplementary estimate of the sums required to replace the amount so advanced shall, as soon as practicable, be laid before and voted on by the House of Assembly and the sums so voted shall be included in a Supplementary Appropriation Bill or a Final Appropriation Bill.

Public Debt.

134. The Public Debt of The Bahamas, including the interest on that debt, sinking fund payments and redemption monies in respect of that debt and the costs, charges and expenses incidental to the management of that debt, is hereby charged on the Consolidated Fund.

Remuneration of Governor-General and certain other officers.

135.—(1) There shall be paid to the holders of the offices to which this Article applies such salaries and allowances as may be prescribed by or under any law.

(2) The salaries payable to the holders of the offices to which this Article applies are hereby charged on the Consolidated Fund.

(3) The salary and allowances payable to the holder of any office to which this Article applies and his other terms of service shall not be altered to his disadvantage after his appointment, and, for the purposes of this paragraph, in so far as the terms of service of any person depend upon the option of that person, the terms for which he opts shall be taken to be more advantageous to him than any other terms for which he might have opted.

(4) This Article applies to the offices of Governor-General, Justice of the Supreme Court, Justice of Appeal, Auditor-General and member of any Commission established by Chapter VIII of this Constitution or of the Public Service Board of Appeal.

Establishment of office and functions of Auditor-General.

136.—(1) There shall be an Auditor-General whose office shall be a public office.

(2) The Auditor-General shall be appointed by the Governor-General, by instrument under the Public Seal, acting on the recommendation of the Public Service Commission made after the Commission has consulted the Prime Minister.

(3) The accounts of the Supreme Court, the Senate, the House of Assembly, all departments and offices of the Government (but excluding the Department of the Auditor-General), the Public Service Commission, the Judicial and Legal Service Commission, the Police Service Commission and all Magistrates' Courts shall, at least once in every year, be audited and reported on by the Auditor-General who, with his subordinate staff, shall at all times be entitled to have access to all books, records, returns and reports relating to such accounts.

(4) The Auditor-General shall submit his reports made under paragraph (3) of this Article without undue delay to the Speaker (or, if the office of Speaker is vacant or the Speaker is for any reason unable to

perform the functions of his office, to the Deputy Speaker) who shall cause them to be laid before the House of Assembly without undue delay.

(5) In the exercise of his functions under the provisions of paragraphs (3) and (4) of this Article, the Auditor-General shall not be subject to the direction or control of any other person or authority.

(6) The accounts of the department of the Auditor-General shall be audited and reported on by the Minister of Finance and the provisions of paragraphs (3) and (4) of this Article shall apply in relation to the exercise by that Minister of those functions as they apply in relation to audits and reports made by the Auditor-General.

(7) Nothing in this Article shall prevent the performance by the Auditor-General of—

(a) such other functions in relation to the accounts of the Government and the accounts of other public authorities and other bodies administering public funds in The Bahamas as may be prescribed by or under any law for the time being in force in The Bahamas ; or

(b) such other functions in relation to the supervision and control of expenditure from public funds in The Bahamas as may be so prescribed.

(8) The Auditor-General may be removed from office only for inability to discharge the functions thereof (whether arising from infirmity of mind or body or any other cause) or for misbehaviour, and shall not be so removed except in accordance with the provisions of paragraph (9) of this Article.

(9) The Auditor-General shall be removed from office by the Governor-General if the question of his removal from office has been referred to a tribunal appointed under paragraph (10) of this Article and the tribunal has recommended to the Governor-General that he ought to be removed from office for inability as aforesaid or for misbehaviour.

(10) If the Prime Minister represents to the Governor-General that the question of removing the Auditor-General from office for inability as aforesaid or for misbehaviour ought to be investigated, then—

(a) the Governor-General shall appoint a tribunal, which shall consist of a chairman and not less than two other members, selected by the Governor-General, acting in accordance with the advice of the Judicial and Legal Service Commission, from among persons who hold or have held or are eligible to hold high judicial office ; and

(b) the tribunal shall enquire into the matter and report on the facts thereof to the Governor-General and recommend to the Governor-General whether the Auditor-General ought to be removed from office for inability as aforesaid or for misbehaviour.

(11) If the question of removing the Auditor-General from office has been referred to a tribunal under paragraph (9) of this Article, the Governor-General, acting in accordance with the advice of the Public Service Commission, may suspend the Auditor-General from performing the functions of his office and any such suspension may at any time be revoked by the Governor-General, and shall in any case cease to have effect if the tribunal recommends to the Governor-General that the Auditor-General should not be removed from office.

CHAPTER X

INTERPRETATION

Interpreta-
tion.

137.—(1) In this Constitution, unless it is otherwise provided or required by the context—

"Act" or "Act of Parliament" means any law made by Parliament ;

"The Bahamas" means The Commonwealth of The Bahamas ;

"the Commonwealth" means, save as otherwise prescribed, The Bahamas, the United Kingdom, Canada, Australia, New Zealand, India, Sri Lanka, Ghana, Malaysia, Nigeria, Cyprus, Sierra Leone, Tanzania, Jamaica, Trinidad and Tobago, Uganda, Kenya, Malawi, Malta, Zambia, The Gambia, Singapore, Guyana, Lesotho, Botswana, Barbados, Mauritius, Swaziland, Tonga, Fiji, Western Samoa, Nauru, Bangladesh and any dependency of any such country ;

"election" means an election of a member or members of the House of Assembly ;

"the Gazette" means the Official Gazette of The Bahamas ;

"House" means either the Senate or the House of Assembly or both, as the context may require ;

"high judicial office" means the office of judge of a court having unlimited jurisdiction in civil and criminal matters in some part of the Commonwealth or a court having jurisdiction in appeals from any such court ;

"law" includes any instrument having the force of law and any un-written rule of law, and "lawful" and "lawfully" shall be construed accordingly ;

"Minister" includes a temporary Minister appointed under Article 76 of this Constitution, except in relation to Articles 72, 73, 76 and 86 of this Constitution ;

"Minister of Finance" means the Minister, by whatever title styled, responsible for Government finance ;

"oath" includes affirmation ;

"Parliament" means the Parliament of The Bahamas ;

"the Police Force" means the Police Force established in and for The Bahamas and maintained under the provisions of the Police Act 1965(**a**) or any law amending or replacing that Act ;

"prescribed" means provided by or under an Act of Parliament ;

"public office" means, subject to the provisions of paragraph (6) of this Article and Article 127 of this Constitution, any office of emolument in the public service ;

"public officer" means the holder of any public office and includes any person appointed to act in any such office ;

"the public service" means, subject to the provisions of Article 127 of this Constitution, the service of the Crown in a civil capacity in respect of the Government of The Bahamas ;

"session" means, in relation to a House, the sittings of that House commencing when it first meets after this Constitution comes

---

(**a**) Statute Law of the Bahama Islands. No. 29 of 1965.

into operation or after any general election or prorogation of Parliament and terminating when Parliament is prorogued or is dissolved without having been prorogued ;

" sitting " means, in relation to a House, a period during which that House is sitting continuously without adjournment and includes any period during which the House is in committee.

(2) For the purposes of this Constitution the territory of The Bahamas shall comprise all the areas that were comprised therein immediately before 10th July 1973 together with such other areas as Parliament may declare to form part thereof.

(3) For the purposes of Articles 42, 43, 48 and 49 of this Constitution—

(a) " government contract " means, subject to such exceptions as Parliament may prescribe, any contract made with the Government of The Bahamas or with a department of that Government or with an officer of that Government contracting as such ; and

(b) a person shall be deemed to be interested in a government contract if—

(i) subject to such exceptions as Parliament may prescribe, he is a party to such a contract or a partner in a firm or director or manager of a company which is a party to such a contract ; or

(ii) he is otherwise interested in such a contract in such manner as Parliament may prescribe.

(4) In this Constitution, unless it is otherwise provided or required by the context—

(a) any reference to the date on which this Constitution comes into operation shall be construed as a reference to the appointed day referred to in section 1(2) of the Order in Council to which this Constitution is scheduled ;

(b) any reference to a law (which term shall, without prejudice to the definition in paragraph (1) of this Article, include an Act) shall be construed as including a reference to a law made at any time before this Constitution comes into operation ;

(c) any reference to power to make appointments to any office shall be construed as including a reference to power to make appointments on promotion and transfer to that office and to power to appoint a person to act in that office during any period during which it is vacant or the holder thereof is unable (whether by reason of absence or of infirmity of body or mind or any other cause) to perform the functions of that office ;

(d) any reference to the holder of an office by a term designating or describing his office shall be construed as including a reference to any person for the time being acting in that office or, to the extent of his authority, otherwise authorised to perform the functions of that office.

(5) Where by this Constitution any person is directed, or power is conferred on any person or authority to appoint a person, to act in or otherwise to perform the functions of an office if the holder thereof is unable to perform the functions of that office, the validity of any performance of those functions by the person so directed or of any appointment made in exercise of that power shall not be called in

question in any court on the ground that the holder of the office is not unable to perform the functions of the office.

(6) For the purposes of this Constitution, a person shall not be considered to hold a public office by reason only that he is in receipt of a pension or other like allowance in respect of public service.

(7) References in this Constitution to the power to remove a public officer from his office shall, subject to the provisions of this Constitution, be construed as including references to any power conferred by any law to require or permit that officer to retire from the public service.

(8) Save as otherwise provided in this Constitution, any provision of this Constitution that vests in any person or authority power to remove any public officer (other than a public officer mentioned in paragraph (9) of this Article) from his office shall be without prejudice to the power of any person or authority to abolish any office or to any law providing for the compulsory retirement of public officers generally or any class of public officer on attaining an age specified therein.

(9) If any circumstances arise that, under the provisions of this Constitution, require the Governor to remove a Justice of the Supreme Court or a Justice of Appeal or the Commissioner of Police, the Deputy Commissioner of Police or the Auditor-General from office for inability to discharge the functions of his office, such removal may be carried out either by dismissing that officer or by requiring him to retire.

(10) Where any power is conferred by this Constitution to make any proclamation, order, rules or regulations or to give any direction, the power shall be construed as including a power exercisable in like manner to amend or revoke any such proclamation, order, rules, regulations or direction.

(11) Any person appointed to an office under any provision in this Constitution may resign that office. Except as otherwise provided in this Constitution such resignation shall be made in writing to the person in whom under this Constitution the power is vested to make appointments to the office concerned.

(12) Where two or more persons are holding the same office by reason of an appointment made in pursuance of paragraph (4) of this Article, then—

(a) for the purposes of any function conferred upon the holder of that office ; and

(b) for the purposes of any reference in this Constitution to the absence, illness or inability to perform the functions of his office or the holder of that office,

the person last appointed to the office shall be deemed to be the sole holder of the office.

(13) The Interpretation Act of The Bahamas(a) and all amendments thereto as in force on 10th July 1973 shall apply, with the necessary adaptations, for the purpose of interpreting this Constitution and otherwise in relation thereto as it applies for the purpose of interpreting and in relation to Acts of Parliament of The Bahamas.

(a) Statute Law of the Bahama Islands, Revised Edition 1965, C. 180.

EXPLANATORY NOTE

(This Note is not part of the Order.)

By virtue of the Bahamas Independence Act 1973, The Bahamas will attain fully responsible status within the Commonwealth on 10th July 1973. This Order makes provision for a Constitution for The Bahamas to come into effect on that day, including provision for the legislature, the executive government, the judicature and the public service. The Constitution also contains provisions relating to citizenship of The Bahamas and fundamental rights and freedoms of the individual.

STATUTORY INSTRUMENTS

1973 No. 1081

JUDICIAL COMMITTEE

The Bahamas (Procedure in Appeals to Privy Council) (Amendment) Order 1973

Made - - - -	*20th June* 1973
Coming into Operation	10*th July* 1973

At the Court at Windsor Castle, the 20th day of June 1973

Present,

The Queen's Most Excellent Majesty in Council

Her Majesty, by virtue and in the exercise of the powers in that behalf by section 1 of the Judicial Committee Act 1844(a) or otherwise in Her Majesty vested, is pleased, by and with the advice of Her Privy Council, to order, and it is hereby ordered, as follows:—

Citation and commencement

1.—(1) This Order may be cited as The Bahamas (Procedure in Appeals to Privy Council) (Amendment) Order 1973 and shall come into operation on 10th July 1973.

(2) This Order shall be construed as one with the Bahama Islands (Procedure in Appeals to Privy Council) Order 1964(b) (hereinafter referred to as " the principal Order ") and that Order and this Order may be cited together as The Bahamas (Procedure in Appeals to Privy Council) Orders 1964 and 1973.

Amendment of section 2 of principal Order

2. Section 2 of the principal Order is amended:—

(a) by substituting for the definition of " Court " the following definition:—

" " Court " means the Court of Appeal for The Bahamas; ";

(b) by substituting the words " The Bahamas " for the words " the Bahama Islands " in the definition of " judgment " ;

(c) by inserting the following definition in its proper alphabetical position:—

" " The Bahamas " means The Commonwealth of The Bahamas ; ".

Revocation of section 21 of principal Order

3. Section 21 of the principal Order is revoked.

(a) 1844 c. 69.   (b) S.I. 1964/2042 (1964 III, p. 5127).

Pending proceedings

4.—(1) In respect of any judgment of the Court of Appeal for the Bahama Islands established by the Bahama Islands (Constitution) Order 1969(a) given in the exercise of any jurisdiction conferred upon it by any law in force in the Bahama Islands before the commencement of this Order, an appeal may be commenced, continued and concluded or continued and concluded, as the case may be, in accordance with the provisions of the principal Order as nearly as may be as if it were an appeal from a judgment of the Court.

(2) Any Order that Her Majesty in Council may see fit to make on any such appeal or any Order made by Her Majesty in Council before the commencement of this Order on an appeal from a judgment of the Court of Appeal for the Bahama Islands given in the exercise of such jurisdiction, but not enforced before such commencement, may be enforced as if it were an Order made on appeal from the judgment of the Court.

W. G. Agnew.

EXPLANATORY NOTE

(This Note is not part of the Order.)

This Order amends the principal Order by substituting references to the new Court of Appeal for The Bahamas established by The Bahamas Independence Order 1973 (S.I. 1973/1080) in place of references to the Court of Appeal for the Bahama Islands. The Order also contains transitional provisions.

(a) S.I. 1969/590 (1969 I, p. 1567).

STATUTORY INSTRUMENTS

1973 No. 1082

DIPLOMATIC SERVICE

The Consular Fees (Amendment) (No. 2) Order 1973

Made - - - -	20*th June* 1973
Coming into Operation	11*th July* 1973

At the Court at Windsor Castle, the 20th day of June 1973

Present,

The Queen's Most Excellent Majesty in Council

Her Majesty, by virtue and in exercise of the powers conferred upon Her by section 2(1) of the Consular Salaries and Fees Act 1891(**a**) and section 8(1) of the Fees (Increase) Act 1923(**b**), or otherwise in Her Majesty vested, is pleased, by and with the advice of Her Privy Council, to order, and it is hereby ordered, as follows:—

1. This Order shall come into operation on 11th July 1973 and may be cited as the Consular Fees (Amendment) (No. 2) Order 1973.

2. Part II of the table of consular fees in the Schedule annexed to the Consular Fees Order 1971(**c**) as amended(**d**) is hereby amended by substituting for Fee 16 the following:—

£

" 16 Renewing a passport issued before the introduction of
passports of 10 years' validity at the office of issue,
a certificate of identity, or other travel document ...   2·00
except where fee 17, 23 or 24 is to be taken   "

W. G. Agnew.

EXPLANATORY NOTE

(*This Note is not part of the Order.*)

This Order fixes a fee for renewing for a further 5 years passports of 5 years' validity which were issued before the introduction of passports of 10 years' validity at the office of issue, and amends the Consular Fees Order 1971 accordingly.

(**a**) 1891 c. 36.   (**b**) 1923 c. 4.   (**c**) S.I. 1971/211 (1971 I, p. 601).
(**d**) The amendments do not relate expressly to the subject matter of this Order.

STATUTORY INSTRUMENTS

1973 No. 1083

DIPLOMATIC AND INTERNATIONAL IMMUNITIES AND PRIVILEGES

The International Cocoa Organization (Immunities and Privileges) Order 1973

Laid before Parliament in draft

Made - - - -	20*th June* 1973
Coming into Operation	*On a date to be notified in the London, Edinburgh and Belfast Gazettes*

At the Court at Windsor Castle, the 20th day of June 1973

Present,

The Queen's Most Excellent Majesty in Council

Whereas a draft of this Order has been laid before Parliament in accordance with section 10 of the International Organisations Act 1968(**a**) and has been approved by a resolution of each House of Parliament:

Now, therefore, Her Majesty, by virtue and in exercise of the powers conferred on Her by section 1 of the said Act or otherwise in Her Majesty vested, is pleased, by and with the advice of Her Privy Council, to order, and it is hereby ordered, as follows:—

1. This Order may be cited as the International Cocoa Organization (Immunities and Privileges) Order 1973. It shall come into operation on the date on which the International Cocoa Agreement, 1972(**b**), opened for signature at New York on 15th November 1972, enters into force in respect of the United Kingdom. This date shall be notified in the London, Edinburgh and Belfast Gazettes.

2. The Interpretation Act 1889(**c**) shall apply for the interpretation of this Order as it applies for the interpretation of an Act of Parliament.

3. The International Cocoa Organization is an organization of which Her Majesty's Government in the United Kingdom and the Governments of foreign sovereign Powers are members.

(**a**) 1968 c. 48.   (**b**) Cmnd. 5263.   (**c**) 1889 c. 63.

4. The International Cocoa Organization shall have the legal capacities of a body corporate.

W. G. Agnew.

EXPLANATORY NOTE
(This Note is not part of the Order.)

This Order confers the legal capacities of a body corporate on the International Cocoa Organization. It will enable the United Kingdom to give effect to Article 21(1) of the International Cocoa Agreement, 1972 (Cmnd. 5263) which the Government of the United Kingdom signed at New York on 15th November 1972. It will come into operation on the date on which the Agreement enters into force with respect to the United Kingdom.

STATUTORY INSTRUMENTS

1973 No. 1084

JUDICIAL COMMITTEE

The Turks and Caicos Islands (Appeal to Privy Council) (Amendment) Order 1973

Made - - - - 20*th June* 1973

Coming into Operation   On a date to be appointed by the Governor of the Turks and Caicos Islands.

At the Court at Windsor Castle, the 20th day of June 1973

Present,

The Queen's Most Excellent Majesty in Council

Her Majesty, by virtue and in the exercise of the powers in that behalf by section 1 of the Judicial Committee Act 1844(a) or otherwise in Her Majesty vested, is pleased, by and with the advice of Her Privy Council, to order, and it is hereby ordered, as follows: —

Citation and commencement

1.—(1) This Order may be cited as the Turks and Caicos (Appeal to Privy Council) (Amendment) Order 1973 and shall come into operation on a date to be appointed by the Governor of the Turks and Caicos Islands.

(2) This Order shall be construed as one with the Turks and Caicos Islands (Appeal to Privy Council) Order 1965(b) (hereinafter referred to as "the principal Order") and that Order and this Order may be cited together as the Turks and Caicos Islands (Appeal to Privy Council) Orders 1965 and 1973.

Amendment of section 2 of principal Order

2. Section 2(1) of the principal Order is amended :—

(*a*) by substituting for the definition of " Court " the following definition :—
" " Court " means the Court of Appeal for the Turks and Caicos Islands ; " ;

(*b*) by inserting the following definition in its proper alphabetical position—
" " the Bahama Islands " means The Commonwealth of The Bahamas ; ".

Revocation of section 22 of principal Order

3. Section 22 of the principal Order is revoked.

(**a**) 1844 c. 69.   (**b**) S.I. 1965/1863 (1965 III, p. 5643).

Pending proceedings

4.—(1) In respect of any judgment of the Court of Appeal for the Bahama Islands, given in the exercise of the jurisdiction conferred upon it by section 41 of the Turks and Caicos Islands (Constitution) Order 1969(a) before the commencement of this Order, an appeal may be commenced, continued and concluded or continued and concluded, as the case may be, in accordance with the provisions of the principal Order as nearly as may be as if it were an appeal from a judgment of the Court.

(2) Any Order that Her Majesty in Council may see fit to make on any such appeal or any Order made by Her Majesty in Council before the commencement of this Order on an appeal from a judgment of the Court of Appeal for the Bahama Islands given in the exercise of such jurisdiction, but not enforced before such commencement, may be enforced as if it were an Order made on appeal from the judgment of the Court.

W. G. Agnew.

EXPLANATORY NOTE

(This Note is not part of the Order.)

This Order amends the principal Order by substituting references to the new Court of Appeal for the Turks and Caicos Islands established by the Turks and Caicos Islands (Constitution) (Amendment) Order 1973 in place of references to the Court of Appeal for the Bahama Islands, (which previously had jurisdiction to hear appeals from the Turks and Caicos Islands). The Order also contains transitional provisions.

(a) S.I. 1969/736 (1969 II, p. 1992).

STATUTORY INSTRUMENTS

1973 No. 1085

SOCIAL SECURITY

The Family Allowances (Jersey) Order 1973

Made - - - *20th June* 1973

At the Court at Windsor Castle, the 20th day of June 1973

Present,

The Queen's Most Excellent Majesty in Council

Her Majesty, in pursuance of section 105(1) of the National Insurance Act 1965(**a**), as extended by section 22(1) of the Family Allowances Act 1965(**b**), and of all other powers enabling Her in that behalf, is pleased, by and with the advice of Her Privy Council, to order, and it is hereby ordered, as follows: —

Citation and interpretation

1.—(1) This Order may be cited as the Family Allowances (Jersey) Order 1973.

(2) The rules for the construction of Acts of Parliament contained in the Interpretation Act 1889(**c**) shall apply in relation to this Order and in relation to the regulations revoked by it as if this Order and the regulations revoked by it were Acts of Parliament, and as if the revocation were a repeal.

Modification of Acts

2. The provisions contained in the Agreement on Family Allowances set out in the Schedule to this Order shall have full force and effect, so far as the same relate to England, Wales and Scotland and provide for reciprocity in any matters specified in section 105(1) of the National Insurance Act 1965 as extended by section 22(1) of the Family Allowances Act 1965; and the Family Allowances Acts 1965 to 1969 and the National Insurance Acts 1965 to 1972 shall have effect subject to such modifications as may be required therein for the purpose of giving effect to any such provisions.

Revocation of Regulations

3. The Family Allowances (Jersey Reciprocal Arrangements) Regulations 1954(**d**) are hereby revoked.

W. G. Agnew.

(**a**) 1965 c. 51.　　　　　　　　(**b**) 1965 c. 53.
(**c**) 1889 c. 63.　　　　　　　　(**d**) S.I. 1954/863 (1954 I, p. 835).

SCHEDULE

AGREEMENT ON FAMILY ALLOWANCES BETWEEN THE SECRETARY OF STATE FOR SOCIAL SERVICES AND THE LIEUTENANT-GOVERNOR OF THE ISLE OF MAN, WITH THE ADVICE AND CONSENT OF THE ISLE OF MAN BOARD OF SOCIAL SECURITY CONSTITUTED UNDER THE ISLE OF MAN BOARD OF SOCIAL SECURITY ACT 1970, OF THE FIRST PART AND THE SOCIAL SECURITY COMMITTEE, WITH THE CONSENT OF THE STATES OF JERSEY, OF THE SECOND PART.

PART I: DEFINITIONS AND SCOPE

ARTICLE 1

For the purposes of this Agreement, unless the context otherwise requires—

(a) "competent authority" means—

  (i) in relation to Great Britain, the Secretary of State for Social Services or the Isle of Man Board of Social Security, as the case may require;

  (ii) in relation to Jersey, the Social Security Committee;

(b) "country" means Great Britain or Jersey, as the case may require;

(c) "family allowance" means a family allowance as defined in the legislation which, in accordance with the provisions of this Agreement, applies in any particular case;

(d) "gainfully occupied" means employed or self employed;

(e) "Great Britain" means England, Scotland, Wales and the Isle of Man;

(f) "legislation" means, in relation to either country, the legislation of that country specified in Article 2 of this Agreement;

and other expressions have the meanings respectively assigned to them in the legislation of Great Britain or Jersey, as the case may require.

ARTICLE 2

(1) The provisions of this Agreement shall apply—

(a) in relation to Great Britain, to—

  (i) the National Insurance Act, 1965, the National Insurance (Isle of Man) Act, 1971 and the legislation repealed or consolidated by, or repealed by enactments consolidated by, those Acts;

  (ii) the Family Allowances Act, 1965 and the Family Allowances (Isle of Man) Act, 1971;

(b) in relation to Jersey, to—

  (i) the Insular Insurance (Jersey) Law, 1950;

  (ii) the Family Allowances (Jersey) Law, 1972.

(2) The Agreement shall apply to any legislation which supersedes, amends, supplements or consolidates the legislation specified in paragraph (1) of this Article.

PART II: PROVISIONS WHICH DETERMINE THE LEGISLATION APPLICABLE

ARTICLE 3

(1) Subject to the provisions of paragraphs (2) and (3) of this Article where a person, and his children, are ordinarily resident in one country and that person is gainfully occupied in the other country, he, and his children shall be treated as resident and present in the territory of the former country and the legislation of that country concerning family allowances shall apply:

Provided that, if his gainful occupation in the latter country has lasted for as long as twenty-four months, this paragraph shall cease to apply to him, unless the competent authorities of the two countries otherwise agree in a particular case.

(2) Where a person in the Government service or in the service of any public corporation of one country goes in the course of that employment to work in the other country and the provisions of paragraph (1) of this Article do not apply to him or have ceased to apply to him, he shall be entitled to choose within three months of the beginning of that employment in the latter country or of the time when those provisions cease to apply to him that, as from the date on which he gives notice to the competent authority of the latter country, the legislation of the former country shall apply to him, in which case he, together with his children, shall be treated as resident and present in the territory of the former country: Provided that his choice of legislation under the provisions of this paragraph shall be the same as his choice of legislation concerning payment of contributions under the provisions of any social security agreement in force between the two countries.

(3) Where a person is ordinarily resident in one country and is employed either—

(a) as master or a member of the crew of a ship, vessel or hovercraft which is registered or owned in the other country and engaged in regular trade between the two countries; or

(b) as pilot, commander, navigator or a member of the crew of an aircraft which is registered in the other country and engaged in regular trade between the two countries;

he shall be treated for the purpose of any claim to family allowances as if he were in and employed in the former country; and if his children are in the other country they shall be treated as if they were in the former country.

(4) Where, but for the provisions of this paragraph, the legislation of both countries would apply in respect of the same children, the legislation of the country where the children are ordinarily resident shall apply, provided that where a child would be treated as included in the family of one parent under the legislation of one country, and in the family of the other parent under the legislation of the other country for the same period, then that child shall be included in one of those families to the exclusion of the other as may be agreed between the parents, or, in default of such agreement in the family which the competent authorities may by agreement determine.

PART III: GENERAL PROVISIONS

ARTICLE 4

For the purposes of all or any of the provisions of the legislation of either country, a child who, by reason of his having been removed from the control of his parents, would be excluded from the family under the legislation of one country shall be so excluded for the purposes of the legislation of the other country.

ARTICLE 5

Subject to the provisions of Article 3, a person who is ordinarily resident in Great Britain shall, for the purposes of any claim to receive a family allowance under the legislation of Great Britain, be treated—

(a) as if his place of birth were in Great Britain if it is in Jersey;

(b) as if he had been resident or present in Great Britain during any period during which he was, respectively, resident or present in Jersey;

Provided that where a person moves from Jersey to Great Britain no payment shall accrue under the provisions of this Article for any period before the first day of presence in Great Britain, or the date on which the legislation of Jersey ceases to apply, whichever is the later.

ARTICLE 6

(1) Subject to the provisions of Article 3, a person who claims a family allowance under the legislation of Jersey—

(a) shall be treated as if any period of residence or presence he has completed in Great Britain had been a period of residence or presence in Jersey;

(b) who becomes ordinarily resident in Jersey and who immediately before his arrival in Jersey was resident in Great Britain and would have satisfied the residence and presence conditions for a family allowance under the legislation of Great Britain, or was in receipt of a family allowance under the legislation of Great Britain, shall be eligible for a family allowance under the legislation of Jersey from the date of the arrival of his family in Jersey or the cessation of family allowance under the legislation of Great Britain, whichever is the later;

(c) who becomes ordinarily resident in Jersey, and who, immediately before his arrival in Jersey was resident in Great Britain, but who did not satisfy the residence and presence conditions for receipt of a family allowance under the legislation of that country, shall be eligible for a family allowance under the legislation of Jersey from the date on which he would have become entitled to a family allowance under the legislation of Great Britain if he had remained in that country, or from the date on which he would be eligible under the legislation of Jersey, whichever is the earlier.

(2) Notwithstanding the provisions of this Article, a family allowance shall not be payable under the legislation of Jersey unless and until the provisions of that legislation concerning the income of the family are satisfied.

ARTICLE 7

A child in respect of whom a Guardian's Allowance is payable under the legislation of one country shall be treated for the purposes of the legislation of the other country as a child in respect of whom a Guardian's Allowance is payable under the legislation of that other country.

PART IV: MISCELLANEOUS PROVISIONS

ARTICLE 8

The competent authorities shall make such financial and administrative arrangements as may appear to them to be necessary for the purpose of giving effect to this Agreement.

ARTICLE 9

The competent authority of one country shall furnish assistance to the competent authority of the other country with regard to any matter relating to the application of this Agreement as if the matter were one affecting the application of the legislation of the former country.

PART V: TRANSITIONAL AND FINAL PROVISIONS

ARTICLE 10

Where a person is entitled to an allowance (or but for the absence of a valid claim would have been so entitled) under the provisions of Article 4(1) of the Memorandum of Reciprocal Arrangements relating to Family Allowances signed by the Minister of Pensions and National Insurance, and the Greffier of the States which came into force on 6 July 1954 an allowance shall continue to be paid for the remainder of the six month period laid down in that Article provided that all other conditions for receipt of the allowance from the country concerned continue to be satisfied. After payment of such an allowance has ceased entitlement to any further allowance shall be determined in accordance with the provisions of this Agreement and the applicable legislation. Nothing in this Article shall confer entitlement to an allowance from both countries for the same period.

ARTICLE 11

Subject to the provisions of Article 10 of this Agreement, the Memorandum of Reciprocal Arrangements relating to Family Allowances which was signed by the Minister of Pensions and National Insurance and the Greffier of the States in 1954 shall be terminated on the date of entry into force of this Agreement.

ARTICLE 12

(1) This Agreement shall enter into force on 8 May 1973 and shall remain in force for an indefinite period unless six months notice of termination is given in writing by the Secretary of State for Social Services and the Lieutenant-Governor of the Isle of Man of the first part or the Social Security Committee of Jersey of the second part.

(2) In the event of termination of this Agreement, any right acquired by a person in accordance with its provisions shall be maintained.

Given under the Official Seal of the Secretary of State for Social Services this 12th day of April 1973.

(L.S.)   *Keith Joseph,*
Secretary of State for Social Services.

Given under the hand of the Lieutenant-Governor of the Isle of Man this 24th day of April 1973.

P. H. G. Stallard,
Lieutenant-Governor.

The consent of the Isle of Man Board of Social Security is hereby given to this Agreement.

(L.S.)   *J. C. Nivison,*
Chairman, Isle of Man Board of Social Security.

Signed on behalf of the Social Security Committee this 7th day of May 1973 and authorised by Act of the States of Jersey this 3rd day of April 1973.

E. J. M. Potter,
Greffier of the States.

EXPLANATORY NOTE
(*This Note is not part of the Order.*)

This Order gives effect in England, Wales and Scotland to the Agreement (set out in the Schedule) made between the Secretary of State for Social Services and the Lieutenant-Governor of the Isle of Man, with the advice of the Isle of Man Board of Social Security, of the first part, and the Social Security Committee, with the consent of the States of Jersey, of the second part, in so far as it relates to matters for which provision is made by the Family Allowances Acts 1965 to 1969 and the National Insurance Acts 1965 to 1972.

STATUTORY INSTRUMENTS

1973 No. 1087

TELEVISION AND LOCAL SOUND BROADCASTING

The Sound Broadcasting Act 1972 (Channel Islands) Order 1973

Made - - - 20*th June* 1973

Coming into Operation 16*th July* 1973

At the Court at Windsor Castle, the 20th day of June 1973

Present,

The Queen's Most Excellent Majesty in Council

Her Majesty, in exercise of the powers conferred on Her by section 13(5) of the Sound Broadcasting Act 1972(**a**), is pleased, by and with the advice of Her Privy Council, to order, and it is hereby ordered, as follows:—

1. This Order may be cited as the Sound Broadcasting Act 1972 (**Channel** Islands) Order 1973 and shall come into operation on 16th July 1973.

2. Sections 1, 4, 6, 12 and 13 of, and Schedules 1 and 2 to, the Sound Broadcasting Act 1972 shall extend to the Channel Islands subject to the exceptions, adaptations and modifications specified in the Schedule to this Order.

W. G. Agnew.

SCHEDULE

EXCEPTIONS, ADAPTATIONS AND MODIFICATIONS IN THE EXTENSION OF PARTS OF THE SOUND BROADCASTING ACT 1972 TO THE CHANNEL ISLANDS

1. Unless the context otherwise requires, any reference to the Sound Broadcasting Act 1972, shall be construed as a reference to that Act as extended to the Channel Islands by this Order and any reference to the Television Act 1964(**b**) (hereinafter referred to as "the Act of 1964") shall be construed as a reference to that Act as extended to the Channel Islands by the Television Act 1964 (Channel Islands) Order 1964(**c**) as amended by the Television Act 1964 (Channel Islands) Order 1969(**d**).

2. Any reference in the Sound Broadcasting Act 1972 to local sound broadcasting shall be construed as local sound broadcasting provided or to be provided by the Authority in the United Kingdom by virtue of the aforesaid Act as it has effect in the United Kingdom.

(**a**) 1972 c. 31. (**b**) 1964 c. 21.
(**c**) S.I. 1964/1202 (1964 II, p. 2786). (**d**) S.I. 1969/1370 (1969 III, p. 4086).

3. In section 6, subsections (3) and (4) and in subsection (1) the words "or subsection (3A)" shall be omitted.

4. In section 13, subsections (4), (5) and (6) shall be omitted.

5. Schedule 1 shall apply only in respect of sections 1, 13, 21 and 28 of the Act of 1964 and to Schedule 1 thereto and—

(a) in the amendment of section 1 for the first semicolon there shall be substituted a full stop and all the following words shall be omitted;

(b) in the amendment of section 13 there shall be omitted the words "In subsection (1)," and the words "in paragraph (a),";

(c) in the amendment of section 28 all the words between "In subsection (1)," and "after the definition" shall be omitted and after the words "Sound Broadcasting Act 1972" in both places where they occur, there shall be inserted the words "as it has effect in the United Kingdom".

6. Schedule 2 shall apply only in respect of the repeal of subsections (1) and (2) of section 21 of the Act of 1964.

EXPLANATORY NOTE

(This Note is not part of the Order.)

This Order extends certain provisions of the Sound Broadcasting Act 1972 to the Channel Islands with necessary modifications.

STATUTORY INSTRUMENTS

1973 No. 1088

TELEVISION AND LOCAL SOUND BROADCASTING

The Sound Broadcasting Act 1972 (Isle of Man) Order 1973

Made - - -	*20th June* 1973
Coming into Operation	*16th July* 1973

At the Court at Windsor Castle, the 20th day of June 1973

Present,

The Queen's Most Excellent Majesty in Council

Her Majesty, in exercise of the powers conferred on Her by section 13(5) of the Sound Broadcasting Act 1972(**a**), is pleased, by and with the advice of Her Privy Council, to order, and it is hereby ordered, as follows:—

1. This Order may be cited as the Sound Broadcasting Act 1972 (Isle of Man) Order 1973 and shall come into operation on 16th July 1973.

2. Sections 1, 4, 12 and 13 of, and Schedules 1 and 2 to, the Sound Broadcasting Act 1972 shall extend to the Isle of Man subject to the exceptions, adaptations and modifications specified in the Schedule to this Order.

W. G. Agnew.

SCHEDULE

EXCEPTIONS, ADAPTATIONS AND MODIFICATIONS IN THE EXTENSION OF PARTS OF THE
SOUND BROADCASTING ACT 1972 TO THE ISLE OF MAN

1. Unless the context otherwise requires, any reference to the Sound Broadcasting Act 1972, shall be construed as a reference to that Act as extended to the Isle of Man by this Order and any reference to the Television Act 1964(**b**) (hereinafter referred to as "the Act of 1964") shall be construed as a reference to that Act as extended to the Isle of Man by the Television Act 1964 (Isle of Man) Order 1965(**c**) as amended by the Television Act 1964 (Isle of Man) Order 1969(**d**).

2. Any reference in the Sound Broadcasting Act 1972 to local sound broadcasting shall be construed as local sound broadcasting provided by the Authority in the United Kingdom by virtue of the aforesaid Act as it has effect in the United Kingdom.

(**a**) 1972 c. 31.	(**b**) 1964 c. 21.
(**c**) S.I. 1965/601 (1965 I, p. 1906).	(**d**) S.I. 1969/1372 (1969 III, p. 4088).

3. In section 13, subsections (4), (5) and (6) shall be omitted.

4. Schedule 1 shall apply only in respect of sections 1, 13, 21 and 28 of the Act of 1964 and to Schedule 1 thereto and—

(a) in the amendment of section 1 for the first semicolon there shall be substituted a full stop and all the following words shall be omitted;

(b) in the amendment of section 13 there shall be omitted the words "In subsection (1)," and the words "in paragraph (a),";

(c) in the amendment of section 28 all the words between "In subsection (1)," and "after the definition" shall be omitted and after the words "Sound Broadcasting Act 1972" in both places where they occur, there shall be inserted the words "as it has effect in the United Kingdom".

5. Schedule 2 shall apply only in respect of the repeal of subsections (1) and (2) of section 21 of the Act of 1964.

EXPLANATORY NOTE

(This Note is not part of the Order.)

This Order extends certain provisions of the Sound Broadcasting Act 1972 to the Isle of Man with necessary modifications.

STATUTORY INSTRUMENTS

1973 No. 1089

COPYRIGHT

The Copyright (International Conventions) (Amendment No. 4) Order 1973

Made - - -	*20th June* 1973
Laid before Parliament	*26th June* 1973
Coming into Operation	*17th July* 1973

At the Court at Windsor Castle, the 20th day of June 1973

Present,

The Queen's Most Excellent Majesty in Council

Her Majesty, by and with the advice of Her Privy Council, and by virtue of the authority conferred upon Her by sections 31, 32 and 47 of the Copyright Act 1956(**a**) and of all other powers enabling Her in that behalf, is pleased to order, and it is hereby ordered, as follows:—

1.—(1) This Order may be cited as the Copyright (International Conventions) (Amendment No. 4) Order 1973, and shall come into operation on 17th July 1973.

(2) The Interpretation Act 1889(**b**) shall apply to the interpretation of this Order as it applies to the interpretation of an Act of Parliament.

2. The Copyright (International Conventions) Order 1972(**c**) (hereinafter referred to as "the principal Order"), as amended(**d**), shall be further amended as follows:—

(*a*) in Schedule 1 (which names the countries of the Berne Copyright Union) Cameroon shall be indicated with an asterisk denoting that it is also party to the Universal Copyright Convention;

(*b*) in Schedule 3 (countries in whose case copyright in sound recordings includes the exclusive right of public performance and broadcasting) there shall be included a reference to Austria;

(*c*) in Schedules 4 and 5 (countries whose broadcasting organisations have copyright protection in relation to their sound and television broadcasts) there shall be included references to Austria and related references to 17th July 1973 in the list of dates in those two Schedules;

(*d*) in paragraph 3 of Schedule 7 (which sets out the modifications of Part III of the principal Order insofar as that Part is part of the law of Gibraltar) in the references in sub-paragraphs (*a*) and (*b*) thereof to the Federal Republic of Germany (and Land Berlin) for "(and Land Berlin)" shall be substituted "(and Berlin West))".

(**a**) 1956 c. 74. (**b**) 1889 c. 63.
(**c**) S.I. 1972/673 (1972 I, p. 2172).
(**d**) The relevant amending Order is S.I. 1973/772 (1973 I, p. 2448).

3. Article 2(b) of the Copyright (International Conventions) (Amendment No. 2) Order 1973(a), so far as it amends Schedules 4 and 5 to the principal Order, shall extend to Gibraltar and Bermuda.

4.—(1) This Order except for Article 2(c) and (d) and Article 3 shall extend to all the countries mentioned in the Schedule hereto.

(2) Article 2(c) shall extend to Gibraltar and Bermuda.

(3) Article 2(d) shall extend to Gibraltar.

W. G. Agnew.

SCHEDULE

Countries to which this Order extends

Bermuda
Belize
Cayman Islands
Falkland Islands and its Dependencies
Gibraltar
Hong Kong
Isle of Man
Montserrat
Seychelles
St. Helena and its Dependencies
Virgin Islands

EXPLANATORY NOTE

(This Note is not part of the Order.)

This Order further amends the Copyright (International Conventions) Order 1972. It takes account of—

(a) the accession of Cameroon to the Universal Copyright Convention;

(b) the ratification by Austria of the International Convention for the Protection of Performers, Producers of Phonograms and Broadcasting Organisations.

The Order extends, so far as is appropriate, to dependent countries of the Commonwealth to which the 1972 Order extends.

(a) S.I. 1973/772 (1973 I, p. 2448).

STATUTORY INSTRUMENTS

1973 No. 1093

MONOPOLIES AND MERGERS

The Regulation of Prices (Tranquillising Drugs) (No. 3) Order 1973

Made - - -	*21st June* 1973
Laid before Parliament	*22nd June* 1973
Coming into Operation	*25th June* 1973

Whereas it appears to the Secretary of State on the facts found by the Monopolies Commission as stated in their report entitled "A report on the supply of chlordiazepoxide and diazepam" that the prices charged in the case of goods of the classes to which the report relates, being goods to which this Order applies, are or have been such as to operate against the public interest:

Now, therefore, the Secretary of State in exercise of the powers conferred by section 3(3)(*a*), and (*d*) and (4)(*c*) of the Monopolies and Mergers Act 1965**(a)** and section 10(3) of the Monopolies and Restrictive Practices (Inquiry and Control) Act 1948**(b)** and now in him vested**(c)** and of all other powers enabling him in that behalf and with a view to remedying or preventing mischiefs which in his opinion result or may be expected to result from the things which according to the said report as laid before Parliament on 11th April 1973 operate or may be expected to operate against the public interest hereby orders as follows:—

1.—(1) This Order may be cited as the Regulation of Prices (Tranquillising Drugs) (No. 3) Order 1973 and shall come into operation on 25th June 1973.

(2) In this Order—

"container" has the same meaning in relation to a preparation mentioned in the Schedule hereto as it has in relation to a medicinal product in the Medicines Act 1968**(d)**; and

references to chlordiazepoxide include references to its salts and references to diazepam include references to its salts.

(3) For the purposes of this Order a body corporate shall be regarded as having a controlling interest in another body corporate if it can—

(i) directly or indirectly determine the manner in which more than one half of the votes which could be cast at a general meeting of the other body corporate are to be cast; or

(ii) by the exercise of a power which does not require the consent or concurrence of any other person appoint or remove the holders of all or a majority of the directorships.

(a) 1965 c. 50.   **(b)** 1948 c. 66.
(c) By the Transfer of Functions (Monopolies, Mergers and Restrictive Practices) Order 1969 (S.I. 1969/1534; 1969 III, p. 4991).   **(d)** 1968 c. 67.

(4) The Interpretation Act 1889(**a**) shall apply to the interpretation of this Order as it applies to the interpretation of an Act of Parliament.

2. This Order applies to F Hoffmann-La Roche and Co. AG, a body corporate incorporated in Switzerland, the SAPAC Corporation Ltd., a body corporate incorporated under the laws of New Brunswick, Canada, to Roche Products Limited, a body corporate incorporated in England, and to any other body corporate (wherever incorporated) in which any of the said bodies corporate has a controlling interest.

3.—(1) Subject to paragraph (2) hereof, the prices charged on the sale in the United Kingdom after the commencement of this Order of any pharmaceutical preparations mentioned in the Schedule hereto shall not exceed the relevant price specified in the third column of the appropriate table in that Schedule, or, if the goods are packed in a container holding a nominal quantity which is not mentioned in that table, the maximum price calculated in accordance with paragraph 2 of that Schedule.

(2) Nothing in paragraph (1) shall apply in relation to—

(*a*) a sale by a person to whom this Order does not apply;

(*b*) a sale of goods which are to be exported from the United Kingdom.

4. It shall be unlawful for any person to whom this Order applies who supplies any pharmaceutical preparation mentioned in the Schedule hereto in the United Kingdom to require as a condition of such supply otherwise than by or for export from the United Kingdom the purchase of any other pharmaceutical preparation.

5.—(1) It shall be unlawful for any person mentioned in Article 4 of this Order to enter into any agreement or arrangement under which any other person is precluded from reselling, or required to preclude any other person from reselling, in the United Kingdom and otherwise than by way of export, except at a price above the price mentioned in paragraph (2) of this Article, any preparation mentioned in the Schedule hereto which has been sold in the United Kingdom on or after 23rd April 1973 by a person to whom this Order applies.

(2) For the purposes of paragraph (1) the highest price at which a person may be required by a minimum resale price condition to resell any goods is—

(*a*) in the case of a resale to a retailer or to any other person purchasing in the course of trade, the relevant price set out in the final column of the appropriate table in the Schedule hereto or, if the goods are not packed in a container in a nominal quantity mentioned in that table, a price which when reduced by $12\frac{1}{2}$ per cent. does not exceed the appropriate maximum selling price calculated in accordance with paragraph 2 of that Schedule;

(*b*) in the case of a resale by retail, a price which does not exceed by more than 50 per cent the highest price which a seller may be required to charge on such a resale as is mentioned in subparagraph (*a*) of this paragraph.

Geoffrey Howe,
Minister for Trade and Consumer Affairs,
Department of Trade and Industry.

Dated 21st June 1973.

(**a**) 1889 c. 63.

SCHEDULE

MAXIMUM PRICES FOR GOODS TO WHICH THE ORDER APPLIES

Standard Packs

1.(a) *Preparations of chlordiazepoxide ("Librium")*

Form of preparation	Nominal quantity in container	Maximum price	Maintainable resale price (wholesale)
		£	£
Tablets or capsules, nominal chlordiazepoxide content 5mg	100	0·28	0·32
	500	1·14	1·30
Tablets or capsules, nominal chlordiazepoxide content 10mg	100	0·35	0·40
	500	1·44	1·64
Tablets (or capsules), nominal chlordiazepoxide content 25mg	100	0·70	0·80
	500	2·87	3·28

(b) *Preparations of diazepam ("Valium")*

Form of preparation	Nominal quantity in container	Maximum price	Maintainable resale price (wholesale)
		£	£
Tablets or capsules, nominal diazepam content 2mg	100	0·18	0·21
	500	0·73	0·83
Tablets or capsules, nominal diazepam content 5mg	100	0·26	0·30
	500	1·08	1·23
Tablets (or capsules), nominal diazepam content 10mg	100	0·39	0·45
	500	1·59	1·82

(c) *Preparations of chlordiazepoxide in combination with theophylline and ephedrine hydrochloride ("Brontrium")*

Form of preparation	Nominal quantity in container	Maximum price	Maintainable resale price (wholesale)
		£	£
Capsules (or tablets), nominal chlordiazepoxide content 10mg	100	0·48	0·55
Capsules (or tablets), nominal chlordiazepoxide content 5mg	100	0·32	0·37

(d) *Preparations of chlordiazepoxide in combination with clidinium bromide ("Libraxin")*

Form of preparation	Nominal quantity in container	Maximum price	Maintainable resale price (wholesale)
		£	£
Tablets (or capsules), nominal chlordiazepoxide content 5mg	100	0·41	0·47
	500	1·69	1·93

(e) *Preparations of chlordiazepoxide in combination with pentaerythritol tetranitrate ("Pentrium")*

Form of preparation	Nominal quantity in container	Maximum price	Maintainable resale price (wholesale)
		£	£
Tablets (or capsules), nominal chlordiazepoxide content 5mg	100	0·42	0·48

(f) Preparations of chlordiazepoxide in combination with amitriptyline ("Limbitrol")

Form of preparation	Nominal quantity in container	Maximum price	Maintainable resale price (wholesale)
		£	£
Capsules (or tablets), nominal chlordiazepoxide content 5mg	100	0·56	0·64
	500	2·32	2·65
Capsules (or tablets), nominal chlordiazepoxide content 10mg	100	0·84	0·97
	500	3·59	4·10

Other Packs

2. For the purposes of Article 3, the maximum price chargeable for any preparations mentioned in the preceding tables when sold in a container holding a nominal quantity which is not so mentioned shall be—

    (i) in a case where only one quantity is mentioned in the relevant table or where two quantities are so mentioned and the nominal quantity in the container is greater than the smaller of those two quantities, a price equal to such a fraction or multiple of the relevant price, or of the greater of the two relevant prices, mentioned in column 3 as appropriately reflects the difference in the quantities;

    (ii) in a case where two quantities are so mentioned and the nominal quantity in the container is less than the smaller of those two quantities, a price equal to such a fraction of the price mentioned in column 3 in relation to the smaller quantity as appropriately reflects the difference between the nominal quantity in the container and that smaller quantity.

EXPLANATORY NOTE

(This Note is not part of the Order.)

This Order reproduces the provisions of the Regulation of Prices (Tranquillising Drugs) (No. 2) Order 1973 (S.I. 1973/925) which in accordance with section 3(11)(b) of the Monopolies and Mergers Act 1965 ceased to have effect on 24th June 1973 for want of approval by resolution of each House of Parliament.

The Order regulates the prices at which certain tranquillising drugs may be sold in the United Kingdom when sold by Roche Products Limited, F Hoffmann-La Roche and Co. AG (a Swiss company) and SAPAC Corporation Ltd. (a Canadian company) and other companies controlled by them.

The Order only relates to drugs sold in the form of tablets or capsules and there are exceptions for exports.

Maximum prices for the quantities in which the drugs are commonly made up are set out in the third column of the tables in the Schedule. For other quantities maximum prices are to be calculated by reference to these prices in accordance with paragraph 2 of the Schedule.

The brand names under which the drugs in question are commonly sold by Roche Products Limited in the United Kingdom are mentioned in the Schedule.

The Order also precludes the companies to which it applies from imposing on the sale of the relevant drugs any condition requiring the buying of other pharmaceutical products, and makes provision as respects the resale prices which can be maintained by minimum resale price conditions.

Copies of the report of the Monopolies Commission referred to in this Order (H.C. 197 Session 1972-73) may be obtained from Her Majesty's Stationery Office.

STATUTORY INSTRUMENTS

1973 No. 1101

ROAD TRAFFIC

The Motor Vehicles (Authorisation of Special Types) General Order 1973

Made	-	-	-	19*th June* 1973
Coming into Operation				18*th July* 1973

ARRANGEMENT OF THE ORDER

PART I

PRELIMINARY

PART II

MISCELLANEOUS VEHICLES

PART III

ABNORMAL INDIVISIBLE LOADS, ENGINEERING PLANT AND OTHER VEHICLES CARRYING WIDE LOADS

Marking of projecting loads and fixed appliances or apparatus which project 25

Approval of the Secretary of State as to the time, date and route of a journey by a vehicle or a vehicle and its load exceeding 4·3 metres in width 26

Notice to police 27

Notice to highway and bridge authorities 28

Restriction on the passage over bridges of vehicles carrying abnormal indivisible loads 29

Breakdown on bridges of vehicles of excessive weight or carrying excessive loads 30

The Secretary of State in exercise of his powers under section 42 of the Road Traffic Act 1972(**a**) and of all other powers him enabling in that behalf, hereby makes the following Order:—

PART I

PRELIMINARY

Commencement and citation

1. This Order shall come into operation on 18th July 1973 and may be cited as the Motor Vehicles (Authorisation of Special Types) General Order 1973.

Revocation

2. The Orders specified in Schedule 3 to this Order are hereby revoked.

Interpretation

3.—(1) In this Order, unless the context otherwise requires, the following expressions have the meanings hereby assigned to them respectively, that is to say—

"Construction and Use Regulations" means the Motor Vehicles (Construction and Use) Regulations 1973(**b**);

"Track Laying Regulations" means the Motor Vehicles (Construction and Use) (Track Laying Vehicles) Regulations 1955(**c**);

"bank holiday", in relation to any provision of this Order requiring notice to be given of the intended use of a vehicle on a road, means a day which is, or is to be observed as, a bank holiday, or a holiday under the Bank Holidays Act 1871(**d**) or the Holidays Extension Act 1875(**e**), either generally or in the locality in which that road is situated;

"controlled by a pedestrian" has the same meaning as in section 193(2) of the Road Traffic Act 1972;

"chief officer of police" and "police area", in relation to England and Wales, have respectively the same meanings as in the Police Act 1964(**f**), and, in relation to Scotland, have respectively the same meanings as in the Police (Scotland) Act 1967(**g**);

(**a**) 1972 c. 20.   (**b**) S.I. 1973/24 (1973 I, p. 93).
(**c**) S.I. 1955/990 (1955 II, p. 2287). (**d**) 1871 c. 17.
(**e**) 1875 c. 13.   (**f**) 1964 c. 48.
(**g**) 1967 c. 77.

"articulated vehicle", "land locomotive", "land tractor", "overall length", "overall width", "overhang", "registered", "straddle carrier", "track laying" and "wheeled" have the same meanings respectively as in the Construction and Use Regulations.

(2) Any reference in this Order to the Construction and Use Regulations shall be construed as a reference to those Regulations as for the time being amended.

(3) Any reference in this Order to the Track Laying Regulations shall be construed as a reference to those Regulations as for the time being amended.

(4) The Interpretation Act 1889(a) shall apply for the interpretation of this Order as it applies for the interpretation of an Act of Parliament, and as if for the purposes of section 38 of that Act this Order were an Act of Parliament and the Orders revoked by Article 2 of this Order were Acts of Parliament thereby repealed.

(5) In so far as any consent, notice, indemnity or dispensation given or any other thing done under a provision of any of the Orders revoked by this Order could have been given or done under a corresponding provision of this Order it shall not be invalidated by the revocation effected by Article 2 of this Order but shall have effect as if given or done under that corresponding provision.

Speed limits

4. Nothing in this Order relating to the speed of vehicles shall be taken to authorise any speed which is in excess of any other speed limit imposed by or under any enactment.

PART II

MISCELLANEOUS VEHICLES

Track laying vehicles

5. The Secretary of State authorises the use on roads of track laying motor vehicles and track laying trailers notwithstanding that such vehicles do not comply in all respects with the requirements of the Construction and Use Regulations or the Track Laying Regulations, subject to the following restrictions and conditions:—

(*a*) a vehicle shall be used only for the purpose of—

(i) demonstration, or

(ii) enabling it to proceed to the nearest suitable railway station for conveyance to a port for shipment or to proceed to a port for shipment from a place in the immediate vicinity of that port where suitable railway facilities are not available;

(*b*) before a vehicle is so used the consent of every highway authority or every person responsible for the maintenance and repair of any road on which it is proposed that the vehicle shall be used shall in each case be obtained in writing; and

(*c*) a vehicle shall not be used for the carriage of goods or burden for hire or reward.

(a) 1889 c. 63.

Naval, military, air force and aviation vehicles

6. The Secretary of State authorises the use on roads of the vehicles specified in Column 1 of Schedule 1 to this Order notwithstanding that such vehicles do not comply in all respects with the requirements of the Regulations of the Construction and Use Regulations or the Track Laying Regulations respectively specified opposite thereto in Column 2 of the said Schedule, subject to the vehicles being the property of, or for the time being under the control of, the persons respectively specified opposite thereto in Column 3 of the said Schedule.

Vehicles used in connection with the saving of life at sea

7. The Secretary of State authorises the use on roads of track laying motor vehicles and track laying trailers notwithstanding that such vehicles do not comply in all respects with the requirements of the Construction and Use Regulations or the Track Laying Regulations, subject to the vehicles being used only for drawing or in connection with the launching of lifeboats which are the property of the Royal National Lifeboat Institution.

Grass cutting machines and hedge trimmers

8. The Secretary of State authorises the use on roads of motor tractors constructed or adapted for use as grass cutters or hedge trimmers (not, in either case, being vehicles controlled by a pedestrian) notwithstanding that such vehicles do not comply with Regulation 48 of the Construction and Use Regulations, subject to the condition that all other relevant requirements of those Regulations are complied with as respects the vehicle and also subject to the following conditions:—

(*a*) the overall width of a vehicle, except when it is actually engaged in grass cutting or hedge trimming operations, must not exceed 2·5 metres; and

(*b*) except when a vehicle is actually engaged in such operations as aforesaid, all cutting or trimming blades which form part of the machinery fitted to the vehicle must be effectively guarded so that no danger is caused or is likely to be caused to any person.

9. The Secretary of State authorises the use on roads of hedge trimmers being vehicles controlled by a pedestrian notwithstanding that such vehicles do not comply in all respects with the requirements of the Construction and Use Regulations, subject to the following conditions:—

(*a*) the requirements of Regulations 22, 28, 31, 90, 98, 101, 106, 107, 109, 114, 115 and 131 of the said Regulations, so far as applicable, must be complied with as respects a vehicle;

(*b*) the unladen weight of a vehicle must not exceed 410 kilograms;

(*c*) the overall width of a vehicle, except when it is actually engaged in hedge trimming operations, must not exceed 2·29 metres; and

(*d*) except when a vehicle is actually engaged in such operations as aforesaid all trimming blades which form part of the machinery fitted to the vehicle must be effectively guarded so that no danger is caused or is likely to be caused to any person.

10. The Secretary of State authorises the use on roads of trailers constructed or adapted for use as grass cutters or hedge trimmers notwithstanding that such trailers do not comply in all respects with such of the requirements of the Construction and Use Regulations as apply to trailers, subject to the following restrictions and conditions:—

(a) the requirements of Regulations 99 and 106 of the said Regulations, so far as they apply to trailers, must be complied with;

(b) the unladen weight of such a trailer must not exceed—

(i) 1020 kilograms if drawn by a locomotive, a motor tractor or a heavy motor car, or

(ii) 815 kilograms in any other case;

(c) the overall width of the motor vehicle by which such a trailer is drawn and, except when it is actually engaged in grass cutting or hedge trimming operations, the overall width of such a trailer must not exceed 2·6 metres;

(d) except when such a trailer is actually engaged in such operations as aforesaid, where it is being drawn in such a manner that its longitudinal axis and that of the drawing vehicle are parallel but lie in different vertical planes, the width of road occupied by both vehicles must not exceed 2·6 metres.

For the purposes of this paragraph, the width aforesaid shall be taken as a distance equivalent to the distance which, if both vehicles were treated as if they were one vehicle at a time when the one is drawing the other in the manner aforesaid, would fall to be measured as its overall width;

(e) except when such a trailer is actually engaged in such operations as aforesaid, all cutting or trimming blades which form part of the machinery fitted to the trailer must be effectively guarded so that no danger is caused or is likely to be caused to any person; and

(f) such a trailer must not be drawn at a speed exceeding 20 miles per hour.

Pedestrian controlled road maintenance vehicles

11.—(1) The Secretary of State authorises the use on roads of motor vehicles constructed or adapted for road maintenance, being vehicles controlled by a pedestrian and not constructed or adapted for use or used for the carriage of a driver or passenger, notwithstanding that such vehicles do not comply in all respects with the requirements of Regulations 11, 13, 34, 50 and 62 of the Construction and Use Regulations, subject to the conditions that all other relevant conditions of those Regulations are complied with as respects a vehicle and also subject to the following restrictions and conditions:—

(a) the weight of a vehicle whether laden or unladen, shall not exceed 410 kilograms,

(b) the vehicle shall be equipped with an efficient braking system capable of being set or with sufficient other means, not being a braking system, whereby it can be brought to a standstill and held stationary.

(2) In this Article "road maintenance" means the gritting of roads, the laying of road markings, the clearing of frost, snow or ice from roads or any other work of maintaining roads.

Vehicles used for experiments or trials

12. The Secretary of State authorises the use on roads of vehicles in or in connection with the conduct of experiments or trials under section 6 of the Roads Improvement Act 1925(**a**) or section 249 of the Highways Act 1959(**b**)

(**a**) 1925 c. 68.   (**b**) 1959 c. 25.

notwithstanding that such vehicles do not comply in all respects with the requirements of the Construction and Use Regulations or the Track Laying Regulations.

Straddle carriers

13.—(1) The Secretary of State authorises the use on roads of straddle carriers notwithstanding that such vehicles do not comply in all respects with the requirements of Regulations 12, 13(2)(b)(ii), 39, 40, 52, 53, 54(5), (6) and (7) and 94 (other than those in paragraph (1)(a) thereof) of the Construction and Use Regulations, subject to the condition that all other relevant requirements of those Regulations are complied with as respects a vehicle and also subject to the following restrictions and conditions:—

(a) a vehicle shall not be used otherwise than for the purpose of demonstration or in the course of delivery on sale or when proceeding to or returning from a manufacturer or repairer for the purpose of repair or overhaul and, when so used, shall carry no load other than its necessary gear or equipment:

Provided that a vehicle which does not comply with the said Regulation 53 may, if it complies with the said Regulations 12 and 52, be used whether laden or unladen in passing from one part of any private premises to any other part thereof or to other private premises in the immediate neighbourhood;

(b) no vehicle shall travel at a speed exceeding 12 miles per hour;

(c) the overall width of a vehicle shall not exceed 2·9 metres;

(d) no vehicle shall be used if the overall length of the vehicle or, where the vehicle is carrying a load, if the overall length of the vehicle together with the length of any forward projection and of any rearward projection of its load exceeds 9·2 metres except with the consent of the chief officer of police of every police area in which it is proposed that the vehicle will be used;

(e) save in so far as the chief officer of police of any police area in which it is proposed that a vehicle will be used dispenses, as respects the use of the vehicle in that area, with any of the requirements contained in this paragraph, the owner of the vehicle shall, not less than two clear days (excluding Sundays, any bank holiday, Christmas Day or Good Friday) before the day on which it is proposed that the vehicle will be used, apply to the chief officer of police of any such area as aforesaid for his consent to the use of the vehicle, and shall, when making the application, furnish to him particulars of the vehicle concerned, of its overall length, of the length of any forward projection or rearward projection of any load proposed to be carried, and of the roads on which it is proposed that the vehicle will be used.

(2) In this Article the expressions "forward projection" and "rearward projection" have the same meanings respectively as in Regulation 130(1) of the Construction and Use Regulations and the provisions of sub-paragraph (e) of the said 130(1) shall apply accordingly.

Land tractors used for reaping and threshing

14. The Secretary of State authorises the use on roads of land tractors constructed for the combined purpose of reaping and threshing notwithstanding that such vehicles do not comply with the requirements of Regulations **48 and 49** of the Construction and Use Regulations, subject to the condition that all other relevant requirements of those Regulations are complied with as respects a vehicle and also subject to the following restrictions and conditions:—

(*a*) no vehicle shall draw a trailer other than a two-wheeled trailer used solely for the carriage of the necessary gear and equipment of the vehicle;

(*b*) the overall width of a vehicle shall not exceed 4·3 metres;

(*c*) where the overall width of a vehicle exceeds 3·5 metres, at least one person in addition to the driver shall be employed in attending to that vehicle to give warning to the driver and to any other person of any danger likely to be caused to any such other person by reason of the presence of the vehicle on the road;

(*d*) no vehicle shall travel at a speed exceeding 12 miles per hour;

(*e*) all cutting blades which form part of the machinery fitted to the vehicle must be effectively guarded so that no danger is caused or is likely to be caused to any person;

(*f*) the three following paragraphs shall apply to the use of a vehicle of which the overall width exceeds 2·9 metres;

(*g*) save in so far as the chief officer of police of any police area in which it is proposed that the vehicle will be used dispenses, as respects the use of the vehicle in that area, with any of the requirements contained in this and the following paragraph as to length of notice or particulars to be given, the owner of the vehicle, before using it on a road for a journey exceeding 5 miles, shall give at least twenty-four hours' notice to the chief officer of police of any such area as aforesaid;

(*h*) the notice referred to in the foregoing paragraph shall contain particulars of the vehicle concerned, of its overall width, and of the time, date and route of the proposed journey; and

(*i*) subject to any variation in the time, date or route of the journey which the owner may be directed to make by any such chief officer of police as aforesaid, the vehicle shall be used only in circumstances which accord with the particulars given in compliance with the foregoing paragraph as to the time, date and route of the journey and only if the overall width of the vehicle does not exceed the width of which particulars have been given as aforesaid.

Mechanically propelled hay and straw balers

15. The Secretary of State authorises the use on roads of motor tractors constructed for the purpose of picking up, baling and binding hay or straw notwithstanding that such vehicles do not comply with the requirements of Regulation 49 of the Construction and Use Regulations, subject to the condition that all other relevant requirements of those Regulations are complied with as respects a vehicle and also subject to the following restrictions and conditions:—

(*a*) the overall width of a vehicle shall not exceed 2·44 metres;

(*b*) the overhang of a vehicle shall not exceed 2·44 metres; and

(*c*) no vehicle shall travel on a road at a speed exceeding 10 miles per hour.

Vehicles for moving excavated material

16. The Secretary of State authorises the use on roads of moveable plant or equipment (other than engineering plant as defined in Article 19 of this Order) being a heavy motor car, trailer or articulated vehicle specially designed and constructed for use in private premises for the primary purpose of moving excavated material and fitted with a tipping body, moving platform or other similar device for discharging its load, and which cannot, owing to the requirements of that purpose, comply in all respects with the requirements of the Construction and Use Regulations, subject, in a case where the overall width of a vehicle exceeds 4·3 metres, to the restrictions and conditions contained in Article 26 of this Order, and also in any case to the following restrictions and conditions:—

(a) a vehicle shall only be used in proceeding to and from private premises or between private premises and a port in either direction and shall carry no load other than its necessary gear or equipment;

(b) a heavy motor car not forming part of an articulated vehicle shall not draw any trailer;

(c) where a trailer is drawn by a motor vehicle the motor vehicle shall not draw any other trailer;

(d) in the case of a heavy motor car not forming part of an articulated vehicle all the Regulations of the Construction and Use Regulations, other than Regulations 12, 13(2)(b)(ii), 39, 40, 52, 54(5), (6) and (7), 56, 79, 83, 86, 87, 88 and 94 (with the exception of paragraph (1)(a) thereof) shall apply;

(e) in the case of a trailer not forming part of an articulated vehicle all the Regulations of the Construction and Use Regulations, other than Regulations 12, 39, 68, 69, 73 and 94 (with the exception of paragraph (1)(a) thereof) shall, subject as provided in paragraph (h) of this Article, apply;

(f) in the case of an articulated vehicle all the Regulations of the Construction and Use Regulations, other than Regulations 9(1), 12, 13(2)(b)(ii), 39, 40, 52, 54(5), (6) and (7), 56, 69, 73, 79, 80, 82, 84 to 88 (inclusive), and 94 (with the exception of paragraph (1)(a) thereof) shall, subject as provided in paragraph (h) of this Article, apply;

(g) in the case of a heavy motor car not forming part of an articulated vehicle and in the case of an articulated vehicle the sum of the weights transmitted to the road surface by any two wheels in line transversely shall not exceed 22,860 kilograms and the sum of the weights so transmitted by all the wheels shall not exceed 50,800 kilograms;

(h) in the case of a trailer, whether or not forming part of an articulated vehicle, sub-paragraphs (b) and (c) of paragraph (1) or paragraph (2) of Regulation 70 of the Construction and Use Regulations shall not apply if the trailer is equipped with an efficient brake or with suitable scotches or similar devices to hold it stationary when necessary;

(i) the overall length of a trailer shall not exceed 8·54 metres and the overall length of an articulated vehicle shall not exceed 13·4 metres;

(j) no vehicle shall travel on any road, other than a special road which is open for use as a special road, at a speed exceeding 12 miles per hour;

(k) every wheel of the vehicle shall be equipped with a pneumatic tyre;

(l) where the overall width of a vehicle exceeds 3·5 metres, at least one person, in addition to the person or persons employed as respects a motor vehicle in driving that vehicle, shall be employed in attending to that vehicle and any load carried thereby and any trailer drawn by that vehicle and any load carried on the trailer and to give warning to the driver of the said motor vehicle and to any other person of any danger likely to be caused to any such other person by reason of the presence of the vehicle or the vehicle and trailer on the road:

Provided that, where three or more vehicles authorised by this Article are travelling together in convoy, it shall be a sufficient compliance with this paragraph if only the foremost and rearmost vehicles in the convoy are attended in the manner prescribed in this paragraph;

(*m*) the three following paragraphs shall apply to the use of a vehicle of which the overall width exceeds 2·44 metres on a road on which a tramcar is operated and to the use of a vehicle of which the overall width exceeds 2·9 metres on any other road;

(*n*) save in so far as the chief officer of police of any police area in which it is proposed that the vehicle will be used dispenses, as respects the use of the vehicle in that area, with any of the requirements contained in this and the following paragraph as to length of notice or particulars to be given, the owner of the vehicle, if its overall width exceeds 2·44 metres, before using it on a road on which a tramcar is operated or, if its overall width exceeds 2·9 metres, before using it on any road, shall give at least two clear days' notice (excluding Sundays, any bank holiday, Christmas Day or Good Friday) to the chief officer of police of any such area as aforesaid;

(*o*) the notice referred to in the foregoing paragraph shall contain particulars of the vehicle concerned, of its overall width, and of the time, date and route of the proposed journey;

(*p*) subject to any variation in the time, date or route of the journey which may be directed by any such chief officer of police as aforesaid, the vehicle shall be used only in circumstances which accord with the particulars given in compliance with the foregoing paragraph as to the time, date and route of the journey and only if the overall width of the vehicle does not exceed the width of which particulars have been given as aforesaid;

(*q*) the four following paragraphs shall apply to the use of a vehicle in respect of which any of the requirements of the Construction and Use Regulations with respect to the weights of vehicles whether laden or unladen or the weights transmitted to the road surface by all or any of the wheels is not complied with or, where a combination of vehicles is used, if any of the said requirements as respects any or all of the vehicles comprised in the combination is not complied with.

For the purposes of this paragraph the reference to a combination of vehicles shall be construed in the same manner as is provided in Regulation 130(1)(*g*) of the Construction and Use Regulations for the purposes of Regulation 131 thereof;

(*r*) save in so far as the highway authority for any road or the bridge authority for any bridge on which it is proposed that the vehicle or, as the case may be, the vehicles will be used dispenses, as respects the use of the vehicle or vehicles on that road or, as the case may be, on that bridge, with the requirements contained in this paragraph as to length of notice or with any of the requirements applicable by virtue of the following paragraph as respects the form of notice or the particulars to be given, the owner of the vehicle, or, as the case may be, of the vehicles, before using the vehicle or vehicles on that road or that bridge, shall give at least two clear days' notice (excluding Sundays, any bank holiday, Christmas Day or Good Friday) as provided by the following paragraph to the highway authority for any such road and to the bridge authority for any such bridge;

(s) the notice referred to in the foregoing paragraph shall, subject to any necessary modification, be in the form and shall contain the particulars specified in Part II of Schedule 2 to this Order and the provisions of Article 28(6) and (7) thereof shall apply as respects any such notice;

(t) before using the vehicle or, as the case may be, the vehicles on any road or bridge the owner of the vehicle or vehicles shall give to the highway authority for the road and to the bridge authority for the bridge an indemnity as provided by the following paragraph; and

(u) the indemnity referred to in the foregoing paragraph shall be in the form specified in Part III of Schedule 2 to this Order and the provisions of Article 28(6) and (7) thereof shall apply as respects any such indemnity.

Motor vehicles and trailers constructed for use outside the United Kingdom or which are new or improved types constructed for tests or trials or are equipped with new or improved equipment or types of equipment

17.—(1) This Article applies to wheeled motor vehicles and trailers not falling within any description of motor vehicle or trailer specified in Article 20 or 21 of this Order and references in this Article to motor vehicles and trailers shall be construed accordingly.

(2) The Secretary of State authorises the use on roads—

(A) of motor vehicles and trailers, or types of motor vehicles and trailers, constructed for use outside the United Kingdom and of new or improved types of motor vehicles and trailers constructed for tests or trials notwithstanding that such vehicles do not comply in all respects with the requirements of the Construction and Use Regulations, and

(B) of motor vehicles and trailers equipped with new or improved equipment or types of equipment notwithstanding that such vehicles do not comply in all respects with such of the requirements of the Construction and Use Regulations as cannot, by reason only of the said equipment, be complied with,

subject, in all cases, to the following restrictions and conditions:—

(a) no vehicle shall be used otherwise than—

(i) for or in connection with the testing or demonstration of the vehicle, or

(ii) in the course of delivery on sale, or

(iii) for proceeding to or returning from a manufacturer or repairer for the purpose of construction, repair or overhaul;

(b) a vehicle shall comply with Regulations 8, 13, 22, 25, 27, 75, 90, 93, 94(1)(a), 95 and 99 to 105 (inclusive) of the Construction and Use Regulations and Regulations 106 to 117 (inclusive) 119 to 123 (inclusive), 125 and 129 to 133 (inclusive) of the said Regulations shall apply thereto;

(c) no vehicle shall be used for the carriage of any load other than its necessary gear or equipment or such apparatus or ballast as may be necessary for the purpose of carrying out a test or trial of that vehicle;

(d) the three following sub-paragraphs shall apply to the use of a vehicle of which the overall width exceeds 2·9 metres or of a vehicle which has an overall length exceeding that specified by any provision of Regulation 9 or 68 of the Construction and Use Regulations as the maximum length for that vehicle;

(e) save in so far as the chief officer of police of any police area in which it is proposed that the vehicle will be used dispenses, as respects the use of the vehicle in that area, with any of the requirements contained in this and the following sub-paragraph as to length of notice or particulars to be given, the owner of the vehicle, before using it on a road, shall give at least two clear days' notice (excluding Sundays, any bank holiday, Christmas Day or Good Friday) to the chief officer of police of any such area as aforesaid;

(f) the notice referred to in the foregoing sub-paragraph shall contain particulars of the vehicle concerned, of its overall width and overall length, of the width and length of any load proposed to be carried, and of the time, date and route of the proposed journey;

(g) subject to any variation in the time, date or route of the journey which may be directed by any such chief officer of police as aforesaid, the vehicle shall be used only in circumstances which accord with the particulars given in compliance with the foregoing sub-paragraph as to the time, date and route of the journey and only if the overall width and overall length of the vehicle and the width and length of any load carried thereon do not exceed the width and length of which particulars have been given as aforesaid;

(h) the four following sub-paragraphs shall apply to the use of a vehicle in respect of which any of the requirements of the Construction and Use Regulations with respect to the weights of vehicles whether laden or unladen or the weights transmitted to the road surface by all or any of the wheels is not complied with or, where a combination of vehicles is used, if any of the said requirements as respects any or all of the vehicles comprised in the combination is not complied with.

For the purposes of this sub-paragraph the reference to a combination of vehicles shall be construed in the same manner as is provided in Regulation 130(1)(g) of the Construction and Use Regulations for the purposes of Regulation 131 thereof;

(i) save in so far as the highway authority for any road or the bridge authority for any bridge on which it is proposed that the vehicle or, as the case may be, the vehicles will be used dispenses, as respects the use of the vehicle or vehicles on that road or, as the case may be, on that bridge, with the requirements contained in this sub-paragraph as to length of notice or with any of the requirements applicable by virtue of the following sub-paragraph as respects the form of notice or the particulars to be given, the owner of the vehicle or, as the case may be, of the vehicles, before using the vehicle or vehicles on that road or that bridge, shall give at least two clear days' notice (excluding Sundays, any bank holiday, Christmas Day or Good Friday) as provided by the following sub-paragraph to the highway authority for any such road and to the bridge authority for any such bridge;

(j) the notice referred to in the foregoing sub-paragraph shall, subject to any necessary modification, be in the form and shall contain the particulars specified in Part II of Schedule 2 to this Order and the provisions of Article 28(6) and (7) thereof shall apply as respects any such notice;

(*k*) before using the vehicle or, as the case may be, the vehicles on any road or bridge the owner of the vehicle or vehicles shall give to the highway authority for the road and to the bridge authority for the bridge an indemnity as provided by the following sub-paragraph; and

(*l*) the indemnity referred to in the foregoing sub-paragraph shall be in the form specified in Part III of Schedule 2 to this Order and the provisions of Article 28(6) and (7) thereof shall apply as respects any such indemnity.

Vehicles fitted with moveable platforms

18.—(1) The Secretary of State authorises the use on roads of a vehicle fitted with a moveable platform notwithstanding that the vehicle does not comply in all respects with the requirements of Regulations 8, 9, 11, 43, 48, 49, 52, 53, 57, 58, or 131 of the Construction and Use Regulations, subject to the condition that all other relevant requirements of those regulations are complied with as respects the vehicle and also subject to the following restrictions and conditions:—

(*a*) no vehicle shall be used on a road unless its special equipment is fully retracted except when the vehicle is at a place where it is being used to facilitate overhead working,

(*b*) any jacks with which the vehicle is fitted for stabilising it while the moveable platform is in use and which project from the sides of the vehicle shall be clearly visible to persons using the road within a reasonable distance of the vehicle, and

(*c*) the vehicle, except in respect of its special equipment when the vehicle is at a place where it is being used to facilitate overhead working, shall—

(i) as respects its overall length, comply with Regulation 9 of the said Regulations,

(ii) as respects its overall width, comply with Regulations 43, 48, 52 or 57 (as the case may be) of the said Regulations,

(iii) in the case of a vehicle other than a locomotive, as respects its overhang, comply with Regulations 49, 53 or 58 (as the case may be) of the said Regulations.

(2) In this Article the expression "moveable platform" means a platform which is attached to, and may be moved by means of, an extensible boom, and the expression "special equipment" means a moveable platform, the apparatus for moving the platform and any jacks fitted to the vehicle for stabilising it while the moveable platform is in use.

Part III

Abnormal Indivisible Loads, Engineering Plant and other Vehicles carrying Wide Loads

Interpretation

19. In this Part of the Order, unless the context otherwise requires, the following expressions have the meanings hereby assigned to them respectively, that is to say—

"abnormal indivisible load" means a load—

(*a*) which cannot without undue expense or risk of damage be divided into two or more loads for the purpose of carriage on roads, and

(b) which—

(i) owing to its dimensions, cannot be carried by a heavy motor car or trailer or a combination of a heavy motor car and trailer complying in all respects with the requirements of the Construction and Use Regulations, or

(ii) owing to its weight cannot be carried by a heavy motor car or trailer or a combination of a heavy motor car and trailer having a total laden weight of less than 24,390 kilograms and complying in all respects with the requirements of the Construction and Use Regulations;

"engineering plant" means—

(a) moveable plant or equipment which consists of a motor vehicle or trailer specially designed and constructed for the special purposes of engineering operations, and which cannot, owing to the requirements of those purposes, comply in all respects with the requirements of the Construction and Use Regulations or the Track Laying Regulations and which is not constructed primarily to carry a load other than excavated material raised from the ground by apparatus on the motor vehicle or trailer or materials which the vehicle or trailer is specially designed to treat while carried thereon, or

(b) a mobile crane which does not comply in all respects with the requirements of the Construction and Use Regulations or the Track Laying Regulations;

"special road" means a special road which is open for use as a special road;

"lateral projection", "forward projection" and "rearward projection" have the same meanings respectively as in Regulation 130(1) of the Construction and Use Regulations and references in this Part of this Order to a special appliance or apparatus in relation to a vehicle, to a forward projection or a rearward projection in relation to a vehicle, to the distance between vehicles in relation to vehicles carrying a load, and to a combination of vehicles in relation to a motor vehicle which is drawing one or more trailers, shall be construed respectively in the same manner as is provided in the said Regulation 130(1) for the purposes of Regulation 131 of the said Regulations, and the provisions of sub-paragraphs (b), (e), (h), (i) and (j) of the said Regulation 130(1) shall apply for the purposes of this Part of this Order as they apply for the purposes of the said Regulations 130(1) and 131;

"tractor" means a motor tractor;

"locomotive" has the same meaning as in the Construction and Use Regulations.

Vehicles for carrying or drawing abnormal indivisible loads

20. The Secretary of State authorises the use on roads of heavy motor cars and trailers specially designed and constructed for the carriage of abnormal indivisible loads and of locomotives and tractors specially designed and constructed to draw trailers specially so designed and constructed notwithstanding that such vehicles do not comply in all respects with the requirements of the Construction and Use Regulations, subject to the restrictions and conditions contained in Articles 23(1) and 29 of this Order and, in a case where Article 24, 25, 27 or 28 of this Order applies, to the restrictions and conditions contained in such of those Articles as are applicable to that case and, in a case where the overall width of a vehicle or of a vehicle together with the width of any lateral projection or projections of its load exceeds 4·3 metres, to the restrictions and conditions contained in Article 26 of this Order and also, in any case, to the following further restrictions and conditions:—

(a) a heavy motor car or trailer which does not comply with Part II of the Construction and Use Regulations shall be used only, save as provided in paragraph (p) of this Article, for or in connection with the carriage of an abnormal indivisible load;

(b) a locomotive or tractor which does not comply with Part II of the Construction and Use Regulations shall be used only for or in connection with the drawing of trailers the use of which on roads is authorised by this Article;

(c) in the case of a heavy motor car all the Regulations of the Construction and Use Regulations, other than Regulations 12, 13(2)(b)(ii), 40, 52, 54(5), (6) and (7), 55, 56, 79, 81 to 89 (inclusive), 94 (with the exception of paragraph (1)(a) thereof), 131 and 142 shall apply;

(d) in the case of a trailer all the Regulations of the Construction and Use Regulations, other than Regulations 9, 12, 20, 69, 70(2), 71 to 73 (inclusive), 77, 80 to 89, 94 (with the exception of paragraph (1)(a) thereof), 131 and 142 shall, subject as provided in paragraph (e) of this Article, apply:

Provided that it shall not be necessary for a trailer constructed before 15th January 1931 to comply with Regulation 11 of the Construction and Use Regulations;

(e) in the case of a trailer whether manufactured before 1st January 1968 or on or after that date, Regulation 70(1) of the Construction and Use Regulations shall apply as it applies to trailers manufactured before 1st January 1968;

(f) in the case of a locomotive or tractor all the Regulations of the Construction and Use Regulations, other than Regulations 12, 40, 43, 48, 77 and 81 shall apply;

(g) the overall width of a heavy motor car shall not exceed 2·9 metres unless it is used for or in connection with the carriage of a load which can only safely be carried on a heavy motor car which exceeds that overall width;

(h) the overall width of a locomotive or tractor shall not exceed 2·9 metres unless it is used for or in connection with the carriage of a load on a trailer which exceeds that overall width, being a load which can only be safely carried on such a trailer;

(i) the overall width of a trailer shall not exceed 2·9 metres unless it is drawn by a locomotive or tractor and is used for or in connection with the carriage of such a load as is mentioned in the foregoing paragraph;

(j) notwithstanding anything in any of the three foregoing paragraphs the overall width of a heavy motor car, locomotive, tractor or trailer shall not exceed 6·1 metres;

(k) where, in relation to the load carried by a vehicle, there is a lateral projection on one or both sides of the vehicle the overall width of the vehicle together with the width of the projection, or as the case may be, of both projections shall not exceed 6·1 metres;

(l) the overall length of a vehicle shall not exceed 27·4 metres;

(i) where a load is carried in such a manner that its weight rests on one vehicle being a heavy motor car or a trailer, the overall length of the heavy motor car or, as the case may be, of the trailer together with the length of any forward and of any rearward projection of its load shall not exceed 27·4 metres; and

(ii) where a load is carried in such a manner that its weight rests on more than one vehicle and the vehicles consist of—

(a) a motor vehicle drawing one trailer whether forming part of an articulated vehicle or not, or

(b) any other combination of vehicles,

then, in the case at (a) above, the overall length of the trailer together with the length of any forward projection of the load extending beyond the foremost point of the trailer and of any rearward projection of the load shall not exceed 27·4 metres and, in the case at (b) above, the overall length of the vehicles together with the distance between vehicles and the length of any forward and of any rearward projection of the load shall not exceed 27·4 metres;

(m) a vehicle shall be so constructed that it is a wheeled vehicle;

(n) every wheel of a vehicle shall be equipped with a pneumatic tyre or a tyre of soft or elastic material;

(o) the following restrictions on weight shall apply to vehicles, including articulated vehicles, carrying an abnormal indivisible load:—

(i) the sum of the weights transmitted to the road surface by all the wheels of the vehicle or vehicles carrying the load shall not exceed 152,400 kilograms,

(ii) the weight transmitted to the road surface by any one wheel shall not exceed 11,430 kilograms,

(iii) the weight transmitted to any strip of road surface upon which the wheels rest contained between any two parallel lines drawn on that surface at right angles to the longitudinal axis of the vehicle or vehicles carrying the load shall not exceed, if the parallel lines are not more than 610 millimetres apart, 45,720 kilograms and, thereafter, additional weight shall be permitted, for any distance apart of the parallel lines in excess of 610 millimetres but not exceeding a total distance apart of 2·13 metres at a rate of 30,000 kilograms per metre and, thereafter, additional weight shall be permitted, for any distance apart of the parallel lines in excess of 2·13 metres, at a rate of 10,000 kilograms per metre, and

(iv) the total weight transmitted to the road surface by any wheels in line transversely not fitted with pneumatic tyres shall be such that the average weight per 25 millimetres width of tyre in contact with the road surface shall not exceed 765 kilograms:

Provided that the restrictions contained in item (ii) of this paragraph shall not apply to any heavy motor car registered on or before 31st December 1951 or any trailer manufactured before 1st January 1952.

For the purposes of item (ii) of this paragraph any two wheels shall be regarded as one wheel if the distance between the centres of the areas of contact between such wheels and the road surface is less than 610 millimetres; and (*p*) no vehicle or combination of vehicles shall carry more than one abnormal indivisible load at any one time:

Provided that—

(i) subject to compliance with all the requirements of the Construction and Use Regulations with respect to the laden weights of vehicles and the weights transmitted to the road surface by all or any of the wheels, it shall be permissible for a vehicle or any vehicles comprised in a combination of vehicles to carry more than one abnormal indivisible load of the same character and, where any abnormal indivisible load is carried, to carry any articles of a similar character;

(ii) in the case of vehicles not falling within the foregoing proviso, it shall be permissible for a vehicle or any vehicles comprised in a combination of vehicles to carry more than one abnormal indivisible load each of the same character if—

(*a*) the sum of the weights transmitted to the road surface by all the wheels of the vehicle or vehicles carrying the loads does not exceed 76,200 kilograms;

(*b*) the overall length in relation to the vehicle or vehicles carrying the loads is such that the provisions of sub-paragraph (i) or (ii) of paragraph (*l*) above would be complied with were "18·3 metres" substituted for "27·4 metres" except that, where such compliance would be impossible by reason of the length of one of the loads if that were the only one carried, the aforesaid distance of 18·3 metres may be increased to such greater distance not exceeding 27·4 metres as may be necessary to permit the carriage of that load;

(*c*) the overall width of any vehicle together with the width of any lateral projection of its load does not exceed 2·9 metres or, where it would be impossible for the aforesaid distance to be complied with by reason of the width of one of the loads if that were the only one carried, such greater distance not exceeding 6·1 metres as may be necessary to permit the carriage of that load; and

(*d*) all the loads carried are loaded at the same place and conveyed to the same destination.

Engineering plant

21. The Secretary of State authorises the use on roads of engineering plant notwithstanding that such vehicles do not comply in all respects with the requirements of the Construction and Use Regulations or the Track Laying Regulations, subject to the restriction contained in Article 23(2) of this Order and, in a case where Article 24, 25, 27 or 28 of this Order applies, to the restrictions and conditions contained in such of those Articles as are applicable to that case and, in a case where the overall width of a vehicle or of a vehicle together with the width of any lateral projection or projections of its load exceeds 4·3 metres to the restrictions and conditions contained in Article 26 of this Order and also, in any case, to the following further restrictions and conditions:—

(*a*) engineering plant other than a mobile crane shall only be used on a road for the purpose of proceeding to or from the site of engineering operations or when actually engaged in such operations and shall carry no load other than its necessary gear or equipment or, in the case of plant when actually engaged on the construction, maintenance and repair of roads, materials which it is specially designed to treat while carried on the vehicle or which have been excavated and raised from the ground by apparatus on the motor vehicle or trailer;

(*b*) a mobile crane shall only be used on a road for the purpose of proceeding from one place to another and not for the purpose of the lifting or transportation of goods or burden otherwise than when actually engaged in engineering operations;

(*c*) no engineering plant other than a mobile crane shall draw any trailer other than a trailer which is engineering plant or a living van or office hut used in connection with the construction, maintenance and repair of roads;

(*d*) no mobile crane shall draw a trailer;

(*e*) a vehicle shall be so constructed that it is either a wheeled vehicle or a track laying vehicle;

(*f*) in the case of a wheeled motor vehicle Regulations 4, 11, 21, 22, 24 to 35 (inclusive), 42, 90, 93, 94(1)(*a*), 95 to 99 (inclusive), 101, 106 to 117 (inclusive), 119 and 120 of the Construction and Use Regulations shall apply:
Provided that—

  (i) in the case of a motor vehicle registered on or before 31st December 1951 Regulations 24 and 25 of the said Regulations shall not apply, and

  (ii) in the case of a machine designed for use and used solely for the purpose of laying materials for the repair or construction of road surfaces if the weight transmitted to the road surface by any two wheels in line transversely does not exceed 11,180 kilograms the said Regulation 11 shall not apply;

  (iii) in the case of a motor vehicle designed for use in work of construction or repair of road surfaces, the wheels of which are equipped with pneumatic tyres specially provided with smooth treads for such use and which is incapable by reason of its construction of exceeding a speed of 20 miles per hour on the level under its own power, Regulation 99(1)(*f*) of the said Regulations shall not apply;

(*g*) in the case of a wheeled trailer Regulations 4, 11, 75, 90, 94(1)(*a*), 95, 99, 106, 114 and 119 of the Construction and Use Regulations shall apply:
Provided that in the case of a trailer designed for use in work of construction or repair of road surfaces and the wheels of which are equipped with pneumatic tyres specially provided with smooth treads for such use, the said Regulation 99(1)(*f*) shall not apply;

(*h*) in the case of a track laying motor vehicle Regulations 4, 6, 9, 13, 14, 16 to 24 (inclusive), 51, 53 to 69 (inclusive), 71, 72 and 78 of the Track Laying Regulations shall apply:
Provided that—

  (i) in the case of a motor vehicle registered on or before 31st December 1951 Regulations 16 and 17 of the said Regulations shall not apply, and

  (ii) in the case of a motor vehicle which is a road roller the said Regulation 9 shall not apply;

(*i*) in the case of a track laying trailer Regulations 4, 6, 9, 22, 23, 44, 51, 54, 56, 57, 59, 67 and 71 of the Track Laying Regulations shall apply:

Provided that in the case of a trailer which is a road roller the said Regulation 9 shall not apply;

(*j*) all the wheels of a vehicle which are not equipped with pneumatic tyres or tyres of soft or elastic material shall be equipped with smooth tyres and have the edges rounded to a radius of not less than 12 millimetres and not more than 25 millimetres:

Provided that in the case of gritting machines designed for use and used for gritting frosted and icebound roads all or any of the tyres may be shod with diagonal cross bars of equal width of not less than 25 millimetres, extending the full breadth of the tyre and so arranged that the distance between adjacent cross bars is not greater than the width of the cross bars;

(*k*) in the case of any vehicle the weight transmitted to the road surface by any one wheel not equipped with pneumatic tyres where no other wheel is in the same line transversely or by all the wheels not equipped with pneumatic tyres in line transversely shall be such that the average weight per 25 millimetres width of tyre in contact with such surface does not exceed 765 kilograms;

(*l*) a motor vehicle shall be equipped with an efficient brake:

Provided that—

(i) in the case of a motor vehicle propelled by steam the engine shall be deemed to be an efficient brake if the engine is capable of being reversed, and

(ii) in the case of a motor vehicle registered on or after 1st January 1952 any brake required by this paragraph shall be capable of being set so as to hold the vehicle when stationary unless another brake fitted to the vehicle is capable of being so set;

(*m*) a trailer shall be equipped with an efficient brake or with suitable scotches or other similar devices to hold the vehicle stationary when necessary;

(*n*) no motor vehicle which exceeds 7·93 metres in overall length shall draw a trailer:

Provided that this paragraph shall not apply to any broken down vehicle which is being drawn by a motor vehicle in consequence of the breakdown;

(*o*) the sum of the weights transmitted to the road surface by all the wheels and tracks of a vehicle shall not exceed 152,400 kilograms;

(*p*) the overall length of a vehicle shall not exceed 27·4 metres;

(*q*) the overall width of a vehicle shall not exceed 6·1 metres;

(*r*) as respects weight—

(i) the weight transmitted to the road surface by any one wheel of a vehicle shall not exceed 11,430 kilograms,

(ii) the weight transmitted to any strip of road surface upon which the wheels of a vehicle rest contained between any two parallel lines drawn on that surface at right angles to the longitudinal axis of the vehicle shall not exceed, if the parallel lines are not more than 610 millimetres apart, 45,720 kilograms and, thereafter, additional weight shall be permitted, for any distance apart of the parallel lines in excess of 610 millimetres but not exceeding a total distance apart of 2·13 metres, at a rate of 30,000 kilograms per metre and, thereafter, additional weight shall be permitted, for any distance apart of the parallel lines in excess of 2·13 metres, at a rate of 10,000 kilograms per metre,

(iii) the total weight transmitted to the road surface by any wheels of a vehicle in line transversely not fitted with pneumatic tyres shall be such that the average weight per 25 millimetre width of tyre in contact with the road surface shall not exceed 765 kilograms:

Provided that the restrictions contained in item (i) of this paragraph shall not apply to any heavy motor car registered on or before 31st December 1951 or any trailer manufactured before 1st January 1952.

For the purposes of item (i) of this paragraph any two wheels shall be regarded as one wheel if the distance between the centres of the areas of contact between such wheels and the road surface is less than 610 millimetres, and

(iv) in the case of a track laying vehicle, in addition to the foregoing restrictions, the weight transmitted by each track thereof to any strip of road surface contained between any two parallel lines drawn on that surface at right angles to the longitudinal axis of the vehicle shall not exceed, if the parallel lines are not more than 610 millimetres apart, 11,430 kilograms, and, thereafter, additional weight shall be permitted, for any distance apart of the parallel lines in excess of 610 millimetres but not exceeding a total distance apart of 2·13 metres, at a rate of 7,500 kilograms per metre and, thereafter, additional weight shall be permitted, for any distance apart of the parallel lines in excess of 2·13 metres, at a rate of 2,500 kilograms per metre.

Other vehicles carrying loads exceeding 4·3 *metres in width*

22. The Secretary of State authorises the use on roads of motor vehicles and trailers carrying loads where the overall width of the vehicle on which the load is carried together with the width of any lateral projection or projections of the load exceeds 4·3 metres but does not exceed 6·1 metres, subject to the restrictions and conditions contained in Articles 23(3), 24, 26 and 27 of this Order and also to the condition that the vehicle complies in all respects with the requirements of the Construction and Use Regulations (other than Regulation 131(1) and (2) thereof).

Speed limits for vehicles authorised by Article 20, 21 *or* 22

23.—(1) A vehicle the use of which on roads is authorised by Article 20 of this Order shall not travel on any road, other than a special road,—

(a) in the case of a vehicle—

(i) which is not carrying a load,

(ii) which has an overall width not exceeding 2·9 metres, and

(iii) which complies with all the relevant requirements of the Construction and Use Regulations with respect to the springs, wings, brakes and tyres with which a vehicle is required to be fitted or equipped, to the weights of vehicles and to the weights transmitted to the road surface by the wheels of vehicles,

at a speed exceeding 20 miles per hour; and

(b) in any other case, at a speed exceeding 12 miles per hour.

(2) A vehicle the use of which on roads is authorised by Article 21 of this Order shall not travel on any road, other than a special road, at a speed exceeding 12 miles per hour.

(3) A vehicle the use of which on roads is authorised by Article 22 of this Order shall not travel on any road, other than a special road, at a speed exceeding 20 miles per hour.

Attendants

24.—(1) This Article applies in the case of a vehicle the use of which on roads is authorised by Article 22 of this Order and in the case where—

(*a*) the overall width of a vehicle the use of which on roads is authorised by Article 20 or 21 of this Order or of the vehicle together with the width of any lateral projection or projections of its load exceeds 3·5 metres, or

(*b*) the overall length of a vehicle the use of which on roads is authorised by the said Article 20 or 21 or of the vehicle together with the length of any forward projection and of any rearward projection of its load exceeds 18·3 metres, or

(*c*) as respects a motor vehicle (whether or not its use is authorised by the said Article 20 or 21) which is drawing a trailer or trailers the use of which is so authorised, a load is carried in such a manner that its weight rests on more than one of the vehicles being—

(i) the motor vehicle and one trailer whether forming part of an articulated vehicle or not, or

(ii) any other combination of vehicles,

and, in the case of (i) above, the overall length of the trailer together with the length of any forward projection of the load extending beyond the foremost point of the trailer and of any rearward projection of the load exceeds 18·3 metres and, in the case at (ii) above the overall length of the vehicles together with the distance between vehicles and the length of any forward and of any rearward projection of the load exceeds 18·3 metres, or

(*d*) a motor vehicle (whether or not its use is authorised by the said Article 20 or 21) is drawing a trailer or trailers the use of which is so authorised and the overall length of the combination of vehicles together with the length of any forward projection of any load extending beyond the foremost point of the drawing vehicle comprised in the combination and the length of any rearward projection of any load extending beyond the rearmost point of the rearmost vehicle comprised therein exceeds 25·9 metres, or

(*e*) a vehicle the use of which is authorised by the said Article 20 or 21 is carrying a load having a forward projection exceeding 1·83 metres in length or a rearward projection exceeding 3·05 metres in length or is fitted with any special appliance or apparatus having such a projection as aforesaid.

(2) As respects a vehicle falling within a case to which this Article applies at least one person, in addition to the person or persons employed as respects a motor vehicle in driving that vehicle, shall be employed in attending to that vehicle and its load and any other vehicle or vehicles drawn by that vehicle and the load carried on the vehicle or vehicles so drawn and to give warning to the driver of the said motor vehicle and to any other person of

any danger likely to be caused to any such other person by reason of the presence of the said vehicle or vehicles on the road:

Provided that, where three or more vehicles to which this paragraph applies are travelling together in convoy, it shall be a sufficient compliance with this paragraph if only the foremost and rearmost vehicles in the convoy are attended in the manner prescribed in this paragraph.

(3) For the purposes of the foregoing paragraph—

(*a*) in a case where a motor vehicle is drawing a trailer or trailers any person employed in pursuance of section 34 of the Road Traffic Act 1972 in attending that vehicle or any such trailer shall be treated as being an attendant required by that paragraph so long as he is also employed to discharge the duties mentioned in that paragraph, and

(*b*) in a case where a motor vehicle is drawing a trailer or trailers and another motor vehicle is used for the purpose of assisting in their propulsion on the road, the person or persons employed in driving that other motor vehicle shall not be treated as a person or persons employed in attending to the first-mentioned vehicle or any vehicle or vehicles drawn thereby.

Marking of projecting loads and fixed appliances or apparatus which project

25.—(1) This Article applies in a case where a vehicle the use of which is authorised by Article 20 or 21 of this Order—

(*a*) carries a load which—

(i) has a forward projection or a rearward projection exceeding 1·83 metres in length, or

(ii) has a rearward projection exceeding 1·07 metres in length but not exceeding 1·83 metres in length, or

(*b*) is fitted with a special appliance or apparatus which—

(i) has a forward projection exceeding 1·83 metres in length or a rearward projection exceeding 3·05 metres in length, or

(ii) has a rearward projection exceeding 1·07 metres in length but not exceeding 3·05 metres in length.

(2) Subject to the provisions of paragraphs (3), (4) and (5) of this Article—

(*a*) as respects a projection mentioned in sub-paragraph (*a*)(i) or in sub-paragraph (*b*)(i) of the foregoing paragraph the conditions specified in paragraph 3 of Schedule 8 to the Construction and Use Regulations shall be complied with, and accordingly the provisions of the said paragraph 3 shall apply in relation to that projection as they apply in relation to a relevant projection as mentioned in that paragraph, and

(*b*) as respects a projection mentioned in sub-paragraph (*a*)(ii) or in sub-paragraph (*b*)(ii) of the foregoing paragraph the conditions specified in paragraph 4 of the said Schedule 8 shall be complied with, and accordingly the provisions of the said paragraph 4 shall apply in relation to that projection as they apply in relation to a relevant projection as mentioned in that paragraph.

(3) Where, in any of the cases mentioned in paragraph (1) of this Article, a vehicle is carrying a load or is fitted with a special appliance or apparatus and the load or the appliance or apparatus has, in relation to the vehicle, a forward projection or a rearward projection, and another vehicle is attached to that end of the vehicle from which the load or, as the case may be, the

appliance or apparatus projects and is attached to that vehicle in such a manner that—

    (a) in the case where there is a forward projection, the foremost point of that other vehicle extends beyond the foremost part of the projection or, in the case where there is a rearward projection, the rearmost point of that other vehicle extends beyond the rearmost part of the projection, or

    (b) in the case where there is a forward projection, the foremost part of the projection extends beyond the foremost point of that other vehicle or, in the case where there is a rearward projection, the rearmost part of the projection extends beyond the rearmost point of that other vehicle, then—

        (i) in either of the cases mentioned in sub-paragraph (a) of this paragraph, the provisions of paragraph (2) of this Article shall not apply as respects any such projection, and

        (ii) in either of the cases mentioned in sub-paragraph (b) of this paragraph, the provisions of the said paragraph (2) shall apply as if each of the references in paragraph (1) of this Article to a rearward projection were treated as a reference to so much of a rearward projection as extends beyond the rearmost point of that other vehicle and as if the reference in the said paragraph (1) to a forward projection were treated as a reference to so much of a forward projection as extends beyond the foremost point of that other vehicle measured, in either case, when the longitudinal axis of each vehicle lies in the same vertical plane between vertical planes at right angles to the said longitudinal axis and passing, in the case of a rearward projection, through the rearmost point of the said other vehicle and that part of the projection furthest from that point or, in the case of a forward projection, through the foremost point of the said other vehicle and that part of the projection furthest from that point.

(4) This Article shall not apply to any motor vehicle or trailer being used—

    (a) for fire brigade, ambulance or police purposes or for defence purposes (including civil defence purposes), or

    (b) in connection with the removal of any obstruction to traffic

if, in any such case, compliance with any provision of this Article would hinder or be likely to hinder the use of the vehicle for the purpose for which it is being used on that occasion.

(5) Notwithstanding that paragraph (2)(a) provides for the conditions specified in paragraph 3 of Schedule 8 to the Construction and Use Regulations to be complied with as respects a load which has a projection to which sub-paragraph (a)(i) of paragraph (1) of this Article applies, those conditions in relation to the exhibition of the end projection surface on that projection need not be complied with in the case of such a load which carries a rear marking in accordance with the Motor Vehicles (Rear Markings) Regulations 1970(a), as amended(b).

(a) S.I. 1970/1700 (1970 III, p. 5577).   (b) S.I. 1972/842 (1972 II, p. 2681).

Approval of the Secretary of State as to the time, date and route of a journey by a vehicle or a vehicle and its load exceeding 4·3 metres in width

26.—(1) This Article applies in the case of a vehicle the use of which on roads otherwise falls to be authorised—

(a) by Article 16 of this Order where the overall width of a vehicle exceeds 4·3 metres;

(b) by Article 20 or 21 of this Order where the overall width of the vehicle or, if it is used for carrying a load, where the overall width of the vehicle together with the width of any lateral projection or projections of its load exceeds 4·3 metres; or

(c) by Article 22 of this Order.

(2) Subject to the provisions of paragraph (3) of this Article, a vehicle mentioned in the foregoing paragraph shall be used only—

(a) for the purpose of making such a journey between specified places as the Secretary of State may have approved by notice in writing given to the owner of the vehicle and only at such times (if any), on such a date or dates (if any) and on such a route (if any) as the Secretary of State may have specified in the said notice or as the chief officer of police of any police area in which it is proposed that the vehicle shall be used may have specified, in relation to the use of the vehicle in that area, in a direction given to the owner of the vehicle, and

(b) if the notice referred to in the foregoing sub-paragraph is carried on the vehicle at all times while it is being used for the purpose of making the journey for which the Secretary of State's approval has been given.

(3) Where the effect of any such direction as is mentioned in sub-paragraph (a) of the foregoing paragraph is to vary, in relation to a time, a date or a route of the journey approved by the Secretary of State under that sub-paragraph, the time, the date or dates or the route of the said journey, the vehicle shall not be used in accordance with that direction unless the Secretary of State has given his further approval that the vehicle shall be so used.

Notice to police

27.—(1) This Article applies in the case of a vehicle the use of which on roads is authorised by Article 22 of this Order and in a case where—

(a) the overall width of a vehicle the use of which on roads is authorised by Article 20 or 21 of this Order or of the vehicle together with the width of any lateral projection or projections of its load exceeds—

(i) if the vehicle is to be used on a road on which a tramcar is operated, 2·44 metres, or

(ii) if the vehicle is not to be used on such a road, 2·9 metres, or

(b) the overall length of a vehicle the use of which on roads is authorised by the said Article 20 or 21 or of the vehicle together with the length of any forward projection and of any rearward projection of its load exceed 18·3 metres, or

(c) as respects a motor vehicle (whether or not its use is authorised by the said Article 20 or 21) which is drawing a trailer or trailers the use of which is so authorised, a load is carried in such a manner that its weight rests on more than one of the vehicles being—

(i) the motor vehicle and one trailer whether forming part of an articulated vehicle or not, or

(ii) any other combination of vehicles,

and, in the case at (i) above, the overall length of the trailer together with the length of any forward projection of the load extending beyond the foremost point of the trailer and of any rearward projection of the load exceeds 18·3 metres and, in the case at (ii) above the overall length of the vehicles together with the distance between vehicles and the length of any forward and of any rearward projection of the load exceeds 18·3 metres, or

(d) a motor vehicle (whether or not its use on roads is authorised by the said Article 20 or 21) is drawing a trailer or trailers the use of which is so authorised and the overall length of the combination of vehicles together with the length of any forward projection of any load extending beyond the foremost point of the drawing vehicle comprised in the combination and the length of any rearward projection of any load extending beyond the rearmost point of the rearmost vehicle comprised therein exceeds 25·9 metres, or

(e) a vehicle the use of which on roads is authorised by the said Article 20 or 21 is carrying a load having a forward projection or a rearward projection exceeding 3·05 metres in length or is fitted with any special appliance or apparatus having such a projection as aforesaid, or

(f) the total weight of a vehicle the use of which on roads is authorised by the said Article 20 or 21 or of such a vehicle and its load or, in a case where a motor vehicle (whether or not its use is so authorised) is drawing a trailer or trailers the use of which is so authorised, the total weight of the combination of vehicles or of the said combination and of any load carried by any vehicle or vehicles comprised therein exceeds 76,200 kilograms.

(2) Save in so far as the chief officer of police of any police area in which it is proposed that the vehicle or, as the case may be, the vehicles, will be used dispenses, as respects the use of the vehicle or vehicles in that area, with the requirements contained in this paragraph as to length of notice or with any of the requirements applicable by virtue of the following paragraph as respects the form of notice or the particulars to be given, the owner of the vehicle or, as the case may be, of the vehicles, before using the vehicle or vehicles on a road, shall give at least two clear days' notice (excluding Sundays, any bank holiday, Christmas Day or Good Friday) as provided by the following paragraph to the chief officer of police of any such area as aforesaid.

(3) The notice referred to in the foregoing paragraph shall, subject to any necessary modification, be in the form and shall contain the particulars specified in Part I of Schedule 2 to this Order.

(4) Subject to any variation in the time, date or route of the journey which may be directed by any such chief officer of police as aforesaid, and subject to any delay which may be occasioned by reason of a direction given by a police constable, in the interests of road safety or to avoid undue traffic congestion, to the driver of a vehicle to halt it in a place on or adjacent to the road on which the vehicle is travelling, the vehicle or vehicles shall be used only in circumstances which accord with the particulars given in compliance with the last foregoing paragraph as to the time, date and route of the journey and only if any dimension or measurement relating to the vehicle or the vehicles (including that relating to a combination of vehicles) or to a special appliance or apparatus or to a load to be carried, being a dimension or measurement of which particulars have been given as aforesaid, is not exceeded.

Notice to highway and bridge authorities

28.—(1) This Article applies in a case where—

(*a*) the total weight of a vehicle the use of which on roads is authorised by Article 20 or 21 of this Order or of such a vehicle and its load or, in a case where a motor vehicle (whether or not its use is so authorised) is drawing a trailer or trailers the use of which is so authorised, the total weight of the combination of vehicles or of the said combination and of any load carried by any vehicle or vehicles comprised therein exceeds 76,200 kilograms, or

(*b*) as respects any vehicle the use of which is authorised as aforesaid any of the requirements of the Construction and Use Regulations or the Track Laying Regulations with respect to the weights of vehicles whether laden or unladen or the weights transmitted to the road surface by all or any of the wheels or tracks or, as the case may be, the wheels and tracks, is not complied with or, where a combination of vehicles is used, if any of the said requirements as respects any or all of the vehicles comprised in the combination is not complied with.

(2) Subject to the provisions of paragraphs (6), (7), (8), (9) and (10) of this Article, save in so far as the highway authority for any road or the bridge authority for any bridge on which it is proposed that the vehicle or, as the case may be, the vehicles, will be used dispenses, as respects the use of the vehicle or vehicles on that road or, as the case may be, on that bridge, with the requirements contained in this paragraph as to length of notice or with any of the requirements applicable by virtue of the following paragraph as respects the form of notice or the particulars to be given, the owner of the vehicle or, as the case may be, of the vehicles, before using the vehicle or vehicles on that road or that bridge, shall give, in a case mentioned in sub-paragraph (*a*) of the foregoing paragraph, at least six clear days' notice as provided by the following paragraph and, in a case mentioned in sub-paragraph (*b*) of the foregoing paragraph, at least two clear days' notice as so provided (in either case excluding Sundays, any bank holiday, Christmas Day or Good Friday) to the highway authority for any such road and to the bridge authority for any such bridge.

(3) The notice referred to in the foregoing paragraph shall, subject to any necessary modification, be in the form and shall contain the particulars specified in Part II of Schedule 2 to this Order.

(4) Before using the vehicle or, as the case may be, the vehicles on any road or bridge the owner of the vehicle or vehicles shall give to the highway authority for the road and to the bridge authority for the bridge an indemnity as provided by the following paragraph.

(5) The indemnity referred to in the foregoing paragraph shall be in the form specified in Part III of Schedule 2 to this Order.

(6) In the case of any part of a trunk road where, by virtue of the provisions of section 10 of the Highways Act 1959, the functions of the Secretary of State with respect to maintenance are exercised in England (excluding Monmouthshire) by the council of a county (including the Greater London Council) the council of a borough (including a London borough) or the council of an urban district or the functions of the Secretary of State with respect to maintenance are exercised in Wales (including Monmouthshire) by the council of a county, borough or urban district or where, by virtue of the provisions of section 5 of the Trunk Roads Act 1936(**a**), as amended or modified by the Trunk Roads

(**a**) 1936 c. 5.

Act 1946(a), the functions of the Secretary of State with respect to maintenance and repair are exercised in Scotland by the council of a county or large burgh or where by virtue of an agreement between or having effect under paragraph 2 of Schedule 6 to the Transport Act 1962(b) as if between the Secretary of State and either the British Railways Board, the London Transport Board, the British Transport Docks Board or the British Waterways Board, the maintenance or, as the case may be, the maintenance and repair of that part are carried out by any such Board, the notice and indemnity required to be given to the Secretary of State by paragraphs (2) and (4) respectively of this Article shall be treated as given in accordance with paragraph (2) of this Article (as respects the said notice) and paragraph (4) thereof (as respects the said indemnity) only if addressed to, or included in any notice and indemnity given to, such Council or Board as the case may be.

(7) Any notice and indemnity in respect of any part of a trunk road required by the foregoing paragraph to be addressed to, or included in any notice and indemnity given to, the British Railways Board shall be addressed to, or included in a notice and indemnity given to, the Board at the Headquarters of the Regional Railways Board responsible for the part of the railway system which is affected by any such agreement as is mentioned in that paragraph by virtue of the agreement applying to that part of the trunk road.

(8) Where in the case of any trailer, being a vehicle falling within a case mentioned in sub-paragraph (a) of paragraph (1) of this Article, at least six days' notice has been given in accordance with paragraph (2) of this Article and it is found impracticable to use any vehicle specified in the notice (not being a vehicle the use of which upon roads is authorised by Article 20 or 21 of this Order) as a vehicle intended to draw the trailer, then any other vehicle similar in type to the vehicle so specified may be substituted for that vehicle if at least two clear days' notice of the substitution is given to every authority to whom the previous notice was given, and thereupon the last-mentioned notice shall have effect as if the substituted vehicle and not the replaced vehicle had always been specified therein as the vehicle intended to draw the trailer.

(9) In the case of a vehicle the use of which on roads is authorised by Article 20 of this Order, being a vehicle in relation to the use of which notice and an indemnity is required respectively by paragraphs (2) and (4) of this Article to be given to any authority but, in connection with a particular journey, cannot be given to that authority in accordance with the said paragraphs (2) and (4) on account of the urgency of the journey in the national interest, it shall be sufficient compliance with the provisions of the said paragraph (2) (as respects the said notice) and of the said paragraph (4) (as respects the said indemnity) as respects that authority if the notice and indemnity be given so as to be received by that authority or, if sent by post, be posted, before the vehicle is used on any road or bridge for the maintenance and repair of which that authority is responsible:

Provided that the provisions of this paragraph shall only apply if—

(a) the vehicle is used solely for carrying any of the vehicles specified in paragraph 1 or 2 in Column 1 of Schedule 1 to this Order, being the property of, or for the time being under the control of, the persons respectively specified opposite thereto in Column 3 of that Schedule;

(a) 1946 c. 30. (b) 1962 c. 46.

(*b*) the owner of the carrying vehicle has previously consulted the Secretary of State on the route proposed to be followed; and

(*c*) it is certified in writing by the proper naval, military or air force authority that the journey is urgent in the national interest.

(10) Notwithstanding anything in the foregoing provisions of this Order, nothing in this Article shall apply to the use on roads of any vehicle which is the property of, or for the time being under the control of, the Secretary of State for Defence.

Restriction on the passage over bridges of vehicles carrying abnormal indivisible loads

29. Where a motor vehicle the use of which on roads is authorised by Article 20 of this Order is so used or where a motor vehicle (whether or not its use is so authorised) is drawing a trailer or trailers the use of which is so authorised and an abnormal indivisible load is being carried by any such vehicle, the driver of the motor vehicle shall not cause or permit either that vehicle or, in the case of a combination of vehicles, any vehicle comprised in the combination—

(*a*) to enter on any bridge whilst there is on that bridge any other vehicle which is either carrying an abnormal indivisible load or is being used to draw a trailer carrying such a load the presence of which is known to or could reasonably be ascertained by him, or

(*b*) to remain stationary on any bridge except in circumstances beyond his control.

Breakdown on bridges of vehicles of excessive weight or carrying excessive loads

30. Where a vehicle (including an articulated vehicle) laden or unladen has a gross weight of more than 32,520 kilograms, and the use on roads of the vehicle or of the trailer forming part of the articulated vehicle is authorised by Article 6, 7, 12, 16, 17, 20 or 21 of this Order, then in the event of that vehicle being caused to stop for any reason while it is on the bridge, the vehicle shall as soon as practicable be moved clear of the bridge by appropriate action on the part of the person in charge of the vehicle if such movement is practicable without applying any concentrated load to the surface of that part of the road carried by the bridge, but if such movement is not so practicable and it becomes necessary to apply any concentrated load to the said surface by means of jacks, rollers or other similar devices, then before any concentrated load is applied to that surface the advice of the bridge authority responsible for the maintenance of the bridge shall be sought by such person as to the use of spreader plates to reduce the possibility of any damage which might be caused by the application of such concentrated load, and that person shall arrange that no such concentrated load shall be applied to the said surface without using any such spreader plates as the bridge authority may have advised to be used.

Signed by authority of the Secretary of State.

N. H. Calvert,
**An Under Secretary of the
Department of the Environment.**

19th June 1973.

SCHEDULE 1
(see Article 6)

SERVICE AND AVIATION VEHICLES

Column 1	Column 2	Column 3
1. Motor vehicles or trailers constructed either for actual combative purposes or for naval, military or air force training in connection therewith or for use with, or for the carriage or drawing of, instruments of war, including guns and machine guns.	Construction and Use Regulations—All. Track Laying Regulations—All.	The Secretary of State for Defence or the Secretary of State for Trade and Industry, or any contractor making such vehicles for the said Secretaries of State or any sub-contractor of such contractor.
2. Track laying motor vehicles or track laying trailers constructed either for actual combative purposes or for use with, or for the carriage or drawing of, instruments of war, including guns and machine guns, ammunition, equipment or stores in connection therewith.	Construction and Use Regulations—All. Track Laying Regulations—All.	The Secretary of State for Defence or the Secretary of State for Trade and Industry, or any contractor making such vehicles for the said Secretaries of State, or any sub-contractor of such contractor.
3. Motor vehicles or trailers constructed for the carriage of tanks.	Construction and Use Regulations—All. Track Laying Regulations—All.	The Secretary of State for Defence or the Secretary of State for Trade and Industry, or any contractor making such vehicles for the said Secretaries of State, or any sub-contractor of such contractor.
4. Motor vehicles or trailers constructed for the carriage of searchlights or the necessary equipment therefor.	Construction and Use Regulation 12. Track Laying Regulation 7.	The Secretary of State for Defence or the Secretary of State for Trade and Industry, or any contractor making such vehicles for the said Secretaries of State, or any sub-contractor of such contractor.
5. Motor vehicles or trailers constructed for the carriage of aircraft or aircraft parts.	Construction and Use Regulations 9, 52, 53, 69 and 131. Track Laying Regulations 5, 30 and 75.	The Secretary of State for Defence or the Secretary of State for Trade and Industry, or any contractor making such vehicles for the said Secretaries of State, or any sub-contractor of such contractor.

Column 1	Column 2	Column 3
6. Motor tractors, heavy motor cars and trailers constructed for naval, military, air force or aviation purposes before 1st January 1949.	Construction and Use Regulations 48, 52, 53, 69 and 70.	The Secretary of State for Defence or the Secretary of State for Trade and Industry, or any contractor making such vehicles for the said Secretaries of State, or any sub-contractor of such contractor.
7. Heavy motor cars or trailers constructed for use and used only in connection with flying operations where the additional width is made necessary by the design of the equipment or its installation on the vehicle.	Construction and Use Regulations 52 and 69.	The Secretary of State for Defence or the Secretary of State for Trade a Industry, or any contractor making such vehicles for the said Secrtearies of State, or any sub-contractor of such contractor.
8. Aircraft drawn by motor vehicles.	Construction and Use Regulations 12 and 68 to 70 (inclusive).	The Secretary of State for Defence.
9. Motor vehicles or trailers used for the carriage of generating equipment, being equipment used for naval, military or air force purposes.	Construction and Use Regulations 43, 68, 69, 76, 77, 80, 88 and 142.	The Secretary of State for the Environment.

SCHEDULE 2

PART I (see Article 27)

Form of Notice to Police

The Motor Vehicles (Authorisation of Special Types) General Order 1973

In pursuance of Article 27 of the above-mentioned Order I/We.........................

..............................of...being the owner(s) of the under-mentioned vehicle(s) to which the Order applies hereby give notice that it is my/our intention to use the said vehicle(s) on the roads specified below from

....to...starting at

approximately...............a.m./p.m. on the..............day of...........................and

completing the journey at approximately............a.m./p.m. on the.......................

day of........................ The route proposed to be followed is:—

...........................to...............................
...........................to...............................   Department of the Environment
            Classification No. ....

                          "   " ....

Note:—Any further particulars of route necessary to define it clearly are to be given overleaf and where a road is unclassified sufficient information is to be given to enable it to be identified.

Particulars
(to be given in respect of each vehicle)

1. Vehicle(s) to which the Order applies.
Registration Mark (if any)..
Operator's licence number (if any)..
Type..
Description of load (if any)...
Dimensions of vehicle(s) and of load (if any)—
  Maximum height of vehicle(s) or of vehicle(s) and load............................
  ....
  Overall width of vehicle(s) inclusive, where a load is to be carried having a lateral
    projection, of the width of any such projection..
  Overall length of vehicle(s)...
  Length of any projection of special appliance or apparatus or load—
    forward projection..
    rearward projection ....
  Distance between vehicles where load is to be carried by more than one vehicle
  ....
  Overall length of any combination of vehicles (inclusive of load)....................
  Total weight of vehicle(s) (inclusive of load, if any)....................................

2. Other vehicle(s) (if any) drawing or drawn by the above-mentioned vehicle(s).
Registration Mark (if any)..
Operator's licence number (if any)..
Type..
Laden weight...
  Date...................................... Signed.............................

PART II (see Articles 16, 17 and 28)
Form of Notice to Highway and Bridge Authorities

The Motor Vehicles (Authorisation of Special Types) General Order 1973
In pursuance of Article 16/17/28 of the above-mentioned Order I/We
.... of...
being the owner(s) of the under-mentioned vehicle(s) to which the Order applies hereby
give notice that it is my/our intention to use the said vehicle(s) on the roads specified
below from..to.............................
starting at approximately.........a.m./p.m. on the.........day of.............................
and completing the journey at approximately ....a.m./p.m. on the....................
day of........................ The route proposed to be followed is:—

............................to............................   Department of the Environment
............................to............................   Classification No. ....
                             "   " ....

Note:—Any further particulars of route necessary to define it clearly are to be given
overleaf and where a road is unclassified sufficient information is to be given to enable
it to be identified.

Particulars
(to be given in respect of each vehicle)

1. Total number of vehicles to be used including not only vehicles the use of which
is authorised only by the Order but also other vehicles to be used in conjunction therewith........................

2. Number of such vehicles the use of which is authorised only by the Order.........

3. Vehicle(s) to which the Order applies.

*(Particulars to be given in respect of each vehicle)

---

*All particulars in respect of an articulated vehicle should be included under 3 as if it
were a single vehicle.

Registration Mark (if any)..
Operator's licence number (if any)...................•..
Type..
Description of load (if any)..

Overall dimensions of vehicle(s) (inclusive of load, if any):—
    Maximum height..
    Maximum width...
    Maximum length..

Weight of vehicle(s) (inclusive of load, if any)...

Spacing and weight of load carrying axles—
    (a) first load carrying axle:
        (i) number of wheels...
        (ii) approximate weight on axle..............................
        (iii) distance to second load carrying axle....................

    (b) second load carrying axle:
        (i) number of wheels...
        (ii) approximate weight on axle..............................
        (iii) distance to third load carrying axle....................

Repeat for all load carrying axles.

In the case of track laying vehicles a dimensioned sketch plan is to be attached showing the number and disposition of all wheels (if any) and tracks in contact with the road surface indicating the weights transmitted by the wheel or tracks of the vehicle(s).

4. Other vehicle(s) (if any) drawing or drawn by the above-mentioned vehicle(s).
Registration Mark (if any)..
Operator's licence number (if any)..
Type..
Laden weight..

PART III (see Articles 16, 17 and 28)

Form of Indemnity

I/We hereby agree to indemnify you and each and every highway or bridge authority responsible for the maintenance and repair of any road or bridge on the journey to which the above notice relates in respect of any damage which may be caused to any such road or bridge—

    (a) by [any of] the above mentioned vehicle[s]—

        (i) by reason of the construction of or weight transmitted to the road surface by [any of] the said vehicle[s], or

        (ii) by reason of the dimensions, distribution or adjustment of the load carried by [any of] the said vehicle[s]; or

    (b) by any other vehicle by reason of the use of [any of] the above-mentioned vehicle[s] on the road or, as the case may be, the bridge except to the extent that the damage was caused or contributed to by the negligence of the driver of the other vehicle:

Provided that any claim in respect of damage so caused by any vehicle shall be made in writing within twelve months from the date on which the vehicle is last used on the journey to which the above notice relates, stating the occasion and place of the damage.

Date....................................   Signed................................

Note:—Paragraph (a)(ii) above only applies where vehicles are carrying an abnormal indivisible load and in other cases should be omitted.

SCHEDULE 3
ORDERS REVOKED BY ARTICLE 2

Title	Year and Number
The Motor Vehicles (Authorisation of Special Types) General Order 1969	S.I. 1969/344 (1969 I, p. 947).
The Motor Vehicles (Authorisation of Special Types) (Amendment) Order 1969	S.I. 1969/1457 (1969 III, p. 4710).
The Motor Vehicles (Authorisation of Special Types) (Amendment) Order 1971	S.I. 1971/980 (1971 II, p. 2848).
The Motor Vehicles (Authorisation of Special Types) (Amendment) Order 1972	S.I. 1972/1609 (1972 III, p. 4730).

EXPLANATORY NOTE
(This Note is not part of the Order.)

This Order, which consolidates with minor amendments the Motor Vehicles (Authorisation of Special Types) General Order and other Orders specified in Schedule 3 to the Order, authorises the use on roads, subject to the restrictions and conditions specified by or under the Order, of certain vehicles which are special, constructed for special purposes, for tests or trials or for use outside the United Kingdom, new or improved types, equipped with new or improved equipment or which carry loads of exceptional dimensions, notwithstanding that they do not comply with all the regulations made under section 40 of the Road Traffic Act 1972 relating to the construction and use of vehicles, or such of them as are specified in the Order. The amendments are principally concerned with up dating references and metricating the measurements based on imperial units (except those expressed by reference to miles).

STATUTORY INSTRUMENTS

1973 No. 1102

HOUSING, ENGLAND AND WALES

The Housing (Contributions for Housing Association Dwellings) Order 1973

Made - - - -	*20th June* 1973
Laid before Parliament	*2nd July* 1973
Coming into Operation	*23rd July* 1973

The Secretary of State for the Environment, in exercise of powers conferred by sections 21(6) and 85 of the Housing Act 1969(a) and now vested in him(b), and of all other powers enabling him in that behalf, hereby makes the following order:—

1.—(1) This order may be cited as the Housing (Contributions for Housing Association Dwellings) Order 1973 and shall come into operation on 23rd July 1973.

(2) The Interpretation Act 1889(c) shall apply for the interpretation of this order as it applies for the interpretation of an Act of Parliament.

2. The sum of £1,500 is hereby specified as the sum to be substituted for that specified by or under subsection (5) of section 21 of the Housing Act 1969 in giving effect to that subsection where subsection (6) of the said section 21 applies.

Geoffrey Rippon,
Secretary of State for the Environment.

20th June 1973.

(a) 1969 c. 33. (b) S.I. 1970/1681 (1970 III, p. 5551).
(c) 1889 c. 63.

EXPLANATORY NOTE

(This Note is not part of the Order.)

Unless the Secretary of State, on being satisfied that there is good reason for doing so, has determined a higher amount in the particular case or in a class of case to which it belongs, section 21(5) of the Housing Act 1969 limits to £1,000, or such other sum as the Secretary of State may by order specify, the amount that may be determined as the allowable cost for the purposes of a contribution by him for a dwelling provided by conversion, or improved, by a housing association under arrangements with a local authority.

Section 21(6) of the Housing Act 1969 provides that where the dwelling is one in which the housing association has acquired an estate or interest for the purpose of converting it or improving it, section 21(5) shall have effect as if for the sum specified by or under it there were substituted £1,250 or such other sum as the Secretary of State may by order specify. This Order, which applies to England and Wales, specifies £1,500 as the sum to be so substituted.

STATUTORY INSTRUMENTS

1973 No. 1103

ROAD TRAFFIC

The Local Authorities' Traffic Orders (Procedure) (England and Wales) (Amendment) Regulations 1973

Made - - -	*20th June* 1973
Laid before Parliament	*2nd July* 1973
Coming into Operation	*23rd July* 1973

The Secretary of State for the Environment (as respects England excluding Monmouthshire) and the Secretary of State for Wales (as respects Wales and Monmouthshire), make these Regulations in exercise of the powers conferred by section 84C of the Road Traffic Regulation Act 1967(a), as amended by Part IX of the Transport Act 1968(b) and as read with section 32 of the Countryside Act 1968(c), and now vested in them(d), and of all other enabling powers, and after consultation with representative organisations in accordance with section 107(2) of the said Act of 1967:—

PART I

GENERAL

Citation and Commencement

1. These Regulations may be cited as the Local Authorities' Traffic Orders (Procedure) (England and Wales) (Amendment) Regulations 1973, and shall come into operation on 23rd July 1973.

Interpretation

2. The Interpretation Act 1889(e) shall apply for the interpretation of these Regulations as it applies for the interpretation of an Act of Parliament.

Amendment

3. The Local Authorities' Traffic Orders (Procedure) (England and Wales) Regulations 1969(f), as amended by Regulation 4 of the Local Authorities' Traffic Orders (Exemptions for Disabled Persons) (England and Wales) Regulations 1971(g), shall have effect as though—

(a) 1967 c. 76.
(b) 1968 c. 73.
(c) 1968 c. 41.
(d) As respects the Secretary of State for the Environment —
(e) 1889 c. 63.   S.I. 1970/1681 (1970 III, p. 5551).
(f) S.I. 1969/463 (1969 I, p. 1318).   (g) S.I. 1971/1493 (1971 III, p. 4185).

(*a*) in Regulation 2(1) of the 1969 Regulations, in the definition of "consolidation order" (substituted by the 1971 Regulations), there were inserted after the words "in respect of a disabled person's vehicle" the words "or of a provision for conferring on a traffic warden functions similar to those conferred by the existing order or orders on a police constable in uniform or of both such exemption and such provision";

(*b*) at the end of Regulation 20 of the 1969 Regulations (which was added by the 1971 Regulations and which contains special provisions for certain variation orders) there were inserted the words "or a provision for conferring on a traffic warden functions similar to those conferred by the order being varied on a police constable in uniform or both such exemption and such provision".

Signed by authority of the Secretary of State.

John Peyton,
Minister for Transport Industries,
Department of the Environment.

20th June 1973.

Peter Thomas,
Secretary of State for Wales.

20th June 1973.

EXPLANATORY NOTE

(This Note is not part of the Regulations.)

These Regulations amend the Local Authorities' Traffic Orders (Procedure) (England and Wales) Regulations 1969 (as amended by Regulation 4 of the Local Authorities' Traffic Orders (Exemptions for Disabled Persons) (England and Wales) Regulations 1971) so as to alter in the 1969 Regulations the definition of "consolidation order" and the special provisions about variation orders, thus enabling a simplified procedure to be adopted in cases where consolidation orders or variation orders include an additional provision for enabling a traffic warden to exercise functions conferred on a police constable in uniform by the orders being consolidated or varied.

STATUTORY INSTRUMENTS

1973 No. 1105

ROAD TRAFFIC

The Goods Vehicles (Plating and Testing) (Amendment) Regulations 1973

Made - - -		21st June 1973
Laid before Parliament		2nd July 1973
Coming into Operation		23rd July 1973

The Secretary of State for the Environment, in exercise of his powers under section 45(1) and (6) of the Road Traffic Act 1972(**a**) and of all other enabling powers, and after consultation with representative organisations in accordance with the provisions of section 199(2) of that Act, hereby makes the following Regulations: —

1.—(1) These Regulations shall come into operation on 23rd July 1973 and may be cited as the Goods Vehicles (Plating and Testing) (Amendment) Regulations 1973.

(2) The Interpretation Act 1889(**b**) shall apply for the interpretation of these Regulations as it applies for the interpretation of an Act of Parliament.

2. The Goods Vehicles (Plating and Testing) Regulations 1971(**c**), as amended(**d**), shall be further amended in accordance with the provisions of these Regulations.

3. Regulation 3 (interpretation) shall have effect as though—

(*a*) in paragraph (1) the following definition were inserted after the definition of "articulated vehicle", " "auxiliary station" means a vehicle testing station which is regularly not open for the carrying out of re-tests on certain normal working days" and in the definition of "the standard lists" in paragraph (*b*) for the words "and the 10th August 1970" there were substituted the words "the 10th August 1970, the 15th July 1971, the 13th August 1971 and the 1st August 1972,";

(*b*) in paragraph (3) for the words "3 feet 4 inches" there were substituted the words "1·02 metres".

4. Regulation 4 (application of regulations) shall have effect as though—

(*a*) in paragraph (1)(*c*) for the words "30 hundredweight" there were substituted the words "1525 kilogrammes";

(*b*) in paragraph (1)(*e*) for the words "1 ton" there were substituted the words "1020 kilogrammes".

(**a**) 1972 c. 20.   (**b**) 1889 c. 63.
(**c**) S.I. 1971/352 (1971 I, p. 1098).
(**d**) The relevant amending instruments are S.I. 1971/2074, 1972/195, 806 (1971 III, p. 6149; 1972 I, p. 679; II, p. 2598).

5. Regulation 16 (examinations for plating) shall have effect as though—

(*a*) in paragraph (*a*) for the words from "then such equivalent weight" to the end of that paragraph there were substituted the words "then all or any of such equivalent weights shall for the purpose of the determination of a plated weight under this Regulation be reduced to such extent as will ensure compliance with any such Regulation;";

(*b*) in the proviso to paragraph (*b*) the references to 32 tons were references to 32520 kilogrammes and the references to 24 tons were references to 24390 kilogrammes.

6. In Regulation 17 (determination of plated weights) for the words "32 tons or, in any other case 24 tons" there shall be substituted the words "32520 kilogrammes or, in any other case 24390 kilogrammes".

7. Regulation 20 (application for Part II re-tests) shall have effect as though for paragraphs (2), (3) and (4) there were substituted the following paragraphs:—

"(2) Where it is desired to submit a vehicle for a Part II re-test, within a period of 14 days after the date it was submitted for its first examination, at the vehicle testing station at which it was submitted for its first examination or, where that station was an auxiliary station, at that or a different testing station, the applicant for the re-test shall first make arrangements with the person in charge of:—

(*a*) the station at which the vehicle was submitted for its first examination, or

(*b*) where that station was an auxiliary station, that or another vehicle testing station,

for a date and a time at which the vehicle is to be submitted for the re-test.

(3) Where it is desired to submit a vehicle for a Part II re-test (not being a re-test mentioned in the last preceding or next following paragraph) the applicant for the re-test shall first make a written application to such vehicle testing station as he shall select for a date and time at which the vehicle may be submitted for the re-test and every such application shall be made not later than 7 days before the date on which the re-test is required on a form approved by the Secretary of State and shall contain the particulars required by that form, and upon receipt of the application the Secretary of State shall send to the applicant a notice stating when the re-test is to take place and in this connection shall have regard so far as is reasonably practicable to any preference expressed by the applicant as to when the re-test should take place.

(4) Where it is desired to submit a vehicle for a further Part II re-test, within a period of 14 days after the date it was submitted for a re-test under the last preceding paragraph, at the vehicle testing station at which it was submitted for its last re-test or, where that station was an auxiliary station, at that or a different testing station, the applicant for the re-test shall make arrangements with the person in charge of:—

(*a*) the station at which the vehicle was submitted for its last re-test, or

(b) where that station was an auxiliary station, that or another vehicle testing station,

for a date and a time at which the vehicle is to be submitted for the re-test.".

8. Regulation 21 (fees for Part II re-tests) shall have effect as though in the definition of "relevant time" after the words "vehicle testing station" there were inserted the words "at which arrangements have been made for the re-test to be carried out".

9. Regulation 35 (application for Part III re-tests) shall have effect as though for paragraphs (2), (3) and (4) there were substituted the following paragraphs: —

"(2) Where it is desired to submit a vehicle for a Part III re-test, within a period of 14 days after the date it was submitted for its last periodical test, at the vehicle testing station at which it was submitted for its last periodical test or, where that station was an auxiliary station, at that or a different testing station, the applicant for the re-test shall first make arrangements with the person in charge of: —

    (a) the station at which the vehicle was submitted for its last periodical test, or

    (b) where that station was an auxiliary station, that or another vehicle testing station,

for a date and a time at which the vehicle is to be submitted for the re-test.

(3) Where it is desired to submit a vehicle for a Part III re-test (not being a re-test mentioned in the last preceding or next following paragraph) the applicant for the re-test shall first make a written application to such vehicle testing station as he shall select for a date and time at which the vehicle may be submitted for the re-test and every such application shall be made not later than 7 days before the date on which the re-test is required on a form approved by the Secretary of State and shall contain the particulars required by that form, and, upon receipt of the application the Secretary of State shall send to the applicant a notice stating when the re-test is to take place and in this connection shall have regard so far as is reasonably practicable to any preference expressed by the applicant as to when the re-test should take place.

(4) Where it is desired to submit a vehicle for a further Part III re-test within a period of 14 days after the date it was submitted for a re-test under the last preceding paragraph, at the vehicle testing station at which it was submitted for its last re-test or, where that station was an auxiliary station, at that or a different testing station, the applicant for the re-test shall make arrangements with the person in charge of: —

    (a) the station at which the vehicle was submitted for its last re-test, or

    (b) where that station was an auxiliary station, that or another vehicle testing station,

for a date and a time at which the vehicle is to be submitted for the re-test.".

10. Regulation 36 (fees for Part III re-tests) shall have effect as though in the definition of "relevant time" in paragraph (1) after the words "vehicle testing station" there were inserted the words "at which arrangements have been made for the re-test to be carried out".

11. Regulation 50 (general provision as to fees) shall have effect as though in paragraph (2) for sub-paragraph (i) there were substituted the following sub-paragraph—

> "(i) the said applicant may make an application in writing to the Secretary of State at the time of the notice given under paragraph 2(*a*) or (*b*) of this Regulation, or within 28 days of the date thereof, for another examination of the same kind for that vehicle or another vehicle to be carried out within three months of the date of the application and in that event the said fee shall be treated as having been paid in respect of that application or examination, unless the fee in respect of that application or examination is greater, in which case the fee already paid shall be treated as having been paid towards the fee payable in respect of that application or examination; or".

12. Paragraph 2 of Schedule 1 (provisions as to braking force for trailers) shall have effect as though each reference to 6 tons were a reference to 6100 kilogrammes.

13. In Schedule 2 (classes of vehicle to which Regulations do not apply) for paragraph 30 there shall be substituted the following paragraph—

"30. Motor vehicles first used before 1st January 1940, used unladen and not drawing a laden trailer, and trailers manufactured before 1st January 1940 and used unladen.

For the purposes of this paragraph any determination as to when a motor vehicle is first used shall be made as provided in Regulation 3(2) of the Motor Vehicles (Construction and Use) Regulations 1973.".

Signed by authority of the Secretary of State.
21st June 1973.

John Peyton,
Minister for Transport Industries,
Department of the Environment.

EXPLANATORY NOTE

(*This Note is not part of the Regulations.*)

These Regulations further amend the Goods Vehicles (Plating and Testing) Regulations 1971. The principal changes are to metricate references to lengths and weights and—

> (*a*) the definition of "standard lists" contained in Regulation 3(1) of the 1971 Regulations is extended by the inclusion in that definition of lists published on the 15th July 1971, 13th August 1971 and 1st August 1972 (Regulation 3),

(*b*) provision is made enabling free re-tests of a vehicle to be carried out in certain circumstances at a different vehicle testing station from the one at which an earlier examination of the vehicle was carried out (Regulations 7 to 10),

(*c*) the circumstances in which a fee paid for an examination which is not carried out may be applied to the fee for a subsequent examination are further restricted to a case where the application for the subsequent examination is made for an examination to be carried out within 3 months of the date of the application (Regulation 11),

(*d*) there are exempted from the plating and testing scheme certain motor vehicles first used, as opposed to registered, before 1st January 1940 (Regulation 13).

STATUTORY INSTRUMENTS

1973 No. 1106

SOCIAL SECURITY

The National Insurance and Industrial Injuries (Collection of Contributions) Amendment Regulations 1973

Made - - -	*22nd June* 1973
Laid before Parliament	*29th June* 1973
Coming into Operation	*19th July* 1973

The Secretary of State for Social Services(a), in exercise of powers conferred by section 12(7) of the National Insurance Act 1965(b) and of all other powers enabling him in that behalf, after considering the report of the National Insurance Advisory Committee on the preliminary draft submitted to them in accordance with section 108 of that Act, hereby makes the following regulations:—

Citation, interpretation and commencement

1. These regulations, which may be cited as the National Insurance and Industrial Injuries (Collection of Contributions) Amendment Regulations 1973, shall be read as one with the National Insurance and Industrial Injuries (Collection of Contributions) Regulations 1948(c), as amended(d) (hereinafter referred to as "the principal regulations"), and shall come into operation on 19th July 1973.

Amendment of the principal regulations

2. In regulation 6A of the principal regulations (recovery by employer of insured person's contributions during period when sale of stamps is interrupted) after the words "to the public" there shall be inserted the words "or the issue of insurance cards or emergency cards".

Revocation of Provisional Regulations

3. The National Insurance and Industrial Injuries (Collection of Contributions) Amendment Provisional Regulations 1973(e) are hereby revoked, but without prejudice to anything duly done or suffered or to any right, privilege, obligation or liability acquired, accrued or incurred, thereunder.

Keith Joseph,
Secretary of State for Social Services.

22nd June 1973.

(a) For transfer of functions from the Minister of Pensions and National Insurance to (eventually) the Secretary of State, *see* Ministry of Social Security Act 1966 (c. 20) and S.I. 1968/1699 (1968 III, p. 4585).
(b) 1965 c. 51.   (c) S.I. 1948/1274 (Rev. XVI, p. 148: 1948 I, p. 3037).
(d) The relevant amending instruments are the National Insurance Act 1965 and S.I. 1971/993 (1971 II, p. 2940).   (e) S.I. 1973/398 (1973 I, p. 1347).

EXPLANATORY NOTE

(This Note is not part of the Regulations.)

These Regulations revoke and replace the National Insurance and Industrial Injuries (Collection of Contributions) Amendment Provisional Regulations 1973. They amend the National Insurance and Industrial Injuries (Collection of Contributions) Regulations 1948, as amended, by adding the non-availability of insurance cards or emergency cards to the circumstances in which paragraph (*b*) of the proviso to section 12(2) of the National Insurance Act 1965 (recovery by employer of insured person's flat-rate contribution) does not apply.

The report of the National Insurance Advisory Committee on the preliminary draft of these Regulations dated 14th May 1973 is contained in House of Commons Paper No. 337 (Session 1972-73) published by Her Majesty's Stationery Office.

STATUTORY INSTRUMENTS

1973 No. 1107

PLANT HEALTH

The Landing of Unbarked Coniferous Timber (Amendment) Order 1973

Made - - -	*22nd June* 1973
Laid before Parliament	*28th June* 1973
Coming into Operation	*1st July* 1973

The Forestry Commissioners, in exercise of the powers vested in them by sections 2 and 3 of the Plant Health Act 1967(**a**) and of all other powers enabling them in that behalf, hereby make the following Order : —

Citation, commencement and extent

1. This Order, which may be cited as the Landing of Unbarked Coniferous Timber (Amendment) Order 1973, shall come into operation on 1st July 1973 and shall apply to Great Britain.

Interpretation

2.—(1) In this Order "the principal Order" means the Landing of Unbarked Coniferous Timber Order 1961(**b**).

(2) The Interpretation Act 1889(**c**) shall apply for the interpretation of this Order as it applies for the interpretation of an Act of Parliament.

Amendment of the principal Order

3. The principal Order shall be amended as follows : —

(*a*) in article 2(1) there shall be inserted after the definition of "importer" the following definition—

"premises" includes any vehicle, vessel, aircraft, hovercraft or freight container;

(*b*) for paragraph (1) of article 3 there shall be substituted the following paragraph—

"(1) The landing in Great Britain of any consignment of unbarked coniferous timber grown in or brought from any of the countries specified in the Schedule to this Order is hereby prohibited unless

---

(**a**) 1967 c. 8.
(**c**) 1889 c. 63.

(**b**) S.I. 1961/656 (1961 I, p. 1395).

it is accompanied by an official certificate of the plant protection service of the country from which it is exported to Great Britain endorsed by or on behalf of that service and certifying that it has been examined and found to be free from *Ips typographus* and *Dendroctonus micans*.".

IN WITNESS whereof the Official Seal of the Forestry Commissioners is hereunto affixed on 22nd June 1973.

(L.S.)

P. Nicholls,
Forestry Commissioner.

EXPLANATORY NOTE
(This Note is not part of the Order.)

This Order amends the Landing of Unbarked Coniferous Timber Order 1961, which imposes an absolute prohibition on the landing in Great Britain of unbarked coniferous timber grown in or brought from Belgium, Denmark, the Federal Republic of Germany or the Netherlands. This Order relaxes that prohibition, and permits the importation of consignments of such timber from those countries, provided that each consignment is accompanied by an official certificate certifying that the consignment has been found free from *Ips typographus* and *Dendroctonus micans*.

STATUTORY INSTRUMENTS

1973 No. 1108

SEEDS

The Forest Reproductive Material (Amendment) Regulations 1973

Made - - -	*20th June* 1973
Laid before Parliament	*28th June* 1973
Coming into Operation	*1st July* 1973

The Minister of Agriculture, Fisheries and Food, the Secretary of State for Scotland and the Secretary of State for Wales, acting jointly, in exercise of the powers vested in them by subsections (1), (1A), (2), (3), (4) and (8) of section 16 of the Plant Varieties and Seeds Act 1964(a) as amended by section 4(1) of, and subparagraphs (1), (2), (3), (4) and (5) of paragraph 5 of Schedule 4 to, the European Communities Act 1972(b), and of all other powers enabling them in that behalf, after consultation with representatives of such interests as appear to them to be concerned, hereby make the following regulations: —

Citation and commencement

1. These regulations may be cited as the Forest Reproductive Material (Amendment) Regulations 1973, and shall come into operation on 1st July 1973.

Interpretation

2.—(1) In these regulations "the principal regulations" means the Forest Reproductive Material Regulations 1973(c).

(2) The Interpretation Act 1889(d) shall apply for the interpretation of these regulations as it applies for the interpretation of an Act of Parliament.

Amendment of the principal regulations

3. For paragraph B of Part II of Schedule 3 of the principal regulations there shall be substituted the following paragraph—

"B. *Maximum Weights of Lots Sampled and Minimum Weights of, or Minimum Numbers of, Seeds in Samples to be Submitted for Testing*

In relation to seed of the species mentioned in the table below, the maximum weight of seed in a lot sampled and the minimum weight or the minimum number of seeds in a sample submitted for testing shall be as set out in the table below: —

(a) 1964 c. 14.   (b) 1972 c. 68.   (c) S.I. 1973/944 (1973 II, p. 2843).
(d) 1889 c. 63.

"

Species	Minimum sample weight (gm)	Maximum lot weight (kg)
(a) *Abies alba* Mill.	240	1000
Fagus sylvatica L.	1000	1000
Larix decidua Mill.	25	1000
Larix leptolepis (Sieb. & Zucc.) Gord.	25	1000
Picea abies Karst.	25	1000
Picea sitchensis Trautv. et Mey.	25	1000
Pinus nigra Arn.	80	1000
Pinus sylvestris L.	40	1000
Pinus strobus L.	90	1000
Pseudotsuga taxifolia (Poir.) Britt.	60	1000

Species	Minimum number of seeds in sample	Maximum lot weight (kg)
(b) *Quercus borealis* Michx.	500	5000
Quercus pedunculata Ehrh.	500	5000
Quercus sessiliflora Sal.	500	5000

".

In Witness whereof the official seal of the Minister of Agriculture, Fisheries and Food is hereunto affixed on

(L.S.)

20th June 1973.

Joseph Godber,
Minister of Agriculture, Fisheries and Food.

Gordon Campbell,
Secretary of State for Scotland.

18th June 1973.

Peter Thomas,
Secretary of State for Wales.

18th June 1973.

EXPLANATORY NOTE
(*This Note is not part of the Regulations.*)

These Regulations amend the Forest Reproductive Material Regulations 1973. They improve the presentation and correct a technical defect in paragraph B of Part II of Schedule 3 of those Regulations (which part sets out rules for the sampling of seed) by substituting for a reference to maximum number of seeds in lots a reference to maximum lot weight.

STATUTORY INSTRUMENTS

1973 No. 1109

CUSTOMS AND EXCISE

The Customs Duties (Quota Relief) (Portugal) Order 1973

Made - - -	*22nd June* 1973
Laid before the House of Commons	*25th June* 1973
Coming into Operation	*1st July* 1973

The Secretary of State, in exercise of the powers conferred on him by section 5(1) and (4) of the Import Duties Act 1958(**a**), as amended by section 5(5) of, and paragraph 1 of Schedule 4 to, the European Communities Act 1972(**b**), and of all other powers enabling him in that behalf, hereby makes the following Order:

1.—(1) This Order may be cited as the Customs Duties (Quota Relief) (Portugal) Order 1973 and shall come into operation on 1st July 1973.

(2) The Interpretation Act 1889(**c**) shall apply for the interpretation of this Order as it applies for the interpretation of an Act of Parliament.

2. In this Order:

(*a*) "goods of Portugal" means goods which under the Agreement, signed on 22nd July 1972, between the European Economic Community and Portugal are to be regarded as originating in Portugal, and

(*b*) the "relevant quota" means, in relation to goods of any description specified in the Schedule hereto, the quantity of such goods which are to be subject to a reduced rate of duty on import into the United Kingdom under the provisions of three Regulations approved by the Council of the European Communities on 18th June 1973.

3.—(1) Up to and including 31st December 1973 any customs duty which is for the time being chargeable on goods of a subheading of the Customs Tariff 1959 specified in column 1 of the Schedule hereto shall be chargeable at the relevant rate specified in column 3 of that Schedule in the case of goods of Portugal which are of a description specified in column 2 thereof and form part of the relevant quota.

(**a**) 1958 c. 6.
(**c**) 1889 c. 63.

(**b**) 1972 c. 68.

(2) Goods shall be treated as forming part of the relevant quota as soon as they are entered for home use (within the meaning of the Customs and Excise Act 1952(**a**)) in the United Kingdom.

4. Any description in column 2 of the Schedule hereto shall be taken to comprise all goods which would be classified under an entry in the same terms constituting a subheading (other than the final subheading) in the relevant heading of the Customs Tariff 1959.

Limerick,
Parliamentary Under Secretary of State,
Department of Trade and Industry.
22nd June 1973.

SCHEDULE

1 *Tariff subheading*	2 *Description of Goods*	3 *Rates of duty within quota*
22.05(C)(III)(*a*)(1)	Port, Madeira and Setubal muscatel of an actual alcoholic strength exceeding 15° [26.2° proof] but not exceeding 18° [31.5° proof] with a registered designation of origin, in containers holding 2 litres or less	£1.975 per gallon
22.05(C)(III)(*a*)(2)(*aa*)(11)	Port, Madeira and Setubal muscatel, of an actual alcoholic strength exceeding 15° [26.2° proof] but not exceeding 18° [31.5° proof] with a registered designation of origin, in containers holding more than 2 litres, not in bottle	£1.875 per gallon
22.05(C)(III)(*a*)(2)(*aa*)(22)	Port, Madeira and Setubal muscatel as described in the entry immediately above but in bottle	£1.975 per gallon
22.05(C)(IV)(*a*)(1)	Port, Madeira and Setubal muscatel, of an actual alcoholic strength exceeding 18° [31.5° proof] but not exceeding 22° [38.4° proof] with a registered designation or origin, in containers holding 2 litres or less	£1.975 per gallon
22.05(C)(IV)(*a*)(2)(*aa*)(11)	Port, Madeira and Setubal muscatel, of an actual alcoholic strength exceeding 18° [31.5° proof] but not exceeding 22° [38.4° proof] with a registered designation of origin, in containers holding more than 2 litres, not in bottle	£1.875 per gallon
22.05(C)(IV)(*a*)(2)(*aa*)(22)	Port, Madeira and Setubal muscatel as described in the entry immediately above but in bottle	£1·975 per gallon

(**a**) 1952 c. 44.

EXPLANATORY NOTE
(This Note is not part of the Order.)

This Order, which comes into operation on 1st July 1973, provides for the implementation and administration of the United Kingdom's shares of the tariff quotas opened by the European Economic Community for certain wines originating in Portugal under the provisions of three Regulations approved by the Council of the European Communities on 18th June 1973. The criteria of Portuguese origin are laid down in the Agreement, signed on 22nd July 1972, between the European Economic Community and Portugal, annexed to Regulation (EEC) No. 2844/72 (OJ No. L301, p.164).

The Order specifies the reduced rates of customs duty applicable up to and including 31st December 1973 to imports of the relevant goods within the United Kingdom's share of each quota. The size of such shares is determined in accordance with the Regulations.

The Order also provides that any goods which form part of the United Kingdom's share of each quota do so as soon as they are entered for home use in the United Kingdom.

STATUTORY INSTRUMENTS

1973 No. 1110

LOCAL GOVERNMENT, ENGLAND AND WALES

The Local Government (Successor Parishes) Order 1973

Made - - - -	*22nd June* 1973
Laid before Parliament	*29th June* 1973
Coming into Operation	*6th July* 1973

The Secretary of State for the Environment, upon consideration of proposals made to him by the Local Government Boundary Commission for England and in exercise of the powers conferred upon him by paragraph 2(1) of Part V of Schedule 1 to the Local Government Act 1972(a) and of all other powers enabling him in that behalf, hereby makes the following order:—

Title, commencement and interpretation

1. This order may be cited as the Local Government (Successor Parishes) Order 1973 and shall come into operation on 6th July 1973.

2. The Interpretation Act 1889(b) shall apply for the interpretation of this order as it applies for the interpretation of an Act of Parliament.

Successor parishes

3. There shall be constituted the parishes named in column (1) of Parts I and II of the Schedule to this order, the boundaries of which are coterminous—

(*a*) in the case of the parishes in Part I, with the boundaries of the existing urban districts or boroughs respectively specified in respect of such parishes in column (2);

(*b*) in the case of the parishes in Part II, with the boundaries of the parts of existing urban districts respectively specified in respect of such parishes in column (2).

Parish councillors

4. In relation to the parishes named in column (1) of the said Part I, 6th July 1973 is hereby specified as the date for the purposes of sub-paragraphs (2) (aldermen and councillors of boroughs or councillors of urban districts to be parish councillors) and (5) (cessation of provision suspending elections, and filling of casual vacancies) of paragraph 13 of Schedule 3 to the Local Government Act 1972.

(a) 1972 c. 70. (b) 1889 c. 63.

SCHEDULE
PART I

(1) Parishes	(2) Existing urban districts or boroughs
County of Avon	
Clevedon	The urban district of Clevedon
Norton-Radstock	The urban district of Norton-Radstock
Portishead	The urban district of Portishead
County of Bedfordshire	
Ampthill	The urban district of Ampthill
Biggleswade	The urban district of Biggleswade
Kempston Urban	The urban district of Kempston
Leighton-Linslade	The urban district of Leighton-Linslade
Sandy	The urban district of Sandy
County of Berkshire	
Wokingham	The borough of Wokingham
Eton	The urban district of Eton
County of Buckinghamshire	
Buckingham	The borough of Buckingham
Beaconsfield	The urban district of Beaconsfield
Chesham	The urban district of Chesham
Marlow	The urban district of Marlow
County of Cambridgeshire	
Huntingdon and Godmanchester	The borough of Huntingdon and Godmanchester
Saint Ives	The borough of St. Ives
Chatteris	The urban district of Chatteris
Ely	The urban district of Ely
March	The urban district of March
Ramsey	The urban district of Ramsey
St. Neots	The urban district of St. Neots
County of Cheshire	
Alderley Edge	The urban district of Alderley Edge
Alsager	The urban district of Alsager
Bollington	The urban district of Bollington
Knutsford	The urban district of Knutsford
Lymm	The urban district of Lymm
Middlewich	The urban district of Middlewich
Nantwich	The urban district of Nantwich
Northwich	The urban district of Northwich
County of Cleveland	
Guisborough	The urban district of Guisborough
Loftus	The urban district of Loftus
Saltburn and Marske-by-the-Sea	The urban district of Saltburn and Marske-by-the-Sea
County of Cornwall	
Bodmin	The borough of Bodmin
Helston	The borough of Helston
Launceston	The borough of Dunheved, otherwise Launceston
Liskeard	The borough of Liskeard
Penryn	The borough of Penryn

(1) Parishes	(2) Existing urban districts or boroughs
St. Ives	The borough of St. Ives
Saltash	The borough of Saltash
Bude-Stratton	The urban district of Bude-Stratton
Looe	The urban district of Looe
St. Just	The urban district of St. Just
Torpoint	The urban district of Torpoint
County of Cumbria	
Appleby	The borough of Appleby
Cockermouth	The urban district of Cockermouth
Grange-over-Sands	The urban district of Grange
Keswick	The urban district of Keswick
Maryport	The urban district of Maryport
Ulverston	The urban district of Ulverston
Windermere	The urban district of Windermere
County of Derbyshire	
Ashbourne	The urban district of Ashbourne
Bakewell	The urban district of Bakewell
Belper	The urban district of Belper
Old Bolsover	The urban district of Bolsover
Clay Cross	The urban district of Clay Cross
Dronfield	The urban district of Dronfield
New Mills	The urban district of New Mills
Ripley	The urban district of Ripley
Staveley	The urban district of Staveley
Whaley Bridge	The urban district of Whaley Bridge
Wirksworth	The urban district of Wirksworth
County of Devon	
Dartmouth	The borough of Clifton Dartmouth Hardness
Great Torrington	The borough of Great Torrington
Honiton	The borough of Honiton
Okehampton	The borough of Okehampton
Totnes	The borough of Totnes
Ashburton	The urban district of Ashburton
Buckfastleigh	The urban district of Buckfastleigh
Budleigh Salterton	The urban district of Budleigh Salterton
Crediton	The urban district of Crediton
Dawlish	The urban district of Dawlish
Ilfracombe	The urban district of Ilfracombe
Kingsbridge	The urban district of Kingsbridge
Lynton and Lynmouth	The urban district of Lynton
Northam	The urban district of Northam
Ottery St. Mary	The urban district of Ottery St. Mary
Salcombe	The urban district of Salcombe
Seaton	The urban district of Seaton
Sidmouth	The urban district of Sidmouth
Teignmouth	The urban district of Teignmouth
County of Dorset	
Blandford Forum	The borough of Blandford Forum
Bridport	The borough of Bridport
Dorchester	The borough of Dorchester
Lyme Regis	The borough of Lyme Regis
Shaftesbury	The borough of Shaftesbury
Wareham Lady St. Mary	The borough of Wareham

(1) Parishes	(2) Existing urban districts or boroughs
Portland	The urban district of Portland
Sherborne	The urban district of Sherborne
Swanage	The urban district of Swanage
Wimborne Minster	The urban district of Wimborne Minster
County of Durham	
Barnard Castle	The urban district of Barnard Castle
Brandon and Byshottles	The urban district of Brandon and Byshottles
Shildon	The urban district of Shildon
Spennymoor	The urban district of Spennymoor
Tow Law	The urban district of Tow Law
County of East Sussex	
Rye	The borough of Rye
Newhaven	The urban district of Newhaven
County of Essex	
Harwich	The borough of Harwich
Saffron Walden	The borough of Saffron Walden
Brightlingsea	The urban district of Brightlingsea
Burnham-on-Crouch	The urban district of Burnham-on-Crouch
Epping	The urban district of Epping
Frinton and Walton	The urban district of Frinton and Walton
Halstead	The urban district of Halstead
Waltham Holy Cross	The urban district of Waltham Holy Cross
West Mersea	The urban district of West Mersea
Wivenhoe	The urban district of Wivenhoe
County of Gloucestershire	
Tewkesbury	The borough of Tewkesbury
Cirencester	The urban district of Cirencester
Nailsworth	The urban district of Nailsworth
County of Greater Manchester	
Blackrod	The urban district of Blackrod
County of Hampshire	
Romsey	The borough of Romsey
Alton	The urban district of Alton
Petersfield	The urban district of Petersfield
County of Hereford and Worcester	
Bewdley	The borough of Bewdley
Droitwich	The borough of Droitwich
Evesham	The borough of Evesham
Leominster	The borough of Leominster
Kington	The urban district of Kington
Ross-on-Wye	The urban district of Ross-on-Wye
Stourport-on-Severn	The urban district of Stourport-on-Severn
County of Hertfordshire	
Berkhamsted	The urban district of Berkhamsted
Chorleywood	The urban district of Chorleywood
Royston	The urban district of Royston
Sawbridgeworth	The urban district of Sawbridgeworth
Tring	The urban district of Tring
Ware	The urban district of Ware

(1) Parishes	(2) Existing urban districts or boroughs
County of Humberside	
Hedon	The borough of Hedon
Barton-upon-Humber	The urban district of Barton-upon-Humber
Brigg	The urban district of Brigg
Hornsea	The urban district of Hornsea
County of Isle of Wight	
Ventnor	The urban district of Ventnor
County of Kent	
Faversham	The borough of Faversham
Hythe	The borough of Hythe
Lydd	The borough of Lydd
New Romney	The borough of New Romney
Sandwich	The borough of Sandwich
Tenterden	The borough of Tenterden
Broadstairs and St. Peters	The urban district of Broadstairs and St. Peter's
Sevenoaks	The urban district of Sevenoaks
Southborough	The urban district of Southborough
Swanscombe	The urban district of Swanscombe
County of Lancashire	
Carnforth	The urban district of Carnforth
Kirkham	The urban district of Kirkham
Longridge	The urban district of Longridge
Preesall	The urban district of Preesall
Whitworth	The urban district of Whitworth
Withnell	The urban district of Withnell
County of Leicestershire	
Ashby-de-la-Zouch	The urban district of Ashby de la Zouch
Ashby Woulds	The urban district of Ashby Woulds
Oakham	The urban district of Oakham
County of Lincolnshire	
Louth	The borough of Louth
Stamford	The borough of Stamford
Alford	The urban district of Alford
Bourne	The urban district of Bourne
Horncastle	The urban district of Horncastle
Mablethorpe and Sutton	The urban district of Mablethorpe and Sutton
Market Rasen	The urban district of Market Rasen
Skegness	The urban district of Skegness
Sleaford	The urban district of Sleaford
Woodhall Spa	The urban district of Woodhall Spa
County of Merseyside	
Rainford	The urban district of Rainford
County of Norfolk	
Thetford	The borough of Thetford
Cromer	The urban district of Cromer
Diss	The urban district of Diss
Downham Market	The urban district of Downham Market
East Dereham	The urban district of East Dereham
Hunstanton	The urban district of Hunstanton
North Walsham	The urban district of North Walsham
Sheringham	The urban district of Sheringham
Swaffham	The urban district of Swaffham

(1) Parishes	(2) Existing urban districts or boroughs
Wells-next-the-Sea	The urban district of Wells-next-the-Sea
Wymondham	The urban district of Wymondham
County of North Yorkshire	
Richmond	The borough of Richmond
Ripon	The city of Ripon
Filey	The urban district of Filey
Knaresborough	The urban district of Knaresborough
Malton	The urban district of Malton
Northallerton	The urban district of Northallerton
Norton-on-Derwent	The urban district of Norton
Pickering	The urban district of Pickering
Scalby	The urban district of Scalby
Selby	The urban district of Selby
Whitby	The urban district of Whitby
County of Northamptonshire	
Brackley	The borough of Brackley
Higham Ferrers	The borough of Higham Ferrers
Burton Latimer	The urban district of Burton Latimer
Desborough	The urban district of Desborough
Irthlingborough	The urban district of Irthlingborough
Oundle	The urban district of Oundle
Raunds	The urban district of Raunds
Rothwell	The urban district of Rothwell
County of Northumberland	
Alnwick	The urban district of Alnwick
Amble	The urban district of Amble
Hexham	The urban district of Hexham
Prudhoe	The urban district of Prudhoe
County of Nottinghamshire	
Eastwood	The urban district of Eastwood
Warsop	The urban district of Warsop
County of Oxfordshire	
Abingdon	The borough of Abingdon
Chipping Norton	The borough of Chipping Norton
Henley-on-Thames	The borough of Henley-on-Thames
Wallingford	The borough of Wallingford
Woodstock	The borough of Woodstock
Bicester	The urban district of Bicester
Thame	The urban district of Thame
Wantage	The urban district of Wantage
Witney	The urban district of Witney
County of Salop	
Newport	The urban district of Newport
County of Somerset	
Chard	The borough of Chard
Glastonbury	The borough of Glastonbury
Wells	The city of Wells
Burnham-on-Sea and Highbridge	The urban district of Burnham-on-Sea
Crewkerne	The urban district of Crewkerne
Frome	The urban district of Frome

(1) Parishes	(2) Existing urban districts or boroughs
Ilminster	The urban district of Ilminster
Shepton Mallet	The urban district of Shepton Mallet
Street	The urban district of Street
Watchet	The urban district of Watchet
Wellington	The urban district of Wellington
County of South Yorkshire	
Penistone	The urban district of Penistone
Stocksbridge	The urban district of Stocksbridge
Tickhill	The urban district of Tickhill
County of Staffordshire	
Biddulph	The urban district of Biddulph
Leek	The urban district of Leek
Stone	The urban district of Stone
Uttoxeter	The urban district of Uttoxeter
County of Suffolk	
Aldeburgh	The borough of Aldeburgh
Beccles	The borough of Beccles
Eye	The borough of Eye
Southwold	The borough of Southwold
Sudbury	The borough of Sudbury
Bungay	The urban district of Bungay
Hadleigh	The urban district of Hadleigh
Halesworth	The urban district of Halesworth
Leiston	The urban district of Leiston-cum-Sizewell
Saxmundham	The urban district of Saxmundham
Stowmarket	The urban district of Stowmarket
Woodbridge	The urban district of Woodbridge
County of Surrey	
Godalming	The borough of Godalming
Haslemere	The urban district of Haslemere
County of Warwickshire	
Stratford-upon-Avon	The borough of Stratford-upon-Avon
Warwick	The borough of Warwick
Kenilworth	The urban district of Kenilworth
County of West Sussex	
Arundel	The borough of Arundel
Burgess Hill	The urban district of Burgess Hill
East Grinstead	The urban district of East Grinstead
Littlehampton	The urban district of Littlehampton
County of West Yorkshire	
Todmorden	The borough of Todmorden
Denholme	The urban district of Denholme
Hebden Royd	The urban district of Hebden Royd
Hemsworth	The urban district of Hemsworth
Otley	The urban district of Otley
Ripponden	The urban district of Ripponden
Silsden	The urban district of Silsden
County of Wiltshire	
Calne	The borough of Calne
Devizes	The borough of Devizes

(1) Parishes	(2) Existing urban districts or boroughs
Malmesbury	The borough of Malmesbury
Marlborough	The borough of Marlborough
Wilton	The borough of Wilton
Bradford-on-Avon	The urban district of Bradford-on-Avon
Melksham	The urban district of Melksham
Warminster	The urban district of Warminster
Westbury	The urban district of Westbury

PART II

(1) Parishes	(2) Parts of existing urban districts
County of Cheshire Culcheth and Glazebury	So much of the urban district of Golborne as is comprised in the district of Warrington
County of Cumbria Lakes	So much of the urban district of Lakes as is comprised in the district of South Lakeland
Patterdale	So much of the urban district of Lakes as is comprised in the district of Eden
County of Lancashire Turton North	So much of the urban district of Turton as is comprised in the district of Blackburn
County of Merseyside Billinge Chapel End	So much of the urban district of Billinge-and-Winstanley as is comprised in the district of St. Helens
Seneley Green	So much of the urban district of Ashton-in-Makerfield as is comprised in the district of St. Helens

22nd June 1973.

Geoffrey Rippon,
Secretary of State for the
Environment.

EXPLANATORY NOTE
(This Note is not part of the Order.)

Part V of Schedule 1 to the Local Government Act 1972 makes provision for the constitution of parishes for areas of existing boroughs and urban districts in England. This Order gives effect to proposals made by the Local Government Boundary Commission for England. It also specifies a date for certain electoral provisions of the 1972 Act (see article 4).

STATUTORY INSTRUMENTS

1973 No. 1114 (L.15)

CRIMINAL PROCEDURE, ENGLAND AND WALES

The Criminal Appeal (Reference of Points of Law) Rules 1973

Made - - -	*22nd June* 1973
Laid before Parliament	*3rd July* 1973
Coming into Operation	*1st October* 1973

We, the Crown Court rule committee, in exercise of the powers conferred upon us by section 99 of the Supreme Court of Judicature (Consolidation) Act 1925(**a**) and section 46 of the Criminal Appeal Act 1968(**b**) as amended by section 56(1) of and paragraph 57(2) of Schedule 8 to the Courts Act 1971(**c**), hereby make the following Rules:—

1. These Rules may be cited as the Criminal Appeal (Reference of Points of Law) Rules 1973 and shall come into operation on 1st October 1973.

2.—(1) In these Rules—

"court" means the Criminal Division of the Court of Appeal;

"reference" means a reference of a point of law to the court in pursuance of section 36 of the Criminal Justice Act 1972(**d**);

"the registrar" means the registrar of criminal appeals;

"respondent", in relation to any reference, means the acquitted person in whose case the point of law referred arose.

(2) The Interpretation Act 1889(**e**) shall apply for the interpretation of these Rules as it applies for the interpretation of an Act of Parliament.

3.—(1) Every reference shall be in writing and shall—

(*a*) specify the point of law referred and, where appropriate, such facts of the case as are necessary for the proper consideration of the point of law;

(*b*) summarise the arguments intended to be put to the court; and

(*c*) specify the authorities intended to be cited:

Provided that no mention shall be made in the reference of the proper name of any person or place which is likely to lead to the identification of the respondent.

(2) A reference shall be entitled "Reference under section 36 of the Criminal Justice Act 1972" together with the year and number of the reference.

(**a**) 1925 c. 49.	(**b**) 1968 c. 19.
(**c**) 1971 c. 23.	(**d**) 1972 c. 71.
(**e**) 1889 c. 63.	

4.—(1) The registrar shall cause to be served on the respondent notice of the reference which shall also—

(a) inform the respondent that the reference will not affect the trial in relation to which it is made or any acquittal in that trial;

(b) invite the respondent, within such period as may be specified in the notice (being not less than twenty-eight days from the date of service of the notice), to inform the registrar if he wishes to present any argument to the court and, if so, whether he wishes to present such argument in person or by counsel on his behalf.

(2) The court shall not hear argument by or on behalf of the Attorney-General until the period specified in the notice has expired unless the respondent agrees or has indicated that he does not wish to present any argument to the court.

5. The Attorney-General may withdraw or amend the reference at any time before the court have begun the hearing, or, after that, and until the court have given their opinion, may withdraw or amend the reference by leave of the court, and notice of such withdrawal or amendment shall be served on the respondent on behalf of the Attorney-General.

6. The court shall ensure that the identity of the respondent is not disclosed during the proceedings on a reference except where the respondent has given his consent to the use of his name in the proceedings.

7. An application under section 36(3) of the Criminal Justice Act 1972 (reference to the House of Lords) may be made orally immediately after the court give their opinion or by notice served on the registrar within the fourteen days next following.

8.—(1) For the purpose of these Rules service of a document on the respondent may be effected—

(a) in the case of a document to be served on a body corporate by delivering it to the secretary or clerk of the body at its registered or principal office or sending it by post addressed to the secretary or clerk of that body at that office;

(b) in the case of a document to be served on any other person by—

(i) delivering it to the person to whom it is directed, or

(ii) leaving it for him with some person at his last known or usual place of abode, or

(iii) sending it by post addressed to him at his last known or usual place of abode.

(2) For the purpose of these Rules, service of a document on the registrar may be effected by—

(a) delivering it to the registrar;

(b) addressing it to him and leaving it at his office in the Royal Courts of Justice, London, W.C.2; or (*c*) sending it by post addressed to him at the said office.

Dated 22nd June 1973.

> *Hailsham of St. Marylebone,* C.
> *Widgery,* C. J.
> *Frederick Lawton,* L. J.
> *George Bean,* J.
> *C. D. Aarvold.*
> *Alan S. Trapnell.*
> *D. R. Thompson.*
> *J. B. Edwards.*
> *Basil Wigoder.*
> *David Calcutt.*
> *A. Crawford Caffin.*
> *G. G. A. Whitehead.*

EXPLANATORY NOTE

(This Note is not part of the Rules.)

These Rules provide safeguards in respect of disclosure of the identity of an acquitted person where a point of law, arising out of the trial in which that person was acquitted, is referred to the Court of Appeal under section 36 of the Criminal Justice Act 1972; section 66 of that Act requires such rules of court to be made before the commencement of section 36.

The Rules also provide for the form of the reference, for notice to be given to the acquitted person and for certain other procedural matters.

STATUTORY INSTRUMENTS

1973 No. 1115

WAGES COUNCILS

The Wages Regulation (Rope, Twine and Net) Order 1973

Made - - - -	*25th June* 1973
Coming into Operation	*23rd July* 1973

Whereas the Secretary of State has received from the Rope, Twine and Net Wages Council (Great Britain) the wages regulation proposals set out in Schedules 1 and 2 hereto;

Now, therefore, the Secretary of State in exercise of powers conferred by section 11 of the Wages Councils Act 1959(a), as modified by Article 2 of the Counter-Inflation (Modification of Wages Councils Act 1959) Order 1973(b), and now vested in him(c), and of all other powers enabling him in that behalf, hereby makes the following Order:—

1. This Order may be cited as the Wages Regulation (Rope, Twine and Net) Order 1973.

2.—(1) In this Order the expression "the specified date" means the 23rd July 1973, provided that where, as respects any worker who is paid wages at intervals not exceeding seven days, that date does not correspond with the beginning of the period for which the wages are paid, the expression "the specified date" means, as respects that worker, the beginning of the next such period following that date.

(2) The Interpretation Act 1889(d) shall apply to the interpretation of this Order as it applies to the interpretation of an Act of Parliament and as if this Order and the Order hereby revoked were Acts of Parliament.

3. The wages regulation proposals set out in Schedules 1 and 2 hereto shall have effect as from the specified date and as from that date the Wages Regulation (Rope, Twine and Net) Order 1972(e) shall cease to have effect.

Signed by order of the Secretary of State.
25th June 1973.

W. H. Marsh,
Assistant Secretary,
Department of Employment.

Article 3   SCHEDULE 1

The following minimum remuneration shall be substituted for the statutory minimum remuneration fixed by the Wages Regulation (Rope, Twine and Net) Order 1972 (Order R. (160)).

(a) 1959 c. 69.   (b) S.I. 1973/661 (1973 I, p. 2141).
(c) S.I. 1959/1769, 1968/729 (1959 I, p. 1795; 1968 II, p. 2108).
(d) 1889 c. 63.   (e) S.I. 1972/782 (1972 II, p. 2549).

STATUTORY MINIMUM REMUNERATION

Part I

GENERAL

1. The minimum remuneration payable to a worker to whom this Schedule applies for all work except work to which a minimum overtime rate applies under Part III of this Schedule is:—

(1) in the case of a time worker, the general minimum time rate, or, where appropriate, the minimum weekly remuneration payable to the worker under Part II of this Schedule;

(2) in the case of a worker employed on piece work—

(a) where a general minimum piece rate applies under Part II of this Schedule, that piece rate increased by 26½ per cent., or

(b) where no general minimum piece rate applies, piece rates each of which would yield, in the circumstances of the case, to an ordinary worker at least the same amount of money as the piece work basis time rate applicable to the worker under paragraph 3(5) of this Schedule.

DEFINITIONS

2. In this Schedule, unless the context otherwise requires,

(1) SHIFT WORKER means a worker employed on a shift system in accordance with which—

(a) a 24-hour period is divided into two or more shifts, one of which is a night shift; or

(b) there is no night shift and the remainder of the day is divided into two or more shifts;

and for the purposes of this definition NIGHT SHIFT means a turn of duty which includes some period of employment between 10 p.m. on one day and 6 a.m. on the next following day.

(2) HARD FIBRES means manilla, sisal, maguey fibre, New Zealand hemp or coir or a mixture thereof;

SHRINK NETTING means that the netting is made by shrinking or gaining, that is to say, the process of putting two meshes into one mesh or vice versa in order to obtain the required taper, shrink or gain;

PLAIN NETTING is ordinary braiding, single selvedge, the net mesh when straight hanging diamond;

A RAN SHORT REEL is the amount of twine wound on a reel 69 inches in circumference in 400 revolutions or 766⅔ yards;

SIZE OF MESH means in the case of all nets, other than the stack nets referred to in paragraph 9, the total length of two adjacent sides of the mesh, measured from the inside of one knot to the outside of the other.

Part II

ALL SECTIONS OF THE TRADE

GENERAL MINIMUM TIME RATES, MINIMUM WEEKLY REMUNERATION AND PIECE WORK BASIS TIME RATES

3.—(1) Subject to the provisions of sub-paragraphs (2) to (4) of this paragraph, the general minimum time rates payable to male and female workers of the categories specified in this sub-paragraph are the rates set out in Columns 2, 4 or 6 as appropriate of the next following Table:

(a) Warehouse and store personnel employed in lifting or carrying packages exceeding 56 lbs in weight;

(b) Bale openers;

(c) Tar house operators (kettle or machine), proofers, dyers and batching makers;

(d) Operators of braiding and plaiting machines producing material in excess of 1″ (24-mm) diameter;

(e) Operators employed in stranding, laying and coiling of ropes and lines in excess of ⅝″ (16-mm) diameter, either by house machine or walk, but not including frame or creel minders;

(f) Operators employed in cutting, splicing, hanking and making up ropes, cords and lines in excess of ⅝″ (16-mm) diameter;

(g) Operators employed in hand braiding, fixing and rigging of netting from any material in excess of ⅝″ (16-mm) diameter;

(h) Fork lift and truck drivers, oilers, greasers and belt menders;

(i) Workers not coming within any of the categories specified in (a) to (h) above.

(2) Where, in any week, the remuneration payable to a worker for the hours worked (excluding overtime) in that week, calculated at the appropriate general minimum time rate, together with any bonus payments or holiday remuneration payable to the worker in that week amounts to less than the minimum weekly remuneration specified for that worker in Columns 3, 5 or 7 as appropriate of the next following Table, the minimum remuneration (exclusive of any amount payable in respect of overtime) payable to that worker in that week shall be the minimum weekly remuneration so specified.

(3) For the purposes of the preceding sub-paragraph the minimum weekly remuneration shall be reduced proportionately according as the number of hours worked (excluding overtime) is less than 40 where—

(a) The worker is a part-time worker who normally works for the employer for less than 40 hours a week by reason only of the fact that

  (i) he does not hold himself out as normally available for work for more than the number of hours he normally works in the week:

  or

  (ii) he was engaged to work under a system of part-time working in operation in the factory or workshop where he is employed.

(b) The worker works for less than 40 hours in any week by reason of absence at any time during that week with the consent of the employer or because of proved incapacity due to illness or injury:

  or

(c) The employer is unable to provide the worker with work by reason of a strike or shortage of work or circumstances beyond his control and gives the worker notice to that effect two clear weeks before the week or weeks in question in the case of a shortage of work and four clear days in any other case:

  or

(d) The worker's employment is terminated before the end of the week.

(4) Except as provided by sub-paragraph (3)(b) of this paragraph, the minimum weekly remuneration specified in Columns 3, 5 or 7 as appropriate of the next following Table shall not be payable to a worker in any week in which that worker at any time in that week is absent from work without the consent of the employer.

TABLE OF GENERAL MINIMUM TIME RATES AND MINIMUM WEEKLY REMUNERATION

TIME WORKERS	WORKERS OTHER THAN SHIFT WORKERS (including homeworkers)		SHIFT WORKERS (WHEN EMPLOYED ON DAY SHIFTS)		SHIFT WORKERS (WHEN EMPLOYED ON NIGHT SHIFTS)	
Column 1	Column 2 General Minimum Time Rate	Column 3 Minimum Weekly Remuneration	Column 4 General Minimum Time Rate	Column 5 Minimum Weekly Remuneration	Column 6 General Minimum Time Rate	Column 7 Minimum Weekly Remuneration
	Per hour p	£	Per hour p	£	Per hour p	£
WORKERS IN THE CATEGORIES SPECIFIED IN (a) TO (h) OF SUB-PARAGRAPH (1) OF THIS PARAGRAPH:—						
WORKERS AGED 18 YEARS OR OVER—						
Male workers	43¾	19·15	49¼	21·55	52½	23·00
Female workers	39¾	17·20	44¼	19·35	—	—
Provided that the following rates shall apply to new entrants who enter or have entered the trade for the first time at or over the age of 18 years:—						
Male workers—for the first eight weeks of employment	43¾	17·50	43¾	17·50	43¾	17·50
Female workers—for the first eight weeks of employment	39¾	15·90	39¾	15·90	—	—
WORKERS AGED UNDER 18 YEARS All workers, being aged—						
17½ years and under 18 years	33½	13·40	37¼	15·10	—	—
17 ,, ,, 17½ ,, ,, ...	30	12·00	33¾	13·50	—	—
16½ ,, ,, 17 ,, ,, ...	26½	10·60	29¾	11·90	—	—
Under 16½ years	23	9·20	26	10·40	—	—

TIME WORKERS	WORKERS OTHER THAN SHIFT WORKERS (including homeworkers)		SHIFT WORKERS (WHEN EMPLOYED ON DAY SHIFTS)		SHIFT WORKERS (WHEN EMPLOYED ON NIGHT SHIFTS)	
	General Minimum Time Rate	Minimum Weekly Remuneration	General Minimum Time Rate	Minimum Weekly Remuneration	General Minimum Time Rate	Minimum Weekly Remuneration
Column 1	Column 2	Column 3	Column 4	Column 5	Column 6	Column 7
	Per hour p	£	Per hour p	£	Per hour p	£
WORKERS SPECIFIED IN (i) OF SUB-PARAGRAPH (1) OF THIS PARAGRAPH:—						
All workers, being aged—						
18 years or over	37¾	16·40	42½	18·45	52½	23·00
17½ and under 18 years	33½	13·40	37¾	15·10	—	—
17 „ „ 17½ „	30	12·00	33¾	13·50	—	—
16½ „ „ 17 „	26½	10·60	29¾	11·90	—	—
Under 16½ years	23	9·20	26	10·40	—	—
Provided that, for the first eight weeks of employment, the following rates shall apply to new entrants who enter or have entered the trade for the first time at or over the age of 18 years	37¾	15·10	37¾	15·10	—	—

(5) The piece work basis time rates applicable to the male or female workers specified in Column 1 of the next following Table, when employed on piece work with the materials specified in Column 2 or 3 as the case may be, are the rates set out in Column 2 or 3 respectively.

TABLE OF PIECE WORK BASIS TIME RATES

WORKERS EMPLOYED ON PIECE WORK	Fibres other than man-made fibres of continuous filament	Man-made fibres of continuous filament
Column 1	Column 2	Column 3
	Per hour p	Per hour p
Workers in the categories specified in (a) to (h) of sub-paragraph (1) of this paragraph:—		
Male workers other than shift workers	44½	—
Female ,, ,, ,, ,, ...	40½	42¼
Male shift workers on day shift	50	—
Female ,, ,, ,, ,, ...	45½	48
Male workers on night shift	53½	—
Workers in the category specified in (i) of sub-paragraph (1) of this paragraph:—		
Workers other than shift workers	38½	40¼
Shift workers on day shift	43¼	45¾
Shift workers on night shift	53½	—

(6) In this paragraph—

"bonus payments" means any production, merit, incentive or similar bonus payments payable at intervals of not more than one month;

"the trade" means the Rope, Twine and Net Trade as specified in paragraph 14.

GENERAL MINIMUM PIECE RATES
MAKING COTTON NORSELLS

4. The general minimum piece rates payable per pound to female home-workers for making cotton norsells are as follows:—

11 inches and upwards:—

	p			p
32s/18 ply norsells	93·055	32s/36 ply norsells	39·584
32s/21 ,, ,, ...	77·084	32s/42 ,, ,, ...	31·500
32s/24 ,, ,, ...	61·705	32s/48 ,, ,, ...	28·819
32s/27 ,, ,, ...	54·514	32s/54 ,, ,, ...	26·042
32s/30 ,, ,, ...	46·527	32s/60 ,, ,, ...	22·395

MAKING HEMP NORSELLS

5. The general minimum piece rates payable per 1,000 to female home-workers for making hemp norsells are as follows:—

	Natural colour	Tanned			Natural colour	Tanned
	p	p			p	p
18 inch	46·527	55·209	36 inch		81·250	93·055
20 ,, ...	47·222	56·510	42 ,, ...		89·757	103·299
22 ,, ...	49·305	59·027	48 ,, ...		103·299	115·320
24 ,, ...	55·989	62·674				

HANDBRAIDING, HANDKNOTTING OR HANDBAITING NETS FROM FIBRES NOT BEING HARD FIBRES OR MAN-MADE FIBRES OF CONTINUOUS FILAMENT

NETS MADE FROM SINGLE TWINE

6.—(1) The general minimum piece rates set out in the next following Table are per dozen rans short reel or per 9,200 yards and are payable, subject to the provisions of this paragraph, to female home-workers employed on handbraiding, handknotting or handbaiting nets made from single twine (of sizes up to and including 36 lbs. per dozen rans short reel or per 9,200 yards) from fibres not being hard fibres or man-made fibres of continuous filament.

(2) The length of the nets referred to in Columns 3 to 8 inclusive of the said Table is the length measured by stretched mesh or through the hand.

(3) Where the twine is of a size larger than 36 lbs. per dozen rans short reel or per 9,200 yards the general minimum piece rates payable to the said workers are the rates set out in the said Table increased as follows:—

Size of Twine	Additions
	£
Over 36 lbs. and up to and including 48 lbs.	0·840
,, 48 ,, ,, ,, ,, ,, ,, 60 ,, ...	1·965
,, 60 ,, ,, ,, ,, ,, ,, 84 ,, ...	2·611
,, 84 ,, ,, ,, ,, ,, ,, 96 ,, ...	2·667
,, 96 ,, ,, ,, ,, ,, ,, 108 ,, ...	3·000
,, 108 ,, ,, ,, ,, ,, ,, 120 ,, ...	3·500
,, 120 ,, ,, ,, ,, ,, ,, 132 ,, ...	4·000
,, 132 ,, ,, ,, ,, ,, ,, 144 ,, ...	4·500
,, 144 ,, ,, ,, ,, ,, ,, 156 ,, ...	5·000
,, 156 ,, ...	5·500

(4) Where the work is double knotted work, the general minimum piece rates payable to the said workers shall be one and two-thirds times the rates payable for single knotted work.

TABLE OF PIECE RATES

Twines of sizes up to and including 36 lbs. per dozen rans short reel or per 9,200 yards

Size of mesh	Plain netting	Shrink or square mesh work irrespective of numbers of meshes begun or ended (single or double selvedge) and plain netting with double selvedge	Netting braided in the form of a hose or bag, including shrimp and landing nets, billiard table pockets and other fancy nets					
			Length 30 inches and over	Length 20 inches and over but under 30 inches	Length 15 inches and over but under 20 inches	Length 10 inches and over but under 15 inches	Length 5 inches and over but under 10 inches	Length under 5 inches
	Column 1	Column 2	Column 3	Column 4	Column 5	Column 6	Column 7	Column 8
	£	£	£	£	£	£	£	£
Over 7 inch	7·47	7·75	8·13	9·32	10·28	10·06	11·61	12·19
5 inch and over up to and including 7 inch	7·69	8·13	8·50	9·77	10·74	11·55	12·13	12·74
4 inch and over up to but not including 5 inch	8·31	8·75	9·15	10·52	11·58	12·44	13·07	13·72

Size of mesh	Plain netting	Shrink or square mesh work irrespective of numbers of meshes begun or ended (single or double selvedge) and plain netting with double selvedge	Netting braided in the form of a hose or bag, including shrimp and landing nets, billiard table pockets and other fancy nets					
			Length 30 inches and over	Length 20 inches and over but under 30 inches	Length 15 inches and over but under 20 inches	Length 10 inches and over but under 15 inches	Length 5 inches and over but under 10 inches	Length under 5 inches
	Column 1	Column 2	Column 3	Column 4	Column 5	Column 6	Column 7	Column 8
	£	£	£	£	£	£	£	£
Rows per yard:— Over 18 and up to and including 21	8·86	9·27	9·74	11·20	12·32	13·24	13·94	14·60
" 21 " " " " 24	9·32	9·78	10·27	11·81	12·99	13·97	14·66	15·40
" 24 " " " " 27	9·78	10·27	10·57	12·38	13·62	14·64	15·37	16·14
" 27 " " " " 30	10·27	10·79	11·30	13·00	14·30	15·37	16·14	16·94
" 30 " " " " 33	10·72	11·27	11·82	13·59	14·95	16·07	16·87	17·72
" 33 " " " " 36	11·21	11·79	12·33	14·26	15·60	16·77	17·60	18·49
" 36 " " " " 39	11·68	12·24	12·84	14·77	16·24	17·46	18·33	19·25
" 39 " " " " 42	12·17	12·72	12·38	15·38	16·92	18·19	19·09	20·06
" 42 " " " " 45	12·61	13·24	13·87	15·95	17·55	18·86	19·81	20·79
" 45 " " " " 48	13·10	13·75	14·41	16·57	18·23	19·59	20·57	21·60
" 48 " " " " 54	14·03	14·75	15·46	17·78	19·56	21·02	22·07	23·18
" 54 " " " " 60	14·99	15·74	16·48	18·95	20·85	22·41	23·53	25·70
" 60 " " " " 66	15·92	16·74	18·20	20·16	21·18	23·84	25·03	26·28
" 66 " " " " 72	16·88	17·05	18·56	21·34	23·48	25·24	26·50	27·82
" 72 " " " " 78	17·81	18·69	19·59	22·53	24·79	26·64	27·97	29·37
" 78 " " " " 84	18·77	19·70	20·64	23·73	26·10	28·06	29·47	30·94
" 84 " " " " 90	19·70	20·69	21·69	24·94	27·43	29·49	30·97	32·51
" 90 " " " " 96	20·63	21·68	22·72	26·13	28·74	30·89	32·44	34·06
" 96 " " " " 108	22·53	23·65	24·78	28·50	31·34	33·70	35·39	37·16
" 108 " " " " 120	24·41	25·65	26·84	30·87	33·96	36·51	38·33	40·25
" 120 " " " " 132	26·31	27·62	28·95	33·30	36·63	39·38	41·34	43·41
" 132 " " " " 144	28·31	29·60	31·03	35·69	39·26	42·20	44·31	46·53
" 144 " " " " 162	31·04	31·84	34·15	39·28	43·20	46·44	48·77	51·20

NETS MADE FROM DOUBLE OR TREBLE TWINE

7. The general minimum piece rates payable to female home-workers employed on handbraiding, handknotting or handbaiting nets made from double or treble twine from fibres not being hard fibres or man-made fibres of continuous filament are respectively three-quarters and two-thirds of the general minimum piece rates which would be payable under paragraph 6 if the nets were made from single twine.

HANDBRAIDING OF TRAWL, SEINE OR OTHER NETS FROM HARD FIBRES

8.—(1) The general minimum piece rates set out in the next following Table are per lb. of twine and are payable, subject to the provisions of this paragraph, to female workers (including home-workers) employed in the handbraiding of trawl, seine or other nets (other than stack nets to which paragraph 9 applies) from hard fibres.

(2) The general minimum piece rates set out in the said Table are payable where the needles are filled at the expense of the worker. Where the needles are filled at the expense of the employer, the said rates shall be reduced by ten per cent.

(3) Where a net section contains meshes of more than one size, the general minimum piece rate payable for the whole section is that for a mesh size ascertained by a weighted average arrived at as follows: Multiply the number of rows of each separate mesh size by the size of the mesh, add the product, and divide the result by the total number of rows in the net section.

For example: The belly of a new trawl net consisting of 75 rows of 3-inch mesh, 50 rows of 4-inch mesh, 25 rows of 5-inch mesh: Calculation of weighted average mesh—

$$
\left.
\begin{array}{rcl}
75 \times 3 &=& 225 \\
50 \times 4 &=& 200 \\
25 \times 5 &=& 125 \\
\hline
150 && 550
\end{array}
\right\}
\text{Weighted average mesh size} = \frac{550}{150} = 3\tfrac{2}{3} \text{ inches.}
$$

The whole net section must be paid for as though the mesh was $3\tfrac{2}{3}$ inches throughout, viz., under Col. 8 of the said Table.

TABLE OF PIECE RATES

Size of mesh: less than / and / not less than

Twine used as { S. = Single, D. = Double }

Twine sizes:—
Up to and including 60 yds. per lb.
Over 60 up to and including 75 yds. per lb.
"   "   "   90   "
"   "   "   105   "
"   "   "   120   "
"   "   "   135   "
"   "   "   150   "
"   "   "   165   "
"   "   "   180   "
"   "   "   195   "
"   "   "   210   "
"   "   "   255   "

Columns 1–6 (all values in pence, p). Size of mesh —
Col. 1: less than 2 in., not less than —;
Col. 2: less than 2¼ in., not less than 2 in.;
Col. 3: less than 2½ in., not less than 2¼ in.;
Col. 4: less than 2¾ in., not less than 2½ in.;
Col. 5: less than 3 in., not less than 2¾ in.;
Col. 6: less than 3¼ in., not less than 3 in.

Twine size	Col. 1 S.	Col. 1 D.	Col. 2 S.	Col. 2 D.	Col. 3 S.	Col. 3 D.	Col. 4 S.	Col. 4 D.	Col. 5 S.	Col. 5 D.	Col. 6 S.	Col. 6 D.
60	41·40	28·05	26·91	18·75	23·35	16·14	20·48	14·15	17·54	12·50	14·76	10·50
75	44·10	29·60	28·55	19·71	24·65	17·02	21·36	14·76	18·40	12·94	15·90	11·03
90	47·30	31·51	30·55	20·75	26·47	18·14	22·65	15·93	19·80	13·97	16·84	11·98
105	51·23	34·03	32·98	22·06	28·31	20·06	24·48	16·75	21·27	14·50	18·40	12·68
120	55·22	36·80	35·85	23·62	30·39	21·18	26·47	17·89	22·65	15·63	19·89	13·38
135	60·15	39·93	39·06	25·88	33·16	24·23	28·64	19·19	24·74	16·58	21·62	14·58
150	66·05	43·31	42·98	28·31	36·73	27·08	31·08	20·75	26·91	17·98	23·44	15·97
165	73·09	47·22	47·48	31·25	40·81	29·78	34·12	22·83	29·60	19·71	25·96	17·37
180	80·81	52·17	52·52	34·30	45·57	32·81	37·85	25·09	32·98	21·88	28·73	19·28
195	90·97	57·98	58·86	37·85	51·14	36·38	42·63	27·96	37·41	24·23	32·56	21·27
210	102·70	64·15	65·81	41·75	57·21	40·81	48·18	31·34	42·63	27·26	37·06	23·79
255	127·70	79·78	81·78	52·00	70·48	44·89	60·33	38·97	52·26	33·33	46·53	29·87

Columns 7–12 (all values in pence, p). Size of mesh —
Col. 7: less than 3½ in., not less than 3¼ in.;
Col. 8: less than 3¾ in., not less than 3½ in.;
Col. 9: less than 4 in., not less than 3¾ in.;
Col. 10: less than 4¼ in., not less than 4 in.;
Col. 11: less than 4½ in., not less than 4¼ in.;
Col. 12: less than 4¾ in., not less than 4½ in.

Twine size	Col. 7 S.	Col. 7 D.	Col. 8 S.	Col. 8 D.	Col. 9 S.	Col. 9 D.	Col. 10 S.	Col. 10 D.	Col. 11 S.	Col. 11 D.	Col. 12 S.	Col. 12 D.
60	12·68	8·86	11·56	8·00	10·60	7·48	9·89	6·95	9·30	6·60	8·86	6·16
75	13·47	9·38	12·50	8·69	11·38	7·99	10·68	7·48	10·26	7·13	9·80	6·69
90	14·59	10·33	13·20	9·21	12·24	8·69	11·56	8·08	11·21	7·72	10·84	7·48
105	15·97	10·86	14·59	9·90	13·38	9·21	12·68	8·78	12·07	8·60	11·73	8·08
120	17·20	11·98	15·97	10·86	14·68	10·25	14·06	9·56	13·38	9·21	12·94	8·86
135	18·67	12·94	17·46	12·07	16·23	11·30	15·64	10·68	14·76	10·25	14·41	9·90
150	20·66	14·24	19·37	13·29	18·23	12·59	17·37	11·98	16·75	11·38	16·15	10·86
165	23·27	15·64	21·45	14·59	19·98	13·82	18·84	13·29	18·49	12·86	17·90	12·50
180	25·27	17·20	23·62	15·97	22·15	15·29	21·19	14·59	20·58	14·15	19·72	13·98
195	28·56	19·28	26·74	17·98	25·09	17·02	23·88	16·23	23·27	15·81	22·15	15·20
210	32·30	21·19	30·22	19·80	28·31	18·84	27·26	18·23	25·97	17·55	25·09	17·02
255	41·23	26·74	37·50	24·83	35·33	23·80	34·04	22·66	32·48	21·97	31·25	21·36

Size of mesh { less than … … …		Col. 13		Col. 14		Col. 15		Col. 16		Col. 17		Col. 18	
less than		5 in.		5¼ in.		5½ in.		5¾ in.		6 in.		—	
not less than		4¾ in.		5 in.		5¼ in.		5½ in.		5¾ in.		6 in.	
Twine used as { S. = Single / D. = Double }		S.	D.	S.	D.	S.	D.	S.	D.	S.	D.	S.	D.
Twine sizes:—		p	p	p	p	p	p	p	p	p	p	p	p
Up to and including 60 yds. per lb. …		8·69	6·08	8·25	5·99	8·08	5·90	7·99	5·55	7·72	5·48	7·48	5·40
Over 60 up to and including 75 yds. per lb.		9·30	6·60	9·13	6·51	8·78	6·16	8·69	6·09	8·25	5·99	8·08	5·90
„ 75 „ „ „ 90		10·26	7·13	9·90	6·95	9·56	6·69	9·30	6·60	9·13	6·51	8·86	6·16
„ 90 „ „ „ 105		11·38	7·72	10·86	7·56	10·68	7·48	10·51	7·30	10·25	7·13	10·07	6·95
„ 105 „ „ „ 120		12·68	8·69	12·07	8·60	11·29	8·08	11·47	7·99	11·30	7·72	11·02	7·56
„ 120 „ „ „ 135		14·15	9·56	13·47	9·21	13·20	8·86	12·86	8·78	12·68	8·69	12·50	8·69
„ 135 „ „ „ 150		15·90	10·68	15·55	10·33	14·76	10·07	14·50	9·90	14·15	9·80	14·06	9·47
„ 150 „ „ „ 165		17·37	11·98	16·85	11·47	16·23	11·30	16·06	11·02	15·81	10·86	16·64	10·77
„ 165 „ „ „ 180		19·37	13·29	18·67	12·94	18·40	12·68	18·05	12·50	17·46	12·24	17·37	12·07
„ 180 „ „ „ 195		21·63	14·59	20·84	14·41	20·07	13·97	19·80	13·82	19·54	13·38	19·37	13·29
„ 195 „ „ „ 210		23·88	16·23	23·27	15·97	22·22	15·64	21·97	15·20	21·62	15·11	21·36	14·76
„ 210 „ „ „ 255		29·78	20·66	28·91	19·80	27·44	18·84	26·65	18·49	25·88	17·98	24·83	17·36

HANDBRAIDING OF STACK NETS

9.—(1) The general minimum piece rates set out in the next following Table are payable to female workers (including home-workers) employed in the handbraiding of stack nets and shall apply to the making by hand of all such nets irrespective of the method of manufacture and the type of material used.

(2) The general minimum piece rates set out in the said Table are payable where the needles are filled at the expense of the worker. Where the needles are filled at the expense of the employer, the said rates shall be reduced by ten per cent.

TABLE OF PIECE RATES

Diamond mesh throughout		Square mesh throughout	
Size of mesh	Per dozen meshes	Size of mesh	Per square yard
	p		p
Less than 16 ins.		Less than 6 ins.	1·055
Not less than 16 ins. but less than 18 ins.	0·693	Not less than 6 ins. but less than 7 ins.	0·902
Not less than 18 ins. but less than 20 ins.	0·824	Not less than 7 ins. but less than 8 ins.	0·869
Not less than 20 ins. but less than 22 ins.	0·902	Not less than 8 ins. but less than 9 ins.	0·825
Not less than 22 ins. but less than 24 ins.	1·085	Not less than 9 ins. but less than 10 ins.	0·782
Not less than 24 ins. but less than 26 ins.	1·215	Not less than 10 ins. but less than 11 ins.	0·739
Not less than 26 ins. but less than 28 ins.	1·389	Not less than 11 ins. but less than 12 ins.	0·652
28 ins. and over	1·475	Not less than 12 ins. but less than 13 ins.	0·607
	1·605	Not less than 13 ins. but less than 14 ins.	0·564
		14 ins. and over	0·520

(3) For the purposes of this paragraph—

(a) Square yardage shall be calculated by multiplying in feet the length by the breadth of the net and dividing the result by nine.

(b) SIZE OF MESH is—

(i) in the case of diamond mesh, the total length of two adjacent sides of the mesh measured from the inside of one knot to the outside of the other;

(ii) in the case of square mesh, the length of one side of the mesh measured from the inside of one knot to the outside of the other.

PART III
OVERTIME AND WAITING TIME

10. This Part of this Schedule applies to a worker in any section of the Trade, not being—

(1) a home-worker employed in the net section on piece work or

(2) a female home-worker employed in a section other than the net section.

MINIMUM OVERTIME RATES

11.—(1) Subject to the provisions of sub-paragraph (2) of this paragraph, minimum overtime rates are payable to any worker to whom this Part of this Schedule applies as follows:—

(*a*) on any day other than a Saturday, Sunday or a customary holiday—
    (i) for the first two hours worked in excess of 8 hours   time-and-a-quarter
    (ii) thereafter   ...   .   time-and-a-half

(*b*) on a Saturday, not being a customary holiday—
    (i) for the first two hours worked   ...   .   time-and-a-quarter
    (ii) thereafter   ...   .   time-and-a-half

(*c*) on a Sunday or a customary holiday—
    for all time worked   ...   .   double time

(2) Where the employer and the worker by agreement in writing fix in respect of each weekday the number of hours after which a minimum overtime rate shall be payable and the total number of such hours amounts to 40 weekly, the following minimum overtime rates shall be payable in substitution for those set out in sub-paragraph (1) of this paragraph:—

(*a*) on any day other than a Saturday, Sunday or a customary holiday—
    (i) for the first two hours worked in excess of the
    agreed number of hours   ...   .   time-and-a-quarter
    (ii) thereafter   ...   .   time-and-a-half

(*b*) on a Saturday, not being a customary holiday—
    for all time worked in excess of the agreed number of
    hours   ...   .   time-and-a-half

Provided that where the said agreement provides that Saturday shall not normally be a working day, the following minimum overtime rates shall apply—
    (i) for the first two hours worked   ...   .   time-and-a-quarter
    (ii) thereafter   ...   .   time-and-a-half

(*c*) on a Sunday or a customary holiday—
    for all time worked   ...   .   double time

12. In this Part of this Schedule—

(1) The expression "customary holiday" means:—

    (*a*) (i)   In England and Wales:—

Good Friday, Easter Monday, *the last Monday in May, the last Monday in August*, Christmas Day, *26th December if it be not a Sunday, 27th December in a year when 25th or 26th December is a Sunday;* or where another day is substituted for any of the said days by national proclamation, that day; or in the case of the last Monday in August, or any day substituted therefor by national proclamation, such day, other than a weekly short day, as may be substituted therefor by the employer, being a day which is by local custom recognised as a day of holiday and which falls within three months of the day for which it is substituted;

(ii) In Scotland:—

> The New Year's holiday (2 days),
> The local Spring holiday (1 day),
> The local Autumn holiday (1 day) and
>> two other weekdays (being days upon which the worker normally attends for work) in the course of a calendar year, to be fixed by the employer and notified to the worker not less than three weeks before the holiday; or

(b) in the case of each of the said days, such weekday falling between 1st April and 30th September as may be substituted therefor by agreement between the employer and the workers.

(2) The expressions "time-and-a-quarter", "time-and-a-half" and "double time" mean respectively:—

(a) in the case of a time worker, one and a quarter times, one and a half times and twice the general minimum time rate otherwise payable to the worker;

(b) in the case where a piece work basis time rate is otherwise applicable to a piece worker,

(i) a time rate equal respectively to one quarter, one half and the whole of the said piece work basis time rate, and, in addition thereto,

(ii) the piece rates otherwise applicable under paragraph 1(2);

(c) in the case where a general minimum piece rate is otherwise payable to a piece worker employed in the net section of the trade on hand net braiding, knotting or baiting,

(i) a time rate equal respectively to one quarter, one half and the whole of the piece work basis time rate which would be applicable to a female worker under the provisions of paragraph 3 if a minimum overtime rate did not apply and, in addition thereto,

(ii) the said general minimum piece rate.

WAITING TIME

13.—(1) A worker is entitled to payment of the minimum remuneration specified in this Schedule for all time during which he is present on the premises of the employer, unless he is present thereon in any of the following circumstances:—

(a) without the employer's consent, express or implied;

(b) for some purpose unconnected with his work and other than that of waiting for work to be given to him to perform;

(c) by reason only of the fact that he is resident thereon;

(d) during normal meal times in a room or place in which no work is being done and he is not waiting for work to be given to him to perform.

(2) The minimum remuneration payable under sub-paragraph (1) of this paragraph to a piece worker when not engaged on piece work is that which would be payable if he were a time worker.

PART IV

APPLICABILITY OF STATUTORY MINIMUM REMUNERATION

14. This Schedule applies to workers in relation to whom the Rope, Twine and Net Wages Council (Great Britain) operates, that is to say, workers employed in Great Britain in the branches of work specified in the Schedule to the Trade Boards (Rope, Twine and Net Trade, Great Britain) (Constitution and Proceedings) Regulations 1933(a), but excluding therefrom the splicing or braiding of rope, cord or twine performed by hand or machine when incidental to, or carried on in association with or

---

(a) S.R. & O. 1933/1023 (1933, p. 2049).

in conjunction with, the operations specified in paragraphs 1 and 2 of the Appendix to the Trade Board (Made-up Textiles) Order 1920(a), or any other processes or operations which are specifically mentioned in the said Appendix.

The Schedule to the said Regulations reads as follows:—

"The Rope, Twine and Net Trade, that is to say—

(1) The making or re-making of (a) rope (including driving rope and banding), (b) cord (including blind and window cord, but excluding silk, worsted and other fancy cords), (c) core for wire-ropes, (d) lines, (e) twine (including binder and trawl twine), (f) lanyards, (g) net and similar articles.

(2) The bleaching, teazing, hackling, carding, preparing and spinning of the materials required for the making or re-making of any of the articles (a) to (g) above when carried on in the same factory or workshop as such making or re-making.

(3) The manufacture of packings, gaskins and spun yarns, when carried on in the same factory or workshop as the making or re-making of any of the articles (a) to (g) above.

(4) The braiding or splicing of articles made from rope, cord, twine or net.

(5) The mending of nets and the winding, twisting, doubling, laying, polishing, dressing, tarring, tanning, dyeing, balling, reeling, finishing, packing, despatching, warehousing and storing of any of the above articles, where these operations or any of them are carried on in a factory or workshop in which any of the articles (a) to (g) above are made or re-made;

but excluding the making of wire rope (unless made in the same factory or workshop as hemp or similar rope or core for wire rope), and also excluding the making of net in connection with the lace-curtain trade and the weaving of cloth."

SCHEDULE 2
Article 3

HOLIDAYS AND HOLIDAY REMUNERATION

The Wages Regulation (Rope, Twine and Net) (Holidays) Order 1970(b) (Order R.(156)) shall have effect as if in the Schedule thereto for sub-paragraph (2) of paragraph 2 (which relates to customary holidays) there were substituted the following:—

"(2) the said customary holidays are:—

(a) (i) in England and Wales—

Good Friday, Easter Monday, *the last Monday in May, the last Monday in August*, Christmas Day, *26th December if it be not a Sunday, 27th December in a year when 25th or 26th December is a Sunday;* or where another day is substituted for any of the said days by national proclamation, that day; or in the case of the last Monday in August, or any day substituted therefor by national proclamation, such day, other than a weekly short day, as may be substituted therefor by the employer, being a day which is by local custom recognised as a day of holiday and which falls within three months of the day for which it is substituted;

(ii) In Scotland:—
The New Year's holiday (2 days),
The local Spring holiday (1 day),
The local Autumn holiday (1 day) and
two other weekdays (being days upon which the worker normally attends for work) in the course of a calendar year, to be fixed by the employer and notified to the worker not less than three weeks before the holiday; or

(b) in the case of each of the said days, such weekday falling between 1st April and 30th September as may be substituted therefor by agreement between the employer and the workers."

(a) S.R. & O. 1920/1901 (1920 II, p. 782).   (b) S.I. 1970/979 (1970 II, p. 3110).

EXPLANATORY NOTE

(This Note is not part of the Order.)

This Order has effect from 23rd July 1973. Schedule 1 sets out the increased statutory minimum remuneration payable in substitution for that fixed by the Wages Regulation (Rope, Twine and Net) Order 1972 (Order R. (160)), which Order is revoked. Schedule 2 amends the provisions of the Wages Regulation (Rope, Twine and Net) (Holidays) Order 1970 (Order R. (156)), relating to customary holidays so as to take account of recent changes in the law and practice relating to public holidays.

New provisions are printed in italics.

STATUTORY INSTRUMENTS

1973 No. 1116 (S.82)

JUSTICES OF THE PEACE

The Justices Allowances (Scotland) Amendment Regulations 1973

Made - - -	*22nd June* 1973
Laid before Parliament	*3rd July* 1973
Coming into Operation	*6th July* 1973

In exercise of the powers conferred on me by section 8(6) and (7) of the Justices of the Peace Act 1949(a), as amended by section 31 of the Administration of Justice Act 1964(b), and of all other powers enabling me in that behalf, I hereby make the following regulations: —

1.—(1) These regulations may be cited as the Justices Allowances (Scotland) Amendment Regulations 1973 and shall come into operation on 6th July 1973.

(2) The Interpretation Act 1889(c) shall apply for the interpretation of these regulations as it applies for the interpretation of an Act of Parliament.

2. In Schedule 3 to the Justices Allowances (Scotland) Regulations 1971(d) as amended(e) (which sets out the rate of financial loss allowance payable to justices of the peace) for the expressions "£2·37½" and "£4·75" there shall be substituted the expressions "£2·75" and "£5·50" respectively.

Gordon Campbell,
One of Her Majesty's Principal
Secretaries of State.

St. Andrew's House,
Edinburgh.
22nd June 1973.

EXPLANATORY NOTE
(This Note is not part of the Regulations.)

These Regulations increase the rate of financial loss allowance payable to justices of the peace.

(a) 1949 c. 101.   (b) 1964 c. 42.
(c) 1889 c. 63.   (d) S.I. 1971/490 (1971 I, p. 1440).
(e) The relevant amending instrument is S.I. 1971/1990 (1971 III, p. 5672).

STATUTORY INSTRUMENTS

1973 No. 1117 (S.83)

SEEDS

The Seeds (EEC) (Scotland) General Licence 1973

Made - - -	*15th June* 1973
Coming into Operation	*1st July* 1973

Whereas I am satisfied that the circumstances connected with the sale or exposure for sale of the seeds described in the Schedule hereto (hereinafter called "the said seeds") in containers labelled and sealed with the official labels and seals of the European Economic Community are such that compliance with the provisions of section 1 of the Seeds Act 1920(a), as amended by section 12 of the Agriculture (Miscellaneous Provisions) Act 1954(b) and section 24 of the Agriculture (Miscellaneous Provisions) Act 1963(c), cannot reasonably be enforced and that an exemption should be granted so as to apply generally to all persons as regards such provisions in relation to such sales or exposures for sale of the said seeds;

Now therefore in exercise of the powers conferred upon me by section 1(7) of the Seeds Act 1920 and of all other powers enabling me in that behalf and in accordance with Regulation 9 of the Seeds (Scotland) Regulations 1961(d) I hereby grant the following licence:—

1. This licence which may be cited as the Seeds (EEC) (Scotland) General Licence 1973 shall come into operation on 1st July 1973 and shall cease to have effect on 30th June 1974.

2. On the sale or exposure for sale of the said seeds in containers labelled and sealed with the official labels and seals of the European Economic Community the seller is hereby exempted from compliance with the provisions of section 1 of the Seeds Act 1920.

Gordon Campbell,
One of Her Majesty's Principal
Secretaries of State.

St. Andrew's House,
Edinburgh.
15th June 1973.

(a) 1920 c. 54.
(c) 1963 c. 11.

(b) 1954 c. 39.
(d) S.I. 1961/274 (1961 I, p. 446).

SCHEDULE

The seeds of the following kinds:—

barley, maize, oats, rye, wheat, cocksfoot, meadow fescue, red fescue, tall fescue, meadow foxtail, smooth-stalked meadowgrass, rough-stalked meadow-grass, hybrid ryegrass, Italian ryegrass, perennial ryegrass, Westerwolds rye-grass, timothy, birdsfoot trefoil, alsike clover, crimson clover, red clover, white clover, lucerne, sainfoin, field pea, field (horse or tic) bean, fodder kale, mustard (black, brown or white) fodder radish, swede rape, turnip rape, swede, flax, linseed, lupin, sunflower, vetch, fodder beet, sugar beet.

EXPLANATORY NOTE

(This Note is not part of the Licence.)

This Licence relieves sellers of seeds from the obligations imposed by the Seeds Act 1920 to test and give prescribed particulars of the kinds of seeds set out in the Schedule to the Licence, provided that the containers of such seeds bear the official labels and seals of the European Economic Community.

STATUTORY INSTRUMENTS

1973 No. 1118 (L.16)

MAGISTRATES' COURTS
The Adoption (Juvenile Court) Rules 1973

Made - - - -	*25th June* 1973
Laid before Parliament	*4th July* 1973
Coming into Operation	*1st August* 1973

The Lord Chancellor, in exercise of the powers conferred on him by section 15 of the Justices of the Peace Act 1949(a), as extended by section 122 of the Magistrates' Courts Act 1952(b), section 9 of the Adoption Act 1958(c) and sections 2(2) and 3(2) of the Welsh Language Act 1967(d), after consultation with the Rule Committee appointed under the said section 15, hereby makes the following Rules:—

1. These Rules may be cited as the Adoption (Juvenile Court) Rules 1973 and shall come into operation on 1st August 1973.

2. In these Rules "the principal Rules" means the Adoption (Juvenile Court) Rules 1959(e) as amended (f).

3. In Rule 8(2)(a) and (3) of the principal Rules (appointment of guardian ad litem) for the words "children's officer" wherever they occur there shall be substituted the words "director of social services".

4. After paragraph (2) of Rule 12 of the principal Rules (service of notice of an application for adoption) there shall be added the following paragraph:—

"(3) Where the court has been requested to dispense with the consent of a parent or guardian of the infant in a case where a serial number has been assigned to the applicant in accordance with Rule 2 of these Rules, the justices' clerk shall omit from the statement of the facts on which the applicant intends to rely which is required to be attached to the notice set out in Form 6 any reference to the applicant other than by that serial number.".

5. For Rule 19 of the principal Rules (form of an adoption order) there shall be substituted the following Rule:—

"**19.**—(1) Subject to paragraphs (2) and (3) of this Rule an adoption order shall be drawn up in Form 9.

(2) Where—

(a) an adoption order is made by a court sitting in Wales or Monmouthshire in respect of an infant who was born in Wales or Monmouthshire or who is treated for the purposes of section 21(3) of the Adoption Act 1958 as born in the registration district and sub-district in which the court sits; and

(b) the adopter so requests before the order is drawn up,

the form of Schedule set out in Form 9A shall be used in place of the Schedule contained in Form 9.

(a) 1949 c. 101.	(b) 1952 c. 55.
(c) 1958 c. 5 (7 & 8 Eliz. 2).	(d) 1967 c. 66.
(e) S.I. 1959/504 (1959 I, p. 1626).	(f) S.I. 1965/2072 (1965 III, p. 6097).

(3) Where, in accordance with paragraph (2) of this Rule, the form of Schedule set out in Form 9A is used, the adoption order shall specify both in English and in Welsh the particulars to be entered under the headings in entries 2 to 6 of that Schedule and, in the case of any discrepancy between the English and Welsh text of any such particulars, the English text shall prevail.".

6. Paragraph (2) of Rule 20 of the principal Rules (size of copy of adoption order to be sent to Registrar General) shall be omitted.

7. For Rule 21 of the principal Rules (abridged copy of adoption order to be served on applicant) there shall be substituted the following Rule:—

"**21.**—(1) Subject to paragraph (2) of this Rule, within 7 days after the making of an adoption order the justices' clerk shall serve on the applicant an abridged copy of the adoption order in Form 10 signed by a member of or the clerk to the court.

(2) Where, in accordance with paragraph (2) of Rule 19 of these Rules, the adoption order contains a Schedule in the form set out in Form 9A, the copy of the order required to be served on the applicant under paragraph (1) of this Rule shall contain a Schedule in that form instead of in the form set out in Form 10 and paragraph (3) of the said Rule 19 shall have effect in relation to the copy as it has effect in relation to the order.".

8. For paragraph 13 of Form 1 in Schedule 1 to the principal Rules (application for adoption order) there shall be substituted the following paragraph:—

"13. I/We request the court to dispense with the consent of the infant's mother/father/guardian on the ground that .... [8] and I/we attach a statement of the facts on which I/we intend to rely.".

9. For paragraph E of the medical report as to the health of the infant set out in Form 3 in Schedule 1 to the principal Rules there shall be substituted the following paragraph:—

"E. (i) (*To be completed in the case of a child at least 6 weeks old at the time of the test—either test (a) or tests (b) (i) and (ii) may be carried out except where test (b)(i) or (ii) is positive, when test (a) must also be carried out*)

   (*a*) Result of a suitable serological test of the child's blood for syphilis (please specify test)............

   (*b*) Result of suitable serological tests of the mother's blood for syphilis—

     (i) reagin (please specify test)

     (ii) verification (please specify test)

   (ii) (*To be completed in the case of a child over 6 complete days (excluding the day of his birth) and under 2 years old at the time of the test*)

Result of test of the child's blood for the purpose of estimating the level of phenylalanine therein............ ".

10. For the entry numbered "(5)" in Form 6 in Schedule 1 to the principal Rules (notice to respondent of application for adoption order) there shall be substituted the following entry:—

"(5) The court has been requested to dispense with your consent on the ground that .... and a statement of the facts on which the applicant[s] intend[s] to rely is attached.".

11. For Form 9 in Schedule 1 to the principal Rules (form of adoption order) there shall be substituted the following Form:—

Rule 19(1)   "Form 9

Adoption Order (Adoption (J.C.) Rules 1959, r. 19)

In the [county of   . Petty Sessional
Division of   ].

Before the Juvenile Court sitting at   .

Whereas an application has been made by
[and   his wife] (more particularly described in the Schedule hereto and hereinafter called the applicant[s]) for an
adoption order in respect of   (*enter names and
surname as shown in birth certificate or Adopted Children Register or, if not
so shown, by which known before being placed for adoption*) an infant of the
                              sex the [adopted] child of
(hereinafter called the child);

And Whereas the name or names and surname by which the child is to be
known are   ;

And Whereas the court is satisfied that the applicant[s] [is] [are] qualified
in accordance with the provisions of the Adoption Act 1958 to adopt the
child and that all conditions precedent to the making of an adoption order
by the court have been fulfilled;

It is ordered that the applicant[s] be authorised to adopt the child;

[And as regards costs, it is ordered that   ;]

[And the court not being satisfied as to the precise date of the child's birth,
it is determined that the probable date thereof was that specified in the
Schedule hereto;]

[And the court not being satisfied as to the country of the child's birth
and it [not] appearing probable that the child was born within the United
Kingdom, the Channel Islands or the Isle of Man the child's country of birth
is [not] specified in the Schedule hereto as ["England"] ["Wales"];]

[And the country of the child's birth being specified in the Schedule hereto
as [England] [Wales] but the court not being satisfied as to the registration
district and sub-district in which the child was born, the district and sub-
district in which the court sits are specified in the Schedule hereto as those
in which the child was born;]

And it is directed that the Registrar General shall, in accordance with the
Adoption Act 1958, enter in the Adopted Children Register the particulars
specified in the Schedule hereto;

[And the court being satisfied that the child is identical with
                              to whom the entry numbered   made on the
                              day of   , 19   , in [the Registers
of Births for the registration district of   and sub-district
of   in the county of   ]
[the Adopted Children Register] relates, it is directed that the said entry be
marked with the word ["Adopted"] ["Re-adopted"].]

[The following payment or reward is sanctioned   .]

Dated the   day of   , 19   .

(Signature)
Justice of the Peace for the [county]
first above-mentioned.

[*or* By order of the Court,

J.C.,
Clerk of the Court.]

SCHEDULE

1. No. of entry	
2. Date .... and country .... of birth of child	*Registration District* .... *Sub-district* ....
3. Name and surname of child	
4. Sex of child	
5. Name and surname, address and occupation of adopter or adopters........	....
6. Date of adoption order and description of court by which made	....
7. Date of entry	
8. Signature of officer deputed by Registrar General to attest the entry	

Notes

1. Entries 1, 7 and 8 should be completed by the Registrar General.

2. *Name and surname of child.* Enter the name or names and surname by which the child is to be known.

3. *Sex of child.* Enter "male" or "female", as the case may be.

4. *Address of adopter or adopters.* If the applicant is not ordinarily resident in Great Britain, enter the place abroad where he ordinarily resides.".

12. After Form 9 in Schedule 1 to the principal Rules there shall be added the following Form:—

Rule 19(2)   "Form 9A

Form of bilingual Schedule for inclusion in adoption orders made by Welsh courts (Adoption (J.C.) Rules 1959, r.19)

SCHEDULE

1. No. of entry Rhif y gofnod	
2. Date .... Dyddiad .... and a'r country of birth of child............................. wlad lle ganwyd y plentyn............................	*Registration District Dosbarth Cofrestru* .... *Sub-district Is-ddosbarth*
3. Name and surname of child Enw a chyfenw y plentyn	
4. Sex of child Rhyw y plentyn	
5. Name and surname, Enw a chyfenw, address cyfeiriad and a occupation of adopter or adopters gwaith y mabwysiadwr neu'r mabwysiadwyr	
6. Date of adoption order... Dyddiad y gorchymyn mabwysiadu .... and description of court by which made .... a disgrifiad o'r llys a'i gwnaeth	
7. Date of entry Dyddiad y gofnod	
8. Signature of officer deputed by Registrar General to attest the entry Llofnod y swyddog a benodwyd gan y Cofrestrydd Cyffredinol i ardystio'r gofnod	

Notes

1. Entries 1, 7 and 8 should be completed by the Registrar General.

2. *Name and surname of child.* Enter the name or names and surname by which the child is to be known.

3. *Sex of child.* Enter "male" or "female", as the case may be.

4. *Address of adopter or adopters.* If the applicant is not ordinarily resident in Great Britain, enter the place abroad where he ordinarily resides.".

Nodiadau

1. Dylid llenwi 1, 7 ac 8 gan y Cofrestrydd Cyffredinol.

2. *Enw a chyfenw'r plentyn.* Rhowch yr enw neu'r enwau ynghyd â'r cyfenw yr adnabyddir y plentyn wrthynt.

3. *Rhyw'r plentyn.* Rhowch "gwryw" neu "benyw", fel y bo'r achos.

4. *Cyfeiriad y person neu'r personau sy'n mabwysiadu.* Os nad yw'r sawl sy'n gwneud y cais yn byw'n arferol ym Mhrydain Fawr, rhowch enw'r lle tramor lle y bydd yn byw'n arferol.".

13. For Form 10 in Schedule 1 to the principal Rules there shall be substituted the following Form:—

"Form 10   Rule 21

Adoption Order (Adoption (J.C.) Rules 1959, r. 21)

In the [county of   . Petty Sessional Division of   ].

Before the Juvenile Court sitting at   .

Whereas an application has been made by   [and his wife] (more particularly described in the Schedule hereto and hereinafter called the applicant[s]) for an adoption order in respect of   (*enter names and surname as shown in birth certificate or Adopted Children Register or, if not so shown, by which infant was known before being placed for adoption*) (hereinafter called the child);

It is ordered that the applicant[s] be authorised to adopt the child;

And it is directed that the Registrar General shall, in accordance with the Adoption Act 1958, enter in the Adopted Children Register the particulars specified in the Schedule hereto.

Dated the   day of   , 19   .

(*Signature*)
Justice of the Peace for the [county] aforesaid.

[*or* By order of the Court,

J.C.,
Clerk of the Court.]

SCHEDULE

1. No. of entry	
2. Date and country of birth of child	*Registration District* .... *Sub-district* ....
3. Name and surname of child	
4. Sex of child	
5. Name and surname, address and occupation of adopter or adopters	
6. Date of adoption order and description of court by which made	
7. Date of entry	
8. Signature of officer deputed by Registrar General to attest the entry	

".

Dated 25th June 1973.

Hailsham of St. Marylebone, C.

EXPLANATORY NOTE

(This Note is not part of the Rules.)

These Rules amend the Adoption (Juvenile Court) Rules 1959.

Rule 3 substitutes in Rule 8 of the Rules of 1959, which provides for the appointment of a guardian ad litem, for references to the children's officer of a local authority references to the director of social services.

Rules 5 and 12 substitute a new Rule for Rule 19 of the Rules of 1959 which requires the Schedule to an adoption order made by a court in Wales or Monmouthshire in respect of an infant born in Wales or Monmouthshire (or treated as having been born in the registration district where the court sits) to be in bilingual form if the adopter so requests and prescribe that form. Where this version of the Schedule is used the particulars entered in the Adopted Children Register will be in both English and Welsh. Rule 7 makes similar provision in relation to the abridged copy of an adoption order which is required to be served on the applicant by Rule 21 of the Rules of 1959.

Rule 6 omits Rule 20(2) of the Rules of 1959, which prescribes the measurements and format of the copy of an adoption order which is required to be sent to the Registrar General.

Rules 8 and 10 amend respectively Forms 1 and 6 in Schedule 1 to the Rules of 1959 and require an applicant for an adoption order to attach a statement of the facts on which he intends to rely where he requests the court to dispense with the consent of the infant's parent or guardian and for a copy of the statement to be attached to the notice of the application which is required to be sent to the respondent. Rule 4 amends Rule 12 of the Rules of 1959 so as to require the copy of the statement not to include any reference to an applicant to whom a serial number has been assigned other than by that number.

Rule 9 substitutes a new paragraph for paragraph E of the medical report as to the health of the infant set out in Form 3 in Schedule 1 to the Rules of 1959. The new paragraph, in the case of a child at least 6 weeks old, enables tests of the blood of the child's mother for syphilis to be carried out as an alternative to a test of the child's blood except where the result is positive when a test of the child's blood must also be carried out. The entry relating to the result of an examination of the child's urine for phenylpyruvic acid is replaced by an entry relating to the result of a test of the child's blood for phenylalanine to be completed in the case of a child over 6 days and under 2 years old.

Rule 11 substitutes a new form of adoption order for that set out in Form 9 of Schedule 1 to the Rules of 1959. The principal changes relate to the format of the Schedule to the adoption order. Rule 13 similarly amends the form of the Schedule contained in the abridged copy of an adoption order which is required to be sent to the applicant.

STATUTORY INSTRUMENTS

1973 No. 1119 (L.17)

JUVENILE COURTS AND OFFENDERS

The Magistrates' Courts (Children and Young Persons) (Welsh Forms) Rules 1973

Made	-	-	-	*25th June* 1973
Laid before Parliament				*6th July* 1973
Coming into Operation				*1st August* 1973

The Lord Chancellor, in exercise of the powers conferred on him by section 15 of the Justices of the Peace Act 1949(a), as extended by section 122 of the Magistrates' Courts Act 1952(b) and section 2 of the Welsh Language Act 1967(c), after consultation with the Rule Committee appointed under the said section 15, hereby makes the following Rules:—

1. These Rules may be cited as the Magistrates' Courts (Children and Young Persons) (Welsh Forms) Rules 1973 and shall come into operation on 1st August 1973.

2.—(1) In these Rules—

(*a*) "English form" means any form prescribed in the Magistrates' Courts (Children and Young Persons) Rules 1970(d) corresponding to a Welsh form;

(*b*) "Welsh form" means any form contained in Schedule 1 to these Rules.

(2) The Interpretation Act 1889(e) shall apply to the interpretation of these Rules as it applies to the interpretation of an Act of Parliament.

3. The Summary Jurisdiction (Children and Young Persons) (Welsh Forms) Rules 1969(f) are hereby revoked.

4. Subject to the provisions of these Rules, Welsh forms may be used, with such variations as the circumstances may require, in connection with proceedings in magistrates' courts in Wales and Monmouthshire.

5. Both a Welsh and an English form may be included in the same document.

(a) 1949 c. 101.   (b) 1952 c. 55.
(c) 1967 c. 66.   (d) S.I. 1970/1792 (1970 III, p. 5803).
(e) 1889 c. 63.   (f) S.I. 1969/259 (1969 I, p. 697).

6.—(1) Where only a Welsh form, specified in Part I of Schedule 1 to these Rules, or only the corresponding English form, is used in connection with proceedings in magistrates' courts in Wales and Monmouthshire, there shall be added the words in Welsh and English contained in Schedule 2 to these Rules; and the clerk of the magistrates' court or other person responsible for the service of the form shall, if any person upon whom that form is served so requests, provide him with the corresponding English or Welsh form.

(2) In this Rule any reference to serving a document shall include the sending, giving or other delivery of it.

7. In the case of any discrepancy between an English and a Welsh text, the English text shall prevail.

Dated 25th June 1973.

Hailsham of St. Marylebone, C.

SCHEDULE 1   Rule 2

INDEX TO WELSH FORMS

PART I

Forms requiring the endorsement in Schedule 2 to the Rules

Number of Form in
Magistrates' Courts
(Children and Young
Persons) Rules 1970

1.	Summons: offence.
2.	Summons for attendance of parent or guardian of child or young person: offence.
4.	Summons: care proceedings and proceedings in respect of supervision order.
5.	Summons for attendance of parent or guardian of child or young person: care proceedings and proceedings in respect of supervision order.
7.	Notice of care proceedings.
8.	Notice to parent under rule 22.
19.	Notice of extended remand.
27.	Notice of fine etc.: criminal proceedings.
30.	Attendance centre order: offence.
43.	Supervision order: criminal proceedings.
44.	Supervision order: care proceedings.
45.	Supervision order: made on discharge of care order.
46.	Order varying or discharging supervision order.
47.	Attendance centre order on failure to comply with supervision order.
53.	Summons to parent etc.: contribution order.

PART II

Forms not requiring the endorsement in Schedule 2 to the Rules

Number of Form in
Magistrates' Courts
(Children and Young
Persons) Rules 1970

3.	Warrant for arrest of child or young person: offence.
6.	Warrant for arrest: care proceedings and proceedings in respect of supervision order.
9.	Authority to remove to a place of safety.
10.	Warrant to search for or remove child or young person.
11.	Order for removal of foster child or protected child to a place of safety.
28.	Offence condition finding: care proceedings.
38.	Order of recognizance to keep proper care, etc.: criminal proceedings.
39.	Order of recognizance to keep proper care, etc.: care proceedings.
40.	Order of recognizance to keep the peace, etc.: care proceedings.
54.	Contribution order.
55.	Arrears order.

PART I

Forms requiring the endorsement in Schedule 2 to the Rules

1

Gwŷs: trosedd

Yn [sir   . Rhanbarth Llys Ynadon   ].

At A.B. (a elwir yma wedi hyn y diffynnydd) [a E.F. tad/mam/gwarcheidwad] o

Cyflwynwyd hysbysiaeth heddiw [ger fy mron i, sydd â'm henw isod] [gerbron (*rhodder yr enw*) [Ynad Heddwch] [Clerc yr Ynadon] gan C.D. eich bod chwi y diffynnydd, a chwithau, fel y credir, yn blentyn/berson ieuanc, ar y
dydd o   fis   , 19 , yn
yn y [sir] a enwyd uchod [neu o   ] wedi (*rhodder yn gryno fanylion am y trosedd*):

[A chyflwynwyd hysbysiaeth ymhellach gan C.D. mai chwi E.F. yw tad neu fam [neu warcheidwad] y diffynnydd.]

Gan hynny gwysir chwi drwy hyn [y naill a'r llall ohonoch] i ymddangos ar ddydd
, y   dydd o fis
19 , am   o'r gloch y bore/prynhawn gerbron y Llys [Ieuenctid]
[Ynadon] a fydd yn eistedd yn   , i ateb i'r hysbysiaeth honno.

Dyddiegig y   dydd o fis   , 19 .

Y.H.,

Ynad Heddwch yn y [sir] a enwyd gyntaf uchod

[neu Rhoddwyd y wŷs hon gan yr Ynad Heddwch a enwyd uchod.

C.Y.,

Clerc Llys yr Ynadon yn eistedd yn .]

[neu C.Y.,

Clerc Ynadon y Rhanbarth Llys Ynadon a enwyd uchod.]

2

Gwŷs yn galw am bresenoldeb tad neu fam neu warcheidwad plantyn neu berson ieuanc:
trosedd

Yn [sir . Rhanbarth Llys Ynadon].

At C.D. o .

Dygir cyhuddiad yn erbyn A.B., y credir mai plentyn/person ieuanc ydyw, ac y
dywedir eich bod chwi yn dad/fam/warchediwad iddo/iddi gan honni ei fod/bod ar y
dydd o fis , 19 ,
yn yn y [sir] a enwyd uchod [*neu* o], wedi
(*rhodder yn gryno fanylion am y trosedd*):

Gan hynny gwysir chwi drwy hyn i ymddangos gerbron y Llys [Ieuenctid] [Ynadon]
a fydd yn eistedd yn ar ddydd , y
dydd o fis , 19 , am o'r
gloch y bore/prynhawn a thrwy gydol y gweithrediadau.

Y.H.,

Ynad Heddwch yn y [sir] a enwyd gyntaf uchod.
[neu Roddwyd y wŷs hon gan yr Ynad Heddwch a enwyd uchod.

C.Y.,

Clerc Llys yr Ynadon yn eistedd yn].

[*neu* C.Y.,

Clerc Ynadon y Rhanbarth Llys Ynadon a enwyd uchod.]

4

Gwŷs: gweithrediadau gofal, a gweithrediadau ynglŷn â gorchymyn goruchwyliad

Yn [sir . Rhanbarth Llys Ynadon].

At A.B. (a elwir yma wedi hyn y plentyn dan sylw) [ac E.F. tad/mam/gwarcheidwad]
o .

Gan fod [cyngor sir/bwrdeistref sirol] [C.D. sy'n gwnstabl/
berson awdurdodedig] [C.D., goruchwyliwr y plentyn dan sylw] wedi cyflwyno hysbysiad fod y plentyn dan-sylw i'w ddwyn gerbron y llys dan adran [1] [15] Deddf Plant
a Phersonau Ieuainc 1969 ar y sail a nodwyd yn yr hysbysiad:

A chan fod cais wedi ei wneud yn rheolaidd i'r pwrpas hwnnw i [mi sydd â'm llofnod isod] [*neu rhodder yr enw*] [Ynad Heddwch] [Glerc yr Ynadon].

Gwysir chwi drwy hyn [y naill a'r llall ohonoch] i ymddangos ar ddydd
y   dydd o fis   , 19 , am
o'r gloch y bore/prynhawn gerbron y Llys Ieuenctid a fydd yn eistedd yn
i fod yn bresennol yn y gweithgariadau a gynhelir yn unol â'r hysbysiad hwnnw.

Dyddiedig y   dydd o fis   , 19 .

Y.H.,

Ynad Heddwch yn y [sir] a enwyd gyntaf uchod.

[*neu* Cyflwynwyd y wŷs hon gan yr Ynad heddwch a enwyd uchod.

C.Y.,

Clerc Llys yr Ynadon yn eistedd yn   .]

[*nei* C.Y.,

Clerc yr Ynadon dros Ranbarth y Llys Ynadon a enwyd uchod.]

5

*Gwŷs yn galw am bresenoldeb tad neu fam neu warcheidwad plentyn neu berson ieuanc:
gweithrediadau gofal a gweithrediadau ynglŷn â gorchymyn goruchwyliad*

Yn [sir   . Rhanbarth Llys Ynadon   ].

At E.F. tad/mam/gwarcheidwad A.B. (a elwir yma wedi hyn y plentyn dan sylw),
y credir mai plentyn/person ieuanc ydyw, o   .

Gan fod cyngor sir   /bwrdeistref sirol   ]
[C.D. sy'n gwnstabl/berson awdurdodedig] [C.D., goruchwyliwr y plentyn dan sylw]
wedi cyflwyno hysbysiad fod y plentyn dan sylw i'w ddwyn gerbron y llys dan adran
[1] [15], Deddf Plant a Phersonau Ieuainc 1969 ar y sail a nodwyd yn yr hysbysiad:

A chan fod cais wedi ei wneud yn rheolaidd i'r pwrpas hwnnw i [mi sydd â'm llofnod isod] [*neu rhodder yr enw*] [Ynad Heddwch] [Glerc yr Ynadon]:

Gwysir chwi drwy hyn i ymddangos ar ddydd   , y
dydd o fis   , 19 , am   o'r gloch y bore/
prynhawn gerbron y Llys Ieuenctid a fydd yn eistedd yn   i fod yn
bresennol yn y gweithrediadau a gynhelir yn unol â'r hysbysiad hwnnw.

Dyddiedig y   dydd o fis   , 19 .

Y.H.,

Ynad Heddwch yn y [sir] a enwyd gyntaf uchod.

[*neu* Cyflwynwyd y wŷs hon gan yr ynad heddwch a enwyd uchod.

C.Y.,

Clerc Llys yr Ynadon yn eistedd yn   .]

[*neu* C.Y.,

Clerc yr Ynadon dros Ranbarth y Llys Ynadon a enwyd uchod.

7

Hysbysiad am weithrediadau gofal

At Glerc y Llys Ieuenctid yn eistedd yn

Bydded hysbys i chwi fod A.B. o   (a elwir yma wedi hyn y plentyn dan sylw), y credir mai plentyn/person ieuanc ydyw, i gael ei ddwyn gerbron y Llys dan adran 1, Deddf Plant a Phersonau Ieuainc 1969 ar y sail a nodir yma wedi hyn.

Honnir fod yr amod canlynol wedi ei gyflawni mewn perthynas â'r plentyn dan sylw, hynny yw (*rhodder manylion yn nhermau adran* 1 (2) (*a*) i (*f*) *gan nodi, yn achos paragraff* (*f*), *y trosedd*).

Honnir ymhellach fod ar y plentyn dan sylw angen gofal neu reolaeth, a'i fod yn annhebyg o'i gael oni wneir gorchymyn dan yr adranl honno.

Yn unol â Rheol 14, Rheolau Llysoedd Ynadon (Plant a Phersonau Ieuainc) 1970, danfonir copi o'r hysbysiad hwn at bob un o'r personau canlynol, hynny yw, at:—

Dyddiedig y   dydd o fis   , 19 .

C.D.,

[Ar ran cyngor sir/bwrdeistref sirol   ].

[Cwnstabl].

[Person awdurdodedig].

8

Hysbysiad i dad neu fam dan reol 22

At C.B. o

Bydded hysbys i chwi fy mod wedi achwyn wrth y Llys Ieuenctid yn eistedd yn
                    er sicrhau gorchymyn yn erbyn cyngor sir/bwrdeistref sirol
                    , yn eu gorfodi i ddyfod â A.B. gerbron y Llys am y rheswm fy mod yn methu ei reoli ef/rheoli hi.

Gwrandewir yr achwyniad gan y Llys ar ddydd   , y   dydd o fis   , 19 , am   o'r gloch y bore/prynhawn.

Os dymunwch, gellwch siarad â'r Llys amdano/amdani cyn i'r Llys ddod i bender-fyniad ar yr achwyniad.

(*Arwyddwyd*) B.B.

19

Hysbysiad am estyn remandiad

At A.B. (a elwir yma wedi hyn y diffynnydd) o   a C.D. o
a E.F. o   (meichiau/meichiafon dros y diffynnydd).

Bydded hysbys i chwi eich bod chwi, y diffynnydd, wedi eich remandio gan y Llys Ieuenctid yn eistedd yn   i ymddangos gerbron y Llys hwnnw ar y   dydd o fis   , 19 , a bod y Llys Ieuenctid a fu'n eistedd yn   heddiw yn eich absen wedi eich remandio chwi, y diffynnydd, i ymddangos gerbron y Llys Ieuenctid a fydd yn eistedd yn   ar ddydd   , y   dydd o fis   .   , 19 , am o'r gloch y bore/prynhawn.

Dyddiedig y dydd o fis , 19 .

C.Y.,

Clerc y Llys Ieuenctid yn eistedd yn

27

Hysbysiad am ddirwy etc: gweithrediadau troseddol

Yn [sir . Rhanbarth Llys Ynadon].

Gerbron y Llys [Ieuenctid] [Ynadon] yn eistedd yn .

At A.B., o .

DYFARNIAD		
Dirwy		
Iawn		
Costau		
Cyfanswm ...		

Dyfarnwyd C.D., o , ac yntau, fel y credir, wedi ei eni ar , yn euog heddiw [*neu* ar y dydd o fis , 19 ,] o drosedd sef, (*rhodder yn gryno fanylion am y trosedd*) a gorchmynnwyd i chwi, gan eich bod yn dad/fam/ warcheidwad i'r C.D. hwnnw, dalu'r swm o , fel y dangosir ar ymyl y ddalen hon, a'r swm hwnnw i'w dalu ar unwaith [neu *erbyn* y dydd o fis , 19] [*neu* yn rhan-daliadau wythnosol [*neu* misol] o , a'r rhandaliad cyntaf i'w wneud erbyn y dydd o fis , 19]. Dylid talu naill ai drwy'r post i mi, Clerc y Llys yn (*rhodder yma'r cyfeiriad*) neu yn bersonol yn (*rhodder yma'r cyfeiriad a hefyd y dyddiau a'r oriau y gellir talu*). Os na thalwch ar unwaith [*neu* erbyn y dydd [iau] a enwyd] gellir [eich carcharu* am (*enwer y cyfnod*) [neu eich restio] neu atafaelu'ch arian a'ch eiddo heb rybudd arall, [oni bai eich bod wedi gofyn am estyn yr amser i dalu, a bod hynny wedi'i ganiatáu i chwi wyn y dydd hwnnw. Gellir gofyn am estyn yr amser naill ai'n bersonol i'r Llys neu drwy lythyr wedi'i gyfeirio ataf fi, Clerc y Llys yn (*rhodder yma'r cyfeiriad*), ac yn mynegi'n llawn y rhesymau dros ofyn].

Dyddiedig y dydd o fis , 19 .

Y.H.

Clerc y Llys.

SYLWER. Rhaid stampio'n briodol unrhyw ohebiaeth a anfonir drwy'r post. Ni ddylid anfon arian drwy'r post mewn amlenni heb eu cofrestru.

---

*Dilëer oni fydd Llys yr Ynadon, wrth ddyfarnu'n euog, wedi pennu tymor o garchar, dan adran 65(2), Deddf Llysoedd Ynadon 1952, am beidio â thalu ac wedi gohirio arwyddo'r warant garcharu.

30

Gorchymyn canolfan fynychu: trosedd

Yn [sir . Rhanbarth Llys Ynadon].

Gerbron y Llys Ieuenctid yn eistedd yn .

Heddiw [*neu* ar y dydd o fis , 19 ,] cafwyd
A.B. o , yn euog o drosedd y gall ynadon gosbi dyn mewn oed
amdano â charchar, am fod y diffynnydd, ar y dydd o fis ,
19 , wedi (*rhodder yn gryno fanylion am y trosedd*).

A chan fod yr Ysgrifennydd Gwladol wedi hysbysu'r Llys fod y ganolfan fynychu
a enwir yma ar gael ar gyfer derbyn o'r Llys bersonau o ddosbarth neu ddisgrifiad
y diffynnydd.

A chan fod y Llys wedi ei fodloni fod y ganolfan fynychu yn un y gall y diffynnydd
ei chyrraedd yn rhesymol o hawdd o ystyried ei oedran, y moddion sydd ar gael iddo
fynd yno, ac unrhyw amgylchiadau eraill:

[A chan fod y Llys o'r fan y byddai mynychu am ddeuddeg awr yn [ormodol, o
ystyried oedran y diffynnydd *neu* yr amgylchiadau canlynol, sef (*rhodder manylion*),
gan fod y diffynnydd dan bedair ar ddeg oed,] [annigonol, o ystyried yr holl amgyl-
chiadau]:]

Gorchmynnir drwy hyn fod y diffynnydd i fynychu'r ganolfan fynychu yn (*rhodder
yma gyfeiriad y ganolfan*) am y tro cyntaf ar y dydd o fis ,
19 , am o'r gloch y bore/prynhawn, ac wedi hynny ar yr adegau a
bennir gan y swyddog sydd â gofal y ganolfan honno, nes iddo gwblhau cyfnod
mynychu o awr.

Dyddiedig y dydd o fis , 19 .

Y.H.,

Ynad Heddwch yn y [sir] a enwyd uchod.

[*neu* Drwy orchymyn y Llys,

C.Y.,

Clerc y Llys].

43

Gorchymyn goruchwyliad: gweithrediadau troseddol

Yn [sir . Rhanbarth Llys Ynadon].

Gerbron y Llys Ieuenctid yn eistedd yn .

Heddiw/*neu* Ar y dydd o fis , 19 ,] cafwyd
A.B. o (a elwir yma wedi hyn y diffynnydd), ac yntau
fel y credir wedi ei eni ar , yn euog o drosedd, sef, (*rhodder yn
gryno fanylion am y trosedd*):

Y mae'n ymddangos i'r Llys fod/y bydd y diffynnydd yn preswylio yn sir/
ym mwrdeistref sirol ac yn rhanbarth llys ynadon :

Gorchmynnir drwy hyn fod y diffynnydd i gael ei roi dan oruchwyliad [cyngor y
sir/fwrdeistref sirol honno] [cyngor sir/bwrdeistref sirol , sydd wedi
cytuno i gael ei benodi'n oruchwyliwr] [swyddog profiannaeth a benodwyd neu a
neilltuwyd ar gyfer y rhanbarth llys ynadon hwnnw] (a elwir yma wedi hyn y goruchwyliwr) [am gyfnod o]:

[Gorchmynnir ymhellach fod y diffynnydd i breswylio gyda G.H. o ,
sydd wedi cytuno â'r gofyniad hwn:]

[Gorchmynnir ymhellach fod y diffynnydd i gydymffurfio ag unrhyw gyfarwyddiadau a roir gan y goruchwyliwr yn unol ag adran 12, Deddf Plant a Phersonau Ieuainc 1969, sy'n ei gwneud yn ofynnol iddo (*rhodder manylion yn nhermau adran* 12(2))] ac mewn perthynas â chyfarwyddiadau o'r fath a'r gorchymyn hwn, bydd adran 12(3)(a)/(b)/(c) o'r Ddeddf 1969 honno yn dod i rym fel petai cyfeiriad at diwrnod wedi ei roi yn lle'r cyfeiriad at 90/30 diwrnod:]

[Gorchmynnir ymhellach fod y diffynnydd, am y cyfnod canlynol, sef, yn derbyn triniaeth (*rhodder manylion am y driniaeth yn nhermau adran* 12(4)), gan fod y Llys wedi ei fodloni, ar dystiolaeth ymarferydd meddygol sy'n gymeradwy at ddibenion adran 28, Deddf Iechyd y Meddwl 1959, fod ei gyflwr meddyliol o'r fath fel bod arno angen triniaeth, ac y gallai ymateb i driniaeth, ond nad yw ei gyflwr yn gwarantu ei gadw yn unol â gorchymyn ysbyty dan Ran V o'r Ddeddf 1959 honno] [ac y mae'r diffynnydd, ac yntau dros bedair ar ddeg oed, wedi cytuno â'r gofyniad hwn:]

[Gorchmynnir ymhellach, er mwyn hwyluso gwaith y goruchwyliwr yn ei ddyletswydd i gynghori, cynorthwyo, a llochesu'r diffynnydd, fod y diffynnydd i gydymffurfio â'r gofynion ychwanegol canlynol:—

1. ei fod i hysbysu'r goruchwyliwr ar unwaith os bydd yn newid ei breswylfod neu ei waith;

2. ei fod i gadw mewn cysylltiad â'r goruchwyliwr yn unol ag unrhyw gyfarwyddiadau a roir o bryd i'w gilydd gan y goruchwyliwr, ac, yn arbennig, ei fod yn derbyn ymweliadau gan y goruchwyliwr yn ei gartref, os bydd y goruchwyliwr yn dymuno hynny:

(*gellir cynnwys y naill neu'r llall o'r gofynion ychwanegol uchod, neu'r ddau*)].

Dyddiedig y   dydd o fis   , 19   .

Y.H.,

Ynad Heddwch yn y [sir] a enwyd gyntaf uchod.

[*neu* Drwy orchymyn y Llys,

C.Y.,

Clerc y Llys.]

44

Gorchymyn goruchwyliad: gweithrediadau gofal

Yn [sir   . Rhanbarth Llys Ynadon   ].
Gerbron y Llys Ieuenctid yn eistedd yn   .

Dygwyd A.B. o   (a elwir yma wedi hyn y plentyn dan sylw), ac yntau, fel y credir, wedi ei eni ar   , gerbron y Llys heddiw [*neu* ar y   dydd o fis   , 19   ,] dan adran 1, Deddf Plant a Phersonau Ieuainc 1969:

Ac y mae'r Llys wedi ei fodloni fod yr amod canlynol wedi ei gyflawni mewn perthynas â'r plentyn dan sylw, hynny yw, (*rhodder manylion yn nhermau adran* 1(2)(*a*) i (*f*) *gan nodi, yn achos* (*f*), *y trosedd*), a hefyd fod angen gofal neu reolaeth arno, a'i fod yn annhebyg o'i gael oni wneir gorchymyn ar ei gyfer dan yr adran honno:

Y mae'n ymddangos i'r Llys fod/y bydd y plentyn dan sylw yn preswylio yn sir/ym mwrdeistref sirol   ac yn rhanbarth llys ynadon   :

Gorchmynnir drwy hyn fod y plentyn dan sylw i gael ei roi dan oruchwyliad [cyngor y sir/fwrdeistref sirol honno] [cyngor sir/bwrdeistref sirol ,
sydd wedi cytuno i gael ei benodi'n oruchwyliwr] [swyddog profiannaeth a benodwyd neu a neilltuwyd ar gyfer y rhanbarth llys ynadon hwnnw] (a elwir yma wedi hyn y goruchwyliwr) [am gyfnod o   ] [nes i'r plentyn dan sylw gyrraedd deunaw oed]:

[Gorchmynnir ymhellach fod y plentyn dan sylw i breswylio gyda G.H. o
, sydd wedi cytuno â'r gofyniad hwn:]

[Gorchmynnir ymhellach fod y plentyn dan sylw i gydymffurfio ag unrhyw gyfarwyddiadau a roir gan y goruchwyliwr yn unol ag adran 12, Deddf Plant a Phersonau Ieuainc 1969, sy'n ei gwneud yn ofynnol iddo (*rhodder manylion yn nhermau adran* 12(2))] [ac mewn perthynas â chyfarwyddiadau o'r fath a'r gorchymyn hwn, bydd adran 12(3)(a)/(b)/(c) o'r Ddeddf 1969 honno yn cael yr effaith fod cyfeiriad at diwrnod wedi ei roi yn lle'r cyfeiriad at 90/30 diwrnod:]

[Gorchmynnir ymhellach fod y plentyn dan sylw, am y cyfnod canlynol, sef
, yn derbyn triniaeth (*rhodder manylion am y driniaeth yn nhermau adran* 12(4)), gan fod y Llys wedi ei fodloni, ar dystiolaeth ymarferydd meddygol sy'n gymeradwy at ddibenion adran 28, Deddf Iechyd y Meddwl 1959, fod ei gyflwr meddyliol o'r fath fel bod arno angen triniaeth, ac y gallai ymateb i driniaeth, ond nad yw ei gyflwr yn gwarantu ei gadw yn unol â gorchymyn ysbyty dan Ran V o'r Ddeddf 1959 honno] [ac y mae'r plentyn dan sylw, ac yntau dros bedair ar ddeg oed, wedi cytuno â'r gofyniad hwn:]

[Gorchmynnir ymhellach, er mwyn hwyluso gwaith y goruchwyliwr yn ei ddyletswydd i gynghori, cynorthwyo, a llochesu'r plentyn dan sylw, fod y plentyn perthnasol i gydymffurfio â'r gofynion ychwanegol canlynol:—

1. ei fod i hysbysu'r goruchwyliwr ar unwaith os bydd yn newid ei breswylfod neu ei waith;

2. ei fod i gadw mewn cysylltiad â'r goruchwyliwr yn unol â chyfarwyddiadau o'r fath a roir o bryd i'w gilydd gan y goruchwyliwr ac, yn arbennig, ei fod yn derbyn ymweliadau gan y goruchwyliwr yn ei gartref, os bydd y goruchwyliwr yn dymuno hynny:

(*gellir cynnwys y naill neu'r llall o'r gofynion ychwanegol uchod, neu'r ddau*)].

Dyddiedig y   dydd o fis   , 19 .

Y.H.,

Ynad Heddwch yn y [sir] a enwyd gyntaf uchod.

[neu Drwy orchymyn y Llys,

C.Y.,

Clerc y Llys.]

45

Gorchymyn goruchwyliad a wneir wrth ddiddymu gorchymyn gofal

Yn [sir   . Rhanbarth Llys Ynadon   ].
Gerbron y Llys Ieuenctid yn eistedd yn   .

Gwnaeth y Llys Ieuenctid yn eistedd yn   ar y
dydd o fis   , 19 , orchymyn gofal yn traddodi A.B. o
(a elwir yma wedi hyn y plentyn dan sylw) ac yntau, fel y credir, wedi ei eni ar
              , i ofal cyngor/sir bwrdeistref sirol   :

Mae [y plentyn dan sylw] [E.F. tad/mam/gwarcheidwad y plentyn dan sylw ar ei
ran] [y cyngor hwnnw] wedi gwneud cais am ddiddymu'r gorchymyn hwnnw:

Y mae'n ymddangos i'r Llys fod/y bydd y plentyn dan sylw yn preswylio yn sir/ym
mwrdeistref sirol   ac yn rhanbarth llys ynadon   :

Gorchmynnir drwy hyn fod y gorchymyn gofal hwnnw yn cael ei ddiddymu ond
bod y plentyn dan sylw yn cael ei roi dan oruchwyliad [cyngor y sir/fwrdeistref sirol
a enwyd ddiwethaf] [cyngor sir/bwrdeistref sirol   , sydd wedi cytuno
i gael ei benodi'n oruchwyliwr] [swyddog profiannaeth a benodwyd neu a neilltuwyd
ar gyfer y rhanbarth llys ynadon hwnnw] (a elwir yma wedi hyn y goruchwyliwr) [am
gyfnod o   ] [nes i'r plentyn dan sylw gyrraedd deunaw oed]:

[Gorchmynnir ymhellach fod y plentyn dan sylw i breswylio gyda G.H. o
           , sydd wedi cytuno â'r gofyniad hwn:]

[Gorchmynnir ymhellach fod y plentyn dan sylw i gydymffurfio ag unrhyw
gyfarwyddiadau a roir gan y goruchwyliwr yn unol ag adran 12, Deddf Plant a
Phersonau Ieuainc 1969, sy'n ei gwneud yn ofynnol iddo (*rhodder manylion yn nhermau
adran* 12(2))] [ac mewn perthynas â chyfarwyddiadau o'r fath a'r gorchymyn hwn,
bydd adran 12(3)(a)/(b)/(c) o'r Ddeddf 1969 yn dod i rym fel petai cyfeiriad at
         diwrnod wedi ei roi yn lle'r cyfeiriad at 90/30 diwrnod:]

[Gorchmynnir ymhellach, er mwyn hwyluso gwaith y goruchwyliwr yn ei ddyletswydd
i gynghori, cynorthwyo, a llochesu'r plentyn dan sylw, fod y plentyn dan sylw yn
cydymffurfio â'r gofynion ychwanegol canlynol:—

1. ei fod i hysbysu'r goruchwyliwr ar unwaith os bydd yn newid ei breswylfod neu
   ei waith;

2. ei fod i gadw mewn cycylltiad â'r goruchwyliwr yn unol ag unrhyw gyfarwyddiadau
   a roir o bryd i'w gilydd gan y goruchwyliwr, ac, yn arbennig, ei fod yn derbyn
   ymweliadau gan y goruchwyliwr yn ei gartref os bydd y goruchwyliwr yn dymuno
   hynny:

(*gellir cynnwys y naill neu'r llall o'r gofynion ychwanegol uchod, neu'r ddau*)].

Dyddiedig y   dydd o fis   , 19 .

Y.H.,

Ynad Heddwch yn y [sir] a enwyd gyntaf uchod.

[*neu* Drwy orchymyn y Llys,

C.Y.,

Clerc y Llys.]

46

Gorchymyn yn amrywio neu'n diddymu gorchymyn goruchwyliad

Yn [sir   . Rhanbarth Llys Ynadon   ].

Gerbron y Llys [Ieuenctid] [Ynadon] yn eistedd yn   .

Gwnaeth y Llys Ieuenctid yn eistedd yn   ar y
dydd o fis   , 19   , orchymyn goruchwyliad o fewn ystyr Deddf Plant
a Phersonau Ieuainc 1969 ar gyfer A.B. o   (a elwir yma wedi hyn y
person dan oruchwyliaeth), ac yntau fel y credir wedi ei eni ar   .

[Amrywiwyd y gorchymyn goruchwyliad hwnnw gan orchymyn a wnaed gan y Llys
Ieuenctid yn eistedd yn   ar y   dydd o fis   ,
19   :]

Mae'r gorchymyn goruchwyliad hwnnw [fel y'i amrywiwyd] yn enwi sir/bwrdeistref
sirol   a rhanbarth llys ynadon   fel y rhanbarthau
lle'r ymddengys fod/y bydd y person dan oruchwyliad yn preswylio, ac yn ei roi ef
dan oruchwyliad [cyngor y sir/fwrdeistref sirol honno] [cyngor sir/bwrdeistref sirol
               ] [swyddog profiannaeth a benodwyd neu a neilltuwyd ar gyfer y
rhanbarth llys ynadon hwnnw], ac oni ddiddymwyd y gorchymyn cyn hynny, bydd yn
peidio â bod mewn grym ar (noder y dyddiad).

Mae'r gorchymyn goruchwyliad hwnnw/fel y'i amrywiwyd], yn unol ag adrannau
12 a 18(2) o'r Ddeddf 1969 honno, yn cynnwys gofynion arbennig, gan gynnwys y
gofyniad/gofynion canlynol (rhodder many ion am y gofyniad/gofynion y bwriedir ei
amrywio/eu hamrywio):]

Mae [y person dan oruchwyliad] [E.F., tad/mam/gwarcheidwad y person dan
oruchwyliad ar ei ran] [y goruchwyliwr] wedi gwneud cais am [amrywio] [ddiddymu]
y gorchymyn goruchwyliad hwnnw.

Mae'r goruchwyliwr wedi cyfeirio at y Llys adroddiad gan ymarferydd meddygol
yn unol ag adran 15(5) o'r Ddeddf 1969 honno, yn cynnig y dylid [dileu] [amrywio]
gofyniad triniaeth iechyd y meddwl am y rhesymau canlynol (rhodder manylion yn
nhermau adran 15(5)):]

Gorchmynnir drwy hyn fod y gorchymyn goruchwyliad hwnnw [a amrywiwyd fel
y nodwyd uchod] yn cael ei [ddiddymu] [amrywio/amrywio ymhellach fel hyn:—
                            ].

Dyddiedig y   dydd o fis   , 19 .

Y.H.,

Ynad Heddwch yn y [sir] a enwyd gyntaf uchod.

[neu Drwy orchymyn y Llys,

C.H.,

Clerc y Llys.]

47

Gorchymyn canolfan fynychu am beidio â chydymffurfio â gofynion
gorchymyn goruchwyliad

Yn [sir   . Rhanbarth Llys Ynadon   ].

Gerbron y Llys [Ynadon] [Ieuenctid] yn eistedd yn   .

Gwnaeth y Llys Ynadon yn eistedd yn   ar y   dydd
o fis 19   , orchymyn goruchwyliad o fewn ystyr Deddf Plant a Phersonau Ieuainc 1969
ar gyfer A.B. o   (a elwir yma wedi hyn y person dan oruchwyliad),
ac yntau, fel y credir, wedi ei eni ar   :

Ni wnaethpwyd y gorchymyn goruchwyliad hwnnw dan awdurdod adran 1 o'r Ddeddf honno nau ar ddiddymiad y gorchymyn gofal.

[Amrywiwyd y gorchymyn goruchwyliad hwnnw gan orchymyn a wnaethpwyd gan y Llys Ieuenctid yn eistedd yn   ar y   dydd o fis   , 19   :]

Mae'r gorchymyn goruchwyliad [fel y'i amrywiwyd] yn enwi sir/bwrdeistref sirol   a rhanbarth llys ynadon   fel y rhanbarthau lle'r ymddengys fod/ y bydd y person dan oruchwyliad yn preswylio, ac yn ei roi ef dan oruchwyliad [cyngor y sir/fwrdeistref sirol honno] [cyngor sir/bwrdeistref sirol   ] [swyddog profiannaeth a benodwyd neu a neilltuwyd ar gyfer y rhanbarth llys ynadon hwnnw] (a elwir yma wedi hyn y goruchwyliwr):

Mae'r gorchymyn goruchwyliad hwnnw [fel y'i amrywiwyd] yn unol ag adrannau 12 a 18(2) o'r Ddeddf 1969 honno yn cynnwys gofynion arbennig gan gynnwys y gofyniad/gofynion canlynol (*rhodder manylion am y gofyniad/gofynion a dorrwyd neu y cynigir ei amrywio/ eu hamrywio*):

Ar gais y goruchwyliwr, mae'r Llys wedi ei fodloni fod y person dan oruchwyliad wedi methu â chydymffurfio â'r [gofyniad/gofynion] [a enwyd] [hwnnw/hynny]:

Gorchmynnir drwy hyn fod y gorchymyn goruchwyliad [a amrywiwyd fel y dynodwyd uchod] yn cael ei [ddiddymu] [amrywio/amrywio ymhellach fel hyn:—
                                    :]

A chan fod yr Ysgrifennydd Gwladol wedi hysbysu'r Llys fod y ganolfan fynychu a enwir yma ar gael ar gyfer derbyn o'r Llys bersonau o ddosbarth neu ddisgrifiad y person dan oruchwyliad:

A chan fod y Llys wedi ei fodloni fod y ganolfan fynychu yn un y gall y person dan oruchwyliad ei chyrraedd yn rhesymol o hawdd o ystyried y moddion sydd ar gael i'r plentyn dan sylw fynd yno, ac unrhyw amgylchiadau eraill:

[A chan fod y Llys wedi ei fodloni y byddai mynychu am ddeuddeg awr yn annigonol o ystyried yr holl amgylchiadau:]

Gorchmynnir [ymhellach] fod y person dan oruchwyliad, oherwydd y methiant hwnnw, i fynychu'r ganolfan fynychu yn   , am y tro cyntaf ar y   dydd o fis   , 19 , am   o'r gloch y bore/prynhawn, ac wedi hynny ar yr adegau a bennir gan y swyddog sydd â gofal y ganolfan honno, nes iddo gwblhau cyfnod mynychu o   awr.

Dyddiedig y   dydd o fis   , 19 .

Y.H.,

Ynad Heddwch yn y [sir] a enwyd gyntaf uchod.

[*neu* Drwy orchymyn y Llys,

C.Y.,

Clerc y Llys.]

53

Gwŷs i dad/mam, etc: gorchymyn cyfrannu

Yn [sir   . Rhanbarth Llys Ynadon   ].

At C.D. o   .

Gwnaed achwyniad heddiw i [mi sydd â'm henw isod] [*neu rhodder yr enw*] [Ynad Heddwch] [Glerc yr Ynadon] gan gyngor sir/bwrdeistref sirol eich bod yn agored i dalu cyfraniadau dan adran 86, Deddf Plant a Phersonau Ieuainc 1933 ar gyfer A.B., person sydd yng ngofal y cyngor hwnnw:

Gwysir chwi, felly, i ymddangos ar ddydd , y
dydd o fis , 19 , am o'r gloch y bore/prynhawn
i ddangos achos pam na ddylid gwneud gorchymyn yn ei gwneud yn ofynnol i chwi gyfrannu swm wythnosol y tybir gan y Llys ei fod yn gymwys, gan ystyried eich adnoddau ac yn unol ag adran 62, Deddf Plant a Phersonau Ieuainc 1969.

Dyddiedig y dydd o fis , 19 .

Y.H.,

Ynad Heddwch yn y [sir] a enwyd gyntaf uchod.

[*neu* Cyflwynwyd y wŷs hon gan yr Ynad Heddwch a enwyd uchod.

C.Y.,

Clerc Llys yr Ynadon yn eistedd yn]
neu C.Y.,
[*neu* C.Y.,

Clerc Ynadon y Rhanbarth Llys Ynadon a enwyd uchod].

PART II

Forms not requiring the endorsement in Schedule 2 to the Rules

3

Gwarant i restio plentyn neu berson ieuanc: trosedd

Yn [sir . Rhanbarth Llys Ynadon].
At bob un o gwnstabliaid .

Cyflwynwyd hysbysiaeth ar lw [*neu* gadarnhad] heddiw ger fy mron i, yr Ynad Heddwch sydd â'i enw isod, gan C.D. fod A.B. (a elwir yma wedi hyn y diffynnydd), y credir mai plentyn/person ieuanc ydyw, ar y dydd
o fis , 19 , yn yn y [sir] a enwyd uchod [*neu* o
], wedi (*rhodder yn gryno fanylion am y trosedd*):

Gan hynny, gorchmynnir chwi drwy hyn i restio'r diffynnydd ar unwaith a'i ddwyn gerbron y Llys [Ieuenctid] [Ynadon] a fydd yn eistedd yn i ateb yr hysbysiaeth honno.

Dyddiedig y dydd o fis , 19 .

Y.H.,

Ynad Heddwch yn y [sir] a enwyd gyntaf uchod.

(*Nodiad lle caniateir mechniaeth*)

Gorchmynnir fod y diffynnydd wedi iddo gael ei restio i'w ryddhau ar fechniaeth, os bydd yn gwneud ymrwymiad yn y swm o   , gyda mechiau/
o feichiafon am   [yr un] ei fod yn ymddangos gerbron y Llys
[Ieuenctid] [Ynadon] am   o'r gloch y bore/prynhawn pan fydd y Llys
yn eistedd nesaf [*neu* ar y   dydd o fis   , 19   .]

[Bydd ymrwymiad y diffynnydd dan yr amod [au] canlynol (*rhodder manylion*).]

Y.H.,

Ynad Heddwch yn y [sir] a enwyd gyntaf uchod.

6

Gwarant i restio: gweithrediadau gofal a gweithrediadau ynglŷn â gorchymyn goruchwyliad

Yn [sir   . Rhanbarth Llys Ynadon   ].

[Gerbron y Llys [Ieuenctid] [Ynadon] yn eistedd yn   ].

At bob un o gwystabliaid   .

[Gan fod cyngor sir/bwrdeistref sirol   ] [C.D. sy'n gwnstabl/berson awdurdodedig] [C.D., goruchwyliwr y plentyn dan sylw a enwir yma wedi hyn] wedi cyflwyno hysbysiad fod A.B. o   (a elwir yma wedi hyn y plentyn dan sylw) i'w ddwyn gerbron y llys dan adran [1] [15], Deddf Plant a Phersonau Ieuainc 1969 ar y sail a nodwyd yn yr hysbysiad:

[A chan fod y plentyn dan sylw wedi ei wysio i ymddangos ar ddydd   ,
y   dydd o fis   , 19 , am   o'r gloch y bore/prynhawn gerbron y Llys [Ieuenctid] [Ynadon] a fydd yn eistedd yn   i fod yn bresennol yn y gweithrediadau a gynhelir yn unol â'r hysbysiad hwnnw:]

[A chan fy mod i, yr Ynad Heddwch sydd â'i enw isod, wedi fy modloni gan dystiolaeth ar lw/gadarnhad na ellir cyflwyno'r wŷs honno:]

[A chan fod y Llys wedi ei fodloni gan dystiolaeth ar lw/gadarnhad fod y plentyn dan sylw heb ymddangos i ateb y wŷs honno, ond bod y wŷs wedi ei chyflwyno iddo o fewn amser a ymddengys i'r Llys yn rhesymol, cyn y gwrandawiad [gohiriedig]:]

[A chan fod y Llys wedi ei fodloni gan dystiolaeth ar lw/gadarnhad fod y plantyn dan sylw, ar ôl bod yn bresennol ar achlysur cynharach mewn gweithrediadau a gynhaliwyd yn unol â'r hysbysiad hwnnw, heb ymddangos yn y gwrandawiad gohiriedig a'i fod wedi cael hysbysiad digonol am amser a lle y gwrandawiad gohiriedig:]

Gorchmynnir chwi drwy hyn i ddod â'r plentyn dan sylw gerbron y Llys [Ieuenctid] [Ynadon] a fydd yn eistedd yn   , neu gerbron ynad heddwch ar unwaith, neu beth bynnag cyn pen deuddeg awr a thrigain.

Y.H.,

Ynad Heddwch yn y [sir] a enwyd gyntaf uchod

[*neu* Drwy orchymyn y Llys,

C.Y.,

Clerc y Llys.]

(*Nodiad lle caniateir mechniaeth*)

Gorchmynnir fod y plentyn dan sylw, wedi iddo gael ei restio, i'w ryddhau ar fechniaeth os bydd yn gwneud ymrwymiad yn y swm o   gyda meichiau/   o feichiafon am   [yr un] ei fod yn ymddangos gerbron y Llys [Ieuenctid] [Ynadon] a fydd yn eistedd yn am   o'r gloch y bore/prynhawn yn eisteddiad nesaf y Llys hwnnw (*neu* ar y   dydd o fis   , 19]. [Bydd ymrwymiad y plentyn dan sylw yn unol â'r amod(au) canlynol (*rhodder manylion*)].

Y.H.,

Ynad Heddwch yn y [sir] a enwyd uchod

[*neu* Drwy orchymyn y Llys,

C.Y.,

Clerc y Llys.]

9

Awdurdod i symud i le diogel

Yn [sir   . Rhanbarth Llys Ynadon   ].

Y mae C.D. o   (a elwir yma wedi hyn yr ymgeisydd) wedi gwneuthur cais heddiw dan adran 28(1), Deddf Plant a Phersonau Ieuainc 1969, am awdurdod i gadw a chymryd i le diogel A.B. o   , plentyn neu berson ieuanc (a elwir yma wedi hyn y plentyn dan sylw):

Ac yr wyf fi, yr Ynad Heddwch sydd â'i enw isod, wedi fy modloni fod gan yr ymgeisydd achos rhesymol dros gredu (*rhodder manylion am yr hyn a gredir yn nhermau adran* 28(1) (*a*), (*b*), *neu* (*c*)), ac yr wyf drwy hyn yn caniatáu'r cais:

A gellir cadw'r plentyn dan sylw mewn lle diogel ar sail yr awdurdod am gyfnod o   diwrnod yn dechrau gyda'r dyddiad hwn.

Dyddiedig y   dydd o fis   , 19 .

Y.H.,

Ynad Heddwch yn y [sir] a enwyd uchod.

10

Warant i chwilio am blentyn neu berson ieuanc, neu i'w symud

Yn [sir   . Rhanbarth Llys Ynadon   ].

At bob un o gwnstabliaid

Cyflwynwyd hysbysiaeth ar lw [*neu* gadarnhad] heddiw ger fy mron i, yr Ynad Heddwch sydd â'i enw isod, gan C.D. o   , person sy'n gweithredu er lles plentyn neu berson ieuanc, sef (*rhodder enw a chyfeiriad neu fanylion eraill digon i'w adnabod*) (a elwir yma wedi hyn y plentyn dan sylw) fod achos rhesymol dros dybio (*rhodder manylion yn nhermau adran* 40(1) (*a*) *neu* (*b*), *Deddf Plant a Phersonau Ieuainc* 1933):

[Awdurdodir chwi drwy hyn i chwilio am y plentyn dan sylw, ac os darganfyddir fod (*rhodder manylion yn nhermau adran* 40(1)), i'w gymryd i le diogel:]

[Awdurdodir chwi drwy hyn i symud y plentyn dan sylw i le diogel wedi chwilio neu heb chwilio amdano:]

[Ac i'r dibenion hyn, awdurdodir chwi drwy hyn i fynd i mewn i (*enwer y tŷ etc*):]

[Gorchmynnir drwy hyn na chiaff C.D. fod yn eich cwmni/fod rhaid i ymarferydd meddygol sydd â'r cymwysterau priodol fod yn eich cwmni wrth weithredu ar y warant hon].

A gellir cadw'r plentyn dan sylw mewn lle diogel dan awdurdod y warant hon nes y gellir ei ddwyn gerbron llys ieuenctid, ond na chaiff y plentyn dan sylw ei gadw felly am gyfnod hwy na   diwrnod.

Dyddiedig y   dydd o fis   , 19 .

Y.G.,

Ynad Heddwch yn y [sir] a enwyd uchod.

11

Gorchymyn i symud plentyn maeth neu blentyn dan ymgeledd i le diogel

Yn [sir   . Rhanbarth Llys Ynadon   ].

[Gerbron y Llys Ieuenctid yn eistedd yn   ].

At bob un o gwnstabliaid   [ac at C.D. o   ,
person a awdurdodwyn i ymweld â phlant maeth/dan ymgeledd.

[Gan fod achwyniad wedi ei wneud heddiw gan gyngor sir/bwrdeistref sirol
                    [gan fod cais wedi ei wneud i mi, yr Ynad Heddwch sydd â'i enw
isod, gan C.D. o   , person a awdurdodwyd i ymweld â phlant
maeth/dan ymgeledd] ar y sail fod A.B. o   , plentyn maeth/dan
ymgeledd (a elwir wedi hyn y plentyn) yn   (*noder yn fyr ar ba sail
y gwneir yr achwyniad neu'r cais*):
[Gan fod prawf wedi ei roi fod iechyd neu les y plentyn yn debyg o fod mewn
perygl:

Gorchmynnir drwy hyn fod y plentyn [a phob plentyn maeth arall a gedwir yn
(*enwer y lle*)] i'w symud i le diogel.

A gellir cadw'r plentyn [ac unrhyw blentyn maeth arall a symudir felly] mewn lle
diogel oherwydd y gorchymyn hwn nes y rhoir ef yn ôl i'w fam neu ei dad, perthynas,
neu warcheidwad, neu nes y gellir gwneud trefniadau eraill, ond na chaiff y plentyn
[ac unrhyw blentyn maeth arall a symudir felly] ei gadw felly am gyfnod hwy na
                    diwrnod.

Dyddiedig y   dydd o fis   , 19 .

Y.H.,

Ynad Heddwch yn y [sir] a enwyd gyntaf uchod.

[*neu* Drwy orchymyn y Llys,

C.Y.,

Clerc y Llys.]

28

Dyfarniad ar amod trosedd: gweithrediadau gofal

Yn [sir   . Rhanbarth Llys Ynadon   ].

Gerbron y Llys Ieuenctid yn eistedd yn   ].

Dygwyd A.B. o   (a elwir yma wedi hyn y plentyn dan sylw), ac yntau, fel y credir, wedi ei eni ar   , gerbron y Llys heddiw [*neu* ar y   dydd o fis   , 19   ,] dan adran 1, Deddf Plant a Phersonau Ieuainc 1969:

A honnwyd fod yr amod canlynol wedi ei gyflawni mewn perthynas â'r plentyn dan sylw, hynny yw, ei fod yn euog o drosedd, sef, (*rhodder yn gryno fanylion am y trosedd*):

Dyfernir drwy hyn fod y plentyn dan sylw yn euog/ddieuog o'r trosedd hwnnw.

Dyddiedig y   dydd o fis   , 19   .

Y.H.,

Ynad Heddwch yn y [sir] a enwyd uchod.
[*neu* Drwy orchymyn y Llys,

C.Y.,
Clerc y Llys.]

38

Gorchymyn ymrwymiad i gadw gofal priodol etc: gweithrediadau troseddol

Yn [sir   . Rhanbarth Llys Ynadon   ].

Gerbron y Llys [Ieuenctid] [Ynadon] yn eistedd yn   .

Dyfarnwyd A.B. o   (a elwir yma wedi hyn y diffynnydd) ac yntau, fel y credir, wedi ei eni ar   , yn euog heddiw [*neu* ar y dydd o fis   , 19   ,] o drosedd, sef, (*rhodder yn gryno fanylion am y trosedd*):

Gorchmynnir drwy hyn fod E.F. o   , tad/mam/gwarcheidwad y diffynnydd sydd wedi cytuno i'r gorchymyn hwn gael ei wneud, yn gwneud ymrwymiad ar unwaith yn y swm o   i gymryd gofal priodol o'r diffynnydd a'i reoli'n briodol [am gyfnod o   ] [nes i'r diffynnydd gyrraedd deunaw oed].

Dyddiedig y   dydd o fis   , 19   .

Y.H.,

Ynad Heddwch yn y [sir] a enwyd uchod.
[*neu* Drwy orchymyn y Llys,

C.Y.,
Clerc y Llys.]

39

Gorchymyn ymrwymiad i gadw gofal priodol, etc: gweithrediadau gofal

Yn [sir   . Rhanbarth Llys Ynadon   ].

Gerbron y Llys Ieuenctid yn eistedd yn   .

Dygwyd A.B. o   (a elwir yma wedi hyn y plentyn dan sylw) ac
yntau, fel y credir, wedi ei eni ar   , gerbron y Llys heddiw [*neu* ar y
            dydd o fis   , 19   ,] dan adran 1, Deddf Plant a
Phersonau Ieuainc 1969.

Ac y mae'r Llys wedi ei fodloni fod yr amod canlynol wedi ei gyflawni mewn
perthynas â'r plentyn dan sylw, hynny yw (*rhodder manylion yn nhermau adran* 1(2)(*a*)
i (*f*) *gan nodi, yn achos* (*f*), *y trosedd*), a hefyd fod angen gofal neu reolaeth arno,
a'i fod yn annhebyg o'i gael oni wneir gorchymyn ar ei gyfer dan yr adran honno:

Gorchmynnir drwy hyn fod E.F. o   , tad/mam/gwarcheidwad y
plentyn dan sylw, sydd wedi cytuno i'r gorchymyn hwn gael ei wneud, yn gwneud
ymrwymiad ar unwaith yn y swm o   i gymryd gofal priodol o'r
plentyn dan sylw a'i reoli'n briodol [am gyfnod o   ] [nes i'r plentyn
dan sylw gyrraedd deunaw oed].

Dyddiedig y   dydd o fis   , 19   .

Y.H.,

Ynad Heddwch yn y [sir] a enwyd uchod.

[*neu* Drwy orchymyn y Llys,

C.Y.,

Clerc y Llys.]

40

Gorchymyn ymrwymiad i gadw heddwch, etc: gweithrediadau gofal

Yn [sir   . Rhanbarth Llys Ynadon   ].

Gerbron y Llys Ieuenctid yn eistedd yn   .

Dygwyd A.B. o   , person ieuanc ac yntau, fel y credir, wedi ei eni
ar   gerbron y Llys heddiw [*neu* ar y   dydd o fis
    , 19   .] dan adran 1, Deddf Plant a Phersonau Ieuainc 1969:

Ac y mae'r Llys wedi ei fodloni fod yr amod canlynol wedi ei gyflawni mewn
perthynas â'r person ieuanc hwnnw, hynny yw, ei fod yn euog o drosedd sef (*rhodder
yn gryno fanylion am y trosedd*) a hefyd fod angen gofal neu reolaeth arno, a'i fod yn
annhebyg o'i gael oni wneir gorchymyn ar ei gyfer dan yr adran honno:

Gorchmynnir fod y person ieuanc hwnnw, sydd wedi cytuno i'r gorchymyn hwn
gael ei wneud, yn gwneud ymrwymiad ar unwaith yn y swm o   , [gadw
heddwch] [ac] [ymddwyn yn weddus] am gyfnod o   o ddyddiad y
gorchymyn hwn.

Dyddiedig y   dydd o fis   , 19   .

Y.H.,

Ynad Heddwch yn y [sir] a enwyd uchod.

[*neu* Drwy orchymyn y Llys,

C.Y.,

Clerc y Llys.]

54

Gorchymyn cyfrannu

Yn [sir   . Rhanbarth Llys Ynadon   ].

Gerbron Llys yr Ynadon yn eistedd yn   .

Gwnaed achwyniad gan gyngor sir/bwrdeistref sirol   fod E.F. o
            (a elwir yma wedi hyn y cyfrannwr) yn agored i dalu cyfraniadau
dan adran 86, Deddf Plant a Phersonau Ieuainc 1933, fel tad/mam A.B., ac yntau,
fel y credir, wedi ei eni ar   ac sydd yng ngofal y cyngor hwnnw (a
elwir yma wedi hyn y plentyn dan sylw):

Awgrymodd y cyngor hwnnw, mewn hysbysiad ysgrifenedig a roddwyd i'r cyfrannwr
ar y   dydd o fis   , 19 , gyfraniad wythnosol o
    [ond nid yw'r cyngor hwnnw a'r cyfrannwr wedi cytuno ar swm y
cyfraniad o fewn un mis wedi'r dyddiad hwnnw] [a chytunodd y cyfrannwr â swm y
cyfraniad ond y mae wedi methu talu'r cyfraniad oedd yn ddyledus ar gyfer (*noder yr
wythnos*):]

Gorchmynnir drwy hyn, yn unol ag adran 87 o'r Ddeddf 1933 honno fod y cyfrannwr
yn talu i'r cyngor hwnnw swm wythnosol o   nes i'r plentyn dan sylw
beidio â bod yng ngofal y cyngor hwnnw, neu iddo gyrraedd un ar bymtheg oed cyn
hynny, ac eithrio ar gyfer cyfnodau, os bydd rhai, y bydd, y cyngor hwnnw yn
caniatáu i'r plentyn fod yng ngofal a than reolaeth tad/mam, gwarcheidwad, perthynas,
neu gyfaill:

[A gorchmynnir ymhellach fod y cyfrannwr yn talu'r swm o   ar
gyfer costau.]

Dyddiedig y   dydd o fis   , 19 .

Y.H.,

Ynad Heddwch yn y [sir] a enwyd gyntaf uchod.

[*neu* Drwy orchymyn y Llys,

C.Y.,

Clerc y Llys.]

55

Gorchymyn Ôl-ddyledion

Yn [sir   . Rhanbarth Llys Ynadon   ].

Gerbron Llys yr Ynadon yn eistedd yn   .

Gwnaed achwyniad gan gyngor sir/bwrdeistref sirol   fod E.F. o
            (a elwir yma wedi hyn y cyfrannwr) yn agored i dalu cyfraniadau
dan adran 86, Deddf Plant a Phersonau Ieuainc 1933 fel tad/mam A.B., ac yntau, fel
y credir, wedi ei eni ar   , ac sydd yng ngofal y cyngor hwnnw, ar
gyfer cyfnod o ddiffygdalu pan nad oedd gorchymyn mewn grym dan adran 86 o'r
Ddeddf 1933 honno, yn ei gwneud yn ofynnol i'r cyfrannwr dalu'r cyfraniadau hynny,
ac y mae'r cyngor hwnnw wedi gwneud cais am orchymyn ôl-ddyledion:

Awgrymodd y cyngor hwnnw, mewn hysbysiad ysgrifenedig a roddwyd i'r cyfrannwr
ar y   dydd o fis   , 19 , gyfraniad wythnosol o
           [ond nid yw'r cyngor hwnnw a'r cyfrannwr wedi cytuno ar swm y
cyfraniad o fewn un mis wedi'r dyddiad hwnnw] [a chytunodd y cyfrannwr â swm y
cyfraniad, ond y mae wedi methu talu'r cyfraniad oedd yn ddyledus ar gyfer (*noder
yr wythnos*):]

Y mae'r Llys wedi penderfynu mai cyfnod y diffygdaliad yw   .

Gorchmynnir drwy hyn, yn unol ag adran 30, Deddf Plant a Phersonau Ieuainc
1963, fod y cyfrannwr yn talu i'r cyngor hwnnw swm wythnosol o   am
gyfnod o   wythnos.

Dyddiedig y   dydd o fis   , 19 .

Y.H.,

Ynad Heddwch yn y [sir] a enwyd gyntaf uchod.

[*neu* Drwy orchymyn y Llys,

C.Y.,

Clerc y Llys.]

SCHEDULE 2
Rule 5

Darperir y ddogfen non yn Gymraeg/Saesneg os bydd arnoch ei heisian. Dylech
wnend cais yn ddi-oed i Glerc Llys yr Ynadon (*rhodder yma'r cyfeiriad*)....................

This document will be provided in Welsh/English if you require it. You should
apply immediately to the Clerk of the Magistrates' Court (address).......................

EXPLANATORY NOTE

(*This Note is not part of the Rules.*)

These Rules replace the Summary Jurisdiction (Children and Young Persons)
Rules 1969. They provide for the use of Welsh forms in proceedings in magistrates' courts in Wales and Monmouthshire involving children and young
persons . They include provision authorising the use of bilingual forms in
connection with such proceedings and provide that in certain cases a person
served with a form in one language may require the form in the other language.

STATUTORY INSTRUMENTS

1973 No. 1120

MEDICINES

The Medicines (Hexachlorophane Prohibition) Order 1973

Made - - -	*25th June* 1973
Laid before Parliament	*4th July* 1973
Coming into Operation	*30th July* 1973

The Secretaries of State respectively concerned with health in England and in Wales, the Secretary of State concerned with health and with agriculture in Scotland, the Secretary of State for Northern Ireland and the Minister of Agriculture, Fisheries and Food, acting jointly, in exercise of the powers conferred by section 62(1) of the Medicines Act 1968(a) and now vested in them (b) and of all other powers enabling them in that behalf, it appearing to them to be necessary in the interests of safety to make the following order, after consulting such organisations as appear to them to be representative of interests likely to be substantially affected by the following order, and after taking into account the advice of the Committee on Safety of Medicines (c) and the advice of the Veterinary Products Committee (d), hereby make the following order:—

Citation, commencement and interpretation

1.—(1) This order may be cited as the Medicines (Hexachlorophane Prohibition) Order 1973 and shall come into operation on 30th July 1973.

(2) In this order unless the context otherwise requires—

"the Act" means the Medicines Act 1968;

"hexachlorophane" means the substance for which such name is shown in the list of names prepared and published under section 100 of the Act, otherwise known as hexachlorophene or 2,2'-Methylenebis(3,4,6-trichlorophenol);

"soap" means any compound of a fatty acid with an alkali or amine;

and other expressions have the same meaning as in the Act.

(3) Except in so far as the context otherwise requires, any reference in this order to any enactment, regulation or order shall be construed as a reference to that enactment, regulation or order, as the case may be, amended or extended by any other enactment, regulation or order.

(a) 1968 c. 67.

(b) In the case of the Secretary of State concerned with health in Wales by virtue of the provisions of Article 2(2) of, and Schedule 1 to, the Transfer of Functions (Wales) Order 1969 (S.I. 1969/388 (1969 I, p. 1070); and in the case of the Secretary of State for Northern Ireland by virtue of the provisions of section 1(1)(a) of the Northern Ireland (Temporary Provisions) Act 1972 (c. 22).

(c) S.I. 1970/1257 (1970 I, p. 4098).   (d) S.I. 1970/1304 (1970 I, p. 4335).

(4) The rules for the construction of Acts of Parliament contained in the Interpretation Act 1889(a) shall apply for the purposes of the interpretation of this order as they apply for the purposes of the interpretation of an Act of Parliament.

Provisions prohibiting sale, supply and importation

2.—(1) Subject to the following provisions of this order, the sale, supply and importation of any medicinal product containing hexachlorophane is hereby prohibited.

(2) The prohibition imposed by paragraph (1) of this Article shall be subject to the exceptions that—

(i) the sale, supply or importation shall not be prohibited in the case of a medicinal product, not being an aerosol, which contains—

    (*a*) where the medicinal product is for use by being administered to human beings, 0·1% or less of hexachlorophane provided that the conditions specified in Article 3(i) of this order are satisfied, or

    (*b*) where the medicinal product is for use by being administered to animals, 0·75% or less of hexachlorophane provided that the conditions specified in Article 3(ii) of this order are satisfied;

(ii) the sale, supply or importation shall not be prohibited in the case of a medicinal product, being an aerosol, the contents of the container of which shall be 0·1% or less of hexachlorophane provided that the conditions specified in Article 3(i) or Article 3(ii) of this order, as the case may be, are satisfied;

(iii) the sale, supply or importation shall not be prohibited in the case of a medicinal product for use by being administered to human beings, not being an aerosol, which contains 0·75% or less of hexachlorophane provided that the conditions specified in Article 3(i) of this order are satisfied and—

    (*a*) the sale or supply is by a person lawfully conducting a retail pharmacy business at a registered pharmacy, or

    (*b*) the sale or supply is by the manufacturer of such medicinal product—

        (1) to a person lawfully conducting a retail pharmacy business, or

        (2) to a person carrying on the business of wholesale dealing for sale to a person lawfully conducting a retail pharmacy business, or

        (3) to a doctor or dentist, or

        (4) to a hospital or health centre, or

    (*c*) the sale is by way of wholesale dealing and is for sale or supply in the circumstances specified in (1) (2) (3) or (4) of (*b*) of this sub-paragraph, or

    (*d*) in the case of importation, where the importation is for the purposes of sale or supply in the circumstances specified in (1) (2) (3) or (4) of (*b*) of this sub-paragraph;

(iv) the sale, supply or importation shall not be prohibited—

    (*a*) in the case of the sale or supply of a medicinal product that is a soap in the form of a cake, tablet or bar which is for use by being administered to human beings, and which contains 2% or less of hexachlorophane provided that the conditions specified in Article

---

(a) 1889 c. 63.

3(i) of this order are satisfied and the label therein referred to contains the further words "Not to be used for whole-body bathing
except on medical advice" and—

    (1) the sale or supply is by a person lawfully conducting a retail
        pharmacy business at a registered pharmacy, or

    (2) the sale or supply is by the manufacturer of such medicinal
        product—

        (*aa*) to a person lawfully conducting a retail pharmacy
             business, or

        (*bb*) to a person carrying on the business of wholesale dealing
             for sale to a person lawfully conducting a retail pharmacy
             business, or

        (*cc*) to a doctor or dentist, or

        (*dd*) to a hospital or health centre, or

    (3) the sale is by way of wholesale dealing and is for sale or supply
        in the circumstances specified in (*aa*) (*bb*) (*cc*) or (*dd*) of (2) of
        this sub-paragraph;

  (*b*) in the case of the sale or supply of a medicinal product that is a
     soap or shampoo, and is for use by being administered to animals,
     and which contains 2% or less of hexachlorophane provided that the
     conditions specified in Article 3(ii) of this order are satisfied;

  (*c*) in the case of importation, where the importation is for the pur-
     poses of sale or supply of medicinal products to which (*a*) or (*b*) of
     this sub-paragraph refers.

(3) the prohibition imposed by paragraph (1) of this Article shall be subject
to the further exceptions that the sale, supply or importation of a medicinal
product containing hexachlorophane shall not be prohibited, provided that the
conditions specified in Article 3(i) or Article 3(ii) of this order, as the case may
be, are satisfied—

  (*a*) where the sale or supply is by a doctor or dentist to a patient of his
     or to a person under whose care such a patient is or by a veterinary
     surgeon or veterinary practitioner for administration by him or under
     his direction to an animal or herd which is under his care, or

  (*b*) where the sale or supply is by a doctor or dentist at the request of,
     and to, another doctor or dentist for administration to a particular
     patient of that other doctor or dentist, or

  (*c*) where the sale or supply is by a veterinary surgeon or veterinary prac-
     titioner at the request of, and to, another veterinary surgeon or veterinary
     practitioner for administration to a particular animal or herd which is
     under the care of that other veterinary surgeon or veterinary practitioner,
     or

  (*d*) where the sale or supply is by a person lawfully conducting a retail
     pharmacy business at a registered pharmacy and is in accordance with
     a prescription given by a practitioner, or

  (*e*) where the sale or supply is in the course of the business of a hospital
     or health centre and the sale or supply is for the purpose of administra-
     tion, whether in the hospital or health centre or elsewhere, in accordance
     with the directions of a doctor or dentist, or

  (*f*) where the sale is by way of wholesale dealing provided that the sale
     is—

    (i) to another person carrying on the business of wholesale dealing, or

(ii) to a person lawfully conducting a retail pharmacy business, or

(iii) to a practitioner, or

(iv) to a hospital or health centre,

and the medicinal product is for sale or supply in any of the circumstances specified in (*a*) to (*e*) of this paragraph, or

(*g*) where the sale or supply is by the manufacturer of such medicinal product and the sale or supply is for the purpose of sale or supply in any of the circumstances specified in (*a*) to (*f*) of this paragraph, or

(*h*) where the sale or supply of a medicinal product is for use by being administered orally to sheep or cattle for the prevention or treatment of liver fluke disease, or

(*i*) in the case of importation, where the importation is for the purpose of sale or supply in the circumstances specified in any of the sub-paragraphs (*a*) to (*h*) of this paragraph, or

(*j*) where the sale or supply is to or by any of the following persons:—

(i) a public analyst appointed under section 89 of the Food and Drugs Act 1955**(a)**, section 27 of the Food and Drugs (Scotland) Act 1956**(b)** or section 31 of the Food and Drugs Act (Northern Ireland), 1958**(c)**;

(ii) a sampling officer within the meaning of the Food and Drugs Act 1955, the Food and Drugs (Scotland) Act 1956 or the Food and Drugs Act (Northern Ireland), 1958;

(iii) a sampling officer within the meaning of Schedule 3 of the Act;

(iv) an inspector appointed by the Pharmaceutical Society of Great Britain under section 25 of the Pharmacy and Poisons Act 1933**(d)**.

(4) The prohibition imposed by paragraph (1) of this Article shall be subject to the additional exception that the sale, supply or importation of a medicinal product containing hexachlorophane shall not be prohibited where the sale or supply involves, or the sale, supply or importation is for the purposes of, exporting the medicinal product.

(5) So long as section 12 of the Pharmacy and Poisons Act 1933 remains in force in its application to Great Britain, paragraphs 2 and 3 of this Article, insofar as those paragraphs relate to a registered pharmacy, shall apply to anything done by an authorised seller of poisons within the meaning of that Act at premises that are entered in the register kept under the said section 12.

(6) So long as section 17 of the Pharmacy and Poisons Act (Northern Ireland) 1925**(e)** remains in force paragraphs 2 and 3 of this Article, insofar as those paragraphs relate to a registered pharmacy, shall apply to anything that is done at premises for which an annual licence is in force under the said section 17.

Conditions

3. The conditions referred to in Article 2 of this order are that—

(i) in the case of a medicinal product for use by being administered to human beings, the container of the medicinal product shall bear a label

---

(a) 1955 (4 & 5 Eliz. 2) c.16.   (b) 1956 c. 30.
(c) 1958 c. 27 (N.I.).   (d) 1933 c. 25.
(e) 1925 c. 8 (N.I.).

which shall contain the words "Not to be used for babies" or a warning that the medicinal product is not to be administered, except on medical advice, to a child under two years of age;

(ii) in the case of a medicinal product for use by being administered to animals, the container of the medicinal product shall bear a label which shall contain the words "For animal treatment only" and, where the medicinal product is for oral administration for the prevention or treatment of liver fluke disease in cattle, shall contain a warning that the medicinal product is not for use in lactating cattle and, where the medicinal product is for oral administration for the prevention or treatment of liver fluke disease in sheep or cattle, a statement that protective clothing must be worn by the operator when the medicinal product is being administered.

Temporary Provisions

4.—(1) The prohibition imposed by Article 2(1) of this order shall not operate during a period of six months from the date of the coming into operation of this order in the case of medicinal products containing hexachlorophane which have before that date been sold or supplied for retail sale or for supply in circumstances corresponding to retail sale, and which, under this order may be sold or supplied otherwise than in accordance with a prescription given by a practitioner.

(2) The conditions imposed by Article 3 of this order shall not operate for a period of six months from the date of the coming into operation of this order in the case of medicinal products containing hexachlorophane, when sold or supplied in accordance with a prescription given by a practitioner, provided that, before that date, such medicinal products have been sold or supplied to a person lawfully conducting a retail pharmacy business or to a hospital or health centre.

Keith Joseph,
Secretary of State for Social Services.

20th June 1973.

Peter Thomas,
Secretary of State for Wales.

20th June 1973.

Gordon Campbell,
Secretary of State for Scotland.

21st June 1973.

W. S. I. Whitelaw,
Secretary of State for Northern Ireland.

23rd June 1973.

In witness whereof the official seal of the Minister of Agriculture, Fisheries and Food is hereunto affixed on 25th June 1973.

(L.S.)   *Joseph Godber,*
Minister of Agriculture, Fisheries and Food.

EXPLANATORY NOTE.

(This Note is not part of the Order.)

This Order prohibits, subject to certain exceptions, the sale, supply and importation of medicinal products containing hexachlorophane. Exceptions are provided for various forms of medicinal product according to the amount of hexachlorophane in the medicinal product or in the container of the medicinal product and according to the channel of distribution, provided that there is compliance with labelling requirements. Further exceptions, not related to the amount of hexachlorophane are made by Article 2(3) provided that the sale, supply or importation takes place in the circumstances prescribed and provided that there is compliance with labelling requirements. Article 2(4) makes an exception for exports and Article 4 permits in certain circumstances and for a limited period, the retail sale of existing stock or its supply in circumstances corresponding to retail sale.

STATUTORY INSTRUMENTS

1973 No. 1121 (S.84)

ROAD TRAFFIC

The Secretary of State's Traffic Orders (Procedure) (Scotland) Regulations 1973

Made - - - -	*19th June* 1973
Laid before Parliament	*5th July* 1973
Coming into Operation	*26th July* 1973

The Secretary of State for Scotland (in relation to all matters other than orders made under section 15 or 33 of the Road Traffic Regulation Act 1967(a)) and the Secretary of State for the Environment (in relation to orders made under the said section 15 or 33) in exercise of their powers under section 84C(5) of the said Act of 1967 as read with section 32 of the Countryside Act 1968(b), and the Secretary of State for the Environment Order 1970(c), and of all other powers enabling them in that behalf, and after consultation with representative organisations in accordance with section 107(2) of the said Act of 1967, hereby make the following regulations:—

PART I

GENERAL

Citation, Extent and Commencement

1. These regulations, which may be cited as the Secretary of State's Traffic Orders (Procedure) (Scotland) Regulations 1973, apply to Scotland and shall come into operation on the 26th July 1973.

Interpretation

2.—(1) The Interpretation Act 1889(d) shall apply for the interpretation of these regulations as it applies for the interpretation of an Act of Parliament.

(2) In these regulations the following expressions have the meanings hereby respectively assigned to them:—

"the Act" means the Road Traffic Regulation Act 1967, as amended by Part IX of the Transport Act 1968(e) and as read with section 32 of the Countryside Act 1968;

(a) 1967 c. 76.   (b) 1968 c. 41.
(c) S.I. 1970/1681 (1970 III, p. 5551).   (d) 1889 c. 63.
(e) 1968 c. 73.

"consolidation order" means an order which revokes provisions of one or more existing orders, reproduces those provisions without any change in substance and makes no other provision, but so, however, that, for the purpose of this definition, the inclusion in the order (by way of addition to the provisions of any existing order or orders) of an exemption in respect of a disabled person's vehicle of the same kind as is mentioned in regulation 4 of the Local Authorities Traffic Orders (Exemptions for Disabled Persons) (Scotland) Regulations 1971(a); or of a provision for conferring on a traffic warden functions similar to those conferred by the existing order or orders on a police constable in uniform or of both such exemption and such provision, shall not be regarded as constituting a change in substance;

"countryside road order" has the meaning given to that expression in regulation 3;

"disabled person's vehicle" means a motor vehicle driven by, or used for the carriage of, a disabled person of a description prescribed in the Disabled Persons (Badges for Motor Vehicles) Regulations 1971(b);

"the notice of proposals" and "the notice of making", in relation to an order, mean respectively the notices required to be published under regulations 5 and 12;

"the objection period" means the period within which objections to an order may be made in accordance with regulation 6;

"the order" means, in relation to anything occurring or falling to be done before its making, the order as proposed to be made, and in relation to anything occurring or falling to be done on or after its making, the order as made;

"the relevant local authority" means—

(a) in relation to a reserve power order—

    (i) where the order is made or proposed to be made by virtue of section 84A(2) of the Act, the local authority to which there has been given a direction under section 84A(1) of the Act, for the purpose of securing the object of which the order is made or proposed to be made,

    (ii) where the order is made or proposed to be made under section 84A(4) of the Act, the local authority whose order is or is proposed to be varied or revoked by the reserve power order,

(b) in relation to a trunk road order the local authority which would have the power under the Act to make the order if the road were not a trunk road,

(c) in relation to a countryside road order, the local authority which has power under section 1 of the Act to make such an order as respects the road to which the countryside road order applies or will apply,

and where under the foregoing provisions of this definition there would in relation to any particular order be more than one relevant local authority, that expression shall in the case of that order include all of those authorities;

"reserve power order" and "trunk road order" have the meanings respectively given to those expressions in regulation 3; and "road" includes any length of road and any part of the width of a road.

(a) S.I. 1971/1521 (1971 III, p. 4270).　　　(b) S.I. 1971/1492 (1971 III, p. 4177).

(3) Any reference in these regulations to an order under any particular section of the Act includes:—

(*a*) a reference to an order (whether made by virtue of section 84D, or under section 84A(4), of the Act) varying or revoking an order made, or having effect as if made, under the section in question, and

(*b*) a reference to an order under the section in question made or proposed to be made by virtue of section 84A(2) of the Act;

(4) Any reference in these regulations to any enactment shall be construed as a reference to that enactment as amended by or under any subsequent enactment;

(5) Any reference in these regulations to a numbered regulation shall, unless the context otherwise requires, be construed as a reference to the regulation bearing that number in these regulations.

Application of regulations

3.—(1) These regulations apply to—

(*a*) orders made or proposed to be made by the Secretary of State by virtue of subsection (2) or under subsection (4) of section 84A of the Act (any such order being referred to in these regulations as a "reserve power order"),

(*b*) orders made or proposed to be made by the Secretary of State with respect to trunk roads under any of the following provisions of the Act, that is to say, sections 1(1) to (7), 9, 73 and 74 (any such order being referred to in these regulations as a "trunk road order"), and

(*c*) orders made or proposed to be made by the Secretary of State with respect to roads which are not trunk roads under section 32(3) of the Countryside Act 1968 (any such order being referred to in these regulations as a "countryside road order").

(2) Except where otherwise stated, each regulation applies to every such order.

(3) Where, in connection with an order to which these regulations apply, procedural steps which accord substantially with the relevant requirements of these regulations have been taken before the coming into operation of these regulations or are in the course of being taken when these regulations come into operation (whether or not they were taken or are being taken in the sequence required by these regulations), but the order has not been made before these regulations come into operation, then those steps need not be repeated, and for the purpose of these regulations they shall be deemed to have been taken under and in accordance with these regulations, and any remaining procedural steps in connection with the order shall be determined by, and carried out or completed in accordance with, these regulations as nearly as may be.

(4) Nothing in these regulations shall apply to any order made before the coming into operation of these regulations.

PART II

PROCEDURE BEFORE MAKING THE ORDER

Consultation with Police

4.—(1) Before making any order to which these regulations apply the Secretary of State shall consult with the chief constable for the police force maintained for the area in which any road or other place to which the order is to relate is situated.

(2) The consultation referred to in paragraph (1) of this regulation is additional to any consultation required by the Act or, in the case of a countryside road order, by section 32 of the Countryside Act 1968.

(3) This regulation has effect subject to regulation 13 below.

Publication of proposals

5.—(1) After any consultation required by regulation 4 above or by the Act and, in the case of a countryside road order, by section 32 of the Countryside Act 1968, but before making any order the Secretary of State shall:—

(a) publish once at least in a local newspaper circulating in the area in which any road or other place to which the order relates is situated a notice of proposals containing the particulars specified in Part I of Schedule 1 to these regulations;

(b) publish a similar notice in the Edinburgh Gazette;

(c) serve upon the relevant local authority a copy of the notice of proposals containing the particulars aforesaid and a copy of the order as drafted;

(d) comply with the relevant requirements of Schedule 2 to these regulations as to the notices to be displayed in each road or other place to which the order relates; and

(e) comply with the relevant requirements of Schedule 3 to these regulations as to the availability of documents for inspection.

(2) Where the order is one which relates to a road, or to roads, situated in more than one locality, it shall be sufficient for the purposes of this regulation if the notice published in each local newspaper states the general nature and effect of the order so far as it affects the road or roads situated in the locality in which that newspaper circulates and names or otherwise describes only the road or roads so affected in that locality, but the notice in the Edinburgh Gazette shall state the general nature and effect of the entire order and name or otherwise describe the whole road, or all the roads, to which the order relates.

(3) This regulation has effect subject to regulations 13 and 14 below.

Objections

6.—(1) The period during which objections to the order can be made shall terminate not earlier than 21 days from the date on which the Secretary of State has complied with the requirements of paragraph (1)(a), (b) and (c), and (where such display is required) has begun to display the notices required by paragraph 1(d), of regulation 5 above.

(2) Any person desiring to object to the Secretary of State's proposals to make the order shall send within the period, and to the address, specified in the notice of proposals published as required by regulation 5 above, a written statement of his objection and of the grounds thereof.

(3) This regulation has effect subject to regulations 13 and 14 below.

Notice of public inquiry

7.—(1) Where the Secretary of State decides, before publishing the notice of proposals under regulation 5 above, that a public inquiry shall be held, the notice of proposals shall contain, in addition to the particulars required by that regulation, the particulars specified in Part II of Schedule 1 to these regulations.

(2) In any case where the Secretary of State decides that a public inquiry shall be held in connection with any objection to an order to which these regulations apply but the published notice of proposals has not contained the particulars specified in Part II of Schedule 1 aforesaid, the Secretary of State shall:—

(a) publish once at least in a local newspaper circulating in the area in which any road or other place to which the order relates is situated a notice of the inquiry containing the particulars specified in Part III of Schedule 1 to these regulations;

(b) publish a similar notice in the Edinburgh Gazette;

(c) serve upon the relevant local authority a copy of the notice of the inquiry containing the particulars aforesaid;

(d) except where the order is an order under section 9 of the Act, comply with the relevant requirements of Schedule 2 to these regulations as to the notices to be displayed in each road or other place to which the order relates;

(e) comply with the relevant requirements of Schedule 3 to these regulations as to the availability of documents for inspection; and

(f) not later than the date of the first publication of the notice required by sub-paragraph (a) of this paragraph, inform in writing any person who has objected to the order in accordance with regulation 6 above and who has not withdrawn the objection, of the date, time and place of the inquiry.

(3) The provisions of paragraph (2) of regulation 5 above shall apply in relation to the publication of a notice under paragraph (2) of this regulation as they apply in relation to the publication of a notice of proposals under the said regulation 5.

(4) Where the notice of proposals announces the holding of a public inquiry there shall be at least 42 days between the date on which the publication of that notice in the local newspaper and the Edinburgh Gazette under the foregoing provisions of these regulations is completed and the date on which the inquiry is due to begin, and in all other cases there shall be at least 21 days between the date on which the publication as aforesaid of the notice announcing the holding of the public inquiry is completed or the date of the expiration of the objection period (whichever is later) and the date on which the inquiry is due to begin.

Procedure at Public Inquiry

8.—(1) Any person interested in the subject matter of a public inquiry may appear at the inquiry in person or may be represented by counsel, solicitor or other representative.

(2) Any person so interested may, whether or not he proposes to appear at the inquiry, send to the address given in the notice of proposals for the receipt of objections, such written representations as he may wish to make in relation to the subject matter of the inquiry with a view to their transmission to and consideration by the person appointed to hold the inquiry.

(3) The person holding the inquiry may refuse to hear any person, or to consider any objection or representation made by any person, if he is satisfied

that the views of that person or the objection or representation are frivolous or that such views have already been adequately stated by some other person at the inquiry.

(4) Subject as aforesaid, the procedure at the inquiry shall be at the discretion of the person holding it.

Consideration of Objections

9. Before making the order the Secretary of State shall consider all objections duly made in accordance with regulation 6 above and not withdrawn and also the report and recommendations (if any) of the person holding any public inquiry in connection with the order.

Modifications

10. The Secretary of State may make the order with modifications (whether in consequence of any objections or otherwise), but where the modifications which the Secretary of State proposes to make appear to him substantially to affect the character of the order as drafted, then, before making the order, he shall take such steps as appear to him to be appropriate for informing any persons likely to be concerned of the effect of the proposed modifications and for giving to those persons an opportunity to make representations in connection therewith, and shall consider any such representations which are made to him.

PART III

MAKING THE ORDER AND SUBSEQUENT PROCEDURE

Operative date of Order

11.—(1) The order shall specify the date on which it comes into operation or, in a case where different operative dates are provided for different provisions of the order, each of the dates on which a provision of the order comes into operation.

(2) No date on which an order, or a provision of an order, comes into operation shall be earlier than the date on which the notice of the making of the order is published in the local newspaper under regulation 12 below.

Notice of the making of the order

12.—(1) When the Secretary of State has made the order, he shall:—

(a) forthwith give notice in writing of the making of the order to the relevant local authority and to the chief constable of the police force maintained for the area in which any road or other place to which the order relates is situated;

(b) except where such notification has previously been given to such person, notify in writing each person who has duly objected to the order in accordance with regulation 6 above and has not withdrawn his objection, of the Secretary of State's decision in relation to the objection and, where the objection has not been, or not wholly been, acceded to, of the Secretary of State's reasons therefor;

(c) within 14 days of the making of the order publish once in a local news-paper circulating in the area in which any road or other place to which the order relates is situated a notice of the making of the order containing the particulars specified in Part IV of Schedule 1 to these regulations;

(d) within the same period publish a similar notice in the Edinburgh Gazette;

(e) comply with the relevant requirements of Schedule 3 to these regulations as to the availability of documents for inspection;

(f) where the order relates to any road, forthwith take such steps as it is practicable for him to take to ensure before the order comes into opera-tion—

    (i) the placing on or near the road of such traffic signs in such positions as he may consider requisite for the purpose of securing that ade-quate information as to the effect of the order is made available to persons using the road, and

    (ii) in a case where the order contains provisions for revoking, or altering the application of a previous order, the removal or replacement of existing traffic signs as he may consider requisite for the purpose of avoiding confusion to users of the road or the continuance of traffic signs in incorrect positions.

(2) The provisions of paragraph (2) of regulation 5 above shall apply in relation to the publication of a notice of making under paragraph (1) of this regulation as they apply in relation to the publication of a notice of proposals under the said regulation 5.

(3) The provisions of paragraph (1)(f) above are without prejudice to section 75 of the Act.

(4) This regulation has effect subject to regulation 13 below.

PART IV

SPECIAL PROCEDURAL PROVISIONS FOR CERTAIN ORDERS

Special provisions for consolidation orders and for certain variation orders

13.—(1) Regulations 4, 5 and 6 above shall not apply to any trunk road order which is a consolidation order and regulation 12 above shall have effect in relation to such an order with the following modifications, namely, that the particulars to be contained in the notice of the making of the order shall consist only of:—

    (i) the title of the order;

    (ii) a statement of the titles of the orders the provisions of which are reproduced in the order;

    (iii) the operative date or dates of the order; and

    (iv) the items numbered 6 and (if necessary) 7 in Part IV of Schedule 1 to these regulations.

(2) A trunk road order which is a consolidation order shall be framed so as to come into operation on a date not less than 14 days after the publication in the local newspaper of the notice of the making of the order.

(3) Regulations 4, 5 and 6 above shall not apply to an order the sole effect of which would be:—

(a) to postpone for a period of not more than 6 months the coming into operation of any provision of an existing order; or

(b) to vary an order under section 1 or 9 of the Act so as to include in the order being varied an exemption in respect of a disabled person's vehicle of the same kind as is mentioned in regulation 4 of the Local Authorities' Traffic Orders (Exemption for Disabled Persons) (Scotland) Regulations 1971, or a provision for conferring on a traffic warden functions similar to those conferred by the order being varied on a police constable in uniform or both such exemption and such provision.

Special provisions for certain experimental traffic orders and other orders

14.—(1) Regulation 5 and 6 above shall not apply to the following orders, that is to say:—

(a) a trunk road order under section 9 of the Act;

(b) a reserve power order under section 84A(4) of the Act which provides only for one or more of the following matters:—

   (i) the revocation of an order made, or having effect as if made, under section 9(1) of the Act;

   (ii) the variation of an order made, or having effect as if made, under the said section 9(1) so as to reduce the extent of its application or the stringency of any prohibition or restriction imposed by it;

(c) a reserve power order under section 9(3) of the Act by virtue of section 84A(2) thereof; and

(d) an order under section 1 of the Act where the sole effect of the order would be to—

   (i) prohibit the riding of cycles or mopeds on a footbridge or in a pedestrian subway or in the approaches to such bridge or subway, or

   (ii) restrict the driving of vehicles into a boxed area, or

   (iii) revoke or vary the provision of an order, being a provision the sole effect of which is as mentioned in (i) or (ii) of this sub-paragraph.

Provided that where the order is a reserve power order the Secretary of State shall, not less than 14 days before making the order, serve upon the relevant local authority a notice of his proposal to make the order, a copy of the order as drafted and a statement of his reasons for proposing to make the order.

(2) In this regulation—

"Boxed area" means an area of the carriageway of a road, at or near its junction with another road, marked or to be marked by a traffic sign consisting of cross hatched yellow lines, bounded by a yellow line, placed on the carriageway to indicate that a vehicle must not be driven into the area at a time when, by reason of the presence of one or more other vehicles in or near to that area, it cannot be driven out of that area without stopping;

"cycle" means a pedal cycle which is not a motor vehicle; and

"moped" means a motor cycle which is equipped with pedals by means whereof it is capable of being propelled and which has an engine with a cylinder capacity not exceeding 50 cubic centimetres.

Gordon Campbell,
One of Her Majesty's Principal
Secretaries of State.

St. Andrew's House,
  Edinburgh.

8th June 1973.

Signed by authority of the Secretary of State.

John Peyton,
Minister for Transport Industries,
Department of the Environment.

19th June 1973.

SCHEDULE 1

PARTICULARS TO BE INCLUDED IN PRESS NOTICES

PART I—PARTICULARS TO BE INCLUDED IN THE NOTICE OF PROPOSALS

1. The title of the order.

2. A statement of the general nature and effect of the order.

3. Where the order relates to any road, the name or other brief description of the road and, in a case where the order is an order under section 73 or 74 of the Act, a statement of the approximate length of that road to which the order will apply.

4. Where the order does not relate to a road, a brief description of the place to which it does relate and of the location of that place.

5. Where the order is a reserve power order to be made under section 84A(4) of the Act, a statement of the title, date and general nature of the order proposed to be varied or revoked and of the name of the authority who made that order.

6. Each address at which a copy of the draft order, a copy of the relevant map and a copy of the Secretary of State's statement of reasons for proposing to make the order can be inspected, and the times when inspection can take place at each such address.

7. The period during which, and the address to which, objections to the order can be made, and a statement that all objections must be made in writing and must specify the grounds thereof.

PART II—ADDITIONAL PARTICULARS TO BE INCLUDED IN THE NOTICE OF PROPOSALS WHICH ANNOUNCES THE HOLDING OF A PUBLIC INQUIRY

1. A statement that a public inquiry will be held in connection with the order.

2. The date, time and place of the inquiry.

PART III—PARTICULARS TO BE INCLUDED IN THE SEPARATE NOTICE OF A PUBLIC INQUIRY

1. The title of the order.

2. A statement which refers to the published notice of proposals for the order and which indicates that a public inquiry will be held in connection with the order.

3. A brief statement of the general nature and effect of the order and of the name or other brief description of any road or other place to which the order will apply.

4. The date, time and place of the inquiry.

5. Each address at which a copy of the draft order, a copy of the relevant map and a copy of the Secretary of State's statement of reasons for proposing to make the order can be inspected, and the times when inspection can take place at each such address.

PART IV—PARTICULARS TO BE INCLUDED IN THE NOTICE OF MAKING THE ORDER

1. The title of the order.

2. A statement of the general nature and effect of the order and of its operative date or dates.

3. Where the order relates to any road, the name or other brief description of the road.

4. Where the order does not relate to a road, a brief description of the place to which it does relate and of the location of that place.

5. Where the order is a reserve power order made under section 84A(4) of the Act, a statement of the title, date and general nature of the order varied or revoked and of the name of the authority who made that order.

6. Each address at which a copy of the order, as made, can be inspected, and the times when inspection can take place at each such address.

7. In the case of an order under section 1, 5, 9, 15, 28, 33 or 35 of the Act, a statement that any person who desires to question the validity of the order or of any provision contained in the order on the ground that it is not within the powers of the relevant section of the Act or on the ground that any requirement of that section or of section 84A, 84B or 84C of the Act or any regulation made under the said section 84C has not been complied with in relation to the order, may, within 6 weeks of the date on which the order is made (such date being stated in the notice), make application for the purpose to the Court of Session.

SCHEDULE 2

REQUIREMENTS AS TO NOTICES TO BE DISPLAYED IN A ROAD OR OTHER PLACE

PART I—PARTICULARS TO BE INCLUDED IN THE NOTICE

1. The title of the order.

2. A brief statement of the effect of the order in relation to the road or other place where it is displayed.

3. Each address at which a copy of the draft order, a copy of the relevant map and a copy of the Secretary of State's statement of reasons for proposing to make the order can be inspected, and the times when such inspection can take place.

4. Where the notice is a notice of proposals, the address to which, and the period during which, objections to the order can be made, and a statement that all objections must be made in writing and must specify the grounds thereof.

5. Where the notice announces the holding of a public inquiry, the date, time and place of the inquiry.

PART II—OTHER REQUIREMENTS AS TO THE DISPLAY OF THE NOTICE

1. Where the order relates to any road the notice shall be displayed in a prominent position at or near each end of the road and in such other positions (if any) as the Secretary of State thinks requisite for securing that adequate information about the subject matter of the notice is made available to persons using the road.

2. Where the order does not relate to a road, the notice shall be displayed in one or more prominent positions in the road or roads giving access to the place to which it does relate, and, where that place is in public use, in that place itself.

3. The notice shall first be displayed as aforesaid not later than the first publication of the corresponding notice in the local newspaper and the Secretary of State shall take all steps which it is reasonably practicable for him to take to ensure that it remains in a legible condition and continues to be so displayed:—

(a) in the case of a notice of proposals not announcing the holding of a public inquiry until the end of the objection period;

(b) in the case of a notice announcing the holding of a public inquiry until the date on which the inquiry begins.

SCHEDULE 3

REQUIREMENTS AS TO THE AVAILABILITY OF DOCUMENTS FOR INSPECTION

1. There shall be available for inspection at such address or addresses, and during such times, as may be specified in the notice in connection with which they are required to be made available (one such address being, so far as practicable, an address in the area in which any road or other place to which the order relates is situated) the following documents:—

(a) a copy of the order as drafted or made (as the case may be);

(b) in the case of an order which varies, revokes, applies or suspends a previous order, a copy of the said previous order;

(c) in the case of a reserve power order made or proposed to be made by virtue of section 84A(2) of the Act, a copy of the direction for the purpose of securing the object of which the order is made or proposed to be made;

(d) in the case of a proposed order, a copy of a statement setting out the Secretary of State's reasons for proposing to make the order and a copy of the relevant map; and

(e) in the case of an order made after the holding of a public inquiry a copy of the report and the recommendations (if any) of the person appointed to hold the inquiry.

2. The said documents shall be made available as aforesaid not later than the date of the first publication in the local newspaper of the notice in connection with which they are required to be made available, and they shall continue to be so available:—

(a) where the notice is a notice of proposals not announcing the holding of a public inquiry until the end of the objection period;

(b) where the notice is one announcing the holding of a public inquiry, until the date on which the inquiry begins, and

(c) where the notice is a notice of making the order, until the end of 6 weeks from the date on which the order is made.

EXPLANATORY NOTE

(*This Note is not part of the Regulations.*)

These Regulations lay down the procedure to be followed in Scotland by the Secretary of State for Scotland and the Secretary of State for the Environment in connection with the making by them of various types of traffic orders under the Road Traffic Regulation Act 1967, as amended by Part IX of the Transport Act 1968 and under section 32(3) of the Countryside Act 1968.

Regulation 3 specifies the orders to which the Regulations apply. These include with respect to trunk roads traffic regulation orders, experimental traffic orders, orders relating to speed limits, and with respect to non trunk roads, orders made under the Countryside Act 1968 or under the reserve powers of the Secretaries of State under section 84A of the 1967 Act.

Regulations 4 to 10 lay down the procedure to be followed before the order is made. They provide for preliminary consultation with the Police (Regulation 4), publication of proposals (Regulation 5), objections to the order (Regulations 6 and 9), public inquiries (Regulations 7 and 8) and the modification of proposals (Regulation 10).

Regulations 11 and 12 contain requirements about the operative date of the order and make provision as to the manner of making the order and as to the giving of notice of its making.

Certain of the above requirements are modified in relation to consolidation and certain variation orders and some experimental traffic orders by Regulations 13 and 14.

Schedules 1 to 3 contain particulars of the details to be included in the press notices of an order, of the requirements as to display of notices of an order in the road itself, and of the requirements about making documents relating to an order available for public inspection.

STATUTORY INSTRUMENTS

1973 No. 1122 (S.85)

SEA FISHERIES

The Sea Fisheries (Scotland) Byelaw (No. 86) 1973

Made	-	-	-	*25th June* 1973
Coming into Operation			*31st August* 1973

The Secretary of State in exercise of the powers conferred upon him by section 7 of the Herring Fishery (Scotland) Act 1889(a) and of all other powers enabling him in that behalf hereby makes the following byelaw: —

Citation, commencement and interpretation

1.—(1) This byelaw may be cited as the Sea Fisheries (Scotland) Byelaw (No. 86) 1973.

(2) This byelaw shall come into operation on 31st August 1973.

(3) The Interpretation Act 1889(b) shall apply for the interpretation of this byelaw as it applies for the interpretation of an Act of Parliament.

Methods of fishing permitted in a defined area of the Moray Firth

2. Notwithstanding the provisions of—

(a) Byelaw (No. 10) made by the Fishery Board for Scotland on 27th September 1892 and confirmed by the Secretary for Scotland on 22nd November 1892(c) (prohibition of trawling in Moray Firth); and

(b) Sea Fisheries (Scotland) Byelaw (No. 81) 1968(d) (conditional permitting of trawling in part of Moray Firth)

it shall be lawful to use the methods of fishing known as beam trawling and otter trawling in that area of the Moray Firth comprising that part lying to the west of a line from Duncansby Head to Rattray Point except such parts thereof as are within the fishery limits of the British Islands appurtenant to the coast of Scotland between Duncansby Head and Rattray Point.

Made by the Secretary of State on 25th June 1973.

Eric Gillett,
Fisheries Secretary.

Department of Agriculture and
   Fisheries for Scotland,
St. Andrew's House,
Edinburgh.

(a) 1889 c. 23.   (b) 1889 c. 63.
(c) S.R. & O.1892, p. 1010 (Rev VII, p. 1029).   (d) S.I. 1968/1011 (1968 II, p. 2674).

EXPLANATORY NOTE
(This Note is not part of the Byelaw.)

This Byelaw permits, unconditionally, the use of the methods of fishing known as beam trawling and otter trawling within that part of the waters in the Moray Firth which is outwith the fishery limits.

STATUTORY INSTRUMENTS

1973 No. 1124

SOCIAL SECURITY

The National Insurance (Death Grant) Regulations 1973

Made - - -	21*st June* 1973
Laid before Parliament	3*rd July* 1973
Coming into Operation	24*th July* 1973

The National Insurance Joint Authority, in exercise of powers conferred by sections 18(2), 39(4), 45 and 49(1) and (2) of the National Insurance Act 1965(a), and now vested in them (b), and the Secretary of State for Social Services(c), in exercise of powers conferred by sections 39(2), 49(1) and 81(3) of, and paragraphs 1, 17, 18 and 19(e) of Schedule 11 to that Act and by section 8 of the National Insurance Act 1969(d), in each case in conjunction with the Treasury so far as relates to matters with regard to which the Treasury have so directed (e), and in exercise of all other powers enabling them in that behalf, and for the purpose only of consolidating the regulations hereby revoked, hereby make the following regulations:—

Citation, commencement and interpretation

1.—(1) These regulations may be cited as the National Insurance (Death Grant) Regulations 1973 and shall come into operation on 24th July 1973.

(2) In these regulations, unless the context otherwise requires:—

"the Act" means the National Insurance Act 1965;

"the New Entrants Regulations" means the National Insurance (New Entrants Transitional) Regulations 1949(f), as amended (g);

"the Residence and Persons Abroad Regulations" means the National Insurance (Residence and Persons Abroad) Regulations 1948(h), as amended (i);

"the General Transitional Regulations" means the National Insurance (General Transitional) Regulations 1948(j);

"the General Benefit Regulations" means the National Insurance (General Benefit) Regulations 1970(k), as amended (l);

(a) 1965 c. 51.
(b) *See* S.I. 1948/211 (Rev. XVI, p. 367: 1948 I, p. 2905) and ss. 104(4)(*b*) and 117(1) of the National Insurance Act 1965 (c. 51).
(c) For transfer of functions from the Minister of Pensions and National Insurance to (eventually) the Secretary of State, *see* Ministry of Social Security Act 1966 (c.20) and S.I. 1968/1699 (1968 III, p. 4585).   (d) 1969 c. 44.
(e) *See* s. 106(5) of the National Insurance Act 1965 (c. 51).
(f) S.I. 1949/352 (1949 I, p. 2737).
(g) The relevant amending instruments are S.I. 1957/2147, 1958/1239, 1960/1210 (1957 I, p. 1694; 1958 II, p. 1661; 1960 II, p. 2234).
(h) S.I. 1948/1275 (Rev. XVI, p. 88: 1948 I, p. 2864).
(i) The relevant amending instruments are S.I. 1950/1946, 1956/2021, 1958/1084, 1960/1210 (1950 II, p. 27; 1956 I, p. 1687; 1958 II, p. 1581; 1960 II, p. 2234).
(j) S.I. 1948/1503 (Rev. XVI, p.2:1948 I, p. 2880). (k) S.I. 1970/1981 (1970 III, p. 6461).
(l) The relevant amending instruments are S.I. 1971/621, 1419, 1972/166 (1971 I, p. 1623; II, p. 3964; 1972 I, p. 588).

"the Existing Contributors Regulations" means the National Insurance (Pensions, Existing Contributors) (Transitional) Regulations 1948(a), as amended (b);

"the Members of the Forces Regulations" means the National Insurance (Members of the Forces) Regulations 1968(c);

"the Mariners Regulations" means the National Insurance (Mariners) Regulations 1967(d);

"the Airmen Regulations" means the National Insurance (Airmen) Regulations 1948(e);

"the Continental Shelf Regulations" means the National Insurance (Continental Shelf) Regulations 1964(f);

"the Overlapping Benefits Regulations" means the National Insurance (Overlapping Benefits) Regulations 1972(g);

"British Islands" means the United Kingdom, the Channel Islands and the Isle of Man;

"the deceased" has the same meaning as in section 39 of the Act;

"contributions" has the same meaning as in the Act save that it does not include graduated contributions;

and other expressions have the same meanings as in the Act.

(3) References in these regulations to any enactment or regulation shall, except in so far as the context otherwise requires, be construed as references to such enactment or regulations as amended or extended by any subsequent enactment, order or regulation and as including references to any enactment or regulation thereby consolidated.

(4) The rules for the construction of Acts of Parliament contained in the Interpretation Act 1889(h) shall apply in relation to this instrument (including any instrument read as one therewith) and in relation to any revocation effected by it as if this instrument, the regulations revoked by it and any regulations revoked by the regulations so revoked were Acts of Parliament, and as if each revocation were a repeal.

Calculation of yearly average of contributions, etc., for death grant

2.—(1) The yearly average of contributions paid by or credited to any person shall, in relation to death grant, be calculated in the same manner as that provided in regulation 3 of the General Benefit Regulations in relation to widow's benefit and retirement pensions, and accordingly that regulation shall also apply as a separate provision in relation to death grant.

(2) Regulation 13(2) of the said regulations (suspension of payment of certain benefits pending appeals to the National Insurance Commissioner) shall apply in relation to death grant as it applies in relation to the benefits referred to in sub-paragraph (*b*) of that regulation; and regulation 13(10) of the said regulations (payment of certain benefits in an emergency under arrangements made by the Secretary of State with the consent of the Treasury), other than paragraph (*b*) of the proviso thereto, shall apply in relation to death grant as it applies in relation to the benefits referred to in that regulation.

(a) S.I. 1948/612 (Rev. XVI, p. 18: 1948 I, p. 2834).
(b) The relevant amending instruments are S.I. 1957/1332, 1960/1210 (1957 I, p. 1706; 1960 II, p. 2234).
(c) S.I. 1968/827 (1968 II, p. 2228).   (d) S.I. 1967/386 (1967 I, p. 1294).
(e) S.I. 1948/1466 (Rev. XVI, p. 108: 1948 I, p. 2616).
(f) S.I. 1964/1855 (1964 III, p. 4047).   (g) S.I. 1972/604 (1972 I, p. 1994).
(h) 1889 c. 63.

Modification of the Act in relation to period over which yearly average of contributions is to be calculated for death grant in the case of certain persons under pensionable age and over 16

3. The period over which the yearly average of contributions paid by or credited to any person is to be calculated shall, in relation to death grant, in the case of any person becoming insured under the Act on or after 5th July 1948 who immediately before that date was under pensionable age and on that date was over the age of 16, be the same as that specified in regulation 2(1) of the New Entrants Regulations, and accordingly that regulation (other than sub-paragraph (*b*) thereof) shall apply in relation to death grant.

Special provisions for men over 55 *and women over* 50 *immediately before 5th July* 1948

4.—(1) The provisions of regulation 4(1)(*a*) and (*b*) of the New Entrants Regulations (postponement of the pensionable age for, and contributions paid by or in respect of, certain persons who immediately before 5th July 1948 were over the age of 55 in the case of men or 50 in the case of women and under pensionable age) shall apply in relation to death grant as they apply for the purposes of retirement pensions and widow's benefit.

(2) The provisions of regulation 10(1)(*a*) and (*b*) of the Existing Contributors Regulations (postponement of pensionable age for, and contributions paid by or in respect of, certain existing pensions contributors) shall apply in relation to death grant as they would apply for the purposes of retirement pensions and widow's benefit if regulation 10(2) of those regulations were omitted.

(3) Where a person attained pensionable age within the period of 26 weeks commencing on 5th July 1948, and by the time he had attained that age had not satisfied the contribution condition for death grant contained in paragraph 5(1)(*a*) of Schedule 2 to the Act, but thereafter further contributions have been or are paid by him, or have been or are credited to him in respect of any period commencing on or after 5th July 1948, which, if taken into account, would satisfy that condition, he shall be deemed to have satisfied that condition as from 5th July 1949, or the end of the week in respect of which the 26th contribution was so paid or credited, whichever is the later.

Children

5. Where the deceased was at death a child but the requirements of section 39(1) of the Act (persons by whom the contribution conditions for death grant may be satisfied) are not satisfied, a death grant shall, subject to the provisions of the Act, be payable in respect of the death of the deceased if the relevant contribution conditions are satisfied by either—

(1) a parent (including a person who has adopted a child pursuant to an order made in the British Islands or an overseas adoption within the meaning of section 4 of the Adoption Act 1968(**a**)) of the deceased, notwithstanding that the deceased was not at death a child of the family of that parent; or

(2) a person who, immediately before the deceased's death, was entitled to an increase of benefit in respect of the deceased under sections 40 or 41 of the Act (increases of benefit for children), or would have been so entitled had he then been entitled to any benefit of which the said section 40 provides an increase:

(a) 1968 c. 53.

Provided that—

(a) subject to the next following paragraph of this proviso, the amount of a death grant payable by virtue of this regulation shall not exceed the amount of the deceased's funeral expenses;

(b) the foregoing paragraph of this proviso shall not apply if the deceased would have been a child of the family of a parent satisfying the relevant contribution conditions but for the provisions of section 20(3) of the Family Allowances Act (condition of a child's being included in a family that the child is in Great Britain).

Deaths occurring outside Great Britain

6.—(1) Subject to the provisions of the Act and these regulations, a death grant shall be payable in respect of a death occurring outside Great Britain if the conditions contained in any one of the following sub-paragraphs are satisfied, namely—

(a) that the deceased immediately before death was, or but for any failure to make a claim would have been, entitled to sickness benefit or invalidity benefit under the Act, or to industrial injury benefit under the Industrial Injuries Act; or

(b) that the deceased immediately before death was, or but for any failure to make a claim would have been, entitled to widow's benefit or a retirement pension under the Act, or to industrial death benefit under the Industrial Injuries Act, or would have been entitled to a retirement pension had he then retired from regular employment and made the necessary claim, or was a child in respect of whom a child's special allowance or a guardian's allowance was payable; or

(c) that the deceased was a widow who was, immediately before her death, entitled to any personal death benefit by way of pension or allowance in respect of the death of her husband under any Personal Injuries Scheme, any Service Pensions Instrument or any 1914-1918 War Injuries Scheme; or

(d) that the deceased immediately before death was entitled to industrial disablement benefit under the Industrial Injuries Act; or

(e) that the deceased immediately before death was liable or entitled, as the case may be, to pay contributions either under the provisions of regulation 3(2) or regulation 5(2) of the Residence and Persons Abroad Regulations, or under regulation 3(3) of the General Transitional Regulations (circumstances in which contributions are payable by or in respect of persons for periods when they are outside Great Britain), and not less than 45 contributions were paid by or credited to him in respect of a contribution year, being either the last complete contribution year before his death or the contribution year immediately preceding that year; or

(f) that the deceased immediately before death was a serving member of the forces within the meaning of regulation 1(2) of the Members of the Forces Regulations; or

(g) that the deceased immediately before death was either—

(i) employed as a mariner within the meaning of regulation 1(2) of the Mariners Regulations (other than a mariner excepted from insurance by regulation 2(2) of those regulations) or as an airman within the meaning of regulation 1(2) of the Airmen Regulations (other than an airman excepted from insurance by regulation 2(2) of those regulations), or

(ii) a person who (then being otherwise entitled to unemployment benefit, or then being so entitled but for any failure to make a claim) by virtue of the relevant provisions of either of the said regulations was not disqualified for receiving any such benefit by reason of his absence from Great Britain; or

(*h*) that the deceased's death occurred in a designated area within the meaning of the Continental Shelf Regulations and that his absence from Great Britain immediately before his death was due to his being or having been in prescribed employment within the meaning of those regulations; or

(*i*) that the deceased immediately before death was either the wife or husband or child (to whom the provisions of section 39(1) of the Act are applicable) of a person who, had he then died, would have satisfied the conditions contained in any one of the foregoing paragraphs, and such wife or husband or child, as the case may be, was then resident with that person, and for this purpose the expression "child of the family" contained in the said section 39(1) shall be deemed to include a child who would be included in that expression but for the provisions of section 20(3) of the Family Allowances Act (condition of a child's being included in a family that the child is in Great Britain); or

(*j*) that the deceased immediately before death was ordinarily resident in Great Britain, and the death occurred within a period of 13 weeks or, in the case of a death occurring in the Channel Islands, within a period of 6 months from the date when he last left Great Britain; or

(*k*) that the deceased was a woman who immediately before death was residing in Great Britain with her husband and he was then an insured person satisfying the relevant contribution conditions; or

(*l*) that the deceased was a child (including a person treated as a child under section 39(3) of the Act) who immediately before death was residing in Great Britain with an insured person by virtue of whose satisfaction of the relevant contribution conditions a death grant is payable in respect of the deceased's death; or

(*m*) that the deceased died during or as the result of a confinement in respect of which she was not, or but for any failure to make a claim would not have been, disqualified for receiving maternity benefit (to which she was otherwise entitled) by reason of her absence from Great Britain.

(2) In this regulation, the expressions "personal death benefit", "Personal Injuries Scheme", "Service Pensions Instrument" and "1914-1918 War Injuries Scheme" have the same meanings as in the Overlapping Benefits Regulations.

Absence from Great Britain

7. A person shall not be disqualified for receiving death grant by reason of being absent from Great Britain.

Imprisonment and detention in legal custody

8. A person shall not be disqualified for receiving a death grant by reason of undergoing a period of imprisonment or detention in legal custody, but the payment of the grant shall be suspended during any such period:

Provided that the grant may nevertheless be paid during any such period to any person appointed by the Secretary of State to receive and deal with any sum payable on behalf of the beneficiary on account of the grant, and the receipt of any person so appointed shall be a good discharge to the Secretary of State and the National Insurance Fund for any sum so paid.

Partial satisfaction of contribution conditions, and reduced amount of death grant

9.—(1) Where a death grant would be payable but for the fact that the relevant contribution conditions are not satisfied as respects the yearly average of contributions paid or credited, the grant shall nevertheless be payable in accordance with the next succeeding paragraph if the yearly average of contributions paid or credited is not less than 13.

(2) Where the full amount of the death grant under Schedule 4 to the Act is one of the amount's first set out in columns (2), (3), (4), (5) and (6) of Schedule 1 to these regulations, then the grant shall be reduced to the amount specified in the appropriate column of the said Schedule 1 which corresponds with the yearly average of contributions paid or credited as shown in column (1) of that Schedule.

Revocation of regulations and general savings

10.—(1) The regulations specified in column (1) of Schedule 2 to these regulations are hereby revoked to the extent mentioned in column (3) of that Schedule.

(2) Anything whatsoever done under or by virtue of any regulation revoked by these regulations shall be deemed to have been done under or by virtue of the corresponding provisions of these regulations, and anything whatsoever begun under any such regulation may be continued under these regulations as if begun under these regulations.

(3) Nothing in paragraph (2) of this regulation shall be taken as affecting the general application by regulation 1(4) of these regulations of the rules for the construction of Acts of Parliament contained in section 38 of the Interpretation Act 1889 (effect of repeal) with regard to the effect of revocations.

Given under the official seal of the National Insurance Joint Authority.

(L.S.)

Keith Joseph,
Secretary of State for Social Services, a member
of the National Insurance Joint Authority.

20th June 1973.

Keith Joseph,
Secretary of State for Social Services.

20th June 1973.

Tim Fortescue,
Oscar Murton,
Two of the Lords Commissioners of Her
Majesty's Treasury.

21st June 1973.

SCHEDULE 1   Regulation 9(2)

Showing reduced amount of death grant payable if the contribution conditions are not fully satisfied.

(1)	(2)	(3)	(4)	(5)	(6)
	and the age of deceased at death was				
	over 18				
Yearly average of contributions paid or credited	and, if a man was under 55 on 4th July 1948 or; if a woman was under 50 at that date	and, if a man was over 55 and under 65 on 4th July 1948 or; if a woman, was over 50 and under 60 at that date	between 6 and 18	between 3 and 6	under 3
	Full amount of death grant payable under Schedule 4 to the National Insurance Act 1965				
	£30·00	£15·00	£22·50	£15·00	£9·00
	Reduced amount of death grant payable:—				
30–44	£22·50	£11·25	£16·87	£11·25	£6·75
13–29	£15·00	£7·50	£11·25	£7·50	£4·50

SCHEDULE 2   Regulation 10(1)

Regulations revoked (1)	Reference (2)	Extent of revocation (3)
The National Insurance (Death Grant) Regulations 1949	S.I. 1949/1204 (1949 I, p. 2708)	The whole regulations
The National Insurance (Death Grant) Amendment Regulations 1949	S.I. 1949/1696 (1949 I, p. 2717)	The whole regulations
The National Insurance (Child's Special Allowance) Regulations 1957	S.I. 1957/1835 (1957 I, p. 1523)	In the Schedule, the entry relating to regulation 5(b) of the National Insurance (Death Grant) Regulations 1949, as amended
The National Insurance (Death Grant) (Consequential Provisions) Regulations 1957	S.I. 1957/2179 (1957 I, p. 1527)	The whole regulations
The National Insurance (Graduated Contributions and Non-participating Employments—Miscellaneous Provisions) Regulations 1960	S.I. 1960/1210 (1960 II, p. 2234)	In the Schedule, the entry relating to the National Insurance (Death Grant) Regulations 1949
The National Insurance (Continental Shelf) Regulations 1964	S.I. 1964/1855 (1964 III, p. 4047)	Regulation 4
The National Insurance (Determination of Claims and Questions) (No. 2) Regulations 1967	S.I. 1967/1570 (1967 III, p. 4350)	In the Schedule the entry relating to the National Insurance (Death Grant) Regulations 1949
The Family Allowances, National Insurance, Industrial Injuries and Miscellaneous Provisions (Decimalisation of the Currency) Regulations 1970	S.I. 1970/46 (1970 I, p. 243)	Regulation 8 and Schedule 6

EXPLANATORY NOTE

(This Note is not part of the Regulations.)

These Regulations are made for the purpose only of consolidating Regulations hereby revoked, and accordingly, by virtue of section 108(9)(*c*) of the National Insurance Act 1965, no reference of them has been made to the National Insurance Advisory Committee.

These Regulations contain miscellaneous provisions affecting death grants. Regulation 1 relates to the citation, commencement and interpretation of the Regulations. Regulations 2-4 contain provisions relating to the contribution conditions for death grant. Regulation 5 contains special provisions relating to death grant in respect of children. Regulation 6 relates to the circumstances in which death grant is payable where the death occurs outside Great Britain. Regulations 7 and 8 relate to exception from disqualification for receiving death grant where the persons concerned are either absent from Great Britain or are imprisoned or detained in legal custody. Regulation 9 and Schedule 1 relate to payment of death grant at reduced rates, where the contribution conditions are only partially satisfied. Regulation 10 and Schedule 2 contain transitional provisions and provisions relating to the revocation of the former Regulations.

STATUTORY INSTRUMENTS

1973 No. 1125 (C.27)

LIBRARIES

The British Library Act (Appointed Day) Order 1973

Made - - - *26th June* 1973

The Secretary of State in exercise of the power conferred on her by section 3(2)(a) of the British Library Act 1972 hereby makes the following Order:—

Citation

1. This Order may be cited as the British Library Act (Appointed Day) Order 1973.

Appointed Day

2. The day appointed for the purposes of the British Library Act 1972 is 1st July 1973.

Given under the Official Seal of the Secretary of State for Education and Science on 26th June 1973.

(L.S.)   *Margaret H. Thatcher,*
Secretary of State for Education and Science.

EXPLANATORY NOTE

(*This Note is not part of the Order.*)

This Order appoints 1st July 1973 as the day for the transfer to the British Library of the collections of the British Museum Library specified in section 3 of the British Library Act 1972 and matters consequential upon that transfer.

(a) 1972 c. 54.

STATUTORY INSTRUMENTS

1973 No. 1126

MUSEUMS

The British Museum (Authorised Repositories) Order 1973

Made - - -	*26th June* 1973
Laid before Parliament	*6th July* 1973
Coming into Operation	*1st August* 1973

The Secretary of State for Education and Science with the agreement of the Trustees of the British Museum, in exercise of the powers conferred by section 10(2) of the British Museum Act 1963(a) and vested in her (b), hereby makes the following Order:—

Citation and commencement

1. This Order may be cited as the British Museum (Authorised Repositories) Order 1973 and shall come into operation on 1st August 1973.

Deletion of references to authorised repositories

2. The references to the sites specified in paragraphs 2, 3, 4, 5 and 7 of Part I (authorised repositories of the British Museum) of schedule 3 to the British Museum Act 1963 as amended (c) shall be deleted.

Given under the Official Seal of the Secretary of State for Education and Science on 26th June 1973.

(L.S.)

Margaret H. Thatcher,
Secretary of State for
Education and Science.

EXPLANATORY NOTE
(This Note is not part of the Order.)

This Order provides that, following the transfer to the British Library of the collections of the British Museum Library specified in section 3 of the British Library Act 1972 (c. 54), the buildings in which those collections are housed shall cease to be authorised repositories of the British Museum.

(a) 1963 c. 24.   (b) S.I. 1965/603 (1965 I, p. 1911).
(c) S.I. 1966/99, 1968/1604, 1970/1956, 1971/82, 1972/653 (1966 I, p. 222; 1968 III, p. 4406; 1970 III, p. 6408; 1971 I, p. 139; 1972 I, p. 2136).

STATUTORY INSTRUMENTS

1973 No. 1129 (S.86)

JURIES

The Jurors' Allowances (Scotland) Amendment Regulations 1973

Made - - -		*26th June* 1973
Coming into Operation		*2nd July* 1973

In exercise of the powers conferred on me by sections 24(1) and 32(1) of the Juries Act 1949(a), as amended by the Juries Act 1954(b), and of all other powers enabling me in that behalf and as read with the Minister for the Civil Service Order 1971(c), I hereby, with the consent of the Minister for the Civil Service, make the following regulations:—

1.—(1) These regulations may be cited as the Jurors' Allowances (Scotland) Amendment Regulations 1973 and shall come into operation on 2nd July 1973.

(2) The Interpretation Act 1889(d) shall apply for the interpretation of these regulations as it applies for the interpretation of an Act of Parliament.

2. In regulation 5 of the Jurors' Allowances (Scotland) Regulations 1971(e) as amended(f) (which relates to compensation for loss of earnings or additional expense) for the expressions "£2·37½", "£4·75" and "£9·50" there shall be substituted the expressions "£2·75", "£5·50" and "£11" respectively.

Gordon Campbell,
One of Her Majesty's Principal
Secretaries of State.

St. Andrew's House,
Edinburgh.
22nd June 1973.

Consent of the Minister for the Civil Service given under his Official Seal on 26th June 1973.

P. M. Blake,
Authorised by the Minister
for the Civil Service.

(a) 1949 c. 27. (b) 1954 c. 41. (c) S.I. 1971/2099 (1971 III, p. 6186).
(d) 1889 c. 63. (e) S.I. 1971/220 (1971 I, p. 651).
(f) The relevant amending instrument is S.I. 1971/2022 (1971 III, p. 5795).

EXPLANATORY NOTE

(This Note is not part of the Regulations.)

These Regulations amend the Jurors' Allowances (Scotland) Regulations 1971. They provide for an increase in the maximum amount payable to a juror as compensation for loss of earnings or additional expense.

1973 No. 1137

MONOPOLIES AND MERGERS

Restriction of Merger (No. 2) Order 1973

Made - - -	*29th June* 1973
Laid before Parliament	*29th June* 1973
Coming into Operation	*30th June* 1973

Whereas the Secretary of State in exercise of powers conferred by section 6(7) of the Monopolies and Mergers Act 1965(a) and now vested in him by virtue of the Transfer of Functions (Monopolies, Mergers and Restrictive Practices) Order 1969(b) has referred to the Monopolies Commission for investigation and report the matter of the proposed acquisition by British Match Corporation Limited of Wilkinson Sword Limited:

Now, therefore, the Secretary of State with a view to preventing action which may prejudice the reference or impede the taking of any remedial action which may be warranted by the Commission's report and in exercise of powers conferred by sections 3(5) and 6(11) of the said Act and now vested in him hereby orders as follows:—

1.—(1) This Order may be cited as the Restriction of Merger (No. 2) Order 1973 and shall come into operation on 30th June 1973.

(2) The Interpretation Act 1889(c) shall apply to the interpretation of this Order as it applies to the interpretation of an Act of Parliament.

2. It shall be unlawful for British Match Corporation Limited or any subsidiary thereof to acquire any shares or any interest in shares of Wilkinson Sword Limited if such acquisition would or might result in British Match Corporation Limited and Wilkinson Sword Limited becoming interconnected bodies corporate:

Provided that this Article shall not apply to anything done in pursuance of a legally enforceable agreement to acquire shares made before the commencement of this Order other than an agreement made in pursuance of any general offer addressed to the members of Wilkinson Sword Limited by Hambros Bank Limited on behalf of British Match Corporation Limited.

Peter Emery,
Parliamentary Under Secretary of State,
Department of Trade and Industry.

Dated 29th June 1973.

(a) 1965 c. 50.   (b) S.I. 1969/1534 (1969 III, p. 4991).
(c) 1889 c. 63.

EXPLANATORY NOTE

(This Note is not part of the Order.)

This Order imposes a standstill on any acquisition by British Match Corporation Limited or its subsidiaries of shares of Wilkinson Sword Limited which would or might result in Wilkinson Sword Limited becoming a subsidiary of British Match Corporation Limited. The proposed merger of these two companies has been referred to the Monopolies Commission.

An exemption is provided for any acquisition of shares in pursuance of an agreement made before the commencement of this Order other than an agreement resulting from a general offer to acquire shares of Wilkinson Sword Limited made by Hambros Bank Limited on behalf of British Match Corporation Limited.

The Order, unless previously revoked, will cease to have effect—

(a) 40 days after the report of the Monopolies Commission on the proposed merger is laid before Parliament; or

(b) on the failure of the Commission to report within the period allowed.

STATUTORY INSTRUMENTS

1973 No. 1138 (S.87)

POLICE

The Police Cadets (Scotland) Amendment Regulations 1973

Made - - -	*26th June* 1973
Laid before Parliament	*6th July* 1973
Coming into Operation	*31st July* 1973

In exercise of the powers conferred on me by section 27 of the Police (Scotland) Act 1967(a), and of all other powers enabling me in that behalf, and after consulting (i) the Police Advisory Board for Scotland in accordance with section 26(9) of the said Act and (ii) the Police Council for the United Kingdom in accordance with section 4(4) of the Police Act 1969(b), I hereby make the following regulations: —

Citation

1. These regulations may be cited as the Police Cadets (Scotland) Amendment Regulations 1973.

Operation and effect

2. These regulations shall come into operation on 31st July 1973 and shall have effect: —

    (*a*) for the purposes of regulation 5 thereof, as from 1st April 1973; and

    (*b*) for the purposes of regulation 6 thereof, as from 1st September 1973.

Interpretation

3. In these regulations any reference to the principal regulations is a reference to the Police Cadets (Scotland) Regulations 1968(c), as amended(d).

4. The Interpretation Act 1889(e) shall apply for the interpretation of these regulations as it applies for the interpretation of an Act of Parliament.

Pay

5. For the Table in Schedule 1 to the principal regulations (which contains scales of pay) there shall be substituted the following Table: —

"TABLE

Age	Annual Pay
under 17 years	£ 594
17 years	£ 642
18 years	£ 723
19 years	£ 789 "

(a) 1967 c. 77.   (b) 1969 c. 63.
(c) S.I. 1968/208 (1968 I, p. 557).
(d) The relevant amending regulations are S.I. 1969/493, 1820, 1970/1413, 1971/810, 1972/778 (1969 I, p. 1402; III, p. 5649; 1970 III, p. 4664; 1971 II, p. 2323; 1972 II, p. 2541).
(e) 1889 c. 63.

6. For paragraph (*a*) of regulation 2 of the principal regulations (which relates to qualifications for appointment) there shall be substituted the following paragraph:—

"(*a*) has attained the age of 16 years;".

Gordon Campbell,
One of Her Majesty's Principal
Secretaries of State.

St. Andrew's House,
Edinburgh.
26th June 1973.

EXPLANATORY NOTE

(*This Note is not part of the Regulations.*)

These Regulations amend the Police Cadets (Scotland) Regulations 1968.

Regulation 5 provides for increases in pay.

Regulation 6 raises the minimum age for appointment as a cadet from 15 to 16 as a consequence of the raising of the school leaving age.

By virtue of Regulation 2 the increases in pay have effect from 1st April 1973. This is provided in exercise of the power conferred by section 27(2) of the Police (Scotland) Act 1967.

STATUTORY INSTRUMENTS

1973 No. 1140

WAGES COUNCILS
The Wages Regulation (Retail Bespoke Tailoring) (England and Wales) Order 1973

Made - - - -	28*th June* 1973
Coming into Operation	6*th August* 1973

Whereas the Secretary of State has received from the Retail Bespoke Tailoring Wages Council (England and Wales) (hereafter in this Order referred to as "the Wages Council") the wages regulation proposals set out in the Schedule hereto;

Now, therefore, the Secretary of State in exercise of powers conferred by section 11 of the Wages Councils Act 1959(a), as modified by Article 2 of the Counter-Inflation (Modification of Wages Councils Act 1959) Order 1973(b), and now vested in him (c), and of all other powers enabling him in that behalf, hereby makes the following Order:—

1. This Order may be cited as the Wages Regulation (Retail Bespoke Tailoring) (England and Wales) Order 1973.

2.—(1) In this Order the expression "the specified date" means the 6th August 1973, provided that where, as respects any worker who is paid wages at intervals not exceeding seven days, that date does not correspond with the beginning of the period for which the wages are paid, the expression "the specified date" means, as respects that worker, the beginning of the next such period following that date.

(2) The Interpretation Act 1889(d) shall apply to the interpretation of this Order as it applies to the interpretation of an Act of Parliament and as if this Order and the Order hereby revoked were Acts of Parliament.

3. The wages regulation proposals set out in the Schedule hereto shall have effect as from the specified date and as from that date the Wages Regulation (Retail Bespoke Tailoring) (England and Wales) Order 1972(e) shall cease to have effect.

Signed by order of the Secretary of State.

28th June 1973.

W. H. Marsh,
Assistant Secretary,
Department of Employment.

(a) 1959 c. 69. (b) S.I. 1973/661 (1973 I, p. 2141).
(c) S.I. 1959/1769, 1968/729 (1959 I, p. 1795; 1968 II, p. 2108).
(d) 1889 c. 63. (e) S.I. 1972/680 (1972 II, p. 2213).

ARRANGEMENT OF SCHEDULE

Article 3

SCHEDULE

The following minimum remuneration shall be substituted for the statutory minimum remuneration fixed by the Wages Regulation (Retail Bespoke Tailoring) (England and Wales) Order 1972 (Order R.B. (77)).

STATUTORY MINIMUM REMUNERATION
Part I
GENERAL

1.—(1) The minimum remuneration payable to a worker to whom this Schedule applies for all work except work to which a minimum overtime rate applies under Part IV is:—

(a) in the case of a time worker, the hourly general minimum time rate applicable to the worker under the provisions of this Schedule;

(b) in the case of a worker employed on piece work, piece rates each of which would yield, in the circumstances of the case, to an ordinary worker (that is to say, a worker of ordinary skill and efficiency of the class in question) at least the same amount of money as the piece work basis time rate applicable to the worker or, where no piece work basis time rate is applicable, at least the same amount of money as the hourly general minimum time rate which would be applicable to the worker if he were a time worker.

(2) In this Schedule, in relation to a worker to whom a weekly general minimum time rate applies, the expression hourly general minimum time rate means the weekly general minimum time rate applicable to the worker divided by 40.

APPLICABILITY OF STATUTORY MINIMUM REMUNERATION

2.—(1) Subject to the provisions of sub-paragraph (2) of this paragraph, this Schedule applies to workers in relation to whom the Retail Bespoke Tailoring Wages Council (England and Wales) operates, that is to say, workers employed in England and Wales in any of the branches of work in the retail bespoke tailoring trade as specified in the Schedule to the Trade Boards (Retail Bespoke Tailoring Trade, England and Wales) (Constitution and Proceedings) Regulations 1924(a), which are set out below, that is to say:—

Those branches of men's, women's, boys' and girls' bespoke tailoring in which the tailor supplies the garment direct to the individual wearer and employs the worker direct.

A worker shall be deemed to be employed by the tailor direct, if employed by another worker in the employ of the tailor, to whom a minimum rate of wages fixed under the Wages Councils Act 1959 is applicable; or if employed by a sub-contractor engaged in cutting, making or finishing garments exclusively for the tailor in the tailor's shop or in a building of which the shop forms part or to which the shop is attached;

including:—

(a) S.R. & O. 1924/835 (1924, p. 1769).

(*a*) (i) The altering, repairing, renovating, or re-making of men's, women's, boys' or girls' tailored garments where carried out for the individual wearer by a tailor who employs the worker direct as defined above;

(ii) The cleaning of such garments where carried on in association with or in conjunction with the repairing, renovating or re-making of the garments;

(*b*) The lining with fur of the above-mentioned garments where carried out in association with or in conjunction with the making of such garments;

(*c*) All processes of embroidery or decorative needlework where carried out in association with or in conjunction with the above-mentioned branches of tailoring;

(*d*) The packing and all other operations incidental to or appertaining to any of the above-mentioned branches of tailoring;

but excluding:—

(*a*) All or any of the above-mentioned operations where carried on in a factory where garments are made up for three or more retail establishments;

(*b*) The making of head-gear.

(2) Notwithstanding the provisions of sub-paragraph (1) of this paragraph, this Schedule does not apply to workers employed as cutters, trimmers or packers.

PART II

GENERAL MINIMUM TIME RATES

3. Subject to the provisions of this Schedule, the general minimum time rates are as follows:—

	per hour p
(1) RETAIL TAILORING CRAFT WORKER (as defined in paragraph 15(2))	48·16
(2) ASSISTANT RETAIL TAILORING CRAFT WORKER GRADE 1 (as defined in paragraph 15 (3))	45·45
(3) ASSISTANT RETAIL TAILORING CRAFT WORKER GRADE 2 (as defined in paragraph 15 (4))	42·33

(4) INDENTURED APPRENTICES whose employment complies with the conditions specified in paragraph 13 during the following periods of apprenticeship:—

	per week £
The 1st year of apprenticeship	6·09
The 2nd year of apprenticeship	7·71
The 3rd year of apprenticeship	9·75

	per hour p
The 4th year of apprenticeship	30·36
The 5th year of apprenticeship	38·61

(5) LEARNERS whose employment complies with the conditions specified in paragraph 15 (5) during the following periods of learnership:—

	per week £
The 1st year of learnership	6·09
The 2nd year of learnership	7·71
The 3rd year of learnership	9·75

	per hour p
The 4th year of learnership	30·36
The 5th year of learnership	37·51

(6) OTHER WORKER (other than the workers specified in sub-paragraphs (1) to (5) inclusive of this paragraph).

		per hour
		p
During the 1st year	... ...	18·81
During the 2nd year	... ...	22·99
During the 3rd year	... ...	27·28
During the 4th year	... ...	31·57
During the 5th year	... ...	35·75
after 5 years employment in the trade	... ...	42·33

PIECE WORK BASIS TIME RATES

4. The piece work basis time rate applicable to a worker, irrespective of experience in the trade, who is employed on piece work shall be a rate equal to the general minimum time rate which would be payable if the worker were a time worker who has completed five years' employment in the trade, increased by twelve per cent., provided that where the worker is of a class specified in sub-paragraph (1), (2) or (3) of paragraph 3, the piece work basis time rate for that worker shall be a rate equal to the appropriate general minimum time rate applicable to that class of worker, increased by twelve per cent.

WORKERS ON SPECIAL CLASSES OF WORK

5. Notwithstanding the provisions of paragraphs 3 and 4, where a worker who has completed five years' employment in the trade is employed in the making of (i) military dress uniforms (other than khaki), (ii) naval frock and dress uniforms, (iii) hunt coats and hunt riding breeches, (iv) frock and dress coats and (v) court and diplomatic garments, or any of those garments, the general minimum time rate or the piece work basis time rate applicable to the worker shall be increased by 1p per hour.

PART III

RECKONING OF EXPERIENCE

PREVIOUS INSTRUCTION IN AN APPROVED TECHNICAL CLASS

6. Where any worker has, after attaining the age of 15 years and prior to his employment on work to which this Schedule applies, received instruction in tailoring processes and related studies in a technical class at any school or other institution and such instruction has been approved by the Wages Council, for the purpose of reckoning the period of his apprenticeship, learnership or other employment in the trade each complete one hundred hours of such instruction shall be treated as four weeks of apprenticeship, learnership or other employment in the trade: Provided that the period to be so treated as employment in the trade shall not exceed the total number of weeks during which the worker attended the technical class.

PREVIOUS EXPERIENCE IN THE TAILORING TRADE

7. Where any worker has at any time been employed as a worker in relation to whom there operated one or more of the following Wages Councils, that is to say, the Retail Bespoke Tailoring Wages Council (England and Wales), the Retail Bespoke Tailoring Wages Council (Scotland), the Ready-made and Wholesale Bespoke Tailoring Wages Council (Great Britain) and the Wholesale Mantle and Costume Wages Council (Great Britain), each such period of employment shall, for the purpose of reckoning the period of the worker's learnership or other employment (not being apprenticeship) in the trade, be treated as though it were an equal period of learnership or other employment in the trade.

EXPERIENCE UNDER THE GOVERNMENT VOCATIONAL TRAINING SCHEME

8. Where any worker has completed the full period of training in retail bespoke tailoring in respect of which training allowances are payable under the Government Vocational Training Scheme, such period of training shall, for the purpose of reckoning the period of the worker's employment in the trade, be treated as though it were a period of five years' employment therein.

PART IV

OVERTIME AND WAITING TIME

NORMAL NUMBER OF HOURS

9. Minimum overtime rates set out in paragraph 10 are payable to any worker as follows:—

(1) in any week,
for all time worked in excess of ... ... 40 hours

(2) on any day other than a Saturday, Sunday or a customary holiday,
for all time worked in excess of ... ... $7\frac{1}{4}$ hours

Provided that where the worker normally attends on five days only in the week, minimum overtime rates shall apply to all time worked in excess of the hours following:—

where the normal working hours exceed $8\frac{1}{2}$ ... ... 9 hours
or
where the normal working hours are more than 8 but not more than $8\frac{1}{2}$ ... ... $8\frac{1}{2}$ hours
or
where the normal working hours are not more than 8 ... 8 hours

(3) on a Saturday, not being a customary holiday—

(a) where the worker normally attends on six days in the week, for all time worked in excess of ... 4 hours

(b) where the worker normally attends on five days only in the week ... ... for all time worked

(4) on a Sunday or a customary holiday ... ... for all time worked

MINIMUM OVERTIME RATES

10.—(1) Minimum overtime rates are payable to any worker as follows:—

(a) on any day other than a Saturday, Sunday or customary holiday—

(i) for the first 2 hours of overtime worked ... ... time-and-a-quarter

(ii) for the next 2 hours ... ... time-and-a-half

(iii) thereafter ... ... double time

(b) on a Saturday, not being a customary holiday—

(i) where the worker normally attends on six days in the week—
for all time worked in excess of 4 hours ... ... double time

(ii) where the worker normally attends on five days only in the week—
for the first 2 hours worked ... ... time-and-a-quarter
for the next 2 hours ... ... time-and-a-half
thereafter ... ... double time

(c) on a Sunday or a customary holiday—

for all time worked ... ... double time

(d) in any week, exclusive of any time in respect of which a minimum overtime rate is payable under the foregoing provisions of this sub-paragraph—

for all time worked in excess of 40 hours ... ... time-and-a-quarter

(2) Where it is the practice in a Jewish undertaking for the employer to require attendance of the worker on Sunday and not on Saturday (except where such attendance on Sunday is unlawful) Saturday shall be treated as a Sunday, and, subject to the provisions of sub-paragraph (3) of this paragraph, Sunday as a Saturday.

(3) Where the worker normally attends on six days in the week and an ordinary week-day is substituted for Saturday, or in a case where the provisions of sub-paragraph (2) of this paragraph apply, for Sunday, as the worker's weekly short day, for the purposes of this Part of this Schedule (except where such substitution is unlawful) that ordinary week-day shall be treated as a Saturday, and Saturday or Sunday, as the case may be, as an ordinary week-day.

(4) Where the worker normally attends on five days only in the week and Saturday is one of his normal working days, the ordinary week-day on which he does not normally attend shall for the purposes of this Part of this Schedule be treated as a Saturday and Saturday as an ordinary week-day.

11. In this Part of this Schedule—

(1) the expression "CUSTOMARY HOLIDAY" means—

(a) Christmas Day; *26th December if it be not a Sunday; 27th December in a year when 25th or 26th December is a Sunday;* Good Friday; Easter Monday; *the last Monday in May; the last Monday in August;* or, *where another day is substituted for any of the above days by national proclamation, that day;* or

(b) in the case of each of the said days, a day substituted by the employer therefor, being a day recognised by local custom as a day of holiday in substitution for the said day;

(2) the expressions "time-and-a-quarter", "time-and-a-half" and "double time" mean, respectively,

(a) in the case of a time worker, one and a quarter times, one and a half times and twice the hourly general minimum time rate otherwise applicable to the worker;

(b) in the case of a worker employed on piece work,

(i) a time rate equal respectively to one quarter, one half, and the whole of the piece work basis time rate otherwise applicable to the worker or, where no piece work basis time rate is otherwise applicable, of the hourly general minimum time rate which would be applicable to the worker if he were a time worker and a minimum overtime rate did not apply, and in addition thereto,

(ii) the piece rates otherwise applicable to the worker under paragraph 1(1).

WAITING TIME

12.—(1) A worker is entitled to payment of the minimum remuneration specified in this Schedule for all time during which he is present on the premises of his employer unless he is present thereon in any of the following circumstances:—

(a) without the employer's consent, express or implied;

(b) for some purpose unconnected with his work and other than that of waiting for work to be given to him to perform;

(c) by reason only of the fact that he is resident thereon;

(d) during normal meal times in a room or place in which no work is being done and he is not waiting for work to be given to him to perform.

(2) The minimum remuneration payable under sub-paragraph (1) of this paragraph to a piece worker when not engaged on piece work is that which would be applicable if he were a time worker.

PART V

APPRENTICES

CONDITIONS AS TO RATES FOR APPRENTICES

13. The general minimum time rates specified in (4) of paragraph 3 apply only to an apprentice in whose case the conditions following are fulfilled:—

(1) the apprentice shall be employed for a period of five years under, and in accordance with, a written contract of apprenticeship which has been duly executed and which contains the following provisions, which the Wages Council considers necessary for the effective instruction of the apprentice, or provisions substantially to the same effect, and no provisions contrary thereto, namely,—

(a) the apprentice, of his own free will and with the consent of his guardian, binds himself to serve the employer as his apprentice in his trade of retail bespoke tailoring for a term of five years;

(b) the employer shall keep the apprentice as his apprentice during the said term and to the best of his power, skill and knowledge shall instruct the apprentice, or cause him to be instructed by a retail tailoring craft worker, in the making throughout of such one or more of the following garments, namely, coats, skirts, trousers, breeches, waistcoats or cassocks as shall be specified in the said contract of apprenticeship and in everything relative to the work of making and completing the same;

(c) during the first three years of apprenticeship the employer shall not require the apprentice to work during any period for which a minimum overtime rate is payable under the provisions of Part IV; and

(d) during the said term of apprenticeship the employer shall not put the apprentice on piece work;

(2) the apprentice shall be the holder of a certificate of registration of apprenticeship issued by or on behalf of the Wages Council, or shall have made application for such a certificate which has been duly acknowledged and is still under consideration:

Provided that the certification of the apprentice may be cancelled by the Wages Council if the other conditions of apprenticeship are not complied with.

PROSPECTIVE APPRENTICES

14.—(1) Notwithstanding the foregoing provisions of this Schedule an employer may employ a worker as a prospective apprentice where all the foregoing conditions of apprenticeship other than those with regard to employment under a written contract of apprenticeship and certification by the Wages Council are fulfilled, for a probationary period:—

(a) not exceeding 12 months where the employer has given to the worker a written undertaking that he will permit the worker to attend a full-time course of instruction in tailoring processes approved by the Wages Council;

(b) not exceeding six months in any other case.

(2) The minimum remuneration applicable to such a prospective apprentice during the probationary period shall be that applicable to an indentured apprentice employed in accordance with the conditions specified in the preceding paragraph.

(3) Where before the expiration of the probationary period the Wages Council has received from the employer written notification of the intention of the employer and worker to enter into a written contract of apprenticeship and has acknowledged the same in writing the probationary period may be extended as the Wages Council considers necessary for the drawing up and execution of the written contract.

(4) If the employer and worker enter into a written contract of apprenticeship at the end of any probationary period then for the purposes of this Schedule such probationary period shall be included in reckoning the period of five years referred to in paragraph 13(1) hereof.

PART VI

DEFINITIONS AND INTERPRETATION

15. For the purposes of the Schedule:—

(1) The expression "OUTWORKER" means a worker who works in his own home or in some other place not under the control or management of the employer.

(2) The expression:—

"RETAIL TAILORING CRAFT WORKER" means a worker who

(a) has completed

    (i) an apprenticeship complying with the conditions specified in paragraph 13, or

    (ii) five years' employment on work to which this Schedule applies (of which at least two years shall have been completed after having attained the age of 18 years), including employment in the trade reckoned in accordance with the provisions of paragraphs 6, 7 and 8; and

(b) is capable of making throughout, without supervision, one or more of the following garments, namely, coats, skirts, trousers, breeches, waistcoats, or cassocks.

(3) The expression:—

"ASSISTANT RETAIL TAILORING CRAFT WORKER GRADE 1" means a worker other than a Retail Tailoring Craft Worker who

(a) has completed

    (i) five years employment as a learner, as defined in sub-paragraph (5) of this paragraph, or

    (ii) five years employment on work to which this Schedule applies (of which at least two years shall have been completed after having attained the age of 18 years), including employment in the trade reckoned in accordance with the provisions of paragraphs 6, 7 and 8; and

(b) is either

    (i) skilled in the general trade of pressing-off, or

    (ii) is capable of carrying out, in the making of coats (including overcoats and ladies' coats) or vests or trousers or breeches or cassocks or skirts, without supervision, three or more of the operations specified below:—

COATS

Fitting up
Baisting for try on
Putting in pockets by hand or machine
Putting in linings by hand or machine
Canvassing
Baisting under
Baisting out
Putting on collars by hand or machine
Working button holes
Stitching edges by hand or machine
Pressing off

VESTS

Fitting up
Baisting for try on
Putting in pockets
Canvassing
Making up edges
Working button holes
Pressing off
Stitching edges by hand or machine

TROUSERS, BREECHES OR SKIRTS

Fitting up
Baisting for try on
Making up fly or placket by hand or machine
Making up tops by hand or machine
Putting in pockets by hand or machine
Making up bottoms by hand or machine
Pressing off

CASSOCKS

Fitting up
Baisting for try on
Putting in pockets by hand or machine
Putting on collars by hand or machine
Working button holes by hand or machine
Pressing off

(4) The expression:—

"ASSISTANT RETAIL TAILORING CRAFT WORKER GRADE 2" means a worker other than a Retail Tailoring Craft Worker or an Assistant Retail Tailoring Craft Worker Grade 1 who

(a) has completed five years employment on work to which this Schedule applies (of which at least two years shall have been completed after having attained the age of 18 years), including employment in the trade reckoned in accordance with the provisions of paragraphs 6, 7 and 8; and

(b) is either:—

(i) skilled in the general trade of under pressing, or

(ii) is capable of carrying out, in the making of coats (including overcoats and ladies' coats) or vests or trousers or breeches or cassocks or skirts, without supervision, one or more of the operations specified below:—

COATS

Marking up
Piecing up by hand or machine
Making sleeves by hand or machine
Making linings by hand or machine
Padding
Making collars
Under pressing

VESTS

Marking up
Making back and putting in linings
Under pressing

TROUSERS, BREECHES OR SKIRTS

Marking up
Piecing up and seaming seams by hand or machine
Making up bottoms by hand or machine (excluding breeches)
Under pressing

CASSOCKS

Marking up
Piecing up by hand or machine
Making collars
Under pressing

(5) The expression "LEARNER" means any worker, who,

   (*a*) not being—

     (i) an apprentice, employed in accordance with the conditions specified in paragraph 13;

     (ii) a worker who has completed the full period of training in retail bespoke tailoring in respect of which training allowances are payable under the Government Vocational Training Scheme;

     (iii) a worker who has been employed for more than five years in the retail bespoke section of the tailoring trade, the ready-made and wholesale bespoke tailoring trade, and the wholesale mantle and costume trade, or in one or more of such trades; or

     (iv) a worker who works in a room used for dwelling purposes unless he is in the employment of his parent or guardian;

   (*b*) is employed by an employer who provides him with reasonable facilities for learning—

     (i) the general trade of under pressing and pressing off, or

     (ii) three or more of the operations specified in sub-paragraph (3)(*b*)(ii) of this paragraph in the making of coats (including overcoats and ladies' coats) or vests or trousers or breeches or cassocks or skirts, and who, until at least three operations on any one garment have been taught, is not employed by the same employer for more than six months on any one operation, and

   (*c*) has received a certificate of registration of learnership from the Wages Council, or has made an application for such certificate which has been duly acknowledged and is still under consideration:

   Provided that the certificate may be cancelled by the Wages Council if the other conditions of learnership are not complied with.

EXPLANATORY NOTE

(This Note is not part of the Order.)

This Order, which has effect from 6th August 1973, sets out the increased statutory minimum remuneration payable in substitution for that fixed by the Wages Regulation (Retail Bespoke Tailoring) (England and Wales) Order 1972 (Order R.B. (77)), which Order is revoked.

New provisions are printed in italics.

STATUTORY INSTRUMENTS

1973 No. 1141

WAGES COUNCILS

The Wages Regulation (Retail Bespoke Tailoring) (England and Wales) (Holidays) Order 1973

Made - - - -	28th June 1973
Coming into Operation	6th August 1973

Whereas the Secretary of State has received from the Retail Bespoke Tailoring Wages Council (England and Wales) the wages regulation proposals set out in the Schedule hereto;

Now, therefore, the Secretary of State in exercise of powers conferred by section 11 of the Wages Councils Act 1959(a), as modified by Article 2 of the Counter-Inflation (Modification of Wages Councils Act 1959) Order 1973(b), and now vested in him (c), and of all other powers enabling him in that behalf, hereby makes the following Order:—

1. This Order may be cited as the Wages Regulation (Retail Bespoke Tailoring) (England and Wales) (Holidays) Order 1973.

2.—(1) In this Order the expression "the specified date" means the 6th August 1973, provided that where, as respects any worker who is paid wages at intervals not exceeding seven days, that date does not correspond with the beginning of the period for which the wages are paid, the expression "the specified date" means, as respects that worker, the beginning of the next such period following that date.

(2) The Interpretation Act 1889(d) shall apply to the interpretation of this Order as it applies to the interpretation of an Act of Parliament and as if this Order and the Order hereby revoked were Acts of Parliament.

3. The wages regulation proposals set out in the Schedule hereto shall have effect as from the specified date and as from that date the Wages Regulation (Retail Bespoke Tailoring) (England and Wales) (Holidays) Order 1967(e) shall cease to have effect.

Signed by order of the Secretary of State.
28th June 1973.

W. H. Marsh,
Assistant Secretary,
Department of Employment.

(a) 1959 c. 69. (b) S.I. 1973/661 (1973 I, p. 2141).
(c) S.I. 1959/1769, 1968/729 (1959 I, p. 1795; 1968 II, p. 2108).
(d) 1889 c. 63. (e) S.I. 1967/1631 (1967 III, p. 4483).

Article 3

SCHEDULE

HOLIDAYS AND HOLIDAY REMUNERATION

The following provisions as to holidays and holiday remuneration shall be substituted for the provisions as to holidays and holiday remuneration set out in the Wages Regulation (Retail Bespoke Tailoring) (England and Wales) (Holidays) Order 1967 (Order R.B. (69)).

PART I

APPLICATION

1. This Schedule applies to every worker for whom statutory minimum remuneration has been fixed other than a worker who has more than two workers in his employment.

PART II

CUSTOMARY HOLIDAYS

2.—(1) An employer shall allow to every worker in his employment to whom this Schedule applies a holiday (hereinafter referred to as a "customary holiday") in each year on each of the days specified in the following sub-paragraph, provided that the worker shall have been in his employment for a period of not less than eight weeks immediately preceding the customary holiday and shall have worked for the employer during the whole or part of that period.

(2) The days of customary holiday are:—

(a) Christmas Day; *26th December if it be not a Sunday; 27th December in a year when 25th or 26th December is a Sunday;* Good Friday; Easter Monday; *the last Monday in May; the last Monday in August*; or,

where another day is substituted for any of the above days by national proclamation, that day; or

(b) in the case of each of the said days, a day substituted by the employer therefor, being a day recognised by local custom as a day of holiday in substitution for the said day.

(3) Notwithstanding the preceding provisions of this paragraph, an employer may (except where in the case of a woman or young person such a requirement would be unlawful) require a worker who is otherwise entitled to any customary holiday under the foregoing provisions of this Schedule to work thereon and, in lieu of any such holiday on which he so works for the employer, the worker shall be entitled to be allowed a day's holiday (hereinafter referred to as a "holiday in lieu of a customary holiday") on a weekday on which he would normally work within the period of three weeks next ensuing.

(4) A worker who is required to work on a customary holiday shall be paid:—

(a) for all time worked thereon the statutory minimum remuneration then appropriate to the worker for work on a customary holiday; and

(b) in respect of the holiday in lieu of the customary holiday, holiday remuneration in accordance with paragraph 7.

PART III

ANNUAL HOLIDAY

3.—(1) Subject to the provisions of this paragraph and of paragraph 4, in addition to the holidays specified in Part II of this Schedule, an employer shall, between the date on which this Schedule becomes effective and 30th September 1973, and in each succeeding year between 6th April and 30th September allow a holiday (hereinafter referred to as an "annual holiday") to every worker in his employment to whom this Schedule applies, who has been employed by him during the 12 months immediately preceding the commencement of the holiday season for any of the periods of employment (calculated in accordance with the provisions of paragraph 11) specified below, and the duration of the annual holiday shall in the case of each such worker be related to that period as follows:—

Workers with a normal working week of 6 days		Workers with a normal working week of 5 days or less	
Period of employment	Duration of annual holiday	Period of employment	Duration of annual holiday
At least 48 weeks	18 days	At least 48 weeks	15 days
,, ,, 46 ,, ...	17 ,,	,, ,, 45 ,, ...	14 ,,
,, ,, 44 ,, ...	16 ,,	,, ,, 42 ,, ...	13 ,,
,, ,, 42 ,, ...	15 ,,	,, ,, 39 ,, ...	12 ,,
,, ,, 40 ,, ...	14 ,,	,, ,, 36 ,, ...	11 ,,
,, ,, 38 ,, ...	13 ,,	,, ,, 33 ,, ...	10 ,,
,, ,, 36 ,, ...	12 ,,	,, ,, 30 ,, ...	9 ,,
,, ,, 33 ,, ...	11 ,,	,, ,, 27 ,, ...	8 ,,
,, ,, 30 ,, ...	10 ,,	,, ,, 24 ,, ...	7 ,,
,, ,, 27 ,, ...	9 ,,	,, ,, 21 ,, ...	6 ,,
,, ,, 24 ,, ...	8 ,,	,, ,, 18 ,, ...	5 ,,
,, ,, 21 ,, ...	7 ,,	,, ,, 15 ,, ...	4 ,,
,, ,, 18 ,, ...	6 ,,	,, ,, 12 ,, ...	3 ,,
,, ,, 15 ,, ...	5 ,,	,, ,, 8 ,, ...	2 ,,
,, ,, 12 ,, ...	4 ,,	,, ,, 4 ,, ...	1 day
,, ,, 9 ,, ...	3 ,,		
,, ,, 6 ,, ...	2 ,,		
,, ,, 3 ,, ...	1 day		

(2) Notwithstanding the provisions of the last foregoing sub-paragraph, the number of days of annual holiday which an employer is required to allow to a worker in respect of a period of employment during the 12 months immediately preceding 6th April 1973 and during the 12 months immediately preceding 6th April in any succeeding year shall not exceed in the aggregate three times the number of days constituting the worker's normal working week.

(3) The duration of the worker's annual holiday in the holiday season ending on 30th September 1973, shall be reduced by any days of annual holiday duly allowed to him by the employer under the provisions of Order R.B. (69) between 6th April 1973 and the date on which this Schedule becomes effective.

(4) In this Schedule the expression "holiday season" means in relation to the year 1973 the period commencing on 6th April 1973 and ending on 30th September 1973 and in relation to each subsequent year, the period commencing on 6th April and ending on 30th September in that year.

4.—(1) Subject to the provisions of this paragraph, an annual holiday under this Schedule shall be allowed on consecutive working days and days of holiday shall be treated as consecutive notwithstanding that a day of holiday allowed to a worker under Part II of this Schedule or a day upon which he does not normally work for the employer intervenes.

(2) (a) Where the number of days of annual holiday for which a worker has qualified exceeds the number of days constituting his normal working week, but does not exceed twice that number, the holiday may be allowed in two periods of consecutive working days; so, however, that when a holiday is so allowed, one of the periods shall consist of a number of such days not less than the number of days constituting the worker's normal working week.

(b) Where the number of days of annual holiday for which a worker has qualified exceeds twice the number of days constituting his normal working week the holiday may be allowed as follows:—

(i) as to two periods of consecutive working days, each such period not being less than the period constituting the worker's normal working week, during the holiday season; and

(ii) as to any additional days, on working days which need not be consecutive, to be fixed by agreement between the employer or his representative and the worker or his representative, either during the holiday season or within the period ending on 15th January immediately following the holiday season.

(3) (*a*) Where an annual holiday is allowed in two periods in accordance with sub-paragraph (2)(*a*) of this paragraph, then notwithstanding paragraph 3, the period which is not required by virtue of sub-paragraph (2)(*a*) of this paragraph to consist of a number of days not less than the number of days constituting the worker's normal working week may be allowed either in the holiday season or, where before 23rd September in any holiday season a worker and his employer so agree in writing, after the end of the holiday season but before 1st January next following.

(*b*) Where an annual holiday is allowed in two or more periods in accordance with the provisions of sub-paragraph (2)(*b*) of this paragraph, then notwithstanding paragraph 3, one of the periods allowed in accordance with sub-paragraph (2)(*b*)(i) of this paragraph may be allowed either in the holiday season or, where before 23rd September in any holiday season a worker and his employer so agree in writing, after the end of the holiday season but before 1st January next following.

(4) Where a day of holiday allowed to a worker under Part II of this Schedule immediately precedes a period of annual holiday or occurs during such a period and the total number of days of annual holiday required to be allowed in the period under the foregoing provisions of this paragraph, together with any such day of holiday allowed under Part II of this Schedule, exceeds the number of days constituting the worker's normal working week then, notwithstanding the foregoing provisions of this paragraph, the duration of that period of annual holiday may be reduced by one day and in such a case one day of annual holiday may be allowed on any working day (not being the worker's weekly short day) in the holiday season (or before 1st January next following the end of the holiday season where the period of annual holiday is allowed in accordance with sub-paragraph (3) of this paragraph).

(5) Subject to the provisions of sub-paragraph (1) of this paragraph, any day of annual holiday under this Schedule may be allowed on a day on which the worker is entitled to a day of holiday or to a half-holiday under any enactment other than the Wages Councils Act 1959.

5. An employer shall give to a worker, other than an outworker, reasonable notice of the commencing date or dates and of the duration of the period or periods of his annual holiday. Such notice may be given individually to the worker or by the posting of a notice in the place where the worker is employed.

6.—(1) An outworker shall give to the employer at least 14 days' notice of the date in the holiday season on which he proposes to commence the annual holiday for which he has qualified under this Schedule, and the holiday shall be allowed by the employer as from that date or, subject to the provisions of paragraphs 3 and 4, from such other date or dates and for such periods as may be substituted therefor by agreement between the employer and the outworker.

(2) Where no notice has been given or agreement made in accordance with sub-paragraph (1) of this paragraph, the employer shall allow the outworker the annual holiday for which he has qualified in the last two weeks of the holiday season.

PART IV

HOLIDAY REMUNERATION

CUSTOMARY HOLIDAYS AND HOLIDAYS IN LIEU OF CUSTOMARY HOLIDAYS

7.—(1) For each day of holiday to which a worker is entitled under Part II of this Schedule he shall be paid by the employer as holiday remuneration one-fifth of the average weekly net earnings of the worker during the eight weeks immediately preceding the holiday, such average weekly net earnings to be determined by dividing, by the number of weeks during the whole or part of which the worker has worked for the employer during the said period, the worker's total net earnings in respect of those weeks.

(2) Notwithstanding the provisions of sub-paragraph (1) of this paragraph, payment of the said holiday remuneration is subject to the condition that the worker (unless excused by the employer or absent by reason of the proved illness of, or accident to, the worker) presents himself for employment at the usual starting hour on the first working day following the holiday:

Provided that when two customary holidays occur on successive days (or so that no working day intervenes) the said condition shall apply only to the second customary holiday.

(3) Where a worker normally works in the week on every weekday except Saturday, he shall be paid in respect of any Saturday on which he would have been entitled to a holiday under Part II of this Schedule if it had been a day on which he normally worked, a sum equivalent to the holiday remuneration he would have been entitled to receive had he been allowed a holiday on that day.

(4) Holiday remuneration in respect of any customary holiday shall be paid by the employer to the worker on the pay-day on which the wages for the first working day following the customary holiday are paid.

(5) Holiday remuneration in respect of any holiday in lieu of a customary holiday shall be paid on the pay-day on which the wages are paid for the first working day following the holiday in lieu of a customary holiday:

Provided that the said payment shall be made immediately upon the termination of the worker's employment if he ceases to be employed before being allowed such holiday in lieu of a customary holiday and in that case the condition specified in sub-paragraph (2) of this paragraph shall not apply.

ANNUAL HOLIDAY

8.—(1) Subject to the provisions of paragraph 9, a worker qualified to be allowed an annual holiday under this Schedule shall be paid as holiday remuneration by his employer in respect thereof, on the last pay-day preceding such annual holiday, an amount equal to six per cent. of the total net earnings of the worker during the 12 months ending on 5th April immediately preceding the commencement of the holiday season.

(2) Where, under the provisions of paragraph 4, an annual holiday is allowed in more than one period the holiday remuneration shall be apportioned accordingly.

9. Where any accrued holiday remuneration has been paid by the employer to the worker (in accordance with paragraph 10 of this Schedule or under the provisions of Order R.B. (69)) in respect of employment during any of the periods referred to in that paragraph or that Order, the amount of holiday remuneration payable by the employer in respect of any annual holiday for which the worker has qualified by reason of employment during the said period shall be reduced by the amount of the said accrued holiday remuneration unless that remuneration has been deducted from a previous payment of holiday remuneration made under the provisions of this Schedule or of Order R.B. (69).

ACCRUED HOLIDAY REMUNERATION PAYABLE ON TERMINATION OF EMPLOYMENT

10.—(1) Where a worker ceases to be employed by an employer after the provisions of this Schedule become effective the employer shall, immediately on the termination of the employment, pay to the worker as accrued holiday remuneration:—

(a) in respect of employment in the 12 months up to and including the preceding 5th April, a sum equal to the holiday remuneration which would be payable for any days of annual holiday for which he has qualified (except days of annual holiday which he has been allowed or has become entitled to be allowed before leaving the employment) if they were allowed at the time of leaving the employment; and

(b) in respect of any employment since the said 5th April, a sum equal to six per cent. of the total net earnings of the worker since that date.

(2) Where an employer has ceased for a continuous period of one calendar month to give out work to an outworker before that worker has become entitled to be allowed an annual holiday or before he has been allowed the whole of any annual holiday for which he has qualified under this Schedule the day on which the said calendar month expires shall be treated for the purposes of this Schedule as the day on which the outworker's employment with the employer is terminated.

PART V

GENERAL

11.—(1) For the purpose of calculating any period of employment qualifying a worker, other than an outworker, for an annual holiday or for any accrued holiday remuneration under this Schedule, the worker shall be treated—

(a) as if he were employed for a week in respect of any week in which—

(i) he has worked for the employer for not less than 24 hours and has performed some work for which statutory minimum remuneration is payable;

(ii) he has worked for the employer for less than 24 hours by reason of the proved illness of, or accident to, the worker or for a like reason has been absent throughout the week:

Provided that the number of weeks which may be treated as weeks of employment for such reason shall not exceed eight in the aggregate in any such period; or

(iii) he has been suspended throughout the week owing to shortage of work: Provided that the number of weeks which may be treated as weeks of employment for such reason shall not exceed six in the aggregate in any such period;

(b) as if he were employed on any day of holiday allowed under the provisions of this Schedule, or of Order R.B. (69), and for the purposes of the provisions of (a) of this sub-paragraph, a worker who is absent on such a holiday shall be treated as having worked thereon for the employer on work for which statutory minimum remuneration is payable for the number of hours ordinarily worked by him on that day of the week.

(2) For the purpose of calculating any period of employment qualifying an outworker for an annual holiday or for any accrued holiday remuneration under this Schedule, the worker shall be treated as if he were employed for a week in respect of any week in which he has worked for the employer and has performed some work for which statutory minimum remuneration is payable.

12. In this Schedule, unless the context otherwise requires, the following expressions have the meanings hereby respectively assigned to them, that is to say:—

"NET EARNINGS" means the remuneration paid or payable by the employer to the worker less any necessary expenditure incurred by the worker in connection with his employment and for the purposes of this definition—

(1) "remuneration" does not include any payment made by the employer to the worker in respect of holidays; and

(2) "necessary expenditure" includes the cost of seat room, light and heat, as well as of sewings and other materials provided by the worker.

"NORMAL WORKING WEEK" means the number of days on which it has been usual for the worker to work in a week in the employment of the employer in the 12 months immediately preceding the commencement of the holiday season:

Provided that—

(1) part of a day shall count as a day;

(2) no account shall be taken of any week in which the worker did not perform any work for which statutory minimum remuneration has been fixed.

"OUTWORKER" means a worker who works in his own home or in some other place not under the control or management of the employer.

"STATUTORY MINIMUM REMUNERATION" means minimum remuneration (other than holiday remuneration) fixed by a wages regulation order.

"WEEK" means "pay week".

13. The provisions of this Schedule are without prejudice to any agreement for the allowance of any further holidays with pay or for the payment of additional holiday remuneration.

EXPLANATORY NOTE

(This Note is not part of the Order.)

This Order, which has effect from 6th August 1973, sets out the holidays which an employer is required to allow to workers in relation to whom the Retail Bespoke Tailoring Wages Council (England and Wales) operates and the remuneration payable for those holidays.

It amends the provisions relating to customary holidays contained in the Wages Regulation (Retail Bespoke Tailoring) (England and Wales) (Holidays) Order 1967 (Order R.B. (69)) so as to take account of recent changes in the law and practice relating to public holidays. Order R.B. (69) is revoked.

New provisions are printed in italics.

STATUTORY INSTRUMENTS

1973 No. 1145 (S.89)

LEGAL AID AND ADVICE, SCOTLAND

Act of Adjournal (Criminal Legal Aid Fees Amendment) 1973

Made - - -	*22nd June* 1973
Coming into Operation	*16th July* 1973

The Lord Justice-General, the Lord Justice-Clerk and the Lords Commissioners of Justiciary, under and by virtue of the powers conferred upon them by section 16 of the Legal Aid (Scotland) Act 1967(a), and of all other powers competent to them in that behalf, do hereby enact and declare as follows:

1. This Act of Adjournal may be cited as the Act of Adjournal (Criminal Legal Aid Fees Amendment) 1973 and shall come into operation on 16th July 1973.

2. The Act of Adjournal (Criminal Legal Aid Fees) 1964(b) as amended by the Act of Adjournal (Criminal Legal Aid Fees Amendment) 1965(c), by the Act of Adjournal (Criminal Legal Aid Fees Amendment) 1968(d), by the Act of Adjournal (Criminal Legal Aid Fees Amendment) 1971(e) and by the Act of Adjournal (Alteration of Criminal Legal Aid Fees) 1973(f) shall be further amended as follows:

(a) by deleting sub-paragraph (2) of paragraph 13 thereof and by substituting a new sub-paragraph as follows—

"(2) In the case of all trials on indictment it shall be competent immediately on conclusion of the trial, or, where the trial is not the last trial of the sitting, at the close of proceedings on the day on which the trial has ended, for the counsel or solicitor who appeared for the accused to make oral application to the Court either in Court or in chambers for a certificate that the case has necessarily been one of exceptional length, complexity or difficulty. Such certificate may be granted or refused forthwith, or the judge may adjourn the application for a further hearing in chambers on a later date This hearing must take place within seven days of such adjournment. In the event of such an adjournment being ordered, written grounds for such application must be lodged within two days of the adjournment being ordered, otherwise the application shall be refused. The prosecutor may be represented at such hearing or adjourned hearing."

(b) by adding new sub-paragraphs (3) and (4) to paragraph 13 as follows—

"(3) In all other cases it shall be competent immediately on conclusion of the trial for the counsel or solicitor who appeared for the accused to make oral application to the Court for a certificate that the case has necessarily been one of exceptional length, complexity

---

(a) 1967 c. 43.

(b) S.I. 1964/1410 (1964 III, p. 3292).

(c) S.I. 1965/1788 (1965 III, p.5461).

(d) S.I. 1968/1933 (1968 III, p. 5241).

(e) S.I. 1971/926 (1971 II, p. 2671).

(f) S.I. 1973/673 (1973 I, p. 2184).

or difficulty. Such certificate may be granted or refused forthwith by the Court, or the judge may adjourn the application for a hearing in chambers. This hearing must take place within seven days of such adjournment. In the event of such an adjournment being ordered, written grounds for such application must be lodged within two days of the adjournment being ordered, otherwise the application shall be refused. The prosecutor may be represented at such hearing."

"(4) If such a certificate as is referred to in the foregoing sub-paragraphs shall be granted, then any limitation contained in the foregoing paragraphs or such of them as are referred to in such certificate, on the amount of any fee payable shall not apply and such fees shall be allowed, after taking into account all the relevant circumstances of the case, in respect of the work done, as appears to represent fair remuneration according to the work actually and reasonably done, due regard being had to economy."

And the Lords appoint this Act of Adjournal to be recorded in the Books of Adjournal, and to be published in the Edinburgh Gazette.

Edinburgh. *G. C. Emslie,*
22nd June 1973. **I. P. D.**

EXPLANATORY NOTE

(This Note is not part of the Act of Adjournal.)

This Act of Adjournal further amends the Act of Adjournal (Criminal Legal Aid Fees) 1964 by providing that in the case of all trials on indictment application for a certificate under paragraph 13(2) of the Act of Adjournal of 1964 as amended may be made to the judge either in Court or in chambers.

STATUTORY INSTRUMENTS

1973 No. 1150

COMPANIES

The Companies (Accounts) Regulations 1973

Made - - -	*2nd July* 1973
Laid before Parliament	*6th July* 1973
Coming into Operation	*31st July* 1973

The Secretary of State, in exercise of his powers under section 454(1) of the Companies Act 1948(a), hereby makes the following Regulations:—

1. These Regulations may be cited as the Companies (Accounts) Regulations 1973 and shall come into operation on 31st July 1973.

2. After paragraph 15(5) of Schedule 8 to the Companies Act 1948 there shall be inserted the following sub-paragraph:—

"(5A) Paragraphs (*b*) and (*c*) of sub-paragraph (4) above shall not apply where the company is a wholly-owned subsidiary of another body corporate incorporated in Great Britain if there is annexed to the balance sheet a statement that in the opinion of the directors of the company the aggregate value of the assets of the company consisting of shares in, or amounts owing (whether on account of a loan or otherwise) from, the company's subsidiaries is not less than the aggregate of the amounts at which those assets are stated or included in the balance sheet."

Limerick,
Parliamentary Under Secretary of State,
Department of Trade and Industry.

2nd July 1973.

EXPLANATORY NOTE

(*This Note is not part of the Regulations.*)

These Regulations amend the requirements of the Companies Acts as to the particulars to be disclosed in company accounts. A wholly-owned subsidiary of a body incorporated in Great Britain which does not submit group accounts is no longer required to give information concerning the profits or losses of its subsidiaries if the directors state that in their opinion the value of the company's investments in its subsidiaries is not less than the amount at which they are stated or included in the balance sheet.

(a) 1948 c. 38.

STATUTORY INSTRUMENTS

1973 No. 1154

EXCHANGE CONTROL

The Exchange Control (Authorised Dealers and Depositaries) (Amendment) (No. 4) Order 1973

Made - - -	*2nd July* 1973
Coming into Operation	*1st August* 1973

The Treasury, in exercise of the powers conferred upon them by sections 36(5) and 42(1) of the Exchange Control Act 1947(**a**), hereby make the following Order: —

1.—(1) This Order may be cited as the Exchange Control (Authorised Dealers and Depositaries) (Amendment) (No. 4) Order 1973, and shall come into operation on 1st August 1973.

(2) The Interpretation Act 1889(**b**) shall apply for the interpretation of this Order as it applies for the interpretation of an Act of Parliament.

2. Schedule 2 to the Exchange Control (Authorised Dealers and Depositaries) Order 1973(**c**), as amended(**d**), (hereinafter called "the said Order") shall be further amended as follows: —

(*a*) by inserting the words "Commerzbank A. G." after the words "Commercial Banking Company of Sydney, Ltd.";

(*b*) by inserting the words "Havana International Bank Ltd." after the words "Harris Trust and Savings Bank.";

(*c*) by inserting the words "Texas Commerce Bank N.A." after the words "Swiss-Israel Trade Bank."; and

(*d*) by inserting the words "Westdeutsche Landesbank Girozentrale." after the words "Wells Fargo Ltd."

3. Paragraph 6 of Schedule 3 to the said Order shall be further amended as follows: —

(*a*) by inserting the words "Australia and New Zealand Banking Group (Channel Islands) Ltd." before the words "Bank of Bermuda (Guernsey) Ltd., The.";

(*b*) by deleting the words "Butterfield & Son (Channel Islands) Ltd., N.T." and substituting the words "Barfield Trust Co. Ltd.";

(**a**) 1947 c. 14.   (**b**) 1889 c. 63.

(**c**) S.I. 1973/42 (1973 I, p. 351).

(**d**) S.I. 1973/451, 615, 775 (1973 I, pp. 1544, 1948, 2454).

(c) by inserting the words "L.B.I. Finance (Guernsey) Ltd." after the words "Joseph & Sons (Guernsey) Ltd., Leopold."; and

(d) by inserting the words "Ocean Finance and Trust Corporation Ltd." and the words "Rea Brothers (Guernsey) Ltd." after the words "New Guarantee Trust of Jersey Ltd., The."

4. This Order shall extend to the Channel Islands, and any reference in this Order to the Exchange Control Act 1947 includes a reference to that Act as extended by the Exchange Control (Channel Islands) Order 1947(**a**).

P. L. Hawkins,
Oscar Murton,

Two of the Lords Commissioners
of Her Majesty's Treasury.

2nd July 1973.

EXPLANATORY NOTE

(*This Note is not part of the Order.*)

This Order amends the list of banks and other persons authorised under the Exchange Control Act 1947 to deal in gold and foreign currencies and to act as authorised depositaries for the purpose of the deposit of securities as required by that Act.

(**a**) S.R. & O. 1947/2034 (Rev. VI, p. 1001: 1947 I, p. 660).

STATUTORY INSTRUMENTS

1973 No. 1155

MONOPOLIES AND MERGERS

The Restriction of Merger (Revocation) (No. 2) Order 1973

Made - - -	*3rd July* 1973
Laid before Parliament	*3rd July* 1973
Coming into Operation	*4th July* 1973

The Secretary of State in exercise of powers conferred by section 10(6) of the Monopolies and Restrictive Practices (Inquiry and Control) Act 1948(**a**), as having effect by virtue of section 3(1) of the Monopolies and Mergers Act 1965(**b**), and now vested in him by virtue of the Transfer of Functions (Monopolies, Mergers and Restrictive Trade Practices) Order 1969(**c**), hereby orders as follows:—

1. This Order may be cited as the Restriction of Merger (Revocation) (No. 2) Order 1973, and shall come into operation on 4th July 1973.

2. The Restriction of Merger (No. 1) Order 1973(**d**) is hereby revoked.

Dated 3rd July 1973.

Geoffrey Howe,
Minister for Trade and Consumer Affairs,
Department of Trade and Industry.

EXPLANATORY NOTE

(*This Note is not part of the Order.*)

This Order revokes the Restriction of Merger (No. 1) Order 1973. The Order which is revoked imposed a temporary standstill on any takeover of Capper-Neill Limited by Whessoe Limited while the Monopolies Commission inquired into the matter. The Secretary of State has consented under section 6(7) of the Monopolies and Mergers Act 1965 to the Monopolies Commission laying aside the reference on the grounds that the proposed merger has been abandoned.

(**a**) 1948 c. 66.	(**b**) 1965 c. 50.
(**c**) S.I. 1969/1534 (1969 III, p. 4991).	(**d**) S.I. 1973/924 (1973 II, p.2801).

STATUTORY INSTRUMENTS

1973 No. 1156

POLICE

The Police Cadets (Amendment) Regulations 1973

Made - - -	*1st July* 1973
Laid before Parliament	*10th July* 1973
Coming into Operation	*1st August* 1973

In exercise of the powers conferred on me by section 35 of the Police Act 1964(**a**), and after consulting the Police Council for the United Kingdom in accordance with section 4(4) of the Police Act 1969(**b**), I hereby make the following Regulations:—

1. These Regulations may be cited as the Police Cadets (Amendment) Regulations 1973.

2. These Regulations shall come into operation on 1st August 1973 and shall have effect as from 1st April 1973.

3. For the Table in Schedule 1 to the Police Cadets Regulations 1968(**c**), as amended(**d**), (scales of pay) there shall be substituted the following Table:—

"TABLE

Age	City of London and metropolitan police forces	Other police forces
Under 17 years	£624 a year	£594 a year
17 years	£672 a year	£642 a year
18 years	£753 a year	£723 a year
19 years	£819 a year	£789 a year"

Robert Carr,
One of Her Majesty's Principal
Secretaries of State.

Home Office,
 Whitehall.
1st July 1973.

(**a**) 1964 c. 48.   (**b**) 1969 c. 63.   (**c**) S.I. 1968/25 (1968 I, p. 31).
(**d**) The relevant amending instrument is S.I. 1972/706 (1972 II, p. 2263).

EXPLANATORY NOTE

(This Note is not part of the Regulations.)

These Regulations amend the Police Cadets Regulations 1968.

Regulation 3 increases the pay of a police cadet by amounts which vary according to his age. By virtue of Regulation 2 (made in exercise of the power conferred by section 33(4), as applied by section 35(2), of the Police Act 1964), these increases have effect from 1st April 1973.

STATUTORY INSTRUMENTS

1973 No. 1158

INDUSTRIAL TRAINING

The Industrial Training Levy (Water Supply) Order 1973

Made - - -	*3rd July* 1973
Laid before Parliament	*13th July* 1973
Coming into Operation	*8th August* 1973

The Secretary of State after approving proposals submitted by the Water Supply Industry Training Board for the imposition of a further levy on employers in the water supply industry and in exercise of powers conferred by section 4 of the Industrial Training Act 1964(a) and now vested in him(b), and of all other powers enabling him in that behalf hereby makes the following Order:—

Title and commencement

1. This Order may be cited as the Industrial Training Levy (Water Supply) Order 1973 and shall come into operation on 8th August 1973.

Interpretation

2.—(1) In this Order unless the context otherwise requires:—

(*a*) "activities of the water supply industry" means any activities (not being agriculture) which, subject to the provisions of paragraph 2 of Schedule 1 to the industrial training order, are specified in paragraph 1 of that Schedule as activities of the water supply industry;

(*b*) "agriculture" has the same meaning as in section 109(3) of the Agriculture Act 1947(c) or, in relation to Scotland, as in section 86(3) of the Agriculture (Scotland) Act 1948(d);

(*c*) "an appeal tribunal" means an industrial tribunal established under section 12 of the Industrial Training Act 1964;

(*d*) "assessment" means an assessment of an employer to the levy;

(*e*) "the eighth base period" means the period of twelve months that commenced on 6th April 1972;

(*f*) "the eighth levy period" means the period commencing with the day upon which this Order comes into operation and ending on 31st March 1974;

(*g*) "emoluments" means all emoluments assessable to income tax under Schedule E (other than pensions), being emoluments from which tax under that Schedule is deductible, whether or not tax in fact falls to be deducted from any particular payment thereof;

(a) 1964 c. 16.
(c) 1947 c. 48.
(b) S.I. 1968/729(1968 II, p. 2108).
(d) 1948 c. 45.

(h) "employer" means an employer in the water supply industry, being on the day upon which this Order comes into operation statutory water undertakers or a regional water board;

(i) "the Industrial Training Board" means the Water Supply Industry Training Board;

(j) "the industrial training order" means the Industrial Training (Water Supply Board) Order 1965(a);

(k) "the levy" means the levy imposed by the Board in respect of the eighth levy period;

(l) "notice" means a notice in writing;

(m) "regional water board" means a regional water board within the meaning of the Water (Scotland) Act 1967(b);

(n) "statutory water undertakers" means any statutory water undertakers within the meaning of the Water Act 1945(c).

(2) The Interpretation Act 1889(d) shall apply to the interpretation of this Order as it applies to the interpretation of an Act of Parliament.

Imposition of the levy

3.—(1) The levy to be imposed by the Industrial Training Board on employers in respect of the eighth levy period shall be assessed in accordance with the provisions of this Article.

(2) The levy shall be assessed by the Industrial Training Board in respect of each employer.

(3) The amount of the levy imposed on an employer shall be a sum equal to 1·6 per cent. of the emoluments of the persons following—

(a) in the case of statutory water undertakers, all persons employed by the employer in the eighth base period in activities of the water supply industry and any other persons employed at any time in that period in a water undertaking or part of a water undertaking that on the day upon which this Order comes into operation forms part of the water undertaking of the employer;

(b) in the case of a regional water board, all persons employed by the board in activities of the water supply industry in the eighth base period.

(4) For the purposes of this Article no regard shall be had to persons wholly engaged in agriculture or in the supply of food or drink for immediate consumption.

Assessment notice

4.—(1) The Industrial Training Board shall serve an assessment notice on every employer.

(2) An assessment notice shall state the address of the said Board for the service of a notice of appeal or of an application for an extension of time for appealing.

(3) An assessment notice may be served on an employer by sending it by post to the employer's registered or principal office.

(a) S.I. 1965/1258 (1965 II, p. 3556).   (b) 1967 c. 78.

(c) 1945 c. 42.   (d) 1889 c. 63.

Payment of the levy

5.—(1) Subject to the provisions of this Article and of Articles 6 and 7, the amount of an assessment appearing in an assessment notice served by the Industrial Training Board shall be payable to the Board in two equal instalments and the said instalments shall be due respectively one month and five months after the date of the assessment notice.

(2) An instalment of an assessment shall not be recoverable by the Industrial Training Board until there has expired the time allowed for appealing against the assessment by Article 7(1) of this Order and any further period or periods of time that the said Board or an appeal tribunal may have allowed for appealing under paragraph (2) or (3) of that Article or, where an appeal is brought, until the appeal is decided or withdrawn.

Withdrawal of assessment

6.—(1) The Industrial Training Board may, by a notice served on the person assessed to the levy in the same manner as an assessment notice, withdraw an assessment if that person has appealed against that assessment under the provisions of Article 7 of this Order and the appeal has not been entered in the Register of Appeals kept under the appropriate Regulations specified in paragraph (4) of that Article.

(2) The withdrawal of an assessment shall be without prejudice to the power of the Industrial Training Board to serve a further assessment notice on the person assessed to the levy.

Appeals

7.—(1) A person assessed to the levy may appeal to an appeal tribunal against the assessment within one month from the date of the service of the assessment notice or within any further period or periods of time that may be allowed by the Industrial Training Board or an appeal tribunal under the following provisions of this Article.

(2) The Industrial Training Board by notice may for good cause allow a person assessed to the levy to appeal to an appeal tribunal against the assessment at any time within the period of four months from the date of the service of the assessment notice or within such further period or periods as the Board may allow before such time as may then be limited for appealing has expired.

(3) If the Industrial Training Board shall not allow an application for extension of time for appealing, an appeal tribunal shall upon application made to the tribunal by the person assessed to the levy have the like powers as the Board under the last foregoing paragraph.

(4) An appeal or an application to an appeal tribunal under this Article shall be made in accordance with the Industrial Tribunals (England and Wales) Regulations 1965(a) as amended by the Industrial Tribunals (England and Wales) (Amendment) Regulations 1967(b) except in the case of a regional water board when the appeal or application shall be made in accordance with the Industrial Tribunals (Scotland) Regulations 1965(c) as amended by the Industrial Tribunals (Scotland) (Amendment) Regulations 1967(d).

(a) S.I. 1965/1101 (1965 II, p. 2805).   (b) S.I. 1967/301 (1967 I, p. 1040).
(c) S.I. 1965/1157 (1965 II, p. 3266).   (d) S.I. 1967/302 (1967 I, p. 1050).

(5) The powers of an appeal tribunal under paragraph (3) of this Article may be exercised by the President of the Industrial Tribunals (England and Wales) or by the President of the Industrial Tribunals (Scotland) as the case may be.

Evidence

8.—(1) Upon the discharge by a person assessed to the levy of his liability under an assessment the Industrial Training Board shall if so requested issue to him a certificate to that effect.

(2) The production in any proceedings of a document purporting to be certified by the Secretary of the Industrial Training Board to be a true copy of an assessment or other notice issued by the Board or purporting to be a certificate such as is mentioned in the foregoing paragraph of this Article shall, unless the contrary is proved, be sufficient evidence of the document and of the facts stated therein.

Signed by order of the Secretary of State.

R. Chichester-Clark,
3rd July 1973.   Minister of State,
                                  Department of Employment.

EXPLANATORY NOTE

(This Note is not part of the Order.)

This Order gives effect to proposals submitted by the Water Supply Industry Training Board to the Secretary of State for Employment for the imposition of a further levy on employers in the water supply industry for the purpose of raising money towards the expenses of the Board.

The levy is to be imposed in respect of the eighth levy period commencing with the date on which this Order comes into operation and ending on 31st March 1974. The levy will be assessed by the Industrial Training Board and there will be a right of appeal against an assessment to an industrial tribunal.

STATUTORY INSTRUMENTS

1973 No. 1159

WAGES COUNCILS

The Wages Regulation (Pin, Hook and Eye, and Snap Fastener) Order 1973

Made - - -		*3rd July* 1973
Coming into Operation		*1st August* 1973

Whereas the Secretary of State has received from the Pin, Hook and Eye, and Snap Fastener Wages Council (Great Britain) the wages regulation proposals set out in the Schedule hereto;

Now, therefore, the Secretary of State in exercise of powers conferred by section 11 of the Wages Councils Act 1959(a), as modified by Article 2 of the Counter-Inflation (Modification of Wages Councils Act 1959) Order 1973(b), and now vested in him(c), and of all other powers enabling him in that behalf, hereby makes the following Order:—

1. This Order may be cited as the Wages Regulation (Pin, Hook and Eye, and Snap Fastener) Order 1973.

2.—(1) In this Order, the expression "the specified date" means the 1st August 1973, provided that where, as respects any worker who is paid wages at intervals not exceeding seven days, that date does not correspond with the beginning of the period for which the wages are paid, the expression "the specified date" means, as respects that worker, the beginning of the next such period following that date.

(2) The Interpretation Act 1889(d) shall apply to the interpretation of this Order as it applies to the interpretation of an Act of Parliament and as if this Order and the Order hereby revoked were Acts of Parliament.

3. The wages regulation proposals set out in the Schedule hereto shall have effect as from the specified date and as from that date the Wages Regulation (Pin, Hook and Eye, and Snap Fastener) Order 1972(e) shall cease to have effect.

Signed by order of the Secretary of State.

3rd July 1973.

W. H. Marsh,
Assistant Secretary,
Department of Employment.

(a) 1959 c. 69.　　　　　　　　　(b) S.I. 1973/661 (1973 I, p. 2141).
(c) S.I. 1959/1769, 1968/729 (1959 I, p. 1795; 1968 II, p. 2108).
(d) 1889 c. 63.　　　　　　　　　(e) S.I. 1972/718 (1972 II, p. 2282).

SCHEDULE   Article 3

The following minimum remuneration shall be substituted for the statutory minimum remuneration fixed by the Wages Regulation (Pin, Hook and Eye, and Snap Fastener) Order 1972 (Order O.(87)).

STATUTORY MINIMUM REMUNERATION

PART I

GENERAL

1.—(1) Subject to the provisions of paragraph 7, which relate to the guaranteed weekly remuneration, the minimum remuneration payable to a worker (including a home-worker) to whom this Schedule applies is as follows:—

(*a*) for all work other than work to which a minimum overtime rate applies under Part III of this Schedule—

   (i) in the case of a time worker, the hourly general minimum time rate applicable to the worker under the provisions of this Schedule;

   (ii) in the case of a male worker employed on piece work, piece rates each of which would yield, in the circumstances of the case, to an ordinary worker at least the same amount of money as the hourly general minimum time rate which would be applicable under the provisions of this Schedule if the worker were a time worker;

   (iii) in the case of a female worker employed on piece work, piece rates each of which would yield, in the circumstances of the case, to an ordinary worker at least the same amount of money as the hourly piece work basis time rate as defined in sub-paragraph (2) of this paragraph or the piece work basis time rate applicable to the worker under paragraph 4 of this Schedule;

(*b*) for all work to which a minimum overtime rate applies under Part III of this Schedule, that rate.

(2) In this Schedule the expression "per week" in Part II means per week of 40 hours, and the expression "hourly general minimum time rate" and "hourly piece work basis time rate" mean respectively the general minimum time rate and the piece work basis time rate applicable to the worker under paragraphs 2 and 3 of this Schedule divided by 40.

PART II

ALL MALE WORKERS

GENERAL MINIMUM TIME RATES

2. The general minimum time rates payable to male workers are as follows:—

	Per week £
(1) Workers aged 20 years or over—	
(*a*) Artificers (including Pinmakers) in charge of automatic machinery, carrying out if required toolmaking, toolsetting, hardening and minor repairs	22·00
(*b*) Toolsetters, other than workers covered by (*a*) above, who are in charge of automatic machinery but who do not make tools ...	22·00
(*c*) (i) Platers and Finishers carrying out (without technical supervision) one or more of the following processes— electro-deposition ... ... chemical deposition ... ... dyeing ... ... enamelling and lacquering ... ... barrel polishing	21·30
(ii) Platers and Finishers carrying out under technical supervision, one or more of the processes specified in (i) above ...	19·45
(iii) Plating and Finishing workers, other than those specified in (i) and (ii) above	17·50

Per week
£

(d) Wire Straighteners wholly or mainly engaged in wire straight-
ening; and Assistant Toolsetters working under the supervision
of artificers or toolsetters   ...   .   19·45

(e) Workers other than those specified in (a) to (d) above   ...   17·50

(2) Workers aged under 20 years, being aged—
19 and under 20 years ...   .   16·25
18 „   „   19 „   ...   .   14·51
17 „   „   18 „   ...   .   12·36
16 „   „   17 „   ...   .   9·14
Under 16 years ...   .   7·53

ALL FEMALE WORKERS (OTHER THAN HOME-WORKERS) GENERAL MINIMUM TIME RATES AND PIECE WORK BASIS TIME RATES

3. The general minimum time rates and piece work basis time rates payable to
female workers other than home-workers are as follows:—

	General minimum Time Rates Per week £	Piece work basis Time Rates Per week £
(1) Charge hands who are responsible for all work and order in the particular section of which they have charge	17·50	—
(2) All other workers		
Aged 20 years or over	15·50	16·00
„ 19 and under 20 years	13·90	14·41
„ 18 „ „ 19 „	12·33	13·78
„ 17 „ „ 18 „	10·51	12·97
„ 16 „ „ 17 „	7·77	12·69
„ 15 „ „ 16 „	6·40	12·25

FEMALE HOME-WORKERS

Per hour
p

4. The piece work basis time rate applicable (irrespective of age) to female
home-workers is 25½

PART III

ALL WORKERS OTHER THAN HOME-WORKERS MINIMUM OVERTIME RATES

5.—(1) Minimum overtime rates are payable to any worker (other than a home-
worker) as follows:—

(a) on a Sunday or a customary holiday—
for all time worked   ...   .   double time

(b) on a Saturday, not being a customary holiday—
for all time worked in excess of 4½ hours   ...   ...   time-and-a-half

(c) in any week exclusive of any time in respect of which a minimum overtime rate is payable under the preceding provisions of this sub-paragraph—

   (i) for the first 10 hours worked in excess of 40 hours   time-and-a-quarter

   (ii) thereafter ...   .   time-and-a-half

(2) The minimum overtime rates set out in sub-paragraph (1)(a) and (b) of this paragraph are payable in any week whether or not a minimum overtime rate set out in sub-paragraph (1)(c) is also payable.

6. In this Part of this Schedule,

(1) the expression "customary holiday" means—

   (a) (i) in England and Wales—
      Christmas Day;
      26th December if it be not a Sunday; 27th December in a year when 25th or 26th December is a Sunday;
      Good Friday;
      Easter Monday;
      the last Monday in May;
      the last Monday in August;
      (*or where a day is substituted for any of the above days by national proclamation, that day*);

      (ii) in Scotland—
      New Year's Day (or, if New Year's Day falls on a Sunday, the following Monday);
      the local Spring holiday;
      the local Autumn holiday; and
      three other days (being days on which the worker normally works) in the course of a calendar year, to be fixed by the employer and notified to the worker not less than three weeks before the holiday;

   or (b) in the case of each of the said days (other than a day fixed by the employer and notified to the worker as aforesaid) such weekday as may be substituted therefor by agreement between the employer and the worker.

(2) the expressions "time-and-a-quarter", "time-and-a-half" and "double time" mean respectively—

   (a) in the case of a time worker, one and a quarter times, one and a half times and twice the hourly general minimum time rate otherwise payable to the worker;

   (b) in the case of a worker employed on piece work—

      (i) a time rate equal respectively to one quarter, one half and the whole of the hourly general minimum time rate which would be payable if the worker were a time worker and a minimum overtime rate did not apply, and, in addition thereto,

      (ii) the piece rates otherwise payable to the worker under sub-paragraph (1)(a) of paragraph 1.

PART IV

GUARANTEED WEEKLY REMUNERATION FOR WORKERS OTHER THAN HOME-WORKERS

7.—(1) Subject to the provisions of this paragraph a worker (other than a home-worker) who ordinarily works for the employer at least 34 hours weekly on work to which this Schedule applies shall be paid in respect of any week in which he works for less than 34 hours on such work not less than the guaranteed weekly remuneration.

(2) The guaranteed weekly remuneration is 34 hours' pay calculated at the hourly general minimum time rate ordinarily applicable to the worker.

(3) The guaranteed weekly remuneration in any week shall be reduced by the amount of any holiday remuneration paid, or payable, by the employer to the worker in respect of any holiday allowed to, and taken by, the worker in that week under the provisions of the Wages Councils Act 1959.

(4) In calculating the number of hours worked in any week for the purposes of this paragraph, a worker shall be treated as though he had worked on any holiday allowed to, and taken by, him in that week under the provisions of the Wages Councils Act 1959, the number of hours ordinarily worked by him on that day of the week, provided that a worker shall not be treated as having worked in any week throughout which he is on holiday.

(5) Payment of the guaranteed weekly remuneration in any week is subject to the condition that the worker throughout the period of his ordinary employment in that week, excluding any day allowed to him as a holiday, is—

    (a) capable of and available for work; and

    (b) willing to perform such duties outside his normal occupation as the employer may reasonably require if his normal work is not available to him in the establishment in which he is employed.

(6) The guaranteed weekly remuneration shall not be payable to a worker—

    (a) in any week in which work is not available to him by reason of a strike or lock-out or circumstances outside the employer's control, if he has given the worker not less than four days' notice of his inability to provide such employment and the notice has expired; or

    (b) in any week in which the worker has been dismissed on the grounds of serious misconduct; or

    (c) if at any time in the week the worker is absent from work by reason of sickness; or

    (d) if at any time in the week or during the preceding four weeks the worker has been otherwise absent from work without the leave of the employer.

(7) The guaranteed weekly remuneration payable to a piece worker shall be the sum to which he would be entitled if he were a time worker.

PART ·V

ALL WORKERS
WAITING TIME

8.—(1) A worker shall be entitled to payment of the minimum remuneration specified in this Schedule for all time during which he is present on the premises of his employer unless he is present thereon in any of the following circumstances: —

    (a) without the employer's consent, express or implied;

    (b) for some purpose unconnected with his work and other than that of waiting for work to be given to him to perform;

    (c) by reason only of the fact that he is resident thereon;

    (d) during normal meal times in a room or place in which no work is being done and he is not waiting for work to be given to him to perform.

(2) The minimum remuneration payable under sub-paragraph (1) of this paragraph to a piece worker when not engaged on piece work, is that which would be payable if the worker were a time worker.

APPLICABILITY OF STATUTORY MINIMUM REMUNERATION

9. This Schedules applies to workers in relation to whom the Wages Council operates, that is to say, workers employed in Great Britain in the trade specified in the Schedule to the Trade Boards (Pin, Hook and Eye, and Snap Fastener Trade, Great Britain) (Constitution and Proceedings) Regulations 1935(a), namely:—

"The manufacture of pins, hairpins, hooks and eyes, hair-curlers, snap fasteners, or safety pins, from the following metals in wire or sheet form:— aluminium, copper, iron, lead, steel, tin, zinc, or alloys of any two or more of the above metals;

INCLUDING:—

(a) the capping of safety pins;

(b) the operation of pin sticking;

(c) packeting, boxing, or carding of any of the above articles wherever carried on;

(d) packing, despatching, warehousing or other operations incidental to or appertaining to the manufacture of any of the above articles.

BUT EXCLUDING:—

(e) the manufacture of steel hatpins or shanks for steel toilet pins, wherever carried on."

EXPLANATORY NOTE

(This Note is not part of the Order.)

This Order, which has effect from 1st August 1973, sets out the increased statutory minimum remuneration payable in substitution for that fixed by the Wages Regulation (Pin, Hook and Eye, and Snap Fastener) Order 1972 (Order O. (87)), which Order is revoked.

New provisions are printed in italics.

(a) S.R. & O. 1935/440 (1935, p. 1680).

STATUTORY INSTRUMENTS

1973 No. 1160

WAGES COUNCILS

The Wages Regulation (Pin, Hook and Eye, and Snap Fastener) (Holidays) Order 1973

Made - - -	*3rd July* 1973
Coming into Operation	*1st August* 1973

Whereas the Secretary of State has received from the Pin, Hook and Eye, and Snap Fastener Wages Council (Great Britain) the wages regulation proposals set out in the Schedule hereto;

Now, therefore, the Secretary of State in exercise of powers conferred by section 11 of the Wages Councils Act 1959(a), as modified by Article 2 of the Counter-Inflation (Modification of Wages Councils Act 1959) Order 1973(b), and now vested in him(c), and of all other powers enabling him in that behalf, hereby makes the following Order:—

1. This Order may be cited as the Wages Regulation (Pin, Hook and Eye, and Snap Fastener) (Holidays) Order 1973.

2.—(1) In this Order the expression the "specified date" means the 1st August 1973, provided that where, as respects any worker who is paid wages at intervals not exceeding seven days, that date does not correspond with the beginning of the period for which the wages are paid, the expression "the specified date" means, as respects that worker, the beginning of the next such period following that date.

(2) The Interpretation Act 1889(d) shall apply to the interpretation of this Order as it applies to the interpretation of an Act of Parliament and as if this Order and the Order hereby revoked were Acts of Parliament.

3. The wages regulation proposals set out in the Schedule hereto shall have effect as from the specified date and as from that date the Wages Regulation (Pin, Hook and Eye, and Snap Fastener) (Holidays) Order 1970(e) shall cease to have effect.

Signed by order of the Secretary of State.
3rd July 1973

W. H. Marsh,
Assistant Secretary,
Department of Employment.

(a) 1959 c. 69. (b) S.I. 1973/661 (1973 I, p. 2141).
(c) S.I. 1959/1769, 1968/729 (1959 I, p. 1795; 1968 II, p. 2108).
(d) 1889 c. 63. (e) S.I. 1970/312 (1970 I, p. 1188).

SCHEDULE Article 3

The following provisions as to holidays and holiday remuneration shall be substituted for the provisions as to holidays and holiday remuneration set out in the Wages Regulation (Pin, Hook and Eye, and Snap Fastener) (Holidays) Order 1970 (hereinafter referred to as "Order O.(83)").

PART I

APPLICATION

1. This Schedule applies to every worker (other than a home-worker) for whom statutory minimum remuneration has been fixed.

PART II

CUSTOMARY HOLIDAYS

2.—(1) An employer shall allow to every worker to whom this Schedule applies a holiday (hereinafter referred to as a "customary holiday") in each year on the days specified in the following sub-paragraph, provided that the worker has been in his employment for a period of not less than four weeks immediately preceding the customary holiday and has worked for the employer during the whole or part of that period and (unless excused by the employer or absent by reason of the proved illness of the worker) has worked for the employer throughout the last working day on which work was available to him prior to the customary holiday.

(2) The said customary holidays are:—

(a) (i) In England and Wales—
Christmas Day;
26th December if it be not a Sunday; 27th December in a year when 25th or 26th December is a Sunday;
Good Friday;
Easter Monday;
the last Monday in May;
the last Monday in August;
(or where a day is substituted for any of the above days by national proclamation, that day);

(ii) in Scotland—
New Year's Day (or, if New Year's Day falls on a Sunday, the following Monday);
the local Spring holiday;
the local Autumn holiday; and
three other days (being days on which the worker normally works) in the course of a calendar year, to be fixed by the employer and notified to the worker not less than three weeks before the holiday;

or (b) in the case of each of the said days (other than a day fixed by the employer and notified to the worker as aforesaid) such weekday as may be substituted therefor by agreement between the employer and the worker.

(3) Notwithstanding the provisions of sub-paragraph (1) of this paragraph, an employer may (unless it is not lawful for him to do so) require a worker who is otherwise qualified to be allowed a customary holiday to work thereon and where he does so the employer shall allow the worker a day's holiday (hereinafter referred to as a "holiday in lieu of a customary holiday") on a weekday on which he normally works for the employer within the four weeks immediately following the customary holiday.

(4) A worker who is required to work on a customary holiday shall be paid:—

(a) for all time worked thereon at the minimum rate then appropriate to the worker for work on a customary holiday; and

(b) in respect of the holiday in lieu of the customary holiday, holiday remuneration in accordance with paragraph 6.

PART III

ANNUAL HOLIDAY

3.—(1) In addition to the holidays specified in Part II of this Schedule and subject to the provisions of paragraph 4, an employer shall, between the date on which the provisions of this Schedule become effective and 30th September 1973, and in each succeeding year between 1st May and 30th September, allow a holiday (hereinafter referred to as an "annual holiday") to every worker in his employment to whom this Schedule applies who has been employed by him during the 12 months immediately preceding the commencement of the holiday season for any of the periods of employment specified below, and the duration of the annual holiday shall in the case of each such worker be related to that period as follows:—

Period of employment	Duration of annual holiday
Column 1	Column 2
At least 48 weeks	16 days
„ „ 44 „	14 „
„ „ 40 „	13 „
„ „ 36 „	11 „
„ „ 32 „	10 „
„ „ 28 „	9 „
„ „ 24 „	8 „
„ „ 20 „	6 „
„ „ 16 „	5 „
„ „ 12 „	4 „
„ „ 8 „	2 „
„ „ 4 „	1 day

(2) Notwithstanding the provisions of the last foregoing sub-paragraph the number of days of annual holiday which an employer is required to allow to a worker in any holiday season shall not exceed in the aggregate *three times* the number of days constituting the worker's normal working week, plus *one* day.

(3) the duration of the worker's annual holiday during the holiday season ending on 30th September 1973 shall be reduced by any days of annual holiday duly allowed to him by the employer under the provisions of Order 0. (83) between 1st May 1973 and the date on which the provisions of this Schedule become effective.

(4) In this Schedule the expression "holiday season" means in relation to the year 1973 the period commencing on 1st May 1973 and ending on 30th September 1973, and in each succeeding year, the period commencing on 1st May and ending on 30th September of the same year.

4.—(1) Subject to the provisions of this paragraph, an annual holiday shall be allowed on consecutive working days, being days on which the worker is normally called upon to work for the employer.

(2) Where the number of days of annual holiday for which a worker has qualified exceeds the number of days constituting his normal working week, the holiday may be

allowed in two or more periods of consecutive working days, provided that one of the periods shall be of not less duration than the number of days constituting the worker's normal working week.

(3) For the purposes of this paragraph, days of annual holiday shall be treated as consecutive notwithstanding that a day of holiday allowed to a worker under Part II of this Schedule or a day upon which he does not normally work for the employer intervenes.

(4) Where an annual holiday is allowed in two or more periods in accordance with sub-paragraph (2) of this paragraph, then notwithstanding paragraph 3, the periods which are not required by virtue of sub-paragraph (2) of this paragraph to consist of a number of days not less than the number of days constituting the worker's normal working week may be allowed either in the holiday season or, by agreement with the worker, after the end of the holiday season but before 30th April next following.

(5) Where a day of holiday allowed to a worker under Part II of this Schedule immediately precedes a period of annual holiday or occurs during such a period and the total number of days of annual holiday required to be allowed in the period under the foregoing provisions of this paragraph, together with any such day of holiday allowed under Part II of this Schedule, exceeds the number of days constituting the worker's normal working week then, notwithstanding the foregoing provisions of this paragraph, the duration of that period of annual holiday may be reduced by one day and in such a case one day of annual holiday may be allowed on any working day (not being the worker's weekly short day) in the holiday season.

(6) Any day of annual holiday under this Schedule may be allowed on a day on which the worker is entitled to a day of holiday or to a half-holiday under any enactment other than the Wages Councils Act 1959.

5. An employer shall give to a worker reasonable notice of the commencing date or dates and duration of the period or periods of his annual holiday. Such notice may be given individually to the worker or by the posting of a notice in the place where the worker is employed.

Part IV

HOLIDAY REMUNERATION

A—CUSTOMARY HOLIDAYS AND HOLIDAYS IN LIEU OF CUSTOMARY HOLIDAYS

6.—(1) For each day of holiday which a worker is allowed under Part II of this Schedule he shall be paid by the employer holiday remuneration equal to the amount to which he would have been entitled, calculated at the general minimum time rate applicable to the worker (or which would be applicable if he were a time worker) increased by one-third, if the day had not been a day of holiday and he had been employed on work entitling him to statutory minimum remuneration for the time normally worked by him on that day of the week:

Provided that payment of the said holiday remuneration is subject to the condition that the worker (unless excused by the employer or absent by reason of the proved illness of the worker) presents himself for employment within one hour of the usual starting hour on the first working day following the holiday.

(2) Holiday remuneration in respect of any holiday allowed under Part II of this Schedule shall be paid to the worker not later than the day on which the wages are paid for the first working day following the holiday: Provided that where a worker ceases to be employed before being allowed a holiday in lieu of a customary holiday, he shall be paid the holiday remuneration for that day immediately upon the termination of his employment and in such a case the condition contained in the proviso to sub-paragraph (1) of this paragraph shall not apply.

B—ANNUAL HOLIDAY

7.—(1) Subject to the provisions of paragraph 8, a worker qualified to be allowed an annual holiday under this Schedule shall be paid by the employer in respect thereof, on the last pay day preceding such annual holiday, one day's holiday pay (as defined in paragraph 11) in respect of each day thereof.

(2) Where under the provisions of paragraph 4 an annual holiday is allowed in more than one period, the holiday remuneration shall be apportioned accordingly

8. Where any accrued holiday remuneration has been paid by the employer to the worker in accordance with paragraph 9 or with Order O. (83) in respect of employment during any of the periods referred to in that paragraph or that Order, the amount of holiday remuneration payable by the employer in respect of any annual holiday for which the worker has qualified by reason of employment during the said period shall be reduced by the amount of the said accrued holiday remuneration unless that re-muneration has been deducted from a previous payment of holiday remuneration made under the provisions of this Schedule or of Order O.(83).

ACCRUED HOLIDAY REMUNERATION PAYABLE ON TERMINATION OF EMPLOYMENT

9. Where a worker ceases to be employed by an employer after the provisions of this Schedule become effective the employer shall, immediately on the termination of the employment (hereinafter referred to as the "termination date") pay to the worker as accrued holiday remuneration:—

(1) in respect of employment in the 12 months ended on the preceding 30th April, a sum equal to the holiday remuneration for any days of annual holiday for which he has qualified, except days of annual holiday which he has been allowed or has become entitled to be allowed before leaving the employment; and

(2) in respect of any employment since the preceding 30th April, a sum equal to the holiday remuneration which would have been payable to him if he could have been allowed an annual holiday in respect of that employment at the time of leaving it.

Part V

GENERAL

10. For the purposes of calculating any period of employment qualifying a worker for an annual holiday or for any accrued holiday remuneration, the worker shall be treated:—

(1) as if he were employed for a week in respect of any week in which—

(a) he has worked for the employer for not less than 20 hours and has performed some work for which statutory minimum remuneration is payable; or

(b) he has been absent throughout the week, or he has worked for the employer for less than 20 hours, solely by reason of the proved illness of, or accident to, the worker, provided that the number of weeks which may be treated as weeks of employment for such reason shall not exceed six in the aggregate in the period of 12 months immediately preceding the comm-encement of the holiday season; or

(c) he is absent from work throughout the week owing to suspension due to shortage of work, provided that the number of weeks which may be treated as weeks of employment for such reason shall not exceed four in the aggre-gate in the period of 12 months last mentioned, and

(2) as if he were employed on any day of holiday allowed under the provisions of this Schedule or of Order O.(83), and for the purposes of the provisions of sub-paragraph (1) of this paragraph, a worker who is absent on such a holiday shall be treated as having worked thereon for the employer for the number of hours ordinarily worked by him on that day of the week on work for which statutory minimum remuneration is payable.

11. In this Schedule, unless the context otherwise requires, the following expressions have the meanings hereby respectively assigned to them, that is to say:—

"NORMAL WORKING WEEK" means the number of days on which it has been usual for the worker to work in a week in the employment of the employer during the 12 months immediately preceding the commencement of the holiday season or, where accrued holiday remuneration is payable under (2) of paragraph 9 on the termination of the employment, during the 12 months immediately preceding the termination date:

Provided that—

(1) part of a day shall count as a day;

(2) no account shall be taken of any week in which the worker did not perform any work for which statutory minimum remuneration has been fixed.

"ONE DAY'S HOLIDAY PAY" means the appropriate proportion of the remuneration which the worker would be entitled to receive from his employer at the date of the annual holiday (or where the holiday is allowed in more than one period at the date of the first period) or at the termination date, as the case may require, for one week's work if working his normal working week and the number of daily hours normally worked by him (exclusive of overtime) and if paid at the general minimum time rate applicable to the worker (or which would be applicable if he were a time worker) increased by one-third, for work for which statutory minimum remuneration is payable and at the same rate (increased as aforesaid) for any work for which such remuneration is not payable, and in this definition "appropriate proportion" means—

where the worker's normal working week is six days ... ... one-sixth

where the worker's normal working week is five days ... ... one-fifth

where the worker's normal working week is four days or less ... one-quarter

"STATUTORY MINIMUM REMUNERATION" means minimum remuneration (other than holiday remuneration) fixed by a wages regulation order made by the Secretary of State to give effect to proposals submitted to him by the Pin, Hook and Eye, and Snap Fastener Wages Council (Great Britain).

"WEEK" in paragraphs 3 and 10 means "pay week".

12. The provisions of this Schedule are without prejudice to any agreement for the allowance of any further holidays with pay or for the payment of additional holiday remuneration.

EXPLANATORY NOTE

(This Note is not part of the Order.)

This Order, which has effect from 1st August 1973, sets out the holidays which an employer is required to allow to workers in relation to whom the Pin, Hook and Eye, and Snap Fastener Wages Council (Great Britain) operates and the remuneration payable for those holidays, in substitution for the holidays and holiday remuneration fixed by the Wages Regulation (Pin, Hook and Eye, and Snap Fastener) (Holidays) Order 1970, (Order O. (83)), which Order is revoked.

It amends the provisions relating to customary holidays contained in Order O. (83), so as to take account of recent changes in the law and practice relating to public holidays.

New provisions are printed in italics.

STATUTORY INSTRUMENTS

1973 No. 1164

MEDICINES

The Medicines (Feeding Stuffs Additives) Order 1973

Laid before Parliament in draft

Made - - - -	*2nd July* 1973
Coming into Operation	1*st August* 1973

The Minister of Agriculture, Fisheries and Food, the Secretary of State concerned with agriculture in Scotland and the Secretary of State for Northern Ireland, acting jointly, in exercise of powers conferred by section 104(1) of the Medicines Act 1968**(a)** and now vested in them**(b)** and of all other powers enabling them in that behalf, having taken into account the advice of the Veterinary Products Committee established by the Medicines (Veterinary Products Committee) Order 1970**(c)** and after consulting such organisations as appear to them to be representative of interests likely to be substantially affected, hereby make the following order, a draft of which has been laid before Parliament and has been approved by resolution of each House of Parliament.

Citation and commencement

1. This order may be cited as the Medicines (Feeding Stuffs Additives) Order 1973 and shall come into operation on 1st August 1973.

Interpretation

2. In this order—

(1) "the Act" means the Medicines Act 1968;

"the Agriculture Ministers" means the Minister of Agriculture, Fisheries and Food, the Secretary of State concerned with agriculture in Scotland and the Secretary of State for Northern Ireland, acting jointly;
and other expressions have the same meaning as in the Act.

(2) The Interpretation Act 1889**(d)** shall apply to the interpretation of this order as it applies to the interpretation of an Act of Parliament.

Extension of the Medicines Act 1968

3. The Agriculture Ministers hereby specify for the purposes of section 104(1) of the Act the substances or articles described in column 1 of the Schedule to this order as appearing to them to be substances or articles which are not medicinal products but are manufactured, sold, supplied, imported or exported

---

(a) 1968 c. 67.

(b) In the case of the Secretary of State for Northern Ireland under the provisions of section 1(1)(*a*) of the Northern Ireland (Temporary Provisions) Act 1972 (c. 22).

(c) S.I. 1970/1304 (1970 III, p. 4335). (d) 1889 c. 63.

for use wholly or partly for a medicinal purpose and hereby direct that the provisions of the Act set out in column 2 of the said Schedule shall have effect in relation to such substances or articles as those provisions have effect in relation to medicinal products.

In Witness whereof the official seal of the Minister of Agriculture, Fisheries and Food is hereunto affixed on 28th June 1973.

(L.S.)   *Joseph Godber,*
                              Minister of Agriculture, Fisheries and Food.

                                              Gordon Campbell,
2nd July 1973.   Secretary of State for Scotland.

                                            W. S. I. Whitelaw,
2nd July 1973.   Secretary of State for Northern Ireland.

SCHEDULE

Column 1	Column 2
Substances or articles appearing to the Agriculture Ministers to be substances or articles which are not medicinal products but are manufactured, sold, supplied, imported or exported for use wholly or partly for a medicinal purpose.	Provisions of the Act applicable to those substances.
Any substance or article other than a medicinal product, intended to be incorporated in any animal feeding stuff for a medicinal purpose with a view to— (a) feeding it, while so incorporated, to one or more animals, or (b) selling, supplying or exporting it, while so incorporated.	The provisions of sections 90 and 91.

EXPLANATORY NOTE

(This Note is not part of the Order.)

This Order, made under section 104(1) of the Medicines Act 1968, extends the application of sections 90 and 91 of the Act (which provide for the application of powers for labelling containers or packages of animal feeding stuffs in which medicinal products have been incorporated) to include application in relation to substances or articles other than medicinal products intended to be incorporated as additives in animal feeding stuffs for a medicinal purpose.

STATUTORY INSTRUMENTS

1973 No. 1165 (S.90)

TOWN AND COUNTRY PLANNING, SCOTLAND
The Town and Country Planning (Use Classes)

(Scotland) Order 1973

Made - - - 29th June 1973

Coming into Operation 1st August 1973

In exercise of powers conferred on me by sections 19 (2)(*f*) and 273 (3) and (4) of the Town and Country Planning (Scotland) Act 1972(**a**), and of all other powers enabling me in that behalf, I hereby make the following order:—

Citation and commencement

1. This order may be cited as the Town and Country Planning (Use Classes) (Scotland) Order 1973 and shall come into operation on 1st August 1973.

Interpretation

2.—(1) The Interpretation Act 1889(**b**) shall apply for the interpretation of this order as it applies for the interpretation of an Act of Parliament.

(2) In this order, unless the context otherwise requires, the following expressions have the meanings respectively assigned to them, namely:—

"Act" means the Town and Country Planning (Scotland) Act 1972;

"betting office" means any building in respect of which there is for the time being in force a betting office licence pursuant to the provisions of the Betting, Gaming and Lotteries Acts 1963 to 1971;

"general industrial building" means an industrial building, other than a light industrial building or a special industrial building;

"industrial building" means a building (other than a building in or adjacent to and belonging to a quarry or mine and other than a shop) used for the carrying on of any process for or incidental to any of the following purposes, namely:—

(*a*) the making of any article or of part of any article, or

(*b*) the altering, repairing, ornamenting, finishing, cleaning, washing, packing or canning, or adapting for sale or breaking up or demolition of any article, or

---

(**a**) 1972 c. 52.   (**b**) 1889 c. 63.

(c) without prejudice to the foregoing paragraphs, the getting, dressing or treatment of minerals,

being a process carried on in the course of trade or business other than agriculture, and for the purpose of this definition the expression "article" means an article of any description, including a ship or vessel;

"launderette" includes any building used for the purpose of washing or cleaning clothes or fabrics in machines available for operation by members of the public;

"light industrial building" means an industrial building (not being a special industrial building) in which the processes carried on or the machinery installed are such as could be carried on or installed in any residential area without detriment to the amenity of that area by reason of noise, vibration, smell, fumes, smoke, soot, ash, dust or grit;

"motor vehicle" means any motor vehicle for the purposes of the Road Traffic Acts 1960 to 1967;

"office" includes a bank and premises occupied by an estate agency, building society or employment agency, or (for office purposes only) for the purpose of car hire or driving instruction, but does not include a post office or betting office;

"post office" does not include any building used primarily for the sorting or preparation for delivery of mail or for the purposes of Post Office administration;

"shop" means a building used for the carrying on of any retail trade or retail business wherein the primary purpose is the selling of goods by retail, and without prejudice to the generality of the foregoing includes a building used for the purposes of a hairdresser, undertaker, travel agency, ticket agency or post office or for the reception of goods to be washed, cleaned or repaired, but does not include a building used as a fun fair, amusement arcade, pin-table saloon, garage, launderette, petrol filling station, office, betting office, hotel, restaurant, snack bar or cafe, or premises licensed for the sale of excisable liquor for consumption on the premises;

"special industrial building" means an industrial building used for one or more of the purposes specified in Classes V, VI, VII, VIII and IX referred to in the Schedule to this order.

(3) References in this order to a building may, except where otherwise provided, include references to land occupied therewith and used for the same purposes.

Use Classes

3.—(1) Where a building or other land is used for a purpose of any class specified in the Schedule to this order, the use of such a building or other land for any other purpose of the same class shall not be deemed for the purposes of the Act to involve development of the land.

(2) Where a group of contiguous or adjacent buildings used as parts of a

single undertaking includes industrial buildings used for purposes falling within two or more of the classes specified in the Schedule to this order as Classes III to IX inclusive, those particular two or more classes may, in relation to that group of buildings, and so long as the area occupied in that group by either general or special industrial buildings is not substantially increased thereby, be treated as a single class for the purposes of this order.

(3) A use which is ordinarily incidental to and included in any use specified in the Schedule to this order is not excluded from that use as an incident thereto merely by reason of its specification in the said Schedule as a separate use.

(4) Nothing in this order shall be construed as limiting or restricting the power of a local planning authority under sections 26 and 27 of the Act to impose conditions on the grant of planning permission.

Revocation

4. The Town and Country Planning (Use Classes) (Scotland) Order 1950(a), the Town and Country Planning (Use Classes) (Scotland) Amendment Order 1960(b) and the Town and Country Planning (Use Classes) (Scotland) Amendment Order 1965(c) are hereby revoked.

Gordon Campbell,
One of Her Majesty's Principal
Secretaries of State.

St. Andrew's House,
Edinburgh.
29th June 1973.

SCHEDULE

Class I.—Use as a shop for any purpose except as: —

(i) a shop for the sale of hot food;

(ii) a tripe shop;

(iii) a shop for the sale of pet animals or birds;

(iv) a cats-meat shop;

(v) a shop for the sale of motor vehicles.

Class II.—Use as an office for any purpose.

(a) S.I. 1950/1133 (1950 II, p. 1140).   (b) S.I. 1960/2014(1960 III, p. 3298).
(c) S.I. 1965/230 (1965 I, p. 585).

Class III.—Use as a light industrial building for any purpose.

Class IV.—Use as a general industrial building for any purpose.

Class V. (Special Industrial Group A)—Use for any work which is registrable under the Alkali &c Works Regulation Act 1906(a) as extended by the Alkali &c Works (Scotland) Order 1972(b) and which is not included in any of Classes VI, VII, VIII or IX of this Schedule.

Class VI. (Special Industrial Group B)—Use for any of the following processes, except a process ancillary to the getting, dressing or treatment of minerals which is carried on in or adjacent to a quarry or mine:—

    (i) smelting, calcining, sintering or reduction of ores, minerals, concentrates or mattes;

    (ii) converting, refining, re-heating, annealing, hardening, melting, carburising, forging or casting of metals or alloys, other than pressure die-casting;

    (iii) recovery of metal from scrap or drosses or ashes;

    (iv) galvanising;

    (v) pickling or treatment of metal in acid;

    (vi) chromium plating.

Class VII. (Special Industrial Group C)—Use for any of the following processes except a process ancillary to the getting, dressing or treatment of minerals which is carried on in or adjacent to a quarry or mine:—

    (i) burning of bricks or pipes;

    (ii) lime or dolomite burning;

    (iii) production of zinc oxide, cement or alumina;

    (iv) foaming, crushing, screening or heating of minerals or slag;

    (v) processing by heat of pulverized fuel ash;

    (vi) production of carbonate of lime and hydrated lime;

    (vii) production of inorganic pigments by calcining, roasting or grinding.

Class VIII. (Special Industrial Group D)—Use for any of the following purposes:—

    (i) distilling, refining or blending of oils (other than petroleum or petroleum products);

    (ii) production or employment of cellulose and employment of other pressure sprayed metal finishes (other than the employment of any such finishes in vehicle repair workshops in connection with minor repairs, and the application of plastic powder by the use of fluidised bed and electrostatic spray techniques).

  (a) 1906 c. 14.   (b) S.I. 1972/1330 (1972 II, p. 4016).

(iii) boiling of linseed oil and the running of gum;

(iv) processes involving the use of hot pitch or bitumen (except the use of bitumen in the manufacture of roofing felt at temperatures not exceeding 220°C and also the manufacture of coated roadstone);

(v) stoving of enamelled ware;

(vi) production of aliphatic esters of the lower fatty acids, butyric acid, caramel, hexamine, iodoform, napthols, resin products (excluding plastic moulding or extrusion operations and production of plastic sheets, rods, tubes, filaments, fibres or optical components produced by casting, calendering, moulding, shaping or extrusion), salicylic acid or sulphonated organic compounds;

(vii) production of rubber from scrap;

(viii) chemical processes in which chlorphenols or chlorcresols are used as intermediates;

(ix) manufacture of acetylene from calcium carbide;

(x) manufacture, recovery or use of pyridine or picolines, any methyl or ethyl amine or acrylates.

Class IX. (Special Industrial Group E)—Use for carrying on any of the following industries, businesses or trades:—

Animal charcoal manufacturer.

Animal hair cleanser, adapter or treater.

Blood albumen maker.

Blood boiler.

Bone boiler or steamer.

Bone burner.

Bone grinder.

Breeder of maggots from putrescible animal matter.

Candle maker.

Catgut manufacturer.

Chitterling or nettlings boiler.

Dealer in rags or bones (including receiving, storing or manipulating rags in or likely to become in an offensive condition, or any bones, rabbit-skins, fat or putrescible animal products of a like nature).

Fat melter or fat extractor.

Fellmonger.

Fish curer.

Fish oil manufacturer.

Fish skin dresser or scraper.

Glue maker.

Gut scraper or gut cleaner.

Maker of feeding stuff for animals or poultry from any meat, fish, blood, bone, feathers, fat or animal offal, either in an offensive condition or subjected to any process causing noxious or injurious effluvia.

Manufacture of manure from bones, fish, offal, blood, spent hops, beans or other putrescible animal or vegetable matter.

Size maker.

Skin drier.

Soap boiler.

Tallow melter or refiner.

Tripe boiler or cleaner.

Class X.—Use as a boarding or guest house or a hotel providing sleeping accommodation (except such a boarding or guest house or a hotel licensed for the sale of excisable liquor to persons other than residents or to persons other than persons consuming meals on the premises).

Class XI.—Use as a residential or boarding school or a residential college.

Class XII.—Use as a building for public worship or religious instruction or for the social or recreational activities of the religious body using the building.

Class XIII.—Use as a home or institution providing for the boarding, care and maintenance of children, old people or persons under disability, a convalescent home, a nursing home, a sanatorium or a hospital.

Class XIV.—Use (other than residentially) as a health centre, a school treatment centre, a clinic, a creche, a day nursery or a dispensary, or use as a consulting room or surgery unattached to the residence of the consultant or practitioner.

Class XV.—Use as an art gallery (other than for business purposes), a museum a public library or reading room, a public hall or an exhibition hall.

Class XVI.—Use as a theatre, a cinema, a concert hall or a music hall.

Class XVII.—Use as a dance hall, a skating rink, a swimming bath, a Turkish bath or any other form of bath, a gymnasium or a sports hall.

EXPLANATORY NOTE

(This Note is not part of the Order.)

This Order revokes and re-enacts with amendments the Town and Country Planning (Use Classes) (Scotland) Order 1950 (as amended by two subsequent orders) which was made under enactments now consolidated in the Town and Country Planning (Scotland) Act 1972.

The Order specifies classes for the purpose of section 19(2)(f) of the Act of 1972. By virtue of section 19 the use of buildings or other land for any other purpose of the same class shall not be taken to involve development within the meaning of that section.

The principal amendments made by the Order to the provisions of the previous Orders are the exclusion of launderettes, cafes, restaurants and the expression "any other purpose appropriate to a shopping area" from the definition of a shop; the recasting of Special Industrial Groups A, B and C; the omission of the former Classes XI and XVII; and the exclusion from Class X of a hotel licensed for the sale of liquor to persons other than residents or persons taking meals. Other amendments are the substitution of hot food for fried fish in Class I; the omission of leather dresser, parchment maker and tanner from class IX; and minor changes of wording in what are now Classes XV, XVI and XVII.

STATUTORY INSTRUMENTS

1973 No. 1166

CUSTOMS AND EXCISE

The Import Duties (General) (No. 5) Order 1973

Made - - -	*5th July* 1973
Laid before the *House of Commons*	*10th July* 1973
Coming into Operation	*1st August* 1973

The Lords Commissioners of Her Majesty's Treasury, by virtue of the powers conferred on them by sections 1, 2 and 13 of the Import Duties Act 1958(a), as amended by section 5(5) of, and paragraph 1 of Schedule 4 to, the European Communities Act 1972(b), and of all other powers enabling them in that behalf, on the recommendation of the Secretary of State(c), hereby make the following Order:—

1.—(1) This Order may be cited as the Import Duties (General) (No. 5) Order 1973 and shall come into operation on 1st August 1973.

(2) The Interpretation Act 1889(d) shall apply to the interpretation of this Order as it applies to the interpretation of an Act of Parliament.

2. In Schedule 1 to the Import Duties (General) (No. 7) Order 1971(e), as amended(f), tariff headings 01.04 (live sheep and goats), 07.05 (dried, shelled leguminous vegetables), 15.02 (fats of bovine cattle, sheep or goats) and 23.03 (beet-pulp and certain other wastes and residues) shall be further amended as specified in the Schedule to this Order.

3. In consequence of the amendments made by Article 2 above, the Import Duties (Developing Countries) Order 1971(g), as amended(h), shall be further amended by substituting in the second column of Schedule 2 thereto:

(a) for the entry relating to tariff heading 07.05, "All goods falling within subheadings (A)(I)(b)(1), (A)(I)(c), (A)(I)(d), (A)(II), (A)(III), (B)(I)(c)(1), (B)(I)(d), (B)(I)(e), (B)(II) and (B)(III)" and

(b) for the entry relating to tariff heading 23.03, "All goods falling within subheadings (A), (B)(I)(b) and (B)(II)".

Tim Fortescue,
P. L. Hawkins,
Two of the Lords Commissioners
of Her Majesty's Treasury.

5th July 1973.

(a) 1958 c. 6.　　　　　　　　　　　　(b) 1972 c. 68.
(c) *See* S.I. 1970/1537 (1970 III, p. 5293).　(d) 1889 c. 63.
(e) S.I. 1971/1971 (1971 III, p. 5330).
(f) The relevant amending Orders are S.I. 1972/1909, 1973/648 (1972 III, p. 5549;
　　1973 I, p. 2015).　　　　　　　　　(g) S.I. 1971/1882 (1971 III, p. 5125).
(h) The relevant amending Order is S.I. 1973/16 (1973 I, p. 71).

SCHEDULE

1. For subheading 01.04(A)(II) there shall be substituted the following:—

"(II)   Goats:

     (a) Pure-bred breeding animals   —   —

     (b) Other   —   —".

2. For heading 07.05 there shall be substituted the following:—

"07.05 Dried leguminous vegetables, shelled, whether or not skinned or split:

(A) For sowing:

     (I)   Peas (including chick peas) and beans (of the species *Phaseolus*):

(a) Whole peas (other than peas of the varieties commonly known as maple peas, dun peas and yellow or white peas)	£0·3750 per cwt or 10%, whichever is the greater	C — E £0·3750 per cwt or 10%, whichever is the greater
(b) Other peas:		
(1) Chick peas (*cicer arietinum*)	5%	C — E 5%
(2) Other	10%	C — E 10%
(c) Beans, dried, white (including haricot) other than butter	4%	C — E 4%
(d) Other beans	5%	C — E 5%
(II) Lentils	5%	C — E 5%
(III) Other	5%	C — E 5%

(B) Other:

     (I)   Peas (including chick peas) and beans (of the species *Phaseolus*):

(a) Split peas	15%	C — E 15%
(b) Whole peas (other than peas of the varieties commonly known as maple peas, dun peas and yellow or white peas)	£0·3750 per cwt or 10%, whichever is the greater	C — E £0·3750 per cwt or 10%, whichever is the greater
(c) Other peas:		
(1) Chick peas (*cicer arietinum*)	5%	C — E 5%
(2) Other	10%	C — E 10%
(d) Beans, dried, white (including haricot) other than butter	4%	C — E 4%
(e) Other beans	5%	C— E 5%
(II) Lentils	5%	C — E 5%
(III) Other	5%	C — E 5%".

3. For subheading 15.02 (B)(II) there shall be substituted the following:—

"(II) Unrendered fats of sheep; rendered or solvent-extracted fats (including "premier jus") obtained from those fats	10%	C — E 10%
(III) Other	10%	C — E 10%".

4. Subheading 23.03(B)(I) there shall be substituted the following:—

"(I)   Beet-pulp, bagasse and other waste of
sugar manufacture:

(*a*) Bagasse	—	—
(*b*) Other	10%	C — E 10%".

EXPLANATORY NOTE

(*This Note is not part of the Order.*)

This Order, which comes into operation on 1st August 1973, further amends the Import Duties (General) (No. 7) Order 1971, which sets out the United Kingdom Customs Tariff and the protective import duties chargeable in accordance with it.

The Order provides for amendments (set out in the Schedule) to the manner in which tariff headings 01.04, 07.05, 15.02 and 23.03 are subdivided. These amendments are made in order to conform with changes in the nomenclature of the Common Customs Tariff of the European Economic Community (made by Regulation (EEC) No. 1014/73—O.J. No. L106, 20.4.73, p. 1). The only effect on the rates of duty actually chargeable is a reduction from 10 per cent to 5 per cent *ad valorem* in the case of chick peas (subheadings 07.05 (A)(I)(*b*)(1) and 07.05 (B)(I)(*c*)(1).

STATUTORY INSTRUMENTS

1973 No. 1167

INDUSTRIAL TRAINING

The Industrial Training Levy (Rubber and Plastics Processing) Order 1973

Made - - -	*4th July* 1973
Laid before Parliament	*13th July* 1973
Coming into Operation	*8th August* 1973

The Secretary of State after approving proposals submitted by the Rubber and Plastics Processing Industry Training Board for the imposition of a further levy on employers in the rubber and plastics processing industry and in exercise of powers conferred by section 4 of the Industrial Training Act 1964(**a**) and now vested in him(**b**), and of all other powers enabling him in that behalf hereby makes the following Order:—

Title and commencement

1. This Order may be cited as the Industrial Training Levy (Rubber and Plastics Processing) Order 1973 and shall come into operation on 8th August 1973.

Interpretation

2.—(1) In this Order unless the context otherwise requires:—

(*a*) "agriculture" has the same meaning as in section 109(3) of the Agriculture Act 1947(**c**) or, in relation to Scotland, as in section 86(3) of the Agriculture (Scotland) Act 1948(**d**);

(*b*) "an appeal tribunal" means an industrial tribunal established under section 12 of the Industrial Training Act 1964;

(*c*) "assessment" means an assessment of an employer to the levy;

(*d*) "the Board" means the Rubber and Plastics Processing Industry Training Board;

(*e*) "business" means any activities of industry or commerce;

(*f*) "charity" has the same meaning as in section 360 of the Income and Corporation Taxes Act 1970(**e**);

(*g*) "emoluments" means all emoluments assessable to income tax under Schedule E (other than pensions), being emoluments from which tax under that Schedule is deductible, whether or not tax in fact falls to be deducted from any particular payment thereof;

(*h*) "employer" means a person who is an employer in the rubber and plastics processing industry at any time in the sixth levy period;

(**a**) 1964 c. 16. (**b**) S.I. 1968/729 (1968 II, p. 2108).
(**c**) 1947 c. 48. (**d**) 1948 c. 45.
(**e**) 1970 c. 10.

(*i*) "the sixth base period" means the period of twelve months that commenced on 6th April 1972;

(*j*) "the sixth levy period" means the period commencing with the day upon which this Order comes into operation and ending on 31st March 1974;

(*k*) "the industrial training order" means the Industrial Training (Rubber and Plastics Processing Board) Order 1967(**a**);

(*l*) "the levy" means the levy imposed by the Board in respect of the sixth levy period;

(*m*) "notice" means a notice in writing;

(*n*) "rubber and plastics processing establishment" means an establishment in Great Britain engaged in the sixth base period wholly or mainly in the rubber and plastics processing industry for a total of twenty-seven or more weeks or, being an establishment that commenced to carry on business in the sixth base period, for a total number of weeks exceeding one half of the number of weeks in the part of the said period commencing with the day on which business was commenced and ending on the last day thereof;

(*o*) "the rubber and plastics processing industry" means any one or more of the activities which, subject to the provisions of paragraph 2 of Schedule 1 to the industrial training order, are specified in paragraph 1 of that Schedule as the activities of the rubber and plastics processing industry.

(2) Any reference in this Order to a person employed at or from a rubber and plastics processing establishment shall in any case where the employer is a company be construed as including a reference to any director of the company (or any person occupying the position of director by whatever name he is called) who is required to devote substantially the whole of his time to the service of the company.

(3) In the case where a rubber and plastics processing establishment is taken over (whether directly or indirectly) by an employer in succession to, or jointly with, another person, a person employed at any time in the sixth base period at or from the establishment shall be deemed, for the purposes of this Order, to have been so employed by the employer carrying on the said establishment on the day upon which this Order comes into operation and any reference in this Order to persons employed by an employer in the sixth base period at or from a rubber and plastics processing establishment shall be construed accordingly.

(4) Any reference in this Order to an establishment that commences to carry on business or that ceases to carry on business shall not be taken to apply where the location of the establishment is changed but its business is continued wholly or mainly at or from the new location, or where the suspension of activities is of a temporary or seasonal nature.

(5) The Interpretation Act 1889(**b**) shall apply to the interpretation of this Order as it applies to the interpretation of an Act of Parliament.

Imposition of the levy

3.—(1) The levy to be imposed by the Board on employers in respect of the sixth levy period shall be assessed in accordance with the provisions of this Article.

(**a**) S.I. 1967/1062 (1967 II, p. 3151).   (**b**) 1889 c. 63.

(2) The levy shall be assessed by the Board separately in respect of each rubber and plastics processing establishment of an employer (not being an employer who is exempt from the levy by virtue of paragraph (5) of this Article), but in agreement with the employer one assessment may be made in respect of any number of such establishments, in which case those establishments shall be deemed for the purposes of that assessment to constitute one establishment.

(3) Subject to the provisions of this Article, the levy assessed in respect of a rubber and plastics processing establishment of an employer shall be an amount equal to 0·75 per cent. of the sum of the emoluments of all the persons employed by the employer at or from that establishment in the sixth base period.

(4) The amount of the levy imposed in respect of a rubber and plastics processing establishment that ceases to carry on business in the sixth levy period shall be in the same proportion to the amount that would otherwise be due under paragraph (3) of this Article as the number of days between the commencement of the said levy period and the date of cessation of business (both dates inclusive) bears to the number of days in the said levy period.

(5) There shall be exempt from the levy—

   (a) an employer in whose case the number of all the persons employed by him on 5th April 1973 at or from the rubber and plastics processing establishment or establishments of the employer was less than twenty-six;

   (b) a charity.

(6) For the purposes of this Article no regard shall be had to any person wholly engaged in agriculture or in the supply of food or drink for immediate consumption.

Assessment notices

4.—(1) The Board shall serve an assessment notice on every employer assessed to the levy, but one notice may comprise two or more assessments.

(2) The amount of any assessment payable under an assessment notice shall be rounded down to the nearest £1.

(3) An assessment notice shall state the Board's address for the service of a notice of appeal or of an application for an extension of time for appealing.

(4) An assessment notice may be served on the person assessed to the levy either by delivering it to him personally or by leaving it, or sending it to him by post, at his last known address or place of business in the United Kingdom or, if that person is a corporation, by leaving it, or sending it by post to the corporation, at such address or place of business or at its registered or principal office.

Payment of the levy

5.—(1) Subject to the provisions of this Article and of Articles 6 and 7, the amount of the levy payable under an assessment notice served by the Board shall be payable to the Board in two instalments equal to one-fifth and four-fifths of the said amount respectively, and the said instalments shall be due respectively on 1st December 1973 and 1st September 1974.

(2) An instalment of an assessment shall not be recoverable by the Board

until there has expired the time allowed for appealing against the assessment by Article 7(1) of this Order and any further period or periods of time that the Board or an appeal tribunal may have allowed for appealing under paragraph (2) or (3) of that Article or, where an appeal is brought, until the appeal is decided or withdrawn.

Withdrawal of assessment

6.—(1) The Board may, by a notice served on the person assessed to the levy in the same manner as an assessment notice, withdraw an assessment if that person has appealed against that assessment under the provisions of Article 7 of this Order and the appeal has not been entered in the Register of Appeals kept under the appropriate Regulations specified in paragraph (5) of that Article.

(2) The withdrawal of an assessment shall be without prejudice to the power of the Board to serve a further assessment notice in respect of any establishment to which that assessment related.

Appeals

7.—(1) A person assessed to the levy may appeal to an appeal tribunal against the assessment within one month from the date of the service of the assessment notice or within any further period or periods of time that may be allowed by the Board or an appeal tribunal under the following provisions of this Article.

(2) The Board by notice may for good cause allow a person assessed to the levy to appeal to an appeal tribunal against the assessment at any time within the period of four months from the date of the service of the assessment notice or within such further period or periods as the Board may allow before such time as may then be limited for appealing has expired.

(3) If the Board shall not allow an application for extension of time for appealing, an appeal tribunal shall upon application made to the tribunal by the person assessed to the levy have the like powers as the Board under the last foregoing paragraph.

(4) In the case of an establishment that ceases to carry on business in the sixth levy period on any day after the date of the service of the relevant assessment notice, the foregoing provisions of this Article shall have effect as if for the period of four months from the date of the service of the assessment notice mentioned in paragraph (2) of this Article there were substituted the period of six months from the date of the cessation of business.

(5) An appeal or an application to an appeal tribunal under this Article shall be made in accordance with the Industrial Tribunals (England and Wales) Regulations 1965(a) as amended by the Industrial Tribunals (England and Wales) (Amendment) Regulations 1967(b) except where the establishment to which the relevant assessment relates is wholly in Scotland in which case the appeal or application shall be made in accordance with the Industrial Tribunals (Scotland) Regulations 1965(c) as amended by the Industrial Tribunals (Scotland) (Amendment) Regulations 1967(d).

(6) The powers of an appeal tribunal under paragraph (3) of this Article may be exercised by the President of the Industrial Tribunals (England and

---

(a) S.I. 1965/1101 (1965 II, p. 2805).
(c) S.I. 1965/1157 (1965 II, p. 3266).

(b) S.I. 1967/301 (1967 I, p. 1040).
(d) S.I. 1967/302 (1967 I, p. 1050).

Wales) or by the President of the Industrial Tribunals (Scotland) as the case may be.

Evidence

8.—(1) Upon the discharge by a person assessed to the levy of his liability under an assessment the Board shall if so requested issue to him a certificate to that effect.

(2) The production in any proceedings of a document purporting to be certified by the Secretary of the Board to be a true copy of an assessment or other notice issued by the Board or purporting to be a certificate such as is mentioned in the foregoing paragraph of this Article shall, unless the contrary is proved, be sufficient evidence of the document and of the facts stated therein.

Signed by order of the Secretary of State.
4th July 1973.

R. Chichester-Clark,
Minister of State,
Department of Employment.

EXPLANATORY NOTE
(This Note is not part of the Order.)

This Order gives effect to proposals submitted to the Secretary of State for Employment by the Rubber and Plastics Processing Industry Training Board for the imposition of a further levy on employers in the rubber and plastics processing industry for the purpose of raising money towards the expenses of the Board.

The levy is to be imposed in respect of the sixth levy period commencing with the day upon which this Order comes into operation and ending on 31st March 1974. The levy will be assessed by the Board and there will be a right of appeal against an assessment to an industrial tribunal.

STATUTORY INSTRUMENTS

1973 No. 1171

JURIES

The Jurors' (Coroners' Courts) Allowances (Amendment) (No. 2) Regulations 1973

Made - - -	*3rd July* 1973
Coming into Operation	*7th August* 1973

In exercise of the powers conferred on me by section 1 of the Juries Act 1949(a), as amended by section 1 of the Juries Act 1954(b), section 36 of the Courts Act 1971(c) and section 27 of the Criminal Justice Act 1972(d), I hereby, with the consent of the Minister for the Civil Service, make the following Regulations:—

1. These Regulations may be cited as the Jurors' (Coroners' Courts) Allowances (Amendment) (No. 2) Regulations 1973 and shall come into operation on 7th August 1973.

2. Regulation 7 of the Jurors' (Coroners' Courts) Allowances Regulations 1972(e), as amended (f), shall be amended by the substitution of the words "£2·75" and "£5·50" for the words "£2·375" and "£4·75" respectively.

Robert Carr,
One of Her Majesty's Principal
Secretaries of State.

Home Office,
Whitehall.
1st July 1973.

Consent of the Minister for the Civil Service given under his official seal on 3rd July 1973.

(L.S.)

P. M. Blake,
Authorised by the Minister
for the Civil Service.

EXPLANATORY NOTE

(This Note is not part of the Regulations.)

These Regulations increase the maximum rates of financial loss allowances payable in respect of jury service in a coroner's court. The new maximum rates are £5·50, if the time involved exceeds 4 hours in a 24 hour period, and £2·75 in other cases.

(a) 1949 c. 27.   (b) 1954 c. 41.   (c) 1971 c. 23.   (d) 1972 c. 71.
(e) S.I. 1972/1001 (1972 II, p. 3084).   (f) S.I.1973/935 (1973 II, p. 2814).

STATUTORY INSTRUMENTS

1973 No. 1172

CRIMINAL PROCEDURE, ENGLAND AND WALES

COSTS AND EXPENSES

The Witnesses' Allowances (Amendment) (No. 2) Regulations 1973

Made - - -	*1st July* 1973
Coming into Operation	*7th August* 1973

In exercise of the powers conferred upon me by section 17 of the Costs in Criminal Cases Act 1973(**a**), I hereby make the following Regulations:—

1. These Regulations may be cited as the Witnesses' Allowances (Amendment) (No.2) Regulations 1973 and shall come into operation on 7th August 1973.

2. In Regulation 7 of the Witnesses' Allowances Regulations 1971(**b**) as amended(**c**), for the words "£4·75" there shall be substituted the words "£5·50" and for the words "£2·375" in both places where they occur there shall be substituted the words "£2·75".

3. In Regulation 10(1)(*a*) of the said Regulations for the words "£4·75" there shall be substituted the words "£5·50".

Robert Carr,
One of Her Majesty's Principal
Secretaries of State.

Home Office,
Whitehall.
1st July 1973.

EXPLANATORY NOTE
(This Note is not part of the Regulations.)

These Regulations provide for an increase in allowances to seamen who miss their ships through being detained on shore to give evidence and to other witnesses (not being professional or expert witnesses).

(**a**) 1973 c. 14. (**b**) S.I. 1971/107 (1971 I, p. 195).
(**c**) The relevant amending instrument is S.I. 1973/922 (1973 II, p. 2797).

STATUTORY INSTRUMENTS

1973 No. 1173

CORONERS

EXPENSES

The Coroners (Fees and Allowances) (Amendment) (No. 2) Rules 1973

Made - - -		*1st July* 1973
Coming into Operation		*7th August* 1973

In exercise of the powers conferred upon me by section 1(1) of the Coroners Act 1954(**a**), I hereby make the following Rules:—

1. These Rules may be cited as the Coroners (Fees and Allowances) (Amendment) (No.2) Rules 1973 and shall come into operation on 7th August 1973.

2. The Coroners (Fees and Allowances) (Amendment) Rules 1972(**b**) are hereby revoked.

3. In Rule 7 of the Coroners (Fees and Allowances) Rules 1971(**c**), as amended(**d**), for the words "£4·75" there shall be substituted the words "£5·50" and for the words "£2·375" in both places where they occur there shall be substituted the words "£2·75".

Robert Carr,
One of Her Majesty's Principal
Secretaries of State.

Home Office,
  Whitehall.
1st July 1973.

(**a**) 1954 c. 31.　　　　　　　　(**b**) S.I. 1972/980 (1972 II, p. 3061).
(**c**) S.I. 1971/108 (1971 I, p. 200).
(**d**) S.I. 1972/980, 1973/921 (1972 II, p. 3061; 1973 II, p. 2795).

EXPLANATORY NOTE

(This Note is not part of the Rules.)

These Rules increase the maximum daily loss allowances which may be paid to a witness attending at an inquest from £4·75 to £5·50 if the time involved exceeds 4 hours or if he necessarily loses more than half a day's remuneration, or if the expense incurred necessarily exceeds £2·75, and from £2·375 to £2·75 in other cases.

STATUTORY INSTRUMENTS

1973 No. 1174

JUSTICE OF THE PEACE

The Justices' Allowances (Amendment) Regulations 1973

Made - - -	*1st July* 1973
Laid before Parliament	*16th July* 1973
Coming into Operation	*7th August* 1973

In exercise of the powers conferred upon me by section 8(6) and (7) of the Justices of the Peace Act 1949(**a**), as extended by section 4 of the Justices of the Peace Act 1968(**b**), I hereby make the following Regulations:—

1. These Regulations may be cited as the Justices' Allowances (Amendment) Regulations 1973 and shall come into operation on 7th August 1973.

2. The Justices' Allowances (Amendment) Regulations 1971(**c**), are hereby revoked.

3. In Regulation 5 of the Justices' Allowances Regulations 1971(**d**), as amended(**c**) for the words "£2·375" and "£4·75" there shall be substituted the words "£2·75" and "£5·50" respectively.

Robert Carr,
One of Her Majesty's Principal
Secretaries of State.

Home Office,
Whitehall.
1st July 1973.

EXPLANATORY NOTE

(This Note is not part of the Regulations.)

These Regulations increase the maximum rates of financial loss allowances payable to justices of the peace. The new maximum rates are £5·50, if the time involved exceeds 4 hours in a 24 hour period, and £2·75 in other cases.

(**a**) 1949 c. 101.   (**b**) 1968 c. 69.
(**c**) S.I. 1971/1975 (1971 III, p. 5648).   (**d**) S.I. 1971/413 (1971 I, p. 1217).

STATUTORY INSTRUMENTS

1973 No. 1175

PROBATION AND AFTER-CARE

The Probation (Allowances) (Amendment) Rules 1973

Made - - -		*1st July* 1973
Coming into Operation		*7th August* 1973

In exercise of the powers conferred upon me by Schedule 5 to the Criminal Justice Act 1948(a), as extended by section 36 of the Justices of the Peace Act 1949(b) (as amended by section 4 of the Justices of the Peace Act 1968(c) and applied by section 52(5) of the Criminal Justice Act 1972(d)), I hereby make the following Rules:—

1. These Rules may be cited as the Probation (Allowances) (Amendment) Rules 1973 and shall come into operation on 7th August 1973.

2. The Probation (Allowances) (Amendment) Rules 1971(e), are hereby revoked.

3. In Rule 5 of the Probation (Allowances) Rules 1971(f), as amended(e), for the words "£2·375" and "£4·75" there shall be substituted the words "£2·75" and "£5·50" respectively.

Robert Carr,
One of Her Majesty's Principal
Secretaries of State.

Home Office,
 Whitehall.
1st July 1973.

EXPLANATORY NOTE

(This Note is not part of the Rules.)

These Rules increase the maximum rates of financial loss allowances payable to members of probation and after-care committees, case committees and community service committees. The new rates are £5·50, if the time involved exceeds 4 hours in a 24 hour period, and £2·75 in other cases.

(a) 1948 c. 58.	(b) 1949 c. 101.
(c) 1968 c. 69.	(d) 1972 c. 71.
(e) S.I. 1971/1976 (1971 III, p. 5649).	(f) S.I. 1971/414 (1971 I, p. 1225).

STATUTORY INSTRUMENTS

1973 No. 1176 (S.91)

EDUCATION, SCOTLAND

The Education Authority Bursaries (Scotland) (Amendment) Regulations 1973

Made - - -		*4th July* 1973
Laid before Parliament		*13th July* 1973
Coming into Operation		*3rd August* 1973

In exercise of the powers conferred upon me by sections 49(3) and 144(5) of the Education (Scotland) Act 1962(a) and of all other powers enabling me in that behalf, I hereby make the following regulations:—

Citation, construction and commencement

1. These regulations, which may be cited as the Education Authority Bursaries (Scotland) (Amendment) Regulations 1973, shall be construed as one with the Education Authority Bursaries (Scotland) Regulations 1969(b) as amended(c) (hereinafter referred to as "the principal regulations") and shall come into operation on 3rd August 1973.

Amendment of principal regulations

2.—(1) Part 1 of Schedule 2 (assessment of estimated expenditure in relation to full-time further education bursaries) to the principal regulations shall be varied as follows:—

(*a*) in paragraph 1(6) for the sums of "£5" and "£8" there shall be substituted respectively the sums of "£5·50" and "£8·67";

(*b*) in paragraph 1(7) for the sum of "£5" there shall be substituted the sum of "£5·50";

(*c*) in paragraph 1(8) for the sum of "£2·55" there shall be substituted the sum of "£2·76";

(*d*) in paragraph 3(i) for the sum of "£3·80" there shall be substituted the sum of "£4·13";

(*e*) in paragraph 3(ii) for the sum of "£2·05" there shall be substituted the sum of "£2·15".

(2) In Part 2 of Schedule 2 (assessment of contribution in relation to full-time further education bursaries) to the principal regulations for paragraph 6(*b*) there shall be substituted—

(a) 1962 c. 47.   (b) S.I. 1969/841 (1969 II, p. 2349).
(c) S.I. 1972/844 (1972 II, p. 2690).

"(*b*) in the assessment of a category B bursary, if the balance of income is not less than £1,500 and not more than £2,000, the contribution shall be £30 with the addition of £1 for every complete £5 by which the balance of income exceeds £1,500; if the balance of income is not less than £2,000 the contribution shall be £130 with the addition of £1 for every complete £10 by which the balance of income exceeds £2,000."

Gordon Campbell,
One of Her Majesty's Principal
Secretaries of State.

St. Andrew's House,
Edinburgh.

4th July 1973.

EXPLANATORY NOTE

(This Note is not part of the Regulations.)

These Regulations amend the bursary rates and the parental contribution scale which are prescribed by the Education Authority Bursaries (Scotland) Regulations 1969, as amended, to be applied by education authorities in the calculation of bursaries for students who are over eighteen and who are attending full-time further education courses.

STATUTORY INSTRUMENTS

1973 No. 1177 (S.92)

REPRESENTATION OF THE PEOPLE

The Representation of the People (Scotland) Regulations 1973

Made - - -	*17th May* 1973
Laid before Parliament	*13th June* 1973
Coming into Operation	*17th July* 1973

In exercise of the powers conferred on me by sections 42 and 171(5) of and Schedule 4 to the Representation of the People Act 1949(a) and of all other powers enabling me in that behalf, I hereby make the following regulations:—

1.—(1) These regulations may be cited as the Representation of the People (Scotland) Regulations 1973 and shall come into operation fourteen days after they have been approved by both Houses of Parliament.

(2) The Interpretation Act 1889(b) shall apply for the interpretation of these regulations as it applies for the interpretation of an Act of Parliament.

2. After regulation 21(*a*) of the Representation of the People (Scotland) Regulations 1969(c) there shall be inserted the following paragraph:—

"(*aa*) one copy of the register for any constituency or part of a constituency included in the registration area to the Member of Parliament for that constituency;".

Gordon Campbell,
One of Her Majesty's Principal
Secretaries of State.

St. Andrew's House,
Edinburgh.
17th May 1973.

(a) 1949 c. 68.   (b) 1889 c. 63.
(c) S.I. 1969/912 (1969 II, p. 2726).

EXPLANATORY NOTE

(This Note is not part of the Regulations.)

These Regulations amend the Representation of the People (Scotland) Regulations 1969 so as to require the registration officer on being requested to supply without fee one copy of the register of electors for any constituency or part of a constituency included in the registration area to the Member of Parliament for that constituency.

STATUTORY INSTRUMENTS

1973 No. 1178

ANIMALS

The Export of Horses and Ponies (Increase in Minimum Values) Order 1973

Made - - - -	*5th July* 1973
Coming into Operation	*1st August* 1973

The Minister of Agriculture, Fisheries and Food and the Secretary of State, acting jointly. in exercise of the powers conferred by sections 37(3), 37(4A) and 85(1) of the Diseases of Animals Act 1950(a), as extended by section 1(*a*) of the Ponies Act 1969(b) and adapted to air transport by section 11 of, and Schedule 2 to, the Agriculture (Miscellaneous Provisions) Act 1954(c), and now vested in them(d), and of all their other enabling powers, hereby order as follows:—

Citation, extent and commencement

1. This order, which may be cited as the Export of Horses and Ponies (Increase in Minimum Values) Order 1973, applies to Great Britain, and shall come into operation on 1st August 1973.

Interpretation

2.—(1) In this order, unless the context otherwise requires—

"the Act" means the Diseases of Animals Act 1950, as amended and extended by the Ponies Act 1969;

"pony" means any horse not more than $14\frac{1}{2}$ hands in height, except a foal travelling with its dam if the dam is over $14\frac{1}{2}$ hands.

(2) The Interpretation Act 1889(e) applies to the interpretation of this order as it applies to the interpretation of an Act of Parliament, and as if this order and the order hereby partly revoked were Acts of Parliament.

Increase in minimum values of certain horses and of ponies for the purposes of section 37 of the Act

3.—(1) For the purposes of section 37(3) of the Act, the minimum value of a horse of a category referred to in that subsection shall be, in the case of—

(*a*) a heavy draft horse, £300

(a) 1950 c. 36.
(c) 1954 c. 39.
(e) 1889 c. 63.

(b) 1969 c. 28.
(d) S.I. 1955/554 (1955 I, p. 1200).

(b) a vanner, mule or jennet,   £250

(c) an ass,   £120

(2) For the purposes of section 37(4A)(a) of the Act, the minimum value of a pony of a category referred to in that paragraph shall be, in the case of a pony—

(a) over 12 hands in height,   £160

(b) not exceeding 12 hands in height (other than a pony of the Shetland breed not exceeding 10½ hands in height),   £120

(c) of the Shetland breed not exceeding 10½ hands in height, £60

Revocation

4. Article 5 of the Export of Horses (Veterinary Examination) Order 1966(a) (prescription of minimum values of certain categories of horses for the purposes of section 37 of the Act) is hereby revoked.

In Witness whereof the Official Seal of the Minister of Agriculture, Fisheries and Food is hereunto affixed on 5th July 1973.

(L.S.)

Joseph Godber,
Minister of Agriculture, Fisheries and Food.

5th July 1973.

Gordon Campbell,
Secretary of State for Scotland.

EXPLANATORY NOTE
(This Note is not part of the Order.)

This order increases the minimum value of certain horses and of ponies for the purposes respectively of section 37(3) and section 37(4A) of the Diseases of Animals Act 1950. In the case of horses to which section 37(3) applies, before exportation from Great Britain will be permitted a veterinary inspector must be satisfied that the horse in question is worth not less than the prescribed minimum value. In the case of ponies, the Minister of Agriculture, Fisheries and Food or (in Scotland) the Secretary of State must be similarly satisfied before authorising the exportation of a pony.

(a) S.I. 1966/507 (1966 I, p. 1071).

STATUTORY INSTRUMENTS

1973 No. 1185 (C.28) (S.93)

NATIONAL HEALTH SERVICE, SCOTLAND

The National Health Service Reorganisation Act 1973 (Commencement No. 1) (Scotland) Order 1973

Made - - -	*5th July* 1973
Laid before Parliament	*2nd August* 1973
Coming into Operation	*5th July* 1973

In exercise of the powers conferred upon me by section 58(3) of the National Health Service Reorganisation Act 1973(a), I hereby make the following Order:—

1. This Order may be cited as the National Health Service Reorganisation Act 1973 (Commencement No. 1) (Scotland) Order 1973.

2. The following provisions of the National Health Service Reorganisation Act 1973 shall come into operation on 5th July 1973:

    (*a*) paragraphs 41, 138 to 140 and 142 to 150 of Schedule 4

    (*b*) the entries in Schedule 5 relating respectively to the National Health Service (Scotland) Act 1947(b) and the National Health Service (Scotland) Act 1972(c).

Gordon Campbell,
One of Her Majesty's Principal
Secretaries of State.

St. Andrew's House,
Edinburgh.
5th July 1973.

EXPLANATORY NOTE
(*This Note is not part of the Order.*)

This Order—

    (*a*) brings into operation the provisions of paragraph 41 of Schedule 4 to the National Health Service Reorganisation Act 1973, under which Regulations made by the Secretary of State relating to the payment of compensation for loss of the right to sell a medical practice may provide for the interest payable on any amount of compensation to be paid at a later date than that compensation;

    (*b*) incorporates in the National Health Service (Scotland) Act 1972 the minor and consequential amendments and repeals made by Schedules 4 and 5 to the National Health Service Reorganisation Act 1973.

(**a**) 1973 c. 32.	(**b**) 1947 c. 27.	(**c**) 1972 c. 58.

STATUTORY INSTRUMENTS

1973 No. 1187 (C.29)

NATIONAL HEALTH SERVICE, ENGLAND AND WALES

The Health Services and Public Health Act 1968 (Commencement No. 6) Order 1973

Made - - - *6th July* 1973

The Secretary of State for Social Services, in exercise of his powers under section 79(2) of the Health Services and Public Health Act 1968(a) and of all other powers enabling him in that behalf, hereby orders as follows:—

1. This Order may be cited as the Health Services and Public Health Act 1968 (Commencement No. 6) Order 1973.

2. The appointed day for the coming into force of the provisions of section 26 of the Health Services and Public Health Act 1968 shall be 1st September 1973.

Keith Joseph,
Secretary of State for Social Services.

6th July 1973.

EXPLANATORY NOTE

(This Note is not part of the Order.)

This Order appoints 1st September 1973 as the appointed day for the coming into force of section 26 of the Health Services and Public Health Act 1968 which relates to enquiries in connection with removals of disqualifications of practitioners and others.

This Order applies to England and Wales only.

(a) 1968 c. 46.

STATUTORY INSTRUMENTS

1973 No. 1189

CIVIL AVIATION

The Carriage by Air (Sterling Equivalents) Order 1973

Made - - -	*6th July* 1973
Coming into Operation	*27th July* 1973

The Secretary of State in exercise of the powers conferred by section 4(4) of the Carriage by Air Act 1961(**a**) and under that provision as applied by Article 6 of the Carriage by Air Acts (Applications of Provisions) Order 1967(**b**) and now vested in him(**c**) and of all other powers enabling him in that behalf hereby orders as follows:

1. This Order may be cited as the Carriage by Air (Sterling Equivalents) Order 1973 and shall come into operation on 27th July 1973.

2. This Order supersedes the Carriage by Air (Sterling Equivalents) Order 1968(**d**).

3. The amounts shown in column 2 of the following Table are hereby specified as amounts to be taken for the purposes of Article 22 in the First Schedule to the Carriage by Air Act 1961 and of that Article as applied by the Carriage by Air Acts (Application of Provisions) Order 1967 as equivalent to the sums respectively expressed in francs on the same line in column 1 of that Table:

TABLE

Amount of francs	Sterling equivalent
	£
250	7·78
5,000	155·47
125,000	3886·72
250,000	7773·43
875,000	27206·98

G. R. Sunderland,
An Assistant Secretary,
Department of Trade and Industry.

6th July 1973.

(**a**) 1961 c. 27.   (**b**) S.I. 1967/480 (1967 I, p. 1475).
(**c**) S.I. 1966/741, 1970/1537 (1966 II, p. 1732; 1970 III, p. 5293).
(**d**) S.I. 1968/1316 (1968 II, p. 3647).

EXPLANATORY NOTE ﹐
(This Note is not part of the Order.)

This Order specifies the sterling equivalents of amounts expressed in gold francs as the limit of the air carriers liability under the Warsaw Convention of 1929, and under that convention as amended by the Hague Protocol of 1955, as well as under corresponding provisions applying to carriage by air to which the Convention and Protocol do not apply.   It supersedes the Carriage by Air (Sterling Equivalents) Order 1968.

The sterling equivalents have been calculated on the basis of current market rates for sterling in terms of the US dollar on the basis of the proposed valuation of gold at US $ 42·222 per fine ounce.

1973 No. 1190

MERCHANT SHIPPING

The Merchant Shipping (Limitation of Liability) (Sterling Equivalents) Order 1973

Made - - - *6th July* 1973

Coming into Operation *27th July* 1973

The Secretary of State, in exercise of the powers conferred by section 1(3) of the Merchant Shipping (Liability of Shipowners and Others) Act 1958(a) and now vested in him(b) and of all other powers enabling him in that behalf, hereby orders as follows:—

1. This Order may be cited as the Merchant Shipping (Limitation of Liability) (Sterling Equivalents) Order 1973 and shall come into operation on 27th July 1973.

2. The Interpretation Act 1889(c) shall apply to the interpretation of this Order as it applies to the interpretation of an Act of Parliament and as if this Order and the Order hereby revoked were Acts of Parliament.

3. For the purposes of section 1 of the Merchant Shipping (Liability of Shipowners and Others) Act 1958, £96·3911 and £31·0939 are hereby specified as the amounts which shall be taken as equivalent to 3,100 and 1,000 gold francs respectively.

4. The Merchant Shipping (Limitation of Liability) (Sterling Equivalents) Order 1972(d) is hereby revoked.

G. R. W. Brigstocke,
An Under-Secretary of
6th July 1973. The Department of Trade and Industry.

(a) 1958 c. 62. (b) S.I. 1970/1537 (1970 III, p. 5293).
(c) 1889 c. 63. (d) S.I. 1972/734 (1972 II, p. 2329).

EXPLANATORY NOTE

(This Note is not part of the Order.)

Under section 503 of the Merchant Shipping Act 1894 (c.60), and section 2 of the Merchant Shipping (Liability of Shipowners and Others) Act 1900 (c.32) as amended by the Merchant Shipping (Liability of Shipowners and Others) Act 1958, shipowners, harbour authorities and others may limit their liability at amounts expressed in gold francs. This Order specifies the sterling equivalents of the gold franc amounts. These have been calculated on the basis of current market rates for sterling in terms of the US dollar on the basis of the proposed valuation of gold at US $42·222 per fine ounce.

STATUTORY INSTRUMENTS

1973 No. 1191

NATIONAL HEALTH SERVICE, ENGLAND AND WALES

The National Health Service (Determination of Regions) Order 1973

Made - - -		*9th July* 1973
Laid before Parliament		16*th July* 1973
Coming into Operation		6*th August* 1973

The Secretary of State for Social Services, in exercise of the powers conferred on him by section 5(1) of the National Health Service Reorganisation Act 1973(**a**) and of all other powers enabling him in that behalf, hereby makes the following Order:—

1. This Order may be cited as the National Health Service (Determination of Regions) Order 1973 and shall come into operation on 6th August 1973.

2. Each of the regions described in column (3) of the Schedule to this Order and respectively numbered 1 to 14 in column (1) of the Schedule shall be a region for which a Regional Health Authority shall be constituted and each such region shall be known by the title set out in column (2) of the Schedule.

3. References in column (3) of the Schedule to a county are references to such county as described in the Local Government Act 1972(**b**) and references therein to a London borough are references to such a borough as incorporated in pursuance of the London Government Act 1963(**c**) and as described in that Act, in the Greater London, Kent and Surrey Order 1968(**d**) and in the Greater London and Surrey Order 1970(**e**).

Keith Joseph,
Secretary of State for Social Services.

9th July 1973.

(**a**) 1973 c. 32.
(**c**) 1963 c. 33.
(**e**) S.I. 1970/397.

(**b**) 1972 c. 70.
(**d**) S.I. 1968/2020.

SCHEDULE

HEALTH AUTHORITY REGIONS

Column (1) No. of Region	Column (2) Name of Region	Column (3) Description of Region
1.	Northern Region	The metropolitan county of Tyne and Wear and the non-metropolitan counties of Cleveland, Cumbria, Durham and Northumberland.
2.	Yorkshire Region	The metropolitan county of West Yorkshire and the non-metropolitan counties of Humberside and North Yorkshire.
3.	Trent Region	The metropolitan county of South Yorkshire and the non-metropolitan counties of Derbyshire, Leicestershire, Lincolnshire and Nottinghamshire.
4.	East Anglia Region	The non-metropolitan counties of Cambridgeshire, Norfolk and Suffolk.
5.	North West Thames Region	The non-metropolitan counties of Bedfordshire and Hertfordshire and the London boroughs of Barnet, Brent, Ealing, Hammersmith, Harrow, Hillingdon, Hounslow, Kensington and Chelsea and Westminster.
6.	North East Thames Region	The non-metropolitan county of Essex, the London boroughs of Barking, Camden, Enfield, Hackney, Haringey, Havering, Islington, Newham, Redbridge, Tower Hamlets and Waltham Forest, and the City of London.
7.	South East Thames Region	The non-metropolitan counties of East Sussex and Kent and the London boroughs of Bexley, Bromley, Greenwich, Lambeth, Lewisham and Southwark.
8.	South West Thames Region	The non-metropolitan counties of Surrey and West Sussex and the London Boroughs of Croydon, Kingston-upon-Thames, Merton, Richmond-upon-Thames, Sutton and Wandsworth.
9.	Wessex Region	The non-metropolitan counties of Dorset, Hampshire, Isle of Wight and Wiltshire.
10.	Oxford Region	The non-metropolitan counties of Berkshire, Buckinghamshire, Northamptonshire and Oxfordshire.
11.	South Western Region	The non-metropolitan counties of Avon, Cornwall, Devon, Gloucestershire and Somerset.
12.	West Midlands Region	The metropolitan county of West Midlands and the non-metropolitan counties of Hereford and Worcester, Salop, Staffordshire and Warwickshire.

Column (1) No. of Region	Column (2) Name of Region	Column (3) Description of Region
13.	Mersey Region	The metropolitan county of Merseyside and the non-metropolitan county of Cheshire.
14.	North Western Region	The metropolitan county of greater Manchester and the non-metropolitan county of Lancashire.

EXPLANATORY NOTE

(This Note is not part of the Order.)

This Order determines regions in England for which Regional Health Authorities are to be established under the National Health Service Reorganisation Act 1973.

STATUTORY INSTRUMENTS

1973 No. 1192

NATIONAL HEALTH SERVICE, ENGLAND AND WALES

The National Health Service (Constitution of Regional Health Authorities) Order 1973

Made - - -	*9th July* 1973
Laid before Parliament	*16th July* 1973
Coming into Operation	*6th August* 1973

The Secretary of State for Social Services, in exercise of the powers conferred on him by section 5(1) of the National Health Service Reorganisation Act 1973(**a**) and. of all other powers enabling him in that behalf, hereby makes the following Order: —

Citation, commencement and interpretation

1.—(1) This Order may be cited as the National Health Service (Constitution of Regional Health Authorities) Order 1973 and shall come into operation on 6th August 1973.

(2) In this Order: —

"The Act of 1973" means the National Health Service Reorganisation Act 1973;

"Authority" means Regional Health Authority;

"The Determination of Regions Order" means the National Health Service (Determination of Regions) Order 1973(**b**).

(3) The rules for the construction of Acts of Parliament contained in the Interpretation Act 1889(**c**) shall apply for the purpose of the interpretation of this Order as they apply for the purpose of the interpretation of an Act of Parliament.

Constitution of Authorities

2. There is hereby constituted an Authority for each of the regions set out in the Schedule to the Determination of Regions Order, and numbered respectively 1 to 14 in that Schedule, for the purpose of exercising any functions exercisable by such an Authority by virtue of any provision of the Health Service Acts and for the purpose of exercising, on behalf of the Secretary of State, such of his functions relating to the health service as are specified in directions given by him under section 7 of the Act of 1973.

Titles of Authorities

3. The Authority for each of the said regions numbered 1 to 14 in the

---

(**a**) 1973 c. 32.   (**b**) S.I. 1973/1191 (1973 II, p. 3566).
(**c**) 1889 c. 63.

Schedule to the Determination of Regions Order and correspondingly numbered in column (1) of the Schedule hereto shall be known by the title set out in column (2) of the Schedule hereto opposite the number in column (1).

Membership of Authorities

4. Each Authority shall consist of a chairman and such number of other members as is shown in column (3) of the Schedule hereto opposite the number of the region in column (1) all of whom shall be appointed by the Secretary of State in accordance with the provisions of Part I of Schedule 1 to the Act of 1973.

Keith Joseph,
Secretary of State for Social Services.

9th July 1973.

SCHEDULE

Column (1) Number of Region	Column (2) Title of Regional Authority	Column (3) Number of Members (Excluding Chairman)
1.	Northern Regional Health Authority	16
2.	Yorkshire Regional Health Authority	16
3.	Trent Regional Health Authority	18
4.	East Anglia Regional Health Authority	14
5.	North West Thames Regional Health Authority	16
6.	North East Thames Regional Health Authority	15
7.	South East Thames Regional Health Authority	15
8.	South West Thames Regional Health Authority	14
9.	Wessex Regional Health Authority	14
10.	Oxford Regional Health Authority	14
11.	South Western Regional Health Authority	15
12.	West Midlands Regional Health Authority	16
13.	Mersey Regional Health Authority	14
14.	North Western Regional Health Authority	16

EXPLANATORY NOTE

(This Note is not part of the Order.)

This Order establishes Regional Health Authorities in England for the purposes of regional administration of the National Health Service as reorganised under the National Health Service Reorganisation Act 1973.

STATUTORY INSTRUMENTS

1973 No. 1193

ROAD TRAFFIC

The Designation of Approval Marks (European Communities) Regulations 1973

Made - - - -	*3rd July* 1973
Laid before Parliament	*20th July* 1973
Coming into Operation	*10th August* 1973

The Secretary of State for the Environment, as the designated Minister under the European Communities (Designation) Order 1972(a), in exercise of the powers conferred by section 2(2) of the European Communities Act 1972(b) and of all other enabling powers, hereby makes the following Regulations:—

1. These Regulations shall come into operation on 10th August 1973, and may be cited as the Designation of Approval Marks (European Communities) Regulations 1973.

2. Section 63(1) of the Road Traffic Act 1972(c) shall have effect as if after the words "is a party" there were inserted the words "or a Community obligation".

Signed by authority of the Secretary of State.

John Peyton,
Minister for Transport Industries,
Department of the Environment.

3rd July 1973.

(a) S.I. 1972/1811 (1972 III, p. 5216).　　(b) 1972 c. 68.
(c) 1972 c. 20.

EXPLANATORY NOTE

(This Note is not part of the Regulations.)

These Regulations amend section 63(1) of the Road Traffic Act 1972, which enables the Secretary of State to designate certain markings as approval marks, with the result that such markings become a trade description for the purposes of the Trade Descriptions Act 1968 (c. 29). The marks to which section 63 applies are markings for which an international agreement, to which the United Kingdom is a party, provides, are to be applied—

    (i) to motor vehicle parts of any description to indicate conformity with a type approved by any country; or

    (ii) to a motor vehicle to indicate that the vehicle is fitted with motor vehicle parts of any description and either that the parts conform with a type approved by any country or that the vehicle is such that as so fitted it conforms with a type so approved,

and in relation to which such an agreement provides for motor vehicle parts or, as the case may be motor vehicles, bearing those markings to be recognised as complying with the requirements imposed by the law of another country. These Regulations extend the power to designate markings to those for which an obligation arising by or under the Treaties (with the meaning of the European Communities Act 1972) makes similar provision.

STATUTORY INSTRUMENTS

1973 No. 1194

MERCHANDISE MARKS
The Motor Vehicles (Designation of Approval Marks) (No. 2) Regulations 1973

Made - - - -	*3rd July* 1973
Laid before Parliament	*20th July* 1973
Coming into Operation	*10th August* 1973

The Secretary of State for the Environment, in exercise of his powers under section 63(1) of the Road Traffic Act 1972(a), as amended by the Designation of Approval Marks (European Communities) Regulations 1973(b) and of all other enabling powers, and after consulation with representative organisations in accordance with the provisions of section 199(2) of the Act, hereby makes the following Regulations:—

1.—(1) These Regulations shall come into operation on 10th August 1973 and may be cited as the Motor Vehicles (Designation of Approval Marks) (No. 2) Regulations 1973.

(2) The Interpretation Act 1889(c) shall apply for the interpretation of these Regulations as it applies for the interpretation of an Act of Parliament.

2. The Secretary of State hereby designates as approval marks the markings which, subject to Part II of the Schedule to these Regulations, are in the same form as, and of sizes not less than, the markings shown in the diagrams in column 1 of Part 1 of that Schedule and are such that the ratios between the dimensions of the said markings are maintained, each of the said markings being a marking for which provision is made by the Directives issued under the EEC Treaty and specified in column 2 of Part I of that Schedule in relation to that marking being such provision as is mentioned in section 63(1)(a) and (b) of the Road Traffic Act 1972 in connection with the motor vehicle part specified in column 3 of Part I of that Schedule in relation to that marking.

Signed by authority of the Secretary of State.

John Peyton,
Minister for Transport Industries,
Department of the Environment.

3rd July 1973.

(a) 1972 c. 20.
(c) 1889 c. 63.

(b) S.I. 1973/1193 (1973 II, p. 3571).

THE SCHEDULE
PART I—DIAGRAMS

1. Diagram showing marking	2. Directive issued under the EEC Treaty	3. Motor Vehicle Part to which marking applied
AUDIBLE WARNING DEVICE — THE DIMENSIONS OF THE APPROVAL MARK ARE IN MILLIMETRES; THEY ARE MINIMUM DIMENSIONS AND THE RATIOS MUST BE MAINTAINED	The European Communities Council Directive of 27th July 1970 on the approximation of the laws of member states relating to audible warning devices for motor vehicles	Audible warning devices
REAR VIEW MIRRORS	The European Communities Council Directive of 1st March 1971 on the harmonisation of Member States' legislation on rear-view mirrors of motor vehicles	Rear-view mirrors

PART II—VARIATIONS OF MARKINGS

1. The number shown inside the rectangle will be varied, where appropriate, so as to be the distinguishing symbol assigned to the country which has granted the approval, that is to say 1 for Germany, 2 for France, 3 for Italy, 4 for the Netherlands, 6 for Belgium, 11 for the United Kingdom, 12 for Luxembourg, IRL for Ireland and DK for Denmark.

2. The number shown outside and immediately below the rectangle shall be varied, where appropriate, to correspond to the number of the approval document issued for the prototype vehicle component concerned.

3. The Roman numeral shown outside and immediately above the rectangle in relation to the marking for rear-view mirrors will be varied, where appropriate, to be the Roman numeral signifying the class of rear-view mirror concerned, that is to say I for interior rear-view mirrors, II for exterior rear-view mirrors for all category A vehicles and III for exterior rear-view mirrors for all category B vehicles. In this paragraph category A vehicles are those with a maximum laden weight exceeding 3·5 metric tons and category B vehicles are those with a maximum laden weight not exceeding 3·5 metric tons.

EXPLANATORY NOTE

(This Note is not part of the Regulations.)

Section 63(1) of the Road Traffic Act 1972, as amended by the Designation of Approval Marks (European Communities) Regulations 1973, provides (inter alia) that where a Community obligation provides for markings to be applied to motor vehicle parts of any description to indicate conformity with a type approved by any country and for motor vehicles parts bearing those markings to be recognised as complying with the requirements imposed by the law of another country the Secretary of State for the Environment may by regulations designate the markings as approval marks. Section 63 of the Road Traffic Act 1972 also provides that any markings so designated shall be deemed for the purpose of the Trade Description Act 1968 (c.29) to be a trade description and that it shall be an offence under that Act to apply an approval mark without proper authority.

These Regulations designate for the purposes of the said section 63 as approval marks, markings complying with the provisions of the Schedule to these Regulations and in respect of which Community Directives of 27th July 1970 (70/388/EEC) and 1st March 1971 (71/127/EEC) make provision for such markings to be applied to audible warning devices and rear-view mirrors being respectively, motor vehicle parts.

STATUTORY INSTRUMENTS

1973 No. 1196

CIVIL AVIATION

The Civil Aviation (Route Charges for Navigation Services) (Amendment) (No. 3) Regulations 1973

Made - - - -	*8th July* 1973
Laid before Parliament	*11th July* 1973
Coming into Operation	*1st August* 1973

Whereas in pursuance of tariffs approved under the Eurocontrol Convention(a) and under the Multilateral Agreement relating to the Collection of Route Charges concluded at Brussels on 8th September 1970(b) (being an international agreement to which the United Kingdom is a party), the Secretary of State has determined that the rates of charges, payable to the Eurocontrol Organisation under the Civil Aviation (Route Charges for Navigation Services) Regulations 1971(c), as amended(d), in respect of the navigation services specified in the said Regulations, shall be further amended as provided in the following Regulations:

Now, therefore, the Secretary of State in exercise of his powers under sections 4 and 7(1) of the Civil Aviation (Eurocontrol) Act 1962(e), section 15(3) of the Civil Aviation Act 1968(f), and paragraph 6 of Schedule 10 to the Civil Aviation Act 1971(g), and of all other powers enabling him in that behalf, hereby makes the following Regulations:

Citation and Operation

1. These Regulations may be cited as the Civil Aviation (Route Charges for Navigation Services) (Amendment) (No. 3) Regulations 1973 and shall come into operation on 1st August 1973.

Interpretation

2. The Interpretation Act 1889(h) applies for the purpose of the interpretation of these Regulations as it applies for the purpose of the interpretation of an Act of Parliament.

Amendment of Regulations

3. The Civil Aviation (Route Charges for Navigation Services) Regulations 1971, as amended, shall be further amended as follows:

(1) In Regulation 6:—

    (*a*) in subparagraph (1) for "2·6734 United States dollars" there shall be substituted "2·9704 United States dollars";

(a) Cmnd. 2114.   (b) Cmnd. 4916.
(c) S.I. 1971/1715 (1971 III, p. 4666).
(d) S.I. 1972/108, 905 (1972 I, p. 285; II, p. 2848).
(e) 1962 c. 8.   (f) 1968 c. 61.
(g) 1971 c. 75.   (h) 1889 c. 63.

(b) in subparagraph (7) for "1·4147 United States dollars instead of 2·6734 United States dollars" there shall be substituted "1·5719 United States dollars instead of 2·9704 United States dollars".

(2) For the Schedule there shall be substituted the Schedule to these Regulations.

Michael Heseltine,
Minister for Aerospace and Shipping,
Department of Trade and Industry.

8th July 1973.

SCHEDULE

(1) Aerodromes of departure (or of first destination) situated	(2) Aerodromes of first destination (or of departure)	(3) Amount of the charge in US dollars
between 14°W and 110°W and North of 55°N (ZONE I)	Belfast	9·86
	Berlin	52·41
	Brussels	38·88
	Coventry	29·02
	Dusseldorf	45·08
	Edinburgh	17·11
	Frankfurt/Main	50·63
	Glasgow	13·90
	Gutersloh	46·28
	Hanover	48·85
	Lahr	46·11
	London	30·03
	Luxembourg	45·35
	Manchester	22·81
	Mildenhall	31·04
	Ostend	36·54
	Prestwick	17·05
	Shannon	2·18
	Wiesbaden	50·30
	Woodbridge	30·57
	Zurich	59·74
West of 110°W and North of 55°N (ZONE II)	Amsterdam	12·33
	Hamburg	3·65
	London	33·57
between 30°W and 110°W and between 28°N and 55°N (ZONE III)	Amsterdam	29·91
	Athens	38·15
	Barcelona	29·44
	Belfast	8·77
	Bordeaux	17·97
	Brize Norton	14·39
	Brussels	28·58
	Casablanca	8·80

(1) Aerodromes of departure (or of first destination) situated	(2) Aerodromes of first destination (or of departure)	(3) Amount of the charge tin US dollars
(ZONE III) *continued*	Copenhagen	23·50
	Cologne-Bonn	33·63
	Dublin	6·08
	East Midlands	16·57
	Frankfurt/Main	36·71
	Geneva	28·85
	Hamburg	41·21
	Hanover	43·30
	Helsinki	19·25
	Lahr	32·75
	Las Palmas (Canary Islands)	11·54
	Lisbon	9·62
	London	18·72
	Luton	16·76
	Luxembourg	29·47
	Lyneham	13·90
	Madrid	21·97
	Malaga	22·72
	Manchester	14·94
	Marham	21·59
	Milan	28·85
	Mildenhall	20·35
	Munich	46·86
	Naples	46·19
	Nice	21·90
	Palma (Majorca)	34·47
	Paris	22·38
	Prague	43·16
	Prestwick	10·49
	Rabat	8·80
	Rome	41·78
	Rota	18·63
	St. Mawgan	11·48
	Shannon	3·41
	Sollingen	31·25
	Stockholm	18·09
	Stuttgart	39·62
	Tel Aviv/Lod	38·15
	Thorney Island	16·65
	Turin	31·71
	Warsaw	28·10
	Vienna	61·43
	Zagreb	56·19
	Zurich	31·27
West of 110°W and between 28°N and 55°N (ZONE IV)	Amsterdam	35·60
	Berlin	52·41
	Brussels	33·04
	Dusseldorf	43·15
	Frankfurt/Main	48·35
	London	29·22
	Paris	30·74
	Prestwick	13·72
	Shannon	2·71

(1) Aerodromes of departure (or of first destination) situated	(2) Aerodromes of first destination (or of departure)	(3) Amount of the charge in US dollars
West of 30°W and between the equator and 28°N (ZONE V)	Amsterdam	29·91
	Casablanca	5·79
	Frankfurt/Main	36·71
	Las Palmas (Canary Islands)	24·79
	Lisbon	10·38
	London	16·62
	Luxembourg	18·56
	Madrid	23·10
	Milan	29·79
	Paris	13·70
	Rome	27·05
	Shannon	3·96
	Zurich	38·96

EXPLANATORY NOTE

(This Note is not part of the Regulations.)

These Regulations amend the Civil Aviation (Route Charges for Navigation Services) Regulations 1971, as amended, so as to give effect to new tariffs in relation to flights which enter the airspace, specified in the 1971 Regulations, where the United Kingdom provides air navigation services. The tariffs have been agreed internationally under the Eurocontrol Convention and the Multilateral Agreement relating to the Collection of Route Charges. They reflect recent changes in the effective parity relationships of currencies.

STATUTORY INSTRUMENTS

1973 No. 1197

INDUSTRIAL TRAINING

The Industrial Training Levy (Cotton and Allied Textiles) Order 1973

Made - - -	*9th July* 1973
Laid before Parliament	*19th July* 1973
Coming into Operation	*15th August* 1973

The Secretary of State after approving proposals submitted by the Cotton and Allied Textiles Industry Training Board for the imposition of a further levy on employers in the cotton and allied textiles industry and in exercise of powers conferred by section 4 of the Industrial Training Act 1964(a) and now vested in him(b), and of all other powers enabling him in that behalf hereby makes the following Order:—

Title and commencement

1. This Order may be cited as the Industrial Training Levy (Cotton and Allied Textiles) Order 1973 and shall come into operation on 15th August 1973.

Interpretation

2.—(1) In this Order unless the context otherwise requires:—

(*a*) "agriculture" has the same meaning as in section 109(3) of the Agriculture Act 1947(c) or, in relation to Scotland, as in section 86(3) of the Agriculture (Scotland) Act 1948(d);

(*b*) "an appeal tribunal" means an industrial tribunal established under section 12 of the Industrial Training Act 1964;

(*c*) "assessment" means an assessment of an employer to the levy;

(*d*) "the Board" means the Cotton and Allied Textiles Industry Training Board;

(*e*) "business" means any activities of industry or commerce;

(*f*) "charity" has the same meaning as in section 360 of the Income and Corporation Taxes Act 1970(e);

(*g*) "cotton and allied textiles establishment" means an establishment in Great Britain engaged in the seventh base period wholly or mainly in the cotton and allied textiles industry for a total of twenty-seven or more weeks or, being an establishment that commenced to carry on

---

(a) 1964 c. 16.   (b) S.I. 1968/729 (1968 II, p. 2108).
(c) 1947 c. 48.   (d) 1948 c. 45.
(e) 1970 c. 10.

business in the seventh base period, for a total number of weeks exceeding one half of the number of weeks in the part of the said period commencing with the day on which business was commenced and ending on the last day thereof;

(*h*) "the cotton and allied textiles industry" means any one or more of the activities which, subject to the provisions of paragraph 2 of Schedule 1 to the industrial training order, are specified in paragraph 1 of that Schedule as the activities of the cotton and allied textiles industry;

(*i*) "emoluments" means all emoluments assessable to income tax under Schedule E (other than pensions), being emoluments from which tax under that Schedule is deductible, whether or not tax in fact falls to be deducted from any particular payment thereof;

(*j*) "employer" means a person who is an employer in the cotton and allied textiles industry at any time in the seventh levy period;

(*k*) "the industrial training order" means the Industrial Training (Cotton and Allied Textiles Board) Order 1966(a);

(*l*) "the levy" means the levy imposed by the Board in respect of the seventh levy period;

(*m*) "notice" means a notice in writing;

(*n*) "the sixth base period" and "the seventh base period" respectively mean the period of twelve months that commenced on the 6th April 1971 and the period of twelve months that commenced on 6th April 1972;

(*o*) "the seventh levy period" means the period commencing with the day upon which this Order comes into operation and ending on 31st March 1974.

(2) Any reference in this Order to an establishment that commences to carry on business or that ceases to carry on business shall not be taken to apply where the location of the establishment is changed but its business is continued wholly or mainly at or from the new location, or where the suspension of activities is of a temporary or seasonal nature.

(3) In the case where a cotton and allied textiles establishment is taken over (whether directly or indirectly) by an employer in succession to, or jointly with, another person, a person employed at any time in the sixth base period or the seventh base period at or from the establishment shall be deemed, for the purposes of this Order, to have been so employed by the employer carrying on the said establishment on the day upon which this Order comes into operation, and any reference in this Order to persons employed by the employer at or from a cotton and allied textiles establishment in the sixth base period or the seventh base period shall be construed accordingly.

(4) Any reference in this Order to a person employed at or from a cotton and allied textiles establishment shall in any case where the employer is a company be construed as including a reference to any director of the company (or any person occupying the position of director by whatever name he is called) who is required to devote substantially the whole of his time to the service of the company.

(a) S.I. 1966/823 (1966 II, p. 1907).

(5) The Interpretation Act 1889(a) shall apply to the interpretation of this Order as it applies to the interpretation of an Act of Parliament.

Imposition of the levy

3.—(1) The levy to be imposed by the Board on employers in respect of the seventh levy period shall be assessed in accordance with the provisions of this Article.

(2) The levy shall be assessed by the Board separately in respect of each cotton and allied textiles establishment of an employer (not being an employer who is exempt from the levy by virtue of paragraph (7) of this Article), but in agreement with the employer one assessment may be made in respect of any number of such establishments, in which case those establishments shall be deemed for the purposes of that assessment to constitute one establishment.

(3) Subject to the provisions of this Article, the levy assessed in respect of a cotton and allied textiles establishment of an employer shall be an amount equal to 0·75 per cent. of the appropriate sum (calculated in accordance with the Schedule to this Order).

(4) In the case of one establishment only of an employer, the appropriate sum shall be treated for the purposes of the assessment of the levy in respect of that establishment as if that sum were reduced by £25,000.

(5) For the purposes of the application of the provisions of the last foregoing paragraph the Board shall, if necessary—

(*a*) select the establishment in relation to which the provisions of the said paragraph are to apply; or

(*b*) aggregate the appropriate sums in respect of any two or more cotton and allied textiles establishments of the employer, in which case the said establishments shall be deemed for the purposes of the assessment to constitute one establishment.

(6) The amount of the levy imposed in respect of a cotton and allied textiles establishment that ceases to carry on business in the seventh levy period shall be in the same proportion to the amount that would otherwise be due under the foregoing provisions of this Article as the number of days between the commencement of the said levy period and the date of cessation of business (both dates inclusive) bears to five times the number of days in the said levy period.

(7) There shall be exempt from the levy—

(*a*) an employer in whose case the appropriate sum, or where there is more than one cotton and allied textiles establishment of the employer, the aggregate of the appropriate sums, is less than £26,334;

(*b*) a charity.

Assessment notices

4.—(1) The Board shall serve an assessment notice on every employer assessed to the levy, but one notice may comprise two or more assessments.

(a) 1889 c. 63.

(2) An assessment notice shall state the amount of the levy payable by the person assessed to the levy, and that amount shall be equal to the total amount (rounded down where necessary to the nearest £1) of the levy assessed by the Board under Article 3 of this Order in respect of each establishment included in the notice.

(3) An assessment notice shall state the Board's address for the service of a notice of appeal or of an application for an extension of time for appealing.

(4) An assessment notice may be served on the person assessed to the levy either by delivering it to him personally or by leaving it, or sending it to him by post, at his last known address or place of business in the United Kingdom or, if that person is a corporation, by leaving it, or sending it by post to the corporation, at such address or place of business or at its registered or principal office.

Payment of the levy

5.—(1) Subject to the provisions of this Article and of Articles 6 and 7, the amount of the levy payable under an assessment notice served by the Board shall be due and payable to the Board one month after the date of the notice.

(2) The amount of an assessment shall not be recoverable by the Board until there has expired the time allowed for appealing against the assessment by Article 7(1) of this Order and any further period or periods of time that the Board or an appeal tribunal may have allowed for appealing under paragraph (2) or (3) of that Article or, where an appeal is brought, until the appeal is decided or withdrawn.

Withdrawal of assessment

6.—(1) The Board may, by a notice served on the person assessed to the levy in the same manner as an assessment notice, withdraw an assessment if that person has appealed against that assessment under the provisions of Article 7 of this Order and the appeal has not been entered in the Register of Appeals kept under the appropriate Regulations specified in paragraph (5) of that Article, and such withdrawal may be extended by the Board to any other assessment appearing in the assessment notice.

(2) The withdrawal of an assessment shall be without prejudice—

(a) to the power of the Board to serve a further assessment notice in respect of any establishment to which that assessment related;

(b) to any other assessment included in the original assessment notice and not withdrawn by the Board, and such notice shall thereupon have effect as if any assessment withdrawn by the Board had not been included therein.

Appeals

7.—(1) A person assessed to the levy may appeal to an appeal tribunal against the assessment within one month from the date of the service of the assessment notice or within any further period or periods of time that may be allowed by the Board or an appeal tribunal under the following provisions of this Article.

(2) The Board by notice may for good cause allow a person assessed to the levy to appeal to an appeal tribunal against the assessment at any time

within the period of four months from the date of the service of the assessment notice or within such further period or periods as the Board may allow before such time as may then be limited for appealing has expired.

(3) If the Board shall not allow an application for extension of time for appealing, an appeal tribunal shall upon application made to the tribunal by the person assessed to the levy have the like powers as the Board under the last foregoing paragraph.

(4) In the case of an establishment that ceases to carry on business in the seventh levy period on any day after the date of the service of the relevant assessment notice, the foregoing provisions of this Article shall have effect as if for the period of four months from the date of the service of the assessment notice mentioned in paragraph (2) of this Article there were substituted the period of six months from the date of the cessation of business.

(5) An appeal or an application to an appeal tribunal under this Article shall be made in accordance with the Industrial Tribunals (England and Wales) Regulations 1965(a) as amended by the Industrial Tribunals (England and Wales) (Amendment) Regulations 1967(b) except where the establishment to which the relevant assessment relates is wholly in Scotland in which case the appeal or application shall be made in accordance with the Industrial Tribunals (Scotland) Regulations 1965(c) as amended by the Industrial Tribunals (Scotland) (Amendment) Regulations 1967(d).

(6) The powers of an appeal tribunal under paragraph (3) of this Article may be exercised by the President of the Industrial Tribunals (England and Wales) or by the President of the Industrial Tribunals (Scotland) as the case may be.

Evidence

8.—(1) Upon the discharge by a person assessed to the levy of his liability under an assessment the Board shall if so requested issue to him a certificate to that effect.

(2) The production in any proceedings of a document purporting to be certified by the Secretary of the Board to be a true copy of an assessment or other notice issued by the Board or purporting to be a certificate such as is mentioned in the foregoing paragraph of this Article shall, unless the contrary is proved, be sufficient evidence of the document and of the facts stated therein.

Signed by order of the Secretary of State.
9th July 1973.

R. Chichester-Clark,
Minister of State,
Department of Employment.

(a) S.I. 1965/1101 (1965 II, p. 2805).   (b) S.I. 1967/301 (1967 I, p. 1040).
(c) S.I. 1965/1157 (1965 II, p. 3266).   (d) S.I. 1967/302 (1967 I, p. 1050).

SCHEDULE

1. The provisions of this Schedule shall have effect for the purpose of calculating the appropriate sum under Article 3 of this Order.

2. For the purposes of this Schedule—

(a) references to an establishment are references to a cotton and allied textiles establishment;

(b) subject to sub-paragraph (c), references to the sum of the emoluments are references to the sum of the emoluments of the persons employed by the employer at or from the establishment;

(c) no regard shall be had to the emoluments of any person wholly engaged in agriculture or in the supply of food or drink for immediate consumption;

(d) "A" is the sum of the emoluments in the seventh base period;

(e) "B" is the sum of the emoluments in the sixth base period.

3. Where $\frac{A}{B}$ is equal to or less than $\frac{1}{4}$ the appropriate sum shall be $\frac{A}{B}$ multiplied by A.

4. In any other case the appropriate sum shall be A.

EXPLANATORY NOTE

(This Note is not part of the Order.)

This Order gives effect to proposals submitted by the Cotton and Allied Textiles Industry Training Board to the Secretary of State for Employment for the imposition of a further levy upon employers in the cotton and allied textiles industry for the purpose of raising money towards the expenses of the Board.

The levy is to be imposed in respect of the seventh levy period commencing with the date upon which this Order comes into operation and ending on 31st March 1974. The levy will be assessed by the Board and there will be a right of appeal against an assessment to an industrial tribunal.

STATUTORY INSTRUMENTS

1973 No. 1198

WAGES COUNCILS

The Wages Regulation (Retail Furnishing and Allied Trades) Order 1973

Made	-	-	-	-	*9th July* 1973
Coming into Operation					*20th August* 1973

Whereas the Secretary of State has received from the Retail Furnishing and Allied Trades Wages Council (Great Britain) the wages regulation proposals set out in the Schedule hereto;

Now, therefore, the Secretary of State in exercise of powers conferred by section 11 of the Wages Councils Act 1959(a), as modified by Article 2 of the Counter-Inflation (Modification of Wages Councils Act 1959) Order 1973(b), and now vested in him (c), and of all other powers enabling him in that behalf, hereby makes the following Order:—

1. This Order may be cited as the Wages Regulation (Retail Furnishing and Allied Trades) Order 1973.

2.—(1) In this Order the expression "the specified date" means the 20th August 1973, provided that where, as respects any worker who is paid wages at intervals not exceeding seven days, that date does not correspond with the beginning of the period for which the wages are paid, the expression "the specified date" means, as respects that worker, the beginning of the next such period following that date.

(2) The Interpretation Act 1889(d) shall apply to the interpretation of this Order as it applies to the interpretation of an Act of Parliament and as if this Order and the Order hereby revoked were Acts of Parliament.

3. The wages regulation proposals set out in the Schedule hereto shall have effect as from the specified date and as from that date the Wages Regulation (Retail Furnishing and Allied Trades) Order 1972(e) shall cease to have effect.

Signed by order of the Secretary of State.

9th July 1973.

W. H. Marsh,
Assistant Secretary,
Department of Employment.

(a) 1959 c. 69. (b) S.I. 1973/661 (1973 I, p. 2141).
(c) S.I. 1959/1769, 1968/729 (1959 I, p. 1795; 1968 II, p. 2108).
(d) 1889. c. 63. (e) S.I. 1972/1116 (1972 II, p. 3298).

ARRANGEMENT OF SCHEDULE

Part I : STATUTORY MINIMUM REMUNERATION

Article 3

SCHEDULE

The following minimum remuneration and provisions as to holidays and holiday remuneration shall be substituted for the statutory minimum remuneration and the provisions as to holidays and holiday remuneration fixed by the Wages Regulation (Retail Furnishing and Allied Trades) Order 1972 (hereinafter referred to as "Order R.F.A. (58)").

Part I : STATUTORY MINIMUM REMUNERATION
APPLICATION

1. Subject to the provisions of paragraphs 2, 7 and 10, the minimum remuneration payable to workers to whom this Schedule applies shall be the remuneration set out in paragraphs 3, 4, 5 and 6: Provided that any increase in remuneration payable under the provisions of paragraphs 5 or 6 shall become effective on the first day of the first full pay week following the date upon which the increase would otherwise become payable under those provisions.

HOURS ON WHICH REMUNERATION IS BASED

2.—(1) The minimum remuneration specified in this Part of this Schedule relates to a week of 40 hours exclusive of overtime and, except in the case of guaranteed weekly remuneration under paragraph 10, is subject to a proportionate reduction according as the number of hours worked is less than 40.

(2) In calculating the remuneration for the purpose of this Schedule recognised breaks for meal times shall, subject to the provisions of paragraph 8, be excluded.

SHOP MANAGERS AND SHOP MANAGERESSES

3. Subject to the provisions of this paragraph, the minimum remuneration payable to Shop Managers and Shop Manageresses employed in the areas specified in Column 2 of Table A or Table B of this paragraph shall be the amount appearing in the said Column 2 against the amount of weekly trade shown in Column 1 of the said Table A or Table B as the case may require.

TABLE A

Up to and including 3rd September 1973

Column 1			Column 2					
			LONDON AREA per week		PROVINCIAL A AREA per week		PROVINCIAL B AREA per week	
			Male	Female	Male	Female	Male	Female
			£	£	£	£	£	£
WEEKLY TRADE								
Under £175	...	...	20·80	19·90	20·40	19·50	19·80	19·00
£175 and under £200		...	21·05	20·15	20·65	19·75	20·05	19·25
£200 „ „ £240		...	21·25	20·35	20·85	19·95	20·25	19·45
£240 „ „ £280		...	21·45	20·55	21·05	20·15	20·45	19·65
£280 „ „ £320		...	21·65	20·75	21·25	20·35	20·65	19·85
£320 „ „ £360		...	21·85	20·95	21·45	20·55	20·85	20·05
£360 „ „ £400		...	22·05	21·15	21·65	20·75	21·05	20·25
£400 „ „ £440		...	22·25	21·35	21·85	20·95	21·25	20·45
£440 „ „ £480		...	22·45	21·55	22·05	21·15	21·45	20·65
£480 „ „ £520		...	22·65	21·75	22·25	21·35	21·65	20·85
£520 „ „ £560		...	22·85	21·95	22·45	21·55	21·85	21·05
£560 „ „ £600		...	23·05	22·15	22·65	21·75	22·05	21·25
£600 „ „ £640		...	23·25	22·35	22·85	21·95	22·25	21·45
£640 „ „ £680		...	23·45	22·55	23·05	22·15	22·45	21·65
£680 „ „ £720		...	23·65	22·75	23·25	22·35	22·65	21·85
£720 „ „ £760		...	23·85	22·95	23·45	22·55	22·85	22·05
£760 „ „ £800		...	24·05	23·15	23·65	22·75	23·05	22·25
£800 „ „ £840		...	24·25	23·35	23·85	22·95	23·25	22·45
£840 „ „ £880		...	24·45	23·55	24·05	23·15	23·45	22·65
£880 „ „ £920		...	24·65	23·75	24·25	23·35	23·65	22·85
£920 „ „ £960		...	24·85	23·95	24·45	23·55	23·85	23·05
£960 „ „ £1,000		...	25·05	24·15	24·65	23·75	24·05	23·25
£1,000 and over	...	...	25·25	24·35	24·85	23·95	24·25	23·45

TABLE B

On and after 4th September 1973

Column 1				Column 2	
			LONDON AREA per week	PROVINCIAL A AREA per week	PROVINCIAL B AREA per week
			£	£	£
WEEKLY TRADE					
Under £175	...	...	20·80	20·40	19·80
£175 and under £200	...	...	21·05	20·65	20·05
£200 „ „ £240	...	...	21·25	20·85	20·25
£240 „ „ £280	...	...	21·45	21·05	20·45
£280 „ „ £320	...	...	21·65	21·25	20·65
£320 „ „ £360	...	...	21·85	21·45	20·85
£360 „ „ £400	...	...	22·05	21·65	21·05
£400 „ „ £440	...	...	22·25	21·85	21·25
£440 „ „ £480	...	...	22·45	22·05	21·45
£480 „ „ £520	...	...	22·65	22·25	21·65
£520 „ „ £560	...	...	22·85	22·45	21·85
£560 „ „ £600	...	...	23·05	22·65	22·05
£600 „ „ £640	...	...	23·25	22·85	22·25
£640 „ „ £680	...	...	23·45	23·05	22·45
£680 „ „ £720	...	...	23·65	23·25	22·65
£720 „ „ £760	...	...	23·85	23·45	22·85
£760 „ „ £800	...	...	24·05	23·65	23·05
£800 „ „ £840	...	...	24·25	23·85	23·25
£840 „ „ £880	...	...	24·45	24·05	23·45
£880 „ „ £920	...	...	24·65	24·25	23·65
£920 „ „ £960	...	...	24·85	24·45	23·85
£960 „ „ £1,000	...	...	25·05	24·65	24·05
£1,000 and over	...	...	25·25	24·85	24·25

For the purposes of this paragraph "weekly trade" shall be calculated half-yearly and based on the period of 12 months immediately preceding the commencement of each half-year in the following manner:—

For the period of 26 weeks beginning (1) with the fifth week or (2) with the 31st week following the accounting date in any year, the weekly trade of a shop shall be one fifty-second of the amount of the total receipts for goods sold at that shop during the 52 weeks immediately preceding the accounting date (in the case of (1) hereof) or the 26th week following the accounting date (in the case of (2) hereof).

Except as provided as aforesaid, the weekly trade in respect of any week shall be the amount of the total receipts for goods sold at the shop in the preceding week.

In this paragraph—

(a) "accounting date" means that date in each year on which the books of accounts of a shop are closed for the purposes of preparing the annual accounts in respect of that shop, or, in the absence of any such date, the 5th April in any year;

(b) the expression "receipts for goods sold" includes receipts in respect of hire purchase transactions;

(c) "shop" includes any part of the shop not engaged in the retail furnishing and allied trades.

TEMPORARY SHOP MANAGERS AND
TEMPORARY SHOP MANAGERESSES

4.—(1) Subject to the provisions of this paragraph, the minimum remuneration payable to Temporary Shop Managers and Temporary Shop Manageresses, for each continuous period of employment as Temporary Shop Manager or Temporary Shop Manageress (reckoned in accordance with the provisions of sub-paragraph (2) of this paragraph), shall be the appropriate minimum remuneration for a Shop Manager or Shop Manageress, as the case may be, under the provisions of paragraph 3.

(2) In reckoning any continuous period of employment as Temporary Shop Manager or Temporary Shop Manageress for the purposes of sub-paragraph (1) of this paragraph, no account shall be taken of any period of employment:—

(a) not exceeding two consecutive working days; or

(b) not exceeding a total of two weeks in any year, being a period when the Shop Manager or Shop Manageress is absent on holiday:

Provided that for the purposes of this paragraph where in any year a worker is employed by the same employer as a Temporary Shop Manager or Temporary Shop Manageress at more than one shop during the absence on holiday of the Shop Manager or Shop Manageress, the first period of such employment and any subsequent periods of such employment in the same year shall be treated as a continuous period of employment.

(3) The minimum remuneration payable to Temporary Shop Managers and Temporary Shop Manageresses for any period of employment mentioned in (a) or (b) of sub-paragraph (2) of this paragraph, shall be not less than the appropriate minimum remuneration for a Sales Supervisor under the provisions of this Schedule.

(4) For the purposes of this paragraph "year" means the 12 months commencing with 1st January and ending with 31st December.

WORKERS OTHER THAN SHOP MANAGERS, SHOP MANAGERESSES, TEMPORARY SHOP MANAGERS, TEMPORARY SHOP MANAGERESSES OR TRANSPORT WORKERS

5. Subject to the provisions of paragraph 1, the minimum remuneration payable to male or female workers of the classes specified in Column 1 of Table A or Table B of this paragraph employed in the London Area, Provincial A Area or Provincial B Area, as the case may be, shall be the appropriate amount set out in Column 2 of the said Table A or Table B as the case may require.

TABLE A

Up to and including 3rd September 1973

Column 1	Column 2					
	LONDON AREA per week		PROVINCIAL A AREA per week		PROVINCIAL B AREA per week	
	Male	Female	Male	Female	Male	Female
	£	£	£	£	£	£
(1) SALES SUPERVISOR ...	18·90	18·05	18·40	17·60	17·80	17·00
(2) CLERK GRADE I	18·40	17·60	17·90	17·10	17·30	16·55
(3) CLERK GRADE II, SALES ASSISTANT, CASHIER, CENTRAL WAREHOUSE WORKER, STOCKHAND OR VAN SALESMAN:—						
Aged 21 years or over	17·40	16·65	16·90	16·15	16·30	15·60
Aged 20 and under 21 years ...	14·80	14·15	14·35	13·75	13·85	13·25
„ 19 „ „ 20 „ ...	13·90	13·30	13·50	12·90	13·05	12·50
„ 18 „ „ 19 „ ...	13·05	12·50	12·70	12·10	12·25	11·70
„ 17 „ „ 18 „ ...	11·30	10·80	11·00	10·50	10·60	10·15
„ 16 „ „ 17 „ ...	10·45	10·00	10·15	9·70	9·80	9·35
„ under 16 years	9·55	9·15	9·30	8·90	8·95	8·60
(4) SHOP WORKER, PORTER OR GENERAL WORKER:—						
Aged 21 years or over	16·90	16·15	16·40	15·70	15·80	15·10
„ 20 and under 21 years ...	14·35	13·75	13·95	13·35	13·45	12·85
„ 19 „ „ 20 „ ...	13·50	12·90	13·10	12·55	12·65	12·10
„ 18 „ „ 19 „ ...	12·70	12·10	12·30	11·80	11·85	11·35
„ 17 „ „ 18 „ ...	11·00	10·50	10·65	10·20	10·25	9·80
„ 16 „ „ 17 „ ...	10·15	9·70	9·85	9·40	9·50	9·05
„ under 16 years	9·30	8·90	9·00	8·65	8·70	8·30

TABLE B

On and after 4th September 1973

Column 1	Column 2		
	LONDON AREA per week	PROVINCIAL A AREA per week	PROVINCIAL B AREA per week
	£	£	£
(1) SALES SUPERVISOR ...	18·90	18·40	17·80
(2) CLERK GRADE I	18·40	17·90	17·30
(3) CLERK GRADE II, SALES ASSISTANT, CASHIER, CENTRAL WAREHOUSE WORKER, STOCKHAND OR VAN SALESMAN:—			
Aged 21 years or over	17·40	16·90	16·30
„ 20 and under 21 years ...	14·80	14·35	13·85
„ 19 „ „ 20 „ ...	13·90	13·50	13·05
„ 18 „ „ 19 „ ...	13·05	12·70	12·25
„ 17 „ „ 18 „ ...	11·30	11·00	10·60
„ 16 „ „ 17 „ ...	10·45	10·15	9·80
„ under 16 years	9·55	9·30	8·95
(4) SHOP WORKER, PORTER OR GENERAL WORKER:—			
Aged 21 years or over	16·90	16·40	15·80
„ 20 and under 21 years ...	14·35	13·95	13·45
„ 19 „ „ 20 „ ...	13·50	13·10	12·65
„ 18 „ „ 19 „ ...	12·70	12·30	11·85
„ 17 „ „ 18 „ ...	11·00	10·65	10·25
„ 16 „ „ 17 „ ...	10·15	9·85	9·50
„ under 16 years	9·30	9·00	8·70

TRANSPORT WORKERS

6. Subject to the provisions of paragraph 1, the minimum remuneration payable to Transport Workers employed in the London Area, Provincial A Area or Provincial B Area, as the case may be, shall be the appropriate amount set out in Column 3 of the next following table:—

Column 1	Column 2	Column 3		
Age of transport worker	Mechanically propelled vehicle with carrying capacity of	LONDON AREA per week	PROVINCIAL A AREA per week	PROVINCIAL B AREA per week
		£	£	£
21 years or over ...	} 1 ton or less {	18·40	17·90	17·30
Under 21 years ...		16·45	16·20	15·60
All ages ...	Over 1 ton and up to 5 tons	18·90	18·40	17·80
	Over 5 tons	19·60	19·10	18·50

MINIMUM OVERTIME RATES

7. Overtime shall be payable at the following minimum rates:—

(1) To any worker, for work on a Sunday or customary holiday,

    (*a*) where time worked does not exceed 4½ hours   ...   double time for 4½ hours

    (*b*) where time worked exceeds 4½ hours but does not exceed 8 hours   ... ...   double time for 8 hours

    (*c*) where time worked exceeds 8 hours   ... ...   double time for all time worked

Provided that—

    (i) Where a worker performs work on a customary holiday which is a day fixed by the employer, being a day on which the worker would normally work, during the period commencing on the last day on which the worker would normally work before Christmas Day and ending on the next following 9th January, overtime rates in accordance with the provisions of this sub-paragraph shall be payable to that worker only if—

        (*a*) he is a worker who normally works for the employer for more than 9 hours in a week; and

        (*b*) he has been in the employment of the employer throughout the period of 8 weeks immediately preceding the week in which Christmas Day falls.

    (ii) Overtime rates in accordance with the foregoing provisions of this paragraph shall be payable to a Shop Manager, Temporary Shop Manager, Shop Manageress or Temporary Shop Manageress only if the overtime worked is specifically authorised in writing by the employer or his representative.

    (iii) Where it is or becomes the practice in a Jewish undertaking for the employer to require the worker's attendance on Sunday instead of Saturday, the provisions of this paragraph shall apply as if in such provisions the word "Saturday" were substituted for "Sunday", except where such attendance on Sunday is unlawful.

(2) To any worker, on the weekly short day in any week during which, under sub-section (3) of section 40 of the Shops Act 1950(a), the employer is relieved of his obligation to allow the worker a weekly half-day,

    for any time worked after 1.30 p.m.   ... ...   double time

(3) To any worker, other than a Shop Manager, Temporary Shop Manager, Shop Manageress or Temporary Shop Manageress—

    (*a*) on the weekly short day (not being a weekly short day to which sub-paragraph (2) of this paragraph applies)

    for any time worked after 1.30 p.m. ...   ...   time-and-a-half

    (*b*) in any week, exclusive of any time in respect of which a minimum overtime rate is payable under the foregoing provisions of this paragraph,

    for all time worked in excess of 40 hours   ... ...   time-and-a-half

---

(a) 1950 c. 28.

Provided that in any week which includes one customary holiday "*33* hours" shall be substituted for "40 hours", in any week which includes two customary holidays "*26* hours" shall be substituted for the said "40 hours", *and in any week which includes three customary holidays "19 hours" shall be substituted for the said "40 hours"*.

WAITING TIME

8. A worker shall be entitled to payment of the minimum remuneration specified in this Schedule for all the time during which he is present on the premises of the employer unless he is present thereon in any of the following circumstances, that is to say—

(1) without the employer's consent, express or implied;

(2) for some purpose unconnected with his work, and other than that of waiting for work to be given to him to perform;

(3) by reason only of the fact that he is resident thereon; or

(4) during normal meal times, and he is not waiting for work to be given to him to perform.

WORKERS WHO ARE NOT REQUIRED TO WORK ON A CUSTOMARY HOLIDAY

9.—(1) Subject to the provisions of sub-paragraph (2) and sub-paragraph (3) of this paragraph, a worker who is not required to work on a customary holiday shall be paid for that holiday not less than the amount to which he would have been entitled under the foregoing provisions had the day not been a customary holiday and had he worked the number of hours ordinarily worked by him on that day of the week.

(2) A worker shall not be entitled to any payment under this paragraph unless he—

(*a*) worked for the employer throughout the last working day on which work was available for him preceding the holiday; and

(*b*) presents himself for employment at the usual starting time on the first working day after the holiday:

Provided that (*a*) or (*b*), as the case may be, of this sub-paragraph shall be deemed to be complied with where the worker is excused by his employer or is prevented by his proved illness or injury from working or presenting himself for employment as aforesaid.

(3) A worker shall not be entitled to any payment under this paragraph in respect of a customary holiday which is a day fixed by the employer, being a day on which the worker would normally work, during the period commencing on the last day on which the worker would normally work before Christmas Day and ending on the next following 9th January unless—

(*a*) he is a worker who normally works for the employer for more than 9 hours in a week; and

(*b*) he has been in the employment of the employer throughout the period of 8 weeks immediately preceding the week in which Christmas Day falls.

GUARANTEED WEEKLY REMUNERATION PAYABLE TO A FULL-TIME WORKER

10.—(1) Notwithstanding the other provisions of this Schedule, where in respect of any week the total remuneration (including holiday remuneration but excluding remuneration in respect of overtime) payable to a full-time worker under those other provisions is less than the guaranteed weekly remuneration provided under this paragraph, the minimum remuneration payable to that worker for that week shall be that guaranteed weekly remuneration with the addition of any amount excluded as aforesaid.

(2) The guaranteed weekly remuneration payable in respect of any week to a full-time worker is the remuneration to which he would be entitled under paragraph 3, 5 or 6 for 40 hours' work in his normal occupation:

Provided that—

(a) where the worker normally works for the employer on work to which this Schedule applies for less than 40 hours in the week by reason only of the fact that he does not hold himself out as normally available for work for more than the number of hours he normally works in the week and the worker has informed the employer in writing that he does not so hold himself out, the guaranteed weekly remuneration shall be the remuneration to which the worker would be entitled (calculated as in paragraph 2) for the number of hours in the week normally worked by the worker for the employer on work to which this Schedule applies;

(b) where in any week a worker at his request and with the written consent of his employer is absent from work during any part of his normal working hours on any day (other than a holiday allowed under Part II of this Schedule or a customary holiday or a holiday allowed to all persons employed in the undertaking or branch of an undertaking in which the worker is employed), the guaranteed weekly remuneration payable in respect of that week shall be reduced in respect of each day on which he is absent as aforesaid by one-sixth where the worker's normal working week is six days or by one-fifth where his normal working week is five days.

(3) Guaranteed weekly remuneration is not payable in respect of any week unless the worker throughout his normal working hours in that week (excluding any time allowed to him as a holiday or during which he is absent from work in accordance with proviso (b) to sub-paragraph (2) of this paragraph) is—

(a) capable of and available for work; and

(b) willing to perform such duties outside his normal occupation as the employer may reasonably require if his normal work is not available in the establishment in which he is employed.

(4) Guaranteed weekly remuneration is not payable in respect of any week if the worker's employment is terminated before the end of that week.

(5) If the employer is unable to provide the worker with work by reason of a strike or other circumstances beyond his control and gives the worker four clear days' notice to that effect, guaranteed weekly remuneration shall not be payable after the expiry of such notice in respect of any week during which or during part of which the employer continues to be unable to provide work as aforesaid:

Provided that in respect of the week in which the said notice expires there shall be paid to the worker, in addition to any remuneration payable in respect of time worked in that week, any remuneration that would have been payable if the worker had worked his normal hours of work on every day in the week prior to the expiry of the notice.

BENEFITS AND ADVANTAGES

11. The following benefits or advantages, being benefits or advantages provided, in pursuance of the terms and conditions of the employment of the worker, by the employer or by some other person under arrangements with the employer and not being benefits or advantages the provision of which is illegal by virtue of the Truck Acts 1831 to 1940(a), or of any other enactment, are authorised to be reckoned as payment of wages by the employer in lieu of payment in cash in the following manner:—

(1) board and lodging for seven days a week, as the appropriate amount set out in the following table—

In the case of a worker aged	LONDON AREA per week	PROVINCIAL A AREA per week	PROVINCIAL B AREA per week
	£	£	£
21 years or over	1·80	1·60	1·35
20 and under 21 years	1·70	1·50	1·25
19 „ „ 20 „	1·60	1·40	1·15
18 „ „ 19 „	1·50	1·30	1·05
17 „ „ 18 „	1·40	1·20	0·95
under 17 years	1·25	1·05	0·80

or, where board and lodging is not so provided,

(2) dinner of good and sufficient quality and quantity provided on each day on which the worker normally works in the week, other than the weekly short day, as an amount of £0.45 per week;

(3) tea of good and sufficient quality and quantity provided as aforesaid, as an amount of £0.15 per week.

Part II: ANNUAL HOLIDAY AND HOLIDAY REMUNERATION

ANNUAL HOLIDAY

12.—(1) Subject to the provisions of sub-paragraph (2) of this paragraph and of paragraph 13, an employer shall, between the date on which the provisions of this Schedule become effective and 31st October 1973, and in each succeeding year between 1st April and 31st October, allow a holiday (hereinafter referred to as an "annual holiday") to every worker in his employment to whom this Schedule applies who has been employed by him during the 12 months immediately preceding the commencement of the holiday season for any one of the periods of employment (calculated in accordance with the provisions of paragraph 19) set out in the first column of the table below and the duration of the annual holiday shall in the case of each such worker be related to that period as follows:—

(a) 1831 c. 37; 1887 c. 46; 1896 c. 44; 1940 c. 38.

Period of employment		Duration of annual holiday			
		Where the worker's normal working week is			
		Six days	Five days	Four days	Three days or less
12 months		12 days	10 days	8 days	6 days
Not less than 11 months but less than 12 months		11 „	9 „	7 „	5 „
„ „ „ 10 „ „ „ „ 11 „ ...		10 „	8 „	7 „	5 „
„ „ „ 9 „ „ „ „ 10 „ ...		9 „	7 „	6 „	4 „
„ „ „ 8 „ „ „ „ 9 „ ...		8 „	7 „	5 „	4 „
„ „ „ 7 „ „ „ „ 8 „ ...		7 „	6 „	5 „	3 „
„ „ „ 6 „ „ „ „ 7 „ ...		6 „	5 „	4 „	3 „
„ „ „ 5 „ „ „ „ 6 „ ...		5 „	4 „	3 „	2 „
„ „ „ 4 „ „ „ „ 5 „ ...		4 „	3 „	3 „	2 „
„ „ „ 3 „ „ „ „ 4 „ ...		3 „	2 „	2 „	1 day
„ „ „ 2 „ „ „ „ 3 „ ...		2 „	2 „	1 day	1 „
„ „ „ 1 month „ „ „ 2 „ ...		1 day	1 day	1 „	nil

(2) Notwithstanding the provisions of the last foregoing sub-paragraph—

(a) the number of days of annual holiday which an employer is required to allow to a worker in any holiday season shall not exceed in the aggregate twice the number of days constituting the worker's normal working week;

(b) where the worker does not wish to take his annual holiday or part thereof during the holiday season in any year and, before the expiration of such holiday season, enters into an agreement in writing with his employer that the annual holiday or part thereof shall be allowed, at a date or dates to be specified in that agreement, after the expiration of the holiday season but before the first day of January in the following year, then any day or days of annual holiday so allowed shall be treated as having been allowed during the holiday season;

(c) the duration of the worker's annual holiday during the holiday season ending on 31st October 1973 shall be reduced by any days of annual holiday duly allowed to him by the employer under the provisions of Order R.F.A. (58) between 1st April 1973 and the date on which this Schedule becomes effective.

(3) In this Schedule the expression "holiday season" means in relation to the year 1973 the period commencing on 1st April 1973, and ending on 31st October 1973, and, in each succeeding year, the period commencing on 1st April and ending on 31st October of the same year.

13. Where at the written request of the worker at any time during the three months immediately preceding the commencement of the holiday season in any year, his employer allows him any day or days of annual holiday and pays him holiday remuneration in respect thereof calculated in accordance with the provisions of paragraphs 16 and 17, then

(1) the annual holiday to be allowed in accordance with paragraph 12 in the holiday season in that year shall be reduced by the day or days of annual holiday so allowed prior to the commencement of that holiday season; and

(2) for the purpose of calculating accrued holiday remuneration under paragraph 18 any day or days of annual holiday deducted in accordance with sub-paragraph (1) hereof shall be treated as if they had been allowed in the holiday season.

14.—(1) An annual holiday shall be allowed on consecutive working days, being days on which the worker is normally called upon to work for the employer.

(2) Where the number of days of annual holiday for which a worker has qualified exceeds the number of days constituting his normal working week, the holiday may be allowed in two periods of consecutive working days; so however that when a holiday is so allowed, one of the periods shall consist of a number of such days not less than the number of days constituting the worker's normal working week.

(3) For the purposes of this paragraph, days of annual holiday shall be treated as consecutive notwithstanding that a customary holiday on which the worker is not required to work for the employer or a day on which he does not normally work for the employer intervenes.

(4) Where a customary holiday on which the worker is not required to work for the employer immediately precedes a period of annual holiday or occurs during such a period and the total number of days of annual holiday required to be allowed in the period under the foregoing provisions of this paragraph, together with any customary holiday, exceeds the number of days constituting the worker's normal working week, then, notwithstanding the foregoing provisions of this paragraph, the duration of that period of annual holiday may be reduced by one day and in such a case one day of annual holiday may be allowed on a day on which the worker normally works for the employer (not being the worker's weekly short day) in the holiday season or after the holiday season in the circumstances specified in sub-paragraph (2)(b) of paragraph 12.

(5) No day of annual holiday shall be allowed on a customary holiday.

(6) A day of annual holiday under this Schedule may be allowed on a day on which the worker is entitled to a day of holiday (not being a customary holiday) or to a half-holiday under any enactment other than the Wages Councils Act 1959:

Provided that where the total number of days of annual holiday allowed to a worker under this Schedule is less than the number of days in his normal working week, the said annual holiday shall be in addition to the said day of holiday or the said half-holiday.

15. An employer shall give to a worker reasonable notice of the commencing date or dates and of the duration of his annual holiday. Such notice may be given individually to the worker or by the posting of a notice in the place where the worker is employed.

REMUNERATION FOR ANNUAL HOLIDAY

16.—(1) Subject to the provisions of paragraph 17, a worker qualified to be allowed an annual holiday under this Schedule shall be paid by his employer, on the last pay day preceding such holiday, one day's holiday pay in respect of each day thereof.

(2) Where an annual holiday is taken in more than one period the holiday remuneration shall be apportioned accordingly.

17. Where any accrued holiday remuneration has been paid by the employer to the worker (in accordance with paragraph 18 of this Schedule or with Order R.F.A. (58)), in respect of employment during any of the periods referred to in that paragraph, the amount of holiday remuneration payable by the employer in respect of any annual holiday for which the worker has qualified by reason of employment during the said period shall be reduced by the amount of the said accrued holiday remuneration, unless that remuneration has been deducted from a previous payment of holiday remuneration made under the provisions of this Schedule or of Order R.F.A. (58).

ACCRUED HOLIDAY REMUNERATION PAYABLE ON
TERMINATION OF EMPLOYMENT

18. Where a worker ceases to be employed by an employer after the provisions of this Schedule become effective, the employer shall, immediately on the termination of the employment (hereinafter referred to as the "termination date"), pay to the worker as accrued holiday remuneration:—

(1) in respect of employment occurring in the 12 months up to 1st April immediately preceding the termination date, a sum equal to the holiday remuneration for any days of annual holiday for which he has qualified except days of annual holiday which he has been allowed or has become entitled to be allowed before leaving the employment; and

(2) in respect of any employment since the said 1st April, a sum equal to the holiday remuneration which would have been payable to him if he could have been allowed an annual holiday in respect of that employment at the time of leaving it:

Provided that—

(a) no worker shall be entitled to the payment by his employer of accrued holiday remuneration if he is dismissed on the grounds of misconduct and is so informed by the employer at the time of dismissal;

(b) where a worker is employed under a contract of service under which he is required to give not less than one week's notice before terminating his employment and the worker, without the consent of his employer, terminates his employment without having given not less than one week's notice, or before one week has expired from the beginning of such notice, the amount of accrued holiday remuneration payable to the worker shall be the amount payable under the foregoing provisions of this paragraph less an amount equal to the statutory minimum remuneration which would be payable to him at the termination date for one week's work if working his normal working week and the normal number of daily hours worked by him;

(c) where during the period or periods in respect of which the said accrued holiday remuneration is payable the worker has at his written request been allowed any day or days of holiday (other than days of holiday allowed by the employer under paragraph 13) for which he has not qualified under the provisions of this Schedule, any accrued holiday remuneration payable as aforesaid may be reduced by the amount of any sum paid by the employer to the worker in respect of such day or days of holiday.

CALCULATION OF EMPLOYMENT

19. For the purpose of calculating any period of employment qualifying a worker for an annual holiday or for any accrued holiday remuneration, the worker shall be treated as if he were employed for a month in respect of any month throughout which he has been in the employment of the employer.

PART III : GENERAL

DEFINITIONS

20. For the purposes of this Schedule—

"BOARD" means not less than three meals a day, of good and sufficient quality and quantity, one of which shall be dinner; and "LODGING" means clean and adequate accommodation and clean and adequate facilities for eating, sleeping, washing and leisure.

"CARRYING CAPACITY" means the weight of the maximum load normally carried by the vehicle, and such carrying capacity when so established shall not be affected either by variations in the weight of the load resulting from collections or deliveries or emptying of containers during the course of the journey, or by the fact that on any particular journey a load greater or less than the established carrying capacity is carried.

"CASHIER" means a worker employed in a shop and engaged wholly or mainly in receiving cash or giving change.

"CENTRAL WAREHOUSE WORKER" means a worker wholly or mainly employed in a central warehouse, that is to say, a warehouse from which an undertaking in the retail furnishing and allied trades supplies its shops.

"CLERK GRADE I" means a worker engaged wholly or mainly on clerical work which includes responsibility for maintaining ledgers or wages books or for preparing financial accounts of the undertaking or of a branch or department thereof.

"CLERK GRADE II" means a worker, other than a Clerk Grade I, engaged wholly or mainly on clerical work.

"CUSTOMARY HOLIDAY" means

(1) (a) In England and Wales—

Christmas Day; *26th December if it be not a Sunday; 27th December in a year when 25th or 26th December is a Sunday;* Good Friday; Easter Monday; *the last Monday in May; the last Monday in August; or, where a day is substituted for any of the above days by national proclamation, that day;*

and any day proclaimed as a public holiday throughout England and Wales; and

(b) one other day (being a day on which the worker would normally work) during the period commencing on the last day on which the worker would normally work before Christmas Day and ending on the next following 9th January to be fixed by the employer and notified to the worker not less than three weeks before the holiday;

(c) in Scotland—

New Year's Day, if it be not a Sunday or, if it be a Sunday, 2nd January;

the local Spring holiday;

the local Autumn holiday;

Christmas Day, if it be not a Sunday or, if it be a Sunday, 26th December; two other days (being days on which the worker would normally work) in the course of a calendar year, to be fixed by the employer and notified to the worker not less than three weeks before the holiday and any day proclaimed as a public holiday throughout Scotland; and

(d) one other day (being a day on which the worker would normally work) during the period commencing on the last day on which the worker would normally work before Christmas Day and ending on the next following 9th January to be fixed by the employer and notified to the worker not less than three weeks before the holiday; or

(2) where in any undertaking it is not the custom or practice to observe such days as are specified in (1)(a) or (1)(c) above as holidays, such other days, not fewer in number, as may by agreement between the employer or his representative and the worker or his representative be substituted for the specified days.

"FULL-TIME WORKER" means a worker who normally works for the employer for at least 36 hours in the week on work to which this Schedule applies.

"GENERAL WORKER" means a worker employed in a shop or in a warehouse operated in connection with a shop and engaged in general duties.

"LONDON AREA", "PROVINCIAL A AREA" and "PROVINCIAL B AREA" have the meanings respectively assigned to them in paragraph 21.

"MONTH" means the period commencing on a date of any number in one month and ending on the day before the date of the same number in the next month or, if the commencing date is the 29th, 30th or 31st day of a month and there is no date of the same number in the next month, then on the last day of that month.

"NORMAL WORKING WEEK" means the number of days on which it has been usual for the worker to work in a week while in the employment of the employer during the 12 months immediately preceding the commencement of the holiday season or, where under paragraph 18 accrued holiday remuneration is payable on the termination of the employment, during the 12 months immediately preceding the date of the termination of the employment:

Provided that—

(1) part of a day shall count as a day;

(2) no account shall be taken of any week in which the worker did not perform any work for which statutory minimum remuneration has been fixed.

"ONE DAY'S HOLIDAY PAY" means the appropriate proportion of the remuneration which the worker would be entitled to receive from his employer at the date of the annual holiday (or where the holiday is taken in more than one period at the date of the first period) or at the termination date, as the case may be, for one week's work—

(1) if working his normal working week, and the number of daily hours normally worked by him (exclusive of overtime),

(2) if the employer were not providing him with meals or board and lodging, and

(3) if he were paid at the appropriate rate of statutory minimum remuneration for work for which statutory minimum remuneration is payable and at the same rate for any work for the same employer for which such remuneration is not payable,

and in this definition "appropriate proportion" means—

where the worker's normal working week is six days						...	one-sixth
,,	,,	,,	,,	,,	,, ,, five days	...	one-fifth
,,	,,	,,	,,	,,	,, ,, four days	...	one-quarter
,,	,,	,,	,,	,,	,, ,, three days	...	one-third
,,	,,	,,	,,	,,	,, ,, two days	...	one-half
,,	,,	,,	,,	,,	,, ,, one day	...	the whole.

"PORTER" means a worker employed wholly or mainly upon one or more of the operations of packing, unpacking, moving, loading, or unloading merchandise or materials.

"SALES ASSISTANT" means a worker who is wholly or mainly engaged in the serving of customers and is normally expected to advise customers on the choice or use of merchandise.

"SALES SUPERVISOR" means a sales assistant other than a shop manager or a shop manageress who either (a) exercises general supervision over not less than 6 sales assistants or (b) exercises supervisory authority under a shop manager or a shop manageress and performs the duties of the shop manager or shop manageress in his or her absence.

"SHOP MANAGER", "SHOP MANAGERESS" means a worker who is employed at, and is normally immediately in charge of the operation of, an undertaking or branch (but not of a department of an undertaking or branch), including the custody of cash and stock, and, if employed in the London Area or in Provincial A Area, has immediate control of staff, if any, or, if employed in Provincial B Area, has immediate control of at least one full-time or two part-time staff; and for the purpose of this definition a worker shall not be deemed not to be immediately in charge of the operation of an undertaking or branch by reason only of being subject to the supervision of the employer or some person acting on his behalf, being in either case a person who is not normally, during the hours when the undertaking or branch is open to the public, wholly or mainly engaged in work at the undertaking or branch.

"SHOP WORKER" means a worker other than a sales assistant, a sales supervisor, a shop manager or a shop manageress who (a) is wholly or mainly engaged in the serving of customers but is not normally expected to advise them in the choice or use of merchandise, or (b) is otherwise wholly or mainly employed in or about a shop in duties other than the serving of customers but involving assistance in the making of sales.

"STOCKHAND" means a worker employed in a shop or in a warehouse operated in connection with a shop, and wholly or mainly engaged in the reception, checking and re-issuing of goods together with the keeping of records in connection therewith.

"TEMPORARY SHOP MANAGER", "TEMPORARY SHOP MANAGERESS" means a worker who, in the absence of the Shop Manager or Shop Manageress, as the case may be, is employed at and is temporarily immediately in charge of the operation of an undertaking or branch (but not of a department of an undertaking or branch) including the custody of cash and stock, whilst the worker is so in charge; and for the purpose of this definition a worker shall not be deemed not to be immediately in charge of the operation of an undertaking or branch by reason only of being subject to the supervision of the employer or some person acting on his behalf, being in either case a person who is not normally, during the hours when the undertaking or branch is open to the public, wholly or mainly engaged in work at the undertaking or branch.

"TIME-AND-A-HALF" and "DOUBLE-TIME" mean, respectively, one and a half times and twice the hourly rate obtained by dividing by 40 the minimum weekly remuneration to which the worker is entitled under the provisions of paragraphs 3, 4, 5 or 6.

"TRANSPORT WORKER" means a worker (other than a van salesman) engaged wholly or mainly in driving a mechanically propelled road vehicle for the transport of goods and on work in connection with the vehicle and its load (if any) while on the road.

"VAN SALESMAN" means a worker wholly or mainly employed in the sale of goods to customers from a van or other vehicle.

"WATCHMAN" means a worker wholly or mainly engaged in guarding the employer's premises for the prevention of theft, fire, damage or trespass.

"WEEK" means "pay week".

"WEEKLY SHORT DAY" means:—

(1) that day in any week on which the worker is, in accordance with the provisions of section 17 of the Shops Act 1950, required not to be employed about the business of a shop after half-past one o'clock in the afternoon, or,

(2) where there is no such day, or where the day falls on a customary holiday, a working day in the week not being a customary holiday, fixed by the employer and notified to the worker not later than the Saturday preceding the week during which it is to have effect; or, failing such notification, the last working day in the week which is not a customary holiday:

Provided that where the day specified in (1) of this definition falls on Christmas Day or Boxing Day in England and Wales or Christmas Day or New Year's Day in Scotland the employer may fix as the weekly short day for that week a working day in the following week not being either a customary holiday or the weekly short day for that following week.

AREAS

21. In this Schedule:—

(1) "LONDON AREA" means the Metropolitan Police District, as defined in the London Government Act 1963(a), the City of London, the Inner Temple and the Middle Temple.

(a) 1963 c. 33.

(2) "PROVINCIAL A AREA" means

(a) in Scotland

(i) the following burghs:—

ABERDEEN COUNTY
Aberdeen (including
part in Kincardine
County)
Fraserburgh
Peterhead

ANGUS COUNTY
Arbroath
Brechin
Dundee
Forfar
Montrose

ARGYLL COUNTY
Dunoon

AYR COUNTY
Ardrossan
Ayr
Irvine
Kilmarnock
Largs
Prestwick
Saltcoats
Stevenston
Troon

BANFF COUNTY
Buckie

BUTE COUNTY
Rothesay

CLACKMANNAN
COUNTY
Alloa

DUMFRIES COUNTY
Dumfries

DUNBARTON
COUNTY
Bearsden
Clydebank
Dumbarton
Helensburgh
Kirkintilloch
Milngavie

EAST LOTHIAN
COUNTY
North Berwick

FIFE COUNTY
Buckhaven and Methil
Burntisland
Cowdenbeath
Dunfermline
Kirkcaldy
Leven
Lochgelly
St. Andrews

INVERNESS COUNTY
Inverness

KINCARDINE
COUNTY
Stonehaven

LANARK COUNTY
Airdrie
Coatbridge
Glasgow
Hamilton
Lanark
Motherwell and
         Wishaw
Rutherglen

MIDLOTHIAN
COUNTY
Dalkeith
Edinburgh
Musselburgh

MORAY COUNTY
Elgin

ORKNEY COUNTY
Kirkwall

PERTH COUNTY
Perth

RENFREW COUNTY
Barrhead
Gourock
Greenock
Johnstone
Paisley
Port Glasgow
Renfrew

ROSS AND
CROMARTY COUNTY
Stornaway

ROXBURGH COUNTY
Hawick

SELKIRK COUNTY
Galashiels

STIRLING COUNTY
Denny and Dunipace
Falkirk
Grangemouth
Kilsyth
Stirling

WEST LOTHIAN
COUNTY
Armadale
Bathgate
Bo'ness

WIGTOWN COUNTY
Stranraer

ZETLAND COUNTY
Lerwick

(ii) the following Special Lighting Districts, the boundaries of which have been defined, namely, Vale of Leven and Renton in the County of Dunbarton, and Larbert and Airth in the County of Stirling, and

(iii) the following areas the boundaries of which were defined as Special Lighting Districts prior to 10th March 1943, namely, Bellshill and Mossend, Blantyre, Cambuslang, Larkhall and Holytown, New Stevenston and Carfin, all in the County of Lanark.

(b) In England and Wales, the areas administered by County Borough, Municipal Borough or Urban District Councils, except where they are included in the London area or are listed in (3)(b) of this paragraph.

(3) "PROVINCIAL B AREA" means

    (a) In Scotland, all areas other than those listed in (2)(a) of this paragraph;

    (b) In England and Wales, all areas not included in the London area administered by Rural District Councils, and the areas administered by the following Municipal Borough and Urban District Councils:—

ENGLAND (excluding Monmouthshire)

BEDFORDSHIRE
Ampthill
Sandy

BERKSHIRE
Wallingford
Wantage

BUCKINGHAMSHIRE
Buckingham
Linslade
Marlow
Newport Pagnell

CHESHIRE
Alsager
Longdendale

CORNWALL
Bodmin
Bude Stratton
Fowey
Helston
Launceston
Liskeard
Looe
Lostwithiel
Padstow
Penryn
St. Just
Torpoint

DERBYSHIRE
Bakewell
Whaley Bridge
Wirksworth

DEVON
Ashburton
Buckfastleigh
Budleigh Salterton
Crediton
Dartmouth
Great Torrington
Holsworthy
Honiton
Kingsbridge
Lynton
Northam
Okehampton
Ottery St. Mary
Salcombe
Seaton
South Molton
Tavistock
Totnes

DORSET
Blandford Forum
Lyme Regis
Shaftesbury
Sherborne
Wareham
Wimborne Minster

DURHAM
Barnard Castle
Tow Law

ELY, ISLE OF
Chatteris

ESSEX
Brightlingsea
Burnham-on-Crouch
Saffron Walden
West Mersea
Wivenhoe

GLOUCESTERSHIRE
Nailsworth
Tewkesbury

HEREFORDSHIRE
Bromyard
Kington
Ledbury

HERTFORDSHIRE
Baldock
Chorleywood
Royston
Sawbridgeworth

HUNTINGDONSHIRE
Huntingdon and
    Godmanchester
Ramsey
St. Ives
St. Neots

KENT
Lydd
New Romney
Queenborough
Sandwich
Tenterden

LANCASHIRE
Carnforth
Grange

LINCOLNSHIRE
Alford
Barton-upon-Humber
Bourne
Brigg
Horncastle
Mablethorpe and Sutton
Market Rasen
Woodhall Spa

NORFOLK
Cromer
Diss
Downham Market
Hunstanton
North Walsham
Sheringham
Swaffham
Thetford
Wells-next-the-Sea
Wymondham

**NORTHAMPTON-
    SHIRE**
Brackley
Burton Latimer
Higham Ferrers
Oundle

NORTHUMBERLAND
Alnwick
Amble

OXFORDSHIRE
Bicester
Chipping Norton
Thame
Woodstock

RUTLAND
Oakham

SHROPSHIRE
Bishop's Castle
Church Stretton
Ellesmere
Market Drayton
Newport
Wem

SOMERSET
  Chard
  Crewkerne
  Glastonbury
  Ilminster
  Portishead
  Shepton Mallet
  Street
  Watchet
  Wellington

SUFFOLK
  Aldeburgh
  Beccles
  Bungay
  Eye
  Hadleigh
  Halesworth
  Haverhill

SUFFOLK—cont.
  Leiston-cum-Sizewell
  Saxmundham
  Southwold
  Sudbury
  Stowmarket
  Woodbridge

SUSSEX
  Arundel
  Rye

WESTMORLAND
  Appleby
  Lakes

WILTSHIRE
  Bradford-on-Avon
  Calne

WILTSHIRE—cont.
  Malmesbury
  Marlborough
  Melksham
  Westbury
  Wilton

WORCESTERSHIRE
  Bewdley
  Droitwich

YORKSHIRE
  Hedon
  Hornsea
  Malton
  Norton
  Pickering
  Richmond
  Tickhill
  Withernsea

WALES AND MONMOUTHSHIRE

ANGLESEY
  Amlwch
  Beaumaris
  Llangefni
  Menai Bridge

BRECONSHIRE
  Builth Wells
  Hay
  Llanwrtyd Wells

CAERNARVONSHIRE
  Bethesda
  Betws-y-Coed
  Criccieth
  Llanfairfechan
  Penmaenmawr
  Portmadoc
  Pwllheli

CARDIGANSHIRE
  Aberayron
  Cardigan
  Lampeter
  New Quay

CARMARTHENSHIRE
  Cwmamman
  Kidwelly
  Llandeilo
  Llandovery
  Newcastle Emlyn

DENBIGHSHIRE
  Llangollen
  Llanrwst
  Ruthin

FLINTSHIRE
  Buckley
  Mold

GLAMORGAN
  Cowbridge

MERIONETHSHIRE
  Bala
  Barmouth
  Dolgellau
  Towyn

MONMOUTHSHIRE
  Caerleon
  Chepstow
  Usk

MONTGOMERYSHIRE
  Llanfyllin
  Llanidloes
  Machynlleth
  Montgomery
  Newtown and
    Llanllwchaiarn
  Welshpool

PEMBROKESHIRE
  Fishguard and
    Goodwick
  Narberth
  Neyland
  Tenby

RADNORSHIRE
  Knighton
  Llandrindod Wells
  Presteigne

(4) Any reference to a local government area shall be construed as a reference to that area as it was on 23rd April 1961, unless otherwise stated.

WORKERS TO WHOM THIS SCHEDULE APPLIES

22.—(1)(i) Subject to the provisions of sub-paragraph (2) of this paragraph the workers to whom this Schedule applies are all workers employed in Great Britain in any undertaking or any branch or department of an undertaking, being an undertaking, branch or department engaged—

  (a) wholly or mainly in the retail furnishing and allied trades; or

  (b) wholly or mainly in those trades and one or more of the groups of retail distributive trades set out in the Appendix to this paragraph, and to a greater extent in the retail furnishing and allied trades than in any one of those groups:

Provided that if a branch or department of an undertaking is not so engaged this Schedule shall not apply to workers employed in that branch or department (notwithstanding that the undertaking as a whole is so engaged), except in the case of workers as respects their employment in a department of that branch if that department is so engaged.

(ii) For the purposes of this sub-paragraph

(a) in determining the extent to which an undertaking or branch or department of an undertaking is engaged in a group of trades, regard shall be had to the time spent in the undertaking, branch or department on work in that group of trades;

(b) an undertaking or branch or department of an undertaking which is engaged in any operation in a group of trades shall be treated as engaged in that group of trades.

(2) This Schedule does not apply to any of the following workers in respect of their employment in any of the following circumstances, that is to say:—

(i) workers in relation to whom the Road Haulage Wages Council operates in respect of any employment which is within the field of operation of that Council;

(ii) workers employed on post office business;

(iii) workers employed on the maintenance or repair of buildings, plant, equipment or vehicles (but not including workers employed as cleaners);

(iv) workers employed on the installation, maintenance or repair of radio or television sets;

(v) workers employed on the repair or renovation of furniture (including mattresses), the making up, planning or laying of carpets, linoleum or similar floor coverings, or the measuring, cutting, sewing, making up or fixing of blinds, curtains, pelmets or loose covers;

(vi) workers employed on the packing, storing or removal of furniture or other household effects in connection with a household removal;

(vii) workers employed in the assembling, installation, maintenance, alteration or repair of electrical or gas appliances and apparatus of all kinds;

(viii) workers employed by a Gas or Electricity Supply Undertaking;

(ix) workers employed as watchmen.

(3) For the purpose of this Schedule the retail furnishing and allied trades consist of:—

(i) the sale by retail of:—

(a) household and office furniture, including garden furniture, mattresses, floor coverings and mirrors, but excluding billiard tables, clocks, pianos, gramophones and pictures;

(b) ironmongery, turnery and hardware, of kinds commonly used for household purposes, including gardening implements;

(c) hand tools;

(d) woodware, basketware, glassware, potteryware, chinaware, brassware, plasticware and ceramic goods, being articles or goods of kinds commonly used for household purposes or as household ornaments;

(e) electrical and gas appliances and apparatus, of kinds commonly used for household purposes (excluding clocks), and accessories and component parts thereof;

(f) heating, lighting and cooking appliances and apparatus, of kinds commonly used for household purposes, and accessories and component parts thereof;

(g) radio and television sets and their accessories and component parts;

(h) pedal cycles and their accessories and component parts;

(i) perambulators, push chairs and invalid carriages;

(j) toys, indoor games, requisites for outdoor games, gymnastics and athletics, but excluding billiard tables and sports clothing;

(k) saddlery, leather goods (other than articles of wearing apparel), travel goods and ladies' handbags;

(l) paint, distemper and wallpaper and oils of kinds commonly used for household purposes (excluding petrol and lubricating oils);

(m) brushes, mops and brooms, used for household purposes, and similar articles;

(n) disinfectants, chemicals, candles, soaps and polishes, of kinds commonly used for household purposes;

(ii) operations in or about the shop or other place where any of the articles specified in (i) of this sub-paragraph are sold by retail, being operations carried on for the purpose of such sale or otherwise in connection with such sale;

(iii) operations in connection with the warehousing or storing of any of the articles specified in (i) of this sub-paragraph for the purpose of the sale thereof by retail, or otherwise in connection with such sale, where the warehousing or storing takes place at a warehouse or store carried on in conjunction with one or more shops or other places where the said articles are sold by retail;

(iv) operations in connection with the transport of any of the articles specified in (i) of this sub-paragraph when carried on in conjunction with their sale by retail or with the warehousing or storing operations specified in (iii) of this sub-paragraph; and

(v) clerical or other office work carried on in conjunction with the sale by retail of any of the articles specified in (i) of this sub-paragraph and relating to such sale or to any of the operations specified in (ii) to (iv) of this sub-paragraph;

and for the purpose of this definition the sale by retail of any of the articles specified in (i) of this sub-paragraph does not include sale by auction (except where the auctioneer sells articles by retail which are his property or the property of his master) but includes the sale of any of the articles therein specified to a person for use in connection with a trade or business carried on by him if such sale takes place at or in connection with a shop engaged in the retail sale to the general public of any of the said articles.

APPENDIX TO PARAGRAPH 22

GROUPS OF RETAIL DISTRIBUTIVE TRADES

Group 1.—The Retail Food Trades, that is to say, the sale by retail of food or drink for human consumption and operations connected therewith including:—

(i) operations in or about the shop or other place where the food or drink aforesaid is sold, being operations carried on for the purpose of such sale or otherwise in connection with such sale;

(ii) operations in connection with the warehousing or storing of such food or drink for the purpose of sale by retail, or otherwise in connection with such sale, where the warehousing or storing takes place at a warehouse or store carried on in conjunction with one or more shops or other places where such food or drink is sold by retail;

(iii) operations in connection with the transport of such food or drink when carried on in conjunction with its sale by retail or with the warehousing or storing operations specified in (ii) above; and

(iv) clerical or other office work carried on in conjunction with the sale by retail aforesaid and relating to such sale or to any of the operations in (i) to (iii) above;

but not including

the sale by retail of bread, pastry or flour confectionery (other than biscuits or meat pastries) or the sale by retail of meat (other than bacon, ham, pressed beef, sausages, or meat so treated as to be fit for human consumption without further preparation or cooking) or the sale by retail of milk (other than dried or condensed milk) or the sale by retail of ice-cream, aerated waters, chocolate confectionery or sugar confectionery, or the sale of food or drink for immediate consumption.

For the purpose of this definition "sale by retail" includes any sale of food or drink to a person for use in connection with a catering business carried on by him, when such sale takes place at or in connection with a shop engaged in the retail sale of food or drink to the general public.

Group 2.—The Retail Drapery, Outfitting and Footwear Trades, that is to say—

(1) the sale by retail of

(a) wearing apparel of all kinds (including footwear, headwear and hand-wear) and accessories, trimmings and adornments for wearing apparel (excluding jewellery and imitation jewellery);

(b) haberdashery;

(c) textile fabrics, in the piece, leather cloth, plastic cloth and oil cloth (but not including carpets, linoleum and other kinds of floor covering);

(d) knitting, rug, embroidery, crochet and similar wools or yarns;

(e) made-up household textiles (but excluding mattresses and floor coverings);

(f) umbrellas, sunshades, walking sticks, canes and similar articles;

(2) operations in or about the shop or other place where any of the articles included in (1) above are sold by retail, being operations carried on for the purpose of such sale or otherwise in connection with such sale;

(3) operations in connection with the warehousing or storing of any of the articles included in (1) above for the purpose of the sale thereof by retail, or otherwise in connection with such sale, where the warehousing or storing takes place at a warehouse or store carried on in conjunction with one or more shops or other places where the said articles are sold by retail;

(4) operations in connection with the transport of any of the articles included in (1) above when carried on in conjunction with their sale by retail or with the warehousing or storing operations specified in (3) above; and

(5) clerical or other office work carried on in conjunction with the sale by retail of any of the articles included in (1) above and relating to such sale or to any of the operations specified in (2) to (4) above;

and for the purpose of this definition the sale by retail of any of the articles in (1) above includes the sale of that article to a person for use in connection with a trade or business carried on by him if such sale takes place at or in connection with a shop engaged in the retail sale to the general public of any of the articles included in (1) above.

Group 3.—The Retail Bookselling and Stationery Trades, that is to say—

(1) the sale by retail of the following articles:—

(a) books (excluding printed music and periodicals);

(b) all kinds of stationery including printed forms, note books, diaries and similar articles, and books of kinds used in an office or business for the purpose of record;

(c) pens, pencils, ink, blotting paper and similar articles;

(d) maps and charts;

(e) wrapping and adhesive paper, string, paste and similar articles;

(2) operations in or about the shop or other place where any of the articles specified in (1) above are sold by retail, being operations carried on for the purpose of such sale or otherwise in connection with such sale;

(3) operations in connection with the warehousing or storing of any of the articles specified in (1) above for the purpose of the sale thereof by retail, or otherwise in connection with such sale, where the warehousing or storing takes place at a warehouse or store carried on in conjunction with one or more shops or other places where the said articles are sold by retail;

(4) operations in connection with the transport of any of the articles specified in (1) above when carried on in conjunction with their sale by retail or with the warehousing or storing operations specified in (3) above; and

(5) clerical or other office work carried on in conjunction with the sale by retail of any of the articles specified in (1) above and relating to such sale or to any of the operations specified in (2) to (4) above;

Group 4.—The Retail Newsagency, Tobacco and Confectionery Trades, that is to say—

(1) the sale by retail of the following articles:—

    (*a*) newspapers, magazines and other periodicals;

    (*b*) tobacco, cigars, cigarettes, snuff and smokers' requisites;

    (*c*) articles of sugar confectionery and chocolate confectionery and ice-cream;

(2) operations in or about the shop or other place where any of the articles specified in (1) above are sold by retail, being operations carried on for the purpose of such sale or otherwise in connection with such sale;

(3) operations in connection with the warehousing or storing of any of the articles specified in (1) above for the purpose of the sale thereof by retail, or otherwise in connection with such sale, where the warehousing or storing takes place at a warehouse or store carried on in conjunction with one or more shops or other places where the said articles are sold by retail;

(4) operations in connection with the transport of any of the articles specified in (1) above when carried on in conjunction with their sale by retail or with the warehousing or storing operation specified in (3) above; and

(5) clerical or other office work carried on in conjunction with the sale by retail of any of the articles specified in (1) above and relating to such sale or to any of the operations specified in (2) to (4) above.

EXPLANATORY NOTE

(*This Note is not part of the Order.*)

This Order, which has effect from 20th August 1973, sets out the statutory minimum remuneration payable and the holidays which an employer is required to allow to workers in relation to whom the Retail Furnishing and Allied Trades Wages Council (Great Britain) operates, in substitution for the remuneration and holidays provided for in the Wages Regulation (Retail Furnishing and Allied Trades) Order 1972 (Order R.F.A. (58)), which Order is revoked.

It increases statutory minimum remuneration and continues the progress towards equal pay for men and women begun in Order R.F.A. (58).

It amends the provisions in Order R.F.A. (58) relating to customary holidays so as to take account of recent changes in the law and practice relating to public holidays.

New provisions are printed in italics.

STATUTORY INSTRUMENTS

1973 No. 1199

ROAD TRAFFIC

The Motor Vehicles (Type Approval) Regulations 1973

Made - - - -	*3rd July* 1973
Laid before Parliament	*20th July* 1973
Coming into Operation	*10th August* 1973

The Secretary of State for the Environment, as the designated Minister under the European Communities (Designation) Order 1972(a), in exercise of his powers under section 2 of the European Communities Act 1972(b) and of all other enabling powers, hereby makes the following Regulations:—

PART I—GENERAL

Commencement and citation

1. These Regulations shall come into operation on 10th August 1973 and may be cited as the Motor Vehicles (Type Approval) Regulations 1973.

Vehicles to which the Regulations apply

2. These Regulations apply in relation to every motor vehicle (other than a land tractor) which is manufactured on or after 1st July 1973, being a vehicle which—

(*a*) has four or more wheels; and

(*b*) is so constructed as to be capable of exceeding a speed of 25 kilometres per hour on the level under its own power,

and to every trailer which is manufactured on or after that date, being a trailer drawn by such a motor vehicle, and references in Parts II and III of these Regulations to a vehicle to which these Regulations apply shall be construed accordingly.

In this Regulation, "land tractor" means a tractor which is designed primarily for work on the land in connection with agriculture or forestry and which is not designed primarily for use on a road (within the meaning of the Road Traffic Act 1972(c)) for the conveyance of any goods or burden other than agricultural or woodland produce or articles required for the purposes of agriculture or forestry.

Interpretation

3.—(1) In these Regulations—

"information document"—

(a) S.I. 1972/1811 (1972 III, p. 5216).　　(b) 1972 c. 68.　　(c) 1972 c. 20.

   (i) in relation to a motor vehicle to which these Regulations apply or to a component of such a vehicle, means a document in the form set out in Part I of Schedule 1 to these Regulations, and

   (ii) in relation to a trailer to which these Regulations apply or to a component of such a trailer, means a document in the form set out in Part II of that Schedule;

"type approval certificate", in relation to a vehicle to which these Regulations apply or to a component of such a vehicle, means a document in the form set out in Part III of Schedule 1 to these Regulations to which there is attached an information document relating to that vehicle or, as the case may be, to that component;

"certificate of conformity", in relation to a vehicle to which these Regulations apply, means a document in the form set out in Part IV of the said Schedule 1;

"conform" means conform in all respects or with any permitted variation;

"the type approval requirements" means the requirements contained in the Community Directives, being requirements with respect to the design, construction, equipment and marking of vehicles or their components;

"the relevant aspects of design, construction, equipment and marking", in relation to a vehicle or to the component of a vehicle, means those aspects of design, construction, equipment and marking which are subject to the type approval requirements;

"the Community Directives" means the Council Directives concerning the approximation of laws of member States for the purposes of the type approval of motor vehicles and trailers and their components in relation to the design, construction, equipment and marking of such vehicles and components, being the Directives mentioned in Schedule 2 to these Regulations;

"member State" means any State which is a member of the European Economic Community;

"component", in relation to a vehicle has the same meaning as the expression "motor vehicle part" as that expression is defined in section 63(4) of the Road Traffic Act 1972;

"vehicle component" has the meaning assigned to that expression in Regulation 4(1) below; and
references to the competent authority of any member State other than the United Kingdom are references to the authority in that State who has functions in relation to the type approval of vehicles and their component scorresponding to those of the Secretary of State under these Regulations.

(2) Any notice required under these Regulations to be given by or to any person shall be given in writing.

(3) The Interpretation Act 1889**(a)** shall apply for the interpretation of these Regulations as it applies for the interpretation of an Act of Parliament.

(a) 1889 c. 63.

Part II—Type Approval of Vehicles and their Components

Application for type approval

4.—(1) An application by or on behalf of a manufacturer for the approval of a vehicle to which these Regulations apply as a type vehicle, or of the component of such a vehicle (hereafter referred to as "a vehicle component") as a type component, shall be made in writing to the Secretary of State and shall be accompanied by an information document duly completed so as to furnish all the information required by the document (being such of that information as is applicable to a vehicle or, as the case may be, a vehicle component of the type in respect of which the application is made), together with such other documents as are mentioned in the said information document as being required in connection with the application.

(2) Where in pursuance of this Regulation an application has been made to the Secretary of State in respect of a vehicle or vehicle component of a particular type, then until that application is disposed of or, where an appeal is made under Regulation 13 below in respect of the decision on that application, until that appeal has been disposed of, no similar application in respect of a vehicle or vehicle component of that type shall be made by or on behalf of the same manufacturer to the competent authority of any other member State.

Approval of type vehicles or type vehicle components

5.—(1) Where the Secretary of State is satisfied on application made to him by or on behalf of the manufacturer of a vehicle to which these regulations apply or of a vehicle component and after examination of the vehicle, or, as the case may be, the vehicle component—

(*a*) that the vehicle or vehicle component is of a type which conforms—

(i) with the information given in relation to the vehicle or vehicle component in the information document which accompanied the application, and

(ii) with such of the type approval requirements as apply in relation to vehicles or vehicle components of that type; and

(*b*) that adequate arrangements have been made to secure that other vehicles or other vehicle components purporting to conform with that vehicle or, as the case may be, that component in the relevant aspects of design, construction, equipment and marking will so conform in all respects or with such variations as are permitted by those requirements,

he shall approve the vehicle as a type vehicle or, as the case may be, the vehicle component as a type vehicle component and shall issue a type approval certificate in respect of it.

(2) A type approval certificate may be issued in respect of a type vehicle where the Secretary of State is satisfied that one or more, but not all, of the type approval requirements applicable to vehicles of that type are complied with in the case of that vehicle and a further type approval certificate may be issued by virtue of this paragraph on the application of any person who manufactures any part of the vehicle or by whom the vehicle is finally assembled, and references in these Regulations to a manufacturer shall be construed accordingly.

(3) Where the Secretary of State on an application under Regulation 4 above decides not to issue a type approval certificate in respect of a vehicle or vehicle component he shall give notice to the applicant of the decision stating the grounds on which it is based and informing the applicant of his right of appeal under Regulation 13 below in respect of the decision and, within a period of one month from the date on which that notice is given, shall give the like notice to the competent authority of every other member State.

(4) Where the Secretary of State issues a type approval certificate in pursuance of an application under Regulation 4 above he shall, within a period of one month from the date on which the certificate is issued, give notice of that fact to the competent authority of every other member State and shall include with that notice a copy of the type approval certificate so issued.

Certificates of conformity to a type vehicle

6.—(1) Subject to paragraph (2) below, a manufacturer of a type vehicle in respect of which a type approval certificate is in force may issue, in respect of each vehicle which is manufactured by him and which conforms with the type vehicle in such of the relevant aspects of design, construction, equipment and marking as are mentioned in the type approval certificate, a certificate of conformity stating that the vehicle does so conform.

(2) Where a certificate of conformity is issued in consequence of any type approval certificate issued by virtue of Regulation 5(2) above, it shall relate only to the type approval requirement or requirements to which that type approval certificate relates.

Conditions of issue of type approval certificates and cancellation or suspension thereof for breach of condition

7.—(1) A type approval certificate may be issued subject to conditions with respect to—

(*a*) the inspection by officers of the Secretary of State of samples of vehicles or vehicle components purporting to conform with the type vehicle or, as the case may be, the type vehicle component in the relevant aspects of design, construction, equipment and marking and of the parts and equipment of any vehicles, and of the parts of any vehicle components, selected for such inspection, and, for that purpose, the entry of premises where any such vehicles or vehicle components are manufactured; and

(*b*) the notification by the manufacturer of differences of design, construction, equipment or marking (other than such variations as are permitted by the type approval requirements) between any such vehicles and the type vehicle or between any such vehicle components and the type vehicle component which might affect those requirements.

(2) If it appears to the Secretary of State that there has been a breach of a condition subject to which a type approval certificate has been issued or if he ceases to be satisfied as to any other matter relevant to a type approval certificate, he may, by notice under Regulation 12 below, cancel or suspend the certificate.

Notice by a manufacturer of cessation of, or alteration in, the manufacture of vehicles or vehicle components of an approved type, or of alterations in the relevant aspects of design etc.

8.—(1) Where a manufacturer of a type vehicle or a type vehicle component in respect of which a type approval certificate is in force—

    (*a*) intends to cease the manufacture of that vehicle or vehicle component; or

    (*b*)intends to make any alteration in that manufacture such that any of the particulars furnished in the relevant information document no longer apply in relation to the vehicle or, as the case may be, the vehicle component; or

    (*c*) intends to make any alteration in any of the relevant aspects of design, construction, equipment or marking (being aspects in relation to which notice has been previously given to the manufacturer by the Secretary of State that they are aspects to which this sub-paragraph applies),

the manufacturer shall, as soon as practicable after forming that intention, give notice of it to the Secretary of State specifying the type vehicle or, as the case may be, the type vehicle component to which it relates and—

    (i) in a case mentioned in sub-paragraph (*a*) above, the date when the manufacture of the vehicle or vehicle component in question is to cease, and

    (ii) in a case mentioned in sub-paragraph (*b*) or (c) above, particulars of the alterations in question and of the date or dates on which they are to be made.

In this paragraph the reference to the relevant information document is a reference to the information document which, in accordance with Regulation 4(1) above, accompanied the application under that Regulation for the type approval certificate in question.

(2) In addition to the notice required under paragraph (1) above the manufacturer concerned shall, not later than fourteen days after the date on which he has ceased the manufacture of the vehicle or vehicle component in question or, as the case may be, after he has made any alterations such as are mentioned in sub-paragraph (*b*) or (*c*) of the said paragraph (1), give notice of that fact to the Secretary of State specifying—

    (i) the date (whether or not it is the same date specified in the notice under the said paragraph (1)) on which the manufacture ceased or, as the case may be, the alterations were made, and

    (ii) where the notice under the said paragraph (1) related to a type vehicle, the frame or chassis number assigned to the vehicle of that type which was last manufactured before that date.

(3) A copy of any notice given by or to a manufacturer under paragraph (1) above or by a manufacturer under paragraph (2) above shall, within a period of one month from the date on which it is given, be sent by the Secretary of State to the competent authority of every other member State.

Cancellation, suspension or modification of a type approval certificate where notice is given under Regulation 8

9.—(1) Where a notice given by a manufacturer under Regulation 8(1) or (2) above is a notice that he intends to cease or, as the case may be, has ceased, the manufacture of a vehicle or a vehicle component of the type referred to in the notice, the Secretary of State may cancel the type approval certificate in force in respect of the type vehicle or, as the case may be, the type vehicle component to which the said notice relates.

(2) Where a notice given by a manufacturer under the said Regulation 8(1) or (2) is a notice that he intends to make or, as the case may be, that he has made alterations such as are mentioned in sub-paragraph (b) or (c) of the said Regulation 8(1) the Secretary of State, if satisfied that the alterations specified in the notice are such as to necessitate doing so, may, by notice under Regulation 12 below—

(a) cancel or suspend the type approval certificate in force in respect of the vehicle or vehicle component to which the notice relates; or

(b) cancel the said type approval certificate and substitute for it, without further application by the manufacturer, a new type approval certificate in respect of the same type vehicle or, as the case may be, the same type vehicle component; or

(c) modify the said type approval certificate.

Cancellation or suspension of type approval certificates where vehicles or vehicle components are not manufactured in conformity with type approval requirements

10.—(1) If the Secretary of State—

(a) after examination of at least two vehicles, being vehicles of a particular type in respect of which a type approval certificate is in force and in respect of each of which a certificate of conformity is in force, or after examination of at least two vehicle components, being components of a particular type in respect of which a type approval certificate is in force, is satisfied that each of those vehicles or, as the case may be, each of those vehicle components has not been manufactured so as to conform with the relevant aspects of design, construction, equipment or marking; or

(b) is notified by the competent authority of any other member State that, in relation to any such vehicles or vehicle components and the manufacturer thereof as may be specified by that authority, the authority, after such examination as aforesaid, is similarly so satisfied, he shall give notice of that fact to the manufacturer specifying—

(i) the particular respects in which the vehicles or vehicle components in question have been found (either by the Secretary of State or, as the case may be, the said competent authority) not so to conform,

(ii) the steps that shall be taken by the manufacturer to ensure that vehicles or vehicle components of that type are manufactured by him so as to conform with the said aspects and the period within which those steps shall be taken, and

(iii) that unless those steps are taken within that period the type approval certificate in question may be cancelled or suspended,

and if, at any time after the expiration of that period, the Secretary of State (whether or not after any or any further examination of any such vehicles or vehicle components) is not satisfied that all the steps so specified have been taken, he may, by notice under Regulation 12 below, cancel or suspend the type approval certificate.

(2) A copy of any notice given to a manufacturer under paragraph (1) above shall, within a period of one month from the date on which it is given, be sent by the Secretary of State, to the competent authority of every other member State.

Suspension of type approval certificates where vehicles having a certificate of conformity are altered

11.—(1) If, after examination of a vehicle in respect of which a certificate of conformity is in force, the Secretary of State is satisfied that an alteration has been made to the vehicle (being an alteration in any of the relevant aspects of design, construction, equipment or marking which, by virtue of Regulation 8(1)(*c*) above, are required to be notified by the manufacturer of the vehicle) he may, by notice under Regulation 12 below, suspend the relevant type approval certificate.

(2) In this Regulation, "the relevant type approval certificate" means the certificate issued under Regulation 5(1) above in respect of a vehicle of the type to which the vehicle mentioned in paragraph (1) above conformed in the respects mentioned in Regulation 6(1) above at the time when that vehicle was manufactured.

Notice of cancellation, suspension or modification of type approval certificates

12.—(1) Where the Secretary of State decides to cancel, suspend or modify a type approval certificate under any provisions of these Regulations, he shall—

(*a*) as soon as practicable, give notice of the decision to the manufacturer to whom the certificate was issued; and

(*b*) within a period of one month from the date on which that notice is given, give the like notice to the competent authority of every other member State.

(2) A notice under paragraph (1) above shall specify the date on which the cancellation, suspension or modification of the certificate to which the notice relates shall take effect and—

(*a*) in the case of cancellation, shall specify the grounds for the decision to cancel;

(*b*) in the case of suspension, shall specify—

(i) the grounds for the decision to suspend,

(ii) the conditions which must be fulfilled before the suspension can cease to have effect; and

(iii) that the suspension shall have effect until such time as the Secretary of State gives notice to the manufacturer under this sub-paragraph that he is satisfied that the said conditions have been fulfilled; and

(*c*) in the case of modification, shall specify particulars of the modifications,

and shall inform the manufacturer concerned of his right of appeal under Regulation 13 below in respect of the decision.

(3) The cancellation, suspension or modification of a type approval certificate under any provision of these Regulations shall not affect the validity of any certificate of conformity previously issued in consequence of that type approval certificate.

Appeals

13.—(1) A person who is aggrieved by a decision given by or on behalf of the Secretary of State with respect to a type approval certificate may, within the time and in the manner respectively specified in paragraphs (2) and (3) below, appeal to the Secretary of State, and on the appeal the Secretary of State—

(*a*) shall have the like powers and duties as he has on an original application for a type approval certificate;

(*b*) may hold an inquiry in connection therewith; and

(*c*) may appoint an assessor for the purpose of assisting him with the appeal or any such inquiry.

(2) An appeal under paragraph (1) above shall be made by notice to the Secretary of State which shall be lodged with him not later than fourteen days from the date on which notice of the decision in respect of which the appeal is made was given.

(3) A notice of appeal under this Regulation shall state the grounds on which the appeal is made and shall be accompanied by the following documents, that is to say:—

(*a*)a copy of the information document which, in accordance with Regulation 4(1) above, accompanied the application under that Regulation for the type approval certificate in question; and

(*b*) where the appeal relates to the cancellation, suspension or modification of a type approval certificate, a copy of that certificate.

PART III—SUPPLEMENTARY PROVISIONS

Provision of testing stations

14. The Secretary of State may provide and maintain stations where examination of vehicles (being vehicles to which these Regulations apply) and the components of such vehicles may be carried out for the purposes of these Regulations and may provide and maintain the apparatus for carrying out such examinations.

Keeping and inspection of records relating to certificates of conformity

15.—(1) A manufacturer of a type vehicle in respect of which a type approval certificate is in force shall keep a record of every certificate of conformity issued by him under Regulation 6 above, being a record of the serial number of the certificate and of the manufacturer's identification number assigned to the vehicle in respect of which the certificate was issued and of the Community reference numbers of the Community Directives with whose requirements the vehicle conformed.

(2) A person authorised for the purpose by the Secretary of State may, on giving any such manufacturer as aforesaid reasonable notice and after production, if so required,of his authority, require the manufacturer to produce for inspection the records kept by him under paragraph (1) above, and the authorised person may inspect and take copies of such records.

(3) In a case where any such manufacturer as aforesaid fails to comply with a requirement under paragraph (2) above or obstructs an authorised person in the exercise of his powers under that paragraph, the Secretary of State may treat the case as if there had been, in relation to the type approval certificate mentioned in paragraph (1) above, a breach of a condition such as is mentioned in Regulation 7(2) above and (without prejudice to the application of the said Regulation 7(2) in respect of any other breach of a condition so mentioned) the provisions of that Regulation and of Regulations 12 and 13 above shall apply accordingly in relation to that certificate.

Signed by authority of the Secretary of State.

John Peyton,
Minister for Transport Industries,
Department of the Environment.

3rd July 1973.

SCHEDULE 1   (*See* Regulation 3(1))
PART I

Form of information document in relation to a motor vehicle to which these Regulations apply or to a component of such a motor vehicle

FOR DOE
USE ONLY

TYPE APPROVAL OF A MOTOR VEHICLE

in accordance with EEC Directive 70/156

INFORMATION DOCUMENT   NUMBER

Items of information heavily outlined to be omitted where application is for a passenger car in category M1

If a component has been approved under an EEC Directive its description shall be replaced by the approval number in this document.

If the space is insufficient for an answer please add further pages.

Notes (*a*) to (*p*) are at page 21

FOR DOE
APPROVAL

0.	**GENERAL**
0.1	Make
0.2	Type and commercial description (include all variants)
0.3	Class (eg private car, estate car goods vehicle, public service vehicle)
0.4	Category (*a*)
0.4.1	Manufacturers vehicle identification code, (if any, explanation of system)
0.5	Name and address of manufacturer
0.6	Name and address of manufacturer's authorised representative (if address at 0.5 is outside United Kingdom)

0.7   Location of identification plates and inscriptions and method of fixing:

0.7.1   on the chassis

0.7.2   on the body

0.7.3   on the engine

0.8   Commencing chassis number

1.   BODYWORK AND CHASSIS (to be shown on drawings 1 & 2, see list on page 20)

1.1   Type of bodywork (material used and construction method)

1.2   Number of axles and wheels [(count twin wheels as one) if tracklaying vehicle, number of tracks]

1.2.1   [Number of twin wheels (if applicable)]

1.2.2   Driving wheels (number, situation, connection to other axles) [count twin wheels as one]

1.3	Position of driving cab	forward/semi-forward/normal

1.4   Number and position of doors (direction of opening, latches & hinges).

1.5   Seats (number, position, type)

1.6   Windscreen and other windows (number and position, material and approval details)

1.6.1   Field of vision (to be shown on drawing 14)

1.6.2   Angle of inclination of windscreen

1.7   Rear view mirrors (number and position)

1.8   Arrangement and identification of controls (to be shown on drawing 15)

1.9   Safety belt and other retention devices (type, number and position)

1.9.1   Safety belt anchorage points (number and position) (to be shown on drawing 16)

1.10   Interior protection for occupants (brief description)

1.11   Chassis frame (if any) (brief description) (to be shown on drawing 3)

1.12   Material used

1.13   Yield point

1.14   Ultimate tensile stress

1.15   Elongation (%)

1.16   Brinell hardness

2.   WEIGHTS AND DIMENSIONS (use metric units) (b)

2.1   Overall length (c)

2.2   Overall height (unladen) (d)

2.3   Overall width (e)

2.4   Wheelbase (f)

2.5   Track of each axle (g) Front | Intermediate
                             Rear | „

2.6   Overhang—Front   (h)

2.7   Overhang—Rear (i)

2.8   Ground clearance (laden) (j)

2.9   In the case of tractive units:

2.9.1   Fifth wheel lead (k)

2.9.2   Maximum height of the fifth wheel (standardised) (l)

2.9.3   Distance between the rear of the cab and the rear axle:

2.9.3.1 Distance between the rear of the cab and the rear
        axle(s) (in cases of a chassis with cab)

2.9.3.2 Distance between the rear of the steering wheel and
        the rear axle(s) (in the case of a bare chassis)

2.10   Weight of vehicle (less coolant, oils, fuel,
        spare wheel, tools, driver and cab)

2.10.1 Distribution of this weight:
            On front axle | On intermediate axle
            On rear axle | „   „   „

2.11   Weight of vehicle in running order
        (with coolant, oils, fuel, spare
        wheel, tools and driver)   (m)

2.11.1 Distribution of this weight:

            On front axle | On intermediate axle
            On rear axle | „   „   „
                                   | On kingpin

2.12   Maximum allowable gross vehicle
        weight permitted by maker

2.12.1 Distribution of this weight:
On front axle
On rear axle

| On intermediate axle |
| " " " |
| On kingpin |

2.13 Maximum allowable weight on each
axle permitted by maker
On front axle
On rear axle

| On intermediate axle |
| " " " |
| On kingpin |

2.14 If the vehicle is used as a drawing vehicle
the maximum allowable laden weight of the
combination permitted by the maker

2.14.1 Maximum allowable weight of trailer permitted
by maker (if applicable)

2.15 Maximum permitted towing weight
(unbraked trailer)

2.16 Maximum permitted towing weight
(braked trailer)

2.17 Maximum gradient fully laden
(stop/start)

2.18 Maximum gradient fully laden
with maximum towing weight
(stop/start)

2.19 Recommended vertical hitch load

2.20 Permissible maximum laden weight

2.20.1 Distribution of this weight
–on front axle
FOR –on rear axle
–intermediate axle
– " "
–on kingpin "

2.21 DOE Permissible maximum weight–on front axle
on each axle
–on rear axle
–intermediate axle
– " "
–on kingpin "

2.22 APPROVAL Where vehicle is used as a drawing vehicle, permissible maximum weight of the combination

2.22.1 Maximum weight of the trailer, where applicable

3. ENGINE (If other than piston engine, give full description at
10.7)

3.1 Manufacturer

3.2   Designation

3.3   Type

3.3.1   Position and arrangement in vehicle

3.4   Number and arrangement of cylinders

3.5   Capacity (cc)

3.6   Bore (mm)

3.7   Stroke (mm)

3.8   Max power, kw @ rpm (to be shown in drawing 17)

3.9   Max torque, Nm @ rpm   „   „   „

3.10   Test standard used

3.11   Compression ratio

3.12   Normal fuel (petrol, diesel)

3.13   Type of carburetter and number fitted

3.14   Injection pump

3.15   Governor

3.16   Injector type

3.17   Fuel pump

3.18   Supercharger (type, pressure etc.)

3.19   Ignition (type of equipment, type
        of advance control)
3.20   Suppression equipment

3.21   FUEL SYSTEM

3.21.1 Location of tank(s) (to be shown on drawing 2)

3.21.2 Capacity (mention reserve if applicable)

3.22   EXHAUST SYSTEM (to be shown on drawings 4 and 5)

3.22.1 Type and number of silencers

3.23   COOLING SYSTEM

3.23.1 Type (air, water, pressurised etc.)

3.24   MEASURES TAKEN AGAINST AIR POLLUTION

3.24.1 Petrol engine

3.24.2 Diesel   „

4.   TRANSMISSION SYSTEM (to be shown on drawings
        6, 7 and 8)

4.1   Type (mechanical, hydraulic etc.)

4.2   Weight of clutch

4.3   Gearbox (type, location, method of control)

4.3.1   Gearbox options

4.3.2   Weight of gearbox

4.4   Transmission from engine to road wheels

4.4.1   Differential lock

4.4.2   Overdrive

4.5   GEAR RATIOS (Show options in separate boxes or continue into next box for additional ratios)

	GEARBOX	FINAL DRIVE	OVERALL		GEARBOX	FINAL DRIVE	OVERALL
1							
2							
3							
4							
5							
6							
R							

	GEARBOX	FINAL DRIVE	OVERALL		GEARBOX	FINAL DRIVE	OVERALL
1							
2							
3							
4							
5							
6							
R							

4.6   VEHICLE ROAD SPEED AT 1000 rpm with Standard tyres
(show variants in separate boxes) (o)

GEAR	Speed km/h	Circum- ference of tyre (p)	GEAR	Speed km/h	Circum- ference of tyre	GEAR	Speed km/h	Circum- ference of tyre
1								
2								
3								
4								
5								
6								
R								

4.7   Maximum vehicle speed in highest gear (a 5% tolerance is
permitted). To be tested on level   ....km/h

4.8   Speedometer

4.9   Tachograph (if fitted) maker and type

5.   SUSPENSION (to be shown on drawings 9 and 10)

5.1   FRONT

5.1.1   Make and type (independent etc.)

5.1.2   If solid axle, state material
characteristics

5.1.3   Tyres (dimensions, characteristics and pressures)

5.1.4   Characteristics of springing
parts (design, characteristsics
of materials and dimensions)

5.1.5   Wheel type and dimensions

5.1.6   Stabilisers   fitted/not fitted

5.1.7   Dampers   fitted/not fitted

5.2   INTERMEDIATE(S)   (1)   (2)

5.2.1   Make and type (independent etc.)

5.2.2   If solid axle state material
characteristics

5.2.3   Tyres (dimensions, characteristics and pressures)

5.2.4	Characteristics of springing parts (design, characteristics of materials and dimensions)		
5.2.5	Wheel type and dimensions		
5.2.6	Stabilisers	fitted/not fitted	fitted/not fitted
5.2.7	Dampers	fitted/not fitted	fitted/not fitted

5.3 REAR

5.3.1 Make and type (independent etc.)

5.3.2 If solid axle state material characteristics

5.3.3 Tyres (dimensions, characteristics and pressures)

5.3.4 Characteristics of springing parts (design, characteristics of materials and dimensions)

5.3.5 Wheel type and dimensions

5.3.6 Stabilisers   fitted/not fitted

5.3.7 Dampers   fitted/not fitted

6. STEERING (to be shown on drawing 11)

6.1 Make and type

6.2 Type of linkage to wheels

6.3 Type of power assistance (if applicable)

6.4 Maximum turning angle of   to left   to right wheels (degrees) in each direction

6.5 Number of turns of steering   to left   to right control in each direction

6.5.1 Force on steering control

6.6 Minimum turning circle, in each direction (n)

6.7 Swept path

7. BRAKING SYSTEM (to be shown on drawing 12)

7.1 SERVICE BRAKE

7.1.1 Description

7.1.2 Master cylinder type and diameter

7.1.3   Outside source of energy if any
         (specify type, eg vacuum, servo etc.)

7.1.4   FRONT

7.1.4.1 Wheel cylinder number and diameter

7.1.4.2 Disc/drum dimensions

7.1.4.3 Friction material (make and type)

7.1.4.4 Total lining area

7.1.5   INTERMEDIATE(S)

7.1.5.1 Wheel cylinder number and diameter

7.1.5.2 Disc/drum dimensions

7.1.5.3 Frictional material (make and type)

7.1.5.4 Total lining area

7.1.6   REAR

7.1.6.1 Wheel cylinder number and diameter

7.1.6.2 Disc/drum dimensions

7.1.6.3 Frictional material (make and type)

7.1.6.4 Total lining area

7.2   SECONDARY BRAKE

7.2.1   Brief description

7.3   PARKING BRAKE

7.3.1   Brief description

7.4   ADDITIONAL BRAKING SYSTEM (if any)

7.4.1   Brief description

7.5   GENERAL

7.5.1   Thrust and transmission of braking forces
         (details of torque reaction arrangements,
         ie. road springs, radius rods etc.)

7.5.2   Calculation of braking systems (attach details, ref. 13)

7.5.3   Test conditions

7.5.4   Test results

FOR DOE
APPROVAL
USE ONLY

8.   LIGHTING SYSTEM/ELECTRICAL
         (Position and dimensions of lights to be
         shown on drawing 2)

8.1   Headlights (Main beam)

8.1.1   Headlights (Dipped beam)

8.2   Front position lights

8.2.1   Rear position lights

8.3   Front direction indicators

8.3.1   Rear direction indicators

8.3.2   Side direction indicators

8.4   Brake lights

8.5   Rear registration plate lights

8.6   Red rear reflex reflectors

8.7   Reverse lights

8.8   Parking lights

8.9   Auxiliary lights

8.9.1   Fog lights

8.10   Side Marker lights

8.11   Amber side reflex reflectors

8.12   Hazard warning

8.13   Additional lighting equipment for
          special vehicles

8.14   Audible warning device (number,
          make, type and location)

8.15   Generator (type and output and
          method of control)

8.16   Voltage of system and ± earth

8.17   Battery (type and capacity)

8.18   FORWARD VISION AIDS

8.18.1   Windscreen wipers (type)

8.18.2   Windscreen washers (type)

8.18.3   Demister (type)

9.   MISCELLANEOUS

9.1   Anti-theft device (make and type)

9.2   Sound level

9.3   Location of registration plate(s)

9.4   Optional equipment

9.5   Special provisions for taxis

9.6   Special provisions for PSV or goods vehicles

9.7   Towing hook

9.8   Connections between drawing vehicles and trailers or semi-trailers (description of mechanical and electrical connections)

10.   ELECTRIC TRACTION MOTOR (if applicable)

10.1   Type (series, shunt, etc. winding)

10.2   Hourly maximum output and operating voltage

10.3   Battery position

10.4   Number of cells

10.5   Weight

10.6   Capacity (according to BSS 2550.71)

10.7   OTHER POWER UNITS (if applicable)

         Particulars of the operating principles
         of such engines or motors

ENCLOSURES TO BE SUBMITTED WITH FORM

1.   ¾ front and ¾ rear photograph of whole vehicle

2.   Dimensional drawing of whole vehicle (following views)
         (a) Front
         (b) Side
         (c) Rear
         (d) Plan

3.   Outline sketch of chassis frame

4.   Exhaust system complete

5.   Sectional view of each silencer

6.   Sketch of transmission layout

7.   Section though gearbox

8.   Section through final drive arrangement

9.   Dimensional scheme of each axle

10.   Sketch of suspension arrangement

11.   Schematic layout of steering system including ratios

12.   Schematic layout of brake system

13.   Calculation of braking systems—determination of the ratio between braking force on pedal and total braking force at circumference of road wheels

14.   Field of vision

15.   Arrangement and identification of controls

16.   Position of safety belt anchorage points

17.   Power curve

Signed   ....
Date   ....

NOTES

(a) Classified according to the following international categories (The gross vehicle weight should be used to determine in which category a drawing vehicle is to be shown):

Category M: Motor vehicles having at least four wheels, or having three wheels when the maximum weight exceeds 1 metric ton, and used for the carriage of passengers.

Category M1: Vehicles used for the carriage of passengers and comprising no more than eight seats in addition to the driver's seat.

Category M2: Vehicles used for the carriage of passengers, comprising more than eight seats in addition to the driver's seat, and having a maximum weight not exceeding 5 metric tons.

Category M3: Vehicles used for the carriage of passengers, comprising more than eight seats in addition to the driver's seat, and having a maximum weight exceeding 5 metric tons.

Category N: Motor vehicles having at least four wheels, or having three wheels when the maximum weight exceeds 1 metric ton, and used for the carriage of goods.

Category N1: Vehicles used for the carriage of goods and having a maximum weight not exceeding 3·5 metric tons.

Category N2: Vehicles used for the carriage of goods and having a maximum weight exceeding 3·5 but not exceeding 12 metric tons.

Category N3: Vehicles used for the carriage of goods and having a maximum weight exceeding 12 metric tons.

(b) Where there is one version with a normal cab and another with a couchette cab, both sets of weights and dimensions are to be stated.

(c) ISO Recommendation 612, term No. 11.

(d) ISO Recommendation 612, term No. 16.

(e) ISO Recommendation 612, term No. 15.

(f) ISO Recommendation 612, term No. 3.

(g) ISO Recommendation 612, term No. 2.

(h) ISO Recommendation 612, term No. 21.

(i) ISO Recommendation 612, term No. 22.

(j) ISO Recommendation 612, term No. 8.

(k) ISO Recommendation 612, term No. 36.

(l) ISO Recommendation 612, term No. 38.

(m) The weight of the driver is assessed at 75 kg.

(n) ISO Recommendation 612, term No. 30 (a and c).

(o) A 5% tolerance is permitted.

(p) Use laden rolling radius x 2π.

PART II

Form of information document in relation to a trailer to which these Regulations apply or to a component of such a trailer

	FOR DOE USE ONLY
TYPE APPROVAL OF A TRAILER in accordance with EEC Directive 70/156 INFORMATION DOCUMENT NUMBER	

If a component has been approved under an EEC Directive its description shall be replaced by the approval number in this document.

If the space is insufficient for an answer please add further pages.

Notes (*a*) to (*j*) are at page 28

		FOR DOE APPROVAL
0.	GENERAL	
0.1	Make	
0.2	Type and commercial description (include all variants)	
0.3	Class (eg semi-trailer, drawbar trailer, caravan, etc.)	
0.4	Category (*a*)	
0.4.1	Manufacturer's vehicle identification code (if any, explanation of system)	
0.5	Name and address of manufacturer	
0.6	Name and address of manufacturer's authorised representative (if address at 0.5 is outside United Kingdom)	
0.7	Location of identification plates and inscriptions and method of fixing:	
0.7.1	On the chassis	
0.7.2	On the bodywork	
0.8	Commencing chassis number	
1.	GENERAL CONSTRUCTIONAL CHARACTERISTICS OF THE TRAILER (to be shown on drawings 1 and 2)	
1.1	Number of axles and wheels (count twin wheels as one)	
1.1.1	Number of twin wheels (if applicable)	

1.2   Chassis frame (if any) brief description (to be shown on draw-
        ing 3)

1.2.1   Material used

1.2.2   Yield point

1.2.3   Ultimate tensile stress

1.2.4   Elongation (%)

1.2.5   Brinell hardness

2.   WEIGHTS AND DIMENSIONS (Use metric units)

2.1   Wheelbase (fully loaded) (b)

2.1.1   In the case of semi-trailers: distance between
        the axis of the fifth wheel kingpin and the
        foremost rear axle

2.2   Track of each axle (c)   Front
                                                  Rear
                                                  Intermediate

2.3   Maximum (or overall) trailer dimensions

	Chassis without body		Chassis with body	
	Max	Min	With fittings	Without fittings
2.3.1 Length (d)				
2.3.2 Width (e)				
2.3.3 Height (unladen) (f)				
2.3.4 Overhang—front (g)				
2.3.5 Overhang—rear (h)				
2.3.6 Ground clearance (Laden) (i)				
2.3.7 Distance(s) between axles				

2.4   Weight of the bare chassis (without spare wheel, tools)

2.4.1   Distribution of this weight   on front axle
                                              „ rear axle
                                              „ intermediate
                                                 axle

2.5   Weight of trailer with bodywork in running order
        or weight of the chassis if the manufacturer does
        not fit the bodywork (including tools, spare wheel)

2.5.1	Distribution of this weight	on front axle „ rear axle „ intermediate axle „ kingpin

2.6	Maximum allowable gross vehicle weight permitted by maker	

2.6.1	Distribution of this weight	on front axle „ rear axle „ intermediate axle „ kingpin

2·7	Maximum allowable weight on each axle permitted by maker	on front axle „ rear axle „ intermediate axle „ kingpin

2.8	Maximum vertical hitch load	

2.9 | Permissible maximum laden weight

2.9.1
FOR

Distribution of this weight on front axle
„ rear axle
„ intermediate axle
„ kingpin

DOE

2.10
APPROVAL

Permissible maximum weight on each axle
on front axle
„ rear axle
„ intermediate axle

3.　　AXLES (to be shown on drawing 4)

4.　　SUSPENSION (to be shown on drawing 5)

4.1　　FRONT

4.1.1　Make and type (independent etc.)

4.1.2　If solid axle, state material and characteristics

4.1.3　Tyres (dimensions, characteristics and pressures)

4.1.4　Characteristics of springing parts (design, characteristics of materials and dimensions)

4.1.5　Wheel type and dimensions

4.1.6　Stabilisers　　　　　　　　　　　　fitted/not fitted

| 4.1.7 | Dampers | fitted/not fitted |

4.2   INTERMEDIATE

4.2.1   Make and type (independent etc.)

4.2.2   If solid axle, state material
        and characteristics

4.2.3   Tyres (dimensions, characteristics
        and pressures)

4.2.4   Characteristics of springing parts (design,
        characteristics of materials and dimensions)

4.2.5   Wheel type and dimensions

| 4.2.6 | Stabilisers | fitted/not fitted |

| 4.2.7 | Dampers | fitted/not fitted |

4.3   REAR

4.3.1   Make and type (independent etc.)

4.3.2   If solid axle, state material
        and characteristics

4.3.3   Tyres (dimensions, characteristcis
        and pressures)

4.3.4   Characteristics of springing parts (design,
        characteristics of materials and dimensions)

4.3.5   Wheel type and dimensions

| 4.3.6 | Stabilisers | fitted/not fitted |

| 4.3.7 | Dampers | fitted/not fitted |

5.   STEERING (to be shown on drawing 6, if applicable)

5.1   Make and type

5.2   Type of linkage to wheels

5.3   Type of power assistance (if applicable)

5.4   Maximum turning angle of wheels   to left   to right
        (degrees) in each direction

5.5.   Minimum turning circle in
        each direction (*j*)

5.6   Swept path

6.   BRAKING SYSTEM (to be shown on drawing 7)

6.1   SERVICE BRAKE

6.1.1   Description

6.1.2   Outside sources of energy if any
          (specify type, eg vacuum, servo, etc.)

6.1.3   FRONT
6.1.3.1   Wheel cylinder, number and diameter

6.1.3.2   Disc/drum dimensions

6.1.3.3   Friction material (make and type)

6.1.3.4   Total lining area

6.1.4   INTERMEDIATE

6.1.4.1   Wheel cylinder, number and diameter

6.1.4.2   Disc/drum dimensions

6.1.4.3   Friction material (make and type)

6.1.4.4   Total lining area

6.1.5   REAR

6.1.5.1   Wheel cylinder, number and diameter

6.1.5.2   Disc/drum dimensions

6.1.5.3   Friction material (make and type)

6.1.5.4   Total lining area

6.2   SECONDARY BRAKE

6.2.1   Brief description

6.3   PARKING BRAKE

6.3.1   Brief description

6.4   ADDITIONAL BRAKING SYSTEM (if any)

6.4.1.   Brief description

6.5   AUTOMATIC BRAKING SYSTEM (which functions
          in the event of coupling breakage)

6.5.1   Brief description

6.6   GENERAL

6.6.1   Thrust and transmission of braking forces
          (details of torque reaction arrangements
          i.e. road springs, radius rods, etc.)

6.6.2   Calculation of braking systems
          (attach details, ref. 8)

6.6.3	FOR DOE APPROVAL	Test conditions
6.6.4	,, ,, ,,	Test results

7.   BODYWORK (to be shown on drawings 1 and 2)

7.1   Type of bodywork (material used and construction method)

7.2   Number and position of doors (direction of opening, latches and hinges)

7.3   Rear protective devices

8.   LIGHTING SYSTEM/ELECTRICAL (Position and dimensions of lights to be shown on drawing 2)

8.1   Front position lights (if fitted)

8.2   Rear position lights

8.3   Direction indicators

8.4   Brake lights

8.5   Rear registration plate lights

8.6   Red rear reflex reflectors

8.7   Front reflex reflectors

8.8   Parking lights

8.9   Reversing lights

8.10   Side marker lights

8.11   Amber side reflex reflectors

8.12   Additional lighting equipment for special vehicles

8.13   Hazard warning lights

9.   MISCELLANEOUS

9.1   Location of registration plate(s)

9.2   Towing hook

9.3   Trailer legs

9.4   Connections between drawing vehicles and trailers or semi-trailers (description of mechanical and electrical connections)

9.5   Details of linkages, couplings, safety devices

9.6   Optional equipment

ENCLOSURES TO BE SUBMITTED WITH FORM

1. ¾ front and ¾ rear photographs of the whole trailer.

2. Dimensional sketch of the whole trailer (following views).

   (*a*) Front
   (*b*) Side
   (*c*) Rear
   (*d*) Plan

3. Outline sketch of chassis frame.

4. Dimensional sketch of each axle.

5. Sketch of suspension arrangement.

6. Schematic layout of steering system (if applicable).

7. Schematic layout of braking system(s).

8. Calculations of braking system(s)—determination of the ratios between the braking force on pedal and total braking force at circumference of road wheels.

Signed.....................................
Dated....................................

NOTES

   (*a*) Classified according to the following international categories:—

   CATEGORY O—Trailers (including semi-trailers).

   CATEGORY O1—Trailers with a maximum weight not exceeding 0·75 metric ton.

   CATEGORY O2—Trailers with a maximum weight exceeding 0·75 metric ton but not exceeding 3·5 metric tons.

   CATEGORY O3—Trailers with a maximum weight exceeding 3·5 but not exceeding 10 metric tons.

   CATEGORY O4—Trailers with a maximum weight exceeding 10 metric tons.

   (*b*) ISO Recommendation 612, Term No. 3.
   (*c*) ISO Recommendation 612, Term No. 2.
   (*d*) ISO Recommendation 612, Term No. 11.
   (*e*) ISO Recommendation 612, Term No. 15.
   (*f*) ISO Recommendation 612, Term No. 16.
   (*g*) ISO Recommendation 612, Term No. 21.
   (*h*) ISO Recommendation 612, Term No. 22.
   (*i*) ISO Recommendation 612, Term No. 8.
   (*j*) ISO Recommendation 612, Term No. 30 (*a* and *c*).

PART III
Form of type approval certificate

The undersigned hereby certifies the accuracy of the manufacturer's description in Information Document No................ of the vehicle having the chassis No................ and engine No................, such vehicle having been submitted by the manufacturer as a prototype of model...............................

The checks carried out at the request of the manufacturer, ..., show that the vehicle specified above, which has been submitted as a series prototype, satisfies all requirements in respect of each and every item in this certificate.

...., ...
       (Place)   (Date)

....
         (Signature)

[1] If this has not been given, another form of identification.

PART IV
FORM OF CERTIFICATE OF CONFORMITY

The undersigned..
        (surname and first names)

of ....
        (name of manufacturer)

hereby certifies that the vehicle:

   1. Class (e.g. private car, goods vehicle)...

   2. Make ....

   3. Type ....

   4. Manufacturer's vehicle Identification and/or chassis No...............................

conforms in all respects to the type approved at ....

on.. by.. and

described in Type Approval Certificate No...............................
The vehicle to which the above Type Approval Certificate relates was granted type approval in respect of the following EEC Directives.

....

....

....

....
       (Place)   (Signature)

....
       (Date)   (Position)

SCHEDULE 2

(*See* Regulation 3(1))

The Council Directives with respect to the design, construction, equipment, and marking of vehicles or their components.

Community Reference Number	Date of Directive	Subject Matter	Official Journal Reference
(1)	(2)	(3)	(4)
70/157/EEC	6th February 1970	The permissible sound level and the exhaust system of motor vehicles.	O.J. L42, 23.2. 1970, p. 16 (S.E. 1970(I), p. 111)
70/220/EEC	20th March 1970	Measures to be taken against air pollution by gases from positive ignition engines of motor vehicles.	O.J. L76, 6.4. 1970, p. 25 (S.E. 1970(I), p. 171)
70/221/EEC	20th March 1970	Liquid fuel tanks and rear protective devices for motor vehicles and their trailers.	O.J. L76, 6.4. 1970, p.23 (S.E. 1970(I), p. 192)
70/222/EEC	20th March 1970	The mounting and fixing of rear registration plates and motor vehicles and their trailers.	O.J. L76, 6.4.1970, p. 25 (S.E. 1970(I), p. 194)
70/311/EEC	8th June 1970	The steering equipment for motor vehicles and their trailers.	O.J. L133, 18.6. 1970, p. 10 (S.E. 1970(II), p. 375).
70/387/EEC	27th July 1970	The doors of motor vehicles and their trailers.	O.J. L176, 10.8. 1970, p.5 (S.E. 1970(II), p. 564)
70/388/EEC	27th July 1970	Audible warning devices for motor vehicles.	O.J. L176, 10.8.1970, p. 12 (S.E. 1970(II), p. 571)
71/127/EEC	1st March 1971	The rear-view mirrors of motor vehicles.	O.J. L68, 22.3.1971, p.1 (S.E. 1971(I), p. 136)
71/320/EEC	26th July 1971	The braking devices of certain categories of motor vehicles and their trailers.	O.J. L202, 6.9. 1971, p. 37 (S.E. 1971(III) p. 746)
72/245/EEC	20th June 1972	The suppression of radio interference produced by spark-ignition engines fitted to motor vehicles.	O.J. L152, 6.7.1972, p.15 (S.E. 1972(II), p. 637)

EXPLANATORY NOTE
(This Note is not part of the Regulations.)

These Regulations make provision, as required by virtue of a Directive of the European Economic Community (Council Directive No. 70/156/EEC of 6th February 1970), for the type approval of certain motor vehicles and trailers and their components. The vehicles in question are those which are manufactured on or after 10th August 1973, being vehicles of the description specified in Regulation 2 of these Regulations.

Part II of the Regulations deals with the procedure for obtaining such type approval and with other related matters. Regulation 4 provides for applications for type approval to be made to the Secretary of State by the manufacturer of the vehicle or vehicle component in question. Under Regulation 5, where the Secretary of State is satisfied that the vehicle or vehicle component is of a type which conforms with the requirements as to design, construction, equipment and marking which are applicable thereto by virtue of the Council Directives specified in Schedule 2 to the Regulations, he is required to approve the vehicle as a type vehicle or, as the case may be, a type vehicle component, and to issue a type approval certificate in respect of it. Regulation 6 provides for the issue by the manufacturer of a type vehicle of a certificate of conformity in respect of each vehicle manufactured by him which conforms to the type vehicle in the relevent aspects of design, construction, equipment and marking.

Regulation 7 provides for the conditions subject to which type approval certificates may be issued, and for the cancellation or suspension of such certificates for breach of condition. Regulations 8 and 9 provide for notice to be given by manufacturers who cease to manufacture type vehicles or type vehicle components, or who make alterations in their manufacture or in any of the relevant aspects of design, construction, equipment or marking, and for the cancellation, suspension or modification of type approval certificates in consequence thereof. Regulation 10 provides for the cancellation or suspension of type approval certificates where vehicle or vehicle components are manufactured otherwise than in conformity with the relevant requirements. Regulation 11 provides for the suspension of type approval certificates where vehicles having a certificate of conformity are altered. Regulation 12 requires the Secretary of State to give due notice of his decisions to cancel, suspend or modify type approval certificates; and Regulation 13 provides for a right of appeal to the Secretary of State against any decision given by him with respect to such certificates.

Part III of the Regulations makes supplementary provisions in this connection. Regulation 14 authorises the Secretary of State to provide testing stations and Regulation 15 requires manufacturers to keep records relating to certificates of conformity issued by them.

STATUTORY INSTRUMENTS

1973 No. 1200

NATIONAL HEALTH SERVICE, ENGLAND AND WALES

The National Health Service (Medical Practices Compensation) Amendment Regulations 1973

Made - - -	*9th July* 1973
Laid before Parliament	*17th July* 1973
Coming into Operation	*7th August* 1973

The Secretary of State for Social Services(**a**), in exercise of the powers conferred by section 36(3) of the National Health Service Act 1946(**b**), as amended by section 1 of the National Health Service (Amendment) Act 1949(**c**) and section 51 of, and paragraph 22 of Schedule 4 to, the National Health Service Reorganisation Act 1973(**d**) and of all other powers enabling him in that behalf, and after consulting such organisations as are recognised by him as representing the medical profession, hereby makes the following regulations:—

1.—(1) These regulations may be cited as the National Health Service (Medical Practices Compensation) Amendment Regulations 1973 and shall come into operation on 7th August 1973.

(2) The Interpretation Act 1889(**e**) applies to the interpretation of these regulations as it applies to the interpretation of an Act of Parliament.

2. In these regulations, unless the context otherwise requires "the principal regulations" means the National Health Service (Medical Practices Compensation) Regulations 1948(**f**) as amended(**g**).

3. The principal regulations shall be further amended as follows:—

(1) In regulation 13 (which provides for payment of compensation) for paragraph (1)(*b*) there shall be substituted the following:—

"(*b*) in the case of a practitioner who retires or dies before 7th August 1973, on the retirement from practice or death of the practitioner concerned, whichever shall first occur:

(*c*) in any other case as soon as may be after 6th August 1973".

(2) In regulation 13(4) there shall be deleted from the table set out therein of the ages specified in column 1 and the dates set against those ages specified in column 2 the ages following the age "64" in column 1 and the dates following the date "1st April 1973" in column 2.

(**a**) For transfer of functions from the Minister of Health to the Secretary of State, *see* S.I. 1968/1699 (1968 III, p. 4585).
(**b**) 1946 c. 81.   (**c**) 1949 c. 93.
(**d**) 1973 c. 32.   (**e**) 1889 c. 63.
(**f**) S.I. 1948/1506 (Rev. XV, p. 758; 1948 I, p. 2183).
(**g**) The relevant amending instruments are S.I. 1949/1248, 1950/1744, 1966/756, 1971/1684 (1949 I, p. 2620; 1950 I, p. 1320; 1966 II, p. 1745, 1971 III p. 4609).

(3) At the end of regulation 14(3) there shall be inserted the following words: —

"(iii) any payment in respect of interest due on the compensation payable to a practitioner under regulation 13(1)(c) shall not after 7th August 1973 be paid on the fifth day of January and the fifth day of July in each year but may be paid at any time and shall be paid not later than 6 months after the date when compensation is paid."

Keith Joseph,
Secretary of State for Social Services.

9th July 1973.

EXPLANATORY NOTE

(This Note is not part of the Regulations.)

These Regulations further amend the National Health Service (Medical Practices Compensation) Regulations 1948 by making provision for all outstanding compensation payable to medical practitioners in respect of the loss of the right to sell the goodwill of a practice to be paid as soon as possible after 6th August 1973 and for the balance of interest payable thereon to be paid at any time, not later than six months after the time of payment.

STATUTORY INSTRUMENTS

1973 No. 1203

CHILDREN AND YOUNG PERSONS
The Adoption Agencies Regulations 1973

Made - - -		*9th July* 1973
Coming into Operation		*1st August* 1973

The Secretary of State for Social Services (as respects England, except Monmouthshire) and the Secretary of State for Wales (as respects Wales and Monmouthshire) in exercise of the powers conferred upon them by section 32 of the Adoption Act 1958(a), hereby make the following Regulations:—

1. These Regulations may be cited as the Adoption Agencies Regulations 1973 and shall come into operation on 1st August 1973.

2. Any reference in these Regulations to the principal Regulations is a reference to the Adoption Agencies Regulations 1959(b) as amended (c).

3. For paragraph (3) of Regulation 6 of the principal Regulations (which, as set out in Regulation 1 of the Adoption Agencies Regulations 1961(c), provides for certain tests and examinations to be carried out in respect of infants placed for adoption by or on behalf of an adoption society) there shall be substituted the following paragraphs:—

"(3) Where an infant has been placed by or on behalf of a registered adoption society in the care and possession of a person proposing to adopt him, then—

    (*a*) if, at the time of the said placing, the infant has not attained the age of six weeks, the society shall make arrangements for a serological test of his blood or his mother's blood for syphilis to be carried out by, and a report thereon obtained from, a fully registered medical practitioner as soon as practicable after the infant has attained that age;

    (*b*) if, at the time of the said placing, the infant has not attained the age of six complete days, the society shall also make arrangements for a test of his blood for the purpose of estimating the level of phenylalanine therein to be carried out by, and a report thereon obtained from, a fully registered medical practitioner as soon as practicable after the infant has attained that age:

Provided that if the result of a test of the blood of the infant's mother carried out in accordance with sub-paragraph (*a*) of this paragraph is positive the society shall also make arrangements for a test of the infant's blood for syphilis to be carried out and a report obtained as soon as practicable in accordance with the provisions of that sub-paragraph.

(4) For the purpose of computing the age of an infant for the purposes of paragraph (3)(*b*) of this Regulation the day of the infant's birth shall be excluded.

(a) 1958 c. 5 (7 & 8 Eliz. 2).   (b) S.I. 1959/639 (1959 I, p. 594).
(c) The relevant amending instrument is S.I. 1961/900 (1961 I, p. 1721).

(5) The society shall furnish a copy of any report obtained under paragraph (3) of this Regulation to the person proposing to adopt the infant to which it related.".

4. For paragraph E of the form of medical report set out in Schedule 5 to the principal Regulations (which sets out the form of the medical report which is required to be obtained by a registered adoption society or local authority on the health of an infant who is placed for adoption by or on behalf of the society or local authority), there shall be substituted the following paragraph:—

"E (i) (*To be completed in the case of a child at least six weeks old at the time of the test—either test (a) or tests (b) (i) and (ii) may be carried out except where test (b) (i) or (ii) is positive, when test (a) must also be carried out*)

(*a*) Result of a suitable serological test of the child's blood for syphilis (please specify test) ....

(*b*) Result of suitable serological tests of the mother's blood for syphilis

(i) reagin (please specify test)
....

(ii) verification (please specify test)
....".

(ii) (*To be completed in the case of a child over six complete days (excluding the day of his birth) and under two years old at the time of the test*)

Result of test of the child's blood for the purpose of estimating the level of phenylalanine therein ....".

Keith Joseph,
Secretary of State for Social Services.

5th July 1973.

Peter Thomas,
Secretary of State for Wales.

9th July 1973.

EXPLANATORY NOTE

(This Note is not part of the Regulations.)

These Regulations amend the provisions of Regulation 6 of and Schedule 5 to the Adoption Agencies Regulations 1959 relating to the tests which a registered adoption society or local authority must arrange to be made in respect of a child who is placed for adoption.

First, the provisions for carrying out a test for syphilis are modified. The medical report which must be obtained before a child at least six weeks old is placed for adoption (set out in Schedule 5 to the Regulations of 1959) may contain the result of tests for syphilis made of the blood of the child's mother instead of the child unless the result is positive, when a test must also be made of the child's blood. Similar amendments are made to Regulation 6 of the Regulations of 1959 to enable a registered adoption society or local authority which places for adoption a child who has not attained the age of six weeks to arrange for a test of the mother's blood and a medical report thereon to be obtained as an alternative to a test of the child's blood as soon as practicable after the child has attained that age, unless the result of the test is positive.

Secondly, the requirement that an examination of the child's urine for phenylpyruvic acid should be made in the case of a child over six weeks and under two years old is omitted. Instead the medical report required by Schedule 5 to the Regulations of 1959 must contain, in the case of a child over six complete days and under two years old, the result of a test of the child's blood to ascertain the level of phenylalanine therein. If a child is placed for adoption before it has attained the age of six complete days the society or local authority must arrange for the blood test for phenylalanine to be made as soon as practicable after he has attained that age. For the purpose of calculating the period of six days the day of the child's birth is excluded.

STATUTORY INSTRUMENTS

1973 No. 1212

ROAD TRAFFIC

The Heavy Goods Vehicles (Drivers' Licences) (Amendment) Regulations 1973

Made - - -	*12th July* 1973
Laid before Parliament	*23rd July* 1973
Coming into Operation	*13th August* 1973

The Secretary of State for the Environment, in exercise of his powers under section 119(1) and (3) of, and paragraph 2 of Schedule 5 to, the Road Traffic Act 1972(a) and of all other enabling powers, and after consultation with representative organisations in accordance with section 199(2) of that Act, hereby makes the following Regulations:—

1. These Regulations shall come into operation on 13th August 1973 and may be cited as the Heavy Goods Vehicles (Drivers' Licences) (Amendment) Regulations 1973.

2. Regulation 28(1) of the Heavy Goods Vehicles (Drivers' Licences) Regulations 1969(b), as amended by the Heavy Goods Vehicles (Drivers' Licences) (Amendment) Regulations 1972(c) (which specifies certain classes of vehicles in relation to which the provisions as to the licensing of drivers of heavy goods vehicles now contained in Part IV of, and in paragraph 1 of Schedule 5 to, the Road Traffic Act 1972, shall not apply) shall be further amended in accordance with paragraphs (2) and (3) below.

(2) The said Regulation 28(1), insofar as it provides that paragraph 1 of Schedule 5 to the said Act (transitional provisions) does not apply to heavy goods vehicles of the classes specified in that Regulation, shall have effect as if sub-paragraph (*o*) (vehicles in the service of a visiting force or headquarters) were omitted.

(3) For sub-paragraph (*t*) of the said Regulation 28(1) there shall be substituted the following sub-paragraph:—

"(*t*) a vehicle fitted with apparatus designed for raising a disabled vehicle partly from the ground and for drawing a disabled vehicle when so raised (whether by partial superimposition or otherwise) being a vehicle which—

(i) is used solely for dealing with disabled vehicles,

(ii) is not used for the conveyance of any load other than a disabled

---

(a) 1972 c. 20.　　　　　　　　　(b) S.I. 1969/903 (1969 II. p. 2582).
(c) S.I. 1972/1956 (1972 III. p. 5831).

vehicle when so raised, water, fuel and accumulators and articles required for the operation of, or in connection with, such apparatus as aforesaid or otherwise for dealing with disabled vehicles, and

(iii) has an unladen weight not exceeding 3 tons.".

3. Regulation 2 of the Heavy Goods Vehicles (Drivers' Licences) (Amendment) Regulations 1972, insofar as it provides for the insertion in the said Regulation 28(1) of a sub-paragraph (*t*), is hereby revoked.
Signed by authority of the Secretary of State.

John Peyton,
Minister for Transport Industries,
Department of the Environment.

12th July 1973.

EXPLANATORY NOTE

(This Note is not part of the Regulations.)

These Regulations amend the Heavy Goods Vehicles (Drivers' Licences) Regulations 1969 so as to provide:—

(*a*) that certain transitional provisions contained in paragraph 1 of Schedule 5 to the Road Traffic Act 1972 and relating to licences to drive heavy goods vehicles shall become applicable to vehicles in the service of a visiting force or headquarters. The effect of this is that persons who have been in the habit of driving such vehicles for any period of, or periods amounting in the aggregate to, six months in the course of the year ending on 1st February 1970 may, on their first application for a heavy goods vehicle driver's licence under Part IV of the Road Traffic Act 1972, obtain a full licence without having to pass the prescribed test of competence; and

(*b*) that the exemption of breakdown vehicles provided for by Regulation 28(1)(*t*) of the said Regulations shall include such vehicles fitted with apparatus designed for raising disabled vehicles partly from the ground and for drawing disabled vehicles when so raised.

STATUTORY INSTRUMENTS

1973 No. 1217

TELEGRAPHS

The Wireless Telegraphy (Control of Interference from Ignition Apparatus) Regulations 1973

Made - - - -	11th July 1973
Laid before Parliament	23rd July 1973
Coming into Operation	1st October 1973

The Minister of Posts and Telecommunications, in exercise of powers conferred by section 10 of the Wireless Telegraphy Act 1949(a), by the said section as extended to the Channel Islands by the Wireless Telegraphy (Channel Islands) Order 1952(b) and by the said section as extended to the Isle of Man by the Wireless Telegraphy (Isle of Man) Order 1952(c) and now vested in him (d), and of every other power enabling him in that behalf and after consultation with the advisory committee referred to in section 9 of the Wireless Telegraphy Act 1949 hereby makes the following Regulations:—

Citation and Commencement

1.—These Regulations may be cited as the Wireless Telegraphy (Control of Interference from Ignition Apparatus) Regulations 1973, and shall come into operation on 1st October 1973.

Interpretation

2.—(1) In these Regulations, except so far as the contrary is provided or the context otherwise requires, the following expressions have the meanings hereby respectively assigned to them:

"ignition apparatus" means equipment assembled for the purpose of providing and conveying electrical energy for igniting gas or vapour in an internal combustion engine;

"suppressor" means a piece of equipment designed to reduce the field-strength of the electro-magnetic energy radiated from the apparatus to which it is fitted when that apparatus is being used, and references to "suppressors" include references to a single suppressor;

"the British Islands" means the area comprised by the United Kingdom, the Channel Islands, and the Isle of Man;

(a) 1949 c. 54.   (b) S.I. 1952/1900 (1952 III, p. 3414).
(c) S.I. 1952/1899 (1952 III, p. 3418).
(d) *See* Post Office Act 1969 (c. 48) s.3; as to the Channel Islands, S.I. 1969/1369 (1969 III, p. 4085) and as to the Isle of Man, S.I. 1969/1371 (1969 III, p. 4087).

"megahertz (MHz)" has the same meaning as megacycles per second, i.e. one million cycles per second;

and other expressions have the same meaning as they have in the Wireless Telegraphy Act 1949.

(2) The Interpretation Act 1889(a) applies to the interpretation of these Regulations as it applies to the interpretation of an Act of Parliament.

Assemblers and Importers

3.—(1) This Regulation applies to ignition apparatus forming part of an internal combustion engine other than an engine which forms part of an aircraft.

(2) The requirement referred to in Regulation 5 shall be complied with in the case of any ignition apparatus to which this Regulation applies if, on or after the date on which these Regulations come into operation, that apparatus is, as being part of a vehicle, vessel or engine, to be sold otherwise than for export, or offered or advertised for sale otherwise than for export, or let on hire or offered or advertised for letting on hire, by any person who in the British Islands in the course of business assembles such apparatus as part of a vehicle, vessel or engine, or who in the course of business imports into the British Islands such apparatus already assembled as part of a vehicle, vessel or engine.

Users

4.—(1) This Regulation applies to:—

(a) ignition apparatus forming part of an internal combustion engine other than an engine which forms part of an aircraft or of a foreign vessel, except ignition apparatus which is proved by the person using it to have been assembled as part of a vehicle, vessel or engine before the date on which these Regulations come into operation; and

(b) apparatus which includes one or more components designed to form part of the ignition apparatus of an internal combustion engine, and which is assembled for the purpose of testing or demonstrating the operation of one or more of those components, and which when used involves sudden changes of current in a high-voltage circuit.

(2) The requirement referred to in Regulation 5 shall be complied with in the case of any apparatus to which this Regulation applies, if the apparatus is to be used within the British Islands or the territorial waters adjacent thereto:—

(a) on land, or

(b) on the sea or in any estuary within one hundred metres of any moored vessel or on the landward side of a line one hundred metres to seaward of low water mark, or

(c) on any water, other than the sea or an estuary:

provided that the use of any apparatus referred to in sub-paragraph (a) of paragraph (1) of this Regulation shall be deemed to comply with the said requirement if the person using the apparatus establishes:—

(a) 1889 c. 63.

(i) that suppressors were fitted to the apparatus by the manufacturer or builder of the vehicle, vessel or engine of which the apparatus forms part or by the importer of that vehicle, vessel or engine into the British Islands, and

(ii) that the suppressors so fitted remained fitted to the apparatus at the time of the use, or that suppressors having equivalent electrical characteristics had been correctly fitted to the apparatus at that time in substitution for those fitted as aforesaid, and in either case that the suppressors were then in good electrical and mechanical repair and condition, and

(iii) that the apparatus at the time of the use consisted of the same components as those which were fitted at the time when the vehicle, vessel or engine was manufactured or built, or that any components which had been substituted for those components had equivalent electrical characteristics and had been correctly fitted.

Requirement

5.—(1) The requirement hereinbefore referred to is that the apparatus shall be so designed, constructed, assembled and installed, and that such precautions shall be taken in relation to it (by means of the fitting of suppressors or otherwise) as to ensure that the field-strength, at any distance of not less than ten metres from the apparatus when it is used, as measured and computed in accordance with paragraph 5(3) and the Schedule hereto, of the electro-magnetic energy radiated at forty megahertz and at any frequency up to seventy-five megahertz does not exceed fifty microvolts per metre and at any frequency between seventy-five and two hundred and fifty megahertz does not exceed fifty microvolts per metre at seventy-five megahertz rising linearly with frequency to one hundred and twenty microvolts per metre at two hundred and fifty megahertz.

(2) For the purpose of this Regulation the apparatus shall be deemed to meet these requirements over the whole frequency range of forty to two hundred and fifty megahertz if it meets them at the following discrete frequencies; forty-five, sixty-five, ninety, one hundred and fifty, one hundred and eighty, and two hundred and twenty megahertz. To avoid interference from transmissions operating on these discrete frequencies each frequency shall be subject to a tolerance of plus or minus five megahertz.

(3) For the purpose of Regulation 3 the apparatus shall be deemed to meet these requirements if measurements for the purpose of type-approval and production conformity in type-approved equipment are carried out in accordance with the procedures set out in paragraphs 3.6 and 3.7 respectively of British Standard 833:1970.

(4) For the purpose of measuring and computing the field-strength of such electro-magnetic energy, the apparatus shall be tested by means of measuring apparatus of the description and having the physical and electrical characteristics and performance set out in Section 1 of British Standard 727:1967 "Specification for Radio-Interference Measuring Apparatus for the Frequency Range 0·015 MHz to 1000 MHz", except that where the apparatus forms part of the engine of a road vehicle measuring apparatus having the physical and electrical characteristics and performance set out in Section 2 of British Standard 727:1967 may be used. The tests shall be made by the method and under the conditions set out in the Schedule hereto.

Dated 11th July 1973.

John Eden,
Minister of Posts and Telecommunications.

THE SCHEDULE

Details of Measuring Site and Test Procedure

1. *Measuring Site*

The site to be used for testing for the purpose of Regulation 5 shall conform to the specification set out in paragraph 3.2 of British Standard 833: 1970 "Specification for Radio Interference Limits and Measurements for the Electrical Ignition Systems of Internal Combustion Engines".

2. *Test Procedure*

(1) The test shall be carried out in accordance with the procedures set out in paragraphs 3.3, 3.4 and 3.5 of British Standard 833: 1970.

(2) Where ignition apparatus is being tested for the purpose of Regulation 3, it shall be tested as installed in the engine. If the engine is to form part of a vehicle, vessel or equipment which is to be sold or let on hire by the assembler or importer, the test shall be made with the engine installed in the vehicle, vessel or equipment.

(3) Where ignition apparatus is being tested for the purpose of Regulation 4, it shall be tested under normal conditions of installation. Where apparatus mentioned in Regulation 4(1)(*b*) is being tested for the purpose of that Regulation it shall be tested under normal conditions of installation and use.

EXPLANATORY NOTE

(*This Note is not part of the Regulations.*)

These Regulations prescribe the requirments to be complied with in relation to certain ignition apparatus, for the purpose of ensuring that the apparatus will not cause undue interference with wireless telegraphy.

Regulation 3 applies to ignition apparatus forming part of an internal combustion engine (except an engine forming part of an aircraft) which, on or after the 1st October 1973, is to be sold or offered or advertised for sale (except for export) or let on hire or offered or advertised for letting on hire by an assembler or importer in the course of his business. In respect of such ignition apparatus, the assembler or importer is required, from the date stated, to comply with Regulation 5.

Regulation 4 applies to ignition apparatus (except ignition apparatus of engines in aircraft or foreign vessels) which is first assembled as part of a vehicle, vessel or engine, on or after the 1st October 1973. Users of such apparatus in the area referred to in paragraph (2) are required to comply with Regulation 5; but the user is deemed to comply with Regulation 5 if the manufacturer or builder of the vehicle, vessel or engine fitted suppressors and these remain fitted and in good condition and the ignition apparatus has not been altered, and in certain other circumstances also. Regulation 4 also applies to apparatus which is used for testing or demonstrating the operation of components of ignition systems.

Regulation 5 prescribes the requirement, in terms of the maximum permitted field-strength of the electro-magnetic energy radiated from the apparatus when in use and the description and specification of the measuring apparatus. The Schedule sets out the method by which the field-strength is to be measured and the conditions under which tests are to be made.

STATUTORY INSTRUMENTS

1973 No. 1218

WAGES COUNCILS

The Wages Regulation (Retail Food) (England and Wales) (Amendment) Order 1973

Made - - -		*12th July* 1973
Coming into Operation		*20th August* 1973

Whereas the Secretary of State has received from the Retail Food Trades Wages Council (England and Wales) the wages regulation proposals set out in the Schedule hereto;

Now, therefore, the Secretary of State in exercise of powers conferred by section 11 of the Wages Councils Act 1959(a), as modified by Article 2 of the Counter-Inflation (Modification of Wages Councils Act 1959) Order 1973(b), and now vested in him(c), and of all other powers enabling him in that behalf, hereby makes the following Order:—

1. This Order may be cited as the Wages Regulation (Retail Food) (England and Wales) (Amendment) Order 1973.

2.—(1) In this Order the expression "the specified date" means the 20th August 1973, provided that where, as respects any worker who is paid wages at intervals not exceeding seven days, that date does not correspond with the beginning of the period for which the wages are paid, the expression "the specified date" means, as respects that worker, the beginning of the next such period following that date.

(2) The Interpretation Act 1889(d) shall apply to the interpretation of this Order as it applies to the interpretation of an Act of Parliament.

3. The wages regulation proposals set out in the Schedule hereto shall have effect as from the specified date.

Signed by order of the Secretary of State.

12th July 1973.

W. H. Marsh,
Assistant Secretary,
Department of Employment.

(a) 1959 c. 69. (b) S.I. 1973/661(1973 I, p. 2141).
(c) S.I. 1959/1769, 1968/729 (1959 I, p. 1795; 1968 II, p. 2108).
(d) 1889 c. 63.

SCHEDULE
STATUTORY MINIMUM REMUNERATION

The Wages Regulation (Retail Food) (England and Wales) Order 1973(a) (Order R.F.C. (57)) shall have effect as if in the Schedule thereto for the last proviso in paragraph 7 there were substituted the following:—

"Provided that in any week which includes one customary holiday '35 hours', '34 hours' or '33 hours' shall be substituted for '42 hours', '41 hours' or '40 hours' respectively, in any week which includes two customary holidays '28 hours', '27 hours' or '26 hours' shall be substituted for the said '42 hours', '41 hours' or '40 hours' *and in any week which includes three customary holidays '21 hours', '20 hours' or '19 hours' shall be substituted for the said '42 hours', '41 hours' or '40 hours'.*"

EXPLANATORY NOTE

(This Note is not part of the Order.)

This Order, which has effect from 20th August 1973, amends the overtime provisions of the Wages Regulation (Retail Food) (England and Wales) Order 1973 (Order R.F.C. (57)) by providing for a week in which three days of customary holiday occur.

New rates are printed in italics.

(a) S.I. 1973/39 (1973 I, p. 325).

STATUTORY INSTRUMENTS

1973 No. 1219 (S.94)

NATIONAL HEALTH SERVICE, SCOTLAND

The National Health Service (Medical Practices Compensation) (Scotland) Amendment Regulations 1973

Made - - -	11*th July* 1973
Laid before Parliament	20*th July* 1973
Coming into Operation	10*th August* 1973

In exercise of the powers conferred on me by section 37 of the National Health Service (Scotland) Act 1947(a), as read with sections 1 and 3 of the National Health Service (Amendment) Act 1949(b) and section 51 of, and Schedule 4 to, the National Health Service Reorganisation Act 1973(c) and of all other powers enabling me in that behalf, and after consulting such organisations as are recognised by me as representing the medical profession, I hereby make the following regulations: —

1.—(1) These regulations may be cited as the National Health Service (Medical Practices Compensation) (Scotland) Amendment Regulations 1973 and shall come into operation on 10th August 1973.

(2) The Interpretation Act 1889(d) shall apply for the interpretation of these regulations as it applies for the interpretation of an Act of Parliament.

2. In these regulations, unless the context otherwise requires "the principal regulations" means the National Health Service (Medical Practices Compensation) (Scotland) Regulations 1948(e) as amended(f).

3. The principal regulations shall be further amended as follows: —

(1) In regulation 15 (which provides for payment of compensation) for paragraph (1)(*b*) there shall be substituted the following: —

"(*b*) in the case of a practitioner who retires or dies before 10th August 1973, on the retirement from practice or death of the practitioner concerned, whichever shall first occur:

(*c*) in any other case as soon as may be after 9th August 1973".

(a) 1947 c. 27.   (b) 1949 c. 93.
(c) 1973 c.32.   (d) 1889 c. 63.
(e) S.I. 1948/1768 (Rev. XV, p. 1021: 1948 I, p. 2441).
(f) The relevant amending instruments are S.I. 1949/1206, 1950/1889, 1966/773, 1971/1833 (1949 I, p. 2667; 1950 I, p. 1454; 1966 II, p. 1785; 1971 III, p. 5001).

(2) In regulation 15(4) there shall be deleted from the Table set out therein of the ages specified in column 1 and the dates set against those ages specified in column 2 the ages following the age "64" in column 1 and the dates following the date "1st April 1973" in column 2.

(3) At the end of regulation 16(3) there shall be inserted the following words:—

"(iii) any payment in respect of interest due on the compensation payable to a practitioner under regulation 15(1)(c) shall not after 10th August 1973 be paid on the fifth day of January and the fifth day of July in each year but may be paid at any time and shall be paid not later than six months after the date when compensation is paid."

Gordon Campbell,
One of Her Majesty's Principal
Secretaries of State.

St. Andrew's House,
Edinburgh.

11th July 1973.

EXPLANATORY NOTE

(This Note is not part of the Regulations.)

These Regulations further amend the National Health Service (Medical Practices Compensation) (Scotland) Regulations 1948 by making provision for all outstanding compensation payable to medical practitioners in respect of the loss of the right to sell the goodwill of a practice to be paid as soon as possible after 9th August 1973 and for the balance of interest payable thereon to be paid at any time, not later than six months after the time of payment.

STATUTORY INSTRUMENTS

1973 No. 1222

EDUCATION, ENGLAND AND WALES

The Remuneration of Teachers (Farm Institutes) Order 1973

Made - - -		*16th July* 1973
Coming into Operation		*17th July* 1973

Whereas—

(1) the Committee constituted under section 1 of the Remuneration of Teachers Act 1965(**a**) ("the Act") for the purpose of considering the remuneration of teachers in farm institutes and teachers of agricultural subjects on the staff of local education authorities ("the Committee") have, in pursuance of section 2(2) of the Act, transmitted to the Secretary of State for Education and Science ("the Secretary of State") recommendations agreed on by them with respect to the remuneration of such teachers;

(2) the Committee have, in pursuance of section 2(2) of the Act as modified by the Counter-Inflation (Modification of the Remuneration of Teachers Act 1965) Order 1973(**b**), also transmitted to the Pay Board established under section 1(1) of the Counter-Inflation Act 1973(**c**) ("the Pay Board") the proposals contained in those recommendations for increases in the remuneration of such teachers;

(3) the Pay Board have approved the said proposals;

(4) the Secretary of State has, as required by section 2(3) of the Act as modified as aforesaid, prepared a draft document setting out the scales and other provisions required for determining the remuneration of such teachers in the form in which, in her opinion, those scales and provisions should be so as to give effect to the recommendations;

(5) the Secretary of State has, as required by section 2(4) of the Act, consulted the Committee with respect to the draft document and has made such modifications thereof as were requisite for giving effect to representations (not being representations involving increases in remuneration in excess of those approved by the Pay Board) made by the Committee;

(**a**) 1965 c. 3.　　　　　　　　　　(**b**) S.I. 1973/616 (1973 I, p. 1950).
(**c**) 1973 c. 9.

(6) the Secretary of State has arranged for a document setting out the requisite scales and other provisions in the form of the draft as modified as aforesaid to be published by Her Majesty's Stationery Office on 16th July 1973 under the title "SCALES OF SALARIES FOR THE TEACHING STAFF OF FARM INSTITUTES AND FOR TEACHERS OF AGRICULTURAL (INCLUDING HORTICULTURAL) SUBJECTS, ENGLAND AND WALES, 1973".

Now therefore the Secretary of State, in pursuance of section 2(4) of the Act, hereby makes the following Order:—

Citation and Commencement

1. This Order may be cited as the Remuneration of Teachers (Farm Institutes) Order 1973 and shall come into operation on 17th July 1973.

Interpretation

2. The Interpretation Act 1889(**a**) shall apply for the interpretation of this Order as it applies for the interpretation of an Act of Parliament.

Remuneration of Teachers

3. The remuneration payable from 1st April 1973 to full-time teachers employed as members of the teaching staff of farm institutes maintained by local education authorities or as teachers of agricultural subjects (including horticultural and related subjects) on the staff of local education authorities shall be determined in accordance with the scales and other provisions set out in the document published by Her Majesty's Stationery Office as aforesaid.

Revocation

4. The Remuneration of Teachers (Farm Institutes) No. 2 Order 1972(**b**) is hereby revoked and section 38(2) of the Interpretation Act 1889 (which relates to the effect of repeals) shall have effect in relation to that Order as if both it and this Order were Acts of Parliament.

Given under the Official Seal of the Secretary of State for Education and Science on 16th July 1973.

(L.S.)   *Margaret Thatcher,*
Secretary of State for Education and Science.

(**a**) 1889 c. 63.   (**b**) S.I. 1972/771 (1972 II, p. 2469).

EXPLANATORY NOTE

(This Note is not part of the Order.)

This Order brings into operation the scales and other provisions relating to the remuneration of full-time teachers in farm institutes and teachers of agricultural subjects on the staff of local education authorities set out in a document published by Her Majesty's Stationery Office. This document contains the recommendations of the Committee constituted under the Remuneration of Teachers Act 1965 for the purpose of considering the remuneration of such teachers.

Increases in remuneration resulting from the Order have been approved by the Pay Board.

The Order has effect from 1st April 1973 by virtue of section 7(3) of the Remuneration of Teachers Act 1965.

STATUTORY INSTRUMENTS

1973 No. 1223

EDUCATION, ENGLAND AND WALES

The Remuneration of Teachers (Further Education) Order 1973

Made	- - -	16*th July* 1973
Coming into Operation		17*th July* 1973

Whereas—

(1) the Committee constituted under section 1 of the Remuneration of Teachers Act 1965(a) ("the Act") for the purpose of considering the remuneration of teachers in establishments for further education (other than farm institutes) maintained by local education authorities ("the Committee") have, in pursuance of section 2(2) of the Act, transmitted to the Secretary of State for Education and Science ("the Secretary of State") recommendations agreed on by them with respect to the remuneration of such teachers;

(2) the Committee have, in pursuance of section 2(2) of the Act as modified by the Counter-Inflation (Modification of the Remuneration of Teachers Act 1965) Order 1973(b), also transmitted to the Pay Board established under section 1(1) of the Counter-Inflation Act 1973(c) ("the Pay Board") the proposals contained in those recommendations for increases in the remuneration of such teachers;

(3) the Pay Board have approved the said proposals;

(4) the Secretary of State has, as required by section 2(3) of the Act as modified as aforesaid, prepared a draft document setting out the scales and other provisions required for determining the remuneration of such teachers in the form in which, in her opinion, those scales and provisions should be so as to give effect to the recommendations;

(5) the Secretary of State has, as required by section 2(4) of the Act, consulted the Committee with respect to the draft document and has made such modifications thereof as were requisite for giving effect to representations (not being representations involving increases in remuneration in excess of those approved by the Pay Board) made by the Committee;

(6) the Secretary of State has arranged for a document setting out the requisite scales and other provisions in the form of the draft as modified as aforesaid to be published by Her Majesty's Stationery Office on 16th July 1973 under the title "SCALES OF SALARIES FOR TEACHERS IN ESTABLISHMENTS FOR FURTHER EDUCATION, ENGLAND AND WALES 1973".

(a) 1965 c. 3.   (b) S.I. 1973/616 (1973 I, p. 1950).   (c) 1973 c. 9.

Now therefore the Secretary of State, in pursuance of section 2(4) of the Act, hereby makes the following Order:—

Citation and Commencement

1. This Order may be cited as the Remuneration of Teachers (Further Education) Order 1973 and shall come into operation on 17th July 1973.

Interpretation

2. The Interpretation Act 1889(a) shall apply for the interpretation of this Order as it applies for the interpretation of an Act of Parliament.

Remuneration of Teachers

3. The remuneration payable from 1st April 1973 to teachers in establishments for further education (other than farm institutes) maintained by local education authorities shall be determined in accordance with the scales and other provisions set out in the document published by Her Majesty's Stationery Office as aforesaid.

Revocation

4. The Remuneration of Teachers (Further Education) No. 2 Order 1972(b) is hereby revoked and section 38(2) of the Interpretation Act 1889 (which relates to the effect of repeals) shall have effect in relation to that Order as if both it and this Order were Acts of Parliament.

Given under the Official Seal of the Secretary of State for Education and Science on 16th July 1973.

(L.S.)

Margaret Thatcher,
Secretary of State for Education and Science.

(a) 1889 c. 63.   (b) S.I. 1972/683 (1972 II, p. 2223).

EXPLANATORY NOTE

(This Note is not part of the Order.)

This Order brings into operation the scales and other provisions relating to the remuneration of full-time teachers in establishments for further education (other than farm institutes) maintained by local education authorities set out in a document published by Her Majesty's Stationery Office. This document contains the recommendations of the Committee constituted under the Remuneration of Teachers Act 1965 for the purpose of considering the remuneration of such teachers.

Increases in remuneration resulting from the Order have been approved by the Pay Board.

The Order has effect from 1st April 1973 by virtue of section 7(3) of the Remuneration of Teachers Act 1965.

STATUTORY INSTRUMENTS

1973 No. 1224

INDUSTRIAL TRAINING

The Industrial Training (Furniture and Timber Industry Board) Order 1965 (Amendment) Order 1973

Made - - - -	13th July 1973
Laid before Parliament	24th July 1973
Coming into Operation	15th August 1973

The Secretary of State after consultation with the Furniture and Timber Industry Training Board and with organisations and associations of organisations appearing to be representative respectively of substantial numbers of employers engaging in the activities hereinafter mentioned and of substantial numbers of persons employed in those activities and in exercise of powers conferred by section 9 of the Industrial Training Act 1964(a) and now vested in him (b), and of all other powers enabling him in that behalf hereby makes the following Order:—

Citation, commencement and interpretation

1.—(1) This Order may be cited as the Industrial Training (Furniture and Timber Industry Board) Order 1965 (Amendment) Order 1973 and shall come into operation on 15th August 1973.

(2) In this Order—

(a) "the Act" means the Industrial Training Act 1964;

(b) "the Board" means the Furniture and Timber Industry Training Board;

(c) "Levy Order" includes the Industrial Training Levy (Furniture and Timber) Order 1966(c), the Industrial Training Levy (Furniture and Timber) Order 1968(d), the Industrial Training Levy (Furniture and Timber) Order 1969(e), the Industrial Training Levy (Furniture and Timber) Order 1970(f), the Industrial Training Levy (Furniture and Timber) Order 1971(g), and the Industrial Training Levy (Furniture and Timber) Order 1972 (h);

(d) "the principal Order" means the Industrial Training (Furniture and Timber Industry Board) Order 1965(i);

(e) "the 1969 Order" means the Industrial Training (Furniture and Timber Industry Board) Order 1969(j);

(f) "the 1970 Order" means the Industrial Training (Furniture and Timber Industry Board) Order 1969 (Amendment) Order 1970(k).

(a) 1964 c. 16.
(b) S.I. 1968/729 (1968 II, p. 2108).
(c) S.I. 1966/1437 (1966 III, p. 3793).
(d) S.I. 1968/1034 (1968 II, p. 2732).
(e) S.I. 1969/820 (1969 II, p. 2317).
(f) S.I. 1970/1273 (1970 II, p. 4157).
(g) S.I. 1971/1392 (1971 II, p. 3907).
(h) S.I. 1972/1157 (1972 II, p. 3435).
(i) S.I. 1965/2028 (1965 III, p. 5998).
(j) S.I. 1969/1290 (1969 III, p. 3820).
(k) S.I. 1970/1634 (1970 III, p. 5372).

(3) The Interpretation Act 1889(a) shall apply to the interpretation of this Order as it applies to the interpretation of an Act of Parliament and as if this Order, the principal Order, the 1969 Order and the 1970 Order were Acts of Parliament.

Amendment of the principal Order

2. The principal Order (as amended by the 1969 Order and the 1970 Order), shall be further amended in accordance with the Schedule to this Order, and accordingly the activities in relation to which the Board exercises the function conferred by the Act upon industrial training boards shall be the activities specified in Schedule 1 to the principal Order, as amended by the 1969 Order, the 1970 Order and this Order.

Transitional provisions

3.—(1) The chairman and other members of the Board on the day upon which this Order comes into operation shall continue to be members of the Board and to hold and vacate their offices in accordance with the terms of the instruments appointing them to be members.

(2) The provisions of this Order shall not—

(*a*) extend the operation of a Levy Order;

(*b*) affect the operation of a Levy Order in relation to the assessment of an employer within the meaning of that Order in respect of an establishment that was engaged in the relevant levy period wholly or mainly in activities included in Schedule 1 to the principal Order as amended by the 1969 Order, the 1970 Order and this Order.

(*c*) affect the operation of any assessment notice served by the Board under the provisions of a Levy Order before the date upon which this Order comes into operation or any appeal or other proceedings arising out of any such notice.

Signed by order of the Secretary of State.

13th July 1973.

R. Chichester-Clark,
Minister of State,
Department of Employment.

(a) 1889 c. 63.

Article 2

SCHEDULE

AMENDMENTS TO THE PRINCIPAL ORDER

(AS AMENDED BY THE 1969 ORDER AND THE 1970 ORDER)

1. In this Schedule the expression "the Schedule" means Schedule 1 to the principal Order (as amended by the 1969 Order and the 1970 Order).

2.—(1) Paragraph 2 of the Schedule shall be amended as follows.

(2) In the Table to sub-paragraph (c) there shall be added the following item—

Item No.	*Activities*	*Group of Products*
31.	Manufacture or repair.	Briar pipes.".

(3) For sub-paragraph (e) (iii) there shall be substituted the following—
"(iii) the British Gas Corporation;".

3.—(1) In the Appendix to the Schedule the following entries shall be substituted for the corresponding entries appearing in that Appendix—

Column 1	Column 2	Column 3
The construction industry	The Industrial Training (Construction Board) Order 1964 as amended by the Industrial Training (Construction Board) Order 1973(a)	Schedule 1 Paragraph 1(h)
The engineering industry	The Industrial Training (Engineering Board) Order 1964 as amended by the Industrial Training (Engineering Board) Order 1971(b)	Schedule 1 Paragraph 1 (m)
The agricultural, horticultural and forestry industry	The Industrial Training (Agricultural Horticultural and Forestry Board) Order 1966 as amended by the Industrial Training (Agricultural, Horticultural and Forestry Board) Order 1970(c)	Schedule 1 Paragraph 1(d)
The road transport industry	The Industrial Training (Road Transport Board) Order 1966 as amended by the Industrial Training (Road Transport Board) Order 1972 and the Industrial Training (Road Transport Board) Order 1966 (Amendment) Order 1973(d)	Schedule 1 Paragraph 1(p)
The chemical and allied products industry	The Industrial Training (Chemical and Allied Products Board) Order 1967 as amended by the Industrial Training (Chemical and Allied Products Board) Order 1970(e)	Schedule 1 Paragraph 1(w)
The distributive industry	The Industrial Training (Distributive Board) Order 1968 as amended by the Industrial Training (Distributive Board) Order 1970 and the Industrial Training (Distributive Board) Order 1970 (Amendment) Order 1971(f)	Schedule 1 Paragraph 1(h)
The food, drink and tobacco industry	The Industrial Training (Food, Drink and Tobacco Board) Order 1968 as amended by the Industrial Training (Food, Drink and Tobacco Board) Order 1971(g)	Schedule 1 Paragraph 1(q)

(a) S.I. 1964/1079, 1973/160 (1964 II, p. 2384; 1973 I, p. 654).
(b) S.I. 1964/1086, 1971/1530 (1964 II, p. 2402; 1971 III, p. 4309).
(c) S.I. 1966/969, 1970/1886 (1966 II, p. 2333; 1970 III, p. 6227).
(d) S.I. 1966/1112, 1972/772, 1973/860 (1966 III, p. 2712; 1972 II. p. 2471; 1973 II, p. 2663).
(e) S.I. 1967/1386, 1970/1743 (1967 III, p. 4049; 1970 III, p. 5706).
(f) S.I. 1968/1032, 1970/1053, 1971/1876 (1968 II, p. 2709; 1970 II, p. 3723; 1971 III, p. 5109).
(g) S.I. 1968/1033, 1971/648 (1968 II, p. 2721; 1971 I, p. 1709).

Column 1	Column 2	Column 3
The footwear, leather and fur skin industry	The Industrial Training (Footwear, Leather and Fur Skin Board) Order 1968 as amended by the Industrial Training (Footwear, Leather and Fur Skin Board) Order 1968 (Amendment) Order 1972(a)	Schedule 1 Paragraph 1(v)

(2) The following entry shall be omitted from the Appendix—

Column 1	Column 2	Column 3
The hairdressing and allied services industry	The Industrial Training (Hairdressing and Allied Services Board) Order 1969(b)	Schedule 1 Paragraph 1(g)

EXPLANATORY NOTE

(This Note is not part of the Order.)

This Order further amends the Industrial Training (Furniture and Timber Industry Board) Order 1965 (which was amended by the Industrial Training (Furniture and Timber Industry Board) Order 1969 and the Industrial Training (Furniture and Timber Industry Board) Order 1969 (Amendment) Order 1970) which specifies the activities in relation to which the Furniture and Timber Industry Training Board exercises its functions.

There will henceforth be excluded from the industry the activities of any establishment engaged wholly or mainly in the manufacture or repair of briar pipes.

(a) S.I. 1968/1763, 1972/597 (1968 III, p. 4785; 1972 I, p. 1966).
(b) S.I. 1969/1634 (1969 III, p. 5133).

STATUTORY INSTRUMENTS

1973 No. 1225

INDUSTRIAL TRAINING

The Industrial Training Levy (Wool, Jute and Flax) Order 1973

Made - - -		*13th July* 1973
Laid before Parliament		*24th July* 1973
Coming into Operation		*15th August* 1973

The Secretary of State after approving proposals submitted by the Wool, Jute and Flax Industry Training Board for the imposition of a further levy on employers in the wool, jute and flax industry and in exercise of powers conferred by section 4 of the Industrial Training Act 1964(a) and now vested in him(b), and of all other powers enabling him in that behalf hereby makes the following Order:—

Title and commencement

1. This Order may be cited as the Industrial Training Levy (Wool, Jute and Flax) Order 1973 and shall come into operation on 15th August 1973.

Interpretation

2.—(1) In this Order unless the context otherwise requires:—

(a) "agriculture" has the same meaning as in section 109(3) of the Agriculture Act 1947(c), or, in relation to Scotland, as in section 86(3) of the Agriculture (Scotland) Act 1948(d);

(b) "an appeal tribunal" means an industrial tribunal established under section 12 of the Industrial Training Act 1964;

(c) "assessment" means an assessment of an employer to the levy;

(d) "the Board" means the Wool, Jute and Flax Industry Training Board;

(e) "business" means any activities of industry or commerce;

(f) "charity" has the same meaning as in section 360 of the Income and Corporation Taxes Act 1970(e);

(g) "emoluments" means all emoluments assessable to income tax under Schedule E (other than pensions), being emoluments from which tax under that Schedule is deductible, whether or not tax in fact falls to be deducted from any particular payment thereof;

(h) "employer" means a person who is an employer in the wool, jute and flax industry at any time in the ninth levy period;

(i) "the industrial training order" means the Industrial Training (Wool, Jute and Flax Board) Order 1968(f);

(a) 1964 c. 16.	(b) S.I. 1968/729 (1968 II, p. 2108).
(c) 1947 c. 48.	(d) 1948 c. 45.
(e) 1970 c. 10	(f) S.I. 1968/898 (1968 II, p. 2376).

(*j*) "the levy" means the levy imposed by the Board in respect of the ninth levy period;

(*k*) "the ninth base period" means the period commencing on 1st April 1972 and ending on 31st March 1973;

(*l*) "the ninth levy period" means the period commencing with the day upon which this Order comes into operation and ending on 5th April 1974;

(*m*) "notice" means a notice in writing;

(*n*) "wool, jute and flax establishment" means an establishment in Great Britain engaged in the ninth base period wholly or mainly in the wool, jute and flax industry for a total of twenty-seven or more weeks or, being an establishment that commenced to carry on business in the ninth base period, for a total number of weeks exceeding one-half of the number of weeks in the part of the said period commencing with the day on which business was commenced and ending on the last day thereof;

(*o*) "the wool, jute and flax industry" means any one or more of the activities which, subject to the provisions of paragraph 2 of the Schedule to the industrial training order, are specified in paragraph 1 of that Schedule as the activities of the wool, jute and flax industry.

(2) In the case where a wool, jute and flax establishment is taken over (whether directly or indirectly) by an employer in succession to, or jointly with, another person, a person employed at any time in the ninth base period at or from the establishment shall be deemed, for the purposes of this Order, to have been so employed by the employer carrying on the said establishment on the day upon which this Order comes into operation, and any reference in this Order to persons employed by an employer at or from a wool, jute and flax establishment in the ninth base period shall be construed accordingly.

(3) Any reference in this Order to an establishment that commences to carry on business or that ceases to carry on business shall not be taken to apply where the location of the establishment is changed but its business is continued wholly or mainly at or from the new location, or where the suspension of activities is of a temporary or seasonal nature.

(4) The Interpretation Act 1889(**a**) shall apply to the interpretation of this Order as it applies to the interpretation of an Act of Parliament.

Imposition of the levy

3.—(1) The levy to be imposed by the Board on employers in respect of the ninth levy period shall be assessed in accordance with the provisions of this Article and of the Schedule to this Order.

(2) The levy shall be assessed by the Board separately in respect of each wool, jute and flax establishment of an employer (not being an employer who is exempt from the levy by virtue of paragraph 3 of the said Schedule), but in agreement with the employer one assessment may be made in respect of any number of such establishments, in which case those establishments shall be deemed for the purposes of that assessment to constitute one establishment.

(**a**) 1889 c. 63.

Assessment notices

4.—(1) The Board shall serve an assessment notice on every employer assessed to the levy, but one notice may comprise two or more assessments.

(2) An assessment notice shall state the amount (rounded down, where necessary, to the nearest £1) of the levy payable by the person assessed thereto, and where the notice comprises two or more assessments the said amount shall, before any such rounding down, be equal to the total amount of the levy assessed by the Board under Article 3 of this Order in respect of each establishment included in the notice.

(3) An assessment notice shall state the Board's address for the service of a notice of appeal or of an application for an extension of time for appealing.

(4) An assessment notice may be served on the person assessed to the levy either by delivering it to him personally or by leaving it, or sending it to him by post, at his last known address or place of business in the United Kingdom or, if that person is a corporation, by leaving it, or sending it by post to the corporation, at such address or place of business or at its registered or principal office.

Payment of the levy

5.—(1) Subject to the provisions of this Article and of Articles 6 and 7, the amount of the levy payable under an assessment notice served by the Board shall be due and payable to the Board one month after the date of the notice.

(2) The amount of an assessment shall not be recoverable by the Board until there has expired the time allowed for appealing against the assessment by Article 7(1) of this Order and any further period or periods of time that the Board or an appeal tribunal may have allowed for appealing under paragraph (2) or (3) of that Article or, where an appeal is brought, until the appeal is decided or withdrawn.

Withdrawal of assessment

6.—(1) The Board may, by notice served on the person assessed to the levy in the same manner as an assessment notice, withdraw an assessment if that person has appealed against that assessment under the provisions of Article 7 of this Order and the appeal has not been entered in the Register of Appeals kept under the appropriate Regulations specified in paragraph (5) of that Article.

(2) The withdrawal of an assessment shall be without prejudice—

    (*a*) to the power of the Board to serve a further assessment notice in respect of any establishment to which that assessment related; or

    (*b*) to any other assessment included in the original assessment notice, and such notice shall thereupon have effect as if any assessment withdrawn by the Board had not been included therein.

Appeals

7.—(1) A person assessed to the levy may appeal to an appeal tribunal against the assessment within one month from the date of the service of the assessment notice or within any further period or periods of time that may be allowed by the Board or an appeal tribunal under the following provisions of this Article.

(2) The Board by notice may for good cause allow a person assessed to the levy to appeal to an appeal tribunal against the assessment at any time within the period of four months from the date of the service of the assessment notice or within such further period or periods as the Board may allow before such time as may then be limited for appealing has expired.

(3) If the Board shall not allow an application for extension of time for appealing, an appeal tribunal shall upon application made to the tribunal by the person assessed to the levy have the like powers as the Board under the last foregoing paragraph.

(4) In the case of an establishment that ceases to carry on business in the ninth levy period on any day after the date of the service of the relevant assessment notice, the foregoing provisions of this Article shall have effect as if for the period of four months from the date of the service of the assessment notice mentioned in paragraph (2) of this Article there were substituted the period of six months from the date of the cessation of business.

(5) An appeal or an application to an appeal tribunal under this Article shall be made in accordance with the Industrial Tribunals (England and Wales) Regulations 1965(a) as amended by the Industrial Tribunals (England and Wales) (Amendment) Regulations 1967(b) except where the establishment to which the relevant assessment relates is wholly in Scotland in which case the appeal or application shall be made in accordance with the Industrial Tribunals (Scotland) Regulations 1965(c) as amended by the Industrial Tribunals (Scotland) (Amendment) Regulations 1967(d).

(6) The powers of an appeal tribunal under paragraph (3) of this Article may be exercised by the President of the Industrial Tribunals (England and Wales) or by the President of the Industrial Tribunals (Scotland) as the case may be.

Evidence

8.—(1) Upon the discharge by a person assessed to the levy of his liability under an assessment the Board shall if so requested issue to him a certificate to that effect.

(2) The production in any proceedings of a document purporting to be certified by the Secretary of the Board to be a true copy of an assessment or other notice issued by the Board or purporting to be a certificate such as is mentioned in the foregoing paragraph of this Article shall, unless the contrary is proved, be sufficient evidence of the document and of the facts stated therein.

Signed by order of the Secretary of State.

R. Chichester-Clark,
Minister of State,
13th July 1973.   Department of Employment.

(a) S.I. 1965/1101 (1965 II, p. 2805).   (b) S.I. 1967/301 (1967 I, p. 1040).
(c) S.I. 1965/1157 (1965 II, p. 3266).   (d) S.I. 1967/302 (1967 I, p. 1050).

Article 3

SCHEDULE

1.—(1) In this Schedule unless the context otherwise requires—

(a) "the appropriate percentage" means, in relation to the emoluments of persons employed at or from a wool, jute or flax establishment that was engaged wholly or mainly in any one or more of the activities comprised in one of the three groups of activities specified in the first and second columns of the Appendix to this Schedule, the percentage specified in relation to that group in the third column of that Appendix;

(b) "arranging for the carrying out on commission" in relation to any activities mentioned in the Appendix to this Schedule means arranging for the carrying out by another person in pursuance of a contract of work or labour (with or without the provision of materials) of those activities wholly or mainly upon or from materials owned in the course of this business by the person for whom such activities are to be carried out;

(c) "production" in relation to any yarn includes any of the processes mentioned in sub-paragraphs (d), (e), (f) and (g) of paragraph 1 of the Schedule to the industrial training order;

(d) "related or administrative activities" means activities of a kind to which paragraph 1(r) of the Schedule to the industrial training order applies;

(e) other expressions have the meanings assigned to them respectively by paragraph 3 or 4 of the Schedule to the industrial training order or by Article 2 of this Order.

(2) The activities in any Group specified in the first and second columns of the Appendix to this Schedule include the activities of arranging either directly or through another person for the carrying out on commission of any activities comprised in that Group, and include also any related or administrative activities undertaken in relation to any activities comprised in such Group.

(3) In reckoning any sum of emoluments for the purposes of this Schedule no regard shall be had to the emoluments of any person wholly engaged in agriculture or in the supply of food or drink for immediate consumption.

2. Subject to the provisions of this Schedule, the amount of levy to be imposed on an employer in respect of a wool, jute and flax establishment shall be equal to the appropriate percentage of the sum of the emoluments of all the persons employed by the employer in the ninth base period at or from the establishment.

3. There shall be exempt from the levy:—

(a) an employer in whose case—

(i) the sum of the emoluments of all the persons employed by him in the ninth base period at or from the wool, jute and flax establishment or establishments of the employer (including any persons employed at or from a wool, jute and flax establishment by an associated company of the employer) did not exceed £17,000; or

(ii) the number of employees employed by him (or by an associated company of the employer) at or from such establishment or establishments on the 31st day of March 1973 did not exceed 15;

(b) a charity.

4. The amount of the levy imposed in respect of a wool, jute and flax establishment that ceases to carry on business in the ninth levy period shall be in the same proportion to the amount that would otherwise be due in accordance with the foregoing provisions of this Schedule as the number of days between the commencement of the said levy period and the date of cessation of business (both dates inclusive) bears to the number of days in the said levy period.

APPENDIX

Group No.	Description of Activities	Appropriate Percentage

1. Dealing in—
  (i) fleeces;
  (ii) textile fibres not being jute, flax, hemp or similar fibres;
  (iii) tops;
  (iv) yarn not consisting of jute, flax, hemp or similar fibres.
		0·50%

2. The activities following or any of them—
  (a) the production of yarn from jute;
  (b) the manufacture of any woven fabric from such yarn; or
  (c) the production of any other yarn or the manufacture of any other woven fabric, being production or manufacture in a textile factory from any textile fibres, yarn or continuous filament and, in any case, by a system commonly employed in the production of jute yarn or in the manufacture of jute fabric or by a system similar thereto.
		0·74%

3. Any other activities of the wool, jute and flax industry not being activities comprised in Group 1 or 2 of this Appendix.		0·65%

EXPLANATORY NOTE

(This Note is not part of the Order.)

This Order gives effect to proposals submitted to the Secretary of State for Employment by the Wool, Jute and Flax Industry Training Board for the imposition of a further levy upon employers in the wool, jute and flax industry for the purpose of raising money towards the expenses of the Board.

The levy is to be imposed in respect of the ninth levy period commencing with the day upon which this Order comes into operation and ending on 5th April 1974. The levy will be assessed by the Board and there will be a right of appeal to an industrial tribunal.

STATUTORY INSTRUMENTS

1973 No. 1226

SOUTHERN RHODESIA

The Southern Rhodesia (Distribution to Creditors) Order 1973

Made - - - -	*16th July* 1973
Laid before Parliament	*17th July* 1973
Coming into Operation	
Articles 1, 2 *and* 16 -	*20th July* 1973
Remainder - -	*On a day to be appointed under Article* 1(2)

At the Court at Buckingham Palace, the 16th day of July 1973

Present,

The Queen's Most Excellent Majesty in Council

Her Majesty, in exercise of the powers conferred on Her by section 2 of the Southern Rhodesia Act 1965(a), is pleased, by and with the advice of Her Privy Council, to order, and it is hereby ordered as follows:—

Citation and Commencement

1.—(1) This Order may be cited as the Southern Rhodesia (Distribution to Creditors) Order 1973.

(2) This Article and Articles 2 and 16 of this Order shall come into operation on 20th July 1973 ; and the other provisions of this Order shall come into operation on a day to be appointed by a Secretary of State by notice published in the London Gazette (in this Order referred to as " the appointed day ").

Temporary prohibition regarding use of certain moneys

2.—(1) So long as this Article is in operation, no person having possession in the United Kingdom of any moneys of the Crown in right of the Government of Southern Rhodesia shall, without the consent of a Secretary of State, use those moneys for the purpose of satisfying, in whole or in part, a liability of the Crown arising in respect of that Government to make a payment to another person ; and the provisions of this paragraph shall have

---

(a) 1965 c. 76.

effect notwithstanding any judgment given after this Article comes into operation in civil proceedings in any part of the United Kingdom to the effect that any moneys in the United Kingdom are moneys of the Crown in right of that Government available in the United Kingdom to satisfy any such liability as aforesaid.

(2) Any person who has possession in the United Kingdom of moneys of the Crown in right of the Government of Southern Rhodesia shall give notice in writing of the amount or nature of those moneys to the Secretary of State for Foreign and Commonwealth Affairs.

(3) The provisions of this Article shall expire on the appointed day.

Certain proceedings not to be instituted

3.—(1) So long as this Article is in operation, no proceedings to which this Article applies shall be instituted ; but any such proceedings commenced before the appointed day may be continued, and for the purposes of this paragraph a proceeding by petition of right shall be deemed to be commenced on the date when the petition is presented.

(2) This Article applies to such civil proceedings as, apart from this Order, might be taken in any part of the United Kingdom against the Crown or any other person for the purpose of obtaining a judgment that the Crown is under a liability arising in respect of the Government of Southern Rhodesia to make a payment to another person.

(3) A certificate of a Secretary of State to the effect that any alleged liability of the Crown arises in respect of the Government of Southern Rhodesia shall, for the purposes of this Order, be conclusive as to the matter so certified.

Use of certain moneys

4. If a judgment is given on or after 20th July 1973 in civil proceedings in any part of the United Kingdom to the effect that any moneys in the United Kingdom are moneys of the Crown in right of the Government of Southern Rhodesia available in the United Kingdom to satisfy any liability such as is mentioned in Article 2(1) of this Order, then those moneys shall not be used to satisfy, in whole or in part, any such liability except in accordance with the following provisions of this Order.

Payment of moneys to the Foreign Compensation Commission

5.—(1) When any judgment given and having effect as mentioned in Article 4 of this Order becomes final the moneys to which it relates shall be paid or transferred to the Foreign Compensation Commission constituted by the Foreign Compensation Act 1950(a) (hereinafter referred to as " the Commission ").

(2) For the purposes of paragraph (1) of this Article a judgment shall be regarded as having become final when any time prescribed or allowed for giving notice of appeal therefrom or for applying for leave to appeal therefrom has expired or for any other reason an appeal does not lie or no longer lies from that judgment.

(a) 1950 c. 12.

(3) Where on or after the appointed day any person has possession in the United Kingdom of moneys to which no judgment given and having effect as mentioned in Article 4 of this Order relates and in relation to which no proceedings for the purpose of obtaining such a judgment have been instituted, he shall, if those moneys are moneys of the Crown in right of the Government of Southern Rhodesia available by law to satisfy, in whole or in part, a liability of the Crown arising in respect of that Government to make a payment to another person, pay or transfer those moneys to the Commission.

Establishment of a fund

6.—(1) The Commission shall establish a fund to be called the Southern Rhodesia Fund (hereinafter referred to as " the Fund ") into which shall be paid all moneys received by the Commission under Article 5 of this Order (including the proceeds of sale of shares or securities so received).

(2) Any moneys standing to the credit of the Fund may be temporarily invested in such manner as the Treasury may authorise ; and where the Commission has received moneys consisting of shares or securities they may, with the authority of the Treasury, hold them as if they had been invested under this paragraph.

(3) All interest, dividends and other sums received by the Commission as a result of the investment of any moneys standing to the credit of the Fund shall be paid into the Fund.

Applications in respect of debts

7.—(1) Subject to the provisions of this Order, any person may make application to the Commission for the purpose of establishing a claim in respect of any debt due to him to which this Article applies.

(2) This Article applies to debts of the following kind, that is to say, any liability of the Crown arising in respect of the Government of Southern Rhodesia—

(a) to make any payment of capital, or of any interest, which has become due before the appointed day or 31st July 1974 (whichever is the later) in respect of any stock to which the Colonial Stock Act 1877(a) applies ;

(b) to make payment of any sum due by virtue of any judgment given in civil proceedings in any part of the United Kingdom.

(3) This Article also applies, as if the sum were a debt due to the Crown in right of the Government of the United Kingdom, to—

(a) any sum which has become due before the date mentioned in paragraph (2)(a) of this Article to the Government of the United Kingdom or any officer or department thereof from the Government of Southern Rhodesia, being a sum described in Schedule 1 to this Order ; and

(b) any sum due to the Government of the United Kingdom or any officer or department thereof in respect of costs and expenses incurred by the Crown or its officers or agents in defending on behalf of the Government of Southern Rhodesia any civil proceedings taken as mentioned in Article 3(2) of this Order ;

and an application to the Commission in respect of any such sum may be made under this Article on behalf of the Government of the United Kingdom or the officer or department concerned by any person duly authorised for the purpose.

(a) 1877 c. 59.

(4) A Secretary of State may by order direct that this Article shall apply to any such additional liability of the Crown arising in respect of the Government of Southern Rhodesia as may be specified in the order, being a liability to make payment of a liquidated sum which has become due before the date mentioned in paragraph (2)(*a*) of this Article, and this Article shall apply to the debt concerned accordingly.

(5) An order made under paragraph (4) of this Article shall, for the purposes of the Statutory Instruments Act 1946(**a**), be a statutory instrument within the meaning of that Act and shall be subject to annulment in pursuance of a resolution of either House of Parliament; and any such order may be revoked or varied by a subsequent order.

(6) An application shall not be entertained by the Commission for the purposes of this Order unless it is made in accordance with the Rules of the Commission and has reached the Commission by 31st October 1974 or by the date which is one year after the appointed day, whichever date is the later.

Determination of applications

8.—(1) The Commission shall, subject to the provisions of this Order, determine whether or not each claim in respect of which an application is made is established and, when a claim is established, the amount thereof.

(2) Where an applicant shows that he is entitled to the benefit of a subsisting judgment given in civil proceedings in any part of the United Kingdom to the effect that the Crown is under any liability arising in respect of the Government of Southern Rhodesia to make any payment, the Commission shall determine that the claim in respect of the liability concerned is established in the amount specified in that judgment unless it appears to them that the liability concerned has, in whole or in part, been discharged or satisfied.

(3) In determining whether a claim is established and the amount thereof the Commission shall treat any payment made since 11th November 1965 by or under the purported authority of any person or body of persons in Southern Rhodesia claiming to be the Government of that country or a Minister or Officer of the Government thereof and purporting to be made in discharge or satisfaction, in whole or in part, of the liability concerned as if it had been lawfully so made.

(4) Each application shall be determined by not less than two members of the Commission; provided that one member of the Commission may provisionally determine any application which is not the subject of an oral hearing unless it is determined that such application be dismissed wholly or in part or the aggregate amount of the claim exceeds £10,000.

Payments out of the Fund

9.—(1) The Commission shall make payments out of the Fund to every person who has established a claim under this Order and who applies to the Commission for payment.

(2) The reference in paragraph (1) of this Article to a person who has established a claim under this Order includes a reference to any person who has become entitled to the payment of the debt to which the claim relates, or any part of it, in consequence of the death of the claimant or of any

---

(a) 1946 c. 36.

devolution in law from the claimant or of any assignment or transfer of the debt and who produces such evidence of his title as may be reasonably required by the Commission ; and in determining whether a person has become entitled to the payment of a debt such as is mentioned in Article 7(2)(a) of this Order the Commission shall act after consultation with the registrar of the stock concerned.

Amount of Payments

10.—(1) The payment in respect of each claim established under this Order shall be a fraction of the distributable amount of the Fund equal to the proportion which the amount of the claim, as determined by the Commission, bears to the total of the amounts so determined with respect to all claims established under this Order.

(2) The distributable amount of the Fund shall be the total of all sums constituting the Fund on such date as the Commission may determine after the deduction of any payments made or to be made therefrom into the Consolidated Fund in accordance with any Order in Council made under section 7(2) of the Foreign Compensation Act 1950(**a**) (as applied by this Order).

Interim Payments

11.—(1) Whether or not all claims under this Order have been finally determined, the Commission may, at such time or times as they may decide, make from the Fund interim payments in respect of any of the claims established under this Order to persons entitled to payments under Article 9 of this Order.

(2) Interim payments made under the provisions of this Article shall be made—

(a) on account of payments to be made under Article 10 of this Order ; and

(b) so that an equal proportion is paid of the amount of the claims concerned, being a proportion that in the opinion of the Commission will not exceed that likely to be payable under Article 10 of this Order.

(3) For the purposes of this Article—

(a) a claim shall be deemed to be established under this Order even though the determination thereof may be provisional and subject to review under the Rules of the Commission ; and

(b) the amount of a claim shall be deemed to be the amount so provisionally determined subject to review unless before the date of payment the Commission shall have made a final determination on review.

Effect of payments on debts

12. A payment from the Fund in respect of any claim established under this Order shall reduce the amount of the debt concerned by the amount of the payment but shall not affect the liability of the Crown in respect of the Government of Southern Rhodesia with regard to any remaining amount of the debt.

Additional provisions relating to stock

13.—(1) Where a claim is established under this Order in respect of any stock mentioned in Article 7(2)(a) of this Order and a certificate of title or proprietorship has been issued in respect of that stock and has not previously been surrendered or cancelled, the Commission shall, as a condition of the making of any payment in respect of that claim, require the person to whom payment is to be made to forward that certificate to the Commission.

(**a**) 1950 c. 12.

(2) Where a claim is established under this Order in respect of any stock mentioned in Article 7(2)(*a*) of this Order and a stock certificate to bearer (within the meaning of the Colonial Stock Act 1877(**a**)) has been issued and is outstanding in respect of that stock (whether or not the certificate has ceased to be transferable by delivery) the Commission shall, as a condition of the making of any payment in respect of that claim, require the person to whom payment is to be made to surrender to the Commission such certificate and any coupons attached thereto.

(3) Where any payment is made from the Fund in respect of any capital or interest due in respect of any stock mentioned in Article 7(2)(*a*) of this Order, the Commission shall send to the registrar of the stock any certificate surrendered under paragraph (1) of this Article and shall give notice in writing of the payment to the registrar ; and thereupon the registrar shall note particulars of the payment on any such certificate and, except in the case of stock in respect of which a certificate to bearer has been surrendered under paragraph (2) of this Article, shall enter the particulars contained in the notice in the register of the stock.

(4) When the registrar has noted particulars of the payment on any certificate in accordance with paragraph (3) of this Article he shall return the certificate to such person as the Commission may direct.

(5) A notice given under paragraph (3) of this Article shall include particulars of the person to whom the payment is made, of the stock in respect of which the payment is made, of the amount of the payment and of any certificate and coupons surrendered under paragraph (2) of this Article and shall state whether the payment has been made in respect of capital or interest and, when it is made in respect partly of capital and partly of interest, the amounts paid in respect of capital and interest respectively.

(6) When the Commission are satisfied that no further payment will be made from the Fund in respect of any stock for which a certificate has been surrendered under paragraph (2) of this Article they shall send the certificate and any coupons attached thereto to the registrar of the stock for cancellation ; and, in so far as any stock to which the certificate relates has not been redeemed by payment of capital from the Fund, the registrar shall enter the holder thereof in the register as the proprietor of the stock, and shall also enter therein particulars of any interest due to the holder in respect of coupons attached to the certificate and which has not been paid from the Fund.

Calculation of time limits

14. In calculating the period prescribed by or under any enactment or rule of law for bringing or taking any step in any proceedings no account shall be taken in relation to any proceedings to which Article 3 of this Order applies of any period beginning on the appointed day and ending when that Article ceases to be in operation.

Application of certain enactments

15. The enactments mentioned in column 1 of Schedule 2 to this Order shall apply in relation to the Commission and its functions under this Order and for that purpose shall have effect as if modified in the manner specified in column 2 of that Schedule.

(**a**) 1877 c. 59.

Interpretation

16.—(1) In this Order the following expressions have the meanings hereby respectively assigned to them, that is to say—

" interest ", in relation to any stock, includes any dividend on such stock ;

" judgment " includes any order or declaration ;

" moneys " includes shares and other securities.

(2) The Interpretation Act 1889(a) shall apply, with the necessary adaptations, for the purpose of interpreting this Order and otherwise in relation thereto as it applies for the purpose of interpreting and in relation to Acts of Parliament.

W. G. Agnew.

Article 7(3)(*a*)   SCHEDULE 1

Sums due to the Government of the United Kingdom, or an officer or department thereof, to which Article 7 applies

1. Any sum due (including interest thereon at such rate as may be fixed in accordance with section 1(3)(*e*) of the Colonial Loans Act 1949(b)) for the repayment of any sum issued on account of default by the Government of Southern Rhodesia out of the Consolidated Fund in fulfilment of any guarantee given as mentioned below by the Treasury in pursuance of the Colonial Loans Acts 1949 to 1962(c)—

(*a*) the guarantee given in respect of a loan to Southern Rhodesia by an agreement between the United Kingdom and the International Bank for Reconstruction and Development dated 27th February 1952 ;

(*b*) the guarantee given in respect of a loan to the Federal Power Board of the Federation of Rhodesia and Nyasaland by an agreement between the United Kingdom and the International Bank for Reconstruction and Development dated 21st June 1956 ;

(*c*) the guarantee given in respect of a loan to the Federation of Rhodesia and Nyasaland by an agreement between the United Kingdom and the International Bank for Reconstruction and Development dated 16th June 1958 ;

(*d*) the guarantee given in respect of a loan to the Federation of Rhodesia and Nyasaland by an agreement between the United Kingdom and the International Bank for Reconstruction and Development dated 1st April 1960 ;

(*e*) the guarantee given in respect of a loan to the Central African Power Corporation of Northern Rhodesia and Southern Rhodesia by an agreement between the United Kingdom and the International Bank for Reconstruction and Development dated 2nd October 1964.

For the purposes of this Order the repayment of any sum issued as mentioned in this paragraph shall be regarded as having become due on the date that sum was issued.

2. Sums due on Promissory Notes issued by the Government of Southern Rhodesia in respect of liabilities of that Government resulting from the apportionment by section 16(1)(*c*) of the Federation of Rhodesia and Nyasaland (Dissolution) Order in Council 1963(d) of liabilities of the Federation incurred under an agreement known as the United Kingdom-Federation of Rhodesia and Nyasaland Credit Agreement 1962.

(a) 1889 c. 63.   **(b)** 1949 c. 50.   **(c)** 1949 c. 50; 1952 c. 1; 1962 c. 41.
                 (d) S.I. 1963/2085 (1963 III, p. 4477).

3. Any sum due in respect of instalments of the purchase price of military aircraft and associated equipment sold by the Government of the United Kingdom to the Government of the Federation of Rhodesia and Nyasaland and allocated, together with liabilities or obligations relating thereto, to the Government of Southern Rhodesia on or in consequence of the dissolution of the Federation.

4. Any sum due by way of interest on, or in repayment of, any loan made to the Government of Southern Rhodesia under section 2 of the Colonial Development and Welfare Act 1959(a).

SCHEDULE 2 Article 15

Enactment	*Modification*
The following provisions of the Foreign Compensation Act 1950(b)—	
Section 4(2)	The omission of the first five words, and the substitution of a reference to this Order for the reference to the Act.
Section 4(3)	The substitution of a reference to this Order for the reference to an Order in Council made under section 2 of the Act, and the omission of the last sixteen words.
Section 5	——
Section 7(2)	The substitution of a reference to this Order for the reference to the Act.
Section 8	——
Subsections (1) to (11) of section 3 of the Foreign Compensation Act 1969(c).	In subsection (1) the substitution of a reference to this Order for the reference to an Order in Council made under section 3 of the Foreign Compensation Act 1950.
	In subsection (9) the substitution of a reference to this Order for the reference to the Foreign Compensation Act 1950.

(a) 1959 c. 71.   (b) 1950 c. 12.   (c) 1969 c. 20.

EXPLANATORY NOTE

(This Note is not part of the Order.)

This Order makes provision for an equitable distribution by the Foreign Compensation Commission to certain creditors of the Government of Southern Rhodesia of moneys of that Government that are or may be found to be available in the United Kingdom to satisfy its debts.

Article 2, which comes into operation on 20th July 1973 and will expire on the coming into operation of the other provisions of the Order on a day to be appointed, prohibits a person possessing such moneys from using them to satisfy such a debt without the consent of a Secretary of State.

Article 3 provides that proceedings may not be commenced after the appointed day for the purpose of establishing the existence of a Southern Rhodesian Government debt. Articles 4, 5 and 6 provide for available moneys of the Government of Southern Rhodesia to be transferred to a Fund established by the Foreign Compensation Commission. Article 7 provides for the making of claims to the Commission in respect of certain debts, including sums due in respect of stocks to which the Colonial Stock Act 1877 applies and certain sums due to the Government of the United Kingdom. Articles 8 to 11 deal with the determination of claims by the Commission, the making of payments from the Fund and the effect of such payments on the debts concerned. Article 13 contains additional provisions relating to stock, including provision for the surrender of certificates and noting by the registrar of particulars of payments, and Article 14 deals with the calculation of time limits for bringing proceedings to which Article 3 applies.

STATUTORY INSTRUMENTS

1973 No. 1232

EDUCATION, ENGLAND AND WALES

The Postgraduate, etc. Courses (Exclusion from Discretionary Awards) Regulations 1973

Made - - -	*12th July* 1973
Laid before Parliament	*24th July* 1973
Coming into Operation	*1st September* 1973

The Secretary of State for Education and Science, in exercise of the powers conferred on her by section 4 of the Education Act 1973(a), hereby makes the following regulations: —

Citation and commencement

1. These regulations may be cited as the Postgraduate, etc. Courses (Exclusion from Discretionary Awards) Regulations 1973 and shall come into operation on 1st September 1973.

Designated courses

2. There are hereby designated for the purposes of section 4 of the Education Act 1973 (exclusion of postgraduate courses from grants under section 2(1) of the Education Act 1962(b) as postgraduate courses or comparable to postgraduate courses—

(*a*) any full-time course at a university or other institution in Great Britain or Northern Ireland in preparation for a doctorate, or a degree of bachelor of letters or bachelor of philosophy;

(*b*) any full-time course at a university or other institution in Great Britain or Northern Ireland in preparation for a master's degree which is not a course to which section 1(1) of the Education Act 1962 applies;

(*c*) any course at the Royal College of Art in preparation for a master's degree or a diploma of the College;

(*d*) any art and design course at an establishment of further education within the meaning of the Further Education Regulations 1969(c)) maintained by a local education authority in preparation for the Higher Diploma in Art or the Higher Diploma in Design; and

(*e*) any other full-time course (whether in Great Britain or elsewhere) which is for the time being designated by the Secretary of State under these regulations.

(a) 1973 c. 16.   (b) 1962 c. 12.
(c) S.I. 1969/403 (1969 I, p. 1138).

Given under the Official Seal of the Secretary of State for Education and
Science on 12th July 1973.

(L.S.)   *Margaret H. Thatcher*,
                        Secretary of State for Education and Science.

EXPLANATORY NOTE

(This Note is not part of the Regulations.)

These Regulations designate the courses to which section 2(1) of the Education Act 1962 (which enables local education authorities to bestow awards
on persons over compulsory school age attending courses of further education) is not to apply.

STATUTORY INSTRUMENTS

1973 No. 1233

EDUCATION, ENGLAND AND WALES

The Awards (First Degree, etc. Courses) (Amendment) Regulations 1973

Made - - -		*12th July* 1973
Laid before Parliament		*24th July* 1973
Coming into Operation		*1st September* 1973

The Secretary of State for Education and Science, in exercise of the powers conferred by section 1 of the Education Act 1962(a) and vested in her(b), hereby makes the following regulations.

Citation, commencement and interpretation

1.—(1) These regulations may be cited as the Awards (First Degree, etc. Courses) (Amendment) Regulations 1973 and shall come into operation on 1st September 1973.

(2) In these regulations "the principal regulations" means the Awards (First Degree, etc. Courses) Regulations 1971(c) as amended by the Awards (First Degree, etc. Courses) (Amendment) Regulations 1972(d).

(3) The Interpretation Act 1889(e) shall apply for the interpretation of these regulations as it applies for the interpretation of an Act of Parliament.

Requirements for ordinary maintenance

2. The provisions of the principal regulations specified in the first column below shall have effect with the substitution for the amounts specified in the second column of the amounts specified in the third column.

Regulation 19(3)	£195	£215
	£265	£285
	£245	£265
Schedule 1		
Paragraph 3(1)	£480	£520
Paragraph 3(2)	£445	£485
Paragraph 3(3)	£355	£390
Paragraph 3(4)	£480	£520
Paragraph 14(2)(*b*)	£445	£485

(a) 1962 c. 12.   (b) S.I. 1964/490 (1964 I, p. 800).
(c) S.I. 1971/1297 (1971 II, p. 3722).   (d) S.I. 1972/1124 (1972 II, p. 3326).
(e) 1889 c. 63.

Resources

3.—(1) At the end of paragraph 1 (student's income) of schedule 2 to the principal regulations there shall be added as a note—

"Note: the reduction for income tax is to be made by calculating the tax payable on the income received in the year as if that year were a year of assessment within the meaning of the Income Tax Acts (the necessary apportionment being made in any case where the relevant provisions of those Acts change during the year)."

(2) In paragraph 4 (parental contribution) of schedule 2, for subparagraph (1) there shall be substituted—

"**4.**—(1) Subject to subparagraph (2) below, the parental contribution shall be—

(*a*) in any case in which the residual income is not less than £1,500 and not more than £1,999, £30 with the addition of £1 for every complete £5 by which it exceeds £1,500; and

(*b*) in any case in which the residual income is not less than £2,000, £130 with the addition of £1 for every complete £10 by which it exceeds £2,000;

and in any case in which the residual income is less than £1,500 the parental contribution shall be nil."

Miscellaneous amendments relating to requirements

4.—(1) The provisions of schedule 1 to the principal regulations specified in the first column below shall have effect subject to the amendments specified in the second column.

Paragraph 2(1)	For the words "maintenance in respect of his attendance at the course during term" there shall be substituted the words "ordinary maintenance".
Paragraph 3(4)	The words "(otherwise than on an exchange basis)" shall be omitted.
Paragraph 4(1)	For the word "fortnight" in each place where it occurs there shall be substituted the word "week" and for the references to £9·80, £19·60 and £16·80 there shall be substituted references to £4·90, £9·80 and £8·40 respectively.
Paragraph 4(2)	For the references to 26 weeks and 31 weeks there shall be substituted references to 25 weeks 3 days and 30 weeks 3 days respectively.
Paragraph 6(1)(*c*)	At the beginning there shall be inserted the words "(in the case of a student attending a course at an establishment which is not a university)" and there shall be omitted the words from "but" to "establishment" (both inclusive).
Paragraph 8(1)(*b*)	There shall be omitted "(*b*) dentistry" and "and (*b*) £60 respectively."

Paragraph 14(2)(b)   For the words after "£485" (as substituted by regulation 2 above) there shall be substituted the words "and any relevant sum specified by paragraph 11".

(2) In paragraph 2 of schedule 4 (sandwich courses), for the references to 31 weeks in subparagraphs (a) and (b) there shall be substituted references to 30 weeks 3 days.

Given under the Official Seal of the Secretary of State for Education and Science on 12th July 1973.

Margaret H. Thatcher,

(L.S.)   Secretary of State for Education and Science.

EXPLANATORY NOTE

(This Note is not part of the Regulations.)

These Regulations increase the rates of ordinary maintenance prescribed by the Awards (First Degree, etc. Courses) Regulations 1971 as amended, modify the provisions in those Regulations relating to the parental contribution and make other amendments of a minor character.

STATUTORY INSTRUMENTS

1973 No. 1234

EDUCATION, ENGLAND AND WALES

The Students' Dependants' Allowances Regulations 1973

Made	- - -	12th July 1973
Laid before Parliament		24th July 1973
Coming into Operation		1st September 1973

The Secretary of State for Education and Science, in exercise of the powers conferred by sections 1 and 3(*a*) of the Education Act 1962(**a**) and section 3 of the Education Act 1973(**b**) and vested in her(**c**), hereby makes the following regulations:—

Citation, commencement, construction and interpretation

1.—(1) These regulations may be cited as the Students' Dependants Allowances Regulations 1973 and shall come into operation on 1st September 1973.

(2) These regulations (except regulation 7) shall be construed together with the Awards (First Degree, etc. Courses) Regulations 1971(**d**) ("the principal regulations") as amended(**e**).

(3) The Interpretation Act 1889(**f**) shall apply for the interpretation of these regulations as it applies for the interpretation of an Act of Parliament.

Power to pay allowances

2.—(1) Subject to regulation 3 below, the Secretary of State may pay an allowance in respect of any eligible dependant to a student to whom paragraph 10 of Schedule 1 to the principal regulations does not apply.

(2) References in these regulations to the eligible dependant of a student mean—

(*a*) a wife with whom the student is living if—

(i) they have a dependent child; and

(ii) she does not hold a statutory award;

(*b*) a wife or husband with whom the student is living and in respect of whom there is for the time being in force a certificate by a registered medical practitioner that she or he is incapable of being gainfully employed for a period of at least eight weeks;

(*c*) a dependent child, unless the parents do not live together and the child resides with the other parent.

(**a**) 1962 c. 12.   (**b**) 1973 c. 16.
(**c**) S.I. 1964/490 (1964 I, p. 800).   (**d**) S.I. 1971/1297 (1971 II, p. 3722).
(**e**) S.I. 1972/1124, 1973/1233 (1972 II, p.3326; 1973 II, p.3683).
(**f**) 1889 c. 63.

Exceptions

3. No allowance shall be payable to a student if by virtue of regulation 20 (students whose parents have not been found) of the principal regulations the minimum payment is paid to or in respect of him or if by virtue of regulation 21 (assisted students) of those regulations no payment is made to or in respect of him under those regulations.

Amount of allowance

4.—(1) Subject to paragraph (4) below, an allowance shall be payable at the weekly rate specified in paragraph (2) below for any week or (where the period in question is not a whole number of weeks) part of a week in which—

(a) the student attends the course at the establishment, or is pursuing any course of study of a kind mentioned in paragraph 5 of Schedule 1 to the principal regulations; and

(b) there is an eligible dependant of the student.

(2) The weekly rate of an allowance shall, subject to paragraph (3) below, be the amount by which the aggregate of—

(a) one fifty-second of the amount for the time being prescribed by any appropriate provision of the principal regulations as the requirements of a student for the maintenance of a wife, husband or child; and

(b) (if the student maintains a home for himself and an eligible dependant in the United Kingdom at a place other than that at which he resides during the course) one thirtieth of the amount for the time being prescribed by the principal regulations as the requirements of a student who maintains such a home for himself and a dependant to whom those regulations apply—

exceeds one fifty second of the annual income of the student's family (within the meaning of regulation 5 below).

(3) In the case of any student to or in respect of whom the minimum payment is paid by virtue of regulation 14, 17 or 18(a)(ii) of the principal regulations, the rate of the allowance shall be reduced—

(a) if his requirements as assessed in accordance with the principal regulations exceed his resources as so assessed, by one fifty-second of the amount by which the excess falls short of £50;

(b) if those requirements do not exceed those resources, by 96p.

(4) No allowance shall be paid for any week in which the capital resources of the student's household (assessed in accordance with Part III of Schedule 2 to the Ministry of Social Security Act 1966(**a**) amount to £800 or more.

(5) For the purposes of this regulation a student shall be treated as having attended at an establishment, or as having pursued a course of study, for a part of a week if he attends at an establishment, or pursues such a course, on four consecutive days; and, in determining whether he has attended the establishment or pursued the course, any period during which he is absent on account of illness shall be ignored.

(**a**) 1966 c. 20.

Income of student's family

5. For the purpose of these regulations the income of the student's family in any year shall be taken to be the aggregate of—

(*a*) any sums which are disregarded in calculating the student's income for the purposes of the principal regulations, except—

(i) the first £100 of any scholarship, bursary or similar endowment awarded in respect of his attendance at the establishment;

(ii) remuneration for work done in vacations;

(iii) any benefit under the Ministry of Social Security Act 1966;

(iv) family allowances; and

(v) (in the case of a sandwich student) any payment made to him by his employer in respect of any period of experience;

(*b*) the income (reduced by income tax, family allowances and national insurance contributions) of a wife, husband or child, or of a person cohabiting with the student as wife or husband, who is a member of the same household; and

(*c*) (in the case of any student to or in respect of whom the minimum payment is paid) the amount (if any) by which his resources as assessed in accordance with the principal regulations exceed his requirements as so assessed.

Supplementary

6.—(1) An allowance may be paid in instalments.

(2) An allowance, and an instalment of an allowance, may be paid before the end of the year by reference to which, in accordance with regulation 4 above, it falls to be assessed; and any overpayment in any year may, and any underpayment in any year shall, be corrected by way of deduction from or addition to any allowance payable in the next following year or, if no such allowance is payable, by repayment to or payment by the Secretary of State.

Application to students training as teachers

7. These regulations shall apply to a person to or in respect of whom a grant is for the time being paid in pursuance of—

(*a*) regulation 34(1) of the Training of Teachers Regulations 1967(**a**) (grants to recognised students); or

(*b*) arrangements approved under section 2(3) (grants for training of teachers) of the Education Act 1962;

and in its application to such a person any reference in the preceding regulations to a provision of the principal regulations shall be construed as a reference to—

(i) that provision as applied by regulation 34(2) of the Training of Teachers Regulations 1967; or

(ii) any provision to the like effect contained in arrangements approved under section 2(3) of the Education Act 1962—

respectively.

(**a**) S.I. 1967/792 (1967 II, p. 2319).

Amendment of principal regulations

8. In paragraph 13 (discretionary payments for maintenance of dependants) of Schedule 1 to the principal regulations subparagraph (*b*) shall be omitted.

Given under the Official Seal of the Secretary of State for Education and Science on 12th July 1973.

(L.S.)   *Margaret H. Thatcher*,
Secretary of State for Education and Science.

EXPLANATORY NOTE

(This Note is not part of the Regulations.)

These Regulations enable the Secretary of State to pay allowances to students attending first degree university etc. courses and courses for the training of teachers. The allowances are payable in respect of the wife or husband, or child, of a student who is not entitled to any payment in respect of his or her dependants under the statutory provisions regulating the payment of grants to students attending such courses.

STATUTORY INSTRUMENTS

1973 No. 1236

INDUSTRIAL TRAINING

The Industrial Training Levy (Road Transport) Order 1973

Made - - - -	16*th July* 1973
Laid before Parliament	25*th July* 1973
Coming into Operation	17*th August* 1973

The Secretary of State after approving proposals submitted by the Road Transport Industry Training Board for the imposition of a further levy on employers in the road transport industry and in exercise of powers conferred by section 4 of the Industrial Training Act 1964(a) and now vested in him (b), and of all other powers enabling him in that behalf hereby makes the following Order:—

Title and commencement

1. This Order may be cited as the Industrial Training Levy (Road Transport) Order 1973 and shall come into operation on 17th August 1973.

Interpretation

2.—(1) In this Order unless the context otherwise requires:—

(*a*) "an appeal tribunal" means an industrial tribunal established under section 12 of the Industrial Training Act 1964;

(*b*) "assessment" means an assessment of an employer to the levy;

(*c*) "the Board" means the Road Transport Industry Training Board;

(*d*) "business" means any activities of industry or commerce;

(*e*) "employer" means a person who is an employer in the road transport industry at any time in the seventh levy period;

(*f*) "the industrial training order" means the Industrial Training (Road Transport Board) Order 1966(c) as amended by the Industrial Training (Road Transport Board) Order 1972(d) and the Industrial Training (Road Transport Board) Order 1966 (Amendment) Order 1973(e);

(*g*) "the levy" means the levy imposed by the Board in respect of the seventh levy period;

(a) 1964 c. 16.   (b) S.I. 1968/729 (1968 II, p. 2108).
(c) S.I. 1966/1112 (1966 III, p. 2712).   (d) S.I. 1972/772 (1972 II, p. 2471).
(e) S.I. 1973/860 (1973 II, p. 2663).

(*h*) "notice" means a notice in writing;

(*i*) "road transport establishment" means an establishment in Great Britain engaged in the seventh base period wholly or mainly in the road transport industry for a total of twenty-seven or more weeks or, being an establishment that commenced to carry on business in the seventh base period, for a total number of weeks exceeding one half of the number of weeks in the part of the said period commencing with the day on which business was commenced and ending on the last day thereof;

(*j*) "the road transport industry" means any one or more of the activities which, subject to the provisions of paragraph 2 of Schedule 1 to the industrial training order, are specified in paragraph 1 of that Schedule as the activities of the road transport industry;

(*k*) "the seventh base period" means the period of twelve months that commenced on 6th April 1972;

(*l*) "the seventh levy period" means the period commencing with the day upon which this Order comes into operation and ending on 5th April 1974.

(2) Any reference in this Order to persons employed at or from a road transport establishment shall in any case where the employer is a company be construed as including a reference to any director of the company (or any person occupying the position of director by whatever name he is called) who devotes substantially the whole of his time to the service of the company.

(3) In the case where a road transport establishment is taken over (whether directly or indirectly) by an employer in succession to, or jointly with, another person, a person employed at any time in the seventh base period at or from the establishment shall be deemed, for the purposes of this Order, to have been so employed by the employer carrying on the said establishment on the day upon which this Order comes into operation, and any reference in this Order to persons employed by the employer at or from a road transport establishment in the seventh base period shall be construed accordingly.

(4) Any reference in this Order to an establishment that commences to carry on business or that ceases to carry on business shall not be taken to apply where the location of the establishment is changed but its business is continued wholly or mainly at or from the new location, or where the suspension of activities is of a temporary or seasonal nature.

(5) The Interpretation Act 1889(a) shall apply to the interpretation of this Order as it applies to the interpretation of an Act of Parliament.

Imposition of the levy

3. The levy to be imposed by the Board on employers in respect of the seventh levy period shall be assessed in accordance with the provisions of the Schedule to this Order.

(a) 1889 c. 63.

Assessment notices

4.—(1) The Board shall serve an assessment notice on every employer assessed to the levy.

(2) The amount payable under an assessment notice shall be rounded down to the nearest £1.

(3) An assessment notice shall state the Board's address for the service of a notice of appeal or of an application for an extension of time for appealing.

(4) An assessment notice may be served on the person assessed to the levy either by delivering it to him personally or by leaving it, or sending it to him by post, at his last known address or place of business in the United Kingdom or, if that person is a corporation, by leaving it, or sending it by post to the corporation at such address or place of business or at its registered or principal office.

Payment of levy

5.—(1) Subject to the provisions of this Article and of Articles 6 and 7, the amount of the levy payable under an assessment notice served by the Board shall be due and payable to the Board on 1st December 1973, or one month after the date of the assessment notice, whichever is the later.

(2) The amount of an assessment shall not be recoverable by the Board until there has expired the time allowed for appealing against the assessment by Article 7(1) of this Order and any further period or periods of time that the Board or an appeal tribunal may have allowed for appealing under paragraph (2) or (3) of that Article or, where an appeal is brought, until the appeal is decided or withdrawn.

Withdrawal of assessment

6.—(1) The Board may, by a notice served on the person assessed to the levy in the same manner as an assessment notice, withdraw an assessment if that person has appealed against that assessment under the provisions of Article 7 of this Order and the appeal has not been entered in the Register of Appeals kept under the appropriate Regulations specified in paragraph (5) of that Article.

(2) The withdrawal of an assessment shall be without prejudice to the power of the Board to serve a further assessment notice on the employer.

Appeals

7.—(1) A person assessed to the levy may appeal to an appeal tribunal against the assessment within one month from the date of the service of the assessment notice or within any further period or periods of time that may be allowed by the Board or an appeal tribunal under the following provisions of this Article.

(2) The Board by notice may for good cause allow a person assessed to the levy to appeal to an appeal tribunal against the assessment at any time within the period of four months from the date of the service of the assessment notice or within such further period or periods as the Board may allow before such time as may then be limited for appealing has expired.

(3) If the Board shall not allow an application for extension of time for appealing, an appeal tribunal shall upon application made to the tribunal by the person assessed to the levy have the like powers as the Board under the last foregoing paragraph.

(4) In the case of an assessment that has reference to an establishment that ceases to carry on business in the seventh levy period on any day after the date of the service of the assessment notice, the foregoing provisions of this Article shall have effect as if for the period of four months from the date of the service of the assessment notice mentioned in paragraph (2) of this Article there were substituted the period of six months from the date of the cessation of business.

(5) An appeal or an application to an appeal tribunal under this Article shall be made in accordance with the Industrial Tribunals (England and Wales) Regulations 1965(a) as amended by the Industrial Tribunals (England and Wales) (Amendment) Regulations 1967(b) except where the assessment relates to persons employed at or from one or more establishments which are wholly in Scotland and to no other persons in which case the appeal or application shall be made in accordance with the Industrial Tribunals (Scotland) Regulations 1965(c) as amended by the Industrial Tribunals (Scotland) (Amendment) Regulations 1967(d).

(6) The powers of an appeal tribunal under paragraph (3) of this Article may be exercised by the President of the Industrial Tribunals (England and Wales) or by the President of the Industrial Tribunals (Scotland) as the case may be.

Evidence

8.—(1) Upon the discharge by a person assessed to the levy of his liability under an assessment the Board shall if so requested issue to him a certificate to that effect.

(2) The production in any proceedings of a document purporting to be certified by the Secretary of the Board to be a true copy of an assessment or other notice issued by the Board or purporting to be a certificate such as is mentioned in the foregoing paragraph of this Article shall, unless the contrary is proved, be sufficient evidence of the document and of the facts stated therein.

Signed by order of the Secretary of State.

16th July 1973.

R. Chichester-Clark,
Minister of State,
Department of Employment.

(a) S.I. 1965/1101 (1965 II, p. 2805).   (b) S.I. 1967/301 (1967 I. p. 1040).
(c) S.I. 1965/1157 (1965 II, p. 3266).   (d) S.I. 1967/302 (1967 I, p. 1050).

SCHEDULE

1.—(1) In this Schedule unless the context otherwise requires—

 (a) "the appropriate percentage", in relation to the emoluments of persons employed at or from the road transport establishment or establishments of an employer means—

   (i) in the case where the employer was, on the relevant date, wholly or mainly engaged in any of the activities comprised in one of the thirteen Groups specified in columns 1 and 2 of the Appendix to this Schedule, the percentage specified in relation to that Group in column 3 or column 4, of that Appendix, whichever is appropriate, in accordance with paragraph 2(2) of this Schedule;

   (ii) in any other case, the lowest percentage specified in column 3 or column 4, whichever is appropriate as aforesaid, in relation to any Group which comprises an activity in which the employer was engaged;

 (b) "emoluments" means all emoluments assessable to income tax under Schedule E (other than pensions), being emoluments from which tax under that Schedule is deductible, whether or not tax in fact falls to be deducted from any particular payment thereof;

 (c) "the relevant date" means the 5th April 1973;

 (d) other expressions have the meanings assigned to them respectively by paragraph 3 or 4 of the Schedule to the industrial training order or by Article 2 of this Order.

 (2) For the purposes of this Schedule no regard shall be had to the emoluments of any person employed as follows:—

 (a) by the London Transport Executive wholly in any activities to which paragraph 1(p) of Schedule 1 to the industrial training order applies, not being activities that are specified in head (ii) (v) or (vi) of the definition of related activities in paragraph 3 of that Schedule and are incidental or ancillary to principal activities of the road transport industry;

 (b) by a local authority or a joint board or joint committee of such authorities in any activities, not being activities carried out for the purpose of a passenger road transport service provided by the authority, board or committee;

 (c) wholly in agriculture;

 (d) wholly as a registered dock worker on dock work; or

 (e) wholly in the supply of food or drink for immediate consumption.

2.—(1) The levy shall be assessed by the Board in respect of each employer, not being an employer who is exempt from the levy by virtue of paragraph 3 of this Schedule, and, subject to the provisions of this Schedule, the amount thereof shall be equal to the appropriate percentage of the sum of the emoluments of all the persons employed by the employer in the seventh base period at or from his road transport establishment or establishments (being an establishment or establishments carrying on business in the seventh levy period).

(2)(*a*) Where the sum of the emoluments referred to in the previous sub-paragraph exceeds £7,500 (£10,000 in the case of an employer wholly or mainly engaged on the relevant date in any of the activities comprised in Group 1 in the Appendix to this Schedule) but is less than £30,000 the appropriate percentage shall be that specified in column 3 of that Appendix;

(*b*) where the sum of such emoluments is £30,000 or more the appropriate percentage shall be that specified in column 4 of the said Appendix.

3. There shall be exempt from the levy an employer—

(*a*) in whose case the sum of the emoluments of all the persons employed by him in the seventh base period at or from his road transport establishment or establishments was £7,500 or less (£10,000 or less in the case of an employer wholly or mainly engaged on the relevant date in any of the activities comprised in Group 1 in the said Appendix);

(*b*) who was wholly or mainly engaged on the relevant date in giving instruction by way of business in the driving of motor vehicles or goods vehicles.

4. Where any persons whose emoluments are taken into account for the purpose of the preceding paragraphs of this Schedule were employed at or from an establishment that ceases to carry on business in the seventh levy period, the sum of the emoluments of those persons shall, for the purposes of the assessment, be reduced in the same proportion as the number of days between the commencement of the said levy period and the date of cessation of business (both dates inclusive) bears to the number of days in the said levy period, but the appropriate percentage shall be determined in accordance with the provisions of the said paragraphs as if the provisions of this paragraph did not apply.

APPENDIX

Column 1 Group No.	Column 2 Description of Activities	Column 3 Appropriate	Column 4 percentage
1.	Dealing in, letting out on hire or the repair by way of business of, agricultural machinery and equipment.	1·4%	1·9%
2.	Dealing in, or the repair of, motor vehicles or goods vehicles.	1·4%	1·9%
3.	Selling by retail, motor spirit, diesel fuel or lubricating or other oils for use in motor vehicles or goods vehicles.	1·4%	1·9%
4.	Dealing in, or letting out on hire, transport service equipment.	1·4%	1·9%
5.	Dealing (not being selling by retail) in components, replacements, spare parts or accessories (not being tyres) for motor vehicles or goods vehicles.	1·2%	1·9%
6.	The carriage of passengers by motor vehicles on roads for hire or reward.	1·2%	1·7%
7.	The letting out on hire (with or without the services of the drivers) of motor vehicles for the conveyance of persons.	1·2%	1·7%

Column 1 Group No.	Column 2 Description of Activities	Column 3 Appropriate	Column 4 percentage
8.	Public warehousing.	1·2%	1·7%
9.	The manufacture, fitting out or repair of vehicle bodies.	1·2%	1·7%
10.	The carriage or haulage of goods by goods vehicles on roads for hire or reward or arranging by way of business the transport of goods by goods vehicles on roads.	1·0%	1·7%
11.	The collection of motor vehicles or goods vehicles and their delivery by road by way of business.	1·0%	1·7%
12.	The letting out on hire (with or without the services of the drivers) of goods vehicles for the carriage or haulage of goods.	1·0%	1·7%
13.	The removal of furniture by way of business.	0·7%	1·1%

EXPLANATORY NOTE

(This Note is not part of the Order.)

This Order gives effect to proposals submitted by the Road Transport Industry Training Board to the Secretary of State for Employment for the imposition of a further levy upon employers in the road transport industry for the purpose of raising money towards the expenses of the Board.

The levy is to be imposed in respect of the seventh levy period commencing with the day upon which this Order comes into operation and ending on 5th April 1974. The levy will be assessed by the Board and there will be a right of appeal against an assessment to an industrial tribunal.

STATUTORY INSTRUMENTS

1973 No. 1237

WAGES COUNCILS

The Wages Regulation (Retail Bread and Flour Confectionery) (England and Wales) (Amendment) Order 1973

Made - - - 16th July 1973
Coming into Operation 20th August 1973

Whereas the Secretary of State has received from the Retail Bread and Flour Confectionery Trade Wages Council (England and Wales) the wages regulation proposals set out in the Schedule hereto;

Now, therefore, the Secretary of State in exercise of powers conferred by section 11 of the Wages Councils Act 1959(a), as modified by Article 2 of the Counter-Inflation (Modification of Wages Councils Act 1959) Order 1973(b), and now vested in him(c), and of all other powers enabling him in that behalf, hereby makes the following Order:—

1. This Order may be cited as the Wages Regulation (Retail Bread and Flour Confectionery) (England and Wales) (Amendment) Order 1973.

2.—(1) In this Order the expression "the specified date" means the 20th August 1973, provided that where, as respects any worker who is paid wages at intervals not exceeding seven days, that date does not correspond with the beginning of the period for which the wages are paid, the expression "the specified date" means, as respects that worker, the beginning of the next such period following that date.

(2) The Interpretation Act 1889(d) shall apply to the interpretation of this Order as it applies to the interpretation of an Act of Parliament.

3. The wages regulation proposals set out in the Schedule hereto shall have effect as from the specified date.

Signed by order of the Secretary of State.
16th July 1973.

> W. H. Marsh,
> Assistant Secretary,
> Department of Employment.

(a) 1959 c. 69.　　　　　　　　　(b) S.I. 1973/661 (1973 I, p. 2141).
(c) S.I. 1959/1769, 1968/729 (1959 I, p. 1795; 1968 II, p. 2108).
(d) 1889 c. 63.

Article 3

SCHEDULE

STATUTORY MINIMUM REMUNERATION

The Wages Regulation (Retail Bread and Flour Confectionery) (England and Wales) Order 1972(a) (Order B.F.C. (34)), shall have effect as if in the Schedule thereto for the proviso at the end of paragraph 11 there were substituted the following:

"Provided that

    (i) overtime rates under this paragraph shall be payable to a manager or manageress only if the overtime worked is specifically authorised by the employer or his representative;

    (ii) where a worker is employed in a shop which is registered under section 53 of the Shops Act 1950 (which relates to persons observing the Jewish Sabbath), the provisions of this paragraph shall apply as if for the word 'Sunday' there were substituted the word 'Saturday';

    (iii) in any week which includes one customary holiday, '33 hours' shall be substituted for '40 hours' where it occurs in the foregoing provisions of this paragraph and in any week which includes two customary holidays, '26 hours' shall be substituted for the said '40 hours' *and in any week which includes three customary holidays '19 hours' shall be substituted for the said '40 hours'.*"

EXPLANATORY NOTE

(This Note is not part of the Order.)

This Order, which has effect from 20th August 1973, amends that provision of the Wages Regulation (Retail Bread and Flour Confectionery) (England and Wales) Order 1972 (Order B.F.C. (34)) which relates to the calculation of overtime worked in a week in which there is or are a day or days of customary holiday.

New provisions are printed in italics.

(a) S.I. 1972/2018 (1972 III, p. 5973).

STATUTORY INSTRUMENTS

1973 No. 1243

WAGES COUNCILS

The Wages Regulation (Licensed Residential Establishment and Licensed Restaurant) (Amendment) Order 1973

Made	- - -		17th July 1973
Coming into Operation		10th September 1973	

Whereas the Secretary of State has received from the Licensed Residential Establishment and Licensed Restaurant Wages Council the wages regulation proposals set out in the Schedule hereto;

Now, therefore, the Secretary of State in exercise of powers conferred by section 11 of the Wages Councils Act 1959(**a**), as modified by Article 2 of the Counter-Inflation (Modification of Wages Councils Act 1959) Order 1973(**b**), and now vested in him(**c**), and of all other powers enabling him in that behalf, hereby makes the following Order: —

1. This Order may be cited as the Wages Regulation (Licensed Residential Establishment and Licensed Restaurant) (Amendment) Order 1973.

2.—(1) In this Order the expression "the specified date" means the 10th September 1973, provided that where, as respects any worker who is paid wages at intervals not exceeding seven days, that date does not correspond with the beginning of the period for which the wages are paid, the expression "the specified date" means, as respects that worker, the beginning of the next such period following that date.

(2) The Interpretation Act 1889(**d**) shall apply to the interpretation of this Order as it applies to the interpretation of an Act of Parliament.

3. The wages regulation proposals set out in the Schedule hereto shall have effect as from the specified date.

Signed by order of the Secretary of State.

17th July 1973.

W. H. Marsh,
Assistant Secretary,
Department of Employment.

(**a**) 1959 c. 69.　　　　　　　　(**b**) S.I. 1973/661 (1973 I, p. 2141).
(**c**) S.I. 1959/1769, 1968/729 (1959 I, p. 1795; 1968 II, p. 2108).
(**d**) 1889 c. 63.

Article 3

SCHEDULE

The Wages Regulation (Licensed Residential Establishment and Licensed Restaurant) Order 1972(a) (Order L.R. (44)) shall have effect as if in the Schedule thereto:—

1. for paragraph 13 there were substituted the following paragraph:—

"PAYMENT FOR SPREADOVER OF HOURS OF WORK

13.—(1) Subject to the provisions of sub-paragraphs (2) and (3) of this paragraph, where the hours of duty on any day of a worker, other than an extra waiter, extra waitress or extra head waiter, are spread over more than 12 hours calculated from the time at which the worker first commences duty on that day, he shall be paid, in addition to the minimum remuneration to which he is entitled under the other provisions of this Part of this Schedule, remuneration in accordance with the following Table:—

Where the hours of duty are spread over—

more than 12 hours and not more than 14 hours	more than 14 hours and not more than 15 hours	more than 15 hours
Column 1	Column 2	Column 3
25p per day	50p per day	75p per day

(2) Where the worker works for less than eight hours on any day and his hours of duty are spread over more than 13 hours, he shall be paid the minimum remuneration to which he would be entitled under the other provisions of this Part of this Schedule if he had worked for eight hours, and in addition the appropriate remuneration set out in Column 1, 2 or 3 of the foregoing Table:

Provided that, in calculating the remuneration to which the worker would be entitled if he had worked for eight hours, overtime rates shall apply only to overtime worked.

(3) The foregoing provisions of this paragraph shall not apply—

(a) during the off-season to a worker employed in a seasonal establishment; and

(b) to a worker on any day on which his hours of duty are spread over not more than 14 hours who is employed either in a seasonal establishment or in a licensed residential establishment which contains not more than 35 rooms ordinarily available as sleeping accommodation for guests or lodgers.

(4) For the purposes of this paragraph—

(a) where a worker commences a turn of duty on any day before midnight and that turn of duty continues beyond midnight, the hours of duty after midnight shall be treated as hours of duty performed on the day upon which the turn of duty commenced; and

(a) S.I. 1972/757 (1972 II, p. 2379).

(b) emergency duty (as defined in paragraph 34) shall not be taken into consideration when calculating the hours over which the hours of duty have been spread.

(5) In this paragraph the following expressions have the meanings hereby respectively assigned to them, that is to say:—

'Seasonal establishment' means a licensed residential establishment at which there is posted up a current certificate signed by a qualified auditor certifying that in his opinion more than 50 per cent. of the annual takings at the establishment in respect of the sale of food and drink (other than intoxicating liquor) and the provision of living accommodation is ordinarily earned during the months of June, July, August and September; and for the purposes of this definition—

(a) a certificate shall be treated as current for a period of 12 months from the date thereof; and

(b) 'qualified auditor' means a member of one or more of the following bodies:—

The Institute of Chartered Accountants in England and Wales;

The Institute of Chartered Accountants of Scotland;

The Association of Certified and Corporate Accountants;

The Institute of Chartered Accountants in Ireland;

any other body of accountants established in the United Kingdom and for the time being recognised for the purposes of paragraphs (a) and (b) of sub-section (1) of section 161 of the Companies Act 1948(a) by the Board of Trade;

'Off-season' means the months of a calendar year except the months June, July, August and September."

2. for the definition of "Customary Holiday" in paragraph 34 there were substituted the following definition:—

" 'CUSTOMARY HOLIDAY' means

(1) In England and Wales—

(a) Christmas Day; *26th December if it be not a Sunday; 27th December in a year when 25th or 26th December is a Sunday;* Good Friday; Easter Monday; *the last Monday in May; the last Monday in August; or, where a day is substituted for any of the above days by national proclamation, that day;* and any day proclaimed as an additional bank holiday or a general holiday; or

(b) in the case of each of the said days, a day substituted by the employer therefor, being a day recognised by local custom as a day of holiday in substitution for the said day.

(2) In Scotland—

(a) New Year's Day (or the following day if New Year's Day falls on a Sunday), the local Spring Holiday, the Local Autumn Holiday and any day proclaimed as an additional bank holiday or a general holiday throughout Scotland; and

(b) three other week-days in the course of a calendar year, to be fixed by the employer and notified to the worker not less than three weeks before the holiday, or any other day or days falling within the same calendar year which may be substituted for such day or days by agreement between the employer and the worker or his representative."

(a) 1948 c. 38.

EXPLANATORY NOTE

(This Note is not part of the Order.)

This Order, which has effect from 10th September 1973, amends the provisions of the Wages Regulation (Licensed Residential Establishment and Licensed Restaurant) Order 1972 (Order L.R. (44)) relating to payment for spreadover of hours of work.

It also amends the provisions relating to customary holidays contained in Order L.R. (44) so as to take account of recent changes in the law and practice relating to public holidays.

New provisions are printed in italics.

STATUTORY INSTRUMENTS

1973 No. 1249 (C.30)

SOCIAL SECURITY

The Social Security Act 1973 (Commencement) Order 1973

Made - - - -	*19th July* 1973
Laid before Parliament	*19th July* 1973
Coming into Operation	*19th July* 1973

The Secretary of State for Social Services, in exercise of powers conferred by section 101 of the Social Security Act 1973(a), hereby makes the following order:—

Citation and commencement

1. This order may be cited as the Social Security Act 1973 (Commencement) Order 1973 and shall come into operation on 19th July 1973.

Appointed days

2. The day appointed for the coming into force of any provision of the Social Security Act 1973 specified in column 1 of the Schedule to this Order shall be the date specified in column 3 of that Schedule in relation to that provision.

3. Where any provision specified in column 1 of that Schedule contains a reference to "the appointed day" that day shall be the day specified in column 3 of that Schedule in relation to that provision.

Keith Joseph,
Secretary of State
for Social Services.

19th July 1973.

_____

(a) 1973 c. 38.

Article 2

SCHEDULE

Provisions of the Social Security Act 1973	Subject matter	Appointed day
Section 1 and Schedule 1	Outline of basic scheme contributory system	6th April 1975
Section 2	Class 1 contributions	6th April 1975
Section 3	Class 2 contributions	6th April 1975
Section 4	Class 3 contributions	6th April 1975
Section 5 and Schedule 2	Class 4 contributions	6th April 1975
Section 6	General power to limit, and otherwise regulate, liability for contributions	6th April 1975
Section 9	Descriptions of benefits; the earnings factor; crediting of contributions	6th April 1975
Schedule 3	Contribution conditions for basic scheme benefit	6th April 1975
Section 36	Review of provision for chronically sick and disabled persons	19th July 1973
Section 42	Married women, widows, etc	6th April 1975
Section 48 and Schedule 12	National Insurance Advisory Committee and its functions	19th July 1973
Section 77	Reserve scheme contributions	6th April 1975
Section 78 and Schedule 19	Reserve scheme premium on termination of recognised pensionable employment	6th April 1975
Section 95(1) in relation only to the following provision	Application of Parts II and III of the Act to Northern Ireland	19th July 1973
Section 96	Orders and regulations (general provisions)	19th July 1973
Section 97	Parliamentary control of orders and regulations	19th July 1973
Section 99	Interpretation	19th July 1973
Section 101	Citation and commencement	19th July 1973

EXPLANATORY NOTE

(This Note is not part of the Order.)

This Order brings into force on 6th April 1975 the provisions of the Social Security Act 1973 relating to basic scheme contributions, the crediting of contributions, the contribution conditions for basic scheme benefit, reserve scheme contributions and premiums, married women and widows, and the review of provision for the chronically sick and disabled. It also brings into operation immediately provisions relating to the making of regulations and orders, the Parliamentary control of them, reference of them to the National Insurance Advisory Committee, and the interpretation, citation and commencement of the Act and the application of Parts II and III of the Act to Northern Ireland.

STATUTORY INSTRUMENTS

1973 No. 1251

CUSTOMS AND EXCISE

The Import Duties (Temporary Exemptions) (No. 18) Order 1973

Made - - -		*18th July* 1973
Laid before the House of Commons		*19th July* 1973
Coming into Operation		*20th July* 1973

The Lords Commissioners of Her Majesty's Treasury, by virtue of the powers conferred on them by sections 1, 3(6) and 13 of the Import Duties Act 1958(a), as amended by paragraph 1 of Schedule 4 to the European Communities Act 1972(b), and of all other powers enabling them in that behalf, on the recommendation of the Secretary of State(c) hereby make the following Order:—

1.—(1) This Order may be cited as the Import Duties (Temporary Exemptions) (No. 18) Order 1973 and shall come into operation on 20th July 1973.

(2) The Interpretation Act 1889(d) shall apply for the interpretation of this Order as it applies for the interpretation of an Act of Parliament.

2.—(1) Up to and including 31st December 1973 or, in the case of goods in relation to which an earlier day is specified in the Schedule to this Order, up to and including that day, any import duty which is for the time being chargeable on goods of a heading of the Customs Tariff 1959 specified in that Schedule shall not be chargeable on goods of any description there specified in relation to that heading.

(2) Any entry in the second column of the Schedule to this Order shall be taken to comprise all goods which would be classified under an entry in the same terms constituting a subheading (other than the final subheading) in the relevant heading in the Customs Tariff 1959.

(3) For the purposes of classification under the Customs Tariff 1959, in so far as that depends on the rate of duty, any goods to which paragraph (1) or paragraph (2) above applies shall be treated as chargeable with the same duty as if this Order had not been made.

Tim Fortescue,

P. L. Hawkins,

Two of the Lords Commissioners of Her Majesty's Treasury.

18th July 1973.

(a) 1958 c. 6.	(b) 1972 c. 68.
(c) See S.I. 1970/1537 (1970 III, p. 5293).	(d) 1889 c. 63.

SCHEDULE

GOODS TEMPORARILY EXEMPT FROM IMPORT DUTY

Tariff Heading	Description
28·38	Zinc sulphate
29·08	2,2-Di-[4-(2-hydroxy-n-propoxy)phenyl]propane
29·34	Di(tri-n-butyltin) oxide (up to and including 31st October 1973)
	Tri-n-butyltin chloride (up to and including 31st October 1973)

EXPLANATORY NOTE

(*This Note is not part of the Order.*)

This Order provides that the goods listed in the Schedule shall be temporarily exempt from import duty up to and including 31st December 1973 or, in the case of certain items, up to and including 31st October 1973.

STATUTORY INSTRUMENTS

1973 No. 1252

POLICE

The Police Federation (Transitory Provisions) Regulations 1973

Made - - -	*17th July* 1973
Laid before Parliament	*26th July* 1973
Coming into Operation	*1st September* 1973

In exercise of the powers conferred on me by section 44 of the Police Act 1964(a), and after consultation with the three Central Committees of the Police Federation for England and Wales sitting as a Joint Committee, I hereby make the following Regulations:—

1. These Regulations may be cited as the Police Federation (Transitory Provisions) Regulations 1973 and shall come into operation on 1st September 1973.

2. These Regulations shall be construed as one with the Police Federation Regulations 1969(b), as amended (c), but shall have effect notwithstanding anything in Regulations 6 and 12 of those Regulations (branch boards and central committees).

3.—(1) In the year 1973 no branch board elections shall be held in pursuance of paragraph (8) of the said Regulation 6.

(2) The members of branch boards serving as such on the date of the coming into operation of these Regulations shall, subject to paragraph (10) of the said Regulation 6, remain members thereof until 1st April 1974.

4.—(1) In the year 1974 no central committee elections shall be held in pursuance of paragraph (2) of the said Regulation 12.

(2) The members of each central committee serving as such at the beginning of the annual meeting in 1974 of the inspectors', sergeants' or, as the case may be, constables' central conference shall remain members of the committee in question as though they had been re-elected at that annual meeting.

Robert Carr,
One of Her Majesty's Principal
Secretaries of State.

Home Office,
Whitehall.
17th July 1973.

(a) 1964 c. 48.   (b) S.I. 1969/1787 (1969 III, p. 5592).
(c) The amending instruments are not relevant to the subject matter of these Regulations.

EXPLANATORY NOTE

(*This Note is not part of the Regulations.*)

Regulations 6 and 12 of the Police Federation Regulations 1969 provide for the election of members of branch boards and central committees of the Police Federation.

The present Regulations make transitory provision as respects the years 1973 and 1974. In 1973 no branch board, and in 1974 no central committee, elections are to be held. The serving members of branch boards are to remain members until 1st April 1974 (the date on which the Local Government Act 1972 becomes fully operative) and the serving members of central committees are to remain members as though re-elected in the year 1974.

STATUTORY INSTRUMENTS

1973 No. 1253 (C.31)

BANKS AND BANKING

The Mercantile Credit Act 1973 (Appointed Day) Order 1973

Made - - -		18*th July* 1973

The Secretary of State, in exercise of his powers under section 3 of the Mercantile Credit Act 1973(a), hereby makes the following Order:—

1. This Order may be cited as the Mercantile Credit Act 1973 (Appointed Day) Order 1973.

2. 1st September 1973 shall be the appointed day for the purposes of the Mercantile Credit Act 1973.

P. A. R. Brown,
An Under Secretary,
Department of Trade and Industry.

18th July 1973.

(a) 1973 c. v.

STATUTORY INSTRUMENTS

1973 No. 1254 (C.32)

BANKS AND BANKING
The Forward Trust Act 1973 (Appointed Day)
Order 1973

Made - - - 18*th July* 1973

The Secretary of State, in exercise of his powers under section 3 of the Forward Trust Act 1973(a), hereby makes the following Order:—

1. This Order may be cited as the Forward Trust Act 1973 (Appointed Day) Order 1973.

2. 31st August 1973 shall be the appointed day for the purposes of the Forward Trust Act 1973.

P. A. R. Brown,
An Under Secretary,
Department of Trade and Industry.

18th July 1973.

(a) 1973 c. viii.

STATUTORY INSTRUMENTS

1973 No. 1255

WAGES COUNCILS

The Wages Regulation (Flax and Hemp) Order 1973

Made - - -		*18th July* 1973
Coming into Operation		*17th August* 1973

Whereas the Secretary of State has received from the Flax and Hemp Wages Council (Great Britain) the wages regulation proposals set out in the Schedule hereto;

Now, therefore, the Secretary of State in exercise of powers conferred by section 11 of the Wages Councils Act 1959(a), as modified by Article 2 of the Counter-Inflation (Modification of Wages Councils Act 1959) Order 1973(b), and now vested in him(c), and of all other powers enabling him in that behalf, hereby makes the following Order:—

1. This Order may be cited as the Wages Regulation (Flax and Hemp) Order 1973.

2.—(1) In this Order the expression "the specified date" means the 17th August 1973, provided that where, as respects any worker who is paid wages at intervals not exceeding seven days, that date does not correspond with the beginning of the period for which the wages are paid, the expression "the specified date" means, as respects that worker, the beginning of the next such period following that date.

(2) The Interpretation Act 1889(d) shall apply to the interpretation of this Order as it applies to the interpretation of an Act of Parliament and as if this Order and the Order hereby revoked were Acts of Parliament.

3. The wages regulation proposals set out in the Schedule hereto shall have effect as from the specified date and as from that date the Wages Regulation (Flax and Hemp) Order 1972(e) shall cease to have effect.

Signed by order of the Secretary of State.

18th July 1973.

W. H. Marsh,
Assistant Secretary,
Department of Employment.

Article 3
SCHEDULE

The following minimum remuneration shall be substituted for the statutory minimum remuneration fixed by the Wages Regulation (Flax and Hemp) Order 1972 (Order F.H. (130)).

(a) 1959 c. 69.   (b) S.I. 1973/661 (1973 I, p. 2141).
(c) S.I. 1959/1769, 1968/729 (1959 I, p. 1795; 1968 II, p. 2108).
(d) 1889 c. 63.   (e) S.I. 1972/928 (1972 II, p. 2916).

STATUTORY MINIMUM REMUNERATION

PART I

GENERAL

1.—(1) The minimum remuneration payable to a worker to whom this Schedule applies for all work except work to which a minimum overtime rate applies under Part III of this Schedule is:—

    (a) in the case of a time worker, the hourly general minimum time rate applicable to the worker under the provisions of this Schedule;

    (b) in the case of a worker employed on piece work, piece rates each of which would yield, in the circumstances of the case, to an ordinary worker (that is to say, a worker of ordinary skill and experience in the work) at least the same amount of money as the hourly piece work basis time rate applicable to the worker or, where no such rate applies, at least the same amount of money as the hourly general minimum time rate which would be applicable if the worker were a time worker:

    Provided that where an hourly guaranteed time rate is applicable to a piece worker under paragraph 6 or under paragraph 7 and the remuneration calculated on a time work basis at that rate exceeds the remuneration calculated on the basis of the said piece rates, the worker shall be paid not less than that guaranteed time rate.

(2) In this Schedule, the expressions "hourly general minimum time rate", "hourly guaranteed time rate" and "hourly piece work basis time rate" mean respectively the general minimum time rate, the guaranteed time rate and the piece work basis time rate applicable to a worker under Part II of this Schedule divided in each case by 40.

PART II

ALL SECTIONS OF THE TRADE

GENERAL MINIMUM TIME RATES AND PIECE WORK BASIS TIME RATES

2.—(1) *Subject to the provisions of this paragraph and of paragraphs 3 and 4 of this Schedule the general minimum time rates payable to male and female workers (in the occupations listed in sub-paragraph (2)) comprised in any of the groups specified in Column 1 of the next following Table are the rates set out in Column 2 or 3 of that Table as the case may be.*

Column 1 Time Workers	Column 2 Adult male workers aged 19 years or over	Column 3 Adult female workers aged 18 years or over
	Per week of 40 hours £	Per week of 40 hours £
Group 1	16·03	12·67
Group 2	16·16	13·00
Group 3	16·28	13·33
Group 4	16·40	13·67
Spinners when employed on night shifts	19·13	—
Group 5	16·52	14·00
During the first six months of employment as a Weaver ...	16·09	14·00
Group 6	17·50	14·85
Group 7	18·50	15·70

(2) *The occupations of workers included in Groups 1 to 7 are as follows:—*

Group 1
Bobbin setter
Can transporter
Sweeper

Group 2
Back ender
Bank filler
Emulsion mixer (*proofing*)
Ingiver
Labourer—General
Lapper
Stamper and Sample cutter
Weft carrier

Group 3
Breaker Card attendant
Canvas darner
Cloth inspector
Cloth Starch Machine attendant
Cropper
Emulsion Machine 2nd operator
  (*proofing*)
Finisher card attendant
Fork lift driver
Hackling machine attendant
Hackling Piecer
Hosepipe darner
Hose warehouseman
Loose stock dyer

Group 3 (*contd.*)
Loose stock pan packer
Oiler
Packer—Press and Hand
Preparer
Tenter's helper
Twister Frame attendant
Warehouseman Tow and Flax
Yarn Examiner and Packer
Yarn Storeman

Group 4
Drawer
Emulsion Machine 1st operator (*proofing*)
Package Boiling plant operator
Reeler
Spinner
Warper
Winder

Group 5
Rubber liner
Weaver

Group 6
Yarn Dresser

Group 7
Tenter

(3) The following general minimum time rates are applicable to junior workers, except learners to whom the minimum rates specified in paragraph 3 apply, being aged:—

	Per week of 40 hours £ Male	Per week of 40 hours £ Female
18 and under 19 years	12·67	—
17½ and under 18 years	11·38	11·38
17 and under 17½ years	10·39	10·39
16½ and under 17 years	9·67	9·67
16 and under 16½ years	9·01	9·01
15½ and under 16 years	8·44	8·44
under 15½ years	7·99	7·99

Provided that:—
  (i) the rate for male spinners aged 18 and under 19
    years when employed on night shift shall be ...   14·78   —
  (ii) the rate for female workers who have com-
    pleted two years' employment (including any
    period of learnership) in some or all of the
    processes of bobbin carrying, doffing, piecing
    or assisting at spinning frame, and who are in
    charge of a frame shall be   ...   .   —   12·76

LEARNERS AND WEAVING TEACHERS

3.—(1) The following general minimum time rates are applicable to female learners:—

	Per week of 40 hours £

(a) Learners employed in weaving, warping, winding, reeling or spinning for one period of learnership not exceeding six months where such learnership is commenced—

(i) At 16 years of age or over	9·01
(ii) At 15½ years and under 16 years of age	8·44
(iii) Under 15½ years of age...	7·99

(b) Learners employed in card-cutting for one period of learnership not exceeding 12 months where such learnership is commenced—

(i) At 16 years of age or over	9·01
(ii) At 15½ years and under 16 years of age	8·44
(iii) Under 15½ years of age...	7·99

(2) For the purposes of this paragraph a learner is a female worker who is employed during the whole or a substantial part of her time in learning weaving, warping, winding, reeling, spinning or card-cutting by an employer who ensures that she receives reasonable and proper facilities for such learning and, in the case of a learner employed in weaving, is placed under a competent worker to be taught.

(3) Notwithstanding the provisions of paragraph 2, the weekly remuneration applicable to a worker who is employed in teaching a learner weaving shall not be less than the sum of the following amounts, that is to say—

(a) the amount obtained by multiplying the worker's average hourly earnings during the previous eight weeks (exclusive of any week during which she was teaching a learner) by the number of hours constituting the worker's normal working week while teaching the learner;

(b) the amount (if any) by which the piece work basis time rate in paragraph 5 exceeds the piece work basis time rate which was applicable at the end of the period of eight weeks specified in (a); and

(c) 60p a week.

APPRENTICES AND IMPROVERS TO TENTING OR DRESSING

	Per week of 40 hours £

4.—(1) The following general minimum time rates are applicable to male workers:—

(a) Apprentices to tenting, aged 16 years or over, whose employment complies with the provisions of Part IV of this Schedule—

During the—

1st six months of apprenticeship	9·01
2nd „ „ „ „	9·67
3rd „ „ „ „	10·39
4th „ „ „ „	11·38
3rd year of apprenticeship	12·67
4th „ „ „	16·09

(b) Improvers to tenting—

During one year of employment as an improver	16·80

(c) Apprentices to dressing aged 16 years or over, whose employment complies with the provisions of Part IV of this Schedule—

During the—

1st six months of apprenticeship	9·01
2nd „ „ „ „	9·67
3rd „ „ „ „	10·39
4th „ „ „ „	11·38
3rd year of apprenticeship	12·67

(d) Improvers to dressing—

During one year of employment as an improver ... ... 16·09

(2) For the purposes of this paragraph:—

(a) an improver to tenting is a male worker who having completed four years' apprenticeship to tenting in accordance with the provisions of Part IV of this Schedule has had thereafter less than two years' employment in tenting and is the holder of a certificate of registration as an improver to tenting issued by, or on behalf of, the Wages Council or has made application for such certificate which has been acknowledged and is still under consideration;

(b) an improver to dressing is a male worker who having completed three years' apprenticeship to dressing in accordance with the provisions of Part IV of this Schedule has had thereafter less than one year's employment in dressing.

PIECE WORK BASIS TIME RATE

Per week
of 40 hours
£

5. The piece work basis time rate applicable to female workers employed on piece work is ... ... 13·21

GUARANTEED TIME RATES FOR PIECE WORKERS

6. The guaranteed time rates applicable to female workers employed on piece work (except learners to whom the minimum rates specified in paragraph 3(1) apply) are as follows:—

Per week
of 40 hours
£

Aged 18 years or over	12·67
„ 17½ years and under 18 years	11·38
„ 17 „ „ „ 17½ „	10·39
„ 16½ „ „ „ 17 „	9·67
„ 16 „ „ „ 16½ „	9·01
„ 15½ „ „ „ 16 „	8·44
„ under 15½ years	7·99

GUARANTEED TIME RATE FOR PIECE WORKERS
WEAVERS

Per week
of 40 hours
£

7. The guaranteed time rates applicable to male weavers employed on piece work are as follows:—

(1) During the first six months of employment as a weaver at or after the age of 19 years ... ... 16·09

(2) Thereafter ... ... 16·52

PART III

OVERTIME AND WAITING TIME

MINIMUM OVERTIME RATES—ALL WORKERS

8.—(1) Subject to the provisions of this paragraph, minimum overtime rates are payable to any worker as follows:—

(a) on any day other than a Saturday, Sunday or a customary holiday—

(i) for the first two hours worked in excess of
8¼ hours ...   .   time-and-a-quarter

(ii) thereafter ...   .   time-and-a-half

> Provided that where the worker normally attends on five days only in the week or on five shifts in the case of a shift worker the said minimum overtime rates of time-and-a-quarter and time-and-a-half shall be payable after 9 and 11 hours' work respectively.

(b) on a Saturday, not being a customary holiday—

for all time worked in excess of 3¼ hours   ...   time-and-a-half

> Provided that where the worker normally attends on five days only in the week or on five shifts in the case of a shift worker the said minimum overtime rate of time-and-a-half shall be payable for all time worked on Saturday.

(c) on a Sunday or a customary holiday—

for all time worked   ...   .   double time

(2) Subject to the provisions of sub-paragraph (3) of this paragraph, where the employer and the worker by agreement in writing fix in respect of each week-day or shift the number of hours after which a minimum overtime rate shall be payable and the total number of such hours amounts to 40 weekly, the following minimum overtime rates shall be payable in substitution for those set out in sub-paragraph (1) of this paragraph—

(a) on any day other than a Saturday, Sunday or a customary holiday—

(i) for the first two hours worked in excess of the
agreed number of hours   ...   .   time-and-a-quarter

(ii) thereafter ...   .   time-and-a-half

(b) on a Saturday, not being a customary holiday—

for all time worked in excess of the agreed number of
hours ...   .   time-and-a-half

> Provided that where the said agreement provides that Saturday shall not normally be a working day, the said minimum overtime rate of time-and-a-half shall be payable for all time worked on Saturday.

(c) on a Sunday or a customary holiday—
for all time worked ...   .   double time

(3) Where a worker is employed on a turn of duty which commences on one day and extends into the following day, the whole of that turn of duty shall, for the purposes of this paragraph, be treated as occurring on the day on which the worker was required to commence such turn of duty:

Provided that where the worker is employed on regular night shifts for five nights in the week, and by agreement between the worker and his employer commences a turn of duty on Sunday, then the whole of that turn of duty shall be treated as occurring on Monday.

9. In this Part of this Schedule:—

(1) The expression "customary holiday" means—

(a) (i) In England and Wales—

Christmas Day; *26th December if it be not a Sunday; 27th December in a year when 25th or 26th December is a Sunday;* Good Friday; Easter Monday; *the last Monday in May; the last Monday in August;* or where another day is substituted for any of the above days by national proclamation, that day:

Provided that in the case of workers who normally work on each week-day except Saturday if Christmas Day falls on a Saturday the holiday shall be the next following Tuesday;

(ii) In Scotland—

New Year's Day and the following day:

Provided that if New Year's Day falls on a Sunday, the holidays shall be the following Monday and Tuesday; if New Year's Day falls on a Saturday then in the case of workers who normally work on each week-day except Saturday the holidays shall be the following Monday and Tuesday and in the case of all other workers, New Year's Day and the following Monday;

the local Spring holiday;

the local Autumn holiday;

and two other days (being days on which the worker normally works for the employer) in the course of a calendar year, to be fixed by the employer in consultation with the worker or his representative and notified to the worker not less than three weeks before the holiday;

or

(b) in the case of each of the said days (other than a day fixed by the employer in Scotland and notified to the worker as aforesaid) a day substituted by the employer therefor, being a day recognised by local custom as a day of holiday in substitution for the said day.

(2) The expressions "time-and-a-quarter", "time-and-a-half" and "double time" mean respectively:—

(a) in the case of a time worker, one and a quarter times, one and a half times and twice the hourly general minimum time rate otherwise applicable to the worker;

(b) in the case of a female worker employed on piece work:—

(i) a time rate equal respectively to one quarter, one half and the whole of the hourly piece work basis time rate otherwise applicable to the worker, and, in addition thereto,

(ii) the minimum remuneration otherwise applicable to the worker under paragraph 1(1)(b);

(c) in the case of a male worker employed on piece work:—

(i) a time rate equal respectively to one quarter, one half and the whole of the hourly general minimum time rate which would be applicable to the worker if he were a time worker and a minimum overtime rate did not apply, and, in addition thereto,

(ii) the minimum remuneration otherwise applicable to the worker under paragraph 1(1)(b).

WAITING TIME

10.—(1) A worker is entitled to payment of the minimum remuneration specified in this Schedule for all the time during which he is present on the premises of the employer, unless he is present thereon in any of the following circumstances, that is to say—

(a) without the employer's consent, express or implied;

(b) for some purpose unconnected with his work and other than that of waiting for work to be given to him to perform;

(c) by reason only of the fact that he is resident thereon; or

(d) during normal meal times in a room or place in which no work is being done, and he is not waiting for work to be given to him to perform.

(2) The minimum remuneration payable under sub-paragraph (1) of this paragraph to a piece worker when not engaged on piece work is that which would be applicable to him if he were employed as a time worker.

PART IV

CONDITIONS AS TO RATES FOR MALE APPRENTICES AND PROSPECTIVE APPRENTICES TO TENTING OR DRESSING

11. Subject to the provisions of this Part of this Schedule, the general minimum time rates applicable to apprentices to tenting or dressing under paragraph 4 apply only where the following conditions are fulfilled:—

(1) The apprentice shall be employed during the whole of his time under a written contract of apprenticeship, for a period of four years in the case of an apprenticeship to tenting or three years in the case of an apprenticeship to dressing, which has been duly executed and which contains the following provisions, or provisions substantially to the same effect, and no provisions contrary thereto:—

(a) the apprentice of his own free will and with the consent of the guardian binds himself to serve the employer as his apprentice in his trade for the term of three or four years as aforesaid;

(b) the employer will employ the apprentice as his apprentice during the said term, and to the best of his power, skill and knowledge instruct the apprentice, or cause him to be instructed, in tenting or dressing as the case may be;

(c) the employer will keep the apprentice under his own supervision or place him under the supervision of one or more fully qualified journeymen; and

(d) the employer will, during the term of the apprenticeship, afford the apprentice reasonable facilities, during working hours if necessary, to attend classes at which technical instruction in the principles of the operation being taught is given, or, if at any time no such class exists in the district in which the apprentice is employed, the employer will place the apprentice under the charge of one of his own workers who need not be a journeyman mentioned in (c) of this sub-paragraph, but is competent to instruct the apprentice in the elementary principles of the operation being taught.

(2) The apprentice shall be the holder of a certificate of registration of apprenticeship issued by, or on behalf of, the Wages Council or shall have made application for such certificate which has been duly acknowledged and is still under consideration:

Provided that the Wages Council may decline to issue a certificate in any case where it is not satisfied that the said conditions have been complied with at the date of the application therefor, and the Wages Council may at any time thereafter cancel the certificate, if, in its opinion, any of the said conditions have not been complied with.

PROSPECTIVE APPRENTICES

12. Notwithstanding the foregoing provisions of this Schedule, where an employer employs a worker as a prospective apprentice to tenting or dressing for a probationary period not exceeding 12 weeks and all the conditions specified in the foregoing paragraph other than those with regard to employment under a written contract of apprenticeship and certification by the Wages Council are fulfilled, the minimum remuneration applicable to that worker during the said period shall be that applicable to an apprentice employed in accordance with the conditions specified in the said paragraph, and in the event of the worker being continued thereafter at his employment as an apprentice, the probationary period shall for the purposes of this Schedule be treated as part of the period of apprenticeship, whether or not it is included therein:

Provided that where the employer does not on or before the last day of the said probationary period enter into with the worker such a contract of apprenticeship as is mentioned in the said paragraph, the employer shall pay to the worker a sum equal to the difference between the minimum remuneration payable to him as a prospective apprentice and the amount that would have been payable to him had the provisions of this paragraph not applied.

PART V

APPLICABILITY OF STATUTORY MINIMUM REMUNERATION

13. This Schedule applies to the workers in relation to whom the Wages Council operates, that is to say, workers employed in Great Britain in the trade specified in the Schedule to the Trade Boards (Flax and Hemp Trade, Great Britain) (Constitution and Proceedings) Regulations 1940(a), that is to say:—

The preparing, spinning, and weaving (a) of scutched flax, (b) of hemp, (c) of a mixture of scutched flax and any other fibre, or (d) of a mixture of hemp and any other fibre;

including:—

(1) The preparing and spinning of waste reclaimed at any stage; and

(2) All packing, despatching, warehousing, storing or other operations incidental to or appertaining to any of the above-mentioned work;

but excluding:—

(1) The calendering, bleaching, dyeing or finishing of any of the above-mentioned materials; and

(2) The preparing or spinning of materials required for the making or re-making of (a) rope (including driving rope and banding), (b) cord (including blind and window cord, but excluding silk, worsted and other fancy cords), (c) core for wire ropes, (d) lines, (e) twine (including binder and trawl twine), (f) lanyards, (g) net and similar articles when such spinning or preparing is carried on in the same factory or workshop as the said making or re-making; and

(3) The making or repair of sacks or bags; and also

(4) The weaving of carpets, rugs and mats.

(a) S.R. & O. 1940/1886 (1940 I, p. 1031).

EXPLANATORY NOTE

(This Note is not part of the Order.)

This Order, which has effect from 17th August 1973, amends the provisions of the Wages Regulation (Flax and Hemp) Order 1972 (Order F.H. (130)) by specifying in detail the occupations of workers for whom statutory minimum remuneration has been fixed.

It sets out the statutory minimum remuneration payable under the revised pay structure in substitution for that fixed by Order F.H. (130), which Order is revoked.

New provisions are printed in italics.

STATUTORY INSTRUMENTS

1973 No. 1256

WAGES COUNCILS

The Wages Regulation (Flax and Hemp) (Holidays)
Order 1973

Made - - -	*18th July* 1973
Coming into Operation	*17th August* 1973

Whereas the Secretary of State has received from the Flax and Hemp Wages Council (Great Britain) the wages regulation proposals set out in the Schedule hereto;

Now, therefore, the Secretary of State in exercise of powers conferred by section 11 of the Wages Councils Act 1959(a), as modified by Article 2 of the Counter-Inflation (Modification of Wages Councils Act 1959) Order 1973(b), and now vested in him (c), and of all other powers enabling him in that behalf, hereby makes the following Order:—

1. This Order may be cited as the Wages Regulation (Flax and Hemp) (Holidays) Order 1973.

2.—(1) In this Order the expression "the specified date" means the 17th August 1973, provided that where, as respects any worker who is paid wages at intervals not exceeding seven days, that date does not correspond with the beginning of the period for which the wages are paid, the expression "the specified date" means, as respects that worker, the beginning of the next such period following that date.

(2) The Interpretation Act 1889(d) shall apply to the interpretation of this Order as it applies to the interpretation of an Act of Parliament and as if this Order and the Order hereby revoked were Acts of Parliament.

3. The wages regulation proposals set out in the Schedule hereto shall have effect as from the specified date and as from that date the Wages Regulation (Flax and Hemp) (Holidays) Order 1969(e), shall cease to have effect.

Signed by order of the Secretary of State.
18th July 1973.

W. H. Marsh,
Assistant Secretary
Department of Employment.

(a) 1959 c. 69.   (b) S.I. 1973/661 (1973 I, p. 2141).
(c) S.I. 1959/1769, 1968/729 (1959 I, p. 1795; 1968 II, p. 2108).
(d) 1889 c. 63.   (e) S.I. 1969/1841 (1969 III, p. 5722).

SCHEDULE

The following provisions as to holidays and holiday remuneration shall be substituted for the provisions as to holidays and holiday remuneration set out in the Wages Regulation (Flax and Hemp) (Holidays) Order 1969 (hereinafter referred to as "Order F.H. (122)").

PART I

APPLICATION

1. This Schedule applies to every worker for whom statutory minimum remuneration has been fixed.

PART II

CUSTOMARY HOLIDAYS

2.—(1) An employer shall allow to every worker to whom this Schedule applies a holiday (hereinafter referred to as a "customary holiday") in each year on the days specified in the next following sub-paragraph, provided that the worker has been in his employment for a period of not less than four weeks immediately preceding the customary holiday and has worked for the employer during the whole or part of that period and (unless excused by the employer or absent by reason of the proved incapacity of the worker due to sickness or injury) has worked for the employer throughout the last working day on which work was available to him prior to the customary holiday.

(2) The said customary holidays are:—

(a) (i) In England and Wales—

Christmas Day; *26th December if it not be a Sunday; 27th December in a year when 25th or 26th December is a Sunday;* Good Friday; Easter Monday; *the last Monday in May; the last Monday in August;* or

where another day is substituted for any of the above days by national proclamation, that day:

Provided that in the case of workers who normally work on each week-day except Saturday if Christmas Day falls on a Saturday the holiday shall be the next following Tuesday;

(ii) In Scotland—

New Year's Day and the following day:

Provided that if New Year's Day falls on a Sunday the holidays shall be the following Monday and Tuesday; if New Year's Day falls on a Saturday then in the case of workers who normally work on each week-day except Saturday the holidays shall be the following Monday and Tuesday and in the case of all other workers, New Year's Day and the following Monday;

the local Spring holiday;

the local Autumn holiday;

and two other days (being days on which the worker normally works for the employer) in the course of a calendar year to be fixed by the employer in consultation with the worker or his representative and notified to the worker not less than three weeks before the holiday;

or (b) in the case of each of the said days (other than a day fixed by the employer in Scotland and notified to the worker as aforesaid) a day substituted by the employer therefor, being a day recognised by local custom as a day of holiday in substitution for the said day.

(3) Notwithstanding the preceding provisions of this paragraph, an employer may (except where in the case of a woman or young person such a requirement would be unlawful) require a worker who is otherwise entitled to any customary holiday under the foregoing provisions of this Schedule to work thereon and, in lieu of any such holiday on which he so works, the employer shall allow to the worker a day's holiday (hereinafter referred to as a "holiday in lieu of a customary holiday") on a week-day on which he would normally work for the employer within the period of four weeks immediately following the customary holiday.

(4) A worker who is required to work on a customary holiday shall be paid:—

    (a) for all time worked thereon at the minimum rate then appropriate to the worker for work on a customary holiday; and

    (b) in respect of the holiday in lieu of the customary holiday, holiday remuneration in accordance with paragraph 6.

PART III

ANNUAL HOLIDAY

3.—(1) Subject to the provisions of this paragraph and of paragraph 4, in addition to the holidays specified in Part II of this Schedule an employer shall between the date on which this Schedule becomes effective and 30th September 1973 and between 6th April and 30th September in each succeeding year, allow a holiday (hereinafter referred to as an "annual holiday") to every worker in his employment to whom this Schedule applies who has been employed by him during the 12 months immediately preceding the commencement of the holiday season for any of the periods of employment (calculated in accordance with the provisions of paragraph 10) set out in the appropriate part of the following table and the duration of the annual holiday shall, in the case of each such worker, be related to his period of employment during that 12 months as follows:—

Period of employment	Duration of annual holiday
Column 1	Column 2
At least 48 weeks	15 days
„ „ 45 „	14 „
„ „ 42 „	13 „
„ „ 39 „	12 „
„ „ 36 „	11 „
„ „ 32 „	10 „
„ „ 29 „	9 „
„ „ 26 „	8 „
„ „ 23 „	7 „
„ „ 20 „	6 „
„ „ 16 „	5 „
„ „ 13 „	4 „
„ „ 10 „	3 „
„ „ 7 „	2 „
„ „ 4 „	1 day

(2) Notwithstanding the provisions of sub-paragraph (1) of this paragraph the number of days of annual holiday which an employer is required to allow to a worker in respect of a period of employment during the 12 months immediately preceding 6th April 1973 and during the 12 months immediately preceding 6th April in each succeeding year shall not exceed in the aggregate three times the number of days constituting the worker's normal working week.

(3) The duration of the worker's annual holiday during the holiday season ending on the 30th September 1973 shall be reduced by any days of annual holiday duly allowed to him by the employer under the provisions of Order F.H. (122) between the 6th April 1973 and the date on which this Schedule becomes effective.

(4) In this Schedule the expression "holiday season" means in relation to the year 1973 the period commencing on 6th April 1973 and ending on 30th September 1973, and, in each succeeding year, the period commencing on 6th April and ending on 30th September of the same year.

4.—(1) Subject to the provisions of this paragraph, an annual holiday shall be allowed on consecutive working days, being days on which the worker is normally called upon to work for the employer.

(2)(a) Where the number of days of annual holiday for which a worker has qualified exceeds the number of days constituting his normal working week, days of holiday not exceeding twice that number may, by agreement in writing between the employer and the worker or his representative, be allowed in two periods of consecutive working days; so, however, that when a holiday is so allowed, one of the periods shall consist of a number of such days not less than the number of days constituting the worker's normal working week.

(b) Where the number of days of annual holiday for which a worker has qualified exceeds twice the number of days consituting his normal working week the holiday may be allowed as follows:—

(i) as to the period comprising twice the number of days constituting the worker's normal working week, in accordance with sub-paragraph (a) of this paragraph; and

(ii) as to any additional days, on working days which need not be consecutive, to be fixed by agreement between the employer and the worker or his representative on any working day or days in the holiday season or before the beginning of the next following holiday season.

(3) For the purposes of this paragraph, days of annual holiday shall be treated as consecutive notwithstanding that a day of holiday allowed to a worker under Part II of this Schedule or a day upon which he does not normally work for the employer intervenes.

(4) Where a day of holiday allowed to a worker under Part II of this Schedule immediately precedes a period of annual holiday or occurs during such a period and the total number of days of annual holiday required to be allowed in the period under the foregoing provisions of this paragraph, together with any such day of holiday allowed under Part II of this Schedule, exceeds the number of days constituting the worker's normal working week then, notwithstanding the foregoing provisions of this paragraph, the duration of that period of annual holiday may be reduced by one day and in such a case one day of annual holiday may be allowed on any working day in the holiday season or before the beginning of the next following holiday season.

(5) Subject to the provisions of sub-paragraph (1) of this paragraph, any day of annual holiday under this Schedule may be allowed on a day on which the worker is entitled to a day of holiday or to a half-holiday under any enactment other than the Wages Councils Act 1959.

5. An employer shall give to the worker reasonable notice of the commencing date or dates and duration of the period or periods of his annual holiday. Such notice may be given individually to the worker or by the posting of a notice in the place where the worker is employed.

PART IV

HOLIDAY REMUNERATION

A—CUSTOMARY HOLIDAYS AND HOLIDAYS IN LIEU OF CUSTOMARY HOLIDAYS

6.—(1) Subject to the provisions of this paragraph, for each day of holiday to which a worker is entitled under Part II of this Schedule he shall be paid by the employer holiday renumeration as follows:—

(a) in the case of a piece worker, an amount equal to the worker's average hourly earnings for the hours worked by him for the employer (exclusive of overtime) in the week immediately preceding that in which the holiday occurs multiplied by the number of hours normally worked by him (exclusive of overtime) on that day of the week;

(b) in the case of a time worker, an amount equal to the sum which would be payable to him by the employer if that day were not a holiday and he worked thereon the number of hours normally worked by him (exclusive of overtime) on that day of the week and if he were paid at the hourly rate payable to him under his contract of employment immediately before the holiday.

(2) Payment of the said holiday remuneration is subject to the condition that the worker presents himself for employment at the usual starting hour on the first working day following the holiday and works throughout that day or, if he fails to do so, failure is by reason of the proved incapacity of the worker due to sickness or injury or with the consent of the employer.

(3) The holiday remuneration in respect of any customary holiday shall be paid by the employer to the worker on the pay day on which the wages for the week including the first working day following the customary holiday are paid.

(4) The holiday remuneration in respect of any holiday in lieu of a customary holiday shall be paid on the pay day on which the wages are paid for the week including the first working day following the holiday in lieu of a customary holiday:

Provided that the said payment shall be made immediately upon the termination of the worker's employment in the case where he ceases to be employed before being allowed a holiday in lieu of a customary holiday to which he is entitled, and in that case sub-paragraph (2) of this paragraph shall not apply.

B—ANNUAL HOLIDAY

7.—(1) Subject to the provisions of this paragraph and of paragraph 8, a worker qualified to be allowed an annual holiday under this Schedule shall be paid as holiday remuneration by his employer in respect of the annual holiday to be allowed during the holiday season commencing on 6th April 1973 and during the holiday season in each succeeding year, an amount equal to 6 per cent of his total remuneration determined in accordance with paragraph 11 during the 12 months immediately preceding the commencement of the holiday season.

(2) Holiday remuneration shall be paid by the employer to the worker—

(a) in respect of a holiday allowed on consecutive days, the number of such days being not less than the number of days constituting the worker's normal working week, on the last pay day preceding the holiday; and

(b) in respect of a day or days of holiday allowed within a week in which the worker also works for the employer, on the first pay day following the holiday.

(3) Where under the provisions of paragraph 4 an annual holiday is allowed in more than one period the holiday remuneration shall be apportioned accordingly.

8. Where any accrued holiday remuneration has been paid by the employer to the worker (in accordance with paragraph 9 of this Schedule or with Order F.H. (122)) in respect of employment during any of the periods referred to in that paragraph or that Order, the amount of holiday remuneration payable by the employer in respect of any annual holiday for which the worker has qualified by reason of employment during the said period shall be reduced by the amount of the said accrued holiday remuneration unless that remuneration has been deducted from a previous payment of holiday remuneration made under the provisions of this Schedule.

ACCRUED HOLIDAY REMUNERATION PAYABLE ON TERMINATION OF EMPLOYMENT

9. Where a worker ceases to be employed by an employer after the provisions of this Schedule become effective, the employer shall, immediately on the termination of the employment (hereinafter called "the termination date"), pay to the worker as accrued holiday remuneration:—

(1) in respect of employment in the 12 months up to and including 5th April immediately preceding the termination date, a sum equal to the holiday remuneration for any days of annual holiday for which he has qualified except days of annual holiday which he has been allowed or has become entitled to be allowed before leaving the employment; and

(2) in respect of any employment of at least four weeks duration since the said 5th April, a sum equal to the holiday remuneration which would have been payable to him if he could have been allowed an annual holiday in respect of that employment at the time of leaving it.

Part V

GENERAL

10. For the purpose of calculating any period of employment qualifying a worker for an annual holiday under this Schedule, the worker shall be treated—

(1) as if he were employed for a week in respect of any week during the qualifying period in which—

(a) in the case of a worker other than a part-time worker, he has worked for the employer for not less than 20 hours and has performed some work for which statutory minimum remuneration is payable;

(b) in the case of a part-time worker, he has worked for the employer and has performed some work for which statutory minimum remuneration is payable;

(c) in the case of a worker other than a part-time worker, he has worked for the employer for less than 20 hours by reason of proved incapacity due to sickness or injury or, in the case of any worker, for a like reason he has been absent throughout the week or has been suspended throughout the week owing to shortage of work:

Provided that the number of weeks which may be so treated as weeks of employment shall not exceed:—

(i) 26 weeks in the case of proved incapacity in respect of which the worker is entitled to injury benefit under the National Insurance (Industrial Injuries) Acts 1965 to 1967; and

(ii) four weeks in the case of any other proved incapacity or of suspension owing to shortage of work.

(2) as if he were employed on any day of holiday allowed under the provisions of this Schedule, or of Order F.H. (122), and for the purposes of the provisions of sub-paragraph (1) of this paragraph, a worker who is absent on any such holiday shall be treated as having worked thereon for the employer on work for which statutory minimum remuneration is payable for the number of hours normally worked by him on that day of the week.

11. A worker's total remuneration shall include:—

(1) all payments paid or payable to the worker by the employer in respect of his employment except:—

(a) payments by way of annual holiday remuneration;

(b) payments by way of accrued holiday remuneration;

    (*c*) payments in respect of overtime; and

    (*d*) payments in respect of any period of absence from work by reason of incapacity due to sickness or injury or by reason of suspension owing to shortage of work; and

(2) in respect of any period of absence which under the provisions of sub-paragraph (1)(*c*) of paragraph 10 is to be treated as a period of employment, the amount to which he would have been entitled if he had worked during that period as a time worker for the number of daily hours (exclusive of overtime) normally worked by him.

DEFINITIONS

12. In this Schedule, unless the context otherwise requires, the following expressions have the meanings hereby respectively assigned to them, that is to say:—

"NORMAL WORKING WEEK" means the number of days on which it has been usual for the worker to work in a week in the employment of the employer in the 12 months immediately preceding the commencement of the holiday season, or, where under paragraph 9 accrued holiday remuneration is payable on the termination of the employment, in the 12 months immediately preceding the termination date:
Provided that—

    (1) part of a day shall count as a day;

    (2) no account shall be taken of any week in which the worker did not perform any work for which statutory minimum remuneration has been fixed.

"PART-TIME WORKER" means a worker who normally works for the employer for less than 20 hours a week by reason only of the fact that he does not hold himself out as normally available for work for more than the number of hours he normally works in the week.

"STATUTORY MINIMUM REMUNERATION" means minimum remuneration (other than holiday remuneration) fixed by a wages regulation order made by the Secretary of State to give effect to proposals submitted to him by the Flax and Hemp Wages Council (Great Britain).

"WEEK" in paragraphs 3, 6 and 10 and in this paragraph means "pay week".
13. The provisions of this Schedule are without prejudice to any agreement for the allowance of any further holidays with pay or for the payment of additional holiday remuneration.

EXPLANATORY NOTE
(This Note is not part of the Order.)

This Order, which has effect from 17th August 1973, sets out the holidays which an employer is required to allow to workers in relation to whom the Flax and Hemp Wages Council (Great Britain) operates and the remuneration payable for those holidays.

It amends the provisions relating to customary holidays contained in the Wages Regulation (Flax and Hemp) (Holidays) Order 1969 (Order F.H. (122)) so as to take account of recent changes in the law and practice relating to public holidays. Order F.H. (122) is revoked.

New provisions are printed in italics.

STATUTORY INSTRUMENTS

1973 No. 1258 (S.97)

EDUCATION, SCOTLAND

Milk and Meals (Education) (Scotland) (Amendment No. 2) Regulations 1973

Made - - -	*18th July* 1973
Laid before Parliament	*27th July* 1973
Coming into Operation	*13th August* 1973

In exercise of the powers conferred on me by sections 53(3) and 144(5) of the Education (Scotland) Act 1962(**a**), and of all other powers enabling me in that behalf, I hereby make the following regulations:—

Citation, commencement and interpretation

1.—(1) These regulations may be cited as the Milk and Meals (Education) (Scotland) (Amendment No. 2) Regulations 1973 and shall be included among the regulations which may be cited together as the Milk and Meals (Education) (Scotland) Regulations 1971 to 1973.

(2) These regulations shall come into operation on 13th August 1973.

(3) The Interpretation Act 1889(**b**) shall apply for the interpretation of these regulations as it applies for the interpretation of an Act of Parliament.

Amendment of principal regulations

2.—(1) Regulation 7 of the Milk and Meals (Education) (Scotland) Regulations 1971(**c**) as amended(**d**) shall have effect subject to—

    (*a*) the substitution for the first paragraph of paragraph (4) of the following paragraph:—

        "Arrangements made by an education authority—

        (*a*) under sub-paragraphs (*a*) and (*b*) of paragraph (2) of this regulation shall include provision for the remission of any charge mentioned in the sub-paragraphs in the case of any parent who satisfies them that he is unable to pay it without financial hardship; and

        (*b*) under paragraph (3) of this regulation may include provision for the remission of the charge in the case of any parent in whose case the charge under sub-paragraph (*b*) of paragraph (2) is remitted."

    (*b*) in the second paragraph of paragraph (4) the insertion after the words

---

(**a**) 1962 c. 47.   (**b**) 1889 c. 63.

(**c**) S.I. 1971/1537 (1971 III, p. 4340).   (**d**) S.I. 1972/1220, 1973/423 (1972 II, p. 3612; 1973 I, p. 1386).

"under the said sub-paragraphs (*a*) and (*b*)" of the words "of paragraph (2) or under the said paragraph (3)".

(2) The Schedule to the Milk and Meals (Education) (Scotland) Regulations 1971 (determination of financial hardship) shall have effect subject to the substitution for the table and the first note of the following table and note.

"PART A   PART B

Size of family	Net weekly income in £ p					
	1	2	3	4	5	6
1	16·05					
2	19·70	19·10				
3	23·35	22·75	22·15			
4	27·00	26·40	25·80	25·20		
5	30·65	30·05	29·45	28·85	28·25	
6	34·30	33·70	33·10	32·50	31·90	31·30

For larger families, in respect of each child—

(*a*) £3·65 is to be added at each incremental point in every additional line; and

(*b*) £0·60 is to be subtracted at each incremental point in every additional column."

Gordon Campbell,
One of Her Majesty's Principal
Secretaries of State.

St. Andrew's House,
Edinburgh.
18th July 1973.

EXPLANATORY NOTE

(*This Note is not part of the Regulations.*)

These Regulations enable an education authority to remit the charge for other meals and refreshments provided in day special schools to pupils to whom the authority give the midday meal free of charge and amend the provisions of the Milk and Meals (Education) (Scotland) Regulations 1971 for the calculation of a parent's income for the purpose of determining his entitlement to remission of the charge for schools meals or refreshments.